CW00918819

Vanished

Vanished

An Unnatural History of Extinction

SADIAH QURESHI

ALLEN LANE
an imprint of
PENGUIN BOOKS

ALLEN LANE

UK | USA | Canada | Ireland | Australia
India | New Zealand | South Africa

Allen Lane is part of the Penguin Random House group of companies
whose addresses can be found at global.penguinrandomhouse.com

Penguin Random House UK
One Embassy Gardens, 8 Viaduct Gardens, London SW11 7BW

penguin.co.uk

First published in Great Britain by Allen Lane 2025
001

Copyright © Sadiah Qureshi, 2025

The moral right of the author has been asserted

Penguin Random House values and supports copyright.
Copyright fuels creativity, encourages diverse voices, promotes freedom
of expression and supports a vibrant culture. Thank you for purchasing
an authorized edition of this book and for respecting intellectual property
laws by not reproducing, scanning or distributing any part of it by any
means without permission. You are supporting authors and enabling
Penguin Random House to continue to publish books for everyone.
No part of this book may be used or reproduced in any manner for the
purpose of training artificial intelligence technologies or systems. In accordance
with Article 4(3) of the DSM Directive 2019/790, Penguin Random House
expressly reserves this work from the text and data mining exception.

Set in 12/14.75pt Dante MT Std
Typeset by Jouve (UK), Milton Keynes
Printed and bound in Great Britain by Clays Ltd, Elcograf S.p.A.

The authorized representative in the EEA is Penguin Random House Ireland,
Morrison Chambers, 32 Nassau Street, Dublin D02 YH68

A CIP catalogue record for this book is available from the British Library

ISBN: 978-0-241-35210-6

Penguin Random House is committed to a sustainable future
for our business, our readers and our planet. This book is made from
Forest Stewardship Council® certified paper.

DEDICATION

امی جی اور ابو جی میری ہر خواہش آپ کی دعاؤں کی وجہ سے قبول ہوئ ہے۔
باجی سعدیہ آپ کانام میری زندگی کی برکت ہے۔ میں دعا کرتی ہوں ہم ایک دن ملیں گے۔

Reader, let us create worthwhile futures.
Amid vanishing possibilities,
we can still choose redress, reciprocity, and renewal.

Contents

List of Illustrations

Prologue
Extinction's Pasts

The Mascarene Islands nestle together in the Indian Ocean. More than four hundred kilometres off the coast of Mozambique sits Madagascar, east of which the trio of Réunion, Mauritius, and Rodrigues islands rise above an underwater plateau of volcanoes whose eruptions 65 million years ago formed India's Deccan traps. Mauritius emerged from the sea between 8 and 10 million years ago, while Rodrigues and Réunion are only about 2 million years old. The islands are known for their azure waters, sunny beaches, and unique wildlife.

Millions of years ago, a pigeon spent time hopping between the Mascarene Islands. The bird's descendants took to the ground, lost the ability to fly, developed large beaks to forage for fruit, grew so tall and heavy they took to nesting on the ground, and diverged enough to become unique to their island homes: the Mauritian Dodo and the Rodrigues Solitaire. These, and many other unique beings, lived without human presence for millions of years. Arab traders knew of Mauritius for at least five centuries, but never settled there. The Portuguese arrived in 1507, while the Dutch used the island as a pit-stop on their oceanic voyages from 1598. They found an island with no mammals and introduced prolifically fertile cats, dogs, monkeys, goats, swine, and rats. Isolation had made the dodo so unafraid of outsiders that sailors took the bird by hand to make easy meals and, occasionally, ship the living curiosity to Europe, Japan, and India. Laying only one egg a year, dodos bred slowly and their population plummeted in the maws of ravenous intruders. A shipwrecked sailor made the last confirmed sighting of a dodo in 1662, and the bird was soon extinct, probably by the 1690s.[1] The solitaire survived a while longer, but was also extinct by the 1770s, and possibly earlier.[2]

Memories of the 'strange fowle' faded so fast that the dodo was dismissed as grotesque imagination until nineteenth-century naturalists meticulously documented the bird's presence in travelogues, museum drawers, and art collections. They concluded that dodos were 'almost contemporaries of our great-grandfathers', and the 'first clearly attested' extinction 'through human agency'.[3] While caches of dodo bones first found in 1865 yielded enough material for the construction of composite skeletons, no complete specimen exists. The only known soft tissue is a mummified head of uncertain provenance, but probably from a bird once exhibited in London.

Around 1638, the politician and writer Sir Hamon L'Estrange observed:

> . . . as I walked London streets, I saw the picture of a strange fowle hung out upon a clothe and myselfe with one or two more in company went in to see it. It was kept in a chamber, and was a great fowle somewhat bigger than the largest Turkey cock, and so legged and footed, but stouter and thicker and of more erect shape, coloured before like the breast of a young cock fesan, and on the back of a dunn or dearc colour. The keeper called it a Dodo . . .[4]

L'Estrange's brief note is the only known record of a living dodo in London. After the bird died, possibly by a gunshot to the back of the head, its skin was preserved and probably sold to a father and son named John Tradescant. A pair of gardeners with a penchant for collecting, their cabinet of curiosities was open to anyone with a sixpence to spare in London and known as the Tradescant Ark. After the elder's death, the son sold the treasures to the keen collector Elias Ashmole in 1659. He later offered his 'rarities', including the Ark, to the University of Oxford on condition that they were housed in a purpose-built museum. The Ashmolean Museum opened in 1683, possibly as the last few dodos eked out their existence in Mauritius. The skin of the Tradescants' dodo suffered damage, probably from handling and gnawing critters, and by the mid-eighteenth century the skin was no longer whole.

In the mid-nineteenth century, the dodo's remnants and other natural history specimens were moved yet again to the Oxford University Museum of Natural History.[5] Founded in 1850, the museum provided a focal point for scholars of the natural sciences in a university then dominated by theology, philosophy, and classics. Fossils, stuffed skins, and mined minerals were showcased in an extraordinary building that opened in 1860. The museum tower houses a colony of swifts whose joyful screeches have marked the summer months for decades. Inside, the light-filled galleries teem with glass cabinets, minerals, and skeletons of extinct and living beasts. One cabinet features a lifesize model of the dodo, while the giftshop features numerous dodo-themed keepsakes. The Oxford Dodo lies away from the public's gaze in a secret location. Only accessible by appointment, the Oxford Dodo is an assortment of precious remains: a skull partially sheathed in a mummified skin, an incomplete eye, a foot, a femur, and a single feather so minuscule it resembles an iridescent needle. I was familiar with the specimen from nineteenth-century drawings in which the light touch of artistic hands made the bird look asleep, but even modern photographs did not prepare me for the shock of encountering its desiccated and brittle skin and frail bill in person. As a historian of science, race, and empire, I have encountered life's relics in museums for as long

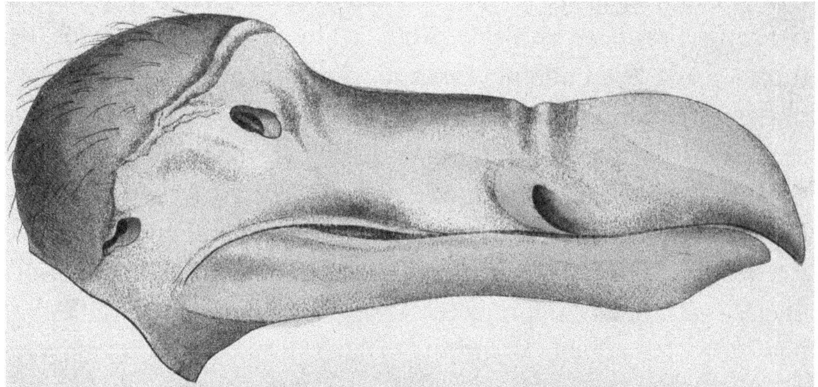

The head of the Oxford dodo.

as I can remember, but seeing one of the world's most distinctive ways of being, and famous victims of extinction, reduced to such grotesque fragility made me gasp and well up with tears.

Extinction extinguishes ways of being: distinct lifeways that might exist for untold millennia, even millions of years, before vanishing. Ways of being are a coalescence of possibilities, a quickening of leaf, wing, scale, and bone into lives we call 'trees', 'bees', 'sharks', 'tigers', or 'human'.[6] Each one is perpetuated by living, reproducing, and growing in communities over innumerable generations. Every way of being is connected to other lives through countless functions, whether as predator, prey, parent, or partner, that create significant relationships between lifeways. Sometimes descendants depart incrementally from ancestral ways, giving rise to new forms, until they appear distinctive enough for us to notice the difference, and perhaps even to designate them a species. The multiple technical definitions used to describe species are a human invention – a way of categorizing life on earth. We usually discuss extinction as the loss of species, but this often obscures how it robs the world of distinctive existences, many far older than any nation, humanity, and even earth's continents.

We will never know how many ways of being once thrived on earth, but you are a survivor of many episodes of catastrophic dying. Geologists currently date the earth to around 4.6 billion years old. The oldest known fossils are dated to about 3.5 billion years old, but carbon residues probably produced by living forms are known from as early as 4.1 billion years ago.[7] Since then innumerable ways of being have found ways to live and flourish, from bacteria living in extreme temperatures in ocean depths, to the birds, plants, and fungi we see and hear around us every day. Earth's past is punctuated by numerous extinctions, meaning all life on earth is descended from just the tenth of species that geologists regard as the survivors of past calamities. A complete catalogue of life is impossible, but fossils provide reliable snapshots of life's diversity and many ways of being before we were ever conscious of their existence. By 2023, biologists had distinguished 2.1 million living species and 250,000 fossil species, but their best estimates for the total number of living species was 8.75 million (including 7.8 million animals, 298,000 plants, and 611,000 fungi), with some suspecting up to 10 million species may once have existed.[8] While birds and mammals are comprehensively named and known, other kinds, such as invertebrates, insects, fungi, or microbes, remain relatively neglected mysteries.

Even if all living species were named, from the blue whale to every microbe, they are a fraction of the once living. Many lives were rendered unknowable in 'dark extinctions': an evocative phrase describing the loss of species before humans were aware of their existence, whether in ancient lost worlds or more recently. In 2021 the scientists Mannfred Boehm and Quentin Cronk used rates of species discovery and known species extinctions to estimate 'the extinction of undescribed species'. They subdivided recent human history into a 'pre-taxonomic period' stretching from 1500 to 1800, essentially including a substantial period of European colonization and collection of species, and a 'taxonomic period' from 1800 to the present day to adjust for variations in the quality of data. They estimated that at least fifty-six unknown species were lost after 1800, whereas another 180 were lost in the previous three centuries. These 'dark extinctions' were in addition to the 178 documented bird extinctions after 1500, and many were caused by humans. Occasionally, those species will appear in the fossil record, in museum drawers, or even found alive, while others leave no trace to be known or named.[9]

Extinction is an important marker of humanity's devastating environmental impact in recent centuries. Fears that we have instigated the sixth mass extinction by overpopulating the earth with our own kind, propagating invasive species, causing pollution, unsustainably harvesting natural resources, causing climate change through destroying natural habitats, and emitting greenhouse gases are familiar to us by now. Responses to earth's plight and the prospect of human extinction range from outright denial and refusal to admit culpability, to sanguine expectations that new technologies will save us, or panic at the prospect of approaching self-annihilation through nuclear war or ecocide. Many fight extinction through conservation or trying to resurrect lost species through 'de-extinction'. The Voluntary Human Extinction Movement (VHEMT, pronounced 'vehement') encourages us to hasten our demise and trigger earth's recovery by choosing not to have children.[10] It is no wonder that so many people feel compelled to take advantage of the last chance to see certain species such as the northern white rhino, or create archives of the dying while trying to make meaning out of loss, grief, panic, and hope. As each way of being slips away from us, we are increasingly likely to be aware of the disappearance as conservation biologists list species in peril and media outlets publish annual updates of the previous year's extinctions.[11] In 2023, for example, the Campo Grande Treefrog of Brazil, Pointed Plateau Loach fish of China, and Java Stingaree stingray of Indonesia were all declared extinct.

Whether playing with toy dinosaurs or visiting natural history museums, even young children are familiar with extinction; encountering such loss is often emotional and upsetting, and remains so as we learn of ever more species doomed to the same fate. Many of us remember the first time we realized a wondrous creature we admired was no longer living, and often that moment involved learning of the dinosaurs' fate. Encountering extinction primarily through prehistoric loss can trick us into imagining extinction as a primarily biological process or catastrophic loss caused by natural disasters. While understandable, this underplays how we contribute to and make sense of extinction. No other species conceives of itself as in danger of extinction. No other species attempts to prevent the extinction of other ways of being, counts them as they disappear, tries to revive those already lost, or frets over its culpability. No other species produces elegiac artforms, or holds ceremonies such as the Remembrance Day for Lost Species, established in 2011 and held every 30 November, to mourn such loss.[12]

How did we come to think of ourselves as survivors in a world where species can vanish for ever, or as capable of plunging our planet into a sixth mass extinction? And how has this understanding of extinction shaped how we imagine our histories, our place in the world, and role in shaping our planet? By tracing how we have made meaning from, and decisions about, extinction, *Vanished* suggests that histories of extinction are a valuable intellectual and ethical endeavour that allow us to understand the entangled roots of extinction, empire, and race in the making of the modern world. Present-day conversations about extinction are dominated by discussions of species loss, but this is a relatively new historical turn. The act of extinguishing was often called 'extinction' in the sixteenth century. From emotional lives to fiery embers, extinction denoted deliberately snuffing out passions or brightness. Likewise, from wills to family trees, extinction might refer to a lineage dying out, perhaps coupled with the loss of a family surname or hereditary title. We might still come across this legacy with someone fretting over carrying on the family name, particularly by those with rare surnames. Occasionally, lists of first names on the verge of extinction circulate on social media or the popular press as parents switch to more fashionable alternatives.[13] Extinction might describe the settling of a debt or score, or an expunging of a moral and political obligation to make good on promises. From the 1700s onwards, and particularly in the nineteenth century, as calls for the abolition of enslavement grew, commentators were increasingly likely to call for the extinction of both the transatlantic trade in enslaved Africans and enslavement itself.[14] Those extinctions were lamentably slow and still demand true reckoning and reparation.[15]

In late eighteenth-century Europe and America, extinction slowly came to mean species loss. Naturalists and theologians of the period usually regarded species as stable, unchanging, natural kinds created by God. The notion they might change, let alone develop into a new species or vanish for ever, was considered implausible at best, and even ungodly or atheistic. When species were believed lost, such as the dodo, their passing was usually attributed to human exploitation leading to 'extirpation', 'eradication', or 'extermination'. Over the nineteenth century, naturalists, theologians, philosophers, and the broader public shifted from primarily blaming humanity to theorizing extinction as a process of routine, recurrent, and ubiquitous loss inherent in the natural world. Extinction shifted from being a theologically perilous idea to a natural law ostensibly ordained by God. By the later nineteenth century, naturalists debating the nature of natural extinction recognized that humanity was also causing profoundly unnatural extinctions of once prolific species, such as the great auk or passenger pigeon, creating new fears about vanishing species. By the mid-twentieth century, biologists were increasingly concerned with counting and categorizing the degrees of threat faced by species on the brink of disappearing. As the environmental movement flourished during the Cold War, geologists suggested life on earth had experienced five catastrophic mass extinctions that annihilated many groups, including the dinosaurs 66 million years ago. By the 1980s, a new generation of conservation biologists reframed species loss as an urgent problem of diminishing diversity of life on earth. Once concerns about biodiversity and the planet's future were intertwined, they helped substantiate terrifying claims that humanity's carelessness meant everyone in the present was living through earth's sixth mass extinction.[16] Tracing the history of extinction as species loss is important, but we should not allow this to overshadow other subjects.

Many white naturalists and colonists in the nineteenth century argued that colonized peoples were on the verge of extinction. Effectively, these writers conflated natural biological extinction with unnatural imperial extermination to suggest that colonized peoples across the world could not, and would not, survive the expansion of European settler colonies. The legacies of those claims are still with us as many colonized peoples are said to be extinct: the Beothuk in Newfoundland, numerous Native nations in North America, and the Aboriginal Tasmanians are among the most frequently named in histories of European imperialism and genocide studies. Yet, colonized peoples and species are rarely discussed together as the subjects of scientific debates about extinction, despite the fact that nineteenth-century writers often conflated extermination with extinction. In some ways this is understandable because it risks implying that colonized peoples are not fully human or are even bestial, which would perpetuate profoundly racist stereotypes that must not be given any credence. However, by treating human extermination and animal extinction as separate historical developments, historians have overlooked an exceptionally important shift. This book argues that the shifting epistemic status of animal extinction helped frame the rapid and violent dispossession of colonized peoples. This cannot be fully appreciated without writing histories about the entangled fates of humans, animals, and plants as new ideas about species loss emerged.

We craft many narratives to make sense of, and wrest meaning from, extinction, yet far too many histories remain untold, forgotten, or erased. Epics in which heroic scientists discover lost species and formulate new theories about their extinction are the most obvious, and common, ways of tracing scientific debates about extinction. In these tales, heroes rooted in entrenched privilege, whether in terms of class, wealth, gender, or race, prevail against the odds to introduce new ideas and change how we view the world. Unfortunately, sweeping accounts of ideas about extinction often fail to recognize women and colonized peoples as producers of meaningful knowledge about the world. In these surveys, marginalized peoples are merely onlookers as history unfolds around them, even as it envelops and destroys their world. This suggests a rather narrow understanding of extinction as a biological process discovered almost exclusively by male scientists, and the nature of history as tales of individualized heroic discovery. Alternatively, we might encounter tragedies in which we lose Edenic bliss and bounty through the sin of earthly over-exploitation that is not slowing even in the gaping maw of an apocalyptic future. Rarity and pre-emptive mourning can also prompt quixotic pilgrimages by intrepid explorers seeking to see the last of their kind. Some extinctions are rendered into exquisite miniatures of endlings, or the last living member of their species, creating a canonical roll-call including Martha the Passenger Pigeon (1914) and Benjamin the Thylacine (1936).[17] While captivating, these perspectives can often lead to histories of climate change, conservation movements, and species loss privileging iconic animals or spectacular wildernesses. However, we need much richer accounts of how ideas of extinction developed, and not just as stories about species and sites we find enchanting, from pandas to national parks.

Vanished traces how naturalists reimagined extinction from acts of wanton human destruction into a scientific idea born of revolution, and the chilling choices facing us today. By exploring concepts of human and ecological loss together, the book provides a broad exploration of how we understand, and make meaning from, extinction. Instead of a sweeping epic, this book is divided into two parts, with each chapter offering kaleidoscopic glimpses of how extinction has been imagined through examples of animals, peoples, and plants over the past three centuries. Part One addresses the challenge of 'Peopling Extinction'. We begin by tracing how eighteenth-century naturalists changed their minds about the nature of extinction. Once regarded as a theologically suspect idea, modern naturalists established the notion of extinction as a providential natural law that governed all life. We continue by exploring how ideas about animal extinction were extended to colonized peoples – from North America to Australia and ancient humans – during the nineteenth and early twentieth centuries. Only by peopling histories of extinction can we fully appreciate how the political processes of colonization, conquest, and extermination were routinely conflated, and recast, as the natural extinction of 'doomed races'. As such, Part One reveals the deep-rooted associations between extinction, empire, genocide, dispossession, and conservation strategies such as the establishment of natural parks, or present-day campaigns for Indigenous land rights. Readers are warned that retracing such connections includes accounts of horrific violence and violations targeting Indigenous peoples, and uses names of the deceased. Part Two explores the making of 'Empire's Endlings'. Between the later nineteenth century and mid-twentieth century, concerns about 'dying races' were joined, and ultimately eclipsed, by concerns about vanishing species. When extinction was first accepted as a pervasive feature of life on earth in the nineteenth century, naturalists tended to think about species loss as historical. When species were eradicated in the modern world, from Steller's sea cow to the great auk, naturalists reimagined extinction as a process creating, and threatening, vanishing species. Part Two traces how ideas about endangerment led to the founding of new international networks of wildlife protection to conserve, and monitor, threatened species, just as ideas about catastrophic mass extinction were established during the Cold War. We end by exploring possibilities for renewal, redress, and restitution, from the chance finding of a tree believed to be extinct, to the challenges of de-extinction, and, finally, the ability of living beings, such as whales, to recover from the brink of annihilation – leaving us with glimmers of hope.

By weaving together histories of science, race, and empire, *Vanished* traces the nature of extinction as a scientific idea, imperial legacy, and political choice. By providing a more compelling account of these past entanglements, this book seeks more worthwhile futures for life on earth. Some ways of being died out long before we existed, but the way we have imagined prehistoric and more recent losses is an unnatural history of our own making that requires fresh historical scrutiny. Extinction may be natural, but it is also a human idea that we use to make meaning from loss in a world that we might be on the verge of destroying – or saving. The choice is ours.

PART ONE

Peopling Extinction

1.
Exit, Pursued by a Mastodon

In spring 1767 the physician William Hunter took a break from ministering to Queen Charlotte, whose husband was George III, and visited the Tower of London. Although the site hosted a menagerie and temporary exhibitions, he travelled there to see the remains of the dead. The Tower had recently acquired the bones, tusks, and teeth of a mysterious beast from North America. Excavators initially believed the fragments were curious minerals moulded in the floodplains, valleys, and flats of a salt lick nicknamed Big Bone Lick, in what is now the state of Kentucky. Over many centuries, animals had visited the site to lick salt, often churning up large bones known to the Shawnee as the father of cattle.[1] As larger fragments accumulated from 1739 onwards, European colonists also recognized them as animal remains, but probably those of a gargantuan monster. Naturalists and fossil connoisseurs disputed the nature of the beast, quickly named the 'Ohio Animal' after the Ohio river. Amid the excitement about a potentially unknown creature, disputes raged about the meaning of the remains. The tusks convinced many it must be elephantine. Imagine an American elephant when only African and Asian varieties were known! Yet, how did the beast reach the Americas? Where had it lived? And, more controversially, was the beast lost for ever?

His curiosity piqued, Dr Hunter met a curator who told him about the fossils' provenance. When Hunter requested an opportunity to examine the relics, the curator obliged by sending him a tusk and teeth for his extended perusal. After an extensive examination, Hunter sought a second opinion. A kinship with elephants seemed obvious at first sight, but he felt the bones were so large that they must have belonged to a more cumbersome creature.

He considered that they might be from a mammoth whose frozen remains were regularly dug up in the Siberian tundra, but this possibility seemed far-fetched as Hunter noted many 'modern philosophers have held the mammoth to be as fabulous as the Centaur'.[2] Given the mystery over whether mammoths even existed, William Hunter showed the bones to his younger brother John Hunter, also a medical man whose anatomical collections eventually formed the Hunterian Museum at the Royal College of Surgeons, London. William tracked down further specimens by visiting collectors with a penchant for the curious, and compared fragments of the Ohio Animal to the teeth and jaws of 'elephants, and hippopotami, and other large animals'. He grew convinced the beast was a gargantuan and carnivorous '*animal incognitum*'.[3]

William Hunter's interest was not limited to naming the unknown. He speculated that the fossils might yield clues to the 'astonishing change' that must have swept the globe causing 'the highest mountains' to have 'lain for many ages in the bottom of the sea' while colder climates must have been home to animals now 'confined to the warm climates'.[4] His excited imagination suggests the mystery of the beast's origins and whereabouts was never merely an issue of classification, but the tantalizing prospect of addressing much bolder questions about earth's past travails. William's researches led him to conclude that the beast was a Siberian mammoth. He presented a paper to the Royal Society the following year where he informed his peers 'we may as philosophers regret it' but 'as men we cannot but thank Heaven that its whole generation is probably extinct'.[5] Hunter's gratitude might seem as odd as his conclusion seems obvious to us. However, both reveal a great deal about the history of ideas about extinction. Mourning loss was not inevitable, while even the most cautious claims about annihilation were bold interventions in broader discussions about the very possibility, and nature, of extinction that remained deeply controversial for decades.

The mystery criss-crossed the Atlantic. In Paris the greatest naturalist of the age, Comte de Buffon, insisted the beast was a type of elephant, but one probably lost for ever. Founding Father, enslaver, and future President of the United States, Thomas Jefferson speculated in his book *Notes on the State of Virginia* (1787) that the incognitum might live in lands untrodden by colonists. A keen naturalist and fossil collector, he started writing his notes in 1781 to contradict European claims that America's fauna was weak and inferior to that of the old world. He observed 'it is well known that on the Ohio, and in many parts of America further north, tusks, grinders, and skeletons of unparalleled magnitude are found in great numbers, some lying on the surface of the earth, and some a little below it'. Drawing on Native knowledge, he insisted that the bones belonged to an animal 'still existing in the northern parts of their country'.[6] As colonization continued westwards from the first thirteen colonies on the east coast of North America, much of the continent remained well known only by Native nations. Jefferson believed it eminently possible that they knew of a living incognitum in their lands. His speculation indicates a broader reluctance to assume apparently absent creatures were extinct, and the difficulty of knowing if they were, even when relying on established Native knowledge stretching further back than any European presence on the continent.

Naturalists knew that declaring the beast extinct required judicious caution. In this period, species were usually regarded as stable, unchanging, natural kinds created by God. The notion they might change, let alone develop or vanish, was considered implausible and possibly even atheistic. Lost natural kinds were Creation's lacunae. If a species was suspiciously absent, three possibilities appeared logically possible in the eighteenth century. First, the species might have migrated and simply remained unknown in new territory. Second, the species might have developed into another, or evolved in modern terms, and survived in an apparently unconnected form, but this was difficult to defend against a broader consensus about the fixity of species. Third, the species had vanished. Extinction was a known possibility, but generally attributed to wanton human destruction. From the three options of migration, development, and extinction, naturalists usually favoured migration. Accepting extinction as a process inherent to life on earth contradicted the belief that God's Creation always exhibited its full range of perfection and diversity, or the principle of plenitude. Regarding natural imperfection as an inherent feature posed significant scientific and theological dangers.[7] William Hunter's cautious description of the incognitum as 'probably extinct' was an important recognition of the claim's gravity. Soon, a political revolution transformed the reticence of naturalists.

Eden's Relics

Parisian revolutionaries stormed the Bastille, a medieval fortress holding just seven quickly liberated prisoners, on 14 July 1789. The overthrow of the old regime ushered in political upheavals credited with the birth of the modern nation and modern sciences. The French Revolution abolished many forms of feudal and aristocratic privilege in an effort to replace the ancient ties of royal subjecthood with the promise of equal citizenship in a new nation.[8] French science already thrived in institutions such as the Académie Royale des Sciences and the Paris Observatory, both founded in the 1660s, but revolution dismantled older hierarchies to found new educational and vocational structures. The royal academies were abolished in 1793 and replaced by the Institut National, dedicated to the three classes of science, moral and political sciences, and literature and art, in 1795. The scientific class was renamed the Académie des Sciences in 1815. The foundation of specialized elite training schools later known as the *grandes écoles*, most notably the École Polytechnique founded in 1794, and new positions in reformed and revolutionary institutions, meant revolutionary upheaval had created fortunate new prospects for ambitious men.[9]

Napoleon Bonaparte seized control of France in 1799, a decade after revolution erupted, moved into the Tuileries Palace in 1800, and crowned himself Emperor in December 1804. Napoleon's early ambitions were evident in his campaign to colonize the ancient kingdom of Egypt; while unsuccessful, he and his men returned with an extraordinary assortment of manuscripts and artefacts collected between 1798 and 1801. Among these, the Rosetta Stone helped scholars decode Egyptian hieroglyphs and, after its seizure by the British, was displayed in the British Museum where it remains. Once home, Napoleon refashioned Paris into an imperial capital with the classical grandeur of ancient Athens or Rome. He commissioned monuments commemorating his military victories, including the Vendôme Column and the Arc de Triomphe. Napoleon's acquisitiveness included the territories of his foes and collections of European elites. Waging near ceaseless war across Europe, he extended France's imperial reach as far as the Kingdom of Prussia along the northern European coast, the Confederacy of the Rhine in central Europe, and into central Italy bordering the Kingdom of Naples. After Napoleon's defeat at the battle of Waterloo in 1815, his success faded and he left France with less territory than when he seized power. However, his exploits permanently swelled with their seized loot the already vast holdings of Parisian museums.[10]

As revolution gripped Paris, the future of the royal garden, the Jardin du Roi, seemed as inauspicious as that of other institutions of the old order. Founded by the royal decree of Louis XIII in May 1635, the royal garden was originally planted as a medicinal herb garden. The site eventually housed the King's personal museum (*Cabinet du Roi*) and menagerie from 1794.[11] In the eighteenth century, the royal garden's intellectual and social fortunes were transformed under the leadership of Georges-Louis Leclerc, Comte de Buffon. Severing the garden from its medicinal roots, he created an important site for botanical research, such as acclimatizing foreign plants sent back to Paris as seeds or living flora by a global network of collectors and correspondents. His stellar reputation rested upon his monumental and encyclopaedic *Natural History* (*Histoire Naturelle*). Lauded as a masterpiece across Europe, this astonishing work comprised thirty-six volumes published during his lifetime, but ultimately sprawled across forty-four volumes published between 1749 and 1804. The magnum opus was posthumously finished by Buffon's protégé, the Comte de Lacépède, who was specifically trained for the task by the elderly author.[12] Buffon presided over the royal garden between 1739 and his death in 1788, a year before the outbreak of revolutionary violence.

When the royal garden's naturalists were summoned before the Revolutionary Assembly they pleaded for a chance to reform. Reprieved, they spent an anxious summer developing a proposal to transform themselves from royally patronized subjects to state-employed professors administering an amalgamated royal botanic garden, menagerie and museum of natural history. In June 1793 revolutionaries abolished the royal garden and rebranded the site a botanic garden (*Jardin des plantes*), while also founding the new Museum of Natural History (*Muséum d'Histoire Naturelle*) alongside twelve professorships. Within weeks, revolutionaries also established an arts museum (*Musée des Arts*) as a state-owned art collection at the Louvre Palace, and the botanic garden was opened to the public the following spring. Amid the political fervour, the professors saved their necks by rebranding their expertise in taming nature as perfectly suited to improving a nation sullied by the worst excesses of the *ancien régime*.[13] In a wonderful history of the garden, the historian

1.1 Jardin des plantes.

Emma Spary suggests that the naturalists tried to create an utopia through nurturing the grounds, and by extension, France into a well-ordered, economically productive garden at the heart of the French Empire.[14] Originally on the outskirts of the city, but eventually enveloped by urban sprawl, the garden was a prominent site for botanical study, innocent walks, and clandestine trysts (Fig. 1.1). The combined effect of revolutionary violence, imperial ambition, and institutional reforms created unrivalled new opportunities to make natural knowledge while gaining power and prestige during the late eighteenth and early nineteenth centuries.

One of the most important careers forged in the wake of these changes was that of a young man interested in geology, anatomy, and natural history. Georges Cuvier made his name as a comparative anatomist whose research transformed the understanding of earth's history and the nature of extinction. Born in 1769, he grew up in the French-speaking principality of Montbéliard, then under the control of the Duke of Württemberg. Cuvier's parents hoped he might become a Lutheran minister, but he proved to be a gifted naturalist, reading his uncle's copy of Buffon's *Histoire Naturelle* at just twelve years old. After completing his education at Caroline University in 1788 he was unable to secure a position in local government. He moved to Normandy and spent six years working as a private tutor while continuing his research in natural history. Cuvier became a French citizen when Montbéliard was subsumed within French territory in 1793. Witnessing revolution erupt from the relative quiet of rural France, he wrote to established professors at the Museum of Natural History seeking new opportunities. He was encouraged to come to Paris by the naturalist Étienne Geoffroy Saint-Hilaire, who was appointed to a professorship at the museum in his early twenties.

Cuvier ventured to Paris hoping to benefit from the dismantling of old patronage networks just after the worst extremes of the Terror in 1795. Amid political disarray, Cuvier was serendipitously recruited to assist an elderly professor of animal anatomy at the new museum. He lived and worked on-site alongside many museum employees and their families. Although appointed as an anatomist, he broadened his research to comparative anatomy, furthered his reputation through public lectures, and achieved a full professorship within seven years. Cuvier believed species were fixed natural kinds that could not change – or evolve in modern terms. He classified life into four main types, or *embranchements*, and privileged inward function over outward form when classifying species. In contrast, his colleague Geoffroy Saint-Hilaire theorized that vertebrates were all based on a single archetypical plan, with higher vertebrates, such as mammals, having descended from simpler forms, such as fish, implying some form of developmental change.[15] Their disagreement over species fixity created a lasting rivalry.

Even as a junior employee, Cuvier's ideas about species and research on fossils proved important. In the pre-modern world any oddly shaped stone might be called a fossil, from the Latin *fossilis* for something dug up from the land. Scholars debated whether fossils were animal, vegetable, or mineral until the sixteenth century. By the eighteenth century, fossilized remnants of marine-dwelling ammonites were considered unlike anything known, but many authorities argued they might be found alive in unexplored territories. As larger beasts were dug up from Siberia to the Americas, naturalists cautiously debated their whereabouts. Cuvier investigated the mystery of apparently vanished beings soon after arriving in Paris, beginning with elephants. Most of his peers regarded Asian and African elephants as the same species. Cuvier suspected otherwise. After the French defeat of the Dutch during the revolutionary wars, the Treaty of the Hague in 1795 committed the removal of Dutch heritage collections to Paris, including important natural history specimens such as elephant skulls from Ceylon, now Sri Lanka, and from the Cape of Good Hope along the South Atlantic coast of southern Africa. Cuvier compared these skulls to a Siberian mammoth's jawbone already in Paris. He presented his findings to colleagues and published a paper on the creatures in 1796. Cuvier already thought the trio were different species, but the Dutch collections allowed him to 'turn the suspicions into certainty'. Cuvier insisted even untrained eyes could discern they were not the same species, but he felt their teeth were especially telling. The Asian elephant's teeth were 'festooned with ribbons', while the African elephant's teeth were 'diamond forms'. He argued the differences were greater 'than the horse from the ass or the goat from the sheep', making the elephants different species.[16]

Cuvier turned his attention to the mammoth. He reminded his readers that mammoths were frequently dug up 'underground in Siberia, Germany, France, Canada, and even Peru', but rejected every explanation for their continued existence. He was unconvinced by local reports that the mammoth was a subterranean beast that resisted capture. Other fossil megafauna appeared ill suited to present-day climates because they were so unlike surviving fauna. If mammoths were lost, Cuvier wondered, what misfortune caused their demise? He considered the three possibilities that naturalists usually entertained when pondering apparent loss: migration, development, and extinction. He was sceptical that such gargantuan animals might roam the earth undiscovered. They were simply too big to survive unnoticed by people even after migrating to pastures new. He was adamant that the mammoth had not developed into another species because he regarded species as unchanging natural kinds. In guarded words, Cuvier proposed that the collection and consideration of 'all these facts, consistent among themselves, and not opposed by any report, seem to prove to me the existence of a world previous to ours, destroyed by some kind of catastrophe'.[17]

A few months later in 1796, Cuvier pondered the strange, and unusually complete, skeleton of the 'Paraguay animal'. Originally revealed a hundred feet below surface rocks near Buenos Aires, then Spanish South America, in 1789 the remains were shipped to Madrid. Juan-Bautista Bru worked at the Royal Cabinet of Natural History of Madrid as a dissector in the royal laboratory. He mounted the bones to conjure a colossal beast twelve feet long and six feet high with broad shoulders, thick thighs, flat feet, and large pointed claws. Bru commissioned engravings of his magnificent prize specimen for future publication. Those images piqued the curiosity of a visiting French official who acquired unpublished proofs and hastily dispatched copies to Paris in 1796. Cuvier pored over the images of individual bones and the mounted skeleton. Not one bone resembled any living animal of similar size while the skull, shoulder blades, pelvis, and pointed claws were utterly peculiar. Cuvier named the beast the *Megatherium americanum* in a paper published in 1798 (Fig. 1.2). He conceded the megatherium's claws and teeth resembled edentates such as sloths, armadillos, pangolins, anteaters and the aardvark, but concluded it must be another long-lost beast, perhaps a gigantic sloth. His paper confidently asserted 'this animal differs, in the ensemble of its characters, from all known animals'. This fact 'adds to the numerous facts that tell us that the animals of the ancient world all differ from those we see on earth today'.[18]

Spurred on by the mammoth and megatherium, Cuvier formulated a new principle of comparative anatomy and made it the cornerstone of his ongoing researches into extinction and earth's history. He hypothesized that if an anatomist found a sharp-toothed jawbone of a carnivore, he could be assured the animal's entire skeleton would enable the rapid and successful hunting of prey and a stomach able to digest meat. On this basis, he believed skilled anatomists could reconstruct whole creatures from fragments because skeletal and visceral forms were interdependent and perfectly suited to the conditions of a creature's existence. Without naming himself and with characteristic bravado, Cuvier elevated his theory about the correlation of parts to the heady levels of disciplinary superiority: 'comparative anatomy has reached such a point of perfection that, after inspecting a single bone, one can often determine the class, and sometimes even the genus of the animal to which it belonged, and above all if the bone belonged to the head of the limbs'.[19] Cuvier's specific claim was about classifying animals, but his devotees insisted that Cuvier's principle allowed him, and his disciples, to summon forth an entire animal from a single bone. The exaggerated claim was repeated in the European and American press for more than a century, elevating the originally pragmatic principle into the natural law of the 'correlation of forms', assuring his subsequent fame.[20]

1.2 Megatherium, Natural History Museum, London.

Cuvier's ideas benefited from the rapid expansion of Paris. As the city's population swelled and new buildings and monuments mushroomed, miners routinely dug up unknown creatures while quarrying for gypsum to mix plaster of Paris, or Lutetian limestone, the distinctive Paris Stone, to render the outside of buildings. Found embedded deep within the stone layers, mysterious forms were routinely sent to the Museum of Natural History. Cuvier wondered: What were they? Why were they deposited so deeply within the strata? What did they reveal about life on earth? Slowly, he interpreted them as 'antiquities of nature', allowing naturalists to disentangle earth's history as effectively as 'ordinary antiquities provide for the political and moral history of nations'.[21] Increasingly convinced that extinct animals perished in a cataclysm affecting a prehuman world, Cuvier compiled a list of extinct species described by himself or other geologists. The twenty-three species included the North American mastodon that baffled so many, Siberian mammoth, megatherium, long-headed rhinoceros, a large German cave bear, a hyena, giant 'Elk' from Irish bogs, fossil turtles, the lizard-like Maastricht crocodile (later named the *Mosasaurus*), a winged Bavarian reptile (which he later named the *ptero-dactyle* or 'wing-fingered animal'), two species of extinct tapir later, and an extinct hippopotamus.[22] Many of these species, such as the crocodile or winged dragon, were widely known geological curiosities when Cuvier compiled his list, but he was confident that they were unlike any living species and so helped to reinterpret their significance. Within a decade, Cuvier used his list to predict that extinct beasts might be found beneath the surface of all nations.

Cuvier was especially intrigued by Parisian fossils that resembled living creatures in far-flung places, such as South American tapirs or Australian marsupials. In 1804 the Parisian gypsum yielded a split rock emblazoned with a tiny skeleton including a visible jaw, ribs, spine, pelvis, and legs. Cuvier suspected it was a marsupial. If true, the remarkable specimen conjured a lost world populated with animals unlike anything surviving in France and known only from New Holland (modern Australia). Imagine, tiny marsupials grazing alongside tapirs in what is now Paris, and rhinos where the Louvre now stands! If the fossil was a marsupial, Cuvier predicted two long, flat bones originally supporting a marsupial pouch were hidden in the pelvis. Typically self-assured, he invited colleagues to watch him chip away at the precious fossil. He carved away the gypsum with delicate strokes, brushed off the debris and, to his satiated delight, found the marsupial bones. As he later noted, such fossils proved the city's plaster quarries were studded with the 'remains of animals that can only be of a genus now confined entirely to America, or else of another confined entirely to New Holland'.[23]

Finding a European marsupial radically shifted scientific thought about the history of the earth, by suggesting an ancient, extinct world in which Europe was home to creatures known only from the Americas or antipodes. Still unique, Cuvier's specimen is so rare that it is kept in secure storage at the museum where he worked. The historian of geology Martin Rudwick suggests the flamboyant demonstration was an attempt to vindicate the predictive powers of comparative anatomy and to argue that it was as scientifically reliable as chemistry or Newtonian mathematics. This was not mere bravado, but a carefully choreographed attempt to establish Cuvier's reputation as the world's foremost authority on fossils and exciting new anatomy that, in turn, was crucial for new ideas about extinction.[24] Cuvier's research can easily be retold as a tale of genius and discovery, but this would misrepresent the broader context in which his research was conducted. In many senses he was a gifted man in the right place at the right time. His unrivalled access to specimens, his position in a stellar research institution, and careful detailed comparisons between fossils and bones all helped to make his claims about extinction and earth's history significantly more compelling than they might have been without such professional and political advantages.

Educated men in world-class institutions are easily acknowledged as makers of new scientific knowledge, but public exhibitions were just as important for circulating and creating knowledge about extinction. The American incognitum was exhibited in America and toured Europe amid continued speculation about its origin and nature (Fig. 1.3).

1.3 Skeleton of the Missouri Leviathan, or American Incognitum.

The American painter and naturalist Charles Willson Peale exhibited the skeleton of an American incognitum at his eponymous museum in Philadelphia. The bones were dug up in Orange County, New York, and heaped in a granary until Peale bought them from the landowner for $200 in 1801. Struck by their commercial potential, Peale secured permission for further excavations and eventually acquired three skeletons. Peale's fabulously named sons, Rembrandt and Rubens, took the second of their father's prized skeletons on tour the following year. Rembrandt wrote an illustrated pamphlet that advertised the 'Great American Incognitum, An Extinct, Immense, Carnivorous Animal', and explicitly used Cuvier's research to promote the beast as a newly discovered scientific marvel. The pamphlet included extensive discussions of the beast's anatomy, the latest scientific literature about life on earth, and legends. These included Shawnee knowledge about a great and ancient destruction, and a rabbi's belief that the mammoth was the Behemoth of the Book of Job and would provide a 'feast for the Jews on their restoration'.[25] Given the incognitum's close resemblance to remains dug up in Siberia and across Britain, Rembrandt advertised the beast as a mammoth and even speculated that Siberia and America were once in 'communication, or that a deluge' deposited the remains in America following the species' disappearance.[26]

Exhibitions, impresarios, and promotional pamphlets may seem peripheral or irrelevant to developing notions of extinction, but they were important in multiple ways. Scholars keen to see the first almost complete reconstruction of an extinct animal exhibited in Britain took advantage of Peale's show for their investigations and wrote scientific papers on the beast. Modern scientific research often occurs in specialist spaces such as laboratories, but natural knowledge was historically made in a much more varied range of venues we might never associate with scientific practice, from royal courts, pubs, and coffee houses, to public exhibitions.[27] Rembrandt Peale's pamphlet made Cuvier's theories about extinction and geological catastrophes accessible far beyond the scientific elite. This introduced Cuvier to a much larger audience, including people with considerable scientific expertise who excerpted the writings for learned publications across Europe. Some of the show's patrons might have known about the incognitum or new research on extinction beforehand, but many first encountered fossil reconstructions through such exhibitions, as we still do by visiting museums. Rembrandt was keenly aware of the value of personal observations of his exhibit: 'Much has been said on the subject of bones found in America by persons who never saw them, but mutilated fragments of them; resting their faith upon what has been said by certain writers of science and respectability . . . and then falling into the error.'[28] These polemical claims were an assertion of authority and an attempt to secure paying custom, but he was not alone, or wrong, in considering the exhibition an important contribution to debates about extinction. Public exhibitions and their accompanying literatures were integral to generating, and circulating, new knowledge about extinction.[29] Rembrandt also left another legacy. He commissioned engravings of the specimen. Copies were sent to Paris where Cuvier worried over them as he revisited his original musings on elephants and catastrophic species loss.

A decade after Cuvier's first investigations into living elephants and their fossilized counterparts, he ruminated at length on the elephantine 'Ohio animal' that so intrigued Hunter, Jefferson, and Buffon. Cuvier was already familiar with elephants, rhinos, tapirs, and the hippos. Vague similarities to elephants aside, on closer inspection Cuvier determined the animal was an extinct species distinct from elephants and mammoths, and named it the Mastodon or 'breast-tooth' to signify the plump mounds sitting above the molars. These helped the beast crush food, unlike the flatter, ribbon-like teeth used for grinding in elephants and mammoths.[30] With a decade's experience of examining fossilized animals and a rapidly growing list of lost species, Cuvier speculated freely about their passing: 'before this catastrophe these animals lived in the [same] climate where their bones are now unearthed. It is this catastrophe that destroyed them there; and since they are no longer found elsewhere, it must indeed have annihilated the species.'[31] Crucially, he believed that the extinct creatures were dug up where they died, rather than far from where they might have been washed away by an ancient deluge, whether Biblical or not. Rather, these beasts were stricken by a mysterious and more sudden calamity, such as climate change.

Cuvier was not the first to suggest animal extinction occurred, so it would be unwise to romanticize him as a lone genius fighting tides of ignorance. However, his careful comparisons between fossilized beasts and living animals, spanning over a decade and covering a multitude of species, yielded so much plausible evidence that megafauna such as the mammoth, mastodon, and megatherium were extinct that even cautious naturalists grew increasingly convinced. Cuvier gathered his papers on fossilized bones and extinct beasts, wrote a new introduction to the collection, and arranged for them to be published in the lavish four-volume *Researches on Fossil Bones of Quadrupeds* (*Recherches sur les ossemens fossiles de quadrupèdes*) in 1812, later superseded by a second edition in seven volumes (1821–4). The work was introduced with a lengthy, and widely distributed 'Preliminary Discourse' (*Discours préliminaire*), which boldly asserted that many calamities caused past extinctions.

Although many naturalists across the Channel read Cuvier's work in French, periodical discussions helped circulate his ideas to a much broader audience and popularized the notion of extinction.[32] Likewise, exhibitions, promotional pamphlets, and reports of his ideas were among the most accessible discussions for anyone beyond the scientific elite. Cuvier's widely circulated research on ancient reptiles and mammals helped confirm that living fauna were radically unlike their predecessors and that an age of reptiles preceded an age of mammals. His investigations were swiftly regarded as irrefutable proof that extinction was not only possible, but an inherent process in life's development. In a decade characterized by revolutionary political violence and European warfare, Cuvier patiently and confidently built his scientific empire through reconstructing lost ancient worlds.

Cuvier's collected works were a 'paper museum of fossil bones' reprinted and circulated in transnational networks, while visitors to the Museum of Natural History in Paris might personally inspect his menagerie of skeletons.[33] His new galleries of comparative anatomy were opened to the public in 1806, the same year he named the American incognitum the mastodon. Situated in a building away from the historic central galleries, Cuvier's displays were a microcosm of his ideas about the fixity of species and classification of life into four main types, or *embranchements*. Stretching over several floors, the galleries showcased his research as the most authoritative explanation of nature's order, much to the chagrin of his dissenting colleagues. Curiously, the extinct beasts so foundational for Cuvier's reputation were either displayed and stored in his private apartments, or in the older, central galleries. A later guidebook to the museum explicitly noted the plethora of extinct species named and reconstructed by the great Monsieur: 'The fossil bones of quadrupeds, birds, and reptiles occupy the twelve glazed cases opposite the windows . . . [they] are arranged according to the order adopted by M. Cuvier in his great work on fossil remains, which contains a description and figure of almost every specimen in this collection.'[34] While the galleries promoted Cuvierian theories of anatomy and taxonomy, the entire site teemed with extinct beasts that affirmed his personal eminence, and the Parisian collections, for understanding extinction.[35]

Cuvier's position within European scientific networks was remarkably significant during his lifetime, but his reputation faded after his death in 1832. His geological research helped establish earth as a subject of historical study, challenging theorists who framed the planet as an abstract timeless world without beginning or end. As evolutionary understandings of life gained ground in the mid-nineteenth century, his steadfast belief in unchanging species meant he fell out of favour with both biologists and historians who caricatured him as on the losing side of the evolutionary debate. His legacy was only revived in the later twentieth century when historians of science used his writings to understand broader themes such as the development of the earth sciences, or the emergence of modern scientific institutions within revolutionary Paris.[36]

Extinction Unbound

In the early nineteenth century, lists of extinct beasts were compiled, lost landscapes recreated, and stellar reputations forged as people imagined and debated the nature of a world before a Biblical flood. Artefacts we consider fossilized remnants of extinct flora and fauna have been encountered by humans for millennia. While ancient peoples used fragments of dinosaur eggs to make jewellery, Native nations were familiar with the large beasts of Big Bone Lick and incorporated them into accounts about the origin of bison long before Europeans worried about the incognitum.[37] These fascinating insights help us trace when petrified beings were first encountered, but we must remember that their finders often invested them with very different meanings. Interpreting these remains as extinct species inhabiting lost worlds only gathered pace in the nineteenth century. The radical surgeon James Parkinson's research on 'shaking palsy' led to the naming of Parkinson's disease. As a keen geologist, he helped found the Geological Society of London in 1807, the world's first national society devoted to the emerging discipline. His beautifully illustrated book *Organic Remains of a Former World* (1804–11) framed fossils as the 'medals of creation', revealing that 'innumerable beings have lived, of which not one of the same kind does any longer exist'. Their sheer abundance must 'excite the highest admiration'. The physician and renowned naturalist Benjamin Smith Barton passionately advocated for the ubiquity of extinction in 1814 when he wrote a book about extinct animals, boldly stating:

> I speak of those animals as *extinct*. In doing this, I adopt the language of the first naturalists of the age. No naturalist, no philosopher; no one tolerably acquainted with the history of nature's works and operations, will subscribe to the puerile opinion, that Nature does not permit any of her species of animals, or vegetables, to perish.[38]

Barton's affirmation of the *latest* natural historical research suggests just how quickly older suspicions about extinction turned into confident assertions.

New understandings of extinction were quickly integrated into Christian theology. Parkinson imagined extinction as a process for 'forming, destroying and reforming the earth', and the perfection of Creation culminating in humans.[39] His discussion of extinction as a cumulative process of development shows how easily new ideas about ubiquitous and recurrent processes of extinction might be incorporated into narratives of developmental progress driven by God's laws. Others drew upon Cuvier's research to reconcile, and recalibrate, new ideas about earth's past with Biblical accounts of Creation.[40] The Reverend William Buckland was appointed the University of Oxford's first Reader in Geology from 1819. He felt Cuvier's catastrophic deluge was easily read as dividing earth's history into an antediluvian age abounding with ancient, fearsome beasts and a post-diluvian world in which Noah's family and animals migrated over the earth to re-establish divinely created abundance. Expectations of conflict between science and religion are often rooted in assumptions that they are separate, incompatible, intellectual endeavours, but this is a modern distinction that makes it difficult to appreciate how past practitioners regarded their faith and scientific research as mutually intelligible. Over the early nineteenth century, many geologists adapted their understanding of Creation as a series of events giving rise to the highest forms of life, and extinction as a God-given law directing, and shaping, a gradual progression to ever more superior beings.[41]

As geologists gained a foothold in elite clubs, new societies, and universities, their ideas about extinction colonized new academic and theological terrain. Reverend Buckland's flamboyant lectures drew crowds of students who learned of strange, extinct beings as they handled depictions of vanished worlds, including a large illustration of Peale's mammoth, paintings of ancient landscapes, and spectacular fossils of ammonites and ichthyosaurs (Fig. 1.4). Buckland also secured fame through his research on extinct British hyenas. In 1821 he visited Kirkdale Cave in North Yorkshire. Geologists knew the site was studded with a pell-mell assortment

1.4 Scholars attending a lecture by Buckland in the Ashmolean Museum, Oxford.

of well-preserved bones from hyenas, elephants, and hippos alongside their ordure. To great acclaim, Buckland vividly reconstructed the hyenas' diet and antediluvian den, making him the first to place an extinct species within the place it once lived, rather than where it perished or was preserved.[42] While Kirkdale Cave teemed with familiar beasts, geologists grappled with accruing revelations about unknown monsters.

The classification of newly unearthed species as extinct kinds created a brisk market for specimens, with some of the most exquisite found by a keen-eyed young girl. The carpenter Richard Anning lived in Lyme Regis in west Dorset, an area well-known for its petrified monsters. He supplemented his income by combing the local beaches for fossils to sell to wealthy collectors. After his death, his wife Mary Anning and their children, Mary and Joseph, became expert fossil hunters in their own right. In 1811 fifteen-year-old Joseph found a peculiar skull, while twelve-year-old Mary found the rest of the skeleton a year later. After its sale to a local collector and an exhibition in London, the specimen caught the attention of many prominent geologists, and was eventually named *Ichthyosaurus* ('fish lizard') in 1817. The young Mary also found a nearly complete skeleton of another lizard-like reptile in 1823, later named *Plesiosaurus* ('almost lizard') by the geologists William D. Conybeare and Henry De La Beche (Fig. 1.5). Unfortunately, the Anning family's precarious finances made selling the treasures an urgent necessity, and for many years Mary's finds were attributed solely to the gentlemen who could afford to buy, keep, display, or donate them, and whose Latin names for the species were suitably accredited by the scientific elite. Mary Anning's fossils ended up in prestigious collections such as the British Museum and Natural History Museum in London, and the Academy of Natural Sciences in Philadelphia. Nonetheless, her personal contribution was largely relegated to children's rhymes about the girl who sold seashells by the seashore or was erased from academic histories of geology despite buyers' private letters referring to her as the curious 'geological Lioness' or 'Princess of palaeontology'.[43] In 2021, following a renaissance of

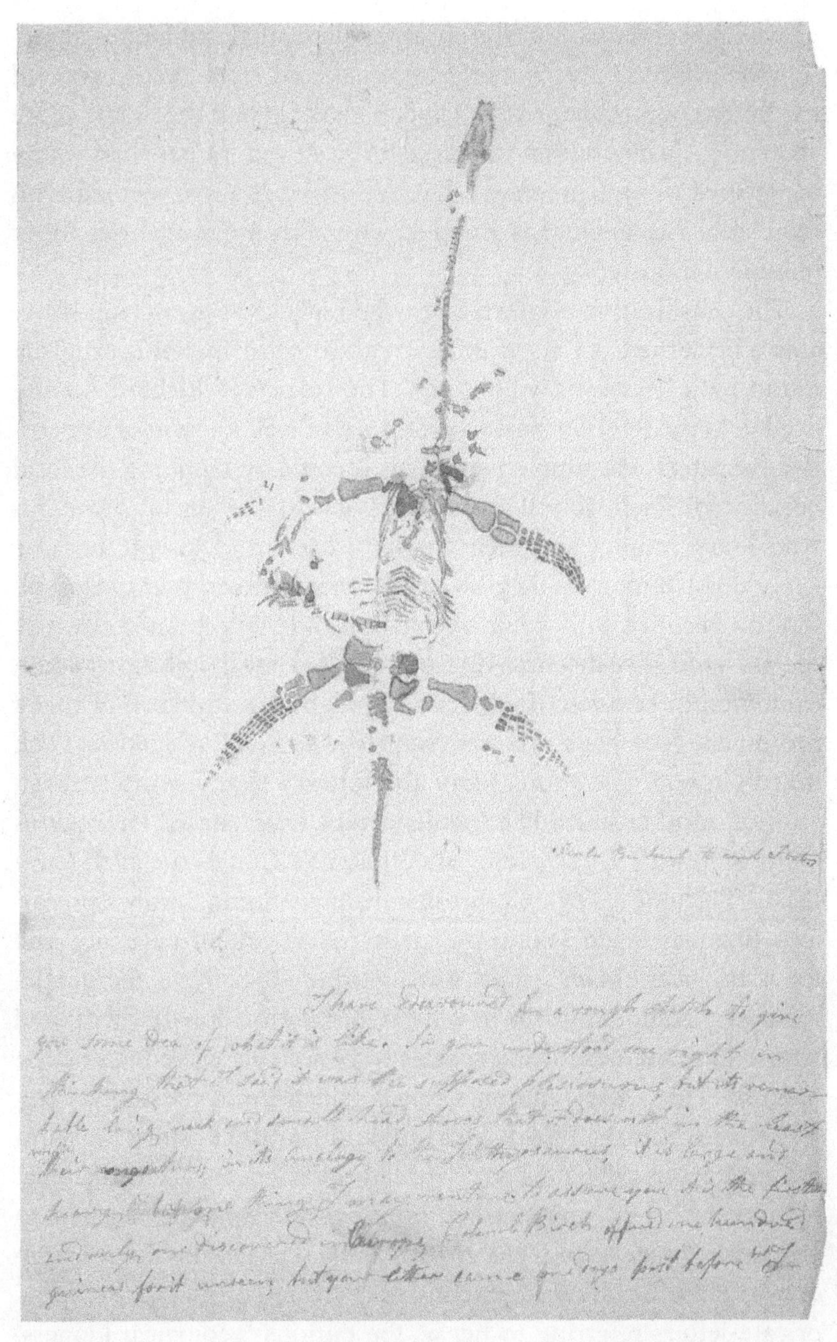

I have drawn you a rough sketch to give
you some idea of what it is like. [illegible] you understand are right in
thinking that I said it was the supposed plesiosaurus but its remarkable long neck and small head shows that it does not in the least
their [struck out] in its analogy to the Ichthyosaurus. It is large and
heavy [illegible] I may venture to assure you it is the first
and only one discovered in Europe. Colonel Birch offered me hundred
guineas for it unseeing but your letter came five days past before [illegible]

1.5 Mary Anning's autograph letter concerning the discovery of plesiosaurus.

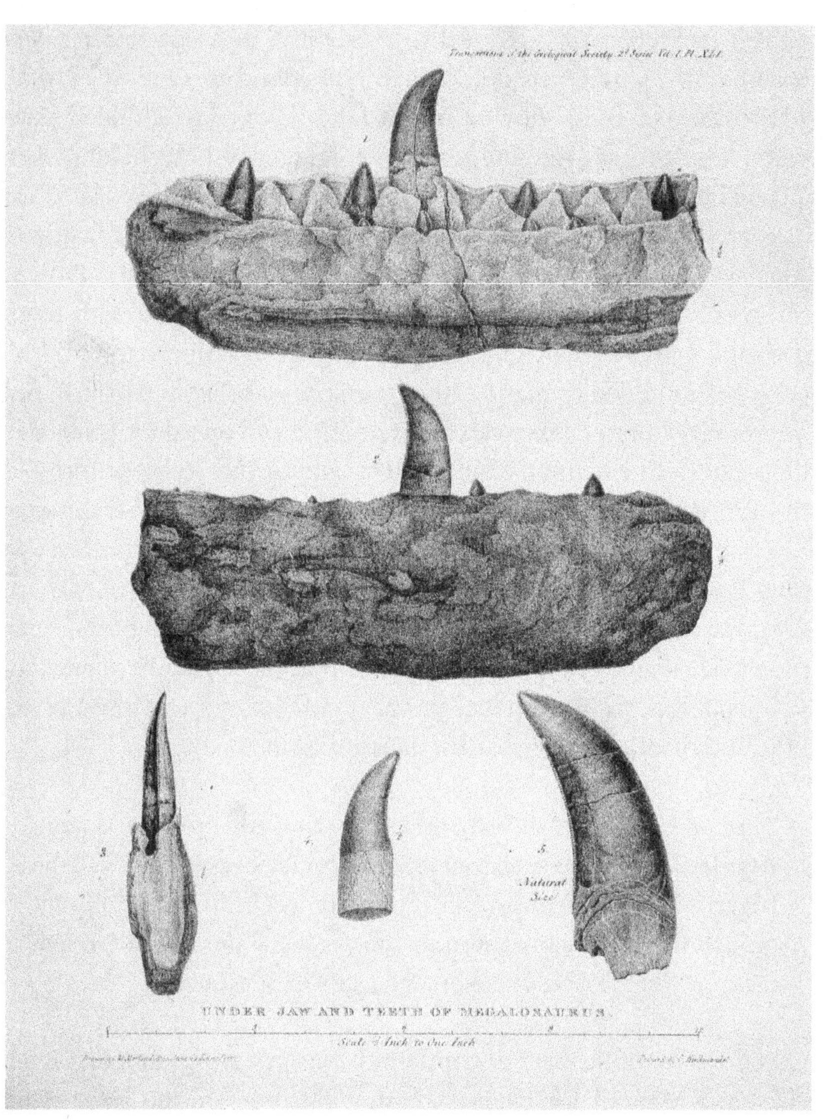

1.6 Megalosaurus teeth and lower jaw.

interest in Anning's finds, Britain's Royal Mint issued commemorative 50-pence coins featuring the *Temnodontosaurus*, *Plesiosaurus*, and *Dimorphodon*, all first unearthed by her geological hammer.

Strange beasts dug up in the craggy coasts, quarries, and wealds of Britain were soon grouped together in a new sub-order called *Dinosauria*.[44] Cuvier visited William Buckland in Oxford in 1818, where the reverend showed him a large lower jaw studded with teeth (Fig. 1.6). Cuvier suggested it might once have belonged to a lizard-like creature, and it was later named the 'great lizard' or *Megalosaurus*.[45] In the same decade, physician and naturalist Gideon Algernon Mantell found many puzzling fragments on the Downs of Sussex. One of his most important finds was a jaw with teeth resembling those of an iguana, but clearly from a much larger herbivore. He intended to name it the *Iguana-saurus* ('iguana-lizard), but eventually shunned the awkward repetition and opted for *Iguanodon* ('iguana-tooth') in 1825. Mantell also named the *Hylaeosaurus* ('of the forest'): a gargantuan lizard identified from stone fragments quarried in Tilgate Forest, Sussex, that he believed might be 200 feet long.[46] As lists of extinct Saurians grew, the palaeontologist Richard Owen tried to make taxonomic sense of the fearsome, antediluvian monsters. In 1842 he proposed gathering *Iguanodon*, *Megalosaurus*, and *Hylaeosaurus* into a new sub-order defined by their fused vertebrae and distinctive pelvis, ribs, hands, and feet:

> The combination of such characters . . . altogether peculiar among Reptiles . . . and all manifested by creatures far surpassing in size the largest of existing reptiles, will, it is presumed, be deemed sufficient ground for establishing a distinct tribe or sub-order of saurian reptiles, for which I would propose the name of *Dinosauria*.[47]

Owen's taxonomic invention inflamed tensions with Mantell. Owen chastised Mantell for over-estimating the size of the beasts and downsized them to no more than 30 feet long. Mantell felt the sting of dishonourable conduct, and their enmity reached new depths of bitterness until Mantell's death in 1852.[48]

Once prised from rocks, fossilized beasts were rehomed in private collections, commercially displayed in exhibition venues, showcased in museum vitrines, or hidden in storage. They also inhabited new literary and visual worlds in beautiful depictions of 'deep time'.[49] Henry De la Beche painted *Duria antiquior* in 1830 to depict the violent waters of ancient Dorset teeming with ravenous ichthyosaurs mauling plesiosaurs under a pair of sparring pterodactyls (Fig. 1.7). The evocative painting is the first to depict this lost world in such vivid, comprehensive, and lifelike detail: De la Beche commissioned his own copies, while many artists followed in his wake, plagiarizing, reworking, or creating their own visions. De La Beche's scene gives us a glimpse into a grotesque, almost comically apocalyptic, vision of earth's past that circulated in this period. Crucially, for many, the extinction of ancient and dangerous monsters elicited not regret, but gratitude for Divine foresight and mercy.[50] Present-day sorrow for endangered and extinct species makes it difficult to appreciate how many nineteenth-century naturalists were unconcerned about or

1.7 Animals and plants of Dorset in the Liassic period.

even grateful for vanished ways of being, but this view dominated early to mid-nineteenth century discussions of extinction.

Extinction was widely promoted as a ubiquitous and recurrent natural process in popular scientific writing by the 1830s. The distinguished geologist Charles Lyell wrote one of the most significant works addressing the subject. Lyell's *Principles of Geology* was published in three volumes appearing annually between 1830 and 1833. The great tome proposed that earth's geological features were best explained by observable processes acting uniformly across time, rather than by uniquely powerful catastrophes.[51] The first volume provided a brief sketch of geology as a discipline and discussed the effects of a changing climate, and innumerable earthquakes, floods and volcanoes, on earth's history. The second volume expanded on Lyell's theories of species extinction and distribution. The final volume addressed the vexatious question of the age of the earth. Lyell regarded species as stable and characterized their extinction as naturally ubiquitous, meaning humans held 'no exclusive prerogative' in gaining 'possession of the earth by conquest'. Instead, he urged his readers to accept 'Every species' must have 'marked its progress by the diminution, or the entire extirpation of some other, and must maintain its ground by successful struggle against the encroachments of other plants and animals'.[52] When writing about flora and fauna, Lyell inferred 'if we wield the sword of extermination as we advance we have no reason to repine at the havoc committed'.[53] Lyell's assertions were rooted in a period when nature was considered plentiful and self-renewing, but can still feel shocking to the modern reader.

Specimens of vanished beings were precious intellectual and economic commodities that helped forge impressive reputations. In the darkening days of October 1839, Richard Owen received a puzzling bone from the surgeon John Rule, resident in New Zealand, which was included in the British colony of New South Wales from 1788, and officially a distinct colony between 1841 and 1907. Rule hoped to sell the bone for ten guineas: it was eventually bought by someone else and loaned to the Hunterian Museum in London, where it was publicly displayed, until it was donated to the British Museum in 1873. Owen believed the bone was a bird's femur, but its size suggested something significantly bigger than any known species. Within a month, he showed the bone to his colleagues at the Zoological Society of London and, appealing to Cuvier's method of the correlation of parts, predicted it belonged to a 'gigantic bird of New Zealand' which was a 'heavier and more sluggish species than the *Ostrich*'.[54] Owen hoped to locate a living specimen, or a complete skeleton if the monumental bird no longer survived. In 1843 a missionary sent a fresh consignment of bones to William Buckland, who passed them on to Owen.[55] He reconstructed a bird towering over his tall frame and, later that month, presented his findings to his peers at the Zoological Society (Fig. 1.8).

Owen's reconstruction of the giant extinct bird drew widespread acclaim and, implicitly, faith in the predictive powers of Cuvier's method. Owen's rising star soon earned him the moniker of the 'British Cuvier', deposing previous holders such as Buckland.[56] Unfortunately, Owen's slipperiness meant he omitted important details, both in his original talk and in subsequent publications. When Rule sent the femur to Owen, he included a note: 'I desire to offer for sale a portion or fragment of a bone . . . Part of the femor [sic] of a bird now considered to be wholly extinct.'[57] Owen's ostensible discovery of the moa was based on Rule's tip as much as Cuvier's principles, but he only acknowledged that Rule supplied the bone. Disenchanted by Owen's misconduct, Rule tried to correct the record, but his contribution remained almost unknown until the 1960s, and was only recently outlined more fully by the literary scholar Gowan Dawson.[58] Owen's conduct was regarded as dishonourable by the few fellows who knew the truth. The sorry episode also reveals a great deal about Owen's ambitious self-regard and position within the metropolitan elite. Collectors in the field, especially within the colonies, had unrivalled access to and knowledge of living specimens. They often sent or sold their specimens to well-connected, often wealthier, men in flagship scientific institutions who regarded themselves as having an exclusive authority to name new species, and therefore claim the rights of discovery. Marginalized collectors seeking credit, such as

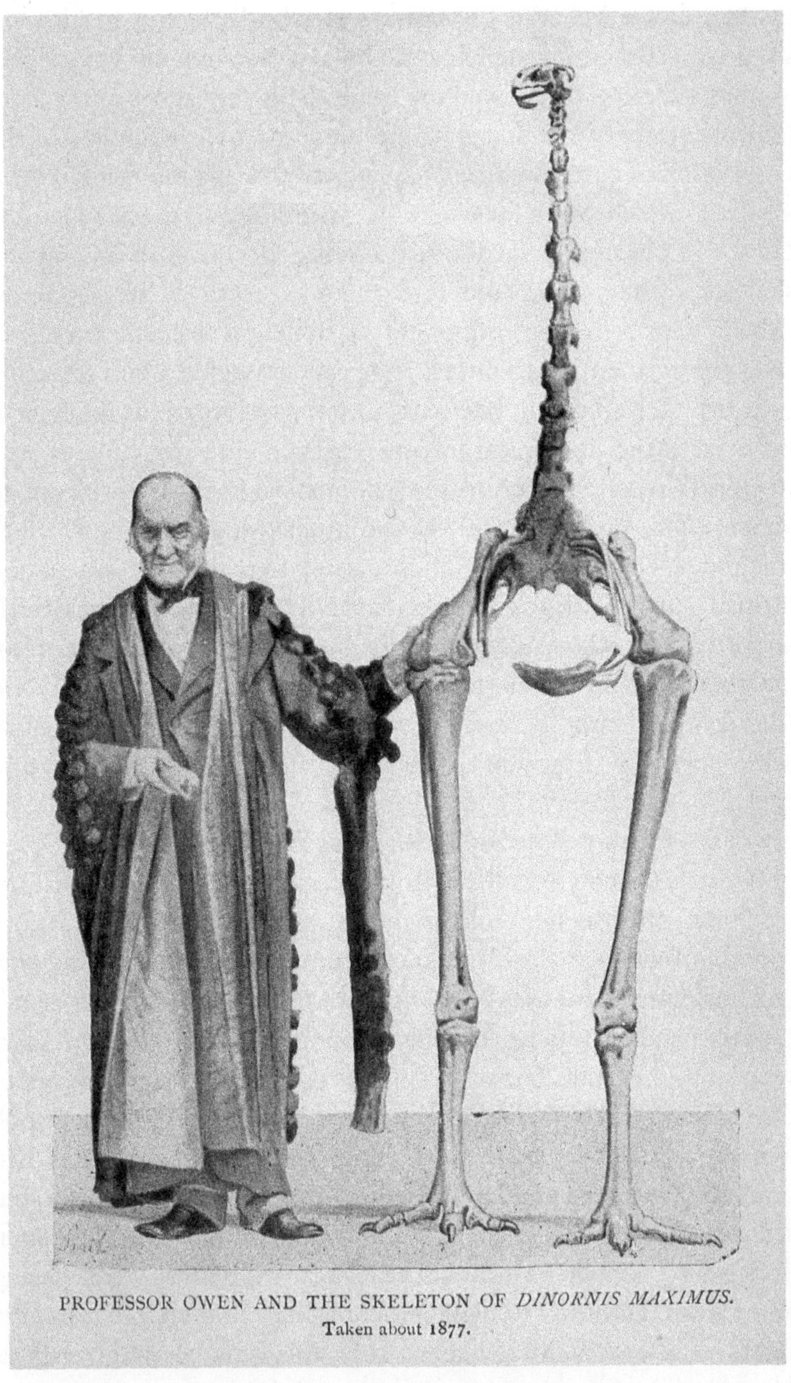

PROFESSOR OWEN AND THE SKELETON OF *DINORNIS MAXIMUS.*
Taken about 1877.

1.8 Richard Owen standing next to the skeleton of the *Dinornis maximus* (the extinct New Zealand moa).

Rule, effectively challenged such entitlement. Sometimes collectors were quite explicit about their expectations. To varying degrees of reciprocity, these fragile relationships of exchange underpinned the collections of many significant scientific collections and institutions in Britain, from Kew Gardens to the British Museum.[59]

The lost worlds of the *Dinosauria* were recreated on Sydenham Hill, London, in 1854 (Fig. 1.9). The landscaped gardens featured spectacular recreations of extinct creatures on three islands emerging from a primeval lake. Models of a hylaeosaur, ichthyosaur, megalosaur, and iguanodon all embellished the middle island. The beasts were fashioned from brick, iron, and cement by the illustrator and sculptor Benjamin Waterhouse Hawkins. His father was an artist, and his mother an heiress to wealth derived from enslaved Africans on a plantation in Jamaica. Hawkins' reputation was founded by illustrating natural history works throughout the 1830s and 1840s. Hawkins had taken up the Sydenham commission in 1852, and was guided by Owen's comments on sketches. Owen reimagined the

1.9 The Crystal Palace at Sydenham.

low-lying crocodilian lizards of earlier writers into more mammal-like positions as reflected in the relatively upright poses of Hawkins' sculptures. On New Year's Eve 1853, Hawkins hosted an eight-course dinner party for twenty-one guests in the *Iguanodon*. Owen sat in the head of the beast, presiding over the table of luminaries. The fanciful revelry was commemorated in the following week's *Illustrated London News*. The image showed a stage constructed around the *Iguanodon*, with waiters climbing a flight of stairs to serve the men nestled like hatchlings literally inside the belly of the beast. The paper observed the 'philosophers' in attendance were 'well pleased with the hospitality of the iguanodon'.[60]

Sydenham also featured a cavernous glass cathedral rising proudly on the hill, which was modelled on the Crystal Palace that housed the Great Exhibition of 1851 three years earlier. The original Crystal Palace showcased arts and manufactures from all over the British Empire to visitors in Hyde Park for months. On closing, a new palace was built in suburban Sydenham, which opened in 1854, and was quickly nicknamed the People's Palace. Both glass edifices were designed by the architect Joseph Paxton, but the Sydenham site was twice the size of the original, featured a substantially different catalogue of exhibits, and was privately owned by the Crystal Palace Company. The original was effectively an international trade fair, but its successor was dedicated to turning a profit by combining private enterprise, national education, entertainment, and spectacle. Effectively a visual encyclopaedia, the People's Palace at Sydenham housed courts devoted to the ancient and classical empires of Egypt, Italy, Greece, Byzantium, and the more modern achievements of the Renaissance and British Empire.[61] Visitors were expected to arrive on site, walk past the scenes of ancient lost worlds, enter the Palace through a court of natural history featuring flora, fauna, and models of colonized peoples, before tracing a progressive history of the rise and fall of civilizations. Anyone following the guidebooks would be encouraged to interpret their journey as retracing a direct path from monsters to imperial Britons. With 1,322,000 visitors in the first year, including 71,000 children, Sydenham proved enormously popular, and remained so, until a fire reduced the site to ashes in 1936.[62] By a stroke of luck, the monsters survived; the Crystal Palace dinosaurs were designated Grade II listed buildings in 1973, and upgraded to Grade I in 2007.[63] Their protected status means they still rise from the waters in the Crystal Palace Park.

Many of Cuvier's reconstructions are still publicly exhibited in the Museum of Natural History in Paris. The landscaped gardens house a zoological park, and two galleries within dedicated buildings. The older collections, including many of Cuvier's specimens, are exhibited in the Gallery of Palaeontology and Comparative Anatomy (*Galerie de Paléontologie et d'Anatomie Comparée*), while the modern displays form a newer Gallery of Evolution (*Grande Galerie de l'Évolution*). Visitors entering the Gallery of Palaeontology and Comparative Anatomy are confronted by a crowd of marching skeletons filed in rows behind a model of a flayed man presiding over the gallery. The rare exhibits include Louis XIV's elephant, Louis XV's rhinoceros, and Steller's sea cow driven to extinction by hunting in 1768. They are exhibited alongside a pod of whales, a herd of giraffes, and other hoofed beasts. On the second floor, the palaeontological specimens include a mammoth, megatherium, dinosaurs, and a glass case showcasing the species that Cuvier identified from the Parisian gypsum.

The newer Gallery of Evolution is an astonishing spectacle of natural history specimens arranged in a central courtyard surrounded by a series of theatrical terraces. One of the side halls displays extinct and endangered species. Entering the grand and sombre hall feels like stepping into a collection of fading sculptures puncturing the darkness. This menagerie of lost ways of being are held captive behind glass under the glare of false suns. Visitors can use virtual-reality glasses to experience extinct beasts around them: Steller's sea cow swims high in the rafters, while dodos peck at the floor, and the thylacine and smilodon (sabre-toothed cat) jump across cabinets as if making their way across uneven high ground. Entranced adults stand marvelling while enthusiastic children desperately try to touch and hold the impossible ghosts. Even though the animals were merely digital flickers, I was still surprised when their vivacious presence triggered a pang of senseless loss as I handed back my glasses.

The theory of extinction gained considerable ground in the late eighteenth and early nineteenth centuries as naturalists shifted from cautious speculation about its possibility to regarding it as an inherent natural process. Cuvier's research on extinct beasts quickly established him as the premier authority on fossils. His important early studies of extinction were focused on megafauna carved from the Parisian rocks, specimens confiscated from European aristocracy, and engravings of beasts he never saw in person. These processes of exchange and circulation among transatlantic and global networks of scientific research helped establish the recurrent and pervasive nature of extinction and changed its epistemic status from a theologically dangerous idea to an ostensibly God-given natural law. Cuvier's legacy encompassed formulating new theories, interpreting evidence, and creating long-standing, publicly accessible museum displays about extinction. Throughout the nineteenth century, ideas of extinction were developed within elite scientific circles, while knowledge about extinction was also created and consumed by an enormous variety of audiences through literature, art, museums, and exhibitions.

Once naturalists acknowledged that mastodons, moas, and dinosaurs all belonged to an ancient lost world, they turned to the fate of the living. Although Cuvier focused on prehistoric animals, naturalists quickly interpreted human encounters, especially within the context of European colonial expansion and the subsequent persecution of many native peoples, as a form of extinction. Many nineteenth-century writers warned that colonized peoples were dying out as a result of colonial contact and conquest. These predictions were issued for decades, particularly in the lands that became Canada, the United States of America, Australia, and Africa. Among the earliest peoples regarded as extinct victims of colonial conquest were those living in Europe's new-found lands.

2.
The Last of Her People

The port city of St John's rises from the eastern side of Newfoundland in the North Atlantic Ocean. The island sits near the Labrador Peninsula at the tip of the Canadian mainland bounded by the Labrador Sea. As North America's closest seaport to Europe, St John's has a long history of transatlantic traffic. In the spring and summer, cruise ships drop anchor and decant their passengers into the city's streets. Most tourists quickly make their way into the bars, restaurants, and boutique gift stores close to the harbour. Others climb Signal Hill for a breathtaking 360-degree view of the ocean and the city's wooden-clad buildings resembling colourful jelly-beans neatly standing to attention. Home to a seventeenth-century fort, Signal Hill is where inventor Guglielmo Marconi first heard the transatlantic radio signal, broadcast from more than two thousand miles away in Poldhu Wireless Station in Cornwall. Tourists often take tours around the island, or to Witless Bay ecological reserve, home to one of the world's largest colonies of puffins. Travel guides enthusiastically recall the island's love of 'God and Cod' in potted histories of migrating settlers who established the local fisheries and numerous churches of different denominations. There is a glaring absence in these practised recollections: the original inhabitants of the island. Their fate is crucial for understanding how new ideas about animal extinction were applied to humans, especially colonized nations.

Islanders and Intruders

The peopling of the Americas is a highly contentious topic among scientists interested in prehistoric human migration. There is a broad consensus that perhaps a few thousand Eurasian people crossed into North America using a long-lost land bridge called Beringia, as well as possible coastal routes along the South Pacific, and that their descendants peopled North and South America. Considerable disagreement remains about when the first crossing of Beringia occurred, how many crossings there might have been, and their exact relationship to coastal routes. From the 1930s, scientists tended towards an estimate of about 13,000 years ago for the first crossings. From the 1970s onwards archaeological finds of older sites in South America raised serious doubts. Within the last decade, DNA evidence has convinced many scientists that North America was extensively settled by at least 15,000 years ago, and the Americas may have been peopled as early as 20,000 to 30,000 years ago.[1]

Many of these ancient migrants settled along the Labrador coast. Archaeologists currently believe that there were three waves of prehistoric peoples who migrated from the Labrador coast and settled on Newfoundland. The first wave of 'Maritime Archaic peoples' flourished on the island between five and three thousand years ago, before disappearing for unknown reasons. The second wave of Early and Late 'Paleo-Eskimos' between 1000 BCE and 800 CE also disappeared for unknown reasons. The third wave of 'Recent Indians' had arrived by 50 BCE and are subdivided into three groups based after the archaeological sites where they were found: 'Cow Head', 'Beaches', and 'Little Passage'.

Islanders formed a small nation enduring into modern times. Attempts to establish how many individuals belonged to this nation is necessarily speculative, but the most cautious and potentially reliable estimates range between 500 and 1,600 individuals descended from the Little Passage peoples by the sixteenth century. Kinship groups probably ranged from thirty to fifty-five individuals, living relatively independently without complicated hierarchies. They adorned their faces and bodies in red ochre in annual ceremonies to mark their ties to each other. Shamans connected the world of spirits to the islanders. Leaders of kinship groups and their closest relatives were laid to rest in burial huts, while others were often wrapped in birchbark or animal skins, laid in the ground, and covered in stones or soil.[2]

Islanders' lives were intimately tied to seasonal bounties and coastlines teeming with seabirds, whales, seals, and fish. The skies formed part of the Atlantic flyway, a path allowing hundreds of migratory bird species to journey between Greenland, the Caribbean, and South America, along the East coast during spring (April to May) and autumn (September to October). Seabirds such as puffins, gannets, razorbills, and the great auk all formed vast breeding communities from May to June. In these months, islanders ventured seawards in canoes, shot birds with arrows, and collected eggs from nearby islands ahead of leaner winters.[3] One writer observed that they ventured 'thither once or twice every year, and return with their canoes laden with birds and eggs; for the number of sea-fowl which resort to this island to breed, are far beyond credibility'.[4] In late summer, Atlantic salmon returned from the sea to spawn a new generation and provide an annual feast. In the autumn, islanders ventured further inland in search of caribou.

Intruding Europeans called the islanders the Beothuk from the 1500s onwards.[5] The name was derived from the islanders' language, but it is impossible to know how accurately Europeans repeated it. Vikings reached the island from Greenland in about 1000 CE, but quickly abandoned the land. The islanders enjoyed centuries of isolation until the Venetian explorer John Cabot sailed across the Atlantic from Bristol in search of a westward route to Asia in May 1497, supported by King Henry VII of England. Cabot sighted a coastline he named New-Found-Land in June. He observed evidence of the Beothuk's lives but never met them.[6] The Portuguese explorer Gasper de Côrte Real made the journey four years later under the auspices of the Portuguese Crown. He captured fifty locals and shipped them to Portugal, but we do not know to which nation they belonged. Cabot's son Sebastian made the same journey eleven years later, seizing more local captives and bringing them back to England.[7] Voyagers routinely enslaved local peoples by sending them to Europe in this period. Explorers and mariners provide the earliest written testimony about life on New-Found-Land. Their words reveal how dangerous it was for the people adorned with red ochre to encounter the Europeans who circulated tales of 'Red Indians'.

Europeans were drawn to the region's waters teeming with fish and whales. English, French, and Iberian seamen hunted for whales and cod along the Labrador coast and around Newfoundland. Initially, they established seasonal fisheries to harvest summer's bounty. With growing traffic between England's southwestern ports and Newfoundland, the English Crown claimed the entire island as a colony in 1610. While Europeans were limited to seasonal presences, the Beothuk took resources they believed were abandoned and reworked them into their own tools. Metal was especially useful, and they often burned abandoned boats and huts to gather nails from the ashes more efficiently, while also taking hooks, axes, and knives. These habits triggered violent reprisals once the English established a permanent settlement, which numbered three thousand by the 1700s. The Beothuk continued taking items they believed were abandoned from coastal settlements and faced severe backlash from irate intruders with very different notions of private property. Competition for resources, especially food, escalated tensions even further. Europeans treated the Beothuk as raiders illegitimately pilfering metal and food, often subjecting them to violent attacks. The Beothuk faced new diseases and were deprived of safe access to their coastal hunting grounds. As a result they increasingly shunned contact with the intruders and endured increasingly precarious lives marked by gnawing hunger. During the early eighteenth century, Europeans moved further inland following the same rivers and waterways to fish for salmon. Progressively more reliant on caribou, the Beothuk grew increasingly desperate to defend their dwindling territory, subsistence, and survival.[8]

Eyewitness testimonies record alarm at the lawlessness of settlers and their treatment of the Beothuk. One of the most detailed and extended accounts was penned by a British colonist named George Cartwright. He entered the military as a fifteen-year-old boy, rose to a captaincy, and accompanied his brother, the naval officer John Cartwright, on voyages around the Newfoundland coast between 1766 and 1768. On these trips George noted of the Beothuk: 'it is thought they were then considerably more numerous than they are at present'.[9] He settled into a life of trading fish and seal while writing a journal. His writing consistently recorded his visceral shock at the actions of settlers:

> I am sorry to add, that the latter are much greater savages than the Indians themselves, for they seldom fail to shoot the poor creatures whenever they can, and afterwards boast of it as a very meritorious action. With horror I have heard several declared, they would rather kill an Indian than a deer![10]

As evidence of settler barbarity, he reported a raiding party killing a Beothuk woman despite her pleas for mercy by pointing to her swollen, pregnant belly; they mutilated her body, then boasted of their violence to their peers. Despite recounting such an 'inhumanity', George Cartwright insisted he knew of actions so 'diabolically shocking' that he refused to discuss them further in print. His euphemistic evasion might have referred to sexual violence, but, even if not, the refusal to disclose further details given the appalling acts he did write about is notable.[11] Believing only 500 Beothuk remained alive, Cartwright wrote to the Colonial Office in London with a proposal on 'The Case of the Wild or Red Indians of Newfoundland with a Plan for their relief' in 1774. He warned that without intervention the Beothuk were an 'unhappy race of mortals' who 'will soon be extirpated'.[12] He suggested removing the Beothuk to a reservation under his supervision, but the British government instead chose inaction. Cartwright's three-volume journal was published in 1792, bringing the Beothuk's plight to a new audience.

Fellow colonists also failed to elicit assistance from the British government. The sailor Christopher Pulling passed through

Newfoundland as he ventured from Halifax, Nova Scotia, to England, in 1785. Pulling suggested that the government establish a new trading relationship with the Beothuk to ameliorate entrenched hostilities, but he was rebuffed. After a prolific career in England authoring legal disquisitions, John Reeves served as Newfoundland's Chief Justice from 1780 until 1792 when he returned to England. Writing to Parliament, he explicitly outlined the appalling violence inflicted upon the Beothuk: 'instead of being traded with, they are plundered, instead of being taught, they are pursued with Outrage and with Murder'.[13] Even this brief catalogue of pleas bears witness to rampant violence targeting the Beothuk, and numerous vain attempts to secure parliamentary intervention. Even while advocating for imperial rule, Newfoundland's colonial administrators explicitly recognized that settlers were persecuting the Beothuk.

Occasionally, officials explicitly articulated the Beothuk's dispossession. Vice Admiral William Waldegrave governed the island between 1797 and 1799 and issued fresh proclamations forbidding ill treatment of the Beothuk. Despite this, the local magistrate John Bland wrote to Waldegrave expressing alarm that Europeans were failing to respect the Beothuk's rights:

> It ought to be remembered that the Savages have a right to this Island, and every invasion of a natural right, is the violation of a Principle of Justice. They have been progressively driven from South to North, and their removal has been produced by a slow and silent operation, it has nevertheless had all the effect of a violent compulsion . . . before the lapse of another Century, the English nation . . . may have affixed to its character the indelible reproach of having extirpated a whole race of people.[14]

Bland beseeched officials to enforce a 'humane plan of rescuing this people from oppression' as soon as possible.[15] He recognized the Beothuk's 'natural right' in terms his contemporaries understood, and possibly shared. Framing his defence as a question of justice and rights makes clear that the assertion of the Beothuk's rights to their land, and by extension the land rights of other colonized peoples, was of concern to early colonists. Bland's questioning is an exceptionally important reminder that we must not assume early colonists were a homogeneous mass who felt unequivocally entitled to land, or that contemporary debates about Indigenous land rights are the sole preserve of present-day activists who misunderstand the historical record. Rather, as Bland's letter suggests, present-day debates often continue precisely because much older arguments and conflicts never established complete consensus, let alone explicit ceding of land based on shared notions of consent or property rights. Waldegrave continued petitioning for government aid without success.[16] Bland's calculation that an entire people might be lost within two or three generations proved disturbingly prescient.

Entangled Fates

In the early nineteenth century the lives of one Beothuk family were entangled with the final bouts of violent dispossession and its legacies more than anyone else from their nation. Demasduit, also known as Mary March, was born in 1796. She married Nonosabasut and they had a child together by 1819. Nonosabasut's year of birth is unknown, but he was probably older than his wife. As leader of his group, he is often called a chief. His niece Shanawdithit, also known as Nancy or Nancy April, was born in about 1801 and possibly as late as 1806. Shanawdithit had one sister whose original name is lost, but was often called Easter Eve, and their mother was called Doodebewshet. Shanawdithit was born into a colony where officials struggled to impose their authority over settlers and to improve relations with the Beothuk, such as Governor John Duckworth who promised to reward anyone who helped with a hundred pounds in 1810.[17] We know exceptionally little about the family's early lives, and far more about their deaths, because they encountered Europeans trying to find the last of the Beothuk before the entire nation was extinct.

In 1811 young Shanawdithit witnessed an inauspicious attempt to contact her people. Governor Duckworth tasked the naval officer Lieutenant David Buchan with leading an expedition to try to track down the Beothuk. In January 1811, Buchan successfully discovered an encampment. He approached the mamateeks (tents), removed the animal skins barring entrance, and found 'groups of men, women and children lying in the utmost consternation; they remained absolutely for some minutes without emotion or utterance.'[18] His narrative gives a sense of the Beothuk's profound fear, his surprise, and attempts to allay their concerns. He spent three and a half hours trying to prove he meant no harm through shaking hands, offering gifts, and food such as cuts of venison. Once the Beothuk acknowledged his presence, he asked if he could collect gifts for them from his base camp. The Beothuk agreed and four of them accompanied Buchan, while two of his party remained behind as a gesture of reciprocity. As Buchan's party neared his camp, three of the accompanying Beothuk grew suspicious and ran away. Fearful of misunderstanding, Buchan trekked back to the hastily deserted Beothuk camp in bitter weather and left blankets, clothing, and pots as gifts. Buchan asked the remaining Beothuk guide to find his people and provide reassurances, but he also grew suspicious and fled when they reached a Beothuk camp where Buchan discovered the decapitated bodies of his two officers in the snow.[19] Buchan hastily retreated, and spent another two years trying to 'bring the natives into civil society' and 'wipe away a certain degree of stigma brought on us by the former barbarity of our countrymen'.[20] He did not realize it, but watchful Beothuk, including Shanawdithit, tracked him as he searched in vain.

Just a few years later, Shanawdithit witnessed the abduction of her aunt Demasduit. John Peyton Junior, and his father John Peyton Senior, ran salmon fisheries from which hungry Beothuk took fish and tools such as knives or traps. Peyton Junior claimed he generally ignored the loss of smaller items, but he retaliated after a group of Beothuk took a large consignment of fish and more valuable articles such as silver watches while damaging some guns. Angered, Junior sought permission from Governor Charles Hamilton to search for the items and those he held responsible. After securing Hamilton's authorization, father, son, and their men hiked up the Exploits River in March 1819, passing abandoned Beothuk camps, before veering northeast towards Red Indian Lake in March. Around the waters, one of the men fired his musket causing hidden Beothuk to flee. Tailing the party, Peyton Junior captured an exhausted Demasduit. Nonosabasut tried freeing his wife. A scuffle ensued and Peyton's men stabbed Nonosabasut with a bayonet and fired several shots terrifying the remainder of the Beothuk. Nonosabasut lost his life. Grief-stricken and separated from her child, Demasduit was led away by captors who believed she was twenty-three years old while the child, said to be a daughter in some testimonies, died two days later. Shanawdithit witnessed the entire affair, later recounting the events in drawings, and providing evidence implying that her nation might have dwindled to seventy-two adults and children.[21]

Demasduit was renamed Mary March and taken to Twillingate, on New World island on the Atlantic coast, where she was held at the home of Reverend John Leigh. As she learned English, Reverend Leigh compiled a Beothuk vocabulary and distributed it to fellow missionaries. Ailing and frail with consumption, Demasduit's health deteriorated. Lieutenant Buchan tried to return her to her people in the hope that she might act as a go-between. Foul weather forced delays, but the party finally set sail in November 1819. Demasduit died on 8 January 1820. Buchan then resolved to return her body to her people. The expedition ventured upriver in treacherous conditions and found few traces of the Beothuk. Buchan found an abandoned camp and, extraordinarily, a body they believed was Nonosabasut in a makeshift Beothuk burial ground. Buchan left Demasduit's coffin suspended in a mamateek along with a doll and ornaments she had received while captive. He observed that 'so little was the change in the features that imagination would fancy life not yet extinct'.[22] After Buchan left, a group of Beothuk tracking him approached Demasduit's coffin and removed the clothing within. A month later, they placed the coffin on the ground and, another two months later, she was buried in the same place as her husband.[23] Shanawdithit was among the group who witnessed Buchan leave her aunt behind.

Shanawdithit, her sister Easter Eve, and their mother Doodebewshet were captured shortly after Demasduit's death. In 1823 settlers hoping to receive the government's reward for capturing Beothuk survivors found a lone elderly woman and her husband. He escaped, but later drowned after falling through ice. They took Doodebewshet to John Peyton Senior. Two weeks later, the men captured Doodebewshet's daughters. The three women were taken to Peyton Senior at Exploits, Burnt Island, but they were moved by Peyton Junior to St John's Courthouse after he alerted Buchan of the prisoners' whereabouts and poor health. Buchan believed the women were about forty-three, twenty-four, and twenty years old. Visitors to the Courthouse observed Doodebewshet was particularly 'morose' and 'looked with dread or hatred on everyone that entered the courthouse'.[24] Today we might interpret her demeanour as profound shock and trauma unrecognized by almost everyone around her.

Buchan arranged for Peyton Junior to return Doodebewshet and her daughters to the Exploits River. Peyton built them a house, provided a boat, and regularly left food for them. Weeks passed. Doodebewshet tended to her daughter's quickening consumption. Eve finally succumbed, followed by her mother. Shanawdithit remained with Peyton Junior's family for five years. She was visited by Bishop John Inglis. He lamented the Beothuk had not been converted to Christianity, which he equated with the progress of civilization, and that Shanawdithit had not learned enough English to be baptized. He noted her fear that her family had probably starved to death. He left beseeching her to convert, and hoping she might convey his faith to her people.[25] She later divulged that she believed only about fifteen of her people remained alive when she was captured. Her precise status, or how she felt about what amounted to house arrest, is difficult to pinpoint. Nicknamed Nancy April after the month of her capture, she occasionally slipped away to visit the graves of her mother and sister and talk to them. A fellow servant described these visits as the result of 'melancholy moods' and called her 'foolish' for believing she was speaking to her mother and sister, but Shanawdithit insisted: 'yes they here, me see them and talk to them'.[26] This minute trace of her ties of kinship is starkly distinctive from so many stories about her. In these words we encounter her refusal to forgo meaningful solace while enduring an isolation barely understood by everyone around her, even those convinced she was the last of her people.[27]

William Epps Cormack founded the Beothuk Institution (originally 'Boeothick') in St John's, Newfoundland, in 1827. A merchant, explorer and natural historian, Cormack hoped his new venture might ensure 'a reconciliation of the Aborigines, to the approaches of civilization'. Despite acknowledging that settler violence made the Beothuk wary of contact with the intruders, he vowed 'I will by degrees have them civilized'.[28] Cormack made several expeditions to find Beothuk in the early years of the nineteenth century, but without success. Given this interest in survivors, he and his peers at the institution resolved that Shanawdithit ought to be 'under the paternal care' of the institution.[29] After Peyton Junior received compensation, Shanawdithit moved to St John's. While she learned English, Cormack continued searching for the Beothuk, but he never found any alive. When he stumbled across the bodies of Demasduit and Nonosabasut, he stole their skulls and various artefacts. After failing to find any living Beothuk on several expeditions, Cormack concluded they were in imminent danger of extirpation – or already extinct.[30]

Shanawdithit remained with Cormack in St John's, where he tried to elicit information about her life and where people were increasingly convinced that she was the last of the Beothuk (Fig. 2.1). He taught her English, methodically interviewed her about Beothuk life, and collected the drawings and artefacts she made with the paper and coloured pencils he provided. Her sketches confirm she witnessed the killing of Lieutenant Buchan's men in 1811, and the capture of her aunt Demasduit. Shanawdithit's recollections are the only surviving testimony from the Beothuk of these events.[31] She confided that her people believed anyone reconciling with settlers would never

2.1 Shanawdithit, c. 1820s.

find happiness in the afterlife or be buried with the material artefacts that they needed for the journey. Moreover, individuals making or seeking contact were often sacrificed to the *munes* (spirits).[32] These confidences reveal the precautions the Beothuk took to protect themselves from colonial encounter and encroachment. It is impossible to know whether such threats were acted upon, but even their circulation suggests that the Beothuk deliberately prohibited contact with the intruders for decades. Cormack's unpublished notes and materials are mostly lost, but some drawings and artefacts survive in the museum vaults at St John's. Shanawdithit's drawings are rarely exposed to light for fear of damage and are only accessible by special request. Delicate pencil sketches, they look fragile enough to be rubbed out with even the lightest of touches. Shanawdithit drew her own people, or details about them, with a red pencil, while outsiders were all drawn in black. They bear Cormack's annotations recording additional details from her. One of the most moving is a map depicting the capture of Demasduit, from the memories of her niece. They are among the most important records of Beothuk life ever produced by a Beothuk individual, and the only records produced by a Beothuk individual that survive in a colonial archive. Viewing them is an exceptionally painful confrontation with the entangled legacies of empire and extinction.

Shanawdithit died on 6 June 1829; she was described in the parish register as 'very probably the last of the aborigines' of Newfoundland.[33] Cormack sent an obituary to *The Times* of London about the 'interesting female [who] lived six years a captive among the English'. He noted 'there has been a primitive nation, once claiming rank as a portion of the human race, who have lived, flourished, and become extinct in their own orbit'. Cormack described the process as being 'dislodged, and disappeared from the earth'.[34] The local doctor, William Carson, conducted a post-mortem, and used the procedure to remove Shanawdithit's scalp and skull. Her remains were buried in a graveyard in St John's harbour. Carson sent her skull to London's Royal College of Physicians as a specimen of presumed scientific interest. The remains were moved to the Royal College of Surgeons in 1938, and are believed to have been destroyed by a German bomb during the Second World War.[35] Sightings of other Beothuk were reported after Shanawdithit's death in 1829, but she quickly gained notoriety as the 'last' of her people.

Enduring Nations

Writers repeatedly described the Beothuk as extinct throughout the nineteenth and early twentieth centuries in scholarly publications, newspapers and periodicals. Seven years after Shanawdithit's death, her biography served as a cautionary tale about 'the last of the Boëothics' in a series on 'Sketches of Savage Life' in *Fraser's Magazine*. Her death was lamented as the extinguishing of a people who 'passed from the face of the earth, ignorant of the good or evil of civilisation; and yet their name will be recorded in the annals of the western world'. The author observed 'it must not be forgotten they were shot by the English and French fishermen and traders, with as little scruple as if the Boëothics were red foxes'.[36] Bishop Inglis wrote about his meeting with Shanawdithit for the Society for the Propagation of the Gospel in Foreign Parts in 1856, and explicitly named her the last of her people. The anthropologist T. G. B. Lloyd conducted significant research on the Beothuk in the 1870s. Lloyd's research was presented at the Anthropological Institute of Great Britain and Ireland in 1875. He was unable to present the paper in person, but it was read out at a meeting by the Director of the Anthropological Institute and later published in the Institute's journal. Lloyd's article outlined a brief history of colonial settlement in Newfoundland and longer summaries of relevant ethnographic information. At the reading, several items were exhibited for the society's fellows, including a lock of Shanawdithit's hair, a tooth taken from a Beothuk woman (presumably without consent after her death, but not specified), and spears. Lloyd reported that the Beothuk were supposedly extinct, but did caution that 'of their ultimate fate nothing is known with certainty'.[37] The geologist James P. Howley compiled an anthology of primary sources over four decades in the late nineteenth and early twentieth centuries, including interviews with Peyton Junior and others who directly encountered the Beothuk. His research was published as a book in 1915, which described the Beothuk as extinct.[38] Howley's book, and claims about extinction, became one of the most important sources for all future histories of the Beothuk.

The anthropologist Frank G. Speck challenged the consensus regarding Beothuk extinction in the early twentieth century. He trained with Franz Boas, who is widely recognized as transforming American anthropology, and the discipline more broadly, in the later nineteenth and early twentieth centuries. Boas argued that culture was not a universal absolute because 'each and every civilization is the outcome of its geographical and historical surroundings'.[39] He urged anthropologists to research peoples, and their cultures, within their own context as this was the only way to understand both humanity's evolution and the nature and meaning of culture. His cultural relativism influenced generations of anthropologists, including Speck, who gained his PhD in 1908 and was an expert in Native languages, and a passionate collector. One obituary of Speck noted that Native nations 'became his life. His office and his home literally became museums filled with material culture of these people.' Moreover, 'From the ashes of destruction he moved about in the north-east salvaging scraps of cultures that everyone else believed to be long dead.'[40] Speck's fieldwork in Newfoundland was published in his book *Beothuk and Micmac* in 1822. Drawing on interviews with local peoples, Speck reasoned that his colleagues' conviction about Beothuk extinction was rooted in a failure to appreciate that interviewees might not want to divulge the true extent of intermarriage among the Beothuk and Mi'kmaq.

Despite Speck's doubts about Beothuk extinction, he was still surprised in 1910 when he met Santu Toney, an elderly woman of Beothuk heritage (Fig. 2.2). He recollected:

> In July, 1910, I happened to talk over ethnological matters with a family of Micmac who were temporarily camped near Gloucester, Mass. The family consisted of an aged woman, her son, his wife and child. They all spoke Micmac. The family name was Toney. On inquiring of the young man, Joe Toney, where he was born, he told me in Newfoundland. Then becoming more interested, I inquired if his mother was a native of Newfoundland, and he replied that she was. After a few minutes' talk with his mother, he said that she was not a true Micmac, but that her father was an *Osa'yan'a* Indian from Red Pond, Newfoundland. This naturally startled me, because it referred indirectly to the supposedly extinct Beothuk.[41]

Knowing that the Mi'kmaq's tongue referred to the Beothuk as *Osa'yan'a*, Speck delved further. He was intrigued by Santu's family ties, both as evidence of movement between Native nations in Newfoundland, and also as a possible insight into the fate of the Beothuk.

2.2 Santu Toney, with her son Joe Toney.

Over several months, Speck interviewed Santu with Joe's help as a translator. Speck established that Santu's mother was a Mi'kmaq from Nova Scotia. Santu's father, named Kop, was raised among the Mi'kmaq, but she believed that he was not a true Mi'kmaq. Instead, she confided he was taken and raised among the Mi'kmaq, but born near Red Pond (Red Indian Lake), and coated in red ochre when a child. Santu's mother died when she was relatively young, and she subsequently moved to Nova Scotia with her father. Santu was married twice: initially to a Mohawk man and, after his death, a Mi'kmaq man with whom she had four or five children, including Joe Toney. Remarkably, Santu remembered a song she learned from her father. Speck recorded her singing and it remains the only known trace of Beothuk song. He regarded Santu's Beothuk descent as entirely plausible given the extent of intermarriage between the Mi'kmaq and Beothuk, but noted: 'My only distrust of the material she was able to give lies in the accuracy of her memory, especially in regard to her vocabulary.'[42] Speck corresponded with Howley about Santu, but Howley dismissed Santu's testimony and framed the Beothuk as extinct in his published work. In recent years, the historian Chris Aylward interviewed Santu's granddaughter and great-granddaughter, Ivy Toney and Ardy Landry, for his documentary *The Beothuk Story* (2021) which traces Beothuk migration and intermingling with other nations.[43] This research is important, but there are even more significant accounts of Beothuk migration and endurance.

Chief Mi'sel Joe of the Miawpukek First Nation in Newfoundland and Labrador is a significant critic of established narratives of Beothuk extinction. He notes: 'Among all of us, there is Beothuk blood somewhere in our genes, through the intermarriage that took place . . . Not only through Conne River, but particularly on the west coast of Newfoundland.'[44] Mi'kmaq oral histories recall Beothuk fleeing to the mainland as settlers encroached on their territories to find new communities. European records of Beothuk intermarrying with Mi'kmaq corroborate Chief Joe's historical knowledge. Even if the imperial archive did not substantiate his history, anyone dismissing his claim in favour of colonial officials documenting extinction would be wise to reflect on whose evidence they are willing to treat as plausible, reliable, or true – and why. Claims of Beothuk extinction favour written histories, especially the preserved paperwork of state bureaucracy, over other forms of historical knowledge, particularly oral histories. Whether implicitly or explicitly, this tendency denies that peoples with long-standing practices of oral record-keeping have reliable ways of transmitting historical knowledge that historians of extinction, and empire more broadly, must acknowledge, respect, and incorporate into their own scholarship.[45]

Scientific research on Beothuk remains has consistently tried to unravel their migration and fate. When William Cormack disturbed the grave of Nonosabasut and Demasduit in 1827, he stole the couple's skulls, a model of a birchbark canoe, clothing, and other artefacts. He sent them to his former university tutor Robert

Jameson, a professor of natural history at the University of Edinburgh for fifty years and curator at the University's Museum. On accession the couple's names were replaced with registration numbers: 1827.25.1 for Nonosabasut and 1825.25.2 for Demasduit. Their individual identities were erased and replaced with attributed codes of scientific cataloguing to seal claims of newly transferred ownership. In the 1850s, the skulls were absorbed into the collections that ultimately became the National Museums of Scotland. The surgeon and naturalist George Busk examined the skulls of Nonosabasut and Demasduit as 'two authentic specimens' of the 'aboriginal Indian inhabitants' of Newfoundland and wrote an illustrated description published in 1876.[46] Cormack publicly acknowledged finding the grave but not his theft.

At some point, perhaps by Cormack's hand or more likely a museum worker, the skulls were desecrated with inscriptions. Nonosabasut's skull was labelled a 'Male Red Indian Newfoundland', 'chief', 'Mr Cormack', and '1827–25', and 'Mongolian' later scratched over. Other annotations were too faded to read when osteologists examined the skulls in 2009. The words 'Female Red Indian Newfoundland' were scrawled across Demasduit's skull.[47] The violation performed multiple functions valued by scientists and museum workers from the nineteenth century to the present day: the text authenticated the bones in terms of geography, racialized them in nineteenth-century scientific terminology, and traced their passage across the Atlantic through Cormack's theft. These processes transformed the bones of Nonosabasut and Demasduit into prized anatomical specimens eagerly examined to understand Beothuk anatomy, evolution, and extinction, rather than their lives, inner worlds, or burials. Their treatment is just one example from a much longer history of Europeans collecting skulls to forge disturbing hierarchies of value between humans.[48]

DNA samples from the stolen skulls of Nonosabasut and Demasduit are still incorporated into scientific studies tracing Beothuk migration and descent.[49] In the early 2000s a group of scientists applied to the National Museums of Scotland for access, and were granted permission to examine the skulls with techniques that make for distressing reading. The team removed a tooth from each skull, cut their roots open, drilled out the inner tissue, dissolved the powdered remains into a liquid solution, extracted mitochondrial DNA, cloned the DNA to 'amplify' the samples, and used them to explore the ancestry of Nonosabasut and Demasduit.[50] Mitochondria are tiny organelles living inside living cells with a nucleus, with their own DNA. Mitochondria provide useful markers to track matrilineal descent because they are only inherited through the maternal line. In an article published in 2007, the team concluded that the Beothuk probably shared ancestors with present-day Mi'kmaq, and that Nonosabasut and Demasduit had no European ancestry. Almost a decade later, after extracting DNA from prehistoric inhabitants of Newfoundland and the Beothuk, another study concluded that northeastern North America and Newfoundland were populated by waves of migration by peoples sharing a common ancestor not in the recent past, but significantly earlier than any arrivals on the island.[51]

Many studies of skulls, from the nineteenth century to the present, were either conducted without consent, or consent from institutions such as museums, with very few securing consent from the closest surviving kin, communities, or nations. In 2019 a new study revisited the issue of the migration and persistence in collaboration with the Miawpukek First Nation. Chief Mi'sel Joe argued that the new research would allow First Nations finally to tell their history from their own perspective. The published article concluded that Beothuk mitochondrial DNA persisted in present-day peoples such as Mi'kmaq. Press reports featured brief histories of colonization, claims of Beothuk extinction, and barely concealed disbelief at the corroboration of oral histories.[52] Historic claims of extinction have created such powerful expectations of total annihilation that many remain shocked by the mere possibility of a continued existence for the Beothuk.

Genetic testing traces Beothuk migration in new ways, but its commercial use is highly controversial. The biotechnology company Viaguard/Accu-Metrics provides commercial forensic services, paternity testing, and genetic screening for cancer. The company originally offered genealogy testing specializing in either 'First Nation, Metis and Native American DNA' or 'African Ancestry DNA'.[53] When the retired teacher Carol Reynolds-Boyce used their services in 2016, they were the only firm claiming the capacity to test for Beothuk ancestry.[54] Boyce sent her DNA to Accu-Metrics and received results suggesting she might have Beothuk ancestors, while her mother and brother were given the same assurances. When the results were reported in the press, geneticists insisted no one had enough information to make direct connections between living people and known Beothuk individuals through DNA testing.[55] Nonetheless, Reynolds-Boyce's declared herself the Chief of the Beothuk First Nation – after her mother and brother elected her – and started a Facebook group dedicated to the 'Beothuk Tribe of Newfoundland and North America Reservation Nation'.[56] Reynolds-Boyce insisted that the DNA test was merely proof of what she already knew, but the company subsequently withdrew their claims about testing for specific racial identities.

The reliability of Viaguard/Accu-Metrics testing has raised broader concerns. In 2018 a Canadian man Louis Côté used the company's services to trace his ancestry. He submitted three samples. Two of them were swabs of his own cheek but labelled with his own name, and his father's. The last sample was taken from a pet chihuahua, but labelled with his adopted son's name. The results were all identical and claimed all three individuals had Indigenous ancestry. Côté sent the samples to the company for testing, including of his dog, because he grew suspicious of the tests while working with the Confederation of Aboriginal People of Canada. The press scandal centred on the possibility that the tests were providing false evidence of Indigenous ancestry.[57] While the case raises exceptionally difficult questions for Viaguard/Accu-Metrics, focusing on reliable testing does not address the more significant issue of what the results might meaningfully prove.

Ancestry services are popular ways of exploring family histories and descent, but their meanings are significantly more uncertain than slick promotional campaigns suggest. Customers' samples are used to create a DNA fingerprint which is compared for its statistical similarity to a database of reference populations using algorithms. Based on these comparisons, companies provide customers with estimates of percentages of the DNA matching different ancestral groups to varying degrees of specificity, including ancient groups, continents, or more specific categories such as countries. DNA fingerprinting is exceptionally accurate, but any claim about *ancestry* depends entirely on the reference populations, which is why many results are supplied with levels of confidence to support the claims. Commercial companies currently use multiple sources for their references: the Human Genome Diversity Project, International HapMap Project, 1000 Genomes Project, and private initiatives. The skulls of Nonosabasut and Demasduit have been reliably identified by a strong trail of independent evidence. Things are much trickier when this is not possible and reference populations rely on individual self-reporting or small sample sizes. Self-reporting is not inherently false, but many customers do not appreciate that ancestry services rely on the self-identification of their *reference* populations as being *a priori* true. At least one commercial company relies on individuals who report their grandparents were all born in the same country to support subsequent claims about ancestry.[58] Ultimately, these problems might be surmounted with better data, but they would still not necessarily establish recognized connections to any Native nation.

Commercial ancestry testing makes it commonplace for customers to claim they belong to a Native nation after receiving their results. Kim TallBear specializes in unravelling the complicated politics of ancestry testing and racial science. Her book *Native American DNA: Tribal Belonging and the False Promise of Genetic Science* (2013) explores how people relying on DNA to claim belonging privilege ancestry testing over other forms of kinship or belonging. Ancestry testing depends on trying to establish, and impose, the authority of DNA testing above other kinds of evidence. This biological essentialism reduces kinship to molecules over relationships, and ignores each nation's own criteria for who belongs, and its sovereign right to decide the boundaries of the nation.[59] As TallBear argues, ancestry testing continues a profoundly harmful history of trying to define race in discrete and concrete biological terms, while ignoring Native sovereignty, kinship, and relations in defining who is Native.

While historic paths of Beothuk migration remain elusive, the journeys of Beothuk bodies and arts to museums and medical collections all over the world are well documented. The skulls of Nonosabasut and Demasduit languished in Edinburgh for nearly two centuries, taken and experimented on without the consent of their closest living communities, until Chief Mi'sel Joe started a campaign to secure their return home in 2015. He visited the skulls and repeatedly asked for their return. A meeting of the Scottish Parliament in the same year discussed possibilities for return. A Member of the Scottish Parliament enquired about the Scottish government's plans for the 'remains of the last two members of the Beothuk tribe'. The Cabinet Secretary confirmed museum officials met campaigners and explained the 'established mechanism for making a formal repatriation request', and noted they expected an official claim soon. The MSP welcomed the news and stated:

> the keeping of skulls is surely not a 21st-century response to the common humanity that we share with these two individuals, who were the last recorded individuals of this tribe, which was wiped out probably because of environmental pressures on their hunting grounds, as well as by cultural pressures. Perhaps it would be an appropriate response to that shared humanity to ensure that, when the request comes, it is dealt with speedily and in a humane fashion, so that we can set the matter to rest.[60]

Early repatriation procedures often required direct descendants to make claims; more recently, this has broadened to include collective requests from communities with established historical connections and cultural continuities.

The Canadian government issued a formal request for the return of Nonosabasut and Demasduit in 2018, with the museum's trustees accepting the claim in 2019. The couple's skulls were initially transferred to the Canadian Museum of History, Ottawa, and moved again to the Museum at St John's.[61] Chief Joe noted that while the Beothuk no longer existed as a distinctive nation, their closest First Nations were ready to welcome them home: 'There is no Beothuk First Nation community, but once they are back in Newfoundland, the government and the First Nations will decide.'[62] Unfortunately, many others will be denied their last rites and eternal rest until they attract the same dedication. Since the 1990s, the theorist Robert Gerald Vizenor has suggested the importance of recognizing 'Survivance' as the 'active sense of presence' that serves to renounce the erasure of Native lives within so many histories of America, as well as accounts of extinction.[63] His insistence on the 'active' nature of survivance is an important reminder that, despite the repeated claims of settlers and scientists, these histories are living legacies that require redress.

Museums are far too often someone's unwanted grave or prison. Countless people were taken, in whole or in part, without consent and incorporated into practices of trade, collection, acquisition, and display. They lie in stores in violation of the wishes of the dead, their descendants, peoples, or beliefs. Museums have acknowledged and wrestled with this inheritance for decades with relatively little public interest beyond those most directly affected, whether descendants or nations. The British government passed the Human Tissue Act in 2004 in response to a scandal in which some hospitals retained organs, primarily of children, for research without consent. Grieving parents and relatives were distraught knowing their children were denied being whole for their last rites. In response to these horrific revelations, the Act established new legal protections for anyone whose death fell within the last century. The Act also included a section allowing museums to deaccession and repatriate people, whole or otherwise, less than a thousand years old, after requests from Australian and Tasmanian peoples for the return of their ancestors.[64] Some museums have already repatriated ancestors, while others are in the process of identifying descendants and nations in the hope of securing their return. Other institutions refuse to countenance repatriation and reparation.

The cemetery where Shanawdithit was laid to rest was marked for redevelopment in 1903. Her original resting place is now marked by a stone landmark bearing a plaque a few hundred feet from where her original grave may have been. A bronze statue of her also stands at the Beothuk Interpretation Centre in Boyd's Cove, Newfoundland. A newer memorial plaque in Bannerman Park, St John's, marks her as a person of national historic significance.[65] First revealed in 2007, the plaque includes inscriptions in English and French that state:

> Shanawdithit is remembered as the last of the Beothuk. Seized by English settlers in 1823, this young woman never regained her freedom. She taught her captors much of what is now known of the decline and dispersal of her people, even though she held no hope for the survival. Aided by her sketches, she described encounters between the British and Beothuk, including the capture of her aunt Demasduit. Shanawdithit died on June 6, 1829 and was buried in St John's. Her legacy gives a unique insight into the final chapter of her people's history.

The plaque adorns a large grey boulder resembling a roughly hewn headstone that is surrounded by flowers. Visiting the memorial feels almost like standing at a grave where anyone might wish Shanawdithit, her uncle, and aunt, the undisturbed rest they were denied by settlers intent on finding the last of the Beothuk.

Shanawdithit's image and biography have served as the face of violent imperial dispossession from the time of her death, but this can easily perpetuate damaging myths of total annihilation. Claims of Beothuk extinction often depend on a range of unwarranted assumptions. Most obviously, it assumes that in the nine years between Shanawdithit's capture and her death, all other Beothuk died. Yet, her family group numbered twelve or thirteen strong and some may have outlived her. It also assumes there was little or no migration between Beothuk and other nations, but multiple forms of evidence suggest otherwise, including genetic testing, colonial archives, and, more reliably, oral histories of First Nations. This is especially true of Santu Toney's testimony, about both her Beothuk heritage, her parents, and other couples.

As the remnants of Nonosabasut, Demasduit, and Shanawdithit traversed the Atlantic Ocean, claims that the Beothuk were extinct grew into broader assumptions about the fate of colonized peoples. Lamenting Beothuk extinction, scholars predicted that other peoples would soon be nothing but a memory. The physician James Cowles Prichard addressed the issue in an article 'On the Extinction of Human Races' in 1839. Best remembered as a founding father of modern anthropology, he spent his life collecting and analysing accounts of human difference to prove humans were a single species. He believed that 'Wherever Europeans have settled, their arrival has been the harbinger of extermination to the native tribes.' Prichard's intellectual concern for the loss of data about human variation was intertwined with moral alarm and calls to 'prevent the extermination of the aboriginal tribes'.[66] While he was sensitive to the contrast between decline through violent persecution and the inherent loss in nature, his peers slowly stopped observing the distinction.[67] Repeatedly reframing dispossession, persecution, and extermination as part of a process of natural extinction created more than just a rhetorical slippage between death and prophesied doom. As the century wore on, the Beothuk were frequently named as early casualties in a lengthening list of peoples doomed, or lost, through European imperial expansion across the world, especially in North America.

3.
The Dispossessor's Lament

As Thomas Jefferson pondered the fate of apparently extinct beasts across the North American continent, his thoughts were also occupied by the rapid decline of Native nations. Jefferson's well-known *Notes on the State of Virginia*, first written in 1781 but only publicly circulated after revisions in 1787, claimed Native peoples were reduced to 'about one-third of their former numbers', including nations reduced to as little as 'three or four men only', '10 or 12 men, tolerably pure from mixture with others colours', and 'A few women constitute the remains of that tribe'.[1] Jefferson lamented the decline partly because he was captivated by the 'noble savage', the romanticized theory that many colonized peoples lived so blissfully attuned to nature that their way of life was preferable to, and innocent of, the corrupting influence of Europeans.[2] Jefferson hoped that Native peoples would assimilate into colonial society by abandoning seasonal occupation, or 'nomadism' in the language of the day, in favour of being settled, independent agriculturalists or merchants, like Europeans. His hopes depended upon a broader belief that European farming was the most productive use of land, and so more highly civilized than noble wanderings.[3] Jefferson imagined a slow process of acculturation and absorption that would create a new kind of citizen. His statistics exaggerated the depletion because he relied on the 1669 census which only included warriors, but his belief in the 'vanishing Indian' was widespread.

After the American Revolutionary War (1775–83) freed the American colonies from British rule, many leaders of the new republic predicted that Native nations were on the verge of dying out. Over the nineteenth century in North America, several major policies were proposed for tackling the perceived decline: removal, reservations, and residential schools. All three contributed to growing Native dispossession. In the later nineteenth century, the establishment of national parks consolidated a much longer process of confiscating Native lands. Claims about doomed races across the United States helped shape much broader debates about empire, land, and the environment, with significant consequences for the meaning of extinction, and the making of the modern world.

Dispossession in the New Republic

Eighteenth-century forays into the interior grew into a rush of colonizers seeking ever more lands by the early nineteenth century. After the Louisiana Purchase of 1803 – involving the acquisition from the French First Republic of Louisiana and considerable land west of the Mississippi – brought a vast new territory under American rule, Jefferson suggested Eastern nations 'exchange for lands beyond the Misip [sic.]'.[4] Rather more brashly, President James Monroe later insisted: 'The hunter of savage state, requires, a greater extent of territory to sustain it, than is compatible with the progress and just claims of civilized life, and must yield to it. Nothing is more certain, than, if the Indian tribes do not abandon that state, and become civilized, that they will decline, and become extinct.'[5] Monroe deemed a 'compulsory process' the only remedy to the upswell in demands for land from European emigrants arriving in the United States in search of new opportunities.

Colonists' dreams of acquiring territory were chastened by the refusal or reluctance of Native nations to cede their homelands to settlers' unslaked thirst for land, whether acquired by conflict, theft, squatting, or state-sanctioned cession. Ned Blackhawk's monumental book *The Rediscovery of America* (2023) beautifully challenges the under-estimation of Native power in American histories. Of this period, he observes: 'despite the bloodshed, native peoples outside the original thirteen colonies maintained control over the majority of North America, which remained in 1783 predominantly Indian Country'. In this period, the possibility of trading furs and taking land attracted colonists further westward into the continent's interior. Sometimes territory was ceded through treaties, but many Native leaders fought to maintain their rightful lands. As Blackhawk argues, treaty-making in the later eighteenth century and 'Indian sovereignty helped to clarify when, where, how, and upon whom American laws operated. The sovereignties of Indian nations and of the United States were interrelated.'[6] When the United States constitution was drawn up in 1787, it granted citizenship only to white men, underpinning the dispossession of Native peoples and enslaved Africans.

The new republic soon passed legislation to wrest land from Native peoples under the guise of humanitarian intervention. In 1830, under the presidency of Andrew Jackson, the United States passed legislation inaugurating the forced removal of peoples east of the Mississippi to the west. Eventually known as the Indian Removal Act, Jackson rationalized the new legal power by claiming that the spectre of certain extinction hovered over the eastern nations unless action was taken to move them to the west. Infamously, in Jackson's first Annual Message to Congress in December 1829, he claimed:

> Our ancestors found them [Indians] the uncontrolled possessors of these vast regions. By persuasion and force, they have been made to retire from river to river, and from mountain to mountain; until some of the tribes have become extinct, and others have left but remnants, to preserve, for a while, their once terrible names. Surrounded by the whites, with their arts of civilization, which, by destroying the resources of the savage, doom him to weakness and decay; the fate of the Mohegan, the Narragansett, and the Delaware, is fast overtaking the Choctaw, the Cherokee, and the Creek. That this fate surely awaits them, if they remain within the limits of the States, does not admit of a doubt. Humanity and national honor demand that every effort should be made to avert such a great calamity.[7]

Jackson faced vigorous opposition. Four months later, Senator Theodore Frelinghuysen delivered a long speech in the Senate opposing removal, and in support of the Native nations who had no desire to move. He maintained that 'God, in his providence, planted these tribes on this Western continent . . . before Great Britain herself had a political existence.' As such, he demanded to know, 'in what code of the law of nations, or by what process of abstract deduction, their rights have been extinguished? Where is the decree or ordinance that has stripped these early and first loads of the soil?' Utterly convinced that Jackson and his supporters were straying beyond any valid claim, the senator insisted that 'from the principles of eternal justice, no argument can shake the political maxim, that, where the Indian always has been, he enjoys an absolute right still to be, in the free exercise of his own modes of thought, government and conduct'.[8] Despite such passionate defences of Native rights, and bitter fights over the principle of removal, the legislation eventually passed with a majority of just one vote.[9] Jackson's commitment to removal is a telling indication that he, and his supporters, were convinced that westward expansion could not be halted, or at least willingly contemplated. The only remedy that Jackson pursued was through expulsion to designated territory of the government's choosing. In this guise, Federal Indian Policy tried regulating relationships already under contestation and negotiation between the new republic and Native nations, while facilitating their rapid dispossession.

In the early to mid-nineteenth century, Americans regarded Eastern Native nations as deeply corrupted by their contact with settlers, as practically non-existent, or in desperate need of paternalistic protection from impending extinction.[10] This implicitly reimagined truly Native peoples as either belonging to a past with more abundant populations, or living west of the then uncolonized Mississippi River. President Jackson simultaneously argued that removal would protect deported nations while presiding over legal provision for future extinction by stating that the 'United States will forever secure and guaranty to them [removed Indians], and their heirs or successors, the country so exchanged with them . . . *Provided always*, That such lands shall revert to the United States, if the Indians become extinct, or abandon the same'.[11] Ultimately, the Indian Removal Act depended upon accepting that extinction was not only possible, but likely enough to require pre-emptive legislation.

Significant westward expansion in the 1840s and 1850s increased pressure on Native nations to cede their lands and a policy shift from removal to reservations. Removal forcibly relocated Native nations to live in a western 'Indian Territory', whereas reservations were areas of land held and governed by federally recognized Nations.[12] Between 1845 and 1850 the Union expanded as Texas, California, and Oregon either gained statehood or came under US control, and Mexico ceded a vast southwestern territory after the Mexican-American War (1846–8).[13] As one historian notes, 'It was not long, however, before the idea of moving a *few* Indians out of the way became a policy of confining *all* Indians in the out-of-the-way places.'[14] The government used reservations to forgo enforced relocation in favour of paternalistic attempts to control and assimilate Native peoples. Supporters of reservations believed confinement and segregation were essential to eventual assimilation. In effect, reservations were an assumed middle ground between colonial encroachment and future citizenship.

Suspected governmental corruption, inefficiency within the Bureau of Indian Affairs, tensions following the American Civil War (1861–5), and events such as the Sand Creek massacre in Colorado Territory of Cheyenne and Arapaho people by the US Army in 1864 prompted a congressional investigation into the state of Native nations in 1865.[15] Senator Doolittle's subsequent report on the *Condition of the Indian Tribes* (1867) summarized the responses to a questionnaire initially circulated to politicians, army officers, agents, and missionaries. Although predominantly concerned with the improvement of the Indian service and future of the Bureau of Indian Affairs (the report recommended it remain with the Department of the Interior rather than be moved to the War Department), it also collated information on the state of Native populations and suggested possible avenues for change. Significantly, twenty of the twenty-seven respondents felt Native populations were decreasing, while only one observed an increase. The demise was attributed to: 'Providence, the encroachment of the white man, civilization in all its forms, inefficient and unfaithful agents, injustice and abuse, want of proper judicious attention – all these cause the extinction of the Indian race.'[16] When asked to propose curative measures, respondents suggested 'there is none' to 'the only practical remedy to prevent the total extinction of the Indian tribes, is to separate them entirely from the white race'.[17] Ultimately, the committee suggested that, as customary 'hunting grounds are taken away, the reservation system, which is the only alternative to their extermination, must be adopted'.[18]

Government policies designed to assimilate Native peoples through allotment were introduced in the 1880s. Senator Henry Dawes guided the General Allotment Act into the statute books in 1887. Essentially, the Act legalized dividing reservations into smallholdings owned by individuals, rather than in common by a Native nation, and made holders of allotted land citizens of the United States. Allotment was designed to transform Native people into settled farmers. Significantly, by stipulating how much land individuals needed, the Dawes Act effectively endorsed the federal redistribution of ostensibly 'surplus' land for purchase by settlers and commercial development, particularly by railway companies. Intended to create a farming nation, supporters of allotment hoped to free up lands they valued but believed 'wasted'. Spurred on by the conviction that hunting and gathering was inherently inefficient compared to farming, allotment's supporters maintained Native nations must be 'civilized' for everyone's benefit.[19] Meanwhile, as noted by its original subjects and subsequent historians, the Act implicitly depended upon the notion of Native extinction, since it made no provision for a future increase in Native populations.[20] Ultimately in 1934, Franklin D. Roosevelt's Indian Reorganization Act, or Indian New Deal, abolished allotment and tried restoring Native self-government on reservations.[21]

Many campaigners regarded forced assimilation as urgent, necessary, and a humanitarian endeavour, especially through residential schools for Native children. The government adopted assimilation as a policy in the 1880s, but some federally funded residential schools were established earlier. Between 1819 and 1969 at least 408 Native boarding schools were established with federal funding across thirty-seven states, but recent research suggests that more than a thousand institutions from day schools to orphanages may have contributed to forced assimilation through education.[22] Native children as young as three were taken from their families and enrolled in residential schools where they were forcibly renamed, reclothed in non-Native garments, forbidden from using their mother tongues, or observing any Native religious or cultural rite in order to convert the children to Christianity and make them 'useful' members of colonial society. Most notoriously, in 1892, General Richard Henry Pratt argued 'all the Indian there is in the race should be dead. Kill the Indian in him, and save the man.'[23] Pratt established the Carlisle Institute in Pennsylvania in 1879 and presided over the school for twenty-four years. Under his leadership, the Institute enrolled 4,903 Native children from seventy-seven Native nations.[24] For crusaders such as Pratt, the intentional and systematic destructiveness inherent in the teaching methods of residential schools was an essential precursor to Native survival.

Residential schools are now formally recognized as institutions of genocide in Canada and the United States. While campaigners for residential schools sincerely believed their motives were humanitarian, there is no doubting the fact that residential schools were deliberately designed to achieve cultural annihilation with profoundly disturbing consequences. In recent years, the hastily buried remains of thousands of Native children have been unearthed in unmarked graves across North America. The most recent finds began with the recovery of 215 children's bodies interred in a mass grave on the site of a former residential school in Kamloops, British Columbia, in May 2021. The bodies of a further 1,300 children were soon found across five sites in Canada. A year later, a preliminary United States government investigation found children buried at fifty-three former residential schools from a total of nearly five hundred sites.[25] The continued use of the historic term 'schools' is increasingly recognized as a euphemism that profoundly understates the genocidal violence underpinning institutions whose survivors report horrific violations such as neglect, physical beatings, or abuse.[26] While the formal recognition of residential schools as genocidal is important, the intergenerational consequences of such harrowing violence remain and demand redress.

Over the nineteenth century, the United States government and campaigners partly justified removal, reservations, and residential schools as essential strategies for tackling declining Native populations. In the later nineteenth century, Native nations experienced new forms of dispossession with the establishment of national parks. Yet, unlike previous policies, national parks were not justified by claiming that they would be of benefit to vanishing peoples or species, but as spectacular sites of national pride for the enjoyment of tourists. Nonetheless, national parks were quickly associated with debates about extinction on an international scale.

Pristine Parks

In the 1830s, the young Pennsylvanian artist George Catlin was so convinced of the imminent extinction of Native peoples that he dedicated himself to publicizing their plight.[27] Born in 1796, he grew up listening to his grandfather's 'thrilling descriptions' of the Battle of Wyoming in 1778, when the British and Haudenosaunee, or Six Nations allies, defeated local opponents during the Revolutionary War. His grandmother and seven-year-old mother were among several hundred prisoners captured during the battle, but later released unharmed. Later in life, Catlin recalled that they were treated 'with the greatest kindness', which he regarded as evidence for 'the honour of the Indian's character'.[28] As a young man, Catlin established himself as a miniature portrait painter in Philadelphia, but moved to bustling New York for better opportunities in 1826. Three years later, he met the painter Charles Bird King, who made his name painting portraits of Native leaders. Within a year, Catlin decided to turn his hand to historical painting and took a steamboat up the Missouri River, starting from St Louis.

Catlin spent six years wandering the Great Plains and Rocky Mountains of North America. He made five treks west of the Mississippi in the summers from 1830 and 1836 and diligently painted the continent's landscapes and peoples while collecting an enormous range of artefacts. Catlin hoped to make his mark, and fortune, by selling his collection of more than six hundred paintings to the American government as a record of the new republic's vanishing nations. When that plan failed, he toured American, European, and British lecture circuits with his 'Indian Gallery'. Catlin publicly exhibited his collection from 1833 onwards, inviting audiences across the United States, including in Pittsburgh, Cincinnati, Louisville, New Orleans, and New York, to hear about his travels. He exhibited his collection alongside Native performers passing through New York in 1837. When profits started to fall, he decided to take his Indian Gallery to London in 1840.

In London, Catlin initially performed wearing Native clothing, or hired Londoners as models-cum-mimics, but a chance encounter enabled him to exhibit his collection alongside travelling Native groups. In 1843 Catlin met the entrepreneur Arthur Rankin, who managed a troupe of Anishinaabe, a nation from the Great Lakes region in the United States, hoping to make money by exhibiting themselves in England. They performed in Manchester and London. At the shows, the group's interpreter Alexander Cadotte, also of native heritage, met the eighteen-year-old English woman Sarah Haynes, and the couple soon married at a church crowded with curious onlookers.[29] Rankin tried to capitalize on the marriage by publicizing the bride's potential appearance in the shows. Infuriated, Cadotte quit the group and the couple departed for Walpole Island, in Ontario bordering Michigan, while Rankin toured Britain independently with the remainder of the group in 1844. In the same year, Catlin entered into a similar arrangement with a group of Báxoje, a Native nation from Iowa, managed by the missionary George Melody while they performed in New

Jersey. Initially, the group performed across Britain, but also ventured to Paris in 1845, before they returned to the United States. A month later, Catlin entered into a third arrangement with another group of Báxoje, managed by a Christian convert named Maungwudaus, or George Henry. He was a government interpreter for a local mission on Walpole Island, southwestern Ontario, before assembling the group of his own people for exhibition abroad. They were exhibited in Paris and London where they also met Queen Victoria.

Catlin spent years regaling patrons with traveller's tales and supplemented his exhibitions with published accounts of his travels, including *Letters and Notes on the Manners, Customs and Conditions of the North American Indians* (1841) and *Life Amongst the Indians: A Book for Youth* (1861). London hosted many exhibitions of foreign peoples. Throughout the 1800s, performers from around the world enacted songs, dances, and rites of passage to showcase their cultures for British audiences keen to observe peoples not easily met in London's already diverse streets. The shows featured men, women, and often children, either as individuals, small groups, or even families, frequently accompanied by a manager giving a lecture, or an interpreter, to facilitate encounters. In the later nineteenth century, displayed peoples were exhibited in much larger groups within world fairs, sometimes living on-site in ostensible 'native villages'. Managers would often showcase warriors from colonial conflicts, presenting them as military foes, or as the last of their race. By exhibiting the Indian Gallery with Native performers, Catlin contributed to a well-established means of profiting from the general public's curiosity about race, empire, and, increasingly, extinction.[30]

Catlin was so captivated by the Native nations he met that he imagined a future when they would be:

> . . . preserved in their pristine beauty and wildness, in a *magnificent park*, where the world could see for ages to come, the native Indian in his classic attire, galloping with his wild horse, with sinewy bow, and shield and lance, amid the fleeting herds of elks and buffaloes.

> What a beautiful and thrilling specimen for America to preserve and hold up to the view of her refined citizens and the world, in future ages! A *nation's Park*, containing man and beast, in all the wild and freshness of their nature's beauty![31]

Catlin hoped that establishing a nation's park would allow Native nations to continue using their lands in customary ways. His landscapes usually included Native individuals as a visual marker of pristine nature (Fig. 3.1). In contrast, by the mid-nineteenth century a new genre of landscape painting emerged in which wilderness was redefined as unpeopled nature. Thomas Moran's *Yellowstone Lake* (1875, Fig. 3.2) is typical of painters who depicted Providence's sublime power through wild landscapes.[32] Catlin is often credited with inventing the notion of a national park, but his dream was markedly different to the eventual reality.

The expectation that Native peoples would soon be extinct contributed to the establishment of national parks. California established Yosemite as the first state park in 1864, and Yellowstone

3.1 George Catlin, *Picturesque Bluffs above Prairie du Chien* (1835–6).

3.2 Thomas Moran, *Yellowstone Lake*, c. 1875.

soon followed as the world's first national park in 1872.[33] Early campaigners routinely claimed that the parks were national monuments of unmatched splendour, but also agriculturally or commercially worthless. In the hopes of securing custom from future visitors to the parks, powerful corporations, such as railway companies, supported the movement.[34] Notably, campaigners promoted national ownership ambiguous the Dawes Act was targeting shared Native ownership because it was regarded as uncivilized and a 'heathen' form of 'socialism' or 'communism'.[35] The crown jewels of American environmental heritage, national parks were consistently carved out from Native territories while perpetuating the notion of an unpeopled American wilderness.

From the outset, national parks helped create a version of wilderness devoid of Native presence. Historians have traced how transferring Native territories into the ownership of the United States of America extinguished subsistence rights, such as for hunting or timber.[36] For example, Yellowstone was regularly used by Crow, Shoshone, Nez Perce Bannock, Flathead, and Blackfeet nations; Yosemite (made a national park in 1890) was home to Miwok groups; Mesa Verde in Colorado, established as a national park in 1906, was associated with the Utes and Anasazi; Glacier National Park in Montana, established in 1910, was home to the Blackfeet; while the Grand Canyon in Arizona, which became a national park in 1919, was used by the Hopi and Navajo. Founding parks often involved coercive strategies. In Yosemite, Miwok villages were strategically razed to the ground while their former inhabitants starved or froze.[37] Native nations who customarily used Yellowstone's geysers to prepare food or for religious worship were systematically denied access.[38] Suppression meant early tourists encountered Native presences as absent, minimal, or heavily stage-managed.[39] Sometimes, Native peoples worked as tour guides or performed for the paying public, such as the Blackfeet at Glacier National Park. These acts reinforced the narrative of Native people as historic ghosts rather than as the presently dispossessed.[40] By promoting a vision of wilderness in which Native use was either systematically denied, suppressed, or erased, the parks movement created a powerful legacy that still holds sway in conservationist circles. Yet, as environmental historians have consistently shown, this presents considerable problems for both historians and policy-makers. By effectively denying human intervention, use, and management of nature as legitimate or desirable, 'wilderness' depended on an unhelpful and unsustainable bind in which the 'natural' and 'artificial' vied against each other in a zero-sum game.[41]

National parks were not established to protect vanishing species, but campaigners for national parks quicky incorporated conservationist rhetoric into their repertoire. Originally, campaigners insisted that parks must be emptied of people to allows tourists to enjoy the landscapes without fear.[42] When Americans began to worry about the dwindling numbers of species such as the bison or grey wolves, campaigners shifted tactics to argue that the parks offered sanctuary for endangered species threatened by any human presence.[43] Environmental concerns about vanishing species created new grounds for removing Native nations and changing customary land use in favour of federal management. Most obviously, officials insisted on Native expulsion because their practices of hunting and lighting fires were blamed for damaging the pristine nature of the American wilderness and possibly causing the extinction of flora and fauna. In 1886 park grounds received military protection, and in 1894 hunting was criminalized there.[44] Protectionist activity systematically redefined customary uses of the land as 'poaching' or 'criminal damage' to enforce dispossession. Persistent resistance left many early conservationists clamouring to confine Native peoples to reservations.[45] By the end of the century, as naturalists increasingly worried about dwindling species, Native nations were frequently dismissed as unfit custodians and ignorant destroyers of wilderness.

America's national parks set precedents that were quickly copied worldwide as countries set up national parks, often on the homelands of Indigenous peoples including in Canada (1887), Australia (1879, 1891, and 1915), and New Zealand (1894). Using military personnel for park management, promoting untouched wilderness, and the development of both a national and international tourist trade, became common features across the world. Significant conservationist efforts in Africa led to the establishment of South Africa's Kruger Park in 1926, and Tanzania's Serengeti Park in 1940. Globally, the national parks movement entrenched forms of wilderness and conservation rooted in the denial and erasure of human use, historically or in the present, as well as widespread dispossession of Native peoples.[46]

Throughout the nineteenth century, presidents, legislators, and reformers partly justified removal, reservations, and residential schools by arguing that they would be for the benefit of Native nations on the verge of extinction. In doing so, campaigners both drew from, and contributed to, broader debates among naturalists about colonized peoples said to be on the verge of extinction while changing the broader meaning of extinction in the modern world.

Dying Races

The British government established the Parliamentary Committee on Aborigines (British Settlement) to explore the treatment of colonized Indigenous peoples ('aborigines' in the report) worldwide just after abolitionists helped secure new legislation to end enslavement across the British Empire in 1833.[47] Thomas Fowell Buxton, one of the period's leading abolitionists, called for a committee to investigate 'what measures ought to be adopted with regard to the native inhabitants of countries where British settlements are made, and to the neighbouring tribes' for their protection and to facilitate their conversion to Christianity.[48] His lobbying was successful. First sitting in 1835, the committee's work prompted the Quaker physician Thomas Hodgkin to found the Aborigines' Protection Society (APS) in 1836. The group pursued reform in the hope of establishing paternalist, humanitarian imperial rule across the British Empire. The APS merged with the abolitionists to form the Anti-Slavery and Aborigines' Protection Society in 1909, which, ultimately, was the forerunner of Anti-Slavery International.

The *Report of the Parliamentary Select Committee on Aboriginal Tribes* (1837) was a catalogue of harm, with recurrent claims about extinction shared and scrutinized. It gathered evidence from North America, South America, the Caribbean, Australia, Tasmania, the Pacific Islands, and South Africa, to assess the nature of British rule. The report noted that colonized peoples faced population declines across the British Empire, but forthrightly challenged fatalistic responses to such loss:

> Not a few, even in the present day, are inclined to the belief, that in spite of all our efforts, the speedy extinction of the Aborigines is inevitable. Their extermination, it would seem, is an appointment of Heaven, and every attempt to avert their doom must, therefore, of necessity prove utterly unavailing. The atrocity of such a sentiment is only surpassed by its impiety. To imagine that there now exists a

> race of men devoted by Providence to destruction, is assuredly to libel the beneficent and merciful character of the Most High.[49]

It might be tempting to dismiss this religious fervour as reformist polemic, especially when even contemporaries dismissed such 'philanthropy'. Charles Dickens beautifully captured the phrase's pejorative implications in *Bleak House* (1852–3). In the novel, Mrs Jellyby ignored the impoverished wretchedness of her family as she tried to provide humanitarian assistance to people living on the banks of the River Niger. Dickens was adamant that such 'philanthropy' was unjust given extensive needs much closer to home. Nonetheless, the report provides important insights for the use of claims of extinction beyond the animal world.

Fatalistic discussions of colonized peoples were widespread within a few decades of new ideas about the ubiquity of animal extinction, and in less than a decade of the reported extinction of the Beothuk in Newfoundland. The refrain of dwindling populations caused by unchecked violence marked the report's discussion of North America, South America, the Caribbean, New Holland (now Australia), Van Diemen's land (now Tasmania), the Pacific Islands, and South Africa. The report began with North America and observed: 'In the colony of Newfoundland it may therefore be stated that we have exterminated the natives.'[50] In Upper Canada, colonized peoples were reportedly 'melting away before the advance of the white population'. Only three lines discussed the West Indies, because 'Of the Caribs . . . we need not speak, as of them little more remains than the tradition that they once existed.' In New Holland only 'devoted missionaries' were considered enough to stop the 'progress of extinction'.[51] The report staunchly noted that culpability lay with the 'guilty ambition and avarice of men professedly civilized and Christian'.[52] This slippage between extermination and extinction gathered strength, especially within North America.

By the mid-nineteenth century, North American theorists touting Native extinction as an inevitable, even desirable by-product of colonization, faced criticism for their malign influence. The

German anthropologist Theodor Waitz accused American theorists of creating an 'American School' promoting extinction as a process of 'higher races' displacing 'lower races' as 'predestined by nature'. Originally published in Germany in 1859, and translated into English four years later, Waitz sarcastically observed:

> . . . it would appear that we must not merely acknowledge the right of the white American to destroy the red man, but perhaps praise him that he has constituted himself the instrument of Providence in carrying out and promoting this law of destruction. The pious manslayer thus enjoys the consolation that he acts according to the laws of nature which govern the rise and extinction of races.[53]

His scathing attack on the conflation of extermination, extinction, and natural laws is revealing. Waitz held the Harvard zoologist and geologist Louis Agassiz, craniometrist Samuel Morton, and their followers responsible for a theory that 'reconciles us both with Providence and the evil dispositions of man', and flattering those lacking moral righteousness. Lest anyone misunderstand his antipathy, he noted that whereas some considered such a natural law evidence for 'a specifically higher mental endowment of the white race', such a position was 'improbable'. In contrast, Waitz contended racial differences 'essentially depended on the natural and social conditions' in which races developed.[54]

Most nineteenth-century scholars of race believed humans were descended from Adam and Eve, and that racial, cultural, and social differences developed as Noah's sons migrated across the world from the moored Ark. As each son's descendants peopled Europe, Asia, and Africa, they encountered different environments which caused new complexions and other racialized differences. Scholars affirming the 'original equality of races', even if later modified by environment, asserted humanity's unity and faith in God's Creation, without implying the racial equality of present-day usage. Waitz's forceful criticism suggests how the notion of providentially doomed races was challenged, dismissed, and even ridiculed within the nineteenth century by those who felt European settlers were expediently, hastily, and falsely claiming moral superiority, or racial advantage.

Despite opposition, extermination was routinely conflated with extinction within the sciences. Like museum relics, some colonized peoples were assumed to be merely historic, and fast-fading, remnants of their nations.[55] A year after the Anthropological Society of London was founded in 1863, the anthropologist Richard Lee presented a paper to the Fellows about 'The Extinction of Races'. He contended:

> The rapid disappearance of aboriginal tribes before the advance of civilisation is one of the many remarkable incidents of the present age. In every new country, from America to New Zealand, from Freemantle to Honolulu, it is observable, and seems to be a necessary result of an approximation of different races, peculiar, however, in degree, at least, to this portion of the world's history. It has been estimated that the Hawaiians have been reduced as much as eighty-five per cent during the last hundred years. The natives of Tasmania are almost, if not quite, extinct. The Maories are passing away at the rate of about twenty-five per cent every fourteen years, and in Australia, as in America, whole tribes have disappeared before the advance of the white man.[56]

Lee characterized extinction as an inevitable feature of global human contact in the same breath as he noted its roots in modern settler colonial expansion. He interpreted observable trends, such as dwindling Indigenous populations, as the 'necessary' consequence of interracial contact leading to endangerment, and, ultimately, extinction. Repeated discussions of dying races like this reframed colonial expansion and settler colonial histories as evidence for a more general natural law, and, implicitly, the will of God. Lee's confidence is typical of nineteenth-century commentators who used species extinction to narrate the history of British imperialism. His chilling list of colonial casualties reveals how quickly dispossession and extermination were disavowed and reframed as a 'necessary result' of imperial encounters subject to the natural law of species extinction.

At the same meeting, a paper 'On the Extinction of Races' was presented by the anthropologist Thomas Bendyshe, known for translating the anthropological treatise of the famous eighteenth-century naturalist Johann Friedrich Blumenbach. Bendyshe condemned his peers for their 'unphilosophical haste' in presuming human extinctions were 'the will of Providence'. The charge might seem innocuous, but it was a serious accusation. Since the seventeenth century, natural philosophers creating scientific knowledge were expected to honour gentlemanly codes of behaviour to distinguish themselves from common artisans, engineers, or labourers. To dismiss a scholar's experiments or investigations as 'unphilosophical' questioned the integrity of his experimental method, scholarly principles, and gentlemanly honour. These considerations persisted into the nineteenth century when Bendyshe issued his warning.

Bendyshe conceded that many colonized populations were declining in North America, Australia, New Zealand, and Tasmania, but he was alarmed by the assumption that extinction would necessarily follow. He observed that 'theories of various kinds have been started to account for what has never yet taken place, at least in a sufficient number of instances to determine whether it is an exceptional or a strictly natural phenomenon'. His distinction between 'exceptional' and 'natural' evoked the contrast between artificial human intervention and God-given laws. Bendyshe insisted that endangerment or extinction only occurred if colonizers encountered populations already in decline and predicted recovery when favourable conditions re-emerged.[57] His caution was a direct challenge to the fatalistic assumptions about colonized peoples' futures. The opposition between Lee and Bendyshe confirms that even when nineteenth-century commentators wrote papers with virtually the same titles and agreed that colonized peoples were declining, they might disagree about the cause and significance. While some scholars deduced that declining populations provided evidence of a more general natural law of extinction equally applicable to animals and humans, others were far more cautious about inferring abstract laws from the available evidence. Such caution recognized that establishing natural laws from empirical data was fraught with philosophical and theological complications because they were not just *descriptions* of natural phenomena, but might potentially be interpreted as *indications* of Providential will.

The tendency to frame imperial encounters as evidence of a natural law of extinction strengthened when combined with new theories of human evolution in the latter half of the nineteenth century. Darwin famously put forward his theory of evolution through natural selection in his most famous book *On the Origin of Species* (1859). Despite outlining animal and plant evolution extensively, he remained famously tight-lipped about our evolutionary past, only hinting in the final pages that in the 'distant future . . . Light will be thrown on the origin of man and his history'. This intimation immediately ignited combative debates on humanity's place in nature.[58] In a well-known twist of fate, natural selection was independently formulated by the naturalist and specimen collector Alfred Russel Wallace. Unlike Darwin, Wallace exempted humans from experiencing natural selection. For him, the 'true grandeur and dignity of man' allowed our species to rise above a natural law that governed 'all other organic beings'. Nonetheless, he maintained:

> It is the same great law of '*the preservation of favoured races in the struggle for life*', which leads to the inevitable extinction of all those low and mentally undeveloped populations with which Europeans come in contact. The red Indian in North America, and in Brazil; the Tasmanian, Australian and New Zealander in the southern hemisphere, die out, not from any one special cause, but from the inevitable effects of an unequal mental and physical struggle.[59]

Moreover, he likened such extinctions to the process that enabled 'the weeds of Europe' to 'overrun North America and Australia, extinguishing native productions . . . by the greater capacity for existence and multiplication'.[60] Given that Wallace explicitly excluded humanity from selection pressures, this passage is a remarkable instance of how colonial violence was reframed as extinction. By describing colonists as vigorous weeds naturally overrunning local flora and peoples, Wallace claimed greater fecundity for imperial whiteness and doomed others to annihilation.

Twelve years later, Darwin finally revealed his own views in his book *The Descent of Man* (1871), with significant consequences for debates about extinction and empire. Equating 'civilisation' with European imperial expansion, Darwin observed that 'Relics of extinct or forgotten tribes have been discovered throughout the civilised regions of the earth, on the wild plains of America, and on the isolated islands in the Pacific Ocean.' He went on: 'Civilised nations are everywhere supplanting barbarous nations, excepting where the climate opposes a deadly barrier.'[61] Darwin concluded: 'Extinction follows chiefly from the competition of tribe with tribe, and race with race.' Crucially, he imagined intercultural encounters as interracial competitions 'settled by war, slaughter, cannibalism, slavery, and absorption'.[62] In Darwinian terms, cultural and social differences determined who would live or die out, whether as individuals, nations, or, ultimately, races. His only concession for ostensibly weaker peoples lay in the competitive advantages of a 'deadly climate'.[63] In arguing so, Darwin conceptualized extinction as an evolutionary pressure driving human evolution and history. The extinction of colonized peoples was predicted long before Darwin committed these words to paper, but they suggest how even the most prominent writers of the age conflated extermination and extinction.

In Darwin's wake, many readers interpreted life's history, including human evolution and modern European colonization, as the extinction of primitive forms supplanted by not just better adapted, but ostensibly more evolved, beings. When combined with notions of progressive development, survival turned into a badge of political, cultural and moral advancement. In this vein, scientists, anthropologists and colonial officials reframed colonial conflicts as intercultural competition subject to natural selection and a form of progressive human development. This politics of progress perpetuated the conflation of extinction and extermination, especially when combined with these new evolutionary ideas, and underpinned fatalistic readings of imperial history as an epic saga in which colonial powers subdued ostensibly weaker races in a vicious struggle for survival. The loss of individuals considered the last of their race, such as Shanawdithit of the Beothuk, fuelled European convictions that many peoples were vanishing or genuinely extinct into the present. In 1924, *Nature* published an editorial about the 'Primitive Races within the British Empire' which confidently asserted: 'Throughout the world, whenever a primitive race is brought into contact with European civilisation, the result is normally, though not invariably, for the inferior race to lose its vitality and to die out.'[64] The wording is remarkably close to Darwin's nearly five decades earlier, but the historical claim is much older and rooted in the violent encounters in settler colonies that were interpreted as scientific evidence for extinction by men like Lee, Wallace, and Darwin. Even more disturbing than naturalists and colonizers framing the past or present in these terms were their attempts to predict the future of colonized peoples as one of certain extinction.

The treatment of many colonized peoples is now regarded as genocidal. The Polish lawyer Raphael Lemkin first defined genocide during the Holocaust, and in the wake of the attempted extermination of Armenians by the Ottoman Empire between 1915 and 1917, and of the Ova Herero and Nama by German colonists in German South West Africa, now Namibia, between 1904 and 1908. Lemkin amassed historical evidence of mass killings over centuries of European colonization, trying to name the 'crime of crimes' after forty-nine members of his own family were murdered for being Jewish. Lemkin coined the word 'genocide' in 1942, from the Greek word 'genos', meaning a people, and the Latin suffix '-cide' for the act of killing.[65] He fought for the recognition of genocide as an international crime, and achieved his ambition remarkably quickly when the United Nations adopted the Convention on the Prevention and Punishment of the Crime of Genocide in 1948.

Lemkin distinguished genocide from mass killing and other

kinds of persecution because it targeted peoples on the basis of their *collective* identity. He regarded attacking collectives as robbing humanity of shared enrichment because 'Our whole cultural heritage is a product of the contributions of all peoples.' Without every unique contribution, humanity's cultural inheritance suffered irretrievable loss. Lemkin defined genocide as a 'coordinated plan aimed at destruction of the essential foundations of the life' of racial, ethnic, religious, national, and political groups.[66] His focus on these groups survives in the convention's definition of genocide as the 'intent to destroy, in whole or in part, a national, ethnical, racial or religious group'. Despite attempts to amend the law and include more groups, such as those based on gender, sexuality, and political beliefs, the original restrictions remain.

Lemkin regarded cultural destruction, biological eradication, and physical killing as genocidal. Despite his broad-ranging definition, genocide is often misunderstood, or more narrowly defined, as primarily, or solely, mass murder. This ambiguity is partly due to the compromises Lemkin made when trying to shepherd the proposed legislation through the United Nations. The final wording of the convention recognizes the following acts as genocidal: 'killing members of the group', 'causing serious bodily or mental harm to members of the group', 'deliberately inflicting on the group conditions of life calculated to bring about its physical destruction in whole or in part', 'imposing measures intended to prevent births within the group', and 'forcibly transferring children of the group to another group'.[67] This wording retained genocidal strategies rooted in biological extermination or mass killing, but jettisoned cultural destruction except for the forcible transfer of children. The differences between Lemkin's original conception and the United Nations definition has created considerable tension and ambiguity over what constitutes genocide in the past or present. Controversies over whether specific mass killings constitute genocide often revolve around establishing the 'intent to destroy'. Specific intent, or *dolus specialis* in legal terms, is notoriously difficult to prove, making successful prosecution on this basis a rarity. Lawyers and political scientists increasingly favour defining, and inferring, intent more broadly. For example, prosecutors might require establishing specific intent only for the architects of genocidal schemes, while perpetrators could be prosecuted on the basis of knowing the purpose of their killing even if they did not plan the extermination. Interpreting intent more broadly would certainly help bring more people to trial, potentially secure more convictions, and bring prosecutions in line with historical practice.

Parsing intent is useful and essential for prosecutions. However, even when not possible or consensus is lacking, we must acknowledge that mass killings, enslavement, starvation, conflict, and new diseases are well-documented features of modern European colonialism. Whether or not these horrors meet the limited definition of genocide established in international law or broader alternatives such as crimes against humanity, arguments about intent should never overshadow the indisputable violence we know was unleashed, and whose legacies still demand acknowledgement, a reckoning, and apology over denial.

Catlin's shows promoted expectations about vanishing nations in a transatlantic context. After his death in 1872, the Smithsonian Institution finally purchased his collection in 1879. By this time, Catlin's paintings were viewed not as a record of decline, but of lost ways of life. Politicians, naturalists, and anthropologists justified government policies of removing Native peoples from their lands, confining them on reservations, and excluding them from national parks. Whether Native extinction was explicitly anticipated, or implicitly planned for, removal deprived Native nations of their rightful homelands, hunting grounds, and natural resources. The establishment of North American national parks created a new strategy for state-sanctioned dispossession that was quickly adopted by conservationists worldwide. National parks in the United States remained under non-Native leadership for over a century until Charles 'Chuck' Sams III was appointed to the directorship of the National Parks Service in 2021. As the first Native person to hold the title, he took up the position hoping to incorporate Native views and knowledge into park management.[68]

Using a newly established language of lost species to discuss human futures is an often overlooked, but important, shift for understanding the unnatural and entangled histories of empire and extinction. Once extinction was regarded as a natural law, predictions about doomed races grew across North America. In this guise, extinction was entwined with narratives of the rise and fall of civilizations in which white, European colonists and new settler states won the spoils.[69] Only by tracing how writers conflated extermination with extinction, and used histories of settler colonialism as evidence for a broadly applicable natural law of extinction, can we appreciate the full significance of new scientific understandings of extinction while challenging the ongoing dispossession they made possible.

There were good reasons to be alarmed. A recent team of scientists, led by the geographer Alexander Koch, tried to quantify the environmental impact of Europeans arriving in the Americas. The team's scientific paper estimated pre-Colombian populations across the Americas numbered around 60 million in 1492, compared to a European population of about 70 to 88 million. The paper estimates that the violent changes caused by European colonization of the Americas, from new diseases to mass killing, had caused the deaths of 56 million people by the 1600s, constituting 90 per cent of the pre-Colombian population and a tenth of the global population. With this 'Great Dying', previously farmed lands grew wild, and absorbed so much carbon from the atmosphere that the average global temperature dropped by 0.15°C contributing to a minor ice age.[70] These numbers and scenarios are one attempt among many to quantify the astonishing violence recorded in the archives of the new American republic.

The genocidal violence was astonishing, and must not be underestimated, or disavowed as simply characteristic of past attitudes. Throughout the nineteenth century, fatalistic claims about colonized peoples' futures were challenged: even when they were the claims of a minority, it is important to note that this is not the preserve of modern-day sensibilities. However, claims about total extinction should be treated with much greater caution, while claims about genocide need to be better understood. Many nations are left battling the assumption that genocide requires total, or near total, annihilation, when there is no ambiguity in Lemkin's original formulation or international law that genocide can be 'in whole, or in part'. Ultimately, despite the most alarming prophecies, Native peoples survived as sovereign nations. Perpetuating myths about their extinction represents a refusal to acknowledge and respect Native forms of defining, and knowing, who they are.[71] In 2017 a dramatic example of these battles culminated in the recognition that the Sinixt First Nation were not extinct. They had been declared extinct by the Canadian government in Canada in 1956 after the death of a Sinixt woman named Annie Joseph. The legal acknowledgement of their survival was only secured after decades of campaigning.[72] Denying people the possibility of knowing they exist is a profound form of epistemic injustice. Rather than enabling such injustice, historians of extinction might facilitate its end.

In the mid-nineteenth century, ideas about human extinction and evolution were transformed by the discovery of human fossils and a new consensus about our ancient origins. Scholars interested in race, extinction, and imperial encounters found novel evidence to fuel their intellectual interests. Suddenly, lost Neanderthals held the key to understanding our past, present, and future.

4.
Humans Before Humans

In June 1840, London's impresarios billed the exhibition of an 'Antediluvian Child' as the first human fossil ever found. Dug up outside Brussels and shown in Leicester Square, its promotional materials invited anyone interested in humanity's origins to come and see the evidence for themselves (Fig. 4.1). Newspaper advertisements confidently announced the child fossil disproved anyone inclined to 'pretend that, previous to the Deluge, the human race had no existence'. Visitors needed to make haste as the fossil was due to be exhibited before the esteemed men of the Academy of Science in Paris within a fortnight. The entry fee of a pound was extraordinarily high compared to many other summer attractions: a shilling gained entry to a concert at the Surrey Zoological Gardens, an exhibition of daguerreotypes, or George Catlin's paintings of the Native nations and landscapes of the Rocky Mountains at the Egyptian Hall.

The Antediluvian Child's fame even reached the Antipodes.[1] William Buckland, twice president of the Geological Society, visited the exhibit with two other men, but was distinctly unimpressed. He dismissed the fossil as 'nothing but concretion of chert in the Brussels sand, something like the head and trunk of a child without legs'.[2] He clearly felt let down, and perhaps even hoaxed. Nevertheless he parted, perhaps even gambled, with such a hefty entrance fee because the exhibition coincided with vigorous debates about our ancient past.

Deciding how to identify, date, and interpret human fossils vexed nineteenth-century geologists. How old were our earliest ancestors? Had humans existed for just a few thousand years as most believed, or did humanity originate in prehistoric times? Despite identifying

EXHIBITION

OF A

HUMAN FOSSIL

18, Leicester Square,

AN ANTE-DILUVIAN CHILD,

Found in a supercritacy soil

At Diehgen, near Brussels, (Belgium.)

There does not perhaps exist in the world a discovery so rare and so wonderful in the matter of Geological science. Until now there never was found but the bones of animals to have turned into a fossil state. Cuvier, the most celebrated of his age, has denied the existence of human fossil remains; and others pretend that previous to the Deluge the human race had no existence.

Here, then, is at once a demonstrative evidence of the falsity of their opinion, and a clear indication of the truth of the Holy Bible.

The Proprietors of this fossil being obliged to return to Paris, where they are called by the Members of the Academy of Science, cannot possibly stay longer than a fortnight in London, as their departure is fixed for the 20th of June, 1840.

Admission £1. each Person.

The Exhibition is open every day from 11 till 4 o'Clock, Sundays excepted.

W. R. Newman, Printer, Widegate-street, Bishopsgate.

4.1 Handbill for the exhibition of the 'Human Fossil'. Reproduced by permission of the Geological Society of London many extinct beasts, Georges Cuvier died eight years before the Antediluvian Child's exhibition, convinced that human fossils had never been found. Geologists knew of many evidently old human bones, but they were wary of defining them as fossils because this implied a startlingly ancient origin. The caution was important for a period when any suggestion that prehistoric people existed was deeply controversial owing to the tricky questions it raised about Biblically calibrated historical timescales. In the mid-nineteenth century, geologists' hammers finally unearthed indisputably ancient human relics, but that did not settle disputes about their meaning. Accepting that ancient humans existed required building a new consensus about how best to date and interpret these strange new remains and artefacts. As scientists debated the peopling of lost worlds, they also tackled troubling new questions. Were ancient humans the same species as modern peoples, or had they died out? Had modern peoples killed off their ancient kin? Did past human extinctions presage more to come? Exploring these questions helped reimagine what it meant to be human, and raised the worrying prospect of both ancient and future human extinctions.

Naming Wise Men

Who counts as human? Philosophers, theologians, and scientists have all proffered answers trying to make sense of our origins, descent, antiquity, and evolution, but we only acquired our scientific name, *Homo sapiens*, in the eighteenth century. In Biblical accounts of Creation, Adam named every living thing before Eve drew breath (Genesis 2:19). Adam's achievement depended on knowing the true essence of living beings, and their relationships to each other. In European traditions, naturalists hoping to know, name, and order living beings faced having to search for a natural system of classification reflecting Adam's order, or accepting artificial systems that provided only imperfect substitutes. Before the mid-eighteenth century, European naturalists named species using a genus and long form of contextual information that allowed experts to distinguish between natural kinds. New discoveries or reclassification entailed updating the contextual evidence to keep names distinctive.

The Swedish botanist and physician Carl Linnaeus proposed two-part names consisting of a genus and species to provide unique references that remained stable and accessible even to ordinary people. His most important works were *Systema Naturae*, or general system of nature, first published in 1735, and *Philosophia Botanica*, first appearing in 1751. He continually revised his general system, which led to the original twelve pages swelling to a three-volume twelfth edition of more than 2,400 pages within his own lifetime, and further editions after his death. He introduced two-part names in the tenth edition of *Systema Naturae* in 1758. Although he was derided as a 'second Adam', plants, animals, bacteria, viruses, and cultivated varieties are still formally named using the Linnaean system.[3]

By naming *Homo sapiens*, Linnaeus defined the limits of humanity. He was especially interested in distinguishing between the *Anthropomorpha*, who he subdivided into *Homo*, or humans; apes and monkeys, or *Simia*; and *Bradypus*, or sloths. Initially, he defined *Homo sapiens* as the sole human species. Derived from the Latin 'homō' for 'human being' and 'sapiēns' meaning 'wise', he further subdivided the species into four continental varieties: *Americanus* (American), *Africanus* (African), *Asiaticus* (Asian), and *Europaeus* (European). The tenth edition of 1758 outlined the natural history of the *Monstrosi*, or monstrous variety, to classify unusual types whether occurring naturally or artificially. He named *Homo troglodytes* by drawing on stories about apes, folk legends about feral people, and medical interest in Amelia Newsham, a young Jamaican girl born to enslaved parents, whose albinism intrigued many scholars in eighteenth-century Britain.[4] By the 1760s, in writings specifically addressing *Anthropomorpha*, Linnaeus also contrasted *Homo sapiens* and *Homo ferus*, a wild man who never gained wisdom, with *Homo caudatus*, a new species named from travellers' tales across the Malay world (Fig. 4.2).[5] The Linnaean system was widely used to classify living beings within a few decades

4.2 The *Anthropomorpha*, as defined by Carl Linnaeus.

of publication, but despite being the archetypical 'wise man', Linnaeus invited considerable ire by naming multiple human species.

In the eighteenth century, most European naturalists assumed humans were one family, or species, descended from Adam and Eve, later known as monogenesis. While respecting the notion of original unity, many scholars subdivided humans into groups called 'varieties' or 'races' depending on the author. Most favoured cleaving humanity into three distinct varieties, namely the 'European', the 'Mongolian', and the 'Ethiopian'. However, the exact number varied: the eighteenth-century comparative anatomist Johann Friedrich Blumenbach favoured five varieties, adding the 'Malayan' and 'American', while the London surgeon John Hunter argued for seven. More rarely, some scholars proposed the existence of humans before Adam, multiple acts of Creation, or numerous groups of survivors following the mooring of Noah's ark, to make sense of observed differences between nations. Isaac de la Peyrère's *Prae-Adamitae* (Pre-Adamites) suggested as early as 1655 that a human race had existed before Adam's creation; however, this remained an alarmingly profane, and marginal, view.[6] Contradicting the Biblical account of a single act of

Creation, shared descent through Adam and Eve, and a single point of migration from Noah's Ark, was a theologically and scientifically risky endeavour – and therefore remained disreputable. Later called 'polygenists', the most vocal dissenters argued 'race' was a fixed character impervious to environment, education, or evolution, and that human races were inherently different species. These extreme views gained ground from the mid-nineteenth century onwards, but they remained in the minority.[7] Ultimately, the Linnaean legacy included the adoption of two-part names and classifying humans as *Homo sapiens*, but did not extend to convincing naturalists there was more than a single species of *Homo*.

Defining humanity as a single family required scholars interested in human variety to trace historic migrations from Noah's Ark, and the subsequent peopling of the world, to piece together our common past. Most theologians believed Noah's Ark moored on Mount Ararat in the Caucasus mountains of Asia after the waters receded, hence the term Caucasian. When Noah's sons journeyed to different regions of the world, each begat the peoples of the world: Japheth and his seven sons wandered across Europe and Asia, Ham and his four sons migrated to Southwest Asia and Africa, while Shem and his five sons journeyed to the Middle East.[8] The calibration of history using strict Biblical timeframes limited human history to literate societies and the age of the earth to about 6,000 years old. The Celts' arrival in Europe was dated to mere centuries before Julius Caesar's expeditions to the British Isles in 55 and 54 BCE expanded the Romans' known world, while Emperor Claudius's invasion from 43 CE led to occupation, conquest, and the start of the Iron Age in Britain.[9] By the mid-nineteenth century, geologists proposed that the slow pace of geological change required much more time than assumed. As geologists reimagined earth's history as a gradually unfolding saga, its past expanded from a few thousand years to unknown millennia. With new timescales for life on earth and lengthening lists of extinct species, writers wondered whether extinct beasts and people had coexisted in lost worlds.[10]

Petrified People

Roman histories of invading and conquering Britain referred to Britons as *barbarus*, Latin for a 'foreigner' or 'savage': in spite of this reputation, nineteenth-century Europeans imagined their ancestors as relatively civilized and skilled metalworkers over the previous two millennia. This self-regard was partially overturned by the reinterpretation of ceraunia, or thunderstones. Highly prized by collectors, ceraunia were originally regarded as the petrified remains of thunderbolts. By the mid-eighteenth century, antiquarians believed they were primitive stone tools made by the earliest Europeans who once lived in a far less exalted, even shockingly lowly, state. Soon, the earliest Europeans were reimagined as barbarous intruders from Asia.[11]

Despite these new histories of European savagery, petrified human bones were regarded with profound caution in the 1820s. Almost two decades before Buckland visited the Antediluvian Child, he found a skeleton dusted in red ochre in Paviland Cave in South Wales in 1823. The fragments included a partial left arm, left leg and foot, partial right foot, several ribs, and the pelvis. Buckland initially suspected a male skeleton, but later described his find as a long-dead witch and, eventually, as the Red Lady of Paviland. While not a literalist interpreter of theological texts, Buckland's geological theories were compatible with relatively short Biblical chronologies and occasional catastrophes such as floods. Buckland contended that the Red Lady was a Roman burial even though her bones were found with much older lost beasts.[12] The geologist Paul Tournal found human remains and pottery intermixed with extinct animal bones in Languedoc, Southern France, in 1827. He published a paper insisting that the people and beasts lived together. Two years later, the well-known excavator Jules de Christol found cave floors scattered with the bones of humans and extinct animal bones near Sommières in France. He reasoned that if geologists admitted the animal bones were fossils, then this must also be true of the human remains. Tournal and Christol published papers challenging Cuvier's insistence that human fossils did not exist, but he remained unconvinced. Cuvier did not rule out the possibility of human fossils, but he doubted whether any of the known finds were truly ancient. Hesitant geologists continued interpreting apparently ancient human bones with the utmost caution.[13]

New finds cumulatively strengthened the case for human antiquity, but scholars remained wary. In 1829 the prehistorian Philippe-Charles Schmerling found two human skulls embedded under a thick cluster of rocks speckled with extinct animals in Engis near Liège in Belgium. The knapped flints and animal bones worked into tools and ornaments convinced him that the skulls belonged to people who had lived among the extinct beasts. Now named Engis 1 and Engis 2, Schmerling's finds attracted enormous interest, partly because of his medical education and his personal excavation of an undisturbed site. Despite his credibility, notable geologists still surmised a later burial for the skulls. The amateur geologist Boucher de Perthes found a thick, blackened fragment of a human jawbone alongside numerous flints in the gravel pits of Abbeville, France, in 1838. He confidently proclaimed the reality of human antiquity, but geologists shrugged off his enthusiasm claiming insufficient evidence.[14]

Geologists and antiquarians expanded the chronology of European history into prehistory even without the formal recognition of human fossils in the 1830s. Dutch and Scandinavian scholars extended human history into three prehistoric ages: the Stone Age, the Bronze Age and the Iron Age. The Three Age system was first developed by C. J. Thomsen, curator of the antiquarian collections at the National Museum of Denmark around 1807. Antiquarians knew that stone, bronze and iron artefacts appeared in repetitive sequence in barrows, mounds, and digs across Europe.[15] Thomsen's system allowed antiquarians to establish the *relative* date of artefacts. even when absolute ages were impossible to establish. The term 'prehistory' (*forhistorisk* in Danish) was first used by Christian Molbech in 1833 in a series of lectures published the following year. The curator of the Museum of the Society of Antiquaries of Scotland, Daniel Wilson, introduced the term prehistory to English speakers in *The Archaeology and Prehistoric*

Annals of Scotland (1851).[16] By the mid-nineteenth century, geologists and antiquarians regarded early Europeans as uncivilized and primitive with histories stretching back a few millennia. This expanded the chronology of European history into prehistory, while *Homo sapiens* remained a singular species.

In August 1856 men quarrying limestone found peculiar bones outside Feldhofer cave, near Düsseldorf in the Neander Valley, Germany. Previously undisturbed for millennia, the shattered remnants were discarded by the workers who continued their task. The site's owner Friedrich Wilhelm Pieper rescued the curiously thick and heavy bones that survived their disposal, including a partial skull cap. Assuming they were the bones of an extinct cave bear, he asked a local teacher and amateur natural historian, Johann Karl Fuhlrott, for help identifying the species. On closer inspection, Fuhlrott suggested they were of a person who once roamed Europe's ancient crags and rivers. Seeking a second opinion, he sent a cast of the skull's remains to Herrmann Schaaffhausen, a professor at the University of Bonn, who asked to examine the original remains. The professor was especially puzzled by the skull's distinctive thickset, continuous brow-ridge. He compared the skull to other skulls in local anatomy collections. None matched. He licked the bones and his tongue stuck. Modern bones were not sticky so the 'tongue test' suggested the bones were fossilized. Had the professor tasted the first human fossil ever found? Despite the tantalizing possibility, sticky tongues are suggestive, not decisive. On 4 February 1857 the professor reported his findings to the Lower Rhine Medical and Natural History Society in Bonn. Almost exactly four months later, both men presented a report on the discovery and condition of the bones to Bonn's scientific men.[17]

Two years later, the excavation of an undisturbed cave in Britain radically changed the meaning of the Neander Valley's mysterious and long-dead resident. News of an undisturbed site at Brixham cave in Devon reached the amateur geologist William Pengelly in 1858. Excited by the pristine site, Pengelly informed members of the Geological Society of London, who formed a committee to supervise the excavation. The cave's floor was marked with a grid and layers of rock were slowly peeled back. Months of painstaking digging generated hundreds of animal bones and, crucially, seven flint tools unquestionably made by people. Several factors convinced geologists that the flint tools were conclusive proof of human antiquity. A pristine site helped defend against potential criticisms of tampering or later occupation by modern peoples. The innovative grid system ensured the dig was exceptionally well documented. Pengelly's foresight in alerting the geologists of London ensured metropolitan interest in directing, and authenticating, the finds. When the results were reported, the scholarly credentials of gentlemanly geologists helped verify the flint tools as genuine.[18] The combination of practical methods and elite validation were essential to widespread interest in the cave's significance.

The geologist Charles Lyell visited the cave and later used his presidential address to the annual meeting of the British Association for the Advancement of Science in September 1859 to make his views public: 'No subject has lately excited more curiosity and general interest among geologists and the public than the question of the antiquity of the human race.' Despite numerous suggestive finds, he noted the 'extreme reluctance' to 'admit the validity of such evidence'. After all, many sites endured floods and multiple occupations making the evidence difficult to interpret. Nonetheless, Lyell vouched for the empirical reliability of the Brixham flints and declared they 'imply a remote antiquity for the human fossil remains, and make it probable that man was old enough to have coexisted, at least, with the Siberian mammoth'.[19] Sceptics remained, but Lyell's address marked an important new consensus that our past receded into unknown millennia. The address also promised his audience that a great work twenty years in the making would soon solve another great mystery about life on earth.

Charles Darwin's *On the Origin of Species by Means of Natural Selection, or the Preservation of Favoured Races in the Struggle for Life* was published by the respectable press of John Murray in November 1859. Many naturalists of the time believed species were immutable natural kinds based on the assumption that God's Creation was perfect from the outset. As early as 1844, Darwin admitted that he no longer believed species were fixed to his botanist friend Joseph Dalton Hooker, who later became the Director of Kew Gardens. Darwin described it as 'like confessing a murder'.[20] As he privately worried over the nature of species, the anonymous publication of *Vestiges of the Natural History of Creation* in 1844 sparked intense controversy for arguing that life on earth developed from cosmologically humble beginnings to our world. Reviewers issued vicious denunciations for contradicting the Biblical account of Creation and fretted about society at large, because they associated such godlessness with the gutter press and the bloodiest horrors of the French Revolution where naturalists such as Jean-Baptiste Lamarck suggested that new species developed through ancestors passing on useful acquired characteristics.[21] British fears that revolutionary political violence might spread like contagion from Europe to Britain ensured that radical ideas such as species change were simply not respectable subjects for legitimate scientific inquiry, or discussion. In a magisterial history of the reception of *Vestiges*, the historian James A. Secord suggests that anonymity made it impossible to dismiss *Vestiges* as a hack job unworthy of any consideration. The book rapidly became a bestseller and previously hushed conversations bloomed into open debates.[22] Even more fearful of public censure, Darwin privately amassed evidence until he rushed to publication.

The *Origin of Species* hinted that in the future 'Light will be thrown on the origin of man and his history': these twelve words triggered immediate, often vitriolic, speculation about our origins. The heretical implication that humans and apes might share a common ancestor suggested a much lowlier origin than being created in God's 'own image' as noted in verse 27 of the first chapter of the Book of Genesis. Despite Darwin's deliberate reticence on human origins, many readers were immediately alert to, and horrified by, the implication that humans were descended from apes, with moral inclinations rooted in bestial instincts. Cartoonists mocked Darwin and his advocates by filling the Victorian press with caricatures of monkey ancestors, or tracing bizarre evolutionary lineages. Darwin was not the first to suggest that species changed or that apes and humans might share ancestry, but several factors made his intervention significant. Just as anonymity protected the author of *Vestiges*, so Darwin's gentlemanly standing, reputation as a gifted naturalist among London's scientific elite, and prestigious publisher ensured his ideas were not summarily dismissed. The startling new prospect of an evolutionary natural history for humans stimulated the search for human fossils as well as the 'missing link' between apes and humans, while Darwin finally addressed human evolution in *The Descent of Man* in 1871.[23]

Meanwhile, the identity of the newly named Neanderthal Man remained a mystery. Lyell visited the Neander Valley in 1860, licked the bones to find his tongue stuck, and carried home a cast of the skull. The cast circulated among London's gentlemanly elite and was carefully pored over by the surgeon George Busk, Hunterian Professor of Comparative Anatomy and Physiology at the Royal College of Surgeons. Busk translated sections of Schaaffhausen's original article from German and added extensive commentary in 1861. Busk suspected the remains were of great antiquity from their stickiness and fine dendritic marks he had only observed in fossilized cave bears, horses, and woolly mammoths.[24] Busk was fascinated by the Neanderthal skull's form, which he interpreted as 'the most savage primitive type of the human race'.[25] He lamented that 'no portions of the facial bones, whose confirmation is so decisive' were preserved'.[26] He took measurements and compared them to other skulls, including published measurements for the skulls of at least two African men, an African woman, individuals from Malaysia and India, and skulls from Italy, Iceland, Norway, and Ireland. Busk failed to find a close match in the 'museums of the College of Surgeons in London, the Jardin des Plantes Paris, of the universities of Göttingen, Berlin, and Bonn'.[27] He concluded that the skull belonged to a 'barbarous and savage race'.[28]

Busk's frustration with an incomplete skull indicated his inability to take standardized anthropological measurements. Craniometrists reduced skulls to numerical data to help make comparisons and create hierarchies using cranial capacity, facial angle, and cephalic index. Cranial capacity, defined as the volume of the brain case, was used to make racialized claims about intelligence based on the twinned assumptions that the measurement was an adequate measure of brain size, and that brain size was directly correlated to intelligence.[29] The facial angle was defined as the angle between a vertical line drawn following the slope of the brow intersecting with a horizontal line drawn from the base of the nostril to the ear. Invented by the physician Petrus Camper to catalogue human proportions in the 1770s, anatomists, anthropologists, and artists quickly used the facial angle to make broader claims about beauty and intelligence. They compared the facial angles of apes, colonized peoples, and Europeans to depict an order that they believed reflected ascending degrees of intelligence and beauty (Fig. 4.3). While apes were presumed to be the lowest and ugliest forms, colonized peoples were depicted as intermediaries, and Europeans classified as the epitome of beauty and intelligence as represented by the Roman sculpture of Apollo Belvedere, whose facial angle was close to 45 degrees.[30] The Swedish professor of anatomy Anders Retzius defined the cephalic

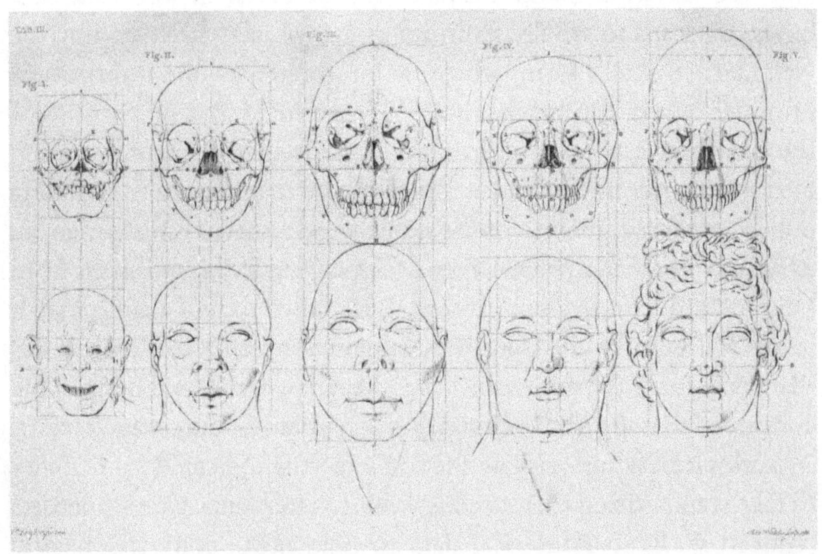

4.3 A human hierarchy constructed using the facial angle from ape to Apollo.

index as the ratio produced by dividing the skull's width by its length, and used it to classify skulls into three types: oval, long and narrow, or broad and short.[31] Whether used alone, or in combination, craniometrists used cranial capacity, facial angle, and the cephalic index to create racist hierarchies with Europeans at the top, other peoples in the middle, and apes as the lowliest of all. Busk's desire to make these measurements on the Neanderthal skull was an empirical and political urge to incorporate the mysterious person into an existing racialized hierarchy of human worth.

In the first few weeks after their finding, the Neanderthal bones were said to be *unlike* any living peoples, but within a few years they were routinely likened to living colonized peoples. Thomas Henry Huxley, an anatomist and staunch defender of Darwin's new evolutionary theories, examined the Neanderthal skull cast procured by Lyell and worried over by Busk. Huxley wrote about the skull in his essay collection on *Man's Place in Nature* (1863). He assured readers that the skull's 'extraordinary form' was 'not known to exist, even in the most barbarous races' (Fig. 4.4).[32] He confirmed the bones were fossils, but emphatically refuted they were a 'missing link' between apes and humans. He compared the Neanderthal cast to four skulls identified only by their origin: an African man, an Aboriginal man from Western Port in Australia, a Mongolian skull held at the Royal College of Surgeons, and an unidentified skull in his own possession from a Constantinople cemetery. He illustrated his essay with a figure comparing the Neanderthal cast to the Aboriginal Australian man, contending that a 'small additional amount of flattening and lengthening, with a corresponding increase of the supraciliary ridge, would convert the Australian braincase into a form identical with that of the aberrant fossil'. Huxley admitted that without the Neanderthal jaw 'any judgement on the relations of the fossil skulls to recent Races must be accepted with a certain reservation'.[33] Despite the qualification, Huxley's implication that Aboriginal peoples were living fossils from the Stone Age dominated nineteenth-century debates about human antiquity and laid the foundations of profoundly racist stereotypes that linger to this day.

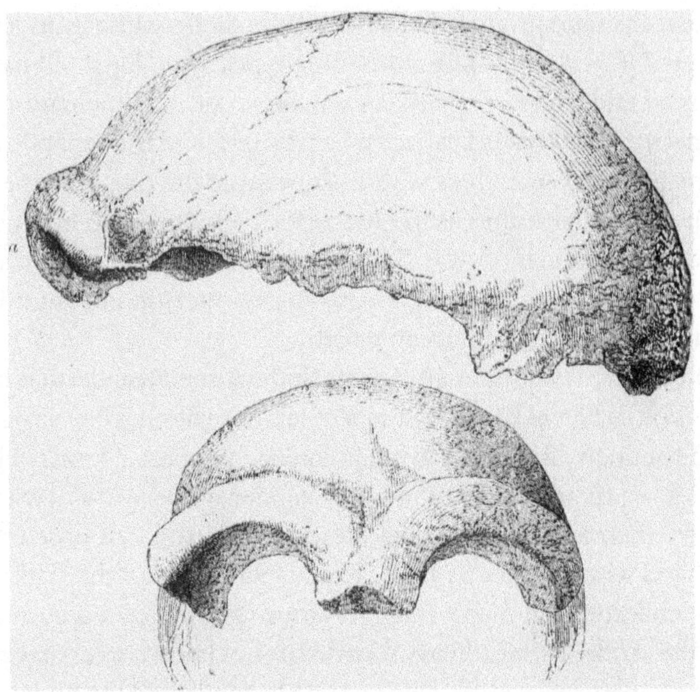

4.4 Huxley's drawing of the Neanderthal skull cast.

Neanderthals were finally given a species name in 1864. In an almost throwaway remark buried in a footnote, the geologist and keen fossil collector William King proposed *Homo neanderthalensis* as a suitable recognition of the first widely accepted new member of the genus since Linnaeus invented *Homo*. King concluded that the Neanderthal was 'not only specifically but generically distinct from Man' by comparing the Neanderthal skull cast to the Andaman islanders.[34] King regarded them as 'next to brute benightedness', yet he reasoned, *even* they had skulls akin to 'the highest intellectual races'.[35] King's comparisons with living peoples he considered as lowly as possible reveals how debates about Neanderthal humanity were utterly dependent on racialized discussions about who counted as a human or animal, and the assumed spectrum from uncivilized to civilized, in the nineteenth century. Such comparisons strengthened King's conviction that 'the Neanderthal skull is eminently simial' and so 'I feel myself constrained to believe that the thoughts and desires which once dwelt within it never soared beyond that of the brute'.[36]

In the same year that *Homo neanderthalensis* was formally named a species in its own right, a skull from Gibraltar captivated London's scientific elite. Dug up in Forbes' quarry by Lieutenant Edmund Flint, the skull was presented to the Gibraltar Scientific Society in 1848.[37] The skull reached London in unclear circumstances, but was quickly examined and compared to the Neanderthal by George Busk. Gratified, he declared it 'of infinitely higher value than the much-disputed [German] relic' because it retained 'nearly the entire face including the upper jaw with most of the much and curiously worn teeth'. Busk finally calculated the facial angle and cephalic index for a fossilized human skull. Using these measurements, he concluded that the Gibraltar skull confirmed that the Neanderthal remains were not 'a mere individual peculiarity' but probably a 'race extending from the Rhine to the Pillars of Hercules'. The geographical range contradicted one naturalist's view that the bones were merely a diseased and wounded horseman taking refuge after fighting in the Russian army against the French in the Napoleonic wars. Busk delighted in clarifying that a grave so far west made it impossible to believe 'a rickety Cossack engaged in the campaign of 1814 had crept into a sealed fissure in the Rock of Gibraltar'.[38] Now known as Gibraltar 1, it was considered the first Neanderthal found until Schmerling's find of Engis 2 was reclassified as a Neanderthal child in 1936. Gibraltar 1 remains the first adult Neanderthal unearthed.[39] In 1886 two nearly complete Neanderthal skeletons were found at Griotte de Spy, Belgium, finally ending speculation on whether they were a new human species.[40]

The debate about who counted as human existed long before our ancient ancestors were found, but it took on new dimensions as nineteenth-century diggers and sifters exposed our fragmented, petrified kin. Geologists, antiquarians, anthropologists, and archaeologists all formulated new theories and methods to make sense of these unique puzzles throughout the nineteenth century.[41] Crucially, scholars compared Neanderthal remains to other skulls in their substantial collections from peoples all over the world, ensuring ancient humans were quickly incorporated into a global, and highly racialized, story about humanity's origins. As Lubbock wrote: 'Not only throughout Europe – not only in Italy and Greece – but even in the so-called cradle of civilisation itself, in Palestine, and Syria, in Egypt, and in India, the traces of a stone age have been discovered.'[42] The disagreement over Neanderthal taxonomy also revolved around the special status of human beings. As the *Anthropological Review* argued: 'Man, in his pride, is so much in the habit of considering himself as the last link, as the epitome of the vegetable and animal world, in short as the lord of the creation, that he conceives it beneath his dignity to appear on the scene until everything has been duly prepared for his reception.'[43] Human antiquity challenged ideas of superiority rooted in Biblical theologies about Adam being created by God in His own image and with dominion over the earth, but this was not due to an inherent conflict between science and theology. Instead, many geologists and theologians created new narratives about human evolutionary progress.

Debates about human antiquity overlapped with much older ideas about political, social, cultural and moral worth. In the most basic terms, eighteenth-century scholars used a four-stage model of human development. The lowliest societies were believed to be nomadic hunter-gatherers, followed by pastoralists with domesticated animals. Next were the agriculturalists whose farming of crops allowed them to settle down. Establishing commerce and permanent settlement was regarded as the highest stage of human civilization. Scholars interested in human classification used a broad range of factors, such as geography, religion, clothing, means of subsistence, and complexion, to distinguish between human varieties and pinpoint stages of development to define 'race' and 'civilization'. This allowed 'race' to function as an elastic category defined by a broad variety of cultural, environmental, and physical factors.[44]

Histories of racial thought often associate the 1860s with the overthrowing of older elastic and developmental difference in favour of theories proposing innate physiological, anatomical, or biological differences between humans. The proposed shift is attributed to many factors, including debates over enslavement, the diminishing importance of environmental ideas about human difference, and the emergence of a new scientific racism exemplified by polygenesis.[45] However, human antiquity allowed scholars arguing over whether humans were a single species, or many, to strengthen their cases. Both factions needed vast tranches of time to explain the development of variation from a single origin or, more controversially, the emergence of multiple human species. Far from disappearing, stadial and developmental classifications persisted well into the late nineteenth century, especially when combined with ideas about social evolution. A narrative of progressive civilization, with some peoples achieving greater advances than others, still resonated with many. As such, the mid-nineteenth century saw a substantial proliferation, not simplification, of theories of human difference, because older classifications did not disappear but competed with newer ways of cleaving humanity into distinct kinds: whether of a single descent or many; savage, barbarous, or civilized; and ancient or modern.

The Ascent of Extinction

Amid debates about the meaning of human difference, geologists popularized the new consensus on human antiquity throughout the 1860s. Charles Lyell's *Geological Evidences of the Antiquity of Man* (1863) discussed the lives of ancient humans alongside the emergence of Europeans. The book shifted the debate from whether men walked among mammoths to when they first met.[46] Two years later, John Lubbock's *Pre-Historic Times* (1865) summarized the latest geological research and introduced new epochs of human history. A baronet, banker, and devoted carer for a pet wasp now preserved in the British Museum, Lubbock was an important member of London's scientific elite who further subdivided the Stone Age, Bronze Age, and Iron Age.[47] He proposed four great epochs: the 'Palaeolithic' Stone Age when ancient humans lived alongside cave bears and woolly mammoths; the 'Neolithic', or 'polished Stone Age', when human metalwork was limited to gold; the Bronze Age when humans used the metal for armaments and implements; and, finally, the Iron Age in which bronze was primarily ornamental and iron used more widely.[48] Lubbock's division of the Stone Age into the Palaeolithic and Neolithic extended, consolidated, and refined the use of the Three Age classification in Britain. When Darwin finally addressed our ancient past in the 1870s, he was keenly aware that vast new timescales made human evolution plausible. As he noted, the 'high antiquity of man has recently been demonstrated . . . this is the indispensable basis for understanding his origin. I shall, therefore, take this conclusion for granted.'[49]

Prehistory captivated scholars exploring humanity's pasts, but the lack of written sources and rarity of artefacts made reconstructing the lives of our ancestors near impossible for historians who depended upon methods rooted in the study of literate societies. The historian Francis Palgrave evocatively captured the scale of the challenge:

> You can no more judge of their age than the eye can estimate the height of the clouds: the shapeless masses impart but one lesson, the impossibility of recovering by induction any knowledge of the speechless past. Waste not your oil. Give it up, that speechless past; whether fact or chronology, doctrine or mythology; whether in Europe, Asia, Africa or America; at Thebes or Palenque, on Lycian shore or Salisbury Plain: lost is lost; gone is gone forever.[50]

An expert on Normandy and England, Palgrave's dour advice proclaimed writing prehistory universally futile, providing a dizzying sense of the expansion of historical time from a few millennia of written sources to time immemorial, and the new challenges facing anyone interested in studying our ancient past.[51]

Geologists soon proposed that ethnographic observations offered solutions to archaeological hindrances. Alert to the empirical paucity of knapped stone or fossilized bones, Lubbock proposed using modern colonized peoples as living proxies of ancient human society.

Since early Europeans lived in uncivilized states, Lubbock reasoned that peoples in similar states of arrested development around the world might facilitate comparisons. Lubbock regarded his comparative method as an essential tool: 'if we wish to clearly understand the antiquities of Europe, we must compare them with the rude implements and weapons still, or until lately, used by savage races in other parts of the world'.[52] His book's title made the archaeological equivalence explicit: *Pre-Historic Times: As Illustrated by Ancient Remains and the Manners and Customs of Modern Savages* (1865). Lubbock's global aspirations were evident in chapters devoted to 'Savages' and discussing the Khoisan, Indians, Andaman Islanders, Aboriginal Australians, Aboriginal Tasmanians, Fijians, Māori, Tahitians, Inuit, Native nations of America, and peoples of Paraguay and Patagonia.[53] While Lubbock, and his contemporaries, almost always referred to specific groups when providing examples, this was usually in the service of much broader categories such as 'savage' and 'civilized'.

Lubbock assembled evidence from 'merchants, philosophers, naval men, and missionaries alike' to provide 'almost universal testimony' about colonized peoples.[54] His list of authorities is revealing. Merchants, missionaries, and mariners were on a par with philosophers precisely because scholars valued in situ knowledge provided by people living, trading, and labouring within colonies and along global shipping routes. Ethnographic observations flowed along the same paths as people and commodities, making scientific knowledge dependent on imperial infrastructure. The comparative method was not a panacea and could reveal unexpected relationships, but it remained a significant way of understanding human prehistory and made the lives of modern colonized peoples into the foundations of nineteenth-century comparative prehistoric archaeology.[55]

Ancient human disappearances were regarded as a consequence of migration, conquest, and extermination, but extinction also became an explanatory tool in the mid-nineteenth century.[56] Discussing human antiquity in the *Anthropological Review*, one writer suspected that 'Premature as the inference may be . . . the conclusion is not altogether unfounded that the original races were inferior to the succeeding immigrants, and also that the primitive race is now extinct in Europe, and has shared the fate of the gigantic animals with which it was contemporaneous.'[57] In these discussions, ancient peoples were believed to have replaced, and probably exterminated, ostensibly inferior races as they migrated across the world. Lubbock regarded Stone Age and Bronze Age Danish archaeological remains as so distinctive that the latter might have 'been introduced by a *new race of men*' who 'rapidly exterminated the previous inhabitants . . . and were all together in a much higher state of civilisation'.[58] In the 1870s, the French anthropologist Paul Broca argued that Neanderthals only survived as a people until 'another stronger and more perfect race' supplanted the former after 'having nearly exterminated it'.[59] The conflation of extermination and extinction continued in the 1880s as the archaeologist William Boyd Dawkins conjectured that Palaeolithic peoples encountering Neolithic invaders found 'there were the same feelings between them as existed in Hearne's times between the Eskimos and the Red Indian, terror and defenceless hatred being, on the one side, met by ruthless extermination on the other'.[60] Dawkins blended evidence of ancient and modern violence to explain why prehistoric humans were 'gradually driven from Europe, without leaving any mark on the succeeding peoples in blood, manners or customs'.[61] Prehistorians effectively recast ancient human exterminations as extinctions while justifying their conflation as evidence of a timeless suspicion of migrants.

Nineteenth-century beliefs that colonized peoples were Stone Age relics were reflected in the museums of the day. Augustus Henry Lane Fox, later Pitt Rivers, is best remembered for his founding bequest to the Pitt Rivers Museum in Oxford, established in 1884 within twenty-five years of the discovery of ancient flint tools at Brixham Cave in Devon.[62] He used his inherited wealth to build an extensive personal collection of ethnographic artefacts, archaeological finds, and European folk art, some of which he excavated personally while holidaying in Europe, Egypt, and North America. Keen to display his treasures to best effect, Pitt Rivers invented a system based on sequences of types to show evolutionary change.

Crucially, he intended his typological system to exhibit progressive human development:

> The resemblance between the arts of modern savages and those of primeval man may be compared to that existing between recent and extinct species of animals. As we find amongst existing animals, species akin to what geology teaches us were primitive species, and as among existing species we find the representatives of successive stages of geological species, so amongst the arts of existing savages we find forms which, being adapted to a low condition of culture, have survived from the earliest times, and also the representatives of many successive stages through which development has taken place in times past.[63]

Pitt Rivers' bequest made his collection, and the evolutionary assumptions underlying it, publicly available for decades, perpetuating interpretations of colonized peoples as lowly vestiges of ancient pasts.

The image of Neanderthals as unintelligent brutes was transformed later in the twentieth century. The remarkably complete skeleton of the Old Man of La Chapelle in central France was dug up in 1908. Found in a limestone cave floor among extinct rhinoceros, reindeer, bison, and hyena, the Old Man appeared to have been deliberately buried. Convinced of the skeleton's importance, the excavators donated it to the National Museum of Palaeontology in Paris.[64] The French palaeontologist Marcellin Boule reconstructed the skeleton and penned an unflattering article conjecturing that Neanderthals walked on two feet, in a hunchbacked, ape-like posture: 'Neanderthal Man must have possessed only a rudimentary psychic nature, superior certainly to that of the anthropoid apes, but markedly inferior to that of any modern race whatever. He had doubtless only the most rudimentary articulate language.'[65] Reports in *Nature* marvelled at the find and compared the Old Man to the peoples of both Australia and Africa. The stooped, inhuman brute that Boule imagined dominated ideas about Neanderthals for decades.[66]

The discovery of Neanderthal children excited twentieth-century prehistorians and archaeologists. In 1915 the archaeologist H. Martin dug up the skull of a young girl, now believed to have been around seven or eight years old, in the La Quina rock shelter of the Charente in western France. Eleven years later, the English archaeologist Dorothy Garrod excavated the Devil's Tower, Gibraltar, close to where Gibraltar 1 was discovered. Using dynamite to blow apart the layers of rock, Garrod and her team recovered fragments of a boy's skull so young that he still had milk teeth.[67] A writer for the *Science News-Letter* could hardly disguise their surprising news with the headline 'WOMAN FINDS NEW CAVE MAN SKULL AT GIBRALTAR'.[68] The omission of Garrod's name is indicative of the historic exclusion of women from both scientific research and histories of science. Garrod's career is remarkable beyond her discovery of the young boy. Thirteen years later, she was the first woman elected to a professorship at the University of Cambridge or the University of Oxford, marking an important milestone for the achingly slow inclusion of women within academia and scientific research, particularly at ancient universities and elite learned societies. The child's skull is known as Gibraltar 2 and believed to have been about three years old at the time of death, providing important evidence of Neanderthal childhood.

Between the two World Wars, significant discoveries of human fossils in Asia and Africa radically transformed reconstructions of human prehistory while scientists still longed to find the missing link between apes and humans.[69] *Australopithecus africanus* was first excavated in Taung, northwest South Africa, in 1925. Indonesian expeditions yielded fossils named *Pithecanthropus* between 1929 and 1937. A skull found in a Chinese cave was eventually named *Sinanthropus* and widely reported in the press as 'Peking Man' in 1929. *Pithecanthropus* and *Sinanthropus* attracted much greater interest than *Australopithecus*, partly because scientists expected to find ancestral fossil humans in Asia owing to much older ideas about our origins rooted in the Biblical story of Noah's Ark mooring in the Caucasus mountains. After the Second World War, attention switched to Africa when numerous fossils were unearthed, including *Homo habilis* in 1960. These finds vastly expanded the human family tree and created new interpretative possibilities for understanding our relationship to Neanderthals. Africa was reimagined as humanity's cradle and palaeoanthropologists reconstructed new patterns of global migration from that continent.

Amid the reorientation of our origins, the stereotype of Neanderthals as slouching, inhuman brutes was challenged.[70] The anthropologist William Straus and anatomist Alexander Cave visited the Old Man at the *Museé de l'Homme* (Museum of Man) in Paris in July 1955. They concluded that Boule had misinterpreted the deformations of an elderly, arthritic skeleton as typical of a healthy Neanderthal. Boule knew that some of the vertebrae were diseased, but Cave and Straus felt he had underestimated the extent of the pathology. Moreover, Boule pieced together an unusually straight spine in stark contrast to the naturally curved spine of modern humans. For Cave and Straus these problems rendered Boule's assertions of a stooped gait and brutish ape-like appearance invalid. Famously, they quipped that if a Neanderthal man was 'reincarnated and placed in a New York subway – provided that he were bathed, shaved, and dressed in modern clothing – it is doubtful whether he would attract any more attention than some of its other denizens'.[71] Straus and Cave were among the earliest scientists to transform our understanding of Neanderthals.

Stereotypes of ancient humans as grunting brutes are common in popular culture, but modern scientists regard Neanderthals as complex, adaptable, and intelligent kin.[72] They are now believed to have been adept hunters who crafted efficient hunting weapons, such as spears, and killed large animals such as aurochs, bison, horses, reindeers, and seals, while trying to outwit predatory hyenas.[73] They also harvested plants and seafood, including cockles, limpets, crabs, mussels, and oysters along the shore of the Mediterranean and the coasts of the Atlantic and Africa.[74] Specialists have interpreted figurative hand prints believed to be over 66,000 years old as evidence that Neanderthals consciously created and appreciated art, in addition to the belief that they might also have used body art and ornaments, from feathers to paint and clothes.[75]

The nature of Neanderthal extinction remains unclear. Ranging across Europe and Asia, Neanderthals appear in the fossil record from around 450,000 years ago and disappear about 40,000 years ago. As early as the 1940s, the geneticist and evolutionary biologist Theodosius Dobzhansky suggested that Neanderthals and modern humans interbred.[76] Discussing fossil remains from Palestine, he noted that the distinctive population 'arose . . . as a result of hybridization of a Neanderthaloid and a modern type, these types having been formed earlier in different geographical regions'.[77] In 1998 a team found the well-preserved skeleton of a four-year-old Neanderthal boy in the limestone cliffs of the Lagar Velho rock shelter, Portugal. They dated his burial to between 28,000 and 30,000 years ago and argued the boy's features were a 'mosaic' of Neanderthal and modern humans. They interpreted this as evidence that the boy descended from populations with substantial intermixing for millennia.[78] The team also interpreted the burial site as indicating that the last Neanderthals took refuge in Iberia, probably Gibraltar, before their extinction.[79]

Neanderthals may no longer survive as a kind, but their DNA may linger in many of us. The Neanderthal genome was sequenced by a team based in Leipzig, Germany, in 2010.[80] They began with twenty-one fossilized Neanderthal bones from Croatia, whittled the collection down to three individuals from which they extracted nine samples of Neanderthal DNA, and compared these larger samples to smaller fragments from three other Neanderthal sites, including the original remains from Neander Valley in Germany. They also compared the Neanderthal DNA to that of chimpanzees and five modern humans, including 'one San from Southern Africa, one Yoruba from West Africa, one Papua New Guinean, one Han Chinese, and one French from Western Europe'.[81] The team inferred that Neanderthals and modern humans diverged between 270,000 and 440,000 years ago while modern humans inherited between 1 per cent and 4 per cent of their genes from Neanderthals. They also concluded that all modern

Eurasians, but only some Africans, share genes with Neanderthals.[82] More recent studies argue that modern humans arrived in Europe 45,000 years ago and overlapped with Neanderthals for at least five thousand years, allowing considerable time for intermixing.[83] Within a year of the Neanderthal genome's reconstructions, commercial ancestry testing gave customers the chance to 'Find Your Inner Neanderthal' and, more recently, to 'Celebrate your Ancient DNA'.[84] Whether we choose to redefine our reflections, blood, or genes as our 'inner Neanderthal' or not, we remain as captivated by our ancient ancestors as did the people who first encountered our petrified kin.

Naming Neanderthals a distinct species radically changed naturalists' sense of human uniqueness. The exact form of humanity's family tree remains heavily disputed, but there are currently thirteen species within the genus *Homo*, and more might be added as new fossils are found.[85] Nineteenth-century writers were horrified that the hideous cranium from the Neander Valley might be anything more than a diseased or deformed oddity. From Sunday schools to learned societies, people scrabbled for answers to troubling questions raised by the prospect of human fossils. Were humans placed on earth by God, or did they share a common ancestor with apes? When did humans first take their place among the beasts? Had some humans died out? If so, how? What was the best way to understand the society and culture of the first humans? From the 1860s onwards, intense debates yielded a consensus that our ancient ancestors had once roamed lost worlds and there were many more ways of being human than previously imagined. Historical and scientific interest in evolution tends to overshadow the importance of the almost parallel debates on human antiquity, but questions about our origins were just as important as those about race, descent, or evolution.[86]

When the first scholars pored over the bones from Neander Valley, they drew on nineteenth-century ideas about race and development to interpret Neanderthals as hideous, apish brutes. They also drew direct comparisons with living peoples routinely vilified as lowly or inferior across Africa, Asia, Australia, and the Americas. Modern palaeoanthropologists have abandoned the language of 'savages', but they still use living peoples as proxies of ancient human behaviour, echoing the nineteenth-century logic that hunter-gatherers represent early stages of human development.[87] Recognizing the origins of these racialized, and often racist, claims about who counts as human and how developed they might be is essential to unravelling the legacies of older ideas about extinction. Our fascination and desire to understand our kin may be harmless, but early debates about what it means to be human have left more disturbing legacies.

The possibility that ancient human extinctions were harbingers of modern colonial encounters created disturbing prophecies and comparisons. Writers such as Lubbock and Dawkins, when considering human antiquity and extinction, inferred that a broader pattern of extinction governed human encounters throughout our existence. These comparisons laid the foundations of racist stereotypes that some peoples, particularly in Australia or the Andaman Islands in the Bay of Bengal, were Stone Age relics in arrested states of development. In Australia, early colonists partly rationalized Aboriginal dispossession through claims that British emigrants were merely replacing peoples who were doomed to extinction.[88]

In the late nineteenth century a young Irish woman read about the prophesied doom of Aboriginal peoples. Stirred by their plight, she set sail for Australia where she preached the creed of extinction to her dying breath.

5.

Daisy's Dying Legacy

Daisy Bates eagerly unwrapped copies of her first published book a few weeks after her seventy-ninth birthday, during a period convalescing in an Adelaide hospital.[1] Sent straight from its London printing press, the book's publication in 1938 marked the culmination of her lifetime's labour – and a narrow escape from oblivion. The plane carrying her manuscript from Australia to London had crashed into the sea en route. Luckily, the mail had been rescued and the manuscript sent on to her publisher John Murray.[2] *The Passing of the Aborigines: A Lifetime Spent Among the Natives of Australia* recounted over forty years that Bates spent camping in the Australian desert, devoted to her 'self-imposed task' of 'making the passing easy' for a dying race.[3] The book included stories of her frequent encounters with individuals she described as the last of their kind.[4]

Bates earned a peculiar fame as the 'Great White Queen of the Never Never': a white woman, dressed in Edwardian fashion, living in the desert. The writer Darcy Niland reminisced:

> The most interesting person I've met in my wanderings around Australia was a woman from the Stone Age who wore a stiff starched white collar, and a black skirt which swept the desert dust. She spoke the barbaric tongue of the most primitive, most neglected people in the world – and she wore on her forehead a little frizzy fringe, just like Queen Alexandria. This was Mrs Daisy Bates . . . [5]

Bates was widely praised as a humanitarian and appointed a Commander of the British Empire (CBE) in 1934. Her fame endures in Australia, but she is largely forgotten in histories of anthropology or extinction despite perpetuating and popularizing the notion of dying races in the twentieth century. Yet, in recent years, Bates's meditations on Aboriginal extinction have finally yielded an unexpected legacy that she would never have dreamed possible.

Invasion

The ancient land mass of Sahul comprised the land masses now known as Australia, New Guinea and Tasmania. Palaeoanthropologists regard the peopling of Sahul as essential for unravelling our ancient past, especially our ancestors' migration out of Africa. The exact timing, route, and number of entry points are heavily disputed. Archaeologists have repeatedly revised their estimates for the Aboriginal occupation of Australia: dates of 10,000 years ago were common in the 1950s, but jumped to 20,000 years by the mid-1960s, to 30,000 years by the end of the 1960s, and even further to 40,000 years by the early 1970s. The most recent estimate stands at 65,000 years ago in an article published in *Nature* in 2017.[6] Despite this long-running dispute, often conducted with little regard for Aboriginal peoples' own histories of their presence, we know that the peopling of Country led to an extraordinarily dynamic flourishing of cultural complexity, trade, language, and art. As peoples radiated across the continent, they spoke of their own becoming using at least 250 known language groups, including 800 dialects.[7]

Aboriginal peoples first encountered Europeans and Southeast Asians in the seventeenth century. The Dutch United East India Company (*VOC*, or *Verenigde Oostindische Compagnie*) was founded in 1602, two years after the English East India Company. The VOC was central to Dutch trade across Southeast Asia, and the crews of VOC ships were the first Europeans to anchor and come ashore on the continent now called Australia in 1606 as they tried to find new trading opportunities. The Dutch surveyed the north and west coasts, while the Dutch explorer Abel Tasman voyaged to the continent in 1642 and 1644, naming it New Holland on his second trip.

Within a few years more local connections were forged. The port city of Makassar lies on the island of Sulawesi, in present-day Indonesia. Between 1650 and 1750, Makassans visited the northern coast of the continent in *praus*, or boats, to catch *trepang*, or sea-cucumbers, as prized foods and medicines in home markets. Their initial forays turned into seasonal stays, sometimes lasting a few months, but the Makassans remained on the coast, and never tried to settle permanently, or impose their customs on the local peoples. The English explorer William Dampier reached New Holland in 1688 and 1699 and wrote in profoundly negative terms about the people he met there in his book *A New Voyage Around the World* (1697). The Dutch, and Dampier, kidnapped locals to serve as guides or interlocutors, leading to Aboriginal peoples facing violence and guns remarkably early in encounters with outsiders.[8]

Exploration, and colonization, followed from the eighteenth century onwards. British naval officer Captain James Cook's three Pacific voyages aboard the ship *Endeavour* in 1768, 1770, and 1779, accompanied by the botanist Joseph Banks, are among the most famous of the twenty European voyages in the late eighteenth century. While Cook's first voyage reached Tahiti, he also made landfall in New Holland. Cook had expected a warm welcome and new opportunities for trade, but he and Banks noticed local people shying away from any approach. Two local men spotted Cook, but warily tried to stop him landing. Cook shot, and hurt, one of the men, and named the place Botany Bay. The crew moved on to the far north coast, where they exchanged items with the residents. As he sailed away from the east coast, Cook stopped at an island, declared himself its first discoverer, named it Possession Island, and claimed the land in the name of King George III.[9] Cook's voyages were essential for expanding British knowledge of the continent, especially for charting the Pacific, collecting natural history specimens, and making ethnographic observations about Aboriginal peoples (Fig. 5.1).

Cook argued that the continent was essentially empty, making it ideal for colonization. The historical Aboriginal population is immensely difficult to quantify as many early records did not include

Engraved for BANKES's New System of GEOGRAPHY Published by Royal Authority.

The KANGUROO an Animal found on the Coast of New Holland.

The OPOSSUM found in the Southern extremity of New Holland.

5.1 Drawings of Australian fauna and flora from the voyages of Joseph Banks. Australia: above, a kangaroo; below, a common ringtail possum.

Aboriginal peoples, or used changing categories of who counted as Aboriginal. This makes any early figures deeply problematic and unreliable. In recent years, population scientists have tried to mathematically model the historical population based on known archaeological sites.[10] Estimates range from a few hundred thousand to the low millions. No matter how well informed these studies are, any speculation about historic numbers requires great caution. Even without exact figures, we know that early European explorers believed the continent was so sparsely populated that it was effectively *Terra Nullius*, or empty land, and regarded Aboriginal peoples as wandering 'nomads' lacking self-government and meaningful ties to the land. These views were rooted in a profound misunderstanding of Aboriginal seasonal occupation, social structures, and belonging to country. Ultimately, European assumptions about empty lands underpinned the rapid dispossession of Aboriginal peoples.

The first British fleet arrived in Botany Bay in 1788 to found a settlement at Sydney Cove, with another following on Van Diemen's Land (now Tasmania) in 1803. Official records indicate that 4,100 men and women had arrived in New South Wales by 1796, swelling to 7,014 by 1802, and 33,543 by 1820.[11] The British government hoped penal colonies would rehabilitate convicts transported from Britain into productive farmers tilling empty, but fertile, soils. The unceded coast proved far less suitable for growing European crops than colonial officials hoped, and settlement encroached further inland fuelled by the transportation of 27,000 convicts between 1788 and 1822, and rising to 160,000 by 1868. Sydney was established as an important port that connected the Australian continent to India, China, the United States, and the Cape of Good Hope in southern Africa by the early 1800s.[12]

From 1803 onwards, Europeans who arrived in the penal colony of Van Diemen's Land, renamed Tasmania in 1856, subjected islanders to horrific state-sanctioned violence. By the early 1820s, escapees and colonists spoke of a 'Black war' against Aboriginal peoples, whom they hunted and murdered with impunity. Estimates of the Aboriginal population before European contact are necessarily speculative, with figures ranging from four to fifteen thousand. Government records provide a chilling record of decline. By the 1830s, the colonial government removed a few hundred Aboriginal peoples to reservations: by 1847 only forty-seven known survivors remained and all of them had passed away by the 1870s. Notoriously, in 1869 William Lanney, widely perceived as the last Tasmanian man, and in 1876 Trukanini, considered the last Tasmanian woman, passed away. Their deaths were widely reported as the complete extinction of their people, forcing surviving Aboriginal Tasmanians to refute claims of their extinction.[13]

The scale and breadth of the everyday violence underpinning these claims of extinction has recently been revealed in an extraordinary project led by the late historian Lyndall Ryan. Defining frontier massacres as the deliberate killing of six or more people, the project created a map pinpointing Australian frontier massacres across the continent between 1788 and 1930. By late 2024 the map showed 438 massacres, with more than 10,000 people killed. Of this total, 419 were massacres by colonists of Aboriginal or Torres Strait Islander people. The map also shows a broadly consistent number of frontier massacres from the 1820s to the 1890s, with a peak in Tasmania in the 1820s, and a peak across the continent in the 1840s. Even this partial archive provides important evidence for the violence underpinning claims of extinction in the nineteenth century.[14]

A rising tide of outsiders and frontier violence led to calls for the greater protection of Aboriginal peoples by the 1830s. One of the most important British parliamentary reports published in 1836 noted: 'In the formation of these settlements it does not appear that the territorial rights of the natives were considered, and very little care has since been taken to protect them from the violence or the contamination of the dregs of our countrymen.'[15] This searing reproach blamed the 'dregs', or former convicts, as a lawless class for committing violent outrages, and ignoring the 'territorial rights' of Aboriginal peoples in the rush to seize land. These accusations clearly betray some class snobbery towards the convicts, but they also openly refer to the pre-existing territorial rights of Aboriginal peoples as a factor that was either carelessly disregarded or even deliberately violated with the arrival of the British. The language of 'territorial rights' is an important indication that people in the nineteenth century, even supporters of imperial rule, were sometimes critical of such dispossession across Australia. The report suggested a policy shift from neglecting frontier violence to establishing paternalistic humanitarian protection. The British government tried to establish protectorates for Aboriginal peoples in the wake of the report, but widespread settler opposition to them as unwarranted metropolitan intervention led to their abolition in the later 1840s. By the mid-nineteenth century, colonial officials, former convicts, entrepreneurs, and swelling numbers of emigrants from Europe, especially those seeking gold or escaping catastrophes such as the Irish Famine (1842–52), formed a settler society that further encroached on Aboriginal lands. By the mid-nineteenth century, expectations of Aboriginal extinction were so rife that colonists freely spoke of the impossibility of Aboriginal assimilation and of their necessary disappearance in due course.[16]

Forging Miss Daisy

Daisy Bates was born in Ireland on 16 October 1859 at a time of rapid colonial expansion in Australia. Her parents named her Margaret Dwyer, but she later adopted the name Daisy and only referred to Margaret as if speaking of a sister. She emigrated to England in 1881 and Australia in 1882.[17] In Australia, Daisy O'Dwyer introduced herself as a twenty-year-old Anglo-Irish Protestant, rather than a twenty-three-year-old Catholic with an affected O' added to her surname. She worked as a governess before marrying Edwin Murrant on 13 March 1884, even though he was two years shy of the legal age of consent of twenty-one. The pair never formally divorced, but the marriage withered, and he later travelled to South Africa. She moved to Sydney and married a second time, to a man named Jack Bates, on 17 February 1885. While Jack went roving in Queensland, Daisy remained in Sydney and married another man named Ernest

Clarke Bagelhole. For unknown reasons, she quickly returned to Jack and never disclosed her bigamy. She gave birth to her only child, Arnold Hamilton Bates, in 1886 within a year of her return. The marriage survived eight years, but disintegrated as Daisy left Jack and sent Arnold to boarding school. Her son occasionally saw her, but died estranged from his mother. Daisy eventually returned to England where she met the journalist W. T. Stead, perhaps best known for publicly campaigning against the use of children in the sex trade and in support of raising the age of consent from thirteen to sixteen in the 1880s, and dying with the sinking of the *Titanic* in 1912.[18] Stead trained Bates as a journalist and hired her as a writer. Little more is known of her life until the end of the century.

Daisy Bates returned to Australia on an urgent, self-imposed mission in 1899. She spent more than forty years visiting and researching Aboriginal peoples, often living in the desert, writing for Australian newspapers, and corresponding with numerous amateur ethnographers. Initially working with varying degrees of governmental support and later at her own expense, she travelled across Western Australia (Fig. 5.2). She visited Rottnest Island prison and went on to the Beagle Bay mission in the remote Kimberley region of Western Australia. She ventured to Broome and Roebuck Plains, the Maamba Reserve outside Perth with peoples of the southwestern districts, the northwest of the state including Bernier and Dorre Islands. She later moved to southern Australia where she spent time at Eucla, Fowlers Bay, Wirilya lying west of Fowlers Bay, Ooldea Soak, and finally Adelaide where she spent her last days.[19]

Bates prioritized learning Aboriginal languages, conducted her own fieldwork, and described her developing proficiency as the process of teaching herself the 'A.B.C. of Anthropology in what I consider was the best way'. She quickly developed her identity as a researcher with unrivalled access to Aboriginal knowledge through linguistic expertise and familiarity with Aboriginal 'go-betweens'.[20] Bates regarded her intensive fieldwork as authoritative experience giving her the freedom to correct the mistakes of others. Between 1904 and 1912 she collected vocabularies from Western Australian

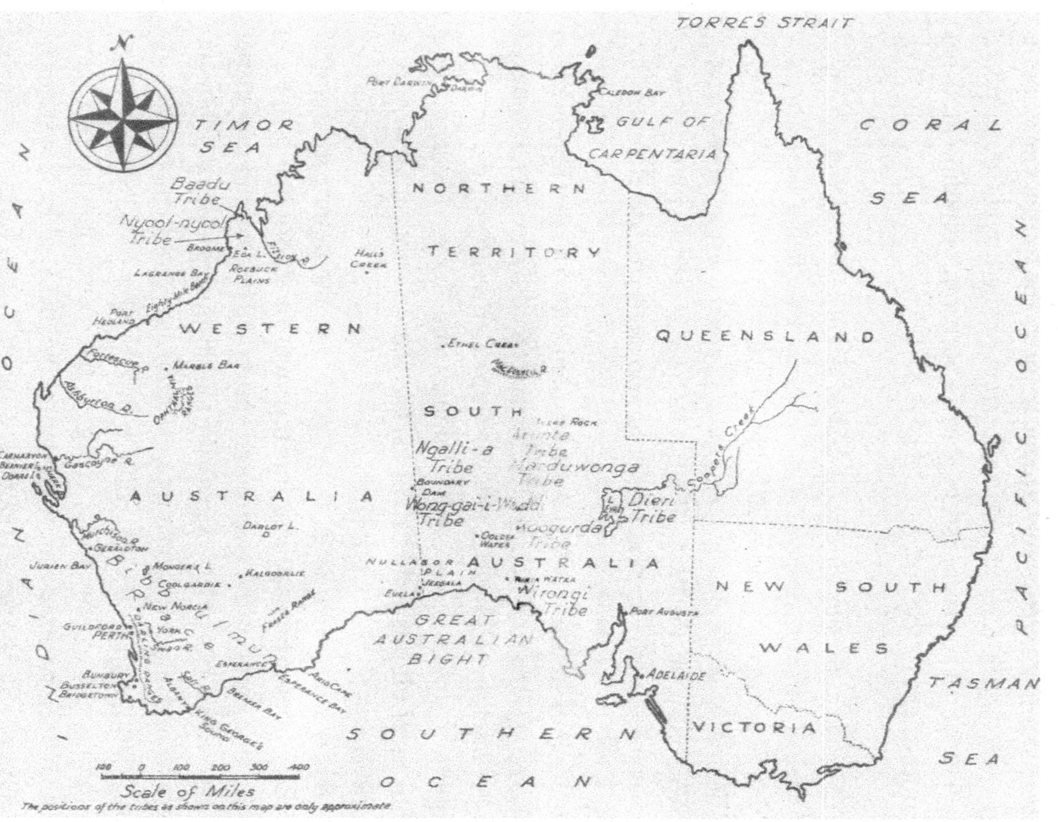

5.2 A map of Australia highlighting the places where Daisy Bates conducted her research.

Aboriginal peoples supported by a commission from Malcolm Fraser, the Registrar-General for Western Australia.[21] She regarded existing vocabularies as 'each contradictory of the other in essentials' (original emphasis). Convinced that 'a faithful record' was only possible by going into 'the Field myself', she marshalled her research into a three-volume manuscript.[22] The founder and honorary secretary of the Queensland branch of the Royal Geographical Society of Australasia, James Park Thomson, complimented her commitment to the task:

> One has to muster up a good deal of courage in undertaking any kind of literary compilation . . . but when we find a lady who is brave enough to sit down in cold blood and tackle the compilation of a work so essentially technical in character as the History and Vocabulary of the W. A. Abo[rigines] then it seems to me that we have reached the highest stage of human intellectual development.[23]

Thomson's almost comical astonishment shows a keen appreciation of the research and betrays the pitfalls faced by women interested in conducting fieldwork. The Australian government declined the expense of publishing Bates's findings and her efforts languished until posthumous publication as *The Native Tribes of Western Australia* in 1985.[24]

When asked why Bates chose her life in the desert, she recalled reading about the appalling mistreatment of Aboriginal peoples in *The Times* early in the twentieth century.[25] The London newspaper published a series of letters in spring 1904 disputing whether white settlers were deliberately trying to exterminate Aboriginal peoples. An early campaigner for Aboriginal rights, Walter Malcolmson, wrote to the paper on 8 April 1904 charging that Aboriginal peoples 'have almost been civilized out of existence'. He believed local systems of indenture left Aboriginal peoples 'worse off' than formerly enslaved Africans in North America. He supported his claim with horrific examples of beating, starvation, and policing.[26] Malcolmson provoked the fury of several writers who categorically denied his claims about enslavement and broader patterns of settler violence. The pastoralist and politician, Henry Bruce Lefroy, denied ever witnessing ill-treatment while tending to his sheep station and alleged: 'The aboriginals of Australia are admitted to be one of the lowest types of humanity. To the higher influence of civilization they have proved unamenable . . . Hence their extinction.'[27] Lefroy's palpable repugnance exemplifies broader, and long-standing, attitudes. A flurry of responses followed, challenging Malcolmson's comparisons with America, and Lefroy's denial, as well as the presumed extinction.[28] Bates contributed to the debate with a characteristically trenchant defence of the British government. She claimed 'equal authority to that of Mr. Malcolmson' rooted in making 'the native question a special study'. She dismissed Malcolmson's letter as 'ridiculous', insisting that 'the natives prefer to be indentured'.[29] Bates carefully used living in the desert as a credential for challenging men, and consistently downplayed any demand for Aboriginal rights by arguing only imperial rule offered suitable protection. Her utter disdain for Aboriginal self-government is transparent. She also claimed *The Times* commissioned her to investigate the abuse further, although proof of the appointment has eluded all her biographers. State concern about how best to manage the situation led to a Royal Commission and report on the 'Condition of the Natives' published in 1905.[30]

Bates's self-reliance and regard for her own research frequently appears in her personal papers. In 1910 she joined the Cambridge Anthropological Expedition in Australia led by Alfred Reginald Brown, who later added his mother's maiden name to become Radcliffe-Brown, and which included the zoologist Grant Watson.[31] Keenly aware she lacked academic accreditations, Bates felt it was a 'huge honour even to be asked to cooperate with such learned professors, and I should love it'. Significantly, she wrote of incorporating herself and Radcliffe-Brown into Aboriginal kinship classifications to secure passage across the land.[32] Radcliffe-Brown read Bates's manuscript for *The Native Tribes of Western Australia*, but a disagreement left Bates alone as Radcliffe-Brown and Watson went on to Bernier Island.[33] Historians tend to neglect Bates's role in the Cambridge Anthropological Expedition by omitting it entirely, or erasing the importance of her expertise. One notable historian of anthropology writes: 'Mrs Daisy Bates, [was] an amateur ethnographer and philanthropist, whom Radcliffe-Brown took on in a show of sexual egalitarianism.' Noting they 'soon quarrelled . . . Radcliffe-Brown decided to leave, and after a row abandoned poor Mrs Daisy Bates on her own'.[34] This account is unusual in acknowledging Bates's presence, but her inclusion is presented as an act of masculine generosity and expulsion as abandonment, rather than presenting 'poor' Bates as an active participant in the expedition's success or the men's gathering of information.

Bates later accused Radcliffe-Brown of plagiarism and rendering her manuscript 'mutilated beyond recovery' at the roving meeting of the British Association for the Advancement of Science that took place across several cities in Australia in 1914.[35] Incontrovertible proof in Bates's favour has never been found, but their contemporaries also questioned Radcliffe-Brown's conduct. Bates's biographer Elizabeth Salter grew suspicious of Radcliffe-Brown's conduct after uncovering letters in which he explicitly noted Bates's manuscript was worth publishing after revision.[36] Salter corresponded with Rodney Needham, a British anthropologist specializing in Southeast Asia, who identified similarities between Radcliffe-Brown's treatment of Bates and of the anthropologist Edward Horace Man. Needham felt that Man's *On the Aboriginal Inhabitants of the Andaman Islands* (1885) was unfairly disparaged and inappropriately credited in Radcliffe-Brown's *The Andaman Islanders* (1922), despite being a better book. Needham also highlighted Radcliffe-Brown's failure to retract his comments despite public rebukes from colleagues.[37] Needham referred Salter to Norman B. Tindale's *Aboriginal Tribes of Australia: The Terrain, Environmental Controls, Distribution, Limits, and Proper Names* (1974). Tindale noted the important work done by Robert Hamilton Mathews, a surveyor working in Paramatta, in correspondence with Daisy Bates: 'Even those versed in Australian literature may not have noticed how often his work was absorbed into the writings of A. R. Brown, one of his detractors, in such a manner as to obscure the fact that he was quoting rather than reporting primary data.'[38] Radcliffe-Brown's contemporaries evidently had reservations regarding his professional conduct and may have regarded Bates with more sympathy in private than they publicly disclosed.

Despite soured relationships with some men, the reputation of unrivalled expertise that Bates fashioned for herself led others to seek her out. The historian of anthropology Isobel White contends that Bates's extensive desert stays enabled her to conduct a different kind of research from that of her male peers. While male colleagues were often fixated on social structures, White suggests that Bates's writings are uniquely textured with details of quotidian life, food, knowledge of the geographical range of languages, descriptions of closely guarded ceremonies, and the first explanation of the geographical differences between matrilineal and patrilineal kinship structures.[39] Bates's surviving letters include many enquiries from amateurs and professionals who valued her research.[40] Surviving enquiries about sexuality are particularly telling. In 1905, Kenneth Young wrote to Bates about his research on body modifications.[41] In the same year, R. H. Mathew (the surveyor praised by Tindale) wrote to Young and Bates. One of his letters marked 'Private' solicited details regarding body modifications with graphic marginalia.[42] Bates's papers do not include a reply. Perhaps respectability made her reticent, but given the discussions of sexuality in her published work and private notes, she may simply have wished to protect her expertise.

Bates frequently claimed she had unparalleled access to Aboriginal knowledge. She asserted that Aboriginal peoples regarded her as a mystical 'Kabbarli', or grandmother: 'I became an "ancestral sorceress" and finally Kabbarli but a magic Kabbarli.'[43] She consistently stressed how readily Aboriginal peoples rewarded her patience with precious confidences:

> My success, thank God, lies and has lain with my forbearance and readiness to serve them in trouble, and never never worrying them. Their time is so short with us – more than 50 of these groups have passed on. They used not to speak of their dead, but here with me,

> they are so keen to let one another know 'all about Kabbarli' that each knows what had been done for sick and dying Mother, sister or child. I hear it all as I remember and name each little grown-up friend.[44]

Bates deliberately lingered over her position within Aboriginal kinship networks and emphasized the willingness of her informants to break with the custom of not naming and speaking of the departed in order to share stories. Her claim that she complied with Aboriginal laws bolstered her assertions of privileged inclusion and ostensible respect. Crucially, this was not 'going native' and living as her subjects, but a calculated choice to observe and participate in some customs all while dressed as a respectable English lady in white gloves, long skirts, cropped jacket, and a wide-brimmed hat. Although Bates often presented herself as a sorceress, she occasionally divulged her more coercive measures to discipline informants or extract information. In particular, she detested Aboriginal people with white heritage and shunned them from her camp.[45] She also insisted on particular manners or protocols for addressing her, such as waiting a certain distance away from her tent for attention. When these were not observed she refused to speak to individuals and would often send them away: 'I had to banish them for the new vices they had adopted during my six years absence, 1935–1941'.[46] More commonly though, she presented herself as a welcome and honoured family member with unrivalled anthropological expertise.

Prophesying Extinction

In 1934, after her last three-year stint in the desert, Daisy Bates decamped to Adelaide to write up her life's work (Figure 5.3).[47] With the help of her amanuensis Ernestine Hill, she edited her manuscript and submitted it to the publisher John Murray, partly attracted by their impressive back catalogue.[48] She considered 'Kabbarli' as a title, but settled on 'My Natives and I'. Her editor solicited peer reviews, and one pointedly distinguished between Bates's

5.3 Darian D. Smith. 'Mrs Daisy Bates at her desk in Adelaide, South Australia' (1941).

undisputed experience and lack of credentials easily available only to men: 'This is a book that requires a Preface by Scientific Expert. It needs such imprimatur: for although she, through living with the aborigines of Australia for over 30 years, witnessed the intimate life & tribal & racial customs, she has rather knowledge than scholarship on the subject.'[49] A second referee also recommended a preface from a suitably eminent expert: 'The author must be individual, and it is of course obvious that she thinks herself marvellous and that various other people are not; this may deprive it of attraction in some quarters . . . It also seems to me essential that the book should have an Introduction by some well-known authority, giving details of her family and her history.'[50] Both reviewers felt the book could not stand on its own merits without being introduced, and therefore officially accredited, by a white male 'Scientific Expert'. This conviction persisted even though one reviewer noted 'quite evidently her studies were true' and that the manuscript 'As a human document . . . has value, and probably has scientific value also.'[51] These reviews both acknowledged and undermined Bates's expertise within a few short lines.

Although Bates originally titled her manuscript 'My Natives and I', John Murray suggested 'The Passing of the Aborigines'. After she approved the change as 'a true title for my book', it was finally published in 1938.[52] Bates asked whether there was anything she could do to help secure reviews in the Australian press and offered extensive lists of potential publications and reviewers.[53] She was partly motivated by economic necessity, but her letters also betray her desire to secure a legacy. Writing to Murray she confided: 'I hope the book will succeed. I don't think I've written a line that will hurt anyone living or dead.'[54] Arthur Mee, a journalist known for writing *The Children's Encyclopaedia*, and a friend of Bates, introduced her to readers as 'one of the least known' but 'most romantic figures in the British Empire'. A woman who gave 'her life and her heart to this dying race, the first people of our southern Dominion', and all for the 'love of humanity and for England'. He stressed her motherly devotion as 'More than once the last member of one of these tribes has died in the arms of Daisy Bates.' In private, she admitted that her life's work had been a 'self-imposed task of "making the passing easy" and doing all I could for their comfort'.[55]

Bates framed Aboriginal peoples in terms of past-tense losses, or present-tense dangers. She characterized settler colonial encroachment as a 'contamination of civilization' that would wipe out Aboriginal peoples despite anyone's best efforts.[56] Bates interviewed individuals she believed to be the last of the Noongar people from southwest Australia, and later wrote of having witnessed the 'Last Perth Native Woman' passing.[57] She frequently referred to the deaths of particular individuals as the last of their kind, whether in terms of kinship, language, or geography. Discussions of sickly individuals, primitivism, and impending loss became intertwined with the leitmotif of extinction:

> One thing runs through my book – the thorough understanding and sympathy and sorrow for the dying peoples . . . for those who I made 'my natives' . . . It will more or less impress every reader of the book in England and here in Australia and help them all to see more and more clearly the inevitable passing of these primitive peoples.[58]

Bates's conviction is an obvious thread in the book, but it also surfaces continually in her private letters. In particular, she dreamt of a colonial governor presiding over the peoples she believed were doomed to die out: 'I wonder if in the days to come they will have a King's Man over them who will understand them and work in their interests and for their "happy passing" as I loved to work? Please God such a man will come.'[59] This particular hope resurfaced in many of her letters, often accompanied by emphatic expressions of her love of King and Empire.[60] She hoped John Murray might publish further work when her subjects had 'become a memory'.[61] Her correspondence is strewn with similar fatalistic predictions, often made as an aside in discussions of other matters. Bates's research was marked by a possessive entitlement to 'my natives', framed by notions of imminent extinction, and her desire for their 'happy passing'.

Bates's life and work bridged older nineteenth-century writing on the shifting nature of extinction and later European colonial fantasies of annihilation. Born in 1859, she first drew breath in a world where debates about extinction, especially with reference to Aboriginal peoples, were rife, and usually expressed in nihilistic terms. Bates first visited Australia, including Tasmania, less than two decades after Trukanini's death in 1876 was noted as that of the last of the Aboriginal Tasmanians. In 1893, Bates stayed in Hobart, Tasmania, and visited Donald MacKinnon, near Launceston, where she saw a photograph of Trukanini.[62] Bates may even have seen Trukanini's stolen skeleton as it was displayed against her wishes in the Hobart Museum until 1947.[63] Like so many other ethnographers and anthropologists of the period, she kept an annotated photograph of Trukanini and photographic postcards of her and William Lanney in her papers.[64] As Bates's encounter and personal papers

5.4 Glass phial labelled as containing the 'Hair of Extinct Tasmanian Aboriginal'. The hair was likely to have been taken without consent, and is just one example of how ostensibly extinct peoples were turned into fragments collected by museums around the world.

show, the 'last Tasmanians' were marketed as popular curios, with images and remains kept by settlers and scientists (Fig. 5.4). From the outset, Bates's research was predicated on fatalistic expectations of the worldwide extinction of dying races. Claiming that Aboriginal peoples were endangered was common, but Bates refused to consider any preventive measures. She was convinced Aboriginal peoples were an 'anachronism . . . withering from contact with the white man's civilization, which can find no place for the primitive'. As such, she believed that nothing could, or should, be done to stave off annihilation. Instead, she observed: 'I realized that they were passing from us. I must make their passing easier.'[65] For a modern reader, encountering her desire feels like meeting a colonizer whose ego can only imagine providing palliative care for a dying race.

Bates's annihilatory pessimism was not universal. Writing in *The Times* just ten months before *The Passing of the Aborigines* was published, Frederic Wood Jones, then Professor of Anatomy at the University of Manchester and formerly of the University of Melbourne, noted that the Aboriginal population was probably over

300,000 when settlers invaded. He estimated that fewer than 55,000 Aboriginal individuals survived, but cautioned against ignoring the growing numbers of people with white and Aboriginal heritage, which were 'increasing in numbers, and they have risen during the last 10 years from 11,000 to 22,000'.[66] He urged governmental intervention to stem further depletion. His alertness to the growing numbers of people descended from Aboriginal peoples and settlers is significant because it did not immediately erase the Aboriginal heritage of anyone who did not fit European notions of who counted as Aboriginal. Many white settlers of this period, including Bates, imposed European notions of kinship and blood purity on Aboriginal peoples by discriminating between ostensibly authentic ('full-blooded') and non-authentic ('half-caste') Aboriginal heritage without much, or any, reference to Aboriginal peoples' own definitions of kinship or belonging. As with other societies, such as the Beothuk in Newfoundland, colonial commentators privileged Europeans' notions of kinship, fixed in fractions of blood, over Aboriginal relations to substantiate claims of imminent extinction.[67]

Bates's stark insistence on the futility of protectionist measures is particularly chilling for an era when Aboriginal population numbers were recovering from the first waves of colonization. Her position contrasted with other colonial activists who campaigned for measures to protect Aboriginal ways of living, not just Aboriginal peoples. Donald Thomson, an anthropologist based in Melbourne, suggested that Aboriginal extinction might be prevented by establishing reservations.[68] Reporting on the conditions in Arnhem Land in the Northern Territory just two years before Bates's book was published, Thomson believed it was an 'undeniable fact that the native population is not only dying out rapidly, but that it is already on the road to extinction'. However, Thomson did not share Bates's resignation. He feared 'prolonged contact' with Europeans or Asians would always cause Aboriginal 'decay, and degradation and racial extinction'. He believed the only solution lay in 'steps of a positive character' (original emphasis).[69] He was particularly concerned about the tendency for government plans to coerce Aboriginal peoples into agricultural subsistence: 'Most of the projects that have so far been advanced for dealing with these natives assume at once that their culture is to be destroyed.' In contrast, Thomson believed protection required 'Absolute segregation with the Arnhem Land reserve. The social structure in toto should be preserved as an essential factor in the life of these people' (original emphasis).[70] Thomson was unusual in calling for extensive in situ protection of Aboriginal peoples and their culture.

White activists in the early 1930s more commonly endorsed segregating Aboriginal peoples on reservations or mission stations for conversion to Christianity.[71] By the later 1930s, the University of Sydney professor of anthropology A. P. Elkin and many other activists were increasingly likely to eschew reservations in favour of granting Aboriginal peoples civil rights and expecting assimilation, sometimes forcibly through child removal. Earlier policies of absorption and systematic whitening gave way to a drive for assimilation after the Second World War. These policies were finally recognized as genocidal by the Australian government in a report in 1997 after decades of campaigning. The government finally issued an apology to the 'Stolen Generations' in 2008.[72]

Aboriginal activists opposed Bates's colonial paternalism throughout the 1920s and 1930s. William Harris founded the Native Union of Western Australia in 1926. He fought for equal civil rights with a particular focus on the discriminatory provisions of the Aborigines Act 1905. These established the position of Chief Protector as legal guardian over all Aboriginal persons until they reached the age of sixteen, including the power to prevent marriages between Aboriginal individuals and white colonizers.[73] Harris publicly rebuked Bates in the *Sunday Times* in 1921 when she reiterated her claims about cannibalism and belief that only strict segregation on the Central Australian Reserve would prevent residents being 'contaminated by those already "within the pale of civilisation"'.[74] She offered to police the reserve to stem any mixing, thereby maintaining the value of Aboriginal residents as human types for ethnologists. Harris responded by correcting her claims about cannibalism and reasoned that 'any one with the brains of an oyster' ought to know that the scheme would be a disgraceful 'imprisonment for those that are in, and perpetual banishment for those that are on the outside of the boundary'. Harris encouraged Bates to focus on doing good 'among the poor and needy white women and children'.[75] A month later, an unrelated James Harris protested against 'being so grossly insulted and libelled in this manner. We would like to know who set Mrs. Bates up to be the accuser, judge and jury over us'.[76]

Aboriginal activists disputed Bates's strongest beliefs about who counted as Aboriginal, the best policies for their future and, significantly, who should administer such protection, nearly two decades before her book was published. Bates's efforts at maintaining strict segregation, her refusals to acknowledge anyone with a fraction of white heritage as Aboriginal, and her insistence that Aboriginal people only needed ministering for easier 'passing' were all challenged by broader shifts in Aboriginal activism during the 1920s and 1930s. The campaigner Fred Maynard Sydney founded the Australian Aboriginal Progressive Association in 1924, and a decade later William Cooper established the Australian Aborigines' League.[77] Despite these fights for civil rights and citizenship, Bates continued in full conviction of the scientific value of her work and remained committed to her belief in the imminent extinction of Aboriginal peoples.

The 'Great White Queen of the Never Never'

Daisy Bates's book received a mixed reception. Australian ethnographers were singularly unconvinced by her accusations that cannibalism was rife among her subjects. As John Murray tried to drum up interest, he received both refusals to help and commendations. One reviewer commented on 'so much in the book that is unconvincing'.[78] Another reviewer for the *Illustrated London News* felt that Bates was a 'wonderful interpreter' whose book contained 'a great deal of information for the anthropologists, not all of whom travel amongst the people they write about'.[79] Although unfavourably received among ethnographers and activists, Bates's book found an eager readership outside academic and missionary circles.

Despite attracting criticism for her tales of promiscuity and cannibalism, Bates stressed in private correspondence to Murray that the book might have been even more sensational:

> If I were not the 'me' I am, I could have written an exciting book, making use of my intimacy with these dying people, to make the book 'sell' but I never looked upon my natives as purely 'copy'. They liked me from the beginning and in their way they 'proved me'; and so gave me their entire trust.[80]

This admission reveals how deliberately Bates cultivated an identity as someone privy to authentic and unparalleled knowledge of Aboriginal customs, while underplaying the controversial and routinely disputed nature of her views. Her declarations also reveal a profound concern with asserting intellectual ownership. In one letter to her publisher, she noted: 'I would like to keep the authorship of these things it cost me so much to obtain.'[81] Bates's substantial personal and economic privations made her sensitive to protecting her findings, but she also wanted to be remembered in specific ways.

Bates crafted her legacy through destroying some papers and making bequests. Despite her 'heartfelt regret', she destroyed the personal diaries she kept from 1899 to 1940 to prevent anyone ever reading them, most likely to protect her privacy.[82] She also longed to be remembered by the Aboriginal peoples among whom she once lived: 'I'm nearly halfway to my 80th milestone, and I want to be sure that my natives will remember "Kabbarli"' (original emphasis).[83] Likewise, Bates intended to donate her papers to the University in Adelaide as early as 1931, expecting them to be 'an asset to university scientists in years to come when conditions are favourable to Scientific Exploration'.[84] Bates's explicit concern with legacy suggests a researcher who was confident in the value of her research in spite of discrimination, and for whom writing became an act of personal and ethnographic memorialization. Her book ended with a characteristic longing: 'if the slightest impression of anything I have said or done, by example or in devotion, remains with them in comfort for the past or hope for the future, I shall be content'.[85]

On 18 April 1951, Bates passed away, survived by so many whose extinction she had foretold. She bequeathed the residue of her estate 'for the relief of poverty and distress and the improvement of the conditions of life in such manner as my trustees may think fit among the Australian Aborigines residing in or resorting to the district of Ooldea and its vicinity in the State of Western Australia'.[86] Inadvertently, she left a far more valuable bequest.

Bates's reputation partly rests upon her linguistic expertise. Her papers in the National Library of Australia contain 4,500 typed pages, alongside notebooks covered with her distinctive spidery handwriting in faded brown ink. Much of her early information was collated through questionnaires she produced when working for the state of Western Australia. The questionnaire pleaded for informants to help with the state's attempt to 'compile, whilst the material is still procurable, a short authentic historical record of the Habits, Customs, and Language of the various tribes of the Aboriginal natives of this State'.[87] Even in the earliest days of listing vocabularies, Bates proceeded on the assumption that she was studying populations doomed to extinction. Her papers include 23,000 pages of notes on languages and world lists. These vocabularies have now been digitized and made publicly available through the Digital Daisy Bates website. The remarkable resource provides access to her research, most importantly for Aboriginal peoples to research their own heritage.[88]

Languages are easily lost forms of knowledge. They capture different ways of knowing the world, and their loss diminishes our heritage. Anyone who has ever tried to translate texts between languages knows how difficult it can be because words and expressions can encapsulate entire concepts for which there may be no equivalent in another tongue. UNESCO has long been associated with the protection of monumental remains and spectacular landscapes, but concern for languages has prompted their recognition as important forms of 'intangible' human heritage. UNESCO warns that around half of the world's 6,000 living languages will be unspoken as everyday languages before the end of the century. Threatened languages were first listed in the *Red Book of Endangered Languages* (1994), but were later replaced by the *Atlas of the World's Languages in Danger* (1996), and are now incorporated into the *World Atlas of Languages* launched online in 2021.[89]

Akin to the Red List of endangered species, UNESCO catalogues and classifies the world's endangered languages as one of the following:

> Vulnerable, when still spoken by children, but often in restricted spaces
>
> Definitely endangered, once children are not taught the language as their 'mother tongue'
>
> Severely endangered, where elders and grandparents speak the language, parents may understand it, but children often don't
>
> Critically endangered, as soon as even the youngest speakers are elders who no longer remain fluent or use the language irregularly
>
> Extinct after there are no known speakers remaining.

Language loss can occur within a couple of generations, particularly when younger children are not taught ancestral tongues. Many first- and second-generation migrants, even if they speak a language with numerous native speakers, are likely to recognize the scenario underpinning 'severely endangered' languages when parents become linguistic bridges between grandparents and grandchildren. While Daisy Bates's research on languages is explored further, her writings have already played an important role in legal cases.

Many colonized peoples who outlived dire prophecies of their extinction have sought restitution, especially of their ancestral lands. In 1992 a landmark ruling in the case of *Mabo v. Queensland* (no. 2) led to the introduction of the Native Title Act 1993.[90] Early campaigns for Aboriginal rights tended to seek civil rights accorded to white settlers; from 1968 onwards, campaigns increasingly focused on Indigenous rights, emphasizing Aboriginal peoples' ancestral connections to the land through historic occupation and their Aboriginality. Eddie Mabo, an Indigenous Torres Strait Islander, fought for the recognition of his rights and those of others. The case dragged on for years. The final ruling in favour of Mabo established that 'native title exists and is recognized by the common law of Australia.'[91] The recognition of native title was significant, but many activists prefer and seek 'Land rights' because they secure specific recognition of ongoing interests in the land and must be granted through separate legal arrangements. Numerous claims from Aboriginal peoples seeking restitution through the recognition of native title and granting of land rights have reached Australian courts. This connects to a broader global shift in recognizing the special status of Indigenous peoples in settler societies such as New Zealand, Canada, and the United States. The United Nations established a Working Group on Indigenous Peoples in 1982, which finally led to the United Nations Declaration on the Rights of Indigenous Peoples in 2007 after many years of drafting and debate.[92] Bates's papers are an important resource for reclaiming Aboriginal rights because they provide historical evidence of ties to the land that are necessary for legal recognition.

Fanny Balbuk Yoreel, a Whadjuk woman born in 1840, lived through the early colonization of Whadjuk country, which she refused to accept throughout her life. Her immediate family connected her to considerable knowledge of Aboriginal ties to the land, including her grandfather, who witnessed the arrival of Europeans, and also her father, mother, and uncle.[93] Bates interviewed Balbuk and wrote about her publicly after her death in 1907, in press reports, journal articles, and her book. Her readers learned that Balbuk was the 'last Perth woman' who 'To the end of her life . . . raged and stormed at the usurping of her beloved home ground.'[94] This included protesting the building of Government House over the grave of her grandmother and breaking fences erected across her walking routes. Bates prized Balbuk's information as 'unspoiled by white influence of any kind'.[95] Bates's correspondents also valued Balbuk's knowledge and body. Writing to Bates in 1902, John

Mathew was keen that she should obtain Balbuk's skull, believing she represented a particularly archaic human type.[96] On Balbuk's death in 1907, Bates lamented her passing as one that extinguished any possibility of reliable information about her people.[97] Bates tried to obtain the skull, but when her request was rebuffed, she fantasized about body-snatching as an alternative.[98] This private correspondence is just one example of a much broader and well-established process. Aboriginal bodies were frequently desecrated by anthropologists, curators, and medical practitioners to secure supplies for museums and medical collections throughout the nineteenth and early twentieth centuries.[99]

Balbuk's refusal of early colonial encroachment makes her an important resistance fighter to present-day Aboriginal peoples, and holds new legal significance.[100] Balbuk's attachment to her land, as recorded and interpreted by Bates, helped support a land-rights claim by the Noongar people in Western Australia, including the state capital Perth. For formal legal recognition of Native Title, the Australian government requires Aboriginal peoples to demonstrate that they have ongoing, largely uninterrupted ties to their ancestral lands, including continued observance of their rites. The state government argued that the Noongar people did not meet these criteria. The Noongar people used Bates's research to challenge the government's position. Court records state:

> The evidence identifies two persons who wrote about the south-west Aborigines in the early 20th century – the latest point of time at which it was possible for any writer to have contact with a person who was alive in 1829, or born shortly thereafter. One of those writers was Professor A. R. Radcliffe-Brown, Professor of Anthropology at Sydney University. His work *The social organisation of Australian tribes* was published in 1930–1931. This work is widely respected by modern anthropologists. However, it is not in evidence. I gather it dealt sparsely with the south-west and casts little light on the issues that call for determination in this case. The other . . . was Daisy Bates . . . Bates was not a trained anthropologist and her writings

> have been criticised, both for their lack of organisation and for Bates' pronounced Eurocentric judgments. However, even her critics acknowledge her great industry and excellent rapport with Aborigines. She is widely regarded as having been a good observer and patient listener. Dr Brunton [an expert witness in the case] said Bates engaged in 'participant observation'.[101]

These records trace an extraordinary twist of fate. Bates was cited alongside Radcliffe-Brown. Qualms about her institutional standing and lack of formal anthropological training were evident, but her use of 'participant observation' rendered her a sufficiently reliable, and even preferable, source to Radcliffe-Brown. The court records also included significant extracts from Bates's posthumously published *The Native Tribes of Western Australia*, including references to Balbuk, her family, their genealogy, and experiences of early colonization. Despite inconsistencies in Bates's notes, court documents show her records of Balbuk's knowledge were critical in establishing that the Noongar had long-standing ties to their land before settlement. In 2006, Judge Justice Murray Wilcox found in favour of the claim to about 200,000 square kilometres. The verdict was overturned on appeal, but ultimately the South West Native Title Settlement was agreed. It recognized the Noongar people as the Traditional Owners of the region and their right to co-manage Crown land with the Western Australian government, a first for a state capital.[102]

The Passing of the Aborigines secured Daisy Bates's infamy. Critics reproached her for writing sensationalist, inaccurate tall tales about cannibalism, murder, and sexual intrigue. Her writings remain deeply controversial. Devotees romanticized her as a compassionate woman doing her best to offer vanishing peoples palliative care. Bates's life and writings are relatively well known within Australia, but often forgotten elsewhere. Her story can be told in multiple ways. Some writers portray her as a romantic, eccentric, and independent woman making a life for herself in the Australian outback, whereas critics emphasize her racism and profoundly damaging views of Aboriginal peoples.[103] Historians of anthropology tend to dismiss Bates as an eccentric amateur of little scientific or anthropological importance in comparison to professional men such as Radcliffe-Brown. In her own lifetime, Bates insisted on the value of her work and wrote that in time 'The "cycle" of half-educated bewhiskered young "ologists" will have passed and steady well-read all-round scientists will come into their own.'[104] Understanding the impediments she faced as a woman, Bates hoped that future generations would recognize her worth.

Bates's research was a form of salvage anthropology conducted in absolute conviction of impending Aboriginal extinction. She left twinned legacies for Aboriginal peoples and historians of extinction. Her writings, especially *The Passing of the Aborigines*, retold the violent invasion of the continent we call Australia, and the subsequent dispossession of Aboriginal peoples as an inevitable process of extinction. In spite of Bates's hopes, the resuscitation of her research as a valuable resource has not come at the hands of scientists or anthropologists, but from the determination of Aboriginal activists. Through reframing the purpose of her archives, Aboriginal peoples are fighting for recognition and recompense. Bates's refusal to accept Aboriginal sovereignty and colonial paternalism means she could never have imagined, let alone welcomed, such a legacy. Yet, in spite of herself, she has helped secure some measure of redress for those she expected to outlive.

PART TWO

Empire's Endlings

6.
Red Alert!

In the bitter winter of 1741, the Danish-born Russian explorer Vitus Jonassen Bering and the German naturalist, physician, and explorer Georg Wilhelm Steller were shipwrecked on a remote island in the North Pacific. Stranded in November, twenty-eight men, including Bering, perished. Forty-six survivors built a boat from the wreckage and set sail for Russia in August 1742. They finally returned home a decade after leaving. The men aboard the stranded *St Peter* were on the Second Kamchatka expedition (1733–43). Before the sudden death of Peter the Great in 1725, the emperor had hoped to settle whether Asia and America were connected by a land bridge through sponsoring a state scientific expedition. Bering duly found a strait, now bearing his name, between Asia and America on the First Kamchatka expedition (1725–7). On the second expedition, Bering and his men became the first Europeans to reach Alaska in July 1741 in an era when the North Pacific and Arctic were barely known, but they were stranded on Bering Island as they returned. Steller occupied his days observing the marine wildlife around him, including a gargantuan manatee-like creature known as the sea cow.[1]

Sea cows once lived across the North Atlantic, but slowly retreated to waters around the Commander Islands in the Bering Sea by the time Steller encountered them (Fig. 6.1). Sea cows were sociable animals that congregated in shallow water to feast on kelp. Hunted by local Aleutian islanders, the beasts were so large and heavy that up to thirty men might be needed to haul an individual cow ashore. Steller found many washed-up carcasses which he dissected. He measured one specimen at just over 7.5 metres (c. 25 feet) long. He described their milk as 'very rich and sweet', and their meat as 'like corned beef

6.1 Steller's sea cow.

and very excellent in flavour'.[2] Steller died in 1746 within a few years of describing the sea cow that was named after him. The creatures fared little better as commercial hunting caused their extinction in less than forty years. The English explorer Martin Sauer noted that the 'Sea cows were very numerous about the coast of Kamchatka, and the Aleutian Islands, at the time when they were first discovered; but the last of this species was killed in 1768 on Bering's island, and none have been ever seen since.'[3] Likewise, the German naturalist and explorer Georg Heinrich von Langsdorff observed that Steller's sea cow 'must now be ranked among the list of beings lost from the animal kingdom, like the dodo, the mammoth, the carnivorous elephant of Ohio, and others'.[4]

When the reality of pervasive natural extinctions was first established during the French Revolution, geologists tended to focus on exploring historical losses, often in deep time; with growing awareness of the extinction of Steller's sea cow in the 1760s, naturalists slowly reimagined the fate of living species as uncertain, and even threatened by unnatural extinctions caused by human exploitation. The loss of a megafaunal species in living memory provided important evidence that extinction was not only an ancient or primarily historical phenomenon, but a present-day possibility. As naturalists and hunters witnessed the decline of once prolific species, from great auks to bison, they issued increasingly urgent and frequent calls to action. Naturalists established the notion of vanishing species as they shifted from debating the nature of extinction to the threat of endangerment. Efforts to save some species, such as the bison, were successful in the later nineteenth century, but the broader notion of international nature protection followed after the Second World War. Listing threatened species emerged as one of the most widely used strategies to inform modern conservation efforts. Understanding how the concept of vanishing species emerged, and why we classify and count the species we worry we might lose, reveals how we have shaped our place within the realms of the extinct, the threatened, and the thriving.

Vanishing Futures

Naturalists in the early nineteenth century rarely thought about dwindling animal populations as threatened, even when they berated humanity for its persecution of the animal world. In 1824 the Reverend John Fleming accused humans of indulging in 'unremitting persecution . . . against the lower animals, during the long term of nearly 6,000 years', ensuring the 'geographical range of many species' was transformed while the 'weapons of the huntsman completed the extinction of many animals'.[5] Fleming lamented the disappearance of birds such as eagles, bustards, and western capercaillie from across the British Isles, and expanded on his list of 'extirpated' and 'extinct' species in *A History of British Animals* (1828). In later decades, the diplomat and antiquarian George Perkins Marsh reprimanded humans for wreaking havoc on the natural world in his book *Man and Nature* (1864): 'Man has too long forgotten that the earth was given to him for usufruct alone, not for consumption, still less for profligate waste.' Significantly, Marsh continued, 'man' alone 'commences an almost indiscriminate warfare upon all the forms of animal and vegetable existence around him, and as he advances in civilization, he gradually eradicates or transforms every spontaneous product of the soil he occupies'.[6] Marsh is often credited with foreshadowing modern ecological science because he imagined nature as an interdependent system. Despite such moral certainty about humanity's profligacy, Fleming and Marsh were unusual in calling attention to the scale of harm.[7] Marsh, in particular, explicitly drew on the fate of the dodo, Steller's sea cow, and the great auk to argue that 'man' alone left a trail of extinctions in his wake.

The great auk, or garefowl, was a sea bird that lived across the North Atlantic. The bird stood proudly at about 70 to 85 centimetres tall (28 to 33 inches). Its white abdomen contrasted with a deep black beak, small head, and back, as if wearing a rather dashing dinner jacket. Although the short stubby wings were useless for flight, they swiftly powered the bird through ocean waters in search of fish. Although the great auk looks remarkably like a small penguin, it is formally classified in the same family as guillemots, razorbills, and puffins. The Beothuk of Newfoundland harvested the great auk, and its eggs, annually, for its meat, oil, and feathers, but the bird's demise was sealed by trade. Europeans hunted the great auk for food, oil, and fish bait for centuries, but they started to harvest great auk feathers for bedding in the eighteenth century. As great auk populations plummeted from the industrialized killing, their skins and eggs were increasingly rare and valuable. Their large pale eggs were mottled with dark inky patterns to help nesting birds identify their own, but that evolutionary advantage also turned each egg into an ornithological treasure. The last pair of great auks was seen, and killed, by collectors hired by a merchant in 1844 on Eldney island, off the coast of southwest Iceland.[8] Skins and eggs were highly prized by collectors, but only about eighty great auk specimens, and some eggs, survive in museum collections around the world.

Extinct birds such as the great auk and dodo captured the public imagination in the 1860s, just as naturalists started to consider extinction as a process. The great auk features in Charles Kingsley's *The Water-Babies* (1862–3) while the dodo appears in Lewis Carroll's

Alice in Wonderland (1865). The books made both birds into the icons of extinction that they are today. Despite suspicions that the species was lost, the ornithologist Alfred Newton and naturalist John Wolley set sail in the hope of seeing a living great auk in 1858. Their interests in natural history were supported by family fortunes made through industrialization and enslavement. Wolley's grandfather Richard Arkwright transformed textile production by inventing the spinning frame, while Newton's family owned West Indian sugar plantations. Wolley's extraordinary bird egg collection was only possible because of his inheritance. Despite voyaging for two months in search of the great auk, the men returned home from Eldney island without success and were forced to console themselves with reams of notes from their conversations with islanders.[9]

As Newton pored over his records, he was convinced that understanding the great auk's demise might help clarify how even the most seemingly inexhaustible species could vanish. He suspected that the great auk was driven to extinction by commercial exploitation. Suggesting that a once abundant species could be exterminated so rapidly was a startling possibility since extinct species, such as the dodo or Steller's sea cow, were known only from significantly smaller ranges. Despite clinging to his hope that great auks might be alive into the 1860s, Newton noted they were effectively 'a thing of the past'. Lamenting that the 'exterminating process' attracted 'little or no attention until the doom of the victim is sealed', Newton began to think of extinction as a progressive process of loss that might be triggered by humanity's destructiveness, but, crucially, one that might be stalled or even halted.[10] Motivated by his new understanding of the 'exterminatory process', Newton turned to wildlife protection. He contributed to writing the first British legislation for protecting sea birds in 1869 and promoted the work of the Society for the Protection of Birds. Emily Williamson founded the society in 1889 to campaign against the use of feathers in fashionable ladieswear, with a royal charter following in 1904. Soon, many more naturalists shared Newton's view of unnatural extinction.

As hunters, naturalists, and collectors across Europe and North

America witnessed the demise of big game in the later nineteenth century, they grew concerned. Bison in North America and the 'big five' prized beasts of Africa (lions, rhinos, cape buffalos, leopards, and elephants) drew particular attention. The declining numbers of these charismatic species attracted dire warnings from hunters about the threat to wild lives. By the 1880s, startled naturalists, hunters, and curators noted the devastating impact of European colonialism across North America. As one writer for the periodical *Science* observed: 'The course of the pioneer has ever been marked by slaughter of animal life, too often recklessly, even for the mere sport of killing, and not merely from necessity or with utilitarian intent.'[11] These claims provided important recognition that, despite extensive hunting by Native nations, many species remained plentiful until European colonizers and pioneers targeted bigger beasts for sport, trade, or as vermin.

North American bison populations plummeted from an estimated 30 million in 1800 to fewer than a hundred before the end of the century. Bison are wild cattle whose magnificent herds once migrated across the Great Bison Belt, a tract of habitat that connected Alaska to the Gulf of Mexico. Adult bulls can easily weigh a metric tonne, reach ten feet long, and stand six feet high at the shoulder, while the cows are slightly smaller. Despite their size, they are remarkably swift and can outrun most horses, reaching speeds of up to 40 miles per hour. Many Native nations used bison for food, furs, and tools. In the nineteenth century, bison hunters slaughtered the beasts on an industrial scale for trade. Bison were often killed just for their tongues, but they were also hunted for skins, while their bones were crushed, burned, and processed into bone china, glue, fertilizer, and ash.[12]

In the late nineteenth century, the killing of bison was deliberately pursued even when the annihilation of the species was predicted. Writing in 1876, the naturalist Joel Asaph Allen observed that the herds of bison once occupying a third of the North American continent had been 'gradually exterminated' in so many regions that there was 'nothing to mark their former presence but their rapidly crumbling skeletal remains and their well-worn trails'.[13] Government officials and military men regarded the extermination of the bison as an ideal means of depriving Native nations of their subsistence and forcing them onto reservations. In this guise, loss was encouraged and equated with civilized progress.[14] By the 1880s, Yellowstone National Park was the last sanctuary of the remaining bison. Building on Allen's early warnings, the taxidermist and hunter William Temple Hornaday penned numerous publications about the bleak prospects facing wild lives, including *The Extermination of the Bison* (1889) and *Our Vanishing Wildlife* (1913). With the 'sting of a rapier thrust', Hornaday noted that there were no grounds to 'hope that a single wild and unprotected individual [bison] will remain alive ten years hence. The nearer the species approaches to complete extermination, the more eagerly are the wretched fugitives pursued to the death whenever found.'[15] Campaigners for bison protection were motivated both by the desire to ensure the survival of a natural resource and by romantic notions of pioneering vigour.

American naturalists often discussed vanishing species within broader conversations about racial peril. In transatlantic debates of the eighteenth century, 'race' described animal varieties, especially within the context of husbandry. Later scholars used 'race' to describe peoples across a broad spectrum of difference, from merely varieties to nations, or in more extreme cases, distinct species. Within broader debates about American colonization, eighteenth-century European naturalists were convinced that North America's cold wilds sustained only under-developed wildlife unable to match the fecund magnitude of European beasts. Writers, such as the future president Thomas Jefferson, defended their new nation so successfully that by the end of the nineteenth century, the continent's deliberately unpeopled wilderness and frontier life was associated with a vigorous racial superiority for 'old-stock' white Americans descended from European colonists. As the environmental historian Miles Powell judiciously notes, white Americans advocating for their own racial 'supremacy believed that their nation's distinctly democratic government owed in part to innate racial characteristics derived from Angle,

Saxon, Jute, and Viking ancestors'. Moreover, these writers insisted that they 'reached their pinnacle by conquering America's wilderness. This process had created a special bond between the continent's wild lands and its white race, a connection that appeared threatened with the closing of the frontier.'[16] These complicated associations between the European colonization of North America and notions of racial vigour were tied to debates about vanishing species by the late nineteenth century. By the early twentieth century, dedicated reservations for the bison were founded and their populations slowly recovered.

Bison were pulled back from the brink of extinction in a period when vanishing species were seldom protected, even when their rarity was widely acknowledged. The lack of conservation measures is probably a shock to modern readers, but such expectations are the product of decades of living in an age when wildlife protection is a well-established international concern. In the early twentieth century, as naturalists grappled with the unnatural extinctions of once abundant species and the plight of threatened species, they helped create new institutions and tools for wildlife conservation.

Penitent Butchers

The international conservationist movement was founded at the start of the twentieth century. In 1900 naturalists, gentlemen, hunters, aristocrats, and colonial officials concerned with the fate of African wildlife attended a specialist conference in London to deliberate over the future of threatened wildlife. After considerable discussion, the Convention for the Preservation of Wild Animals, Birds and Fish in Africa (also known as the London Convention of 1900) was signed by states with African colonial territories, including Great Britain, France, Germany, Spain, Portugal, and Italy. The convention was neither ratified nor implemented. Three years later, frustrated by inaction, many of the same men formed the British Society for the Preservation of Wild Fauna of the Empire, just before Christmas in a meeting held at the Natural History Museum in London. Quickly dubbed the 'penitent butchers', they campaigned for the 'protection of the wild fauna in all British possessions' as the 'the heritage of Empire, which if it be once lost, can never be replaced'.[17] These men were primarily concerned with preserving big game in Africa by establishing pristine nature parks, devoid of local peoples, and regulating hunting. After Yellowstone was established as the world's first national park in 1872, the subsequent rush to establish national parks and stimulate tourism dispossessed Native nations of their lands. Later lobbyists shifted strategies by arguing that parks were sanctuaries for endangered species. The American model proved immensely powerful as preservationists who favoured maintaining ostensibly untouched wilderness clashed for decades with conservationists who sought to actively manage protected landscapes for human use.[18]

Nature protection gained an institutional foothold after the First World War. In 1913 concerned officials discussed founding a new international organization for the protection of nature at a conference convened in Bern, Switzerland, but the outbreak of the Great War in 1914 halted plans. Almost exactly a decade after the Armistice of 11 November 1918, the International Office of Documentation and Correlation for the Protection of Nature was finally founded in Brussels in October 1928. Six years later, the name was changed to the International Office for the Protection of Nature, or IOPN, but its activities remained rather limited compared to its founding members' ambitions.[19] Across the Atlantic, the American Committee for International Wild Life Protection, or ACIWLP, was founded in 1930 by the naturalists John C. Phillips and Harold, or 'Hal', J. Coolidge, partly motivated by their experiences of hunting diminishing numbers of trophies or museum specimens in Africa.[20] Both Phillips and Coolidge were adamant that nature protection was an 'international obligation'.[21] It may seem obvious that protecting nature is, and ought to be, of international concern, particularly since species do not observe political borders, whether because of migration or living in territories across nations, but this argument had to be made and won. Early discussions between organizations such as the IOPN and ACIWLP made conservation into the global political project of today. Experts forged new career paths as 'nature's diplomats' within interwar and post-war governance structures such as the League of Nations, founded in 1920, the United Nations, or UNESCO (United Nations Educational, Scientific, and Cultural Organization), both founded in 1945.[22] The success of these men, and it was largely men, in wresting wildlife protection from national control fundamentally shaped international wildlife management to the present day.

Older inventories of extinct beasts were complemented by new lists of endangered species between the World Wars. In 1933 conservationists met in London to continue the diplomatic work of the pre-war years. They produced the 'London Convention', which proved influential by defining new classes of threatened animals. Class A species were defined as needing extensive protection to survive and included twenty-one species, predominantly focused on large mammals such as several species of antelope, the okapi, pigmy hippopotamus, mountain zebra, white rhinoceros, hartebeest, and elephant alongside gorillas, lemurs, wolves; as well as birds such as the whale-headed stork, bald-headed Ibis, and white-breasted guineafowl, and one plant, *Welwitschia mirabilis*, found in the Namib Desert in Southern Africa. Class B species were defined as in need of some protection and included twenty-two species of mammals and birds including the chimpanzee, colobus monkey, giraffe, giant eland, black rhinoceros, pangolin, ostrich, and several species of egret.[23]

The American naturalist John C. Phillips returned home from the meeting brimming with ideas. He was especially keen that the ACIWLP create an 'authoritative inventory' of extinct and endangered species.[24] Phillips drummed up the funding to commission the naturalist Francis Harper to begin the project in 1936. He was expected to complete the project in a year, but everyone underestimated the task ahead. Phillips died within two years and never saw the list published. The naturalist Glover M. Allen was hired to help complete the list. Allen's report was eventually published as *Extinct and Vanishing Mammals of the Western Hemisphere with the Marine Species of All the Oceans* in 1942 and Harper's report was published as *Extinct and Vanishing Mammals of the Old World* in 1945. Almost a decade later, James Greenaway's *Extinct and Vanishing Birds of the World* was published in 1954. These three reports inspired lists of threatened species published after the Second World War.[25]

As the immediate shock of the Second World War receded, a delegation of diplomats, government officials, and naturalists congregated at the Palace of Fontainebleau outside Paris. François I had transformed the original medieval hunting lodge amid ancient forest into a palace where French kings held court from the sixteenth century, until the Revolution robbed them of their titles and heads. In autumn 1948 the palace teemed with delegates from nation states and non-governmental organizations gathered to discuss the future of endangered wildlife.[26] The idea of an international organization dedicated to nature conservation was raised two years earlier, and European delegates were keen for these conversations to bear fruit. On Thursday, 5 October 1948 delegates signed the constitution of the newly founded International Union for the Protection of Nature (IUPN), which superseded the older IOPN.[27]

The IUPN quickly took on the task of monitoring endangered species. Within a year, the American government hosted a meeting of the new organization at Lake Success, near New York, in late summer and early autumn 1949 alongside a UNESCO conference on natural resources.[28] Coolidge presented a paper proposing 'Emergency Action for the Preservation of Vanishing Species' and calling for an 'International Survival Office' to co-ordinate 'periodic reports' on the 'present status of all patent and vanishing species'.[29] Coolidge had aired his ideas for a Survival Office earlier that year, and his proposal was adopted as a key task for the IUPN.[30] As Chairman of the new Survival Service, Coolidge hoped to update existing lists of vanishing mammals and extend the same coverage to endangered 'flora, and eventually to reptiles, amphibians and fishes, as well as to invertebrates'.[31] Driven by his desire to update the Harper and Allen reports on vanishing mammals, Coolidge's ambitions for more comprehensive lists were kick-started when delegates of the conference at Lake Success created two preliminary lists of vanishing species for 'immediate and vigorous action'.[32] The species listed were as follows:

Birds

1. Arabian Ostrich (*Struthio camelus syriacus*)
2. Hawaiian Goose (*Nesochen sandvicensis*)
3. New Caledonian Kagou (*Rhinochethus jubatus*)
4. Indian Pink-Headed Duck (*Rhodenessa caryophyllacea*)
5. Australian Ground Parakeet (*Pezoporus wallicus*)
6. Laysan Duck (*Anas laysanensis*)
7. Marianas Mallard (*Anas oustaleti*)
8. Cuban Ivory-billed Woodpecker (*Campephilus principalis bairdii*)
9. Bermuda Petrel (*Pterodroma cahow*)
10. Marianas Megapode (*Megapodius laperouse*)
11. California Condor (*Gymnogyps californianus*)
12. Eskimo Curlew (*Numenius borealis*)
13. North American Whooping Crane (*Grus americana*)

Mammals

1. Javan One-Horned Rhinoceros (*Rhinoceros sondaicus*)
2. Indian One-Horned Rhinoceros (*Rhinoceros unicornis*)
3. Asiatic Lion (*Leo leo persicus*)
4. Burmese Brow-Antlered Deer (*Rucervus eldii eldii*)
5. Giant Sable Antelope (*Hippotragus variani*)
6. North African Bubal (*Alcelaphus buselaphus*)
7. Tasmanian Wolf (*Thylacinus cynocephalus*)
8. Marsupial Banded Anteater (*Myrmecobius fasciatus fasciatus*)
9. Wisent (*Bison bonasus bonasus*)
10. Chinchilla (*Chinchilla*, all species)
11. Mountain Zebra (*Equus zebra zebra*)
12. Caribbean Monk Seal (*Monachus tropicalis*)
13. Addo Bush Elephant (*Loxodonta africana africana*)
14. Cuban Solenodon (*Solenodon cubanus*)

Even if these names are unfamiliar, the lists reveal the bias towards birds and mammals, and the preoccupation of early conservationists for emergency action to be taken regarding well-known, often large, charismatic species. Coolidge acknowledged the limitations of the lists, but he still felt they were worthwhile preliminary indicators of the need for more authoritative and comprehensive lists of species targeted for 'emergency action'. Delegates also resolved that the IUPN should promote and sponsor ecological research to best advise governments about protecting wildlife. The listed species faced diverging fates. Some such as the Caribbean monk seal were extinct within a few years, others such as whooping cranes survived with intensive efforts, while the last known thylacine had already passed away.

Thylacines, also known as the Tasmanian tiger or Tasmanian wolf, once roamed across the lands now known as Australia, New Guinea, and Tasmania. Thylacines arrived in Australia and Tasmania far more recently than people. These curiously beautiful and shy wolf-like carnivores had short, tawny fur, and darker brown stripes across their backs (Fig. 6.2). Despite resembling dogs, thylacine mothers raised their young in a pouch, so biologists classify them as marsupials, like the kangaroo or possum. Aboriginal art depicts thylacines on rocks across the continent, but they died out on the mainland long ago. Scientists exploring the thylacine's demise suspect that a number of

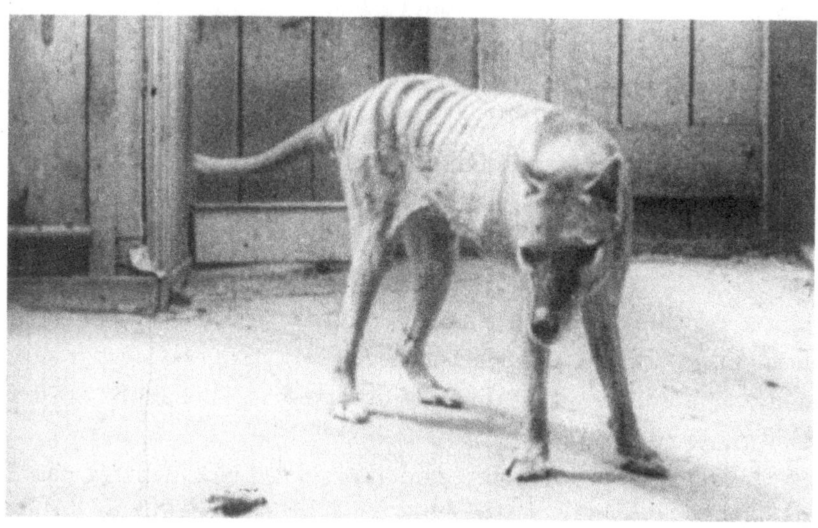

6.2 A thylacine, probably in Hobart Zoo (1930).

factors, such as competition with dingoes or climate change, caused their local extinction around three thousand, perhaps three and a half thousand, years ago, with only a remnant of anywhere between two and five thousand surviving in Tasmania into the nineteenth century.[33] These scenarios and numbers are hotly debated, but Aboriginal records prove that thylacines lived across a much larger range than the 'Tasmanian' moniker suggests, and in much larger numbers than when they were added to the list of threatened species at Lake Success. The last known thylacine died in Hobart Zoo on 7 September 1936. Often called Benjamin, she died fifty-six days after the Tasmanian government named her a protected species and twelve years before her species was listed at Lake Success.

Thylacines lived alongside Aboriginal Tasmanians for millennia, but they were driven to extinction in little more than a century after European colonizers reached Tasmania in 1803. As colonists settled on the island, they established farms, reared sheep, and introduced dogs. When farmers lost livestock to local predators, they blamed thylacines and killed them as pests. In 1830 the Van Diemen's Land Company offered a bounty for every thylacine killed, and the state followed in 1888, offering £1 for every dead carcass. Government records show thousands of bounties were paid, and the persecution of thylacines led to plummeting numbers. Thylacines were considered rare when Benjamin died, but her death was only marked retrospectively. Until the 1960s, reports of thylacine sightings were common, but none were confirmed. As hunters, zoos, and collectors failed to find living thylacines, Benjamin's death gained significance, as it dawned on conservationists that she was the last known of her species. Despite extensive searching by amateur enthusiasts and biologists, conclusive proof, such as the body of a thylacine, has never been found.[34] The IUCN officially declared thylacines extinct in 1986, and 7 September is now officially observed as Threatened Species Day in Australia.

The listing of thylacines, and the subsequent debates about whether they survive, reveal many aspects of the nature of listing. For all its limitations, early conservationists welcomed listing as an important means of recognizing and tracking the state of vanishing species, but listing provided little protection on its own. As campaigners developed their new surveillance tool, it was embedded within policy-making and public-awareness campaigns. This entrenched both listing as a practice and species as the preferred taxonomic unit of modern international conservation.

Endangered!

The Survival Service developed listing into one of its most important modern conservation tools from 1948 onwards. Conservationists working for the Survival Service kept a card index to collate and track any information they received about 'threatened species'.[35] Keen to update the Lake Success lists, the Survival Service drafted a questionnaire on vanishing mammals to collate information on the history and ecology of endangered mammals alongside suggestions for protective measures. Sent to numerous specialists, the questionnaire is an early example of the Survival Service proactively collecting and compiling new information on endangered species.[36] In 1952 responsibility for maintaining a list of endangered birds was transferred to the International Council for Bird Preservation (ICBP, later BirdLife International).[37] In the same year, the young ecologist Lee Merriam Talbot conducted fieldwork on threatened species in the Middle East, India, Nepal, and Southeast Asia. Talbot ventured across the world seeking information from scientists, government officials, and conservationists while also exploring the forests, deserts, and savannahs where the threatened species made their homes.[38] Meanwhile, botanists within the IUPN created a system for classifying endangered plants based on the categories used for animals.[39] Extending categories developed to define threatened animals towards plants allowed the Survival Service to proactively develop ways to classify *degrees of endangerment* for all life on earth.

Threatened species were regarded as a pressing priority in the 1950s, while listing reached a much wider audience in the 1960s. The newly rebranded International Union for the Conservation of Nature and Natural Resources (IUCN) established the Survival Service as a permanent commission in 1956 led by the retired army officer Charles Leofrick Boyle.[40] Boyle started a card index of endangered species which included thirty-four mammals and was reprinted in the proceedings of the IUCN's Seventh General Assembly.[41] By the end of the decade, the Lake Success list of mammals had swollen to twenty-six species including the addition of the Arabian oryx, Angolan giraffe, Sumatran rhinoceros, and Black-footed ferret. During the 1960s, the Survival Service's card index was published as a series of Red Data Books with support from the World Wildlife Fund (WWF). Lee Talbot's report, *A Look at Threatened Species* (1960), fanned enthusiasm for publicly accessible reports on endangered species.[42] Published by the Fauna Preservation Society, the report provided biographies of endangered species illustrated by images and maps, alongside geographical essays surveying the fauna of the Middle East and Asia. Coolidge's foreword placed Talbot's report as the latest offspring in a lineage that had begun under the auspices of the American Committee for International Wild Life Protection and the meetings at Lake Success. Shortly after, between 1960 and 1962, Boyle transferred his card index to typed sheets in a red binder titled *Animals and Plants Threatened with Extinction.*[43] Intended for specialists, fewer than fifty copies were produced and most no longer survive.

When Peter Scott took over the reins of the Survival Service in 1963, he colour-coded the lists and led efforts to broaden their coverage and reach the public. A founding member of the WWF and son of the explorer Captain Robert Falcon Scott, Peter Scott hit upon the idea of red colour-coding to signal danger. He kept personal notes from the Survival Service's card index in notebooks, including a 'Red Book' on endangered species.[44] Within five years of its founding in 1961, the WWF raised $1.9 million which it used to support international conservation projects, including the IUCN's development of the Red List.[45] Scott's Red Book was developed for internal use, but strong external demand promoted a new approach. In 1964 updated versions of the card index of mammals and a list of birds prepared by the International Council for Bird Preservation were published in the *IUCN Bulletin*. With a readership of roughly 10,000, these lists reached an unprecedentedly broad readership and are now recognized as the first official Red Lists.[46] The first Red Data Books, volume one on mammals and volume two on birds, were published in 1966.[47] Initially, a thousand copies were produced and nearly all were sold within three years.[48] The original Red Data Books were intended for specialists, but Scott enthusiastically supported mass-market publications. The hugely popular *The Red Book: Wildlife in Danger* (1969) soon followed and sold 35,000 copies in Europe and the United States within months.[49] Looking back on their publication just eight years later, one reviewer was clear about their impact: 'Quickly the RDBs became Holy Writ in this field.'[50]

The first Red Data Books were custom-printed ring binders containing loose-leaf sheets organized with plastic dividers. They were chosen to allow routine updates: readers were expected to remove and destroy out-of-date sheets, to replace them with new reports. The cycle of destruction and updates means no one is certain whether copies of the original Red Data Books with only, or at least all, the original sheets still exist. The historian Jon Agar believes the original Red Data Books might be the rarest scientific books of the twentieth century.[51] The sheets were also colour-coded: pink for those species in the greatest peril and green for species with improving outlooks. Reviewers were generally positive about the technical benefits, but wrote in surprisingly emotional terms about their use. While reviewing the volumes on mammals and birds, one ecologist and keen birder was moved by the 'regrettable pink tinge to the edges of the book when closed' and 'happily' noted the 'few green pages'. As new sheets were added, he hoped 'a greenish tinge will appear on the edge of each volume'.[52] Another reviewer regarded the colour-coding as a great saga: 'here a small triumph for the conservationist, a more optimistic note about the possibilities of ensuring survival; there, alas more often, a setback to record, or even the final closing of accounts and transfer of the creature to a black sheet In Memoriam'.[53] James Fisher, who edited the popular version of the Red List, noted that the Survival Service had another list: 'Black for death, or rather extinction.'[54] The Black List was the cumulative knowledge created by notices of species known or believed to be extinct since 1600 in the *IUCN Bulletin*. One reader fervently hoped that publishing lists would finally convince others of the true extent of 'the crimes of genocide against man's environment and the state of the combat against them, hitherto drily hidden in official communiqués'.[55] Public education and mass-market versions of the Red Data Books were a crucial element of early conservationists' campaigns as public awareness and support could not be taken for granted.

The original card indexes were replaced by electronic databases in the 1970s. Staff were trained to use computers in the IUCN headquarters at Morges, Switzerland, in 1976.[56] Two years later, the ring binders and loose sheets were replaced with bound volumes. The first bound Red Data Books listed plants, quickly followed by another on birds.[57] The Survival Service appointed the biologist Jane Thornback to set up the Species Conservation Monitoring Unit in Cambridge, England, just as the computers were installed. She led on the compilation and publication of a series of regional Red Data Books.[58] The introduction of bound volumes, regional publications, and computerized databases were all important shifts for the Survival Service as they made Red Data Books available to a much wider audience than the original card indexes.

The first Red Lists were arranged by taxonomic categories such as Order, Family, Genus, and Species.[59] When published as Red Data Books, the lists of species were also divided into four categories based on perceived threat, including:

1. Very rare and believed to be decreasing in numbers.
2. Less rare but believed to be threatened – requires watching.
3. Very rare but believed to be stable or increasing.
4. Status inadequately known – survey required or data sought.[60]

In addition, species and subspecies were assigned a starred listing:

- *** Giving cause for very grave anxiety.
- ** Giving cause for considerable anxiety.
- * Giving cause for some anxiety.[61]

Perhaps the most intriguing sheet was dedicated to the thylacine and printed on a pink sheet and rated '1(a)***p'. This denoted (a) a 'full species' that was (1) 'very rare and believed to be decreasing in numbers and (***) cause for 'very grave anxiety', but (p) 'legally protected, at least in some parts of its range'.[62] The criteria were quickly amended to make them more comprehensive for the second volume on birds in which a fifth category was added: '5 depleted = severely reduced in abundance and still decreasing'.[63] Qualitative criteria are not inherently inaccurate or undesirable, but conservationists' concerns about applying these criteria accurately and consistently ruffled feathers.

Endangerment was recategorized in quantitative terms in the 1980s. The recently renamed Species Survival Commission met in Madrid in 1984 to consider new approaches to defining endangerment.[64] Attendees felt listing was useful, but they wanted more precise terminology for signalling degrees of threat to remove subjective inconsistencies.[65] The Commission asked the evolutionary ecologist Georgina Mace in April 1989 to develop proposals for redefining endangerment. A researcher based at London Zoo exploring how genetics could be used to manage wildlife, Mace took on the challenge early in her career.[66] She produced a draft system using three categories – Extinct, Endangered, and Vulnerable – and defined an endangered species as 'those that are estimated to have at least a 10% chance of going extinct in the next 100 years if current conditions prevail'.[67] A few months later she was joined by Russell Lande, an established scholar whose research used quantitative studies of genes to explore large-scale problems in evolution, such as natural selection, sexual selection, inbreeding, and extinction.

Mace and Lande proposed overhauling the categories of threatened species in a landmark scientific article. Published in 1991, their paper 'Assessing Extinction Threats' incorporated emerging ideas in population ecology to provide the most radical overhaul of the Red List categories in decades. Biologists increasingly hypothesized that species needed a minimum viable population to survive, determined by a population viability analysis, to determine the true health of a population. One of the most famous rules of thumb was the 50/500 rule based on the proposal that a species required a minimum population of 50 to survive without inbreeding, but a population of 500 was needed to ensure genetic variability and long-term survival.[68] Mace and Lande proposed four quantitative categories:

1. Extinct species
2. Critical species, defined as those with a '50% probability of extinction within 5 years or 2 generations', and a population of less than 250
3. Endangered species, defined as those with a '20% probability of extinction within 20 years or 10 generations', and a population of less than 2,500
4. Vulnerable species, defined as those with a '10% probability of extinction within a hundred years', and a population of less than 10,000.[69]

Recognizing that a universally applicable metrics system was probably impossible, the team still recommended their system as suitable for mammals, birds, and reptiles. The Mace-Lande criteria were redrafted numerous times in response to criticism and feedback, with the final criteria adopted in 1994.[70] The *1996 Red List of Threatened Animals* was the first to use the new categories.[71] Listing gained an even stronger foothold when the IUCN established a dedicated Red List Unit and shifted to producing an electronic version in 1998. Going digital made listing an even bigger global endeavour.

In the new millennium, the Red Data Books were replaced by Red Lists in an ambitious strategy to catalogue a phenomenon increasingly called a 'biodiversity crisis' or 'extinction crisis'.[72] The

2000 IUCN List of Threatened Species was the first publicly available online Red List.[73] Released on the IUCN's website, the new Red List unified the work of the Species Survival Commission into a searchable database and sealed the fate of printed Red Data Books. Instead of publishing hard copies of the Red List, the IUCN now publishes analyses of the latest developments, from newly defined extinctions to success stories about recovery. In 2010 the United Nations launched an International Year of Biodiversity and the IUCN launched an ambitious strategic plan to make the Red List into a 'Barometer of Life' over the next decade.[74] The IUCN aimed to expand the Red List's coverage from 48,000 species to 160,000 species, increase the number of trained experts conducting classification, and increase the rate at which new species were included. By the end of the decade, the IUCN Red lists covered 134,400 species, with the numbers growing constantly as the IUCN aims to establish the Red List as a 'Barometer of Life' – one to complement the *Encyclopedia of Life*, an attempt to classify every known species.

Living in the Red, Surviving in the Green

The Red List is a vast compendium of species amassed in just a few decades, but what might it mean for the Red List to serve as a barometer of life? Biologists currently recognize 1.9 million living species and 250,000 fossil species, but the most widely used estimate for the total number of species stands at 8.75 million. By 2024 the Red List included 163,040 species, with the goal of expanding to 260,000.[75] Assessing the remainder requires vast funds, and the IUCN encourages people to donate money to help complete the Red List. The current Red List covers a fraction of known species: these include all known mammals, birds, and amphibians, but other kinds such as fish, insects, plants, fungi, and microbes are woefully under-represented.[76] The uneven coverage is partly the historical legacy of early lists focusing on mammals and birds, but it also reflects which species conservationists regard as charismatic, interesting, or important. The IUCN's decade-long push to train more evaluators and improve the rate at which species were added to the Red List has attempted to remedy this situation, but many species have not been fully assessed or remain unlisted.

The Red List's comprehensiveness matters far beyond the pleasure of a finished task. Early conservationists working in the Survival Service proved remarkably effective at establishing listing species as a conservation tool with relevance to policy-making. Once governments used lists to allocate resources for conservation or protect species against hunting, trade, and other threats, inclusion effectively demarcated between lives worth protecting and those whose loss would be regrettable, but allowable.[77] Listing creates other unintended consequences. Despite the best efforts of global wildlife regulators, illegal trade and trafficking remain rampant, and are estimated to be outdone in value only by the drug trade. On the multi-billion-dollar black market, trade bans and listing can enhance the desirability of a species precisely because they provide official recognition of endangerment and, in turn, rarity.[78] Rhino horns, elephant ivory, and tiger parts are perhaps the best-known examples of illegal commodities whose value rises with increased rarity. Rhino horns are so sought after that museums with stuffed rhinos frequently replace their horns with synthetic substitutes to deter thieves.[79] Given the limited nature of conservation resources, listing inevitably privileges certain species for protection, but it can also create new targets for traffickers.

The IUCN aims to make the Red List into a continuous assessment of extinction threats.[80] The current Red List arranges species along a spectrum of threat of loss: species are categorized as Not Evaluated, Data Deficient, Least Concern, Near Threatened, Vulnerable, Endangered, Critically Endangered, Extinct in the Wild, and Extinct. Potentially every species might be included, for even the most unfamiliar might be tagged as 'Not Evaluated' with an implicit call for further investigations to be reclassified into another category. Meanwhile, tracking threat is so ingrained in the Red List that there is no category indicating safety: the best possible outlook for an evaluated species is of 'Least Concern'. What does this mean for the lives most thoroughly catalogued by the Red List? All known mammals, birds, and amphibians are listed, meaning they have already been incorporated into a state of living in the Red. Perhaps unsurprisingly for a species with an enormous ego, self-evaluating *Homo sapiens* is listed as of 'Least Concern'. *Homo sapiens* is the only species to list itself. Our egotism and propensity for destruction might eventually trigger our self-annihilation but, for now, our future is rosier than many species eking out slow deaths in captivity, such as the Hawaiian crow or the last two northern white rhinos.

The IUCN has developed a 'Green Status' to track species recovery rates and complement the Red List. In 2012 the IUCN held a World Conservation Congress in Jeju, Republic of Korea. Delegates wanted to build on the success of the Red List in assessing 'extinction risk' by developing an additional measure for recovery and celebrate success stories whether of protected areas, ecosystems, or species. After years of debating the criteria for assessment, in 2017 the IUCN developed a global standard for listing protected areas. Red List assessors were able to include the 'Green Status' of species as an optional element from 2020. The Green Status currently categorizes species into: 'indeterminate', 'non-depleted', 'fully recovered', 'slightly depleted', 'moderately depleted', 'largely depleted', 'critically depleted', and 'extinct in the wild', based on calculations of a species rate of recovery.[81] By 2024 thirty-eight species were listed with a Green Status. These include success stories such as the saiga antelope and Iberian lynx, whose populations are increasing, or the pink pigeon and alpine ibex whose numbers are stable. The Green Status echoes the Red Lists' categories, creating a spectrum of existence from Black, or 'extinct', to living in the Red in varying degrees of threat, to Green and perhaps thriving to the point of being 'fully recovered'. Meanwhile, the inclusion of mathematical criteria for expressing species recovery builds on the legacy of Mace and Lande, who incorporated theories of population ecology into listing.

One promising candidate for demonstrating recovery is the whooping crane, which was included on the first lists of threatened species produced at Lake Success. Whooping cranes are tall white migratory birds, with a distinct red crown, black forehead, and distinctive sweep of black curving around the eye and onto the lower jaw, and wings tipped with black. The bird was once native to Canada, the United States, and Mexico. Ornithologists estimate there was a historical population of more than 10,000 whooping cranes before the colonization of the Americas, which dropped to a couple of thousand by the start of European settlement. Although notional, these figures suggest an uncommon bird whose numbers quickly plummeted in the later nineteenth century to about 1,300–1,400 whooping cranes by the 1870s as they lost their habitat to farmers and their lives to hunters. Their increased rarity made them especially valuable to commercial hunters, collectors, and curators. By 1939, only fourteen whooping cranes were known to exist, all living on the Aransas National Wildlife Refuge, founded in Texas in 1937. In the late 1940s, the US Fish and Wildlife Service tried to establish the species' migratory patterns so that nesting sites could be identified. A service employee serendipitously identified nesting sites in Wood Buffalo National Park, Canada, in 1954. Meanwhile, whooping-crane numbers fluctuated with modest breeding success and fifty-six birds were living on the refuge by 1970, and nearly 150 by 1990.[82]

Whooping cranes were saved from extinction through extraordinary efforts from the 1960s onwards. The US Fish and Wildlife Service tried to establish a flock of whooping cranes in captivity by taking one egg from nests in the wild, leaving at least one or more eggs, and using sandhill cranes as surrogate parents in the 1960s, with a second flock established in the 1990s. Unfortunately, the flocks never reached more than a few dozen and the captive birds were all dead by 2002. Further efforts to establish a flock of captive birds that were not free to migrate achieved modest success from the 1990s, but conservationists' efforts turned towards training captive whooping cranes in the behaviours they needed to live as closely as possible to their wild kin. Newly hatched birds often form a special attachment to their mothers, known as imprinting. The process is innate and the precise details vary: hatchlings can imprint on the first object they see, or the first thing to move or make a sound around them. To avoid chicks imprinting on humans, carers wore costumes to mimic adult cranes and were silent around the birds. The young whooping cranes were also socialized by sandhill cranes, and taught migratory routes by a pilot in crane costume flying an aircraft with the whooping cranes between 1997 and 2015. These strategies were intended to teach the birds behaviours they would have learned from their parents in order to establish a self-sustaining stock of birds outside captivity. As the ecologist and historian Laura Martin observes, these birds were 'wild by design'.[83] By 2020, 483 whooping cranes were counted living in the wild, but they still face perilous journeys across landscapes dotted with power lines, or hunters with loaded rifles.[84] In spite of these trials, the whooping cranes living and migrating between Texas and Canada appear to be sustaining their ways of being, raising hopes that they might eventually thrive again.

In the later nineteenth century, geologists' ideas about pervasive extinctions in the natural world were soon accompanied by naturalists' concerns for vanishing species. Naturalists and colonial officials warned of the impending extinction of colonized peoples long before they conceived of species as subject to the same threats. Naturalists and hunters bore witness to declining populations of numerous species in multiple ways. Biologists and collectors on scientific expeditions found capturing specimens, from gorillas to migratory birds, increasingly difficult.[85] We might expect rarity to trigger protective measures, but museum curators or naturalists were more likely to hunt, and collect, specimens to ensure continued access. Rarity often made species far more valuable, and therefore profitable, to the commercial collectors who tracked down and sold the last of their kinds to acquisitive naturalists, as in the case of the great auk. As naturalists accumulated evidence of extinctions in living memory, from Steller's sea cow to the great auk, they feared many other species were on the brink of extermination. Naturalists, especially Alfred Newton, added the possibility of unnatural extinctions to the widely known reality of natural extinctions in life's great drama. By the later nineteenth century, naturalists developed the new category of vanishing species and their understanding of extinction as a process that could be quickened, stalled, or stopped through humanity's interventions, from wanton slaughter to preservation.

Concerns about vanishing species underpinned new forms of wildlife protection in the post-war world. Conservationists forged new career paths as they helped establish non-governmental organizations dedicated to wildlife protection, such as the forerunners of the IUCN. In this context, listing emerged as one of the most important, and favoured, tools to count and classify vanishing species. Reading the first lists drawn up by the IUPN at Lake Success in 1948, readers might recognize a variety of fates. The Caribbean monk seal was extinct within four years of its listing. The Tasmanian wolf, or thylacine, was listed twelve years after the last known endling died. The American whooping crane and North American bison were pulled back from the brink, but many of the species remain threatened despite decades of warnings.

Listing has blossomed into a gargantuan international initiative with the Red List firmly established as a 'barometer of life'. Campaigners for modern nature protection could have chosen to protect threatened habitats or landscapes, or selected broader taxonomic categories, such as Order or Family, but they chose species.[86] Species remain privileged in how we identify, and protect, threatened lives. Originally, species were most likely to capture the attention of conservationists if they were furry or feathered. This historical bias towards mammals and birds remains despite conservationists' efforts to expand the coverage of the Red List. The philosophical peculiarities of the Red List have recently shifted with the adoption of the Green Status for measuring species recovery. Originally, assessed species could only live in the Red and the best-case scenario for even the most abundant species, such as humans, was being classified as of 'Least Concern'. The IUCN has now allowed for the possibility of recovering, and even thriving, in the Green, paving the way for a significant, and welcome, philosophical and practical revolution. Yet, the Green Status has further entrenched our focus on species, and listing as a surveillance tool, and degrees of threat as the most common way of allocating resources. Listing is a political act that never produced a neutral inventory of endangered lives. From its inception, listing was the outcome of countless political and philosophical choices that reveal how we imagine our relationship to other ways of being, and whose ways of being we allow to wither, and whose we value enough to defend and, perhaps, save.

7. *Catastrophe Strikes*

One day, 66 million years ago, spawning fish, blossoming lilies, and unsuspecting dinosaurs were wiped out by a 7-kilometre-wide rock smashing into the Yucatán Peninsula, Mexico. The ferocious speed, intensity, and heat of the impact vaporized the rock in less than a second and tore into the earth's crust, leaving a crater about 40 kilometres across. Within a couple of seconds, the shockwave blasted underlying rocks into the air and the crater widened to between 150 and 200 kilometres. The furious heat melted rock into glass droplets. They vaporized and cooled on contact with air, forming billions of miniature glass spheres blasted into the air alongside dust and debris. Life inside the crater was instantly annihilated. The impact triggered tsunamis in the nearby Gulf of Mexico. Intense tidal waves engulfed the coastline, forcing water inland for hundreds of kilometres through waterways connected to the coast. A fireball soon ripped across the land sterilizing it of life. Within hours, the impact's energy transformed countless ways of being into fragmented debris strewn across North America and the Caribbean. Over the next few days, winds encircled earth's northern hemisphere in lethal dust, blotting out the sun's warmth and light for months.[1] Many lives were lost on contact, while other creatures slowly suffocated or starved in the charred aftermath. Only the smallest creatures survived, eventually giving rise to birds and mammals.

Geologists and palaeontologists knew almost nothing about this calamity until remarkably recently. They knew some species suddenly vanished from the fossil record, such as trilobites at the end of the Permian Period (251.9 million years ago) – the largest extinction event in earth's history – and dinosaurs at the end of the Cretaceous

Period (66 million years ago). Nevertheless, they were far more likely to be interested in calculating the age of the earth, or investigating the formation of geological wonders such as coral reefs and mountain ranges, than oddities such as disappearing species. When Georges Cuvier claimed that some species no longer existed, he believed that past catastrophes might be the cause, but his peers and successors dismissed tumultuous disasters as the cause of extinctions. Instead, generations of geologists were trained to theorize earth's history as an achingly slow development. In the 1980s shocking theories about the death of the dinosaurs and other species in mass extinctions changed the attitudes of palaeontologists and geologists to catastrophic change. As geologists reimagined the history of our planet and life's evolution, the broader public were captivated and alarmed by the possibility that we might have triggered a mass extinction in the present day.

Slow Formations

As a young man, Charles Darwin voyaged around the world aboard HMS *Beagle*. He set sail from Plymouth docks the day after Boxing Day in 1831. Captain Robert Fitzroy and the crew were tasked with surveying the coasts of South America, to measure longitude, observe weather conditions, and map coral reefs to make maritime navigation substantially safer for British sailors. Darwin observed the volcanic mountain ranges of Cape Verde, tropical forests of South America, craggy islands and subtly varying finches of the Galapagos, marsupials of Hobart and Sydney, coral reefs in the Pacific and Indian oceans from Tahiti to Mauritius, and from the Cape of Good Hope to the Azores.[2] He returned to Falmouth in chilly October five years later and wended his way home to Kent, where he lived in relative seclusion with his wife Emma and their children. Ensconced in his library, he continued reading voraciously and relied on an extraordinary correspondence network with experts for scientific information.[3] Darwin was especially influenced by Charles Lyell's recent masterpiece *Principles of Geology* (1830–3). Many of their peers believed the earth was no more than a few thousand years old and relied on catastrophes to explain how mountains or the continents formed in the geological blink of an eye. Lyell contended that the earth's most spectacular geological features, from volcanoes to glaciers, were formed by almost imperceptible forces, such as the movement of the earth's surface and fluctuating seas. Such slow forces required time to act, so Lyell reasoned that earth's history must stretch deep into unknown pasts.[4] Darwin deliberated over the origins of geological formations and species with Lyell's gift of near unlimited time.

Most naturalists regarded species as immutable natural kinds, but Darwin grew doubtful. He suspected that individuals of a species better suited for prevailing conditions were more likely to survive and leave descendants. Over countless generations, minute modifications accumulated in a species, which improved the chances of its survival. Ultimately, he developed his theory that 'descent with modification' created new species better adapted for survival through a process he called natural selection.[5] Upon publication of his ideas, Darwin benefited from decades of debates about whether species could 'transmute', or 'develop'. While many readers were shocked by his ideas about natural selection, his broader ideas about evolution were easily incorporated into a developmental story about life's progress by geologists and theologians. A younger generation of biologists adopted Darwin's mechanism of natural selection, but many peers did not regard it as essential to evolutionary change. When biologists identified genes as the building blocks of inheritance in the twentieth century, natural selection allowed them to model the inheritance of genes in populations. This 'modern synthesis' helped pave the way for a new consensus that life on earth evolved through natural selection, and embedded evolution and extinction into life's history.[6]

Darwin imagined extinction as the necessary by-product of natural selection. In his view, living beings better adapted to any set of conditions would successfully compete for resources and reproduce. Over time, if any descendants were better suited to those conditions, no matter how minutely, they would survive, thrive, and 'continually take the places of and exterminate their parent-forms'. Darwin knew that curious readers were likely to ask about transitional forms in the geological record. This created a significant dilemma because he knew of none. This apparent absence created the 'gravest objection which can be urged against my theory'.[7] In his defence, he likened the fossil record to a tatty book:

> I look at the natural geological record, as a history of the world imperfectly kept, and written in a changing dialect; of this history we possess the last volume alone, relating only to two or three countries. Of this volume, only here and there a short chapter has been preserved; and of each page, only here and there a few lines. Each word of the slowly-changing language, in which the history is supposed to be written, being more or less different in the interrupted succession of chapters, may represent the apparently abruptly changed forms of life, entombed in our consecutive, but widely separated formations.[8]

When fossils of *Archaeopteryx* were found in Germany in 1861, they finally provided a transitional form from dinosaurs to birds, but this was hardly enough to lay doubt to rest. Darwin knew of 'the apparently sudden extermination of whole families or orders', such as trilobites and ammonites, in the fossil record, and inferred that the best explanation was imperfection of the fossil record.[9] His metaphor of the shabby, torn book prompted geologists to shun catastrophic explanations for evolutionary change for over a century.

Periodic Calamities

Palaeontologists routinely assumed that the fossil record provided no meaningful evidence of evolutionary processes, and evolutionary biologists commonly dismissed mass extinctions as evolutionarily irrelevant until after the Second World War.[10] As the world grappled with the genocidal horrors of the war, one palaeontologist's misgivings grew. In the 1950s, the American geologist Norman D. Newell urged geologists to recognize that the fossil record was far more reliable than they assumed. Determined to understand rapid change in the geological record, he tracked the appearance and disappearance of genera such as corals, trilobites, and ammonites. When he produced timelines comparing the origins and deaths of marine genera, he noticed numerous precipitous declines in life's diversity coinciding with the end of several geological periods. Instead of dismissing these as artefacts caused by an unreliable data set, he ventured into unfamiliar territory. He suggested that life on earth experienced periodic 'wholesale extinctions' caused by catastrophic events, such as seas receding from continental land masses.[11] Writing for *Scientific American* in the early 1960s, Newell predicted: 'If we may judge from the fossil record, eventual extinction seems to be the lot of all organisms', with the cause of mass extinctions remaining a 'major problem of evolutionary history'.[12]

Newell's research provided the strongest evidence that abrupt losses in the geological record were reliable signals. Hypothesizing that mass extinctions were observable phenomena challenged disciplinary caution. Newell's ideas helped to establish mass extinction and catastrophic causes as legitimately useful subjects for geological research and encouraged others to devote their careers to understanding the nature of extinction. Newell's graduate students were initially exasperated by these irritating diversions from evolution. The American palaeontologist Niles Eldredge recalls 'as acolytes' in Newell's 'graduate student seminars, we used to despair of hearing Norman discuss evolution. Extinction to us was the "down side" – we wanted to talk about evolution!'[13] The American historian of palaeobiology David Sepkoski suggests that Newell's research contributed to a revolution that established palaeobiology as a distinctive and important field in its own right between the 1950s and 1980s. This stimulated research into the nature of extinction. In the 1970s, a new generation of scientists asked where, when, and how often did mass extinctions occur? Was it possible to distinguish between an imperfect geological record and meaningful loss? Might mathematical models yield new ways of understanding the fossil record? By pursuing these questions, palaeobiologists reconceptualized extinction as an independent evolutionary phenomenon. Eldredge notes of Newell's legacy: 'Norman's focus on mass extinction may well prove to be his most lasting gift to us all.'[14]

Niles Eldredge was among the new generation in the 1970s who helped reinterpret the geological record in terms of rapid change. For his doctoral dissertation in the 1960s he explored the evolution of trilobites, concentrating on the species *Phacops rana*, once widespread around 380 million years ago (Fig. 7.1). After collecting his specimens, Eldredge grew concerned as his trilobites did not appear to be evolving, but he soon noticed that their eyes told a different story. *Phacops rana* has distinctive large eyes made from numerous compound lenses, and the number of those lenses did change. As Eldredge explored the eyes, he noticed that the species existed for long periods with the number of compound lenses making up the eyes changing suddenly. This pattern was completely unexpected according to the traditional model of slow, iterative evolutionary change. Eldredge collaborated with the American palaeobiologist Stephen J. Gould, now fondly remembered as a well-known popular scientific writer. In a paper

7.1 A fossil of the Devonian trilobite *Phacops rana*.

published in 1972, the pair argued that scientists were too wedded to visions of gradual evolution and that species often survived in stable states for long periods, but then evolved in rapid bursts, as with the trilobites. Their radical new theory of 'punctuated equilibria' was deeply controversial, but it forced palaeobiologists to reconsider the possibility of rapid changes in the geological record as meaningful signals, not misleading anomalies.[15]

In the same year, John 'Jack' Sepkoski was studying evolution at Harvard University with luminaries such as Stephen Jay Gould and Edward O. Wilson, a biologist whose stellar reputation rested on his theories about species evolution on islands. Within four years, Sepkoski met David Raup, a geologist with considerable expertise in extinction and mathematical modelling. Biologists classify species into a hierarchical system of increasingly specific categories until they reach a distinctive name: each name designates a species, which also belongs to a genus, family, order, class, phylum, and kingdom. The geological record rarely provides sufficient data to analyse the past history of species, but is significantly more reliable for broader categories. Sepkoski tried to pinpoint the origins of families. Choosing families as the basic unit for tracking evolution made it significantly easier to harvest reliable information and spot larger evolutionary patterns.

Jack Sepkoski realized that extant datasets barely addressed millions of years of evolutionary change. Modern geologists divide life on earth into four eons: the Hadean (from 4.6 billion years ago) witnessed the earth's formation; the earth cooled enough for the formation of continents and the earliest signs of life during the Archean (from 4 billion years ago); simple bacteria, algae, and jellyfish emerged in the Proterozoic (from 2.5 billion years ago); finally, the Phanerozoic, spanning the last 541 million years, included the emergence of invertebrate animals, early bony fish, the earliest land animals, the first plants with seeds, and eventually the emergence of insects, birds, dinosaurs, mammals, and humans. Sepkoski kept track of the origins and disappearance of families within the Phanerozoic in notebooks during the 1970s. He hoped his data might illuminate global patterns of life's diversification from the earliest organisms. Sepkoski and Raup collaborated on a paper published in *Nature* in 1981 that argued Sepkoski's data represented 'a strong evolutionary signal' of increased biodiversity in marine families.[16] Building on this important defence of the fossil record's reliability, they repurposed Sepkoski's data for 3,300 marine families, including 2,400 extinct lineages, to study extinction. When they used the data to track extinction rates for families against time for the entire Phanerozoic, they noticed five large drops in the number of families. They quickly wrote a paper, published by *Science*, which proposed that life on earth experienced five mass extinctions.[17] Their identification of five mass extinctions changed how we understand our past, and present.

Mass extinctions signpost the history of life on earth. Early geologists used vanished species to mark breaks between periods in the fossil record, making it easy to align new theories of mass extinction with much older practices of defining geological boundaries. When Georges Cuvier first claimed extinct beasts were eradicated by unknown catastrophes, the principle of extinction was quickly embedded within geological theories, but his explanation for their loss faded into obscurity. Generations of geologists regarded catastrophism as a joke. Raup and Sepkoski's publications provided the clearest evidence that mass extinctions were tangible events of evolutionary significance. Throughout the 1970s palaeobiologists were already divided into two camps: one group hoped to create idealized mathematical laws to describe life's evolution, while the other group hoped to incorporate more literal readings of the fossil record into geological research, and included important figures such as Stephen Jay Gould and Raup. Identifying mass extinctions helped Raup and Sepkoski create fruitful new avenues for combining ideas about random events, selective pressures, and empirical evidence from the fossil record.[18] In doing so, they established catastrophic extinctions as momentous geological events that permanently changed lifeways.

We are all stardust, and survivors of the Great Dying. Geologists believe that every living being is descended from the mere tenth of species that survived previous mass extinctions. About 444 million years ago, the first mass extinction caused the deaths of approximately 85 per cent of marine life at the end of the Ordovician. About 372 million years ago, the second mass extinction also caused widespread loss of 75 per cent of marine life in the late Devonian. The third mass extinction proved the deadliest at the end of the Permian, 252 million years ago, known as the Great Dying when at least 90 per cent of species went extinct. While land dwellers lost 70 per cent of their species, marine species bore the brunt of the loss. The fourth mass extinction caused the loss of 80 per cent of life at the end of the Triassic about 201 million years ago. Many mammals died out, but the dinosaurs, which originated in the Triassic, flourished during the subsequent Jurassic. The dinosaurs were wiped out in the fifth mass extinction at the end of the Cretaceous Period, which killed off 50 per cent of all species 66 million years ago.[19] Higher death rates leave a smaller pool of species to live on, slowing down life's rate of recovery in the aftermath. When encountering mass extinction and its consequences, many of us understandably worry about a future calamity that might wipe out all life. Yet life has always persisted after such catastrophes and flourished into new ways of being, including our own.[20]

In the Asteroid's Wake

Doomed dinosaurs are the most famous marker of any mass-extinction event, well known to us through museums, novels, soft toys, memes, and Hollywood blockbusters. Their cultural ubiquity emerged alongside new ideas about mass extinction in the 1980s. The demise of the prehistoric, lizard-like monsters was well known in the nineteenth century, but the cause of their extinction attracted little attention.[21] In the twentieth century, a slew of papers tackled the mystery, with suggestions ranging from plausible scenarios to fanciful guesses. As late as 1963, Norman Newell noted, 'If mass extinctions were not brought about by changes in atmospheric oxygen, by disease, by cosmic radiation, by trace-element poisoning, by climatic changes or by violent upheavals of the Earth's crust, where is one to look for a satisfactory – and testable – hypothesis?'[22] Seventeen years later, an infamous paper ignited bitter controversies over the answer.

The Apennine mountains stretch along the length of Italy, but their stratigraphy is peculiarly exposed in the lower slopes near the medieval Umbrian town of Gubbio.[23] There, reddish limestone known as *Scaglia rossa* brims with tiny, often microscopic, intricate shells of fossilized plankton called *foraminifera*, or forams. These past sea-dwellers allow geologists to date rocks and observe changes in earth's magnetic field. During summer fieldwork in the late 1970s, as the American geologist Walter Alvarez chipped away at these rocks he noticed that the forams were abundant during the late Cretaceous deposits, above which there was a centimetre-thick layer of clay with few fossils, and then a new tertiary layer where the forams were almost extinct.[24] He suspected that the rocks preserved an unbroken record of the transition from the end of the Cretaceous Period to the start of the Paleogene Period (or the K-Pg transition, 66 million years ago). Alvarez hoped the site would yield insights into bigger mysteries, because the forams vanished at the same time as dinosaurs, and rocks spanning the K-Pg transition were then unknown. Intrigued, he worried over the clay layer in conversation, then collaboration, with his father, Luis Alvarez, winner of the Nobel Prize in Physics in 1968.

Walter and Luis were keen to date the clay layer: the quicker it formed, the earlier the forams died out. Unfortunately, thickness is an unreliable guide to the rate of formation, so they needed an alternative means of measuring time. Luis suggested using radioactivity as a molecular clock. Radioactive elements decay at known rates, measured in half-lives, or the time it takes for half a given quantity of an element to lose its radioactivity. Comparing traces of radioactivity in rocks or organic matter to naturally occurring levels of those elements allows scientists to date materials. The most promising element seemed to be iridium. In 1977 they asked the chemist Frank Asaro to analyse samples of the Gubbio clay for iridium. Expecting only to find traces of around one part per billion, Asaro found nine parts per billion. This infinitesimal number was still thirty times more than the 0.3 parts per billion in the layers below the clay. Was the spike an anomaly, or a meaningful exception? The pair might easily have dismissed using iridium as a molecular clock, or argued that the clay layer must have taken thirty times as long as the lower layers to be deposited, but they worried over its exceptional concentration. Iridium is nearly absent in the earth's crust, but highly concentrated in the meteor dust constantly showering us with cosmic rain. Was the iridium extraterrestrial? The team searched for other sites spanning the K-Pg transition, and eventually found another dark clay layer in the white chalk of Stevns Klint cliffs near Copenhagen in Denmark. Asaro found another iridium spike in the Danish samples. The team expanded to include the chemist Helen V. Michel, and they continued taking measurements as they reflected on possible causes, before finding another iridium spike in Woodside Creek on South Island in New Zealand.

Science published the team's bombshell in 1980. They proposed that the most likely cause of dinosaur extinction was a 10-kilometre-wide asteroid smashing into earth, creating a 200-kilometre-wide crater, which ejected dust plumes into the air that encircled the globe, darkened the skies, stopped plants photosynthesizing thereby causing the collapse of food chains and, finally, the death of the dinosaurs.[25] Luis Alvarez modelled the sequence of explosion, dust clouds, and death on the volcanic eruption of Krakatoa in 1883. The violent blast in Indonesia was heard as far away as Australia, and volleyed so much ash into the skies that London's artists spent months painting exceptionally vivid red sunsets. The eruption might even have been the source of the bloody painted sky in Edvard Munch's painting *The Scream* (1893).[26] Luis suspected that the eruption provided a useful model for the aftermath of a giant asteroid strike. The team finished the paper by urging colleagues to find the impact crater and making the grand claim that other asteroid impacts might also have caused mass extinctions.[27] Newspapers circulated the sensational theory around the world. Some reporters dutifully noted yet another theory for the death of the dinosaurs. Others conjured more lurid scenarios of death and destruction. The *Boston Globe* vaguely claimed 'Long ago, something happened', while the *Christian Science Monitor* derided the Alvarez team for founding 'fantasies' on a mere 'bit of space debris'. The *New York Times* ran a series of articles exploring the asteroid impact as one theory among many, such as volcanic eruptions, debated by the world's dinosaur experts. Beyond the details of the hypothesis, the press attention created widespread interest in the dinosaurs and the broader phenomena of mass extinctions.[28]

Geologists were convinced the Alvarez team was wrong. David Raup, who worked with John 'Jack' Sepkoski on mass extinctions, peer-viewed the paper before publication. He made several suggestions for improvement, but warned:

> The potential impact of this paper has cosmic proportions. If the hypothesis is correct, it will have profound influence on geology and evolution – not to mention philosophy. The paper will probably change the basic thinking of many people. This is fine if the hypothesis is correct. But if it turns out (later) to be wrong, a lot of damage will have been done and it will take years to recover.[29]

Raup rejected the paper as 'sloppy and incomplete, however brilliant'.[30] His misgivings were echoed by many scientists upon publication; years later, he recalled the paper's publication 'was met with nearly universal derision'.[31] Objections included the lack of palaeontological expertise among the Alvarez team, a lack of evidence for the asteroid strike and subsequent dust clouds, questioning the presence of iridium in stratigraphical sections not at the K-Pg boundary, and general suspicion of any appeals to catastrophic and extra-terrestrial causes.[32]

Incredulous palaeontologists were infuriated by the Alvarez team's audacity in stepping so far beyond their disciplinary expertise. The *New York Times* regularly updated readers about the twists and turns in the debates. Despite widespread scepticism, sympathetic readers started testing the Alvarez team's predictions. Testing meant the paper was not dismissed as quickly as previous catastrophic musings. In just over a decade, nearly a thousand times more iridium than the average concentrations in earth's crust was found at more than a hundred sites.[33] The impact site eluded scientists until a team led by the geologist Alan R. Hildebrand found the 'largest probable impact crater on earth' in 1991.[34] Buried under the Yucatán Peninsula in Mexico, the dimensions of the 180-kilometre-wide Chicxulub crater were remarkably consistent with the predicted 10-kilometre-wide asteroid. Subsequent research confirmed the crater is 66 million years old and the epicentre of the dinosaurs' demise.

As news of the crater circulated globally, scientists, historians, philosophers, and sociologists attended a conference near Chicago about the mass-extinction controversies. In conference proceedings, the American geologist and historian William Glen felt it was difficult to 'overstate' the effects of the Alvarez paper:

> The past 13 years have seen the publication of more than two and half thousand papers and books touching on various aspects of the controversy, and the tide of publications continues to rise. Career goals have been refocused, dormant areas of research rejuvenated, tacit assumptions hastily re-examined, and scientists in widely separated fields swept into an unprecedented array of collaborative efforts. Ingenious experiments, field studies, and the development of new instruments now undergird an effort to resolve the many questions raised in these far-flung debates.

Glen's enthusiasm captures the intellectual and disciplinary shockwaves caused by the Alvarez team's findings. Several antecedents imagined catastrophic explanations for dinosaur extinction, from cosmic rays or meteorites, but this paper was the first to offer more than a just-so story. The Alvarez team faced ridicule for entertaining catastrophic extinction, but their imaginative leap transformed our ideas about the multiple paths to life's extirpation. Their ideas have been so successful that many now worry we have triggered another catastrophic mass extinction.

The Apocalyptic Anthropocene

The desert lit up with a fiery dome that bloomed into a mushroom cloud 12 kilometres high. The intensely hot fireball mutated from purple, to green, and blinding white light, visible for 160 miles. The blast carved a crater 80 metres wide and 1.4 metres deep into the desert while the sand melted into green radioactive glass encircling the epicentre for almost 300 metres. The scar marked the successful detonation of the world's first nuclear weapon, 'The Gadget', at 5:29 a.m. on 16 July 1945, in New Mexico. Code-named Trinity, the test was the culmination of the American military's Manhattan project to build an atomic bomb in the midst of the Second World War. For three years, the physicist Robert J. Oppenheimer, now immortalized in a Hollywood blockbuster, led the Los Alamos laboratory in New Mexico where research into nuclear fission and its application made the weapon possible. With hundreds of personnel cheering and cameras capturing the moment for posterity, their mission bore monstrously lethal fruit.[35] White 'snow' blanketed areas of Mexico as much as 250 miles away. This toxic fallout blighted the lives of local people, many of whom developed severe illnesses such as cancer.[36] Twenty-one days later, on 6 August, the US military detonated an atomic bomb over the city of Hiroshima, and three days later an atomic bomb targeted Nagasaki. Japan surrendered on 10 August and the Second World War drew to a close on 2 September. The atomic bomb hastened the end of the Second World War while ushering in the spectre of a self-inflicted mass extinction.

Scientists developed ideas of mass extinction as Cold War tensions ramped up and fears of nuclear war pervaded daily life, with school safety drills and televised digests of political tensions between the United States and the Soviet Union. The two shifts are intimately connected. It would be easy to write about mass extinctions as becoming scientifically palatable once the fossil record was better understood, or mathematical modelling made broader patterns of evolution significantly easier to see, particularly by younger men eager to make their own names in conflict with existing authorities. It would certainly be an attractive story of discovery against the odds, but it would underplay the broader social and cultural factors that shaped theories of extinction, as well as scientific research more broadly.

Jack Sepkoski's son, David, is a historian of science specializing in palaeontology and scientific ideas about extinction. He suggests that broader fears of nuclear war plausibly resonated with scenarios of mass extinction. Recollecting repeated nightmares about atomic bombs, he writes:

> It didn't occur to me at the time to wonder whether there was any connection between the way scientists like my father understood mass extinction, and the pervasive anxiety we all felt about nuclear war . . . I came to be convinced that it was no accident that catastrophic mass extinction became an object of scientific study and popular fascination at precisely the moment when we imagined a similar fate for ourselves.[37]

As knowledge of the horrific consequences of dropping nuclear bombs accumulated, this exacerbated fears of the Americans or Soviets using nuclear arsenals to settle broader ideological and political conflicts. Advocates for battling communism claimed that using nuclear weapons would only cause targeted devastation, making a nuclear war winnable. Opponents warned that no one might survive, let alone win.

The public learned of their impending extinction in 1983. Carl Sagan, a distinguished astrophysicist, Pulitzer-prize-winning popular science writer and presenter of *Cosmos*, America's most popular television science series at the time, wondered whether the Alvarez hypothesis might illuminate the atmospheric climate change following a nuclear war. Sagan and a team including several of his former students modelled the effects of nuclear war on earth's atmosphere. In October 1983 an impatient Sagan wrote about their ideas for the popular press, with the team's co-authored scientific paper following in December's issue of *Science*. They estimated that the world's nuclear arsenal amounted to about 12,000 megatons concentrated in 17,000 warheads with the firepower of '1 million Hiroshima bombs'. They modelled the effects of detonating anything between 5,000 and 25,000 megatons and predicted that unleashing even the lower ranges of that firepower would trigger immense conflagrations, releasing blackened palls of noxious gas and incinerating materials amounting to about 225 million tonnes. The sun would warm the soot and smoke still further and carry them into the upper stratosphere. Rain might wash away the soot in a couple of months, but finer dust storms would swirl around the globe hindering sunlight for years. A cold, endless night would visit crop failures and famine across the world. The radically reduced ozone layer would expose humans to unbearable levels of ultraviolet radiation.[38] Humans were on the verge of inflicting their own extinction through playing Star Wars chicken.

While Cold War threats have faded in recent years, our fears continue in new guises. As scientists ushered in the spectre of nuclear war, they may have also inaugurated a new geological epoch. Trinity's fallout, and the flurry of atomic-bomb testing in this period, littered earth's atmosphere with radioactive debris. Soil samples and ice cores worldwide captured a 'bomb spike' of radioactive Carbon-14 and Plutonium-239 beginning in 1945 and up to 1951, with radioactive molecules peaking in 1964.[39] They are likely permanent scars. Even if you've never seen a geological chart subdividing earth's existence into units of time, you're likely familiar with at least a couple of periods, such as the Jurassic or Triassic. Geologists currently believe our planet warmed over the last 11,700 years after the last Ice Age during the Holocene epoch. In the intervening millennia, human societies have flourished, but also wreaked havoc on the planet.

The Nobel Laureate Paul Crutzen suggested recognizing humanity's intervention in earth systems with a new geological epoch named the Anthropocene. The term derives from the root 'anthropo' meaning human and 'cene' signalling a geological epoch. Since 2009, the Anthropocene Working Group has analysed the case for formally recognizing a new geological division. Their preliminary reports suggested that the new epoch had begun – raising the issue of when. Many beginnings vied for the grim accolade. The earliest starting point suggested is the extinction of Pleistocene fauna such as mammoths through human predation about 14,000 years ago, while the beginnings of human agricultural cultivation around 5,000 years ago has also been proposed. Others argue that the starting point should be recognized as the early colonization of the Americas and subsequent destruction of ecosystems, extinctions, and profound violence visited upon Native nations known as the 'Colombian exchange'.

Extinction looms large in debates about the origins, nature, and future dangers of the Anthropocene. Originally, Crutzen and other members of the Working Group favoured fossil-fuel-powered industrialization in the 1800s and the increasingly rapid release of greenhouse gases as their preferred starting point. Advocates of recognizing an early date single out human hunting and the loss of beloved megafauna such as the mammoth. Supporters for recognizing the 1500s as the start of the Anthropocene epoch hope to account for catastrophic environmental destruction and genocide resulting from the colonization of the Americas.[40] This also overlaps with the historical period of ecosystems collapse covered by the IUCN's globally used Red Lists of extinct and endangered species. Extinction may not always have scarred the geological record enough to leave global signals sufficient to determine the start of the Anthropocene, but it is a recurrent theme in debates about the wounds we have inflicted on earth and such destruction has quickened the pace of exterminating countless ways of being. In 2023 the Anthropocene Working Group recommended that geologists recognize the mid-twentieth century as the start of the Anthropocene. Against all expectations, geologists rejected the proposal in the first formal vote following years of debate in 2024. The surprise decision drew immediate, and ongoing, controversy with accusations that the vote was invalid.[41]

Scientists, environmental activists, and writers started categorizing species loss as a biodiversity crisis requiring new conservation strategies in the late 1970s. Conservation biology emerged as a distinctive discipline in this period, as conservationists moved on from trying to specify desirable sizes for wildlife refuges to considering minimum viable populations of species. The first international congresses in conservation biology were held in 1978 and 1985, spanning the same years in which new ideas about mass extinction reached the wider scientific community. Stark warnings about rapidly increasing rates of species extinction circulated in mass-market books such as Norman Myers' *The Sinking Ark* (1979). The environmental campaigner warned that 'within the twinkling of an evolutionary eye' humans risked creating 'a biological débâcle greater than all mass extinctions of the geological past put together'. He assured readers:

> . . . by tomorrow morning we shall almost certainly have one less species on planet Earth than we had this morning. It will not be a charismatic creature like the Tiger. It could well be an obscure insect in the depths of some remote rainforest. It may even be a creature that nobody has ever heard of. But it will have gone. A unique form of life would have been driven from the face of the earth forever.[42]

Many warnings focused on charismatic species and the potential harm of losing undiscovered medicines and natural resources. Myers did not shy away from these arguments, but this passage outlines his hope that readers would empathize with the loss of ways of being. Within two years, further warnings about the ecological consequences of accelerating extinctions circulated in *Extinction: The Causes and Consequences of the Disappearance of Species* (1981), written by the biologists Paul and Anne Ehrlich.

Books, films, and television documentaries consistently warned of ubiquitous endangerment in the late twentieth century, creating new languages of loss. In the mid-1980s biologists adopted the term biodiversity as shorthand for biological diversity, and by the late 1980s loss was reconceived from the problem of vanishing individual species to a crisis of waning biodiversity.[43] The sense of environmental urgency gathered pace when that crisis was reframed as the beginning of a sixth mass extinction. The anthropologists Richard Leakey and Roger Lewin first popularized the term in their book *The Sixth Extinction: Biodiversity and Its Survival* (1995). More recently, the journalist Elizabeth Kolbert's *The Sixth Extinction: An Unnatural History* (2014) has reached a new generation of readers. The evocative phrasing would not make sense without the theoretical shifts of the 1980s.

Our sense of crisis is well justified, but it is just as important to choose wisely amid the panic as it is to avoid being petrified into inaction or sleepwalking into a crisis we might have prevented. We are clearly losing many ways of being, although there is disagreement over just how much faster extinctions are now taking place.[44] Suggestions for halting the sixth mass extinction include devoting immense portions of earth to wildlife refuges to allow our planet to recover. The United Nations adopted the new Global Biodiversity Framework at the UN Biodiversity Conference, or COP 15, in Montreal, Canada, in December 2022. Often called '30 by 30', the framework commits to protecting and renewing 30 per cent of the planet by 2030. The '30 by 30' plan is an important effort to address the destruction of irreplaceable ancient ecosystems and related species decline, Yet, without understanding the historic roots of such conservation measures, we risk exacerbating historical injustices.

The '30 by 30' policy is predicated upon the same questionable divisions between humanity and nature that have underpinned harmful conservation practices in the modern world. As we have seen, early European colonizers often imagined Indigenous peoples as noble savages at one with nature, or even as elements of local flora and fauna. By the end of the nineteenth century, sublime wilderness was redefined as devoid of all human habitation. Following the designation of Yellowstone as the world's first national park in 1872, the model was adopted across America, Africa, Europe, and the rest of the world. National parks were originally created as wonderlands for tourists and only tied to environmental protection in the later nineteenth and early twentieth centuries. They promoted a version of wilderness predicated on the forced relocation and territorial dispossession of many nations. Conservationists treated wildlife reservations as fortresses to be protected from all humans, even Indigenous peoples with a history of using the land sustainably for centuries, or millennia.[45]

While ambitious, the '30 by 30' policy might be an interim measure as future policies may attempt to call for a much bigger expansion of protected areas.[46] The '30 by 30' policy was partly inspired by the biologist E. O. Wilson's proposal that half of earth be protected for the benefit of wildlife.[47] About 250 million people are believed to live in protected areas; however, one team of scientists estimates that over a billion people might be directly affected if Wilson's dream was implemented and, crucially, that already marginalized communities would face a disproportionate impact.[48] This may seem exaggerated, but the proposed areas will probably be expansions of existing protected areas. Forced removal is worrying enough, but it also potentially targets communities with unrivalled expertise of local biodiversity. Removal on the assumption that outsiders know best is a worrying form of cultural arrogance with deep roots in colonialism.

Writing specifically about Canada, but with broader implications, the philosopher Zoe Todd maintains that 'First Nations, Inuit, and Métis communities and nations across the country deserve conservation approaches and policies' that protect their sovereignty without pressuring them to acquiesce in externally imposed conservation strategies.[49] Unfortunately, given the harmful roots of wilderness protection, the expansion of protected areas might easily perpetuate dispossession of Indigenous peoples worldwide. The '30 by 30' plan might also perpetuate conservation practices that have already caused harm. When the plan was published, an open letter was circulated raising the prospect of significant human-rights abuses and signed by forty-nine signatories. The open letter stated that 'Egregious human rights violations including wholesale involuntary removal of entire communities have been abundantly documented for decades by academics, investigative journalism and civil society organizations.' Moreover, treating protected areas as fortresses excludes the very people who might help protect biodiversity.[50]

These criticisms are exceptionally important for acknowledging the widespread dispossession that might result from expanding fortress-style wildlife reservations based on past experiences. In 2019 a media investigation alleged that ecoguards working for the World Wildlife Fund had used physical violence, torture, sexual assault, and even murder in protected areas within India, Nepal, Cameroon, the Republic of Congo, and the Democratic Republic of Congo. The WWF commissioned an independent report led by Judge Navi Pillay, a former commissioner for human rights at the United Nations. The report clarified that the WWF's own staff had not committed any of the alleged crimes, but they did find evidence for abuses committed by park rangers appointed by governments. It concluded that the WWF had failed to act on previous allegations, and had taken insufficient steps to prevent crimes and abuses by associates, even though its 'own human rights commitments' were often 'higher than those applied nationally'. The organization issued a statement outlining changes to their working practices to address the situation. While the WWF's employees were not found guilty, the report highlights how easily fortress-style conservation practices can cause broader injustices even in the pursuit of laudable aims.

The worry that we are living through the sixth mass extinction of life on earth is commonplace in discussions about saving life on earth. The theories that the dinosaurs were wiped out by an extraterrestrial body hitting earth, and that earth has suffered five mass extinctions, are exceptionally recent theories of geological and palaeontological research in the 1980s. Until the Second World War, caution dominated our understanding of earth's history and the role of extinction within life's evolution. Notions of mass extinction had far-reaching consequences both for the emergence of new scientific disciplines, such as palaeobiology, and for approaches to conservation. In particular, mass extinction made scenarios of apocalyptic annihilation, whether of ourselves or of other beings, plausible and ubiquitous.

Extinction may be natural, but it is also how we make sense of the changes humanity has caused to life on earth. That makes extinction both a human idea and a political choice. The five mass extinctions of life on earth were unavoidable, but the current crisis in which we stand to lose countless ways of being is an unnatural extinction of our making. Debates over protecting our own future alongside the species with whom we share this planet will continue. Instead of addressing our panic and widespread loss with policies that perpetuate historical dispossession, we stand to gain far more by imagining new forms of conservation and asking more from those who bear far greater culpability and responsibility for our current predicament than the Indigenous nations wrestling with the details of the '30 by 30' plan. In our current panic, having the courage to imagine differently will help ensure that every way of being that has escaped past catastrophes might still survive and thrive.

8.
Pinosaur Redux

Trees can outlive other beings by an astonishing magnitude. The bristlecone pine Methuselah lives in the White Mountains of California, a land known only to Native nations for more than the first four millennia of the tree's 4,850-year existence. Yet Methuselah is not even the oldest known tree in the world. Another unnamed bristlecone pine in the same mountain range is believed to be at least 5,070 years old, but even this does not match the age of Prometheus, a bristlecone pine that stood in Nevada, but was dated to 5,200 years old after it was felled in 1963. This trio of pines existed even before humans developed writing around 4,600 years ago.

While these pines are the oldest living individual trees, older communities thrive. Some trees live a couple of centuries as individuals, but regenerate through cloning themselves and last for millennia. A creosote bush in California has survived 11,700 years, while Pando is the world's largest plant, and one of the world's oldest living organisms at about 14,000 years old. Pando is a grove of 48,000 quaking aspen trees sharing a single root system across 106 acres near Fish Lake, Utah, creating an extraordinarily beautiful sea of autumnal yellow leaves. Pando's exact age remains disputed, but this ancient being probably existed before the Quaternary extinction event 10,000 years ago, which killed some of the most famous prehistoric megafauna such as most mammoths, megatheriums, and sabre-toothed cats.[1] Even common species can live for millennia. The Bowthorpe Oak in Lincolnshire is believed to be Britain's oldest oak, having lived for more than a millennium. Britain's, and possibly even Europe's, oldest tree is most likely the Fortingall Yew. It thrives in a Perthshire churchyard in Scotland, and cautious estimates age it to between 2,000 and 3,000 years old, but the yew might be as old as 9,000 years.[2] Yews are among the longest-living species in Europe. Often planted in churchyards, they are associated with death. The lifespans of these pines, oaks, and yews far outstrip the survival capacity of most living beings.

Respecting such ancient lifeways honours life itself, yet plants rarely feature in histories of extinction. Whether in post-war conservation efforts or in historical accounts of broader environmental movements, plants are commonly neglected in conservation projects and historical narratives. Such disregard is a shame, as incorporating plants into histories of extinction challenges us to think beyond anthropocentric and animal-centric policy-making and history writing. Just before the new millennium, one man's chance encounter with an unknown and ancient tree sparked worldwide interest in botanical conservation. As botanists realized that the tree's origins stretched back into a world still inhabited by dinosaurs, they hoped for new insights into earth's past climate and biodiversity. Promoted as the botanical find of the last century, the tree's journey from wild endangerment to global celebrity is a rare tale of an endangered plant attracting global conservation efforts.

Like 'Finding a Small Dinosaur Still Alive'

The jagged mountain vertebrae of Australia's Great Dividing Range entwine into a spine along the continent's southeast and eastern coastline. A million hectares of this astonishing landscape form the Greater Blue Mountains Area, including seven national parks and a conservation reservation on the unceded lands of the Gandangara people. Designated a UNESCO World Heritage site at the turn of the millennium, it attracts millions of visitors every year keen to see a sliver of wilderness, especially the Three Sisters. These mountain peaks tower more than 900 metres over a valley dominated by eucalypt forest and suffused with blue haze.[3] Wending away from tourist hotspots leads to unfamiliar territory riven with deep fissures that expose the underlying sandstone. No one knows the precise number of canyons amid these uplands, but estimates range as high as five hundred for Wollemi National Park alone. Reputedly named after the Darkinjung word *wollumnii* meaning 'look out' or 'watch your step', the name acknowledges, albeit inadequately, the land's first guardians.

The ancient landscape attracts millions of visitors every year. In September 1994 three experienced local hikers found a canyon previously unknown to them in Wollemi National Park. One of them was a field officer for the New South Wales National Parks and Wildlife Service (NPWS) named David Noble. He noticed a small grove of peculiar trees that were unfamiliar to him, despite his considerable knowledge of the area. From mounds of leaf debris rose tall slender trunks with strangely bubbled bark and bottlebrush-shaped crowns chasing sunlight high into the canopy. Intrigued, Noble took some leaf cuttings and headed home with his friends. A few days later, Noble showed the cuttings to his equally puzzled father. They sought a second opinion from the botanist Wyn Jones who also worked for the NPWS. He could not name the tree despite his comprehensive acquaintance with the local flora. The fernlike leaves led Jones to assume they were from a bush, and he was utterly shocked when Noble confirmed the cuttings were in fact from tall trees. Jones consulted a botanist based at the Royal Botanical Gardens of Sydney, who was similarly stumped. The trees remained a mystery.

Jones nurtured a suspicion that the trees belonged to the ancient conifer family Araucariaceae, but he needed further specimens to confirm the hunch. Nearly five weeks after Noble's chance find, he and Jones visited the canyon to take photographs and collect samples. Jones also started collaborating with the botanist Jan Allen to identify the species. They quickly realized that leaf samples were insufficient as members of the family are distinguished by their female seed cones. Within a week of the second trip, Jones and Noble visited the trees again. Reaching the seed cones required dangling precariously above the canopy from an overhead aircraft. Jones and Allen confirmed that the tree belonged within an ancient family of pines by dissecting the seed cone, but they hit a dead end when trying to be any more specific about the genus or species. They wondered if they were on the cusp of a major botanical find.[4]

The Araucariaceae family of conifers are thought to have originated in the Triassic Period between 230 and 190 million years ago, with wild-forest communities scattered across the southern hemisphere in Australia, New Zealand, New Caledonia, and South America. In the mid-1990s botanists identified two living genera within the family: *Araucaria* and *Agathis*. The spiky monkey puzzle tree was the first described member of the *Araucaria,* with its name honouring the tree's native Arauco province in Chile. *Araucaria* also includes the bunya-pine, whose cones can easily weigh 10 pounds (4.5 kilograms); the Cook pine, named after Captain James Cook; the hoop pine, widely cultivated for its timber; and the strikingly symmetrical Norfolk Island pine. *Agathis* includes species such as the black kauri, Sulawesi kauri, Sabah kauri, and Sarawak kauri, also grown for their timber. Although characteristically southern inhabitants now, fossil remains confirm the family thrived globally from around 200 million years ago until the same mass extinction leading to the death of the dinosaurs wiped out northern communities, except in pockets of Southeast Asia, 66 million years ago. The genus includes nineteen species. Five species are endangered, and three considered vulnerable to extinction.[5]

Seed-bearing conifers existed long before flowers and appear in the fossil record about 300 million years ago. Conifer seed cones are distinctive enough to define species in formal classification. Although commonly called pines, none of the family feature seed cones with the *paired* winged seeds characteristic of true pines. *Araucaria* seeds are all fused to the female cone, and they fall as fragments of scale and seed as the cone disintegrates. *Agathis* is defined by winged seeds that fall freely from, rather than with, seed cones. When Jones and Allen dissected the female cones of the mystery tree, they found seeds fell freely from the cone as with *Agathis*, but they lacked its wing. The tree's visible peculiarities and seeds were distinctive enough to classify it as a new genus with only one known, or monotypic, species. Jones and Allen informally nicknamed the tree the Wollemi pine and co-wrote a scientific article with Hill, formally naming it *Wollemia nobilis* honouring its wild sanctuary and Noble's role.[6] The scientific paper also detailed its etymology, structure, seeds, and ecology, categorized it as endangered, and called for its conservation.[7] Their fears were well founded.

Wollemi pines are curious ways of being. They might reach a height of 40 metres (131 feet) in the wild. Their resinous dark-brown bark resembles bubbling chocolate, giving rise to the 'Coco Pops tree' nickname. The tree has a unique double crown, with mature foliage at the top and juvenile foliage below. Wollemi pine leaves begin as bright-green foliage closer to a fresh lime, or apple, maturing into a slate blue-green. The branches whorl around their trunks and bear flat leaves in even rows. The soft juvenile leaves arranged in two rows look remarkably like ferns. Darker, stiffer mature leaves are arranged in four rows in the upper crown and are tipped with either male or female cones. Male and female cones are found on the same trees, making them bisexual, or monoecious. Many trees salvage nutrients after reproducing and redirect the energy and resources to grow fruits and seeds. We experience this rhythmic senescence as spectacular autumnal shades before leaf fall reveals woody skeletons that sleep until spring. Wollemi pines shed entire branches, forming a coppery bed of debris around emerging trunks. The trees regenerate through 'coppicing', when new trunks grow from old bases or burnt stumps, allowing the trees to survive periodic wildfires or injury. Wild individuals might have dozens of younger trunks surrounding a lost original stem, making them difficult to date. Given that individual stems may easily survive for centuries, a whole tree might live for many centuries or even beyond a millennium. David Noble first stumbled into a grove of about forty trees at different stages of growth, but three further sites were subsequently found. By 2021, forty-six adult trees were producing seed-bearing cones, while eleven older juveniles, and thirty-two younger saplings survived across four sites.[8]

Wollemi pines were called 'living fossils' almost immediately. Locating their genuine fossils took years, but it solved two botanical mysteries stretching back to the 1960s. Pollen grains are abundant in the fossil record because they have tough outer casings that make them significantly hardier than any other remains of parent plants. When the palaeobotanist Wayne Harris encountered an unfamiliar and profuse pollen type in 1965, he named it *Dilwynites*. Traces were scattered from Tasmania to Perth, Antarctica to New Zealand, dating between 91 million to 2 million years ago. Hearing of the Wollemi pine, the palaeobotanist Mike Macphail revisited specimens of *Dilwynites* and realized they closely matched the Wollemi pine's historic range. He first confirmed the link in 1995 and later found pollen traces in South America.[9] While Harris pored over microscopic pollen remains, the palaeobotanists Carrick Chambers and his doctoral student Andrew Drinnan explored fossilized plant remains from the Australian state of Victoria. They were particularly puzzled by a conifer apparently within the Araucariaceae family, but not fitting into the two known genera *Araucaria* and *Agathis*. Without naming the curious tree, they described it as an intermediary. When news of the Wollemi pine broke, they revisited the unnamed fossils and realized they were of the same tree.[10]

Lifeways known only from the fossil record, but then found living, are called 'Lazarus Taxa' or 'Lazarus species' after the Biblical tale of the dead brother mourned by his sisters Martha and Mary, but miraculously returned to the living by Jesus.[11] The miracle of the dead rising again, with grief capitulating to joy, captures the shock and exhilaration of encountering a way of being thought lost.

Living Fossils

The 'dinosaur pine' made international headlines from Melbourne to New York, and Mumbai to Japan. New species are named every year without public fanfare. Larger fauna might attract attention, but flora rarely make headlines. The Wollemi pine was a rare exception. The National Parks and Wildlife Service press release proclaimed a 'Jurassic Pine Discovered in Blue Mountains'. Press reports, popular science articles, and sober bulletins of learned societies all characterized the 'Jurassic Pine' as a 'living fossil', 'back from the dead', with roots in the 'dinosaur age'.[12] The Director of Sydney's Royal Botanic Gardens maintained the 'discovery is the equivalent of finding a small dinosaur still alive on earth', while the gardens' scientific director ranked the find as 'one of the most outstanding discoveries of the century'. Ferns and mosses are evolutionarily older, and Ginkgo trees are the only known living connection between ferns and conifers, but finding an unknown plant of such size and ancient origins is extraordinary. Botanists were clearly overawed and compared finding the Wollemi pine to an earlier discovery in China.

As the school principal Lung-Hsing Yang admired the *shuishan* tree towering over a place of worship, he eagerly sought its scientific name. The deciduous bright-green leaves congregated in small branchlets, seed-bearing cones, and fissured dark-grey bark, flaking away in ribbons and revealing inner brown hues that were unlike any other tree in the area. When he met Chan Wang, an employee of the Bureau of Forest Research conducting fieldwork in the forests of Enshi, western China, in 1943, Yang hoped he might finally have an answer, but he was disappointed. Intrigued by news of this strange tree, Wang visited Moudao, in Sichuan province, where he found the tree and collected specimens he later identified as a cypress. Three years later he gave a specimen to a colleague, who showed the herbarium sheet to his botanical colleague Wan-Chun Cheng at the National Central University. Convinced the species was not a common conifer, Cheng examined the original specimens collected by Wang, arranged for a student to collect further specimens, and shared his suspicions with his colleague Hsen-Hsu Hu, Director of Beijing's Fan Memorial Institute of Biology. Hu reclassified the tree within the *Metasequoia* genus first described by Shigeru Miki at Kyoto University in 1941. Miki had worked from fossils widely believed to represent an extinct species more than 100 million years old. Hu first described the species as a living fossil in print in 1946 without formally naming the species. Two years later, Hu and Cheng formally named *Metasequoia glyptostroboides*, making headlines around the world.[13]

Finding a living *Metasequoia* has also been proclaimed 'As remarkable as discovering a living dinosaur'.[14] Locally known as *shuishan*, initial press reports either used the Latin name, or called it Chinese water fir, but the tree was quickly nicknamed the Dawn Redwood by the botanist Ralph W. Chaney, who wrote about the species for American audiences. *The Times* reported the overwhelming scientific and public interest revealed in the 'romantic unexpectedness with which natural history, after centuries of investigation, still enchants its devotees'.[15] While Hu prepared his publications, Cheng's colleague Ching-Tsan Hwa returned to the only known tree to gather more specimens. Exploring further, he found a valley with a large community of mature trees. He gathered seeds that were later shared with the Arnold Arboretum at Harvard University, from where they were distributed to researchers and botanic gardens across the world. These seeds grew into the oldest individuals of the species now living outside China, many now towering over the crowns of native trees worldwide. In 1948 the founding of the Chinese Shuishan Preservation Committee led to the population count of known trees rising from a few dozen to at least 1,219 adults after an expedition led by Chinese and Californian botanists.[16] By the 1970s, 5,746 wild trees were known. A further 5 million trees were planted to create the City of Metasequoia, including the longest tree avenue in the world, in 1996.[17] The *shuishan* was listed in the Register of Major National Protected Wild Plants in 1999, while propagation and celebration of the tree ensured it grew into a native 'national treasure', rooting modern Chinese identity in the tree's past.[18]

When the *Sydney Morning Herald* reported that the Wollemi pine was a living tree from the 'Dinosaur Age', it provided readers with a brief chronology of other finds including the lungfish in 1870, the coelacanth fish in 1938, and the 'Dawn Redwood' tree in 1941. The appeal of these romantic narratives of discovery is understandable, but they also leave a great deal out. Most obviously, they erase the knowledge of local people and their historical interaction with a species. The *shuishan* already shared a home with people, and botanists were only alerted to its existence by the curiosity of an ordinary school principal about an alternative name. Yet, retellings frequently begin with Wang's first encounter with the tree.[19] Historians of science have long cautioned against narratives of discovery and lone scientific geniuses precisely because they obscure much richer stories of exchange and collaboration across global networks, and professional practices dependent on people often not recognized as makers of scientific knowledge in their own right, whether lab technicians, skilled artisans, or local field guides.[20]

When botanists described the Wollemi pine as a living fossil from the age of the dinosaurs, they hoped that the tree would provide new clues to earth's past. Wollemi pines first thrived in landscapes so ancient that they exceeded many previous estimates for earth's antiquity. By the end of the nineteenth century, geologists contemplated an earth aged 100 million years old, whereas physicists favoured estimates ranging from 40 to 50 million years old. After William Röntgen identified X-rays in 1895 and Marie and Pierre Curie's research on 'radio-activity' in the same decade, estimates for earth's age expanded by an astonishing order of magnitude. Before the First World War, the first cohorts of physicists and chemists used radioactive decay as a molecular clock and increased estimates for earth's age to at least 1,600 million years. After the Second World War, increasingly precise molecular clocks underpinned a new consensus around the absolute figure of 4.5 billion years for the age of the earth.[21] Meanwhile, geologists also puzzled over apparently broken threads of rock traversing oceans. Why did the stratigraphy of the Appalachians mirror the Scottish Highlands? Why did the coasts of South America and Africa look like a sheet of rock torn in half? The geologist Alfred Wegener's book *On the Origin of Continents and Oceans* (1915) suggested that present-day continents were not immobile entities formerly connected by land bridges as often imagined, but continually displaced fragments of earth's crust. Wegener's theory of 'continental drift' proved controversial for decades. In his book *Principles of Physical Geology* (1944), the geologist Arthur Holmes argued that continents were not freely floating flotsam, but had been tugged apart by vast underlying movements. By the 1960s, geophysicists divided earth's crust into 'tectonic plates', slowly parted by sea-floor spreading, to explain the fracturing of earth's land mass.

Geologists now believe that 250 million years ago the supercontinent Pangea included earth's entire land mass. About 180 million years ago Pangea fractured into the twinned supercontinents of Laurasia in the northern hemisphere and Gondwanaland in the southern. They also splintered into fragments that Europeans named North America, Europe and Asia from Laurasia; and Antarctica, India, Australia, South America, and Africa from Gondwanaland. The labour of the Atlantic Ocean's birth cleaved apart Africa and South America, and the emerging sea floor divided Madagascar and Africa during the Jurassic Period. Pangea's parts are thought to have drifted until their shapes and relationships were almost recognizable from a modern map by 65 million years ago, although North and South America were independent while Australia and Antarctica were united. About 34 million years ago Australia split from Gondwanaland to form the world's largest island, and remained so even after Tasmania drifted into isolation from Australia and Antarctica by around 30 million years ago. Moving across the continent from Western Australia to New South Wales means crossing from the oldest rocks (Archean, 4,500–2,000 million years ago) to newer formations (Palaeozoic, 542–251 million years ago). As the continent heated and dried, much of Australia's lush green and temperate climate transformed into sparse bush and outback.[22]

Gondwanaland's rainforests retreated to the eastern boundaries of the continent and endured as tiny prehistoric microcosms where Wollemi pines survived. The scientific paper naming the tree withheld their location because the authors feared avaricious collectors would pilfer specimens while even honest admirers might trample seedlings or accidentally introduce deadly pathogens. Fortuitously, the trees' home in a national park made it considerably easier to incorporate them into existing conservation practices and provide extra security. Within a year, the New South Wales government trademarked the Wollemi pine to prevent anyone collecting, cloning, or selling specimens.[23] Declaring the trees 'critically endangered' on the IUCN's Red List, and their home a 'critical habitat', offered national and international legal protection. The Wollemi pine was also the first threatened species to be provided with a formal recovery plan by the state government. It outlined measures to protect the wild trees and precautionary conservation strategies to create translocated and domesticated populations.[24] With these protections, the Wollemi pine was quickly assimilated into well-established national and international mechanisms for the surveillance and protection of endangered beings, while also inaugurating new practices. Of these, the rush to clone and grow the trees is perhaps the most globally visible. Unlike many endangered beasts, the trees are relatively easy to clone and grow. Making the trees commercially available protected the wild population and ensured their descendants soon thrived in gardens the world over.

Jurassic Gardening

Sydney sits on the unceded lands of the Gadigal at the ragged eastern edge of the Australian continent. The harbour opens into the Tasman Sea, leading into the South Pacific Ocean. The Royal Botanic Garden occupies 30 hectares, cupping one of the inlet's numerous coves, and sits alongside the opera house, giving visitors spectacular views over the water. The Royal Botanic Garden, founded in 1816 and walled into an enclosed space by 1818, is the oldest scientific institution in Australia, and earned its Royal appellation in 1959. A commemorative plaque marks the site of the garden's first Wishing Tree, a Norfolk Island pine planted in 1818 and felled in 1915 over fears its decay might trigger a disastrous collapse.

Botanical gardens are important places for the public to learn about and enjoy a wide variety of plants, and centres of scientific research. In modern Europe their roots often lay in older physic gardens or aristocratic collections, while many new gardens were established in the colonies. From the tea and coffee we drink to the spices we use as seasoning, the cotton and linen clothes we wear, and the hardwood furniture we use, our everyday lives are shaped by a global trade in plants stretching back centuries which shaped modern empires. Some plant commodities, such as sugar and cotton, have well-known links to empire and enslavement, but the colonial and ecologically devastating harvesting of other commodities, such as teak or mahogany from tropical forests, is less well known. The economic value of some species made botanical research, and its associated institutions, immensely important within expanding European empires.

The global connections of the Royal Botanic Gardens at Kew in London, especially with newly established collectors and gardens in colonies such as Australia and New Zealand, are examples of the broader imperial networks that were essential for the development of botanic gardens. As Director of the Royal Botanic Gardens at Kew between 1865 and 1885, the botanist Joseph Dalton Hooker solicited botanical specimens from all over the world. His correspondents included the New Zealand missionary William Colenso, who sent Hooker many antipodean specimens. Hooker was indebted to Colenso for specimens, but also assumed that his own position within London's elite scientific circles gave him the authority to name, and claim discovery rights for, plants sent to him by correspondents. To Hooker's surprise, Colenso tried to name plants and used his knowledge of plants living in situ to critique Hooker's classifications.[25] Both men used colonial infrastructures to collect and exchange specimens while navigating uneasy power relations to pursue their research. Like so many other botanic gardens, Kew depended on empire to exist.

As Sydney's botanic garden expanded into scientific research, it was incorporated within global networks of specimen exchange and scientific research. The garden's impressive herbarium includes many specimens prepared by the naturalist Joseph Banks while voyaging aboard the Royal Navy's HMS *Endeavour* under the captaincy of James Cook between 1768 and 1771.[26] Botanic gardens were often sites for exploring the acclimatization of plants, and the use of plants in agriculture or medicine, so they were important sites for developing resource extraction. Initial efforts to farm crops such as corn might have failed in Sydney, but these attempts show the high priority given to cultivating economically important staples. Between the 1830s and 1850s the garden was run by two superintendents with experience of working at Kew, the brothers Allan and Richard Cunningham. They exchanged precious local plants for imported crops and seeds with Kew. As well as trying to grow crops in the garden, seeds and plants were given away so that settlers could till the soil. Early colonists regarded establishing agriculture as a practical necessity to provide food staples, but it also allowed them to tame wilderness and create valuable agricultural land. Europeans regarded such productivity as justification for the dispossession of Aboriginal peoples because they were regarded as unproductive, and therefore less deserving, occupants of the land. The intertwining of naval power, colonial prospecting, scientific collecting, and establishing agriculture is a common thread in the emergence and role of botanic gardens within European empires.

Botanic gardens were vital for exploring the Wollemi pine's natural history and domestication. Wild Wollemi pines scatter their pollen in the spring winds of October and November, with seed cones reaching maturity the following summer and autumn, from January to March in a cycle of sixteen to nineteen months. Birds, such as the gorgeous crimson rosella, or ground feeders, such as rats, gorge on the seeds, and wild seedlings seldom reach maturity. They must fight through heaped debris on the forest floor, and usually remain saplings for decades before new canopy openings provide enough light for them to reach their full potential. The retreat of Gondwanaland's forests and the challenges that saplings must overcome mean fewer than a hundred wild Wollemi pine trees are known, across three sites all within a relatively small area. A single fire or pathogen could wipe out every wild Wollemi pine. Fearful of such a calamity, botanists rushed to create ex situ conservation collections. The first Wollemi pine we know to have been planted has thrived at Sydney's Royal Botanic Garden since 1998. Fears of unscrupulous collectors meant the tree was initially imprisoned in a cage. Eventually freed, it now towers above visitors.

Botanists tried to propagate the Wollemi pine before the public were even aware it existed. Expeditions by the New South Wales National Parks and Wildlife Service collected cuttings from branches and leaves, seeds, and a seedling. Large white nets placed under the canopy harvested seeds in 1996 and 1997, while cones could only be reached by dangling from a helicopter, and were collected in February 1995 and March 1998. The seedling was watched over at Sydney's Royal Botanic Garden with such caution that an official noted 'anyone even breathing on it makes the garden's staff nervous'.[27] Fortunately, researchers realized that the natural tendency of Wollemi pines to regenerate made domestication through cloning possible.[28] In the new millennium, an assortment of specimens raised at Mount Annan in New South Wales were moved to Queensland under the auspices of the state's Department of Primary Industries and Fisheries in the hope they could be sold within six years. The founding collection included 300 plants raised from cuttings from wild plants, 500 seedlings raised from seed collected from the wild, and 200 plants raised from cuttings taken from trees grown in the gardens. These 1,000 plants were descended from twenty-six individuals from the first site and eighteen from the second site, and they are the parents of almost every domesticated Wollemi pine.[29] Eleven years after the survival of 'Pinosaur' made headlines, nearly 300 mature-looking trees were the first Wollemi pines ever sold.

The days leading up to the auction in October 2005 were marked by thunderstorms, but the sun finally broke over Sydney's Royal

Botanical Garden for Sotheby's 'sale of the century'. Better known for selling the world's finest art and antiquities, the auction house strayed into botanical territory when it provided collectors with a chance to bid for the Jurassic pine. More than four hundred people eagerly took their seats or stood, while the press gathered. Reports claimed the auction was the most anticipated since 'the sale of the late Marilyn Monroe's belongings'.[30] Sotheby's marketed the trees as the 'First Generation Collector's Edition'. Publicly exhibited at the gardens beforehand, the 292 trees were split into 148 lots. The lavishly illustrated catalogue included panoramic photographs of the sandstone gorges in which the wild trees survived, carefully labelled maps showing the location of each parent tree, and individual photographs of every sapling. Each sapling was named: some after the wild parent from which cuttings were taken, others from classical heroes such as Hercules or the Egyptian god Geb to the Three Explorers, honouring the first three Europeans to cross the Blue Mountains. Some saplings were auctioned as collections named after famous European naturalists and explorers, such as Joseph Banks and Charles Darwin. Most were named after men, and none was given a name from an Aboriginal language.

Spirited bidding ensured the gavel first fell at AU$6,000 for a tree propagated from the tallest wild tree nicknamed King Billy. Brisk bidding ensured the sale of every lot within three hours. Prices ranged from AU$1,680 to over AU$200,000. A family of twenty trees from the same parent sold for AU$21,000. A collection named after Joseph Banks sold for AU$135,625, and went to a private bidder who bought a total of forty-seven trees for AU$230,000. The auction raised AU$1,059,165, to fund further research and conservation efforts.[31] Many bidders were representatives of botanic gardens hoping to secure a prized specimen. Less than a decade after the auction, a survey of ex-situ conifer collections found the Wollemi pine growing in nearly a hundred botanic gardens and arboretums across the world.[32] Domestic gardeners faced a longer wait, but soon snapped up trees from commercial nurseries for a fraction of the cost.

Botanic gardens conserved the Wollemi pine by using seed

banking, cloning, and ex situ conservation to protect against future loss. A global survey of conifer collections found nearly 80 per cent of the world's threatened conifers were present in 800 botanical collections, but approximately 130 threatened taxa were either barely present or entirely absent from these collections.[33] Botanic gardens are important sites for many ways of conserving plants, from growing threatened trees to seed banking. A few years after the Sotheby's auction, Australia's Black Summer dramatically affirmed the importance of ex situ safeguards.

Lightning pierced the skies above the Blue Mountains weeks into the scorching October of 2019. On the 26th, fiery light hit the ground near Gospers Mountain causing desiccated debris to ignite. The flames swelled into a ferocious blaze that devoured the forests of Wollemi National Park for weeks, while hundreds of fires scorched neighbouring regions. By mid-November, 90,000 hectares were charred. Worse followed when the Gospers Mountain fire combined with other wildfires to create a mega-fire. Nearly three months later, the flames subsided after having burned more than a million hectares in Australia's largest recorded wildfire. Global news outlets streamed footage of charred communities and ecosystems. The fire was the fiercest among 15,000 of the Black Summer. Wildfires burned more than 19 million hectares between 2019 and 2020, including 3.5 million hectares of protected environments.[34] Thirty-three people died and 3,000 homes were obliterated, while an estimated one billion animals perished during the fires and another two billion in the aftermath. Across the Pacific Ocean, wildfires raged through California. Fires are common in both regions, but the scale and ferocity of the Black Summer's conflagrations were extraordinary, and they raised the spectre of recurrent mega-fires caused by human-induced climate change.[35]

As the fires threatened Gondwanaland's survivors, firefighters risked their lives to protect the Wollemi pine from extinction. Initially, they hoped to stop the flames reaching the trees. When that proved impossible, they tried to minimize the damage. Aerial firefighters dropped fire retardant onto the wild trees and surrounding areas, while other specialists were lowered from helicopters to work on the ground. They installed a bespoke irrigation system to soak the undergrowth and stop leaf litter igniting. Despite heroic efforts, fire enveloped the gorge and hid the wild trees in palls of smoke. This lingered for days before clearing and restoring enough light for experts to assess the damage. The species survived, but the community was scarred. Two trees died, forty-two adult trees were singed, and of the others only four escaped unscathed. Forty-three juvenile trees survived, but only eleven were well established. All the juveniles were burned, while smaller saplings in the undergrowth suffered so badly they showed little sign of recovery even two years later.[36] The remarkable mission prevented extinction and highlighted the precariousness of these trees. Official estimates warned that nearly half of the Gondwanaland reserves were burned.[37]

Two years after wild Wollemi pines were almost reduced to ashes, their home acquired new forms of protection. After the Black Summer, the New South Wales government conducted an inquiry to review protections against bushfires. It proposed identifying the state's most important natural and cultural assets for special conservation measures. The last haven for wild Wollemi pines was the first area to be declared an 'asset of intergenerational significance'. Another 279 sites were later offered the same protection, which also benefited species such as the koala, brush-tailed rock-wallaby, eastern bristlebird, crimson spider orchid, dwarf mountain pine, and regent honey eater.[38] The remarkable dedication to conserving the wild Wollemi pine makes clear the work that governments, conservationists, and ordinary people are sometimes willing to do to protect some ways of being. Unfortunately, most trees never enjoy such celebrity despite their desperate need for conservation and care.

Life's Elders

Light is life. Almost all earthly life depends on those living beings able to turn sunlight into edible energy. Plants, phytoplankton, and cyanobacteria use light, carbon dioxide, and water to create oxygen, sugars, and starches, through the near magical process of photosynthesis. It is a gift infinitely more precious than the alchemists' dream of turning base metals into gold. Photosynthesis is the first step in almost every food chain on earth that helps bind us all into communities of eating and excreting. Like many other ways of being, from gargantuan whales to dung beetles, we are so dependent on plants that we could not exist without them. Yet plants received little notice in the conservation regimes that emerged in the post-war world. While endangered birds, mammals, and landscapes were focal points for conservation efforts, botanists were left frustrated by the lack of attention to and funding for protecting plants.[39] Whereas rhinos, elephants, lions, cranes, woodpeckers, thylacines, and condors were among the earliest species to be listed as threatened in the late 1940s, plants found few advocates.

As we have seen, the first lists of endangered species collated by international organizations from the late 1940s were eventually superseded from the 1960s by the Red Data Books, later the Red List, compiled by the International Union for Conservation of Nature (IUCN). Delegates at early meetings hoped for a listing of plants, but the first four Red Data Books were dedicated to mammals, birds, amphibians and reptiles, and freshwater fish. At the IUCN's third general meeting in 1952, attendees argued 'the sooner' the organization directed 'its attention to threatened plants, the greater will be the chances of saving some of them'.[40] By 1954 a botanical subcommittee created a system for classifying endangered plants modelled on the categories used for animals: Class A included 'Vanishing species'; Class B, 'Threatened species'; Class C, 'Species which need local protection to preserve representatives in certain areas'; and Class D, 'Species restored through reforestation or management'.[41] Unfortunately, the subcommittee's work stalled for lack of funds.[42] Following the IUCN's Ninth General Assembly in 1966, the Royal Botanic Gardens at Kew led renewed efforts to document endangered plants supported by the Royal Society in London.

The efforts at Kew were led by the botanist Ronald Melville. Originally a pharmacist, Melville retrained and gained an honours degree in botany in 1931. He worked in the museum at Kew for sixteen years. He became a specialist on elms and served on the British government's Vegetable Drugs Committee. When stocks of vitamin C derived from citrus fruits were jeopardized during the Second World War, he suggested using rose hips: soon, a rich rose syrup was in production. In 1950 Melville transferred to Kew's herbarium, where he specialized in Australian plants and the evolution of flowering plants (formally known as angiosperms). He retired in 1968 and started to list endangered flowering plants. Melville eventually wrote a Red Data Book dedicated to flowering plants, which was published in 1970.[43] The *New York Times* celebrated the addition of plants to the 'bible of wild animal conservationists', which already listed nearly '800 animal species . . . believed to be going the way of the dodo'.[44] The focus on flowering plants, however, left swathes of the plant kingdom such as algae, mosses, cycads, ferns, and trees unlisted.

The success of listing flowering plants spurred the pursuit of more comprehensive coverage of the plant kingdom. Botanists asserted that comprehensive lists would provide the 'world's decision-makers' with 'the facts' as they developed suitable 'action plans'.[45] Following the first global conference on the environment in 1972, the United Nation's Stockholm Declaration identified four priorities of relevance to plants: the creation and management of reserves to conserve plants and their genetics; surveys of wild plants to establish suitable plans for further research; providing lists of plants in the wild and in ex situ collections to track their existence and population health; and finally the conservation of plants as living specimens or seed banks.[46] As with so many species, conservation measures were justified not because of the inherent value of plants, but because of their possible benefit to humans in the present and future. Early reports discussed species, including plants, as present and future sources of commercially traded goods, drugs, food, or natural resources such as oils and timber. As a result, early conservation efforts often depended on debates about future human security and ensuring continued resource extraction, rather than the rights or well-being of any species, from whales to trees.

The IUCN's Species Survival Commission, which managed listing, appointed a Threatened Plants Committee (TPC) in 1974. Based at the Royal Botanic Gardens in Kew, the TPC challenged the systematic neglect of plants in the post-war period.[47] Kew was the central node in a much broader network of regional groups, specialists, and botanic gardens where data was collated and assessed for as many species as possible. The committee noted that agricultural production, resource extraction, habitat loss, human destruction, pollution, climate change, pests, and diseases all threatened plants. The first Red Data Book which expanded coverage beyond flowering plants listed 250 species and appeared in 1978. The IUCN collated and published a revised version as the *IUCN Red Data Book of Threatened Plants* in 1997, which finally listed plants internationally.[48] That volume provided sufficient global coverage of the plant kingdom to complement, and expand, decades of work on animals.

The plight of threatened trees soon drew dedicated attention. Botanists Sara Oldfield, Charlotte Lusty, and Amy MacKinven consulted more than 300 expert foresters, field researchers, taxonomists, conservation biologists, and botanists, through a questionnaire. They held four international workshops in the Netherlands, Costa Rica, Zimbabwe, and Vietnam to discuss the results. They also used the most recent lists of threatened plants from the IUCN and numerous regional lists to provide data. The trio marshalled their results into a landmark report that provided the world's first dedicated assessment of threatened trees in 1998. They estimated that nearly 7,300, or 9 per cent, of the world's 21,000 species of trees were threatened from among 100,000 species of plants worldwide.[49]

Botanists soon called for a global assessment of all trees. Over five years, 500 scientists based at sixty institutions collaborated to produce the first *State of the World's Trees* report, published in 2021.[50] The report established there were at least 58,497 tree species, and it revealed that 30 per cent were in danger of extinction, with 142 species already extinct in the wild. Trees face numerous threats including: the loss of their homes as people destroy habitats; rapacious exploitation for consumer goods from timber to fragrant resins for luxury scents; and pests and diseases. The new data underpins the Global Tree Portal. This open-source database allows users to explore the distribution and conservation status of every tree species, as well as the conservation strategies reviewed for the report.[51] In direct contrast to the historical neglect of the botanical status and endangerment of tree species, the project required the 'largest initiative in the history of the IUCN Red List of Threatened Species'.[52] Such dedicated attention is long overdue, and might be the first step to addressing many forms of neglect and erasure that have consequences for all life on earth.

Almost all life ultimately depends on plants, but they are consistently overlooked in conservation circles. Few plants achieve the celebrity status of the World Wildlife Fund's panda logo, or other charismatic megafauna such as tigers, elephants, or whales. This neglect creates significant problems for policy-makers. Plants are of enormous environmental, economic, and political significance, and protecting them is essential to life's survival.[53]

Paying greater attention to plants also raises important challenges for writing histories of extinction. It requires historians to radically rethink common divisions of time, place, and assumptions about which lives are historically interesting or significant. Exploring the lives of plants holds enormous potential for understanding the interconnectedness of past and present life, and perhaps even respecting plants for their own sake, not just for our self-interest.[54]

Trees prefer to live in communities, but far too many are lonely survivors. Whether flourishing or threatened, most ways of being, especially plants, never receive the attention or protection devoted to the Wollemi pine. The 'Pinosaur' is among the world's rarest trees in the wild, but many other species fare much worse. A lone *Hyophorbe amaricaulis* palm survives in the Curepipe Botanic Gardens in Mauritius but every effort to harvest seeds and grow more such palms has failed.[55] A single male *Encephalartos woodii* cycad survives in Kew Gardens, but despite extensive searching, a wild female plant of the same species has never been found in its home territory of South Africa. Nicknamed the world's loneliest plant, there is every chance Kew's spectacular specimen will be the last of its kind.[56] The critically endangered Wollemi pine faces a more positive future precisely because botanists, government officials, and gardeners all cherish the tree.

Efforts to conserve the Wollemi pine are a reminder that extinction is a political choice. Post-war and Cold War conservation efforts were usually predicated on using 'fuller knowledge and wiser action' to 'leave for ourselves and our posterity a better life'.[57] These endeavours protected many species, but they were rooted in the economic desire to maximize harvests of valuable commodities, such as whale oil or timber, rather than a concern with the rights of living beings. Considering the lifeways of trees allows us to move beyond privileging our own needs to a future of genuine justice for every way of being. Our choices matter more than ever for life's astonishing elders.

9.
Martha's Resurrection

Passenger pigeons once congregated in the largest flocks ever known. The males' bluish head and back were interrupted by iridescent necks glittering in greens, purples, and bronze, earning them the moniker Blue Meteor. The breast and throat were splashed with a wine-red patch. Roughly sixteen and a half inches in length for males, the birds were elegant, swift, and gregarious. About an inch smaller, females had less vivid plumage, but they had the same deep-red feet and piercing red eyes. Their scientific name *Ectopistes migratorius*, meaning migrating wanderer, evokes the vast journeys they would make in search of food, often stripping forests bare as they gorged on the nuts of beech, oak, or horse chestnut in spring, and fruit such as cherries, strawberries, blueberries, cranberries, and raspberries in summer. Roosting in woodlands or swamps, flocks blanketed the forest floor in a layer of snow-like dung. The combined heft of perched birds often broke tree limbs, leaving behind canopy openings into which tree saplings raced upwards. The bird's peak population probably ranged between 3 and 5 billion birds, meaning their kind constituted 25 to 40 per cent of all birdlife across the North American continent.[1] Within a human lifespan, these flocks had vanished.

The ferocious speed and number of birds lost makes their demise peculiarly astonishing. Until recently, the passenger pigeon's fate was an arresting tale of human exploitation, but attempts to resurrect the bird raise numerous questions about how we treat fellow ways of being and the very meaning of extinction.

De-extinction conjures up fantasies of reviving creatures that no one alive has encountered: dinosaurs, mammoths, and dodos. Although understandable, this creates a sense that we live in a world where species are either alive, in however precarious a situation, or gone for ever. Yet extinction proceeds by degrees of peril and loss. Local populations, genetically distinct populations (ecotypes), subspecies, or species might all be subject to numerous local extinctions. Over time, suitable habitat might be lost and territorial range shrink. When multiple varieties of a species exist, any one of those might be lost. Many regard losing a subspecies, such as the Javan tiger native to the Indonesian island until the 1970s, as local extinction, despite the fact that tigers survive as a species. If a species is locally extinct or extinct in the wild, recovery might be achieved through reintroducing living relatives or captives and protecting them until they flourish. Such ecological restoration is 'the process of assisting the recovery of an ecosystem that has been degraded, damaged, or destroyed'.[2] Species might also be declared functionally extinct, when the species survives but can no longer play an ecological role, or declared extinct in the wild, when the only known survivors remain in captivity,.

De-extinction cannot be a singular act of bringing a species back into existence, because extinction covers a broad spectrum of possibilities. Instead, de-extinction might describe multiple forms of recovery, from back-breeding and artificial selection to genetically engineering new hybrids.[3] New and extraordinary opportunities for ecological recovery have prompted an explosion of interest in de-extinction. With rapid technological developments, genetic engineering is transforming how de-extinction might be achieved. As these new techniques redefine what counts as extinction in technical, philosophical, and emotional terms, these multiple threads create an important story of humans struggling with loss – and grief.

Lost Billions

In 1534 the French King Francis I ordered an expedition to North America hoping to discover lucrative spices and a route to Asia. Charged with leading the voyage, the French explorer Jacques Cartier made two expeditions over the next few years. On the first voyage, Cartier sailed through the strait between the lands now known as Labrador and Newfoundland, along the west coast of Newfoundland, around the Gulf of St Lawrence, passing Prince Edward Island, the Gaspé Peninsula and Anticosti Island. Cartier achieved fame for 'discovering' Prince Edward Island and coining the name Canada, probably from the Huron-Iroquois word 'kanata' denoting a settlement.[4] Near Anticosti Island he spotted an apparently infinite number of 'wood pigeons'. His sightings provide the first known written records of the passenger pigeon. In 1663 a man hunting in Québec reportedly killed 132 birds with a lone gunshot. Five decades later, a local bishop reportedly summoned God's help in excommunicating the birds to prevent them from damaging crops. These early testimonies teem with a sense of inexhaustible multitudes.[5]

Centuries later, passenger pigeons inspired awe in ornithologists surveying the birds of North America. In autumn 1813, John James Audubon, an ornithologist and enslaver best remembered for his exquisite drawings of birds later published in *The Birds of America* (1827–38), travelled across Kentucky from his home in Henderson to Louisville, the largest city in the state. He witnessed a migrating kit so prolific that 'The air was literally filled with Pigeons; the light of noonday was obscured as by an eclipse.' Audubon continued his journey mesmerized by the 'extreme beauty of their aerial evolutions, when a Hawk chanced to press upon the rear of a flock. At once, like a torrent, and with a noise like thunder, they rushed into a compact mass.' By sunset he reached Louisville, but the pigeons took three days to pass in 'undiminished numbers'. Audubon estimated the flock numbered 1,115,136,000 strong.[6] In the same decade, Scotsman Alexander Wilson witnessed a 'living torrent' of passenger pigeons he believed numbered at least 2,230,272,000 birds.[7] As one writer notes: 'Assuming each pigeon was about 16 inches long . . . if Wilson's flock had flown beak to tail in a single file the bird would have stretched around the Earth's equatorial circumference *22.6 times*.'[8] These numbers are near unimaginable yet, within fifty years, these flocks were but memories.

The conviction of colonists that passenger pigeons were inexhaustible resources encouraged shocking wastefulness. They were killed for food, feathers, and sport, as hunters shot the bird by day, tucked into pigeon pie in the evening, and slept on passenger-pigeon feather bedding at night. In 1822 one family alone killed 4,000 pigeons for their feathers near Lake Erie in New York, while Audubon observed a hunt in which so many birds were slain that their abandoned corpses littered the ground for hog feed.[9] Until the mid-nineteenth century, the birds were killed indiscriminately. In spite of these pressures, Audubon believed only the loss of forest habitat would diminish the numbers of passenger pigeons. In the 1830s and 1840s new railway networks provided hunters with access to fresh mass markets and the violence escalated into wanton slaughter, tipping the passenger pigeon into decline.[10]

By the 1880s, the sky no longer darkened with meandering feathered rivers: flocks of even a few hundred were rare.[11] Writing in 1895, Chief Simon Pokagon of the Neshnabé nation recalled spending his boyhood 'admiring the movements of these birds . . . like some great river, ever varying in hue'. Lamenting their decline in the intervening six decades, he compared flights of passenger pigeons to the greatest wonders of the landscape: 'I have stood by the grandest waterfall of America . . . yet never have my astonishment, wonder, and admiration been so stirred as when I have witnessed these birds drop from their course like meteors from heaven.' He noted that, despite Native nations hunting the pigeon, 'under our manner of securing them they continued to increase'.[12] Five years later, in the year of Chief Pokagon's death, the last known wild passenger pigeon, a female, was shot by fourteen-year-old Press Clay Southworth in Ohio. She was later stuffed and nicknamed Buttons after the black shoe buttons substituted for her fiery red eyes.[13] Sightings continued, but none were reliable and usually misidentifications of turtle or mourning doves.[14]

The last known passenger pigeons died in captivity. Unfortunately, these birds passed away when naturalists were more likely to capture, study, and preserve the remains of threatened ways of being than to protect survivors. Soon after opening in 1875, Cincinnati Zoo assembled an assortment of passenger pigeons. By 1909, only two birds remained there, nicknamed George and Martha Washington after the First President and First Lady.[15] George died on 10 July 1910 in such a terrible condition that he was not preserved. Martha was suddenly the world's first celebrity endling. Ornithologists wended their way to her cage as if it was hallowed ground. Martha died on 1 September 1914 – just weeks after the assassination of Archduke Franz Ferdinand and his wife Sophie triggered diplomatic turmoil and, ultimately, the First World War.[16]

Martha was suspended in water, frozen into a block of ice, and shipped to the Smithsonian Institution for an autopsy. Robert Wilson Shufeldt, an ethnographer otherwise known for his racist screeds on Black Americans as a 'menace to American civilization', dissected Martha's corpse.[17] Shufeldt carefully unpeeled her skin and, before detaching it for preservation, laid out her remains for some viscerally gruesome photographs. Nobody knows the exact date of Martha's birth, but Shufeldt guessed she was twenty-nine years old based on the testimony of a general manager at Cincinnati Zoo. Shufeldt noted her body was in good condition, but found blood in her abdominal cavity, and observed that the right lobe of her liver and intestine had almost disappeared. He pickled her innards in alcohol, and they remain in the museum's collection to this day. One after another, he examined her internal organs, noting the liver, gizzard, spleen, ovaries, adrenal glands, pancreas, eventually reaching her heart. In a sentimental moment, he cut no further, 'preferring to preserve it in its entirety . . . as the heart of the last "Blue Pigeon" . . . the last representative of countless millions and unnumbered generations of its kind practically exterminated through man's agency'.[18] Shufeldt's sense of loss is palpable, but dwelling on Martha's significance as 'the last living representative of its race' indicated a broader racial anxiety. While Shufeldt's laments are often recited in accounts of Martha's autopsy, writers seldom acknowledge his desire to maintain white supremacy despite its broader significance.

When scientists suggested tackling perceived racial degeneration through selective 'breeding' and prohibiting racial intermingling, such as immigration or marriage, in the later nineteenth century, discussions about white American futures were intimately tied to apprehensions about racial extinction.[19] The anthropologically minded statistician Francis Galton, a cousin of Charles Darwin's, wrote a book called *Hereditary Genius* (1869) that explored his family's success as evidence that intelligence and beauty were inherited. He implored readers to improve their 'race' through choosing mates carefully. While common in animal and plant husbandry, the term 'eugenics' was coined by Galton in 1883 for the selective breeding of people. Eugenic principles underpinned new policies controlling immigration, marriage, and forced sterilization, and targeted the lives of vulnerable people regarded as undesirable, whether poor, disabled, or not white; eugenic laws and policies were most widespread and well established in the United States, but eugenic ideas were influential worldwide. Significantly, eugenics, fears of racial decline, and annihilatory antisemitism underpinned the genocidal crimes of the Holocaust.[20]

In the later nineteenth century, as eugenicists confidently deemed certain people worthier of survival, marriage, and bearing children than others, some naturalists regarded threatened species as ancient, racial lineages in need of swift preservation. By the time naturalists sounded the alarms for bison, declining from more than 30 million to just a few hundred, and passenger pigeons, from billions to mere dozens, by the end of the nineteenth century, their past abundance was associated with a fast-disappearing pioneering colonial vitality.[21] By the time Martha took her last breath, protecting wildlife and securing America's whiteness were often intertwined threads.

Martha has rarely been in the public eye since her death. Her skin was mounted by Nelson R. Wood, a Smithsonian taxidermist, and remained in the museum's storage vaults for many years (Fig. 9.1). Martha has flown twice in death, once in first class chaperoned by a flight attendant. On that first flight, in 1966, she was flown to San Diego, California, for the Zoological Society's Golden Jubilee Conservation Conference. Upon her return to the Smithsonian, she was displayed alongside a sign announcing her historical significance:

9.1 Martha's afterlife as a museum specimen.

MARTHA
Last of her species, died at 1 p.m.,
1 September 1914, age 29, in the
Cincinnati Zoological Garden.
EXTINCT

Martha also flew to her home state, to be displayed in the Reptile House at Cincinnati Zoo in 1974. She was returned to storage in the Smithsonian when it erected a new Hall of Mammals in 1999. On the centenary of her death, she was displayed in the exhibition *Once There Were Billions: Vanished Birds of North America* (2014–16), where she shared the limelight with a great auk (extinct c. 1852), Carolina parakeet (extinct 1918), and Heath hen (extinct c. 1932). Confined to storage ever since, Martha is only accessible by special request for scientific research.[22]

Two memorials to the passenger pigeon were erected in 1947, but they say more about human grief than avian life. Boy Scouts established the first memorial in Pigeon Hills, Pennsylvania, while the Wisconsin Society for Ornithology instituted the second in Wyalusing State Park, with a plaque identifying the harm caused as a consequence of 'the avarice and thoughtlessness of man'.[23] Ruminating on the second memorial, conservationist Aldo Leopold wrote a pre-emptively mournful elegy in expectation of the day when only ancient oaks and hills would bear any trace of the passenger pigeon's memory. Crucially, he identified the historical and human peculiarity of his anguish:

> For one species to mourn the death of another is a new thing under the sun . . . we, who have lost our pigeons, mourn the loss. Had the funeral been ours, the pigeons would hardly have mourned us.[24]

Leopold's pain captures the shock of losing one of the world's most prolific lifeways, and it expresses why species loss is not just a singular event or a barren absence.[25] Extinction is the loss of a way of being endured by the dead, the dying, and the living.

A century after Martha's lonely departure, plans are afoot to resurrect her kind. De-extinction projects are much more likely to succeed for recently lost species as the necessary DNA is probably better preserved. Stewart Brand and Danny Hills co-founded The Long Now Foundation in 1996 (or 01996 in their preferred notation). They aim to think beyond human lifetimes or even our presence on earth, and 'foster responsibility in the framework of the next 10,000 years'.[26] The Foundation's major projects currently include building a clock designed to chime once every 10,000 years and archiving more than 1,500 of the world's languages in the Rosetta Project. In 2013, Brand founded Revive and Restore as a non-profit organization devoted to making de-extinction a reality. Originally an offshoot of the Long Now Foundation, Revive and Restore is now independent. [27] Brand's TED talk 'The Dawn of De-Extinction. Are you ready?' debuted the project as part of a larger TED event on de-extinction and has amassed more than 2.2 million views.[28] Brand's talk was a passionate manifesto for de-extinction with the goal of transforming the 'Sorrow, anger, mourning' of extinction. His solution: 'Don't mourn. Organize.' Brand envisages reviving lost species to rethink our relationship with the natural world. He predicts a century in which children are filled with wonder and trips to Pleistocene Park so they might grow up without 'a view of the relation of humans with nature that is not tragic, for a change'. Such hopefulness is rare in discussions of extinction; we are more likely to encounter elegies for the dead, yet it does raise the question of whether we need to learn meaningful ways to mourn, and honour lost lives, rather than refusing to grieve.[29]

The Great Passenger Pigeon Comeback, led by scientist Ben Novak, is a flagship project for Revive and Restore.[30] Novak promotes the de-extinction of the passenger pigeon because it is an 'engineer species' whose behaviour plays a crucial role in creating habitats for other species. Immense flocks of passenger pigeons used to clear and nourish the ground with guano. Their sheer weight and numbers and damage to trees created gaps in forest canopies. In combination, these behaviours helped regenerate forests and benefited other species. With declining populations, other species did not fulfil the same ecological role as passenger pigeons and so forests, and their inhabitants, suffered.[31] The impact of any hybridized species is probably impossible to predict, but, as Emily Dickinson wrote, '"Hope" is the thing with feathers', and given the current enthusiasm for rewilding, it is entirely possible that generations of people who have never seen a passenger pigeon would welcome its return.[32]

Significantly, Novak's research goes beyond trying to bring back the passenger pigeon to attempting to redefine the very meaning of extinction. In recent years, exploding interest in de-extinction has created multiple, and conflicting, meanings of the term. Novak recently intervened, suggesting that practising de-extinction scientists, rather than scholars working in the humanities and social sciences, should lead the way in defining the term. His preferred definition for de-extinction is 'the ecological replacement of an extinct species by means of purposefully adapting a living organism to serve the ecological function of the extinct species'.[33] According to Novak's definition, the first successful de-extinction is the American peregrine falcon's return as those birds were selectively bred to replace a lost genetic lineage and ecological function. Novak discounts cloned species as true de-extinctions because they are direct copies of an existing genetic lineage, and he also discounts selective breeding to recreate lost species because the process involves recombining elements of ancestral DNA inherited by cross-breeding direct descendants. He also argues that species which survive as frozen specimens are not truly extinct because they survive as genetic lineage, even if only in chilly suspension. In contrast, he defines frozen lineages with no living individuals as 'evolutionarily torpid' because they no longer evolve or perform an ecological function. Whether Novak's definition is widely adopted or not, it is a recent example of privileging genetic lineages as the best way to define a species, among numerous other possibilities.[34] Despite Novak's preferred definition, many forms of recovery are possible whether or not they are formally defined as de-extinction.

Rewilding Spectres

In the 1960s many birds of prey were on the verge of extinction worldwide. In America the peregrine falcon's numbers declined owing to the widespread use of the chemical pesticide DDT from the 1940s onwards. Once in the food chain and consumed by the birds, the toxin caused the thinning of eggshells. Brooding birds shattered their eggs. Decades of unsuccessful breeding eradicated the original population of peregrine falcons. In the 1970s, the Peregrine Fund bred captive birds in efforts to return the birds to the wild. These birds were crosses between seven subspecies and, once released in 1974, thrived after public outcry led to the banning of DDT. In many cases of ecological restoration, such as the beaver, there is genetic continuity between the former population and the restored animals. The resurgence of the American peregrine falcon is a striking example of de-extinction through creating a new genetic lineage.[35]

The most famous example of ecological restoration remains the grey wolf. Once widely distributed throughout North America, grey wolves were persecuted throughout the eighteenth and nineteenth centuries leading to a deeply uncertain future; after the federal government introduced a policy of deliberate extermination in the late 1800s, their numbers crashed to fewer than a thousand wolves scattered across the continent by the 1950s.[36] Food chains are characterized by energy moving through different stages, or trophic levels: plants are the first level, herbivores the second, carnivores next, and apex predators last. Within these networks, keystone species are those that exert an outsized effect on stabilizing the ecosystem, even when present in relatively small numbers, as with apex predators. Removing a keystone species can trigger a series of unexpected and often undesirable effects lower down the food chain, known as a trophic cascade. Reduced wolf populations triggered such a trophic cascade, benefiting other species including trees such as aspen and willow, scavenging birds like eagles and ravens, and even other large carnivores such as grizzly bears. In Yellowstone, populations of coyotes, elk, bison, and pronghorn antelope all increased. Wolves were reintroduced into the wild in 1995 to check abundant grazers. Although deeply controversial at the time, the reintroduction has proved successful in rebalancing the ecosystem. From just 20 wolves in 1995, the wild population reached a peak of nearly 180 wolves in the early 2000s, while hovering around 100 in more recent years.[37]

Rewilding, or projects to reintroduce species to their former ranges, was first proposed as a conservation strategy by Conservation biologist Michael Soulé, founder in 1985 of the Society for Conservation Biology, and the environmentalist David Foreman in the late 1980s. Their collaboration led to the founding of the Wildlands Project, renamed the Wildlands Network, in 1991. Seven years later, Soulé and another conservation biologist, Reed Noss, penned an article on 'Rewilding and Biodiversity' that served as a project manifesto and foundation for the present-day movement.[38] Soulé and Noss advocated protecting wilderness areas with a focus on three Cs: establishing *core* wilderness areas, linked through *corridors* to establish interlinked protected habitats providing species free passage, and allowing large *carnivores* to flourish. Their interest in carnivores stemmed from the large territories they needed for survival. If the large habitats of these umbrella species were successfully protected, many other species would indirectly benefit as if sheltered under their protection. In recent years, rewilding has gained new meanings as it is used to describe numerous conservation strategies beyond the original focus on the three Cs.

American rewilding projects privileged carnivores while European rewilding focused on reintroducing large herbivores. Numerous rewilding projects returned locally extinct species to their former habitats. One of the most long-standing and successful is the European beaver. Once spread across Northern Europe, beavers suffered from loss of habitat, persecution for fur and, ultimately, extinction in Sweden by the 1870s. Norwegian beavers were reintroduced to Sweden in 1922.[39] Other reintroduction projects are continuing, including in Scotland where beavers disappeared in the 1600s. Similarly, the last wild European bison died in 1927. Kent Wildlife Trust and the Wildwood Trust hope that the reintroduction of the European bison in England will serve as a proxy for the steppe bison which once roamed across the continent. Advertisements for a bison herder, described in the British press as 'the job of a lifetime', appeared in January 2021. The herd of four were released in Blean Woods in Kent, in 2022.[40] Rewilding Europe, founded in 2011, is interested in numerous other species such as lynx, elk, ibex, and white-tailed eagle.[41] In these examples, the reintroduced animals are usually translocated from surviving populations to areas they formerly inhabited. For some people, these projects are ecological restoration, not de-extinction, because they are usually returning a surviving species to its former range.[42]

The Netherlands is home to one of Europe's most controversial rewilding projects. The Dutch government reclaimed land from Lake Ijssel in 1968. Now known as the *Oostvaardersplassen* (OVP), the 6,000 hectares lay undeveloped and eventually attracted greylag geese and other beings seeking respite. As the geese flourished, their grazing prevented woodland species succeeding. The area developed into a patchwork of marshes, grasslands, open water, dotted with occasional trees, and now hosts rare birdlife including white egrets, a nesting pair of white-tailed eagles, and lapwings. Formally designated a nature reserve in the 1970s, the OVP attracted the interest of ecologist Frans Vera a decade later. He argued that modern conservationists incorrectly assumed forests once dominated Europe because they were accustomed to the landscapes created by abandoned agricultural land colonized by trees in the absence of large herbivores. In contrast, he suggested that ancient European landscapes were more likely open savannah because they were grazed by deer or extinct herbivores such as aurochs, the ancestors of domesticated cows, or tarpans, the ancestors of wild horses. Vera lamented that agriculture had turned European landscapes into large fragmented and disconnected areas of wilderness.[43]

Drawing on Vera's ideas, the Dutch government introduced Heck cattle, Konik horses, and red deer to the reserve. Left to run wild, the animals flourished, but severe weather killed a third of the cattle in the winter of 2005–6, triggering public fury. A year later, an official inquiry published a report with numerous recommendations that were never implemented. Four years later, another inquiry reiterated the findings of the first report and suggested limited culling. Thirteen years later, another devastating winter destroyed the population with further public outrage over the unfed and emaciated animals. The horses were subsequently removed and limited culling now takes place. For Vera, the OVP is explicitly an open-air laboratory experimenting with rewilding, and humans must allow nature to reach a balance without intervening. For many, the experiment is valuable precisely because it allows conservationists to study open-ended ecological recovery, rather than prescriptive preservation, albeit without apex predators. Critics argue that the OVP should be more proactively managed so animals are not left to die without intervention.[44] These debates will continue as the site develops and is keenly watched by proponents of rewilding. For those interested in histories of extinction, one of the most intriguing aspects of the OVP is Vera's choice of cattle.

Heck cattle were originally bred to recreate aurochs in efforts that recall the troubling origins of some conservation projects. Hunting caused wild aurochs numbers to plummet. As perhaps the earliest recorded extinction, the last known auroch died in a Polish zoo in 1627. In the early twentieth century, brothers Lutz and Heinz Heck were keen to selectively breed close living relatives of aurochs to recreate them. The brothers followed in the footsteps of their father, Berlin zookeeper Ludwig Heck. Heinz managed Munich's Hellabrunn Zoo from 1928 and Lutz succeeded his father at Berlin Zoo four years later. The brothers conducted extensive personal research into the various 'races' of aurochs, and then searched for living cattle with thick horns, muscular bodies, long legs, and an aggressive disposition. Through selective breeding they hoped to recreate an animal with the same appearance and traits as the extinct Ur-bovine, in a process also called back-breeding. Each brother recreated a herd. Heinz began in 1921 and claimed to have succeeded in spring 1932. He also tried to back-breed tarpans and quaggas, taking particular pride in rearing a zebra foal without a stripey rear in 1940. Meanwhile, Lutz secured the patronage of the National Socialist Hermann Göring, who asked Lutz to breed endangered European bison in 1935 and, three years later, to lead Germany's Nature Protection Authority. Göring hoped the collaboration would forge a new Aryan wilderness replete with ostensibly native species to fit within the broader project of Aryanization that ultimately led to the Holocaust.

The close connections between back-breeding aurochs, mythologized Aryan pasts, and genocide reveal the profoundly complicated roots of modern Heck cattle.[45] This darker history shows that de-extinction is not simply a scientific puzzle. Rather, animals, particularly those believed to *belong* to a nation or landscape, become important ways for humans to negotiate the pangs of absence and nationalist pride. In contrast, modern rewilders are not fastidiously concerned with replicating vanished landscapes with pure-bred, native animals. Rather, they aim to create new ecosystems to help life to thrive in unexpected ways, even if that means translocating species or creating new hybrids to find proxies for lost kinds. Since 2008 the Tauros Programme has used modern genetic advances to help recover aurochs and rewild Europe.[46] This intervention is an important expansion of the Heck brothers' early attempts.

Quaggas were a subspecies of zebra endemic to South Africa until they were hunted to extinction, especially for luxury shoe leather in the 1870s. The endling died in Amsterdam Zoo on 12 August 1883. Quaggas are striped like zebras on their forequarters, but these fade out to a uniform dark background on the hindquarters. In 1984, Reinhold E. Rau, a taxidermist and quagga enthusiast based at the South African Museum in Cape Town, now the Iziko South African Museum, obtained a dried sample of muscle and connective tissue from a quagga skin in the collections of the Museum of Natural History in Mainz, West Germany. He sent the sample to a team of scientists in California led by Russell Higuchi. From just 0.7 grams of tissue, the team managed to clone one-hundredth of the DNA of fresh muscle. Their experiment was the first to clone DNA from an extinct species. The team also recovered DNA from a mammoth frozen in Siberia 40,000 years ago. They predicted that 'If the long-term survival of DNA proves to be a general phenomenon, several fields, including palaeontology, evolutionary biology, archaeology and forensic science may benefit.'[47] In 1987 conservationists established a selective breeding programme to recreate quaggas from zebras. Named Rau quaggas, they bear the distinctive faded stripe pattern of quaggas, but they lack the chestnut background of their extinct relatives.[48] Rau's DNA sample came from a salt-preserved hide, but, following the Second World War, freezing DNA created novel possibilities and potentially redefined the meaning of life, death, and extinction.

Technologies using frozen biological material, such as in vitro fertilization, are now so commonplace that it is easy to forget how recently cold storage transformed scientific research, particularly for those interested in reproduction and replication. In 1949 the scientific journal *Nature* published a paper by Chris Polge, Audrey Smith and Alan Parkes, reporting on their experiments mixing glycerol with frog, poultry, and human semen. Freezing biological tissues usually creates ice crystals that can irreparably damage samples, but the team avoided crystallization by adding glycerol, allowing sperm to be frozen at exceptionally low temperatures and thawed. The breeder Rockefeller Prentice, who founded the American Breeders Service eight years earlier, wondered whether frozen semen could be used for the artificial insemination of cattle. His hunch paid off when Frosty, the world's first calf born of frozen bull semen, was born in 1953.[49] Within a decade, the journalist Ann Ewing speculated in the *Science News-Letter* about an impending future when scientists might 'preserve samples of species about to become extinct, store cell or tissue cultures and antibiotic-producing organisms, and stop life processes, in disease as well as in health'.[50] Ewing accurately predicted the opportunities created by suspending 'life processes' for endangered species and beyond.

Biologists quickly created frozen archives of threatened lives. In the 1970s, Kurt Benirschke explored using frozen samples for conservation.[51] After founding the Frozen Zoo in 1972, he served as Director of the San Diego Zoo between 1975 and 1985, and the Center for the Reproduction of Endangered Species (now San Diego Institute for Conservation Research) in 1979.[52] Benirschke urged colleagues to create 'genomic libraries' with haste. For him, every animal's arrival, surgery, birth or death at the zoo was an opportunity to harvest cells and suspend life in glass vials stored in liquid nitrogen. Benirschke believed this would protect against future unknowns and pleaded with his colleagues: 'You must collect things for reasons we don't understand.'[53] The Frozen Zoo was the first of its kind and now holds over 10,000 samples of tissue and blood representing nearly 1,000 taxa, including an extinct species.[54] Following in Benirschke's icy footsteps, multiple international projects now archive endangered species as frozen samples of DNA. In 1996 the Frozen Ark was established as an international consortium of projects preserving endangered species by freezing their DNA and creating a database of existing specimens.[55]

The potential for recovering extinct species from frozen cells was dramatically confirmed when the bucardo, also known as the Pyrenean ibex, was declared extinct in 2000. Once native to the mountainous regions of Spain, the ibex was hunted extensively, which led to severely depleted populations by the mid-twentieth century. With conservation efforts failing, in 1989 the remaining bucardos were rounded up but only three females were found. By 1999 only one survived: tissue samples were collected from her ear and frozen in liquid nitrogen. Encouraged by previous cloning experiments, a team of Spanish, French, and Belgian scientists led by José Folch used the tissue samples to clone bucardo DNA. They transferred the cloned DNA to domestic goat eggs without nuclei to create embryos. Over the course of two experiments, 792 embryos were created, 74 of which were transferred to captive surrogate goats. Seven pregnancies resulted, but only one goat gave birth to a kid, born through a caesarean in 2009. Although the tiny Pyrenean ibex appeared healthy, she died within a few minutes because of a defective lung. She was genetically identical to the last living bucardo, making her a direct clone. Despite her death, the team encouraged scientists to preserve 'tissues and cells of all endangered species or suitable animals, as they may be useful for future cloning-based conservation programs'.[56]

Freezing endangered species raises questions about who or what counts as alive, dead, or extinct. The IUCN declares a species extinct 'when there is no reasonable doubt that the last individual has died'.[57] But are frozen remains dead? The Frozen Ark and similar projects place thousands of species in a liminal state, making declaring a way of being extinct significantly more complicated. In the case of the bucardo, the kid's brief existence raises many questions. For some, the experiment might suggest a successful de-extinction. For others, those brief moments suggest the possibility of de-extinction, but do not yet count as success.[58] As long as species remain in frozen arks, the possibility of resurrecting their kind might mean we are reluctant to define them as truly lost. Yet, this process also risks reducing species to little more than genetic information, rather than appreciating them as living ways of being with their own forms of kinship and community rooted in particular places. These are not merely abstract philosophical distinctions because archiving species in frozen libraries raises significant questions about how we collect, store, and value ways of being.

In recent years the press has often carried stories of sensational technological successes that may pave the way for de-extinction by bringing back mammoths.[59] These were originally believed to have disappeared about 12,000 years ago, but a few survived until as late as 4,000 years ago on Wrangel Island, off the east coast of Russia in the Arctic Ocean, and close to the Bering Strait. This astonishing find means the last known mammoths were alive when the pharaohs ruled ancient Egypt and built the Great Pyramid at Giza (2580–2560 BCE) and the Great Sphinx (2520 BCE). The prospect of bringing back mammoths has created some of the most sensationalist reporting on de-extinction. Beyond attention-grabbing headlines, the reality is clear: if their de-extinction occurs, it will involve creating new hybrid animals through genetic engineering. Ancient DNA can be extracted from museum specimens and fossils up to half a million years old, and this window will probably grow as extraction techniques are improved. Although DNA can survive for thousands of years, it rapidly deteriorates after death and so even the best-preserved specimens provide only fragments of long-lost genomes. Scientists can splice together fragments of ancient and living DNA to create hybrid animals with traits of both living and extinct species, as with woolly mammoths. The geneticist George Church leads a team at Harvard University trying to recreate the mammoth by engineering mammoth DNA into the cells of Asian elephants. If successful, the hybridization will yield an animal that will be heralded as the de-extinction of the mammoth worldwide.[60]

Meanwhile, the Russian scientist Sergey Zimov founded a nature reserve called Pleistocene Park in 1989, where he aims to recreate the grasslands of the last Ice Age home for de-extinct mammoths. The

Siberian reserve is split relatively evenly into meadow, forest, and willow shrubland, and is home to Yakutian horses, reindeer, moose, muskoxen, wolves, bears, lynxes, foxes, hares, ground squirrels, and marmots. Zimov also plans to reintroduce Canadian bison, Siberian tigers, and ultimately, mammoths. He originally argued that grasslands would stabilize the soil and, in turn, prevent the release of sequestered carbon which might quickly follow the ground thawing. In this scenario, rewilding Pleistocene Park with large herbivores would contribute to mitigating the worst effects of human-induced climate change, although its ultimate success remains to be seen.[61]

Pleistocene Park exemplifies the controversial strategy of Pleistocene rewilding. In 2000 the ecologist Josh Donlan and geoscientist Paul Martin met at a conference. They were interested in the role of megafauna in conservation. In 2005 they co-authored a paper published in *Nature* that ignited immediate controversy. A year later, they expanded on their ideas in a paper also co-authored with Michael Soulé and published in the American *Naturalist*. Donlan and his colleagues proposed a plan for rewilding North America with charismatic megafauna such as mastodons, lions, and cheetahs lost over 12,000 years ago during the Ice Age, or Pleistocene. Martin argued these extinctions were caused by human 'overkill', as ancient human hunters crossed the Bering Strait and took unhindered advantage of the continent's bounty. Donlan and the team proposed a three-phase 'Pleistocene rewilding' of America. First, they advocated reintroducing Bolson tortoises, allowing feral horses to roam wild rather than managed as pests, and importing camels. They expected these animals to browse on woody plants in an arid ecosystem. Second, they suggested reintroducing African cheetahs, Asian and African elephants, and lions as substitutes for extinct megafauna. They argued that many of these were already captive in the United States and, although not exact equivalents of ancient beasts, might serve as functional proxies within ecosystems if released. Finally, they planned to establish a series of 'ecological history parks', creating a local tourist industry.[62]

Advocates believe Pleistocene rewilding allows conservationists to shift from 'managing extinction to actively restoring natural processes', thereby offering an alternative to landscapes dominated by 'pests and weeds' such as 'rats and dandelions'.[63] These plans require important shifts in conservation practices. First, planning any kind of recovery requires conservation projects to work towards a baseline. Within America, Columbus's invasion in 1492 is usually used as the preferred baseline. Donlan and his team rejected this timeframe in favour of prehuman time. Second, the team sought an alternative to the sense of doom and gloom in environmental activism. They contended that Pleistocene rewilding offered radical hope amid the current biodiversity crisis, most obviously through creating wondrous parks teeming with enthralling megafauna. Finally, the team insisted that humans were ethically obliged to make amends for harming ancient biodiversity.

Opponents quickly marshalled numerous criticisms. They pointed out potential problems including the immense cost of fencing, unpredictable ecological consequences of releasing megafauna, and the economic damage likely to follow from reduced tourism to African reserves.[64] These reproaches are important attempts to think through the practical challenges of Pleistocene rewilding. Yet far less attention is devoted to accounting for the differential impact of human occupation.[65] After all, arguing that modern humans bear an ethical responsibility for the actions of our ancestors fails to acknowledge that some peoples have caused considerably more damage to American biodiversity, particularly after the continent's colonization by Europeans. It also fails to address the unequal distribution of natural resources, within North America or globally. The question of who bears responsibility directly impacts who will be asked to make sacrifices in the search for a more equitable future. One of the most concerning aspects of Pleistocene rewilding is that there is so little discussion of which losses are imagined as the responsibility of everyone and the most urgent. By advocating a return to prehuman time, the rights of extinct megafauna are effectively given priority over both surviving flora and fauna and the rights of dispossessed peoples.[66] By deploying the undifferentiated category of 'human', and the timeframe of prehumanity, Pleistocene rewilding raises profound questions of justice, for other species and dispossessed peoples. Debating the ethics of de-extinction goes beyond mammoths, to how we treat all life.

Advocates for de-extinction argue that it has many potential benefits. One of the strongest arguments is the ethical obligation we owe to species exterminated by humans. It is difficult to admit, but extinction inevitably follows from inter-species competition. When new species arise, they vie with existing species for resources such as food and territory. Competition leads some species to survive and others to die out. Although extinction is a by-product of geological and ecological processes, humans have clearly contributed to, and accelerated, many extinctions. The geoscientist Paul Martin's theory that humans caused the mammoths' extinction through 'overkill' is still controversial, with many archaeologists disagreeing over the evidence, but it seems increasingly likely that a combination of climate change, loss of habitat, and human predation contributed to the loss of ancient megafauna. More recently, we know that many species such as the dodo, Steller's sea cow, great auk, thylacine, passenger pigeon and countless others were lost through human exploitation and persecution. For de-extinction advocates, restoring these species provides a form of inter-species justice.

Alternatively, de-extinction might help conservation efforts. Advocates are keen on engineering extinct traits into living species in order to create proxies of lost species to help preserve certain habitats or recreate others. The best example is of mammoth rewilding and the hope that frozen tundra might be renewed into grassy savannahs. Scientists also argue that the same gene-editing techniques could be used to reintroduce genetic diversity into living populations. One option might be to use museum specimens to reintroduce extinct diversity into heavily inbred populations. Such de-extinctions would enable humans to direct evolution more precisely than ever.[67]

Opponents of de-extinction implore caution and the focusing of our attention and resources on stopping further extinctions. They worry that species revival will either divert resources from protecting endangered species and their habitats, or prevent humans from making the choices required to reduce the environmental impact of modern, industrialized life. Genome sequencing is getting cheaper, but the cost of making even a single species de-extinct will be astronomical. As de-extinction scientists point out, this may not necessarily divert resources from conserving endangered species because their funding predominantly comes from private donors who might not otherwise fund conservation projects.[68] This may be true, but we should be aware of the intimate, and sometimes deeply problematic, connections between science, capitalism, and philanthropy that can be disavowed by assuming that private funding renders the economic aspects of less concern.[69] In 2019 elite institutions such as Harvard University, Stanford University, and MIT were forced to apologize when news broke that they partially funded many scientific projects, including mammoth de-extinction, by accepting donations from a wealthy donor even after his conviction for horrific sexual violence.[70] The question of private funding is especially pressing for de-extinction projects: after all, how much sway should wealthy people have in potentially reshaping what it means for us all to be alive, dead, or extinct?

Even if mammoths return to Pleistocene Park, many other complicated ethical and political questions remain unresolved. De-extinct species will probably be highly valuable intellectual property able to attract tourists, environmentalists, philanthropists, investors, commercial hunters, and traffickers. That discomforting list reflects the fact that species on the precipice of extinction already attract the interests of multiple groups, and not always in the best interests of the species themselves. In the case of the mammoth, one firm has already cultured cells from the beast to create meatballs. Eating extinct beasts no longer requires the whole animal even to live any kind of life.[71] Assuming de-extinction projects are inherently beneficial to either the species or the environment is unwarranted. As new legal frameworks to regulate de-extinction are explored, it is imperative that the broader public becomes aware of, and participates in, these changes and the potential reshaping of who or what counts as alive, or worthy of revival.

⋆

If you could bring an extinct species back to life, would you? Which species would you pick, and why? Your answers reveal a great deal about you and the broader cultural meanings of extinction. Whenever I have asked friends, students, and strangers these questions, their responses are often ambivalent. Some choose a dinosaur out of a desire to please their younger selves (or their children). Others choose a species lost owing to human actions, such as the dodo and great auk. Very rarely, someone might suggest Neanderthals. Almost no one ever chooses a plant or insect. Everyone finds the choice difficult because they are acutely aware of picking charismatic species rather than choosing what might be best for the species or environment, and they feel ill equipped to judge. Many also worry about whether de-extinction would only create unexceptional substitutes rather than anything resembling the lost way of being. Frequent questions include: What quality of life would these beings have? Would we have learned lessons, or would the species simply become extinct again? These conversations often reveal pangs of loss, anxiety, unresolved grief, and deep uncertainties.

From rewilding degraded ecosystems to bioengineering ancient beasts, de-extinction has already changed conservation practices, and our relationship to other ways of being. De-extinction raises profound questions about the meaning of extinction and the ethics of how we treat lifeways, whether living, endangered, liminal, latent, dead, or extinct. In these debates, we need to consider what we mean by justice, and for whom or what. Whether you oppose de-extinction or not, it is already a reality. In that light, it is important for everyone to be informed about these developing technologies and consider their own ethical position. Meanwhile, aurochs, quaggas, mammoths, moas, heath hens, Floreana Island giant tortoises, thylacines and passenger pigeons are all the subject of multiple de-extinction schemes.[72] These projects will yield new life forms, potentially within our own lifetimes. Whether this constitutes justice or not is another much trickier and more open question.

Birds are among the most visible sentinels of the Anthropocene. Some years ago, I moved to the countryside. A city-dweller at heart, I was rather apprehensive, but my reservations evaporated once I acquainted myself with my fellow residents, including foxes, badgers, bats, swallows, owls, kestrels, and buzzards. Every spring, as the swallows return from their epic journey across the Sahara Desert and the buzzards start mewing in the sky, my spirits soar. In late summer, as the sea of long grass is harvested for animal feed, the buzzards feast on the surprised animals denuded of cover, and kestrels hover in search of their next kill. Occasionally, red kites loom overhead. Remarkably, over the last couple of years local birders have spotted a migrating osprey and white-tailed eagle within a short drive. Just a few decades ago, these skies were markedly different as raptor populations plummeted. As they return, once common birds such as sparrows, swifts, and starlings are all increasingly rare. Seeing lone starlings arrive on these shores when they prefer to live in flocks that can number millions feels like a repetition of the passenger pigeon's decline and extinction.

Recovery is possible, but this depends on knowing that the birds we hear at dawn or see in our skies are remnants of once larger flocks. Historically, birdwatchers have borne witness to the decline of many once abundant species in our gardens, landscapes, and skies. Most of us cannot imagine the past abundance of the passenger pigeon, but we can offer recovery to other ways of being.

10.

Hope for Leviathan

London's Natural History Museum in South Kensington is a Romanesque cathedral rejoicing in God's Creation. First opened to the public on Easter Monday, 1881, the building's warm terracotta tiles, striated with blue, contrast sharply with the surrounding white neo-classical buildings (Fig. 10.1). Carved extinct and living species replace traditional gargoyles on the front façade. Visitors arriving by train and on foot pass through dark-red railings topped with golden lions, cross through gardens landscaped to represent earth's natural history, and

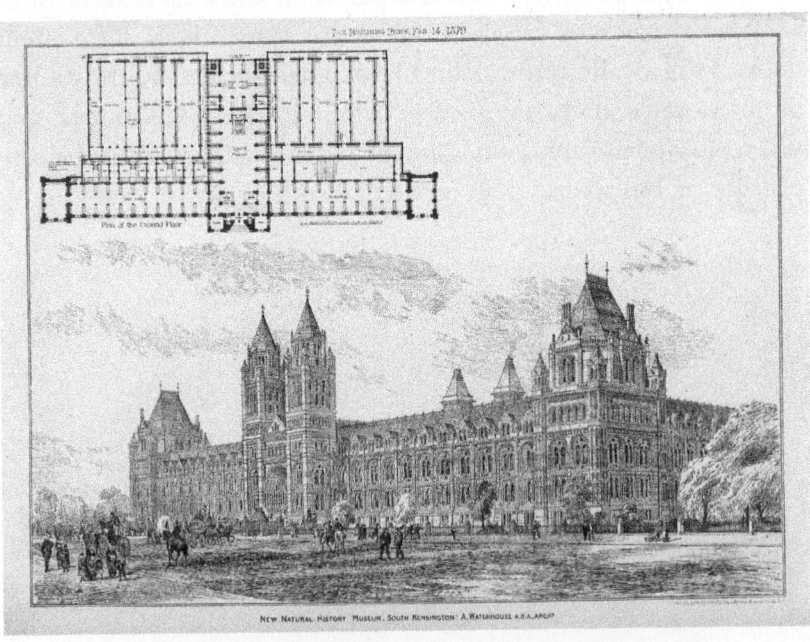

10.1 The Natural History Museum, South Kensington: plan, above, and the street elevation, below.

walk up a large external staircase to the main entrance. The doors might easily be carved into a cliff face. Visitors enter a dark vestibule and proceed to a vast, luminous central hall, where a blue whale called Hope greets all entrants (Fig. 10.2).

Hope dives towards the crowds in an astonishingly beautiful display. Amazed onlookers queue along the staircases and jostle each other as they capture her likeness either alone or in a selfie. Visitors on the first-floor balconies observe the crowds below ebb and

10.2 Hope, the blue whale, Natural History Museum, London.

flow. Hope looms over many important episodes in the history of extinction. Ten side-chapels house specimens tracing the history of the universe and life on earth below Hope.[1] The easterly chapels host an American mastodon, *Mantellisaurus*, fossilized trees, a 2.5-tonne banded-iron formation, and an Imliac meteorite tracing ancient beginnings and extinctions. The westerly chapels showcase two giraffes, an Atlantic blue marlin, a Turbinaria coral, seaweeds, and a swarm of insects representing contemporary endangerment.[2]

Hope's biography is significant, whether as an individual whale, evolutionary lineage, or way of being prized by hunters. By exploring the ancient origins of her kind, their merciless persecution in the modern world to near extinction and ongoing recovery as a species, as well as her individual journey from a mothered calf to museum artefact, we can appreciate how Hope's life is tied to much broader stories of the development of commercial whaling and its international regulation, the emergence of the conservation movement, or the imperial origins of public museums. While each of these threads is crucial, we can also learn how to write about, and appreciate, other ways of being for who they are, rather than what they might provide for us. In doing so, we might finally connect historically and ethically important threads for understanding Hope's life, kin, endangerment, and the possibilities for choosing redress and renewal for life on earth.

Emptying the Deep Blue

What is a whale? Philosophers and naturalists puzzled over this question for centuries. Were they fish or mammals? How did they originate? How did they move, live, and survive underwater? The Greek philosopher Aristotle formally named baleen and toothed whales 'sea monsters', or Cetacea. Despite sympathizing with those who felt the fishiness of whales meant they were fish, he grouped them independently because they had hair, drew breath with lungs rather than gills, gave birth to live young, and fed their calves with milk. Aristotelian categories remained significant until the seventeenth century when his classical authority was challenged by naturalists such as John Ray, who dissected a porpoise in 1671 and felt it resembled swine much more closely than any fish. The Swedish naturalist Carl Linnaeus, who invented the way we name species, created the new class of *Mammalia*, from the Latin 'mammae' or breasts, in 1758. He initially classified whales as fish, but later decided they were mammals; it is possible that worrying about how to classify whales might have led Linnaeus to coin the class of mammals.[3] Modern naturalists accepted whales were mammals and started to ask questions about their evolutionary lineage. In the last few decades a combination of fossil finds and genetic analysis has underpinned new reconstructions of a remarkable story.

Millions of years ago, the decision of a hoofed, land-dwelling creature to take to the water led to new ways of being. According to evolutionary biologists, we know the animal's modern kin as bison, giraffes, alpacas, camels, hippos, goats, and cows. Originating in the early Eocene starting 56 million years ago, these animals all bear down on two of five toes that have evolved into hoofs. By the middle Eocene nearly 48 million years ago, the descendants of the one-hoofed herbivore went from living, loving, and birthing on land, to splashing about at the sea's edge eating fish, and often swimming around the coasts of the region we know as South Asia. Although adept at powering through the water with just its feet, the wolf-sized creature coupled and gave birth to live young on land. No one knows why the water first drew the creature's attention, but hunger and the promise of food seems a likely reason. Future descendants permanently inhabited South Asian waters for about 4 million years, before slowly moving to new coasts around Africa, and then further afield to the Americas. By 38 million years ago, the land-dweller's descendant was fully adapted to a life aquatic. Later named *Dorudon*, the animal's bones were cocooned in blubber in a relatively streamlined body with tiny vestigial legs. A powerful swimmer aided by a tail fanned into a fluke, *Dorudon* supplemented a fishy diet with other sea-dwelling creatures, while courting, mating, and giving birth in the water. This archaic creature migrated throughout the world's waters, with kin and descendants leaving fossil remains in present-day Pakistan, Egypt (where they were first found), Western Sahara, the United States, and New Zealand.[4]

Dorudon's descendants survived an extinction event between 33.9 and 33.4 million years ago marking the new Oligocene epoch, and shaped the new lifeways we call whales. These beautiful creatures are streamlined, almost hairless, with no visible hind limbs, and rely on powerful tails to speed through deep waters – they are therefore a far cry from their hoofed ancestor. They split into baleen whales, formally Mysticeti, and toothed whales, formally Odontoceti, whose closest living land relative is the hippopotamus.[5] Baleen whales are named after the bristly plates lining their mouths. Made from keratin, the same protein as your fingernails, rhino horns, and bird claws, this 'whalebone' forms an intricate filter-feeding system. Feeding baleen whales open their mouths, capture large gulps of water, and then force this water outwards to extract krill and plankton for ingestion. Despite subsisting on such tiny organisms, one of their kind grows into the largest animal ever known: the blue whale. Toothed whales feast on ocean dwellers such as fish, seals, and penguins, and include orcas, dolphins, and sperm whales. For millions of years, whales turned the energy they ate into bone, baleen, and blubber, helping them survive ocean life. Unfortunately, those adaptations were more highly valued by humans than were living whales.

Whales were so vulnerable to human acquisitiveness that modern hunting almost eradicated innumerable ways of being a whale. The historian Graham Burnett traces scientific interest in whales throughout the twentieth century in his monumental book *The Sounding of the Whale* (2012). He identifies several distinctive phases in 'intensive commercial whaling' that almost led to their extinction.[6] He notes, from the medieval period onwards, but particularly between the seventeenth and nineteenth centuries, that the French, Dutch, and British commercially hunted bowhead and right whales in northern waters around Western Europe. By the eighteenth and nineteenth centuries, particularly between the 1820s and

1860s, whalers hunted sperm whales and right whales in southern waters across the Indian and Atlantic oceans, as made infamous by Herman Melville's novel tracing Captain Ahab's disastrous obsession with killing a sperm whale in *Moby Dick* (1851). Until the mid-nineteenth century most whale species survived human predation. Right whales in the Northern Atlantic were the exception because they were hunted to commercial extinction, meaning they were no longer a viable species for making a profit.

Many ways of being a whale were on the brink of extinction in the later nineteenth century as whalers gained a devastating new advantage. For centuries, whales met their deaths when caught off-guard by hunters at close quarters, but new technologies expanded the hunters' range. In 1870 the Norwegian shipping magnate Svend Foyn patented the grenade harpoon. Shot from a cannon aboard the ship, the barbed harpoon embedded itself in whale flesh before releasing a lethal blast. Whales increasingly faced an enemy equipped with greater firepower striking from a bigger distance. Rorquals are a subset of baleen whales that include fin, humpback, minke, and blue whales. They evaded early whalers through speed but could not outpace grenade harpoons. Soon, the North Atlantic brimmed with ships commercially hunting rorquals. Once struck, whales were pumped full of air, tied to the side of ships, and towed to coastline factories for processing, turning entire harbours red with blood. Men stripped whales of their blubber by cutting it away from the inner muscle, and specialist slaughterers further dismembered the half-stripped bodies. For decades, harvesting whales was checked by how quickly bodies were taken ashore for processing before they putrefied. This constraint disappeared when whaling ships were turned into gargantuan floating factories in the 1920s. Harpooned whales were winched through a gaping rear orifice, via a slipway on to the deck, rid of their blubber, butchered, and boiled, in unchecked, industrialized slaughter. The process preserved blubber into fat stable enough for storage, transportation, and profitable exchange. Even the biggest species were rendered into commodities with brutal efficiency: a mature blue whale could be sliced up into saleable fragments within an hour. Freed from shorelines, whalers roamed the high seas in search of diminishing quarry.

Whales faced increasingly perilous journeys through Northern Atlantic waters teeming with armed men. Many hunted species migrate from tropical waters where they were born in winter, to spend summers feeding in much colder northern and polar regions. Whales' bodies archived the increasingly distressing and dangerous journeys. The hormone cortisol is released under stress, making its presence a useful way to track how bodies respond to perceived threats, whether predators or environmental pressures. One recent study tracked cortisol levels in fin, humpback, and blue whales over the twentieth century. Scientists observed cortisol levels were higher during the Second World War and years when whalers successfully caught substantial numbers, such as the 1920s, 1950s, and 1960s, suggesting much higher levels of stress in these years of intense exploitation.[7] Whales survived the onslaught through luck and, remarkably, changing migration routes and intergenerational learning. Recently, a group of biologists examined the logbooks of American whaling ships to analyse sperm-whale kills. Collating data from nearly 78,000 days of voyaging, the logbooks revealed that whalers entering new waters were relatively successful at first, but within a few years their strike rates declined by as much as 58 per cent. Experienced hunters believed whales defended their lives by attacking aggressors or hurtling through the waters upwind of approaching ships. The study corroborates these accounts and suggests sperm whales were learning to avoid whalers, and sharing this knowledge among themselves.[8]

The responses of whales to human exploitation offer ethical and historical lessons. Even if we recognize other living beings as sentient and complex, we still potentially underestimate their abilities in many senses. We need to recognize the resulting ethical compromises and violations we make, especially when living beings face uncertain futures caused by our own lifestyles. As historians, it also challenges us to write about animals as historical agents whose ways of being are worthwhile in their own right, with important consequences for our shared histories.

Unfortunately, despite whales developing strategies to avoid human exploitation, the expansion of commercial whaling endangered many species in the nineteenth century. Humans turned whales into a remarkable variety of profitable commodities including corsets, fertilizer, pet food, lamp oil, margarine, scrimshaw, perfume, car wax, lipstick, shoe polish, animal feed, machine lubricants, and scientific specimens. Scientists and whalers alike worried about depleting stocks, but the trade continued. Within decades, humans hunted to near extinction lifeways that had endured for millions of years. Whales were prized scientific specimens coveted by museum curators, owing to their sheer size and imperilled status, including at the Natural History Museum in London.

London's Ark

Richard Owen dreamed of presiding over a dead ark.[9] A renowned naturalist and anti-Darwinian, he took up a post curating at the British Museum in 1856.[10] At 'every opportunity' he solicited donations from contacts 'travelling abroad' and 'intelligent settlers' in 'several colonies', leading to acquisitions of 'the Aye-Aye, the Gorilla, the Dodo, the Notornis, the maximised and elephant-footed species of Dinornis, the representatives of the various orders and genera of extinct Reptilia from the Cape of Good Hope, and the equally rich and numerous evidences of the extinct Marsupialia from Australia, beside such smaller rarities as the animals of the Nautilus and Spirula'.[11] Owen was exasperated by the difficulty of showcasing his triumphs in the museum's cramped quarters and diligently campaigned for either a cavernous two-storey extension to the British Museum or a new building in South Kensington.[12] He regarded the lack of a dedicated national Museum of Natural History as a scientific and political disgrace.[13] He insisted a national collection ought to provide a comprehensive visual encyclopaedia of the entire natural world, including male, female, and juvenile specimens of every species. His ideal ark would exhibit the fullest 'extent and variety of the Creative Power'.[14]

Owen's natural history fused science, faith, and empire. After bitter public spats with politicians and scientists who criticized the plans, Owen's dreams were largely fulfilled with a new building in South Kensington. Originally known as the British Museum (Natural History), London's Natural History Museum is the best-known building by the architect Alfred Waterhouse.[15] On its opening in 1881, the *Saturday Review* praised Waterhouse for his 'beautiful Romanesque building' and explicitly singled out the megatherium and plesiosaurus as noteworthy specimens, because 'few objects [are] so exciting to the imagination as these colossal fragments of antediluvian life'.[16] The building's imposing façade still dominates its urban landscape, even without the statue of Adam which once adorned the gable, but was toppled during the Second World War. Eve was due to join him, but never did. In its opening year, Owen delivered the Presidential Address of the British Association for the Advancement of Science. He traced the museum's origins to 'Sir Hans Sloane, M.D.' and the 'lucrative practice of his profession in the then flourishing colony of Jamaica'.[17] Owen was right to pinpoint the museum's early Caribbean roots.

The origins of London's Natural History Museum lie in the covetous passions of a wealthy physician. Hans Sloane settled in London a year after qualifying as a physician in 1683.[18] Tending London's wealthy and learned gentlemen helped Sloane create new social and intellectual networks with distinguished men such as the natural philosopher Robert Boyle, a founding member of the Royal Society. Sloane quickly acquired fellowships of the Royal Society and Royal College of Physicians. In 1685 he served as personal physician to the new governor of Jamaica, the Duke of Albemarle. The duke, duchess, and Sloane were met with a gun salute as they arrived on the island in 1687. Sloane managed the duke's health while treating other colonists, and enslaved West Africans, although he frequently dismissed their medical complaints as work-shy fabrications.[19] He roamed across the island, collecting as many natural history specimens as possible, including human bones from burial sites he believed were used by the Taíno.[20] His collector's thirst might never have been slaked, but the duke died within a year on the island. Sloane, the embalmed duke, and widowed duchess set sail for England in March 1689.[21]

Sloane's Caribbean connections were erased for decades by historians, with one account describing his Jamaican sojourn as his 'greatest adventure'.[22] More recently, the historian James Delbourgo's painstaking research reconstructs the multiple ways in which Sloane's collecting of flora, fauna, and 'humana' depended upon empire and enslavement.[23] From the fifteenth century onwards, Spanish colonial powers devastated Jamaica's first inhabitants, the Taíno, who called the island Xamayca, and established the practice of importing and enslaving Akan peoples, from present-day Ghana and Côte d'Ivoire, to cultivate cotton, Indigo, and tobacco. Caribbean English colonies were established throughout the seventeenth century. In quick succession, the English claimed St Christopher in 1624, Barbados in 1627, Nevis in 1628, Montserrat and Antigua in 1632, and Jamaica in 1655.[24] Sloane arrived in a colony with a rapidly increasing population of English colonists and enslaved West Africans, forced to till the island's rapidly expanding sugar plantations. Enslaved peoples were legally transformed into chattel property that might be bought, sold, and inherited by a series of Slave Codes. First passed in Barbados in 1661, with further legislation in 1676, 1682, and 1688, these codes created a racist complexion-based dichotomy between Europeans and Africans, facilitated the expansion of Britain's violent trade in trafficked peoples and new plantation-based economies, all during Sloane's lifetime.[25]

As Sloane settled back into London life, his earnings, marriage, and investments funded his collecting. The heiress and widow Elizabeth Langley Rose married Sloane in 1695. She inherited the estates of her father and her first husband, who owned extensive Jamaican properties tilled by enslaved West Africans. Marriage legally transferred her wealth into Sloane's ownership. Delbourgo's analysis of surviving household accounts reveals a direct income for

Sloane of over £7,145, more than £600,000 in today's terms, from sugar plantations, but notes this is probably a conservative estimate due to incomplete records. He argues that Elizabeth's total share of her father's estate was probably closer to £40,000, or over £3 million today, given that her husband's estate received about £4,000 per year, or nearly £480,000 in today's money. Sloane's coffers also swelled with profits from imperial investments in ventures such as the South Sea Company, which sold enslaved peoples in Spanish America, and the East India Company, which informally controlled India until the Company was dissolved following the Indian uprisings of 1857.[26] Sloane corresponded with middlemen across the British Empire, who redirected treasures to his home as gifts, favours, and reciprocal exchanges.[27] His research was published in two folio volumes as *Voyage to the Islands Madeira, Barbados, Nieves, S. Christophers in Jamaica with the Natural History of the Herbs and Trees, Four-Footed Beasts, Fishes, Birds, Insects, Reptiles, etc. of the Last of Those Islands* (1707–25). Sloane profited from empire in multiple ways, even when comfortably ensconced at home, and contemplating his collection's afterlife.

Sir Hans Sloane died in 1753 after amassing an immense personal collection. His executors' tally noted a library of 50,000 books and manuscripts, and more than 78,000 artefacts including a herbarium of 334 volumes, about 32,000 medals and coins, prints and drawings, precious stones, antiquities, shells, crystals, fossils, minerals, crustaceans, serpents, birds, stuffed animals, insects, curios from peoples all over the world, human remains, and over 2,000 'Miscellaneous Things'.[28] Sloane bequeathed his treasures to the nation on condition that they were housed together in a free public museum, with his heirs paid a fraction of the collections' worth in the total sum of £20,000 by the government. His plans were so unusual they are often credited with giving rise to the concept of the public museum. Parliament pleaded empty coffers and Sloane's desire lingered unfulfilled for months until a public lottery finally raised the funds. His collections formed the core of the new British Museum.[29] God's works of Creation and humanity's works of artifice resided together in the British Museum until the arrival of its first Superintendent of Natural History, Richard Owen.

Owen foregrounded extinct and endangered species as sources of political and imperial pride. The connection to Sloane and Jamaica simply facilitated 'The greatest commercial and colonizing empire of the world' in representing 'the march of civilisation which a Public Museum of Natural History embodies'.[30] Convinced that extinct beasts were among the most popular attractions, Owen wished visitors 'the easiest transit from the specimens of existing to those of extinct animals'.[31] His preferred centrepiece was an imperilled whale. A devout man, perhaps Owen was inspired by the Book of Genesis, in which God created great whales and other fish and fowl on the fifth day of Creation after the waters miraculously burst forth.[32] Owen believed the sheer size of whales exemplified 'the power of the creator'. Acquiring a specimen was an urgent task owing to their 'rapidly diminishing numbers' and likelihood of 'utter extinction'.[33] Owen predicted an endangered cetacean would rival any extinct species in other national collections: 'Saint Petersburg justly boasts of the stuffed skin of its unique Mammoth: Madrid was as famous for its once unique Megatherium. Any capital in Europe would be eagerly visited by the Naturalist if a single specimen of the extinct Dodo were preserved in its national museum . . . '[34] The naturalist William Henry Flower succeeded Owen and served as the museum's first Director from 1884. He rejected Owen's dated grand schemes and quickly used the galleries to tell novel stories of empire, evolution, and extinction.

In the mid-1870s an Atlantic blue whale gave birth to a daughter after a year-long pregnancy. The mother nursed her daughter with rich milk, and she rapidly gained weight for months in warm southern waters. Once ready, the closely bonded pair travelled to colder North Atlantic waters, probably taking about six weeks to migrate over 6,000 kilometres (3,728 miles). Their journey was a practical necessity and opportunity for the mother to teach her daughter the migratory routes she would traverse annually for life. When roughly fifteen years old, the daughter may have birthed and tended her own calf as she explored warmer waters, possibly around the Azores, Cape Verde Islands, and Mauritanian coast.[35] Wandering north one spring, the young whale skimmed too closely to Irish shorelines and beached in Wexford Harbour.[36] She struggled to free herself for days as the locals watched over her and a flurry of press reports tracked her plight. The fisherman Edward Wickham spotted her 'rolling and beating the waves in a struggle apparently to get off the sandbank' on Wednesday, 25 March 1891.[37] Despite desperate efforts she remained stranded. On Friday, Wickham used a makeshift harpoon to 'end her troubles' and the sea was 'dyed with the blood'.[38]

Reports of the young whale's demise quickly reached Flower, who eagerly took advantage of the chance to add a blue whale to the museum's collections.[39] Observers estimated that her length reached 25 metres (82 feet), with flippers of around 3.2 metres in length by 0.7 metres wide (10.5 by 2.5 feet).[40] A whaler for the Anglo-Norwegian Fishing company believed her valuable carcass might yield 'eight and a half tonnes of oil, three tons of guano, and five hundred weight of whalebone' worth over £200, or more than £16,000 in today's terms.[41] Quickly named the 'Wexford Whale', she was auctioned in April. The chairman of the Wexford Harbour Board made the winning bid of £111, but further enquiries secured the whale for the Natural History Museum. The baleen and skeletal remains were sold for an offer of £200, with final settlement of only £178. In May 1891 the Wexford Whale arrived in London.

Flower reconfigured the central hall to showcase whales in peril within broader chronicles of life's evolution. The Wexford Whale languished in storage for decades, while Flower placed a sperm-whale skeleton in the centre of the nave and filled the side-chapels with specimens designed to showcase evolutionary variation among species, including plants, a cross-section of sequoia, pigeons, fowls, insects, mammalian skeletons including a human, sloth, porpoise, baboon, horse, teeth, and a stuffed black leopard exhibiting melanism.[42] Flower's interest in cetaceans extended beyond their magnificent visual appeal. His contemporaries were intrigued by the origin of cetaceans and contemplated two distinct possibilities:

carnivorous, placental mammals or hoofed herbivores. Flower hesitantly favoured extinct hoofed ancestors with a seal-like intermediary, but recognized the debate was shrouded in 'the greatest obscurity'.[43] He admired how evolution granted whales a remarkable 'perfection of their structure and their magnitude', but worried these 'fatal gifts' would rapidly lead 'to their extinction' at the hands of 'civilised man'.[44] Flower's concern was unusual. Many species, whether whales, bison, or passenger pigeons, were once so abundant that their extermination seemed implausible. As their populations waned, rarity made specimens more difficult to procure, profitable to sell, and desirable to acquire among collectors, while protective measures were rarely implemented. After the First World War, whales acquired new guardians.[45]

Fighting for Hope

The plight of whales alarmed few in the early twentieth century as much as the zoologist Sidney Frederick Harmer. The fourth Director of the Natural History Museum between 1919 and 1927, Harmer considered commercial whaling the chief threat to whales and serious enough to lead to their extermination. He had founded the Stranded Whales Programme in 1913 to systematically collect beached whales for scientific study. Harmer's initiative established the museum as a significant site for cetacean research, and it continues to be a globally important resource. Renamed the UK Cetacean Strandings Investigation Programme in 1990, it holds 6,000 skeletons and tissue samples, amassed from hundreds of strandings and expeditions, in an off-site storage facility designed to accommodate the colossal skeletal fragments.[46] Harmer penned official reports warning the British government of declining numbers of whales. In 1915 one report submitted to the Colonial Office identified a rapid decline in the number of humpback whales caught, and an increase in the number of fin and blue whales. Harmer inferred whalers were increasingly pursuing fin and blue whales after nearly exterminating humpbacks. The Colonial

Office regarded Harmer's gloomy predictions with scepticism and cited more optimistic experts to counter his claims. Undeterred, Harmer called for fresh research to assess extant whale populations. While officially downplaying Harmer's predictions, the Colonial Office understood that the *whaling* industry might be endangered. It supported several research expeditions in the 1920s to assess numbers, noting they would be useful 'from an imperial point of view'.[47]

Harmer regarded government-sponsored expeditions to protect commercial whaling as important opportunities for scientific research. Scientific links with industry or the military are hardly rare within the history of science; in Harmer's case, he was dependent upon a governmental desire to protect stocks of a natural resource, and the broader economic value of whales, to unravel even basic questions about cetacean life. Naturalists bitterly disputed the origin of whales and knew little about their natural history. Government-sponsored expeditions developed new techniques to age hunted whales, and used estimated ages to predict population health. This research established that hunters were routinely catching immature whales by the 1930s. Just as Harmer feared, shifts in the species and age profiles of commercial catches suggested profoundly harmful industrial over-exploitation and plummeting numbers.[48] Graham Burnett argues that such close associations created a 'commensal relationship' between commercial whaling and scientific research. As a record annual harvest of 28,000 whales were caught between 1930 and 1931, Harmer fought to convince others of impending extermination, and the Wexford Whale was removed from storage.[49]

The Wexford Whale was the first specimen suspended from the ceiling of the museum's new Whale Hall in 1934.[50] The hall was commissioned in 1929 and completed in 1932, but the economic woes of the Great Depression forced delays. The Whale Hall exhibited its occupants as endangered from the outset. The spine of the Wexford Whale was articulated into a lifeless straight line, in a pose commonly used by museums. She was accompanied by a bowhead whale, grey whale, North Atlantic right whale, and sperm whale.[51] Press reports enthusiastically approved of the 'new quarters' as 'more suited' to the cetaceans' 'vast size and dignity'.[52] Just four years after the opening, a bottlenose whale found in the River Trent was shot and taken to the Natural History Museum. The museum was reportedly keen on the acquisition because it was 'a rare specimen of a species which is fast becoming extinct'.[53]

A painted model of a blue whale hung below the Wexford Whale's skeleton. The model stretched to 93 feet (28.3 metres) and was built by the taxidermist and modeller Percy Stammwitz and his son Stuart. Percy confessed 'It has been my ambition to have a go at the blue whale for some time . . . and I have worried the officials to make one. Now that I'm going to do it I feel a little appalled by the undertaking.'[54] Percy's apprehension was well founded. Stuffing and modelling whales was exceptionally tricky. Whale skin is a delicate sheath that is notoriously difficult to remove and preserve because it deteriorates so quickly after death. In 1865 a young blue whale was stranded on the Swedish coast, near Gothenburg. August Wilhelm Malm managed to procure the carcass and spent weeks preparing the skin and skeleton. The Malm Whale remains one of the few mounted whale specimens with real skin in the world, and the only blue whale. These difficulties made realistic models difficult to make and highly valued. In 1907 the American Museum of Natural History in New York unveiled a model of a blue whale. Scientists used a carcass in Newfoundland to make casts, photographs, paper templates, scale models, and innumerable measurements, to recreate the model. It was unveiled to great fanfare as the museum proudly announced the manufacture of an authentic leviathan.[55] In contrast, Percy Stammwitz modelled his blue whale on site. The Wexford Whale and Percy's rendition of her living form remained in the Whale Hall, later renamed the Mammal Hall, for decades.

Awareness of declining whale populations prompted new regulatory measures. The Geneva Convention for the Regulation of Whaling was signed under the auspices of the League of Nations in 1931. Taking four years to come into force, the legislation tried to license whaling vessels, enforce the collection of statistics from all catches, and protect baleen whales by ensuring hunters were paid by the overall value of their catch, rather than by the total number of carcasses. The Convention was relatively ineffective, especially as some nations ignored it altogether, but it remains a landmark for establishing the principle of the international regulation of whaling. The League of Nations added further restrictions in 1938, including on killing humpback whales in the Antarctic and protecting whales in Antarctic waters from all hunting. Maximum catch limits were first introduced in 1944. They were measured in Blue Whale Units (BWU): a single blue whale equated to two fin whales, 2.5 humpbacks, and six sei whales, with hunters allowed to catch up to 16,000 BWU.

Early efforts yielded the signing of the International Convention for the Regulation of Whaling (ICRW) in December 1946. It established the International Whaling Commission (IWC) to secure international cooperation in 'safeguarding' the 'great natural resources represented by whale stocks' for 'future generations'. The language of management and future harvests reveals the preoccupation of diplomats with protecting a valuable commodity in order to ensure 'maximum sustainable yields'.[56] The ICRW exempted the killing of whales for scientific research, without specifying the limits of legitimate enquiry, thus creating an easily exploited ambiguity. The IWC was founded amid broader optimism about wildlife conservation after the Second World War, but the Commission lost credibility as whale populations continued declining in the 1960s.[57] Modern nations initially regulated whaling to guard the economic value they extracted from cetaceans, but attention slowly turned to protecting ways of being a whale.

Perceptions of whales as gargantuan brutes of great economic value were transformed during the Cold War. Eagerness to understand communist enemies stimulated research in the human sciences, some of it funded by the United States military. The physician and psychoanalyst John C. Lilly established his research career by studying the subjectivity and consciousness of enemy combatants, and he used the same techniques on bottlenose dolphins from the mid-1950s onwards. Lilly was convinced that dolphins possessed near-human intelligence and penned the book *Man and Dolphin: Adventures of a*

New Scientific Frontier (1961). The book made extraordinarily grand claims about the possibilities of us communicating with other beings: 'Within the next decade or two the human species will establish communication with another species: nonhuman, alien, possibly extra-terrestrial, more probably marine; but definitely highly intelligent, perhaps even intellectual.'[58] These claims reflected a profound desire to understand consciousness, and quickly captured the public imagination as Lilly's research hit the headlines.[59] Significantly, it helped establish that cetaceans were intelligent, sentient beings.

Researching whale communication revealed they were songsmiths. In quiet waters, whalers occasionally heard whales as their calls reverberated through wooden hulls. Humpback whales were first recorded making sounds in 1952. New underwater listening technologies confirmed that whales made sounds falling into 'three rough categories: short broad-band clicks, longer narrowband squeals, and complex sounds' usually made up of 'rapidly repeated clicks'.[60] As further recordings accumulated, scientists tried deciphering the purpose of those sounds. The biologists Roger S. Payne and Scott McVay noticed that whales used 'long, fixed sequences' and argued they were not making 'an almost endless variety of sounds', but singing. Unlike birds whose singing lasts a few seconds interspersed with silence, humpbacks sang repeatedly without 'breaking the rhythm of singing' for many minutes.[61] Payne and McVay were baffled by the songs' purpose, but were also convinced of their existence and beauty. *Songs of the Humpback Whale* was released as a commercial recording in 1970 and climbed the bestseller charts.[62] Whale songs further popularized the notion of these creatures as highly sociable, intelligent, and even wise beyond human capability. New perceptions of cetacean intelligence and communication changed why we value their ways of being.

Demands to 'Save the Whales' grew into the first global campaign of the modern environmental movement.[63] In the early 1960s, hippies, Quakers, pacifists, and anti-nuclear activists found common cause in an anti-nuclear protest group called Greenpeace.[64] There is no founding moment for the group, but the early efforts of campaigners Irving

Stowe, Jim Bohlen, and Bob Hunter stand out. Moulded in the anti-nuclear and anti-Vietnam protest movements of the United States and disgusted with their country's military belligerence, they crossed paths in Vancouver fighting for a future without nuclear weapons. They focused on protesting against the American military testing of explosives around the Aleutian Islands. As a new generation of activists joined Greenpeace in the 1960s, tensions sprang up about the group's purpose. Although registered as the Greenpeace Foundation in 1971, the formalization belied considerable disagreement between an older guard intent on exclusively pursuing anti-nuclear campaigns, and a newer generation hoping to address broader environmental damage. Bob Hunter worried that tales of nuclear annihilation created only terrified inaction, and he sought an alternative focal point to motivate and inspire genuine change. He suspected that whales were ideal beings to inspire revolution. In 1973 he met the cetologist Paul Spong, an expert in whale communication who privately regarded their songs as language. Spong confided his belief to a sympathetic Hunter. Spong suggested chartering a boat to bear witness to the mechanized slaughter of whales and circulating the footage to global mass media.[65] In the same year, politicians considered establishing a decade-long moratorium on commercial whaling to protect stocks, but the measure did not gain enough votes at the IWC. A year later, Irving Stowe passed away.

Greenpeace reconfigured itself as a broader group committed to environmental protection in the 1970s, beginning with whales. After weeks in search of Soviet whalers in the Pacific, Greenpeace activists aboard the *Phyllis Cormack* challenged Soviet whalers aboard the *Dalniy Vostok* in 1975. Greenpeace positioned themselves in between the floating factory and a group of whales. Hunter later recalled the gut-wrenching smell, streams of blood, and the 'peculiar obscenity' of realizing the floating factory 'was a beast that fed itself through its anus, and it was into this inglorious hole that the last of the world's whales were vanishing – before our eyes'.[66] The activists assumed the Soviets would hold fire if blocked and so hoped to save the whales' lives. They miscalculated. A harpoonist fired past them and the barbed weapon flew above their heads hitting a whale. Eventually, the Soviets left to pursue other quarry. The whole encounter was filmed by the Greenpeace activists, and later broadcast on the CBS evening news. The dramatic footage shows the harpoon within touching distance of the men as it hits the whale. Beamed into homes across the United States, the protest helped publicize the group's activism across the world.

'Save the Whales' served as an environmental cause célèbre for more than a decade until the global moratorium on commercial whaling in 1982. The legislation signals a dramatic shift in why we protect whales. Regarded as little more than a natural resource for centuries, by the second half of the twentieth century whales were increasingly valued as ways of being intrinsically worthy of protection and of living their lives free of human interference. Despite continued killing on a much smaller scale, legislative protection and respite has pulled many species back from the brink of extinction. The populations of humpbacks and southern right whales have secured the greatest recoveries, but many species remain classified as Threatened, Endangered, or Critically Endangered on the IUCN's Red List. Blue whales remain Endangered. Whales may no longer face industrialized global over-exploitation, but they do endure numerous other threats. Commercial whaling has largely stopped, but Russia, Norway, Iceland, and Japan have all reported to the IWC catching thousands of whales since 1985.[67] Whales also suffer accidental entanglement in commercial fishing nets, noise pollution from increasingly busy marine highways, the loss and deterioration of habitats coupled with dwindling food supplies, and mortal wounds from collisions with ships. The global moratorium on whaling provides clear evidence that sustained and co-ordinated action can stall and reverse decline, but empire's endlings need much more from us.

Curators at the Museum of Natural History in London renamed the Wexford Whale as Hope and moved her to a refurbished central hall. She replaced Dippy, the beloved plaster cast of *Diplodocus carnegii* who towered over visitors from 1979 until departing for a British tour of eight cities including Birmingham, Belfast, Cardiff,

Newcastle-upon-Tyne, and Glasgow between 2018 and 2021.[68] The museum announced Dippy's demotion after securing a £5 million donation from the billionaire hedge-fund manager Sir Michael Hintze and Lady Dorothy Hintze to refurbish the central hall.[69] Hintze Hall evokes several aspects of Richard Owen's original plan for the museum. He imagined the East Wing as dedicated to palaeontology and the West Wing as showcasing zoology, with the central hall featuring an Index Museum brimming with typological specimens. The Index Museum is gone, but the division between extinct and living species resonates with the eastern Wonder Bays that trace the history of our planet, while the western Wonder Bays showcase endangered species.

The eastern Wonder Bays showcase a mastodon, *Mantellisaurus*, fossil trees, a banded-iron formation, and an Imliac meteorite. Among the largest animals alive during the Ice Age, the mastodon was assembled from a series of excavations in Missouri by Albert C. Koch in 1840.[70] Koch's articulated specimen was deliberately exaggerated in size, even adding extra vertebrae, and had tusks facing horizontally outwards. Initially nicknamed the 'Missourium', the beast was later promoted by Koch as the 'Missouri Leviathan', referring to the colossal beast described in the Biblical Book of Job. Koch argued that Native peoples remembered a 'time when the first white settlers emigrated to the Osage country' and the ground yielded 'many large and monstrous animals . . . along and up the Mississippi and Missouri rivers', and he often included Native figures in promotional posters to lend credence to his claims.[71] The beast was exhibited across America before moving on to Europe, and was sold to Owen for £1,300 after a London sojourn in 1843. Owen removed Koch's embellishments and reclassified the mastodon in the museum catalogue that records the acquisition: 'The skeleton of the mastodon exhibited by Mr Koch with the rest of his collection, but set up anew with restorations.'[72] Originally exhibited in the Fossil Mammals gallery, the mastodon was moved to the Mammal Hall with Hope in the 1980s, until both were transferred to Hintze Hall (Fig. 10.3).[73] A *Mantellisaurus* is elegantly poised next to the mastodon.

10.3 Koch's Missouri Leviathan, or the American mastodon.

Living approximately 122 to 129 million years ago, this dinosaur specimen is the holotype, the original specimen from which a new species is named and described.[74] Amateur palaeontologist Reginald Walter Hooley discovered 'this very fine fossil' in the 'débris of Wealden Shales, after a fall of the cliff' on the Isle of Wight in the same year as the outbreak of the First World War'.[75] He classified it within the *Iguanodon* genus, but following a re-evaluation of its taxonomy, it was placed in the *Mantellisaurus* genus in 2007.[76]

The western Wonder Bays showcase species at risk from humans with a pair of giraffes, a blue marlin, Turbinaria coral, seaweeds, and a swarm of insects. The fronds of seaweed stand alert, while the insects swarm in a multi-species rainbow. An estimated 4 to 6 million species of insects exist, but only about a quarter or a third are classified. Even with this partial knowledge we know that many ecosystems would collapse without insects.[77] They are crucial pollinators, as well as food for other species, yet insects are often neglected. The intricately folded Turbinaria coral is delicately studded with corralites, the tiny, usually invisible, indentations that hold individual polyps in living corals. The label informs visitors: 'Coral reefs are among the most biologically diverse ecosystems on the planet, vital for life in the oceans and for many human communities.' Nonetheless, 'Environmental change, pollution and overfishing are disturbing the finely-tuned balance of reefs in unprecedented ways.' Coral bleaching transforms once thriving reefs into threatened habitats, as with the Great Barrier Reef in the coastal waters of Queensland, Australia. The reef is slowly dying and losing its vibrant colours, most likely due to ocean acidification caused by climate change. The bleached Turbinaria represents this broader environmental destruction.[78]

The refurbishment of the central hall evokes Richard Owen's plans for the national museum of natural history he so desperately wanted, while creating significant new conversations about extinction. The spectacular mastodon and *Mantellisaurus* honour Owen's own contributions to British palaeontology, especially in naming the dinosaurs. The broad division between palaeontology and zoology is visible, but the strict division no longer remains. When Waterhouse designed the building he chose carvings of the extinct coelacanth and living passenger pigeon, but the bird became extinct while living coelacanths were found in 1938. There are also elisions between species that are extant and those extinct.

Humanity's wake of extinctions and imperial dispossession are only implicit within the displays. The exact cause of the mastodon's demise remains controversial, so the hall does not exhibit a single species indisputably eradicated by humans. This effectively underplays human culpability in the recent past, although the displays do make clear that environmental change is a factor and endangered species need help to recover. The giraffes silently call to mind this history. From the 1870s until the outbreak of the First World War, lions, elephants, leopards, rhinos, and Cape buffaloes were especially prized as trophies, as colonial officials, sportsmen, and collectors decimated African species.[79] Giraffes were not among these 'big five' species, but hunting still diminished their numbers. In recent years, hunting has come under renewed public scrutiny as enthusiasts boast of their kills on social media to an often disgusted public. One of the most high-profile scandals erupted when an American dentist, Walter Palmer, killed Cecil the lion in Hwange National Park, Zimbabwe, in 2015, having reputedly paid $50,000 for the opportunity.[80] Hunting continues to commodify and endanger many ways of being.

Richard Owen's imperial chauvinism is clearly inappropriate for present-day audiences, but it would be unwise to forget or erase the imperial origins and connections of the collections in London's Museum of Natural History. The banded-iron formation hints at extractive imperialism and environmental degradation. Banded iron is a major source of commercial iron and the museum's sample was unearthed in Pilbara, northwestern Australia, by the multinational company Rio Tinto. It was sent to the museum after it was categorized as a commercially unviable source of iron ore.[81] Rio Tinto faced considerable criticism for their devastation of the Aboriginal site of Juunkan Gorge. Their website features a prominent apology to the Puutu Kunti Kurrama and Pinikura people and explicitly addresses the obligation to protect Aboriginal heritage in a recent report.[82] Unfortunately, Aboriginal dispossession is only implicit in the displays. It is especially important that the imperial connections of museums are not forgotten or obscured to maintain a fantasy of authoritative political neutrality.

Museums were never politically neutral. In the early modern world, cabinets of curiosities helped collectors showcase their wealth and social standing, but only to a chosen elite. Hans Sloane's desire to establish the British Museum as a state-owned public institution was a radical departure from the elitist private museums of the past, but it remained an attempt to keep his treasured collection intact and secure his legacy. Nineteenth-century campaigners hoped new civic museums would educate mass audiences. While a laudable aim, these campaigns were predicated on assumptions that the poorer classes required moral uplift and saving from their own vices. Museum champions believed educational and moral improvement depended on presenting museums as authoritative institutions. Writing in 1880 and just a year before the Natural History Museum opened in London, the art critic John Ruskin proposed that the 'first function of a museum' was 'to give example of perfect order and perfect elegance, in the true sense of that test word, to the disorderly and rude populace'. Moreover, he continued, a 'museum, primarily, is to be for *simple* persons. Children, that is to say, and peasants. For your student, your antiquary, or your scientific gentleman, there must be separate accommodation, or they must be sent elsewhere' (original emphasis).[83] Ruskin was influential in the debates about what a museum should be, and whom it should serve. As the museum movement expanded, exhibited artefacts were often incorporated into broader narratives about national and imperial success. Modern museums might not claim they are serving the 'rude populace', but their functions as educational spaces for the masses are historically rooted in past assumptions about class. Moreover, whereas some museums have tried proactively to address the imperial legacies they have inherited by being open about their roots or returning loot, others have been desperately slow to acknowledge their profoundly and inherently political nature.[84]

Renaming the central hall in the Museum of Natural History after the Hintze family reflects a complicated relationship between capitalism, philanthropy, and heritage tourism. Many wealthy donors have avoided criticism of exploitation, corporate bad behaviour, and unfettered capitalist accumulation under the guise of philanthropy.[85] The backlash against the Sackler family is just one recent example. The family acquired an astonishing fortune from pharmaceuticals and donated extensively to some of the most prestigious cultural institutions around the world. However, they faced intense criticism and lawsuits for profiting from the over-prescription of addictive drugs such as OxyContin, and accusations of reputation laundering through high-profile donations. Likewise, the British Museum has faced controversy over its decision to accept donations from British

Petroleum. Not only is BP one of the world's largest companies trading in fossil fuels, its origins lie in imperial extraction. Established in 1909 as the Anglo-Persian Oil Company to exploit natural resources in Persia, now Iran, it was ultimately renamed British Petroleum in 1954.[86] These historically and politically significant connections are often disavowed by institutions, sometimes in a fight for survival, but they are of increasing interest to a new generation of visitors and campaigners. Hintze Hall encapsulates the difficult choices curators and institutions face as they decide how best to interrogate the roots of their collections for current and future audiences.

In 2019, Extinction Rebellion held a series of die-ins across the globe on Monday 22 April as Earth Day followed Easter Sunday. At 12:05 p.m. a hundred protestors lay under Hope, scattered around the floor of Hintze Hall, while about three hundred protestors lay under Dippy in Kelvingrove Gallery, Glasgow.[87] Extinction Rebellion's choice to die-in under Hope and Dippy indicates that both are international celebrities. As Hope hovers above the museum's visitors, she shows what is possible when we forgo valuing species for their economic significance and instead consider them as ways of being worthy of life.

Epilogue
Extinction's Futures

Imagine a way of life, taking millennia to come into being, and once embodied in thousands, millions, or billions of living bodies. Then imagine it reduced to a tentacle, dismembered wing, or stuffed skin. The indignity of a solitary relic is all that remains of many ways of being. Scientists fear many stored specimens 'will often turn out to be all that remains of organisms that once thrived'.[1] Our best hopes of knowing some lifeways ever existed lie entombed in museums and herbaria. Too many lifeways have already met that fate at human hands, including one I visited during a sweltering, record-breaking heatwave of the kind that is increasingly familiar.

Liverpool is well known to people the world over as the home of The Beatles. The beautifully preserved architectural heritage, particularly along the waterfront featuring the Three Graces – namely the Royal Liver Building, the Cunard Building, and Port of Liverpool Building at Pier Head – earned it UNESCO World Heritage site status in 2004. The Royal Albert Dock once buzzed with stevedores and merchants earning profits from trading cloth, coal, tobacco, sugar, and enslaved Africans during industrial development that quickened the pace of troubling interventions in earth's geological processes. Their stories occupy the Maritime Museum, Museum of Liverpool, and International Slavery Museum along waterways leading to the 'frayed Atlantic edge'.[2] Within a short walk from the waterside, the city's World Museum features an impressive range of artefacts bequeathed by nineteenth- and twentieth-century collectors, showcasing global cultures. One of the most important specimens usually resides away from the public's gaze, but it is available to visit by appointment.

I met one of the museum's curators in the foyer, who quickly led me through a side door to get away from crowds. After winding through flights of stairs and long corridors, we passed places brimming with the dead. One room featured two freezers named 'Dodo' and 'Great Auk', chilling their contents to minus 79°C, while other rooms were filled with rows of locked cabinets and shelves full of specimens. The museum is the final resting place of the Liverpool Pigeon. It is a unicum, or the only known specimen of a species. The curators kindly discussed the collections while I examined the pigeon. I asked if many people asked to see the bird and was surprised to learn it was a relatively common request. Recently, a local boy had asked to see the 'real thing' after learning about the bird's final home in his city. The curators kindly, and carefully, removed the pigeon from its wrappings and laid the remains on a table for me.

To my untrained eye, the pigeon's iridescent colours were reminiscent of the starlings whose murmurations transform the gloaming into an astounding sight. Glossy dark-green feathers adorned the back, while darker and duller feathers lined the underside. The elongated feathers around the neck formed a delicate ruff fit for a royal courtier. Along the back, the feathers turn from dark cinnamon to iridescent green, spotted with pale wedges shaped like guitar picks, giving rise to its informal name of spotted green pigeon. The wings still shimmered, intimating living vibrancy. The eye was eerily lifeless. White fibres filled the eye socket with only a tiny fleck of red hinting at the presence of the false red eye chosen by former handlers. The black beak tipped with dull yellow looked uncannily like a miniature dodo bill. Threads from two labels encircled a detached leg. Later, I learned that the original taxidermist mistakenly swapped the right and left legs, compounding the indignity.[3] Originally mounted for show, the bird was later deposed and reconfigured into the less elaborate pose of a research skin. Sorrow rarely evades me when I encounter extinct lifeways, but realizing how little we know about this solitary specimen left me aghast.

The spotted green pigeon was first described by the physician and naturalist John Latham (Fig. 11.1). He helped establish the Linnean Society of London and was well known to the city's scientific elite,

11.1 The spotted green pigeon.

such as the naturalist Joseph Banks who served as President of the Royal Society. Latham made his name classifying many well-known Australian birds, such as the emu, and studying the birds of India, Australia, and the Pacific with specimens he bought through connections with gentlemen like Banks. Latham's ornithological enthusiasm sustained him as he wrote and illustrated *A General Synopsis for Birds* in his early forties and published it in three volumes between 1783 and 1785. Four decades later, a swollen compendium of ten volumes was published as *A General History of Birds* (1821–8) and dedicated to King George IV. Latham died thirteen years later aged ninety-six.[4] Of the spotted green pigeon he observed:

> LENGTH twelve inches. Bill black, tipped with pale yellow: general colour of the plumage dark green, and glossy: the head and neck are darker than the rest, and of one plain colour: the feathers of the neck long and narrow, like the hackles of a Cock; every feather of

> the wings and scapulars tipped with a spot of very pale cinereous white, with a point running upwards, somewhat triangular: quills and tail black; the feathers of the first tipped with cinereous white, those of the last with ferruginous white, and even at the end: belly, thighs, and vent, dusky black: the legs are brown, and the shins covered half way with downy feathers: claws black.[5]

Intriguingly, Latham noted that two pigeon skins existed in the collections of Banks and General Major Davies. An army officer and dab hand with a paintbrush, Davies was a self-taught taxidermist with a passion for feathered souls. His collection included bird skins acquired through personal travel in North America and contacts in the Pacific. Auctioned after his death, the spotted green pigeon drew the keen eye and winning bid of the thirteenth Earl of Derby, Lord Stanley. In his personal copy of *General Synopsis of Birds*, where Latham notes the skin in Davies' collection, the earl triumphantly scrawled 'now in mine!'[6] Ultimately, Stanley's collections were donated to the city of Liverpool, forming the core of a new museum and forerunner of the current World Museum. Despite the acquisitive glee of a satiated collector, Stanley knew almost nothing of the spotted green pigeon.

No one knew where the Spotted Green pigeon once chanted its song, or who consigned it to an afterlife as dead treasure. Latham described the bird in English, losing the chance to name the species in Latin. Five years later, the naturalist Johann Friedrich Gmelin formally named the species *Columba maculata*. Despite these early efforts, not everyone was convinced the bird was even a species. Some proposed it was just a juvenile Nicobar pigeon. Others were convinced it was a rare abnormality rather than a natural kind. In 1898 the bird was formally reclassified as *Caloenas maculata*, which remains its scientific name. The shift placed the bird in the same genus as the flamboyantly tinted Nicobar pigeon, and the extinct Kanaka pigeon known only from partially fossilized remnants.[7] The skin's two labels memorialize the confusion (Fig. 11.2). One label classifies the bird as a Nicobar pigeon (*Caloenas nicobarica*) and traces the bird's journey

11.2 Labels tracing the collection and classification of the Liverpool pigeon.

from the collection of a 'Gen Davies' to the Museum of Derby, now the World Museum in Liverpool. The ornate cursive script of the other label names the 'spotted green pigeon' (*Columba maculata*) on the authority of 'Lath'. The contradictory labels highlight disagreement about the bird's rightful place among its kin, and the processes by which living beings become prized commodities and material currency among global networks of collectors and curators.

Growing scientific and historical interest in the spotted green pigeon yield only scant clues to the bird's origins and first human name. In 2014 a team of scientists harvested the pigeon's DNA from two feathers and used it to reconstruct the bird's family tree. Historically, evolutionary family trees, or phylogenies, were based on observable characteristics such as outward appearance, physiology, and function. Phylogenies are now more commonly based on computerized statistical analysis of DNA to create numerous family trees and test which best explains the genetic similarity between organisms. Using that technique, the team proposed that the bird was a distinctive species, and that its closest relative is the Nicobar pigeon, and, at one remove, the extinct Rodrigues Solitaire and dodo, all originally from the Indian Ocean.[8] The trio of extinctions also makes the Nicobar pigeon the closest living relative of the dodo. The team inferred the birds shared a common ancestor flying from island to island across the Indian and Pacific oceans. During the spotted green pigeon's subsequent isolation, descendants formed the *Columbidae* family which includes all four species. Which islands? Early naturalists often presumed a Pacific origin for the spotted green pigeon based on the lost specimen owned by Joseph Banks, which is even more plausible given the relationship with the Nicobar pigeon.

Another clue suggests Pacific origins for the spotted green pigeon. The linguist and ethnologist Teuira Henry drew on her grandfather's life to write about the history of Tahiti. Her grandfather, the Reverend John Muggeridge Orsmond, spent decades researching ancient Tahitians during his missionary work. He compiled his observations into a lost manuscript. Henry used her memories and grandfather's notes to reconstruct the work and ensure its publication in a book called *Ancient Tahiti* in 1928. In discussions of local birds, she named one called 'The titi, which cried "titi", now extinct in Tahiti, was speckled green and white, and it was the shadow of the mountain gods.'[9] The spotted green pigeon was probably extinct by the mid-nineteenth century, and perhaps as early as the 1820s, but Henry's observation came from her grandfather's notes so it might be the testimony of someone who saw, and heard, the living bird. After combing through dictionaries compiled by early missionaries, the conservationist Philippe Raust believes Henry's description plausibly matches the little we know of the spotted green pigeon. If so, Tahitians may have named it *tītī* and ascribed it religious or cosmological meaning.[10] Despite this possibility, the pigeon's family connection to the Rodrigues Solitaire and dodo offers the intriguing possibility of South or Southeast Asian roots. Historical and scientific sleuthing provides tantalizing clues, but the pigeon's origins will probably remain obscure until undisturbed remains are found and matched with the skin in Liverpool. The mystery of the bird's origins is compelling, but to know so little about any way of being consigns it to a remarkably miserable fate.

Writing histories of extinction raises profound historical and ethical challenges. In the post-war era, as the history of science was established as a discipline, narratives of progressive enlightenment in which scientists made discoveries to draw closer to abstract truths about the natural world were the most common way of writing about scientific research. Historical theories that did not chime with modern scientific understandings were deemed wrong, while those that fell foul of present-day moral codes, such as racist or sexist ideas, were also often dismissed as pseudoscience. This approach is understandable. Narratives of discovery provide satisfying stories, but dismissing past scientific ideas as simply wrong or pseudoscientific creates two significant difficulties for understanding the history of such ideas. First, it assumes that past scientific knowledge must be judged according to current theories, instead of in its own historical context. Second, it protects the reputation of scientific knowledge as objective, or abstract, truth instead of as a means of making knowledge always rooted in specific, and shifting, historical circumstances. These assumptions make it virtually impossible to understand science historically, including the nature of extinction as an idea. In recent decades, and from the 1980s onwards in particular, historians of science have shown that placing science within its historical context provides a significantly richer understanding of how scientific knowledge was formed, circulated, and transformed.

Vanished has drawn on these insights to trace extinction as a shifting idea shaped as much by theology or global politics as by new scientific methods or evidence. That may feel like an uncomfortable or counter-intuitive approach, especially for anyone used to thinking about 'real' science as objective. For centuries, people contributing to scientific knowledge have claimed that they are objective observers using inductive reasoning to make sense of empirical findings. While this might seem superficially plausible, historians and philosophers of science have spent decades exploring how observing, collecting data, and theorizing are not neutral acts. Rather they are theory laden because they always depend on pre-existing expectations even by the most sincere and earnest truth seekers. When we explore the world around us, our expectations and assumptions shape the questions we ask, where we seek evidence, whose knowledge we regard as reliable enough to constitute answers, and the explanations that we are willing to entertain as making sense of the world. Claims of objectivity were, and can still be, an attempt to seek and assert authority; rather than taking these for granted, historians and philosophers of science have interrogated how scientific knowledge is made to reveal the profound importance of the cultural, social, and political contexts to which all knowledge is inextricably tied. Histories of extinction provide just one example of how intimately connected making natural knowledge was to deeply disturbing ideas about race, being human, life's worth, and imperial politics.

Tracing how scientists, colonial officials, and writers used theories of animal extinction to narrate important historical shifts, from the expansion of European settler colonies to the loss of numerous ways of being, reveals an astonishing but often neglected thread in the making of the modern world. The later nineteenth century has often been associated with the rise of Social Darwinism, and the belief that races and nations were locked in a bloody struggle for survival. While Darwin's legacy is crucial, many writers, scientists, and colonial officials discussed the future of humanity as a natural process of competition, conquest, and extinction long before Darwin's ideas about natural selection were made public in 1859. By then, new ideas about extinction as a process inherent in the natural world were already well established and used to justify European settler colonialism as the outcome of the natural law of extinction. The dispossession of the original nations of Newfoundland, North America, and Australia were all written about as extinctions by naturalists and colonists steeped in a profound disavowal of violence. That erasure shapes the lives of nations forced to prove they still exist, like the Sinixt or Aboriginal Tasmanians, or Indigenous peoples across the world fighting for the return of their lands.

Tracing these connections reveals how extinction-making, and scientific knowledge more broadly, were deeply entwined with, and embedded in, appalling intellectual and moral violence with legacies that still require reckoning and redress.

Many episodes of extinction, from prehistoric losses to more recent eradications, cast long shadows today. The historical conflation of animal extinction, colonial persecution, and the imposition of alien forms of kinship created lasting dispossession for Indigenous peoples in settler colonies across the Americas, Africa, and the Pacific. Many peoples struggle with the consequences of severed relationships with their rightful homelands and are campaigning for restitution. Others fight to prove they even exist as myths of extinction ossified into systematic neglect and political policies of removal or lack of state recognition. Meanwhile, the extraction and exploitation of natural resources, whether fur, feathers, coal, rubber, natural gas, petroleum, palm oil, or timber, generated extraordinary wealth for imperial powers while creating lasting ecological damage. Environmental catastrophes are already here for many nations who, historically or in the present, have contributed little to climate change but are now at the mercy of rising sea levels, flooding, extreme heat, and fires. We saw the urgency of that with the catastrophic flooding in Pakistan in 2022. This raises the pressing issue of whether heavily polluting nations or corporations will contribute fairly to offer reparation for their historically disproportionate contributions to creating our extreme climate and damaged worlds.

We are living through the extinction of many ways of being. The Baiji, or Yangtze dolphin, was declared functionally extinct in 2006. Lonesome George, the last Pinta Island tortoise, died on the Galapagos Islands in 2012. The West African black rhino, Holdridge's toad, golden toad of Costa Rica, and ivory-billed woodpecker were among the many species declared extinct as I wrote this book. We face losing many more kinds without taking action; yet, spurred by panic, it would be exceptionally easy to continue historical dispossession without profound care in the rush to act. In the lead-up to the COP 15 summit in 2022, the United Nations launched a marketing campaign featuring Frankie the dinosaur. Advertisements showed Frankie gate-crashing a UN summit and begging for humanity to avert annihilation with the tagline 'Don't Choose Extinction'.

Recognizing that extinction is a choice is essential. Every time we save a way of being or mourn the passing of a natural kind, whether a species or otherwise, we make decisions rooted in our emotional attachments, or our perceptions of that natural kind's value – whether commercial, aesthetic, or ecological. One of the best examples of that conundrum is the new Global Biodiversity Framework, committed to protecting 30 per cent of the planet by 2030. The policy might be rooted in laudable aims, but whether it truly constitutes justice for humanity or other species will depend on many other decisions about which 30 per cent will be protected and whether historically dispossessed peoples are expected to lose even more land in the process. Conservationists need to adopt radically different approaches informed by the history of their present practice to truly secure just policies.

Writing about extinction means living with restless ghosts. I began this book with more than a decade's experience of reading scientific literature on race debating who counted as human, and insisting that some lives were worth less or worthless. Yet even this familiarity did not lessen the shock of encountering writers who proclaimed that extinction, especially of colonized peoples, was necessary, inevitable, or even desirable. Reading authors disavowing breathtaking slaughter as an inevitable, even providential, process meant confronting an extremely powerful fatalism, and tracing its afterlives. Reading scientific reports, newspapers, and colonial accounts was painful enough, but on many occasions I encountered traces of ostensibly vanished lives that only existed because their creators violated the wishes of the dead. I will never forget the moment of turning the page of a scientific article on extinction to face the horrific photograph of a woman's corpse denied a burial because anthropologists believed she was the last of her race, or looking through an archival box full of documents and realizing that it also served as a casket for hair samples taken without consent from people barely acknowledged as human by anthropologists. Understanding the unnatural histories of extinction and empire that have created these archives and shaped our present means bearing witness to profound intellectual, moral, and physical violence, tracing its legacies, and acknowledging that redress is long overdue and necessary.

Everyone will have an endangered species or cultural practice whose loss they would grieve for more than any other. Whose loss would you mourn? What would you change in order to prevent that loss? As a young child, I wanted to *be* an osprey, meet the ancient trees of the world, and swim with whales and sharks, but nothing compared to the joy of living in a world with tigers. Deliberate persecution, hunting, and habitat destruction contributed to the extinction of Balinese, Caspian, and Javan tigers between the 1930s and 1980s, while the remaining six subspecies occupy just 5 per cent of their former range. Conservation efforts have led to glimmers of hope as tiger populations slowly rise in Nepal, China, and Thailand, but they are still declining elsewhere and fewer than 4,000 mature individuals are known to exist in the present.[11] Knowing they might disappear, and potentially in my lifetime, has always been painful. Such cultural and emotional judgements underpin efforts to conserve any site, practice, or way of being. Untangling these concerns, and being aware of their roots in histories of extractive dispossession, indiscriminate consumption, and denial of Indigenous peoples' rights, helps us to understand why extinction matters to us, and how best to tackle it with just policies.

Extinction is a political choice: histories of extinction offer opportunities to choose wisely. Writing more compelling accounts of the unnatural histories of extinction and empire making provides us with a crucial opportunity to avoid perpetuating dispossession and injustice in the rush to salvage and protect what remains. Despite the accelerating loss of lifeways, hope endures, but it requires a much more critical awareness of our inheritance and present responsibilities. Some of our predecessors bear greater culpability for past wrongs, while many shoulder larger obligations in the present by living lives on unceded lands or causing significantly greater harm

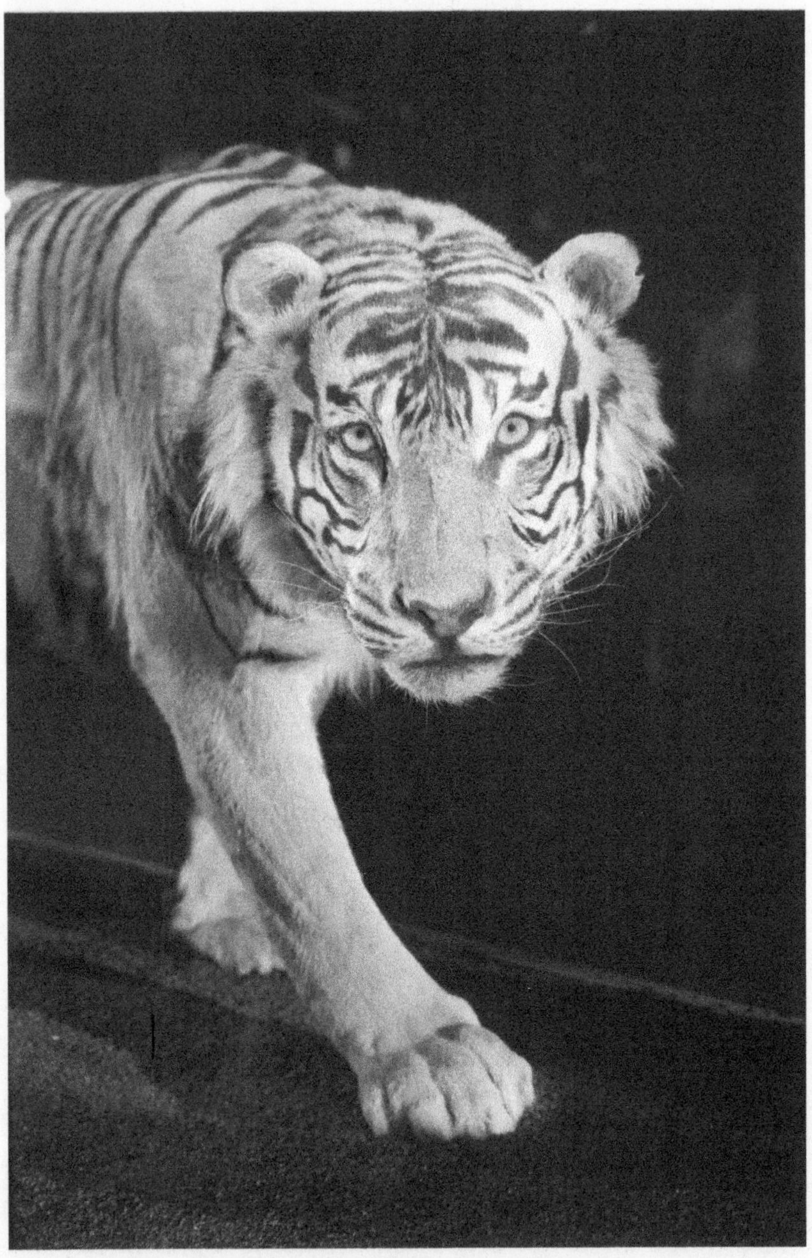

11.3 An endangered Sumatran tiger in the hall of extinct species, Museum of Natural History, Paris.

to life on earth through our lifestyles. Yet, we all have a reason to choose a better future, whether through personal action, holding those with power to account, or supporting policies that honour multiple forms of recovery and redress. Recognizing the roots of the present moment is essential to securing justice not for the few, but for life itself. Transforming the current politics of crisis to an ethics of reciprocal care offers us a rare chance to imagine, and create, worthwhile futures.

For I cannot bear that one day the jungles of my ancestral homeland may no longer resound with the roar of the tigress.

Acknowledgements

Writing a book is a collaborative venture that always depends on the love, faith, support, and inspiration of others. I am profoundly grateful to an astonishing number of wonderful people who have crossed paths with me, or kept me company, as I wrote this book, especially in the shadow of horrific, even genocidal, violence in the global political arena.

Vanished began as a project on the notion of endangered peoples and grew into a much broader exploration of extinction. My ideas about extinction were nurtured as a postdoctoral research fellow within the Cambridge Victorian Studies Group. The late Peter Lipton was the first person to send me the job advert and encourage me to apply. His act of kindness came at a moment when I was deeply unsure of my future and it made all the difference. I remain grateful to him for helping to make the Department of History and Philosophy of Science such a wonderful community where I flourished, from my undergraduate studies right through to my postdoctoral research. Within the Department, I was profoundly conscious of how fortunate I was to be Jim Secord's student. From the moment I first stepped into his office, his intellectual generosity, guidance, and unfailing kindness have helped many of my most cherished dreams come true. I first met him as an undergraduate studying the sciences and convinced that I would leave academia as soon as possible. His teaching inspired me to stay, and I eventually transitioned from being his doctoral student to working alongside him. For more than two decades Jim has transformed my life in the most beautifully unexpected ways, and crossing paths with him stands out as one of the greatest blessings of my life.

The Cambridge Victorian Studies Group was led by Mary Beard, Simon Goldhill, Peter Mandler, Clare Pettitt, and Jim Secord. My postdoctoral peers were Adelene Buckland, David Gange, Michael Ledger-Lomas, Astrid Swenson, Anna Vaninskaya, Daniel Wilson, and David McCallister. The doctoral scholars were Helen Brookman, Jocelyn Betts, and Rachel Bryant-Davies. I'm immensely grateful to them all for contributing to a truly exceptional and formative intellectual space and, in the case of David Gange, for the years we spent teaching and working together after the project ended. Without the group, I doubt I would have remained in academia or found the space and time to develop my interests in race, empire, and extinction in ways that mean so much to me.

I'm honoured and fortunate that so many wonderful people have offered invaluable advice and support over the years. Simon Schaffer and Sujit Sivasundaram have shaped and transformed my intellectual interests from my first encounters with them as a student to this project's inception, and throughout its long gestation. I remain in awe of their many kindnesses for more than two decades. Ralph O'Connor has been as unfailingly generous and perceptive as ever at several turning points. Many people offered important insights and advice on individual themes or career advice, some without even knowing how important our correspondence or conversations were. I am thankful to Sara Ahmed, Jonathan Saha, Kate Nichols, Jim Endersby, Helen Macdonald, Stephanie Pratt, Anne Secord, Jesse Olszynko-Gryn, Surekha Davies, Julia Laite, Catherine Hall, Margot Finn, Lucy Delap, Miranda Lowe, Dirk Moses, Heather Goodall, Martin Rudwick, Chris Manias, Lukas Rieppel, David Sepkoski, Jon Agar, Tara J. Hamling, Sara Butler, Nikesh Shukla, Alice Te Punga Somerville and Tom Stammers. I'm delighted that so many people invited me to speak about my research, especially Jenny Rampling, Joanna Radin, Persephone Pearl, and Rohan Deb Roy. They all invited me to present my research at crucial points in my writing. I'm also indebted to Daisy Larios at the IUCN archives, and Miguel Garcia at the Royal Botanical Gardens in Sydney, for their help in making my archival trips so valuable.

In recent years, two events helped me to finish writing this book after long periods of fearing it might never happen. In the summer of 2023 I joined the University of Manchester to begin a much longed-for new chapter in my life. I'm especially thankful to Anindita Ghosh, Kerry Pimblott, Charlie Wildman, and Max Jones for helping me settle in to such a welcoming department. Shortly after I began, I organized an event called 'In Her Wake' to celebrate an extraordinary cohort of women who were the first of their heritage to be promoted to professorships in Britain. Early in my career, I realized how few women, especially like me, existed in British academia let alone the professoriate. As I searched for my sisterly predecessors, I found many women whose historic achievements were neglected or unknown even to themselves. I especially want to honour Mel Chevannes who in 1990 I believe was the first woman of her heritage to be promoted to a professorship in any discipline within Britain. In her wake, Elizabeth Anionwu, Lola Young, Heidi Safia Mirza, Olivette Otele, Naomi Standen, and Katherine Harloe were all the first of their heritage to be promoted to chairs in their disciplines. All kindly participated in the event, except Lola who was supportive but unable to attend. Each of these women, and likely many others who I do not know about, paved the path for my own success in being the first woman of my heritage to be a history professor within a British university. I also want to thank Claire Langhammer, Deanna Lynn Cook, Imaobong Umoren, and Saima Nasar who were wonderful co-hosts and made the event of 'In Her Wake' as special as it was.

I am obliged to the Leverhulme Trust and British Academy for supporting my research career, and especially for this book. The Leverhulme Trust funded my postdoctoral fellowship and awarded me a Philip Leverhulme Prize. The prize helped broaden the scope of the book, both through supporting my international archival research and providing the time to reconfigure the project from one focused on human extinction to a much broader range of subjects. The British Academy's Mid-Career Fellowship provided the time I needed to recast the manuscript after a period of numerous obstacles prevented any progress. It was also my good fortune to be a Visiting Fellow at the Bodleian Libraries, at the University of Oxford, where I completed the manuscript. I'm especially grateful to Rachel Naismith whose kindness during my visit helped make it so fruitful.

I am thrilled that my agent Andrew Gordon, editors Laura Stickney and Kim Walker, and Penguin Press showed such faith in this project. Andrew and Laura were especially important for supporting this book in its most embryonic stages. Their expertise was invaluable in transforming my ideas into a proposal and complete manuscript, while Kim shepherded the book through the final hurdles. I'm also thankful to Fahad Al-Amoudi, Ruth Pietroni, Gavin Read, Richard Green, Eleni Lawrence, Richard Mason, and the entire publishing team for helping make my ideas into a tangible reality. Like so many young children who discovered the magic of reading, I treasured my Puffin books. My library still contains many volumes I bought as a child exploring new worlds. I could not be more thrilled that this book found its first home with Penguin Press.

Many of the most important people who helped make this book possible have never read a word of the manuscript, but their conversations, hugs, support (often over decades), and general 'roarsomeness' kept my own roars and refusals powerful and enduring in ways that they will likely never fully appreciate. With loving joy, I thank Benjamin Thomas White, Shahmimah Akhtar, Saima Nasar, Michell Chresfield, Kennetta Hammond Perry, Olivette Otele, Fariha Shaikh, Christienna Fryar, Meleisa Ono-George, Caroline Bressey, Gavin Schaffer, David Olusoga, Sarah Qidwai, Mobeen Hussain, Bal, Rosslyn Nelson, the late and much missed Tim Brighouse, Salina Begum, Noreen Jahangir, Uzma Mukhtar, Kev and Vicky Levell. I hope this book might help make the future better for the next generation, especially my niblings Ted, Rose, Jacob, Yusuf, Ruqayyah, Jibreel, Layaal and Rawaan.

My final, and greatest, thanks are to my family, especially Bob, Denise, Mamu, Umair, Atti, Umar, Khalid, and Sumera. Sumayyah and Sidrah have reminded me of, and kept me to, my purpose even when at my lowest ebb. Beloved Sufyan has kept my soul company through tribulations that only he understands. *Vanished* is dedicated to my late *baji*, *abbu ji*, and *ammi ji*, who are the root of my every blessing. Words cannot do them justice, but I pray my duas might.

Notes

Prologue

1 Anthony S. Cheke, 'Speculation, Statistics, Facts and the Dodo's Extinction Date', *Historical Biology* 27, no. 5 (2015): 624–33; Julian P. Hume, 'The Dodo: From Extinction to the Fossil Record', *Geology Today* 28, no. 4 (2012): 147–51; Andrew Jackson, 'Added Credence for a Late Dodo Extinction Date', *Historical Biology* 26, no. 6 (2014): 699–701; David L. Roberts and Andrew R. Solow, 'When Did the Dodo Become Extinct?', *Nature* 426, no. 6964 (2003): 245.

2 On the natural history of the dodo and solitaire consult Jolyon C. Parish, *The Dodo and the Solitaire: A Natural History* (Bloomington, IN: Indiana University Press, 2012).

3 Hugh E. Strickland and A. G. Melville, *The Dodo and Its Kindred; or, the History, Affinities, and Osteology of the Dodo, Solitaire, and Other Extinct Birds of the Islands Mauritius, Rodriguez and Bourbon* (London: Reeve, Benham, and Reeve, 1848), 22, 5; A. Iwanow, 'An Indian Picture of the Dodo', *Journal für Ornithologie* 99, no. 4 (1958): 438–40; Ria Winters and Julian P. Hume, 'The Dodo, the Deer and a 1647 Voyage to Japan', *Historical Biology* 27, no. 2 (2015): 258–64; Emmanuel Richon and Ria Winters, 'The Intercultural Dodo: A Drawing from the School of Bundi, Rājasthān', *Historical Biology* 28, no. 3 (2016): 415–22.

4 Cited in M. Nowak-Kemp and J. P. Hume, 'The Oxford Dodo. Part 1: The Museum History of the Tradescant Dodo: Ownership, Displays and Audience', *Historical Biology* 29, no. 2 (2017): 235.

5 This history of the Oxford Dodo draws from Nowak-Kemp and Hume, 'The Oxford Dodo. Part 1'; M. Nowak-Kemp and J. P. Hume, 'The Oxford Dodo. Part 2: From Curiosity to Icon and Its Role in Displays, Education and Research', *Historical Biology* 29, no. 3 (2017): 296–307; J. M. Warnett et al., 'The Oxford Dodo. Seeing More Than

Ever Before: X-Ray Micro-Ct Scanning, Specimen Acquisition and Provenance', *Historical Biology* 33, no. 10 (2021): 2247–55. For photographs of the Oxford Dodo consult Warnett's article or the Oxford University Museum of Natural History, 'The Oxford Dodo', accessed 22 May 2023, https://oumnh.ox.ac.uk/learn-the-oxford-dodo

6 I am drawing on the discussion of species in Thom Van Dooren, *Flight Ways: Life and Loss at the Edge of Extinction* (New York: Columbia University Press, 2014).

7 Elizabeth A. Bell et al., 'Potentially Biogenic Carbon Preserved in a 4.1 Billion-Year-Old Zircon', *Proceedings of the National Academy of Sciences of the United States of America* 112, no. 47 (24 November 2015): 14518–21.

8 John J. Wiens, 'How Many Species Are There on Earth? Progress and Problems', *PLOS Biology* 21, no. 11 (20 November 2023): e3002388; Camilo Mora et al., 'How Many Species Are There on Earth and in the Ocean?', *PLOS Biology* 9, no. 8 (August 2011): e1001127. Each year the International Union for Conservation of Nature (IUCN) publishes summary statistics of how many species it has evaluated as a proportion of the total number of known species, providing one of the most consistently updated routes to knowing how many species are known. For figures consult IUCN, 'Summary Statistics: The IUCN Red List of Threatened Species', *IUCN Red List of Threatened Species*, 2023, https://www.iucnredlist.org/en. Known species can be explored on a digital tree of life at OneZoom, 'Tree of Life', *OneZoom Tree of Life Explorer*, accessed 21 April 2024, https://www.onezoom.org/introduction

9 Mannfred M. A. Boehm and Quentin C. B. Cronk, 'Dark Extinction: The Problem of Unknown Historical Extinctions', *Biology Letters* 17, no. 3 (2021): rsbl.2021.0007, 20210007. On the potential of museum collections consult Christopher Kemp, *The Lost Species: Great Expeditions in the Collections of Natural History Museums* (Chicago, IL: University of Chicago Press, 2017).

10 James S. Ormrod, '"Making Room for the Tigers and the Polar Bears": Biography, Phantasy and Ideology in the Voluntary Human Extinction Movement', *Psychoanalysis, Culture & Society* 16, no. 2 (2011): 142–61.

11 IUCN, 'The IUCN Red List of Threatened Species', *IUCN Red List of Threatened Species*, 2021, https://www.iucnredlist.org/en; Ana Ratner, 'What the Extinction Crisis Took from the World in 2022', *The Nation*, 22 December 2022, https://www.thenation.com/article/environment/extinct-species-2022; Mark Kaufman, 'These Animals Went Extinct in 2023', *Mashable*, 27 December 2023, https://mashable.com/article/extinct-species-animals-2023

12 Clara de Massol de Rebetz, 'Remembrance Day for Lost Species: Remembering and Mourning Extinction in the Anthropocene', *Memory Studies* 13, no. 5 (2020): 875–88.

13 Anonymous, 'Names Going Extinct: These Are the Baby Names that Are Dying Out . . . ', *Cosmopolitan*, 4 February 2022, https://www.cosmopolitan.com/uk/body/a28347489/uncommon-baby-names-going-extinct; Rachel Avery, '40 Baby Names Set to Go Extinct in 2023', *HELLO!*, 24 October 2022, https://www.hellomagazine.com/healthandbeauty/mother-and-baby/20221024155022/baby-names-going-extinct-in-2023

14 'Extinction', *Oxford English Dictionary*. Even a cursory search for 'extinct' or 'extinction' in archival catalogues exhibits these usages in wills, letters, and pamphlets stretching back centuries.

15 In the wake of the Black Lives Matter movements, much older conversations about acknowledgement and reparations are gaining unprecedented momentum. The literature on these themes is vast, but some important histories of the moral and economic debt include: Eric E. Williams, *Capitalism & Slavery* (London: Andre Deutsch, 1964); Christopher Leslie Brown, *Moral Capital: Foundations of British Abolitionism* (Chapel Hill, NC: University of North Carolina Press, 2006); Hilary Beckles, *Britain's Black Debt: Reparations for Caribbean Slavery and Native Genocide* (Kingston, Jamaica: University of West Indies Press, 2013). For an articulation of these claims in the present consult Ta-Nehisi Coates, 'The Case for Reparations', *The Atlantic*, 22 May 2014, https://www.theatlantic.com/magazine/archive/2014/06/the-case-for-reparations/361631

16 The best summaries of scientific theories of extinction are Mark V. Barrow, *Nature's Ghosts: Confronting Extinction from the Age of*

Jefferson to the Age of Ecology (Chicago, IL: University of Chicago Press, 2009); David Sepkoski, *Catastrophic Thinking: Extinction and the Value of Diversity from Darwin to the Anthropocene* (Chicago, IL: University of Chicago Press, 2020).

17 For examples of epic narratives consult Barrow, *Nature's Ghosts*; Sepkoski, *Catastrophic Thinking*. In combination, Barrow and Sepkoski provide among the most detailed and authoritative histories on the idea of extinction within the life sciences. Barrow's book is particularly commendable as the most exhaustive and nuanced history of the idea of extinction. Yet, precisely because those life sciences were deeply exclusionary, these narratives are centred on white male scientists. For examples of tragedy consult Norman Myers, *The Sinking Ark: A New Look at the Problem of Disappearing Species* (Oxford: Pergamon Press, 1980); Edward O. Wilson, *Half-Earth: Our Planet's Fight for Life* (New York: Liveright, W. W. Norton & Company, 2016); David Wallace-Wells, *The Uninhabitable Earth: A Story of the Future* (London: Allen Lane, 2019). The sense of a lost Eden looms large in many works calling for us to change our ways. The sense of urgency is well founded, as is the sense that humans may well have sown the seeds of their own destruction. For examples of travelogues consult David Quammen, *The Song of the Dodo: Island Biogeography in an Age of Extinctions* (New York: Scribner, 1996); Elizabeth Kolbert, *The Sixth Extinction: An Unnatural History* (New York: Henry Holt and Company, 2014); Jules N. Pretty, *The Edge of Extinction: Travels with Enduring People in Vanishing Lands* (Ithaca, NY: Cornell University Press, 2014); Van Dooren, *Flight Ways*. Here, the authors combine broader meditations on extinction with accounts of their travels to see endangered species, or the last known sites of extinct species. Thom Van Dooren's book is a particularly beautiful example of the environmental humanities, bringing together philosophies and anthropologies of extinction to think about our relationship with species at the 'dull edge of extinction' (passim). Microhistories of extinction focusing on individuals, whether single species or the last remaining individual, are common. For example, consult Mark Avery, *A Message from Martha: The Extinction of the Passenger Pigeon and Its Relevance Today*

(London: Bloomsbury, 2014); Tom Lawson, *The Last Man: A British Genocide in Tasmania* (London: I. B. Tauris, 2014). For the most magnificent account of the shifting meanings of extinction consult Ursula K. Heise, *Imagining Extinction: The Cultural Meanings of Endangered Species* (Chicago, IL: University of Chicago Press, 2016).

Chapter 1

1 On the geology of Big Bone Lick consult Kenneth Barnett Tankersley et al., 'Quaternary Chronostratigraphy and Stable Isotope Paleoecology of Big Bone Lick, Kentucky, USA', *Quaternary Research* 83, no. 3 (2015): 479–87. Keith Stewart Thomson, *The Legacy of the Mastodon: The Golden Age of Fossils in America* (Berkeley, CA: Yale University Press, 2008), 13.

2 William Hunter, 'Observations on the Bones, Commonly Supposed to Be Elephants Bones, Which Have Been Found Near the River Ohio in America: By William Hunter, M. D. F. R. S.', *Philosophical Transactions of the Royal Society* 58 (1768): 35.

3 Ibid., 35, 40.

4 Ibid., 36.

5 Ibid., 45.

6 Thomas Jefferson, *Notes on the State of Virginia* (London: John Stockdale, 1787), 65–6; Barrow, *Nature's Ghosts*, 15–29.

7 M. J. S. Rudwick, *Bursting the Limits of Time: The Reconstruction of Geohistory in the Age of Revolution* (Chicago, IL: University of Chicago Press, 2005), 244.

8 Malcolm Crook, ed., *Revolutionary France: 1788–1880* (Oxford: Oxford University Press, 2002).

9 On the importance of the French Revolution for the sciences consult: Maurice Crosland, *Science under Control: The French Academy of Sciences 1795–1914* (Cambridge: Cambridge University Press, 1992); Charles Coulston Gillispie, *Science and Polity in France: The End of the Old Regime* (Princeton, NJ: Princeton University Press, 2009); Robert Fox and George Weisz, 'France: During the Long Nineteenth Century', in *Modern Science in National, Transnational, and Global Context*, ed. Hugh

Richard Slotten, Ronald L. Numbers, and David N. Livingstone, vol. 8, The Cambridge History of Science (Cambridge: Cambridge University Press, 2020), 192–216; Martin S. Staum, *Minerva's Message: Stabilizing the French Revolution* (Montreal: McGill-Queen's University Press, 1996); and Mary Ashburn Miller, *A Natural History of Revolution: Violence and Nature in the French Revolutionary Imagination, 1789–1794* (Ithaca, NY: Cornell University Press, 2011).

10 Crook, *Revolutionary France.*

11 J. P. F. Deleuze, *History and Description of the Royal Museum of Natural History: Published by Order of the Administration of That Establishment* (Paris: A. Royer, 1823).

12 For the most important history of the garden during the eighteenth century, including the revolutionary reforms, consult E. C. Spary, *Utopia's Garden: French Natural History from Old Regime to Revolution* (Chicago, IL: University of Chicago Press, 2000).

13 Ibid., 92–3, 158–221.

14 Ibid.; Dorinda Outram, 'New Spaces and Natural History', in *Cultures of Natural History*, ed. Nicholas Jardine, James A. Secord, and E. C. Spary (Cambridge: Cambridge University Press, 1996), 249–65.

15 Dorinda Outram, *Georges Cuvier: Vocation, Science, and Authority in Post-Revolutionary France* (Manchester: Manchester University Press, 1984); Dorinda Outram, 'Uncertain Legislator: Georges Cuvier's Laws of Nature in Their Intellectual Context', *Journal of the History of Biology* 19, no. 3 (1986): 323–68; Toby Appel, *The Cuvier-Geoffroy Debate: French Biology in the Decades Before Darwin* (Oxford: Oxford University Press, 1987); Outram, 'New Spaces and Natural History'; M. J. S. Rudwick, *Georges Cuvier, Fossil Bones, and Geological Catastrophes: New Translations & Interpretations of the Primary Texts* (Chicago, IL: University of Chicago Press, 1997).

16 Rudwick, *Georges Cuvier, Fossil Bones, and Geological Catastrophes*, 19; M. J. S. Rudwick, *The Meaning of Fossils: Episodes in the History of Palaeontology*, repr. (Chicago, IL: University of Chicago Press, 1985); Barrow, *Nature's Ghosts*.

17 Georges Cuvier, 'Mémoire sur les espèces d'éléphant tant vivantes que fossiles', *Académie des Sciences, Mémoire 2* (1799): 1–22. Translated

and reprinted in Rudwick, *Georges Cuvier, Fossil Bones, and Geological Catastrophes*, 13–24, 22, 24.

18 Cuvier, 1796, in Ibid., 28, 32. José M. López Piñero, 'Juan Bautista Bru (1740–1799) and the Description of the Genus Megatherium', *Journal of the History of Biology* 21, no. 1 (1988): 147–63; Helen Cowie, 'Sloth Bones and Anteater Tongues: Collecting American Nature in the Hispanic World (1750–1808)', *Atlantic Studies* 8, no. 1 (2011): 5–27.

19 Cuvier, 1798, in Rudwick, *Georges Cuvier, Fossil Bones, and Geological Catastrophes*, 36.

20 Gowan Dawson, *Show Me the Bone: Reconstructing Prehistoric Monsters in Nineteenth-Century Britain and America* (Chicago, IL: University of Chicago Press, 2016).

21 Cuvier, 6 October 1798, in Rudwick, *Georges Cuvier, Fossil Bones, and Geological Catastrophes*, 35.

22 The pterodactyl would now be regarded as a pterosaur. Cuvier, 17 November 1800, in Ibid., 53–5.

23 Cuvier, 1804, in Ibid., 71.

24 Ibid., 68–73.

25 Rembrandt Peale, *An Historical Disquisition on the Mammoth, or, Great American Incognitum, an Extinct, Immense, Carnivorous Animal Whose Fossil Remains Have Been Found in North America*, 2nd ed. (London: E. Lawrence, 1803), 88.

26 Ibid., title page, 69; Barrow, *Nature's Ghosts*, 35–8; Ralph O'Connor, *The Earth on Show: Fossils and the Poetics of Popular Science, 1802–1856* (Chicago, IL: University of Chicago Press, 2007), 31–69. After Peale's museum went into decline, most of his collection was bought by P. T. Barnum and this particular specimen, known as the Masten mastodon, ended up in Europe and is now in the collections of the State Museum of Hesse, Germany, where it can still be seen by visitors. For the most complete history of the specimen, consult Paul Semonin, *American Monster: How the Nation's First Prehistoric Creature Became a Symbol of National Identity* (New York, NY: New York University Press, 2000).

27 Mario Biagioli, *Galileo, Courtier: The Practice of Science in the Culture of Absolutism* (Chicago, IL: University of Chicago Press, 1993); Anne

Secord, 'Science in the Pub: Artisan Botanists in Early Nineteenth-Century Lancashire', *History of Science* 32 (1994): 269–315; Larry Stewart, 'Other Centres of Calculation, Or, Where the Royal Society Didn't Count: Commerce, Coffee-Houses and Natural Philosophy in Early Modern London', *British Journal for the History of Science* 32 (1999): 133–53; Sadiah Qureshi, *Peoples on Parade: Exhibitions, Empire, and Anthropology in Nineteenth-Century Britain* (Chicago, IL: University of Chicago Press, 2011).

28 Peale, *An Historical Disquisition on the Mammoth, or, Great American Incognitum*, 62.

29 O'Connor, *The Earth on Show*, 31–46.

30 Cuvier did not realize that Johann Friedrich Blumenbach's classification of the beast as a pachyderm and species name *Mammut americanum* preceded him in 1799. Blumenbach's placement of the beast in the new genus *Mammut* that year remains used, but the term 'mastodon' is no longer used as the species does not share a common ancestor with elephants.

31 Cuvier, 1806, in Rudwick, *Georges Cuvier, Fossil Bones, and Geological Catastrophes*, 96.

32 Georges Cuvier, *Recherches sur les ossemens fossiles de quadrupèdes*, 4 vols (Paris: Deterville, 1812). Cuvier used an obsolete spelling for bones, which is now usually spelled 'ossements'.

33 M. J. S. Rudwick, 'Georges Cuvier's Paper Museum of Fossil Bones', *Archives of Natural History* 27, no. 1 (2000): 51–68. Also consult Richard Owen, 'Report to the Board of Curators of the Royal College of Surgeons on the Muséum D'Anatomie Comparée in the Garden of Plants, Paris' (London: Royal College of Surgeons, n.d.), Royal College of Surgeons Archives.

34 Deleuze, *History and Description of the Royal Museum of Natural History*, 250–1.

35 In the final decade of the nineteenth century, a new gallery of palaeontology and comparative anatomy was built and explicitly organized around evolutionary theories; it retains much of its original organization to this day, with the beasts marching as they silently retrace the march of life in their deaths. In 1994 another vast gallery of evolution

was added to the site, which theatrically tells the story of nature's biodiversity. On the history and layout of the museum consult Claudine Cohen, 'Exhibiting Life History at the Paris Muséum d'Histoire Naturelle (Nineteenth–Twenty-First Centuries)', in *Museums at the Forefront of the History and Philosophy of Geology: History Made, History in the Making*, ed. G. D. Rosenberg and R. M. Clary, vol. 535, GSA Special Papers (The Geological Society of America, 2018), 117–29, https://doi.org/10.1130/2018.2535(08)

36 Outram, *Georges Cuvier*; Rudwick, *The Meaning of Fossils*; Appel, *The Cuvier-Geoffroy Debate*.

37 Roy Chapman Andrews, 'Explorations in Mongolia: A Review of the Central Asiatic Expeditions of the American Museum of Natural History', *The Geographical Journal* 69, no. 1 (1927): 1–19; Adrienne Mayor, 'The First Fossil Hunters: Dinosaurs, Mammoths, and Myth in Greek and Roman Times', in *The First Fossil Hunters* (Princeton, NJ: Princeton University Press, 2011); Adrienne Mayor, *Fossil Legends of the First Americans* (Princeton, NJ: Princeton University Press, 2013).

38 Cited in Barrow, *Nature's Ghosts*, 42; Benjamin Smith Barton, *Archaeologiae Americanae Telluris Collectanea et Specimina, or, Collections, with Specimens, for a Series of Memoirs on Certain Extinct Animals and Vegetables of North-America: Together with Facts and Conjectures Relative to the Ancient Condition of the Lands and Waters of the Continent* (Philadelphia, PA: Printed for the Author, 1814).

39 Barrow, *Nature's Ghosts*, 43; James Parkinson, *Organic Remains of a Former World: An Examination of the Mineralized Remains of the Vegetables and Animals of the Antediluvian World; Generally Termed Extraneous Fossils*, vol. 1 (London: J. Robson etc., 1804), 6–14, 8, 11, 13; Michel Goedert and Alastair Compston, 'Parkinson's Disease – the Story of an Eponym', *Nature Reviews Neurology* 14, no. 1 (2018): 57–62.

40 Cuvier hinted at the possibility for reconciliation. This was made explicit by Robert Jameson who edited Robert Kerr's translation in 1813 of the *Discours Préliminaire*. Buckland affirmed the possibility while adding arguments of his own. O'Connor, *The Earth on Show*.

41 Ibid., 51–9, 63.

42 Ibid., 71–117.

43 M. J. S. Rudwick, *Worlds Before Adam: The Reconstruction of Geohistory in the Age of Reform* (Chicago, IL: University of Chicago Press, 2008), 25–34; Tom Sharpe, *The Fossil Woman: A Life of Mary Anning* (Wimborne Minster: Dovecote Press, 2020). Mary the fossil hunter was the third daughter to bear the name after the death of two older sisters both called Mary. The monikers are from Gideon Mantell and Ludwig Leichhardt, respectively, cited in Hugh Torrens, 'Mary Anning (1799–1847) of Lyme; "the Greatest Fossilist the World Ever Knew" ', *British Journal for the History of Science* 28 (1995): 257–84.

44 Dennis R. Dean, *Gideon Mantell and the Discovery of Dinosaurs* (Cambridge: Cambridge University Press, 1999); Nicolaas A. Rupke, *Richard Owen: Biology Without Darwin*, rev. ed. (Chicago, IL: University of Chicago Press, 2009); Hugh Torrens, 'Politics and Palaeontology: Richard Owen and the Invention of Dinosaurs', in *The Complete Dinosaur*, ed. Michael K. Brett-Surman et al., 2nd ed. (Bloomington, IN: Indiana University Press, 2012).

45 William Buckland, 'Notice on the Megalosaurus or Great Fossil Lizard of Stonesfield', *Transactions of the Geological Society of London* Series 2, 1 (1824): 390–6.

46 Gideon Mantell, 'Discovery of the Bones of the Iguanodon in a Quarry of Kentish Rag (a Limestone Belonging to the Later Greensand Formation) Near Maidstone, Kent', *Edinburgh New Philosophical Journal* 18 (1834): 200–1; Gideon Mantell, *On the Structure of the Iguanodon, and on the Fauna and Flora of the Wealden Formation* (London: Royal Institution of Great Britain, 1852), https://wellcomecollection.org/works/qx9x8b4w; Dean, *Gideon Mantell and the Discovery of Dinosaurs*; Rupke, *Richard Owen*; Rudwick, *Worlds Before Adam*, 59–72.

47 Richard Owen, 'Report on British Fossil Reptiles. Part II', *Report of the Eleventh Meeting of the British Association for the Advancement of Science; Held at Plymouth in July 1841* (1842), 103.

48 Adrian J. Desmond, 'Designing the Dinosaur: Richard Owen's Response to Robert Edmond Grant', *Isis* 70 (1979): 224–34; Dean, *Gideon Mantell and the Discovery of Dinosaurs*; Torrens, 'Politics and Palaeontology'.

49 M. J. S. Rudwick, *Scenes from Deep Time: Early Pictorial Representations of the Prehistoric World* (Chicago, IL: University of Chicago Press, 1992).

50 O'Connor, *The Earth on Show*, 44.

51 For the best introduction to the work consult James A. Secord, ed., 'Introduction', in *Principles of Geology* by Charles Lyell, Penguin Classics (London; New York: Penguin Books, 1997), ix–xliii. Also, Rudwick, *Worlds Before Adam*; Rudwick, *Bursting the Limits of Time*; O'Connor, *The Earth on Show*, 163–87.

52 Charles Lyell, *Principles of Geology*, vol. 2 (London: John Murray, 1830–3), 150. Also cited and discussed in Barrow, *Nature's Ghosts*, 44–6.

53 Lyell, *Principles of Geology*, vol. 2, 162–3.

54 Richard Owen, 'Notice of a Fragment of the Femur of a Gigantic Bird of New Zealand', *Transactions of the Zoological Society* 3 (1842): 29–32.

55 Dawson, *Show Me the Bone*, 95–132.

56 Rupke, *Richard Owen*.

57 Rule to Owen, October 1839, cited in Dawson, *Show Me the Bone*, 99.

58 On Rule's full involvement, I am indebted to Ibid., 95–132.

59 Richard H. Drayton, *Nature's Government: Science, Imperial Britain, and the 'Improvement' of the World* (New Haven, CT: Yale University Press, 2000); Jim Endersby, *Imperial Nature: Joseph Hooker and the Practices of Victorian Science* (Chicago, IL: University of Chicago Press, 2008). The Tasmanian naturalist Morton Allport sent specimens of thylacines and Aboriginal Tasmanians to national institutions, learned societies, and individuals all over the world in exchange for his admittance to prestigious scientific institutions. For more on Allport's negotiations consult Jack Ashby, 'How Collections and Reputation Were Built out of Tasmanian Violence: Thylacines (*Thylacinus Cynocephalus*) and Aboriginal Remains from Morton Allport (1830–1878)', *Archives of Natural History* 50, no. 2 (2023): 244–64.

60 The islands roughly represented the Palaeozoic, Mesozoic, and Cenozoic eras. Anonymous, 'The Crystal Palace, at Sydenham', *The Illustrated London News* (7 January 1854), The Illustrated London News Historical Archive, 1842–2003; James A. Secord, 'Monsters at the

Crystal Palace', in *Models: The Third Dimension of Science*, ed. Soraya Chadarevian and Nick Hopwood (Stanford, CA: Stanford University Press, 2004), 138–9; O'Connor, *The Earth on Show*, 279–88; Dawson, *Show Me the Bone*, 168–208.

61 For a broader history, including visitor figures, consult, Jan R. Piggott, *Palace of the People: The Crystal Palace at Sydenham 1854–1936* (London: Hurst, 2004); Kate Nichols, *Greece and Rome at the Crystal Palace: Classical Sculpture and Modern Britain, 1854–1936* (Oxford: Oxford University Press, 2015).

62 For visitor figures consult, Piggott, *Palace of the People*. On the court of natural history, Qureshi, *Peoples on Parade*, 185–221.

63 Richard Vaughan, 'Hodge Upgrades Crystal Palace Park Dinosaurs to Grade I Status', *The Architects' Journal*, 7 August 2007, https://www.architectsjournal.co.uk/news/hodge-upgrades-crystal-palace-park-dinosaurs-to-grade-i-status

Chapter 2

1 Timothy D. O'Connor, 'Native American Genomic Diversity through Ancient DNA', *Cell* 175, no. 5 (2018): 1173–4; Ruth Gruhn, 'Evidence Grows that Peopling of the Americas Began More than 20,000 Years Ago', *Nature* 584, no. 7819 (2020): 47–8; Giulia Colombo et al., 'Overview of the Americas' First Peopling from a Patrilineal Perspective: New Evidence from the Southern Continent', *Genes* 13, no. 2 (2022): 220.

2 Unless otherwise indicated this history of Newfoundland settlement, colonization, and Beothuk ethnography draws heavily from James P. Howley, *The Beothucks, or Red Indians: The Aboriginal Inhabitants of Newfoundland* (Cambridge: Cambridge University Press, 1915); Ingeborg Marshall, *A History and Ethnography of the Beothuk* (Montreal: McGill-Queen's University Press, 1996); Sean T. Cadigan, *Newfoundland and Labrador: A History* (Toronto, ON: University of Toronto Press, 2009). Many of the primary sources were also collected and republished in Howley, *The Beothucks*. On Beothuk culture consult Marshall, *A History and Ethnography of the Beothuk*, 278–9, 286–8, 393–411.

3 Melanie Kuch et al., 'A Preliminary Analysis of the DNA and Diet of the Extinct Beothuk: A Systematic Approach to Ancient Human DNA', *American Journal of Physical Anthropology* 132, no. 4 (2007): 594–604; Todd J. Kristensen, 'Seasonal Bird Exploitation by Recent Indian and Beothuk Hunter-Gatherers of Newfoundland', *Canadian Journal of Archaeology/Journal Canadien d'Archéologie* 35, no. 2 (2011): 292–322.

4 George Cartwright, *A Journal of Transactions and Events, During a Residence of Nearly Sixteen Years on the Coast of Labrador. Containing Many Interesting Particulars, Both of the Country and Its Inhabitants, Not Hitherto Known*, vol. 1 (Newark [England]: Allin and Ridge, 1792), 10.

5 Howley, *The Beothucks*, 1–27; Marshall, *A History and Ethnography of the Beothuk*, 13–14.

6 Ibid., 15.

7 Marshall, *A History and Ethnography of the Beothuk*, 15.

8 Cadigan, *Newfoundland and Labrador*, 45–71. Although dated, one of the most detailed accounts of the English colony can be found in Gillian T. Cell, *English Enterprise in Newfoundland 1577–1660* (Toronto, ON: University of Toronto Press, 1969).

9 Cited in Howley, *The Beothucks*, 15.

10 Cartwright, *A Journal of Transactions and Events, During a Residence of Nearly Sixteen Years on the Coast of Labrador*, 1:6.

11 Howley, *The Beothucks*, 34; Cartwright, *A Journal of Transactions and Events, During a Residence of Nearly Sixteen Years on the Coast of Labrador*, 1:11.

12 Marshall, *A History and Ethnography of the Beothuk*, 113. For Cartwright's population estimate see Ibid., 280–1.

13 Marshall, *A History and Ethnography of the Beothuk*, 118.

14 Reprinted in Howley, *The Beothucks*, 58.

15 Ibid.

16 Marshall, *A History and Ethnography of the Beothuk*, 127.

17 Reprinted in Howley, *The Beothucks*, 70.

18 Ibid., 77.

19 Buchan's writings were not published, but extracts were reprinted in Ibid., 72–90.

20 Ibid., 89.

21 Ibid., 91–108. The daughter is mentioned in Ibid., 174. A brief census is provided in Ibid., 226.

22 Howley, *The Beothucks*, 123.

23 Ibid., 95–6, 121–6, f. 241; Marshall, *A History and Ethnography of the Beothuk*, 173–80.

24 Howley, *The Beothucks*, 172.

25 Bishop John Inglis, 'Shanawdithit, the Last of the Bœothicks', *Monthly Record of Church Missions in Connection with the Society for the Propagation of the Gospel in Foreign Parts*, 1856, Nineteenth Century UK Periodicals.

26 Howley, *The Beothucks*, 181.

27 Peyton's own testimony was recorded by J. P. Howley, and published in Ibid., 91–6.

28 Ibid., 184, 198.

29 Ibid., 186.

30 Cormack's papers appear to have been lost and were mainly unpublished. Some substantial extracts were published in Ibid., 130–68. W. E. (William Epps) Cormack, 'Account of a Journey across the Island of Newfoundland, by W. E. Cormack, Esq. in a Letter Addressed to the Right Hon. Earl Bathurst, Secretary of State for the Colonies &c. &c.,—with a Map of Mr. Cormack's Journey across the Island of Newfoundland', *Edinburgh Philosophical Journal* 10 (1824): 156–62; W. E. (William Epps) Cormack, 'Civilization of the Aborigines of Newfoundland', *Edinburgh New Philosophical Journal* 4 (1827): 205–6; W. E. (William Epps) Cormack, 'Report of Mr. W. E. Cormack's Journey in Search of the Red Indians in Newfoundland. Read Before the Boeothick Institution at St John's, Newfoundland. Communicated by Mr. Cormack', *Edinburgh New Philosophical Journal* 20 (1829): 318–29; [Cormack, William], 'Died, at St. John's, Newfoundland', *The Times* (14 September 1829).

31 For Cormack's only published notes on Shanawdithit's testimony consult Howley, *The Beothucks*, 225–30. For the drawings consult Fiona Polack, 'Reading Shanawdithit's Drawings: Transcultural Texts in the North American Colonial World', *Journal of Colonialism and Colonial*

History 14, no. 3 (2013); Nicholas Chare, 'Shanawdithit's Drawings', in *History and Art History: Looking Past Disciplines*, ed. Nicholas Chare and Mitchell B. Frank, 1st ed. (New York, NY: Routledge, 2020).

32 Marshall, *A History and Ethnography of the Beothuk*, 128.

33 Howley, *The Beothucks*, 231.

34 [Cormack, William], 'Died, at St. John's, Newfoundland'.

35 Marshall, *A History and Ethnography of the Beothuk*, 219–21.

36 [McGregor, James], 'Shaa-Naan-Dithit, or the Last of the Boëothics', *Fraser's Magazine* 13 (1836): 316.

37 T. G. B. Lloyd, 'On the "Beothucs", a Tribe of Red Indians, Supposed to Be Extinct, Which Formerly Inhabited Newfoundland', *Journal of the Anthropological Institute of Great Britain and Ireland* 4 (1875): 36; Inglis, 'Shanawdithit, the Last of the Bœothicks'.

38 Christopher Aylward, 'Historical Narrative Perspective in Howley and Speck', in *Tracing Ochre*, ed. Fiona Polack, Changing Perspectives on the Beothuk (Toronto, ON: University of Toronto Press, 2018), 220–44, https://www.jstor.org/stable/10.3138/j.ctv2fjwqbf.16

39 Franz Boas, 'Museums of Ethnology and Their Classification', *Science* 9, no. 228 (1887): 589; Franz Boas, 'The Occurrence of Similar Inventions in Areas Widely Apart', *Science* 9 (1887): 485–6.

40 A. Irving Hallowell, 'Frank Gouldsmith Speck, 1881–1950', *American Anthropologist* 53, no. 1 (3 January 1951): 67–87; Horace P. Beck, 'Frank G. Speck, 1881–1950', *Journal of American Folklore* 64, no. 254 (1951): 415–18.

41 Frank Gouldsmith Speck, *Beothuk and Micmac* (New York, NY: Museum of the American Indian, Heye Foundation, 1922), 55–70, 56.

42 Ibid., 58.

43 *The Beothuk Story* (Zamura Films, 2021), https://www.thebeothukstory.com

44 Tristan Hopper, 'Extinction of Newfoundland's "Lost People" Is a Myth, First Nations Chief Says', *National Post* (18 April 2013), https://nationalpost.com/news/canada/local-post

45 Ned Blackhawk's monumental *The Rediscovery of America* places Native peoples at the heart of five centuries of American history to show: 'Inhabited by approximately 75 million Native peoples in 1492,

the Americas were not so much discovered by Spanish colonialists as created by the generations of Spanish-Indian relations that followed.' Blackhawk's book is a powerful challenge to centuries of historical writing dependent on myths of extinction, and the systemic erasure of Native agency and power. Ned Blackhawk, *The Rediscovery of America: Native Peoples and the Unmaking of U.S. History* (New Haven, CT: Yale University Press, 2023).

46 George Busk, 'Description of Two Beothuc Skulls', *Journal of the Anthropological Institute of Great Britain and Ireland* 5 (1876): 230–3; [Flower, William Henry], 'Obituary Notice of the Late Professor Busk', *Journal of the Anthropological Institute of Great Britain and Ireland* 16 (1887): 403–8.

47 S. M. Black, I. C. L. Marshall, and A. C. Kitchener, 'The Skulls of Chief Nonosabasut and His Wife Demasduit – Beothuk of Newfoundland', *International Journal of Osteoarchaeology* 19, no. 6 (November 2009): 659–77; John Harries, 'Of Bleeding Skulls and the Postcolonial Uncanny: Bones and the Presence of Nonosabasut and Demasduit', *Journal of Material Culture* 15, no. 4 (December 2010): 403–21.

48 Alice L. Conklin, *In the Museum of Man: Race, Anthropology, and Empire in France, 1850–1950* (Ithaca, NY: Cornell University Press, 2013); Samuel J. Redman, *Bone Rooms: From Scientific Racism to Human Prehistory in Museums* (Cambridge, MA: Harvard University Press, 2016).

49 Kuch et al., 'A Preliminary Analysis of the DNA and Diet of the Extinct Beothuk'; Black, Marshall, and Kitchener, 'The Skulls of Chief Nonosabasut and His Wife Demasduit – Beothuk of Newfoundland'; Ana T. Duggan et al., 'Genetic Discontinuity between the Maritime Archaic and Beothuk Populations in Newfoundland, Canada', *Current Biology* 27, no. 20 (23 October 2017): 3149–3156.e11; Ashley Collier and Steven M. Carr, 'On the Persistence and Detectability of Ancient Beothuk Mitochondrial DNA Genomes in Living First Nations Peoples', *Mitochondrial DNA Part A* 30, no. 1 (2 January 2019): 68–74; Steven M. Carr, 'Evidence for the Persistence of Ancient Beothuk and Maritime Archaic Mitochondrial DNA Genome Lineages Among Modern Native American Peoples', *Genome* 63, no. 7 (July 2020): 349–55.

50 Kuch et al., 'A Preliminary Analysis of the DNA and Diet of the Extinct Beothuk'.

51 Duggan et al., 'Genetic Discontinuity between the Maritime Archaic and Beothuk Populations in Newfoundland, Canada'.

52 Carr, 'Evidence for the Persistence of Ancient Beothuk and Maritime Archaic Mitochondrial DNA Genome Lineages Among Modern Native American Peoples'; Ibid.; Holly McKenzie, 'Miawpukek First Nation to Study Genetic Links with Ancient Beothuk', *CBC News*, 18 December 2019, https://www.cbc.ca/news/canada/newfoundland-labrador/dna-testing-beothuk-1.5400540; Anonymous, 'Thought to Be Extinct, Beothuk DNA Is Present in Living Families, Genetics Researcher Finds', *CBC News*, 8 May 2020, https://web.archive.org/web/20230313211303/https://www.cbc.ca/news/canada/newfoundland-labrador/beothuk-dna-steven-carr-1.5559913

53 All claims about tracing ancestry with reference to specific ethnicities or Nation have been removed from the website. Compare the archived version of their homepage with the current one at Anonymous, 'Accu-Metrics – DNA Testing', *Accu-Metrics.Com*, n.d., https://web.archive.org/web/20131013223353/http://www.accu-metrics.com/dna-tests; Accu-metrics, 'Genetic', *Accu-Metrics.Com*, n.d., https://www.accu-metrics.com/c/genetic. These changes were made after the company's results were dismissed as bogus: Chris O' Neill-Yates, CBC News, 'DNA Test Claiming Woman Is Member of Extinct Beothuk First Nation Called Bogus | CBC News', *CBC* (27 January 2017), https://www.cbc.ca/news/canada/newfoundland-labrador/beothuk-dna-ancestry-genetics-1.3953668

54 Tara Bradbury, 'Woman Says DNA Test Proves She Is Beothuk', *Saltwire* (26 January 2017), https://web.archive.org/web/20230515113912/https://www.saltwire.com/newfoundland-labrador/news/local/woman-says-dna-test-proves-she-is-beothuk-16608

55 CBC News, 'DNA Test Claiming Woman Is Member of Extinct Beothuk First Nation Called Bogus | CBC News'; Chris O' Neill-Yates, 'Company's Test for Beothuk DNA Called Bogus by Geneticists', *CBC News* (27 January 2017), https://web.archive.

org/web/20221206195417/https://www.cbc.ca/news/canada/newfoundland-labrador/beothuk-dna-ancestry-genetics-1.3953668

56 [Reynolds-Boyce, Carol], 'Beothuk First Nation Tribe of Canada and North America Reservation INC', n.d., https://www.facebook.com/iambeothuk

57 Jorge Barrera, 'Lab in Dog DNA Debacle Used Phoney Facebook Identity to Recruit Sixties Scoop, Motherisk Plaintiffs', *CBC* (15 September 2018), https://www.cbc.ca/news/indigenous/lab-in-dog-dna-debacle-used-phoney-facebook-identity-to-recruit-sixties-scoop-motherisk-plaintiffs-1.4815401; Jorge Barrera and Tiffany Foxcroft, 'Lab's DNA Results Say This Chihuahua Has 20% Indigenous Ancestry' (13 June 2018), https://newsinteractives.cbc.ca/longform/dna-ancestry-test

58 Eric Y. Durand et al., 'Ancestry Composition: A Novel, Efficient Pipeline for Ancestry Deconvolution' (bioRxiv, 18 October 2014).

59 Kimberly TallBear, *Native American DNA: Tribal Belonging and the False Promise of Genetic Science* (Minneapolis, MN: University of Minnesota Press, 2013).

60 Scottish Parliament, 'Official Report: Meeting of the Parliament' (17 June 2015), 17.

61 Maureen Googoo, 'Miawpukek Chief Leads Effort to Have Beothuk Skulls Returned from Scottish Museum', *Ku'ku'kwes News* (13 July 2017), https://kukukwes.com/2017/07/13/miawpukek-chief-leads-effort-to-have-beothuk-skulls-returned-from-scottish-museum; Anonymous, 'No Formal Request for Return of Native American Skulls', *BBC News* (2017), sec. Scotland, https://www.bbc.com/news/uk-scotland-40131082; Anonymous, 'Museum to Return First Nation Skulls', *BBC News* (2019), https://www.bbc.com/news/uk-scotland-edinburgh-east-fife-46952065; Anonymous, 'National Museum of Scotland to Reach Decision on Return of Beothuk Remains to Newfoundland', *The Herald* (20 January 2019), https://www.heraldscotland.com/news/17371218.will-returned-national-museum-scotland-reach-decision-return-beothuk-remains-newfoundland; Mark Quinn, 'Beothuk Remains Returned to

Newfoundland after 191 Years in Scotland', *CBC News* (12 March 2020), https://web.archive.org/web/20221119054010/https://www.cbc.ca/news/canada/newfoundland-labrador/beothuk-remains-returned-nl-1.5494373

62 Anonymous, '"Bring Them Home and Put Them to Rest": How Museums Are Working with Indigenous Communities to Repatriate Human Remains', *The Globe and Mail*, 9 August 2019, https://web.archive.org/web/20221103072226/https://www.theglobeandmail.com/arts/art-and-architecture/article-repatriating-indigenous-remains-key-to-preserve-privacy-of-communities

63 Gerald Robert Vizenor, *Manifest Manners: Postindian Warriors of Survivance* (Hanover, ON: Wesleyan University Press, 1994); Gerald Robert Vizenor, *Fugitive Poses: Native American Indian Scenes of Absence and Presence*, The Abraham Lincoln Lecture Series (Lincoln, NE: University of Nebraska Press, 1998).

64 UK Government, 'Human Tissue Act 2004' (2004), https://www.legislation.gov.uk/ukpga/2004/30/contents; David Price, 'The Human Tissue Act 2004', *Modern Law Review* 68, no. 5 (2005): 798–821.

65 Parks Canada, 'Shanawdithit National Historic Person', n.d., https://www.pc.gc.ca/apps/dfhd/page_nhs_eng.aspx?id=1936

66 [James Cowles] Prichard, 'On the Extinction of Human Races', *Edinburgh New Philosophical Journal* 28 (1839): 166–70.

67 Even in the twentieth century, scientific papers and imperial histories were written in the full conviction that Aboriginal Tasmanians were completely exterminated, with many characterizing the loss as an imperial genocide. Claims of total extinction are founded on European notions of kinship that ignore Indigenous accounts of their own descent. For decades, Aboriginal Tasmanians have been forced to prove that they have not died out and have continued attachments to their ancestral lands. Rebe Taylor, 'Genocide, Extinction and Aboriginal Self-Determination in Tasmanian Historiography: Genocide, Extinction and Aboriginal Self-Determination', *History Compass* 11, no. 6 (2013): 405–18; Lawson, *The Last Man*.

Chapter 3

1 Jefferson, *Notes on the State of Virginia*, 153–5.

2 Christian B. Keller, 'Philanthropy Betrayed: Thomas Jefferson, the Louisiana Purchase, and the Origins of Federal Indian Removal Policy', *Proceedings of the American Philosophical Society* 144 (2000): 43.

3 Ronald Lindley Meek, *Social Science and the Ignoble Savage* (Cambridge: Cambridge University Press, 1976).

4 Keller, 'Philanthropy Betrayed', 53, 49.

5 James Monroe, cited in Ibid., 50.

6 Blackhawk, *The Rediscovery of America*, 180, 199. For more on Federal Indian Policy in this period, consult Ibid., 176–247; Claudio Saunt, *Unworthy Republic: The Dispossession of Native Americans and the Road to Indian Territory* (New York, NY: W. W. Norton & Co., Inc., 2021); Christina Snyder, *Great Crossings: Indians, Settlers, and Slaves in the Age of Jackson* (Oxford, England; New York, NY: Oxford University Press, 2017); Ronald N. Satz, *American Indian Policy in the Jacksonian Era* (Norman, OK: University of Oklahoma Press, 2002); United States, 'An Act to Provide for an Exchange of Lands with the Indians Residing in Any of the States or Territories, and for Their Removal West of the River Mississippi' (1830).

7 Andrew Jackson, 'First Annual Message, December 8, 1829', in *Messages of Gen. Andrew Jackson: With a Short Sketch of His Life*, ed. N. H. Concord (J. F. Brown and W. White, 1837), 61.

8 Francis Paul Prucha, ed., 'Senator Theodore Freylinghuysen on Indian Removal, April 9, 1830', in *Documents of United States Indian Policy*, 3rd ed. (Lincoln, NE: University of Nebraska Press, 2000), 49–52.

9 Snyder, *Great Crossings*; R. Douglas Hurt, *The Indian Frontier, 1763–1846* (Albuquerque, NM: University of New Mexico Press, 2002); Satz, *American Indian Policy in the Jacksonian Era*.

10 Brian W. Dippie, *The Vanishing American: White Attitudes and US Indian Policy* (Middletown, CT: Wesleyan University Press, 1982).

11 'Indian Removal Act, 28 May 1830', reprinted in Francis Paul Prucha, ed., *Documents of United States Indian Policy*, 52–3.

12 On the development of reservations consult Joel R. Hyer, *We Are Not Savages: Native Americans in Southern California and the Pala Reservation, 1840–1920* (East Lansing, MI: Michigan State University Press, 2001); George Harwood Phillips, *Indians and Indian Agents: The Origins of the Reservation System in California, 1849–1852* (Norman, OK: University of Oklahoma Press, 1997); Brad Asher, *Beyond the Reservation: Indians, Settlers, and the Law in Washington Territory, 1853–1889* (Norman, OK: University of Oklahoma Press, 1999); Richard John Perry, *Apache Reservation: Indigenous Peoples and the American State* (Austin, TX: University of Texas Press, 1993); David J. Wishart, *An Unspeakable Sadness: The Dispossession of the Nebraska Indians* (Lincoln, NE: University of Nebraska Press, 1994).

13 Blackhawk, *The Rediscovery of America*; Ned Blackhawk, *Violence over the Land: Indians and Empires in the Early American West* (Cambridge, MA: Harvard University Press, 2006); Benjamin Madley, *An American Genocide: The United States and the California Indian Catastrophe, 1846–1873* (New Haven, CT: Yale University Press, 2016).

14 Phillips, *Indians and Indian Agents*, 4.

15 Donald Chaput, 'Generals, Indian Agents, Politicians: The Doolittle Survey of 1865', *The Western Historical Quarterly* 3 (1972): 269–82; Blackhawk, *The Rediscovery of America*; Blackhawk, *Violence over the Land*.

16 United States, *Condition of the Indian Tribes: Report of the Joint Special Committee, Appointed Under Joint Resolution of March 3, 1865: With an Appendix* (Washington, DC: Government Printing Office, 1867), 428.

17 Ibid., 472, 440.

18 Ibid., 7.

19 Anthony F. C. Wallace, *Jefferson and the Indians: The Tragic Fate of the First Americans* (Cambridge, MA: Belknap Press, 1999).

20 Dippie, *The Vanishing American*; Philip Burnham, *Indian Country, God's Country: Native Americans and the National Parks* (Washington, DC: Island Press, 2000).

21 Samuel Lyman Tyler, *A History of Indian Policy* (Washington, DC: Bureau of Indian Affairs, 1973), 23.

22 Bryan Newland, 'Federal Indian Boarding School Initiative Investigative Report' (Department of the Interior, United States, May 2022).

23 Richard Henry Pratt, 'The Advantages of Mingling Indians with the Whites', in *Proceedings of the National Conference of Charities and Correction, at the Nineteenth Annual Session Held in Denver, Col., June 23–29, 1892* (Boston, MA: Geo. H. Ellis, 1892), 46.

24 Margaret D. Jacobs, *White Mother to a Dark Race: Settler Colonialism, Maternalism, and the Removal of Indigenous Children in the American West and Australia, 1880–1940* (Lincoln, NE: University of Nebraska Press, 2009), 28, https://hdl-handle-net.manchester.idm.oclc.org/2027/heb08861.0001.001

25 Newland, 'Federal Indian Boarding School Initiative Investigative Report'.

26 Truth and Reconciliation Commission of Canada, *Canada's Residential Schools: Reconciliation: The Final Report of the Truth and Reconciliation Commission of Canada, Volume 6* (Montreal: McGill-Queen's University Press, 2016); Newland, 'Federal Indian Boarding School Initiative Investigative Report'.

27 This account of Catlin's travels draws upon Benita Eisler, *The Red Man's Bones: George Catlin, Artist and Showman* (London: W. W. Norton & Co., 2013); Kate Flint, *The Transatlantic Indian, 1776–1930* (Princeton, NJ: Princeton University Press, 2008); John Hausdoerffer, *Catlin's Lament: Indians, Manifest Destiny, and the Ethics of Nature* (Lawrence, KS: University Press of Kansas, 2009).

28 George Catlin, *Life Amongst the Indians: A Book for Youth* (London: Sampson Low, Son & Co., 1861), 14.

29 Flint, *The Transatlantic Indian, 1776–1930*; Qureshi, *Peoples on Parade*.

30 Qureshi, *Peoples on Parade*.

31 George Catlin, *Letters and Notes on the Manners, Customs, and Condition of the North American Indians*, vol. 1 (London: By the Author, 1841), 262.

32 My discussion draws heavily from Mark David Spence, *Dispossessing the Wilderness: Indian Removal and the Making of the National Parks* (New York, NY, and Oxford: Oxford University Press, 2000).

33 Burnham, *Indian Country, God's Country*, 20.

34 Ibid., 19.

35 Ibid., 37.

36 Robert H. Keller and Michael F. Turek, *American Indians and National Parks* (Tucson, AZ: University of Arizona Press, 2005); Spence, *Dispossessing the Wilderness*; Burnham, *Indian Country, God's Country.*

37 Keller and Turek, *American Indians and National Parks*, 21.

38 Ibid., 22.

39 Burnham, *Indian Country, God's Country.*

40 Spence, *Dispossessing the Wilderness*, 71–82, at 71; Keller and Turek, *American Indians and National Parks*, 56–64.

41 William Cronon, 'The Trouble with Wilderness: Or, Getting Back to the Wrong Nature', *Environmental History* 1 (1996): 7–28.

42 Spence, *Dispossessing the Wilderness*, 54–6.

43 Barrow, *Nature's Ghosts*; Spence, *Dispossessing the Wilderness*.

44 Spence, *Dispossessing the Wilderness*, 55–70.

45 Ibid., 62–70.

46 Daniel Brockington, James Igoe et al., 'Eviction for Conservation: A Global Overview', *Conservation and Society* 4 (2006): 424–70. It should be added that the numbers of people evicted in these reports are often omitted; however, where included they ranged from 'five families . . . to tens of thousands of people', p. 437.

47 Catherine Hall et al., *Legacies of British Slave-Ownership: Colonial Slavery and the Formation of Victorian Britain* (Cambridge: Cambridge University Press, 2014); C. Hall, 'Gendering Property, Racing Capital', *History Workshop Journal* 78, no. 1 (1 October 2014): 22–38.

48 Cited in James Heartfield, *The Aborigines' Protection Society: Humanitarian Imperialism in Australia, New Zealand, Fiji, Canada, South Africa, and the Congo, 1836–1909* (London: Hurst, 2011), 9.

49 Aborigines' Protection Society, 'Report of the Parliamentary Select Committee on Aboriginal Tribes (British Settlements)', 1837, ix.

50 Ibid., 5. The remark drew directly from the writings of Captain Buchan about the Beothuk (consult chapter 2).

51 Ibid., 7, 10, 11.

52 Ibid., 5.

53 Theodor Waitz, *Introduction to Anthropology*, trans. J. Frederick Collingwood (London: Longman, Green, Longman and Roberts, 1863), 351.

54 Ibid. For broader accounts of anti-colonial writing in this period consult Priyamvada Gopal, *Insurgent Empire: Anticolonial Resistance and British Dissent* (London: Verso, 2019).

55 Jacob W. Gruber, 'Ethnographic Salvage and the Shaping of Anthropology', *American Anthropologist* 72, no. 6 (1970): 1289–99.

56 Richard Lee, 'The Extinction of Races', *Journal of the Anthropological Society of London*, vol. 2 (1864): xcv.

57 T. Bendyshe, 'On the Extinction of Races', *Journal of the Anthropological Society of London*, vol. 2 (1864): xcix; Steven Shapin and Simon Schaffer, *Leviathan and the Air-Pump: Hobbes, Boyle, and the Experimental Life* (Princeton, NJ: Princeton University Press, 1985).

58 Charles Darwin, *On the Origin of Species by Means of Natural Selection, or the Preservation of Favoured Races in the Struggle for Life* (London: John Murray, 1859), 488.

59 Alfred R. Wallace, 'The Origin of Human Races and the Antiquity of Man Deduced from the Theory of Natural Selection', *Journal of the Anthropological Society of London*, vol. 2 (1864): clxiv–clxv, clxviii.

60 Ibid.

61 Charles Darwin, *The Descent of Man, and Selection in Relation to Sex*, vol. 1 (London: John Murray, 1871), 160.

62 Ibid., 238.

63 Ibid.

64 Anonymous, 'Primitive Races within the British Empire: A Problem in Adaptation', *Nature* 113, no. 2850 (1924): 846.

65 Raphaël Lemkin, 'Tasmania', *Patterns of Prejudice* 39, no. 2 (2005): 170–96; Ann Curthoys, 'Raphaël Lemkin's "Tasmania": An Introduction', *Patterns of Prejudice* 39, no. 2 (2005): 162–9; A. Dirk Moses, 'Raphael Lemkin, Culture, and the Concept of Genocide', in *The Oxford Handbook of Genocide Studies*, ed. Donald Bloxham and A. Dirk Moses (Oxford: Oxford University Press, 2010), 19–41.

66 Raphaël Lemkin, 'Genocide – A Modern Crime', *Free World* (April 1945).

67 United Nations, 'Convention on the Prevention and Punishment of the Crime of Genocide' (1948).

68 Anonymous, 'CTUIR's Sams Honored, Thankful after Historic Confirmation for National Park Service Director Position – Confederated Umatilla Journal', *Confederated Umatilla Journal* (19 November 2021), https://cuj.ctuir.org/2021/11/4690; Aaron McDade, 'First Native American National Park Service Director Unanimously Confirmed', *Newsweek* (19 November 2021), sec. News, https://www.newsweek.com/senate-unanimously-confirms-first-native-american-leader-national-park-service-1651552

69 David Sepkoski characterizes this view as the first 'extinction imaginary' of many that have framed extinction within the modern world through a 'co-construction of scientific and cultural values'. Sepkoski, *Catastrophic Thinking*, 6.

70 Alexander Koch et al., 'Earth System Impacts of the European Arrival and Great Dying in the Americas after 1492', *Quaternary Science Reviews* 207 (March 2019): 13–36; Alexander Koch et al., 'European Colonisation of the Americas Killed 10% of World Population and Caused Global Cooling', *The Conversation* (31 January 2019), http://theconversation.com/european-colonisation-of-the-americas-killed-10-of-world-population-and-caused-global-cooling-110549

71 TallBear, *Native American DNA*.

72 Ashifa Kassam, 'Sinixt First Nation Wins Recognition in Canada Decades after "Extinction"', *The Guardian* (30 March 2017), sec. World news, https://www.theguardian.com/world/2017/mar/30/canada-sinixt-first-nation-extinct-recognition; Sinixt Nation, 'Not Extinct', n.d., https://keepingthesinixtway.ca

Chapter 4

1 Handbill advertising an exhibition of a 'Human Fossil', 1840, Geological Society of London, LDGSL/547, image 10-03. The text of the handbill was reproduced almost entirely in newspaper advertisements such as Anonymous, 'Human Fossil, Alleged to Be Ante-Diluvian', *The Colonist* (7 November 1840); Anonymous, 'EXHIBITION of a HUMAN FOSSIL', *Morning Post* (9 June 1840).

2 William Buckland, note written on a promotional handbill for the exhibition, cited in Francis Buckland, *Curiosities of Natural History*, 4th ed. (New York: Rudd & Carleton, 1860), 104.

3 This account of Linnaean taxonomy draws from Lisbet Koerner, 'Carl Linnaeus in His Time and Place', in *Cultures of Natural History*, ed. Nicholas Jardine, James A. Secord, and E. C. Spary (Cambridge: Cambridge University Press, 1996), 145–62; Peter Harrison, 'Linnaeus as a Second Adam? Taxonomy and the Religious Vocation', *Zygon®* 44, no. 4 (2009): 879–93; Staffan Müller-Wille and Isabelle Charmantier, 'Natural History and Information Overload: The Case of Linnaeus', *Studies in History and Philosophy of Science Part C: Studies in History and Philosophy of Biological and Biomedical Sciences*, Data-Driven Research in the Biological and Biomedical Sciences, 43, no. 1 (2012): 4–15; S. Müller-Wille, 'Systems and How Linnaeus Looked at Them in Retrospect', *Annals of Science* 70, no. 3 (2013): 305–17.

4 Consult the forthcoming book by Meleisa Ono-George, *My Name Is Amelia Newsham: Science, Art and the Making of Race* (Viking, forthcoming). Also consult Christina Skott, 'Linnaeus and the Troglodyte: Early European Encounters with the Malay World and the Natural History of Man', *Indonesia and the Malay World* 42, no. 123 (4 May 2014): 141–69; Christina Skott, 'Human Taxonomies: Carl Linnaeus, Swedish Travel in Asia and the Classification of Man', *Itinerario* 43, no. 2 (2019): 218–42.

5 Skott, 'Linnaeus and the Troglodyte'; Skott, 'Human Taxonomies'; David Notton and Chris Stringer, 'Who Is the Type of Homo Sapiens?', *International Commission on Zoological Nomenclature*, accessed 3 April 2024, http://iczn.org/content/who-type-homo-sapiens; Gunnar Broberg, 'Homo Sapiens', in *The Man Who Organized Nature* (Princeton, NJ: Princeton University Press, 2023), 294–300. On earlier histories of being human consult Surekha Davies, *Renaissance Ethnography and the Invention of the Human: New Worlds, Maps and Monsters* (Cambridge: Cambridge University Press, 2016).

6 David N. Livingstone, *Adam's Ancestors: Race, Religion, and the Politics of Human Origins* (place Johns Hopkins University Press, 2008).

7 Nancy Stepan, *The Idea of Race in Science: Great Britain, 1800–1960* (Hamden, CT: Archon Books, 1982); Hannah Franziska Augstein, *James Cowles Prichard's Anthropology: Remaking the Science of Man in the Early Nineteenth Century* (Amsterdam, GA: Rodopi, 1999); Chris Manias, *Race, Science, and the Nation: Reconstructing the Ancient Past in Britain, France and Germany* (London: Routledge, 2013); Efram Sera-Shriar, *The Making of British Anthropology, 1813–1871* (Pittsburgh, PA: Pickering & Chatto, 2013).

8 Respectively, Japheth in Genesis 10:2–5, Ham in Genesis 10:6–20 and Shem in Genesis 10:21–30. For an excellent guide to the importance of Biblical ideas of race consult Colin Kidd, *The Forging of Races: Race and Scripture in the Protestant Atlantic World, 1600–2000* (Cambridge: Cambridge University Press, 2006).

9 Peter Salway, *A History of Roman Britain* (Oxford: Oxford University Press, 1997); Richard Hingley, *Conquering the Ocean: The Roman Invasion of Britain* (New York, NY: Oxford University Press, 2022).

10 The literature on human antiquity in this period is growing. The best overviews remain Rudwick, *Worlds Before Adam*; A. Bowdoin Van Riper, *Men Among the Mammoths: Victorian Science and the Discovery of Human Prehistory* (Chicago, IL: University of Chicago Press, 1993); Manias, *Race, Science, and the Nation*; Marianne Sommer, *Bones and Ochre: The Curious Afterlife of the Red Lady of Paviland* (Cambridge, MA: Harvard University Press, 2007).

11 The naturalist Michele Mercati first suggested they were stone tools in the sixteenth century, but his ideas remained unpublished until discovered in his manuscripts after his death in 1593. Matthew R. Goodrum, 'The Meaning of Ceraunia: Archaeology, Natural History and the Interpretation of Prehistoric Stone Artefacts in the Eighteenth Century', *The British Journal for the History of Science* 35 (2002): 255–69; Matthew R. Goodrum, 'Questioning Thunderstones and Arrowheads: The Problem of Recognizing and Interpreting Stone Artifacts in the Seventeenth Century', *Early Science and Medicine* 13 (2008): 482–508; Matthew R. Goodrum, 'Recovering the Vestiges of Primeval Europe: Archaeology and the Significance of Stone Implements, 1750–1800', *Journal of the History of Ideas* 72 (2011): 51–74.

12 Marianne Sommer, '"An Amusing Account of a Cave in Wales": William Buckland (1784–1856) and the Red Lady of Paviland', *The British Journal for the History of Science* 37, no. 1 (2004): 53–74; Sommer, *Bones and Ochre*.

13 Rudwick, *Worlds Before Adam*, 228–32.

14 William Benjamin Carpenter, 'On the Fossil Human Jawbone Recently Discovered in the Gravel Near Abbeville', *Proceedings of the Royal Society of London* 12 (1863): 524–9; Rudwick, *Worlds Before Adam*, 407–22; Van Riper, *Men Among the Mammoths*, 62–73.

15 Peter Rowley-Conwy, *From Genesis to Prehistory: The Archaeological Three Age System and its Contested Reception in Denmark, Britain, and Ireland* (Oxford: Oxford University Press, 2007).

16 Adopted relatively quickly in Scandinavia, the Three Age system was also promoted by J. J. A. Worsaae as he travelled between London, Edinburgh and Dublin from 1846 to 1847. Wilson probably learned of the term from his friend Peter Andreas Munch. On the development of the Three Age system consult Ibid.; Peter Rowley-Conwy, 'The Concept of Prehistory and the Invention of the Terms "Prehistoric" and "Prehistorian": The Scandinavian Origin, 1833–1850', *European Journal of Archaeology* 9, no. 1 (2006): 103–30. On Daniel Wilson's importance also consult Alice B. Kehoe, 'The Invention of Prehistory', *Current Anthropology* 32 (1991): 467–76.

17 The discovery of the Neanderthal bones is well rehearsed in the literature. For the best summary of the circumstances and contested meanings of the bones refer to Paige Madison, 'The Most Brutal of Human Skulls: Measuring and Knowing the First Neanderthal', *The British Journal for the History of Science* 49, no. 03 (2016): 411–32; Paige Madison, 'Characterized by Darkness: Reconsidering the Origins of the Brutish Neanderthal', *Journal of the History of Biology*, 2020.

18 Charles Lyell, 'Introductory Address by the President, Sir C. Lyell. On the Occurrence of Works of Human Art in Post-Pliocene Deposits', *Report of the Twenty-Ninth Meeting of the British Association for the Advancement of Science; Held at Aberdeen in September 1859*, 1860, 93–5; Van Riper, *Men Among the Mammoths*.

19 Lyell, 'Introductory Address', 93.

20 Charles Darwin to Joseph Dalton Hooker, 11 January 1844, MS DAR 114: 3, Darwin Correspondence Project, University Library, Cambridge.

21 Adrian J. Desmond, *The Politics of Evolution: Morphology, Medicine, and Reform in Radical London*, Science and its Conceptual Foundations (Chicago, IL: University of Chicago Press, 1989).

22 The most authoritative and magisterial account of the publication and reception of this bestseller remains James A. Secord, *Victorian Sensation: The Extraordinary Publication, Reception, and Secret Authorship of Vestiges of the Natural History of Creation* (Chicago, IL: University of Chicago Press, 2003).

23 Peter C. Kjærgaard, '"Hurrah for the Missing Link!": A History of Apes, Ancestors and a Crucial Piece of Evidence', *Notes and Records of the Royal Society* 65 (2011): 83–98.

24 S. Schaaffhausen and George Busk, 'On the Crania of the Most Ancient Races of Man. With Remarks, and Original Figures, Taken from a Cast of the Neanderthal Cranium', *Natural History Review* 1 (1861): 155–76.

25 Ibid., 160.

26 Ibid., 162.

27 Ibid., 163, 165.

28 Ibid., 172.

29 Stephen Jay Gould, *The Mismeasure of Man* (New York: W. W. Norton, 1981).

30 David Bindman, *Ape to Apollo: Aesthetics and the Idea of Race in the 18th Century* (Ithaca, NY: Cornell University Press, 2002). On racialization more broadly during the period, consult Roxann Wheeler, *The Complexion of Race: Categories of Difference in Eighteenth-Century British Culture* (Philadelphia, PA: University of Pennsylvania Press, 2000).

31 Formally the skull types are: long and narrow, or dolichocephalic; oval, or mesaticephalic; and brachycephalic or short and broad. Anders Retzius and William Daniel Moore, 'A Glance at the Present State of Ethnology, with Reference to the Form of the Skull', *The British and Foreign Medico-Chirurgical Review* 26, no. 51 (1860): 215–30; Eva Åhrén, 'Figuring Things Out: Visualizations in the Work of

Swedish Anatomists Anders and Gustaf Retzius, 1829–1921', *Nuncius* 32, no. 1 (2017): 166–211; Rowley-Conwy, *From Genesis to Prehistory: The Archaeological Three Age System and its Contested Reception in Denmark, Britain, and Ireland*, 63, 120. The best-known exploration of the legacies of the cephalic index remains Gould, *The Mismeasure of Man*. For more recent explorations of craniometry and the collection of skulls consult Ann Fabian, *The Skull Collectors: Race, Science, and America's Unburied Dead* (Chicago, IL: University of Chicago Press, 2010).

32 Thomas Henry Huxley, *Evidence as to Man's Place in Nature* (London: Williams and Norgate, 1863), 129.

33 Ibid., 155–6.

34 Despite King's casual aside, the name stands according to scientific conventions of priority. William King, 'The Reputed Fossil Man of the Neanderthal', *Quarterly Journal of Science* 1 (1864): 96.

35 Ibid., 93, 96. Also consult William King, 'The Neanderthal Skull', *Anthropological Review* 1 (1863): 393–4. On imperial encounters with the Andaman Islands consult C. Wintle, 'Model Subjects: Representations of the Andaman Islands at the Colonial and Indian Exhibition, 1886', *History Workshop Journal* 67, no. 1 (1 March 2009): 194–207; Clare Anderson, Madhumita Mazumdar, and Vishvajit Pandya, *New Histories of the Andaman Islands: Landscape, Place and Identity in the Bay of Bengal, 1790–2012* (Cambridge: Cambridge University Press, 2016).

36 King, 'The Reputed Fossil Man of the Neanderthal', 96. Also consult Madison, 'Characterized by Darkness'.

37 This history of the Gibraltar skull draws from Alex Menez, 'The Gibraltar Skull: Early History, 1848–1868', *Archives of Natural History* 45 (2018): 92–110; Alex Menez, 'Custodian of the Gibraltar Skull: The History of the Gibraltar Scientific Society', *Earth Sciences History* 37, no. 1 (2018): 34–62.

38 George Busk, 'Pithecoid Priscan Man from Gibraltar', *The Reader. A Review of Literature, Science, and Art* 4 (1864): 110. In 1868 the Gibraltar skull was presented to the Royal College of Surgeons and ultimately transferred to the Natural History Museum where it remains.

39 In 1936, Charles Fraipoint freshly examined the skulls from Engis cave. Fraipoint's research led to Schmerling being recognized as the

first person to discover Neanderthal remains in 1829. Anonymous, 'Research Items: Fossil Men of Engis', *Nature* 138, no. 3491 (1936): 553.

40 The problem of a singular specimen was recognized by later writers such as William Johnson Sollas, 'On the Cranial and Facial Characters of the Neandertal Race', *Philosophical Transactions of the Royal Society of London. Series B, Containing Papers of a Biological Character* 199 (1908): 281.

41 The best analysis of this is Madison, 'The Most Brutal of Human Skulls'.

42 John Lubbock, 'The Early Condition of Man', *Anthropological Review* (1868), 337.

43 Anonymous, 'Notes on the Antiquity of Man', *Anthropological Review* 1 (1863): 61.

44 Wheeler, *The Complexion of Race.*

45 Stepan, *The Idea of Race in Science*; Seymour Drescher, 'The Ending of the Slave Trade and the Evolution of European Scientific Racism', *Social Science History* 14, no. 3 (1990): 415.

46 Van Riper, *Men Among the Mammoths*; Rudwick, *Worlds Before Adam.*

47 Lubbock collected the wasp from the Spanish Pyrenees and donated the insect to the Natural History Museum in London in 1873, where she remains. The wasp's passing was commemorated in *Nature*, and a local newspaper: Anonymous, 'Notes', *Nature* 7, no. 177 (1873): 391; Anonymous, 'Sir John Lubbock's Pet Wasp', *Morpeth Herald*, 8 October 1898.

48 Charles Lyell, *The Geological Evidences of the Antiquity of Man with Remarks on Theories of the Origin of Species by Variation*, vol. 1 (London: John Murray, 1863); John Lubbock, *Pre-Historic Times: As Illustrated by Ancient Remains, and the Manners and Customs of Modern Savages* (London: Williams and Norgate, 1865). On Lubbock's reception consult Clive Gamble and Theodora Moutsiou, 'The Time Revolution of 1859 and the Stratification of the Primeval Mind', *Notes and Records of the Royal Society* 65 (2011): 43–63.

49 Darwin, *The Descent of Man, and Selection in Relation to Sex*, vol. 1, 3.

50 Francis Palgrave, *The History of Normandy and of England*, vol. 1 (London: John W. Parker & Sons, 1851–64), 469–70.

51 Adelene Buckland and Sadiah Qureshi, eds, *Time Travelers: Victorian Encounters with Time and History* (Chicago, IL: University of Chicago Press, 2020).

52 Lubbock, *Pre-Historic Times*, 336.

53 Ibid., 335–91, 392–439, 440–72.

54 Lubbock, 'The Early Condition of Man', 333.

55 Chris Manias, 'The Problematic Construction of "Palaeolithic Man": The Old Stone Age and the Difficulties of the Comparative Method, 1859–1914', *Studies in History and Philosophy of Science Part C: Studies in History and Philosophy of Biological and Biomedical Sciences* (2015).

56 Lubbock, *Pre-Historic Times*; William Boyd Dawkins, *Early Man in Britain and His Place in the Tertiary Period* (London: Macmillan and Co., 1880); Manias, 'The Problematic Construction of "Palaeolithic Man"'.

57 Anonymous, 'Notes on the Antiquity of Man', 106.

58 Lubbock, *Pre-Historic Times*, 99.

59 Anonymous, 'The French Association at Havre', *Nature* 16, no. 410 (1877): 384.

60 Dawkins, *Early Man in Britain and His Place in the Tertiary Period*, 243.

61 Ibid. Accounts of conquest and extermination are striking, but we must remember that displacement, intermingling or co-existence were all recognized responses to prehistoric interethnic encounters. Chris Manias, '"Our Iberian Forefathers": The Deep Past and Racial Stratification of British Civilization, 1850–1914', *Journal of British Studies* 51 (2012): 910–35; Simon John Cook, 'The Making of the English: English History, British Identity, Aryan Villages, 1870–1914', *Journal of the History of Ideas* 75, no. 4 (2014): 629–49.

62 On the development of the typological system and foundation of the Pitt Rivers Museum in Oxford consult B. A. L. Cranstone, 'The Pitt Rivers Museum: Past, Present and Future', *Newsletter (Museum Ethnographers Group)* (1984), 1–8; William Chapman, 'The Organizational Context in the History of Archaeology: Pitt Rivers and Other British Archaeologists in the 1860s', *The Antiquaries Journal* 69, no. 01 (March 1989): 23–42; Alison Petch, 'Collecting Immortality: The Field Collectors Who Contributed to the Pitt Rivers Museum, Oxford', *Journal of*

Museum Ethnography 16 (2003): 127–39; Alison Petch, 'A Typology of Benefactors: The Relationships of Pitt Rivers and Tylor to the Pitt Rivers Museum at the University of Oxford', *Forum for Anthropology and Culture* (2006), http://anthropologie.kunstkamera.ru/files/pdf/eng004/eng4_petch.pdf; A. Petch, 'Chance and Certitude: Pitt Rivers and His First Collection', *Journal of the History of Collections* 18, no. 2 (29 June 2006): 257–66; F. Larson, A. Petch, and D. Zeitlyn, 'Social Networks and the Creation of the Pitt Rivers Museum', *Journal of Material Culture* 12, no. 3 (1 November 2007): 211–39; F. Larson, 'Anthropological Landscaping: General Pitt Rivers, the Ashmolean, the University Museum and the Shaping of an Oxford Discipline', *Journal of the History of Collections* 20, no. 1 (1 May 2008): 85–100.

63 A. H. Lane Fox, 'On the Principles of Classification Adopted in the Arrangement of his Anthropological Collection, Now Exhibited in the Bethnal Green Museum', *Journal of Anthropological Institute* 4 (1874): 307.

64 The Old Man was dug up by Abbés F. and J. Bouyssonie. Anonymous, 'Fossil Man', *Nature* 91 (1913): 91.

65 Marcellin Boule, translated by and cited in William L. Straus and A. J. E. Cave, 'Pathology and the Posture of Neanderthal Man', *The Quarterly Review of Biology* 32, no. 4 (1957): 358. Also consult Anonymous, 'Fossil Man'; Michael Hammond, 'The Expulsion of the Neanderthals from Human Ancestry: Marcellin Boule and the Social Context of Scientific Research', *Social Studies of Science* 12, no. 1 (1982): 1–36; Madison, 'The Most Brutal of Human Skulls'.

66 By the 1920s, Aleš Hrdlička was one of the few people still considering Neanderthals to be a direct ancestor and arguing that humans had undergone a Neanderthal phase. Aleš Hrdlička, 'The Neanderthal Phase of Man', *Journal of the Royal Anthropological Institute of Great Britain and Ireland* 57 (1927): 249–74.

67 The boy, named Gibraltar 2, is now considered to have been about three years old when he died. The girl is known as La Quina 18. Anonymous, 'Woman Finds New Cave Man Skull at Gibraltar', *The Science News-Letter* 9 (1926): 1; Anonymous, 'The Recently Discovered Gibraltar Skull', *Nature* 118, no. 2965 (1926): 320; Anonymous,

'The Gibraltar Skull', *Nature* 120, no. 3028 (1927): 710; Dorothy A. E. Garrod, L. H. Dudley Buxton, and G. Elliot Smith, 'Excavation of a Mousterian Rock-Shelter at Devil's Tower, Gibraltar', *Journal of the Royal Anthropological Institute of Great Britain and Ireland* (1928): 33–113; M. C. Dean, C. B. Stringer, and T. G. Bromage, 'Age at Death of the Neanderthal Child from Devil's Tower Gibraltar and the Implications for Studies of General Growth and Development in Neanderthals', *American Journal of Physical Anthropology* 70 (n.d.): 301–9.

68 Anonymous, 'Woman Finds New Cave Man Skull at Gibraltar'. Compare with the mentions of 'Miss Garrod' in Anonymous, 'The Recently Discovered Gibraltar Skull', *Science* 64, no. 1660 (1926): 397–8.

69 For an introductory account of significant fossil finds, consult Ian Tattersall, *The Fossil Trail: How We Know What We Think We Know About Human Evolution* (New York: Oxford University Press, 1995). On the broader historiography, consult Matthew R. Goodrum, 'The History of Human Origins Research and its Place in the History of Science: Research Problems and Historiography', *History of Science* 47, no. 3 (2009): 337–57.

70 Straus and Cave, 'Pathology and the Posture of Neanderthal Man'.

71 Ibid., 359.

72 Scientific views of human prehistory have shifted dramatically even since the publication of Clive Finlayson, *The Humans Who Went Extinct: Why Neanderthals Died Out and We Survived* (Oxford: Oxford University Press, 2009). For the best overviews of modern scientific views consult João Zilhão, 'The Neanderthals: Evolution, Palaeoecology, and Extinction', in *The Oxford Handbook of the Archaeology and Anthropology of Hunter-Gatherers*, ed. Vicki Cummings, Peter Jordan, and Marek Zvelebil (Oxford: Oxford University Press, 2013), 192–214; Rebecca Wragg Sykes, *Kindred: Neanderthal Life, Love, Death and Art* (London: Bloomsbury Sigma, 2020); Thomas Higham, *The World Before Us: How Science Is Revealing a New Story of Our Human Origins* (New Haven, CT: Yale University Press, 2021).

73 In 2021 the discovery of nine Neanderthal skeletons among hundreds of bones of extinct beasts in Guattari Cave near Rome sparked excitement. The Italian Ministry released a statement suggesting

that many of the bones showed signs of gnawing, probably by the hyenas also found onsite. Lorenzo Tondo, 'Remains of Nine Neanderthals Found in Cave South of Rome', *Guardian*, 8 May 2021, sec. Science,http://www.theguardian.com/science/2021/may/08/remains-of-nine-neanderthals-found-in-cave-south-of-rome

74 J. Zilhão et al., 'Last Interglacial Iberian Neandertals as Fisher-Hunter-Gatherers', *Science* 367, no. 6485 (2020): eaaz7943; Manuel Will, 'Neanderthal Surf and Turf', *Science* 367 (2020): 1422–3.

75 D. L. Hoffmann et al., 'U-Th Dating of Carbonate Crusts Reveals Neandertal Origin of Iberian Cave Art', *Science* 359, no. 6378 (2018): 912–15. For an accessible summary of the latest scientific research on Neanderthal culture consult Wragg Sykes, *Kindred*.

76 Theodosius Dobzhansky, 'On Species and Races of Living and Fossil Man', *American Journal of Physical Anthropology* 2, no. 3 (1944): 262–3.

77 Ibid., 258.

78 C. Duarte et al., 'The Early Upper Paleolithic Human Skeleton from the Abrigo Do Lagar Velho (Portugal) and Modern Human Emergence in Iberia', *Proceedings of the National Academy of Sciences* 96 (1999): 7604–9; I. Tattersall and J. H. Schwartz, 'Hominids and Hybrids: The Place of Neanderthals in Human Evolution', *Proceedings of the National Academy of Sciences* 96 (1999): 7117–19.

79 Duarte et al., 'The Early Upper Paleolithic Human Skeleton from the Abrigo Do Lagar Velho (Portugal) and Modern Human Emergence in Iberia'; Tattersall and Schwartz, 'Hominids and Hybrids'; Clive Finlayson et al., 'Late Survival of Neanderthals at the Southernmost Extreme of Europe', *Nature* 443 (2006): 850–3.

80 Richard E. Green et al., 'A Draft Sequence of the Neandertal Genome', *Science* 328, no. 5979 (2010): 710–22.

81 Ibid., 8.

82 The original research concluded that few Africans carried Neanderthal DNA, but subsequent studies suggested it is far more common than originally imagined. Michael Price, 'Africans, Too, Carry Neanderthal Genetic Legacy', *Science* 367 (2020): 497.

83 Tom Higham et al., 'The Timing and Spatiotemporal Patterning of Neanderthal Disappearance', *Nature* 512 (2014): 306–9; Mateja

Hajdinjak et al., 'Initial Upper Palaeolithic Humans in Europe Had Recent Neanderthal Ancestry', *Nature* 592 (2021): 253–7.

84 ScottH, 'Find Your Inner Neanderthal', *23andMe Blog*, 15 December 2011, https://blog.23andme.com/ancestry-reports/find-your-inner-neanderthal; 23andMe, 'Celebrate your Ancient DNA with a New Neanderthal Report', *23andMe Blog* (23 April 2020), https://blog.23andme.com/ancestry-reports/new-neanderthal-report

85 Tattersall and Schwartz, 'Hominids and Hybrids'.

86 I have previously argued that questions of antiquity, evolution, and descent need to be ranked together as histories of the human sciences in the nineteenth century. Sadiah Qureshi, 'Looking to Our Ancestors', in *Time Travelers: Victorian Encounters with Time and History*, ed. Adelene Buckland and Sadiah Qureshi (Chicago, IL: University of Chicago Press, 2020), 3–23.

87 Compare the nineteenth-century use of ethnographic observations with those in Zilhão, 'The Neanderthals: Evolution, Palaeoecology, and Extinction', 300. Likewise, ethnographic comparisons are consistently made in Wragg Sykes, *Kindred*. This legacy is also explored in Pratik Chakrabarti, *Inscriptions of Nature: Geology and the Naturalization of Antiquity* (Baltimore, MD: Johns Hopkins University Press, 2020).

88 Alison Bashford, *Global Population: History, Geopolitics, and Life on Earth* (New York: Columbia University Press, 2014).

Chapter 5

1 Daisy Bates, letter to John Murray, 2 February 1939, Daisy Bates Papers, John Murray Archive, National Library of Scotland, Acc. 13451, henceforth abbreviated to NLS13451.

2 Bob Reece, *Daisy Bates: Grand Dame of the Desert* (Canberra, ACT: National library of Australia, 2007), 121.

3 Daisy Bates, letter to John Murray, 17 August 1938, NLS13451.

4 For the most important discussion of this theme in Australia, consult Russell McGregor, *Imagined Destinies: Aboriginal Australians and*

the Doomed Race Theory, 1880–1939 (Carlton South, VI: Melbourne University Press, 1998).

5 Darcy Niland, 'Stone Age Woman', *Braidwood Review and District Advocate* (30 January 1951). Bates was called the 'white queen of the never never' in the press, and the 'great white queen of the never never' in Salter's biography. Anonymous, 'Women's World', *Avon Gazette and York Times* (15 June 1923); Elizabeth Salter, *The Great White Queen of the Never Never* (Sydney: Angus and Robertson, 1972).

6 Chris Clarkson et al., 'Human Occupation of Northern Australia by 65,000 Years Ago', *Nature* 547, no. 7663 (2017): 306–10; Shaun Adams et al., 'Early Human Occupation of Australia's Eastern Seaboard', *Scientific Reports* 14, no. 1 (2024): 2579.

7 Australian Institute of Aboriginal and Torres Strait Islander Studies, 'Languages Alive', Australian Institute of Aboriginal and Torres Strait Islander Studies (24 March 2023), https://aiatsis.gov.au/explore/languages-alive; 'AustLang', *Austlang*, n.d., c 2019, https://collection.aiatsis.gov.au/austlang/search

8 Marshall Clark and Sally K. May, *Macassan History and Heritage: Journeys, Encounters and Influences* (ANU Press, 2013); Lyndon Ormond-Parker, 'Aboriginal Trade with Macassan Seafarers', *Agora* 55, no. 3 (2020): 3–7.

9 Alison Bashford and Stuart Macintyre, eds, *The Cambridge History of Australia* (Cambridge: Cambridge University Press, 2013).

10 Tim Rowse, 'Notes on the History of Aboriginal Population of Australia', in *Genocide and Settler Society* (New York: Berghahn Books, 2004); Alan N. Williams et al., 'The First Australians Grew to a Population of Millions, Much More than Previous Estimates', *The Conversation* (29 April 2021), http://theconversation.com/the-first-australians-grew-to-a-population-of-millions-much-more-than-previous-estimates-142371

11 Australian Bureau of Statistics, 'Historical Population, 2016', 2016, https://www.abs.gov.au/statistics/people/population/historical-population/latest-release. All further population statistics for the settler population are taken from this source.

12 Heather Goodall, *Invasion to Embassy: Land in Aboriginal Politics in New South Wales, 1770–1972* (Sydney, NSW: Allen & Unwin, 1996); Bashford and Macintyre, eds, *The Cambridge History of Australia*.

13 Lyndall Ryan, *The Aboriginal Tasmanians*, 2nd ed. (St Leonards, NSW: Allen & Unwin, 1996); Henry Reynolds, *A History of Tasmania* (Cambridge [England] and New York: Cambridge University Press, 2012); Lyndall Ryan, 'Colonial Frontier Massacres in Australia, 1788–1930', *Colonial Frontier Massacres in Australia, 1788–1930* (2022, 2017), https://c21ch.newcastle.edu.au/colonialmassacres; Lawson, *The Last Man*; Taylor, 'Genocide, Extinction and Aboriginal Self-Determination in Tasmanian Historiography'; Benjamin Madley, 'From Terror to Genocide: Britain's Tasmanian Penal Colony and Australia's History Wars', *Journal of British Studies* 47, no. 1 (2008): 77–106; McGregor, *Imagined Destinies*.

14 The map and data are available on the Colonial Frontier Massacres in Australia, 1788–1930 website at https://c21ch.newcastle.edu.au/colonialmassacres. The first release of the data was in 2017, and it was updated until October 2024.

15 Aborigines Protection Society, 'Report of the Parliamentary Select Committee on Aboriginal Tribes (British Settlements)', 10.

16 Ann Curthoys and Jessie Mitchell, 'The Advent of Self-Government, 1840s–90', in *The Cambridge History of Australia*, ed. Bashford and Macintyre, 149–69; Zoë Laidlaw, ' "Aunt Anna's Report": The Buxton Women and the Aborigines Select Committee, 1835–37', *Journal of Imperial and Commonwealth History* 32, no. 2 (2004): 1–28; Heartfield, *The Aborigines' Protection Society*; A. Lester, 'Settler Colonialism, George Grey and the Politics of Ethnography', *Environment and Planning D: Society and Space* 34, no. 3 (1 June 2016): 492–507; Alan Lester and Fae Dussart, 'Trajectories of Protection: Protectorates of Aborigines in Early 19th Century Australia and Aotearoa New Zealand', *New Zealand Geographer* 64, no. 3 (2008): 205–20; Alan Lester and Fae Dussart, *Colonization and the Origins of Humanitarian Governance: Protecting Aborigines across the Nineteenth-Century British Empire*, Critical Perspectives on Empire (Cambridge: Cambridge University Press, 2014).

17 Unless otherwise stated, all biographical details are from Reece, *Daisy Bates*.

18 On Stead's campaign consult Judith R. Walkowitz, *City of Dreadful Delight: Narratives of Sexual Danger in Late-Victorian London* (Chicago, IL: University of Chicago Press, 1992), 81–134.

19 This summary of her travels is condensed from Isobel White, 'Daisy Bates: Legend and Reality', in *First in Their Field: Women and Australian Anthropology*, ed. Julie Marcus (Melbourne: Melbourne University Press, 1993), 46–65; Reece, *Daisy Bates*.

20 Daisy Bates, letter to John Murray, 25 July 1938, NLS13451. On go-betweens consult Simon Schaffer, *The Brokered World: Go-Betweens and Global Intelligence, 1770–1820* (Sagamore Beach, MA: Science History Publications, 2009).

21 Reece, *Daisy Bates*, 45.

22 Bates, letter to John Murray, 25 August 1938, NLS13451.

23 J. P. Thomson, letter to Bates, 30 April 1905, Bates Papers, MS365, NLA, F97/546.

24 Daisy M. Bates, *The Native Tribes of Western Australia*, ed. Isobel White (Canberra, ACT: National Library of Australia, 1985).

25 Bates, letter to John Murray, 4 February 1944, NLS13451.

26 Walter Malcolmson, 'The People of Australia and The Aborigines', *The Times* (8 April 1904).

27 H. B. Lefroy, 'The People of Australia and The Aborigines', *The Times* (12 April 1904).

28 A full list of articles is not possible, but some of the most useful are H. R. Fox Bourne, 'Aborigines of Western Australia', *The Times* (9 May 1904); Henry Copeland, 'The People of Australia and the Aborigines', *The Times* (28 March 1904); Ibid. (21 March 1904); Harold Finch-Hatton and J. F. Hogan, 'The People of Australia and the Aborigines', *The Times* (23 March 1904); J. F. Hogan, 'The People of Australia and the Aborigines', *The Times* (31 March 1904); Finch-Hatton and Hogan, 'The People of Australia and the Aborigines'; Lefroy, 'The People of Australia and The Aborigines'; Walter Malcolmson, 'The Aborigines In Western Australia', *The Times* (8 March 1905); Ibid.

29 Daisy M. Bates, 'The People of Australia and The Aborigines', *The Times* (24 May 1904).

30 Western Australia, Parliament, *Royal Commission on the Condition of the Natives Report* (Perth, WA: W. M. Alfred Watson, Government Printer, 1905).

31 Bates, letter to John Murray, 4 February 1944, NLS13451.

32 Bates, letter to John Mathew, 3 February 1910, MS3197, NLA.

33 Bates, *The Native Tribes of Western Australia*.

34 Adam Kuper, *Anthropology & Anthropologists: The Modern British School*, 3rd ed. (London and New York: Routledge, 1996), 42.

35 Daisy Bates, letter to John Mathew, MS3197, NLA. The original manuscript is in the Bates Papers, MS365, NLA, and has been cut into smaller sections that have been reassembled. BAAS annual report.

36 Elizabeth Salter, correspondence, *Man*, n.s., 10 (1975): 473–4.

37 Rodney Needham, letter to Elizabeth Salter, 16 May 1975, MS6481, Box 4, 2/10, NLA, and Rodney Needham, letter to Elizabeth Salter, 26 September 1975, Box 4, 2/10, NLA. Also consult Isobel White, 'Mrs Bates and Mr Brown: An Examination of Rodney Needham's Allegations', *Oceania* 51, no. 3 (1981): 193–210; Isobel White, 'Isobel White Replies to Professor Needham', *Oceania* 53 (1982): 139–40.

38 Norman B. Tindale, *Aboriginal Tribes of Australia: Their Terrain, Environmental Controls, Distribution, Limits, and Proper Names* (Canberra, ACT: Australian National University Press, 1974), xii. Rodney Needham, letter to Elizabeth Salter, 26 September 1975, Box 4, 2/10, NLA, referred to Tindale's note.

39 White, 'Daisy Bates: Legend and Reality', 60–1.

40 John Mathew, letter to Bates, 23 April 1902, Bates Papers, MS365, NLA, F97/304–5. Bates and Mathew exchanged books, photographs of Aboriginal peoples, and theories about linguistic development, and how closely related Aboriginal peoples were to other Indigenous groups such as the Papuans. Also consult Bob Reece, '"You Would Have Loved Her for Her Lore": The Letters of Daisy Bates', *Australian Aboriginal Studies*, no. 1 (2007): 51–70.

41 Kenneth Young, letter to Bates, 1 August 1905, Bates Papers, MS365, NLA, F97/621–3.

42 R. H. Mathew, letter to Bates, 29 August 1905, Bates Papers, MS365, F97/355–6. See also R. H. Mathew, letter to Bates, 16 July 1905, F 97/353, and 25 September 1905, F97/354.

43 Bates, letter to Murray, 22 July 1944, NLS13451, 165, and Bates, letter to Mr Bartholomew, 2 October 1945, NLS13451, 173.

44 Daisy Bates, letter to Mrs Hosking, 21 December 1944, Salter Papers, MS6481 NLA, box 4-2 (7)-99.

45 'As to the half-castes, however early they may be taken and trained, with very few exceptions the only good half-caste is a dead one.' From Daisy M. Bates, 'Aboriginal Reserves and Women Patrols', *Sunday Times (Perth, WA)*, 2 October 1921, 18.

46 Bates, letter to John Murray, undated, NLS13451.

47 Reece, *Daisy Bates*, 138–41.

48 Throughout the article and footnotes, 'John Murray' refers to the publisher while 'Murray' refers to Bates's editor, John G. Murray. The most detailed published analysis of the book's publication is Bob Reece's 'Introduction' to Daisy Bates, *My Natives and I: Incorporating the Passing of the Aborigines: A Lifetime Spent among the Natives of Australia*, ed. P. J. Bridge (Carlisle, WA: Hesperian Press, 2004), xii–xxxiii.

49 [Andrew Lang], report on the MS of *My Natives and I*, NLS13451.

50 E. M. L., referee's report on the MS of *My Natives and I*, 2 February 1938, NLS13451.

51 Lang, report on MS, NLS13451.

52 Daisy Bates, letter to John Murray, 17 August 1938, NLS13451. To Ernestine Hill's disappointment, she was not credited either as co-author or even editor despite her extensive involvement. Reece, *Daisy Bates*.

53 Bates, letter to Murray, 1 September 1938, NLS13451, 22 and 24 October 1938, NLS13451.

54 Ibid., 15 October 1938, NLS13451.

55 Ibid., 17 August 1938, NLS13451.

56 Daisy Bates, *The Passing of the Aborigines: A Lifetime spent among the Natives of Australia* (London: John Murray, 1938) , p. 207.

57 In the language of the time, these were the 'Bibbulmun'. Bates, *My Natives and I*, ed. Bridge, 64–5, 84–5, 95–6; Daisy M. Bates, 'A Few

Notes on Some South-Western Australian Dialects', *Journal of the Royal Anthropological Institute of Great Britain and Ireland* 44 (1914): 65–82.

58 Bates, letter to John Murray, 16 January 1939, NLS13451.

59 Ibid.

60 'These are such delicate times for us and our Empire. I can only read Headlines in The Advertiser and as I lie awake at night I think of the awful havoc that would issue if by any dreadful circumstance Russia, Germany and Italy would lose their Dictators.' Bates, letter to Murray, 22 September 1938, NLS13451.

61 Bates, letter to Murray, 17 July 1938, NLS13451.

62 Bates, letter to [Allan], 11 November 1940, Adelaide, Salter MS6481 NLA, Box 3-2(4)-47. Reece, *Daisy Bates*.

63 In the present day, Trukanini's image is used within the Tasmanian Museum and Art Gallery as part of a much broader exhibition on the continued existence of Aboriginal Tasmanians.

64 Bates Papers, MS365, F94/28, F94/115 and F94/116.

65 Bates, *The Passing of the Aborigines*, 49, 115.

66 F. Wood Jones, 'The Aborigines: Fate of the Passing People', *The Times* (26 January 1938), viii.

67 Bain Atwood, *Rights for Aborigines* (Crows Nest, NSW: Allen & Unwin, 2003), 22–3.

68 Aboriginal reservations have existed since the nineteenth century when settlers often recognized Aboriginal peoples as having some prior claim to the land, but this recognition faded in the twentieth century. Henry Reynolds, *The Law of the Land*, 2nd ed. (Ringwood: Penguin Books, 1992); Goodall, *Invasion to Embassy*.

69 Donald Fergusson Thomson, *Interim General Report of Preliminary Expedition to Arnhem Land, Northern Territory of Australia, 1935–36* (Canberra, ACT: Department of the Interior, 1936), 42.

70 Ibid., 45; Donald Fergusson Thomson, *Report on Expedition to Arnhem Land, 1936–37* (Canberra, ACT: Department of the Interior, 1939).

71 Atwood, *Rights for Aborigines*; Bain Atwood and Andrew Markus, *Thinking Black: William Cooper and the Australian Aborigines' League* (Canberra, ACT: Aboriginal Studies Press, 2004).

72 Australia and Human Rights and Equal Opportunity Commission, *Bringing Them Home: Report of the National Inquiry into the Separation of Aboriginal and Torres Strait Islander Children from Their Families* (Sydney: Human Rights and Equal Opportunity Commission, 1997); Tony Barta, 'Sorry, and Not Sorry, in Australia: How the Apology to the Stolen Generations Buried a History of Genocide', *Journal of Genocide Research* 10 (2008): 201–14.

73 Such policies and the subsequent forcible child removals are now formally recognized as genocide. Consult Australia and Meredith Wilkie, eds, *Bringing Them Home: Report of the National Inquiry into the Separation of Aboriginal and Torres Strait Islander Children from Their Families*, Parliamentary Paper, no. 128 of 1997 (Sydney: Human Rights and Equal Opportunity Commission, 1997).

74 Daisy Bates, 'New Aboriginal Reserve', *Sunday Times* (Perth) (12 June 1921): 8.

75 William Harris, 'Proposed Aboriginal Reserve', *Sunday Times* (Perth) (4 September 1921): 6. Although Reece does not connect the episode to broader shifts in Aboriginal activism and international recognition of Indigenous rights, see also Reece, *Daisy Bates*, 89–90.

76 James Harris, 'Native Immorality', *Sunday Times* (Perth) (30 October 1921), 12, in response to Daisy Bates, 'Aboriginal Reserves and Women Patrols', *Sunday Times* (Perth) (2 October 1921), 18.

77 Atwood, *Rights for Aborigines*, 32–3.

78 W. Morley to J. G. Murray, 21 February 1939, NLS13451.

79 'A White Woman Among Australian Blacks', *Illustrated London News* (26 November 1938).

80 Bates, letter to Murray, 15 October 1938, NLS13451, P 43.

81 Ibid., 17 July 1938, NLS13451.

82 Ibid., undated, NLS13451.

83 Ibid., undated, NLS13451.

84 Bates, Mr [F. W.] Eardley (University of Adelaide's registrar), Ooldea, MS365, NLA, F87-35–40.

85 Bates, *The Passing of the Aborigines*, 243.

86 Bates, copy of last will and testament, NLS13451.

87 The questionnaire is now publicly available as part of the Digital Daisy Bates project: Anonymous, 'Digital Daisy Bates – the Questionnaire', n.d., http://www.bates.org.au/quest.html

88 Nick Thieberger, 'Digital Daisy Bates', 2017, http://www.bates.org.au; Nick Thieberger, 'Daisy Bates in the Digital World', *Language, Land and Song: Studies in Honour of Luise Hercus.* London (EL Publishing), 2016, 102–14; William B. McGregor, 'Daisy Bates' Documentations of Kimberley Languages', *Language & History* 55, no. 2 (November 2012): 79–101.

89 Christopher Moseley, *The UNESCO List of the World's Languages in Danger: Context and Process: World Oral Literature Project, Occasional Paper Five* (Cambridge: World Oral Literature Project, 2012), https://api.repository.cam.ac.uk/server/api/core/bitstreams/f3539634-2d6a-4522-ba05-c3c7899dc743/content; Stephen Wurm, ed., *Atlas of the World's Languages in Danger* (Paris: UNESCO, 1996); UNESCO, 'The World Atlas of Languages', *UNESCO World Atlas of Languages*, 2021, https://en.wal.unesco.org/world-atlas-languages

90 *Mabo* v. *Queensland* (No. 2) ('Mabo case'), No. 23 (High Court of Australia, 3 June 1992).

91 Ibid.

92 Atwood, *Rights for Aborigines*. In 1967 campaigns for civil rights secured a successful referendum that finally included Aboriginal people in the census and allowed the government to make specific laws for them, thus counteracting decades of assimilationist policies. Also consult United Nations, 'UN Declaration on the Rights of Indigenous Peoples (UNDRIP)' (2017), https://en.unesco.org/indigenous-peoples/undrip; Erica-Irene A. Daes, 'An Overview of the History of Indigenous Peoples: Self-Determination and the United Nations', *Cambridge Review of International Affairs* 21, no. 1 (1 March 2008): 7–26.

93 The Whadjuk people belong to the Noongar group in southwestern Australia. On Balbuk's family, consult Gina Pickering and the National Trust of Australia (WA), *Fanny Balbuk Yoreel: Realising a Perth Resistance Fighter* (Perth, WA: National Trust of Australia, 2017).

94 Bates, *The Passing of the Aborigines*, 69–70.

95 Daisy Bates, 'Aboriginal Sketch: Balbuk, Last of the Perth Tribe', *The Australasian* (Melbourne) (29 September 1923), 64. Also Bates, 'Fanny Balbuk-Yoreel: The Last Swan River (Female) Native', *Western Mail* (Perth) (1 June 1907), 44, and Daisy Bates, 'Hooper's Fence – A Query', *Western Mail* (Perth) (18 April 1935), 9. Some of this material was later repurposed as Daisy Bates, 'Fanny Balbuk-Yoreel: The Last Swan River (Female) Native', *Science of Man*, 13.5 (1911): 100–1, continued in 13.6 (1911): 119–21.

96 John Mathew, letter to Bates, 23 April 1902, Bates Papers, MS365, NLA, F97/304–5.

97 Bates, 'Balbuk, Last of the Perth Tribe', 64. Also Bates, 'Fanny Balbuk-Yoreel', 44, and Bates, 'Hooper's Fence – A Query', 9.

98 Bates, letter to John Mathew, 12 April 1907, p. 1011, MS3197, NLA.

99 Bates noted that the skull of Balbuk's grand-uncle and Yalgoonga's brother, Ya'gan, was in the British Museum. Bates, 'Fanny Balbuk-Yoreel [continued]', 120. After a search lasting twenty years, the head was located in Liverpool, exhumed and returned in 1997 as related in H. McGlade, 'The Repatriation of Yagan: A Story of Manufacturing Dissent', *Law Text and Culture* 4 (1998): 245–55.

100 Pickering and National Trust of Australia (WA), *Fanny Balbuk Yoreel*.

101 Bennell v Western Australia, No. 1243 (Federal Court of Australia, 19 September 2006). Bates's research is also explicitly used alongside Radcliffe-Brown in the court records for Roberts v State of Western Australia, No. 257 (Federal Court of Australia, 21 February 2011).

102 Government of Western Australia, 'South West Native Title Settlement', *Government of Western Australia*, 21 February 2024, https://www.wa.gov.au/organisation/department-of-the-premier-and-cabinet/south-west-native-title-settlement. On the case's complexity and dissent consult Hannah McGlade, 'The McGlade Case: A Noongar History of Land, Social Justice and Activism', *Australian Feminist Law Journal* 43, no. 2 (3 July 2017): 185–210.

103 Unusually, Bates is mentioned, but quickly glossed over, in Kuper, *Anthropology & Anthropologists*. For other writings compare Salter, '*The Great White Queen of the Never Never*'; Julia Blackburn, *Daisy Bates in the Desert* (London: Vintage, 1997); Reece, *Daisy Bates*; White, 'Daisy

Bates: Legend and Reality'; Cynthia Coyne, '"Bye and Bye When All the Natives Have Gone": Daisy Bates and Billingee', in *Uncommon Ground: White Women in Aboriginal History*, ed. Anna Cole, Victoria Haskins, and Fiona Paisley (Canberra, ACT: Aboriginal Studies Press, 2005), 199–216.

104 Bates, letter to Murray, 17 December 1938, NLS13451.

Chapter 6

1 Kristina Küntzel-Witt, 'Georg Wilhelm Steller and Carl Heinrich Merck: German Scientists in Russian Service as Explorers in the North Pacific in the Eighteenth Century', in *Explorations and Entanglements: Germans in Pacific Worlds from the Early Modern Period to World War I*, ed. Hartmut Berghoff, Frank Biess, and Ulrike Strasser, Studies in German History, vol. 22 (New York: Berghahn Books, 2019); Ryan Tucker Jones, *Empire of Extinction: Russians and the North Pacific's Strange Beasts of the Sea, 1741–1867* (Oxford: Oxford University Press, 2014).

2 Georg Wilhelm Steller, 'The Beasts of the Sea (1751)', in *The Fur Seals and Fur-Seal Islands of the North Pacific Ocean*, ed. Paul Royster and David Starr Jordan, trans. Walter Miller and Jennie Emerson Miller (Washington, DC: Government Printing Office, 1899), 26, 47.

3 Martin Sauer, *An Account of a Geographical and Astronomical Expedition to the Northern Parts of Russia* (London: T. Cadell, 1802), 181.

4 Georg Heinrich von Langsdorff, *Bemerkungen auf einer Reise um die Welt in den Jahren 1803 bis 1807*, vol. 2 (Frankfurt: F. Wilmans, 1812), 23.

5 John Fleming, 'Remarks Illustrative of the Influence of Society on the Distribution of British Animals', *Edinburgh Philosophical Journal* 11 (1824): 290–1, 304; John Fleming, *History of British Animals, Exhibiting the Descriptive Characters and Systematical Arrangement of the Genera and Species of Quadrupeds, Birds, Reptiles, Fishes, Mollusca, and Radiata of the United Kingdom; Including the Indigenous, Extirpated, and Extinct Kinds, Together with Periodical and Occasional Visitants* (Edinburgh: Bell & Bradfute, 1828).

6 George Perkins Marsh, *Man and Nature; Or, Physical Geography as Modified by Human Action* (London: Sampson Low, Son & Marston, 1864), 35.

7 On Marsh's legacy consult Barrow, *Nature's Ghosts*, 88–9, 93.

8 Gísli Pálsson, *The Last of Its Kind: The Search for the Great Auk and the Discovery of Extinction* (Princeton, NJ: Princeton University Press, 2024).

9 Ibid.

10 Alfred Newton, 'The Gare-Fowl and Its Historians', *The Natural History Review* 12, N.S.5 (1865): 467, 487; Alfred Newton, 'On the Zoological Aspect of Game Laws', in *Report of the Thirty-Eighth Meeting of the British Association for the Advancement of Science; Held at Norwich in August 1868* (London: John Murray, 1868), 108–9; Henry M. Cowles, 'A Victorian Extinction: Alfred Newton and the Evolution of Animal Protection', *The British Journal for the History of Science* 46, no. 04 (2013): 695–714; Pálsson, *The Last of Its Kind*.

11 Ernest Ingersoll, 'The Effect of the Settlement of North America Upon Its Wild Animals', *Science* n.s. 6, no. 144S (1885): 417.

12 Andrew C. Isenberg, *The Destruction of the Bison: An Environmental History, 1750–1920*, Studies in Environment and History (Cambridge: Cambridge University Press, 2000).

13 J. A. Allen, *The American Bisons, Living and Extinct* (Cambridge, MA: Cambridge University Press, 1876), 176.

14 Isenberg, *The Destruction of the Bison*; Miles A. Powell, *Vanishing America: Species Extinction, Racial Peril, and the Origins of Conservation* (Cambridge, MA: Harvard University Press, 2016).

15 Fairfield Osborn, 'William Temple Hornaday', *Science* 85, no. 2210 (1937): 445–6; William Temple Hornaday, *The Extermination of the American Bison, with a Sketch of Its Discovery and Life History* (Washington, DC: Government Printing Office, 1889), 521; William Temple Hornaday, *Our Vanishing Wild Life: Its Extermination and Preservation* (New York, NY: Charles Scribner's Sons, 1913); William Temple Hornaday and Alwin K. Haagner, *The Vanishing Game of South Africa: A Warning and an Appeal* (New York, NY, 1922).

16 Some of the more famous individuals include William Temple Hornaday, Madison Grant, and Theodore Roosevelt. Powell, *Vanishing America*, 54.

17 Anonymous, 'Memorial to the Right Hon. Earl Cromer, K.C.B. and the Governor-General of the Sudan', *Journal of the Society for the Preservation of the Wild Fauna of the Empire* 1 (1904): 10. On the broader history of the society consult C. W. Hobley, 'The Preservation of Wild Life in the Empire', *Journal of the Royal African Society* 34, no. 137 (1935): 403–7; John M. MacKenzie, *The Empire of Nature: Hunting, Conservation, and British Imperialism*, Studies in Imperialism (Manchester: Manchester University Press, 1997); David K. Prendergast and William M. Adams, 'Colonial Wildlife Conservation and the Origins of the Society for the Preservation of the Wild Fauna of the Empire (1903–1914)', *Oryx* 37, no. 2 (2003): 251–60; William M. Adams, *Against Extinction: The Story of Conservation* (London: Earthscan, 2004).

18 Spence, *Dispossessing the Wilderness*; Burnham, *Indian Country, God's Country*; Keller and Turek, *American Indians and National Parks*.

19 For the best account of the early history of nature conservation consult Raf De Bont, *Nature's Diplomats: Science, Internationalism & Preservation, 1920–1960* (Pittsburgh, PA: University of Pittsburgh Press, 2021). In the original French, the society's original names were the 'International de documentation et de corrélation pour la protection de la nature' and 'Office International pour la protection de la nature (1934–1948)'.

20 Barrow, *Nature's Ghosts*, 139–49.

21 John C. Phillips and Harold J. Coolidge, Jr, *The First Five Years: The American Committee for International Wild Life Protection* (Cambridge, MA: American Committee for International Wildlife Protection, 1934), 3, https://hdl.handle.net/2027/mdp.39015079999960

22 De Bont, *Nature's Diplomats*.

23 Anonymous, 'Convention Relative to the Preservation of Fauna and Flora in Their Natural State' (1933); Anonymous, 'The London Convention for the Protection of African Flora and Fauna', *The Auk* 52, no. 4 (1935): 473–4; Barrow, *Nature's Ghosts*, 151.

24 Barrow, *Nature's Ghosts*, 159–66.

25 Ibid., 161–6.

26 IUPN, *International Union for the Protection of Nature, Established at Fontainebleau, 5 October 1948* (Paris and Brussels: IUPN, 1948).

27 Unless otherwise stated the institutional history of the IUPN and later IUCN draws from Martin Holdgate, *The Green Web: A Union for World Conservation* (London: Earthscan, 1999); Barrow, *Nature's Ghosts*; De Bont, *Nature's Diplomats*.

28 The American government hosted UNESCO's Conference on the Conservation and Utilization of Resources and, concurrently, the International Technical Conference on the Protection of Nature. IUPN, *International Technical Conference on the Protection of Nature: Lake Success, 22–29 VIII 1949, Proceedings and Papers* (Paris: Brussels: International Union for the Protection of Nature, 1950). On the history of the Red Lists consult Peter Scott, John A Burton, and Richard Fitter, 'Red Data Books: The Historical Background', in *The Road to Extinction: Problems of Categorizing the Status of Taxa Threatened with Extinction. A Symposium Held by the Species Survival Commission, Madrid, 7 and 9 November, 1984*, ed. Richard Fitter and Maisie Fitter (Gland, Switzerland: IUCN, 1987), 1–6; N. J. Collar, 'The Reasons for Red Data Books', *Oryx* 30, no. 2 (1996): 121–30; Craig Hilton-Taylor, 'A History of the IUCN Red List', in *The IUCN Red List: 50 Years of Conservation*, ed. Jane Smart, Craig Hilton-Taylor, and Russell A Mittermeier (Washington, DC: Earth in Focus, 2014), 9–27.

29 Coolidge was also keen to create a 'situation map' detailing the 'location of seriously threatened species, and calling attention to parks and reserves established by local governments to assure the preservation of such species'. Harold J. Coolidge, 'Emergency Action for the Preservation of Vanishing Species', in *International Technical Conference on the Protection of Nature: Lake Success, 22–29 VIII 1949, Proceedings and Papers* (Paris: Brussels: International Union for the Protection of Nature, 1950), 486. For further information on the history of the Survival Service consult C. L. Boyle, 'The Survival Service Commission', *Oryx* 5, no. 1 (1959): 30–5; R. S. R. Fitter, 'The Survival Service Commission', *Oryx* 7, no. 4 (1964): 157–9; Anonymous, 'Survival Service Commission', *Oryx* 7, no. 5 (1964): 217–217; H. J. Coolidge, 'The

Development of the Survival Service of the International Union for the Conservation of Nature and Natural Resources', in *Proceedings of the Sixth General Assembly, Athens, 11–19 September, 1958* (Brussels: IUCN, 1960), 133–4.

30 'Whereas: The world is faced with an increasing list of threatened and vanishing species of fauna and flora, The Conference Resolves: the International Union for the Protection of Nature should establish a "survival service" for the assembling, evaluation, and dissemination of information on and the study of, all species of fauna and flora that appear to be threatened with extinction, in order to assist governments and appropriate agencies in assuring their survival.' IUPN, *International Technical Conference on the Protection of Nature: Lake Success, 22–29 VIII 1949, Proceedings and Papers*, 183. For the early years, I refer to the Survival Service for consistency but it did change names. Originally established as the Survival Service, it was later renamed the Survival Service Committee and then again to the Survival Service Commission. In 1981, from the Union's Fifteenth General Assembly, in Christchurch, New Zealand, onwards the name used in official documents changed to the Species Survival Commission. IUCN, *Proceedings of the 15th Session of the General Assembly of the IUCN and 15th IUCN Technical Meeting, Christchurch, New Zealand, 11–23 October, 1981* (Gland, Switzerland: IUCN, 1983), passim, http://data.iucn.org/dbtw-wpd/edocs/GA-15th-009.pdf

31 Coolidge, 'Emergency Action for the Preservation of Vanishing Species', 486–7.

32 Resolution 16 in IUPN, *International Technical Conference on the Protection of Nature: Lake Success, 22–29 VIII 1949, Proceedings and Papers*, 183–5. Also consult resolutions 15 and 17 on these pages.

33 A. A. Burbidge and J. Woinarski, '*Thylacinus Cynocephalus*. The IUCN Red List of Threatened Species 2016: E.T21866A21949291', 2016; Erwin H. Bulte, Richard D. Horan, and Jason F. Shogren, 'Is the Tasmanian Tiger Extinct? A Biological–Economic Re-Evaluation', *Ecological Economics* 45, no. 2 (2003): 271–9; Charles Y. Feigin et al., 'Genome of the Tasmanian Tiger Provides Insights into the Evolution and Demography of an Extinct Marsupial Carnivore', *Nature Ecology &*

Evolution 2, no. 1 (11 December 2017): 182–92; Melanie Fillios, Mathew S. Crowther, and Mike Letnic, 'The Impact of the Dingo on the Thylacine in Holocene Australia', *World Archaeology* 44, no. 1 (1 March 2012): 118–34; Barry W. Brook et al., 'Resolving When (and Where) the Thylacine Went Extinct', *Science of The Total Environment* 877 (2023): 162878.

34 Brook et al., 'Resolving When (and Where) the Thylacine Went Extinct'.

35 The card index was begun by Colonel Hoier, and later kept up to date by Jean-Jacques Petter, a naturalist based at the Natural History Museum in Paris, who took over from J.-M. Vrydagh in 1953. For Vrydagh's full report, see IUPN, *Proceedings and Reports of the Second Session of the General Assembly, held in Brussels, 18–23 October, 1950* (Brussels: IUPN, 1951), 24–8, 25; IUPN, *Proceedings and Reports of the Fourth General Assembly, Held at Copenhagen (Denmark), 25 August to 3 September 1954* (Brussels: IUPN, 1955), 43. In the 1960s many of the early records of the IUCN were lost in a fire and it is likely that the card index was also destroyed.

36 For the draft questionnaire consult IUPN, *Proceedings and Reports of the Second Session of the General Assembly, held in Brussels, 18–23 October, 1950*, 29–30.

37 IUPN, *Proceedings and Reports of the Third General Assembly, Held in Caracas (Venezuela), 3–9 November 1952* (Brussels: IUPN, 1952), 52.

38 The donation was made by M. Russell and M. Arundel. At the same General Assembly, Coolidge called for the Survival Service to be established as a permanent Commission. IUCN, *Proceedings of the Fifth General Assembly, Edinburgh, 20–28 June 1956* (Brussels: IUCN, 1957), 86–9.

39 IUPN, *Proceedings and Reports of the Fourth General Assembly, Held at Copenhagen (Denmark), 25 August to 3 September 1954*, 59.

40 The shift from 'preservation' to 'conservation' in the union's name indicates a broader shift away from preserving pristine wildernesses on the model of American national parks to managing wildlife, landscapes, and natural resources in an effort to reduce overall destruction. IUCN, *Proceedings of the Fifth General Assembly, Edinburgh, 20–28 June*

1956, 89; IUCN, *Proceedings of the Sixth General Assembly, Athens, 11–19 September 1958* (Brussels: IUCN, 1960), 134; Coolidge, 'The Development of the Survival Service of the International Union for the Conservation of Nature and Natural Resources'. Resolutions 233 and 252, IUCN, *Proceedings of the Sixth General Assembly, Athens, 11–19 September 1958*, 69, 77.

41 IUCN, *Proceedings of the Seventh General Assembly, Warsaw, 15–24 June 1960* (Brussels: IUCN, 1960), 101–20.

42 Lee M. Talbot, *A Look at Threatened Species: A Report on Some Animals of the Middle East and Southern Asia Which Are Threatened with Extermination* (London: Fauna Preservation Society, 1960). The illustrations and maps were the work of Gene Christman, staff illustrator at the University of California's Museum of Vertebrate Zoology.

43 Boyle informed his colleagues of his card index at the Seventh General Assembly in Warsaw, Poland. IUCN, *Proceedings of the Seventh General Assembly, Warsaw, 15–24 June 1960*, 99–100. Hilton-Taylor, 'A History of the IUCN Red List', 14.

44 Barrow, *Nature's Ghosts*, 313–17.

45 Barrow, *Nature's Ghosts*.

46 The updated versions of Boyle's sheets were written by the naturalists John H. Calaby, James Fisher, Ronald Melville, Noel Simon, and Jack Vincent. IUCN Operations Intelligence Centre, 'List of Rare Birds, Including Those Thought to Be so but of Which Detailed Information Is Still Lacking', *IUCN Bulletin, New Series* 10 (March 1964): Special Supplement; IUCN Operations Intelligence Centre, 'A Preliminary List of Rare Mammals Including Those Believed to Be Rare but Concerning Which Detailed Information Is Still Lacking', *IUCN Bulletin, New Series* 11 (June 1964): Special Supplement between 4–5; Hilton-Taylor, 'A History of the IUCN Red List', 15. The lists were quickly amalgamated into a 'Preliminary List of Rare Mammals and Birds' featuring 204 mammals and 312 birds and published in the World Wildlife Fund's first annual report: [IUCN Operations Intelligence Centre], 'Preliminary List of Rare Mammals and Birds', in *The Launching of a New Ark: First Report of the President and Trustees of the World Wildlife Fund, an International Foundation for Saving the World's*

Wildlife and Wild Places, 1961–1964, ed. Peter Scott (London: Collins, 1965), 155–207.

47 Noel Simon, ed., *Red Data Book, Volume 1: Mammalia* (Morges, Switzerland: IUCN, 1966); Jack Vincent, ed., *Red Data Book, Volume 2: Aves* (Morges, Switzerland: IUCN, 1966); Robert Rush Miller, ed., *Red Data Book, Volume 4: Pisces* (Morges, Switzerland: IUCN, 1969); René Honegger, ed., *Red Data Book, Volume 3: Amphibia and Reptilia* (Morges, Switzerland: IUCN, 1975).

48 IUCN, *Proceedings of the Tenth General Assembly, Vigyan Bhavan, New Delhi, 24 November–1 December 1969, Volume II* (Morges, Switzerland: IUCN, 1970), 48.

49 James Fisher, Noel Simon, and Jack Vincent, *The Red Book: Wildlife in Danger* (London: Collins, 1969); IUCN, *Proceedings of the Tenth General Assembly, Vigyan Bhavan, New Delhi, 24 November–1 December 1969, Volume II*, 48.

50 Tom Harrisson, 'The New Red Data Book', *Oryx* 12, no. 3 (1974): 321.

51 Jon Agar, 'What Counts as Threatened? Science in the Sixth Extinction', in *Global Transformations in the Life Sciences*, ed. Patrick Manning and Mat Savelli (Pittsburgh, PA: Pittsburgh University Press, 2016), 180–94.

52 F. Fraser Darling, 'Red Data Book, 1. Mammalia, compiled by Noel Simon. 2. Aves, compiled by Jack Vincent. Survival Service Commission, IUCN, Morges, Vaud, Switzerland, 70s. each.', *Oryx* 9, no. 1 (1967): 41–2; Ivor Montagu, 'The Red Book: The World's Endangered Mammals and Birds', *Oryx* 8, no. 5 (1966): 281; Ivor Montagu, 'The Red Book for All', *Oryx* 10, no. 2 (1969): 103–5.

53 Montagu, 'The Red Book for All', 103.

54 Fisher, Simon, and Vincent, *The Red Book: Wildlife in Danger*, 11.

55 Montagu, 'The Red Book for All', 104.

56 IUCN, *Proceedings of the Thirteenth (Extraordinary) General Assembly, Geneva, Switzerland, 19–21 April 1977* (Morges, Switzerland: IUCN, 1977), 86; Hilton-Taylor, 'A History of the IUCN Red List'.

57 Gren Lucas and Hugh Synge, *The IUCN Plant Red Data Book: Comprising Red Data Sheets on 250 Selected Plants Threatened on a World*

Scale (Morges, Switzerland: IUCN, 1978), https://portals.iucn.org/library/node/5780; Warren B. King, *Endangered Birds of the World: The ICPB Bird Red Data Book* (Washington, DC: Smithsonian Institution Press, 1981), https://portals.iucn.org/library/node/6491

58 The Species Conservation Monitoring Unit (SCMU) was superseded by the World Conservation Monitoring Centre (WCMC), which is now the UN Environment Programme World Conservation Monitoring Centre (UNEP-WCMC). Martin Jenkins and Jane Thornback, *The IUCN Mammal Red Data Book: Part 1, Threatened Mammalian Taxa of the Americas and the Australasian Zoogeographic Region (excluding Cetacea)* (Gland, Switzerland: IUCN, 1982), https://portals.iucn.org/library/node/5841; Hilton-Taylor, 'A History of the IUCN Red List', 17.

59 Birds were arranged by Order, Family, and Species, while mammals were arranged by Order.

60 Simon, *Red Data Book, Volume 1: Mammalia*, 1/7.

61 Ibid.

62 The original Red Data Books do not have page numbers, with each species given a reference code instead. The thylacine was species 1/18 in Simon, *Red Data Book, Volume 1: Mammalia.*

63 Vincent, *Red Data Book, Volume 2: Aves*, 2/4.

64 Richard Fitter and Maisie Fitter, eds, *The Road to Extinction: Problems of Categorizing the Status of Taxa Threatened with Extinction. A Symposium Held by the Species Survival Commission, Madrid, 7 and 9 November 1984* (Gland, Switzerland: IUCN, 1987). The name changes after IUCN, *Proceedings of the 15th Session of the General Assembly of the IUCN and 15th IUCN Technical Meeting, Christchurch, New Zealand, 11–23 October, 1981*. For a bibliography of lists in this period consult John A. Burton, 'Bibliography of Red Data Books (Part 1, Animal Species)', *Oryx* 18, no. 1 (1984): 61–4.

65 By 1969, species were classified as Endangered, Rare, Depleted, and Indeterminate. Three years later, these were amended again with new colour coding to Endangered (red), Vulnerable (amber), Rare (white), Out Of Danger (green), and Indeterminate (grey). Later, new possibilities were added when 'Extinct, Insufficiently Known,

Commercially Threatened, and Not Threatened' were used to make sense of threat or loss. For an example of this system in use see the revised version of the Red Data Book on Fishes. The proceedings were later published as *The Road to Extinction* edited by Richard and Maisie Fitter. Richard served as Honorary Secretary of the Fauna Preservation Society, while Maisie edited the Society's journal *Oryx* for nearly twenty years from 1963, before editing the Commission's *Newsletter*. Fitter and Fitter, *The Road to Extinction: Problems of Categorizing the Status of Taxa Threatened with Extinction. A Symposium Held by the Species Survival Commission, Madrid, 7 and 9 November 1984*. 'Richard and Maisie Fitter', in IUCN, *Proceedings of the 16th Session of the General Assembly of the IUCN and 16th Technical Meeting, Madrid, Spain, 5–14 November 1984* (Gland, Switzerland: IUCN, 1984), 182. Hilton-Taylor, 'A History of the IUCN Red List', 18.

66 Nathalie Pettorelli, 'Georgina Mace (1953–2020)', *Nature* 586 (2020): 495. This account draws heavily from the most detailed account of this shift to quantitative criteria in Agar, 'What Counts as Threatened? Science in the Sixth Extinction'.

67 Cited in Agar, 'What Counts as Threatened? Science in the Sixth Extinction'.

68 Quammen, *The Song of the Dodo*, 525–6, 571.

69 Georgina M. Mace and Russell Lande, 'Assessing Extinction Threats: Toward a Reevaluation of IUCN Threatened Species Categories', *Conservation Biology* 5, no. 2 (1991): 151.

70 The final categories were Extinct, Extinct In The Wild, Critically Endangered, Endangered, Vulnerable, Lower Risk, Data Deficient, and Not Evaluated. Lower Risk had three subcategories: 'conservation dependent', 'near threatened', and 'least concern'. Of the final categories, Critically Endangered, Endangered, and Vulnerable were all defined quantitatively, with the rest providing room for qualitative judgements. Agar, 'What Counts as Threatened? Science in the Sixth Extinction'.

71 IUCN Species Survival Commission, *IUCN Red List Categories* (Gland, Switzerland: IUCN, 1994).

72 Sepkoski, *Catastrophic Thinking*, 229–93.

73 Hilton-Taylor, 'A History of the IUCN Red List', 22.

74 Ibid., 27.

75 For the hypothetical total number of species consult Camilo Mora et al., 'How Many Species Are There on Earth and in the Ocean?', *PLOS Biology* 9, no. 8 (23 August 2011): e1001127. For discussion and other figures consult Wiens, 'How Many Species Are There on Earth?'; S. N. Stuart et al., 'The Barometer of Life', *Science* 328, no. 5975 (2010): 177; Cynthia S. Parr et al., 'The Encyclopedia of Life volume 2: Providing Global Access to Knowledge About Life on Earth', *Biodiversity Data Journal*, no. 2 (2014): e1079; 'Encyclopedia of Life', *Encyclopedia of Life*, accessed 1 July 2021, https://eol.org. For figures of the numbers of species listed consult IUCN, 'Barometer of Life', *IUCN Red List of Threatened Species*, 2024, https://www.iucnredlist.org/en

76 Stuart et al., 'The Barometer of Life'; Parr et al., 'The Encyclopedia of Life volume 2'.

77 Irus Braverman, 'En-Listing Life: Red Is the Color of Threatened Species Lists', in *Critical Animal Geographies: Politics, Intersections and Hierarchies in a Multispecies World*, ed. Kathryn Gillespie and Rosemary-Claire Collard (London: Routledge, 2015), 17, https://doi.org/10.4324/9781315762760; Irus Braverman, 'The Regulatory Life of Threatened Species Lists', in *Animals, Biopolitics, Law: Lively Legalities* (Abingdon: Routledge, 2015), 39–58.

78 Anna Santos and Thitikan Satchabut, 'Do Wildlife Trade Bans Enhance or Undermine Conservation Efforts?', *Applied Biodiversity Perspective* 1, no. 3 (2011): 1–15; Michael Hoffmann et al., 'The Impact of Conservation on the Status of the World's Vertebrates', *Science* 330, no. 6010 (10 December 2010): 1503–9.

79 I'm grateful to Nicky Reeves for alerting me to this practice. Rebecca Atkinson, 'Twenty Thefts of Rhino Horn in Six Months', *Museums Association*, 9 August 2011, https://www.museumsassociation.org/museums-journal/news/2011/08/10082011-rhino-horn; Anonymous, 'Rhino Horn Raiders Steal Replicas from Tring Museum', *BBC News* (27 August 2011), https://www.bbc.com/news/uk-england-beds-bucks-herts-14693144

80 For the most elegant discussion of the meaning of Red Lists consult Heise, *Imagining Extinction*.

81 After the initial resolution, the first Green List related to protected areas. IUCN, 'World Conservation Congress: Resolution 041' (IUCN, 2012), 041, https://portals.iucn.org/library; IUCN, 'IUCN Green List of Protected Areas and Conserved Areas: Standard Version 1.1' (Gland, Switzerland: IUCN, 2017); IUCN, 'IUCN Green List: Explore', *IUCN Green List*, 2024, https://iucngreenlist.org/explore. On the Green Status of species: IUCN, 'The IUCN Green Status of Species', *IUCN Red List of Threatened Species*, n.d., https://www.iucnredlist.org/en; H. Resit Akçakaya et al., 'Quantifying Species Recovery and Conservation Success to Develop an IUCN Green List of Species', *Conservation Biology* 32, no. 5 (October 2018): 1128–38.

82 Paul A. Johnsgard, *A Chorus of Cranes* (Denver, CO: University Press of Colorado, 2015), 100–54.

83 Laura J. Martin, *Wild by Design: The Rise of Ecological Restoration* (Cambridge, MA: Harvard University Press, 2022).

84 Birdlife International, '*Grus Americana*. The IUCN Red List of Threatened Species 2020: E.T22692156A18124285' (2020).

85 Barrow, *Nature's Ghosts*, 384; De Bont, *Nature's Diplomats*, 33–6.

86 De Bont, *Nature's Diplomats*.

Chapter 7

1 This account of the impact draws from Walter Alvarez, *T rex and the Crater of Doom* (Princeton, NJ: Princeton University Press, 1997), 7; Michael J. Benton, *The Dinosaurs Rediscovered: How a Scientific Revolution Is Rewriting History* (London: Thames & Hudson, 2019), 254–6; Robert A. DePalma et al., 'A Seismically Induced Onshore Surge Deposit at the Kpg Boundary, North Dakota', *Proceedings of the National Academy of Sciences* 116, no. 17 (23 April 2019): 8190–9.

2 G. R. Chancellor and John Van Wyhe, eds, *Charles Darwin's Notebooks from the Voyage of the Beagle* (Cambridge: Cambridge University Press, 2009).

3 The Darwin Correspondence Project, based at the University Library at the University of Cambridge where Darwin studied, took nearly fifty years of transatlantic collaboration to track down surviving letters written by, or to, Darwin, and publish them in scholarly editions. The full correspondence is available online at https://www.darwinproject.ac.uk, and represents one of the most outstanding academic collaborations relevant to nineteenth-century science.

4 For the best overview of the work's publication history consult Secord, 'Introduction'. Also, Rudwick, *Worlds Before Adam*; Rudwick, *Bursting the Limits of Time*; O'Connor, *The Earth on Show*, 163–87.

5 Darwin, *On the Origin of Species by Means of Natural Selection, or the Preservation of Favoured Races in the Struggle for Life*, passim.

6 Paul Elliott, 'Erasmus Darwin, Herbert Spencer, and the Origins of the Evolutionary Worldview in British Provincial Scientific Culture, 1770–1850', *Isis* 94, no. 1 (2003): 1–29; M. J. S. Hodge and Gregory Radick, eds, *The Cambridge Companion to Darwin*, 2nd ed., Cambridge Companions to Philosophy (Cambridge, England, and New York: Cambridge University Press, 2009).

7 Darwin, *On the Origin of Species by Means of Natural Selection, or the Preservation of Favoured Races in the Struggle for Life*, 281.

8 Ibid., 310–11.

9 Ibid., 321–2. On the lasting legacies of Darwin's claim about the imperfection of the geological record consult David Sepkoski, *Rereading the Fossil Record: The Growth of Paleobiology as an Evolutionary Discipline* (Chicago, IL: University of Chicago Press, 2012).

10 This section is heavily indebted to David Sepkoski. As the son of Jack Sepkoski, a palaeontologist who made important contributions to understanding mass extinctions in the 1980s and a historian of palaeobiology, David's research provides the most detailed and authoritative account of the shifting relationships between biology, geology, and palaeontology. References are given throughout this chapter as the

most relevant, but the most exhaustive account is Sepkoski, *Rereading the Fossil Record*.

11 Norman D. Newell, 'Periodicity in Invertebrate Evolution', *Journal of Paleontology* 26 (1952): 381, 384. Also consult Norman D. Newell, 'Catastrophism and the Fossil Record', *Evolution* 10, no. 1 (1956): 97–101; Norman D. Newell, 'Paleontological Gaps and Geochronology', *Journal of Paleontology* 36 (1962): 592–610; Norman D. Newell, 'Crises in the History of Life', *Scientific American* 208, no. 2 (1963): 76–93.

12 Newell, 'Crises in the History of Life', 76.

13 Niles Eldredge, 'Norman Dennis Newell, 1909–2005', *The Geological Society of London*, 2005, https://www.geolsoc.org.uk/About/History/Obituaries-2001-onwards/Obituaries-2005/Norman-Dennis-Newell-1909--2005

14 Ibid.; Sepkoski, *Rereading the Fossil Record*.

15 Sepkoski, *Rereading the Fossil Record*, 142–84.

16 J. John Sepkoski et al., 'Phanerozoic Marine Diversity and the Fossil Record', *Nature* 293, no. 5832 (1981): 435–7. For Sepkoski and Raup's careers and contributions as summarized here consult J. John Sepkoski, Jr, 'What I Did with My Research Career: Or How Research and Biodiversity Yielded Data on Extinction', in *The Mass-Extinction Debates: How Science Works in a Crisis*, ed. William Glen (Stanford, CA: Stanford University Press, 1994), 132–44; David M. Raup, 'The Extinction Debates: A View from the Trenches', in *The Mass-Extinction Debates*, ed. Glen, 144–51; Derek E. G. Briggs, 'J. John Sepkoski Jr (1948-99)', *Nature* 400, no. 6744 (1999): 514; Douglas H. Erwin, 'David M. Raup (1933–2015)', *Nature* 524, no. 7563 (2015): 36; Sepkoski, *Rereading the Fossil Record*.

17 Formally, in the Late Ordovician, Late Devonian, Late Permian, Late Triassic, and Late Cretaceous periods. D. M. Raup and J. J. Sepkoski, 'Mass Extinctions in the Marine Fossil Record', *Science* 215, no. 4539 (1982): 1501–3; D. M. Raup and J. J. Sepkoski, 'Periodicity of Extinctions in the Geologic Past', *Proceedings of the National Academy of Sciences* 81, no. 3 (1984): 801–5; David M. Raup, *The Nemesis Affair: A Story of the Death of Dinosaurs and the Ways of Science*, rev. and expanded ed. (New York: Norton, 1999).

18 Sepkoski, *Rereading the Fossil Record*, 319–23.

19 Michael J. Benton, *When Life Nearly Died: The Greatest Mass Extinction of All Time*, new ed. (2003; repr., London: Thames & Hudson, 2015), and Michael J. Benton, *Extinctions: How life Survives, Adapts and Evolves* (London: Thames and Hudson, 2023).

20 Chris D. Thomas, *Inheritors of the Earth: How Nature Is Thriving in an Age of Extinction* (London: Allen Lane, 2017).

21 Michael J. Benton, 'Scientific Methodologies in Collision: The History of the Study of the Extinction of the Dinosaurs', *Evolutionary Biology* 24 (1990): 371–400; William Glen, ed., *The Mass-Extinction Debates: How Science Works in a Crisis* (Stanford, CA: Stanford University Press, 1994), 237–8; Sepkoski, *Rereading the Fossil Record*, 71.

22 Newell, 'Crises in the History of Life', 91–2. More recently, the palaeontologist Michael Benton has identified more than a hundred published hypotheses with theories ranging from the outlandish to the plausible, including reduced libido, sexual promiscuity causing AIDS, psychological disorders leading to suicide, predation, changes in climate, and major volcanic eruptions. Benton, 'Scientific Methodologies in Collision'; Benton, *The Dinosaurs Rediscovered*, 258, 290–3.

23 Walter Alvarez, 'The Historical Record in the Scaglia Limestone at Gubbio: Magnetic Reversals and the Cretaceous-Tertiary Mass Extinction', *Sedimentology* 56 (2009): 137–48.

24 The story is well rehearsed in the literature. This account draws from Alvarez, *T rex and the Crater of Doom*; Benton, *When Life Nearly Died*.

25 Luis W. Alvarez et al., 'Extraterrestrial Cause for the Cretaceous-Tertiary Extinction', *Science* 208, no. 4448 (1980): 1095–1108.

26 John W. (John Wesley) Judd et al., *The Eruption of Krakatoa, and Subsequent Phenomena: Report of the Krakatoa Committee of the Royal Society*, ed. G. J. (George James) Symons (London: Trübner & Co., 1888); Marilynn S. Olson, Donald W. Olson, and Russell L. Doescher, 'Marilynn S. Olson, Donald W. Olson, and Russell L. Doescher on the Blood-Red Sky of Munch's the Scream', *Environmental History* 12, no. 1 (2007): 131–5.

27 Three years later, another landmark paper argued that the explosion of a nuclear bomb would trigger a nuclear winter contributing to

mass death. R. P. Turco et al., 'Nuclear Winter: Global Consequences of Multiple Nuclear Explosions', *Science* 222 (1983): 1283–93.

28 For a selection of the coverage consult Clive Cookson, 'Mass Extinction of Life', *The Times* (11 July 1980), The Times Digital Archive; Robert C. Cowen, 'Comets: A Bit of Space Debris Sparks Fantasies', *Christian Science Monitor* (1 October 1980), sec. NEWS; Walter Sullivan, 'Two New Theories Offered on Mass Extinctions in Earth's Past', *New York Times*, 1980, sec. Science Times; Derek York, 'DINOSAURS Clay "Sandwich" May Hold Answer to Mass Extinctions', *Globe and Mail* (15 September 1980); Walter Sullivan, 'Mass Extinctions Increasingly Blamed on Catastrophes from the Sky', *New York Times, Late Edition (East Coast)* (19 January 1982), sec. C; Robert Cooker, 'LONG AGO, SOMETHING HAPPENED', *Boston Globe* (6 January 1982); Anonymous, 'The Meteor Did It', *Boston Globe* (7 November 1983), sec. SCIENCE & TECHNOLOGY; Malcolm W. Browne, 'Dinosaur Experts Resist Meteor Extinction Idea', *New York Times*, 1985, sec. Science.

29 Raup's peer review is reprinted in Raup, *The Nemesis Affair*, 68.

30 Ibid., 69.

31 Raup, 'The Extinction Debate', 145.

32 Raup, *The Nemesis Affair*, 70–1.

33 Glen, *The Mass-Extinction Debates*, 9.

34 Alan R. Hildebrand et al., 'Chicxulub Crater: A Possible Cretaceous/Tertiary Boundary Impact Crater on the Yucatán Peninsula, Mexico', *Geology* 19, no. 9 (1991): 867–71.

35 The most detailed history of the Manhattan Project remains Richard Rhodes, *The Making of the Atomic Bomb* (New York, NY: Simon & Schuster, 1986).

36 Thomas Widner et al., 'Final Report of the Los Alamos Historical Document Retrieval and Assessment (LAHDRA) Project' (Atlanta, GA: Centers for Disease Control and Prevention, 2010).

37 Sepkoski, *Catastrophic Thinking*, 8.

38 Turco et al., 'Nuclear Winter: Global Consequences of Multiple Nuclear Explosions'; Carl Sagan and Richard P. Turco, 'Nuclear Winter in the Post-Cold War Era', *Journal of Peace Research* 30, no. 4 (1993): 369–73.

39 Colin N. Waters et al., 'The Anthropocene Is Functionally and Stratigraphically Distinct from the Holocene', *Science* 351, no. 6269 (2016): aad2622.

40 Koch et al., 'Earth System Impacts of the European Arrival and Great Dying in the Americas after 1492'.

41 Jan Zalasiewicz et al., 'The Working Group on the Anthropocene: Summary of Evidence and Interim Recommendations', *Anthropocene* 19 (2017): 55–60; Will Steffen et al., 'The Trajectory of the Anthropocene: The Great Acceleration', *The Anthropocene Review* 2, no. 1 (2015): 81–98; Erle C. Ellis et al., 'Dating the Anthropocene: Towards an Empirical Global History of Human Transformation of the Terrestrial Biosphere', ed. Joel D. Blum, *Elementa: Science of the Anthropocene* 1 (2013): 000018; Simon L. Lewis and Mark A. Maslin, 'Defining the Anthropocene', *Nature* 519, no. 7542 (March 2015): 171–80; Colin N. Waters et al., 'Candidate Sites and Other Reference Sections for the Global Boundary Stratotype Section and Point of the Anthropocene Series', *The Anthropocene Review* 10, no. 1 (2023): 3–24; Francine M. G. McCarthy et al., 'The Varved Succession of Crawford Lake, Milton, Ontario, Canada as a Candidate Global Boundary Stratotype Section and Point for the Anthropocene Series', *The Anthropocene Review* 10, no. 1 (1 April 2023): 146–76. For coverage of the rejection consult Alexandra Witze, 'Geologists Reject the Anthropocene as Earth's New Epoch – after 15 Years of Debate', *Nature* 627, no. 8003 (6 March 2024): 249–50. On planetary scars see David Farrier, *Footprints: In Search of Future Fossils* (London: 4th Estate, 2020).

42 Myers, *The Sinking Ark*, ix, 5, 3.

43 The term's coinage is usually attributed to Walter G. Rosen in 1985, but, more recently, Sahotna Sarkar has found earlier usages. Quammen, *The Song of the Dodo*, 529–41, 570–1; Barrow, *Nature's Ghosts*, 353–6; Sepkoski, *Catastrophic Thinking*; Sahotra Sarkar, 'Origin of the Term Biodiversity', *BioScience* 71, no. 9 (2021): 893.

44 Sepkoski, *Catastrophic Thinking*; Federica Bocchi et al., 'Are We in a Sixth Mass Extinction? The Challenges of Answering and Value of Asking', *The British Journal for the Philosophy of Science*, 2022, 722107; John C Briggs, 'Emergence of a Sixth Mass Extinction?', *Biological*

Journal of the Linnean Society 122, no. 2 (2017): 243–8; Robert H. Cowie, Philippe Bouchet, and Benoît Fontaine, 'The Sixth Mass Extinction: Fact, Fiction or Speculation?', *Biological Reviews* 97, no. 2 (2022): 640–63.

45 Spence, *Dispossessing the Wilderness*; Sadiah Qureshi, 'Dying Americans', in *From Plunder to Preservation: Britain and the Heritage of Empire, c.1800–1940*, ed. Astrid Swenson and Peter Mandler, Proceedings of the British Academy (Oxford: Oxford University Press, 2013), 267–86.

46 Working Group on the Post-2020 Global Biodiversity Framework, 'Convention on Biological Diversity: First Draft of the Post-2020 Global Biodiversity Framework' (United Nations, 2021); Wilson, *Half-Earth*; E. Dinerstein et al., 'A Global Deal For Nature: Guiding Principles, Milestones, and Targets', *Science Advances* 5, no. 4 (5 April 2019): aaw2869; E. Dinerstein et al., 'A "Global Safety Net" to Reverse Biodiversity Loss and Stabilize Earth's Climate', *Science Advances* 6, no. 36 (2020): abb2824.

47 Wilson, *Half-Earth*.

48 Judith Schleicher et al., 'Protecting Half of the Planet Could Directly Affect over One Billion People', *Nature Sustainability* 2, no. 12 (December 2019): 1094–6.

49 Zoe Todd, 'Respect for Autonomy and Sovereignty of Indigenous and Local Peoples, Not Arbitrary Protection Targets, a Key to Protecting Global Biodiversity', *Critical Indigenous Fish Philosophy*, 1 December 2022, https://fishphilosophy.org/2022/12/01/indigenous-sovereignty-and-autonomy-not-arbitrary-protection-targets-a-key-to-protecting-global-biodiversity

50 Survival International et al., 'NGO Concerns over the Proposed 30% Target for Protected Areas and Absence of Safeguards for Indigenous Peoples and Local Communities', 2020, https://assets.survivalinternational.org/documents/1959/final-en-ngo-concerns-the-proposed-30-target-for-protected-areas-and-absence-of-safeguards-for-indigenous-people-and-local-communities-200901.pdf; Survival International et al., 'Concerns about Protected Areas Targeted in Post-2020 Global Biodiversity Framework', 11 August 2021, https://redd-monitor.org/wp-content/uploads/2021/08/Philan

thropic-Statement-on-CBD-30x30-INITIATIVE-FINAL-2021.Aug_.13-submitted-to-Mr.-Francis-Ogwal-Mr.-Basile-van-Havre-Co-Chairs-of-GBF.pdf

Chapter 8

1 Anonymous, 'Oldest Living Individual Tree', *Guinness World Records*, accessed 24 May 2023, https://www.guinnessworldrecords.com/world-records/oldest-living-individual-tree

2 Anonymous, 'Fortingall', *Scotland's Yew Tree Heritage Initiative*, 2022, https://scotlands-yew-trees.org/yewtree/fortingall/; Anonymous, 'The Tree', *Visit Lincolnshire*, n.d., https://bowthorpeparkfarm.co.uk/the-tree

3 National Parks and Wildlife Service (NPWS, NSW), 'World Heritage Site Nomination for the Greater Blue Mountains Area', 2000, https://whc.unesco.org/uploads/nominations/917.pdf

4 James Woodford, *The Wollemi Pine: The Incredible Discovery of a Living Fossil from the Age of the Dinosaurs*, new ed. (Melbourne: Text Publishing, 2005), 1–44.

5 Marie-Pierre Ledru and Janelle Stevenson, 'The Rise and Fall of the Genus Araucaria: A Southern Hemisphere Climatic Connection', in *Peopled Landscapes: Archaeological and Biogeographic Approaches to Landscapes*, ed. Simon G. Haberle and Bruno David, 1st ed. (ANU Press, 2012); Ruth A. Stockey, 'The Araucariaceae: An Evolutionary Perspective', *Review of Palaeobotany and Palynology* 37, nos 1–2 (July 1982): 133–54; Rod L. Bieleski and Mike D. Wilcox, eds, *Araucariaceae: Proceedings of the 2002 Araucariaceae Symposium, Araucaria-Agathis-Wollemia, International Dendrology Society, Auckland, New Zealand, 14–17 March 2002* (Dunedin, NZ: International Dendrology Society, 2009).

6 Wyn Jones, Kenneth Hill, and Jan Allen, 'Wollemia Nobilis, a New Living Australian Genus and Species in the Araucariaceae', *Telopea* 6 (1995): 173–6. For more on the Araucariaceae, see Bieleski and

Wilcox, *Araucariaceae: Proceedings of the 2002 Araucariaceae Symposium*; Ibid.

7 Jones, Hill, and Allen, 'Wollemia Nobilis, a New Living Australian Genus and Species in the Araucariaceae', 176.

8 These numbers reflect the population distribution after the Black Summer of wildfires. Dominic A. DiPaolo and John C. Villella, 'Ecology and Conservation of a Living Fossil: Australia's Wollemi Pine (Wollemia Nobilis)', in *Imperiled: The Encyclopedia of Conservation*, ed. Dominick A. DellaSala and Michael I. Goldstein (Oxford: Elsevier, 2022), 884–94.

9 Mike Macphail et al., 'Australia: "Wollemi Pine": Old Pollen Records for a Newly Discovered Genus of Gymnosperm', *Geology Today* 11, no. 2 (1995): 48–50; Mike Macphail et al., 'First Evidence for Wollemi Pine-Type Pollen (Dilwynites: Araucariaceae) in South America', ed. Lee A. Newsom, *PLOS ONE* 8, no. 7 (2013): e69281; Mike Macphail and Raymond J. Carpenter, 'New Potential Nearest Living Relatives for Araucariaceae Producing Fossil Wollemi Pine-Type Pollen (*Dilwynites Granulatus* W. K. Harris, 1965)', *Alcheringa: An Australasian Journal of Palaeontology* 38, no. 1 (2014): 135–9.

10 T. Carrick Chambers, Andrew N. Drinnan, and Stephen McLoughlin, 'Some Morphological Features of Wollemi Pine (Wollemia Nobilis: Araucariaceae) and Their Comparison to Cretaceous Plant Fossils', *International Journal of Plant Sciences* 159, no. 1 (1998): 160–71; Cheryl Jones, 'Triumph of the Coneheads', *Bulletin* (3 March 1998).

11 John 11:1–44 (King James Version).

12 Roger Maynard, 'Jurassic Era Relics Found in Remote Australian Forest', *The Times* (15 December 1994); Tom Anderson, 'Aussies Find Tree from the Dinosaur Age', *United Press International* (13 December 1994); Anonymous, '"Living Fossil" Trees a Scientific Sensation', *The Age* (15 December 1994); Barbara G. Briggs, 'From 50 Million Years Ago – the Wollemi Pine', *American Conifer Society Bulletin* 12, no. 1 (1995): 8–9; Randy Bayes, 'New Conifer Found in Australia', *American Conifer Society Bulletin* 12, no. 1 (1995): 6–7; Anonymous, 'Wollemi Pine Thought to Be Living Relic of Dinosaur Age', *Technology Index* 8, no.

1 (1995): 3–4; Ken D. Hill, 'Wollemi Pine: Discovering a Living Fossil', *Nature & Resources* 32 (1996): 20–5.

13 H. H. Hu and W. C. Cheng, 'On the New Family Metasequoiaceae and on *Metasequoia Glyptostroboides*, a Living Species of the Genus Metasequoia Found in Szechuan and Hupeh', *Bulletin of the Fan Memorial Institute of Biology*, n.s., 1 (1948): 154–61; H. H. Hu, 'How Metasequoia, the "Living Fossil", Was Discovered in China', *Arnoldia* 58/59, no. 4/1 (1998): 4–7.

14 Ralph W. Chaney, '"As Remarkable as Discovering a Living Dinosaur": Redwoods in China', *Arnoldia* 58/59, no. 4/1 (1998): 23–32.

15 Anonymous, 'Out of the Past', *The Times* (4 November 1948).

16 J. Linsley Gressitt, 'The California Academy-Lingnan Dawn-Redwood Expedition', *Arnoldia* 58/59, no. 4/1 (1998): 35–9; Yuheng Zhang, '"The Panda of Plants": The Discovery of Dawn Redwood and National Identity Construction in Modern China', *International Journal for History, Culture and Modernity* 7, no. 1 (2019): 271–300.

17 Ralph W. Chaney, 'Redwoods in China', *Natural History Magazine* 47 (1948): 440–4; Chaney, 'As Remarkable as Discovering a Living Dinosaur'; Mike Browell, 'The Creation of the Longest Tree Avenue in the World', *Arboricultural Journal* 35, no. 1 (2013): 50–4.

18 Zhang, '"The Panda of Plants"'.

19 This happened almost immediately, as in Chaney, 'Redwoods in China'.

20 Arun Agrawal, 'Dismantling the Divide Between Indigenous and Scientific Knowledge', *Development and Change* 26, no. 3 (1995): 413–39; Sujit Sivasundaram, 'Sciences and the Global: On Methods, Questions, and Theory', *Isis* 101, no. 1 (March 2010): 146–58.

21 M. J. S. Rudwick, *Earth's Deep History: How It Was Discovered and Why It Matters* (Chicago, IL: University of Chicago Press, 2014), 228–37. According to the latest Iteration of the International Chronostratigraphic Chart, the earth is 4.567 billion years old.

22 This account of Australia's geological formation draws from Richard S. Blewett, Brian L. N. Kennett, and David L. Huston, 'Australia in Time and Space', in *Shaping a Nation: A Geology of Australia*, ed. Richard S. Blewett (Canberra, ACT: Australian National University Press, 2012), 46–119.

23 Anonymous, 'Prehistoric Wollemi Pine Trademarked', *Times of India* (3 August 1995), sec. World; Associated Press, 'Australia Puts Trademark on Prehistoric Pine Trees', *Columbian* (1995), sec. Discovery.

24 Department of Environment and Conservation, New South Wales, *Declaration of Critical Habitat for the Wollemi Pine (Wollemia Nobilis)* (Hurstville, NSW: Dept. of Environment and Conservation, NSW, 2007); Department of Environment and Conservation, 'Wollemia Nobilis: Wollemi Pine Recovery Plan' (Department of Environment and Conservation, NSW, 2007); IUCN, 'Wollemia Nobilis: Thomas, P.: The IUCN Red List of Threatened Species 2011: E.T34926A9898196' (International Union for Conservation of Nature, 20 October 2010).

25 Endersby, *Imperial Nature*; Drayton, *Nature's Government*.

26 Lionel Gilbert, *The Royal Botanic Gardens, Sydney: A History 1816–1985* (Melbourne: Oxford University Press, 1986); Drayton, *Nature's Government*; Jim Endersby, 'A Garden Enclosed: Botanical Barter in Sydney, 1818–39', *The British Journal for the History of Science* 33, no. 3 (September 2000): 313–34; Endersby, *Imperial Nature*.

27 Tom Anderson, ' "Dinosaur Plants" for the Home', *United Press International* (15 December 1994).

28 K. E. Pohio et al., 'Cuttings of Wollemi Pine Tolerate Moderate Photoinhibition and Remain Highly Capable of Root Formation', *Trees* 19, no. 5 (2005): 587–95.

29 Stephen J. Trueman, Geoff S. Pegg, and Judith King, 'Domestication for Conservation of an Endangered Species: The Case of the Wollemi Pine', *Tree and Forestry Science and Biotechnology* 1 (2007): 1–10.

30 Cited prices include buyer's premium and sales tax. Chris Callaghan, 'Botanical Sale of the Century Wollemi Pine Auction', n.d.

31 Callaghan, 'Botanical Sale of the Century Wollemi Pine Auction'; Anonymous, 'Jurassic Bark Fetches Big Bucks'; Richard Macey, 'Living Fossils Grow into Pots of Money', *Sydney Morning Herald* (30 August 1996), sec. NEWS AND FEATURES.

32 Kristy Shaw and Abby Hird, *Global Survey of Ex Situ Conifer Collections* (Richmond: BGCI, 2014).

33 Ibid., 4.

34 Albert Van Dijk, 'Australia's Environment: Mid-Year Update 2019/2020' (Canberra, ACT: Australian National University & TERN, 2021).

35 For official figures of the damage caused, consult Lesley Hughes et al., 'Summer of Crisis' (Climate Council of Australia, 2020); Natural Hazards Research Australia, 'Understanding the Black Summer Bushfires Through Research: A Summary of Key Findings from the Bushfire and Natural Hazards CRC' (Natural Hazards Research Australia, 2023).

36 Sara Spary, 'Australia's Prehistoric Wollemi Pine Trees Saved from Bushfires in Secret Government Mission', *CNN* (15 January 2020), https://www.cnn.com/2020/01/15/australia/dinosaur-pines-rescued-scli-intl/index.html; Brigit Katz, 'Australian Firefighters Have Saved the Last Groves of a Rare, Prehistoric Tree', *Smithsonian Magazine* (17 January 2020), https://www.smithsonianmag.com/smart-news/australian-firefighters-have-saved-last-groves-rare-prehistoric-tree-180974013; John Pickrell and Elizabeth Pennisi, 'Record U.S. and Australian Fires Raise Fears for Many Species', *Science* 370, no. 6512 (2020): 18–19; Peter Hannam, '"Dinosaur Trees" Survived Black Summer, but They Haven't Recovered Enough for the next Bushfire', *The Sydney Morning Herald* (13 January 2021), sec. Conservation, https://www.smh.com.au/environment/conservation/dinosaur-trees-survived-black-summer-but-they-haven-t-recovered-enough-for-the-next-bushfire-20210113-p56tty.html

37 For official figures of the damage caused, consult John Pickrell, 'Australia's Vulnerable Species Hit Hard by Fires', *Science* 366, no. 6472 (2019): 1427–8; John Pickrell, 'As Fires Rage Across Australia, Fears Grow for Rare Species', *Science* 366, no. 6468 (2019): 937; John Pickrell, 'Australian Blazes Will "Reframe Our Understanding of Bushfire"', *Science* 366, no. 6468 (2019): 937–937; Hughes et al., 'Summer of Crisis'; Natural Hazards Research Australia, 'Understanding the Black Summer Bushfires Through Research: A Summary of Key Findings from the Bushfire and Natural Hazards CRC'.

38 Lisa Cox, 'Wollemi Pines Given Special Protected Status after Being Saved from Bushfire Disaster', *The Guardian* (15 January 2021), sec. Environment, https://www.theguardian.com/environment/2021/

jan/15/nsw-wollemi-pines-given-special-protected-status-after-being-saved-from-bushfire-disaster; NSW National Parks and Wildlife Service, 'Assets of Intergenerational Significance (AIS)', *NSW National Parks and Wildlife Service*, n.d., https://www.nationalparks.nsw.gov.au/conservation-programs/assets-of-intergenerational-significance; Ibid. NSW National Parks and Wildlife Service, 'Assets of Intergenerational Significance Conservation Action Plans Consultation', *NSW National Parks and Wildlife Service*, 2023, https://www.environment.nsw.gov.au/topics/parks-reserves-and-protected-areas/park-management/assets-of-intergenerational-significance/assets-of-intergenerational-significance-conservation-action-plans

39 De Bont, *Nature's Diplomats*; Holdgate, *The Green Web*.

40 IUPN, *Proceedings and Reports of the Third General Assembly, Held in Caracas (Venezuela), 3–9 September 1952*, 53.

41 IUPN, *Proceedings and Reports of the Fourth General Assembly, Held at Copenhagen (Denmark), 25 August to 3 September 1954*, 59.

42 Ibid., 43, 59.

43 IUCN, *Proceedings of the Tenth General Assembly, Vigyan Bhavan, New Delhi, 24 November–1 December 1969, Volume II*, 49; Ronald Melville, *Red Data Book 5: Angiospermae* (Morges, Switzerland: IUCN, 1970); Martin J. S. Sands, 'Ronald Melville: 1903–1985', *Kew Bulletin* 41, no. 4 (1986): 761–8.

44 Bayard Webster, 'Plants Called Endangered, Along With Rare Animals', *New York Times* (11 November 1971), sec. Archives.

45 Grenville Lucas, 'Threatened Plants – How to Save Them', *Oryx* 13, no. 3 (1976): 257.

46 United Nations, 'Report of the United Nations Conference on Human Environment: Stockholm, 5–16 June 1972' (New York, NY: United Nations, 1973).

47 Grenville L. Lucas and A. H. M. Synge, 'The IUCN Threatened Plants Committee and Its Work Throughout the World', *Environmental Conservation* 4, no. 3 (October 1977): 179–87.

48 Lucas and Synge, *The IUCN Plant Red Data Book*; Lucas, 'Threatened Plants – How to Save Them'; Kerry S. Walter and Harriett J. Gillett, *The IUCN Red Data Book of Threatened Plants* (Gland, Switzerland:

IUCN, 1998), https://portals.iucn.org/library/node/5780. For contemporary discussion of the importance of this research consult Hugh Synge, Harry Townsend, and Royal Botanic Gardens, Kew, eds, *Survival or Extinction: Proceedings of a Conference Held at the Royal Botanic Gardens, Kew, Entitled the Practical Role of Botanic Gardens in the Conservation of Rare Plants and Threatened Plants, 11–17 September 1978* (Royal Botanic Gardens, Kew: Bentham-Moxon Trust, 1979).

49 Sara Oldfield, Charlotte Lusty, and Amy MacKinven, *The World List of Threatened Trees* (Cambridge: World Conservation Press, 1998), 7. The authors defined a tree as a '*woody plant growing on a single stem usually to a height of over two metres*' (original emphasis), but they acknowledged a precise figure for the number of tree species was made more difficult by lack of consensus on how to define a tree.

50 Botanic Gardens Conservation International, 'State of the World's Trees' (Richmond, UK: Botanic Gardens Conservation International, 2021).

51 Botanic Gardens Conservation International, 'GlobalTree Portal', *Botanic Gardens Conservation International*, accessed 8 May 2023, https://www.bgci.org/resources/bgci-databases/globaltree-portal; Emily Beech, Ryan Hills, and Malin Rivers, 'GlobalTree Portal: Visualizing the State of the World's Trees', *Oryx* 56, no. 3 (2022): 332.

52 Botanic Gardens Conservation International, 'State of the World's Trees', 4.

53 For an excellent study of an endangered crop consult Helen Anne Curry, *Endangered Maize: Industrial Agriculture and the Crisis of Extinction* (Oakland, CA: University of California Press, 2022).

54 Anna Tsing, 'Unruly Edges: Mushrooms as Companion Species', *Environmental Humanities* 1 (2012): 141–54; Anna Lowenhaupt Tsing, *The Mushroom at the End of the World: On the Possibility of Life in Capitalist Ruins* (Princeton, NJ: Princeton University Press, 2021); Eduardo Kohn, *How Forests Think: Toward an Anthropology Beyond the Human* (Berkeley, CA: University of California Press, 2013); Anna M. Lawrence, 'Listening to Plants: Conversations between Critical Plant Studies and Vegetal Geography', *Progress in Human Geography* 46, no. 2 (2022): 629–51.

55 V. Bachraz and W. Strahm, 'Hyophorbe Amaricaulis: The IUCN Red List of Threatened Species 2000: E.T38578A10125958' (2000), https://dx.doi.org/10.2305/IUCN.UK.2000.RLTS.T38578A10125958.en

56 J. D. Bosenberg, 'Encephalartos Woodii: The IUCN Red List of Threatened Species 2022: E.T41881A51057496', 2022, https://dx.doi.org/10.2305/IUCN.UK.2022-1.RLTS.T41881A51057496.en

57 United Nations, 'Report of the United Nations Conference on Human Environment: Stockholm, 5–16 June 1972', 3.

Chapter 9

1 Unless otherwise indicated, this account of the passenger pigeon draws primarily on the authoritative text available: A. W. Schorger, *The Passenger Pigeon: Its Natural History and Extinction*, reprint of 1st ed. (Caldwell, NJ: Blackburn Press, 2004), 14–53. For population estimates, see p. 205.

2 The Society for Ecological Restoration International Science & Policy Working Group, 'The SER International Primer on Ecological Restoration' (2004), 3, https://www.ser-rrc.org/resource/the-ser-international-primer-on

3 My aim here is not to promote one definition over another but to showcase the different meanings that de-extinction has been assigned by both scientists and other scholars. Within the literature, the varied uses have given rise to conflicting claims about the nature of de-extinction. A spirited account of these conflicts from the perspective of a de-extinction scientist can be found in Ben Novak, 'De-Extinction', *Genes* 9, no. 11 (2018): 548.

4 John L. Allen, 'From Cabot to Cartier: The Early Exploration of Eastern North America, 1497–1543', *Annals of the Association of American Geographers* 82, no. 3 (1992): 500–21; Jacques Cartier, *The Voyages of Jacques Cartier*, ed. by Ramsay Cook (Toronto, ON: University of Toronto Press, 1993); Peter Pope, 'The Many Landfalls of John Cabot', in *The Many Landfalls of John Cabot* (Toronto, ON: University of Toronto Press, 1997).

5 Schorger, *Passenger Pigeon*, 3–4.

6 John James Audubon, *Ornithological Biography, or an Account of the Habits of the Birds of the United States of America; Accompanied by Descriptions of the Objects Represented in the Work Entitled the Birds of America, and Interspersed with Delineations of American Scenery and Manners*, vol. 1 (Edinburgh: Adam Black, 1831–9), 319–27.

7 Alexander Wilson, *American Ornithology; Or, the Natural History of the Birds of the United States*, vol. 3 (New York: Collins and Co., 1829), 1–11.

8 Christopher Cokinos, *Hope Is the Thing with Feathers: A Personal Chronicle of Vanished Birds* (New York: J. P. Tarcher/Putnam, 2000), 197.

9 On harvesting feathers consult Schorger, *Passenger Pigeon*, 132; Audubon, *Ornithological Biography*, 1:325.

10 Barrow, *Nature's Ghosts*.

11 Schorger, *Passenger Pigeon*, 155–6, 186; Barrow, *Nature's Ghosts*, 98–9.

12 Simon Pokagon, 'The Wild Pigeon of North America', *The Chautauquan* 22, no. 20 (1895): 202–6, at p. 204.

13 Cokinos, *Hope Is the Thing with Feathers*, 228–9, 244.

14 Ruthven Deane, 'The Passenger Pigeon (*Ectopistes migratorius*) in Confinement', *The Auk* 25, no. 2 (1908): 181–3.

15 Schorger, *Passenger Pigeon*, 20–9; Barrow, *Nature's Ghosts*, 124–6.

16 Schorger, *Passenger Pigeon*, 28–9; Barrow, *Nature's Ghosts*, 126–7; Cokinos, *Hope Is the Thing with Feathers*, 264–71; Powell, *Vanishing America*. The couple were assassinated on 28 June 1914 in Sarajevo. The precise route to war is debated, but, for an accessible survey, consult Christopher M. Clark, *The Sleepwalkers: How Europe Went to War in 1914* (London: Penguin, 2013).

17 Robert Wilson Shufeldt, *The Negro: A Menace to American Civilization* (Boston, MA: Gorham Press, 1907); Robert Wilson Shufeldt, *America's Greatest Problem: The Negro* (Philadelphia, PA: F. A. Davis, 1915).

18 Schorger, *Passenger Pigeon*; R. W. Shufeldt, 'Anatomical and Other Notes on the Passenger Pigeon (*Ectopistes migratorius*) Lately Living in the Cincinnati Zoological Gardens', *The Auk* 32, no. 1 (1915): 29–41; R. W. Shufeldt, 'Published Figures and Plates of the Extinct Passenger Pigeon', *The Scientific Monthly* 12, no. 5 (1921): 458–81.

19 Alison Bashford and Philippa Levine, eds, *The Oxford Handbook of the History of Eugenics* (Oxford: Oxford University Press, 2010).

20 John Connelly, 'Gypsies, Homosexuals, and Slavs', in *The Oxford Handbook of Holocaust Studies*, ed. John Roth and Peter Hayes (Oxford: Oxford University Press, 2010), 274–90.

21 Powell, *Vanishing America*.

22 Dolly Jørgensen, *Recovering Lost Species in the Modern Age: Histories of Longing and Belonging*, History for a Sustainable Future (Cambridge, MA: MIT Press, 2019), 129–30.

23 Ibid., 109–11; Schorger, *Passenger Pigeon*, 230.

24 Aldo Leopold, *A Sand County Almanac* (Oxford: Oxford University Press, 1949).

25 The historian Dolly Jørgensen has provided the first account of extinction from the perspective of a history of emotions. In her fascinating analysis, overwhelming grief for the loss of the passenger pigeon underpins its memorialization and possible de-extinction. Consult Jørgensen, *Recovering Lost Species*, 89–117.

26 The Long Now Foundation, 'About Long Now', *The Long Now Foundation*, n.d., https://longnow.org/about

27 Revive and Restore was founded by Ryan Phelan, its current executive director, and Stewart Brand, and has functioned independently since 2017. Revive and Restore, 'Report on the First De-Extinction Meeting and Other Revivalist News', *Long Now Blog* (7 January 2013), https://blog.longnow.org/02013/01/07/report-on-the-first-de-extinction-meeting-and-other-revivalist-news; Revive & Restore, 'About Us: Revive & Restore', *Revive & Restore*, n.d., https://reviverestore.org/about-us

28 *The Dawn of De-Extinction. Are You Ready?*, Ted Talks, 2013, https://www.ted.com/talks/stewart_brand_the_dawn_of_de_extinction_are_you_ready; Revive & Restore, 'TEDxDeExtinction | Revive & Restore', *Revive & Restore*, n.d., https://reviverestore.org/events/tedxdeextinction. Accessed 21 October 2025.

29 Jørgensen, *Recovering Lost Species*.

30 M. R. O'Connor, *Resurrection Science: Conservation, De-Extinction and the Precarious Future of Wild Things* (New York: St Martin's Press, 2015), 177–206.

31 Novak, 'De-Extinction'.

32 '"Hope" is the thing with feathers–/That perches in the soul–/And sings the tune without the words–/And never stops–at all–.' Emily Dickinson, 'Poem 254', c. 1861.

33 Novak, 'De-Extinction', 5.

34 Ernst Mayr, 'What Is a Species, and What Is Not?', *Philosophy of Science* 63, no. 2 (1996): 262–77; James Mallet, 'A Species Definition for the Modern Synthesis', *Trends in Ecology & Evolution* 10, no. 7 (1 July 1995): 294–9.

35 Harrison B. Tordoff and Patrick T. Redig, 'Role of Genetic Background in the Success of Reintroduced Peregrine Falcons', *Conservation Biology* 15, no. 2 (2001): 528–32.

36 Michael K. Phillips et al., 'Grey Wolves – Yellowstone', in *The Biology and Conservation of Wild Canids*, ed. David W. Macdonald and Claudio Sillero-Zubiri, Oxford Biology (Oxford: Oxford University Press, 2004), 297–310; Dave Foreman, 'The Wildlands Project and the Rewilding of North America', *Denver University Law Review* 76 (1999): 535–53.

37 For a detailed population report consult K. A. Cassidy et al., 'Yellowstone National Park Wolf Project Annual Report 2022' (USA: United States National Park Service, 2022), https://www.nps.gov/yell/learn/nature/wolf-reports.htm

38 Foreman, 'The Wildlands Project and the Rewilding of North America'. The article by Soulé and Noss was essentially a manifesto for the Wildlands Project. Consult Michael E. Soulé and Reed Noss, 'Rewilding and Biodiversity: Complementary Goals for Continental Conservation', *Wild Earth* 8 (1998): 19–26. On the history of the term 'rewilding' consult Dolly Jørgensen, 'Rethinking Rewilding', *Geoforum* 65 (2015): 482–8; Jamie Lorimer et al., 'Rewilding: Science, Practice, and Politics', *Annual Review of Environment and Resources* 40, no. 1 (2015): 39–62. Jørgensen notes the first use of the term was in 1991 in *Wild Earth* magazine. The earliest usage I have found is John Davis, 'A Minority View', *Wild Earth* 1, no. 4 (1991): 5–6.

39 For European examples and discussions of the emotional connections consult Jørgensen, *Recovering Lost Species*; Dolly Jørgensen, 'Reintroduction and De-extinction', *BioScience* 63, no. 9 (2013): 719–20.

40 Patrick Barkham, 'Wanted: UK Bison Rangers, No Previous Experience Expected', *The Guardian* (13 January 2021), http://www.theguardian.com/environment/2021/jan/13/wildlife-rangers-in-uk-jobs-offer-no-bison-experience-required; Anonymous, 'Wilder Blean', *Kent Wildlife Trust*, n.d., https://www.kentwildlifetrust.org.uk/wilderblean

41 'Rewilding Europe: Making Europe a Wilder Place', *Rewilding Europe*, accessed 9 January 2021, https://rewildingeurope.com.

42 Novak, 'De-Extinction'.

43 Frans W. M. Vera, 'Large-Scale Nature Development – The Oostvaardersplassen', *British Wildlife*, (June 2009): 28–36.

44 Ibid. For more on the history and development of the OVP consult Bert Theunissen, 'The Oostvaardersplassen Fiasco', *Isis* 110 (2019): 341–5; Jamie Lorimer and Clemens Driessen, 'Wild Experiments at the Oostvaardersplassen: Rethinking Environmentalism in the Anthropocene', *Transactions of the Institute of British Geographers* 39, no. 2 (2014): 169–81; Jamie Lorimer and C. P. G. Driessen, 'Back-Breeding the Aurochs: The Heck Brothers, National Socialism and Imagined Geographies for Nonhuman Lebensraum', in *Hitler's Geographies: The Spatialities of the Third Reich*, ed. Paolo Giacarria and Claudio Minca (Chicago, IL: University of Chicago Press, 2016), 138–59; Jamie Lorimer and Clemens Driessen, 'From "Nazi Cows" to Cosmopolitan "Ecological Engineers": Specifying Rewilding Through a History of Heck Cattle', *Annals of the American Association of Geographers* 106, no. 3 (2016): 631–52.

45 Lorimer and Driessen, 'From "Nazi Cows" to Cosmopolitan "Ecological Engineers" '; Lorimer and Driessen, 'Back-Breeding the Aurochs'; Heinz Heck, 'The Breeding-Back of the Aurochs', *Oryx* 1, no. 3 (1951): 117–22; Heinz Heck, 'The Breeding-Back of the Tarpan', *Oryx* 1, no. 7 (1952): 338–42.

46 Ronald Goderie, 'The Tauros Programme: The Search for a New Icon for European Wilderness', *The Tauros Programme*, n.d., https://taurosproject.com

47 Russell Higuchi et al., 'DNA Sequences from the Quagga, an Extinct Member of the Horse Family', *Nature* 312, no. 5991 (1984): 284; J. A.

Miller, 'Gene Samples from an Extinct Animal Cloned', *Science News* 125, no. 23 (1984): 356; Peter Heywood, 'The Micro-Politics of Macromolecules in the Taxonomy and Restoration of Quaggas', *Kronos* 41 (2021): 314–37.

48 Heywood, 'The Micro-Politics of Macromolecules in the Taxonomy and Restoration of Quaggas'.

49 C. Polge, A. U. Smith, and A. S. Parkes, 'Revival of Spermatozoa after Vitrification and Dehydration at Low Temperatures', *Nature* 164, no. 4172 (1949): 666; Joanna Radin, *Life on Ice: A History of New Uses for Cold Blood* (Chicago, IL: University of Chicago Press, 2017), 35–9.

50 Ann Ewing, 'Live Cells Frozen Alive', *The Science News-Letter* 81, no. 16 (1962): 246–7.

51 Kurt Benirschke, 'The Frozen Zoo Concept', *Zoo Biology* 3, no. 4 (1984): 325–8; Oliver A. Ryder et al., 'DNA Banks for Endangered Animal Species', *Science* 288, no. 5464 (2000): 275–7; Joanna Radin, 'Planned Hindsight: The Vital Valuations of Frozen Tissue at the Zoo and the Natural History Museum', *Journal of Cultural Economy* 8, no. 3 (2015): 361–78.

52 Benirschke, 'The Frozen Zoo Concept'; K. Benirschke and A. T. Kumamoto, 'Mammalian Cytogenetics and Conservation of Species', *Journal of Heredity* 82, no. 3 (1991): 187–91; Shawna Williams, 'Conservation Biologist and Placenta Expert Kurt Benirschke Dies', *The Scientist Magazine*, (14 September 2018), https://www.the-scientist.com/news-opinion/conservation-biologist-and-placenta-expert-kurt-benirschke-dies-64809

53 Benirschke, 'The Frozen Zoo Concept', 326, 327.

54 Anonymous, 'Frozen Zoo®', *San Diego Zoo: Institute for Conservation Research*, n.d., https://institute.sandiegozoo.org/resources/frozen-zoo%C2%AE

55 Matthew Chrulew, 'Freezing the Ark: The Cryopolitics of Endangered Species Preservation', in *Cryopolitics*, ed. Joanna Radin and Emma Kowal (Cambridge, MA: MIT Press, 2017), 283–305. The Frozen Ark's website is available at https://www.frozenark.org, and the files registering it as a charity are available at https://register-of-charities.charitycommission.gov.uk/charity-search/-/charity-details/4025884, accessed 17 January 2021.

56 J. Folch et al., 'First Birth of an Animal from an Extinct Subspecies (Capra pyrenaica pyrenaica) by Cloning', *Theriogenology* 71, no. 6 (2009): 1033.

57 IUCN, 'The IUCN Red List of Threatened Species'.

58 The historian Joanna Radin suggests that new freezing techniques in the mid-twentieth century created a latent state of existence between life and death. Latency holds the potential for life grounded in the refusal to allow death. Radin, *Life on Ice*. On de-extinction consult Beth Alison Shapiro, *How to Clone a Mammoth: The Science of De-Extinction* (Princeton, NJ: Princeton University Press, 2015), 142–8; Novak, 'De-Extinction'.

59 There is already a substantial literature on de-extinction. Some of the best introductions to the concept, scientific research, and ethics include George M. Church and Edward Regis, *Regenesis: How Synthetic Biology Will Reinvent Nature and Ourselves* (New York: Basic Books, 2012); Shapiro, *How to Clone a Mammoth*; Britt Wray, *Rise of the Necrofauna: The Science, Ethics, and Risks of De-Extinction* (Vancouver, B.C.; Berkeley, CA: Greystone Books, 2017); Helen Pilcher, *Bring Back the King: The New Science of De-Extinction* (London: Bloomsbury, 2016).

60 Shapiro, *How to Clone a Mammoth*, 109–40; Paul S. Martin and Anthony J. Stuart, 'Mammoth Extinction: Two Continents and Wrangel Island', *Radiocarbon* 37, no. 1 (1995): 7–10.

61 Church and Regis, *Regenesis*; S. A. Zimov, 'Pleistocene Park: Return of the Mammoth's Ecosystem', *Science* 308, no. 5723 (2005): 796–8.

62 John Carey, 'Rewilding', *Proceedings of the National Academy of Sciences* 113, no. 4 (26 January 2016): 806–8; Josh Donlan et al., 'Re-Wilding North America', *Nature* 436, no. 7053 (2005): 913–14; Josh Donlan et al., 'Pleistocene Rewilding: An Optimistic Agenda for Twenty-First Century Conservation', *The American Naturalist* 168, no. 5 (November 2006): 660–81; Paul S. Martin, *Twilight of the Mammoths: Ice Age Extinctions and the Rewilding of America* (Berkeley, CA: University of California Press, 2007).

63 Donlan et al., 'Re-Wilding North America', 913.

64 Tim Caro, 'The Pleistocene Re-Wilding Gambit', *Trends in Ecology & Evolution* 22, no. 6 (June 2007): 281–3; Matthew Chrulew, 'Reversing

Extinction: Restoration and Resurrection in the Pleistocene Rewilding Projects', *Humanimalia* 2, no. 2 (2011): 4–27; David Nogués-Bravo et al., 'Rewilding Is the New Pandora's Box in Conservation', *Current Biology* 26, no. 3 (February 2016): R87–91.

65 One of the few examples of such broader critiques is Chrulew, 'Reversing Extinction'. Similar arguments have been made in discussions of the Anthropocene, for instance Donna Haraway, 'Anthropocene, Capitalocene, Plantationocene, Chthulucene: Making Kin', *Environmental Humanities* 6, no. 1 (2015): 159–65; Janae Davis et al., 'Anthropocene, Capitalocene . . . Plantationocene?: A Manifesto for Ecological Justice in an Age of Global Crises', *Geography Compass* 13, no. 5 (May 2019): e12438; James W. Moore, 'Capitalocene & Planetary Justice', *Études digitales* 9 (2021): 53–65.

66 Keller and Turek, *American Indians and National Parks*; Burnham, *Indian Country, God's Country*; Spence, *Dispossessing the Wilderness*.

67 Shapiro, *How to Clone a Mammoth*; Novak, 'De-Extinction'.

68 Ibid.

69 Lukas Rieppel, *Assembling the Dinosaur: Fossil Hunters, Tycoons, and the Making of a Spectacle* (Cambridge, MA: Harvard University Press, 2019).

70 Ibid.; Erika Lorraine Milam, *Creatures of Cain: The Hunt for Human Nature in Cold War America* (Princeton, NJ: Princeton University Press, 2019); Alexandra A. Chaidez and Aidan F. Ryan, '"I Profoundly Regret Harvard's Past Association With Him": Bacow Announces University Will Donate Unspent Epstein Gifts', *The Harvard Crimson* (13 September 2019), https://www.thecrimson.com/article/2019/9/13/harvard-reviews-epstein-gifts; Jeffrey Mervis, 'What Kind of Researcher Did Sex Offender Jeffrey Epstein Like to Fund? He Told Science Before He Died', *Science, AAAS* (19 September 2019), https://www.sciencemag.org/news/2019/09/what-kind-researcher-did-sex-offender-jeffrey-epstein-fund-he-told-science-before-he-died; Adam Rogers, 'How Rich Donors Like Epstein (and Others) Undermine Science', *Wired* (15 September 2019), https://www.wired.com/story/the-problem-with-rich-people-funding-science; Sharon Begley, 'Biologist George Church Apologizes for Contacts with Jeffrey Epstein', *STAT* (5 August 2019),

https://www.statnews.com/2019/08/05/citing-nerd-tunnel-vision-biologist-george-church-apologizes-for-contacts-with-jeffrey-epstein

71 Damian Carrington, 'Meatball from Long-Extinct Mammoth Created by Food Firm', *The Guardian* (28 March 2023), sec. Environment, https://www.theguardian.com/environment/2023/mar/28/meatball-mammoth-created-cultivated-meat-firm; Smithsonian Magazine and Alex Chun, 'This Massive Meatball Was Made With Woolly Mammoth DNA', *Smithsonian Magazine* (30 March 2023), https://www.smithsonianmag.com/smart-news/this-massive-meatball-was-made-with-woolly-mammoth-dna-180981908

72 Novak, 'De-Extinction'.

Chapter 10

1 On the refurbishment of Hintze Hall, consult Pandora Syperek et al., 'Curating Ocean Ecology at the Natural History Museum: Miranda Lowe and Richard Sabin in Conversation with Pandora Syperek and Sarah Wade', *Science Museum Group Journal* 13, no. 13 (2020).

2 You can visit Hintze Hall virtually at https://tinyurl.com/y5gzvag8 and listen to David Attenborough discussing these specimens via the museum's SoundCloud at https://soundcloud.com/nhmlondon/sets/hintze-hall

3 John Ray, 'An Account of the Dissection of a Porpess', *Philosophical Transactions (1665–1678)* 6 (1671): 2274–9; Londa Schiebinger, 'Why Mammals are Called Mammals: Gender Politics in Eighteenth-Century Natural History', *American Historical Review* 98 (1993): 382–411; Philip D. Gingerich, 'Evolution of Whales from Land to Sea', in *Great Transformations in Vertebrate Evolution*, ed. Kenneth P. Dial, Neil Shubin, and Elizabeth L. Brainerd (Chicago, IL: University of Chicago Press, 2015), 239–56.

4 The wolf-sized, semi-aquatic ancestor is formally called *Pakicetus* and was first named in the 1980s. Its descendants included the semi-aquatic *Maiacetus* and the fully aquatic *Dorudon* from which modern baleen and toothed whales descend. Unfortunately, while I'm thrilled

that whales descend from my ancestral homeland, their ancestor's name also brings to mind awful racial slurs, so I have not used the name here. For the evolution and naming of cetaceans, consult Philip D. Gingerich et al., 'Origin of Whales in Epicontinental Remnant Seas: New Evidence from the Early Eocene of Pakistan', *Science* 220, no. 4595 (1983): 403–6; Annalisa Berta, 'What Is a Whale?', *Science* 263, no. 5144 (1994): 180–1; J. G. M. Thewissen et al., 'Whales Originated from Aquatic Artiodactyls in the Eocene Epoch of India', *Nature* 450, no. 7173 (December 2007): 1190–4; Philip D. Gingerich, 'Evolution of Whales from Land to Sea', *Proceedings of the American Philosophical Society* 156, no. 3 (2012): 309–23; Gingerich, 'Evolution of Whales from Land to Sea' (2015); Jonathan H. Geisler, 'Whale Evolution: Dispersal by Paddle or Fluke', *Current Biology* 29 (2019): R280–99; Michael R. McGowen et al., 'Phylogenomic Resolution of the Cetacean Tree of Life Using Target Sequence Capture', ed. Hernam López-Fernández, *Systematic Biology* 69, no. 3 (2020): 479–501. Gingerich's articles are particularly important as they clearly recognize the contributions of his collaborators in the global South, particularly Pakistan and Egypt. For instance, he notes that the type specimen of *Maiacetus inuus* was found by Iyad Zalmout. Such participation and co-discoveries are routinely erased in the history of science more broadly.

5 Gingerich, 'Evolution of Whales from Land to Sea' (2012); Gingerich, 'Evolution of Whales from Land to Sea' (2015).

6 D. Graham Burnett, *The Sounding of the Whale: Science & Cetaceans in the Twentieth Century* (Chicago, IL: University of Chicago Press, 2012).

7 Stephen J. Trumble et al., 'Baleen Whale Cortisol Levels Reveal a Physiological Response to 20th Century Whaling', *Nature* 9, no. 1 (2018): 1–8. Cortisol levels were at their lowest between 1970 and 1999, coinciding with increased protections, including the global moratorium on whaling of 1986.

8 Hal Whitehead, Tim D. Smith, and Luke Rendell, 'Adaptation of Sperm Whales to Open-Boat Whalers: Rapid Social Learning on a Large Scale?', *Biology Letters* 17, no. 3 (2021): rsbl.2021.0030, 20210030. For historians reporting whalers' accounts consult Bathsheba Demuth,

Floating Coast: An Environmental History of the Bering Strait (New York: W. W. Norton & Co., 2019); Ryan Tucker Jones, 'A Whale of a Difference: Southern Right Whale Culture and the Tasman World's Living Terrain of Encounter', *Environment and History* 25 (2019): 185–218.

9 Unless otherwise cited, all discussion of Owen's career draws from Rupke, *Richard Owen*.

10 Carla Yanni, *Nature's Museums: Victorian Science and the Architecture of Display* (New York: Princeton Architectural Press, 2005), 111–15.

11 Richard Owen, 'Presidential Address', *Report of the Fifty-First Meeting of the British Association for the Advancement of Science; Held at York in August and September 1881* 51 (1882): 656.

12 Richard Owen, *On the Extent and Aims of a National Museum of Natural History* (London: Saunders, Otley, & Co, 1862), 75, 99.

13 Unless otherwise indicated, this history of the Natural History Museum draws from F. W. Sheppard, ed., *Survey of London: Volume 38, South Kensington Museums Area*, 47 vols (London: London County Council, 1975), http://www.british-history.ac.uk/survey-london/vol38; Yanni, *Nature's Museums*; William T. Stearn, *The Natural History Museum in South Kensington: A History of the British Museum (Natural History) 1753–1980* (London: Heinemann, 1981); Mark Girouard, *Alfred Waterhouse and the Natural History Museum* (London: Natural History Museum, 1981).

14 Owen, *Extent and Aims of a National Museum*, 11.

15 Yanni, *Nature's Museums*, 117–26.

16 'The Natural History Museum', *Saturday Review* (23 April 1881), 517–18.

17 Owen, 'Presidential Address', 658.

18 Unless otherwise indicated, this account of Sloane's collecting draws from James Delbourgo, *Collecting the World: Hans Sloane and the Origins of the British Museum* (London: Allen Lane, 2017).

19 Ibid., 49–53, 78.

20 Ibid., 67.

21 Ibid., 34–9, 55–7, 132.

22 On the centenary of the Natural History Museum's opening, Stearn's official account does not reflect on the importance of Sloane's trip to

Jamaica or his widow's wealth. Consult Stearn, *The Natural History Museum in South Kensington*, 3–8, at 5.

23 On Sloane's death, his executors recorded 756 human remains catalogued as 'Humana'. Delbourgo, *Collecting the World*, 260.

24 Ibid., 40–4.

25 Hilary M. Beckles, 'The Caribbean and Britain', in *The Origins of Empire*, ed. Nicholas P. Canny, vol. 1, 5 vols, *The Oxford history of the British Empire* (Oxford: Oxford University Press, 1998), 218–40. For more on the crucial links between the Caribbean and British Isles, consult Christienna Fryar's forthcoming book *Entangled Lands*, in press with Allen Lane.

26 Delbourgo, *Collecting the World*, 185–92.

27 Ibid., 156–62.

28 Ibid., 260.

29 Yanni, *Nature's Museums*, 21.

30 Owen, *Extent and Aims of A National Museum*, 126.

31 Ibid., 7.

32 Genesis 1:21 (King James Version).

33 Owen, 14–15. In Owen's language, a Great Whalebone whale of the 'Mysticete'.

34 Ibid., 18–19.

35 Clive N. Trueman et al., 'Combining Simulation Modeling and Stable Isotope Analyses to Reconstruct the Last Known Movements of One of Nature's Giants', *PeerJ* 7 (2019): e7912; Christopher W. Clark and Ellen C. Garland, eds, *Ethology and Behavioral Ecology of Mysticetes*, Ethology and Behavioral Ecology of Marine Mammals (Cham, Switzerland: Springer International Publishing, 2022).

36 This account of Hope's acquisition and early display draws on Richard Sabin and Lorraine Cornish, *Hope: The Story of the Blue Whale* (London: Natural History Museum, 2019), 8–17.

37 'A Huge Whale Killed on the Wexford Coast', *Belfast News-Letter* (30 March 1891): 6.

38 Ibid.

39 Flower served as Director, and Owen's successor, from 1888. On Flower's Directorship consult Stearn, *The Natural History Museum in South Kensington*, 67–77.

40 F. C. Fraser, 'The Blue Whale Skeleton in the Whale Hall', *Natural History Magazine* 4 (1934): 229.

41 J. Wilson, 'The Wexford Whale', *Standard* (4 April 1891): 2. For estimated contemporary values consult the National Archives Currency Converter, 1270–2017, https://www.nationalarchives.gov.uk/currency-converter/#, accessed 13 October 2020.

42 'View of the Central Hall (1888)', British Museum and [Flower, W. H.], *A General Guide to the British Museum (Natural History)* (London: British Museum, 1887), 13, 22–34.

43 W. H. Flower, 'On Whales, Past and Present, and Their Probable Origin I', *Nature* 28, no. 713 (1883): 200.

44 W. H. Flower, 'On Whales, Past and Present, and Their Probable Origin II', *Nature* 28, no. 714 (1883): 229. Flower also gave these papers as a lecture at the Royal Institution in 1883, which was reprinted as William Henry Flower, *On Whales, Past and Present and Their Probable Origin. A Discourse* (London: [n.p.], 1883).

45 Barrow, *Nature's Ghosts*.

46 R. Deaville et al., 'Annual Report for the Period 1st January–31 December 2018 (Contract Number ME6008)' (London: UK Cetacean Strandings Investigation Programme, 2018); Anna Turns, 'A Rare Glimpse Inside Britain's Secret Vault of Whale Skeletons', *Guardian* (21 January 2023), https://www.theguardian.com/environment/2023/jan/21/natural-history-museum-vault-whale-skeletons-cetacean-collection

47 Burnett, *The Sounding of the Whale*, 109–34.

48 Ibid., 150–1.

49 Ibid., 178.

50 Sabin and Cornish, *Hope*, 23, 36; Fraser, 'The Blue Whale Skeleton in the Whale Hall'; G. F. Herbert Smith, 'Note on the Method of Suspension', *Natural History Magazine* 4 (1934): 230–2.

51 Sabin and Cornish, *Hope*.

52 'New Home for Whales', *Nottingham Evening Post* (3 January 1934): 8. Also consult '91 Feet Model Whale', *Evening Telegraph* (24 December 1938): 8.

53 'Rare Whale for Exhibition', *Gloucestershire Echo* (19 August 1938): 6.

54 'The "Ghost" Of a Whale On View', *Gloucester Citizen* (7 June 1937), 8, and Stearn, *The Natural History Museum in South Kensington*, 131–2.

55 Michael Rossi, 'Fabricating Authenticity: Modeling a Whale at the American Museum of Natural History, 1906–1974', *Isis* 101, no. 2 (June 2010): 338–61.

56 International Whaling Commission, 'International Convention for the Regulation of Whaling' (1946), 1, https://archive.iwc.int/?r=3607; Ray Gambell, 'International Management of Whales and Whaling: An Historical Review of the Regulation of Commercial and Aboriginal Subsistence Whaling', *Arctic* 46 (1993): 97–107; Burnett, *The Sounding of the Whale*, 341–409.

57 Burnett, *The Sounding of the Whale*, 328.

58 John C. Lilly, *Man and Dolphin: Adventures of a New Scientific Frontier* (New York: Pyramid Books, 1961), 7.

59 Burnett, *The Sounding of the Whale*.

60 Roger S. Payne and Scott McVay, 'Songs of Humpback Whales', *Science* 173 (1971): 585.

61 Ibid., 590.

62 Burnett, *The Sounding of the Whale*, 628–9.

63 Ibid.; Frank S. Zelko, *Make It a Green Peace! The Rise of Countercultural Environmentalism* (New York: Oxford University Press, 2013).

64 Zelko, *Make It a Green Peace!*

65 Ibid.

66 Hunter's testimony cited in Ibid., 217.

67 International Whaling Commission, 'Total Catches Since the Moratorium Came into Place in 1985', *International Whaling Commission* (2021), https://iwc.int/management-and-conservation/whaling/total-catches

68 Dippy was donated by Andrew Carnegie in 1905. The original specimen stands in Pittsburgh's Carnegie Museum of Natural History while replicas occupy museums in Berlin, Bologna, Madrid, Mexico City, Munich, La Plata, Paris, and Vienna. Rieppel, *Assembling the Dinosaur*, 73–109.

69 Arianna Bernucci, Lorraine Cornish, and Cheryl Lynn, 'Blue Whale on the Move: Dismantling a 125-Year-Old Specimen', in *Green Museum:*

How to Practice What We Preach? 2016 SPNHC Conference, 31st Annual Meeting, June 20–25, 2016, Berlin, Germany (2016); Anonymous, 'Natural History Museum Receives £5m Donation', *BBC News* (8 May 2014), https://www.bbc.com/news/uk-27319973

70 On the history of this specimen consult Albert Koch, *Description of Missourium, or Missouri Leviathan: Together with Its Supposed Habits and Indian Traditions Concerning the Location from Whence It Was Exhumed; Also, Comparisons of the Whale, Crocodile and Missourium with the Leviathan, as Described in 41st Chapter of the Book of Job, And a Catalogue of the Whole Fossil Collection* (London: E. Fisher, 1841); Richard Owen, 'Report on the Missourium Now Exhibiting at the Egyptian Hall, with an Inquiry into the Claims of the Tetracaudodon to Generic Distinction', *Proceedings of the Geological Society of London* 3 (1842): 689–95; P. R. Hoy, 'Dr. Koch's Missourium', *The American Naturalist* 5 (1871): 147–8; James D. Dana, 'On Dr Koch's Evidence With Regard To the Contemporaneity of Man and the Mastodon In Missouri', *American Journal of Science and Arts* 9 (1875): 335–46; William Lindsay, '"Mammoth" Task', *Curator: The Museum Journal* 34, no. 4 (1991): 261–72.

71 Koch, *Description of Missourium, or Missouri Leviathan*, 14.

72 NHM Catalogue number PV OR 15913, https://data.nhm.ac.uk/object/27776c58-61a8-4d27-9771-8091d3d03c60, and Owen, 'Report on the Missourium Now Exhibiting at the Egyptian Hall, with an Inquiry into the Claims of the Tetracaudodon to Generic Distinction'; R. McMillan, 'The Discovery of Fossil Vertebrates on Missouri's Western Frontier', *Earth Sciences History* 29, no. 1 (2010): 26–51.

73 Lindsay, '"Mammoth" Task'; Lu Allington-Jones, 'Mastodon and On and On . . . a Moving Story', *Journal of Natural Science Collections* 5 (2018): 110–14.

74 Reginald Walter Hooley, 'On the Skeleton of Iguanodon atherfieldensis sp. nov., from the Wealden Shales of Atherfield (Isle of Wight)', *Quarterly Journal of the Geological Society* 81 (1925): 1–61; Mantell, 'Discovery of the Bones of the Iguanodon in a Quarry of Kentish Rag (a Limestone Belonging to the Later Greensand Formation) Near Maidstone, Kent'; Mantell, *On the Structure of the Iguanodon, and on the*

Fauna and Flora of the Wealden Formation; Dean, *Gideon Mantell and the Discovery of Dinosaurs*, 52–85.

75 Hooley, 'On the Skeleton of Iguanodon atherfieldensis', 1.

76 Gregory S. Paul, 'A Revised Taxonomy of the Iguanodont Dinosaur Genera and Species', *Cretaceous Research* 29, no. 2 (April 2008): 192.

77 Carlos Roberto Fonseca, 'The Silent Mass Extinction of Insect Herbivores in Biodiversity Hotspots', *Conservation Biology* 23, no. 6 (2009): 1507–15; Simon R. Leather, Yves Basset, and Bradford A. Hawkins, 'Insect Conservation: Finding the Way Forward', *Insect Conservation and Diversity* 1, no. 1 (February 2008): 67–9.

78 Kerry Lotzof, 'Highlighting Coral Reefs at Risk', *Natural History Museum (London)*, n.d., https://www.nhm.ac.uk/discover/highlighting-coral-reefs-at-risk.html; Syperek et al., 'Curating Ocean Ecology at the Natural History Museum'.

79 On imperial hunting and its connections to both extinction and conservation consult Prendergast and Adams, 'Colonial Wildlife Conservation and the Origins of the Society for the Preservation of the Wild Fauna of the Empire (1903–1914)'; MacKenzie, *The Empire of Nature*.

80 Anonymous, 'Cecil the Lion: Zimbabwe Hunter Bailed Over Killing', *BBC News* (29 July 2015), sec. Africa, https://www.bbc.com/news/world-us-canada-33699346

81 Kerry Lotzof, 'The Heavy Metal Rock Bands Charting Life on Early Earth', *Natural History Museum (London)*, n.d., https://www.nhm.ac.uk/discover/the-heavy-metal-rock-bands-charting-life-on-early-earth.html

82 Bruce Harvey and Simon Nish, 'Rio Tinto and Indigenous Community Agreement Making in Australia', *Journal of Energy & Natural Resources Law* 23, no. 4 (2005): 499–510; Thomas F. King, 'Rio Tinto Talks the Talk', *The Historic Environment: Policy & Practice* 3, no. 2 (October 2012): 166–9; Rio Tinto, 'Why Cultural Heritage Matters', n.d., 132; Anonymous, 'Rio Tinto: Church of England Condemns Aboriginal Destruction', *BBC News* (9 September 2020), sec. Business, https://www.bbc.com/news/business-54075614

83 John Ruskin, 'A Museum or Picture Gallery: Its Functions and Its Formation', *The Art Journal (1875–1887)* 6 (1880): 215–17; Amy Woodson-Boulton, *Transformative Beauty: Art Museums in Industrial Britain* (Stanford, CA: Stanford University Press, 2012).

84 The relevant literature is vast, but the following provide helpful context: Donna Haraway, 'Teddy Bear Patriarchy: Taxidermy in the Garden of Eden, New York City, 1908–1936', *Social Text* (1984), 20–64; Paula Findlen, *Possessing Nature: Museums, Collecting, and Scientific Culture in Early Modern Italy*, Studies on the History of Society and Culture 20 (Berkeley, CA: University of California Press, 1994); Conklin, *In the Museum of Man*; Sarah Longair and John McAleer, eds, *Curating Empire: Museums and the British Imperial Experience*, Studies in Imperialism (Museums, material culture and the British Empire) (Manchester: Manchester University Press, 2016); Delbourgo, *Collecting the World: Hans Sloane and the Origins of the British Museum*; Dan Hicks, *The Brutish Museums: The Benin Bronzes, Colonial Violence and Cultural Restitution* (London: Pluto Press, 2020); Adam Kuper, *The Museum of Other People* (London: Profile Books, 2024).

85 Rieppel, *Assembling the Dinosaur*.

86 Patrick Radden Keefe, *Empire of Pain: The Secret History of the Sackler Dynasty* (New York: Doubleday, 2021); Katayoun Shafiee, *Machineries of Oil: An Infrastructural History of BP in Iran* (Cambridge, MA: MIT Press, 2018); Esther Addley, 'British Museum Ends BP Sponsorship Deal after 27 Years', *The Guardian* (2 June 2023), sec. Culture, https://www.theguardian.com/culture/2023/jun/02/british-museum-ends-bp-sponsorship-deal-after-27-years

87 Martha Busby, 'Extinction Rebellion Activists Stage Die-in Protests Across Globe', *The Guardian* (27 April 2019), sec. Environment, http://www.theguardian.com/environment/2019/apr/27/extinction-rebellion-activists-stage-die-in-protests-across-globe; Jen Mills, 'Extinction Rebellion Stage Mass "Die-in" at Natural History Museum', *Metro* (22 April 2019), sec. News, https://metro.co.uk/2019/04/22/extinction-rebellion-stage-mass-die-in-natural-history-museum-9286098; James Morris, 'XR Activists Hold

Dramatic "Die-in" at Natural History Museum', *Evening Standard* (23 April 2019), sec. News, https://www.standard.co.uk/news/london/hundreds-of-extinction-rebellion-protesters-stage-dramatic-diein-at-london-s-natural-history-museum-a4123166.html

Epilogue

1 Peter H. Raven and Scott E. Miller, 'Here Today, Gone Tomorrow', *Science* 370, no. 6513 (2020): 149; Kemp, *The Lost Species*.

2 David Gange, *The Frayed Atlantic Edge: A Historian's Journey from Shetland to the Channel* (London: William Collins, 2020).

3 The swapped legs are noted in Hein van Grouw, 'The Spotted Green Pigeon Caloenas Maculata: As Dead as a Dodo, but What Else Do We Know About It?', *Bulletin of the British Ornithologists' Club* 134, no. 4 (2014): 291–301.

4 On Latham, consult Yolanda Foote, 'Latham, John (1740–1837), Naturalist', in *Oxford Dictionary of National Biography* (Oxford: Oxford University Press, 2004); John Latham, *A General Synopsis of Birds*, vol. 2, 3 vols (London: Leigh & Sotheby, 1783), https://doi.org/10.5962/bhl.title.62572; John Latham, *A General History of Birds*, vol. 8, 10 vols (Winchester: Jacob and Johnson, 1823).

5 Latham, *A General Synopsis of Birds*, 2.2:642.

6 Cited in van Grouw, 'The Spotted Green Pigeon Caloenas Maculata', 292. Stanley's copy of Latham is in the collections of the World Museum, Liverpool.

7 H. Forbes, 'On the Type of the Spotted Green Pigeon of Latham, in the Derby Museum', *Bulletin of the Liverpool Museums* 1 (1898): 83. On historical disagreement about the bird's classification consult van Grouw, 'The Spotted Green Pigeon Caloenas Maculata'.

8 Tim H. Heupink, Hein van Grouw, and David M. Lambert, 'The Mysterious Spotted Green Pigeon and Its Relation to the Dodo and Its Kindred', *BMC Evolutionary Biology* 14, no. 1 (2014): 1–7; van Grouw, 'The Spotted Green Pigeon Caloenas Maculata'.

9 Teuira Henry, *Ancient Tahiti* (Honolulu, HI: Bernice Pauahi Bishop Museum, 1928), 386. Also cited and discussed at length in Philippe Raust, 'On the Possible Vernacular Name and Origin of the Extinct Spotted Green Pigeon Caloenas Maculata', *Bulletin of the British Ornithologists' Club* 140, no. 1 (2020): 3–6.

10 Raust, 'On the Possible Vernacular Name and Origin of the Extinct Spotted Green Pigeon Caloenas Maculata'.

11 J. Goodrich et al., 'Panthera Tigris. The IUCN Red List of Threatened Species 2022: E.T15955A214862019', *IUCN Red List of Threatened Species* (15 December 2021).

Select Bibliography

Archives

Edinburgh, Scotland: National Library of Scotland
Papers of Daisy Bates, John Murray Archive, Acc.13451

Gland, Switzerland
IUCN Archives

Canberra, Australia: National Library of Australia
Daisy Bates Papers, MS365
Bates Letters to Lang, MS2300
Bates Letters to Mathews, MS3197
Bates Memorial, NK7469
Elizabeth Salter Papers, MS6481
Ernestine Hill Papers, MS8392
Hurst Papers, MS7987

Hobart, Tasmania: State Library of Tasmania
Barron Field, 'The Aborigines of New South Wales & Van Diemen's Land', PETHpam4
Mathew, 'On the Origin of Tasmanian Aborigines', MS2296
Thylacine archives, PH30/1/6817

St Johns, Newfoundland: The Rooms
Colonial Secretary's Office, Outgoing Correspondence, G.N.2/1/a
Duckworth Collection, MG205
James Patrick Howley, MG105
Howley's Book on the Beothucks, File 307
John Peyton Jr and Thomas Peyton, MG323

Books and Articles

Abeli, Thomas, Giulia Albani Rocchetti, Zoltan Barina, Ioannis Bazos, David Draper, Patrick Grillas, José María Iriondo, Emilio Laguna, Juan Carlos Moreno-Saiz, and Fabrizio Bartolucci. 'Seventeen "Extinct" Plant Species Back to Conservation Attention in Europe'. *Nature Plants* 7, no. 3 (2021): 282–6.

Aborigines Protection Society. 'Report of the Parliamentary Select Committee on Aboriginal Tribes (British settlements)'. London: 1837.

—'Report of the Parliamentary Select Committee on Aboriginal Tribes (British settlements)'. London: 1838.

Adams, William M. *Against Extinction: The Story of Conservation*. London: Earthscan, 2004.

Adhikari, Mohamed. 'Europe's First Settler Colonial Incursion into Africa: The Genocide of Aboriginal Canary Islanders'. *African Historical Review* 49, no. 1 (2017): 1–26.

—' "Now We Are Natives": The Genocide of the Beothuk People and the Politics of "Extinction" in Newfoundland'. In *Genocidal Violence: Concepts, Forms, Impact*, ed. Frank Jacob and Kim Sebastian Todzi, 115–36. Oldenbourg: Walter de Gruyter GmbH, 2023.

—*The Anatomy of a South African Genocide: The Extermination of the Cape San Peoples*. Cape Town: University of Cape Town Press, 2014.

—' "We Will Utterly Destroy Them . . . and We Will Go in and Possess the Land": Reflections on the Role of Civilian-Driven Violence in the Making of Settler Genocides'. *Acta Academica* 52, no. 1 (2020): 142–64.

Agar, Jon. 'What Counts as Threatened? Science in the Sixth Extinction'. In *Global Transformations in the Life Sciences*, ed. Patrick Manning and Mat Savelli, 180–94. Pittsburgh, PA: Pittsburgh University Press, 2016.

Agrawal, Arun. 'Dismantling the Divide Between Indigenous and Scientific Knowledge'. *Development and Change* 26, no. 3 (1995): 413–39.

Akçakaya, H. Resit, Elizabeth L. Bennett, Thomas M. Brooks, Molly K. Grace, Anna Heath, Simon Hedges, Craig Hilton-Taylor, et al. 'Quantifying Species Recovery and Conservation Success to Develop an IUCN Green List of Species'. *Conservation Biology* 32, no. 5 (October 2018): 1128–38.

Allen, E. A. *The Prehistoric World: Or, All Vanished Races*. Cincinnati, OH: Central Publishing House, 1885.

Allen, Francis A. 'Thoreau's Notes on the Passenger Pigeon'. *The Auk* 27 (1911): 111.

Allen, J. A. 'The Present Wholesale Destruction of Bird-Life in the United States'. *Science* n.s. 7, no. 160S (1886): 191–5.

—'The Right Whale of the North Atlantic'. *Science* n.s. 1, no. 21 (1883): 598–9.

Allen, John L. 'From Cabot to Cartier: The Early Exploration of Eastern North America, 1497–1543'. *Annals of the Association of American Geographers* 82, no. 3 (1992): 500–21.

Allington-Jones, Lu. 'Mastodon and On and On . . . a Moving Story'. *Journal of Natural Science Collections* 5 (2018): 110–14.

Alvarez, Luis W., Walter Alvarez, Frank Asaro, and Helen V. Michel. 'Extraterrestrial Cause for the Cretaceous-Tertiary Extinction'. *Science* 208, no. 4448 (1980): 1095–108.

Alvarez, Walter. *T rex and the Crater of Doom*. Princeton, NJ: Princeton University Press, 1997.

—'The Historical Record in the Scaglia Limestone at Gubbio: Magnetic Reversals and the Cretaceous-Tertiary Mass Extinction'. *Sedimentology* 56 (2009): 137–48.

Anderson, Kay, and Colin Perrin. 'How Race Became Everything: Australia and Polygenism'. *Ethnic and Racial Studies* 31, no. 5 (2008): 962–90.

—' "The Miserablest People in the World": Race, Humanism and the Australian Aborigine'. *The Australian Journal of Anthropology* 18, no. 1 (2007): 18–39.

Anderson, Paul K. 'Competition, Predation, and the Evolution and Extinction of Steller's Sea Cow, *Hydrodamalis Gigas*'. *Marine Mammal Science* 11, no. 3 (1995): 391–4.

Andrews, Edmund. 'Dr. Koch and the Missouri Mastodon'. *American Journal of Science and Arts* 10, no. 55 (1875): 32.

Andrews, Roy Chapman. 'Explorations in Mongolia: A Review of the Central Asiatic Expeditions of the American Museum of Natural History'. *The Geographical Journal* 69, no. 1 (1927): 1–19.

—*On the Trail of Ancient Man: A Narrative of the Field Work of the Central Asiatic Expeditions*. New York: G. P. Putnam's Sons, 1926.

Anonymous. 'A Lost Neanderthal Tooth'. *Nature* 140, no. 3553 (1937): 961.

—'An Appeal to the Women of the Country in Behalf of the Birds'. *Science* n.s. 7, no. 160S (1886): 204–5.

Anonymous [Chambers, Robert]. *Vestiges of the Natural History of Creation*. London: John Churchill, 1844.

—'Comment and Criticism'. *Science* n.s. 3, no. 67 (1884): 585–6.

—'Comment and Criticism'. *Science* n.s. 3, no. 71 (1884): 699–700.

—'Comment and Criticism'. *Science* n.s. 8, no. 178 (1886): 1–3.

—Convention Relative to the Preservation of Fauna and Flora in Their Natural State (1933).

—'Dr D. A. E. Garrod'. *Nature* 143, no. 3628 (1939): 813.

—'Fossil Man'. *Nature* 91 (1913): 662–4.

—'Gibraltar Man'. *Nature* 140, no. 3553 (1937): 961–2.

—'Imperial Botanical Conference'. *Nature* 136, no. 3436 (1935): 402–4.

—'Imperial Botanical Conference, 1924'. *New Phytologist* 22, no. 3 (1923): 149.

—'Instruction in Natural History at the Jardin des Plantes, Paris'. *Science, New Series* 4 (1896): 65–7.

—'International Office for the Protection of Nature'. *Nature* 135, no. 3408 (1935): 301.

Anonymous. 'Mystery Bird Is Dodo Relative'. *Nature* 511, no. 7510 (2014): 387.

—'Notes on the Antiquity of Man'. *Anthropological Review* 1 (1863): 60–106.

—'On Animals Which Have Become Totally Extinct Through Human Agency During the Nineteenth Century'. *Journal of the Society for the Preservation of the Wild Fauna of the Empire, New Series* 7 (1928): 108–9.

—'Prehistoric Man and Racial Characters'. *Nature* 105, no. 2631 (1920): 153.

—'Primitive Races within the British Empire: A Problem in Adaptation'. *Nature* 113, no. 2850 (1924): 845–7.

—'Priorities Action Statement: Wollemi Pine'. n.d., n.p.

—'Research Items: Fossil Men of Engis'. *Nature* 138, no. 3491 (1936): 553.

—'Species of the Day: Wollemia Pine'. IUCN, n.d., n.p.

—'Survival Service Commission'. *Oryx* 7, no. 5 (1964): 217.

—'The Beothucks or Red Indians, the Aboriginal Inhabitants of Newfoundland'. *Athenaeum*, no. 4578 (1915): 63–4.

—'The French Association at Havre'. *Nature* 16, no. 410 (1877): 409–10.

—'The Gibraltar Skull'. *Nature* 120, no. 3028 (1927): 710.

—'The International Union for Conservation of Nature and Natural Resources, African Special Project, Stage I'. *Oryx* 6, no. 3 (1961): 143–70.

—'The London Convention for the Protection of African Flora and Fauna'. *The Auk* 52, no. 4 (1935): 473–4.

—'The Recently Discovered Gibraltar Skull'. *Nature* 118, no. 2965 (1926): 320.

—'The Recently Discovered Gibraltar Skull'. *Science* 64, no. 1660 (1926): 397–8.

—'Wollemi Pine Thought to Be Living Relic of Dinosaur Age'. *Technology Index* 8, no. 1 (1995): 3–4.

—'Woman Finds New Cave Man Skull at Gibraltar'. *The Science News-Letter* 9 (1926): 1.

Appel, Toby. *The Cuvier-Geoffroy Debate: French Biology in the Decades Before Darwin*. Oxford: Oxford University Press, 1987.

Archibald, David J. 'Dinosaur Extinction: Past and Present Perceptions'. In *The Complete Dinosaur*, ed. Michael K. Brett-Surman, Thomas R. Holtz, James Orville Farlow, and Bob Walters, 2nd ed. Bloomington, IN: Indiana University Press, 2012.

Ardelean, Ciprian F., Lorena Becerra-Valdivia, Mikkel Winther Pedersen, Jean-Luc Schwenninger, Charles G. Oviatt, Juan I. Macías-Quintero, Joaquin Arroyo-Cabrales, et al. 'Evidence of Human Occupation in Mexico Around the Last Glacial Maximum'. *Nature* 584, no. 7819 (August 2020): 87–92.

Ashby, Jack, and Rebecca Machin. 'Legacies of Colonial Violence in Natural History Collections'. *Journal of Natural Science Collections* 8 (2021): 44–54.

Asher, Brad. *Beyond the Reservation: Indians, Settlers, and the Law in Washington Territory, 1853–1889*. Norman, OK: University of Oklahoma Press, 1999.

Atwood, Bain. *Rights for Aborigines*. Crows Nest, NSW: Allen & Unwin, 2003.

Atwood, Bain, and Andrew Markus. *Thinking Black: William Cooper and the Australian Aborigines' League*. Canberra, ACT: Aboriginal Studies Press, 2004.

Audubon, John James. *Ornithological Biography, or an Account of the Habits of the Birds of the United States of America; Accompanied by Descriptions of the Objects Represented in the Work Entitled the Birds of America, and Interspersed with Delineations of American Scenery and Manners*. Vol. 1. 5 vols. Edinburgh: Adam Black, 1831–9.

Augstein, Hannah Franziska. *James Cowles Prichard's Anthropology: Remaking the Science of Man in Early Nineteenth-Century Britain*. Amsterdam, GA: Rodopi, 1999.

Australia and Human Rights and Equal Opportunity Commission. *Bringing Them Home: Report of the National Inquiry into the Separation of Aboriginal and Torres Strait Islander Children from Their Families*. Sydney: Human Rights and Equal Opportunity Commission, 1997.

Aylward, Christopher. 'Historical Narrative Perspective in Howley and Speck'. In *Tracing Ochre: Changing Perspectives on the Beothuk*, ed. Fiona Polack, 220–44. Toronto, ON: University of Toronto Press, 2018.

Aylward, Christopher, and Chief Mi'Sel Joe. 'Beothuk and Mi'kmaq: An Interview with Chief Mi'sel Joe'. In *Tracing Ochre: Changing Perspectives on the Beothuk*, ed. Fiona Polack, 117–32. Toronto, ON: University of Toronto Press, 2018.

Baber, Zaheer. 'The Plants of Empire: Botanic Gardens, Colonial Power and Botanical Knowledge'. *Journal of Contemporary Asia* 46, no. 4 (2016): 659–79.

Baillie, Jonathan, and Ellen R. Butcher. *Priceless or Worthless? The World's Most Threatened Species*. London: Zoological Society of London, 2012.

Baillie, Jonathan E. M., Craig Hilton-Taylor, and Simon N. Stuart, eds. *2004 IUCN Red List of Threatened Species: A Global Species Assessment*. Gland, Switzerland: IUCN, 2004.

Banks, Peter B., and Dieter F. Hochuli. 'Extinction, De-Extinction and Conservation: A Dangerous Mix of Ideas'. *Australian Zoologist* 38, no. 3 (January 2017): 390–4.

Barrow, Mark V. *Nature's Ghosts: Confronting Extinction from the Age of Jefferson to the Age of Ecology*. Chicago, IL: University of Chicago Press, 2009.

Barta, Tony. 'Discourses of Genocide in Germany and Australia: A Linked History'. *Aboriginal History* 25 (2001): 37.

—'Sorry, and Not Sorry, in Australia: How the Apology to the Stolen Generations Buried a History of Genocide'. *Journal of Genocide Research* 10 (2008): 201–14.

—' "They Appear Actually to Vanish from the Face of the Earth." Aborigines and the European Project in Australia Felix'. *Journal of Genocide Research* 10, no. 4 (2008): 519–39.

Barton, Benjamin Smith. *Archaeologiae Americanae Telluris Collectanea et Specimina, or, Collections, with Specimens, for a Series of Memoirs on Certain Extinct Animals and Vegetables of North-America*. Philadelphia, PA: Printed for the Author, 1814.

Basedow, Herbert. 'Relic of the Lost Tasmanian Race. Obituary Notice of Mary Seymour'. *Man* 14 (1914): 161.

Bashford, Alison, Pratik Chakrabarti, and Jarrod Hore. 'Towards a Modern History of Gondwanaland'. *Journal of the British Academy* 9.s6 (2021): 5–26.

Bashford, Alison, and Peter Hobbins. 'Science and Medicine'. In *The Cambridge History of Australia*, ed. Alison Bashford and Stuart Macintyre, 263–83. Cambridge: Cambridge University Press, 2013.

Bashford, Alison, and Philippa Levine, eds. *The Oxford Handbook of the History of Eugenics*. Oxford: Oxford University Press, 2010.

Bashford, Alison, and Stuart Macintyre, eds. *The Cambridge History of Australia*. Cambridge: Cambridge University Press, 2013.

Bates, Daisy. *My Natives and I: Incorporating the Passing of the Aborigines: A Lifetime Spent Among the Natives of Australia*, ed. P. J. Bridge. Carlisle, WA: Hesperian Press, 2004.

Bates, Daisy M. 'A Few Notes on Some South-Western Australian Dialects'. *Journal of the Royal Anthropological Institute of Great Britain and Ireland* 44 (1914): 65–82.

—'Fanny Balbuk-Yoreel: The Last Swan River (Female) Native [Part I]'. *Science of Man and Journal of the Royal Anthropological Society of Australasia* 13, no. 5 (1911): 100–1.

—'Fanny Balbuk-Yoreel: The Last Swan River (Female) Native [Part II]'. *Science of Man and Journal of the Royal Anthropological Society of Australasia* 13, no. 6 (1911): 119–21.

—*The Native Tribes of Western Australia*, ed. Isobel White. Canberra, ACT: National Library of Australia, 1985.

—*The Passing of the Aborigines: A Lifetime Spent Among the Natives of Australia*. London: John Murray, 1938.

Bayes, Randy. 'New Conifer Found in Australia'. *American Conifer Society Bulletin* 12, no. 1 (1995): 6–7.

Beche, H. T. De la, and W. D. Conybeare. 'Notice of the Discovery of a New Fossil Animal, Forming a Link Between the Ichthyosaurus and Crocodile, Together with General Remarks on the Osteology of the Ichthyosaurus'. *Transactions of the Geological Society of London* Series 1, no. 5 (1821): 559–94.

Beck, Horace P. 'Frank G. Speck, 1881–1950'. *Journal of American Folklore* 64, no. 254 (1951): 415–18.

Beebe, C. William. 'A Last Attempt to Locate and Save from Extinction the Passenger Pigeon'. *Wilson Bulletin* 21 (1909): 223.

Beech, Emily, Ryan Hills, and Malin Rivers. 'GlobalTree Portal: Visualizing the State of the World's Trees'. *Oryx* 56, no. 3 (2022): 332.

Belhabib, Dyhia. 'Ocean Science and Advocacy Work Better When Decolonized'. *Nature Ecology & Evolution* 5 (2021): 709–10.

Bello, Silvia M. 'Boning up on Neanderthal Art'. *Nature Ecology & Evolution* 5, no. 9 (2021): 1201–2.

Bendyshe, T. 'On the Extinction of Races'. *Journal of the Anthropological Society of London* 2 (1864): xcix.

Benirschke, K., and A. T. Kumamoto. 'Mammalian Cytogenetics and Conservation of Species'. *Journal of Heredity* 82, no. 3 (1991): 187–91.

Benirschke, Kurt. 'The Frozen Zoo Concept'. *Zoo Biology* 3, no. 4 (1984): 325–8.

Bennell v. *Western Australia*, No. 1243 (Federal Court of Australia, 19 September 2006).

Bennett, Matthew R., David Bustos, Jeffrey S. Pigati, Kathleen B. Springer, Thomas M. Urban, Vance T. Holliday, Sally C. Reynolds, et al. 'Evidence of Humans in North America during the Last Glacial Maximum'. *Science* 373, no. 6562 (2021): 1528–31.

Benson, John, and Chris Allen. 'Vegetation Associated with *Wollemia Nobilis* (Araucariaceae)'. *Cunninghamia* 10 (2007): 255–62.

Benton, M. J. *Extinctions: How Life Survives, Adapts and Evolves*. London: Thames and Hudson, 2023.

Benton, Michael J. 'Origin and Early Evolution of Dinosaurs'. In *The Complete Dinosaur*, ed. Michael K. Brett-Surman, Thomas R. Holtz, James Orville Farlow, and Bob Walters, 2nd ed. Bloomington, IN: Indiana University Press, 2012, 333–45.

—'Scientific Methodologies in Collision: The History of the Study of the Extinction of the Dinosaurs'. *Evolutionary Biology* 24 (1990): 371–400.

—'Stems, Nodes, Crown Clades, and Rank-Free Lists: Is Linnaeus Dead?' *Biological Reviews* 75, no. 4 (2000): 633–48.

—*Extinctions: How Life Survives, Adapts and Evolves*. London: Thames and Hudson, 2023.

—*The Dinosaurs Rediscovered: How a Scientific Revolution Is Rewriting History*. London: Thames & Hudson, 2019.

—*When Life Nearly Died: The Greatest Mass Extinction of All Time*. New ed., 2003. Reprint, London: Thames & Hudson, 2015.

Berglund, Oscar, and Daniel Schmidt. *Extinction Rebellion and Climate Change Activism: Breaking the Law to Change the World*. London: Palgrave Macmillan, 2020.

Bernucci, Arianna, Lorraine Cornish, and Cheryl Lynn. 'Blue Whale on the Move: Dismantling a 125-Year-Old Specimen'. In *Green Museum: How to Practice What We Preach? 2016 SPNHC Conference, 31st Annual Meeting, June 20–25, 2016, Berlin, Germany* (2016).

Bernucci, Arianna Lea, Lorraine Cornish, and Cheryl Lynn. 'A Modern Approach to Dismantling and Redisplaying a Historic Blue Whale Skeleton'. *ICOM-CC Locations Online* (2017).

Betts, Jessica, Richard P. Young, Craig Hilton-Taylor, Michael Hoffmann, Jon Paul Rodríguez, Simon N. Stuart, and E. J. Milner-Gulland. 'A Framework for Evaluating the Impact of the IUCN Red List of Threatened Species'. *Conservation Biology* 34, no. 3 (2020): 632–43.

Bieleski, Rod L., and Mike D. Wilcox, eds. *Araucariaceae: Proceedings of the 2002 Araucariaceae Symposium, Araucaria-Agathis-Wollemia, International Dendrology Society, Auckland, New Zealand, 14–17 March 2002*. Dunedin, NZ: International Dendrology Society, 2009.

Bindman, David. *Ape to Apollo: Aesthetics and the Idea of Race in the 18th Century*. Ithaca, NY: Cornell University Press, 2002.

Bischoff, Eva. *Benevolent Colonizers in Nineteenth-Century Australia*. Basingstoke: Palgrave Macmillan, 2020.

Black, S. M., I. C. L. Marshall, and A. C. Kitchener. 'The Skulls of Chief Nonosabasut and His Wife Demasduit – Beothuk of Newfoundland'. *International Journal of Osteoarchaeology* 19, no. 6 (November 2009): 659–77.

Blackhawk, Ned. 'Currents in North American Indian Historiography'. *Western Historical Quarterly* 42, no. 3 (1 August 2011): 319–24.

Blake, C. Carter. 'On Recent Evidences of Extreme Antiquity of the Human Race'. *Transactions of the Anthropological Society of London* 1 (1863): xxvi–xxxiv.

—'On the Alleged Peculiar Characters, and Assumed Antiquity of the Human Cranium from the Neanderthal'. *Journal of the Anthropological Society of London* 2 (1864): cxxxix–clvii.

Blake, Edith. 'The Beothuks of Newfoundland'. *The Nineteenth Century: A Monthly Review* 24 (1888): 899–918.

Blewett, Richard S., ed. *Shaping a Nation: A Geology of Australia*. Canberra, ACT: Australian National University Press, 2012.

Boas, Franz. 'Museums of Ethnology and Their Classification'. *Science* 9, no. 228 (1887): 587–9.

Bocchi, Federica, Alisa Bokulich, Leticia Castillo Brache, Gloria Grand-Pierre, and Aja Watkins. 'Are We in a Sixth Mass Extinction? The Challenges of Answering and Value of Asking'. *The British Journal for the Philosophy of Science* (2022): 722107.

Boehm, Mannfred M. A., and Quentin C. B. Cronk. 'Dark Extinction: The Problem of Unknown Historical Extinctions'. *Biology Letters* 17, no. 3 (2021): 20210007.

Borgelt, Jan, Martin Dorber, Marthe Alnes Høiberg, and Francesca Verones. 'More than Half of Data Deficient Species Predicted to Be Threatened by Extinction'. *Communications Biology* 5, no. 1 (2022): 679.

Botanic Gardens Conservation International. 'State of the World's Trees'. Richmond, UK: Botanic Gardens Conservation International, 2021.

Boucher, Christophe. '"The Land God Gave to Cain": Jacques Cartier Encounters the Mythological Wild Man in Labrador'. *Terrae Incognitae* 35, no. 1 (1 June 2003): 28–42.

Bourdier, Franck. 'Cuvier, Georges'. In *Complete Dictionary of Scientific Biography*, ed. Charles Coulston Gillispie, vol. 3, 521–8. Detroit, MI: Charles Scribner's Sons, 2008.

Bowers, Stephen. 'The Recent Origin of Man'. *Annual Publication of the Historical Society of Southern California, Los Angeles* 3, no. 3 (1895): 51–8.

Bowler, Peter J. *Progress Unchained: Ideas of Evolution, Human History and the Future*. Cambridge: Cambridge University Press, 2021.

Boyce, Mark S. 'Wolves for Yellowstone: Dynamics in Time and Space'. *Journal of Mammalogy* 99, no. 5 (10 October 2018): 1021–31.

Boyle, C. L. 'The Survival Service Commission'. *Oryx* 5, no. 1 (1959): 30–5.

Braverman, Irus. 'En-Listing Life: Red is the Color of Threatened Species Lists'. In *Critical Animal Geographies: Politics, Intersections and Hierarchies in a Multispecies World*, ed. Kathryn Gillespie and Rosemary-Claire Collard, 17. London: Routledge, 2015.

Breithoff, Esther, and Rodney Harrison. 'From Ark to Bank: Extinction, Proxies and Biocapitals in Ex-Situ Biodiversity Conservation Practices'. *International Journal of Heritage Studies* 26, no. 1 (2 January 2020): 37–55.

Brem, Gottfried, and Birgit Kühholzer. 'The Recent History of Somatic Cloning in Mammals'. *Cloning and Stem Cells* 4, no. 1 (2002): 57–63.

Brett-Surman, Michael K., Thomas R. Holtz, James Orville Farlow, and Bob Walters, eds. 'Glossary'. In *The Complete Dinosaur*, 2nd ed., 1075–81. Bloomington, IN: Indiana University Press, 2012.

Briggs, Barbara G. 'From 50 Million Years Ago – the Wollemi Pine'. *American Conifer Society Bulletin* 12, no. 1 (1995): 8–9.

—'What Is Significant – The Wollemi Pine or the Southern Rushes?', *Annals of the Missouri Botanical Garden* 87 (2000): 72–80.

Briggs, Derek E. G. 'J. John Sepkoski Jr (1948–99)'. *Nature* 400, no. 6744 (1999): 514.

British Museum. *The History of the Collections Contained in the Natural History Departments of the British Museum*. Vol. 2. 3 vols. London: Longmans & Co., 1904 and 1906.

British Museum, and [Flower, W. H.]. *A General Guide to the British Museum (Natural History)*. London: British Museum, 1887.

Broberg, Gunnar. 'Homo Sapiens'. In *The Man Who Organized Nature*, 294–300. Princeton, NJ: Princeton University Press, 2023.

Browell, Mike. 'The Creation of the Longest Tree Avenue in the World'. *Arboricultural Journal* 35, no. 1 (2013): 50–4.

Buckland, Francis. *Curiosities of Natural History*. 4th ed. New York: Rudd & Carleton, 1860.

Buckland, William. 'Notice on the Megalosaurus or Great Fossil Lizard of Stonesfield'. *Transactions of the Geological Society of London*, Series 2, 1 (1824): 390–6.

Bulte, Erwin H., Richard D. Horan, and Jason F. Shogren. 'Is the Tasmanian Tiger Extinct? A Biological–Economic Re-Evaluation'. *Ecological Economics* 45, no. 2 (2003): 271–9.

Burbidge, A. A., and J. Woinarski. '*Thylacinus Cynocephalus*. The IUCN Red List of Threatened Species 2016: E.T21866A21949291', 2016.

Burnham, Philip. *Indian Country, God's Country: Native Americans and the National Parks*. Washington, DC: Island Press, 2000.

Burton, John A. 'Bibliography of Red Data Books (Part 1, Animal Species)'. *Oryx* 18, no. 1 (1984): 61–4.

Busk, George. 'Description of Two Beothuc Skulls'. *Journal of the Anthropological Institute of Great Britain and Ireland* 5 (1876): 230–3.

—'On a Very Ancient Human Cranium from Gibraltar'. *Report of the Thirty-Fourth Meeting of the British Association for the Advancement of Science; Held at Bath in September 1864* (1865): 91–2.

—'Pithecoid Priscan Man from Gibraltar'. *The Reader. A Review of Literature, Science, and Art* 4 (1864): 109–10.

—'President's Address'. *Journal of the Anthropological Institute of Great Britain and Ireland* 4 (1875): 476–502.

Cadigan, Sean. 'The Moral Economy of the Commons: Ecology and Equity in the Newfoundland Cod Fishery, 1815–1855'. *Labour/Le Travail* 43 (1999): 9–42.

Cadigan, Sean T. *Newfoundland and Labrador: A History*. Toronto, ON: University of Toronto Press, 2009.

Callaghan, Chris. 'Botanical Sale of the Century Wollemi Pine Auction', n.d., n.p.

Caram, Marguerite. 'Sidelights of an Assembly'. In *Proceedings and Reports of the Second Session of the General Assembly, held in Brussels, 18–23 October 1950*, ed. IUPN, 80–1. Brussels: IUPN, 1951.

Carey, John. 'Rewilding'. *Proceedings of the National Academy of Sciences* 113, no. 4 (26 January 2016): 806–8.

Caro, Tim. 'The Pleistocene Re-Wilding Gambit'. *Trends in Ecology & Evolution* 22, no. 6 (June 2007): 281–3.

Carpenter, Kenneth. 'Dinosaurs as Museum Exhibits'. In *The Complete Dinosaur*, ed. Michael K. Brett-Surman, Thomas R. Holtz, James Orville Farlow, and Bob Walters, 2nd ed., 285–302. Bloomington, IN: Indiana University Press, 2012.

Carpenter, William Benjamin. 'On the Fossil Human Jawbone Recently Discovered in the Gravel Near Abbeville'. *Proceedings of the Royal Society of London* 12 (1863): 524–9.

Carr, Steven M. 'Evidence for the Persistence of Ancient Beothuk and Maritime Archaic Mitochondrial DNA Genome Lineages Among Modern Native American Peoples'. *Genome* 63, no. 7 (July 2020): 349–55.

Carson, Rachel. *Silent Spring*, ed. Linda Lear. Reprint. Penguin Classics. London: Penguin, 2000.

Cartwright, George. *A Journal of Transactions and Events, During a Residence of Nearly Sixteen Years on the Coast of Labrador. Containing Many Interesting Particulars, Both of the Country and Its Inhabitants, Not Hitherto Known.* Vol. 1. 3 vols. Newark [England]: Allin and Ridge, 1792.

Cassidy, K. A., D. W. Smith, E. Stahler, M. Metz, J. SunderRaj, T. Rabe, W. Binder, et al. 'Yellowstone National Park Wolf Project Annual Report 2022'. United States National Park Service (2022).

Castile, George Pierre, and Robert L. Bee, eds. *State and Reservation: New Perspectives on Federal Indian Policy*. Tucson, AZ: University of Arizona Press, 1992.

Catlin, George. *Letters and Notes on the Manners, Customs, and Condition of the North American Indians*. Vols 1 and 2. London: By the Author, 1841.

Cell, Gillian T. *English Enterprise in Newfoundland 1577–1660*. Toronto, ON: University of Toronto Press, 1969.

Chakrabarti, Pratik. *Inscriptions of Nature: Geology and the Naturalization of Antiquity*. Baltimore, MD: Johns Hopkins University Press, 2020.

Chakrabarty, Dipesh. 'Anthropocene Time'. *History and Theory* 57, no. 1 (2018): 5–32.

—'The Climate of History: Four Theses'. *Critical Inquiry* 35, no. 2 (2009): 197–222.

Challender, Daniel, Patricia Cremona, Kelly Malsch, Janine Robinson, Alyson Pavitt, Janet Scott, Rachel Hoffmann, et al. 'Identifying Species Likely Threatened by International Trade on the IUCN Red List Can Inform CITES Trade Measures'. *Nature Ecology & Evolution* 7 (2023): 1211–20.

Chancel, Lucas. 'Global Carbon Inequality over 1990–2019'. *Nature Sustainability* 5, no. 11 (2022): 931–8.

Chancellor, G. R., and John Van Wyhe, eds. *Charles Darwin's notebooks from the voyage of the Beagle*. Cambridge: Cambridge University Press, 2009.

Chaney, Ralph W. ' "As Remarkable as Discovering a Living Dinosaur": Redwoods in China'. *Arnoldia* 58/59, no. 4/1 (1998): 23–32.

—'Redwoods in China'. *Natural History Magazine* 47 (1948): 440–4.

Chapman, John. 'The Colonial and Indian Exhibition'. *Westminster Review* 126 (1886): 29–59.

Chaput, Donald. 'Generals, Indian Agents, Politicians: The Doolittle Survey of 1865'. *The Western Historical Quarterly* 3 (1972): 269–82.

Chen, Lu, Aaron B. Wolf, Wenqing Fu, Liming Li, and Joshua M. Akey. 'Identifying and Interpreting Apparent Neanderthal Ancestry in African Individuals'. *Cell* 180, no. 4 (February 2020): 677–87.

Christenhusz, Maarten J. M., and James W. Byng. 'The Number of Known Plants Species in the World and Its Annual Increase'. *Phytotaxa* 261, no. 3 (20 May 2016): 201.

Chrulew, Matthew. 'Freezing the Ark: The Cryopolitics of Endangered Species Preservation'. In *Cryopolitics*, ed. Joanna Radin and Emma Kowal, 283–305. Cambridge, MA: MIT Press, 2017.

—'Managing Love and Death at the Zoo: The Biopolitics of Endangered Species Preservation – AHR'. *Australian Humanities Review*, no. 50 (2011): 137–57.

—'Reversing Extinction: Restoration and Resurrection in the Pleistocene Rewilding Projects'. *Humanimalia* 2, no. 2 (2011): 4–27.

Church, George M., and Edward Regis. *Regenesis: How Synthetic Biology Will Reinvent Nature and Ourselves*. New York, NY: Basic Books, 2012.

Clarke, A. G. 'The Frozen Ark Project: The Role of Zoos and Aquariums in Preserving the Genetic Material of Threatened Animals'. *International Zoo Yearbook* 43, no. 1 (January 2009): 222–30.

Clubb, Joseph. *Handbook and Guide to the British Birds on Exhibition in the Lord Derby Natural History Museum, Liverpool*. Liverpool: C. Tinling, 1914.

Codrington, Tracy, Leon J. Scott, Kirsten D. Scott, Glenn C. Graham, Maurizio Rosetto, Mary Ryan, Trevor Whiffin, Robert J. Henry, and Ken Hill. 'Unresolved Phylogenetic Position of *Wollemia, Araucaria* and *Agathis*'. In *Araucariaceae: Proceedings of the 2002 Araurariaceae Symposium, Araucaria-Agathis-Wollemia, International Dendrology Society, Auckland, New Zealand, 14–17 March 2002*, ed. Rod L. Bieleski and Mike D. Wilcox, 69–73. Dunedin, NZ: International Dendrology Society, 2009.

Cohen, Claudine. 'Exhibiting Life History at the Paris Muséum D'Histoire Naturelle (Nineteenth–Twenty-First Centuries)'. In *Museums at the Forefront of the History and Philosophy of Geology: History Made, History in the Making*, ed. G. D. Rosenberg and R. M. Clary, 535: 117–29. GSA Special Papers. The Geological Society of America (2018).

Cokinos, Christopher. *Hope Is the Thing with Feathers: A Personal Chronicle of Vanished Birds*. New York, NY: J. P. Tarcher/Putnam, 2000.

Cole, Anna, Victoria Haskins, and Fiona Paisley, eds. *Uncommon Ground: White Women in Aboriginal History*. Canberra, ACT: Aboriginal Studies Press, 2005.

Collar, N. J. 'Species Are a Measure of Man's Freedom: Reflections After Writing a Red Data Book on African Birds'. *Oryx* 20, no. 1 (1986): 15–19.

—'The Reasons for Red Data Books'. *Oryx* 30, no. 2 (1996): 121–30.

Collette, Bruce, Kent Carpenter (USA), Russell Nelson (The Billfish Foundation, USA), William Fox (World Wildlife Fund, Spain), Maria José Juan Jorda (Recursos Marinos y Pesquerias, Italy), Antonio Di Natale (AQUASTUDIO Research Institute, Japan), Yuji Uozumi (National Research Institute of Far Seas Fisheries), et al. 'Makaira nigricans. The IUCN Red List of Threatened Species 2011: e.T170314A6743776' (2010).

Colley, Sarah, Sally Brockwell, Tom Gara, and Scott Cane. 'The Archaeology of Daisy Bates' Campsite at Ooldea, South Australia'. *Australian Archaeology* 28 (1989): 79–91.

Collier, Ashley, and Steven M. Carr. 'On the Persistence and Detectability of Ancient Beothuk Mitochondrial DNA Genomes in Living First Nations Peoples'. *Mitochondrial DNA Part A* 30, no. 1 (2 January 2019): 68–74.

Colombo, Giulia, Luca Traverso, Lucia Mazzocchi, Viola Grugni, Nicola Rambaldi Migliore, Marco Rosario Capodiferro, Gianluca Lombardo, et al. 'Overview of the Americas' First Peopling from a Patrilineal Perspective: New Evidence from the Southern Continent'. *Genes* 13, no. 2 (2022): 220.

Conklin, Alice L. *In the Museum of Man: Race, Anthropology, and Empire in France, 1850–1950*. Ithaca, NY: Cornell University Press, 2013.

Cook, Simon. 'The Tragedy of Cambridge Anthropology: Edwardian Historical Thought and the Contact of Peoples'. *History of European Ideas* 42, no. 4 (18 May 2016): 541–53.

Cook, Simon John. 'The Making of the English: English History, British Identity, Aryan Villages, 1870–1914'. *Journal of the History of Ideas* 75, no. 4 (2014): 629–49.

Coolidge, H. J. 'International Union for the Protection of Nature'. *Science* 119, no. 3100 (1954): 3A.

—'The Development of the Survival Service of the International Union for the Conservation of Nature and Natural Resources'. In *Proceedings of the Sixth General Assembly, Athens, 11–19 September 1958*, 133–4. Brussels: IUCN, 1960.

Coolidge, Harold J. 'Emergency Action for the Preservation of Vanishing Species'. In *International Technical Conference on the Protection of Nature: Lake Success, 22–29 VIII 1949, Proceedings and Papers*, 479–89. Paris and Brussels: International Union for the Protection of Nature, 1950.

Cormack, W. E. (William Epps). 'Account of a Journey across the Island of Newfoundland, by W. E. Cormack, Esq. in a Letter Addressed to the Right Hon. Earl Bathurst, Secretary of State for the Colonies &c. &c.,—with a Map of Mr. Cormack's Journey across the Island of Newfoundland'. *Edinburgh Philosophical Journal* 10 (1824): 156–62.

—'Civilization of the Aborigines of Newfoundland'. *Edinburgh New Philosophical Journal* 4 (1827): 205–6.

—*Narrative of a Journey across the Island of Newfoundland.* Saint John's, Newfoundland: Morning Chronicle, 1873.

—*Narrative of a Journey across the Island of Newfoundland, the Only One Ever Performed by a European.* St John's: Office of the Morning Post and Commercial, 1856.

—'Report of Mr. W. E. Cormack's Journey in Search of the Red Indians in Newfoundland. Read before the Boeothick Institution at St John's, Newfoundland. Communicated by Mr. Cormack'. *Edinburgh New Philosophical Journal* 20 (1829): 318–29.

Cowie, Helen. 'Sloth Bones and Anteater Tongues: Collecting American Nature in the Hispanic World (1750–1808)'. *Atlantic Studies* 8, no. 1 (2011): 5–27.

Cowie, Robert H., Philippe Bouchet, and Benoît Fontaine. 'The Sixth Mass Extinction: Fact, Fiction or Speculation?' *Biological Reviews* 97, no. 2 (2022): 640–63.

Cowles, Henry M. 'A Victorian Extinction: Alfred Newton and the Evolution of Animal Protection'. *The British Journal for the History of Science* 46, no. 04 (2013): 695–714.

Coyne, Cynthia. "'Bye and Bye When All the Natives Have Gone": Daisy Bates and Billingee'. In *Uncommon Ground: White Women in Aboriginal History*, ed. Anna Cole, Victoria Haskins, and Fiona Paisley, 199–216. Canberra, ACT: Aboriginal Studies Press, 2005.

Crates, Ross, Dejan Stojanovic, and Robert Heinsohn. 'The Phenotypic Costs of Captivity'. *Biological Reviews* 98 (2022): brv.12913.

Cronon, William. 'The Trouble with Wilderness: Or, Getting Back to the Wrong Nature'. *Environmental History* 1 (1996): 7–28.

Crowther, William L. 'Notes on the Habits of the Extinct Tasmanian Race'. *Papers and Proceedings of the Royal Society of Tasmania* (1924): 136–9.

—'Notes on the Habits of the Extinct Tasmanian Race, No. 2'. *Papers and Proceedings of the Royal Society of Tasmania* (1926): 165–9.

—'Notes on the Habits of the Extinct Tasmanian Race, No. 3'. *Papers and Proceedings of the Royal Society of Tasmania* (1933): 22–5.

—'Notes on the Habits of the Extinct Tasmanian Race, No. 4'. *Papers and Proceedings of the Royal Society of Tasmania* (1938): 202–12.

Crutzen, Paul J. 'Geology of Mankind'. *Nature* 415 (2002): 23.

Cui, Da-Fang, Yemao Hou, Pengfei Yin, and Xin Wang. 'A Jurassic Flower Bud from China'. *Geological Society, London, Special Publications* (2021), SP521-2021–2122.

Cuvier, Georges. *Recherches sur les ossemens fossiles de quadrupèdes*. 4 vols. Paris: Deterville, 1812.

—*Researches into Fossil Osteology*, trans. Edward Pidgeon. London: George B. Whittaker, 1826.

Dalrymple, Sarah E., and Thomas Abeli. 'Ex Situ Seed Banks and the IUCN Red List'. *Nature Plants* 5, no. 2 (2019): 122–3.

Dana, James D. 'On Dr Koch's Evidence With Regard To the Contemporaneity of Man and the Mastodon In Missouri'. *American Journal of Science and Arts* 9 (1875): 335–46.

Darling, F. Fraser. 'Red Data Book, 1. Mammalia, compiled by Noel Simon. 2. Aves, compiled by Jack Vincent. Survival Service Commission, IUCN, Morges, Vaud, Switzerland, 70s. each'. *Oryx* 9, no. 1 (1967): 41–2.

Darwin, Charles. *Geological Observations on the Volcanic Islands, Visited During the Voyage of HMS Beagle: Together with Some Brief Notices on the Geology of Australia and the Cape of Good Hope. Being the Second Part of the Geology of the Voyage of the Beagle, Under the Command of Capt. Fitzroy, R.N. During the Years 1832–1836*. London: Smith Elder and Co., 1844.

—*On the Origin of Species by Means of Natural Selection, or the Preservation of Favoured Races in the Struggle for Life*. London: John Murray, 1859.

—*The Descent of Man, and Selection in Relation to Sex*. Vol. 1. 2 vols. London: John Murray, 1871.

Das, S., and M. Lowe. 'Nature Read in Black and White: Decolonial Approaches to Interpreting Natural History'. *Journal of Natural Science Collections* 6 (2018): 4–14.

David, Tannatt William Edgeworth. 'Geological Evidence of the Antiquity of Man in the Commonwealth, with Special Reference to the Tasmania Aborigines'. *Papers & Proceedings of the Royal Society of Tasmania* (1923), 109–50.

Davis, Janae, Alex A. Moulton, Levi Van Sant, and Brian Williams. 'Anthropocene, Capitalocene . . . Plantationocene?: A Manifesto for Ecological Justice in an Age of Global Crises'. *Geography Compass* 13, no. 5 (May 2019): e12438.

Davis, Joseph Barnard. *On the Osteology and Peculiarities of the Tasmanians, a Race of Man Recently Become Extinct*. Haarlem: De Erven Loosjes, 1874.

—*The Neanderthal Skull: Its Peculiar Conformation Explained Anatomically*. London: Taylor & Francis, 1864.

Davis, Marc, Piet Hut, and Richard A. Muller. 'Extinction of Species by Periodic Comet Showers'. *Nature* 308, no. 5961 (1984): 715–17.

Dawkins, William Boyd. *Early Man in Britain and His Place in the Tertiary Period*. London: Macmillan and Co., 1880.

Dawson, Gowan. *Show Me the Bone: Reconstructing Prehistoric Monsters in Nineteenth-Century Britain and America*. Chicago, IL: University of Chicago Press, 2016.

De Bont, Raf. *Nature's Diplomats: Science, Internationalism & Preservation, 1920–1960*. Pittsburgh, PA: University of Pittsburgh Press, 2021.

—' "Primitives" and Protected Areas: International Conservation and the "Naturalization" of Indigenous People, ca. 1910–1975'. *Journal of the History of Ideas* 76, no. 2 (2015): 215–36.

Dean, Dennis R. *Gideon Mantell and the Discovery of Dinosaurs*. Cambridge: Cambridge University Press, 1999.

Dean, M. C., C. B. Stringer, and T. G. Bromage. 'Age at Death of the Neanderthal Child from Devil's Tower Gibraltar and the Implications for Studies of General Growth and Development in Neanderthals'. *American Journal of Physical Anthropology* 70 (n.d.): 301–9.

Deane, Ruthven. 'The Passenger Pigeon – Only One Bird Left'. *The Auk* 28 (1911): 262.

—'The Passenger Pigeon (*Ectopistes migratorius*) in Confinement'. *The Auk* 25, no. 2 (1908): 181–3.

Dehler, Gregory J. *The Most Defiant Devil: William Temple Hornaday and His Controversial Crusade to Save American Wildlife*. Charlottesville, VA: University of Virginia Press, 2013.

Demuth, Bathsheba. *Floating Coast: An Environmental History of the Bering Strait*. New York, NY: W. W. Norton & Co., 2019.

—'What Is a Whale? Cetacean Value at the Bering Strait, 1848–1900'. *RCC Perspectives*, no. 5 (2019): 73–80.

Department of Environment and Conservation. 'Wollemia Nobilis: Wollemi Pine Recovery Plan'. Hurstville, NSW: Department of Environment and Conservation, 2007.

Department of Environment and Conservation, NSW. *Declaration of Critical Habitat for the Wollemi Pine (Wollemia Nobilis)*. Hurstville, NSW: Department of Environment and Conservation, 2007.

Department of Planning and Environment. 'Wollemi Pine (Wollemia Nobilis): Conservation Action Plan'. Hurstville, NSW: Department of Planning and Environment, 2022.

Desmond, Adrian. 'Richard Owen's Reaction to Transmutation in the 1830s'. *The British Journal for the History of Science* 18, no. 1 (1985): 25–50.

Desmond, Adrian J. 'Designing the Dinosaur: Richard Owen's Response to Robert Edmond Grant'. *Isis* 70 (1979): 224–34.

—*The Politics of Evolution: Morphology, Medicine, and Reform in Radical London*. Science and Its Conceptual Foundations. Chicago, IL: University of Chicago Press, 1989.

Diamond, Beverley. 'Santu Toney, a Transnational Beothuk Woman'. In *Tracing Ochre: Changing Perspectives on the Beothuk*, ed. Fiona Polack, 247–68. Toronto, ON: University of Toronto Press, 2018.

DiPaolo, Dominic A., and John C. Villella. 'Ecology and Conservation of a Living Fossil: Australia's Wollemi Pine (Wollemia Nobilis)'. In *Imperiled: The Encyclopedia of Conservation*, ed. Dominick A. DellaSala and Michael I. Goldstein, 884–94. Oxford: Elsevier, 2022.

Dippie, Brian W. *The Vanishing American: White Attitudes and US Indian Policy*. Middletown, CT: Wesleyan University Press, 1982.

Dobzhansky, Theodosius. 'On Species and Races of Living and Fossil Man'. *American Journal of Physical Anthropology* 2, no. 3 (1944): 251–65.

Dollman, Captain Guy. 'Mammals Which Have Recently Become Extinct and Those on the Verge of Extinction'. *Journal of the Society for the Preservation of the Wild Fauna of the Empire, New Series* 30 (1937): 67–74.

Donlan, Josh, Joel Berger, Carl E. Bock, Jane H. Bock, David A. Burney, James A. Estes, Dave Foreman, et al. 'Pleistocene Rewilding: An Optimistic Agenda for Twenty-First-Century Conservation'. *The American Naturalist* 168, no. 5 (November 2006): 660–81.

Dooren, Thom van. 'Banking the Forest: Loss, Hope, and Care in Hawaiian Conservation'. In *Cryopolitics*, ed. Joanna Radin and Emma Kowal, 259–82. Cambridge, MA: MIT Press, 2017.

Dooren, Thom van, and Deborah Bird Rose. 'Keeping Faith with the Dead: Mourning and De-Extinction'. *Australian Zoologist* 38, no. 3 (January 2017): 375–8.

Drayton, Richard H. *Nature's Government: Science, Imperial Britain, and the 'Improvement' of the World*. New Haven, CT: Yale University Press, 2000.

Duarte, C., J. Mauricio, P. B. Pettitt, P. Souto, E. Trinkaus, H. van der Plicht, and J. Zilhão. 'The Early Upper Paleolithic Human Skeleton from the Abrigo Do Lagar Velho (Portugal) and Modern Human Emergence in Iberia'. *Proceedings of the National Academy of Sciences* 96 (1999): 7604–9.

Dudley, Nigel, and Hannah Timmins, eds. *A Survey of User Attitudes Towards the Proposed IUCN Green Status of Species*. IUCN, International Union for Conservation of Nature, 2021.

Ehrlich, Anne. 'Nuclear Winter'. *Bulletin of the Atomic Scientists* (15 September 2015).

Ehrlich, Paul R. *Extinction: The Causes and Consequences of the Disappearance of Species*. New York: Random House, 1981.

Eldredge, Niles. 'Reflections on Punctuated Equilibria'. *Paleobiology* (2024): 1–5.

Eldredge, Niles, and Michelle J. Eldredge. 'A Trilobite Odyssey'. In *The Natural History Reader in Evolution*, ed. Niles Eldredge, 61–8. New York: Columbia University Press, 1987.

Eldredge, Niles, and Stephen J. Gould. 'Punctuated Equilibria: An Alternative to Phyletic Gradualism'. In *Models in Paleobiology*, ed. T. J. M. Schopf, 82–115. San Francisco, CA: Freeman, Cooper & Co, 1972.

Endersby, Jim. *Imperial Nature: Joseph Hooker and the Practices of Victorian Science*. Chicago, IL: University of Chicago Press, 2010.

Enright, Kelly. 'Dreaming of Rediscovery: Botanists, Extinction, and the Tree That Sets the Brain on Fire'. *Environmental History* 27, no. 4 (2022): 665–91.

Erwin, Douglas H. 'David M. Raup (1933–2015)'. *Nature* 524, no. 7563 (2015): 36.

Ewing, Ann. 'Live Cells Frozen Alive'. *The Science News-Letter* 81, no. 16 (1962): 246–7.

Farlow, James O., and Michael K. Brett-Surman. 'Dinosauria'. In *The Complete Dinosaur*, ed. Michael K. Brett-Surman, Thomas R. Holtz, James Orville Farlow, and Bob Walters, 2nd ed., ix. Bloomington, IN: Indiana University Press, 2012.

Farrington, Oliver C., and Henry Field. *Neanderthal (Mousterian) Man*. Chicago, IL: Field Museum of Natural History, 1929.

Fay, Charles. 'Life and Labour in Newfoundland: Based on Lectures Delivered at the Memorial University of Newfoundland'. In *Life and Labour in Newfoundland*. Toronto, ON: University of Toronto Press, 1956.

Fernández-Armesto, Felipe. *The Canary Islands after the Conquest: The Making of a Colonial Society in the Early Sixteenth Century*. Oxford Historical Monographs. Oxford and New York: Clarendon Press and Oxford University Press, 1982.

Fernández-Llamazares, Álvaro, Julia E. Fa, Dan Brockington, Eduardo S. Brondízio, Joji Cariño, Esteve Corbera, Maurizio Farhan Ferrari, et al. 'A Baseless Statistic Could Harm the Indigenous Peoples It Is Meant to Support'. *Nature* 633 (2024): 32–5.

Fillios, Melanie, Mathew S. Crowther, and Mike Letnic. 'The Impact of the Dingo on the Thylacine in Holocene Australia'. *World Archaeology* 44, no. 1 (1 March 2012): 118–34.

Finlayson, Clive. *Neanderthals and Modern Humans: An Ecological and Evolutionary Perspective*. Cambridge: Cambridge University Press, 2004.

—*The Humans Who Went Extinct: Why Neanderthals Died Out and We Survived*. Oxford: Oxford University Press, 2009.

Finlayson, Clive, Francisco Giles Pacheco, Joaquín Rodríguez-Vidal, Darren A. Fa, José María Gutierrez López, Antonio Santiago Pérez, Geraldine Finlayson, et al. 'Late Survival of Neanderthals at the Southernmost Extreme of Europe'. *Nature* 443 (2006): 850–3.

Fisher, James, Noel Simon, and Jack Vincent. *The Red Book: Wildlife in Danger*. London: Collins, 1969.

Fitter, R. S. R. 'The Survival Service Commission'. *Oryx* 7, no. 4 (1964): 157–9.

Fitter, Richard. '25 Years On: A Look at Endangered Species'. *Oryx* 12, no. 3 (1974): 341–6.

Fitter, Richard, and Maisie Fitter, eds. *The Road to Extinction: Problems of Categorizing the Status of Taxa Threatened with Extinction. A Symposium Held by the Species Survival Commission, Madrid, 7 and 9 November 1984*. Gland, Switzerland: IUCN, 1987.

Fitter, Richard, and Jacqui Morris. 'The Fauna and Flora Preservation Society – Conserving Wildlife for 90 Years'. *Journal of Biological Education* 27, no. 2 (1993): 103–6.

Fleming, Andrew. 'The Last of the Great Auks: Oral History and Ritual Killings at St Kilda'. *Scottish Studies* 40 (24 January 2024): 29–40.

Fleming, John. *History of British Animals, Exhibiting the Descriptive Characters and Systematical Arrangement of the Genera and Species of Quadrupeds, Birds, Reptiles, Fishes, Mollusca, and Radiata of the United Kingdom; Including the Indigenous, Extirpated, and Extinct Kinds, Together with Periodical and Occasional Visitants*. Edinburgh: Bell & Bradfute, 1828.

—'Remarks Illustrative of the Influence of Society on the Distribution of British Animals'. *Edinburgh Philosophical Journal* 11 (1824): 287–305.

Flint, Kate. *The Transatlantic Indian, 1776–1930*. Princeton, NJ: Princeton University Press, 2008.

Folch, J., M. J. Cocero, P. Chesné, J. L. Alabart, V. Domínguez, Y. Cognié, A. Roche, et al. 'First Birth of an Animal from an Extinct Subspecies (*Capra pyrenaica pyrenaica*) by Cloning'. *Theriogenology* 71, no. 6 (2009): 1026–34.

Fonseca, Carlos Roberto. 'The Silent Mass Extinction of Insect Herbivores in Biodiversity Hotspots'. *Conservation Biology* 23, no. 6 (2009): 1507–15.

Foote, Yolanda. 'Latham, John (1740–1837), Naturalist'. In *Oxford Dictionary of National Biography*. Oxford: Oxford University Press, 2004.

Forbes, H. 'On the Type of the Spotted Green Pigeon of Latham, in the Derby Museum'. *Bulletin of the Liverpool Museums* 1 (1898): 83.

Fraser, F. C. 'The Blue Whale Skeleton in the Whale Hall'. *Natural History Magazine* 4 (1934): 228–30.

Fuller, Errol. *The Passenger Pigeon*. Princeton, NJ: Princeton University Press, 2014.

Gannett, Lisa. 'Theodosius Dobzhansky and the Genetic Race Concept'. *Studies in History and Philosophy of Science Part C: Studies in History and Philosophy of Biological and Biomedical Sciences* 44, no. 3 (2013): 250–61.

Garrod, Dorothy A. E., L. H. Dudley Buxton, and G. Elliot Smith. 'Excavation of a Mousterian Rock-Shelter at Devil's Tower, Gibraltar'. *Journal of the Royal Anthropological Institute of Great Britain and Ireland* (1928), 33–113.

Gatschet, Albert S. 'The Beothuk Indians'. *Proceedings of the American Philosophical Society* 22, no. 120 (1885): 408–24.

—'The Beothuk Indians'. *Proceedings of the American Philosophical Society* 23, no. 123 (1886): 411–32.

—'The Beothuk Indians: Third Article'. *Proceedings of the American Philosophical Society* 28, no. 132 (1890): 1–16.

GenBank. 'Complete Mitochondrial DNA Sequences'. GenBank, n.d.

Gersh, Gabriel. 'Australia's Vanishing Prehistoric People: Review of The Passing of the Aborigines, by Daisy Bates'. *Southwest Review* 52 (1967): 307–11.

Gibbons, Ann. 'When Modern Humans Met Neanderthals'. *Science* 372, no. 6358 (2021): 115–16.

Gibbs, David, Eustace Barnes, and John Cox. 'Spotted Green Pigeon, *Caloenas Maculata*'. In *Pigeons and Doves: A Guide to the Pigeons and Doves of the World*, 394–5. London: Christopher Helm, 2001.

Gilbert, Lionel. *The Royal Botanic Gardens, Sydney: A History 1816–1985*. Melbourne: Oxford University Press, 1986.

Gilbert, William. 'Beothuk-European Contact in the 16th Century: A Re-Evaluation of the Documentary Evidence'. *Acadiensis* 40 (2011): 24–44.

Gillette, Robert. 'Endangered Species: Diplomacy Tries Building an Ark'. *Science* 179, no. 4075 (1973): 777–80.

Gilmore, Simon, and Kenneth Hill. 'Relationships of the Wollemi Pine (*Wollemia Nobilis*) and a Molecular Phylogeny of the Araucariaceae'. *Telopea* 7, no. 3 (17 December 1997): 275–91.

Girouard, Mark. *Alfred Waterhouse and the Natural History Museum*. London: Natural History Museum, 1981.

Gißibl, Bernhard. 'German Colonialism and the Beginnings of International Wildlife Preservation in Africa'. *GHI Bulletin Supplement* 3 (2006), 121–43.

Glen, William, ed. *The Mass-Extinction Debates: How Science Works in a Crisis*. Stanford, CA: Stanford University Press, 1994.

—'What the Impact/Volcanism/Mass-Extinction Debates Are About'. In *The Mass-Extinction Debates: How Science Works in a Crisis*, ed. William Glen, 7–38. Stanford, CA: Stanford University Press, 1994.

Glen, William, and William Glen, eds. 'On the Mass-Extinction Debates: An Interview with Stephen Jay Gould'. In *The Mass-Extinction Debates: How Science Works in a Crisis*, 253–67. Stanford, CA: Stanford University Press, 1994.

—, eds. 'On the Mass-Extinction Debates: An Interview with William A. Clemens, Conducted and Compiled by William Glen'. In *The Mass-Extinction Debates: How Science Works in a Crisis*, 237–52. Stanford, CA: Stanford University Press, 1994.

Goedert, Michel, and Alastair Compston. 'Parkinson's Disease – the Story of an Eponym'. *Nature Reviews Neurology* 14, no. 1 (2018): 57–62.

Goodenough, William, Prince Reginald de Croy, Albert Kitson, and C. W. Hobley. 'Proposed British National Parks for Africa: Discussion'. *The Geographical Journal* 77, no. 5 (1931): 423.

Goodrum, Matthew R. 'Biblical Anthropology and the Idea of Human Prehistory in Late Antiquity'. *History and Anthropology* 13, no. 2 (2002): 69–78.

—'Crafting a New Science: Defining Paleoanthropology and its Relationship to Prehistoric Archaeology, 1860–1890'. *Isis* 105, no. 4 (2014): 706–33.

—'Questioning Thunderstones and Arrowheads: The Problem of Recognizing and Interpreting Stone Artifacts in the Seventeenth Century'. *Early Science and Medicine* 13 (2008): 482–508.

—'Recovering the Vestiges of Primeval Europe: Archaeology and the Significance of Stone Implements, 1750–1800'. *Journal of the History of Ideas* 72 (2011): 51–74.

—'The Beginnings of Human Palaeontology: Prehistory, Craniometry and the "Fossil Human Races"'. *The British Journal for the History of Science* 49 (2016): 387–409.

—'The History of Human Origins Research and Its Place in the History of Science: Research Problems and Historiography'. *History of Science* 47, no. 3 (2009): 337–57.

—'The Idea of Human Prehistory: The Natural Sciences, the Human Sciences, and the Problem of Human Origins in Victorian Britain'. *History and Philosophy of the Life Sciences* 34 (2012): 117–45.

—'The Meaning of Ceraunia: Archaeology, Natural History and the Interpretation of Prehistoric Stone Artefacts in the Eighteenth Century'. *The British Journal for the History of Science* 35 (2002): 255–69.

Gopal, Priyamvada. *Insurgent Empire: Anticolonial Resistance and British Dissent*. London: Verso, 2019.

Grace, Molly K., Elizabeth L. Bennett, H. Reşit Akçakaya, Craig Hilton-Taylor, Michael Hoffmann, Richard Jenkins, E. J. Milner-Gulland, Ana Nieto, Richard P. Young, and Barney Long. 'IUCN Launches Green Status of Species: A New Standard for Species Recovery'. *Oryx* 55, no. 5 (2021): 651–2.

Green, Richard E., Johannes Krause, Adrian W. Briggs, Tomislav Maricic, Udo Stenzel, Martin Kircher, Nick Patterson, et al. 'A Draft Sequence of the Neandertal Genome'. *Science* 328, no. 5979 (2010): 710–22.

Greenway, James C. (James Cowan). *Extinct and Vanishing Birds of the World*. New York, NY: Dover Publications, 1967.

Greenway Jr, James. 'Remarks on the Preservation of Birds'. In *International Technical Conference on the Protection of Nature: Lake Success, 22–29 VIII 1949, Proceedings and Papers*, ed. IUPN, 515–24. Paris and Brussels: International Union for the Protection of Nature, 1950.

Gressitt, J. Linsley. 'The California Academy-Lingnan Dawn-Redwood Expedition'. *Arnoldia* 58/59, no. 4/1 (1998): 35–9.

Grinnell, J. 'A Conservationist's Creed as to Wild-Life Administration'. *Science* 62, no. 1611 (1925): 437–8.

—'Conserve the Collector'. *Science* 41, no. 1050 (1915): 229–32.

Grinnell, J., and T. I. Storer. 'Animal Life as an Asset of National Parks'. *Science* 44, no. 1133 (1916): 375–80.

Grouw, Hein van. 'The Spotted Green Pigeon Caloenas Maculata: As Dead as a Dodo, but What Else Do We Know About It?' *Bulletin of the British Ornithologists' Club* 134, no. 4 (2014): 291–301.

Gruber, Jacob W. 'Ethnographic Salvage and the Shaping of Anthropology'. *American Anthropologist* 72, no. 6 (1970): 1289–99.

Haddon, A. C. 'Nature and Man in Australia'. *Nature* 89, no. 2233 (1912): 608–9.

Hajdinjak, Mateja, Fabrizio Mafessoni, Laurits Skov, Benjamin Vernot, Alexander Hübner, Qiaomei Fu, Elena Essel, et al. 'Initial Upper Palaeolithic Humans in Europe Had Recent Neanderthal Ancestry'. *Nature* 592 (2021): 253–7.

Hallam, A. 'Mass Extinctions in the Fossil Record'. *Nature* 251, no. 5476 (October 1974): 568–9.

Hallam, Anthony. 'Evolution: The Causes of Mass Extinctions'. *Nature* 308, no. 5961 (1984): 686–7.

Haller, John S. 'The Species Problem: Nineteenth-Century Concepts of Racial Inferiority in the Origin of Man Controversy'. *American Anthropologist* 72, no. 6 (1970): 1319–29.

Halliday, T. R. 'The Extinction of the Passenger Pigeon Ectopistes migratorius and its Relevance to Contemporary Conservation'. *Biological Conservation* 17, no. 2 (1980): 157–62.

Hammond, Michael. 'The Expulsion of the Neanderthals from Human Ancestry: Marcellin Boule and the Social Context of Scientific Research'. *Social Studies of Science* 12, no. 1 (1982): 1–36.

Haraway, Donna. 'Anthropocene, Capitalocene, Plantationocene, Chthulucene: Making Kin'. *Environmental Humanities* 6, no. 1 (2015): 159–65.

Haresnape, Geoffrey. 'No Fish, but an Islander: An Early Portrayal of Caliban as a First Nation Beothuk of Newfoundland'. *Shakespeare in Southern Africa* 11 (1998): 1–13.

Harman, Kristyn. 'Protecting Tasmanian Aborigines: American and Queensland Influences on the Cape Barren Island Reserve Act, 1912'. *Journal of Imperial and Commonwealth History* 41, no. 5 (December 2013): 744–64.

Harmer, Sidney F. 'Presidential Address, 24th May, 1928'. *Proceedings of the Linnean Society of London* 140, no. 1 (1928): 51–95.

Harries, John. 'Of Bleeding Skulls and the Postcolonial Uncanny: Bones and the Presence of Nonosabasut and Demasduit'. *Journal of Material Culture* 15, no. 4 (2010): 403–21.

Harrisson, Tom. 'The New Red Data Book'. *Oryx* 12, no. 3 (1974): 321–31.

—'The Turtle Tragedy'. *Oryx* 10, no. 2 (1969): 112–15.

Hauptman, Laurence M., and George Hamell. 'George Catlin: The Iroquois Origins of His Indian Portrait Gallery'. *New York History* 84, no. 2 (2003): 125–51.

Hausdoerffer, John. *Catlin's Lament: Indians, Manifest Destiny, and the Ethics of Nature*. Lawrence, KS: University Press of Kansas, 2009.

Headrick, Daniel R. *Humans Versus Nature: A Global Environmental History*. New York, NY: Oxford University Press, 2020.

Heady, Roger. 'The Wollemi Pine 16 Years On'. In *Australia's Ever-Changing Forests VI: Proceedings of the Eighth National Conference on Australian Forest History*, ed. Brett J. Stubbs, 1–16, 2012.

Heck, Heinz. 'The Breeding-Back of the Aurochs'. *Oryx* 1, no. 3 (1951): 117–22.

—'The Breeding-Back of the Tarpan'. *Oryx* 1, no. 7 (1952): 338–42.

Heise, Ursula K. *Imagining Extinction: The Cultural Meanings of Endangered Species*. Chicago, IL: University of Chicago Press, 2016.

—'Lost Dogs, Last Birds, and Listed Species: Cultures of Extinction'. *Configurations* 18, nos 1–2 (2010): 49–72.

—'The Environmental Humanities and the Futures of the Human'. *New German Critique* 43, no. 2, 128 (August 2016): 21–31.

Herbert, Eugenia W. 'Flora's Empire: British Gardens in India'. In *Flora's Empire*. Philadelphia, PA: University of Pennsylvania Press, 2012.

Herman, William C. 'The Last Passenger Pigeon'. *The Auk* 65, no. 1 (1948): 77–80.

Hermansen, Ralph D. 'Homo Sapiens'. In *Down from the Trees: Man's Amazing Transition from Tree-Dwelling Ape Ancestors*. New York, NY: Apple Academic Press, 2018.

Heupink, Tim H., Hein van Grouw, and David M. Lambert. 'The Mysterious Spotted Green Pigeon and Its Relation to the Dodo and Its Kindred'. *BMC Evolutionary Biology* 14, no. 1 (2014): 1–7.

Hewson, John, and Beverley Diamond. 'Santu's Song'. *Newfoundland Studies* 22, no. 1 (2007): 227–57.

Higham, Thomas. *The World Before Us: How Science Is Revealing a New Story of Our Human Origins*. New Haven, CT: Yale University Press, 2021.

Higham, Tom, Katerina Douka, Rachel Wood, Christopher Bronk Ramsey, Fiona Brock, Laura Basell, Marta Camps, et al. 'The Timing and Spatiotemporal Patterning of Neanderthal Disappearance'. *Nature* 512 (2014): 306–9.

Hight, Kathryn S. '"Doomed to Perish": George Catlin's Depictions of the Mandan'. *Art Journal* 49, no. 2 (1990): 119–24.

Hildebrand, Alan R., Glen T. Penfield, David A. Kring, Mark Pilkington, Antonio Camargo, Z., Stein, B. Jacobsen, and William V. Boynton. 'Chicxulub Crater: A Possible Cretaceous/Tertiary Boundary Impact Crater on the Yucatán Peninsula, Mexico'. *Geology* 19, no. 9 (1991): 867–71.

Hill, Ken D. 'Wollemi Pine: Discovering a Living Fossil'. *Nature & Resources* 32 (1996): 20–5.

Hilton-Taylor, Craig. 'A History of the IUCN Red List'. In *The IUCN Red List: 50 Years of Conservation*, ed. Jane Smart, Craig Hilton-Taylor, and Russell A. Mittermeier, 9–27. Washington, DC: Earth in Focus, 2014.

Hingston, R. W. G. 'Proposed British National Parks for Africa'. *The Geographical Journal* 77, no. 5 (1931): 401.

Hobley, C. W. 'The Preservation of Wild Life in the Empire'. *Journal of the Royal African Society* 34, no. 137 (1935): 403–7.

Hoffmann, D. L., C. D. Standish, M. García-Diez, P. B. Pettitt, J. A. Milton, J. Zilhão, J. J. Alcolea-González, et al. 'U-Th Dating of Carbonate Crusts Reveals Neandertal Origin of Iberian Cave Art'. *Science* 359, no. 6378 (2018): 912–15.

Holden, Constance. 'Ancient Trees Down Under'. *Science* 267, no. 5196 (1995): 334.

Holly, Donald. 'A Historiography of an Ahistoricity: On the Beothuk Indians'. *History and Anthropology* 14, no. 2 (2003): 127–40.

Holly, Donald H. 'Environment, History and Agency in Storage Adaptation: On the Beothuk in the 18th Century'. *Canadian Journal of Archaeology/Journal Canadien d'Archéologie* 22, no. 1 (1998): 19–30.

—'Social Aspects and Implications of "Running to the Hills": The Case of the Beothuk Indians of Newfoundland'. *Journal of Island and Coastal Archaeology* 3, no. 2 (27 October 2008): 170–90.

Holly, Donald H., Christopher Wolff, and John Erwin. 'The Ties That Bind and Divide: Encounters with the Beothuk in Southeastern Newfoundland'. *Journal of the North Atlantic* 3 (December 2010): 31–44.

Holly Jr, Donald H. 'The Beothuk on the Eve of Their Extinction'. *Arctic Anthropology* (2000), 79–95.

Holmes, William H. 'Sketch of the Origin, Development, and Probable Destiny of the Races of Men'. *American Anthropologist* 4, no. 3 (1902): 369–91.

Home, Everard. 'Some Account of the Fossil Remains of an Animal More Nearly Allied to Fishes Than Any of the Other Classes of Animals'. *Philosophical Transactions of the Royal Society of London* 104 (1814): 571–7.

Hooley, Reginald Walter. 'On the Skeleton of Iguanodon atherfieldensis sp. nov., from the Wealden Shales of Atherfield (Isle of Wight)'. *Quarterly Journal of the Geological Society* 81 (1925): 1–61.

Hornaday, William Temple. *Our Vanishing Wild Life: Its Extermination and Preservation*. New York, NY: Charles Scribner's Sons, 1913.

—*The Extermination of the American Bison, with a Sketch of its Discovery and Life History*. Washington, DC: Government Printing Office, 1889.

—*Wild Life Conservation in Theory and Practice: Lectures Delivered before the Forest School of Yale University, 1914*. New Haven, CT: Yale University Press, 1914.

Hornaday, William Temple, and Alwin K. Haagner. *The Vanishing Game of South Africa: A Warning and an Appeal*. New York, NY, 1922.

Horrall, Andrew. *Inventing the Cave Man: From Darwin to the Flintstones*. Manchester: Manchester University Press, 2017.

Host, John T., and Chris Owens, eds. *'It's Still in My Heart This Is My Country': The Single Noongar Claim History*. Crawley, WA: UWA Press, 2009.

Howley, James P. *The Beothucks, or Red Indians: The Aboriginal Inhabitants of Newfoundland*. Cambridge: Cambridge University Press, 1915.

Howorth, H. H. 'Strictures on Darwinism. Part II. The Extinction of Types'. *Journal of the Anthropological Institute of Great Britain and Ireland* 3 (1874): 208–29.

Hoy, P. R. 'Dr. Koch's Missourium'. *The American Naturalist* 5 (1871): 147–8.

Hrdlička, Aleš. 'The Neanderthal Phase of Man'. *Journal of the Royal Anthropological Institute of Great Britain and Ireland* 57 (1927): 249–74.

HRH the Prince of the Netherlands. 'Plants and the Future of Man'. *Environmental Conservation* 3, no. 1 (April 1976): 23–6.

Hu, H. H. 'How Metasequoia, the "Living Fossil", Was Discovered in China'. *Arnoldia* 58/59, no. 4/1 (1998): 4–7.

Hu, H. H., and W. C. Cheng. 'On the New Family Metasequoiaceae and on *Metasequoia Glyptostroboides*, a Living Species of the Genus Metasequoia Found in Szechuan and Hupeh'. *Bulletin of the Fan Memorial Institute of Biology*, n.s., 1 (1948): 154–61.

Huang, Shi. 'Ancient Fossil Specimens of Extinct Species Are Genetically More Distant to an Outgroup than Extant Sister Species Are'. *Nature Precedings* (2008), 553.

Hubbard, Tasha. 'The Call of the Buffalo: Exploring Kinship with the Buffalo in Indigenous Creative Expression'. Doctoral thesis, University of Calgary, 2016.

Hughes, Lesley, Will Steffen, Greg Mullins, Annika Dean, Ella Weisbrot, and Martin Rice. 'Summer of Crisis'. Climate Council of Australia, 2020.

Hui, Alexandra. 'Listening to Extinction: Early Conservation Radio Sounds and the Silences of Species'. *The American Historical Review* 126, no. 4 (2022): 1371–95.

Hume, Julian P. 'The Dodo: From Extinction to the Fossil Record'. *Geology Today* 28, no. 4 (2012): 147–51.

—'The History of the Dodo *Raphus Cucullatus* and the Penguin of Mauritius'. *Historical Biology* 18, no. 2 (2006): 69–93.

Hume, Julian P., and Christine Taylor. 'A Gift from Mauritius: William Curtis, George Clark and the Dodo'. *Journal of the History of Collections* 29 (2016): 467–79.

Hume, Julian Pender, David M. Martill, and Christopher Dewdney. 'Dutch Diaries and the Demise of the Dodo'. *Nature* 429, no. 6992 (2004): 245.

Hunter, William. 'Observations on the Bones, Commonly Supposed to Be Elephant's Bones, Which Have Been Found Near the River Ohio in

America: By William Hunter, M. D. F. R. S.' *Philosophical Transactions of the Royal Society* 58 (1768): 34–45.

Hurt, R. Douglas. *The Indian Frontier, 1763–1846*. Albuquerque, NM: University of New Mexico Press, 2002.

Huxley, Thomas Henry. *Evidence as to Man's Place in Nature*. London: Williams and Norgate, 1863.

Hyer, Joel R. *We Are Not Savages: Native Americans in Southern California and the Pala Reservation, 1840–1920*. East Lansing, MI: Michigan State University Press, 2001.

Ingersoll, Ernest. 'The Effect of the Settlement of North America Upon Its Wild Animals'. *Science* n.s. 6, no. 144S (1885): 416–17.

Inglis, Bishop John. 'Shanawdithit, the Last of the Bœothicks'. *Monthly Record of Church Missions in Connection with the Society for the Propagation of the Gospel in Foreign Parts*, no. 12 (1856): 265–9.

Irwin, Aisling. 'No Tree Left Behind'. *Nature* 609 (2022): 24–7.

Isenberg, Andrew C. *The Destruction of the Bison: An Environmental History, 1750–1920*. Studies in Environment and History. Cambridge: Cambridge University Press, 2000.

IUCN. 'Endangered Mammals and Birds of the World: Summary Statements of Status and Action Treatment: Based on IUCN Supplementary Papers 13 and 14'. IUCN, 1970.

—*IUCN Status and Regulations, and Last Amended 10 September 2016, Including Rules of Procedure of the World Conservation Congress, Last Amended on 10 September 2016, and Regulations Revived on 22 October 1996 and Last Amended on 17 August 2016*. IUCN, 2016.

—*Les Fossiles de Demain*. Brussels: IUCN, 1954.

—*Motions of the World Conservation Congress, Bangkok, Thailand, 17–25 November 2004*. Gland, Switzerland: IUCN, 2004.

—*Motions, World Conservation Congress, Barcelona, October 2008*. Gland, Switzerland: IUCN, 2008.

—*Motions, World Conservation Congress, Honolulu, Hawaii, 2016*. Gland, Switzerland: IUCN, 2016.

—*Motions, World Conservation Congress, Jeju, Republic of Korea, 6–15 September 2012*. Gland, Switzerland: IUCN, 2012.

—*Proceedings of the Fifth General Assembly, Edinburgh, 20–28 June 1956*. Brussels: IUCN, 1957.

—*Proceedings of the Sixth General Assembly, Athens, 11–19 September 1958*. Brussels: IUCN, 1960.

—*Proceedings of the Seventh General Assembly, Warsaw, June 15–24 1960*. Brussels: IUCN, 1960.

—*Proceedings of the Eighth General Assembly, Nairobi, Kenya, September 16–24 1963*. Brussels: IUCN, 1964.

—*Proceedings of the Ninth General Assembly, Lucerne, Switzerland, 25 June–2 July 1966*. Morges, Switzerland: IUCN, 1967.

—*Proceedings of the Tenth General Assembly, Vigyan Bhavan, New Delhi, 24 November–1 December 1969, Volume II*. Morges, Switzerland: IUCN, 1970.

—*Proceedings of the Eleventh General Assembly, Banff, Alberta, Canada, 11–16 September 1972*. Morges, Switzerland: IUCN, 1972.

—*Proceedings of the Twelfth General Assembly, Kinshasa, Zaire, 8–18 September 1975*. Morges, Switzerland: IUCN, 1975.

—*Proceedings of the Thirteenth (Extraordinary) General Assembly, Geneva, Switzerland, 19–21 April 1977*. Morges, Switzerland: IUCN, 1977.

—*Proceedings of the 14th General Assembly of IUCN and 14th IUCN Technical Meeting, Ashkhabad, USSR, 26 September–5 October 1978*. Morges, Switzerland: IUCN, 1979.

—*Proceedings of the 15th Session of the General Assembly of the IUCN and 15th IUCN Technical Meeting, Christchurch, New Zealand, 11–23 October 1981*. Gland, Switzerland: IUCN, 1983.

—*Proceedings of the 16th Session of the General Assembly of the IUCN and 16th Technical Meeting, Madrid, Spain, 5–14 November 1984*. Gland, Switzerland: IUCN, 1984.

—*Proceedings of the 17th General Assembly, San José, Costa Rica, 1988*. Brussels: IUCN, 1988.

—*Proceedings of the 19th General Assembly, Buenos Aires, Argentina, 1994*. Brussels: IUCN, 1994.

—*Proceedings of the Members' Assembly, World Conservation Congress, Jeju, Republic of Korea, 6–15 September 2012*. Gland, Switzerland: IUCN, 2012.

—*Proceedings of the Members' Assembly, World Conservation Congress, Barcelona, October 2008*. Gland, Switzerland: IUCN, 2009.

—*Proceedings of the World Conservation Congress, Amman, Jordan, 4–11 October 2000*, ed. Tim Jones. Gland, Switzerland, and Cambridge: IUCN, 2001.

—*Proceedings, World Conservation Congress, Honolulu, Hawaii, 2016*. Gland, Switzerland: IUCN, 2016.

—, ed. *Proceedings of the 18th General Assembly, Perth, Australia, 1990*. Gland, Switzerland: IUCN, 1991.

—, ed. *Proceedings, World Conservation Congress, Montreal, Canada, 13–23 October 1996*. Norwich: IUCN, 1997.

—*Statutes of 5 October 1948, Revised on 22 October 1996 and Last Amended on 13 October 2008 (including Rules of Procedure of the World Conservation Congress Last Amended on 5 October 2008) and Regulations Revised on 22 October 1996 and Last Amended on 13 October 2008*. Gland, Switzerland: IUCN, 2008.

—*Statutes of 5 October 1948, Revised on 22 October (including Rules of Procedure of the World Conservation Congress, Last Amended 14 September 2012)*. Gland, Switzerland: IUCN, 2012.

—*The Impact of IUCN Resolutions on International Conservation Efforts: An Overview*. Gland, Switzerland: IUCN, n.d.

—'Wollemia Nobilis: Thomas, P.: The IUCN Red List of Threatened Species 2011: E.T34926A9898196'. International Union for Conservation of Nature (20 October 2010).

—'World Conservation Congress: Resolution 041'. IUCN, 2012.

IUCN Operations Intelligence Centre. 'A Preliminary List of Rare Mammals Including Those Believed to Be Rare but Concerning Which Detailed Information Is Still Lacking'. *IUCN Bulletin, New Series* 11 (June 1964): Special Supplement between 4–5.

—'List of Rare Birds, Including Those Thought to Be So But Of Which Detailed Information Is Still Lacking'. *IUCN Bulletin, New Series* 10 (March 1964): Special Supplement.

IUCN Species Survival Commission. *IUCN Species Survival Commission Guidelines on the Use of Ex-Situ Management for Species. Version 2.0*. Gland, Switzerland: IUCN, 2014.

IUCN Species Survival Commission. *IUCN Red List Categories*. Gland, Switzerland: IUCN, 1994.

IUCN Standards and Petitions Subcommittee. 'Guidelines for Using the IUCN Red List Categories and Criteria' (2022).

IUCN, UNEP, and WWF. *World Conservation Strategy*. IUCN, 1980.

IUPN. 'Inquiry on Vanishing Mammals: Draft Questionnaire'. In *Proceedings and Reports of the Second Session of the General Assembly, Held in Brussels, 18–23 October 1950*, 29–30. Brussels: IUPN, 1951.

—*International Technical Conference on the Protection of Nature: Lake Success, NY, 22–29 VIII 1949, Proceedings and Papers*. Paris and Brussels: International Union for the Protection of Nature, 1950.

—*International Union for the Protection of Nature, Established at Fontainebleau, 5 October 1948*. Paris and Brussels: IUPN, 1948.

—*Proceedings and Papers: International Technical Conference on the Protection of Nature, Lake Success, NY, 22–29 VIII, 1949*. Paris and Brussels: IUCN, 1950.

—*Proceedings and Reports of the Fourth General Assembly, Held at Copenhagen (Denmark), 25 August to 3 September 1954*. Brussels: IUPN, 1955.

—*Proceedings and Reports of the Second Session of the General Assembly, held in Brussels, 18–23 October 1950*. Brussels: IUPN, 1951.

—*Proceedings and Reports of the Third General Assembly, Held in Caracas (Venezuela), 3–9 November 1952*. Brussels: IUPN, 1952.

—, ed. 'The Survival Service'. In *Proceedings and Reports of the Second Session of the General Assembly, Held in Brussels, 18–23 October 1950*, 24–8. Brussels: IUPN, 1951.

Jackson, Andrew. 'Added Credence for a Late Dodo Extinction Date'. *Historical Biology* 26, no. 6 (2014): 699–701.

—'First Annual Message, December 8, 1829'. In *Messages of Gen. Andrew Jackson: With a Short Sketch of His Life*, Concord, NH, 39–68. J. F. Brown and W. White, 1837.

Jacob, Frank, and Kim Sebastian Todzi, eds. *Genocidal Violence: Concepts, Forms, Impact*. Oldenbourg: De Gruyter, 2023.

Jacobs, Margaret D. 'After One Hundred Winters: In Search of Reconciliation on America's Stolen Lands'. In *After One Hundred Winters*. Princeton, NJ: Princeton University Press, 2021.

Jardine, Nicholas, James A. Secord, and E. C. Spary, eds. *Cultures of Natural History*. Cambridge: Cambridge University Press, 1996.

Jarvis, C., C. Leon, and S. Oldfield. 'Bibliography of Red Data Books and Threatened Plant Lists'. In *Biological Aspects of Rare Plant Conservation*, ed. H. Synge, 513–29. Chichester: Wiley, 1981.

Jefferson, Thomas. *Notes on the State of Virginia*. London: John Stockdale, 1787.

Jenkins, Martin, and Jane Thornback. *The IUCN Mammal Red Data Book: Part 1, Threatened Mammalian Taxa of the Americas and the Australasian Zoogeographic Region (excluding Cetacea)*. Gland, Switzerland: IUCN, 1982.

Jepson, Paul, and Cain Blythe. *Rewilding: The Radical New Science of Ecological Recovery*. Hot Science. London: Icon Books Ltd, 2020.

John Millard. *Liverpool's Museum: The First 150 Years*. n.p., 2010.

Johnson, E. 'List of Vanishing Gambian Mammals'. *Journal of the Society for the Preservation of the Wild Fauna of the Empire*, n.s. 31 (1937): 62–6.

Jones, Charles C. 'Antiquity of the North American Indians'. *The North American Review*, 1874, 70–87.

Jones, Ryan Tucker. *Empire of Extinction: Russians and the North Pacific's Strange Beasts of the Sea, 1741–1867*. Oxford: Oxford University Press, 2014.

—*Red Leviathan: The Secret History of Soviet Whaling*. Chicago, IL: University of Chicago Press, 2022.

Jones, Wyn, Kenneth Hill, and Jan Allen. '*Wollemia Nobilis*, a New Living Australian Genus and Species in the Araucariaceae'. *Telopea* 6 (1995): 173–6.

Jones, Wyn R., Ken D. Hill, and Jan M. Allen. *Wollemi Nobilis Holotype*. Sydney: Royal Botanic Gardens, Sydney, 1994.

Jørgensen, Dolly. 'Reintroduction and De-Extinction'. *BioScience* 63, no. 9 (2013): 719–20.

—'Rethinking Rewilding'. *Geoforum* 65 (2015): 482–8.

Jørgensen, Dolly, and Isla Gladstone. 'The Passenger Pigeon's Past on Display for the Future'. *Environmental History* 27, no. 2 (2022): 347–53.

Jørgensen, Dolly, Libby Robin, and Marie-Theres Fojuth. 'Slowing Time in the Museum in a Period of Rapid Extinction'. *Museum and Society* 20 (2022): 1–12.

Kaskes, P., S. Goderis, J. Belza, P. Tack, R. A. DePalma, J. Smit, L. Vincze, F. Vanhaecke, and Ph. Claeys. 'Caught in Amber: Geochemistry and Petrography of Uniquely Preserved Chicxulub Microtektites from the Tanis K-Pg Site from North-Dakota (USA)'. *Large Meteorite Impacts* 6 (2019): 1–2.

Kehoe, Alice B. 'The Invention of Prehistory'. *Current Anthropology* 32 (1991): 467–76.

Keith, A. 'Mankind – From the Pliocene to the Present'. *Nature* 87, no. 2190 (1911): 522–3.

—'The Early History of the Gibraltar Cranium'. *Nature* 87, no. 2184 (September 1911): 313–14.

Keith, Arthur. 'A New Theory of the Descent of Man'. *Nature* 85, no. 2146 (1910): 206.

—'Discovery of Neanderthal Man in Malta'. *Nature* 101, no. 2543 (1918): 404–5.

—*The Antiquity of Man*. London: Williams and Norgate, 1915.

Keller, Robert H., and Michael F. Turek. *American Indians and National Parks*. Tucson, AZ: University of Arizona Press, 2005.

Kemp, Christopher. *The Lost Species: Great Expeditions in the Collections of Natural History Museums*. Chicago, IL: University of Chicago Press, 2017.

Kerr, R. A. 'Asteroid Theory of Extinctions Strengthened'. *Science* 210, no. 4469 (1980): 514–17.

Kidd, Colin. *The Forging of Races: Race and Scripture in the Protestant Atlantic World, 1600–2000*. Cambridge: Cambridge University Press, 2006.

King, Warren B. *Endangered Birds of the World: The ICPB Bird Red Data Book*. Washington, DC: Smithsonian Institution Press, 1981.

King, William. 'The Neanderthal Skull'. *Anthropological Review* 1 (1863): 393–4.

—'The Reputed Fossil Man of the Neanderthal'. *Quarterly Journal of Science* 1 (1864): 88–97.

Kirksey, S. Eben, and Stefan Helmreich. 'The Emergence of Multispecies Ethnography'. *Cultural Anthropology* 25, no. 4 (2010): 545–76.

Kjærgaard, Peter C. '"Hurrah for the Missing Link!": A History of Apes, Ancestors and a Crucial Piece of Evidence'. *Notes and Records of the Royal Society* 65 (2011): 83–98.

Kneeland, Jonathan. 'On Some Causes Tending to Promote the Extinction of the Aborigines of America'. *The Transactions of the American Medical Association* 15 (1865): 253–60.

Koch, Albert. *Description of Missourium, or Missouri Leviathan: Together with Its Supposed Habits and Indian Traditions Concerning the Location from whence It Was Exhumed; Also, Comparisons of the Whale, Crocodile and Missourium with the Leviathan, as Described in 41st Chapter of the Book of Job, and a Catalogue of the Whole Fossil Collection*. London: E. Fisher, 1841.

Koch, Alexander, Chris Brierley, Mark M. Maslin, and Simon L. Lewis. 'Earth System Impacts of the European Arrival and Great Dying in the Americas after 1492'. *Quaternary Science Reviews* 207 (March 2019): 13–36.

Koerner, Lisbet. 'Carl Linnaeus in His Time and Place'. In *Cultures of Natural History*, ed. Nicholas Jardine, James A. Secord, and E. C. Spary, 145–62. Cambridge: Cambridge University Press, 1996.

Kohn, Eduardo. *How Forests Think: Toward an Anthropology beyond the Human*. Berkeley, CA: University of California Press, 2013.

Kontler, László. 'Inventing "Humanity": Early-Modern Perspectives'. In *Passions, Politics and the Limits of Society*, ed. Heikki Haara, Koen Stapelbroek, and Mikko Immanen, 25–46. Berlin: De Gruyter, 2020.

Kowal, Emma. *Trapped in the Gap: Doing Good in Indigenous Australia*. New York, NY: Berghahn Books, 2015.

Kowal, Emma, and Joanna Radin. 'Indigenous Biospecimen Collections and the Cryopolitics of Frozen Life'. *Journal of Sociology* 51, no. 1 (2015): 63–80.

Kristensen, Todd J. 'Seasonal Bird Exploitation by Recent Indian and Beothuk Hunter-Gatherers of Newfoundland'. *Canadian Journal of Archaeology/Journal Canadien d'Archéologie* 35, no. 2 (2011): 292–322.

Kristensen, Todd J., and Reade Davis. 'The Legacies of Indigenous History in Archaeological Thought'. *Journal of Archaeological Method and Theory* 22, no. 2 (2015): 512–42.

Kristensen, Todd J., and Donald H. Holly. 'Birds, Burials and Sacred Cosmology of the Indigenous Beothuk of Newfoundland, Canada'. *Cambridge Archaeological Journal* 23, no. 1 (2013): 41–53.

Kroeber, Theodora. *Ishi in Two Worlds*. Berkeley, CA: University of California Press, 1961.

Kuch, Melanie, Darren R. Gröcke, Martin C. Knyf, M. Thomas, P. Gilbert, Ban Younghusband, Terry Young, Ingeborg Marshall, Eske Willerslev, Mark Stoneking, and Hendrik Poinar. 'A Preliminary Analysis of the DNA and Diet of the Extinct Beothuk: A Systematic Approach to Ancient Human DNA'. *American Journal of Physical Anthropology* 132, no. 4 (2007): 594–604.

Kuklick, Henrika. '"Humanity in the Chrysalis Stage": Indigenous Australians in the Anthropological Imagination, 1899–1926'. *Third British Journal for the History of Science* 39 (2006): 535–68.

Kuser, John. 'Metasequoia Keeps On Growing'. *Arnoldia* 42, no. 3 (1982): 130–8.

Kyne, Peter M., and Vanessa M. Adams. 'Extinct Flagships: Linking Extinct and Threatened Species'. *Oryx* 51, no. 3 (2017): 471–6.

Laidlaw, Z. 'Heathens, Slaves and Aborigines: Thomas Hodgkin's Critique of Missions and Anti-Slavery'. *History Workshop Journal* 64, no. 1 (1 January 2007): 133–61.

Laidlaw, Z., Kenneth A. Loparo. *Indigenous Communities and Settler Colonialism: Land Holding, Loss and Survival in an Interconnected World*. London: Palgrave Macmillan UK, 2015.

Laidlaw, Zoë. '"Aunt Anna's Report": The Buxton Women and the Aborigines Select Committee, 1835–37'. *Journal of Imperial and Commonwealth History* 32, no. 2 (2004): 1–28.

—'Breaking Britannia's Bounds? Law, Settlers, and Space in Britain's Imperial Historiography'. *The Historical Journal* 55, no. 3 (September 2012): 807–30.

—'"Justice to India – Prosperity to England – Freedom to the Slave!" Humanitarian and Moral Reform Campaigns on India, Aborigines and American Slavery'. *Journal of the Royal Asiatic Society* 22, no. 2 (April 2012): 299–324.

—*Protecting the Empire's Humanity: Thomas Hodgkin and British Colonial Activism 1830–1870*. Critical Perspectives on Empire. Cambridge and New York, NY: Cambridge University Press, 2021.

—'Slavery, Settlers and Indigenous Dispossession: Britain's Empire through the Lens of Liberia'. *Journal of Colonialism and Colonial History* 13, no. 1 (2012).

Lane Fox, A. H. 'On the Principles of Classification Adopted in the Arrangement of his Anthropological Collection, Now Exhibited in the Bethnal Green Museum'. *Journal of the Anthropological Institute* 4 (1874): 293–308.

Langsdorff, Georg Heinrich von. *Bemerkungen auf einer Reise um die Welt in den Jahren 1803 bis 1807*. 2 vols. Frankfurt: F. Wilmans, 1812.

Lanza, Robert P., Jose B. Cibelli, Francisca Diaz, Carlos T. Moraes, Peter W. Farin, Charlotte E. Farin, Carolyn J. Hammer, Michael D. West, and Philip Damiani. 'Cloning of an Endangered Species (*Bos gaurus*) Using Interspecies Nuclear Transfer'. *Cloning* 2, no. 2 (2000): 79–90.

Latham, John. *A General History of Birds*. Vol. 8. 10 vols. Winchester: Jacob and Johnson, 1823.

—*A General Synopsis of Birds*. Vol. 2.2. 3 vols. London: Leigh & Sotheby, 1783.

Laubenfels, M. W. 'Dinosaur Extinction: One More Hypothesis'. *Journal of Paleontology* 30 (1956): 207–12.

Lauer, Nicolaas Rupke, Gerhard, ed. *Johann Friedrich Blumenbach: Race and Natural History, 1750–1850*. London: Routledge, 2018.

Laundré, John W., Lucina Hernández, and Kelly B. Altendorf. 'Wolves, Elk, and Bison: Reestablishing the "Landscape of Fear" in Yellowstone National Park, U.S.A.' *Canadian Journal of Zoology* 79, no. 8 (2001): 1401–9.

Lawrence, Anna M. 'Listening to Plants: Conversations between Critical Plant Studies and Vegetal Geography'. *Progress in Human Geography* 46, no. 2 (2022): 629–51.

Leather, Simon R., Yves Basset, and Bradford A. Hawkins. 'Insect Conservation: Finding the Way Forward'. *Insect Conservation and Diversity* 1, no. 1 (February 2008): 67–9.

Lee, Richard. 'The Extinction of Races'. *Journal of the Anthropological Society of London* 2 (1864): xcv–xcix.

Leela, N. S. 'Wollemi Pine: Living Fossil from Jurassic Landscape'. *Resonance* 8, no. 8 (2003): 43–7.

Lemkin, Raphaël. 'Genocide – A Modern Crime'. *Free World* 4 (April 1945): 39–43.

Leopold, Aldo. *A Sand County Almanac*. Oxford: Oxford University Press, 1949.

Lester, Alan, and Fae Dussart. 'Trajectories of Protection: Protectorates of Aborigines in Early 19th Century Australia and Aotearoa New Zealand'. *New Zealand Geographer* 64, no. 3 (2008): 205–20.

Levin, Simon Asher, ed. *Encyclopedia of Biodiversity*. 1st ed. Vol. 1: San Diego, CA: Academic Press, 2001.

Levy, Sharon. *Once & Future Giants: What Ice Age Extinctions Tell Us about the Fate of Earth's Largest Animals*. Oxford and New York: Oxford University Press, 2011.

Lewin, R. 'A Mass Extinction without Asteroids'. *Science* 234 (1986): 14–15.

Lindsay, William. ' "Mammoth" Task'. *Curator: The Museum Journal* 34, no. 4 (1991): 261–72.

Litoff, Judy Barrett. 'Gunther's Travels: The Odyssey of Metasequoia Seeds from the 1920s?' In *The Geobiology and Ecology of Metasequoia*, ed. Ben A. LePage, Christopher J. Williams, and Hong Yang, 187–94. Topics in Geobiology. Dordrecht: Springer Netherlands, 2005.

Liverpool Museum (Liverpool, England). *A Companion to the Liverpool Museum, Containing a Brief Description of upwards of Seven Thousand Natural and Foreign Curiosities, Antiquities, and Production of the Fine Arts, Collected during Several Years of Arduous Research, and at an Expense of upwards of Twenty Thousand Pounds, by Willam Bullock of Liverpool; and Now Open for Public Inspection, in the Great Room, No. 22, Piccadilly, London, Which Has Been Fitted for the Purpose in a Manner Entirely New.* Bath: Richard Cruttwell, 1809.

Livingstone, David N. *Adam's Ancestors: Race, Religion, and the Politics of Human Origins*. Baltimore, MD: Johns Hopkins University Press, 2008.

Lloyd, Natasha A., Laura M. Keating, Alyssa J. Friesen, Dylan M. Cole, Jana M. McPherson, H. Resit Akçakaya, and Axel Moehrenschlager. 'Prioritizing Species Conservation Programs Based on IUCN Green Status and Estimates of Cost-Sharing Potential'. *Conservation Biology* 37, no. 3 (2023): e14051.

Lloyd, T. G. B. 'A Further Account of the Beothucs of Newfoundland'. *Journal of the Anthropological Institute of Great Britain and Ireland* 5 (1876): 222–30.

—'Notes on Indian Remains Found on the Coast of Labrador'. *Journal of the Anthropological Institute of Great Britain and Ireland* 4 (1875): 39–44.

—'On the "Beothucs", a Tribe of Red Indians, Supposed to Be Extinct, Which Formerly Inhabited Newfoundland'. *Journal of the Anthropological Institute of Great Britain and Ireland* 4 (1875): 21–39.

—'On the Stone Implements of Newfoundland'. *Journal of the Anthropological Institute of Great Britain and Ireland* 5 (1876): 233–48.

Lorimer, Jamie, and Clemens Driessen. 'Experiments with the Wild at the Oostvaardersplassen'. *Ecos* 35 (2014): 44–52.

—'From "Nazi Cows" to Cosmopolitan "Ecological Engineers": Specifying Rewilding Through a History of Heck Cattle'. *Annals of the American Association of Geographers* 106, no. 3 (2016): 631–52.

Lorimer, Jamie, and C. P. G. Driessen. 'Back-Breeding the Aurochs: The Heck Brothers, National Socialism and Imagined Geographies for Nonhuman Lebensraum'. In *Hitler's Geographies: The Spatialities of the Third Reich*, ed. Paolo Giacarria and Claudio Minca, 138–59. Chicago, IL: University of Chicago Press, 2016.

Lubbock, John. *Fifty Years of Science: Being the Address Delivered at York to the British Association*. 2nd ed. London: Macmillan and Co., 1882.

—*Pre-Historic Times: As Illustrated by Ancient Remains, and the Manners and Customs of Modern Savages*. London: Williams and Norgate, 1865.

—'The Early Condition of Man'. *Anthropological Review* (1868): 328–41.

—*The Origin of Civilization and the Primitive Condition of Man*. 5th ed. London: Longman, Green and Co., 1889.

Lucas, Charles Prestwood. *Native Races in the British Empire. Memorandum. Miscellaneous, no. 217*. London: Colonial Office, 1907.

Lucas, Gren, and Hugh Synge. *The IUCN Plant Red Data Book: Comprising Red Data Sheets on 250 Selected Plants Threatened on a World Scale*. Morges, Switzerland: IUCN, 1978.

Lucas, Grenville. 'Threatened Plants – How to Save Them'. *Oryx* 13, no. 3 (1976): 257–8.

Lucas, Grenville, and A. H. M. Synge. 'The IUCN Threatened Plants Committee and its Work Throughout the World'. *Environmental Conservation* 4, no. 3 (October 1977): 179–87.

Lyell, Charles. 'Introductory Address by the President, Sir C. Lyell. On the Occurrence of Works of Human Art in Post-Pliocene Deposits.' *Report of the Twenty-Ninth Meeting of the British Association for the Advancement of Science; Held at Aberdeen in September 1859*, 1860, 93–5.

—*Principles of Geology*. 3 vols. London: John Murray, 1830–3.

—*The Geological Evidences of the Antiquity of Man with Remarks on Theories of the Origin of Species by Variation*. Vol. 1. London: John Murray, 1863.

Lyster, Simon. *International Wildlife Law: An Analysis of International Treaties Concerned with the Conservation of Wildlife*. Cambridge: Grotius Publications Ltd, 1985.

Ma, Jinshuang. 'The Chronology of the "Living Fossil" *Metasequoia Glyptostroboides* (Taxodiaceae): A Review (1943–2003)'. *Harvard Papers in Botany* 8, no. 1 (2003): 9–18.

—'The History of the Discovery and Initial Seed Dissemination of *Metasequoia Glyptostroboides*, a "Living Fossil" '. *Aliso* 21 (2002): 65–75.

Mabo v. Queensland, No. 2 ('Mabo case'), No. 23 (High Court of Australia, 3 June 1992).

Mace, G., N. Collar, J. Cmke, K. Gaslon, J. Ginsberg, and M. Maunder. 'The Development of New Criteria for Listing Species on the IUCN Red List'. *Species* 19 (1992): 16–22.

Mace, Georgina M. 'The Role of Taxonomy in Species Conservation', ed. H. C. J. Godfray and S. Knapp. *Philosophical Transactions of the Royal Society of London. Series B: Biological Sciences* 359, no. 1444 (2004): 711–19.

Mace, Georgina M., and Russell Lande. 'Assessing Extinction Threats: Toward a Reevaluation of IUCN Threatened Species Categories'. *Conservation Biology* 5, no. 2 (1991): 148–57.

Mace, Georgina M, and W. Kunin. 'Classifying Threatened Species: Means and Ends [and Discussion]'. *Philosophical Transactions of the Royal Society B: Biological Sciences*, 1994, 91–7.

Mace, Georgina M., Nigel J. Collar, Kevin J. Gaston, Craig Hilton-Taylor, H. Resit Akçakaya, Nigel Leader-Williams, E. J. Milner-Gulland, and Simon N. Stuart. 'Quantification of Extinction Risk: IUCN's System for Classifying Threatened Species'. *Conservation Biology* 22, no. 6 (December 2008): 1424–42.

MacGregor, Arthur. 'Sloane, Sir Hans, baronet (1660–7053)'. In *The Oxford Dictionary of National Biography*, ed. H. C. G. Matthew and B. Harrison. Oxford: Oxford University Press, 2004.

Mackenzie, Berin D. E., Steve W. Clarke, Heidi C. Zimmer, Edward C. Y. Liew, Maureen T. Phelan, Catherine A. Offord, Lisa K. Menke, et al. 'Ecology and Conservation of a Living Fossil: Australia's Wollemi Pine (*Wollemia Nobilis*)'. In *Imperiled: The Encyclopedia of Conservation*, ed. Dominick A. DellaSala and Michael I. Goldstein, 884–94. Oxford: Elsevier, 2022.

MacKenzie-Dodds, Jacqueline, Ann Clarke, Dominik Lermen, Isabel Rey, Jonas J. Astrin, Ole Seberg, and Christian C. Oste. 'Recent Initiatives in Biodiversity Biobanking: Summary of Presentations from the ESBB 2012 Conference'. *Biopreservation and Biobanking* 11, no. 3 (2013): 182–8.

Macklem, Patrick. *Indigenous Difference and the Constitution of Canada*. Toronto, ON: University of Toronto Press, 2001.

Macphail, Mike, Ken Hill, Alan Partridge, Elizabeth Truswell, and Clinton Foster. 'Australia: "Wollemi Pine": Old Pollen Records for a Newly Discovered Genus of Gymnosperm'. *Geology Today* 11, no. 2 (1995): 48–50.

Macphail, Mike, Raymond J. Carpenter, Ari Iglesias, and Peter Wilf. 'First Evidence for Wollemi Pine-Type Pollen (*Dilwynites*: Araucariaceae) in South America', ed. Lee A. Newsom. *PLOS ONE* 8, no. 7 (2013): e69281.

Madison, Paige. 'Characterized by Darkness: Reconsidering the Origins of the Brutish Neanderthal'. *Journal of the History of Biology* 53 (2020): 493–519.

—'The Most Brutal of Human Skulls: Measuring and Knowing the First Neanderthal'. *The British Journal for the History of Science* 49, no. 03 (2016): 411–32.

Madley, Benjamin. *An American Genocide: The United States and the California Indian Catastrophe, 1846–1873*. New Haven, CT: Yale University Press, 2016.

—'From Africa to Auschwitz: How German South West Africa Incubated Ideas and Methods Adopted and Developed by the Nazis in Eastern Europe'. *European History Quarterly* 35, no. 3 (2005): 429–64.

—'From Terror to Genocide: Britain's Tasmanian Penal Colony and Australia's History Wars'. *Journal of British Studies* 47, no. 1 (2008): 77–106.

—'Patterns of Frontier Genocide 1803–1910: The Aboriginal Tasmanians, the Yuki of California, and the Herero of Namibia'. *Journal of Genocide Research* 6, no. 2 (2004): 167–92.

—'Reexamining the American Genocide Debate: Meaning, Historiography, and New Methods'. *The American Historical Review* 120, no. 1 (2015): 98–139.

Malm, Andreas, and Alf Hornborg. 'The Geology of Mankind? A Critique of the Anthropocene Narrative'. *The Anthropocene Review* 1, no. 1 (2014): 62–9.

Manias, Chris. '"Our Iberian Forefathers": The Deep Past and Racial Stratification of British Civilization, 1850–1914'. *Journal of British Studies* 51 (2012): 910–35.

—*Race, Science, and the Nation: Reconstructing the Ancient Past in Britain, France and Germany*. London: Routledge, 2013.

—'Sinanthropus in Britain: Human Origins and International Science, 1920–1939'. *The British Journal for the History of Science* 48, no. 02 (June 2015): 289–319.

—*The Age of Mammals: Nature, Development, and Palaeontology in the Long Nineteenth Century*. Pittsburgh, PA: University of Pittsburgh Press, 2023.

—'The Growth of Race and Culture in Nineteenth-Century Germany: Gustav Klemm and the Universal History of Humanity'. *Modern Intellectual History* 9, no. 01 (April 2012): 1–31.

—'The Problematic Construction of "Palaeolithic Man": The Old Stone Age and the Difficulties of the Comparative Method, 1859–1914'. *Studies in History and Philosophy of Science Part C: Studies in History and Philosophy of Biological and Biomedical Sciences* 51 (2015): 32–43.

Mantell, Gideon. 'Discovery of the Bones of the Iguanodon in a Quarry of Kentish Rag (a Limestone Belonging to the Later Greensand Formation) Near Maidstone, Kent'. *Edinburgh New Philosophical Journal* 18 (1834): 200–1.

—'Notice of the Discovery by Mr Walter Mantell in the Middle Island of New Zealand, of the Living Specimen of the Notornis, a Bird of the Rail Family, Allied to Brachypteryx, and Hitherto Unknown to Naturalists Except in a Fossil State'. *Proceedings of the Zoological Society of London* 214 (1850): 209–14.

—*On the Structure of the Iguanodon, and on the Fauna and Flora of the Wealden Formation*. London: Royal Institution of Great Britain, 1852.

Margócsy, Dániel. '"Refer to Folio and Number": Encyclopedias, the Exchange of Curiosities, and Practices of Identification before Linnaeus'. *Journal of the History of Ideas* 71, no. 1 (January 2010): 63–89.

Marsh, George Perkins. *Man and Nature; Or, Physical Geography as Modified by Human Action*. London: Sampson Low, Son & Marston, 1864.

Marsh, O. C. 'Restoration of Mastodon Americanus, Cuvier'. *Geological Magazine* 10, no. 4 (1893): 164.

Marshall, Ingeborg. *A History and Ethnography of the Beothuk*. Montreal: McGill-Queen's University Press, 1996.

Marshall, Ingeborg, and Alan Macpherson. 'William Eppes Cormack (1796–1868): The Later Years'. *Newfoundland and Labrador Studies* 32, no. 1 (2017): 86–150.

Marshall, Ingeborg, and Alan G. Macpherson. 'William Eppes Cormack (1796–1868): A Biographical Account of the Early Years'. *Newfoundland and Labrador Studies* 31, no. 1 (2016): 78–109.

Martin, Paul S. *Twilight of the Mammoths: Ice Age Extinctions and the Rewilding of America*. Berkeley, CA: University of California Press, 2007.

Martin, Paul S., and Anthony J. Stuart. 'Mammoth Extinction: Two Continents and Wrangel Island'. *Radiocarbon* 37, no. 1 (1995): 7–10.

Martin, Robert D. 'Primates'. *Current Biology* 22, no. 18 (2012): R785–90.

Mathews, R. H., and Martin Thomas. *Culture in Translation: The Anthropological Legacy of R. H. Mathews*. Aboriginal History Monograph Series, no. 15. Acton, ACT: ANU E Press, 2007.

Mawson, Stephanie. 'The Deep Past of Pre-Colonial Australia'. *The Historical Journal* 64, no. 5 (2021): 1477–99.

Mayor, Adrienne. *Fossil Legends of the First Americans*. Princeton, NJ: Princeton University Press, 2013.

McCune, Amy Reed. 'On the Fallacy of Constant Extinction Rates'. *Evolution* 36 (1982): 610–14.

McDonnell, Michael A., and A. Dirk Moses. 'Raphael Lemkin as Historian of Genocide in the Americas'. *Journal of Genocide Research* 7, no. 4 (2005): 501–29.

McGlade, Hannah. 'The McGlade Case: A Noongar History of Land, Social Justice and Activism'. *Australian Feminist Law Journal* 43, no. 2 (3 July 2017): 185–210.

[McGregor, James]. 'Shaa-Naan-Dithit, or the Last of the Boëothics'. *Fraser's Magazine* 13 (1836): 316–23.

McGregor, Russell. '"Breed out the Colour" or the Importance of Being White'. *Australian Historical Studies* 33, no. 120 (2002): 286–302.

—*Imagined Destinies: Aboriginal Australians and the Doomed Race Theory, 1880–1939*. Carlton South, VI: Melbourne University Press, 1998.

—'The Doomed Race: A Scientific Axiom of the Late Nineteenth Century'. *Australian Journal of Politics & History* 39, no. 1 (1993): 14–22.

McGregor, William B. 'Daisy Bates' Documentations of Kimberley Languages'. *Language & History* 55, no. 2 (November 2012): 79–101.

McKay, David I., Arie Staal Armstrong, Jesse F. Abrams, Ricarda Winkelmann, Boris Sakschewski, Sina Loriani, Ingo Fetzer, Sarah E. Cornell, Johan Rockström, and Timothy M. Lenton. 'Exceeding 1.5°C Global Warming Could Trigger Multiple Climate Tipping Points'. *Science* 377, no. 6611 (2022): 1–10.

McKenzie, C., and J. A. Mangan. 'Imperial Masculinity Institutionalized: The Shikar Club'. *The International Journal of the History of Sport* 25, no. 9 (2008): 1218–42.

McLaren, D. J. 'Time, Life, and Boundaries'. *Journal of Paleontology* 44 (1970): 801–15.

McLoughlin, Stephen, and Vivi Vajda. 'Ancient Wollemi Pines Resurgent'. *American Scientist* 93 (2005): 540–7.

McMillan, R. 'The Discovery of Fossil Vertebrates on Missouri's Western Frontier'. *Earth Sciences History* 29, no. 1 (2010): 26–51.

McMillan, R. Bruce. 'Man and Mastodon: A Review of Koch's 1840 Pomme de Terre Expeditions'. In *Prehistoric Man and His Environments*, ed. W. Raymond Wood and R. Bruce McMillan, 81–96. San Diego, CA: Academic Press, 1976.

McNab, David T. 'The Perfect Disguise: Frank Speck's Pilgrimage to Ktaqamkuk, the Place of Fog, in 1914'. *The American Review of Canadian Studies* 31 (2001): 85–104.

McNiven, Ian J., and Lynette Russell. *Appropriated Pasts: Indigenous Peoples and the Colonial Culture of Archaeology*. Archaeology in Society series. Lanham, MD: AltaMira Press, 2005.

Melville, Ronald. 'Plant Conservation and the Red Book'. *Biological Conservation* 2, no. 3 (1 April 1970): 185–8.

Menez, Alex. 'Custodian of the Gibraltar Skull: The History of the Gibraltar Scientific Society'. *Earth Sciences History* 37, no. 1 (2018): 34–62.

—'The Gibraltar Skull: Early History, 1848–1868'. *Archives of Natural History* 45 (2018): 92–110.

Mershon, W. B. *The Passenger Pigeon*. New York, NY: Outing Publishing Company, 1907.

Milam, Erika Lorraine. *Creatures of Cain: The Hunt for Human Nature in Cold War America*. Princeton, NJ: Princeton University Press, 2019.

Milam, Erika Lorraine, and Suman Seth. 'Descent of Darwin: Race, Sex, and Human Nature'. *BJHS Themes* 6 (2021): 1–8.

Miller, J. A. 'Gene Samples from an Extinct Animal Cloned'. *Science News* 125, no. 23 (1984): 356.

Miller, Mary Ashburn. *A Natural History of Revolution: Violence and Nature in the French Revolutionary Imagination, 1789–1794*. Ithaca, NY: Cornell University Press, 2011.

Miller, Robert Rush, ed. *Red Data Book,* vol. 4: *Pisces*. Revised. Morges, Switzerland: IUCN, 1977.

Milne, John. *Relics of the Great Auk*. London: n.p., 1875.

Mitchell, Audra. 'Beyond Biodiversity and Species: Problematizing Extinction'. *Theory, Culture & Society* 33, no. 5 (September 2016): 23–42.

—'Is IR Going Extinct?' *European Journal of International Relations* 23, no. 1 (March 2017): 3–25.

—*Revenant Ecologies Defying the Violence of Extinction and Conservation*. Minneapolis, MN: University of Minnesota Press, 2024.

—'Revitalizing Laws, (Re)-Making Treaties, Dismantling Violence: Indigenous Resurgence against "The Sixth Mass Extinction"'. *Social & Cultural Geography* 21, no. 7 (1 September 2020): 909–24.

Mitchell, Audra, and Aadita Chaudhury. 'Worlding beyond "the" "End" of "the World": White Apocalyptic Visions and BIPOC Futurisms'. *International Relations* 34, no. 3 (September 2020): 309–32.

Mitchell, Audra, Zoe Todd, and Pitseolak Pfeifer. 'SSHRC Knowledge Research Report: "How Can Aboriginal Knowledge Systems in Canada Contribute to Interdisciplinary Research on the Global Extinction Crisis?"' Social Sciences and Humanities Research Council of Canada (2017).

Mitchell, Chantelle, and Jaxon Waterhouse. 'Pine-Ing for a Voice: Vegetal Agencies, New Materialism and State Control through the Wollemi Pine'. *Performance Philosophy* 6, no. 2 (2021): 100–16.

Monahan, Erika L. 'Eastbound through Siberia: Observations from the Great Northern Expedition by Georg Wilhelm Steller'. *Ab Imperio* 2022, no. 3 (2022): 311–14.

Monbiot, George. *Feral: Rewilding the Land, the Sea, and Human Life*. London: Penguin Books, 2014.

Mondry, Henrietta. 'Selecting Candidates for De-Extinction and Resurrection: Mammoths, Lenin's Tomb and Neo-Eurasianism'. *Animal Studies Journal* 6 (2017): 12–39.

Montagu, Ivor. 'The Red Book for All'. *Oryx* 10, no. 2 (1969): 103–5.

—'The Red Book: The World's Endangered Mammals and Birds'. *Oryx* 8, no. 5 (1966): 281.

Moodie, R. L. 'The Influence of Disease in the Extinction of Races'. *Science* 45, no. 1151 (1917): 63–4.

Mora, Camilo, Derek P. Tittensor, Sina Adl, Alastair G. B. Simpson, and Boris Worm. 'How Many Species Are There on Earth and in the Ocean?' *PLOS Biology* 9, no. 8 (23 August 2011): e1001127.

Moreno-Mayar, J. Víctor, Ben A. Potter, Lasse Vinner, Matthias Steinrücken, Simon Rasmussen, Jonathan Terhorst, John A. Kamm, et al. 'Terminal Pleistocene Alaskan Genome Reveals First Founding Population of Native Americans'. *Nature* 553, no. 7687 (2018): 203–7.

Moses, A. Dirk. 'An Antipodean Genocide? The Origins of the Genocidal Moment in the Colonization of Australia'. *Journal of Genocide Research* 2, no. 1 (2000): 89–106.

—'Conceptual Blockages and Definitional Dilemmas in the "Racial Century": Genocides of Indigenous Peoples and the Holocaust'. *Patterns of Prejudice* 36, no. 4 (2002): 7–36.

—'Moving the Genocide Debate Beyond the History Wars'. *Australian Journal of Politics & History* 54, no. 2 (25 May 2008): 248–70.

—'Raphael Lemkin, Culture, and the Concept of Genocide'. In *The Oxford Handbook of Genocide Studies*, ed. Donald Bloxham and A. Dirk Moses, 19–41. Oxford: Oxford University Press, 2010.

—*The Problems of Genocide: Permanent Security and the Language of Transgression*. Cambridge: Cambridge University Press, 2021.

Moses, Dirk A. 'Introduction to Special Issue on Colonial Genocide'. *Patterns of Prejudice* 39, no. 2 (2005): 93–6.

—'Race and Indigeneity in Contemporary Australia'. In *Racism in the Modern World: Historical Perspectives on Cultural Transfer and Adaptation*, 329–52. New York, NY, and Oxford: Berghahn Books, 2011.

Moses, Dirk, ed. *Empire, Colony, Genocide: Conquest, Occupation, and Subaltern Resistance in World History*. New York, NY, and Oxford: Berghahn Books, 2008.

Muller, Z., F. Bercovitch, R. Brand, D. Brown, D. Bolger, K. Carter, F. Deacon, et al. 'Giraffa camelopardalis: The IUCN Red List of Threatened Species 2018: e.T9194A136266699'. International Union for Conservation of Nature, 2016.

Murphy, R. C. 'Conservation and Scientific Forecast'. *Science* 93, no. 2426 (1941): 603–9.

Müller-Wille, Staffan. 'Collection and Collation: Theory and Practice of Linnaean Botany'. *Studies in History and Philosophy of Science Part C: Studies in History and Philosophy of Biological and Biomedical Sciences* 38, no. 3 (2007): 541–62.

—'Race and History: Comments from an Epistemological Point of View'. *Science, Technology, & Human Values* 39, no. 4 (2014): 597–606.

Myers, N. 'An Expanded Approach to the Problem of Disappearing Species'. *Science* 193, no. 4249 (1976): 198–202.

Myers, Norman. *The Sinking Ark: A New Look at the Problem of Disappearing Species*. Oxford: Pergamon Press, 1980.

Naish, Darren. 'Birds'. In *The Complete Dinosaur*, ed. Michael K. Brett-Surman, Thomas R. Holtz, James Orville Farlow, and Bob Walters, 2nd ed., 379–424. Bloomington, IN: Indiana University Press, 2012.

National Parks and Wildlife Service (NPWS, NSW). 'World Heritage Site Nomination for the Greater Blue Mountains Area', 2000.

Natural Hazards Research Australia. 'Understanding the Black Summer Bushfires Through Research: A Summary of Key Findings from the Bushfire and Natural Hazards CRC'. Natural Hazards Research Australia, 2023.

Needham, Rodney, and Adam Kuper. 'Radcliffe-Brown, Daisy Bates and Others'. *Man* 11 (1976): 284–5.

Nemser, Daniel. *Infrastructures of Race: Concentration and Biopolitics in Colonial Mexico*. Austin, TX: University of Texas Press, 2017.

Newell, Norman D. 'Catastrophism and the Fossil Record'. *Evolution* 10, no. 1 (1956): 97–101.

—'Crises in the History of Life'. *Scientific American* 208, no. 2 (1963): 76–93.

—'Periodicity in Invertebrate Evolution'. *Journal of Paleontology* 26 (1952): 371–85.

Newton, Adrian, Sara Oldfield, Malin Rivers, Jennifer Mark, George Schatz, Natalia Tejedor Garavito, Elena Cantarello, Duncan Golicher, Luis Cayuela, and Lera Miles. 'Towards a Global Tree Assessment'. *Oryx* 49, no. 3 (2015): 410–15.

Nic Lughadha, Eimear, Barnaby E. Walker, Cátia Canteiro, Helen Chadburn, Aaron P. Davis, Serene Hargreaves, Eve J. Lucas, et al. 'The Use and Misuse of Herbarium Specimens in Evaluating Plant Extinction Risks'. *Philosophical Transactions of the Royal Society B: Biological Sciences* 374, no. 1763 (2019): 20170402.

Noetling, Fritz. 'The Antiquity of Man in Tasmania'. *Papers and Proceedings of the Royal Society of Tasmania* (1910), 231–61.

Nogués-Bravo, David, Daniel Simberloff, Carsten Rahbek, and Nathan James Sanders. 'Rewilding Is the New Pandora's Box in Conservation'. *Current Biology* 26, no. 3 (February 2016): R87–91.

Norman, Colin. 'The Threat to One Million Species'. *Science* 214, no. 4525 (1981): 1105–7.

Norman, David B. 'A Taxonomy of Iguanodontians (dinosauria: Ornithopoda) from the Lower Wealden Group (cretaceous: Valanginian) of Southern England'. *Zootaxa* 2489, no. 1 (2010): 47.

Novak, Ben. 'De-Extinction'. *Genes* 9, no. 11 (2018): 548.

Novak, Ben J. 'The Great Comeback: Bringing a Species Back from Extinction'. *The Futurist* 47, no. 5 (2013): 40–4.

Nowak-Kemp, M., and J. P. Hume. 'The Oxford Dodo. Part 1: The Museum History of the Tradescant Dodo: Ownership, Displays and Audience'. *Historical Biology* 29, no. 2 (2017): 234–47.

—'The Oxford Dodo. Part 2: From Curiosity to Icon and Its Role in Displays, Education and Research'. *Historical Biology* 29, no. 3 (2017): 296–307.

NSW Scientific Committee. 'Final Determination to List the Wollemi Pine'. NSW Scientific Committee, 2015.

Oberle, M. W. 'Endangered Species: Congress Curbs International Trade in Rare Animals'. *Science* 167, no. 3915 (1970): 152–4.

O'Connor, M. R. *Resurrection Science: Conservation, De-Extinction and the Precarious Future of Wild Things*. New York, NY: St Martin's Press, 2015.

O'Connor, Ralph. *The Earth on Show: Fossils and the Poetics of Popular Science, 1802–1856*. Chicago, IL: University of Chicago Press, 2007.

O'Connor, Timothy D. 'Native American Genomic Diversity through Ancient DNA'. *Cell* 175, no. 5 (2018): 1173–4.

Office of Environment and Heritage, NSW. 'Help Save the Wollemi Pine'. Office of Environment and Heritage, NSW, 2015.

—'Iconic Species Project, Wollemi Pine'. Office of Environment and Heritage, NSW, 2014.

—'Saving Our Species Project, Annual Report Card, Wollemi Pine'. Office of Environment and Heritage, NSW, 2014.

—'Saving Our Species Project, Annual Report Card, Wollemi Pine'. Office of Environment and Heritage, NSW, 2016.

—'Saving Our Species Project, Annual Report Card, Wollemi Pine'. Office of Environment and Heritage, NSW, 2021.

Offord, C. A., C. L. Porter, P. F. Meagher, and G. Errington. 'Sexual Reproduction and Early Plant Growth of the Wollemi Pine (*Wollemia Nobilis*), a Rare and Threatened Australian Conifer'. *Annals of Botany* 84, no. 1 (1999): 1–9.

Offord, Catherine A., Patricia F. Meagher, and Heidi C. Zimmer. 'Growing Up or Growing Out? How Soil pH and Light Affect Seedling Growth of a Relictual Rainforest Tree'. *AoB PLANTS* 6 (2014): plu011.

Ogden, Lesley Evans. 'The IUCN's Green List'. *Frontiers in Ecology and the Environment* 16, no. 9 (2018): 497.

Olusoga, David, and Casper W. Erichsen. *The Kaiser's Holocaust: Germany's Forgotten Genocide*. London: Faber and Faber, 2011.

Ormrod, James S. '"Making Room for the Tigers and the Polar Bears": Biography, Phantasy and Ideology in the Voluntary Human Extinction Movement'. *Psychoanalysis, Culture & Society* 16, no. 2 (2011): 142–61.

Outram, Dorinda. *Georges Cuvier: Vocation, Science, and Authority in Post-Revolutionary France*. Manchester: Manchester University Press, 1984.

—'New Spaces and Natural History'. In *Cultures of Natural History*, ed. Nicholas Jardine, James A. Secord, and E. C. Spary, 249–65. Cambridge: Cambridge University Press, 1996.

—'Scientific Biography and the Case of Georges Cuvier: With a Critical Biography'. *History of Science* 14 (1976): 101–37.

—'Uncertain Legislator: Georges Cuvier's Laws of Nature in Their Intellectual Context'. *Journal of the History of Biology* 19, no. 3 (1986): 323–68.

Owen, Richard. *Memoir of the Dodo: With An Historical Introduction by the Late William John Broderip*. London: Taylor and Francis, 1866.

—'Notice of a Fragment of the Femur of a Gigantic Bird of New Zealand'. *Transactions of the Zoological Society* 3 (1842): 29–32.

—*On the Classification and Geographical Distribution of the Mammalia*. London: J. W. Parker, 1859.

—*On the Extent and Aims of a National Museum of Natural History*. London: Saunders, Otley, & Co., 1862.

—'On the Extinction of Species'. In *On the Classification and Geographical Distribution of the Mammalia, Being the Lecture on Sir Robert Read's Foundation, Delivered Before the University of Cambridge in the Senate-House, May 10, 1859.*, 55–63. London: J. W. Parker, 1859.

—'Presidential Address'. *Report of the Fifty-First Meeting of the British Association for the Advancement of Science; Held at York in August and September 1881* 51 (1882): 651–61.

—'Report on British Fossil Reptiles. Part II'. *Report of the Eleventh Meeting of the British Association for the Advancement of Science; Held at Plymouth in July 1841*, 1842, 60–204.

—'Report on the Missourium Now Exhibiting at the Egyptian Hall, with an Inquiry into the Claims of the Tetracaudodon to Generic Distinction'. *Proceedings of the Geological Society of London* 3 (1842): 689–95.

Owen, Suzanne. 'The Demise of the Beothuk as a Past Still Present'. *Journal of the Irish Society for the Academic Study of Religions* 1/2 (2015): 119–39.

Palgrave, Francis. *The History of Normandy and of England*. 4 vols. London: John W. Parker & Sons, 1851–64.

Pálsson, Gísli. *The Last of Its Kind: The Search for the Great Auk and the Discovery of Extinction*. Princeton, NJ: Princeton University Press, 2024.

Parish, Jolyon C. *The Dodo and the Solitaire: A Natural History*. Bloomington, IN: Indiana University Press, 2012.

Parker, Johanna. 'The Appeal of Urgency: Extinction Discourses, Myths and the Private Collectors of Australian Aboriginal Human Remains'. *Museum and Society* 20 (2022): 118–30.

Parkinson, James. *Organic Remains of a Former World: An Examination of the Mineralized Remains of the Vegetables and Animals of the Antediluvian World; Generally Termed Extraneous Fossils*. Vol. 1. 3 vols. London: J. Robson etc., 1804.

—*Organic Remains of a Former World: An Examination of the Mineralized Remains of the Vegetables and Animals of the Antediluvian World; Generally Termed Extraneous Fossils*. Vol. 3. 3 vols. London: J. Robson etc., 1811.

Pastore, Ralph. 'The Collapse of the Beothuk World'. *Acadiensis* 19, no. 1 (1989): 52–71.

Paul, Gregory S. 'A Revised Taxonomy of the Iguanodont Dinosaur Genera and Species'. *Cretaceous Research* 29, no. 2 (April 2008): 192–216.

Peale, Rembrandt. *An Historical Disquisition on the Mammoth, or, Great American Incognitum, an Extinct, Immense, Carnivorous Animal Whose Fossil Remains Have Been Found in North America*. 2nd ed. London: E. Lawrence, 1803.

Penney, Gerald. 'Frank Speck and the Newfoundland Micmac: A Summary'. *Algonquian Papers-Archive* 21 (1990): 295–302.

Pennisi, Elizabeth. 'Linnaeus's Last Stand?' *Science* 291, no. 5512 (23 March 2001): 2304–7.

Perkins, Sid. 'Back from the Dead? "Resurrections" of Long-Missing Species Lead to Revelations'. *Science News* 172, no. 20 (17 November 2007): 312–14.

Pettorelli, Nathalie. 'Georgina Mace (1953–2020)'. *Nature* 586 (2020): 495.

Phillips, George Harwood. *Indians and Indian Agents: The Origins of the Reservation System in California, 1849–1852*. Norman, OK: University of Oklahoma Press, 1997.

Phillips, John C. 'The Work of the American Committee for International Wildlife Protection'. In *Wildlife Restoration and Conservation: Proceedings of the North American Wildlife Conference . . . February 3–7, 1936*, 51–6. Washington, DC: United States Government Printing Office, 1936.

Phillips, John C., and Harold J. Coolidge, Jr. *The First Five Years: The American Committee for International Wildlife Protection*. Cambridge, MA: American Committee for International Wildlife Protection, 1934.

Pickering, Gina, and National Trust of Australia (WA). *Fanny Balbuk Yoreel: Realising a Perth Resistance Fighter*. Perth, WA: National Trust of Australia, 2017.

—'Australia's Vulnerable Species Hit Hard by Fires'. *Science* 366, no. 6472 (2019): 1427–8.

Pickrell, John. 'Australia's Vulnerable Species Hit Hard by Fires'. *Science* 336 (2019): 1427–8.

—'Australian Blazes Will "Reframe Our Understanding of Bushfire" '. *Science* 366, no. 6468 (2019): 937–7.

Pickrell, John, and Elizabeth Pennisi. 'Record U.S. and Australian Fires Raise Fears for Many Species'. *Science* 370, no. 6512 (2020): 18–19.

Piggott, Jan R. *Palace of the People: The Crystal Palace at Sydenham 1854–1936*. London: Hurst, 2004.

Pilcher, Helen. *Bring Back the King: The New Science of De-Extinction*. London: Bloomsbury, 2016.

Piña-Aguilar, Raul E., Janet Lopez-Saucedo, Richard Sheffield, Lilia I. Ruiz-Galaz, Jose de J. Barroso-Padilla, and Antonio Gutiérrez-Gutiérrez. 'Revival of Extinct Species Using Nuclear Transfer: Hope for the Mammoth, True for the Pyrenean Ibex, But Is It Time for "Conservation Cloning"?' *Cloning and Stem Cells* 11, no. 3 (2009): 341–6.

Piñero, José M. López. 'Juan Bautista Bru (1740–1799) and the Description of the Genus Megatherium'. *Journal of the History of Biology* 21, no. 1 (1988): 147–63.

Pitelka, Frank A., and Monroe D. Bryant. 'Available Skeletons of the Passenger Pigeon'. *Condor* 44, no. 2 (1942): 74–5.

Pitman, C. R. S. 'The Balance of Nature'. *Oryx* 2, no. 1 (1953): 9–15.

Pohio, K. E., H. M. Wallace, R. F. Peters, T. E. Smith, and S. J. Trueman. 'Cuttings of Wollemi Pine Tolerate Moderate Photoinhibition and Remain Highly Capable of Root Formation'. *Trees* 19, no. 5 (2005): 587–95.

Pokagon, Simon. 'The Wild Pigeon of North America'. *The Chautauquan* 22, no. 20 (1895): 202–6.

Polack, Fiona. 'Reading Shanawdithit's Drawings: Transcultural Texts in the North American Colonial World'. *Journal of Colonialism and Colonial History* 14, no. 3 (2013).

—'Shanawdithit and Truganini: Converging and Diverging Histories'. In *Tracing Ochre: Changing Perspectives on the Beothuk*, ed. Fiona Polack, 321–44. Toronto, ON: University of Toronto Press, 2018.

Polge, C., A. U. Smith, and A. S. Parkes. 'Revival of Spermatozoa after Vitrification and Dehydration at Low Temperatures'. *Nature* 164, no. 4172 (1949): 666.

Pope, Peter. *The Many Landfalls of John Cabot*. Toronto, ON: University of Toronto Press, 1997.

Poskett, James. *Materials of the Mind: Phrenology, Race, and the Global History of Science, 1815–1920*. Chicago, IL: University of Chicago Press, 2019.

Prance, Ghillean T. 'A Brief History of Conservation at the Royal Botanic Gardens, Kew'. *Kew Bulletin* 65, no. 4 (2010): 501–8.

—'Threatened Plants: The Biological Aspects of Rare Plant Conservation'. Proceedings of a Conference, Cambridge, England, July 1980. Hugh Synge, ed. Wiley-Interscience, New York, NY: 1981.' *Science* 216, no. 4549 (1982): 977–8.

Prendergast, David K., and William M. Adams. 'Colonial Wildlife Conservation and the Origins of the Society for the Preservation of the Wild Fauna of the Empire (1903–1914)'. *Oryx* 37, no. 2 (2003): 251–60.

Price, David. 'The Human Tissue Act 2004'. *Modern Law Review* 68, no. 5 (2005): 798–821.

Price, Michael. 'Africans, Too, Carry Neanderthal Genetic Legacy'. *Science* 367 (2020): 497.

Prichard, [James Cowles]. 'On the Extinction of Human Races'. *Edinburgh New Philosophical Journal* 28 (1839): 166–70.

Quammen, David. *The Song of the Dodo: Island Biogeography in an Age of Extinctions*. New York, NY: Scribner, 1996.

Quatrefages, A. De, and George Frederick Rolph. 'On the Abbeville Jaw'. *Anthropological Review* 1, no. 2 (1863): 312–35.

Quinn, J. F. 'Mass Extinctions in the Fossil Record'. *Science* 219, no. 4589 (1983): 1239–40.

Qureshi, Sadiah. 'Dying Americans'. In *From Plunder to Preservation: Britain and the Heritage of Empire, c.1800–1940*, ed. Astrid Swenson and Peter Mandler, 267–86. Proceedings of the British Academy. Oxford: Oxford University Press, 2013.

—'Looking to Our Ancestors'. In *Time Travelers: Victorian Encounters with Time and History*, ed. Adelene Buckland and Sadiah Qureshi, 3–23. Chicago, IL: University of Chicago Press, 2020.

Raby, Megan. *American Tropics: The Caribbean Roots of Biodiversity Science. Flows, Migrations, and Exchanges*. Chapel Hill, NC: University of North Carolina Press, 2017.

Radin, Joanna. 'Collecting Human Subjects: Ethics and the Archive in the History of Science and the Historical Life Sciences'. *Curator* 57, no. 2 (April 2014): 249–58.

—*Life on Ice: A History of New Uses for Cold Blood*. Chicago, IL: University of Chicago Press, 2017.

—'Planned Hindsight: The Vital Valuations of Frozen Tissue at the Zoo and the Natural History Museum'. *Journal of Cultural Economy* 8, no. 3 (2015): 361–78.

Radin, Joanna, and Emma Kowal, eds. *Cryopolitics: Frozen Life in a Melting World*. Cambridge, MA: MIT Press, 2017.

Raja, Nussaïbah B., Emma M. Dunne, Aviwe Matiwane, Tasnuva Ming Khan, Paulina S. Nätscher, Aline M. Ghilardi, and Devapriya Chattopadhyay. 'Colonial History and Global Economics Distort Our Understanding of Deep-Time Biodiversity'. *Nature Ecology & Evolution*, 2021.

Raup, D. 'Biological Extinction in Earth History'. *Science* 231, no. 4745 (1986): 1528–33.

Raup, D. M. 'Approaches to the Extinction Problem: Presidential Address to the Society November 8, 1977'. *Journal of Palaeontology* 52 (n.d.): 517–23.

—'Size of the Permo-Triassic Bottleneck and Its Evolutionary Implications'. *Science* 206, no. 4415 (1979): 217–18.

—'Taxonomic Diversity during the Phanerozoic'. *Science* 177, no. 4054 (1972): 1065–71.

Raup, D. M., and J. J. Sepkoski. 'Mass Extinctions in the Marine Fossil Record'. *Science* 215, no. 4539 (1982): 1501–3.

—'Periodicity of Extinctions in the Geologic Past'. *Proceedings of the National Academy of Sciences* 81, no. 3 (1984): 801–5.

Raup, David M. *Extinction: Bad Genes or Bad Luck?* New York, NY: W. W. Norton, 1991.

—'The Extinction Debates: A View from the Trenches'. In *The Mass-Extinction Debates: How Science Works in a Crisis*, ed. William Glen, 144–51. Stanford, CA: Stanford University Press, 1994.

—*The Nemesis Affair: A Story of the Death of Dinosaurs and the Ways of Science*. Rev. and expanded edn. New York, NY: W. W. Norton, 1999.

Raup, David M., Stephen Jay Gould, Thomas J. M. Schopf, and Daniel S. Simberloff. 'Stochastic Models of Phylogeny and the Evolution of Diversity'. *Journal of Geology* 81, no. 5 (1973): 525–42.

Raust, Philippe. 'On the Possible Vernacular Name and Origin of the Extinct Spotted Green Pigeon *Caloenas Maculata*'. *Bulletin of the British Ornithologists' Club* 140, no. 1 (2020): 3–6.

Raven, Peter H., and Scott E. Miller. 'Here Today, Gone Tomorrow'. *Science* 370, no. 6513 (2020): 149.

Reece, Bob. *Daisy Bates: Grand Dame of the Desert*. Canberra, ACT: National Library of Australia, 2007.

—'"Killing with Kindness": Daisy Bates and New Norcia'. *Aboriginal History* (2008): 128–45.

—'"You Would Have Loved Her for Her Lore": The Letters of Daisy Bates'. *Australian Aboriginal Studies*, no. 1 (2007): 51–70.

Rees, Amanda. 'Stories of Stones and Bones: Disciplinarity, Narrative and Practice in British Popular Prehistory, 1911–1935'. *The British Journal for the History of Science* 49, no. 3 (2016): 433–51.

Reid, John G. 'British Colonisation in an Atlantic Canadian Context'. In *Reappraisals of British Colonisation in Atlantic Canada, 1700–1930*, ed. S. Karly Kehoe and Michael E. Vance, 11–22. Edinburgh: Edinburgh University Press, 2020.

Rhodes, Richard. *The Making of the Atomic Bomb*. New York, NY: Simon & Schuster, 1986.

Richards, Evelleen. *Darwin and the Making of Sexual Selection*. Chicago and London: University of Chicago Press, 2017.

Richon, Emmanuel, and Ria Winters. 'The Intercultural Dodo: A Drawing from the School of Bundi, Rājasthān'. *Historical Biology* 28, no. 3 (2016): 415–22.

Rieppel, Lukas. *Assembling the Dinosaur: Fossil Hunters, Tycoons, and the Making of a Spectacle*. Cambridge, MA: Harvard University Press, 2019.

—'Hoaxes, Humbugs, and Frauds: Distinguishing Truth from Untruth in Early America'. *Journal of the Early Republic* 38 (2018): 501–29.

Rieppel, Lukas, and Yu-chi Chang. 'Locating the Central Asiatic Expedition: Epistemic Imperialism in Vertebrate Paleontology'. *Isis* 114, no. 4 (2 December 2023): 725–46.

Rival, Laura, ed. *The Social Life of Trees: Anthropological Perspectives on Tree Symbolism*. Materializing Culture. Oxford: Berg, 1998.

Rivers, Malin, Adrian C. Newton, Sara Oldfield, and Global Tree Assessment Contributors. 'Scientists' Warning to Humanity on Tree Extinctions'. *Plants, People, Planet* (2022): 1–17.

Roberts, David L., and Ivan Jarić. 'Inferring the Extinction of Species Known Only from a Single Specimen'. *Oryx* 54, no. 2 (2020): 161–6.

Roberts v State of Western Australia, No. 257, Federal Court of Australia (21 February 2011).

Robertson, Sean. 'Extinction Is the Dream of Modern Powers: Bearing Witness to the Return to Life of the Sinixt Peoples?', *Antipode* 46, no. 3 (2014): 773–93.

Robinson, Angela. 'Enduring Pasts and Denied Presence: Mi'kmaw Challenges to Continued Marginalization in Western Newfoundland'. *Anthropologica* 56, no. 2 (2014): 383–97.

Rodríguez, N. 'National Red Lists: The Largest Global Market for IUCN Red List Categories and Criteria'. *Endangered Species Research* 6 (2008): 193–8.

Roe, Dilys, and Tien Ming Lee. 'Possible Negative Consequences of a Wildlife Trade Ban'. *Nature Sustainability* 4, no. 1 (2021): 5–6.

Rose, Deborah Bird, and Thom Van Dooren, eds. 'Unloved Others: Death of the Disregarded in the Time of Extinctions (Special Issue)'. *Australian Humanities Review* 50 (2011): 1–4.

Ross, Andrew J. 'An Icy Feud in Planetary Science: Carl Sagan, Edward Teller, and the Ideological Roots of the Nuclear Winter Debates, 1980–1984'. *Historical Studies in the Natural Sciences* 52, no. 2 (2022): 190–222.

Roth, H. Ling. 'Is Mrs. F. C. Smith a "Last Living Aboriginal of Tasmania"?' *Journal of the Anthropological Institute of Great Britain and Ireland* 27 (1898): 451.

Rothschild, Walter. *Extinct Birds*. London: Hutchinson & Co., 1907.

Rowe, Frederick William. *Extinction: The Beothuks of Newfoundland*. Toronto, ON: McGraw-Hill Ryerson, 1977.

Rowe, Michael. 'French Revolution, Napoleon, and Nationalism in Europe'. In *The Oxford Handbook of the History of Nationalism*, ed. John Breuilly. Oxford: Oxford University Press, 2013.

Rowley-Conwy, Peter. *From Genesis to Prehistory: The Archaeological Three Age System and Its Contested Reception in Denmark, Britain, and Ireland*. Oxford: Oxford University Press, 2007.

—'The Concept of Prehistory and the Invention of the Terms "Prehistoric" and "Prehistorian": The Scandinavian Origin, 1833–1850'. *European Journal of Archaeology* 9, no. 1 (2006): 103–30.

Rudwick, M. J. S. *Bursting the Limits of Time: The Reconstruction of Geohistory in the Age of Revolution*. Chicago, IL: University of Chicago Press, 2005.

—'Cuvier, Georges'. In the *Complete Dictionary of Scientific Biography*, ed. Charles Coulston Gillispie, 20: 221–7. Detroit, MI: Charles Scribner's Sons, 2008.

—*Earth's Deep History: How It Was Discovered and Why It Matters*. Chicago, IL: University of Chicago Press, 2014.

—*Georges Cuvier, Fossil Bones, and Geological Catastrophes: New Translations & Interpretations of the Primary Texts*. Chicago, IL: University of Chicago Press, 1997.

—'Georges Cuvier's Paper Museum of Fossil Bones'. *Archives of Natural History* 27, no. 1 (2000): 51–68.

—*Scenes from Deep Time: Early Pictorial Representations of the Prehistoric World*. Chicago, IL: University of Chicago Press, 1992.

—*The Meaning of Fossils: Episodes in the History of Palaeontology*. Repr. Chicago, IL: University of Chicago Press, 1985.

—*Worlds before Adam: The Reconstruction of Geohistory in the Age of Reform*. Chicago, IL: University of Chicago Press, 2008.

Rupke, Nicolaas A. *Richard Owen: Biology without Darwin*. Rev. ed. Chicago, IL: University of Chicago Press, 2009.

—'The Road to Albertopolis: Richard Owen (1804–92) and the Founding of the British Museum of Natural History'. In *Science, Politics and the Public Good: Essays in Honour of Margaret Gowing*, ed. Nicolaas A. Rupke, 63–89. London: Palgrave Macmillan, 1988.

Ryder, Oliver A., Anne McLaren, Sydney Brenner, Ya-Ping Zhang, and Kurt Benirschke. 'DNA Banks for Endangered Animal Species'. *Science* 288, no. 5464 (2000): 275–7.

Sabin, Richard, and Lorraine Cornish. *Hope: The Story of the Blue Whale*. London: Natural History Museum, 2019.

Sagan, Carl. *The Nuclear Winter: The World after Nuclear War*. London: Sidgwick & Son, 1985.

Sagan, Carl, and Richard P. Turco. 'Nuclear Winter in the Post-Cold War Era'. *Journal of Peace Research* 30, no. 4 (1993): 369–73.

Sagan, Carl, Richard Turco, George W. Rathjens, Ronald H. Siegel, Stanley L. Thompson, and Stephen H. Schneider. 'The Nuclear Winter Debate'. *Foreign Affairs* 65, no. 1 (1986): 163–78.

Saha, Jonathan. 'Accumulations and Cascades: Burmese Elephants and the Ecological Impact of British Imperialism'. *Transactions of the Royal Historical Society* (2022): 1–21.

Salvadori, T. *Catalogue of the Birds in the British Museum*. Vol. 21. 27 vols. London: Longmans & Co., 1893.

Sand, Peter H. 'The Evolution of International Environmental Law'. In *The Oxford Handbook of International Environmental Law* by Peter H. Sand, ed. Daniel Bodansky, Jutta Brunnée, and Ellen Hey. Oxford: Oxford University Press, 2008.

Sand, Susan. 'The Dawn Redwood: East and West Cooperated to Save This Living Fossil from Extinction'. *American Horticulturalist* (October 1992): 40–4.

Sandler, Ronald. 'De-Extinction and Conservation Genetics in the Anthropocene'. *Hastings Center Report* 47 (2017): S43–7.

Sandom, Christopher J., and David W. Macdonald. 'What Next? Rewilding as a Radical Future for the British Countryside'. In *Wildlife Conservation on Farmland*. Vol. 1, ed. David W. Macdonald and Ruth E. Feber, 291–316. Oxford: Oxford University Press, 2015.

Santos, Anna, and Thitikan Satchabut. 'Do Wildlife Trade Bans Enhance or Undermine Conservation Efforts?' *Applied Biodiversity Perspective* 1, no. 3 (2011): 1–15.

Satz, Ronald N. *American Indian Policy in the Jacksonian Era*. Norman, OK: University of Oklahoma Press, 2002.

Schaaffhausen, Hermann. 'Darwinism and Anthropology'. *Journal of the Anthropological Society of London* 6 (1868): cviii–cxviii.

Schaaffhausen, S., and George Busk. 'On the Crania of the Most Ancient Races of Man. With Remarks, and Original Figures, Taken from a Cast of the Neanderthal Cranium'. *Natural History Review* 1 (1861): 155–76.

Schaafhausen [sic], Prof. 'On the Development of the Human Species, and the Perfectibility of Its Races'. *Anthropological Review* 7, no. 27 (1869): 366–75.

Schaffer, Simon. 'Newton on the Beach: The Information Order of Principia Mathematica'. *History of Science* 47, no. 3 (2009): 243–76.

Schatz, George E. 'Plants on the IUCN Red List: Setting Priorities to Inform Conservation'. *Trends in Plant Science* 14 (2009): 638–42.

Scheffler, Harold W., and Rodney Needham. 'Radcliffe-Brown and Daisy Bates'. *Man* 10 (1975): 310–13.

Schiebinger, Londa. 'Why Mammals Are Called Mammals: Gender Politics in Eighteenth-Century Natural History'. *American Historical Review* 98 (1993): 382–411.

Schleicher, Judith, Julie G. Zaehringer, Constance Fastré, Bhaskar Vira, Piero Visconti, and Chris Sandbrook. 'Protecting Half of the Planet Could Directly Affect Over One Billion People'. *Nature Sustainability* 2, no. 12 (December 2019): 1094–6.

Schorger, A. W. *The Passenger Pigeon: Its Natural History and Extinction*. Reprint of 1st ed. Caldwell, NJ: Blackburn Press, 2004.

Scott, Peter, ed. *The Launching of a New Ark: First Report of the President and Trustees of the World Wildlife Fund, and International Foundation for Saving the World, Wildlife and Wild Places, 1961–1964*. London: Collins, 1965.

Scott, Peter, John A. Burton, and Richard Fitter. 'Red Data Books: The Historical Background'. In *The Road to Extinction: Problems of Categorizing the Status of Taxa Threatened with Extinction. A Symposium Held by the Species Survival Commission, Madrid, 7 and 9 November 1984*, ed. Richard Fitter and Maisie Fitter, 1–6. Gland, Switzerland: IUCN, 1987.

Seal, Alexa N., James E. Pratley, Terry J. Haig, Min An, and Hanwen Wu. 'Plants with Phytotoxic Potential: Wollemi Pine (Wollemia Nobilis)'. *Agriculture, Ecosystems & Environment* 135 (2010): 52–7.

Sebastiani, Silvia. 'Monboddo's "Ugly Tail": The Question of Evidence in Enlightenment Sciences of Man'. *History of European Ideas* 48, no. 1 (2 January 2022): 45–65.

Secord, Anne. 'Botany on a Plate'. *Isis* 93, no. 1 (2002): 28–57.

—'Science in the Pub: Artisan Botanists in Early Nineteenth-Century Lancashire'. *History of Science* 32 (1994): 269–315.

Secord, James A. 'How Scientific Conversation Became Shop Talk'. *Transactions of the Royal Historical Society* 17 (December 2007): 129–56.

—'Knowledge in Transit'. *Isis* 95, no. 4 (2004): 654–72.

—'Monsters at the Crystal Palace'. In *Models: The Third Dimension of Science*, ed. Soraya Chadarevian and Nick Hopwood, 138–9. Stanford, CA: Stanford University Press, 2004.

—*Victorian Sensation: The Extraordinary Publication, Reception, and Secret Authorship of Vestiges of the Natural History of Creation*. Chicago, IL: University of Chicago Press, 2003.

—, ed. 'Introduction'. In *Principles of Geology*, ix–xliii. Penguin Classics. London and New York, NY: Penguin Books, 1997.

Semonin, Paul. *American Monster: How the Nation's First Prehistoric Creature Became a Symbol of National Identity*. New York, NY: New York University Press, 2000.

Sepkoski, David. *Catastrophic Thinking: Extinction and the Value of Diversity from Darwin to the Anthropocene*. Chicago, IL: University of Chicago Press, 2020.

—*Rereading the Fossil Record: The Growth of Paleobiology as an Evolutionary Discipline*. Chicago, IL: University of Chicago Press, 2012.

Sepkoski, J. John. 'A Kinetic Model of Phanerozoic Taxonomic Diversity Ii. Early Phanerozoic Families and Multiple Equilibria'. *Paleobiology* 5, no. 3 (1979): 222–51.

—'Some Implications of Mass Extinction for the Evolution of Complex Life'. In *The Search for Extraterrestrial Life: Recent Developments*, ed. Michael D. Papagiannis, 223–32. Dordrecht: Springer Netherlands, 1985.

Sepkoski, J. John, Richard K. Bambach, David M. Raup, and James W. Valentine. 'Phanerozoic Marine Diversity and the Fossil Record'. *Nature* 293, no. 5832 (1981): 435–7.

Sepkoski, Jr, J. John. 'What I Did with My Research Career: Or How Research and Biodiversity Yielded Data on Extinction'. In *The Mass-Extinction Debates: How Science Works in a Crisis*, ed. William Glen, 132–44. Stanford, CA: Stanford University Press, 1994.

Seritrakul, P., and C. Laosutthipong. 'A Non-Invasive Molecular Genetic Technique for Sex Identification of Nicobar Pigeon (Caloenas Nicobarica), the Last Living Relative of Dodo Bird'. *International Journal of Agricultural Technology* 17 (2021): 713–26.

Seth, Suman. 'Darwin and the Ethnologists: Liberal Racialism and the Geological Analogy'. *Historical Studies in the Natural Sciences* 46, no. 4 (2016): 490–527.

—*Difference and Disease: Medicine, Race, and the Eighteenth-Century British Empire*. Global Health Histories. Cambridge: Cambridge University Press, 2018.

Shapiro, Beth Alison. *How to Clone a Mammoth: The Science of De-Extinction*. Princeton, NJ: Princeton University Press, 2015.

Sharko, Fedor S., Eugenia S. Boulygina, Svetlana V. Tsygankova, Natalia V. Slobodova, Dmitry A. Alekseev, Anna A. Krasivskaya, Sergey M. Rastorguev, Alexei N. Tikhonov, and Artem V. Nedoluzhko. 'Steller's Sea Cow Genome Suggests This Species Began Going Extinct before the Arrival of Paleolithic Humans'. *Nature Communications* 12 (13 April 2021): 2215.

Sharpe, Tom. *The Fossil Woman: A Life of Mary Anning*. Wimborne Minster: Dovecote Press, 2020.

Shaw, Kristy, and Abby Hird. *Global Survey of Ex Situ Conifer Collections*. Richmond, UK: BGCI, 2014.

Sheppard, F. W., ed. *Survey of London: Volume 38, South Kensington Museums Area*. 47 vols. London: London County Council, 1975.

Sherwin, Oscar. 'A Man with a Tail – Lord Monboddo'. *Journal of the History of Medicine and Allied Sciences* 13, no. 4 (1958): 435–68.

Shufeldt, R. W. 'Anatomical and Other Notes on the Passenger Pigeon (*Ectopistes migratorius*) Lately Living in the Cincinnati Zoological Gardens'. *The Auk* 32, no. 1 (1915): 29–41.

—'Published Figures and Plates of the Extinct Passenger Pigeon'. *The Scientific Monthly* 12, no. 5 (1921): 458–81.

Singer, Ronald. 'The Neandertal Centenary'. *The South African Archaeological Bulletin* 12, no. 47 (1957): 79–86.

Sivasundaram, Sujit. 'Sciences and the Global: On Methods, Questions, and Theory'. *Isis* 101, no. 1 (March 2010): 146–58.

Skott, Christina. 'Human Taxonomies: Carl Linnaeus, Swedish Travel in Asia and the Classification of Man'. *Itinerario* 43, no. 2 (2019): 218–42.

—'Linnaeus and the Troglodyte: Early European Encounters with the Malay World and the Natural History of Man'. *Indonesia and the Malay World* 42, no. 123 (4 May 2014): 141–69.

Smart, Jane, Craig Hilton-Taylor, and Russell A. Mittermeier. *The IUCN Red List: 50 Years of Conservation*. Washington, DC: Earth in Focus, 2014.

Smits, David D. 'The Frontier Army and the Destruction of the Buffalo: 1865–1883'. *The Western Historical Quarterly* 25, no. 3 (1994): 312.

Society for Ecological Restoration International Science & Policy Working Group. 'The SER International Primer on Ecological Restoration', 2004.

Sollas, William Johnson. 'On the Cranial and Facial Characters of the Neandertal Race'. *Philosophical Transactions of the Royal Society of London. Series B, Containing Papers of a Biological Character* 199 (1908): 281–339.

Sommer, Marianne. ' "An Amusing Account of a Cave in Wales": William Buckland (1784–1856) and the Red Lady of Paviland'. *The British Journal for the History of Science* 37, no. 1 (2004): 53–74.

—*Bones and Ochre: The Curious Afterlife of the Red Lady of Paviland*. Cambridge, MA: Harvard University Press, 2007.

Sotheby's. *The First-Generation Wollemi Pines*. Sydney: Sotheby's, 2005.

Soulé, Michael E. 'What Is Conservation Biology?' *BioScience* 35, no. 11 (1985): 727–34.

Soulé, Michael E., and Reed Noss. 'Rewilding and Biodiversity: Complementary Goals for Continental Conservation'. *Wild Earth* 8 (1998): 19–26.

Spalding, David A. E., and William A. S. Sarjeant. 'Dinosaurs: The Earliest Discoveries'. In *The Complete Dinosaur*, ed. Michael K. Brett-Surman, Thomas R. Holtz, James Orville Farlow, and Bob Walters, 2nd ed., 3–23. Bloomington, IN: Indiana University Press, 2012.

Spamer, Earle E. 'Know Thyself: Responsible Science and the Lectotype of Homo Sapiens Linnaeus, 1758'. *Proceedings of the Academy of Natural Sciences of Philadelphia* 149 (1999): 109–14.

Spary, E. C. *Utopia's Garden: French Natural History from Old Regime to Revolution*. Chicago, IL: University of Chicago Press, 2000.

Speck, Frank G. 'Culture Problems in Northeastern North America'. *Proceedings of the American Philosophical Society* 65, no. 4 (1926): 272–311.

—'Review of The Beothucks or Red Indians, the Aboriginal Inhabitants of Newfoundland by J. P. Howley'. *American Anthropologist* n.s. 19 (1917): 272–80.

Speck, Frank Gouldsmith. *Beothuk and Micmac*. New York, NY: Museum of the American Indian, Heye Foundation, 1922.

Spence, Mark David. *Dispossessing the Wilderness: Indian Removal and the Making of the National Parks*. New York, NY: Oxford: Oxford University Press, 2000.

SPWFE. *Journal of the Society for the Preservation of the Wild Fauna of the Empire, Volumes 1–3*, 1904.

—*Journal of the Society for the Preservation of the Wild Fauna of the Empire: Volume 4*, 1908.

Staum, Martin S. *Minerva's Message: Stabilizing the French Revolution*. Montreal: McGill-Queen's University Press, 1996.

Stearn, W. T. 'The Background of Linnaeus's Contributions to the Nomenclature and Methods of Systematic Biology'. *Systematic Biology* 8, no. 1 (1 March 1959): 4–22.

Stearn, William T. *The Natural History Museum in South Kensington: A History of the British Museum (Natural History) 1753–1980*. London: Heinemann, 1981.

Stebbins, G. L. 'International Biological Program'. *Science* 137, no. 3532 (1962): 768–70.

Stern, Richard A., and Wouter Bleeker. 'Age of the World's Oldest Rocks Refined Using Canada's SHRIMP: The Acasta Gneiss Complex, Northwest Territories, Canada'. *Geoscience Canada* 25 (1998): 27–31.

Stork, Nigel E. 'Re-Assessing Current Extinction Rates'. *Biodiversity and Conservation* 19, no. 2 (2010): 357–71.

Straus, William L., and A. J. E. Cave. 'Pathology and the Posture of Neanderthal Man'. *The Quarterly Review of Biology* 32, no. 4 (1957): 348–63.

Strickland, Hugh E., and A. G. Melville. *The Dodo and Its Kindred; or, The History, Affinities, and Osteology of the Dodo, Solitaire, and Other Extinct Birds of the Islands Mauritius, Rodriguez and Bourbon*. London: Reeve, Benham, and Beeve, 1848.

Stringer, Chris. *The Origin of Our Species*. London: Penguin Books, 2012.

Stringer, Chris, and Lucile Crété. 'Mapping Interactions of H. Neanderthalensis and Homo Sapiens from the Fossil and Genetic Records'. *PaleoAnthropology* 2022, no. 2 (2022): 401–12.

Stuart, S. N., E. O. Wilson, J. A. McNeely, R. A. Mittermeier, and J. P. Rodríguez. 'The Barometer of Life'. *Science* 328, no. 5975 (2010): 177.

Swaisland, Charles. 'The Aborigines Protection Society, 1837–1909'. *Slavery & Abolition* 21, no. 2 (2000): 265–80.

Sweet, Timothy. *Extinction and the Human: Four American Encounters*. Philadelphia, PA: University of Pennsylvania Press, 2021.

Swenson, Astrid, and Peter Mandler, eds. *From Plunder to Preservation: Britain and the Heritage of Empire, c.1800–1940*. 1st ed. London: British Academy, 2013.

Synge, Hugh, Harry Townsend, and Royal Botanic Gardens, Kew, eds. *Survival or Extinction: Proceedings of a Conference Held at the Royal Botanic Gardens, Kew, Entitled the Practical Role of Botanic Gardens in the Conservation of Rare Plants and Threatened Plants, 11–17 September 1978*. Royal Botanic Gardens, Kew: Bentham-Moxon Trust, 1979.

Syperek, Pandora, Sarah Wade, Miranda Lowe, and Richard Sabin. 'Curating Ocean Ecology at the Natural History Museum: Miranda Lowe and Richard Sabin in Conversation with Pandora Syperek and Sarah Wade'. *Science Museum Group Journal* 13, no. 13 (2020).

Talbot, Lee M. *A Look at Threatened Species: A Report on Some Animals of the Middle East and Southern Asia Which Are Threatened with Extermination*. London: Fauna Preservation Society, 1960.

Tallbear, Kim. 'Beyond the Life / Not-Life Binary: A Feminist-Indigenous Reading of Cryopreservation, Interspecies Thinking, and the New Materia'. In *Cryopolitics*, ed. Joanna Radin and Emma Kowal, 179–202. Cambridge, MA: MIT Press, 2017.

Tarr, R. S. 'The English Sparrow'. *Science* n.s. 6, no. 144S (1885): 416.

Tattersall, Ian. *The Fossil Trail: How We Know What We Think We Know about Human Evolution*. New York, NY: Oxford University Press, 1995.

—'The Genus *Homo*'. *Inference: International Review of Science* 2 (2016): 1–9.

—*Understanding Human Evolution*. Understanding Life. Cambridge: Cambridge University Press, 2022.

Tattersall, I., and J. H. Schwartz. 'Hominids and Hybrids: The Place of Neanderthals in Human Evolution'. *Proceedings of the National Academy of Sciences* 96 (1999): 7117–19.

Tatz, Colin. 'Genocide in Australia'. *Journal of Genocide Research* 1 (1999): 315–52.

The Beothuk Story. Zamura Films, 2021.

The Dawn of De-Extinction. Are You Ready? Ted Talks, 2013.

Theunissen, Bert. 'The Oostvaardersplassen Fiasco'. *Isis* 110 (2019): 341–5.

Thewissen, J. G. M., Lisa Noelle Cooper, Mark T. Clementz, Sunil Bajpai, and B. N. Tiwari. 'Whales Originated from Aquatic Artiodactyls in the Eocene Epoch of India'. *Nature* 450, no. 7173 (December 2007): 1190–4.

Thieberger, Nick. 'Daisy Bates in the Digital World'. In *Language, Land and Song: Studies in Honour of Luise Hercus*, 102–14. London: EL Publishing, 2016.

Thomas, Chris D. *Inheritors of the Earth: How Nature Is Thriving in an Age of Extinction*. London: Allen Lane, 2017.

Thomas, Martin. *Culture and Translation: Recovering the Legacy of R. H. Mathews*. Canberra, ACT: ANU Press, 2007.

Thomson, Donald Fergusson. *Interim General Report of Preliminary Expedition to Arnhem Land, Northern Territory of Australia, 1935–36*. Canberra, ACT: Department of the Interior, 1936.

—*Report on Expedition to Arnhem Land, 1936–37*. Canberra, ACT: Department of the Interior, 1939.

Thomson, Keith Stewart. *The Legacy of the Mastodon: The Golden Age of Fossils in America*. New Haven, CT: Yale University Press, 2008.

Thurner, Mark, and Juan Pimentel. *New World Objects of Knowledge: A Cabinet of Curiosities*. London: University of London Press, 2021.

Tillier, Anne-Marie. 'The Earliest *Homo Sapiens (Sapiens)*: Biological, Chronological and Taxonomic Perspectives'. *Diogenes* 54, no. 2 (May 2007): 110–21.

Tim Rowse. 'Notes on the History of Aboriginal Population of Australia'. In *Genocide and Settler Society*. New York, NY: Berghahn Books, 2004.

Tordoff, Harrison B., and Patrick T. Redig. 'Role of Genetic Background in the Success of Reintroduced Peregrine Falcons'. *Conservation Biology* 15, no. 2 (2001): 528–32.

Torrens, Hugh. 'Politics and Palaeontology: Richard Owen and the Invention of Dinosaurs'. In *The Complete Dinosaur*, ed. Michael K. Brett-Surman, Thomas R. Holtz, James Orville Farlow, and Bob Walters, 2nd ed. Bloomington, IN: Indiana University Press, 2012.

Trudel, Marcel. 'Cartier, Jacques (1491–1557)'. In *Dictionary of Canadian Biography*. Toronto, ON: University of Toronto/Université Laval, 2014.

Trueman, Clive N., Andrew L. Jackson, Katharyn S. Chadwick, Ellen J. Coombs, Laura J. Feyrer, Sarah Magozzi, Richard C. Sabin, and Natalie Cooper. 'Combining Simulation Modeling and Stable Isotope Analyses to Reconstruct the Last Known Movements of One of Nature's Giants'. *PeerJ* 7 (2019): e7912.

Trueman, Stephen J., Geoff S. Pegg, and Judith King. 'Domestication for Conservation of an Endangered Species: The Case of the Wollemi Pine'. *Tree and Forestry Science and Biotechnology* 1 (2007): 1–10.

Trumble, Stephen J., Stephanie A. Norman, Danielle D. Crain, Farzaneh Mansouri, Zach C. Winfield, Richard Sabin, Charles W. Potter, Christine M. Gabriele, and Sascha Usenko. 'Baleen Whale Cortisol Levels Reveal a Physiological Response to 20th Century Whaling'. *Nature* 9, no. 1 (2018): 1–8.

Tsing, Anna Lowenhaupt, ed. *Arts of Living on a Damaged Planet*. Minneapolis, MN: University of Minnesota Press, 2017.

Tuck, James A., and Ralph T. Pastore. 'A Nice Place to Visit, but . . . Prehistoric Human Extinctions on the Island of Newfoundland'. *Canadian Journal of Archaeology/Journal Canadien d'Archéologie* (1985): 69–80.

Turco, R. P., O. B. Toon, T. P. Ackerman, J. B. Pollack, and Carl Sagan. 'Nuclear Winter: Global Consequences of Multiple Nuclear Explosions'. *Science* 222 (1983): 1283–93.

Turco, Richard, and Carl Sagan. 'Policy Implications of Nuclear Winter'. *Ambio* 18, no. 7 (1989): 372–6.

Turnbull, Paul. 'Australian Museums, Aboriginal Skeletal Remains, and the Imagining of Human Evolutionary History, c. 1860–1914'. *Museum and Society* 13, no. 1 (2015): 72–87.

Twomey, Christina. 'Protecting Slaves and Aborigines: The Legacies of European Colonialism in the British Empire'. *Pacific Historical Review* 87, no. 1 (2018): 10–29.

Tyler, Samuel Lyman. *A History of Indian Policy*. Washington, DC: Bureau of Indian Affairs, 1973.

Tylor, Edward B. 'On the Tasmanians as Representatives of Palaeolithic Man'. *Journal of the Anthropological Institute of Great Britain and Ireland* 23 (1894): 141–52.

Ulrich, John M. 'Thomas Carlyle, Richard Owen, and the Paleontological Articulation of the Past'. *Journal of Victorian Culture* 11, no. 1 (2006): 30–58.

UNESCO. *Preparatory Documents to the International Technical Conference on the Protection of Nature, August 1949, USA. Edited by the Secretariat of the International Union for the Protection of Nature.* Paris and Brussels: UNESCO, 1949.

United Nations. Convention on the Prevention and Punishment of the Crime of Genocide (1948).

—*Proceedings of the United Nations Scientific Conference on the Conservation and Utilization of Resources, 17 August–6 September 1949, Lake Success, New York. Volume I: Plenary Meetings*. New York, NY: United Nations, 1950.

—*Proceedings of the United Nations Scientific Conference on the Conservation and Utilization of Resources, 17 August–6 September 1949, Lake Success, New York. Volume VII: Wildlife and Fish Resources*. New York, NY: United Nations, 1950.

United States. 'An Act to Provide for an Exchange of Lands with the Indians Residing in Any of the States or Territories, and for Their Removal West of the River Mississippi' (1830).

Urey, Harold C. 'Cometary Collisions and Tektites'. *Nature* 197, no. 4864 (1963): 228–30.

Urus, Arianne Sedef. '"A Spirit of Encroachment": Trees, Cod, and the Political Ecology of Empire in the Newfoundland Fisheries, 1763–1783'. *Environmental History* 28, no. 1 (2023): 85–108.

Van Dooren, Thom. *Flight Ways: Life and Loss at the Edge of Extinction*. New York, NY: Columbia University Press, 2014.

Van Riper, A. Bowdoin. *Men among the Mammoths: Victorian Science and the Discovery of Human Prehistory*. Chicago, IL: University of Chicago Press, 1993.

Vartanyan, S. L., Kh. A. Arslanov, T. V. Tertychnaya, and S. B. Chernov. 'Radiocarbon Dating Evidence for Mammoths on Wrangel Island, Arctic Ocean, until 2000 BC'. *Radiocarbon* 37, no. 1 (1995): 1–6.

Vermeulen, Hans, and Arturo Alvarez Roldán. *Fieldwork and Footnotes: Studies in the History of European Anthropology*. European Association of Social Anthropologists. London and New York, NY: Routledge, 1995.

Vié, Jean-Christophe, Craig Hilton-Taylor, Caroline M. Pollock, James Ragle, Jane Smart, Simon Stuart, and Rashila Tong. 'The IUCN Red List: A Key Conservation Tool'. In *The 2008 Review of the IUCN Red List of Threatened Species*, ed. Jean-Christophe Vié, Craig Hilton-Taylor, and Simon N. Stuart. Gland, Switzerland: IUCN, 2008.

Vié, Jean-Christophe, Craig Hilton-Taylor, and Simon N. Stuart, eds. *Wildlife in a Changing World: An Analysis of the 2008 IUCN Red List of Threatened Species*. Gland, Switzerland: IUCN, 2008.

Wagstaffe, R[eginald]. *Type Specimens of Birds in the Merseyside County Museums (Formerly City of Liverpool Museums)*. Liverpool: Merseyside County Museum, 1978.

Waitz, Theodor. *Introduction to Anthropology*, trans. J. Frederick Collingwood. London: Longman, Green, Longman and Roberts, 1863.

Wakeham, Pauline. 'The Slow Violence of Settler Colonialism: Genocide, Attrition, and the Long Emergency of Invasion'. *Journal of Genocide Research* 24 (2021): 337–56.

Wallace, Alfred R. 'The Origin of Human Races and the Antiquity of Man Deduced from the Theory of Natural Selection'. *Journal of the Anthropological Society of London* 2 (1864): clviii–clxxxvii.

Wallace-Wells, David. *The Uninhabitable Earth: A Story of the Future*. London: Allen Lane, 2019.

Walter, Kerry S., and Harriett J. Gillett. *The IUCN Red Data Book of Threatened Plants*. Gland, Switzerland: IUCN, 1998.

Warnett, J. M., Mark A. Williams, Paul F. Wilson, and M. Paul Smith. 'The Oxford Dodo. Seeing More Than Ever before: X-Ray Micro-Ct Scanning, Specimen Acquisition and Provenance'. *Historical Biology* 33, no. 10 (2021): 2247–55.

Waters, Colin N., Jan Zalasiewicz, Colin Summerhayes, Anthony D. Barnosky, Clément Poirier, Agnieszka Gałuszka, Alejandro Cearreta, et al. 'The Anthropocene Is Functionally and Stratigraphically Distinct from the Holocene'. *Science* 351, no. 6269 (2016): aad2622.

Watson, Richard T. 'Using Birds of Prey as an Environmental Conservation Tool: The Peregrine Fund's World Programme'. *Environmental Conservation* 18, no. 3 (1991): 269–70.

Webb, Jeff A. 'A Few Fabulous Fragments: Historical Methods in James P. Howley's The Beothucks'. *Histoire Sociale/Social History* 50, no. 101 (2017): 89–111.

Webber, George. *The Last of the Aborigines: A Poem Founded on Facts in Four Cantos*. St John's, Newfoundland: George Webber, 1851.

Weeks, Pris, and Shalina Mehta. 'Managing People and Landscapes: IUCN's Protected Area Categories'. *Journal of Human Ecology* 16, no. 4 (2004): 253–63.

WEF. 'The Global Risks Report 2020', 2020.

Weidenreich, Franz. 'The "Neanderthal Man" and the Ancestors of "Homo Sapiens"'. *American Anthropologist* 45, no. 1 (1943): 39–48.

Western Australia, Parliament. *Royal Commission on the Condition of the Natives Report*. Perth, WA: W. M. Alfred Watson, Government Printer, 1905.

Whatmore, Sarah. 'Hybrid Geographies: Author's Responses and Reflections'. *Antipode* 37, no. 4 (2005): 842–5.

Wheeler, Roxann. *The Complexion of Race: Categories of Difference in Eighteenth-Century British Culture*. Philadelphia, PA: University of Pennsylvania Press, 2000.

White, Isobel. 'Daisy Bates: Legend and Reality'. In *First in Their Field: Women and Australian Anthropology*, ed. Julie Marcus, 46–65. Melbourne: Melbourne University Press, 1993.

—'Isobel White Replies to Professor Needham'. *Oceania* 53 (1982): 139–40.

—'Mrs Bates and Mr Brown: An Examination of Rodney Needham's Allegations'. *Oceania* 51, no. 3 (1981): 193–210.

White, Sam. *A Cold Welcome: The Little Ice Age and Europe's Encounter with North America*. Cambridge, MA: Harvard University Press, 2018.

Widner, Thomas, Joseph Shonka, Robert Burns, Susan Flack, Jack Buddenbaum, James O'Brien, Kate Robinson, and Jeff Knutsen. 'Final Report of the Los Alamos Historical Document Retrieval and Assessment (LAHDRA) Project'. Centers for Disease Control and Prevention, 2010.

Wiens, John J. 'How Many Species Are There on Earth? Progress and Problems'. *PLOS Biology* 21, no. 11 (20 November 2023): e3002388.

Will, Manuel. 'Neanderthal Surf and Turf'. *Science* 367 (2020): 1422–3.

Willerslev, Eske, and David J. Meltzer. 'Peopling of the Americas as Inferred from Ancient Genomics'. *Nature* 594, no. 7863 (2021): 356–64.

Wilson, Alexander. *American Ornithology; Or, the Natural History of the Birds of the United States*. Vol. 1. 3 vols. New York, NY: Collins and Co., 1828–9.

Wilson, Daniel. *Prehistoric Man*. London: Macmillan, 1862.

—*Synopsis of the Museum of the Society of Antiquaries of Scotland*. Edinburgh: Society of Antiquaries of Scotland, 1849.

Wilson, Edward O. *Half-Earth: Our Planet's Fight for Life*. New York, NY: Liveright, W. W. Norton & Co., 2016.

Wilson, Etta S. 'Personal Recollections of the Passenger Pigeon'. *The Auk* 51 (1934): 157–68.

Winters, Ria, and Julian P. Hume. 'The Dodo, the Deer and a 1647 Voyage to Japan'. *Historical Biology* 27, no. 2 (2015): 258–64.

Wolf, Christopher, and William J. Ripple. 'Rewilding the World's Large Carnivores'. *Royal Society Open Science* 5, no. 3 (March 2018): 172235.

Wood, David. 'Homo Sapiens'. In *The Edinburgh Companion to Animal Studies*, ed. Lynn Turner, Undine Sellbach, and Ron Broglio. Edinburgh: Edinburgh University Press, 2022.

Woodford, James. *The Wollemi Pine: The Incredible Discovery of a Living Fossil from the Age of the Dinosaurs*. New ed. Melbourne: Text Publishing, 2005.

Woolford, Andrew, Jeff Benvenuto, and Alexander Laban Hinton, eds. *Colonial Genocide in Indigenous North America*. Durham, NC: Duke University Press, 2014.

Working Group on the Post-2020 Global Biodiversity Framework. 'Convention on Biological Diversity: First Draft of the Post-2020 Global Biodiversity Framework'. United Nations, 2021.

World Economic Forum. 'The Global Risks Report 2022, 17th Edition'. World Economic Forum, 2022.

—'WEF Global Risk Report 2020', 2020.

Wragg Sykes, Rebecca. *Kindred: Neanderthal Life, Love, Death and Art*. London: Bloomsbury Sigma, 2020.

Wray, Britt. *Rise of the Necrofauna: The Science, Ethics, and Risks of De-Extinction*. Vancouver, B.C., and Berkeley, CA: Greystone Books, 2017.

WWF. 'Living Planet Report 2020'. World Wildlife Fund, 2020.

Yanni, Carla. 'Divine Display or Secular Science: Defining Nature at the Natural History Museum in London'. *Journal of the Society of Architectural Historians* 55, no. 3 (1996): 276–99.

—*Nature's Museums: Victorian Science and the Architecture of Display*. New York, NY: Princeton Architectural Press, 2005.

Zalasiewicz, Jan, Colin N. Waters, Colin P. Summerhayes, Alexander P. Wolfe, Anthony D. Barnosky, Alejandro Cearreta, Paul Crutzen, et al. 'The Working Group on the Anthropocene: Summary of Evidence and Interim Recommendations'. *Anthropocene* 19 (2017): 55–60.

Zelko, Frank S. *Make It a Green Peace! The Rise of Countercultural Environmentalism*. New York, NY: Oxford University Press, 2013.

Zhang, Yuheng. '"The Panda of Plants": The Discovery of Dawn Redwood and National Identity Construction in Modern China'. *International Journal for History, Culture and Modernity* 7, no. 1 (2019): 271–300.

Zilhão, J., D. E. Angelucci, M. Araújo Igreja, L. J. Arnold, E. Badal, P. Callapez, J. L. Cardoso, et al. 'Last Interglacial Iberian Neandertals as Fisher-Hunter-Gatherers'. *Science* 367, no. 6485 (2020): eaaz7943.

Zilhão, João. 'The Neanderthals: Evolution, Palaeoecology, and Extinction'. In *The Oxford Handbook of the Archaeology and Anthropology of Hunter-Gatherers*, ed. Vicki Cummings, Peter Jordan, and Marek Zvelebil, 191–213. Oxford: Oxford University Press, 2013.

Zimmer, Heidi, Patrick Baker, Catherine Offord, Jessica Rigg, Greg Bourke, and Tony Auld. '"Wollemia Nobilis" (Wollemi Pine), Araucariaceae'. *Australasian Plant Conservation: Journal of the Australian Network for Plant Conservation* 27, no. 3 (2019): 13–15.

Zimmerer, Jürgen. 'Climate Change, Environmental Violence and Genocide'. *International Journal of Human Rights* 18, no. 3 (3 April 2014): 265–80.

Zimov, S. A. 'Pleistocene Park: Return of the Mammoth's Ecosystem'. *Science* 308, no. 5723 (2005): 796–8.

Index

Page references in *italics* indicate images.

Greg Perry & Marcus Johnson

CW00918598

Turbo C++ By Example

© 1992 by Que

All rights reserved. Printed in the United States of America. No part of this book may be used or reproduced, in any form or by any means, or stored in a database or retrieval system, without prior written permission of the publisher except in the case of brief quotations embodied in critical articles and reviews. Making copies of any part of this book for any purpose other than your own personal use is a violation of United States copyright laws. For information, address Que, 11711 N. College Ave., Carmel, IN 46032.

Library of Congress Catalog Card Number: 92-81021

ISBN: 0-88022-812-1

This book is sold *as is,* without warranty of any kind, either express or implied, respecting the contents of this book, including but not limited to implied warranties for the book's quality, performance, merchantability, or fitness for any particular purpose. Neither Que Corporation nor its dealers or distributors shall be liable to the purchaser or any other person or entity with respect to any liability, loss, or damage caused or alleged to be caused directly or indirectly by this book.

95 94 93 92 8 7 6 5 4 3 2

Interpretation of the printing code: the rightmost double-digit number is the year of the book's printing; the rightmost single-digit number, the number of the book's printing. For example, a printing code of 92-1 shows that the first printing of the book occurred in 1992.

The examples in this book should work with versions of Turbo C++ through 3.0.

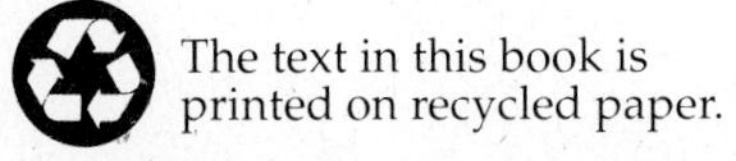

Publisher
Richard Swadley

Publishing Manager
Joseph Wikert

Managing Editor
Neweleen A. Trebnik

Acquisitions Editor
Gregory Croy

Development Editor
Stacy Hiquet

Technical Editor
Andrew Rieger

Production Editors
Jodi Jensen
Virginia Noble

Editorial Assistant
Rosemarie Graham

Project Coordinator
San Dee Phillips

Editorial Coordinator
Becky Freeman

Production Director
Jeff Valler

Production Manager
Corinne Walls

Page Layout Coordinator
Matthew Morrill

Proofreading/Indexing Coordinator
Joelynn Gifford

Production Analyst
Mary Beth Wakefield

Book Design
Michele Laseau

Cover Design
Jean Bisesi

Graphic Image Specialists
Dennis Sheehan
Jerry Ellis

Indexer
Joy Dean Lee

Production
Keith Davenport, Book Shepherd
Paula Carroll, Michelle Cleary, Christine Cook, Terri Edwards, Mark Enochs, Carrie Keesling, Jay Lesandrini, Linda Quigley, Linda Seifert, Louise Shinault, Kevin Spear, Angie Trzepacz, Kelli Widdifield, Allan Wimmer, Phil Worthington

Composed in Palatino and MCPdigital by Prentice Hall Computer Publishing.
Screen reproductions in this book were created by means of the program Collage Plus from Inner Media, Inc., Hollis, NH.

Dedication

Thanks to Dr. Richard Burgess and his wife, Ellen, who taught me lots over the years. I am who I am partly because of them.

G.M.P.

To the growing number of users turned programmers, this book is dedicated.

M.J.

About the Authors

Greg Perry has been a programmer and trainer for the past 14 years. He received his first degree in computer science and then a Masters in corporate finance. He is currently a professor of computer science at Tulsa Junior College, as well as a computer consultant and lecturer. Greg Perry is the author of 10 other computer books. In addition, he has written articles for several publications, including *PC World*, *Data Training*, and *Inside First Publisher*. He has traveled in several countries, attending computer conferences and trade shows, and is fluent in nine computer languages.

Marcus Johnson has been working with computers since the mid-'70s and with microprocessors since the early '80s. He is currently a member of the technical staff at Precision Systems in Clearwater, Florida.

Acknowledgments

The C++ programming language continues to grow stronger daily. I have taught hundreds of students the C++ programming language, and I grow fonder of the language with each course. The C++ programming language is now the mainstream computer course in colleges and a much-needed language for use in the computer industry. I hope that this book helps fill a niche not found in the vast number of C++ books currently in print—that niche being a straightforward, friendly, and comfortable feel that provides a stepping-stone style for beginners to C++.

I appreciate Stacy Hiquet and Joseph Wikert at Prentice Hall for trusting me completely with the direction and style of this book.

G. M. P.

To Stacy Hiquet and Joseph Wikert at Prentice Hall, my deepest appreciation for the opportunity to do this book; to Joan, Chelsea, and Trevor, my love and thanks for giving me the space to do it in.

M. J.

Trademark Acknowledgments

Que Corporation has made every attempt to supply trademark information about company names, products, and services mentioned in this book. Trademarks indicated below were derived from various sources. Que Corporation cannot attest to the accuracy of this information.

ANSI is a registered trademark of American National Standards Institute.

DEC is a registered trademark of Digital Equipment Corporation.

DR DOS is a registered trademark of Digital Research, Inc.

IBM and OS/2 are registered trademarks of International Business Machines Corporation.

Intel is a registered trademark of Intel Corporation.

Microsoft and MS-DOS are registered trademarks of Microsoft Corporation. Windows and QBasic are trademarks of Microsoft Corporation.

Turbo C and Turbo C++ are registered trademarks of Borland International, Inc.

UNIX is a trademark of AT&T.

X Window System is a trademark of The Massachusetts Institute of Technology.

Overview

Contents

Part III C++ Constructs

Part IV Variable Scope and Modular Programming

Part V Character, Input, Output, and String Functions

Part VI Arrays and Pointers

Introduction

Turbo C++ By Example is one of several books in Que's new line of *By Example* titles. The philosophy of these books is a simple one: computer programming concepts are best taught with multiple examples. Command descriptions, format syntax, and language references are not enough for a newcomer to learn a programming language. Only by looking at many examples, where new commands are used immediately, and by running sample programs can programming students get more than just a "feel" for the language.

Who Should Use This Book?

This book teaches on three levels of examples: beginning, intermediate, and advanced. Text accompanies the many examples at each level. If you are new to C++, and even if you are new to computers, this book attempts to put you at ease and gradually builds your C++ programming skills. If you are an expert at C++, this book tries to provide a few extras for you along the way.

The Book's Philosophy

This book focuses on programming *correctly* in C++ by teaching structured programming techniques and proper program design. Emphasis is always placed on a program's readability instead of "tricks of the trade" code examples. In this changing world, programs should be clear, properly structured, and well documented, and this book does not waver from the importance of this philosophy.

The book teaches you C++ by using a holistic approach; you learn the mechanics of the language, tips and warnings, how to use C++ for different types of applications, as well as a little of the history and interesting "sidebars" of the computing industry.

Although many other books build single applications, adding to them a little at a time with each chapter, the chapters of this book are stand-alone chapters showing you complete programs that fully illustrate the commands discussed. There is a program for every level of reader, from beginning to advanced.

Over 200 sample program listings are provided. These programs show ways that C++ can be used for personal finance, school and business record keeping, math and science, and general-purpose applications that almost everybody with a computer can use. This wide variety of programs shows you that C++ is a very powerful language which is easy to learn and use.

At the end of the book (Appendix F), you will find a complete application, much longer than any of the other programs in the book, which tries to bring together your entire working knowledge of C++. The application is a computerized mailing list manager. You learn how each command in the program works throughout the chapters that come before it. You might want to modify the program to suit your needs better. (The comments in the program suggest changes you might want to make.)

Overview of This Book

Turbo C++ By Example is divided into eight parts. Part I introduces you to the C++ environment and introductory programming concepts. Starting with Part II, the book presents the C++

programming language commands and library functions. After mastering the language, you can then use the book as a handy reference. When you need help with a specific C++ programming problem, turn to the appropriate area which describes that part of the language to see various examples of code.

The following sections describe the parts of this book.

Part I: Introduction to C++

Part I explains what C++ is by describing a brief history of the C++ programming language and then presenting an overview of C++'s advantages over other languages. This part of the book describes your computer's hardware, how you develop C++ programs, and the steps you follow to enter and run programs. You will write your first C++ program in the fourth chapter.

Part II: Using C++ Operators

Part II covers the entire set of C++ operators. The rich assortment of operators (more than in any other programming language except APL) makes up for the fact that the C++ programming language is very small. The operators and their order of precedence are more important to C++ than to most programming languages.

Part III: C++ Constructs

C++ data processing is most powerful because of the looping, comparison, and selection constructs that C++ offers. This part of the book shows you how to write programs that correctly flow with control computations to produce accurate and readable code.

Part IV: Variable Scope and Modular Programming

To support true structured programming techniques, C++ must allow for local and global variables, as well as offer several ways to pass and return variables between functions. These subjects are the focus of Part IV. C++ is a very strong structured language that attempts, if the programmer is willing to "listen to the language," to protect local variables by making them visible only to the parts of the program that need those variables.

Part V: Character, Input, Output, and String Functions

C++ contains no commands that perform input or output. To make up for this apparent oversight, C++ compiler writers supply several useful input and output functions, described in this part of the book. By separating input and output functions from the language, C++ achieves better portability between computers; if your program runs on one computer, it should work on any other.

In addition, Part V describes several of the math, character, and string library functions available with C++. These functions keep you from having to write your own routines to perform common tasks.

Part VI: Arrays and Pointers

C++ offers single-dimensional arrays and multidimensional arrays—the subjects of Part VI. A multidimensional array holds multiple occurrences of repeating data but does not require lots of effort on your part to process.

Unlike many other programming languages, C++ uses pointer variables a great deal. Pointer variables and arrays work together to give you flexible data storage, allowing for easy sorting and searching of data.

Part VII: Data Structures

Variables, arrays, and pointers are not enough to hold the types of data your programs will require. Structures and classes, discussed in

Part VII, allow for more powerful grouping of many different kinds of data into manageable units.

Your computer would be too limiting if you could not store data to disk and retrieve that data back into your programs. Disk files are required by most "real world" applications. This part of the book describes how C++ processes sequential and random access files, as well as teaches the fundamental principles needed to save data to the disk effectively.

Part VIII: Appendixes

The appendixes provide support information for the rest of the book. You will find there a review of binary and hexadecimal numbers, answers to the Review Questions for each chapter, a comprehensive ASCII table, a C++ precedence table, a keyword and function reference, and a complete mailing list application.

Conventions Used in This Book

The following typographic conventions are used in this book:

- Code lines, variable names, and any text that you see on the screen are in `monospace`.
- Placeholders on format lines are in *`italic monospace`*.
- User input following a prompt is in **`bold monospace`**.
- File names are in regular text.
- Optional parameters on format lines are enclosed in flat brackets (`[ ]`). You do not type the brackets when you include these parameters.
- New terms, which can be found in the Glossary, are in *italic*.

Index to the Icons

The following icons appear throughout this book:

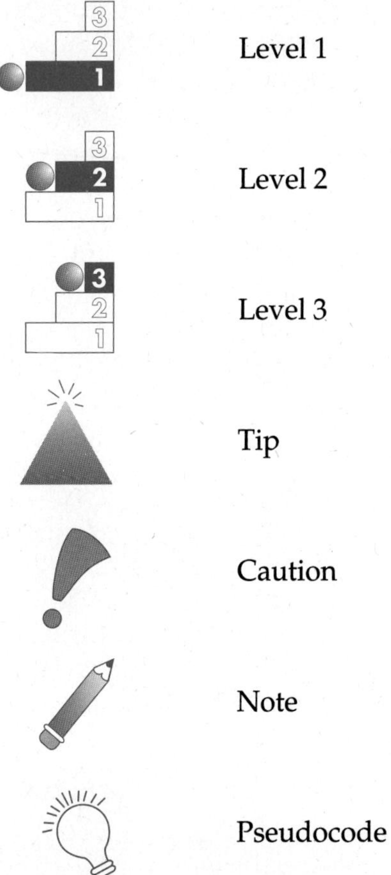

The pseudocode icon appears beside pseudocode, which is typeset in *italic* just after the program. The pseudocode consists of one or more sentences indicating what the program instructions would say if their functions could be stated aloud, in English. Pseudocode appears for selected programs.

The Book's Diagrams (Margin Graphics)

To help your understanding of Turbo C++, this book includes many diagrams, or *margin graphics*. These are similar to flowcharts you might have seen before. Both use standard symbols to represent program logic. Remember the adage "A picture is worth a thousand words"? Instead of wading through a lot of code, you can sometimes glance at the margin graphics to get a feel for the overall logic before dissecting the programs one line at a time.

Throughout this book, these margin graphics are used in two places. Some graphics appear when a new command is introduced, showing you how the command works. Other graphics are placed where new commands appear in sample programs for the first time.

No attempt is made to give you complete, detailed graphics of every statement in each program. The margin graphics are kept simple just to give you an overview of the statements you are reading about at the time.

The symbols used are shown on the following page. The meanings are listed beside the symbols.

You will find the graphics presented here easy to interpret. Their goal is to be self-explanatory, even if you have not fully learned the commands they represent. The margin graphics, the program listings, the program comments, and the program descriptions presented in this book should give you many vehicles for learning the C++ programming language.

Terminal symbol ({,}, Return...)

Assignment statement
(`total = total + newvalue;`
`ctr = ctr + 1;...`)

Input/output
(`cout, cin`)

Calling a function

Small circle; loop begin

Large dot; beginning and end
of `IF-THEN, IF-THEN-ELSE,`
and `SWITCH`

Input/output of arrays;
assumes implied `FOR` loop(s) needed
to deal with array I/O

Comment bracket; used for
added info such as name
of a function

Part I

Introduction to C++

Welcome to Turbo C++

Introduction

This is a book that will help teach you how to use Turbo C++ to write programs. In this chapter, you learn about the history of Turbo C++ and of C and C++. You review the PC system, and you learn how Turbo C++ supports programming for IBM PC systems.

What is Turbo C++?

Turbo C++ is Borland International's implementation of a compiler for the C and C++ computer languages designed to execute on MS-DOS-based systems. It can create programs that will execute under either MS-DOS or Windows. If you are already familiar with C or C++, you may want to skip this section.

What Is a Computer Language?

Remember that a computer, for all its ever-increasing speed and power, is only a device that manipulates numbers. Some of the numbers are interpreted by the computer as instructions; other numbers are interpreted as data. A *program* is a set of instructions that causes the computer to manipulate data. A *programming language* is a means for you, a human, to generate those instructions so that the computer can manipulate the data in the way you want it manipulated. Programming languages must be translated into the set of instructions; this is usually done by another program called a *compiler*, such as Turbo C++.

Low-Level Languages

Computer languages are sometimes categorized as either low-level or high-level. Low-level languages work closely with the computer's native set of instructions; the computer is viewed as being at a lower level than a human, and rightly so. Because such languages are so close to the computer's native set of instructions, a program written in a low-level language can achieve a high degree of efficiency. The program can be written to minimize the amount of time it needs to manipulate data, or to minimize the number of instructions required. The trade-off is that a program written in a low-level language is very difficult to read and write; the program may use several lines of code to do something as simple as "print a character," and it is not at all obvious that that's what is being done.

Furthermore, low-level languages are tailored to the computer. A program written in a low-level language for a Motorola 68000 would have to be completely rewritten in a low-level language for an Intel 80386. The ability to take a program written on one computer and make it run, as written, on a completely different computer is called portability. Low-level languages offer no portability. Because of the bond between a low-level language and its computer, there are no formal standards a low-level language may be expected to meet. Thus, there are usually subtle barriers to portability even between similar low-level languages implemented on a given computer. Assembly language and machine language are examples of low-level languages.

High-Level Languages

High-level languages work more closely with the human programmer and often attempt to emulate human language or activity. Programs written in high-level languages are not generally as efficient as programs written in low-level languages but are often more readable and easier to write. High-level languages are usually hardware-independent; a program written in a high-level language on one hardware platform will generally run, as written, on another hardware platform. High-level languages also have a high degree of portability. Many high-level languages have been standardized by organizations such as ANSI or industry organizations, and this standardization aids in writing portable programs. Examples of high-level languages are FORTRAN, COBOL, and Pascal.

What is C?

C is a programming language that falls somewhere between a low-level language and a high-level language. Programs written in C are not glorified lists of machine instructions; C is a block-structured, procedural language. A well-written program in C can be very readable, and writing programs in C is easy. The authors of the first C implementation, Brian W. Kernighan and Dennis M. Ritchie, wrote C to exploit the native capabilities of the computer they were working on, and further specified that C should always exploit the native capabilities of the computer on which it is implemented. Thus, C can be used to write very efficient programs—although not quite as efficient as programs written in a low-level language (but sometimes very close), and usually more efficient than programs written in a classical high-level language. An ANSI standard for the C language now exists, and writing portable programs in C is not too difficult.

What is C++?

In the last few years, a new method of programming came into existence: *object-oriented programming*. Instead of manipulating numbers, programs manipulate data objects. The basic idea is that when a new data object is to be manipulated, the new object will share some characteristics with an existing object, and a program that manipulates the existing object can be used as the basis of a program that manipulates the new, similar object.

C++, as an extension of C, implements object-oriented programming practices. C++ allows C programmers a migration path into object-oriented programming; programs written in C should compile correctly under a C++ compiler. C++ inherits much of the efficiency of its parent, as well as the readability and ease of writing programs. Although no standard exists for C++ yet, a de facto standard does exist, and the industry is generally tracking the AT&T specifications. Consequently, programs written in C++ may not be quite as portable, but generally the differences between implementations are minor, and porting a program from one implementation to another requires little effort.

The History of Turbo C++

Turbo C was the first C offering from Borland. Patterned after its very successful Turbo Pascal compiler, Turbo C offered PC-based programmers a C programming environment. Previous implementations of C compilers on PCs were patterned after their UNIX-based predecessors, offering a complex and bewildering command-line interface to the programmer. Programs written in C had to be written with a text editor and then compiled separately. These C compilers were so tied to UNIX that they were often bundled with a small version of the UNIX programmer's workbench, a collection of utility programs used by programmers. Turbo C not only provided the traditional command-line interface but also exploited the PC's unique capabilities, offering an environment with a built-in text editor from which you could compile your program. If an error occurred during the compilation, the programmer was returned to the file, with the offending line of code identified and a description of the error given. Within a few years of Turbo C's introduction, Borland had caught up with Microsoft, then the industry leader.

Turbo C++ followed Turbo C as Borland's C++ offering. Although many competing C++ vendors were offering C++ as a

```
DRIVE:
CD\PATH
```

where DRIVE is the letter designating the drive on which you installed Turbo C++, and PATH is the directory on that drive in which you installed the Turbo C++ executable file (TC.EXE). If you don't know what drive and directory contains TC.EXE, there are a number of commercial packages that can find a specified file. Now you can type TC to load Turbo C++ into memory.

If the Turbo C++ path is not in your path, you should add it to your PATH in AUTOEXEC.BAT. After adding the proper directory to your path, you can start Turbo C++. See Que's *Using MS-DOS 5* for more information on using the PATH command.

Power-Up Properly

There is a proper sequence to follow when turning on your computer. The sequence is easy to remember with the following rule: *The boss always comes to work last and is the first to go home.*

Have you had bosses like that? Your computer's power-up sequence should follow a similar rule: *The system unit (the "boss" that holds the CPU) should come to work last.*

In other words, turn on everything else first, including the printer, monitor, and modem. Only then should you turn on the system unit. This keeps system-unit power surges to a minimum and protects the circuits inside the unit.

When you are ready to turn off the computer, turn off the system unit first (the boss goes home first). Then turn off the rest of the equipment in whatever order is most convenient.

TIP: If your computer equipment is plugged into a switched surge protector, it is fine to use the single switch for all your equipment, including the system unit. The surge protector ensures that power gets to the system unit as evenly as possible.

You can add several options to the Turbo C++ start-up command. These options, listed in Table 2.1, affect the Turbo C++ environment, changing the way it starts. Some of the options will make more sense as you learn more about Turbo C++.

Table 2.1. Turbo C++ start-up command-line options.

Option	*Meaning*
/b	Use this option to recompile and link all the files in your project. Compiler messages are printed to the screen and can be redirected to a file or the printer. You should specify the name of a project file or an executable file.
/d	Use this option if you have two monitors on your system. The active monitor receives your program's output; Turbo C++ runs on the inactive monitor. This option is useful in debugging your code.
/e	Use this option to tell Turbo C++ to swap memory in and out of expanded memory. This is much faster than the hard disk, which Turbo C++ uses by default.
/l	Use this option if you are running Turbo C++ on a system with an LCD screen.
/m	Use this option to recompile and link only the outdated files in your project. Compiler messages are printed to the screen and can be redirected to a file or the printer. You should specify the name of a project file or an executable file. This is faster than the /b option, which rebuilds everything.
/p	Use this option to control palette swapping on EGA video adapters. This is useful only if your program is modifying the EGA palette registers or is using the Borland Graphics Interface (BGI) to change the palette.
/r*x*	Use this option to tell Turbo C++ to swap memory in and out of a RAM disk. This is much faster than the hard disk, which Turbo C++ uses by default. The drive letter of the RAM disk is the *x* in /r*x*; for example, you would use /rF if F is your RAM disk.

Option	*Meaning*
/x	Use this option to tell Turbo C++ to swap memory in and out of extended memory. This is much faster than the hard disk, which Turbo C++ uses by default. If you can choose among the three swap options (/e, /rx, and /x), /x is best, followed by /e, and finally /rx.

Examples

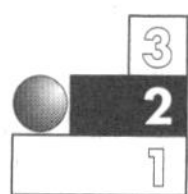

1. To start Turbo C++ and load a program called MYFILE.CPP into the Turbo C++ editor, type the following at the DOS prompt:

```
TC MYFILE.CPP
```

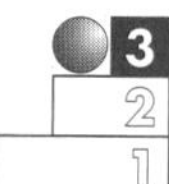

2. To start Turbo C++ on an LCD laptop that does not have color, you might choose to make Turbo C++ more readable by starting it with

```
TC /1
```

The Turbo C++ Screen

Figure 2.2 shows the parts of the Turbo C++ screen. From this screen, you create, modify, and execute Turbo C++ programs. Start the Turbo C++ program, and you see the Turbo C++ screen. If you have a mouse, move it around on your desk so that you can see the mouse pointer.

Using the Mouse

You use the mouse to move the cursor around on the screen quickly. Before mouse devices became common, users had to press the arrow keys continually to move the cursor from one location to another. Now you can move the cursor by moving the mouse across the desk and clicking the mouse when the pointer is at the desired position.

To *click* the mouse, you press and immediately release the left mouse button. Clicking the mouse might select an item from a menu or move the text cursor around the screen. Sometimes you click the mouse after moving the mouse pointer over a Yes or No answer in response to a question.

To *double-click* the mouse, you press the left mouse button twice in rapid succession. You might need to double-click the mouse to execute a menu command.

To *drag* the mouse, you press and hold down the left mouse button and then move the mouse pointer across the screen. Usually, the area you drag the mouse across is highlighted on the screen so that you can see the path the mouse leaves. When you are finished marking the path, release the mouse button. This is one way to select several lines from a Turbo C++ program so that you can move or erase them.

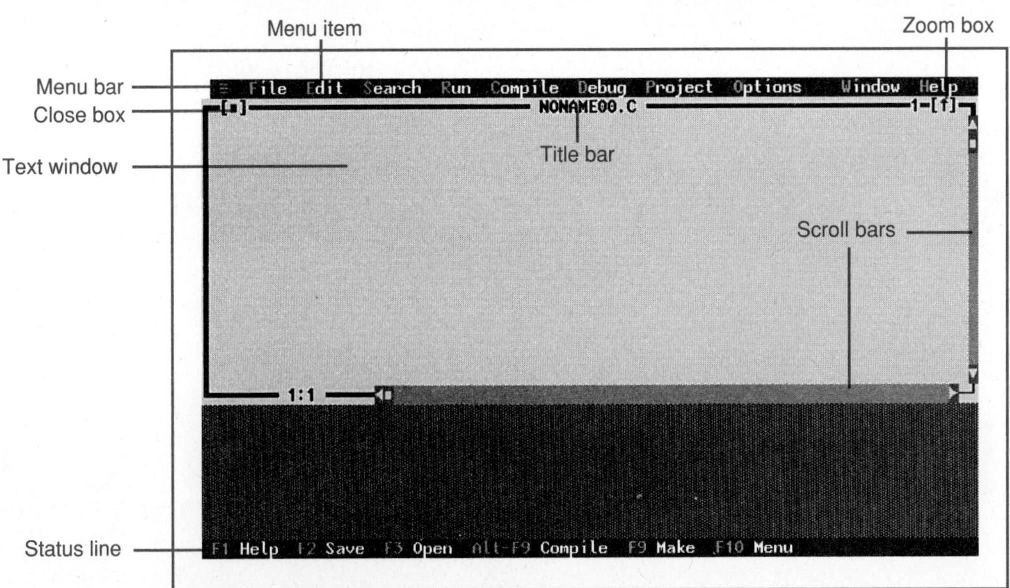

Figure 2.2. **The parts of the Turbo C++ screen.**

The most important part of the screen is the *program-editing window,* where you work with Turbo C++ programs. The window acts like a word processor's document-editing area. You can move the cursor with the arrow keys or mouse and make any necessary changes to the text. The number of windows that can be open is limited by available memory, but only one window is active at a time.

Selecting from Turbo C++'s Menus

How do you know what to order when you go to a new restaurant? You choose from a menu. Restaurant owners know that people who eat in their restaurants have not memorized everything the restaurant serves. Likewise, the authors of Turbo C++ understood that users would not want to memorize the commands that control Turbo C++. They would rather look at a list of possible commands and select the ones they want. The *menu bar* at the top of the screen makes using Turbo C++ easy.

The Turbo C++ menu bar displays the symbol ≡ and the words **F**ile, **E**dit, **S**earch, **R**un, **C**ompile, **D**ebug, **P**roject, **O**ptions, **W**indow, and **H**elp. You can select these items from the Turbo C++ screen. They are not commands but are headings for additional menus. These menus are called *pull-down menus* because they resemble a window shade being pulled down. For example, Figure 2.3 shows what happens if you select the **F**ile pull-down menu.

When you want to look at any of the pull-down menus, you can use either the mouse or the keyboard. To display a pull-down menu with the mouse, move the mouse pointer over a menu bar item and click (see the earlier sidebar "Using the Mouse"). If you click the rest of the items on the menu bar, you see the other pull-down menus in succession.

Displaying a pull-down menu from the keyboard is just as easy as displaying the menu with the mouse. Press the Alt key and the highlighted letter of the menu you want to see. For example, to display the **E**dit pull-down menu, press Alt+E. You pull down the system menu (the ≡ menu) by pressing Alt+spacebar.

If you change your mind, you can press Esc to remove a displayed menu. You are, in effect, escaping from the option you selected.

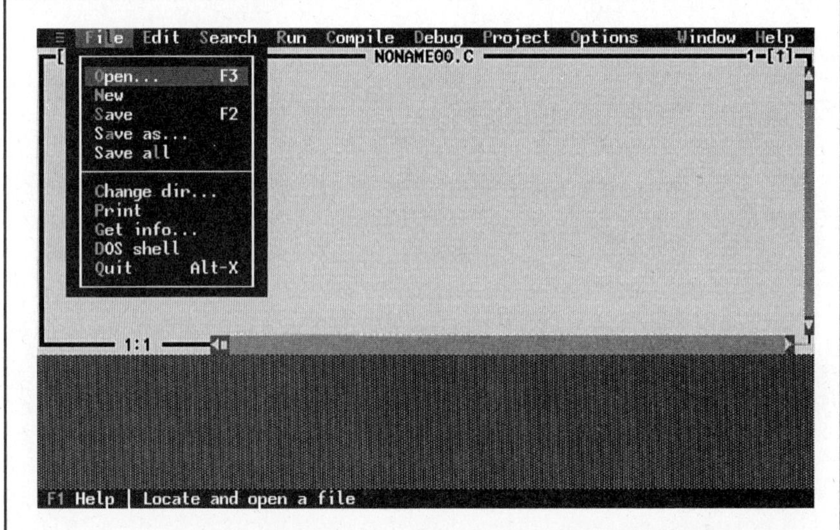

Figure 2.3. Viewing the **F**ile pull-down menu.

TIP: To display a menu, mouse users sometimes prefer the keyboard's Alt+key combination to clicking the mouse. Because your hands are already on the keyboard, pressing Alt+S for **S**earch might be faster than pointing with the mouse and clicking.

Choosing an Option

When you display a pull-down menu, you must tell Turbo C++ which command on the menu to perform. For example, the **F**ile pull-down menu lists several commands. You can request a command in one of three ways:

- Click the command with the mouse.
- Highlight the command with the arrow keys and then press Enter.
- Press the command's highlighted letter.

For example, to request the **New** command, mouse users move the mouse pointer until it rests anywhere on the word **New**. One click of the mouse executes the **New** command. Keyboard users press the down-arrow key until the **New** command is highlighted. Pressing the Enter key carries out the command. Keyboard users also have a shortcut: simply typing the highlighted letter of the command. By typing `N` or `n`, the keyboard user can execute the **New** command. Note that you can use an uppercase letter or a lowercase letter to select any command or option.

If you begin to select from a menu but then change your mind, press Esc to close the menu and return to the program-editing window. Mouse users just click the mouse outside the pull-down menu area to close the menu.

> **TIP:** The best way to learn how to choose from Turbo C++'s pull-down menus is to experiment. As long as you don't save anything to disk, you don't harm existing Turbo C++ program files or data.

Sometimes commands appear in gray and are not as readable as others. For example, notice in Figure 2.4 that most of the options on the **Edit** pull-down menu are in gray and have no highlighted letter. You cannot choose any of these commands. Turbo C++ displays the unavailable commands so that you will remember where they are when you need them. These commands return to their normal colors when they make more sense in the context of your Turbo C++ session.

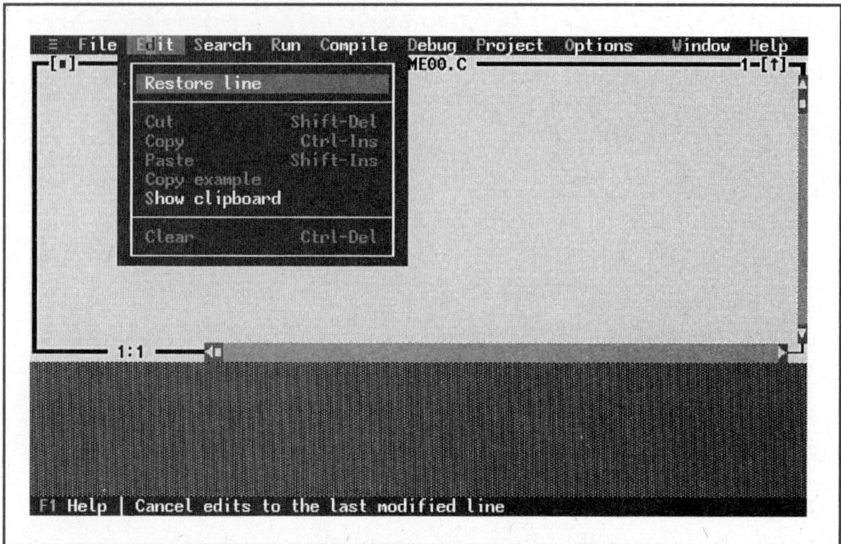

Figure 2.4. The **E**dit pull-down menu.

The Menu Shortcut Keys

After using Turbo C++ for a while, you will become familiar with the commands on the pull-down menus. Despite the ease of using Turbo C++ menus, there is a faster way to select some of the commands. Turbo C++'s *shortcut keys* are easier to use than the menus, whether you use a mouse or the keyboard.

Many of the function keys execute menu commands when you press those keys. Table 2.2 lists these shortcuts. For instance, to choose **R**un **P**rogram reset, you could display the **R**un pull-down menu and then select **P**rogram reset. The **R**un **P**rogram reset menu option, however, has Ctrl-F2 listed to the right of it. The key or key combination listed beside the menu option is the shortcut key for that option. Instead of going through the menu steps, you can press Ctrl-F2 and immediately run the **P**rogram reset command. You will understand the function of each of these shortcut keys as you learn more about Turbo C++.

Table 2.2. Turbo C++ menu shortcut keys.

Key(s)	*Menu Command*
F1	**H**elp
F1+F1	None; provides help on **H**elp
F2	File **S**ave
F3	File **O**pen
F4	**R**un **G**o to cursor
F5	**W**indow **Z**oom
F6	**W**indow **N**ext
F7	**R**un **T**race into
F8	**R**un **S**tep over
F9	Compile **M**ake EXE file
F10	None; takes you to the menu bar
Alt+0	**W**indow **L**ist
Alt+(1-9)	None; displays window 1 through window 9
Alt+F1	**H**elp **P**revious topic
Alt+F3	**W**indow **C**lose
Alt+F4	**D**ebug **I**nspect
Alt+F5	**W**indow **U**ser screen
Alt+F7	**S**earch **P**revious error
Alt+F8	**S**earch **N**ext error
Alt+F9	**C**ompile **C**ompile to OBJ
Ctrl+Del	**E**dit **C**lear
Ctrl+F1	**H**elp **T**opic search
Ctrl+F2	**R**un **P**rogram reset
Ctrl+F3	**D**ebug **C**all stack

continues

Table 2.2. Continued.

Key(s)	*Menu Command*
Ctrl+F4	**D**ebug **E**valuate/modify
Ctrl+F5	None; changes size or position of the active window
Ctrl+F7	**D**ebug **A**dd watch
Ctrl+F8	**D**ebug **T**oggle breakpoint
Ctrl+F9	**R**un **R**un
Ctrl+Ins	**E**dit **C**opy
Ctrl+L	**S**earch **S**earch again
Shift+Del	**E**dit **C**ut
Shift+F1	**H**elp **I**ndex
Shift+Ins	**E**dit **P**aste

Using Dialog Boxes

Not all menu commands execute when you select them. Some are followed by an ellipsis (. . .), such as the **F**ile **O**pen command. If you choose one of these commands, a *dialog box* opens on the screen. You must type more information before Turbo C++ can carry out the command. This extra information might be a number, a word, a file name, or the selection of an option from several that are offered. Sometimes a dialog box requires several actions from you.

Figure 2.5 shows the Options Make dialog box. This is a good time to practice using a dialog box. Select **M**ake from the **O**ptions menu. Notice that each of the first four options (**W**arnings, **E**rrors, **F**atal errors, and **L**ink) is preceded by a set of parentheses and that one of the four sets has a dot in it. These parentheses are called *radio buttons*. You can select only one radio button from a group of buttons; when you select a button, the previously selected button's dot is cleared. You select a radio button by using the arrow keys, pressing Alt plus the selection's highlighted letter, or clicking the radio button or its text.

Another option in this dialog box is preceded by a set of square brackets. These brackets are called a *check box*. You may select any or all of the check boxes, or none of them. A selected check box is indicated by an x in the brackets. You select check boxes in the same way you select radio buttons.

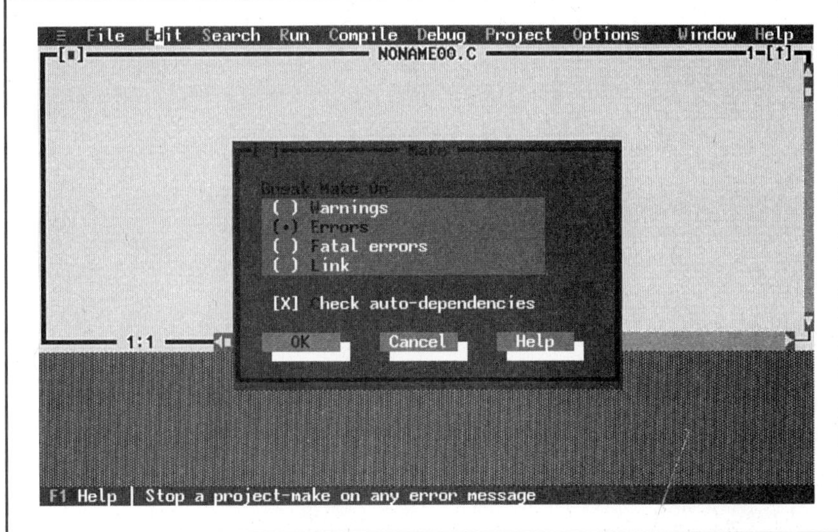

Figure 2.5. The Options Make dialog box.

Getting Help

When using Turbo C++, you can get help at any time by using the online Help feature. Help explains virtually every aspect of Turbo C++. The Turbo C++ Help system gives several kinds of help. Depending on your request, Turbo C++ helps you with whatever you need and even offers sample programs that you can merge into your own programs.

Help Contents

Selecting **Help Contents** gives the beginning Turbo C++ user a "road map" to the various categories of help available. When you double-click a topic shown, you get a help screen specific to that topic. The Help Contents screen is shown in Figure 2.6.

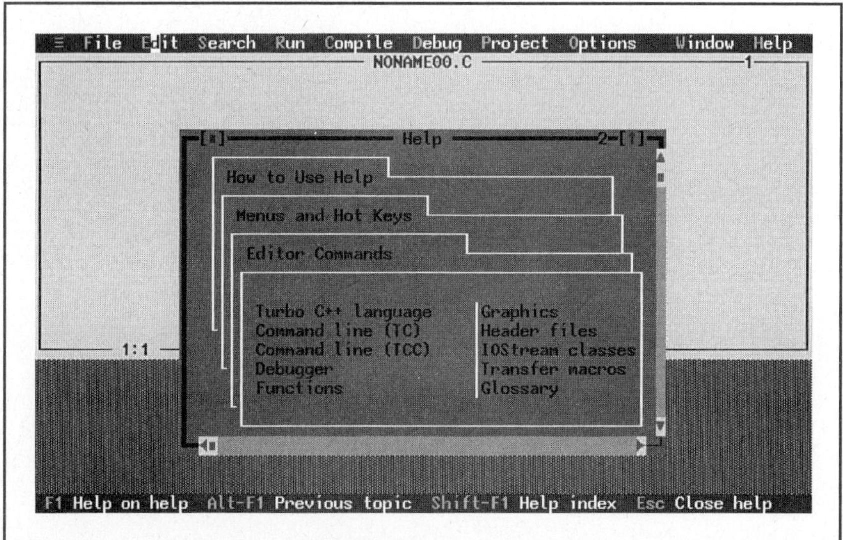

Figure 2.6. The Help Contents screen.

Help about Help

The Turbo C++ online Help system is so complete that it even gives you help about using Help. Press F1 to bring up the **Help** menu and then press F1 again. A window appears that walks you through all aspects of using the Help system (see Figure 2.7). You can press the up- and down-arrow keys, the PgUp key, and the PgDn key to scroll through the text on the screen. Mouse users can click the scroll bar to scroll the text.

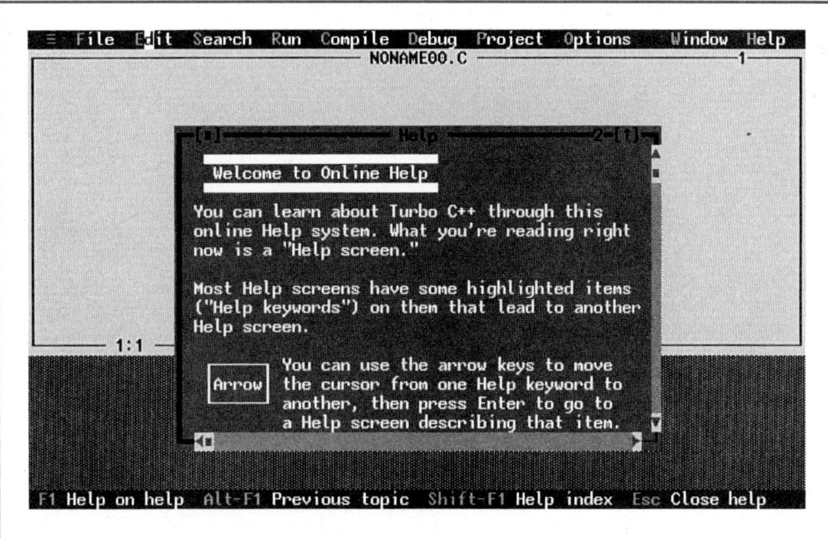

Figure 2.7. Getting help with the Help system.

Help Index

Choosing **I**ndex from the **H**elp menu displays a list of more than 1,000 functions, constants, variables, and topics used in Turbo C++. At this point, most of the entries probably make little sense to you. As you learn more about the Turbo C++ programming language, you will understand these topics better. Notice in Figure 2.8 that only a few of the topics fit on the screen at one time.

Topic and Context-Sensitive Help

When you become familiar with Turbo C++, the *context-sensitive help* feature relieves some of your programming frustration. Whenever you request context-sensitive help by pressing Ctrl+F1 or choosing **H**elp **T**opic search, Turbo C++ "looks" at what you are doing and gives you help with your problem. For example, if you are working on the Turbo C++ `strcpy()` function and the cursor is on the word `strcpy` when you press Ctrl+F1, Turbo C++ displays help on the `strcpy()` function. If you want help on the **S**earch menu, display the **S**earch menu and press F1.

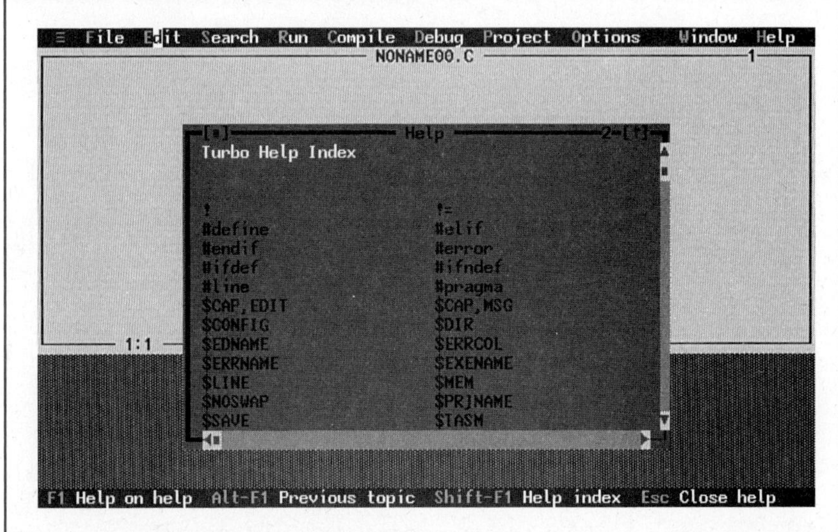

Figure 2.8. The Help Index screen.

About

Selecting **A**bout from the system menu (the ≡ menu) displays a dialog box in the center of the screen that shows the version number of Turbo C++ you are using. This is helpful if you call Borland for support and need to supply this version number. Pressing Esc or clicking OK removes this dialog box from the screen and returns you to the program-editing window.

Quitting Turbo C++

When you finish your Turbo C++ session, you can exit Turbo C++ and return to DOS by choosing **F**ile Exit. It is important to exit to DOS before turning off your computer; if you don't, you could lose some of your work. If you made changes to a Turbo C++ program and you try to exit to DOS without saving the changes to disk, Turbo C++ displays the warning message in the dialog box shown in Figure 2.9.

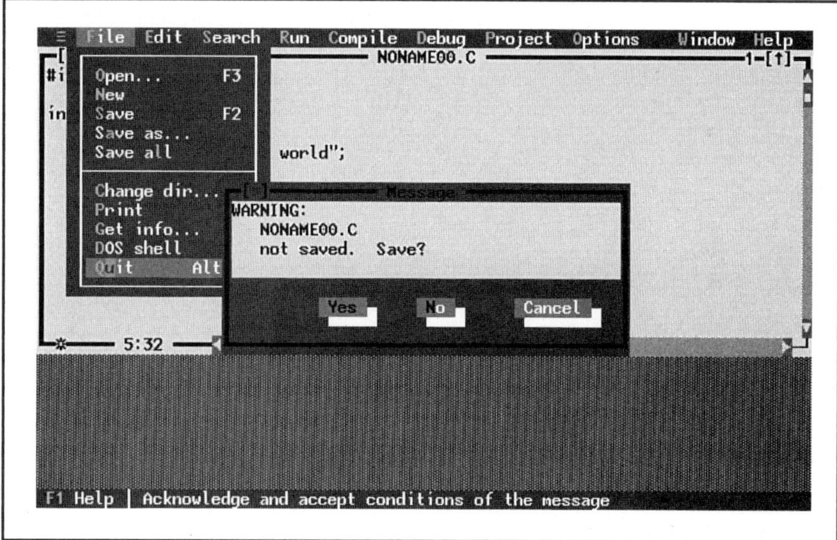

Figure 2.9. The Turbo C++ warning message to save a file.

If you choose **Y**es, Turbo C++ prompts you for a file name under which to save the file (if you haven't named it previously). Choosing **N**o instructs Turbo C++ that you want to exit to DOS without saving the file, although the latest changes are not recorded. Cancel instructs Turbo C++ to return to the program-editing window.

Summary

This chapter familiarized you with the Turbo C++ environment. The major advantages of Turbo C++ over its predecessors are the screen's menus and online Help system. You learned how to start Turbo C++, use the menus, request online help, and exit the program. With its intuitive interface, Turbo C++ makes working easy, whether you use a mouse or the keyboard.

Review Questions

Answers to Review Questions are in Appendix B.

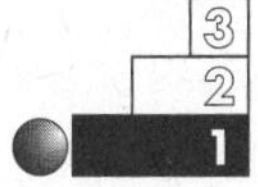

1. True or false: You can find Turbo C++ in your \DOS subdirectory.
2. Which part of the Turbo C++ screen retains the program as you type it?
3. What are the differences in clicking, double-clicking, and dragging a mouse?
4. Do you need to remember command names so that Turbo C++ can execute them? Why or why not?
5. How do you display the Help Contents screen?
6. What does *context-sensitive help* mean?
7. Why should you exit Turbo C++ and return to DOS before turning off your computer?

8. What are two ways to get help in Turbo C++?
9. What are command-line options used for?
10. What are the keyboard shortcut keys used for?

What Is a Program?

This chapter introduces you to fundamental programming concepts. The task of programming computers has been described as rewarding, challenging, easy, difficult, fast, and slow. It is all of these, and more. Programming your computer takes some time to do well, but you will have fun along the way, especially with the rich assortment of features offered by C++. Writing complex programs to solve advanced problems takes time and can be frustrating, but once you get a complex program working, the feeling is gratifying.

In this chapter, you learn about the concept of programming, from a program's design to its execution on your computer. The most difficult part of programming is to break up the problem into logical steps that the computer can carry out. Before you finish the chapter, you will have typed and executed a simple C++ program.

This chapter covers the following topics:

- The concept of programming
- Running C++ programs
- The program's output
- Program design

- Using the Turbo C++ editor
- Using the Turbo C++ compiler

After completing this chapter, you will be ready for the remaining chapters, which explain in detail the elements of the C++ programming language.

Computer Programs

Before you can make C++ work for you, you must write a C++ program. As you learned in Chapter 1, a program is a set of instructions that causes the computer to manipulate data.

Keep in mind that computers are just machines; they are not smart—quite the opposite! They will not do anything until they are given very detailed instructions. If you use your computer for word processing, the word processor is actually a program that someone wrote (in a language such as C++) which tells the computer exactly how to behave when you type words into it.

You are familiar with the concept of programming if you have ever followed a recipe. A recipe is just a program (a set of instructions) that tells the cook how to make a certain dish. A good recipe gives the instructions in the proper order and provides a complete description so that the cook can make everything successfully and with no assumptions.

If you want your computer to help with your budget, keep track of names and addresses, or compute gas mileage for your car travel, the computer needs a program that tells it how to do those things. There are two ways to supply that program for your computer:

- Buy a program written by somebody else that does the job you want.
- Write the program yourself.

Writing the program yourself has a big advantage for many applications: the program will do exactly what you want it to do. If you buy one that is already written, you will have to adapt your needs to those of the designers of the program. That is where C++

comes into the picture. With the C++ programming language (and a little study), you can make your computer perform any task needed.

To create a C++ program for your computer, you must have an *editor* and a C++ *compiler*. Similar to a word processor, an editor is a program that lets you type a C++ program into memory, make changes (such as moving, copying, inserting, and deleting text), and save that program more permanently in a disk file.

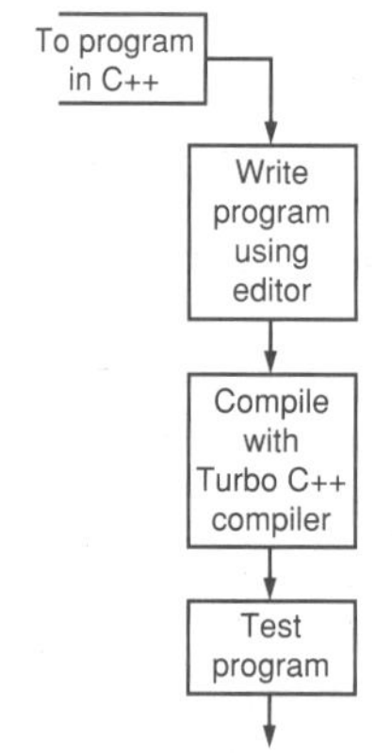

After you type the program by using the editor, you must compile the program before you run it. C++ is usually implemented as a *compiled* language. You usually cannot write a C++ program and run it on your computer unless you have a C++ compiler. A C++ compiler translates the C++ instructions into a form executable by your computer. Turbo C++ comes with its own built-in editor and compiler.

The process of compiling a program before running it may seem like an added and meaningless step to beginning programmers. If you know the BASIC programming language, you may not have heard of a compiler, or understand the need for one. That is because BASIC (as well as APL and some versions of other computer languages) is not a compiled language but an *interpreted* language. Instead of translating the entire program into machine-executable form (as a compiler does), an interpreter translates each program instruction and then executes it before translating the next one. The difference between a compiler and an interpreter is subtle, but the bottom line is not: compilers produce *much* more efficient and faster-running programs than interpreters do. In addition, the program you've written does not require that the user have a copy of the interpreter in order to run the program; the compiler will produce an independently executable program. The seemingly extra step of compiling is worth the effort (and with today's compilers, there is not much extra effort needed).

Because computers are machines that do not think, the instructions you write in C++ must be very detailed. You cannot assume that the computer understands what to do if it is not in your program, or if you give an instruction that does not conform to the C++ language requirements.

Once you write a C++ program, you then must *run*, or *execute*, it. Otherwise, your computer will not know that you want it to follow the instructions in the program. Just as a cook must follow a recipe's instructions before the dish is made, your computer must execute the program instructions before it can accomplish what you want it to do. When you run a program, you instruct the computer to start performing the instructions in the program.

The Program and Its Output

While programming, remember the difference between the program and its output. Your program contains the instructions you write by using C. Only after you run the program does the computer actually follow your instructions.

Throughout this book, you will often see a program listing (the C++ instructions in the program) followed by the program's results (what occurs when you run it). The results, which are the output of the program, go to an output device, such as the screen, the printer, or a disk file.

Program Design

You must plan your programs before typing them in your C++ editor. When a carpenter builds a house, he or she does not get a hammer and nails and start building! The carpenter first finds out what the owner of the house wants, draws up the plans, orders the materials, gathers the workers, and *then* starts hammering the nails.

Design your programs before typing them into the computer.

The hardest part of writing a program is to break it into logical steps the computer can follow. Learning the C++ language is a requirement, but that is not the only thing to consider. There is a method of writing programs, a formal procedure you should learn, that makes your programming job easier. To write a program, you should follow these steps:

1. Define the problem to solve with the computer.
2. Design the output of the program (what the user sees).
3. Break the program into logical steps to achieve the program's output.
4. Write the program (this is where the editor is useful).

5. Compile the program.
6. Test the program to make sure that it performs as expected.

As you can see, the actual typing of the program occurs toward the end of programming. The order of these steps is important, as you must plan how to tell a computer the way to perform a certain task.

Your computer can perform instructions only step-by-step. You must assume that the computer has no previous knowledge of the problem, and it is up to you to supply it with that knowledge. That is what good recipes do. It would be foolish if a recipe for baking a cake simply said, "Bake the cake." Why? Because it assumes way too much on the part of the cook. Even if the recipe is written out step-by-step, care must be taken (through advance planning) that the steps are in the proper sequence. Putting the ingredients in the oven *before* stirring them would not be prudent!

Throughout this book, as programs are presented, this programming process is adhered to. Before seeing a program, you will read about its design. The goals of the program will be presented, those goals will be broken down into logical steps, and then the program will be written.

Designing the program in advance makes the entire program structure more accurate and keeps you from having to make many changes. A builder knows that a room is much harder to add after the house is built. If you do not properly plan and think out every aspect of your program's steps, it will take you longer to create the final, working program. Making major changes to programs is more difficult after they are written.

Using these six steps to develop programs will become more important to you as you write longer and more complicated programs. Throughout this book, you will see tips for program design. Now is the time to launch into C++ so that you can see what it's like to type your own program and watch it run.

Using the Turbo C++ Editor

The instructions in your C++ program are called the *source code*. You type source code into your computer's memory with your editor. Once you type the C++ source code (your program), you should save it to a disk file before compiling and running the program. Most C++ compilers expect C++ source programs to be stored in files with names ending in CPP. All the following are valid filenames for most C++ compilers:

MYPROG.CPP	SALESACT.CPP
ACCREC.C	EMPLYEE.CPP

Figure 3.1 shows a Turbo C++ screen. Across the top of the screen is a menu bar that offers pull-down menus for editing, compiling, and running options. The middle of the screen is the body of the program editor; the program goes in this area. From this screen, you type, edit, compile, and run your C++ source programs. Without Turbo C++'s integrated environment, you would have to start an editor, type your program, save the program to disk, exit the editor, run the compiler, and only then run the compiled program from the operating system. With this integrated environment, you just type the program into the editor and then select the proper menu option that compiles and runs the program in one step.

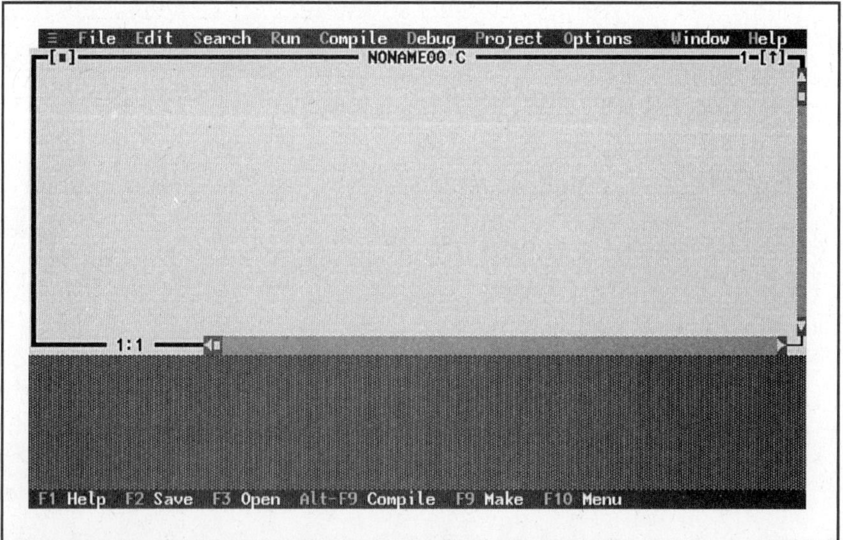

Figure 3.1. Turbo C++'s integrated environment.

Using the Turbo C++ Compiler

Once you type and edit your C++ program's source code, you must compile the program. All you do is press Alt-R to compile and run the program. When you compile the program on your PC, the compiler will eventually produce an executable file whose name begins with the same name as the source code but ends in an EXE file extension. For example, if your source program is named GRADEAVG.CPP, you will wind up with a compiled file called GRADEAVG.EXE, which you could execute from the DOS prompt by typing the name GRADEAVG.

NOTE: Each program in this book contains a comment that specifies a recommended filename for the source program. You do not have to follow the file-naming conventions used in this book. The filenames in the program listings are only suggestions for you. If, however, you decide to obtain the sample diskette that contains a listing of each program in this book, the filenames of the program listings will match those on the diskette you receive.

Unlike many other programming languages, your C++ program is normally routed through a *preprocessor* before it is compiled. C++ source code can contain *preprocessor directives*, which control the way your programs compile. The preprocessor step is performed automatically by Turbo C++, so it requires no additional effort or commands to learn on your part.

There is actually one additional step your program must go through after compiling and before running. This step is called the *linking* stage. When your program is linked, needed runtime information (which is not always available to the compiler) is supplied to your program. You can also take several compiled programs and combine them into one executable program by linking them together. Turbo C++ initiates the linking stage automatically, and you do not have to worry about the process.

Figure 3.2 shows the steps that Turbo C++ performs to produce an executable program.

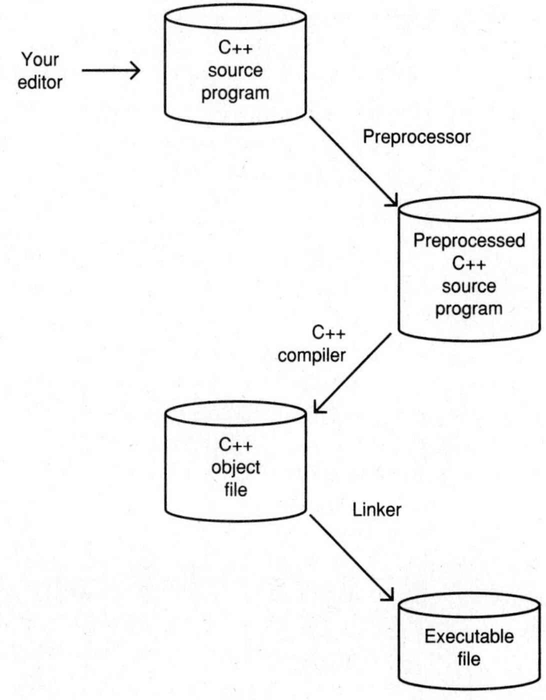

Figure 3.2. Compiling C++ source code into an executable program.

Running a Sample Program

Before delving into the specifics of the C++ language, you should take a few moments to get familiar with the Turbo C++ editor and compiler. Starting in the next chapter, "Your First C++ Program," you should concentrate all your efforts on the C++ programming language.

Therefore, start up Turbo C++ by typing `TC C3SAMPLE.CPP` at the DOS prompt and then type the following program into your computer. Be as accurate as possible, because a single typing error can cause the C++ compiler to generate a series of errors. You do not have to understand the program's content at this point; its purpose is simply to give you practice in using the Turbo C++ editor and compiler.

Comment your program with the program name and description.
Include the header file iostream.h.
Define the variable `BELL` *as the character code* `\a`*, which is a beep.*
Start of the `main()` *function.*
Initialize the integer variable `ctr` *to a zero.*
Define the character array `fname` *to hold 20 elements.*
Print to the screen `What is your first name?`
Accept a string from the keyboard.
Process a loop while the variable `ctr` *is less than 5.*
Print the string accepted from the keyboard.
Increment the variable `ctr` *by one.*
Print to the screen the character code that will make the beep.
Return out of the `main()` *function.*

NOTE: The preceding description is the design of the C3SAMPLE.CPP program. This is called *pseudocode*. Pseudocode is one of several design methods you might use; it is particularly good for writing code in C++.

```
// Filename: C3SAMPLE.CPP
// Requests a name, rings a bell, and prints the name
// 5 times

#include  <iostream.h>

#define   BELL '\a'

main()
     {
     int  ctr = 0;          // Integer variable to count
                            // through loop
     char fname[ 20 ];      // Define character array to hold
                            // name

     cout << "What is your first name? "; // Prompt the user
     cin >> fname;                        // Get the name from
                                          // the keyboard
     while (ctr < 5)                      // Loop to print the
```

```
      {                                  // name exactly 5 times
      cout << fname << "\n";
      ctr++;
      }
   cout << BELL;                         // Ring the bell
   return 0;                             // Return status
   }
```

Again, be as accurate as possible. In most programming languages, and especially in C++, the characters you type in a program must be accurate. In this sample C++ program, there are parentheses (`()`), brackets (`[]`), and braces (`{}`), and none of them can be used interchangeably.

Although the comments to the right of some of the lines (the words after `//`) do not have to end in the same columns as shown in this listing, if you enter the program exactly as shown, you will familiarize yourself with the editor and learn to be accurate with the characters you type.

Compile the program and execute it by pressing Alt-R (hold down the Alt key and then press R).

If There Are Errors

You are typing instructions for a machine, so you must be very accurate. If you misspell a word, leave out a quotation mark, or make another mistake, your C++ compiler will inform you with an error message. The error will appear in a separate message window, as shown in Figure 3.3. The most common error is a *syntax error*, which usually implies a misspelled word.

When you get an error message (or more than one), you should return to the editor window and fix the problem. The error message usually will tell you what line contains the error, and double-clicking the mouse (pressing the left button twice rapidly) on the error message will put the cursor on the offending line in the editor window. If you don't understand the error, you may have to check your reference manual or simply scour your program's source code until you find the offending problem.

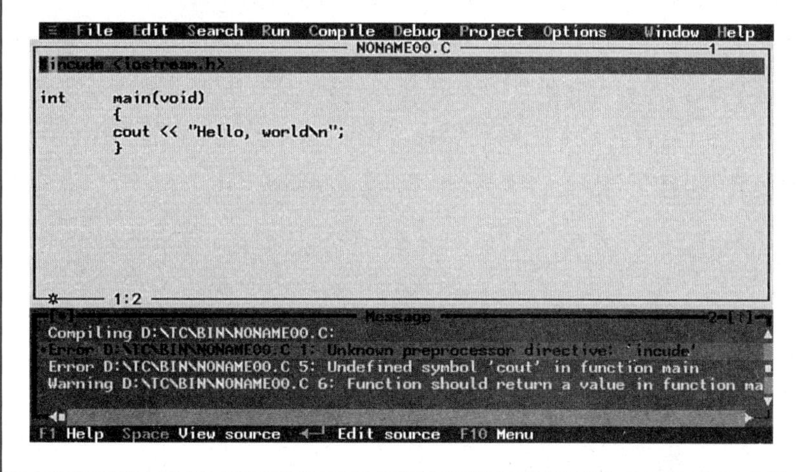

Figure 3.3. The compiler reporting a program error.

Getting the Bugs Out

One of the first computers, owned by the military, refused to print some important data one day. After programmers tried for many hours to find the solution within the program, a lady named *Grace Hopper* decided to check out the printer.

She found a small moth lodged between two important wires. When she removed the moth, the printer started working perfectly (although the moth did not have as much luck).

The late Grace Hopper retired as an admiral from the Navy, and although she is responsible for developing many important computer concepts (she is the author of the original COBOL), she may be best known for discovering the very first computer *bug*.

Since Admiral Hopper discovered the bug, errors in computer programs have been known as *computer bugs*. When you test your programs, you may have to *debug* them—get the bugs (errors) out by fixing your typing mistakes and changing the logic so that it does exactly what you want.

Once you have typed your program correctly and you get no compile errors, it will run properly by asking for your first name and then printing it five times on the screen. After the fifth name is printed, your computer's bell will ring.

This sample program helps illustrate the difference between the program and its output. You must type the program (or load it from disk) and then run the program to see its output.

Summary

After reading this chapter, you should understand the steps necessary to write a C++ program with Turbo C++. You know that advanced planning makes the program writing much easier and that the program's instructions produce the output only after you run the program.

You also saw how to use Turbo C++'s editor and compiler. Now that you know how to run a C++ program, it is time to start learning the actual C++ programming language.

Review Questions

Answers to Review Questions are in Appendix B.

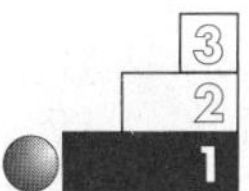

1. What is a program?
2. What are the two ways to obtain a program that you want?
3. True or false: Computers can think.
4. What is the difference between a program and its resulting output?
5. What do you use to type C++ programs into the computer?

6. What filename extension do C++ programs typically have?
7. Why is typing the program one of the *last* steps in the programming process?

8. What does the term *debug* mean?
9. True or false: You must link a program before compiling it.

Your First C++ Program

Before looking at the specifics of the C++ language, many people like to walk through a few simple programs to get a feel for what a C++ program is like. This chapter introduces you to a few C++ language commands and elements.

The following topics are covered:

- An overview of C++ programs and their structure
- C++ comments (the `/*...*/` and `//` language symbols)
- Variables and constants: what they are and their types
- Simple math operators
- Screen output

The rest of the book covers more formally some of the commands mentioned in this chapter.

Looking at a C++ Program

Figure 4.1 shows the outline of a typical small C++ program. No C++ commands are shown in the figure. Although there is much more to a program than the outline suggests, this is the general format of the early programs in this book.

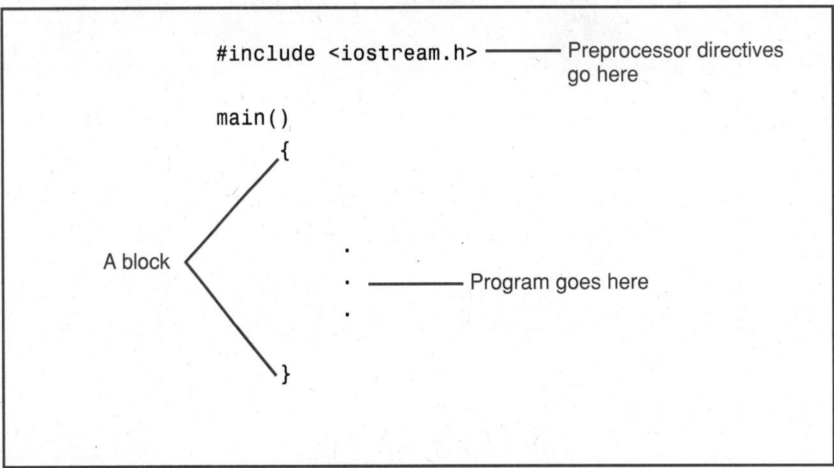

Figure 4.1. **A skeleton outline for a simple C++ program.**

To get acquainted with C++ programs as fast as possible, you should begin to look at a C++ program in its entirety. Here is a listing of a very simple C++ program. It does not do much, but it lets you get started looking at the general format of the C++ language. The next few sections discuss elements from this program. You may not understand everything in the program, even after finishing this chapter, but it is a good place to start. If there is something specific that you do not understand, that is okay for now.

```
// Filename: C4FIRST.CPP
// Initial C++ program that demonstrates the C++ comments
// and shows a few variables and their declarations

#include     <iostream.h>

main()
    {
    int       i;   // These 4 lines declare 4 variables
    int       j;
    char      c;
```

```
float     x;

i = 4;        // i and j are assigned integer constants

j = i + 7;

c = 'A';      // All character constants are enclosed in
              // single quotes

x = 9.087;    // x requires a floating-point value
              // since it was declared as a
              // floating-point variable

x = x * 4.5;    // Change what was in x with a formula

// Send the values of the variables to the screen
cout << i << j << c << x;

return 0;     // ALWAYS end programs and functions with
              // return
}
```

For now, just familiarize yourself with the overall program. Look through it to see whether you can understand part or all of it. If you are new to programming, you should know that the computer will look at each line of the program, starting with the first line and working its way down, until all the instructions given in the program have been performed. (Of course, the program first has to be compiled, as described in the last chapter.)

The output of this program is minimal; it simply displays four values on the screen after performing some assignments and calculations of arbitrary values. Just concentrate on the general format at this point.

The Format of C++ Programs

Unlike some other programming languages, such as COBOL, C++ is a *free-form* programming language. This means that programming statements can start in any column of any line. You can insert blank lines in a program if you want. This sample program, called

C4FIRST.CPP, contains several blank lines. (You can find the name of each program in this book in the first line of each listing.) These blank lines help separate parts of the program. In a simple program such as this, the separation is not as critical as it might be in a longer, more complex program.

C++ is a free-form language.

Generally, spaces within C++ programs are free-form as well. Your goal should not be to make your programs as compact as possible but as readable as possible. For example, the C4FIRST.CPP program *could* be rewritten as the following:

```
// Filename: C4FIRST.CPP Initial C++ program that
// demonstrates the C++ comments and shows a few variables
// and their declarations
#include <iostream.h> main() {int i;
// These 4 lines declare 4 variables
int j;char c;float x;i=4;//i and j are assigned integer
// constants
j=i+7;c='A';// All character constants are enclosed in single
// quotes
x=9.087;// x requires a floating-point value since
// it was declared as a floating-point variable
x=x*4.5;// Change what was in x with a formula
cout<<i<<j<<c<<x; // Send the values of the variables
// to the screen
return 0;}// ALWAYS end programs and functions with return
```

To your C++ compiler, these two programs are exactly the same and will produce the same results. However, to people who must read the program, the first style is *much* more readable. Granted, this is an extreme example.

Readability Is the Key

As long as programs do their job and produce correct output, who cares how well they are written? In today's world of fast computers, abundant memory, and disk space, you should care. Even if nobody else will ever look at your C++ program, you might need to make a change to it at a later date. The more readable you make it, the faster you will be able to find what needs changing and make those changes.

If you work as a programmer for a company, you will almost certainly be expected to modify someone else's source code, and others will modify your programs. In programming departments, it is said that long-term employees write readable programs. Given this new global economy, and all the changes that face businesses in the years ahead, companies are seeking programmers who write for the future; that is, their programs are straightforward, readable, contain lots of white space (separating lines and spaces), and don't include hard-to-read programming tricks that make for messy programs.

Put lots of *white space* in your programs. As noted, white space consists of the separating lines and spaces throughout a program. Notice that the first few lines in C4FIRST.CPP start in the first column, but the body of the program is indented a few spaces. This helps programmers "zero in" on the important code. When you write programs that contain several sections (called *blocks*), white space helps the programmer's eye drop down more easily to the next indented block.

Using Uppercase and Lowercase

Use lowercase abundantly in C++!

Your uppercase and lowercase letters are much more significant in C++ than in most other programming languages. You will find that most of C4FIRST.CPP is in lowercase letters. The entire C++ language itself is in lowercase. For example, you must type the keywords `int`, `char`, and `return` in lowercase characters into your programs. If you used uppercase, your C++ compiler would produce many errors and refuse to compile the program until you fixed them. Appendix E shows a list of every single command in the C++ programming language. You will find that none of the commands are in uppercase letters.

Most C++ programmers reserve uppercase characters for some of the words and messages sent to the screen, printer, and disk files, and use lowercase letters for almost everything else. One exception is discussed in Chapter 7, "Preprocessor Directives," covering the `#define` preprocessor directive.

Braces and `main()`

All C++ programs require the following lines:

```
main()
     {
```

The statements following `main()` will be the first statements executed. The section of a C++ program that begins with `main()`, followed by an opening brace, `{`, is called the *main function*. A C++ program is actually a bunch of functions (small sections of code), and the function called `main()` is required and is always the first function executed.

A C++ block is enclosed between a pair of braces.

In the sample program shown here, almost the entire program is `main()` because the closing brace, `}`, that follows `main()`'s opening brace is at the end of the program. Everything between the two braces is called a *block*. You will read more about blocks later. For now, you should realize that this sample program contains only a single function, `main()`, and that the entire function is a single block because there is only one pair of braces.

All executable C++ statements must end with a semicolon (`;`).

In addition, you should realize that many statements have a semicolon (;) after them. Every executable C++ statement must be followed by a semicolon so that C++ will know where the statements end. The computer ignores all comments, so you don't need to put semicolons after comments. The lines with `main()` and braces do not end with semicolons either; these lines simply define the beginning and ending of the function and do not actually execute.

As you become better acquainted with C++, you will learn when to include the semicolon and when to leave it off. Many beginning C++ programmers learn quickly when semicolons are required. Your compiler will certainly let you know if you forget to include a semicolon where one is needed.

Figure 4.2 repeats the sample program and contains additional markings to help acquaint you with these new terms. Also included are a few other items that are described later in the chapter.

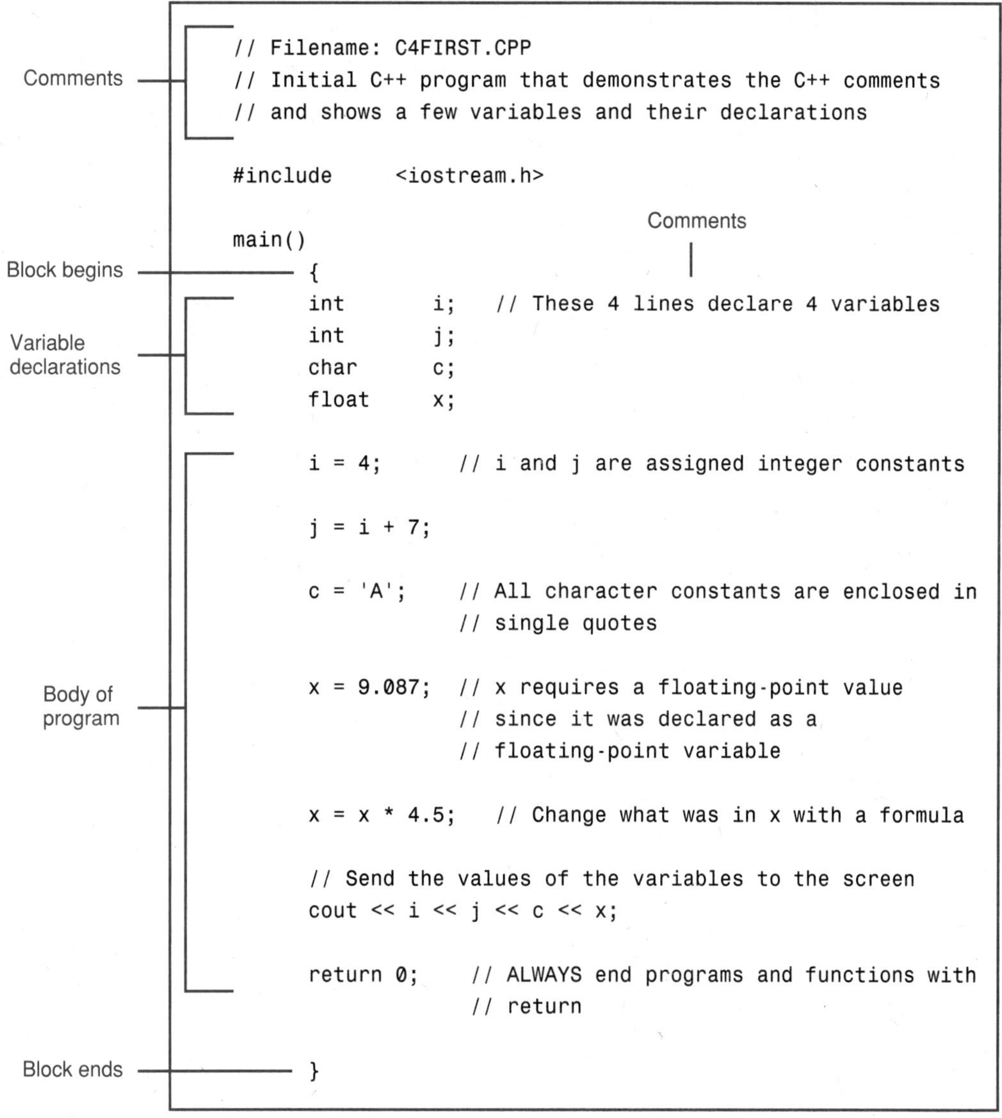
Comments
// Filename: C4FIRST.CPP
// Initial C++ program that demonstrates the C++ comments
// and shows a few variables and their declarations
#include <iostream.h>
Comments
main()
Block begins
{
Variable declarations
int i; // These 4 lines declare 4 variables
int j;
char c;
float x;
Body of program
i = 4; // i and j are assigned integer constants
j = i + 7;
c = 'A'; // All character constants are enclosed in
// single quotes
x = 9.087; // x requires a floating-point value
// since it was declared as a
// floating-point variable
x = x * 4.5; // Change what was in x with a formula
// Send the values of the variables to the screen
cout << i << j << c << x;
return 0; // ALWAYS end programs and functions with
// return
Block ends
}

Figure 4.2. The parts of the sample program.

Comments in C++

In Chapter 3, you learned the difference between a program and its output. Most users of a program do not see the program itself; they see the output from the execution of the program's instructions. Programmers, however, look at the program listings, add new routines, change old ones, and update for new advancements in computer equipment.

As explained earlier, the readability of a program is important so that you and other programmers can look through it without a lot of effort. Nevertheless, no matter how clearly you write C++ programs, you can always improve readability by putting *comments* throughout the program listings.

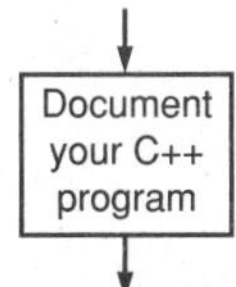

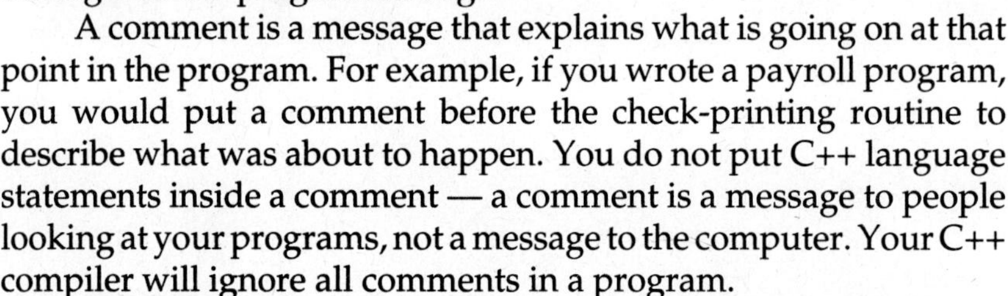

A comment is a message that explains what is going on at that point in the program. For example, if you wrote a payroll program, you would put a comment before the check-printing routine to describe what was about to happen. You do not put C++ language statements inside a comment — a comment is a message to people looking at your programs, not a message to the computer. Your C++ compiler will ignore all comments in a program.

Comments can span more than one line. Notice in the sample program, C4FIRST.CPP, that the first three lines are actually a single comment. This comment explains the filename and a little about the program.

Comments can also share lines with C++ commands. There are several comments out to the right of much of the C4FIRST.CPP program. These comments explain what the individual lines do. Use abundant comments but remember who they are for: *people, not computers.* Use comments if they help explain the code but do not *over*comment. For example, even though you may not be familiar with C++ yet, the following statement is easy; it prints `Turbo C++ By Example` on the screen:

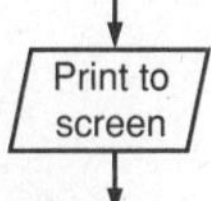


```
cout << "Turbo C++ By Example"; // Print Turbo C++ By
                                // Example on the screen
```

Comments describe to people what the program is doing.

This comment is redundant and adds nothing to the understanding of the line of code. It would be much better in this case to leave the comment out completely. If you find yourself almost repeating the C++ code, leave out that particular comment. Not every line of a C++ program should be commented. Comment only when a line or group of lines needs explaining, in English terms, to the people looking at the program.

If a comment does not span more than one line in your program file, you can start the comment with `//`. The comment is read from the `//` to the end of the line. If the comment does span more than one line, you can either start each subsequent line with a `//`, or you can wrap the comment by starting it with `/*` and ending it with `*/`. The following example shows the use of `/*` and `*/` as comments:

```
/* Print Turbo C++ By Example
   on the screen */
cout << "Turbo C++ By Example";
```

NOTE: C++ comments usually begin with the `//` symbol.

Of course, it does not matter if you use uppercase letters, lowercase letters, or a mix of both in comments because C++ ignores comments. Most C++ programmers capitalize the first letter of sentences in comments, just as they would in everyday writing. Since people, not computers, read comments, use whatever case seems most appropriate to the message in the comment.

CAUTION: C++ comments cannot be nested. That is, you cannot put a comment within another comment. If you do, the C++ compiler will get confused when it sees the first comment end in the middle of the second one.

The following section of a C++ program is illegal because one comment resides within another:

```
sales = 3456.54 * bonus;
// This is an example of a C++ program
   // It does NOT
      comment correctly!
   The first comment did not end before the second began.
```

This sometimes confuses programmers who are just learning C++ but who know another programming language. In C++, you cannot comment out large sections of code just by inserting `//` at the beginning of the section if *any* lines within that section have comments on them. Sometimes programmers like to comment out several lines in a program so that the lines do not execute. This lets the programmer test the remaining lines independently of those commented out. If you were to try this, and nested comments result, your compiler would get confused.

Comment As You Go

Put comments in your programs *as you write them*. You are most familiar with your program logic at the time you are typing the program in the editor. Some people put off including comments until after the program is written. More often than not, the comments never get put in, or only a half-hearted attempt is made.

If you comment as you write your code, you can glance up at the comments while working on later sections of the program, instead of having to decipher the previous code. This greatly helps when you want to look at something earlier in the program.

Examples

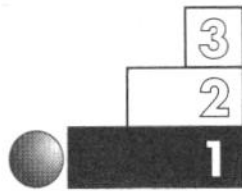

1. Suppose that you want to write a C++ program to produce a fancy, boxed title with your name and flashing dots around it (like a marquee). The C++ code to do this may be difficult to understand and may not, by itself, be understandable to others who look at the program. Before such code, you might want to insert the following comment:

```
// The following few lines draw a fancy box around
// a name and then display flashing dots around the
// name to look like a Hollywood movie marquee.
```

This would not tell C++ to do anything, because a comment is not a C++ command. The comment would, however, make the next few lines of code more understandable to you and others. The comment explains in English, for the people reading the program, exactly what the program is getting ready to do.

2. You should put the disk filename of the program in an early comment. For example, in the C4FIRST.CPP program shown earlier, the first line is the beginning of a comment:

```
// Filename: C4FIRST.CPP
```

The comment continues on the next two lines, but this part of it explains to anyone who might look at the program listing exactly which disk file it is in. Throughout this book, each program has a comment that includes a suggested filename under which the program can be stored. Each filename begins with C*x*, where *x* is the chapter number in which the program appears—for example, C6VARPR.CPP and C10LNIN.CPP. This will help you find the programs in case another section of the book refers to them later.

TIP: It also may be a good idea to put your name in a comment at the top of a program. If someone has to modify your program at a later date, that person may need to speak with you, the original programmer, before changing it.

The Sample Program Summarized

Now that you have an overview of a C++ program, its structure, and its comments, the rest of this chapter walks you through the entire sample program. Do not attempt to become a C++ expert after you complete this section—that is what the rest of the book is for! Just sit back and follow the discussion of the code.

As described earlier, the C4FIRST.CPP program contains several comments. The first three lines of the program are

```
// Filename: C4FIRST.CPP
// Initial CPP program that demonstrates the C++ comments
// and shows a few variables and their declarations
```

This comment gives the filename and explains the purpose of the program. This is not the only comment in the program; others appear throughout the rest of the code.

The next line is the `#include` preprocessor directive:

```
#include     <iostream.h>
```

The next two lines (following the blank separating line) are

```
main()
    {
```

This begins the `main()` function. Basically, the `main()` function's opening and closing braces enclose the body of this program and the instructions that actually execute. Many times, C++ programs contain more than one function, but they always contain one called `main()`. The `main()` function does not have to be the first one, but it usually is. The opening brace begins the first and only block of this program.

When this program is compiled and run, the computer looks for `main()` and starts executing whatever instruction follows `main()`'s opening brace. Here are the next four lines:

```
int      i;     // These 4 lines declare 4 variables
int      j;
char     c;
float    x;
```

These four lines declare variables. A *variable declaration* describes all variables used in that block of code. A C++ program takes data and processes it into meaningful results. All C++ programs include the following:

- ♦ Commands
- ♦ Data

The data is made up of *variables* and *constants*. As the name implies, a *variable* is data that can change (it is *variable*) as the program runs. A *constant* remains the same. In real life, a variable might be your age or salary. Both increase over time (if you are lucky!). Your first name and social security number are constants because they remain with you throughout your life and do not change.

Chapter 5, "Variables and Constants," fully explains these concepts. However, just for an overview of the sample program's elements, the following discussion explains variables and constants in this program.

C++ allows several kinds of constants. For now, you simply need to understand that a C++ constant is any number, character, word, or phrase. All the following are valid C++ constants:

```
5.6     -45     'Q'     "Mary"  18.67643     0.0
```

As you can see, some constants are numeric, and some are character-based. The single and double quotation marks around two of the constants are not part of the constants themselves. A single-character constant requires single quotes around it, whereas a string of characters, such as `"Mary"` requires double quotes.

If you look for the constants in the sample program, you will find the following:

```
4       7       'A'     9.087   4.5
```

A variable is like a box inside your computer that holds something. That something might be a number or character. You can have as many variables as your program needs in order to hold data that changes in the program. Once you put a value into a variable, it stays in that variable until you change it or put something else in it.

Variables have names so that you can tell them apart. You use the *assignment operator*, the equal sign (=), to assign values to variables. The statement

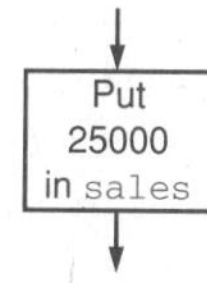


```
sales = 25000;
```

puts the constant value `25000` into the variable named `sales`. In the sample program, you will find the following variables:

```
i      j      c      x
```

The four lines of code that follow the opening brace of the sample program declare these variables. This variable declaration lets the rest of the program know that two integer variables named `i` and `j`, as well as a character variable called `c` and a floating-point variable called `x`, will appear throughout the program. If the terms *integer* and *floating point* are new to you, they are basically two different types of numbers. Integers are whole numbers, and floating-point numbers contain decimal points.

You can see the variables being assigned values in the next few statements in the sample program:

```
i = 4;        //   i and j are assigned integer constants

j = i + 7;

c = 'A';      //   All character constants are enclosed in
              //   single quotes

x = 9.087;    //   x requires a floating-point value
              //   since it was declared as a
              //   floating-point variable

x = x * 4.5;  // Change what was in x with a formula
```

The first line puts a 4 in the integer variable `i`. The second line adds a 7 to the variable `i`'s value to get an 11, which then gets assigned to (put into) the variable called `j`. The plus sign (+) in C++ works the same as on calculators. The other primary math operators are shown in Table 4.1.

Table 4.1. The primary math operators.

Operator	*Meaning*	*Example*
+	Addition	`4 + 5`
-	Subtraction	`7 - 2`
*	Multiplication	`12 * 6`
/	Division	`48 / 12`

The character constant `A` is assigned to the `c` variable. The number 9.087 is assigned to the variable called `x`, and then `x` is immediately overwritten with a new value: itself (9.087) times 4.5. This helps illustrate why computer designers use an asterisk (`*`) for multiplication and not a small *x* as people do when multiplying. The computer would confuse the variable `x` with the multiplication symbol *x* if both were allowed.

TIP: If there are mathematical operators on the right side of the equal sign, the math is completely done before the assignment is performed.

The next line (after the comment) includes the following special, and at first confusing, statement:

```
cout << i << j << c << x;
```

When the program runs and gets to this line, it prints the contents of the four variables to the screen.

The actual output from this line is

```
4 11 A 40.891499
```

Because the `cout` is the only one in the program, this is the only output the program produces. You might think that the program is rather long for such a small line of output. Once you learn more about C++, you will see much more useful programs.

The `cout` is not a C++ command but is actually the name of the *console output stream*; the <<s are overloaded operators defined by the stream classes. You'll learn about classes in Chapter 31; for now, `cout`

is treated as if it were a function. The same applies to `cin`, which is the *console input stream.*

```
return 0;     // ALWAYS end programs and functions with
              // return
}
```

The `return` statement simply tells C++ that this function is finished and to return a value of zero to DOS.

Put a `return` statement at the end of each function.

The `return` statement is optional. C++ would know when it reached the end of the program without a `return`. It is a good programming practice, however, to put a `return` statement at the end of every function, including `main()`. Because some functions require a `return` statement (if you are returning values) but others do not, you will be better off learning the habit of using this statement instead of leaving one out when you really need it.

The closing brace after the `return` does three things in this program. It signals the end of a block (which was begun earlier with the opening brace), the end of the `main()` function, and the end of the program.

Summary

Now that you have a feel for what a C++ program looks like, it is time to begin considering the specifics of commands. This chapter focused on commenting your programs well. You also learned a little about variables and constants. The variables and constants hold the program's data; without them, the term *data processing* would no longer be meaningful.

Starting with the next chapter, you begin to write your own programs. Chapter 5 takes a detailed look at constants and variables, describes their uses, and explains how you choose names for them.

Review Questions

Answers to Review Questions are in Appendix B.

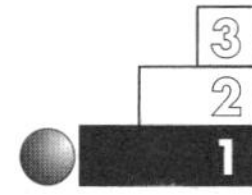

1. What must go before and after each multiline comment in a C++ program?
2. What is a variable?
3. What is a constant?

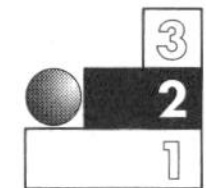

4. True or false: You can put a comment within another comment.
5. What are four C++ math operators?
6. What operator puts a value into a variable? (HINT: It is called the *assignment operator*.)

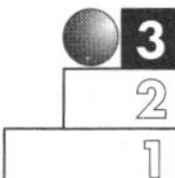

7. True or false: A variable can consist of only two types: integer and character.
8. What is the built-in function that writes output to the screen?
9. Is the following a variable name or a string constant?

```
city
```

10. What, if anything, is wrong with the following C statement?

```
RETURN;
```

Variables and Constants

To understand data processing with C++, you must understand how C++ creates, stores, and manipulates data. This chapter introduces the following topics:

- What variables and constants are
- Naming and using C++ variables
- The types of C++ variables
- Declaring variables
- Assigning values to variables
- The types of C++ constants
- Special constants

Now that you have an overview of C++, you can begin to write your own programs. Before you are done with this chapter, you will be writing your very own C++ programs from scratch.

Garbage in, garbage out!

You learned in the last chapter that C++ programs consist of commands and data. Data is the heart of all C++ programs; if you do not correctly declare or use variables and constants, your data will be inaccurate, and your results will be too. An old computer adage says that if you put "Garbage in, you will get garbage out!" This is very true. Most of the time, people blame computers for mistakes that are made. The computers themselves are probably not to blame, but the data was most likely entered into the programs incorrectly.

This chapter focuses on numeric variables and numeric constants. If you are not a "numbers" person, don't fret. Working with numbers is the computer's job. You just have to understand how to let the computer know what you want it to do.

Variable Characteristics

Variables have characteristics. When you decide that your program needs another variable, you simply declare a new variable, and C++ makes sure that you get it. You declare all C++ variables at the top of whatever block of code needs them. To declare a variable, you must understand its characteristics:

- Each variable has a name.
- Each variable has a type.
- A variable holds a value that you assign to it.

The following sections explain these characteristics.

Naming Variables

Because you can have many variables in a single program, you must assign names to them so that you can keep track of them. Variable names are unique, just as house addresses are unique. If two variables had the same name, C would not know which variable you wanted when you requested one of them.

Variable names can be as short as a single letter or as long as 31 characters. Their names must begin with a letter of the alphabet or an underscore (_). After the first letter or underscore, they can contain letters, numbers, and additional underscores.

TIP: The underscore (_) helps separate parts of the variable name because spaces are not allowed in the name.

The following variable names are valid:

```
salary   aug91_sales   _i   index_age   amount
```

It is traditional to use lowercase letters for C++ variable names. You do not have to follow this tradition, but you should know that uppercase letters in variable names are very different from lowercase letters. Therefore, each of the following four variables are completely different to your C++ compiler:

```
sales   Sales   SALES   sALES
```

Be very careful with the Shift key when you type a variable name. Do not inadvertently change the case of a variable name throughout a program; if you do, C++ will think that they are distinct and separate variables and will not operate on them properly.

Do not give a variable the name of a command or library function.

Variables cannot have the same name as a C++ command or library function. Appendix E shows a list of all C++ command names and library function names. Watch out for these when naming variables.

Here are some *invalid* variable names:

```
81_sales   Aug91+Sales   MY AGE   cout
```

Use Meaningful Variable Names

Although you can call a variable any name that fits the naming rules (as long as the name is not being used by another variable in the program), you should always use meaningful variable names. Use names that help describe the values held by the variables.

For example, keeping track of total payroll in a variable called `total_payroll` is more descriptive than using the variable name `XYZ34`. Even though both names are valid, `total_payroll` is easier to remember, and you have a good idea of what the variable holds by looking at its name.

Variable Types

Variables can hold different *types* of data. Table 5.1 lists the different types of C++ variables. For instance, if a variable holds an integer, C++ assumes that no decimal point or fractional part (the part to the right of the decimal point) exists for the variable's value. Many types are possible in C++. For now, the most important types that you should concentrate on are `char`, `int`, and `float`. You can append the prefix `long` to make some variables hold larger values than they would otherwise. Using the `unsigned` prefix lets them hold positive numbers only.

Table 5.1. Possible C++ variable types.

Declaration Name	*Type*
`char`	Character
`unsigned char`	Unsigned character
`signed char`	Signed character (same as `char`)
`int`	Integer
`unsigned int`	Unsigned integer
`signed int`	Signed integer (same as `int`)
`short int`	Short integer
`unsigned short int`	Unsigned short integer
`signed short int`	Signed short integer (same as `short int`)
`long`	Long integer
`long int`	Long integer (same as `long`)
`signed long int`	Signed long integer (same as `long int`)
`unsigned long int`	Unsigned long integer
`float`	Floating-point
`double`	Double floating-point
`long double`	Long double floating-point

Declare all variables in a C++ program before you use them.

The next section describes each of these types in more detail. For now, you need to concentrate on the importance of declaring them before using them. You can declare a variable in two places:

- After the opening brace of a block of code (usually at the top of a function)
- Before a function name, such as before `main()`

The first of these locations is the most common and is used throughout much this book. (If you declare a variable before a function name, the variable is called a *global* variable. Later chapters address the pros and cons of global variables.) To declare a variable, you must state its type followed by its name. In the last chapter, you saw a program that declared four variables in the following way.

Start of the `main()` *function.*
Declare the variables `i` *and* `j` *as integers.*
Declare the variable `c` *as a character.*
Declare the variable `x` *as a floating-point variable.*

```
main()
     {
     int        i;    // These 4 lines declare 4 variables
     int        j;
     char       c;
     float      x;
     // Rest of program follows
```

This declares two integer variables named `i` and `j`. You have no idea what is inside those variables, however. You generally cannot assume that a variable holds zero or any other number until you assign a value to the variable. The first two lines basically tell C++ the following:

> "I am going to use two integer variables somewhere in this program. Be expecting them. I want them named `i` and `j`. When I put a value into `i` or `j`, I will ensure that the value is an integer and not a floating-point number or anything else."

The third line in this example declares a character variable called `c`. Only single characters should be placed there. A floating-point variable called `x` is declared next.

Examples

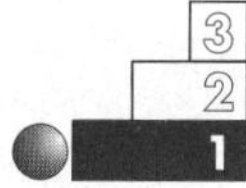

1. Suppose that you have to keep track of a person's first, middle, and last initials. Because an initial is obviously a character, it would be prudent to declare three character variables to hold the three initials. In C++, you can do that with the following statement:

```
main()
     {
     char      first, middle, last;
     // Rest of program follows
```

   This statement can go after the opening brace of `main()` and lets the rest of the program know that you will require these three character variables.

2. You can also declare these three variables on three separate lines, improving readability and maintainability:

```
main()
     {
     char      first;
     char      middle;
     char      last;
     // Rest of program follows
```

3. Suppose that you want to keep track of a person's age and weight. If you want to store these values as whole numbers, they can probably go into integer variables. The following statement declares these variables:

```
main()
     {
     int      age, weight;
     // Rest of program follows
```

4. The next section explores each of the variable types in detail. Despite the fact that there are so many types, you typically use character, integer, and floating-point variables more than any other. In short, character variables hold single characters, integer variables hold whole numbers, and floating-point variables hold numbers that contain decimal points.

   Suppose that a teacher wants to keep track of a class average score, the average letter grade, and the number of students in the class. Note how all three common types of variables are used here:

```
main()
     {
     char      letter_grade;
     float     class_avg;
     int       class_size;
     // Rest of program follows
```

Looking at Data Types

You may be wondering why it is important to have so many variable types. After all, a number is just a number. C++ has more data types than almost any other programming language. It turns out that the type of variable is very critical, but knowing what type to use is not as difficult as it may first seem.

The character variable is easy to understand. This variable can hold only a single character. You cannot put more than a single character into a character variable.

NOTE: C++ does not have a string variable, as do many other programming languages. You cannot hold more than a single character in a C++ character variable. To store a string of characters, you must use an *aggregate* variable type, which combines other fundamental types from Table 5.1, to create an array. Chapter 6, "Character Strings and Character Arrays," explains this more fully.

Integer variables hold whole numbers. Although mathematicians may cringe at this definition, an *integer* is really just any number that does not contain a decimal point. All the following are integers:

```
45      -932   0      12      5421
```

Floating-point numbers contain decimal points. They are known as *real* numbers to mathematicians. Whenever you need to store a salary, a temperature, or any other number that may have a fractional part (a decimal portion), you must store the number in a floating-point variable. All the following are floating-point numbers, and any of the floating-point variables can hold them:

```
45.12   -2344.5432    0.00    .04594
```

Sometimes you have to keep track of very large numbers or very small numbers. Table 5.2 shows a list of ranges that each C++ variable type might hold. *Use this table only as a guide*; different compilers and different computers may allow for different ranges.

Table 5.2. Typical ranges that C++ variables hold.

Type	*Range*
`char`	–128 to 128
`unsigned char`	0 to 255
`signed char`	–128 to 127
`int`	–32768 to 32767
`unsigned int`	0 to 65535
`signed int`	–32768 to 32767
`short int`	–32768 to 32767
`unsigned short int`	0 to 65535
`signed short int`	–32768 to 32767
`long int`	–2147483648 to 2147483647
`signed long int`	–2147483648 to 2147483647
`unsigned long int`	0 to 4294967295

Type	*Range*
`float`	–3.4E+38 to 3.4E+38
`double`	–1.7E+308 to 1.7E+308
`long double`	–1.7E+308 to 1.7E+308

Note: The floating-point ranges are shown in scientific notation. To determine the actual range, take the number before the E (meaning exponent) and multiply it by 10 raised to the power after the plus sign. For instance, a floating-point number (a type `float`) can contain a number as small as $-3.4 * 10^{38}$.

CAUTION: All true C++ programmers know that they cannot count on using this exact table on every computer that uses C++. These ranges may be much different on another computer. Remember to use this table only as a guide.

Notice that long integers and long doubles tend to hold larger numbers (and therefore higher precision) than regular integers and regular double floating-point variables. This is true because of the larger number of memory locations used by many of the C++ compilers for these data types. Again, you cannot count on this always being the case, but it generally is.

Use Variables That Accommodate the Size of the Data

If the long variable types hold larger numbers than the regular ones, you might initially want to use long variables for all your data. This is not required in most cases and will slow down your program's execution.

> As Appendix A explains, the more memory locations used by data, the larger that data can be. However, every time your computer has to access more storage for a single variable (which is usually the case for long variables), the CPU takes much longer to access it, calculate with it, and store it. As designed by Kernighan and Ritchie, the basic data types (`char`, `int`, and `float`) should be optimized for the computer, and in Turbo C++, they are.
>
> Use long variables only if you suspect your data will overflow the typical data type ranges. Although the ranges will vary on other computers, you should have an idea of whether your numbers may exceed the computer's storage ranges. If you are working with extremely large numbers (or extremely small and fractional numbers), consider using long variables so that they hold the extra data width.

Generally, all numeric variables should be signed (the default) unless you know for certain that your data will contain only positive numbers. Some values, such as age and distance, are always positive. Other data can be negative. By making a variable an unsigned variable, you gain a little extra storage range (as explained in Appendix A), but that extra range of values must always be positive.

Obviously, you must be aware of what kinds of data your variables will hold. You certainly do not always know exactly what all of them will hold, but you will have a general idea. For example, if you want to store a person's age, you know that a long integer variable would probably be a waste of space because nobody would live longer than a regular integer could hold.

At first, it may seem strange that Table 5.2 states that character variables can hold numeric values. In C++, integers and character variables can be used interchangeably in many cases. As explained in Appendix A, each of the ASCII table characters has a unique number that corresponds to the character's location in the table. If you store a number in a character variable, C++ will actually treat the data as if it were the ASCII character which matched that number in the table. Conversely, you can store character data in an integer variable. C++ will find that character's ASCII number and store it instead of the character. Examples that help illustrate this appear a little later in this chapter.

Designating Long, Unsigned, and Floating-Point Constants

When you type a number, C++ interprets its type as the smallest type that can hold the number. For example, if you type `63`, C++ knows that this number will fit into a signed integer memory location. C++ will not treat the number as a long integer because 63 is not large enough to warrant a long integer constant size.

You can, however, append a suffix character to numeric constants to override the default type. If you put an `L` at the end of an integer, C++ interprets that integer as a long integer. The number `63` is an integer constant, whereas the number `63L` is a long integer constant.

Assign the `U` suffix to designate an unsigned integer constant. The number `63` is, by default, a signed integer constant. If, however, you type `63U`, C++ treats it as an unsigned integer. The suffix `UL` indicates an unsigned long constant.

C++ interprets all floating-point constants (numbers that contain decimal points) as double floating-point constants. This ensures the maximum accuracy in such numbers. If you used the constant `6.82`, C++ treats it as a double floating-point data type, even though it would fit in a regular float. You can append the floating-point suffix, `F`, or the long double floating-point suffix, `L`, to constants that contain decimal points in order to represent either a floating-point constant or a long double floating-point constant instead of the default double constant value.

You may rarely use these suffixes, but if you have to assign a constant value to an extended or unsigned variable, you may gain a little more accuracy if you append the `U`, `L`, `UL`, or `F` (their lowercase equivalents work too) at the end of the constant.

Assigning Values to Variables

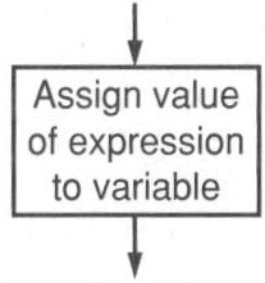

Now that you know about the C++ variable types, you are ready to learn how to put values into those variables. You do this with the *assignment* statement. The equal sign (=) is used for assigning values to variables. The format of the assignment statement is

```
variable = expression;
```

The `variable` is any variable you declared earlier. The `expression` is any variable, constant, expression, or combination that produces a resulting data type which is the same as the `variable`'s data type.

> **TIP:** Think of the equal sign (=) as a left-pointing arrow. Loosely, the equal sign means that you want to take whatever number, variable, or expression is on the right side of the equal sign and put it into the variable on the left side of the equal sign.

Examples

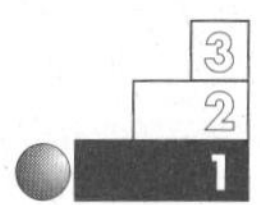

1. If you want to keep track of your current age, salary, and dependents, you can store these values in three C++ variables. You first declare the variables by deciding on correct types and good names for them. You then assign values to them. Later in the program, these values may change — for example, if the program calculates a new pay increase for you.

   Good variable names are `age`, `salary`, and `dependents`. To declare these three variables, the first part of the `main()` function might look like this:

```
// Declare and store three values
main()
     {
     int       age;
     float     salary;
     int       dependents;
```

Notice that you do not have to declare all integer variables together, but you can if you want to. Once these variables are declared, the next three statements can assign them values, as in

```
age = 32;
salary = 25000.00;
dependents = 2;
```

Note that this program is not complete. After these assignment statements come other statements and then a closing brace.

2. The preceding example is not very long, and it does not do much. It does, however, illustrate using values and assigning them to variables. Do not put commas in values you assign to variables. Numeric constants should *never* contain commas. The following statement is *invalid*:

```
salary = 25,000.00;
```

3. You can assign variables to other variables, or mathematical expressions to other variables. Suppose that you stored your tax rate in a variable called `tax_rate` earlier in a program, and you decide to use your tax rate for your spouse's rate as well. At the proper point in the program, you can code the following:

```
spouse_tax_rate = tax_rate;
```

Putting the spaces around the equal sign is okay with the C++ compiler, but you do not have to include them. Use whatever is more comfortable for you.

The value in `tax_rate` will, at this line's point in the program, be copied to a new variable named `spouse_tax_rate`. The value in `tax_rate` will still be there after this line finishes. Of course, an assumption is that the variables were declared earlier in the program.

If your spouse's tax rate is going to be 40 percent of yours, you can assign an expression to the spouse's variables, as in

```
spouse_tax_rate = tax_rate * .40;
```

Any of the four mathematical symbols you learned in the last chapter, as well as all those you will learn later in this book, can be part of the expression you assign to a variable.

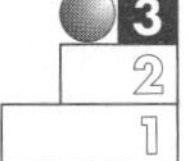

4. If you want to assign character data to a character variable, you must enclose the character in single quote marks. All C++ character constants must be enclosed in single quote marks.

   The following section of a program declares three initial variables and then assigns three initials to them. The initials are character constants because they are enclosed within single quotes.

```
main()
     {
     char     first, middle, last;
     first = 'G';
     middle = 'M';
     last = 'P';
     // Rest of program follows
```

   Of course, you can later put other values into these variables if the program warrants it.

CAUTION: Do not mix types. In most cases, C++ will let you, but the results are unpredictable. For instance, you could have stored a floating-point constant in `middle`, as shown here:

```
middle = 345.43244;    // Do not do this!
```

If you did so, `middle` would hold a strange value that seems to be meaningless garbage. Make sure that values you assign to variables match the variable's type. The only major exception to this occurs when you assign an integer to a character variable, or a character to an integer variable, as you will see shortly.

5. C++ gives you the ability to declare *and* initialize variables with values at the same time. For example, the following section of code declares an integer `age`, a floating-point `salary`, and three character variables, and initializes them at the time of declaration:

```
main()
     {
     int       age = 30;
     float     salary = 25000.00;
     char      first = 'G', middle = 'M', last = 'P';
     // Rest of program follows
```

   This is a little easier than first declaring them and then initializing them with values. As the preceding chapter discussed, `cout` is used to print the values of variables and constants. Chapter 8, "Simple Input and Output," explains `cout` in more detail. Just as a preview, the following `cout` statements will print the variables declared in the preceding section of code:

```
cout << age << ' ' << salary << ' ';
cout << first << ' ' << middle << ' ' << last;
```

   Putting all of these together into one commented program (albeit a short one), produces the following code:

```
// Filename: C5VAR.CPP
// Program that initializes and prints five variables

#include  <iostream.h>

main()
     {
     int     age = 30;
     float   salary = 25000.00;
     char    first = 'G', middle = 'M', last = 'P';

     cout << age << ' ' << salary << ' ';
     cout << first << ' ' << middle << ' ' << last;
     return 0;
     }
```

If you were to compile and run this program, you would see the following output:

```
30 25000 G M P
```

The numbers are not formatted very well (especially `salary`), but you will soon see how to produce output that looks the way you want it to look.

Special Constants

As with variables, C++ has several types of constants. Remember that a constant does not change. Integer constants are whole numbers that do not contain decimal points. Floating-point constants are numbers that contain a fractional portion (a decimal point with an optional value to the right of the decimal point).

Special Integer Constants

You already know that an integer is any whole number without a decimal point. C++ lets you assign integer constants to variables, use integer constants for calculations, and print integer constants with `cout`.

An octal integer constant contains a leading `0`, and a hexadecimal constant contains a leading `0x`.

A regular integer constant cannot begin with a leading `0`. To C++, the number `012` is *not* the number twelve. If you precede an integer constant with a leading `0`, C++ thinks that it is an *octal* constant. An octal constant is a base-8 number. The octal numbering system is not used much in today's computer systems. The newer versions of C++ retain octal capabilities for compatibility with previous versions when octal played a more important role in computers.

Another special integer that is possible in C++ *is* still greatly used today. It is a base-16 or *hexadecimal* constant. Appendix A describes the hexadecimal numbering system. If you want to represent a hexadecimal integer constant, append the 0x prefix to it. In other words, all the following numbers are hexadecimal numbers:

```
0x10   0x2C4   0xFFFF  0X9
```

Notice that it does not matter if you use a lowercase `x` or an uppercase `X` after the leading zero, or a lowercase or an uppercase hexadecimal digit (for hex numbers `A` through `F`). If you write business application programs in C++, you might think that you'll never have the need for using hexadecimal, and you might be correct. However, for a complete understanding of C++, and your computer in general, you should be familiar with the fundamentals of hexadecimal numbers.

Table 5.3 shows a few integer constants represented in their regular decimal, hexadecimal, and octal notations. Each row contains the same number in all three bases.

Table 5.3. Integer constants represented in three different bases.

Base-10 Decimal	*Base-16 Hexadecimal*	*Base-8 Octal*
8	0x08	010
10	0x0A	012
16	0x10	020
65536	0x10000	0200000
25	0x19	031

NOTE: Floating-point constants may begin with a leading zero. They will be properly interpreted by C++ because only integers are possible hexadecimal and octal constants.

Your Computer's Word Size Is Important

If you write many system programs that use hexadecimal numbers, you will probably want to store those numbers in unsigned variables. This keeps C++ from improperly interpreting positive numbers as negative ones.

For example, your computer stores integers in two-byte words. The hexadecimal constant `0xFFFF` represents either –1 or 65535, depending on how the sign bit is interpreted. If you declare an unsigned integer, such as

```
unsigned int i_num = 0xFFFF;
```

C++ knows that you want it to use the sign bit as data and not as the sign. If, however, you declare the same value as a signed integer, as in

```
int i_num = 0xFFFF;     // The word "signed" is optional
```

C++ thinks that this is a negative number (–1) because the sign bit is turned on (if you were to convert `0xFFFF` to binary, you would get 16 ones). Appendix A describes these concepts in more detail.

String Constants

A string constant is always enclosed in double quotes.

One type of C++ constant, called the *string constant*, does not have a matching variable. A string constant is *always* enclosed within double quote marks. Here are examples of string constants:

```
"C++ Programming"    "123"    " "     "4323 E. Oak Road"     "x"
```

Any string of characters between double quotes, as well as single characters between double quotes, is considered to be a string constant. A single space, word, or group of words between double quotes is a C++ string constant. If the string constant contains only numeric digits, it is *not* a number, but a string of numeric digits that you cannot perform math with. You can perform math with numbers only—not with string constants that contain numbers, or even a character constant that might contain a number (enclosed in a single quote).

> **NOTE:** A string constant is *any* character, digit, or group of characters enclosed in double quotes. A character constant is any character enclosed in single quotes.

The double quotes are never considered part of the string constant. The double quotes surround the string and simply inform your C++ compiler that the constant is a string constant, not some other type of constant.

You can print string constants easily. Simply put the string constants in a `cout` call, as in the following line.

Print `Turbo C++ By Example` *to the screen.*

```
cout << "Turbo C++ By Example";
```

Examples

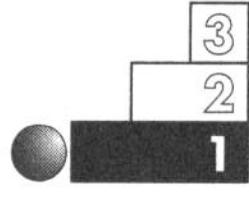

1. The following program displays a simple message to the screen. No variables are needed because no data is stored or calculated.

```
// Filename: C5ST1.CPP
// Displays a string on the screen

#include  <iostream.h>

main()
     {
     cout << "C++ programming is fun!";
     return 0;
     }
```

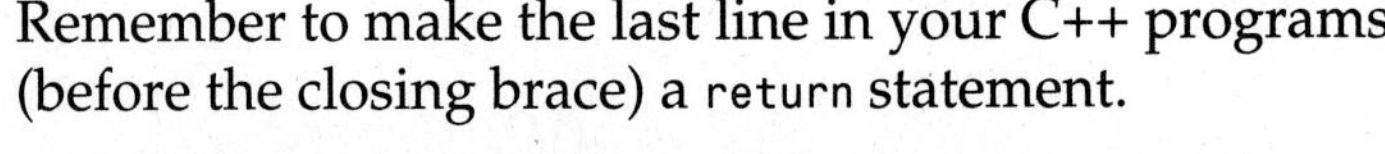

Remember to make the last line in your C++ programs (before the closing brace) a `return` statement.

2. You will want to label the output from your programs. Do not print the value of a variable unless you also print a string constant that describes the variable. The following program computes sales tax for a sale and then prints the tax. Notice that a message is printed first, which tells the user of the program what the next number means.

BEGIN → Compute sales tax → Print sales tax on screen → END

```
// Filename: C5ST2.CPP
// Computes sales tax and with an appropriate message

#include      <iostream.h>

main()
     {
     float     sale, tax;
     float     tax_rate = .08;      // Sales tax percentage

     // Determine the amount of the sale
     sale = 22.54;

     // Compute the sales tax
     tax = sale * tax_rate;

     // Print the results
     cout << "The sales tax is: " << tax;

     return 0;
     }
```

The Tail of String Constants

An additional aspect of string constants sometimes confuses beginning C++ programmers. All string constants end with a zero. You do not see the zero, but C++ makes sure that the zero is stored at the end of the string in memory. Figure 5.1 shows what the string "C++ Program" looks like in memory.

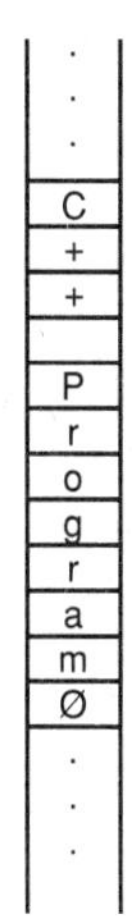

Figure 5.1. A string constant always ends with a zero in memory.

You do not have to worry about putting the zero at the end of a string constant; C++ does this for you whenever it stores a string. If your program were to contain the string "C++ Program", the compiler would recognize it as a string constant (from the double quotes) and store the zero at the end.

The zero, called the *string delimiter*, is important to C++. Without this delimiter, C++ would not know where the string constant ended in memory. (Remember that the double quotes are not stored as part of the string, so C++ cannot use them to determine where the string ends.)

All string constants end in a null zero, sometimes called the binary zero or ASCII zero.

The string-delimiting zero is *not* the same as a character zero. If you look at the ASCII table in Appendix C, you will see that the first entry, ASCII number 0, is the *null* character. This is actually what delimits strings in C++: the null, ASCII zero. (If you are unfamiliar with the ASCII table, read Appendix A for a review.) Sometimes you will hear that C++ string constants end in *ASCII 0*, or the *null zero*. This differentiates the string-delimiting zero from the character `'0'`, whose ASCII value is 48.

As explained in Appendix A, all memory locations in your computer hold bit patterns for characters. If the letter A is stored in memory, an A is not really there, but the binary bit pattern for the ASCII A (01000001) is stored there. Because the binary bit pattern for the null zero is 00000000, the string-delimiting zero is also called a *binary zero.*

To illustrate this concept further, Figure 5.2 shows the bit patterns for the following string constant when stored in memory:

```
"I am 30."
```

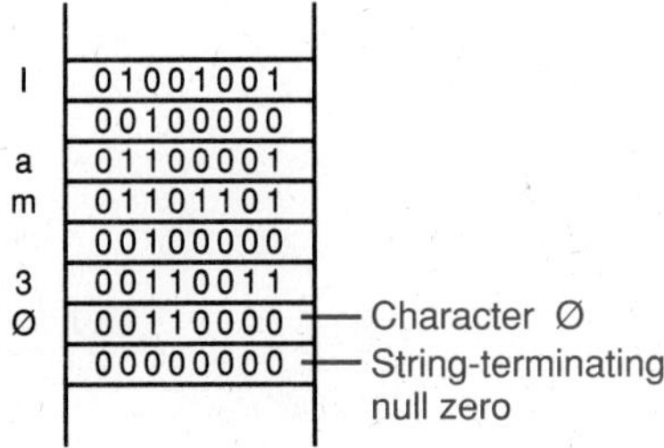

Figure 5.2. **The bit pattern showing the difference between the null zero and the character zero.**

This concept is fairly advanced, but you need to understand it before you continue. If you are new to computers, you should read Appendix A. Figure 5.2 shows how a string is stored in your computer's memory at the binary level. It is important for you to recognize that the character 0 inside the number 30 is not the same zero (at the bit level) as the string-terminating null zero. If it were, C++ would think that this string ended early (after the 3), which is incorrect.

The Length of Strings

Many times, your program needs to know the length of a string. This will become critical when you learn how to accept string input from the keyboard.

NOTE: The length of a string is the number of characters up to, but not including, the delimiting null zero.

In other words, when you need to know how long a string constant is, or when you need to tell C++ how long it is (as you will see a little later), you need to count the number of characters in the string. Do not include the null character in that count, even though you know that C++ will add it to the end of the string.

Examples

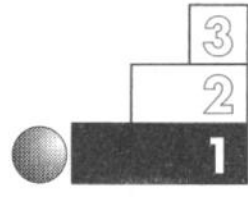

1. Here are some string constants:

```
"0"     "C++"   "A much longer string constant"
```

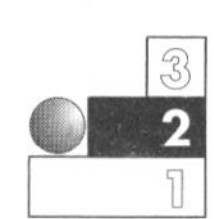

2. Note these string constants and their corresponding string lengths:

String	*Length*
`"C++"`	1
`"0"`	1
`"Hello"`	5
`""`	0
`"30 oranges"`	10

Special Character Constants

All C++ character constants should be enclosed within single quotes. The single quotes are not part of the character, but they serve to delimit it. All the following are valid C++ character constants:

```
'w'     'W'     'C'     '7'     '*'     '='     '.'     'K'
```

C++ does not append a null zero to the end of character constants. Be aware that the following constants are very different to C++:

```
'R'     "R"
```

The first `'R'` is a single character constant. It is one character long, as *all* character constants (and variables) are one character long. The second `"R"` is a string constant because it is delimited by double quotes. Its length is also one, but it includes an extra null zero in memory so that C++ knows where the string ends. Because of this difference, you cannot mix character constants and character strings. Figure 5.3 shows how these two constants are stored in memory.

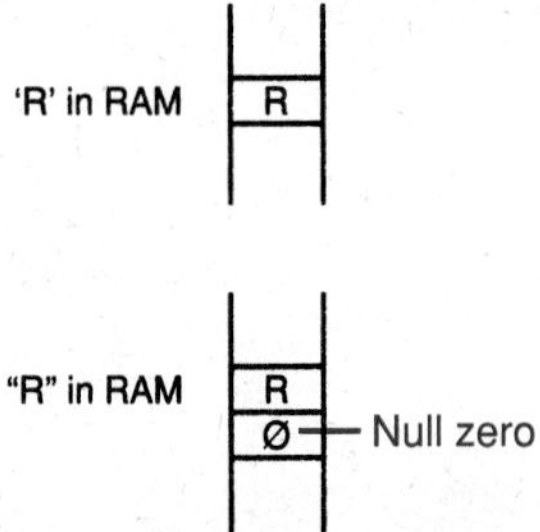

Figure 5.3. The character constant `'R'` and the string constant `"R"` stored in memory.

All the alphabetic, numeric, and special characters on your keyboard can be character constants. There are some characters, however, that cannot be represented with your keyboard. These include some of the higher ASCII characters, such as the Spanish Ñ. Because you do not have keys for every character in the ASCII table, C++ provides a way for you to represent these characters by typing the character's ASCII hex number inside the single quotes.

For example, to store the Spanish Ñ in a variable, look up its hexadecimal ASCII number in Appendix C. You will find that it is A5. Append the prefix `\x` to it and enclose it in single quotes. Then C++ will know to use the special character. You can do this with the following code:

```
char sn='\xA5';        // Puts the Spanish N into the variable
                       // called sn
```

This is the way to store (or print) any character from the ASCII table, even if the character does not have a key on your keyboard.

The single quote marks still tell C++ that a *single* character is inside the quotes. Even though `'\xA5'` contains four characters inside the quotes, those four characters represent a single character, not a character string. If you were to include these four characters inside a string constant, C++ would treat them as a single character within the string. The string constant

```
"An accented a is \xA0"
```

is a C++ string that is 18 characters long. C++ will interpret the `\xA0` character as the á, just as it should.

> **CAUTION:** If you are familiar with entering ASCII characters by typing their ASCII numbers with the Alt-*number* key (from the keypad), do not use this method in your C++ programs. Although the Turbo C++ compiler supports the method, your program might not be portable to another C++ compiler.

Any character interpreted with a backslash (\), such as those in this discussion, are called *escape sequences* or *escape characters*. Table 5.4 shows some additional escape sequences that come in handy when you want to print special characters.

Table 5.4. Special C++ escape sequence characters.

Escape Sequence	*Meaning*
`\a`	Alarm (the terminal's bell)
`\b`	Backspace
`\f`	Formfeed (for the printer)
`\n`	Newline (carriage return and linefeed)
`\r`	Carriage return
`\t`	Tab
`\v`	Vertical tab
`\\`	Backslash (\)
`\?`	Question mark
`\'`	Single quote
`\"`	Double quote

Table 5.4. Continued.

Escape Sequence	*Meaning*
`\ooo`	Octal number
`\xhh`	Hexadecimal number
`\0`	The null zero (or binary zero)

TIP: Include `\n` in a `cout` if you want it to skip to the next line.

Math with C++ Characters

Because C++ links characters so closely with their ASCII numbers, you can actually perform arithmetic on character data. Note the following section of code:

```
char c;
c = 'T' + 5;      // Add 5 to the ASCII character
```

This actually stores a Y in `c`. The ASCII value of the letter T is 84. Adding 5 to 84 produces 89. Because the variable `c` is not an integer variable but is a character variable, C++ knows to put the ASCII character for 89 in `c` and not the number itself.

Conversely, you can store character constants in integer variables. If you do, C++ actually stores the matching ASCII number for that character. Note this section of code:

```
int i = 'P';
```

This does *not* put a letter P in `i`, because `i` is not a character variable. C++ assigns the number 80 to the variable, as 80 is the ASCII number for the letter P.

Examples

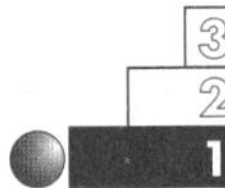

1. To print two names on two different lines, you include `\n` between them.

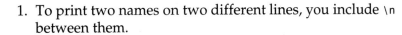

Print `Harry` *to the screen, drop cursor down to newline, and print* `Jerry`.

```
cout << "Harry" << '\n' << "Jerry";
```

When the program gets to this line, it prints

```
Harry
Jerry
```

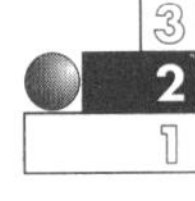

2. The following short program rings the bell on your computer because the program assigns the `\a` escape sequence to a variable and then prints that variable:

BEGIN
Store bell character
Print bell character
END

```
// Filename: C5BELL.CPP
// Rings the bell

#include  <iostream.h>

main()
     {
     char     bell='\a';

     cout << bell;
     return 0;
     }
```

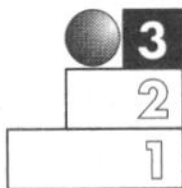

3. Without these escape sequences, you would have no way to print double quote marks. Because double quote marks delimit strings, C++ would think that the string you were printing ended too early. The backslash and single quote cannot print regularly either; C++ interprets the backslash as an escape sequence prefix, and the single quote as a

character constant delimiter. Therefore, the three escape sequences `\"`, `\\`, and `\'` let you print these characters as the following program shows:

```
// Filename: C5SPEC2.CPP
// Prints quotes and a backslash

#include  <iostream.h>

main()
     {
     cout << "Albert said, \"I will be going now.\" \n";
     cout << "The backslash character looks like this: \\ \n";
     cout << "I\'m learning C++ \n";
     return 0;
     }
```

The `\n` is included to send the cursor to the next line after each `cout`. The output from this program looks like this:

```
Albert said, "I will be going now."
The backslash character looks like this: \
I'm learning C++
```

Summary

A firm grasp of C++'s foundation is critical to covering the material in more detail. This is one of the last general-topic chapters in this book. You learned about variable types and constant types, how to name variables, and how to assign values to them. These issues are important to your understanding of the rest of C++.

This chapter showed you how to store in variables almost every type of constant. There is no string variable, so you cannot store string constants in string variables, as you can in other programming languages. However, you can "fool" C++ into thinking that it has a string variable by using a character array to hold strings. The next chapter teaches this important concept.

Review Questions

Answers to Review Questions are in Appendix B.

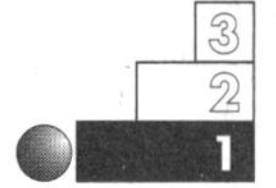

1. Which of the following variable names are valid?

```
my_name          89_sales          sales_89          a-salary
```

2. Which of the following constants are characters, strings, integers, and floating-point constants?

```
0     -12.0     "2.0"     "X"     'X'     65.4     -708     '0'
```

3. How many variables do the following statements declare, and what are their types?

```
int        i, j, k;
char       c, d, e;
float      x = 65.43;
```

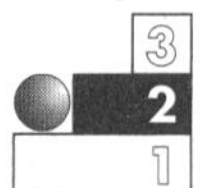

4. What do all string constants end with?

5. True or false: An unsigned variable can hold a larger value than a signed variable.

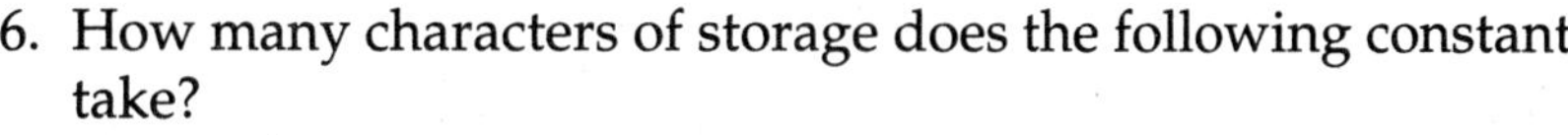

6. How many characters of storage does the following constant take?

```
'\x41'
```

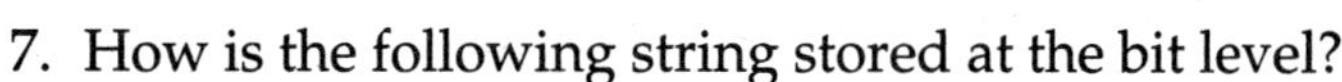

7. How is the following string stored at the bit level?

```
"Order 10 of them."
```

8. How is the following string (called a *null string*) stored at the bit level? (HINT: The length is zero, but there is still a terminating character.)

```
""
```

Review Exercises

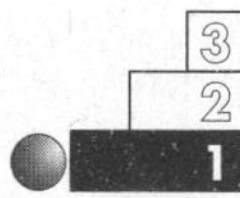

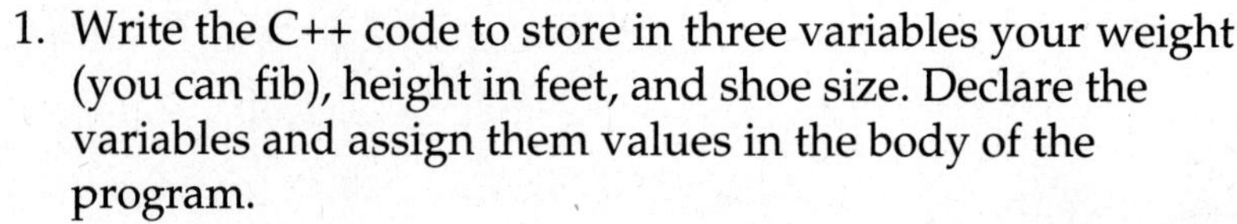

1. Write the C++ code to store in three variables your weight (you can fib), height in feet, and shoe size. Declare the variables and assign them values in the body of the program.

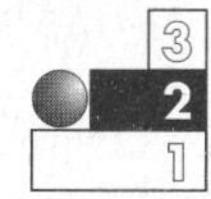

2. Rewrite the program in the preceding exercise, adding proper `cout` statements to print the values to the screen. Use appropriate messages (by printing string constants) to describe the numbers that are printed.

3. Write a program that stores a value in every type of variable C++ allows. You must first declare each variable at the top of the program. Put numbers in the variables and print them out to see how C++ stores and prints them.

Character Strings and Character Arrays

Even though C++ has no string variables, you can make C++ think that it has them by using character arrays. The concept of arrays may be new to you, but this chapter shows how easily you can declare and use them. Once you declare arrays, they can hold character strings, as if they were actual string variables.

This chapter introduces the following topics:

- Character arrays
- Assigning string values to character arrays
- Printing character arrays
- How character arrays differ from strings

After you finish this chapter, you'll be on your way to manipulating almost every type of variable C++ offers. Being able to manipulate characters and words is one thing that separates your computer from powerful calculators, giving the computer true data processing capabilities.

Character Arrays

A string constant can be stored in an array of characters.

There's a variable for almost every type of data in C++, but no variable exists that will hold character strings. The authors of the C++ language realized that users needed some way to store strings in variables. Instead of storing strings in string variables (some languages, such as BASIC and Pascal, have string variables), you must store them in an *array* of characters.

If you have never programmed before, an array will be new to you. Most programming languages allow the use of arrays. An *array* is a list (sometimes called a *table*) of variables. Suppose that you have to keep track of the sales of 100 salespersons. You could make up 100 variable names and assign each one a different salesperson's sales. All those variable names, however, would be difficult to keep track of. If you were to put them into an array of floating-point variables, you would have to keep track of only a single name (the array name) and then reference each of the 100 values with a numeric subscript.

Chapter 28, "Pointers and Arrays," covers processing arrays in more detail than this chapter. However, to work with character string data in your early programs, you need to become familiar with the concept of an array of characters, called a *character array*.

Because a string is simply a list of one or more characters, a character array is a perfect place to hold strings of information. Suppose that you want to keep track of a person's full name, age, and salary by placing them in variables. The age and salary are easy; there are variable types to hold those. You can code the following to declare those variables:

```
int      age;
float    salary;
```

There is no string variable that can hold the name, but you can create an array of characters (one or more character variables next to each other in memory) with the following declaration:

```
char name[ 15 ];
```

This reserves an array of characters. An array declaration always includes brackets (`[ ]`), which declare the storage that C++ needs to reserve for the array. This array will be 15 characters long, and the array name is `name`. You can also assign a value to the character array at the time you declare it. The following declaration statement not only declares the character array but also puts the name "Michael Jones" into it.

Declare the character array name as 15 characters long and assign `Michael Jones` *to that array.*

```
char name[ 15 ] = "Michael Jones";
```

Figure 6.1 shows what this array looks like in memory. Each of the 15 boxes of the array is called an *element*. Notice that there is a null zero (the string-terminating character) at the end of the string. Notice also that the last character of the array, the 15th element, has no data in it. There is a value there, even though the program didn't place any data there. It is not necessary to be concerned with what follows the string's null zero.

	.
name [0]	M
[1]	i
[2]	c
[3]	h
[4]	a
[5]	e
[6]	l
[7]	
[8]	J
[9]	o
[10]	n
[11]	e
[12]	s
[13]	\Ø
[14]	
	.

Figure 6.1. A character array after being declared and assigned a string value.

You can access individual elements in an array, or the array as a whole. This is the primary advantage of an array over a bunch of variables with different names. You can assign values to individual array elements by putting each element's location, called a *subscript*, in brackets. Note an example:

```
name[ 3 ] = 'k';
```

This overwrites the `h` in the name with a `k`. The string now looks like the one in Figure 6.2.

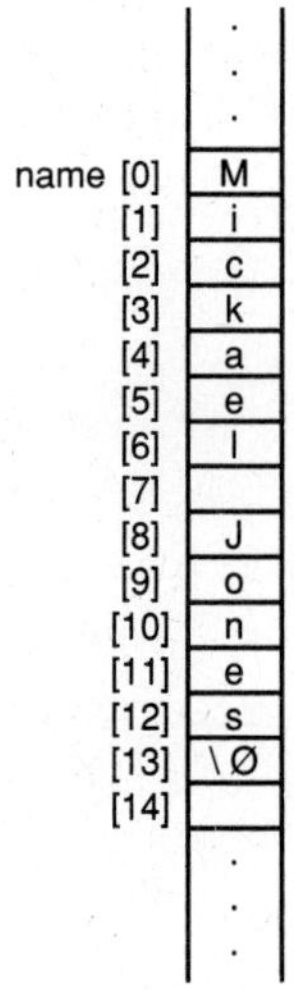

name	
	.
	.
	.
[0]	M
[1]	i
[2]	c
[3]	k
[4]	a
[5]	e
[6]	l
[7]	
[8]	J
[9]	o
[10]	n
[11]	e
[12]	s
[13]	\Ø
[14]	
	.
	.
	.

Figure 6.2. The array contents after changing one of the elements.

All array subscripts begin with 0.

All array subscripts start at zero. Therefore, to overwrite the first element, you have to use a 0 as the subscript. Assigning `name [ 3 ]`, as just shown, changes the fourth value in the array.

You can print the entire string, or more accurately, the entire array, with a single `cout`:

```
cout << name;
```

Notice that when you print an array, you don't put the brackets after the array name.

You must be sure that you reserve enough characters in the array to hold the entire string, including the terminating null zero. For example, the following won't work:

```
char name[ 5 ] = "Michael Jones";
```

This reserves only 5 characters for the array, but the name and its null zero take 14 characters. C++ will not give you an error if you try to do this; instead, C++ overwrites whatever follows the array `name` in memory. This will cause unpredictable results and is certainly not correct.

Always reserve enough array elements to hold the string plus its terminating null character. It's easy to forget the null zero at the end, but don't. If your string contains 13 characters, it must have a 14th null zero, or the string will never be treated as a string. To help eliminate this error, C++ provides a shortcut. The following character array statements are exactly the same:

```
char horse[ 9 ] = "Stallion";
char horse[ ] = "Stallion";
```

If you assign a value to a character array at the same time you declare the character array, C++ counts the string's length, adds one for the null zero, and reserves that much array space for you.

Never declare a character array (or any other type of array) with empty brackets if you don't also assign values to the array at the same time. The statement

```
char people[ ];
```

does *not* reserve any space for the array called `people`. Because you did not assign the array a value when you declared it, C++ assumes that this array contains 0 elements. Therefore, there isn't enough room to put values into the array later.

Character Arrays versus Strings

In the last section, you saw how to put a string in a character array. In C++, strings can exist only as string constants or be stored in character arrays. As you read through this book, familiarizing yourself with the use of arrays and strings, you will become more comfortable with them. At this point, you should understand the following fundamental rule about C++ character arrays and character strings:

> Strings must be stored in character arrays, but not all character arrays contain strings.

To understand this point, look at the two arrays illustrated in Figure 6.3. The first one, called `cara1`, does *not* contain a string. It is, however, a character array, containing a list of several characters. The second array, called `cara2`, does contain a string because there is a null zero at the end.

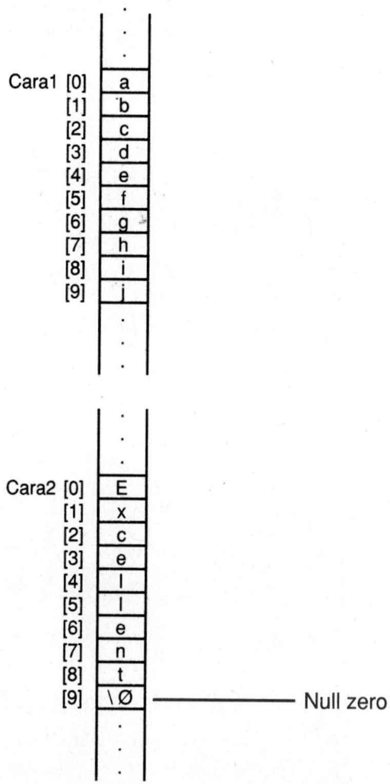

Figure 6.3. Two character arrays, one containing characters and the other containing a character string.

These arrays could be initialized with the following declaration statements.

Declare the array `cara1` with 10 individual characters.
Declare the array `cara2` with the character string `Excellent`.

```
char cara1[ 10 ] = { 'a', 'b', 'c', 'd', 'e', 'f', 'g',
                     'h', 'i', 'j' };
char cara2[ 10 ] = "Excellent";
```

If you want to put individual characters into an array, you must enclose the list of characters in braces, as shown in the preceding statements. You could also initialize `cara1` later in the program, using assignment statements, such as

Initialize each element of array

```
char cara1[ 10 ];
cara1[ 0 ] = 'a';
cara1[ 1 ] = 'b';
cara1[ 2 ] = 'c';
cara1[ 3 ] = 'd';
cara1[ 4 ] = 'e';
cara1[ 5 ] = 'f';
cara1[ 6 ] = 'g';
cara1[ 7 ] = 'h';
cara1[ 8 ] = 'i';
cara1[ 9 ] = 'j';    // Last element possible, since started
                     // with 0 subscript
```

This character array doesn't contain a null zero, so it does not contain a string of characters. It contains characters that can be stored there and used individually, but they cannot be treated as if they were a string in a program.

CAUTION: You cannot assign string values to character arrays in a regular assignment statement, except when you declare them. A character array is not a string variable (the array is used only to hold a string), so the array cannot go on the left side of an equal sign.

The following program is *invalid*:

```
main()
    {
    char     petname[ 20 ];         // Reserve space for
                                    // the pet's name
    petname = "Alfalfa";            // INVALID!
    cout << petname;
    return 0;
    }
```

Because the pet's name was not assigned *at the time the character array was declared*, `petname` cannot be assigned a value later. The following is allowed, however, since you can assign values individually to a character array:

```
main()
    {
    char     petname[ 20 ];        // Reserve space for
                                   // the pet's name
    petname[ 0 ] = 'A';            // Assign values one
                                   // element at a time
    petname[ 1 ] = 'l';
    petname[ 2 ] = 'f';
    petname[ 3 ] = 'a';
    petname[ 4 ] = 'l';
    petname[ 5 ] = 'f';
    petname[ 6 ] = 'a';
    petname[ 7 ] = '\0';            // Needed to ensure that
                                    // this is a string!
    cout << petname;                // Now the pet's name
                                    // prints properly
    return 0;
    }
```

The `petname` character array now holds a string since the last character is a null zero. How long is the string in `petname`? It is 7 characters long because the length of a string never includes the null zero.

You cannot assign more than 20 characters, which is this array's reserved space. However, you can store any string of 19 or fewer characters (leaving one for the null zero) in the array. If you put the `"Alfalfa"` string into the array and then assign a null zero to `petname[ 3 ]`, as in

```
petname[ 3 ] = '\0';
```

the string in `petname` is now just 3 characters long. You have, in effect, shortened the string. There are still 20 characters reserved for `petname`, but the data inside it is the string `"Alf"`, ending with a null zero.

There are many other ways to assign a string a value, such as using a `strcpy()` function. This is a library function that lets you copy a string constant into a string. To copy the `"Alfalfa"` pet name into the `petname` array, you could type

```
strcpy(petname, "Alfalfa"); // Copy Alfalfa into the array
```

The `strcpy()` function puts string constants in string arrays.

The `strcpy()` function (for "string copy") assumes that the first value in its parentheses is a character array name and that the second value is a valid string constant, or another character array that holds a string. You must be sure that the first character array in the parentheses is long enough (has enough elements reserved) to hold whatever string you copy into it.

Other methods of initializing arrays are explored throughout this book.

Examples

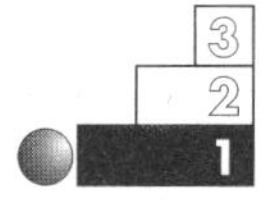

1. Suppose that you want to keep track of your aunt's name in a program so that you can print the name. If your aunt's name is Ruth Ann Cooper, you have to reserve at least 16 elements — 15 to hold the name and another element to hold the null character. The following statement properly reserves a character array to hold the name:

   ```
   char aunt_name[ 16 ];
   ```

2. If you want to put your aunt's name in the array at the same time you reserve the array storage, you can do so like this:

   ```
   char aunt_name[ 16 ] = "Ruth Ann Cooper";
   ```

You could leave out the array size and let C++ count the number needed:

```
char aunt_name[ ] = "Ruth Ann Cooper";
```

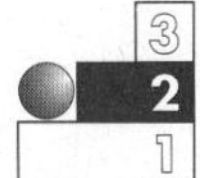

3. Suppose that you want to keep track of three friends' names. The longest name is 20 characters (including the null zero). You just have to reserve enough character array space to hold each friend's name:

```
char friend1[ 20 ];
char friend2[ 20 ];
char friend3[ 20 ];
```

These declarations can go toward the top of the block, along with any integer, floating-point, or character variables you need to declare.

4. The following program asks the user for his or her first and last name. It then prints the user's initials to the screen by printing the first character in each name array. The program must print each array's 0 subscript because the first subscript of any array begins at 0, not 1.

```
// Filename: C6INIT.CPP
// Prints the user's initials

#include <iostream.h>

main()
     {
     char     first[ 20 ];     // Holds the first name
     char     last[ 20 ];      // Holds the last name

     cout << "What is your first name? ";
     cin >> first;
     cout << "What is your last name? ";
     cin >> last;

     // Print the initials
     cout << "Your initials are " << first[0] << '.'
          << last[0] << '.';
     return 0;
     }
```

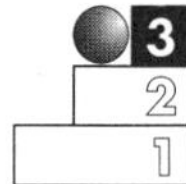

5. The following program takes three friend character arrays and assigns them string values in the three ways shown in this chapter:

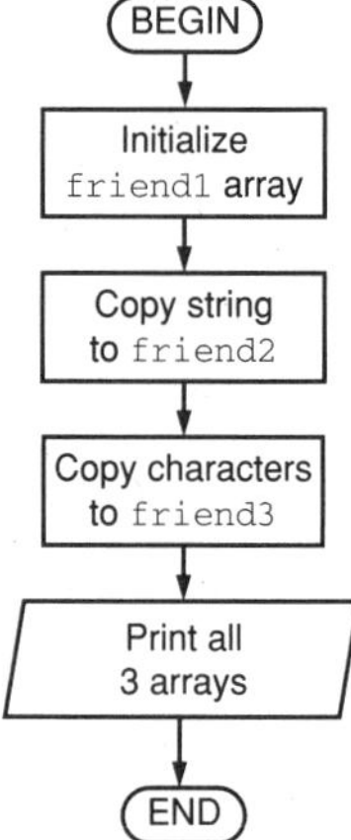


```
// Filename: C6STR.CPP
// Stores and initializes 3 character arrays for 3 friends

#include     <iostream.h>
#include     <string.h>

main()
     {
     // Declare all arrays and initialize the first one
     char     friend1[ 20 ] = "Johann Paul Johnson";
     char     friend2[ 20 ];
     char     friend3[ 20 ];

     // Use a function to initialize the second array
     strcpy(friend2, "Julie L. Roberts");

     friend3[ 0 ] = 'A';     // Initialize the last string
                             // an element at a time
     friend3[ 1 ] = 'd';
     friend3[ 2 ] = 'a';
     friend3[ 3 ] = 'm';
     friend3[ 4 ] = ' ';
     friend3[ 5 ] = 'G';
     friend3[ 6 ] = '.';
     friend3[ 7 ] = ' ';
     friend3[ 8 ] = 'S';
     friend3[ 9 ] = 'm';
     friend3[ 10 ] = 'i';
     friend3[ 11 ] = 't';
     friend3[ 12 ] = 'h';
     friend3[ 13 ] = '\0';

     // Print all three names out
     cout << friend1 << '\n';
     cout << friend2 << '\n';
     cout << friend3 << '\n';
     return 0;
     }
```

Obviously, the last method of initializing a character array with a string one element at a time is not used as often as the other ways.

Summary

This has been a short but powerful chapter. You learned about character arrays that hold strings. Even though C++ has no string variables, character arrays can hold string constants. Once you put a string into a character array, you can print it or manipulate it as if it were a string.

Starting with the next chapter, you will begin to hone the C++ skills you are building. Chapter 7 introduces preprocessor directives. They are not really part of the C++ language itself, but they help you work with your source code as a whole before your program is compiled.

Review Questions

Answers to Review Questions are in Appendix B.

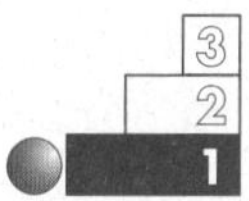

1. How would you declare a character array, called `my_name`, that will hold the following string constant?

```
"This is C++"
```

2. How long is the preceding string?
3. How many bytes of storage does this string take?

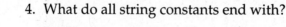

4. What do all string constants end with?
5. How many variables do the following statements declare, and what are their types?

```
char name[ 25 ];
char address[ 25 ];
```

6. True or false: The following statement assigns a string constant to a character array.

```
myname[]="Kim Langston";
```

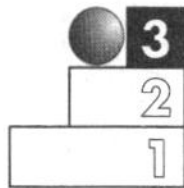

7. True or false: The following declaration puts a string into the character array called `city`.

```
char city[ ] = { 'M', 'i', 'a', 'm', 'i', '\0' };
```

8. True or false: The following declaration puts a string into the character array called `city`.

```
char city[ ] = { 'M', 'i', 'a', 'm', 'i' };
```

Review Exercises

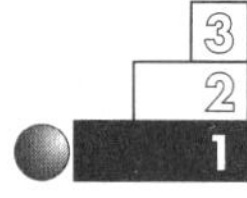

1. Write the C++ code to store your weight (you can fib), height in feet, shoe size, and name in four variables. Declare the variables and then assign them values in the body of the program.

2. Rewrite the program in exercise 1 by adding proper `cout` statements to print the values to the screen. Use appropriate messages (by printing string constants) to describe the values that are printed.

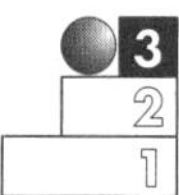

3. Write a program to store and print the names of your two favorite television programs. Store these programs in two character arrays. Initialize one of the strings (assign it the first program's name) at the time you declare the array. Initialize the second value in the body of the program with the `strcpy()` function.

4. Write a program that puts 10 different initials into 10 elements of a single character array. Do not store a string-terminating null zero. Print the list backward, one initial on each line.

Preprocessor Directives

As you might recall from Chapter 3, the C++ compiler routes your programs through a *preprocessor* before compiling your programs. The preprocessor could be called a "precompiler" because it changes your source code before the compiler ever sees it.

The preprocessor is so important to the C programming language that you should familiarize yourself with it before learning more commands within the language itself. Regular C++ commands do not affect the preprocessor. You must supply special non-C++ commands, called *preprocessor directives,* that the preprocessor looks at. These directives make changes to your source code before the C++ compiler looks at it.

This chapter introduces the following topics:

- What preprocessor directives are
- The `#include` preprocessor directive
- The `#define` preprocessor directive

Almost every proper C++ program contains preprocessor directives. In this chapter, you learn about the two most common directives: `#include` and `#define`.

What Are Preprocessor Directives?

As indicated, preprocessor directives are commands you supply to the preprocessor. All preprocessor directives begin with a pound sign (#). Because they are not C++ commands but are C++ preprocessor commands, never put a semicolon at the end of a preprocessor directive. These directives typically begin in column 1 of your source program. They can begin in any column, but in the interest of code portability, stay with tradition and start each one in the first column on the line where the directive appears. Figure 7.1 shows a program that contains three preprocessor directives.

Preprocessor directives

```
// Filename: C7PRE.CPP
// C++ program that demonstrates preprocessor directives

#include <iostream.h>
#define AGE 28
#define MESSAGE "Hello, world."

main()
{
   int i = 10, age;  // i is assigned a value at declaration
                     // age is still UNDEFINED

   age = 5;          // Put 5 in the variable age

   i = i * AGE;   // AGE is not the same as the variable age

   cout << i << age << AGE;   // Print 280 5 28
   cout << MESSAGE;   // Hello, world gets printed on screen

   return;
}
```

Figure 7.1. A program that contains three preprocessor directives.

Preprocessor directives temporarily change your source code.

Preprocessor directives are commands that you give to your C++ preprocessor to change your source code. These changes last only as long as the compile takes. Once you look at your source code again, the preprocessor will be through with your file, and its changes will no longer be in the file. Your preprocessor does not in any way compile your program or look at your actual C++ commands. Some beginning C++ students tend to get confused by this, but you won't be confused if you understand that your program has yet to be compiled when your preprocessor directives execute.

Similar to a word processor or an editor, a preprocessor does what these kinds of programs might do with your program. This analogy applies throughout this chapter.

The `#include` Preprocessor Directive

The `#include` preprocessor directive merges a disk file into your source program. Remember that a preprocessor directive is like a word processing command. Word processors are capable of file merging, just as the `#include` directive is. The `#include` preprocessor directive takes one of the following formats:

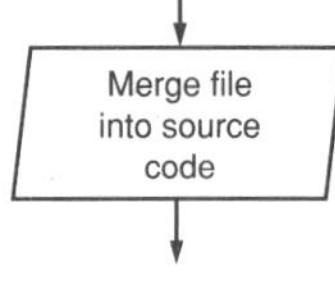


```
#include <filename>
#include "filename"
```

In the `#include` directive, the *`filename`* must be an ASCII text file (as your source file is) that resides on your disk. Take a look at Figure 7.2, which shows the contents of two files on disk. One file is called OUTSIDE, and the other file is called INSIDE. Notice that OUTSIDE includes the following preprocessor directive.

Include in your source file the file INSIDE.

```
#include <INSIDE>
```

The file called OUTSIDE contains the following text:

```
Now is the time for all good men

#include INSIDE

to come to the aid of their country.
```

The file called INSIDE contains the following text:

```
A quick brown fox jumped
over the lazy dog.
```

Figure 7.2. Two files that illustrate the `#include` directive.

Assume that you are able to run the OUTSIDE file through the C++ preprocessor. The preprocessor finds the `#include` directive and replaces it with the entire file called INSIDE. In other words, the C++ preprocessor directive merges the INSIDE file into the OUTSIDE file, at the place of the `#include`. OUTSIDE is expanded to include its original text *plus* the merged text. Figure 7.3 shows what OUTSIDE looks like after the preprocessor gets through with it.

OUTSIDE now includes the INSIDE file:

```
Now is the time for all good men

A quick brown fox jumped
over the lazy dog.

to come to the aid of their country.
```

Figure 7.3. The OUTSIDE file after the preprocessor finishes with the `#include`.

The INSIDE file remains in its original form on the disk. Only the file that contains the `#include` directive is changed. Note that this change is *temporary*; that is, OUTSIDE is expanded by the included file only as long as it takes to compile the program.

Because the OUTSIDE and INSIDE files are not C++ programs, consider a few examples that are more usable to the C++ programming language. You might want to `#include` a file that contains common code you use often. Suppose that you print your name and address many times in your C++ programs. You *could* type the following few lines of code, which print your name and address, into each of your programs:

```
cout << "Kelly Jane Peterson\n";
cout << "Apartment #217\n";
cout << "4323 East Skelly Drive\n";
cout << "New York, New York\n";
cout << "                10012\n";
```

Instead of typing the same five lines everywhere you want your name and address printed, you can type them *once* and then save them in a file called MYADD.CPP. Afterward, you just type the following line when you want your name and address printed:

```
#include <myadd.cpp>
```

This method not only saves keystrokes but also maintains consistency and accuracy. (Sometimes this kind of repeated text is known as *boilerplate* text.)

You usually can use angle brackets (`<>`) or double quotes (`""`) around the included file's name and get the same results. The angle brackets tell the preprocessor to look for the included file in a default include directory set up by your compiler. The double quotes inform the preprocessor to look for the included file first in the directory where the source code is stored, and if not found there, to look in the system include directory.

Most of the time, you will see angle brackets around the included filename. If you want to include sections of code in other programs, be sure to store that code in the system include directory if you use angle brackets. Even though `#include` works well for inserted source code, there are more efficient ways to include common source code. You learn about these methods, called *external functions*, in Part IV of this book.

The `#include` directive is most often used for system header files.

The preceding `#include` example for source code has served well in explaining what the `#include` preprocessor directive does. However, `#include` is not often used to include source code text, but to include special system files called *header* files. Header files inform C++ how it is to interpret the many library functions you use. Your C++ compiler comes with its own header files. When you installed your compiler, these header files were automatically stored on your disk in the system include directory. Their filenames always end in .h to distinguish them from regular C++ source code.

The most common header file is named iostream.h. This gives your C++ compiler needed information about the library `cout` and `cin` functions, as well as other common library routines that perform input and output.

At this point, you do not have to understand fully the iostream.h file. You should, however, place this file before `main()` in every program you write. It is rare when a C++ program does *not* need iostream.h included, and it doesn't harm anything if you include iostream.h when it isn't needed.

Throughout this book, whenever a new library function is described, the matching header file for that function is also given. Because almost every C++ program that you write includes a `cout` to print to the screen, almost every program contains the following line:

```
#include <iostream.h>
```

In the last chapter, you saw the `strcpy()` function. Its header file is called string.h. Therefore, if you write a program that contains `strcpy()`, you should also include its matching header file at the time you include `<iostream.h>`. These items should go on separate lines:

```
#include <iostream.h>
#include <string.h>
```

The order of your include files does not matter as long as you include them before the functions that need them. Most C++ programmers include all their needed header files before the first function in the file.

These header files are nothing more than text files. You may want to search your disk with the editor and find one of them, such as iostream.h, so that you can look at it. It may seem very complex at this point, but there is nothing unusual about these files. If you do look at some of these files, do *not* change them in any way. If you make any changes, you may have to reload them from scratch to get them back.

Examples

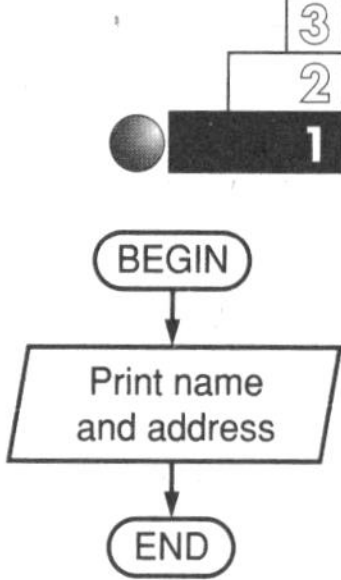

1. The following program is very short. It includes the printing routine for name and address, which was just described. After printing the name and address, the program ends.

```
// Filename: C7INC1.CPP
// Illustrates the #include preprocessor directive

#include  <iostream.h>

main()
     {
#include "myadd.cpp"
     return 0;
     }
```

The double quotes are used because the file named MYADD.CPP is stored in the same directory as the source file. You should realize that if you type this program into your computer (after typing and saving the MYADD.CPP file) and then compile the program, the MYADD.CPP file is included only as long as it takes to compile the program. Your compiler will not see the file as shown here. The compiler will see (and think you typed) the following:

```
// Filename: C7INCL1.CPP
// Illustrates the #include preprocessor directive

#include  <iostream.h>

main()
     {
     cout << "Kelly Jane Peterson\n";
```

```
     cout << "Apartment #217\n";
     cout << "4323 East Skelly Drive\n";
     cout << "New York, New York\n";
     cout << "                10012\n";
     return 0;
     }
```

This explains what is meant by a preprocessor; the changes are made to your source code *before* it is compiled. Your original source code is restored as soon as the compile is finished. When you look at your program again, it is back in its original form, as originally typed, with the `#include` statement.

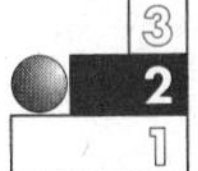

2. The following program copies a message into a character array and prints it to the screen. Because `cout` and `strcpy()` library functions are used, both of their header files should be included as well.

```
// Filename: C7INCL3.CPP
// Uses two header files

#include <iostream.h>
#include <string.h>

main()
     {
     char message[ 20 ];

     strcpy(message, "This is fun!");
     cout << message;
     return 0;
     }
```

The #define Preprocessor Directive

The #define preprocessor directive is also commonly used in many C++ programs. The #define directive may seem strange at first, but it really does nothing more than a word processor's find-and-replace command. The format of #define is

```
#define ARGUMENT1 argument2
```

where *ARGUMENT1* is a single word, containing no spaces. Use the same naming rules for the #define statement's first argument as for variables (refer to Chapter 4). It is traditional to use uppercase characters for *ARGUMENT1*; this is one of the few uses of uppercase in the C++ language. At least one space separates *ARGUMENT1* from *argument2*, which can be any character, word, or phrase. *argument2* can contain spaces or anything else you can type at the keyboard. Because #define is a preprocessor directive and not a C++ executable statement, do not put a semicolon at the end of it.

#define replaces every occurrence of the first argument with the second argument.

The #define preprocessor directive replaces the occurrence of *ARGUMENT1* everywhere in your program with the contents of *argument2*. In most cases, the #define directive should go before main(), along with the #include directive. Look at the following #define directive.

Define the constant AGELIMIT *to 21.*

```
#define AGELIMIT 21
```

If your program includes one or more occurrences of the word AGELIMIT, the preprocessor replaces every one of them with the number 21. Your compiler will think that you actually typed 21 instead of AGELIMIT, because the preprocessor finishes before your compiler sees the source code. Again, though, the change is temporary. After your program is compiled, you will see it as you originally typed it, with the #define and AGELIMITs still intact.

AGELIMIT is *not* a variable. Variables get declared and assigned values only when your program is compiled and run. The preprocessor changes your source file *before* it gets compiled.

You might wonder why you should go to this much trouble. If you wanted `21` everywhere `AGELIMIT` occurs, you could have typed `21` to begin with! The advantage to using `#define` instead of constants is that if the age limit ever changes (is reduced, for example, to 18), you have to change only one line in the program; you do not have to look for every occurrence of `21` and change each one — and maybe miss one in the process.

`#define` creates defined constants.

Because the `#define` preprocessor directive lets you easily define and change constants, the replaced arguments of the `#define` are sometimes called *defined constants*. You can define any type of constant, including string constants. The following program contains a defined string constant that replaces a string in two places:

```
// Filename: C7DEF1.CPP
// Defines a string constant and uses it twice

#include <iostream.h>
#define MYNAME "Phil Ward"

main()
     {
     char name[ ] = MYNAME;
     cout << "My name is " << name << '\n'; // Print the
                                            // array
     cout << "My name is " <<  MYNAME << '\n';  // Print the
                                             // defined constant
     return 0;
     }
```

The reason that the first argument of the `#define` is in uppercase is to distinguish it from variable names in the program. Variables are usually entered in lowercase. Although your preprocessor and compiler would not get confused, people who look at your program can quickly scan it and tell which items are defined constants and which items are not. When they see an uppercase word (if you follow the recommended standard for the first `#define` argument), they will know to look at the top of the program for its actual defined value.

The fact that defined constants are not variables is made even clearer in the following program, which prints five values. Try to guess what those five values are before looking at the answer following the program.

```
// Filename: C7DEF2.CPP
// Illustrates that #define constants are not variables

#include <iostream.h>

#define X1 (b + c)
#define X2 (X1 + X1)
#define X3 (X2 * c + X1 - d)
#define X4 (2 * X1 + 3 * X2 + 4 * X3)

main()
     {
     int  b = 2;     // Declare and initialize 4 variables
     int  c = 3;
     int  d = 4;
     int  e = X4;

     cout << e << "   " << X1 << "   " << X2 << "   " << X3
          << "   " << X4;
     return 0;
     }
```

Here is the output from this program:

```
164   5   10   31   164
```

If you treated X1, X2, X3, and X4 as variables, you would not get the correct answers. X1 through X4 are not variables but defined constants. Before your program is compiled, the preprocessor looks at the first line and knows to change every occurrence of X1 to `(b + c)`. This happens before the next `#define` is processed. Therefore, after the first `#define`, the source code looks like this:

```
// Filename: C7DEF2.CPP
// Illustrates that #define constants are not variables

#include <iostream.h>

#define X2 ((b + c) + (b + c))
#define X3 (X2 * c + (b + c) - d)
#define X4 (2 * (b + c) + 3 * X2 + 4 * X3)

main()
     {
     int  b = 2;     // Declare and initialize 4 variables
     int  c = 3;
     int  d = 4;
     int  e = X4;

     cout << e << "   " << (b + c) << "   " << X2 << "   "
          << X3 << "   " << X4;
     return 0;
     }
```

After the first `#define` finishes, the second one takes over and changes every occurrence of `X2` to `((b + c) + (b + c))`. At that point, your source code looks like this:

```
// Filename: C7DEF2.CPP
// Illustrates that #define constants are not variables

include <iostream.h>

#define X3 (((b + c) + (b + c)) * c + (b + c) - d)
#define X4 (2 * (b + c) + 3 * ((b + c) + (b + c)) + 4 * X3)

main()
     {
     int  b = 2;     // Declare and initialize 4 variables
```

```
     int  c = 3;
     int  d = 4;
     int  e = X4;

     cout << e << "   " << (b + c) << "   " << ((b + c) +
             (b + c)) << "   " << X3 << "   " << X4);
     return 0;
     }
```

After the second `#define` finishes, the third one takes over and changes every occurrence of `X3` to `(((b + c) + (b + c) * c + (b + c) - d)`. Your source code then looks like this:

```
// Filename: C7DEF2.CPP
// Illustrates that #define constants are not variables

#include <iostream.h>

#define X4 (2 * (b + c) + 3 * ((b + c) + (b + c)) + 4 *
        (((b +c) + (b + c)) * c + (b + c) - d))


main()
     {
     int  b = 2;      // Declare and initialize 4 variables
     int  c = 3;
     int  d = 4;
     int  e = X4;

     cout << e << "   " << (b + c) << "   " << ((b + c) +
             (b + c) << "   " << (((b + c) + (b + c)) * c +
             (b + c) - d) << "   " << X4;
     return 0;
     }
```

The source code is growing rapidly! After the third `#define` finishes, the fourth and last one takes over and changes every occurrence of `X4` to `(2 * (b + c) + 3 * ((b + c) + (b + c)) + 4 *` `(((b + c) + (b + c)) * c + (b + c) - d))`. Your source code looks like this at this point:

```
// Filename: C7DEF2.CPP
// Illustrates that #define constants are not variables

#include <iostream.h>

main()
     {
     int  b = 2; // Declare and initialize 4 variables
     int  c = 3;
     int  d = 4;
     int  e = (2 * (b + c) + 3 * ((b + c) + (b + c)) + 4 *
          (((b + c) + (b + c)) * c + (b + c) - d))

     cout << e << "  " << (b + c) << "  " << ((b + c) +
             (b + c) << "  " << (((b + c) + (b + c)) * c +
             (b + c) - d) << "  " << (2 * (b + c) + 3 *
             ((b + c) + (b + c)) + 4 * (((b + c) +
             (b + c)) * c + (b + c) - d));
     return 0;
     }
```

This is what your compiler actually sees. You did not type this complete listing; you typed only the original listing that was first shown. The preprocessor expanded the source into this longer form, as though you *had* typed it this way.

Turbo C++ has an alternative to `#define` for defining constants. The keyword `const` placed before a variable accomplishes the same thing. Note the following lines:

```
const int      i = 12;
const char     c = 'A';
const float    f = 3.1415926;
```

`i`, `c`, and `f` are now constants and cannot be changed.

What are the advantages of using `#define` instead of `const`? They have to do with several points that haven't been made yet.

First, a `#define` allocates no storage, but a `const` variable does. This is important if you're trying to keep your executable program size to a minimum.

Second, a `#define` is visible from where it is in the source file all the way to the end of the file. That is, when the compiler does its search and replace, it will replace every instance from the point of definition on. A `const` variable has visibility only within the program block in which it is defined. In other words, if a `const` is defined inside a block bounded by braces (`{ }`), the `const` has no visibility outside its block. The search and replace is restricted.

The third point has to do with arrays. You can create an array, which is a list of values, by using a `#define` or a `const` variable. With arrays, the first point in favor of `#define` over `const` is reversed. Every time you use an array created by the `#define`, that array is duplicated. Every time you use an array created as a `const` variable, a reference to the variable is created; this takes less room in memory than making another copy of the array.

This example may be extreme, yet it illustrates how `#define` works on your source code and does not define any variables at all. The `#define` does nothing more than a word processor's find-and-replace command. Because of this, you can even rewrite the C++ language. If you are used to BASIC, you might be more comfortable by typing `PRINT` instead of C++'s `cout` when printing to the screen. The `#define` statement

```
#define PRINT cout
```

allows you to print in C++ with the following statements:

```
PRINT << "This is a new printing technique\n";
PRINT << "I could have used cout instead.\n";
```

This works because your compiler, by the time it sees the program, will see the following:

```
cout << "This is a new printing technique\n";
cout << "I could have used printf() instead.\n";
```

You cannot replace a defined constant if it resides in another string constant. For example, you cannot use the `#define` statement

```
#define AGE 15
```

to replace information in the following `cout`:

```
cout << "AGE";
```

`AGE` is a string constant and will print literally as it appears inside the double quotes. As long as the defined constant does not reside between double quotes, the processor will make the replacement.

Do Not Overuse `#define`

Many early C++ programmers enjoy redefining parts of the language to suit what they are used to in another language. The `cout`-to-`PRINT` example is just one illustration. You can virtually redefine any C++ statement or function so that it "looks" the way you like.

There is a danger here, and you should be wary of using `#define` for this purpose. Redefining the language becomes very confusing to others who may need to modify your programs later. In addition, as you become familiar with C++, you will start to use the true C++ language more and more. Any older programs that you redefined will be confusing to you.

If you are going to program in C++, use the language elements supplied by C++. Shy away from redefining commands in the language. The `#define` directive is a great way to define numeric and string constants. If those constants change, you have to change only one line in your program. Resist the temptation to define commands and built-in functions.

Examples

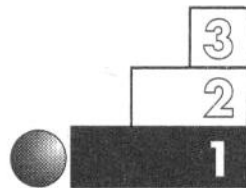

1. Suppose that you want to keep track of your company's target sales amount of $55,000.00. That target amount has not changed for the last two years. Since it probably will not change in the near future (sales are flat), you decide to start using a defined constant to represent the target sales amount. Then, if the target amount does change, you have to change it only on the `#define` line. The `#define` would look like this:

   ```
   #define TARGETSALES 55000.00
   ```

   This line defines a floating-point constant. You can then assign `TARGETSALES` to floating-point variables and print it, just as if you had typed `55000.00` throughout your program.

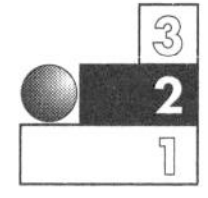

2. If you find yourself defining the same constants in many programs, you might consider putting them in their own file on disk and then include them. This saves typing the defined constants at the top of every program. If you stored that file in a file called MYDEFS.CPP in your program's directory, you could include it with the following `#include` statement:

   ```
   #include "mydefs.cpp"
   ```

   (To use angle brackets, you would have to store the file in your system's include directory.)

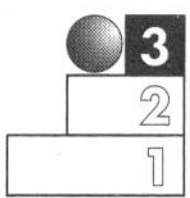

3. Defined constants are good for array sizes. Suppose, for example, that you declare an array for a customer's name. When you write the program, you know that you do not have any customer whose name is longer than 22 characters (including the null zero). Therefore, you can use the following:

   ```
   #define CNMLENGTH 22
   ```

   When you define the array, you could use this:

   ```
   char cust_name[ CNMLENGTH ]
   ```

   Other statements that need to know the array size can also use `CNMLENGTH`.

4. Many C++ programmers define a list of error messages. Once the messages are defined with easy-to-remember names, you can print those constants if an error occurs, while maintaining consistency throughout your programs. You might see something like the following toward the top of C++ programs:

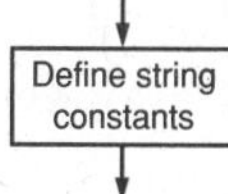


```
#define DISKERR "Your disk drive seems not to be working"
#define PRNTERR "Your printer is not responding"
#define AGEERR  "You cannot enter an age that small"
#define NAMEERR "You must enter a full name"
```

Summary

This chapter covered the `#include` and `#define` preprocessor directives. Although these are the only two preprocessor directives you know so far, they are the two used in most C++ programs. Although these directives are not executed, they change your source file by merging and defining constants in your programs.

The next chapter explains `cout` in more detail. There are many `cout` options that you will want to use as you write programs. You will also see a way to get keyboard input into your C++ programs.

Review Questions

Answers to Review Questions are in Appendix B.

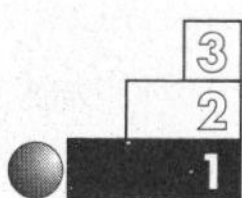

1. True or false: You can define variables with the preprocessor directives.
2. Which preprocessor directive will merge another file into your program?
3. Which preprocessor directive will define constants throughout your program?

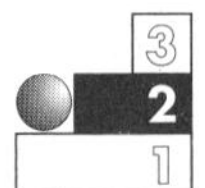

4. True or false: You can define character, string, integer, and floating-point constants with the `#define` directive.
5. Which happens first: your program is compiled or preprocessed?

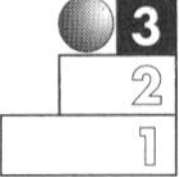

6. When would you use the angle brackets in an `#include`, and when would you use double quotes?
7. Which are easier to change: defined constants or constants you type throughout a program? Why?
8. Which header file should be included in almost every C++ program you write?
9. True or false: The line

   ```
   #define MESSAGE "Please press Enter to continue..."
   ```

   would change the statement

   ```
   cout << "MESSAGE";.
   ```

10. What is the output from the following program?

```
// Filename: C7EXER.CPP

#include <iostream.h>
#define AMT1 a+a+a
#define AMT2 AMT1 - AMT1

main()
     {
     int  a = 1;

     cout << "Amount is " << AMT2;
     return 0;
     }
```

Review Exercises

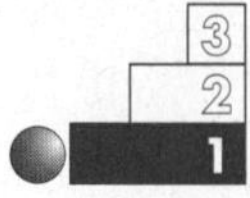

1. Write a program that prints your name to the screen. Use a defined constant for the name. Do not use a character array and do not type your actual name inside the `cout`.

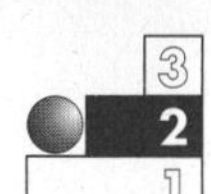

2. Suppose that your boss wants you to write a program which produces an exception report. If the company's sales are lower than $100,000.00 or more than $750,000.00, your boss wants the program to print a message accordingly. You will learn how to produce this type of report later in this book, but for now, write the `#define` statements that define these two floating-point constants.

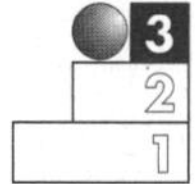

3. Write the `cout` statements that print your name and birth date to the screen. Store these statements in a separate file. Write a second program that includes the first file to print your name and birth date. Be sure to include `<iostream.h>`, because the included file contains `cout` statements.

4. Write a nonsense program that defines 10 digits — 0 through 9 — as constants `ZERO` through `NINE`. Add these 10 defined digits together and print the results.

Simple Input and Output

You have already seen the `cout` operator, which prints values to the screen. There is much more to `cout` than you have learned. Because the screen is such a common output device, you need to understand how to take advantage of `cout` to print data the way you want to see it. In addition, your programs will become more powerful if you learn to get input from the keyboard. `cin` is an operator that mirrors `cout`. Instead of sending output values to the screen, `cin` accepts values the user types at the keyboard.

The `cout` and `cin` operators enable the beginning C++ programmer to send output from and receive input into programs with relative ease.

This chapter covers the following topics:

- Using the `cout` operator
- Using manipulators
- Using the `cin` operator

You will be surprised at how much more advanced your programs can be after you learn these input/output operators.

The cout Operator

cout sends output to the screen.

The cout operator sends data to the standard output device. This is the screen, unless you have redirected the standard output to another device. If you are unfamiliar with device redirection at the operating system level, you learn more about it in Part V of this book. At this point, if you do nothing special, cout sends all output to the screen.

The format of cout is a little different from that of regular C++ commands:

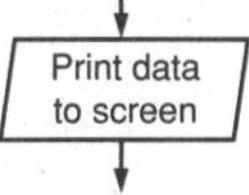


```
cout << data [ << data ];
```

The *data* can be variables, constants, expressions, or a combination of all three.

Note that in this book it is sometimes necessary to define C++ constructs that have an indefinite number of parameters or arguments, or that have optional parameters which may or may not be present. In such cases, the optional parameter appears in square brackets, [ ]. The text enclosed in square brackets may be present one or more times, or not at all.

Printing Strings

The easiest data to print with cout is a string. To print a string constant, you simply put the string constant after the cout operator. For example, to print the string "The rain in Spain", you type the following cout.

Print the phrase The rain in Spain *to the screen.*

```
cout << "The rain in Spain";
```

You must remember, however, that cout does *not* perform an automatic carriage return. This means that the screen's cursor will be left after the last character that is printed. Subsequent couts begin right next to the last character printed. To understand this better, try to predict the output from the following three cout operators:

```
cout << "Line 1";
cout << "Line 2";
cout << "Line 3";
```

These couts produce the output

```
Line 1Line 2Line 3
```

which is probably not what was intended. You must include the newline character, `\n`, whenever you want to move the cursor to the next line. The following three cout operators produce a three-line output:

```
cout << "Line 1\n";
cout << "Line 2\n";
cout << "Line 3\n";
```

Here is the output from these couts:

```
Line 1
Line 2
Line 3
```

The `\n` character sends the cursor to the next line no matter where you insert the character. The following three cout operators also produce the correct three-line output:

```
cout << "Line 1";
cout << "\nLine 2\n";
cout "Line 3";
```

The second cout prints a newline before it prints anything else. It then prints its string followed by another newline. The third string prints on that new line.

You can also print strings stored in character arrays by putting the array name inside the cout. If you were to store your name in an array defined as

```
char my_name[ ] = "Lyndon Harris";
```

you could print the name with the following cout:

```
cout << my_name;
```

Examples

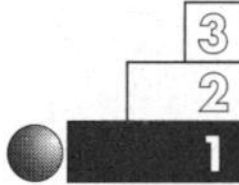

1. The following section of code prints three string constants on three different lines:

```
cout << "Nancy Carson\n";
cout << "1213 Oak Street\n";
cout << "Fairbanks, Alaska\n";
```

2. The following program stores a few values in three variables and prints the result:

```
// Filename: C8PRNT1.CPP
// Prints values in variables

#include <iostream.h>

main()
     {
     char          first = 'E';      // Store some character,
     char          middle = 'W';     // integer, and
     char          last = 'C';       // floating-point
                                     // variables
     int       age = 32;
     int       dependents = 2;
     float     salary = 25000.00;
     float     bonus = 575.25;

     // Print the results
     cout << first << middle << last;
     cout << age << dependents;
     cout << salary << bonus;
     return 0;
     }
```

3. The preceding program does not help the user at all. The output is not labeled, and all of it prints on a single line. Here is the same program with a few messages printed before the numbers and some newline characters placed where they are needed.

```
// Filename: C8PRNT2.CPP
// Prints values in variables with appropriate labels

#include <iostream.h>

main()
     {
     char           first = 'E';       // Store some character,
     char           middle = 'W';      // integer, and
     char           last = 'C';        // floating-point
                                       // variables
     int       age = 32;
     int       dependents = 2;
     float     salary = 25000.00;
     float     bonus = 575.25;

     // Print the results
     cout << "Here are the initials:\n";
     cout << first << middle << last\n\n;
     cout << "The age and number of dependents are:\n";
     cout << age << "   " << dependents << "\n\n";
     cout << "The salary and bonus are:\n";
     cout << salary << ' ' << bonus;
     return 0;
     }
```

Note the output from this program:

```
Here are the initials:
EWC

The age and number of dependents are:
32   2

The salary and bonus are:
25000.000000 575.250000
```

The floating-point values print with too many zeros, but the numbers are correct. The next section shows you how to limit the number of leading and trailing zeros that are printed.

4. The `cout` is often used to label output. Before printing an age, an amount, a salary, or any other numeric data, you should print a string constant that tells the user what the number means. The following `cout` lets the user know that the next number printed will be an age. Without this `cout`, the user may not know that the number is an age.

```
cout << "Here is the age that was found in our files:";
```

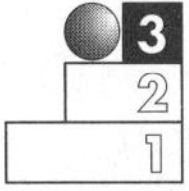

5. All four of the following `cout`s produce different output because all four string constants are different:

```
cout << "Come back tomorrow\n";
cout << "Come  back  tomorrow\n";
cout << "cOME BACK TOMORROW\n";
cout << "C o m e   b a c k   t o   m o r r o w\n";
```

6. You can print a blank line by printing two newline characters next to each other (`\n\n`) after your string:

```
cout << "Prepare the invoices...\n\n";
```

7. If you need to print a table of numbers, you can use the `\t` tab character. Place the tab character between the numbers that print. The following program prints a list of team names and number of hits for the first three weeks of the season:

Print columns of data

```
// Filename: C8TEAM.CPP
// Prints a table of team names and hits for three weeks

#include <iostream.h>

main()
     {
     cout << "Parrots\tRams\tKings\tTitans\tChargers\n";
     cout << "3\t5\t3\t1\t0\n";
     cout << "2\t5\t1\t0\t1\n";
     cout << "2\t6\t4\t3\t0\n";
     return 0;
     }
```

This program produces the following table. You can see that even though the names have different widths, the numbers print correctly beneath them. The `\t` character forces the next name or value into the next tab position (every eight characters).

```
Parrots Rams    Kings   Titans  Chargers
3       5       3       1       0
2       5       1       0       1
2       6       4       3       0
```

The hex and oct Manipulators

The `hex` and `oct` manipulators are used to print hexadecimal and octal numbers. Even if you store a hexadecimal number in an integer variable (with the leading `0x` characters, such as `0x3C1`), that variable will print as a decimal value. To print the value in hex, you must use the `hex` manipulator.

TIP: You can print any integer value as a hexadecimal number if you use the `hex` conversion character. You do not have to store the integer as a hex number first.

Examples

1. Suppose that you are working on a systems program and need to add five hexadecimal values together to test the results. You can write a short C++ program that does just that. You can then print the answer as a hexadecimal

number by using the hex manipulator. Note the following program:

```
// Filename: C8HEX.CPP
// Adds five hexadecimal numbers and prints the answer

#include <iostream.h>

main()
     {
     // Store the five numbers to add together
     int     num1 = 0x4c, num2 = 0x52, num3 = 0xd1,
             num4 = 0xdc, num5 = 0x1f;
     int     hex_ans;      // This will hold the result

     hex_ans = num1 + num2 + num3 + num4 + num5;

     // Print the answer
     cout << "The hexadecimal numbers add up to:"
          << hex << hex_ans << " \n";
     return 0;
}
```

This program produces a single line of output:

```
The hexadecimal numbers add up to: 26a
```

2. If you use octal, you might need this type of routine to add octal (base-8) numbers. The preceding program can be rewritten with octal numbers and printed with the oct manipulator:

```
// Filename: C8OCT.CPP
// Adds five octal numbers and prints the answer

#include <iostream.h>

main()
     {
     // Store the five numbers to add together
     int     num1 = 054, num2 = 067, num3 = 011, num4 = 031,
             num5 = 056;
     int     oct_ans;   // This will hold the result
```

```
     oct_ans = num1 + num2 + num3 + num4 + num5;

     // Print the answer
     cout << "The octal numbers add up to:"
          << oct << oct_ans << " \n";
     return 0;
}
```

This program produces the following output:

```
The octal numbers add up to: 263
```

The answer, `263`, is an octal number (not a decimal) because you printed it with the `oct` manipulator.

3. Use of the `hex` or `oct` manipulator sets integer output to octal or hexadecimal until another `oct`, `hex`, or `dec` manipulator is encountered. The `dec` manipulator returns output to decimal.

Other Manipulators

You have already seen the need for additional program output control. All floating-point numbers print with too many decimal places for most applications. What if you want to print only dollars and cents (two decimal places), or print an average with a single decimal place? If you want to control the way these conversion characters produce output, you need to use a parameterized manipulator.

The `setiosflags` and `resetiosflags` manipulators are used to set certain global flags that the C++ iostream class uses in establishing the default behavior of its input and output. `setiosflags` sets the flags indicated; `resetiosflags` clears (or resets) them. These manipulators take as arguments any of the values shown in Table 8.1. You may add these together.

Table 8.1. Arguments for *`setiosflags`* and *`resetiosflags`*.

Value	*Meaning If Set*
`ios::skipws`	Skip white space on input
`ios::left`	Left-adjust output
`ios::right`	Right-adjust output
`ios::internal`	Pad after the sign or base indicator
`ios::dec`	Decimal conversion
`ios::oct`	Octal conversion
`ios::hex`	Hexadecimal conversion
`ios::showbase`	Show base indicator on output
`ios::showpoint`	Show decimal point
`ios::uppercase`	Uppercase hexadecimal output
`ios::showpos`	Show `'+'` with positive integers
`ios::scientific`	Use scientific notation
`ios::fixed`	Use fixed notation
`ios::unitbuf`	Flush all streams after insertion
`ios::stdio`	Flush `stdout`, `stderr` after insertion

You can modify the way numbers print.

You can specify how many print positions to use in printing a number. For example, the following `cout` prints the number `456`, using three positions (the length of the data):

```
cout << 456;
```

If 456 were stored in an integer variable, it would still use three positions to print, because the number of digits printed is 3. However, you can specify how many positions will print. The following `cout` prints the number `456` in 5 positions (with two leading spaces):

```
cout << setw(5) << setfill(' ') << 456;
```

You typically will use the `setw` manipulator when you want to print data in uniform columns. The following program shows you the importance of the width number. Each `cout` output is shown in the comment to its left.

```
// Filename: C8MOD1.CPP
// Illustrates various integer width cout modifiers

#include <iostream.h>
#include <iomanip.h>

main()
     {                               // The output appears below
     cout << 456 << 456 << 456;      // 456456456
     cout << setw(5) << 456 << setw(5) << 456 << setw(5)
          << 456;                    //   456  456  456
     cout << setw(7) << 456 << setw(7) << 456 << setw(7)
          << 456 << " \n";           //     456    456    456
     return 0;
     }
```

When you use a `setw` manipulator inside a conversion character, C++ right-justifies the number in the width you specify. When you specify an 8-digit width, C++ prints a value inside the 8 digits, padding the number with leading blanks if it does not fill the whole width.

> **NOTE:** If you do not specify a width large enough to hold the number, C++ ignores your width request and prints the number in its entirety.

You can control the width of strings in the same manner, again with the `setw` manipulator. If you don't specify enough width to print the full string, C++ ignores the width. The mailing list application in the back of this book uses this technique to print names on mailing labels.

> **NOTE:** `setw()` becomes more important when you want to print floating-point numbers.

`setprecision(2)` tells C++ to print a floating-point number with two decimal places. If C++ has to round the fractional part, it will do so. The line

```
cout << setw(6) << setprecision(2) << 134.568767;
```

produces the following output:

```
134.57
```

Without the `setw` or `setprecision` manipulator, C++ would print this:

```
134.568767
```

> **TIP:** When printing floating-point numbers, C++ always prints the entire portion to the left of the decimal (to maintain as much accuracy as possible), no matter how many positions wide you specify. Therefore, many C++ programmers ignore the `setw` manipulator for floating-point numbers and specify only the precision, as in `setprecision(2)`.

Examples

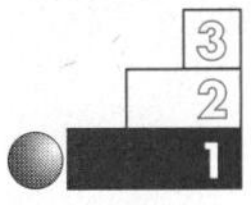

1. You saw earlier how the `\t` (tab character) can be used to print columns of data. The tab character is limited to eight columns. If you want more control of the width of your data, use a `setw` manipulator. The following program is a modified version of C8TEAM.CPP, using the width specifier instead

of the tab character. This specifier ensures that each column is 10 characters wide.

```
// Filename: C8TEAMMD.CPP
// Prints a table of team names and hits for three weeks,
// using width-modifying conversion characters

#include <iostream.h>
#include <iomanip.h>

main()
     {
     cout << setw(10) << "Parrots" << setw(10) << "Rams"
          << setw(10) << "Kings" << setw(10) << "Titans"
          << setw(10) << "Chargers << "\n";
     cout << setw(10) << 3 << setw(10) << 5 << setw(10) << 2
          << setw(10) << 1 << setw(10) << 0 << "\n";
     cout << setw(10) << 2 << setw(10) << 5 << setw(10) << 1
          << setw(10) << 0 << setw(10) << 1 << "\n";
     cout << setw(10) << 2 << setw(10) << 6 << setw(10) << 4
          << setw(10) << 3 << setw(10) << 0 << "\n";
     return 0;
     }
```

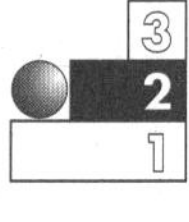

2. The following program is a payroll program. The output prints dollar amounts (to two decimal places).

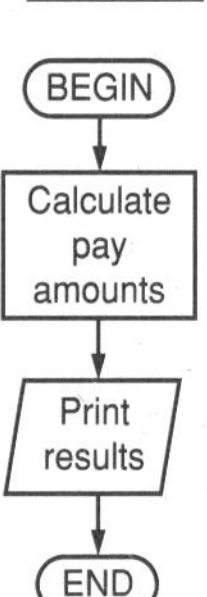


```
// Filename: C8PAY1.CPP
// Computes and prints payroll data properly
// in dollars and cents

#include <iostream.h>
#include <iomanip.h>

main()
     {
     char          emp_name[ ] = "Larry Payton";
     char          pay_date[ ] = "03/09/92";
```

```
int          hours_worked = 40;
float     rate = 7.50;         // Pay per hour
float     tax_rate = .40;      // Tax percentage rate
float     gross_pay, taxes, net_pay;

// Compute the pay amount
gross_pay = hours_worked * rate;
taxes = tax_rate * gross_pay;
net_pay = gross_pay - taxes;

// Print the results
cout << "As of: " << pay_date << "\n";
cout << emp_name << " worked " << hours_worked
     << " hours\n";
cout << "and got paid " << setw(2) << setprecision(2)
     << gross_pay << "\n";
cout << "After taxes of: " << setw(5) << setprecision(2)
     << taxes << "\n";
cout << "his take-home pay was: " << setw(6)
     << setprecision(2) << net_pay << "\n";
return 0;
}
```

The following is the output from this program. You should remember that the floating-point variables still hold the full precision (to six decimal places) as they did in the last program. The modifying `setw` manipulators affect only how the variables are printed, not what is stored in them.

```
As of: 03/09/92
Larry Payton worked 40 hours
and got paid 300.000000
After taxes of: 120.000000
his take-home pay was: $180.000000
```

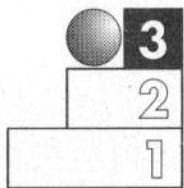

3. Most C++ programmers do not use the `setw` manipulator to the left of the decimal point when printing dollars and cents. Here is the payroll program again, using the shortcut floating-point width method. Notice that the last three `cout` statements include no `setw` manipulator. C++ knows to print the full number to the left of the decimal, but only two places

to the right.

```
// Filename: C8PAY2.CPP
// Computes and prints payroll data properly, using the
// shortcut modifier

#include <iostream.h>
#include <iomanip.h>

main()
     {
     char      emp_name[ ] = "Larry Payton";
     char      pay_date[ ] = "03/09/92";
     int       hours_worked = 40;
     float     rate = 7.50;         // Pay per hour
     float     tax_rate = .40;      // Tax percentage rate
     float     gross_pay, taxes, net_pay;

     // Compute the pay amount
     gross_pay = hours_worked * rate;
     taxes = tax_rate * gross_pay;
     net_pay = gross_pay - taxes;

     // Print the results
     cout << "As of: " << pay_date << "\n";
     cout << emp_name << " worked " << hours_worked
          << " hours\n";
     cout << "and got paid " << setiosflags(ios::fixed)
          << setprecision(2) << gross_pay << "\n";
     cout << "After taxes of: " << setprecision(2) << taxes
          << "\n";
     cout << "his take-home pay was: " << setprecision(2)
          << net_pay << "\n";
     return 0;
     }
```

This program's output is the same as that of the last program.

The `cin` Operator

You now understand how C++ represents data and variables, and you know how to print that data. There is one additional part of programming that you have not seen: inputting data into your programs.

Until this point, every program has had no input of data. All data you worked with was assigned to variables within the program. However, this is not always the best way to get the data into your programs; you rarely know what your data is going to be when you write your programs. The data is known only when you run the programs (or another user runs them).

The `cin` operator stores keyboard input in variables.

You can use the `cin` operator to get input from the keyboard. When your programs reach the line with a `cin`, the user at the keyboard can enter values directly into variables. Your program can then process those variables and produce output. Figure 8.1 illustrates the difference between `cout` and `cin`.

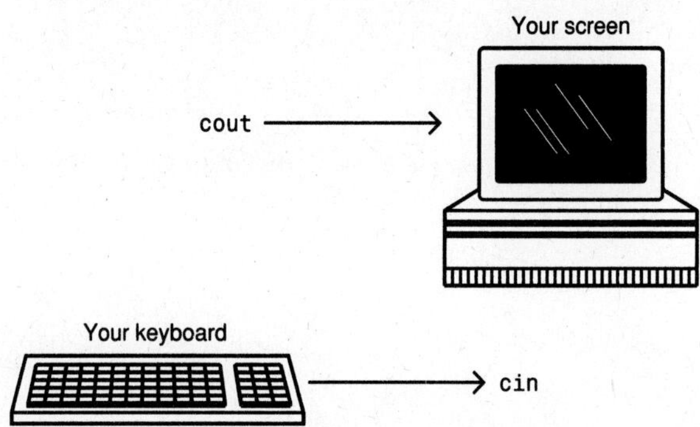

Figure 8.1. The actions of `cout` and `cin`.

> **The `cin` Fills Variables with Values**
>
> There is a major difference between `cin` and the assignment statements (such as `i = 17;`) you have seen. Both fill variables with values. However, an assignment statement is assigned specific values to variables *at programming time*. When you run a program with assignment statements, you know from the program's listing exactly what values will go into the variables, because you wrote the program to store those values there. Every time you run the program, the results are exactly the same since the same values go into (are *assigned* to) the same variables.
>
> When you write programs that use `cin`, you have no idea what values will go into the `cin`'s variables because the values are not known *until the program is run and the user enters those values.* This means more flexible programs that can be used by a variety of people. Whenever the program is run, different results are printed, depending on what is typed at each `cin` in the program.

The `cin` has its drawbacks. However, if you understand the `cout` operator, `cin` should not pose much of a problem. Therefore, the next few chapters make use of `cin`, until you learn the more powerful (and flexible) input methods. The `cin` operator looks very much like `cout`, containing one or more variables to the right of the operator name. The format of `cin` is

```
cin [>> values];
```

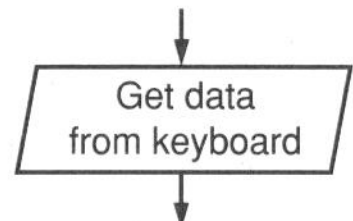

The iostream.h header file contains the information C++ needs for `cin`, so include that file when using `cin`. The `cin` operator uses the same manipulators as the `cout` operator. The *`values`* are the variables into which the data will be placed.

As mentioned, `cin` poses a few problems. The `cin` operator requires that your user type the input *exactly* as `cin` expects it. Because you cannot control the user's typing, its accuracy cannot be ensured. You might want the user to enter an integer value followed by a floating-point value, which your `cin` operator call might expect, yet your user decides to enter something else! If that happens, there is not much you can do; the resulting input will be incorrect, and your C++ program has no reliable method for testing user accuracy.

The `cin` operator requires that the user type correct input. This is not always possible to guarantee!

For the next few chapters, you can assume that the user knows to enter the proper values. But for your own programs used by others, you will want to be on the lookout for additional methods to get better input, starting in Part V of this book.

Examples

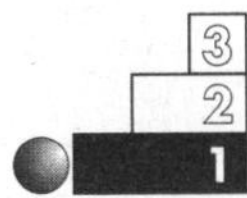

1. If you want a program that computes a 7 percent sales tax, you can use the `cin` statement to get the sales, compute the tax, and print the results. The following program shows you how to do this:

```
// Filename: C8SLTX1.CPP
// Gets a sales amount and prints the sales tax

#include <iostream.h>
#include <iomanip.h>

main()
     {
     float     total_sale;    // User's sales amount
                              // will go here
     float     stax;

     // Get the sales amount from user
     cin >> total_sale;

     // Calculate sales tax
     stax = total_sale * .07;

     cout << "The sales tax for " << setprecision(2)
          << total_sale << " is " << setprecision (2)
          << stax;
     return 0;
     }
```

If you run this program, it will wait for you to enter a value for the total sale. After you press the Enter key, the program calculates the sales tax and prints the results.

If you entered `10.00` as the sales amount, you would see the following output:

```
The sales tax for 10.00 is 0.70
```

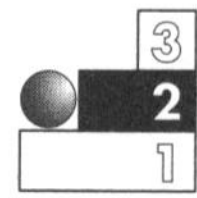

2. The preceding program is fine for introducing `cin` but contains a serious problem. The problem is not in the code itself but in the assumption made about the user. The program does not indicate what it expects the user to enter. The `cin` assumes too much already, so your programs that use `cin` should inform the user exactly what should be typed. The following revision of this program prompts the user with an appropriate message before getting the sales amount:

BEGIN
Prompt for amount
Get amount from keyboard
Calculate sales tax
Print sales tax
END

```
// Filename: C8SLTX2.CPP
// Prompts for a sales amount and prints the sales tax

#include <iostream.h>
#include <iomanip.h>

main()
     {
     float      total_sale;      // User's sales amount
                                 // will go here
     float      stax;

     // Display a message for the user
     cout << "What is the total amount of the sale? ";

     // Get the sales amount from user
     cin >> total_sale;

     // Calculate sales tax
     stax = total_sale * .07;

     cout << "The sales tax for " << setprecision(2)
          << total_sale << " is " << setprecision (2)
          << stax;
     return 0;
     }
```

Because the first `cout` does not contain a newline character, `\n`, the user's response to the prompt will appear directly to the right of the question mark.

3. In inputting keyboard strings into character arrays with `cin`, you are limited to getting one word at a time. The `cin` will not let you type more than one word at a time into a single character array. The following program asks for the user's first and last names. It has to store those two names in two different character arrays because `cin` cannot get both names at once. The program then prints the names in reverse order.

```
// Filename: C8PHON1.CPP
// Program that gets the user's name and prints it
// to the screen as it would appear in a phone book

#include <iostream.h>
#include <iomanip.h>

main()
     {
     char     first[ 20 ], last[ 20 ];

     cout << "What is your first name? ";
     cin >> first;
     cout << "What is your last name? ";
     cin >> last;
     cout << "\n\n";      // Print 2 blank lines
     cout << "In a phone book, your name would look this:\n";
     cout << last << ", " << first;
     return 0;
     }
```

Figure 8.2 shows a sample run from this program.

```
What is your first name? Martha
What is your last name? Roberts


In a phone book, your name would look like this:
Roberts, Martha
```

Figure 8.2. Getting strings from the keyboard.

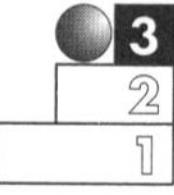

4. Suppose that you want to write a program which does simple addition for your seven-year-old daughter. The following program prompts her for two numbers and then waits for her to type an answer. When she gives her answer, the program displays the correct result so that she can see how well she did. (Later you will learn how you can let her know immediately whether her answer is correct.)

```
// Filename: C8MATH.CPP
// Program to help children with simple addition
// Prompts child for 2 values, after printing a title message
#include <iostream.h>
#include <iomanip.h>

main()
     {
     int     num1, num2, ans;
     int     her_ans;

     cout << "*** Math Practice ***\n\n\n";
     cout << " What is the first number? " );
     cin >> num1;
     cout << "What is the second number? ";
     cin >> num2;

     // Compute answer and give her a chance to wait for it
     ans = num1 + num2;

     cout << "\nWhat do you think is the answer? ";
     cin >> her_ans);      // Nothing is done with this

     // Print answer after a blank line
     cout << "\n" << num1 << " plus " << num2 << " is: "
          << ans << "\n\nHope you got it right!";
     return 0;
     }
```

Summary

You now can print almost anything to the screen. By studying the manipulators and how they behave, you can control your output more thoroughly than ever before. Furthermore, because you can receive keyboard values, your programs are much more powerful. No longer do you have to know your data values when you write the program. You can ask the user to enter values into variables for you with `cin`.

You have the tools to begin writing programs that fit the data processing model of input -> process -> output. This chapter concludes the preliminary discussion of the C++ language. This part of the book provided an overview of the language and showed you enough of its elements so that you can begin writing useful programs as soon as possible.

The next chapter begins a new kind of discussion. You learn how C++'s math and relational operators work on data, and you learn the importance of the precedence table of operators.

Review Questions

Answers to Review Questions are in Appendix B.

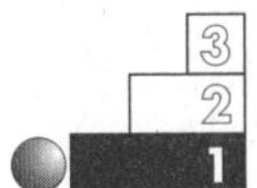

1. What is the difference between `cout` and `cin`?
2. Why is displaying a prompt message important before using `cin` for input?
3. How many values are entered with the following `cin`?

```
cin >> i >> j >> k >> l;
```

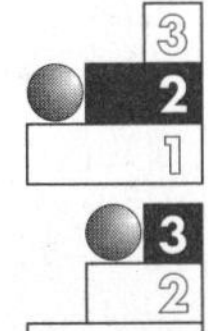

4. Because both methods put values into variables, is there any difference between assigning values to variables and using `cin` to give them values?
5. What is the output produced by the following `cout`?

```
cout << "The backslash, \"\\\" character is special";
```

6. What is the result of the following `cout`?

```
cout << setw(8) << setprecision(3) << 123.456789;
```

Review Exercises

1. Write a program that prompts for the user's name and weight. Store these values in separate variables and print them to the screen.

2. Assume that you are a college professor who needs to average grades for 10 students. Write a program that prompts for 10 different grades and displays an average of them.

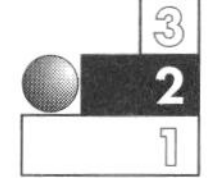

3. Modify the program in exercise 2 to ask for each student's name as well as grade. Print the grade list to the screen, with each student's name and grade in two columns. Make sure that the columns align by using a `setw` manipulator on the grade. At the bottom, print the average of the grades. (HINT: Store the 10 names and 10 grades in different variables with different names.) This program is easy but takes about 30 lines, plus appropriate comments and prompts. Later you learn ways to streamline this program.

4. Write a program that prompts for the user's full name, hours worked, hourly rate, and tax rate, and then displays the taxes and net pay in the appropriate dollars and cents. (Store the first, middle, and last names in three separate character arrays.)

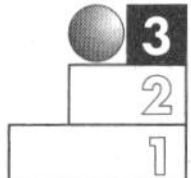

5. Modify the child's math program (C8MATH.CPP), shown earlier in this chapter, so that it practices subtraction, multiplication, and division after it finishes the addition.

6. This exercise tests your understanding of the backslash conversion character. Write a program that uses `cout` operators to produce the following illustration on the screen:

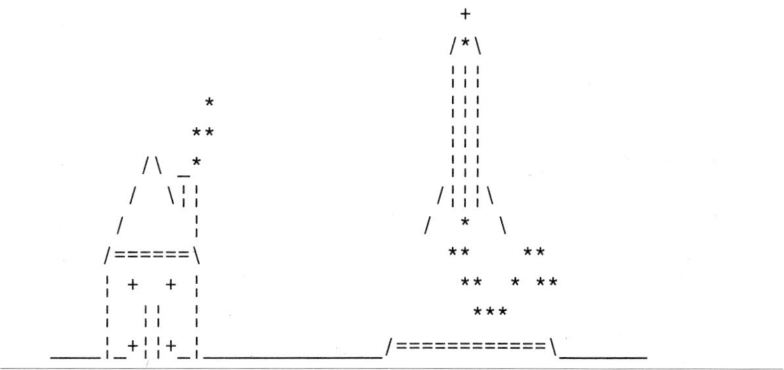

Part II

Using C++ Operators

Using C++ Math Operators and Precedence

You may be dreading this chapter if you don't like math. Relax! C++ does all your math for you. It's a misconception that you have to be good at math to understand how to program computers. The opposite is true. The computer is there to be your slave, follow your instructions, and do all the calculations.

This chapter shows how C++ computes by introducing these topics:

- C++'s primary math operators
- The operator precedence table
- Multiple assignments
- Compound operators
- Mixed data type conversions
- Type casting

Many people who dislike math actually enjoy learning how the computer does calculations. After seeing the operators and a few simple ways in which C++ uses them, you will feel comfortable putting calculations in your programs. Computers are very fast, and they can perform math operations many times faster than people.

The Primary Math Operators

C++ *math operators* are symbols used for addition, subtraction, multiplication, and division, as well as other similar operations. C++ operators are not always mathematical in nature, but many are. Table 9.1 lists the primary C++ operators and their meanings.

Table 9.1. The C++ primary operators and their meanings.

Symbol	*Meaning*
*	Multiplication
/	Division and integer division
%	Modulus or remainder
+	Addition
-	Subtraction

Most of these operators work in ways familiar to you. Multiplication, addition, and subtraction produce the same results (and the division operator usually does) that you get when you do these math functions with a calculator. Table 9.2 shows examples that illustrate four of these simple operators.

Table 9.2. Some typical results of using operators.

Formula	*Result*
`4 * 2`	`8`
`64 / 4`	`16`
`80 - 15`	`65`
`12 + 9`	`21`

Table 9.2 contains examples of *binary operations* performed with four operators. Do not confuse this term with binary numbers. When an operator is used between two constants or variables (or a combination of both), it is called a binary operator because it operates on two values. When you use these operators (as in assigning their results to variables), C++ does not care whether or not you put spaces around the operators.

NOTE: Use the asterisk (`*`) for multiplication and not an *x*, which you normally use when you multiply by hand. An *x* cannot be used because C++ would confuse it with a variable called `x`. C++ would not know whether you wanted to multiply or to use the value of that variable.

The Unary Operators

You can use the addition and subtraction operators by themselves. When you do, they are called *unary operators*. A unary operator operates on, or affects, a single value. For instance, you can assign a variable a positive or negative number by using a unary `+` or `-`. In addition, you can assign a variable another positive or negative variable by using a unary `+` or `-`.

Examples

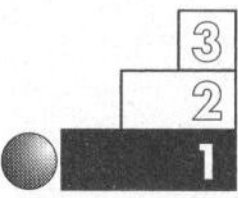

1. The following section of code assigns four variables a positive or negative number. All the plus signs (+) and minus signs (-) are unary because they are not used between two values.

The variable a *becomes equal to negative 25.*
The variable b *becomes equal to positive 25.*
The variable c *becomes equal to negative* a.
The variable d *becomes equal to positive* b.

```
a = -25;     // Assign 'a' a negative 25
b = +25;     // Assign 'b' a positive 25 (The plus sign is
             // unneeded)
c = -a;      // Assign 'c' the negative of 'a' (25)
d = +b;      // Assign 'd' the positive of 'b' (The plus sign
             // is unneeded)
```

2. You generally don't have to use the unary plus sign. C++ assumes that a number or variable is positive even if you don't put a + in front of it. The following four statements are equivalent to the last ones, except that these don't contain plus signs:

```
a = -25;     // Assign 'a' a negative 25
b =  25;     // Assign 'b' a positive 25
c = -a;      // Assign 'c' the negative of 'a' (25)
d =  b;      // Assign 'd' the positive of 'b'
```

3. The unary negative comes in handy when you want to negate a single number or variable. The negative of a negative is positive. Therefore, the following short program assigns a negative number (using the unary -) to a variable and then prints the negative of that variable. Because it had a negative number to begin with, the cout produces a positive result.

```
// Filename: C9NEG.CPP
// The negative of a variable that contains a negative value

#include <iostream.h>

main()
     {
     signed int     temp = -12;     // 'signed' is unneeded
                                    // since that is default

     cout << -temp;     // Produce a 12 on the screen
     return 0;
     }
```

The variable declaration did not need the `signed` prefix because all integer variables are `signed` by default.

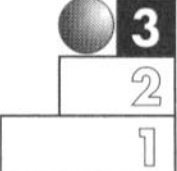

4. If you want to subtract the negative of a variable, make sure that you put a space before the unary minus sign. For example, the line

```
new_temp = old_temp - -inversion_factor;
```

temporarily negates the `inversion_factor` and then subtracts that negated value from `old_temp`.

Division and Modulus

The division operator (`/`) and the modulus operator (`%`) may operate in ways unfamiliar to you. They are usually as easy to use, though, as the other operators just discussed.

The forward slash (`/`) always divides. However, it produces an integer division if integer values (constants, variables, or a combination of both) appear on both sides of the `/`. If there is a remainder, C++ discards it.

The modulus operator (`%`) computes the remainder of division.

The percent sign (`%`) produces a modulus, or a remainder, of an integer division. This operator requires integers on both sides and will not work otherwise.

Examples

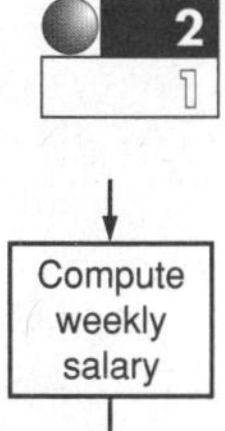

1. Suppose that you want to compute your weekly pay. The following program asks for your yearly pay, divides it by 52, and prints the results to two decimal places:

```
// Filename: C9DIV.CPP
// Displays user's weekly pay

#include <iostream.h>
#include <iomanip.h>

main()
     {
     float     weekly, yearly;

     cout << "What is your annual pay? ";  // Prompt user
     cin >> yearly;

     weekly = yearly / 52;  // Compute the weekly
     cout << "\n\nYour weekly pay is "
          << setprecision(2) << weekly;
     return 0;
     }
```

Because a floating-point number is used in the division, C++ produces a floating-point result. Here is a sample run from this program:

```
What is your annual pay? 38000.00
Your weekly pay is $730.77
```

2. Integer division does not round its results. If you divide two integers and the answer is not a whole number, C++ ignores the fractional part. The following `cout`s help show this. The output that would result from each `cout` appears in the comment to the right of each line.

```
cout << 10 / 2 << " \n";      // 5  (no remainder)
cout << 300 / 100 << " \n";   // 3  (no remainder)
cout << 10 / 3 << " \n";      // 3  (discarded remainder)
cout << 300 / 165 << " \n";   // 1  (discarded remainder)
```

3. The modulus operator produces an integer remainder. If the preceding four couts used the modulus operator, the output would show only the remainder of each division, as in the following:

```
cout << 10 % 2 << " \n";      // 0  (no remainder)
cout << 300 % 100 << " \n";   // 0  (no remainder)
cout << 10 % 3 << " \n"; // 1 (Answer: 3 with '1' remaining)
cout << 300 % 165 << " \n";   // 135 (Answer: 1 with '135'
                              // remaining)
```

The modulus operator will come in handy for several types of applications once you learn a few more commands. You can use the modulus to make sure that the user entered an odd or even number and to check whether a year is a leap year, as well as test for several other helpful values.

The Order of Precedence

Knowing the meaning of the math operators is the first of two steps toward understanding C++ calculations. You must also understand the *order of precedence*. This order (sometimes called the *math hierarchy* or *order of operators*) determines exactly how C++ computes formulas. The precedence of operators is the same as that used in high school algebra courses. (Oops, don't be frightened — this is the easy part of algebra!) To see how the order of precedence works, try to determine the result of the following simple calculation:

```
2 + 3 * 2
```

If you said 10, you would not be alone; many people would respond with 10. However, 10 is correct only if you interpret the formula from left to right. But what if you calculated the multiplication first? If you took the value of `3 * 2` and got an answer of 6, and then added 2 to it, you would end up with 8. This is exactly the answer — 8 — that C++ computes!

Perform multiplication, division, and modulus before addition and subtraction.

C++ always performs multiplication, division, and modulus first, and then performs addition and subtraction. Table 9.3 shows the order of the operators you have seen so far. There are many more levels to C++'s precedence table of operators than those shown in

Table 9.3. Unlike most computer languages, C++ has 15 levels of precedence. Appendix D contains the complete table of precedence. Notice in Appendix D's precedence table that multiplication, division, and modulus reside on level 3, one level higher than level 4's addition and subtraction. In the next few chapters, you learn how to use the rest of the precedence table in your C++ programs.

Table 9.3. The order of precedence for the primary operators.

Order	*Operators*
First	Multiplication, division, modulus remainder (*, /, %)
Second	Addition, subtraction (+, -)

Examples

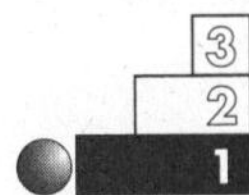

1. Following C++'s order of operators is easy if you look at the intermediate results one at a time. The three calculations in Figure 9.1 show you how to do this.

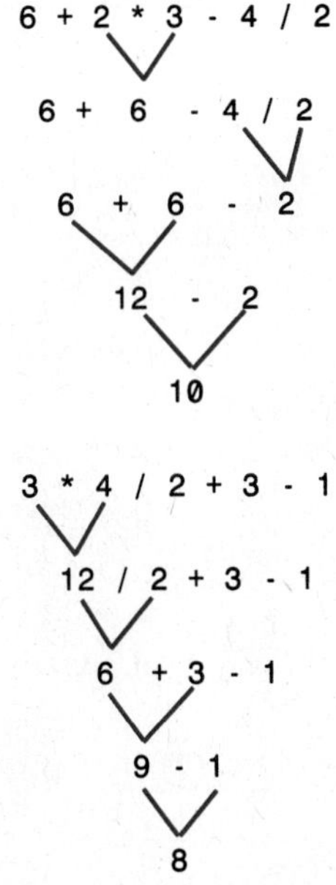

figure continues

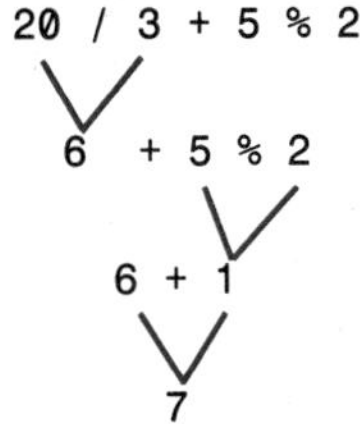

Figure 9.1. Sample calculations showing C++'s order of operators.

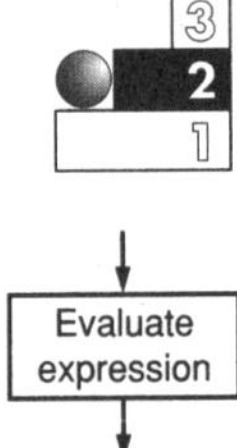

2. Looking back at the order of precedence table again, you will notice that multiplication, division, and modulus are on the same level. This implies that there is no hierarchy on that level. If more than one of these operators appear in a calculation, C++ performs the math from left to right. The same is true of addition and subtraction; the leftmost calculation will be done first. Figure 9.2 shows an example.

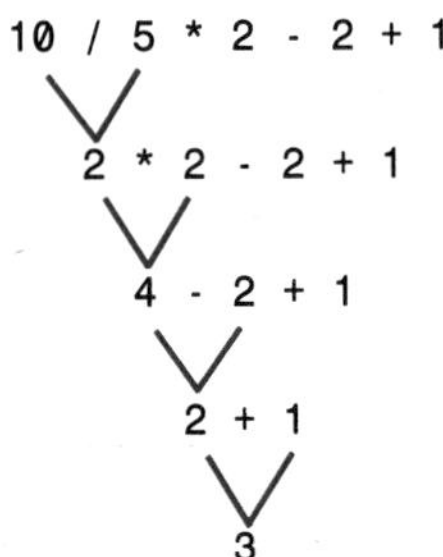

Figure 9.2. Sample calculation showing C++'s order of operators from left to right.

Because the division appears to the left of the multiplication, the division is computed first because both are on the same level in the precedence table (Appendix D).

You now should be able to follow the order of these C++ operators. You really do not need to worry about the math because C++ does all the work. However, you should understand the order of operators so that you will know how to structure your calculations. Now you are ready to see how you can override the order of precedence with parentheses.

Using Parentheses

If you want to override the order of precedence, put parentheses in your calculations. The parentheses actually reside on a level above the multiplication, division, and modulus in the precedence table. In other words, any calculation in parentheses — whether it is addition, subtraction, division, or something else — is always performed before the rest of the line. The other calculations are performed in their normal operator order.

Parentheses override the normal precedence of math operators.

The first formula in this section, `2 + 3 * 2`, produced an 8 because the multiplication was performed before addition. However, by adding parentheses around the addition, as in `(2 + 3) * 2`, the answer becomes 10.

In the precedence table shown in Appendix D, the parentheses reside on level 1, the highest level in the table. Being higher than the other levels means that the parentheses take precedence over multiplication, division, and all the other operators you have seen.

Examples

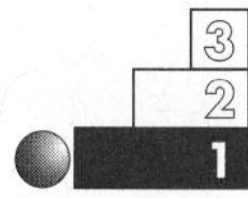

1. The calculations in Figure 9.3 illustrate how parentheses override the regular order of operators. These are the same three formulas shown in the last section, except that their results are calculated differently because of the use of parentheses.

```
6 + 2 * (3 - 4) / 2
6 + 2 * -1 / 2
6 + -2 / 2
6 + - 1
5
```

figure continues

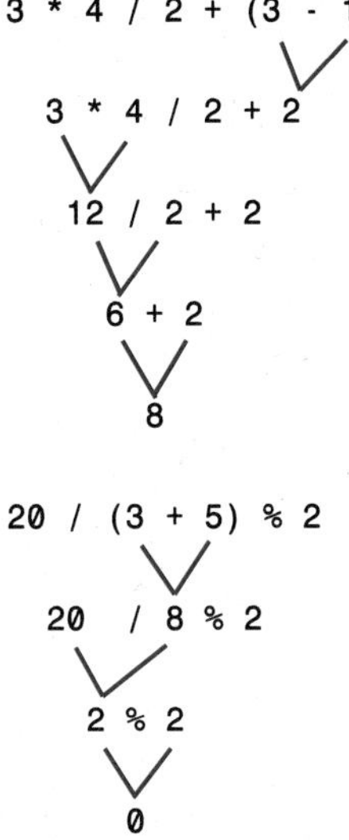

Figure 9.3. The use of parentheses as the highest level of precedence.

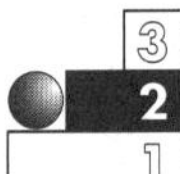

2. If an expression contains parentheses within parentheses, C++ evaluates the contents of the innermost parentheses first. The expression in Figure 9.4 illustrates this.

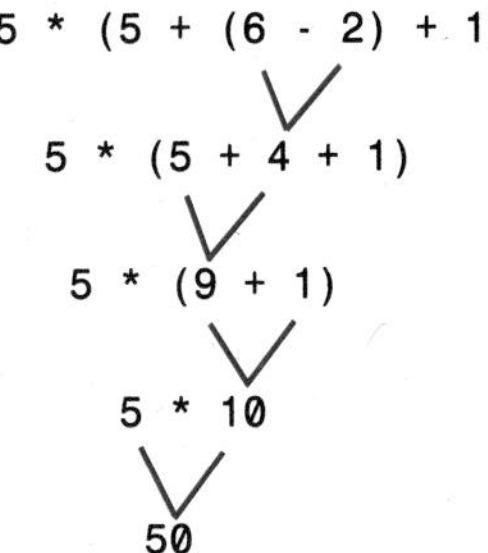

Figure 9.4. The use of parentheses within parentheses.

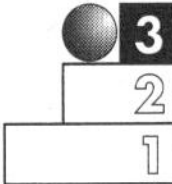

3. The following program produces an incorrect result, even though it looks as if it should work. See if you can spot the error.

Comments to identify your program.
Include the header file iostream.h.
Include the header file iomanip.h.
Start of the `main()` *function.*

> *Declare the variables* `avg`, `grade1`, `grade2`, *and* `grade3` *as floating-point integers.*
> *Set the variable* `grade1` *to 85.0.*
> *Set the variable* `grade2` *to 80.0.*
> *Set the variable* `grade3` *to 75.0.*
> *The variable* `avg` *becomes equal to* `grade1` *plus* `grade2` *plus* `grade3` *divided by 3.0.*
> *Print to the screen* `The average is` *and the average of the 3 grade variables.*
> *Return from the* `main()` *function.*

```
// Filename: C9AVG1.CPP
// Computes the average of three grades

#include <iostream.h>
#include <iomanip.h>

main()
     {
     float     avg, grade1, grade2, grade3;

     grade1 = 85.0;
     grade2 = 80.0;
     grade3 = 75.0;
     avg = grade1 + grade2 + grade3 / 3.0;
     cout << "The average is " << setprecision(1) << avg;
     return 0;
     }
```

The problem is that division is performed first. Therefore, the third grade is first divided by three, and then the other two grades are added to that result. To fix the problem, you just need to add one set of parentheses, as shown here:

```
// Filename: C9AVG2.CPP
// Computes the average of three grades
```

```
#include <iostream.h>
#include <iomanip.h>

main()
     {
     float     avg, grade1, grade2, grade3;

     grade1 = 85.0;
     grade2 = 80.0;
     grade3 = 75.0;
     avg = (grade1 + grade2 + grade3) / 3.0;
     cout << "The average is " << setprecision(1) << avg;
     return 0;
     }
```

TIP: Use plenty of parentheses in your C++ programs to make the order of operators clearer, even when you don't have to override their default order. It sometimes makes the calculations easier to understand when you later modify the program.

Shorter Is Not Always Better

When you program computers for a living, it is much more important to write programs that are easy to understand than to write programs that are short or include tricky calculations.

Maintainability is the computer industry's word for changing and updating programs originally written in a simple style. The business world is changing rapidly, and the programs that companies used for years must be updated to reflect the changing environment. Businesses do not always have the resources to write programs from scratch, so they have to make do with modifying the ones they have.

Years ago, when computer hardware was much more expensive, and when computer memories were much smaller, it was important that you write small programs, despite the problems they caused when they needed to be changed. This was aggravated when the original programmers left and someone else (you!) had to step in and modify another person's code.

Companies are realizing the importance of spending time to write programs that are easy to modify and that do not rely on tricks or "quick and dirty" routines that are hard to follow. You will be a more valuable programmer if you write clean programs, with lots of white space, many remarks, and straightforward code. Put parentheses around formulas to make them clearer, and use variables for storing results in case you need the same answer later in the program. Break long calculations into several smaller ones.

Throughout this book, you will see tips on writing maintainable programs. You and your colleagues will appreciate these tips when you incorporate them into your own C++ programs.

The Assignment Statement

In C++, the assignment operator, =, is used more extensively than in other languages. So far, you have seen this operator used for the simple assignment of values to variables. This is consistent with its use in most programming languages. In C++, the assignment operator can also be used in other ways, such as for multiple assignment and compound assignment. This discussion illustrates these additional uses.

Multiple Assignment

If more than one equal sign appears in an expression, each = performs an assignment. This multiple use introduces a new aspect of the precedence order. Consider the following expression:

```
a = b = c = d = e = 100;
```

This may seem confusing at first, especially if you know other computer languages. To C++, the equal sign always means to "assign the value on the right to the variable on the left." This right-to-left order is described in Appendix D's precedence table. The third column in the table is labeled *Associativity*. The Associativity column describes the direction of the operation. The assignment operator associates from right to left, whereas some of the other operators associate from left to right.

Because the assignment associates from right to left, the preceding expression first assigns the 100 to the variable named `e`. This produces a value, 100, of the expression. In C++, all expressions produce values, typically the result of assignments. Therefore, this value (100) is then assigned to the variable `d`. The value of that, 100, is assigned to `c`, then to `b`, and finally to `a`. Whatever values were in the five variables previous to this statement are replaced by 100 after the statement finishes.

C++ does not automatically set variables to zero before you use them, so you might want to zero them out before you use them with a single assignment statement. The following section of variable declarations and initialization is performed with multiple assignment statements:

Initialize several variables

```
#include <iostream.h>
main()
    {
    int       ctr, num_emp, num_dep;
    float     sales, salary, amount;

    ctr = num_emp = num_dep = 0;
    sales = salary = amount = 0;
    // Rest of program follows
```

In C++, you can include the assignment statement almost anywhere in a program, even within another calculation. For example, note this statement:

```
value = 5 + (r = 9 - c);
```

This is a perfectly legal C++ statement. The assignment operator resides on the first level of the precedence table and always produces a value. Because its associativity is from right to left, the `r` is first assigned `9 - c`, because the equal sign on the right is evaluated first. The subexpression `(r = 9 - c)` produces a value — whatever is placed into `r` — which is added to 5 before that result is stored in `value`.

Examples

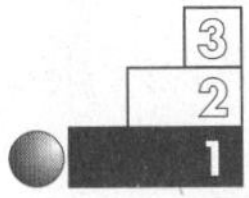

1. Because C++ does not initialize variables to zero before you use them, you may want to include a multiple assignment operator to zero them out before using them. The following section of code ensures that all variables are initialized before the rest of the program uses them:

```
#include <iostream.h>
main()
     {
     int       num_emp, dependents, age;
     float     salary, hr_rate, taxrate;

     // Initialize all variables to zero
     num_emp = dependents = age = hours = 0;
     salary = hr_rate = taxrate = 0.0;

     // Rest of program follows
```

2. The two statements

```
gross = hr_rate * hours;
salary = taxrate * gross;
```

can be combined into one with the multiple assignment operator, as in

```
salary = taxrate * (gross = hr_rate * hours);
```

Use these types of statements judiciously. Even though combining statements may be more efficient than using two statements, combined statements are not necessarily clearer to use.

Compound Assignment

Many times in programming, you will want to update the value of a variable. That is, you will need to take a variable's current value, add or multiply that value by an expression, and then assign it back to the original variable. The following assignment statement demonstrates this:

```
salary = salary * 1.2;
```

This expression multiplies the old value of `salary` by 1.2 (in effect, raising the value in `salary` by 20 percent) and then assigns it back to `salary`. C++ provides several operators, called *compound operators*, that you can use whenever the same variable appears on both sides of the equal sign. The compound operators are shown in Table 9.4.

Table 9.4. The compound operators.

Operator	*Example*	*Equivalent*
`+=`	`bonus += 500;`	`bonus = bonus + 500;`
`-=`	`budget -= 50;`	`budget = budget - 50;`
`*=`	`salary *= 1.2;`	`salary = salary * 1.2;`
`/=`	`factor /= .50;`	`factor = factor / .50;`
`%=`	`daynum %= 7;`	`daynum = daynum % 7;`

The compound operators are low in the precedence table. They are typically evaluated very late in equations that use them.

Examples

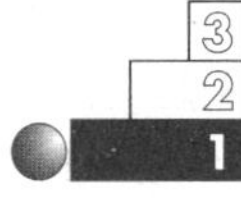

1. Suppose that you have been storing your factory's production amount in a variable called `prod_amt`, and your supervisor has just informed you of a new addition that needs to be applied to that production value. You could code this update in a statement that looks like this:

```
prod_amt = prod_amt + 2.6;  // Add 2.6 to current production
```

Instead of this formula, you should use C++'s compound addition operator by coding the update in this way:

```
prod_amt += 2.6;  // Add 2.6 to current production
```

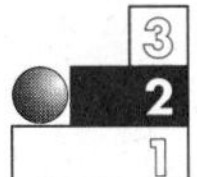

2. Suppose that you are a high school teacher who wants to adjust your students' grades upward. You gave a test that seemed too difficult, and the grades were not up to your expectations. If you had stored each student's grade in variables named `grade1`, `grade2`, `grade3`, and so on, you could update the grades from within a program with the following section of compound assignments:

```
grade1 *= 1.1;     // Increase each student's grade by 10%
grade2 *= 1.1;
grade3 *= 1.1;
// Rest of grade changes follow
```

3. The precedence of the compound operators requires important consideration when you decide how to code compound assignments. Notice in Appendix D that the compound operators are on level 14, much lower than the regular math operators. This means that you must be careful how you interpret them.

   Suppose, for example, that you want to update the value of a sales variable with the following formula:

```
4 - factor + bonus
```

   You could update the sales variable with the statement

```
sales += 4 - factor + bonus;
```

   This applies the new formula, `4 - factor + bonus`, to sales. This is *not* the same as

```
sales = sales + 4 - factor + bonus;
```

   Because the `+=` operator is much lower in the precedence table than `+` or `-`, `+=` is performed last and with right-to-left associativity. Therefore, the following two statements *are* equivalent:

```
sales += 4 - factor + bonus;
sales = sales + (4 - factor + bonus);
```

4. To give you a better idea of the compound operators and their precedence level, the following program uses each compound operator and prints a result based on the operators. The program and its output will help you understand how to use the compound operators and their levels in the precedence table.

```
// Filename: C9CMP.CPP
// Illustrates each compound operator

#include <iostream.h>

main()
     {
     int     i = 4;
     int     j = 8;
     int     k = 12;
     int     ans;           // Will hold various results

     ans = i + j;
     cout << ans << " \n";     // Print a 12
     ans += k;
     cout << ans << " \n";     // Print a 24
     ans /= 3;
     cout << ans << " \n";     // Print an 8
     ans -= 5;
     cout << ans << " \n";     // Print a 3
     ans *= 2;
     cout << ans << " \n";     // Print a 6
     ans %= 4;
     cout << ans << " \n";     // Print a 2

// Order of precedence affects the following
     ans *= 5 + 3;
     cout << ans << " \n";     // Print a 16
     ans += 4 - 2;
     cout << ans << " \n";     // Print an 18

     return 0;
     }
```

Mixing Data Types in Calculations

You can mix data types in C++, such as adding together an integer and a floating-point value. C++ will generally convert the smaller type to the larger type. For instance, if you add a double to an integer, C++ first converts the integer to a double value and then performs the calculation. This produces the most accurate result possible. The automatic conversion of data types is only temporary; the converted value is back in its original data type as soon as the expression is finished.

C++ attempts to convert the smaller data type to the larger one in a mixed data type expression.

If C++ converted two different data types to the smaller value's type, the higher-precision value would be truncated (shortened) too much, and accuracy would be lost. For example, in the following short program, the floating-point value of `sales` is added to an integer called `bonus`. Before computing the answer, C++ converts `bonus` to a floating-point value, which results in a floating-point answer.

Compute bonus

```
// Filename: C9DATA.CPP
// Demonstrates mixed data type in an expression

#include <iostream.h>
#include <iomanip.h>

main()
     {
     int       bonus = 50;
     float     salary = 1400.50;
     float     total;

     total = salary + bonus;    // bonus becomes
                                // floating-point temporarily
     cout << "The total is " << setprecision(2) << total;
     return 0;
     }
```

Type Casting

Most of the time, you will not have to worry about C++'s automatic conversion of data types. However, problems can occur if you mix unsigned variables with variables of other data types. Because of differences between computer architecture, unsigned variables do not always convert to the larger data type. Therefore, loss of accuracy may result, and even incorrect results are possible.

You can override C++'s default conversions by specifying your own temporary type change. This is called *type casting*. When you type cast, you temporarily change a variable's data type from its declared data type to a new one. The format of a type cast is

```
(data type) expression
```

where `data type` can be any valid C++ data type, and the `expression` can be a variable, a constant, or an expression that combines both. The following line of code type casts the integer variable `age` into a double floating-point variable temporarily, so that it can be multiplied by the double floating-point `factor`.

Assign the variable `age_factor` *the value of the variable* age *(now a double floating-point variable) and multiply by the variable* `factor`*.*

```
age_factor = (double)age * factor;    // Temporarily change
                                      // age to double
```

Examples

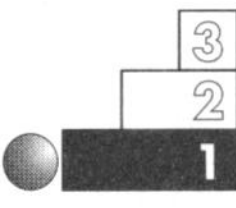

1. Suppose that you want to verify the interest calculation used by your bank on a loan. The interest rate is 15.5 percent, stored as `0.155` in a floating-point variable. The amount of interest you owe is computed by multiplying the interest rate by the amount of the loan balance, and then multiplying that by the number of days in the year since the loan was originated. The following program finds the daily interest rate by dividing the annual interest rate by 365, the number of days in a year. C++ must convert the integer `365` to a

floating-point constant automatically, because it is used in combination with a floating-point variable.

```
// C9INT1.CPP
// Calculates interest on a loan

#include <iostream.h>
#include <iomanip.h>

main()
     {
     int       days = 45;  // Days since loan origination
     float     principal = 3500.00;   // Original loan amount
     float     interest_rate = 0.155; // Annual interest rate
     float     daily_interest;        // Daily interest rate

     daily_interest = interest_rate / 365;   // Compute
                                        // floating-point value

     // Since days is an integer, it too will be converted
     // to float next
     daily_interest = principal * daily_interest * days;
     principal += daily_interest;    // Update the principal
                                     // with interest
     cout << "The balance you owe is "
          << setiosflags(ios::fixed) << setprecision(2)
          << principal;
     return 0;
     }
```

Here is the output of this program:

```
The balance you owe is 3566.88
```

2. Instead of letting C++ perform the conversion, you may want to type cast all mixed expressions to ensure that they convert to your liking. Here is the same program that appears in example 1, except that type casts are used to convert the integer constants to floating-point values before they are used.

```
// C9INT2.CPP
// Calculates interest on a loan using type casting

#include <iostream.h>
#include <iomanip.h>

main()
     {
     int       days = 45;  // Days since loan origination
     float     principal = 3500.00;    // Original loan amount
     float     interest_rate = 0.155; // Annual interest rate
     float     daily_interest;        // Daily interest rate

     // Type cast days to float
     daily_interest = interest_rate / (float)365;

     // Since days is an integer, convert it to float too
     daily_interest = principal * daily_interest *
(float)days;
     principal += daily_interest;     // Update the principal
                                      // with interest
     cout << "The balance you owe is "
          << setiosflags(ios::fixed) << setprecision(2)
          << principal;
     return 0;
     }
```

The output from this program will be exactly the same as the output from the first program.

Summary

You now understand C++'s primary math operators and the important precedence table. Parentheses group operations together so that they override the default precedence levels. Unlike some operators in other programming languages, every operator in C++ has a meaning, no matter where the operator appears in an expression. You can therefore use the assignment operator (=) in the middle of other expressions.

When performing math with C++, you must be aware of how C++ interprets data types, especially when you mix them within the same expression. You can temporarily type cast a variable or constant in order to override its default data type.

This chapter introduced you to C++ operators. The next two chapters extend this discussion to include relational and logical operators, which enable you to compare data and compute accordingly.

Review Questions

Answers to Review Questions are in Appendix B.

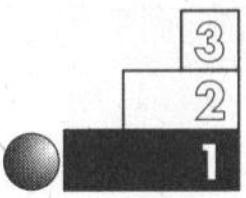

1. What is the result of each of the following expressions?

   A. `1 + 2 * 4 / 2`

   B. `(1 + 2) * 4 / 2`

   C. `1 + 2 * (4 / 2)`

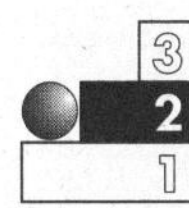

2. What is the result of each of these expressions?

   A. `9 % 2 + 1`

   B. `(1 + (10 - (2 + 2)))`

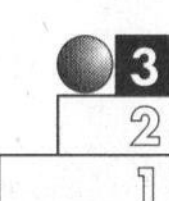

3. Convert each of the following formulas into its C++ assignment equivalents:

   A. $a = \frac{3 + 3}{4 + 4}$

   B. $x = (a - b) * (a - c)2$

   C. $f = \frac{a1/2}{b1/3}$

   D. $d = \frac{(8 - x2)}{(x - 9)} - \frac{(4 * 2 - 1)}{x3}$

4. Write a short program that prints the area of a circle with a radius of 4 and pi = 3.14159. (The area of a circle is computed by `pi * radius²`.)

5. Write the assignment and `cout` statement that prints the remainder of 100 / 4.

Review Exercises

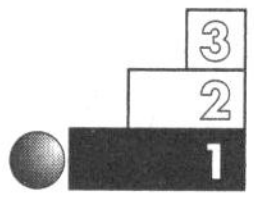

1. Write a program that prints each of the first 8 powers of 2 — that is, $2^1, 2^2, 2^3, \ldots, 2^8$. Please include a comment to indicate your name at the top of the program. Print string constants that describe each answer printed. The first two lines of your output should look like this:

```
2 raised to the first power is: 2
2 raised to the second power is: 4
```

2. Change C8DIV.CPP, shown in the preceding chapter, so that it computes and prints a bonus of 15 percent of the gross pay. Taxes are not to be taken out of the bonus. After printing the four variables `gross_pay`, `tax_rate`, `bonus`, and `net_pay`, print a check on the screen that looks like a printed check. Add string constants so that it prints the name of the payee, and put your name as the payor at the bottom of the check.

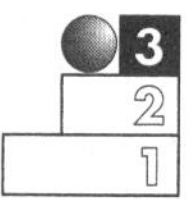

3. Store in variables the weights and ages of three people. Print a table, with titles, of the weights and ages. At the bottom of the table, print the average of the weights and heights as well as their totals.

4. Assume that a video store employee worked 50 hours. She gets paid $4.50 for the first 40 hours, gets time and a half (1.5 times the regular pay rate) for the first 5 hours over 40, and gets double time for all hours over 45. Assuming a 28% tax rate, write a program that prints her gross pay, taxes, and net pay to the screen. Label each amount with appropriate titles (using string constants) and add appropriate comments in the program.

Relational Operators

At times, you don't want every statement in your C++ program to execute whenever the program runs. So far, each program you have seen began executing at the top of the program and continued, line by line, until the last statement executed. Depending on your application, you may not always want this to happen.

Your programs are known as *data-driven* programs. That is, the data should dictate what the program does. You would not want the computer to print paychecks for all employees every pay period; some employees may have taken a leave of absence, or they may be on a sales commission and didn't make a sale during a particular pay period. Printing paychecks with zero dollars would be ridiculous. You want the computer to print checks to employees who have pay coming to them but not to others.

In this chapter, you learn how to create data-driven programs. Such programs do not execute the same way every time they are run. The use of *relational operators* makes this possible. These operators conditionally control other statements. The relational operators look at the constants and variables in the program and operate based on what they find. This may sound difficult, but it is very straightforward and intuitive.

This chapter introduces the following topics:

- Relational operators
- The `if` statement
- The `else` statement

Besides introducing these comparison commands, the chapter prepares you for much more powerful programs that are possible once you learn them.

Looking at Relational Operators

Relational operators compare data.

In addition to using the math operators discussed in the last chapter, you can use other operators to make data comparisons. These operators are called *relational operators*. They compare data, letting you know whether two variables are equal or not equal, or which one is less or more than the other. Table 10.1 lists the relational operators and their meanings.

Table 10.1. The relational operators.

Operator	*Description*
==	Equal to
>	Greater than
<	Less than
>=	Greater than or equal to
<=	Less than or equal to
!=	Not equal to

The six operators in Table 10.1 provide the foundation for comparing data in C++. Each operator always appears with two constants, variables, expressions, or a mix of these — one on each side of the operator. Many of the relational operators are probably familiar to you. You should learn them as well as you know the +, -, *, /, and % mathematical operators.

> **NOTE:** Unlike many programming languages, C++ tests for equality with a double equal sign (==). The single equal sign (=) is reserved for assignment of values only.

Examples

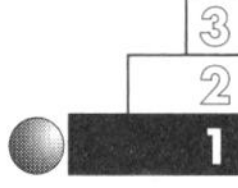

1. Assume that a program initializes four variables in this way:

```
int  a = 5;
int  b = 10;
int  c = 15;
int  d = 5;
```

The following statements are then true:

`a` is equal to `d` so `a == d`.

`b` is less than `c` so `b < c`.

`c` is greater than `a` so `c > a`.

`b` is greater than or equal to `a` so `b >= a`.

`d` is less than or equal to `b` so `d <= b`.

`b` is not equal to `c` so `b != c`.

These are not C++ statements but are statements of relational fact about the values in the variables. Relational logic is easy.

Relational logic always produces a *True* or *False* result. In some programming languages, you cannot directly use the True or False result of relational operators inside other expressions, but in C++ you can. You will soon see how to do this, but for now, the following True and False evaluations are correct:

A *True* relational result evaluates to 1.

A *False* relational result evaluates to 0.

Each of the examples presented earlier in this example evaluate to a 1, or True, result.

2. Assuming the values in the last example's four variables, each of the following statements about those values is False (0):

```
a == b

b > c

d < a

d > a

a != d

b >= c

c <= b
```

You should study these statements to see why each one is False and evaluates to 0. The variables a and d are exactly equal to the same value (5), so neither is greater or less than the other.

You deal with relational logic in everyday life. Think of the following statements you might make:

"The generic butter costs less than the name brand."

"My child is younger than Johnny."

"Our salaries are equal."

"The dogs are not the same age."

Each of these statements is either True or False. There is no other possible outcome.

Watch the Signs!

Many people say that they are "not math-inclined" or "not very logical," and you may be one of them. As mentioned earlier, you do not have to be good in math to be a good computer programmer. And you should not be frightened by the term "relational logic" because you just saw that you use it all the time. Nevertheless, some people get confused about its meaning.

The two primary relational operators, less than (<) and greater than (>), are easy to remember. You may have been taught which is which in school, but you may have forgotten them. Actually, their symbols tell you what they mean.

The "arrow points" of the < and > indicate the smaller of the two values. Notice in the True statements in example 1 that the point of each < and > always goes toward the smaller number. The large, open part of the operators points to the larger values.

The relation is False if the point goes in the wrong direction. In other words, `4 > 9` is False because the point of the operator is pointing to the 9. Or, in English, "4 is greater than 9 is a False statement because 4 is really less than 9."

The `if` Statement

You incorporate relational operators in C++ programs with the `if` statement. This statement is called a *decision statement* because it tests a relationship, using the relational operators, and makes a decision about which statement to execute next, based on the result of that decision. The `if` statement has the following format:

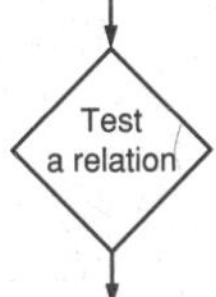


```
if (condition)
     { A block of 1 or more C++ statements }
```

The *`condition`* includes any relational comparison and must be enclosed within parentheses. You saw several relational comparisons earlier, such as `a == d` and `c < d`. The *`block of one or more C++ statements`* is any possible C++ statement, such as an assignment or the `cout` operator, enclosed within braces. The block of the `if`, sometimes called the `body` of the `if` statement, is usually indented a few spaces for readability. This lets you see at a glance exactly what executes if the *`condition`* is True.

If only one statement follows the `if`, the braces are not required, but they are helpful to include. The block will execute *only if the condition is True.* If the condition is False, C++ ignores the block and simply executes the next statement in the program following the `if` statement.

Basically, you can read an `if` statement in the following way: "If the condition is True, perform the block of statements inside the braces. Otherwise, the condition must be False, so do *not* execute the block but continue execution as though the `if` did not exist."

The `if` statement makes a decision.

The if statement is used to make a decision. The block of statements following the if executes if the decision (the result of the relation) is True, and the block does not execute otherwise. As with relational logic, you use "if" logic every day. Consider the following:

"If the day is warm, I will go swimming."

"If I make enough money, we will build a new house."

"If the light is green, go."

"If the light is red, stop."

Each of these statements is *conditional*. That is, if and only *if* the condition is True will you complete the statement.

CAUTION: Do not put a semicolon after the parentheses of the relational test. Semicolons go after each statement inside the block.

Expressions as Conditions

C++ always interprets any nonzero value as True and interprets zero as False. This lets you insert regular nonconditional expressions within the `if` logic. To see this, consider the following section of code:

```
main()
     {
     int      age = 21;      // Declare and assign age a
                             // value of 21
     if (age = 85)
          {
          cout << "You have lived through a lot!";
          // Rest of program goes here
```

At first, it may seem as though the `cout` does not execute, *but it does*. Because a regular assignment operator, `=`, is used and not a relational operator, `==`, C++ performs the assignment of 85 to `age`. As in all the assignments you saw in the last chapter, this produces a value for the expression of 85. Since 85 is nonzero, C++ interprets the `if` condition as True and performs the body of the `if` statement.

NOTE: Mixing the relational equality test (==) and the regular assignment operator (=) is a common error made in C++ programs. The nonzero True test makes this bug even more difficult to find.

The designers of C++ did not intend for this to confuse you. They wanted you to take advantage of this feature when you could. Instead of putting an assignment before an `if` and then testing the result of that assignment, you can combine the assignment and the `if` into a single statement.

To test your understanding, would C++ interpret the following condition as True or False?

```
if (10 == 10 == 10) ...
```

Be careful. At first glance, it seems True, but C++ thinks that the expression is False! The == operator associates from left to right, so the first 10 is compared to the second 10. Because they are equal, the result is 1 (for True) and the 1 is then compared to the third 10, which results in a 0 (False) result!

Examples

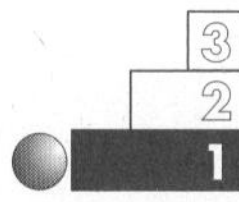

1. All the statements in this example are valid C++ `if` statements.

If (the variable `sales` is greater than 5000),
the variable `bonus` becomes equal to 500.

```
if (sales > 5000)
     {
     bonus = 500; }
```

If this were part of a C++ program, the value inside the variable `sales` determines what happens next. If `sales` contains more than 5000, the next statement that executes is the one inside the block that initializes `bonus`. If, however, `sales` contains 5000 or less, the block will not execute, and the line following the `if`'s block will execute.

If (the variable `age` *is less than or equal to 21),*
print `You are a minor.` *to the screen and go to a newline,*
print `What is your grade?` *to the screen,*
and accept an integer from the keyboard.

```
if (age <= 21)
     {
     cout << "You are a minor.\n";
     cout << "What is your grade?";
     cin >> grade;
     }
```

If the value in `age` is less than or equal to 21, the lines of code in the block will execute next. Otherwise, C++ skips the entire block and continues with the program.

If (the variable `balance` *is greater than the variable* `low_balance`*),*
print `Past due!` *to the screen and move the cursor to a newline.*

```
if (balance > low_balance)
     {
     cout << "Past due!\n";
     }
```

If the `balance` is more than `low_balance`, execution of the program continues at the block, and the message `Past due!` prints to the screen. You can compare two variables as in this example, a variable to a constant as in previous examples, a constant to a constant (although that is rarely done), or an expression in place of any variable or constant. The following `if` statement shows an expression included in the `if`.

If (the variable `pay` *multiplied by the variable* `tax_rate` *equals the variable* `minimum`*),*
the variable `low_salary` *becomes equal to 1400.60.*

```
if (pay * tax_rate == minimum)
    {
    low_salary = 1400.60;
    }
```

The precedence table of operators in Appendix D includes the relational operators. They are on levels 6 and 7, lower than the other primary math operators. When using expressions such as this one, you can make them much more readable if you use parentheses, even though they are not required, around the expressions. Here is a rewrite of this `if` statement with ample parentheses.

If ((the variable `pay` *multiplied by the variable* `tax_rate`*) equals the variable* `minimum`*),*
the variable `low_salary` *becomes equal to 1400.60.*

```
if ((pay * tax_rate) == minimum)
    {
    low_salary = 1400.60;
    }
```

2. Here is a simple program that computes the pay of a salesperson. The salesperson gets a flat pay of $4.10 per hour. In addition, if the sales are more than $8,500, the salesperson gets an additional $500. This is a good introductory example of conditional logic that depends on a relation of two values: `sales` and $8,500.

```
// Filename: C10PAY1.CPP
// Calculates a salesperson's pay based on that person's
// sales

#include <iostream.h>
#include <iomanip.h>
```

```
main()
     {
     char      sal_name[ 20 ];
     int       hours;
     float     total_sales, bonus, pay;

     cout << "\n\n";     // Print 2 blank lines
     cout << "Payroll Calculation\n";
     cout << "------------------\n";

     // Ask the user for needed values
     cout << "What is salesperson's last name? ";
     cin >> sal_name;
     cout << "How many hours did the salesperson work? ";
     cin >> hours;
     cout << "What were the total sales? ";
     cin >> total_sales;

     bonus = 0;     // Initially, there is no bonus

     // Compute the base pay
     pay = 4.10 * (float)hours;     // Type cast the hours

     // Add bonus only if sales were high
     if (total_sales > 8500.00)
          {
          bonus = 500.00;
          }

     cout << sal_name << " made " << setiosflags(ios::fixed)
          << setprecision(2) << pay << " \n";
     cout << "and got a bonus of " << setprecision(2)
          << bonus << "\n";

     return 0;
     }
```

Now take a look at the results of running this program twice, each time with different input values. Notice what the program does: it computes a bonus for one employee, but does not for the other. The $500 bonus is a direct result of the `if` statement. The assignment of $500 to `bonus` is executed only if the `total_sales` is more then $8,500.

```
Payroll Calculation
-----------------
What is salesperson's last name? Harrison
How many hours did the salesperson work? 40
What were the total sales? 6050.64
Harrison made 164.00
and got a bonus of 0.00
Payroll Calculation
-----------------
What is salesperson's last name? Robertson
How many hours did the salesperson work? 40
What were the total sales? 9800
Robertson made 164.00
and got a bonus of 500.00
```

3. When getting input from users, it is often wise to perform *data validation* on the values they type. If a user enters a bad value — for instance, a negative number when you know the input cannot be negative — you can inform the user of the problem and ask that the input be reentered.

   Not all data can be validated, but most of it can be checked to be certain that it's reasonable. For example, if you were writing a student record-keeping program to track each student's name, address, age, and other pertinent data, you could check to see whether the age falls within a reasonable range. If the user enters `213` for the age, you know that the value is incorrect. If the user enters `-4` for the age, you know that the input value is incorrect also. Not all incorrect input can be checked. If the student is 21 and the user types `22`, your program would have no way of knowing whether the age is correct, because 22 falls within a reasonable range.

The following program is a routine that requests an age and checks to make sure that it is more than 10. This is certainly not a foolproof test, as the user can still enter incorrect ages, but it does take care of extremely low values. If the user enters a bad age, the user is requested for it again, inside the `if` statement.

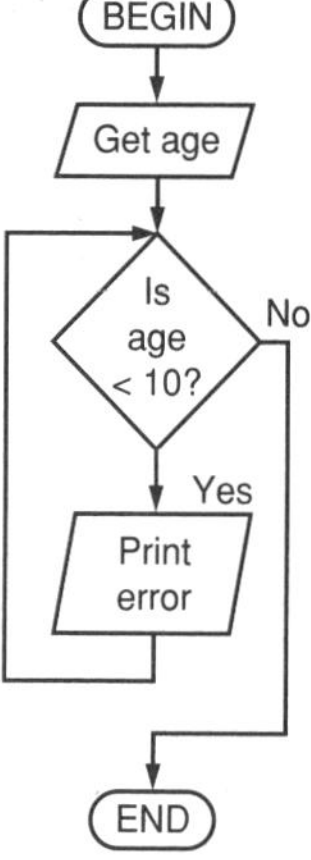


```
// Filename: C10AGE.CPP
// Program to help ensure that age values are reasonable

#include <iostream.h>

main()
     {
     int     age;

     cout << "\nWhat is the student's age? ";
     cin >> age;

     if (age < 10)
          {
          cout << '\x07';     // BEEP
          cout << "*** The age cannot be less than 10 ***\n";
          cout << "Try again...\n\n";
          cout << "What is the student's age? ";
          cin >> age;
          }

     cout << "Thank you.  You entered a valid age.\n";
     return 0;
     }
```

This routine could be a section of a longer program. Later you learn how to prompt repeatedly for a value until a valid input is given. This program takes advantage of the bell (ASCII 7) to warn the user that a bad age was entered.

If the entered `age` is less than 10, the user gets an error message. The program beeps and warns the user about the bad `age` before asking for it again.

Look at the result of running this program. Notice that the program knows, because of the `if` statement, whether `age` is more than 10.

```
What is the student's age? 3
*** The age cannot be less than 10 ***
Try again...

What is the student's age? 21
Thank you.  You entered a valid age.
```

4. Unlike many languages, C++ does not include a square operator. You can take the square of a number by multiplying it by itself. Because many computers don't allow integers to hold more than the square of 180, this program uses `if` statements to make sure that the number fits in an integer answer when it is computed.

   The following program takes a value from the user and prints the square of it, unless it is more than 180. The message `Square is not allowed for numbers over 180` appears if the user types too large a number.

```
// Filename: C10SQRT1.CPP
// Prints the square of the input value
// if the input value is less than 180

#include <iostream.h>

main()
    {
    int     num, square;

    cout << "\n\n";     // Print 2 blank lines
    cout << "What number do you want to see the square of?";
    cin >> num;

    if (num < 180)
```

```
     {
     square = num * num;
     cout << "The square of " << num << " is "
          << square;
     }

if (num >= 180)
     {
     cout << '\x07';      // BEEP
     cout << "\n*** Square is not allowed for ";
     cout << "numbers over 180 ***";
     cout << "\nRun this program again and try ";
     cout << "a smaller value.";
     }

cout << "\nThank you for requesting squares.";
return 0;
}
```

Here are the results of a couple of sample runs from this program. Notice that both conditions work: if the user enters a number below 180, the user sees the square. If the user enters a larger number, an error message appears.

```
What number do you want to see the square of? 45
The square of 45 is 2025
Thank you for requesting squares.

What number do you want to see the square of? 212
*** Square is not allowed for numbers over 180 ***
Run this program again and try a smaller value.
Thank you for requesting squares.
```

This program will be improved when you learn to use `else` later in this chapter. The program's problem is its redundant check of the user's input. The variable `num` has to be checked once to print the square if it is below 180, and checked again for the error message if it is above 180.

5. The value of 1 for True or 0 for False can help save you an extra programming step that other languages do not necessarily allow you. To see how, look at the following section of code:

```
commission = 0;                    // Initialize commission

if (sales > 10000)
     {
     commission = 500.00;
     }

pay = net_pay + commission;       // commission is 0
                                  // unless high sales
```

This program can be streamlined and made more efficient by combining the `if`'s relational test with the assignments to `commission` and `pay`, knowing that it will return 1 or 0:

```
pay = net_pay + (commission = (sales > 10000) * 500.00);
```

This single line does what the previous four lines did. Because the rightmost assignment has precedence, it gets computed first. The variable `sales` is compared to 10000. If it is more than 10000, a True result of 1 is returned. That 1 is multiplied by 500.00 and stored in `commission`. If, however, `sales` is not more than 10000, 0 is the result, and 0 multiplied by 500.00 still leaves 0.

The value (500.00 or 0) that is assigned to `commission` becomes the value of that expression. That value is then added to `net_pay` and stored in `pay`.

The `else` Statement

The `else` statement never appears in a program without an `if` statement. This section introduces the `else` statement by showing you the popular `if-else` combination statement. Here is its format:

```
if (condition)
     {
     A block of 1 or more C++ statements
     }
else
     {
     A block of 1 or more C++ statements
     }
```

The first part of the `if-else` is identical to the `if` statement. If the *`condition`* is True, the block of C++ statements following the `if` executes. However, if the *`condition`* is False, the block of C++ statements following the `else` executes. Although the simple `if` statement determines only what happens when the *`condition`* is True, the `if-else` determines what happens if the *`condition`* is False. No matter what the outcome, the statement following the `if-else` executes next.

NOTE: The following describe the nature of `if-else`:

If the *`condition`* is True, the entire block of statements following the `if` is performed.

If the *`condition`* is False, the entire block of statements following the `else` is performed.

TIP: You can compare characters, not just numbers. When you compare characters, C++ uses the ASCII table to determine which character is "less than" (lower in the ASCII table) the other. You cannot compare character strings or arrays of character strings directly with the relational operators.

Examples

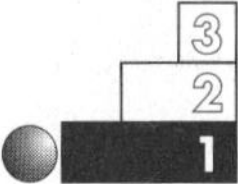

1. The following program asks the user for a number. The program then prints a line indicating that the number is greater than zero or that it is not, using the `if-else` statement.

```
// Filename: C10IFEL1.CPP
// Demonstrates if-else by printing whether an input value
// is greater than zero or not

#include <iostream.h>

main()
     {
     int     num;

     cout << "What is your number? ";
     cin >> num;     // Get the user's number

     if (num > 0)
          {
          cout << "More than 0\n";
          }
     else
          {
          cout << "Less or equal to 0\n";
          }

    // No matter what the number was, the following executes
     cout << "\n\nThanks for your time!\n";
     return 0;
     }
```

There is no need to test for *both* possibilities when you use an `else`. The `if` tests to see whether the number is greater than zero, and the `else` takes care of all other possibilities automatically.

2. The following program asks for the user's first name and stores it in a character array. The first character of the array is then checked to see whether it falls in the upper half of the alphabet. If it does, an appropriate message is displayed.

```
// Filename: C10IFEL2.CPP
// Tests the user's first initial and prints a message

#include <iostream.h>

main()
     {
     char     last[ 20 ];     // Holds the last name

     cout << "What is your last name? ";
     cin >> last;

     // Test the initial - must be uppercase
     if (last[ 0 ] <= 'P')
          {
          cout << "Your name is early in the alphabet.\n";
          }
     else
          {
          cout << "You have to wait a while ";
          cout << "for YOUR name to be called!";
          }
     return 0;
     }
```

Notice that because a character array element is being compared to a character constant, you must enclose the character constant in single quotes. The data types on both sides of each relational operator must match.

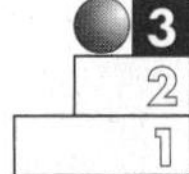

3. The following program is a more complete payroll routine than you have seen. It uses the `if` statement to illustrate how to compute overtime pay. The logic goes something like this:

   If an employee works 40 hours or fewer, the employee gets paid regular pay (the hourly pay times the number of hours worked). If the employee works between 40 and 50 hours, the employee gets one and a half times the hourly rate for the hours over 40. The employee still gets regular pay for the first 40 hours. All hours over 50 earn double time.

```
// Filename: C10PAY2.CPP
// Computes the full overtime pay possibilities

#include <iostream.h>
#include <iomanip.h>

main()
     {
     int          hours;
     float     dt, ht, rp, rate, pay;

     cout << "\n\nHow many hours were worked? ";
     cin >> hours;
     cout << "\nWhat is the regular hourly pay?";
     cin >> rate;

     // Compute pay here
     // Double-time possibility
     if (hours > 50)
          {
          dt = 2.0 * rate * (float)(hours - 50);
          ht = 1.5 * rate * 10.0; // Time + 1/2 for 10 hours
          }
     else
          {
          dt = 0.0;
          } // Either none or double for those hours over 50

     // Time and a half
     if (hours > 40)
          {
```

```
          ht = 1.5 * rate * (float)(hours - 40);
          }

     // Regular pay
     if (hours >= 40)
          {
          rp = 40 * rate;
          }
     else
          {
          rp = (float)hours * rate;
          }

     pay = dt + ht + rp;    // Add up 3 components of payroll

     cout << "\nThe pay is " << setprecision(2) << pay
          << '\n';
     return 0;
     }
```

4. The block of statements following the `if` can contain any valid C++ statement, even another `if` statement. This sometimes comes in handy.

   The following program could be run to give an award to employees based on their years of service to your company. You are giving a gold watch to those with more than 20 years, a paperweight to those with more than 10 years, and a pat on the back to everyone else.

```
// Filename: C10SERV.CPP
// Prints a message depending on years of service

#include <iostream.h>

main()
     {
     int      yrs;

     cout << "How many years of service? ";
     cin >> yrs;      // Get the years employee has worked
```

```
if (yrs > 20)
     {
     cout << "Give a gold watch\n";
     }
else
     {
     if (yrs > 10)
          {
          cout << "Give a paperweight\n";
          }
     else
          {
          cout << "Give a pat on the back\n";
          }
     }
return 0;
}
```

You should probably not rely on `if-else-if` to take care of too many conditions, because more than three or four conditions add confusion. You get into messy logic like this: "If this is True, then if this is True, then do something else if this is True, and so on. . . ." The `switch` statement in a later chapter handles these types of multiple `if` selections better than a long `if-else`.

Summary

You now have the tools to write powerful data-driven programs. This chapter showed you how to compare constants, variables, and combinations of both by using the relational operators. The `if` and `if-else` statements rely on these comparisons of data to determine which code to execute next. You can now *conditionally execute* statements within your programs.

The next chapter goes one step further by combining relational operators to create logical operators (sometimes called compound conditions). These logical operators improve your program's ability to make selections based on data comparisons.

Review Questions

Answers to Review Questions are in Appendix B.

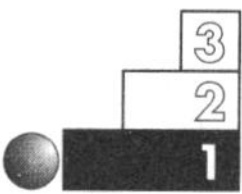

1. What operator tests for equality?

2. Please state whether the following relational tests are True or False:

   A. `4 >= 5`

   B. `4 == 4`

   C. `165 >= 165`

   D. `0 != 25`

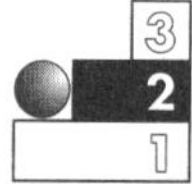

3. True or false: `C++ is fun` will print on the screen when the following statement is executed.

```
if (54 <= 54)
     {

     cout << "C++ is fun";

     }
```

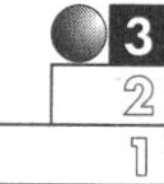

4. What is the difference between an `if` statement and an `if-else` statement?

5. Will the following `cout` execute?

```
if (3 != 4 != 1)
     {

     cout << "This will print";

     }
```

6. Using the ASCII table in Appendix C, please state whether these character relational tests are True or False:

   A. `'C' < 'c'`

   B. `'0' > '0'`

   C. `'?' > ')'`

Review Exercises

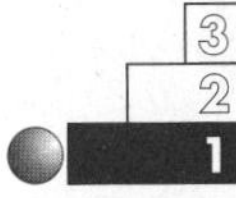

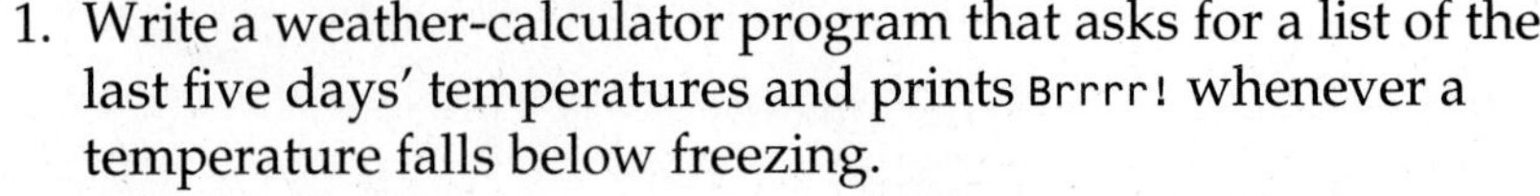

1. Write a weather-calculator program that asks for a list of the last five days' temperatures and prints `Brrrr!` whenever a temperature falls below freezing.

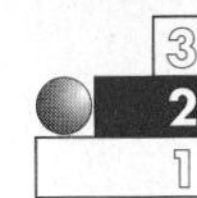

2. Write a program that asks for a number and prints the square and cube (the number multiplied by itself three times) of the input number if that number is more than 1. Otherwise, print nothing.

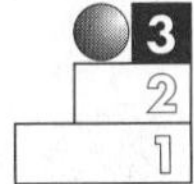

3. Ask the user for two numbers. Print a message telling how the first one relates to the second. In other words, if the user entered `5` and `7`, you would print `5 is less than 7`.

4. Prompt the user for an employee's pretax salary. Print the employee's salary taxes. The taxes are 10 percent if the employee made less than $10,000, 15 percent if the employee earned between $10,000 and $20,000, and 20 percent if the employee earned more than 20 percent.

11

Logical Operators

By combining *logical operators* with relational operators, you can create more powerful data-testing statements. The logical operators are sometimes called *compound relational operators*. As C++'s precedence table shows, the relational operators take precedence over the logical operators when you combine them. The precedence table plays an important role in these types of operators.

In this chapter, you learn about the following topics:

- The `&&` AND operator
- The `||` OR operator
- The `!` NOT operator

This chapter concludes your learning of the conditional testing that C++ allows. Presented here are many examples of `if` statements in programs that work on compound conditional tests.

Defining Logical Operators

There may be times when you need to test more than one set of variables. You can combine more than one relational test into a *compound relational test* by using C++'s logical operators, shown in Table 11.1.

Table 11.1. The logical operators.

Operator	*Meaning*
`&&`	AND
`¦¦`	OR
`!`	NOT

Logical operators are used for compound relational tests.

The first two logical operators, `&&` and `¦¦`, never appear by themselves. They typically go between two or more relational tests.

Tables 11.2, 11.3, and 11.4 illustrate how each of the logical operators work. These tables are called *truth tables*, as they show how to achieve True results from an `if` statement that uses them. Take a minute to study the tables.

Table 11.2. The `&&` AND truth table. Both sides of the operator must be True.

True AND True = True

True AND False = False

False AND True = False

False AND False = False

Table 11.3. The `¦¦` OR truth table. One or the other side of the operator must be True.

True OR True = True

True OR False = True

False OR True = True

False OR False = False

Table 11.4. The ! NOT truth table. An opposite relation is produced.

NOT True =	False
NOT False =	True

The Use of Logical Operators

The True and False on each side of the operators represent a relational `if` test. For instance, the following tests are valid `if` tests that use logical operators (sometimes called *compound relational operators*).

If ((the variable `a` *is less than the variable* `b`*) AND (the variable* `c` *is greater than the variable* `d`*)),*
print `Results are invalid.` *to the screen.*

```
if ((a < b) && (c > d))
     {

     cout << "Results are invalid.";

     }
```

The variable `a` must be less than `b` and, at the same time, `c` must be greater than `d`, for the `cout` to execute. The `if` statement still requires parentheses around its complete conditional test.

The || is sometimes called the "inclusive or."

```
if ((sales > 5000) || (hrs_worked > 81))
     {

     bonus = 500;

     }
```

Here the `sales` must be more than 5000 or the `hrs_worked` must be more than 81 before the assignment executes.

```
if (!(sales < 2500))
     {

     bonus = 500;

     }
```

In this example, if `sales` is greater than or equal to 2500, `bonus` will be initialized. This illustrates an important programming tip: "Use `!` sparingly." (Or, as some so wisely state, "Do not use `!` or your programs will not be `!(unclear)`.") It would be much clearer to rewrite the preceding example by turning it into a positive relational test:

```
if (sales >= 2500)
     {

     bonus = 500;

     }
```

The `!` operator is sometimes helpful, especially when testing for end-of-file conditions later. Most of the time, you can avoid `!` by using reverse logic:

`!(var1 == var2)` is exactly the same as `(var1 != var2)`

`!(var1 <= var2)` is exactly the same as `(var1 > var2)`

`!(var1 >= var2)` is exactly the same as `(var1 < var2)`

`!(var1 != var2)` is exactly the same as `(var1 == var2)`

`!(var1 > var2)` is exactly the same as `(var1 <= var2)`

`!(var1 < var2)` is exactly the same as `(var1 >= var2)`

Notice that the overall format of the `if` statement is retained when you use logical operators, but the relational test has been expanded to include more than one relation. You can even have three or more tests:

```
if ((a == B) && (d == f) || (l = m) || !(k != 2)) ...
```

This is a little too much, however, and good programming practice dictates using, at most, two relational tests inside a single `if` statement. If you need to combine more than two tests, use more than one `if` statement.

As with other relational operators, you use these logical operators in everyday conversation. Note some examples:

> "If my pay is high *and* my vacation time is long, we can go to Italy this summer."
>
> "If you take the trash out *or* clean your room, you can watch TV tonight."
>
> "If you are *not* good, you will be punished."

Internal Truths

The True or False results of relational tests occur internally at the bit level. For example, consider the following `if` test:

```
if (a == 6) ...
```

To determine the truth of the relation, `(a == 6)`, the computer takes a binary 6, or 00000110, and compares it, bit by bit, to the variable `a`. If `a` contains 7, a binary 00000111, the result of the equal test is False because the right bit (called the least significant bit) is different.

C++'s Logical Efficiency

C++ attempts to be more efficient than other languages. If you combine multiple relational tests with one of the logical operators, C++ will not always interpret the full expression. This ultimately makes your programs run faster, but you should be aware of some dangers. Given the conditional test

```
if ((5 > 4) || (sales < 15) && (15 != 15)) ...
```

C++ "looks at" only the first condition, `(5 > 4)`, and realizes that it doesn't have to look further. Because `(5 > 4)` is True, and because True ¦¦ (or) anything that follows is still True, C++ will not bother with the rest of the expression. The same holds for the following:

```
if ((7 < 3) && (age > 15) && (initial == 'D')) ...
```

C++ looks only at the first condition, which is False. Because False `&&` (and) anything else that follows will also be False, C++ does not interpret the expression to the right of `(7 < 3)`. Most of the time, this will not pose a problem, but you should be aware that the following expression may not fulfill your expectations:

```
if ((5 > 4) ¦¦ (num = 0)) ...
```

The `(num = 0)` assignment will never execute because C++ has to interpret only the `(5 > 4)` to see whether the entire expression is True or False. Because of this danger, do not include assignment expressions in the same condition as a logical test. The single `if` condition

```
if ((sales > old_sales) ¦¦ (inventory_flag = 'Y')) ...
```

should be broken into two statements, such as

```
inventory_flag = 'Y';
if ((sales > old_sales) ¦¦ (inventory_flag)) ...
```

so that `inventory_flag` will always be assigned the `'Y'` value, no matter how `(sales > old_sales)` tests.

Examples

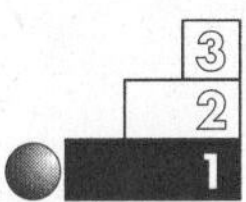

1. The Summer Olympics are held every four years, each year that is divisible evenly by 4. The U.S. Census is taken every 10 years, at the start of each decade, in each year that is evenly divisible by 10. The following short program asks for a year and then tells the user whether it is a year of the Summer Olympics or the year of the census, or both. The program uses relational operators, logical operators, and the modulus operator to determine the output.

```
// Filename: C11YEAR.CPP
// Determines if it is Summer Olympics year, US Census year,
// or both

#include <iostream.h>

main()
     {
     int     year;

     // Ask for a year
     cout << "What is a year for the test? ";
     cin >> year;

     // Test the year
     if ((year % 4) == 0 && (year % 10) == 0)
          {
          cout << "\nBoth Olympics and US Census!\n";
          }
     else
          {
          if ((year % 4) == 0)
               {
               cout << "\nSummer Olympics only\n";
               }
          else
               {
               if ((year % 10) == 0)
                    {
                    cout << "\nUS Census only\n";
                    }
               else
                    {
                    cout << "\nNeither\n";
                    }
               }
          }
     return 0;
     }
```

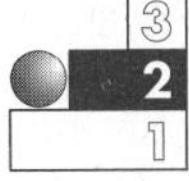

2. Now that you know about compound relations, you can write an age-checking program like C10AGE.CPP, presented in the last chapter. C10AGE.CPP ensured that the age was above 10. There is another way that you can validate input to be sure that it's reasonable. The following program includes a logical operator in its `if` statement to see if the age is greater than 10 and below 100. If both are True, the program knows that the user entered a valid age.

```
// Filename: C11AGE.CPP
// Program to help ensure that age values are reasonable

#include <iostream.h>

main()
     {
     int      age;

     cout << "What is your age? ";
     cin >> age;
     if ((age > 10) && (age < 100))
          {
          cout << "\nYou entered a valid age.\n";
          }
     else
          {
          cout << " \x07 \x07 \n";     // Beep twice
          cout << "\n*** The age must be ";
          cout << "between 10 and 100 ***\n";
          }
     return 0;
     }
```

Compare this program to C10AGE.CPP in Chapter 10. This one is clean and easy to follow.

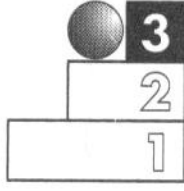

3. The following program might be used by a video store to calculate a discount based on the number of rentals a customer makes and the customer's status. Customers are classified as R for Regular or as S for Special Status. Special Status customers have been members of the rental club for more than one year. They automatically get a 50-cent discount on all rentals. The store also holds value days several times a year. On value days, all customers get the 50-cent discount. Special Status customers do not get an additional 50 cents off during value days because every day is a discount for them.

   The program asks for the customer status and whether it is a value day. The program then uses the `||` operator to test for the discount. Even before you started learning C++, you might look at this problem with the following idea:

   If a customer has Special Status or if it is a value day, deduct 50 cents from the rental.

   This is basically the idea of the `if` decision in the program. Even though Special Status customers do not get an additional discount on value days, there is one final `if` test for them that prints an extra message at the bottom of the screen's bill.

```
// Filename: C11VIDEO.CPP
// Program to compute video rental amounts and give
// appropriate discounts based on the day or customer status

#include <iostream.h>
#include <iomanip.h>

main()
     {
     float          tape_charge, discount, rental_amt;
     char           first_name[ 15 ];
     char           last_name[ 15 ];
     int            num_tapes;
     char           val_day, sp_stat;

     cout << "\n\n *** Video Rental Computation ***\n";
```

```
cout << "     ------------------------\n";
// Underline title

tape_charge = 2.00;     // The before-discount tape fee
                        // per tape

// Get input data
cout << "\nWhat is customer's first name? ";
cin >> first_name;

cout << "What is customer's last name? ";
cin >> last_name;

cout << "\nHow many tapes are being rented? ";
cin >> num_tapes;

cout << "Is this a Value day (Y/N)? ";
cin >> val_day;

cout << "Is this a Special Status customer (Y/N)? ";
cin >> sp_stat;

// Calculate rental amount
discount = 0.0;     // Increase the discount IF they
                    // are eligible
if ((val_day == 'Y') || (val_day == 'y')
     || (sp_stat == 'Y') || (sp_stat == 'y'))
     {
     discount = 0.5;
     rental_amt = (num_tapes * tape_charge)
     - (discount * num_tapes);
     }
else
     {
     rental_amt = num_tapes * tape_charge;
     }

// Print the bill
cout << "\n\n** Rental Club **\n\n";
cout << first_name << ' ' << last_name
     << " rented " << num_tapes << " tapes\n";
cout << "The total was "
```

```
          << setiosflags(oios::fixed) << (setprecision(2)
          << rental_amt << "\n";
     cout << "The discount was " << setprecision(2)
          << discount << " per tape\n";

     // Print extra message for Special Status customers
     if (sp_stat == 'Y') || (sp_stat == 'y')
          {
          cout << "\nThank them for being ";
          cout << "a Special Status customer";
          }
     return 0;
     }
```

Figure 11.1 shows the output from a sample run of this program. Notice that Special Status customers get the extra message at the bottom of the screen. This program, because of its `if` statements, will perform differently depending on the data entered. No discount is applied for Regular customers on nonvalue days.

```
 *** Video Rental Computation ***
     ------------------------

What is customer's first name? Diane
What is customer's last name? Moore

How many tapes are being rented? 3
Is this a Value day (Y/N)? N
Is this a Special Status customer (Y/N)? Y


** Rental Club **

Diane Moore rented 3 tapes
The total was 4.50
The discount was 0.50 per tape

Thank them for being a Special Status customer
```

Figure 11.1. The logical `if` helps give special discounts to certain customers.

The Precedence of Logical Operators

The math precedence order you read about in Chapter 9 did not include the logical operators. To be thorough, you should be familiar with the entire order, presented in Appendix D. As you can see, the math operators take precedence over the relational operators, and the relational operators take precedence over all the logical operators except the logical `!`.

You might wonder why the relational and logical operators are included in a precedence table. The following statement helps show why:

```
if (sales < min_sal * 2 && yrs_emp > 10 * sub) ...
```

Without the complete order of operators, it would be impossible to determine how such a statement would execute. According to the precedence order, the `if` statement executes like this:

```
if ((sales < (min_sal * 2)) && (yrs_emp > (10 * sub))) ...
```

This still may be confusing, but it is less so. The two multiplications are performed first, followed by the operators < and >. The `&&` is performed last because it is lowest in the order of operators.

To avoid such ambiguity problems, use plenty of parentheses, even if the default precedence order is intended. It is also wise to resist combining too many expressions inside a single `if` relational test.

Notice that `||` (OR) has lower precedence than `&&` (AND). Therefore, the following `if` tests are equivalent:

```
if ((first_initial == 'A') && (last_initial == 'G')
    || (id == 321)) ...

if (((first_initial == 'A') && (last_initial == 'G'))
    || (id == 321)) ...
```

The second test is clearer because of the parentheses, but the precedence table makes the tests identical.

Summary

This chapter extended the `if` statement to include the `&&`, `||`, and `!` logical operators. These operators allow you to combine more than one relational test into a single test. C++ does not always have to look at every relational operator when you combine several in an expression. This chapter concludes the explanation of the `if` statement.

The next chapter explains the rest of the regular C++ operators. As you saw in this chapter, the precedence table is very important to the C++ language. When evaluating expressions, keep the precedence table in mind (or at your fingertips) at all times.

Review Questions

Answers to Review Questions are in Appendix B.

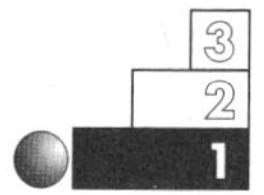

1. What are the three logical operators?

2. The following compound relational tests produce True or False comparisons. Determine which are True and which are False.

   A. `! (true || false)`

   B. `(true && false) && (false || true)`

   C. `! (true && false)`

   D. `true || (false && false) || false`

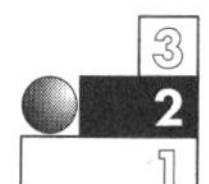

3. Consider the following statement:

   ```
   int i = 12, j = 10, k = 5;
   ```

   What are the results (True or False) of the following statements? (HINT: Remember that C++ interprets *any* nonzero statement as True.)

   A. `i && j`

   B. `12 - i || k`

   C. `j != k && i != k`

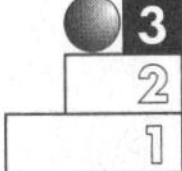

4. What is the value printed in the following program? (HINT: Do not be confused by the assignment operators on each side of the ¦¦.)

```
// Filename: C11LOGO.CPP
// Logical operator test

#include <iostream.h>

main()
     {
     int     f, g;

     g = 5;
     f = 8;
     if ((g = 25) ¦¦ (f = 35))
          {
          cout << "g is " << g << " and f got changed to: "
               << f << '\n';
          }
     return 0;
     }
```

Review Exercises

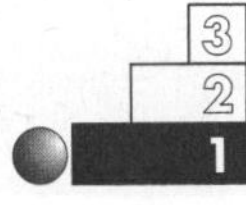

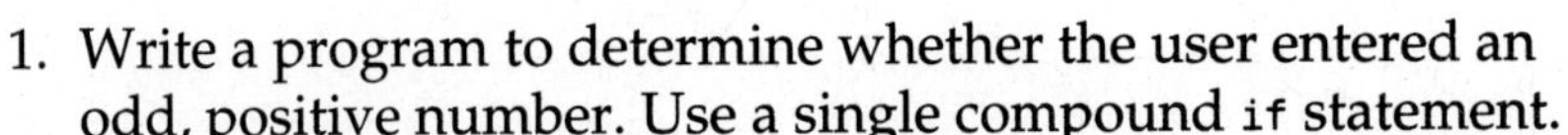

1. Write a program to determine whether the user entered an odd, positive number. Use a single compound `if` statement.

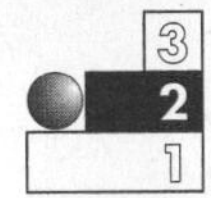

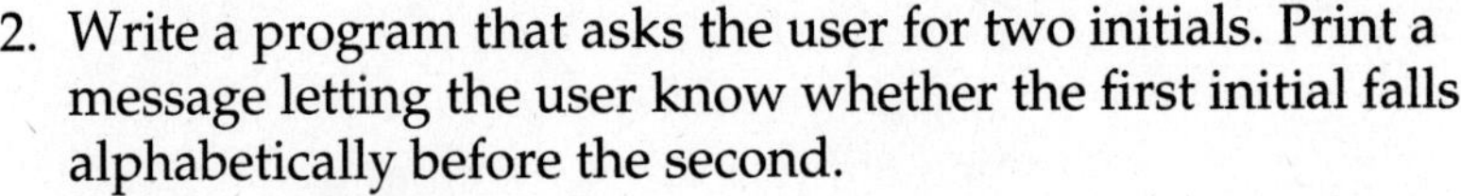

2. Write a program that asks the user for two initials. Print a message letting the user know whether the first initial falls alphabetically before the second.

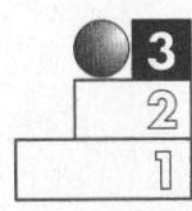

3. Write a number-guessing game. Assign a variable called `number` a value at the top of the program. Give a prompt that asks for five guesses. Get the user's five guesses with a single `cin`. See whether any guess matches the `number` and print an appropriate message if one does.

4. Write a tax-calculation routine. A family pays no tax if its members' combined salaries are less than $5,000. The family pays a 10 percent tax if the combined salaries are between $5,000 and $9,999, and a 20 percent tax if the combined salaries are between $10,000 and $19,999. Otherwise, the family pays a 30 percent tax.

12

Additional C++ Operators

There are several other C++ operators that you should learn. C++ has more operators than most programming languages. If you are not familiar with all the operators, you might think that C++ programs are cryptic and difficult to follow. C++'s heavy reliance on its operators and operator precedence makes it efficient, which means that your programs run smoother and faster.

This chapter introduces the following topics:

- The `?:` conditional operator
- The `++` increment operator
- The `--` decrement operator
- Postfix and prefix operation
- The `sizeof` operator
- The , sequence point operator

Most of the operators described in this chapter are unlike those found in any other programming language. Even if you have programmed in other languages for many years, you may be surprised at the power of some of these operators.

The ?: Conditional Operator

The conditional operator is a ternary operator.

The conditional operator, `?:`, is C++'s only ternary operator. A *ternary* operator requires three operands (instead of the single and double operands of unary and binary operators). The conditional operator is used to replace `if-else` logic in some situations. The format of the conditional operator is

```
conditional_expression ? expression1 : expression2;
```

where *`conditional_expression`* is any expression in C++ that results in a True (nonzero) or False (zero) answer. If the result of the *`conditional_expression`* is True, *`expression1`* executes. If the result of the *`conditional_expression`* is False, *`expression2`* executes. Only one of the expressions following the question mark ever executes. Put a single semicolon at the end of *`expression2`*. The internal expressions, such as *`expression1`*, should not have a semicolon.

Figure 12.1 shows the conditional operator a little more clearly.

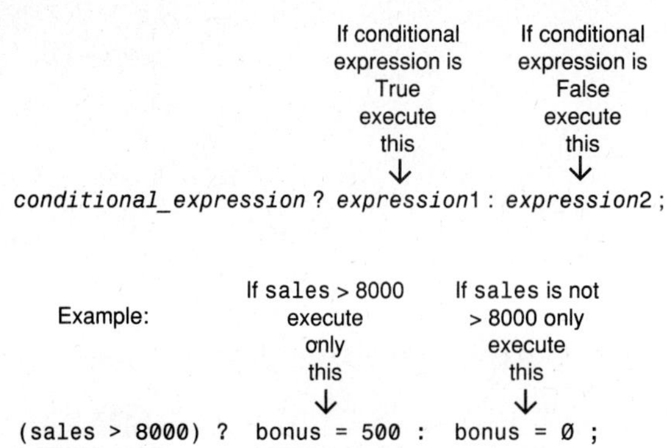

Figure 12.1. The format of the conditional operator.

If you require simple `if-else` logic, the conditional operator usually provides a more direct and succinct method, although you should always prefer readability over compact code.

To get a glimpse of how useful the conditional operator is, consider the following section of code.

If (the variable `a` is greater than the variable `b`), the variable `ans` becomes equal to 10.
Otherwise, the variable `ans` becomes equal to 25.

```
if (a > b)
     {
     ans = 10;
     }
else
     {

     ans = 25;

     }
```

You can easily rewrite this kind of `if-else` code with a single conditional operator, as in the following example.

If the variable `a` is greater than the variable `b`, the variable `ans` becomes equal to 10; otherwise, `ans` becomes equal to 25.

```
a > b ? (ans = 10) : (ans = 25);
```

Because the conditional operator has very low precedence, parentheses are not required around the *`conditional_expression`* to make this work. However, they usually improve readability. This statement could be rewritten, using parentheses, as

```
(a > b) ? (ans = 10) : (ans = 25);
```

Because each C++ expression has a value — in this case, the value being assigned — this statement can be made even more succinct, without loss of readability, by assigning `ans` the answer to the left of the conditional:

```
ans = (a > b) ? (10) : (25);
```

This expression now says the following: if `a` is more than `b`, assign `ans` a 10; otherwise, assign `ans` a 25. Almost any `if-else` statement can be rewritten as a conditional, and a conditional can be rewritten as an `if-else`. You should practice converting one to the other to acquaint yourself with the conditional operator's purpose.

TIP: Any valid C++ statement can be the `conditional_expression`, including all relational and logical operators, as well as any combination of them.

Examples

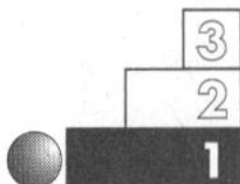

1. Suppose that you are looking over your early C++ programs and you notice the following section of code:

```
if (production > target)
     {
     target *= 1.10;
     }
else
     {
     target *= .90;
     }
```

You realize that such a simple `if-else` statement can be rewritten with a conditional operator and that more efficient code will result. You can change the code to this single statement:

```
(production > target) ? (target *= 1.10) : (target *= .90);
```

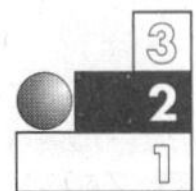

2. Using a conditional operator, you can write a routine to find the lowest value between two variables. This is sometimes called a *minimum routine*. The statement to do this is

```
minimum = (var1 < var2) ? var1 : var2;
```

If `var1` is less than `var2`, the value of `var1` is assigned to `minimum`. If `var2` is less, it is assigned to `minimum`. If the variables are equal, `var2` is assigned to `minimum` (because it doesn't matter which one is assigned).

3. A maximum routine can be written just as easily:

```
maximum = (var1 > var2) ? var1 : var2;
```

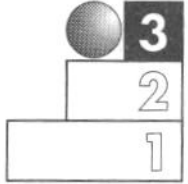

4. Taking the preceding examples a step further, you can test for the sign of a variable. The following conditional expression assigns `-1` to the variable called `sign` if `testvar` is less than 0, `0` to `sign` if `testvar` is 0, and `+1` to `sign` if `testvar` is more than 1:

```
sign = (testvar < 0) ? -1 : (testvar > 0);
```

It might be easy to spot why the less-than test results in `-1`, but the second part may be confusing. This technique works well because of C++'s 1 (True) and 0 (False) return values from a relational test. If `testvar` is 0 or greater, `sign` is assigned the answer to `(testvar > 0)`. The value of `(testvar > 0)` will be 1 if True (therefore, `testvar` is more than 0) or 0 if `testvar` is equal to 0.

This technique takes advantage of C++'s efficiency and conditional operator very well. It may be helpful to rewrite this statement with a typical `if-else`. Here is the same problem written with a typical `if-else` statement:

```
if (testvar < 0)
     {
     sign = -1;
     }
else
     {

     sign = (testvar > 0);

     }     // testvar can be only 0 or more here
```

The ++ and -- Increment and Decrement Operators

C++ offers two unique operators that add 1 to variables or subtract 1 from variables. These are the increment (++) and decrement (--) operators. Table 12.1 shows how these operators relate to other types of expressions you have seen. Notice that the ++ or -- can go on either side of the variable it modifies. If the ++ or -- appears on the left, it is known as a *prefix* operator. If the operator appears on the right, it is a *postfix* operator.

Whenever you need to add 1 to a variable or subtract 1 from a variable, use one of these operators. As Table 12.1 shows, if you need to increment or decrement just a single variable, these operators provide the means to do so.

Table 12.1. The ++ and -- operators.

Operator	*Example*	*Description*	*Equivalent Statements*	
`++`	`i++;`	Postfix	`i = i + 1;`	`i += 1;`
`++`	`++i;`	Prefix	`i = i + 1;`	`i += 1;`
`--`	`i--;`	Postfix	`i = i - 1;`	`i -= 1;`
`--`	`--i;`	Prefix	`i = i - 1;`	`i -= 1;`

Increment and Decrement Efficiencies

The increment (++) and decrement (--) operators are straightforward, efficient methods to add 1 to a variable or subtract 1 from a variable. Often you need to do this when counting or processing loops, which are covered in Part III of this book.

These two operators compile directly into their assembly language equivalents. Almost all computers include, at their lowest binary machine-language commands, increment and decrement instructions. If you use C++'s increment and decrement operators, you ensure that they will compile into these low-level equivalents.

If, however, you code expressions to add or subtract 1, such as `i = i - 1`, as you would in other programming languages, you do not ensure that the C++ compiler will compile this instruction into its machine-language efficient equivalent.

The choice you use, prefix or postfix, does not matter if you are incrementing or decrementing single variables on lines by themselves. However, when you combine these two operators with other operators in a single expression, you must be aware of their differences. Consider the following section of a program. (All variables in the next few examples are integers because the increment and decrement work only on integer variables.)

The variable `a` *becomes equal to 6.*
The variable `b` *becomes equal to the variable* `a` *incremented once* `- 1`.

```
a = 6;
b = ++a - 1;
```

++ adds 1 to a variable, and - - subtracts 1 from a variable.

What are the values of `a` and `b` after these two statements finish? The value of `a` is easy to determine; it gets incremented in the second statement, so the value is 7. However, `b` is either 5 or 6, depending on *when* the variable `a` increments. To determine when `a` increments, consider the following rules:

- If a variable is incremented or decremented with a prefix operator, the increment or decrement occurs *before* the variable's value is used in the rest of the expression.
- If a variable is incremented or decremented with a postfix operator, the increment or decrement occurs *after* the variable's value is used in the rest of the expression.

In the preceding code, `a` contains a prefix increment. Therefore, its value is first incremented to 7, and then the 1 gets subtracted from the 7. The result, 6, is assigned to `b`. If a postfix increment had occurred, as in

```
a = 6;
b = a++ - 1;
```

the `a` would still be 7, but a 5 would be assigned to `b` because `a` did not increment until after its value was used in the expression. The precedence table in Appendix D shows that prefix operators contain higher precedence than almost every other operator, especially postfix increments and decrements that occur last.

TIP: If the order of prefix and postfix confuses you, break your expressions into two lines of code, putting the increment or decrement before or after the expression that uses it. The preceding example could be rewritten as

```
a = 6;
b = a - 1;
a++;
```

There is now no doubt as to when a gets incremented. Despite this tip, you should learn how these operators work because they are efficient and easy to use.

Even parentheses cannot override the postfix rule. Consider the following statement:

```
x = p + (((amt++)));
```

There are some unnecessary parentheses here, but even the redundant parentheses are not enough to increment `amt` before adding its value to `p`. Postfix increment and decrement *always* occur after their variables are used in the surrounding expression.

CAUTION: Do not attempt to increment or decrement an expression. You can apply these operators only to variables. The following expression is *invalid*:

```
sales = ++(rate * hours);   // NOT ALLOWED!
```

Examples

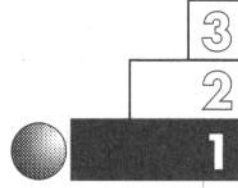

1. As with all other C++ operators, keep the precedence table in mind when evaluating expressions that use increment and decrement. Figure 12.2 shows some examples that illustrate these operators.

```
int i = 1;
int j = 2;
int k = 3;
ans = i++ + j - --k;

      i++ + j - 2

        2  - 2

          0
```

Then i increments by 1 to its final value of 2.

```
int i = 1;
int j = 2;
int k = 3;
ans = ++i * j - k--

       2 * j - k--

         4  -  k--

            1
```

Then k decrements by 1 to its final value of 2.

Figure 12.2. Examples of C++ operators and the precedence table.

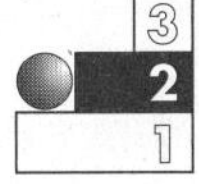

2. The precedence table takes on even more meaning when you see a section of code like that shown in Figure 12.3.

```
int i = 0;
int j = -1;
int k = 0;
int l = 1;

ans = i++ && ++j || k || l++
          i++ && 0 || k || l++
                0 || k || l++
                   0 || l++
                       1
```

Then i and l increment by 1 to their final values of 1 and 2.

Figure 12.3. Another example of C++ operators and the precedence table.

3. Considering the precedence table, and more important, what you know about C++'s relational efficiencies, what is the value of ans in the following section of code?

```
int    i=1, j=20, k=-1, l=0, m=1, n=0, o=2, p=1;
ans = i || j-- && k++ || ++l && ++m || n-- & !o || p--;
```

At first, this seems to be extremely complicated. Nevertheless, you can simply glance at it and determine the value of ans, as well as the ending value of the rest of the variables.

Recall that when C++ performs a relation || (OR), it ignores the right side of the || if the value on the left is True (any nonzero value is True). Because True or any other value is still True, C++ does not think that it has to look at the values on the right. Therefore, C++ performed this expression in the following way:

```
ans = i || j-- && k++ || ++l && ++m || n-- & !o || p--;
        |
        1 (true)
```

Because `i` is true, C++ knows that the entire expression is True and ignores the rest of it after the first `||`. Therefore, *any other increment and decrement expression is ignored.* The result is that only `ans` is changed by this expression, and the rest of the variables, `j` through `p`, are never incremented or decremented, even though several of them contain increment and decrement operators. If you use relational operators, be aware of this problem and break out all increment and decrement operators into statements by themselves before relational statements.

The `sizeof` Operator

Another operator in C++ does not look like an operator at all but looks like a library function. It is the `sizeof` operator. If you think of `sizeof` as a function call, you will not get too confused, because `sizeof` works in a similar way. The `sizeof` operator has one of the following formats:

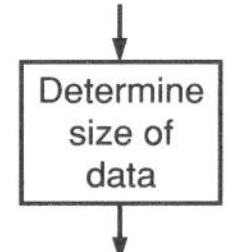


```
sizeof data
sizeof(data type)
```

The `sizeof` operator is a unary operator because it operates on a single value. This operator produces a result that is the size, in bytes, of the `data` or `data type` specified. Because most data types and variables require different amounts of internal storage on different computers, the `sizeof` operator was provided to allow for consistent programs across different kinds of computers.

> **TIP:** Most C++ programmers use parentheses around the `sizeof` argument, whether that argument is `data` or `data type`. Because parentheses are required around `data type` arguments and are optional around `data`, you may want to get in the habit of using parentheses all the time.

The `sizeof` operator is sometimes called a *compile-time operator*. At compile time, not runtime, the compiler replaces each occurrence of `sizeof` in your program with an `unsigned` integer value. The `sizeof` is used in advanced C++ programming.

The `sizeof` operator returns the size, in bytes, of its argument.

If you use an array as the `sizeof` argument, C++ returns the size, in bytes, of the number of bytes you originally reserved for the array. The data in the array, even if it is a short string inside a character array, has nothing to do with the array's size.

Example

Suppose that you want to know the size, in bytes, of floating-point variables for your computer. You can determine this by putting the word `float` in parentheses, as shown in the following program:

```
// Filename: C12SIZE1.CPP
// Prints the size of floating-point values

#include <iostream.h>

main()
     {
     cout << "The size of floating-point variables ";
     cout << "on this computer is " << sizeof(float) << '\n';
     return 0;
     }
```

This program will produce different results on different kinds of computers. You can use any valid data type as the `sizeof` argument. When you directly print `sizeof` results, as shown here, type cast the `sizeof` to an integer in order to print it properly. Compiled under Turbo C++, this program produces the following output:

```
The size of floating-point variables on this computer is 4
```

The Comma Operator

An additional operator (`,`), sometimes called a *sequence point*, is used a little differently from most C++ operators. The comma operator does not directly operate on data but produces a left-to-right evaluation of expressions. The comma allows you to put more than one expression, separated by commas, on a single line.

You have already seen one use of the comma when you learned how to declare and initialize variables. In the following section of code, the comma separates statements. Because the comma associates from left to right, the first variable, `i`, is declared and initialized before the second variable, `j`.

```
main()
    {
    int     i = 10, j = 25;


    // Rest of program follows
```

The comma is *not* a sequence point when used inside function parentheses but is said to *separate arguments*.

Examples

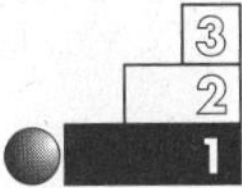

1. You can put more than one expression on a line, using the comma as a sequence point. Note the following program:

```
// Filename: C12COM1.CPP
// Illustrates the sequence point

#include <iostream.h>

main()
     {
     int     num, sq, cube;

     num = 5;

     // Calculate the square and cube of the number
     sq = (num * num), cube = (num * num * num);

     cout << "The square of " << num << " is " << sq
          << " and the cube is " << cube << "\n";
     return 0;
     }
```

   This technique is not necessarily recommended, as it does not add anything to the program and even decreases readability. The square and cube are probably better computed on two separate lines.

2. The comma allows for some interesting statements. Consider the following section of code:

```
i = 10;
j = (i = 12, i + 8);
```

   When this section of code finishes, `j` has the value of 20, even though this is not necessarily clear. In the first statement, `i` is assigned 10. In the second statement, the comma causes the `i` to be assigned a value of 12, and then `i + 8`, or 20, is assigned to `j`.

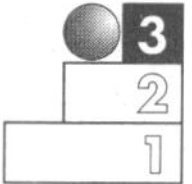

3. In the following section of code, `ans` is assigned the value of 12, because the assignment before the comma is performed first. Despite the right-to-left associativity of the assignment operator, the comma's sequence point lastly forces the assignment of 12 into `x` before `x` is assigned to `ans`.

```
ans = (y = 8, x = 12);
```

When this completes, `y` contains an 8, `x` contains a 12, and `ans` contains a 12 also.

Summary

You now have learned almost every operator in the C++ language. The conditional, increment, and decrement operators make C++ stand apart from many other programming languages. As with all operators, you must be aware of the precedence table at all times when using these operators.

The `sizeof` and sequence point operators are unlike most other operators. The `sizeof` is a compile-time operator that works in a manner similar to the `#define` preprocessor directive; `sizeof` is replaced by its value at compile time. The sequence point operator (`,`) lets you put multiple statements on a line or within a single expression. However, you should reserve this operator for initializing variables because it may be unclear if combined with other expressions.

The next chapter discusses the *bitwise* operators. They operate on a very low binary level on your computer's variables. There are programmers who have programmed in C++ for years but have yet to learn the bitwise operators. If you are just learning C++ and are not interested in doing bit-level operations, you may want to skim the next chapter and come back to it later when you need those operators.

Review Questions

Answers to Review Questions are in Appendix B.

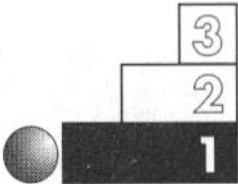

1. Which set of statements does the conditional operator replace?

2. Why is the conditional operator called a ternary operator?

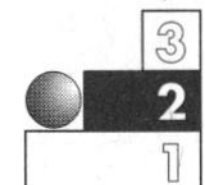

3. Rewrite the following conditional operator as an `if-else`:

```
ans = (a == b) ? c + 2 : c + 3;
```

4. True or false: The following statements produce the same result.

```
var++;
var = var + 1;
```

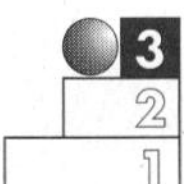

5. Why is using the increment and decrement operators more efficient than using the addition and subtraction operators?

6. What is a sequence point?

7. Can the output of the following section of code be determined?

```
age = 20;
cout << "You are now " << age << ", and will be "
     << age++ << " in one year";
```

8. What is the output of the following section of a program?

```
char   name[ 20 ] = "Mike";
cout << "The size of name is: " << sizeof(name);
```

Review Exercises

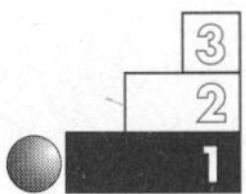

1. Write a program that prints the numbers 1 to 10. Use 10 different `cout`s and only one variable called `result` to hold the value before each `cout`. Use the increment operator to add 1 to `result` before each `cout`.

2. Write a program that asks for the user's age. Using a single `cout` that includes a conditional operator, print the following if the age is over 21:

   ```
   You are not a minor.
   ```

   Otherwise, print the following:

   ```
   You are still a minor.
   ```

   This `cout` may be long, but it helps illustrate how the conditional operator can be used within other statements when the `if-else` cannot.

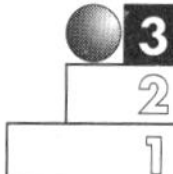

3. Use the conditional operator, not `if-else` statements, to write a tax-calculation routine. A family pays no tax if the members' combined salaries are less than $5,000. The family pays a 10 percent tax if the combined salaries are between $5,000 and $9,999, and 20 percent tax if the combined salaries are between $10,000 and $19,999. Otherwise, the family pays a 30 percent tax. This is similar to an exercise in the preceding chapter, except for the conditional operator.

13

Bitwise Operators

This chapter introduces the *bitwise operators*. They operate on internal representations of data, not just "values in variables," as the other operators do. Bitwise operators require an understanding of Appendix A's binary numbering system and of your PC's memory. If you don't think that you are ready to tackle the bitwise operators, you can skim this chapter and come back to it later.

Some people program in C++ for years and don't know the bitwise operators. Nevertheless, understanding them can help improve the efficiency of your programs and let you operate at a level deeper than many programming languages allow.

In this chapter, you learn about the following topics:

- The bitwise logical operators
- Performing bitwise operations internally
- The bitwise shift operators

This chapter concludes the discussion of C++ operators for a while. After you master this chapter, you will be able to perform almost any operation on your C++ variables and constants.

Bitwise Logical Operators

There are four bitwise logical operators, shown in Table 13.1. Because these operators work on the binary representation of integer data, systems programmers can manipulate internal bits in memory and variables. The bitwise logical operators are not just for systems programmers, however. Application programmers can also improve portions of their programs by learning how to use these operators.

Table 13.1. The bitwise logical operators.

Operator	*Meaning*
`&`	Bitwise AND
`¦`	Bitwise inclusive OR
`^`	Bitwise exclusive OR
`~`	Bitwise 1's complement

Bitwise logical operators perform bit-by-bit operations on internal data.

Each bitwise logical operator performs a bit-by-bit operation on internal data. Bitwise operators apply only to `char`, `int`, and `long` variables and constants, not to floating-point data. Because binary numbers consist of 1s and 0s, these 1s and 0s (called *bits*) are manipulated to produce the desired result of each bitwise operator.

Before looking at examples, you should understand Tables 13.2 through 13.5. They contain truth tables that describe the actions of the bitwise operators on the internal bit patterns of an `int` (or `char` or `long`).

Table 13.2. The bitwise `&` (AND) truth table.

First Bit	*AND*	*Second Bit*	*Result*
1	`&`	1	1
1	`&`	0	0
0	`&`	1	0
0	`&`	0	0

In bitwise truth tables, you can replace the 1 and 0 with TRUE and FALSE, respectively, to understand the result better. For the & (AND) bitwise truth table, both bits being operated on with & must be TRUE for the result to be TRUE. In other words, "TRUE AND TRUE is equal to TRUE."

TIP: By replacing the 1s and 0s with TRUE and FALSE, you might be able to relate the bitwise operators to the regular logical operators `&&` and `||`, which you used with `if` comparisons.

Table 13.3. The bitwise | (OR) truth table.

First Bit	*OR*	*Second Bit*	*Result*
1	|	1	1
1	|	0	1
0	|	1	1
0	|	0	0

The | bitwise operator is sometimes called the *inclusive bitwise OR operator*. Either side of the | operator, or both sides, must be 1 (TRUE) for the result to be 1 (TRUE).

Table 13.4. The bitwise ^ (exclusive OR) operator.

First Bit	*XOR*	*Second Bit*	*Result*
1	^	1	0
1	^	0	1
0	^	1	1
0	^	0	0

For bitwise ^, one side or the other must be 1, but not both sides.

The ^ bitwise operator is called the *exclusive bitwise OR* operator. Either side of the ^ operator must be 1 (TRUE) for the result to be 1 (TRUE), but both sides cannot be 1 (TRUE) at the same time.

Table 13.5. The bitwise ~ (1's complement) operator.

1's Complement	*Bit*	*Result*
~	1	0
~	0	1

The ~ bitwise operator, called the *bitwise 1's complement* operator, reverses each bit to its opposite value.

NOTE: The bitwise 1's complement does *not* negate a number. As Appendix A shows, the PC uses a 2's complement to negate numbers. The bitwise 1's complement reverses the bit pattern of numbers but does not add the additional 1, as the 2's complement requires.

You can test and change individual bits inside variables to check for patterns of data. The examples in the next section help illustrate the bitwise logical operators.

Examples

1. If you apply the bitwise & operator to the numbers 9 and 14, you get a result of 8. Figure 13.1 shows why this is so. When the binary values of 9 (1001) and 14 (1110) are operated on with a bitwise &, the resulting bit pattern is 8 (1000).

```
  1 0 0 1 (9)
  ↓ ↓ ↓ ↓
  & & & &
  1 1 1 0 (14)
  -------
= 1 0 0 0 (8)
```

Figure 13.1. Performing the bitwise & on two numbers.

In a C++ program, you could code this bitwise operation in the following way.

`result` becomes equal to the binary value of 9, which is 1001, AND the binary value of 14, which is 1110.

```
result = 9 & 14;
```

The `result` variable will hold 8, which is the result of the bitwise `&`. The 9 or 14 (or both) could also be stored in variables, with the same result.

2. When applying the bitwise `¦` operator to the numbers 9 and 14, you get 15. When the binary values of 9 (1001) and 14 (1110) are operated on with a bitwise `¦`, the resulting bit pattern is 15 (1111). The reason is that the result's bits are 1 (True) in every position in which a bit is 1 in either of the two numbers.

   In a C++ program, you could code this bitwise operation like this:

   ```
   result = 9 ¦ 14;
   ```

   The `result` variable will hold 15, which is the result of the bitwise `¦`. The 9 or 14, or both, could also be stored in variables, with the same result.

3. The bitwise `^`, when applied to 9 and 14, produces a 7. The bitwise `^` will set the resulting bit to 1 if one number's bit or the other number's bit is on, but not both.

   In a C++ program, you could code this bitwise operation like this:

   ```
   result = 9 ^ 14;
   ```

   The `result` variable holds 7, which is the result of the bitwise `^`. The 9 or 14, or both, could also be stored in variables, with the same result.

4. The bitwise `~` simply negates each bit. `~` is a unary bitwise operator because you can apply it to only a single value at one time. The bitwise `~` applied to 9 will result in several values, depending on the size of the 9 and whether the 9 is a `signed` value or not, as shown in Figure 13.2.

```
~ 1  0  0  1  (9)
= 0  1  1  0  (6)
```

Figure 13.2. Performing the bitwise ~ on the number 9.

In a C++ program, you could code this bitwise operation like this:

```
unsigned char  uc_result = ~9;

signed char    sc_result = ~9;

unsigned int   ui_result = ~9;

signed int     si_result = ~9;

unsigned long  ul_result = ~9;

signed long    sl_result = ~9;
```

The `uc_result` variable will hold 246, the result of the bitwise ~ on the `unsigned char` 9. The `sc_result` variable will hold –10, the result of the bitwise ~ on the `signed char` 9. The `ui_result` variable will hold 65526, the result of the bitwise ~ on the `unsigned int` 9. The `si_result` variable will hold –10, the result of the bitwise ~ on the `signed int` 9. The `ul_result` variable will hold 4294967286, the result of the bitwise ~ on the `unsigned long` 9. The `sl_result` variable will hold –10, the result of the bitwise ~ on the `signed long` 9. In any case, the 9 could have been stored in a variable, with the same result.

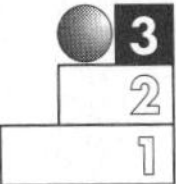

5. You can take advantage of the bitwise operators to perform tests on data that you couldn't perform as efficiently in other ways.

Suppose, for example, that you want to know whether the user typed an odd or even number (assuming that the input is integers). You could use the modulus operator (`%`) to see whether the remainder, after dividing the input value by 2, is 0 or 1. If the remainder is 0, the number is even. If the remainder is 1, the number is odd.

The bitwise operators are more efficient than other operators because bitwise operators directly compare bit patterns without using any mathematical operations. Since a number is even if its bit pattern ends in 0, and odd if its bit pattern ends in 1, you can also test for odd or even numbers by applying the bitwise `&` to the data and to a binary 1. This technique is more efficient than using the modulus operator. The following program tells the user whether the input value is odd or even.

Comments to identify the file.
Include the header file iostream.h.
Start of the `main()` *loop.*

Declare the variable `input` *as an integer.*
Print the statement `What number do you want me to test?` *on the screen.*
Obtain a value for `input` *from the user.*
If the least-significant bit of `input` *is 1, print the statement* `The number <the actual number that the user entered> is odd.`
If the least-significant bit of `input` *is 0, print the statement* `The number <the actual number that the user entered> is even.`

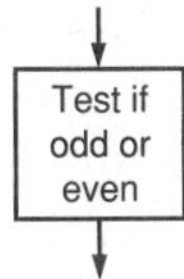


```
// Filename: C13ODEV.CPP
// Uses a bitwise & to see if a number is odd or even

#include <iostream.h>

main()
     {
     int  input;    // Will hold user's number

     cout << "What number do you want me to test? ";
     cin >> input;

     if (input & 1) // True if result is 1; otherwise, it is
                    // False (0)
          {
          cout << "The number " << input << " is odd\n";
          }
     else
          {
          cout << "The number " << input << " is even\n";
          }
return 0;
}
```

6. The only difference between the bit patterns for uppercase and lowercase characters is bit number 5 (the third bit from the left, as shown in Appendix A). For lowercase letters, bit 5 is a 1. For uppercase letters, bit 5 is a 0. Figure 13.3 shows how `A` and `B` differ from `a` and `b` by a single bit.

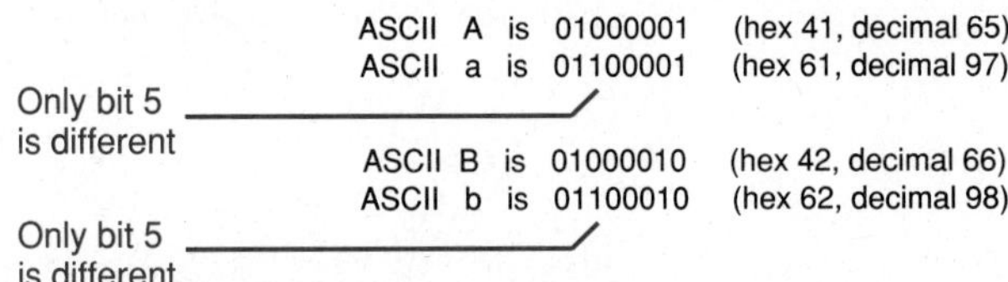

Figure 13.3. The difference between uppercase and lowercase ASCII letters.

To convert a character to uppercase, you have to turn off (change to a 0) bit number 5. You can apply a bitwise & to the input character and 223 (which is 11011111 in binary) to turn off bit 6 and convert any input character to its uppercase equivalent. If the number is already in uppercase, this bitwise & will not change it.

The 223 (binary 11011111) is called a *bit mask* because it masks off (just as masking tape masks off areas to be painted) bit 6 so that it becomes 0, if it isn't already. The following program does this to ensure that the user typed uppercase characters when asked for initials:

Print initials

```
// Filename: C13UPCS1.CPP
// Converts the input characters to uppercase if they aren't
// already

#include <iostream.h>

#define   BITMASK   (0xDF)       // 11011111 in binary

main()
     {
     char      first, middle, last;  // Will hold user's
                                     // initials

     cout << "What is your first initial? ";
     cin >> first;
     cout << "What is your middle initial? ";
     cin >> middle;
     cout << "What is your last initial? ";
     cin >> last;

     // Ensure that initials are in uppercase
     first = first & BITMASK;      // Turn off bit 6 if
     middle = middle & BITMASK;    // it isn't already
     last = last & BITMASK;        // turned off

     cout << "Your initials are: " << first << ' '
          << middle << ' ' << last << '\n';
     return 0;
     }
```

The following output shows what happens when two of the initials are typed with lowercase letters. The program converts them to uppercase before printing them again. Although there are other ways to convert letters to lowercase, none are as efficient as using the & bitwise operator.

```
What is your first initial? g
What is your middle initial? M
What is your last initial? p
Your initials are: G M P
```

Compound Bitwise Operators

As with most of the mathematical operators, you can combine the bitwise operators with the equal sign (=) to form *compound bitwise operators*. When you want to update the value of a variable, using a bitwise operator, you can shorten the expression by using the compound bitwise operators, shown in Table 13.6.

Table 13.6. The compound bitwise operators.

Operator	*Description*
&=	Compound bitwise AND assignment
|=	Compound bitwise inclusive OR assignment
^=	Compound bitwise exclusive OR assignment

The preceding example for converting lowercase initials to their uppercase equivalents can be rewritten with compound bitwise & operations:

```
// Filename: C13UPCS2.CPP
// Converts the input characters to uppercase if they aren't
// already

#include <iostream.h>

#define   BITMASK   (0xDF)      // 11011111 in binary

main()
     {
     char   first, middle, last;  // Will hold user's initials

     cout << "What is your first initial? ";
     cin >> first;
     cout << "What is your middle initial? ";
     cin >> middle;
     cout << "What is your last initial? ";
     cin >> last;

     // Ensure that initials are in uppercase
     first &= BITMASK;      // Turn off bit 6 if it isn't
     middle &= BITMASK;     // already turned off
     last &= BITMASK;

     cout << "Your initials are: " << first << ' '
          << middle << ' ' << last << '\n';
     return 0;
     }
```

Mathematics of the Binary Bitwise Operators

There are three important mathematical properties of the binary bitwise operators. The first property is associativity: the action of any of the binary bitwise operators on any three objects does not depend on how the three objects are grouped. Note the following examples:

(A | B) | C = A | (B | C)

(A & B) & C = A & (B & C)

(A ^ B) ^ C = A ^ (B ^ C)

The second property is commutativity: the action of any of the binary bitwise operators on any two objects does not depend on the order in which the objects are given. Note these examples:

A | B = B | A

A & B = B & A

A ^ B = B ^ A

The third property is that of having an identity value: each of the binary bitwise operators has an identity, which is a value e for which A ° e = e ° A = A, where ° represents the operator. Note some examples:

A | 0 = 0 | A = A

A & 1 = 1 & A = A

A ^ 0 = 0 ^ A = A

The important thing to remember about this last property is that it applies, as the binary bitwise operators do, bit by bit. Although this isn't a problem for the inclusive and exclusive OR operators, it can be a problem for the AND operator. When applying the AND operator, don't forget to include enough 1 bits for the bits you don't want to touch.

Bitwise Shift Operators

The bitwise shift operators are shown in Table 13.7. They shift bits inside a number to the left or right. The number of bits shifted depends on the value to the right of the bitwise shift operator. The formats of the bitwise shift operators are

```
value << number_of_bits

value >> number_of_bits
```

The `value` can be an integer or character variable, or a constant. The `number_of_bits` determines how many bits will be shifted. Figure 13.4 shows what happens when the number 29 (binary 00011101) is left-shifted three bits with a bitwise left shift (<<). Notice that each bit "shifts over" to the left three times, and 0s fill in from the right. If this were a bitwise right shift (>>), the 0s would fill in from the left as the rest of the bits are shifted to the right three times.

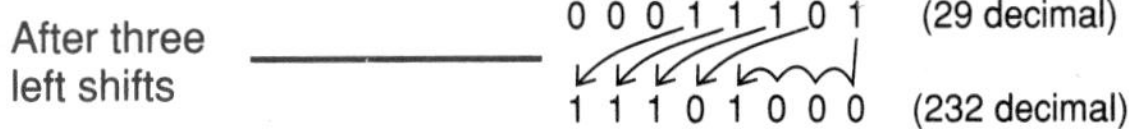

Figure 13.4. Shifting the bits in binary 29 to the left.

Table 13.7. The bitwise shift operators.

Operator	*Description*
<<	Bitwise left shift
>>	Bitwise right shift

CAUTION: The results of bitwise shift operators are not consistent when applied to signed values. On the PC, the sign bit *propagates* with each shift. That is, for every shift position, the sign bit shifts, but the original sign is retained as well. The end result is that negative numbers fill in from the left with 1s and not with 0s, when a bitwise right shift is applied to them.

You've probably noticed that the bitwise shift operators are the same operators used in cout and cin. This advanced feature of C++ is called *operator overloading*. Although the concept of operator overloading is beyond the scope of this book, rest assured that the Turbo C++ compiler can understand from context which meaning you intend.

Examples

1. The following program takes two values and shifts them three bits to the left and then to the right. This program illustrates how to code the bitwise left- and right-shift operators.

```
// Filename: C13SHFT1.CPP
// Demonstrates bitwise left- and right-shift operators

#include <iostream.h>

main()
     {
     int      num1 = 25;          // 00011001 binary
     int      num2 = 102;         // 01100110 binary
     int      shift1, shift2;     // Will hold shifted numbers

     shift1 = num1 << 3;      // Bitwise left shift
     cout << "25 shifted left 3 times is " << shift1
          << " \n";
     shift2 = num2 << 3;      // Bitwise left shift
     cout << "102 shifted left 3 times is " << shift2
          << " \n";
```

```
shift1 = num1 >> 3;      // Bitwise right shift
cout << "25 shifted right 3 times is " << shift1
     << " \n";
shift2 = num2 >> 3;      // Bitwise right shift
cout << "102 shifted right 3 times is " << shift2
     << " \n";

return 0;
}
```

Here is the output for this program:

```
25 shifted left 3 times is 200
102 shifted left 3 times is 816
25 shifted right 3 times is 3
102 shifted right 3 times is 12
```

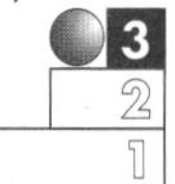

2. You should know another useful feature of bitwise shifting. If you bitwise left-shift a variable by a certain number of bit positions, the result will be the same as multiplying that same number by a power of 2. In other words, 15 left-shifted 4 times results in the same value as 15 times 2^4, or 15 times 16, which equals 240.

   If you bitwise right-shift a number by a certain number of bit positions, the result will be the same as dividing that same number by a power of 2. In other words, 64 right-shifted by 2 results in the same value as 64 divided by 2^2, or 64 divided by 4, which equals 16. This property is retained in signed arithmetic by the sign propagation feature mentioned earlier. For this reason, a shift right on an `unsigned` value is often referred to as a logical shift right, and a shift right on a `signed` value is often referred to as an arithmetic shift right.

   If you have to multiply or divide a variable by a power of 2, you can do it much faster by simply shifting the number. In fact, this is an optimization frequently used internally by the Turbo C++ compiler. The following program illustrates this:

```
// Filename: C13SHFT2.CPP
// Demonstrates multiplication and division by
// bitwise shifting

#include <iostream.h>

main()
     {
     signed int     num1 = 15;      // Numbers to be shifted
     signed int     num2 = -15;
     unsigned int   num3 = 15;
     unsigned int   num4 = 0x8000;

     num1 = num1 << 4;     // Multiply num1 by 16
     num2 = num2 >> 3;     // Divide num2 by 8
     num3 = num3 << 2;     // Multiple num3 by 4
     num4 = num4 >> 1;     // Divide num4 by 2

     cout << "15 multiplied by 16 is " << num1 << " \n";
     cout << "-15 divided by 8 is " << num2 << " \n";
     cout << "15 multiplied by 4 is " << num3 << " \n";
     cout << "0x8000 divided by 2 is 0x" << hex << num4
          << " \n";

     return 0;
     }
```

Compound Bitwise Shift Operators

As with most of the mathematical operators, you can combine the bitwise operators with the equal sign (=) to form *compound bitwise shift operators*. When you want to update the value of a variable, using a bitwise shift operator, you can shorten the expression by using the compound bitwise operators, shown in Table 13.8.

Table 13.8. The compound bitwise shift operators.

Operator	*Description*
`<<=`	Compound bitwise left shift
`>>=`	Compound bitwise right shift

The preceding example that demonstrates math by use of shift operators can be rewritten with compound bitwise & operations:

```
// Filename: C13SHFT3.CPP
// Demonstrates multiplication and division by
// bitwise shifting

#include <iostream.h>

main()
     {
     signed int      num1 = 15;       // Numbers to be shifted
     signed int      num2 = -15;
     unsigned int    num3 = 15;
     unsigned int    num4 = 0x8000;

     num1 <<= 4;      // Multiply num1 by 16
     num2 >>= 3;      // Divide num2 by 8
     num3 <<= 2;      // Multiple num3 by 4
     num4 >>= 1;      // divide num4 by 2

     cout << "15 multiplied by 16 is " << num1 << " \n";
     cout << "-15 divided by 8 is " << num2 << " \n";
     cout << "15 multiplied by 4 is " << num3 << " \n";
     cout << "0x8000 divided by 2 is 0x" << hex << num4
          << " \n";

     return 0;
     }
```

Summary

Because the bitwise operators work at the bit level, they are not often used in application programs. You must be comfortable with the binary numbering system before you can fully understand their operations. However, the bitwise operators offer a very efficient method of changing individual bits or groups of bits in variables. With these operators, you can test for odd and even numbers, multiply and divide by powers of two, and perform other tasks for which you would normally use less efficient operators and commands.

The bitwise operators, despite their efficiency, do not always lend themselves to readable code. Generally, most people reserve them for systems-level programming and use the easier-to-read, higher-level operators for most data processing.

Review Questions

Answers to Review Questions are in Appendix B.

1. What are the four bitwise logical operators, the three compound bitwise logical operators, and the two bitwise shift operators?
2. What is the result of each of the following bitwise True/False expressions?

   A. `1 ^ 0 & 1 & 1 | 0`

   B. `1 & 1 & 1 & 1`

   C. `1 ^ 1 ^ 1 ^ 1`

   D. `~(1 ^ 0)`

3. True or false: 7 (binary 111) can be used as a bit mask to test whether the rightmost three bits in a variable are 1s.
4. What is the difference between the bitwise ~ (1's complement) and 2's complement?

Part III

C++ Constructs

14

while Loops

The capabilities to repeat tasks make computers good tools for processing large amounts of information. This chapter and the next few chapters present C++ constructs. *Constructs* are the control and looping commands in programming languages. C++ constructs include powerful but succinct and efficient looping commands similar to those of other programming languages you may already know.

The `while` loops let your programs repeat a series of statements, over and over, as long as a certain condition is met. Computers don't get bored when performing the same tasks repeatedly. That's one reason why they are so important in business data processing.

This chapter introduces the following topics:

- The `while` loop
- The `do-while` loop
- The `exit()` function
- The `break` statement
- Counters and totals

After completing this chapter, you will know the first of several methods available in C++ for repeating sections of a program. This chapter's discussion of loops includes one of the most important uses for looping: creating counter and total variables.

The `while` Statement

The `while` statement is one of several C++ construct statements. A construct (from *construct*ion) is a programming language statement or a series of statements that controls looping. The `while` is a looping statement. Looping statements control execution of a series of other statements, causing parts of a program to execute repeatedly as long as a certain condition is met.

The format of the `while` statement is

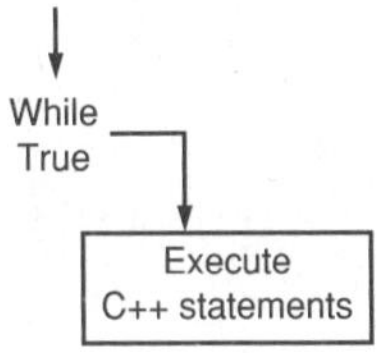

While True → Execute C++ statements

```
while (test expression)
    {
    block of one or more C++ statements;
    }
```

The parentheses around the *`test expression`* are required. As long as the *`test expression`* is True (nonzero), the *`block of one or more C++ statements`* will execute repeatedly until the *`test expression`* becomes False (evaluates to zero). If you want to execute just one statement in the body of the `while` loop, you do not have to enclose the statement in braces. Each statement within the body of the `while` loop requires semicolons at the end.

The body of the `while` loop executes repeatedly as long as the *`test expression`* is True.

The *`test expression`* usually contains relational and possibly logical operators. These operators provide the True-False condition checked for in the *`test expression`*. If the *`test expression`* is False when the program reaches the `while` loop for the first time, the entire body of the `while` loop will not execute at all. Whether the body of the `while` loop executes zero times, one time, or many times, the statements following the `while` loop's closing brace execute when the *`test expression`* becomes False.

Because the *`test expression`* determines when the loop finishes, the body of the `while` loop *should* change variables used in the *`test expression`*. Otherwise, the *`test expression`* will never change, and the `while` loop will repeat forever. This is known as an *infinite loop* and should be avoided.

TIP: If the body of the `while` loop contains only one statement, the braces surrounding it are not required. It is a good habit, however, to enclose all `while` loop statements with braces. If you later have to add more statements to the body of the `while` loop, the braces will already be there.

The Concept of Loops

You use the loop concept throughout your day-to-day life. Whenever you have to repeat a certain procedure several times, you are performing a loop, just as your computer does with the `while` construct. Suppose that you are wrapping holiday gifts. Here are the looping steps, in a `while`-like format, that you go through to wrap them:

```
while (There are still unwrapped gifts)
     {
     Get the next gift;
     Cut the wrapping paper;
     Wrap the gift;
     Put a bow on the gift;
     Fill out a name card for the gift;
     Put the wrapped gift with the others;
     }
```

If you had 3, 15, or 100 gifts to wrap, you would go through this procedure (loop) repeatedly until every gift was wrapped. For a less physical example that might be more easily computerized, suppose that you want to add up all the checks you wrote last month. You perform the following step:

While there are still checks from last month, add the amount of the next check to the total.

The body of the pseudocode `while` loop has only one statement, but that statement must be performed until you have added up all the checks from last month. When this loop ends (when there are no more checks from last month), you will have the total.

The body of the `while` loop can contain one or more C++ statements, even additional `while` loops. Your program will be more readable if you indent the body of a `while` loop a few spaces to the right. The following examples illustrate this.

Examples

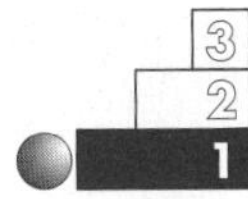

1. Some of the programs you saw in earlier chapters required user input with `cin`. If the user did not enter the appropriate values, the programs displayed an error message and asked the user once more. This was fine, but now that you understand the `while` loop construct, you should put the error message inside a loop, so that the user sees it not once but continually, until the user types the proper input values.

   The following program is short, but it demonstrates a `while` loop used to ensure valid user input. The program asks the user whether to continue with the program. You might want to incorporate this program into a larger one that needs the user's permission to continue. Put a prompt, such as the one shown here, at the bottom of a screenful of text. The text will remain on the screen until the user tells the program to continue with the rest of the execution.

Comments to identify the program.
Include the header file iostream.h.
Start of the `main()` *function.*
  Declare the variable `ans` *as a character.*
  Print to the screen `Do you want to continue (Y/N)?`
  Obtain a character from the keyboard.
  While the character typed is not a `Y` *or an* `N` *(or a* `y` *or an* `n`*), go through the loop.*
    Print to the screen `You must type a Y or an N.`
    Print to the screen `Do you want to continue (Y/N)?`
    Obtain another character from the keyboard.
  Return.

Keep asking while answer is not yes

```
// Filename: C14WHIL1.CPP
// Input routine to ensure that user types a correct response
// This routine might be part of a larger program.

#include <iostream.h>

main()
     {
     char     ans;

     cout << "Do you want to continue (Y/N)? ";
     cin >> ans;      // Get user's answer

     while ((ans != 'Y') && (ans != 'y') && (ans != 'N')
            && (ans != 'n'))
          {
          cout << "\nYou must type a Y or an N\n";
               // Warn and ask again
          cout << "Do you want to continue (Y/N) ?";
          cin >> ans;
          }    // Body of while loop ends here

     return 0;
     }
```

Notice that there are two `cin` functions which do the very same thing. An initial `cin`, outside the `while` loop, must be used to get an answer that the `while` loop can check for. If the user types something other than `Y` or `N` (or `y` or `n`), the program prints an error message, asks for another answer, and loops back to check the answer again. This method of data-entry validation is preferred to giving the user only one additional chance to get it right.

The `while` loop tests the expression at the top of the loop. This is why the loop may never execute; if the test is initially False, the loop will not execute even once. Notice the following output from this program. The program will repeat indefinitely, until the relational test is True (until the user types `Y`, `y`, `N`, or `n`).

```
Do you want to continue (Y/N)? k

You must type a Y or an N
Do you want to continue (Y/N)? c

You must type a Y or an N
Do you want to continue (Y/N)? s

You must type a Y or an N
Do you want to continue (Y/N)? 5

You must type a Y or an N
Do you want to continue (Y/N)? Y
```

2. The following program is an example of an *invalid* `while` loop. See if you can find the problem.

```
// Filename: C14WHBAD.CPP
// Bad use of a while loop

#include <iostream.h>

main()
     {
     int      a = 10, b = 20;

     while (a > 5)
          {
          cout << "a is " << a << ", and b is " << b
               << " \n";
          b = 20 + a;
          }
     return 0;
     }
```

This `while` loop is an example of an infinite loop. It is vital that at least one of the statements inside the `while` changes a variable in the *`test expression`* (in this example, the variable `a`); otherwise, the condition will always be True. Because `a` does not change inside the `while` loop, the program will never end without the user's intervention.

> **TIP:** If you inadvertently write an infinite loop, you will have to stop the program yourself. This typically means pressing Ctrl-Break, if not Ctrl-Alt-Del.

3. The following program asks for the user's first name and then uses a `while` loop to count the characters in the name. This is a string-length program. That is, it counts the number of characters in the name until it reaches the null zero. The length of a string is the number of characters in a string up to, but not including, the null zero.

```
// Filename: C14WHIL2.CPP
// Counts the number of letters in the user's first name

#include <iostream.h>

main()
     {
     char     name[ 15 ];    // Will hold user's first name
     int      count = 0;     // Will hold total characters in
                             // name

     // Get the user's first name
     cout << "What is your first name? ";
     cin >> name;

     while (name[ count ] != 0)      // Loop until the null
                                     // zero is reached
          {
          count++;                   // Add 1 to the count
          }

     cout << "Your name has " << count << " characters\n";
     return 0;
     }
```

The loop continues as long as the value of the next character in the `name` array is more than zero. Because the last character in the array will be a null zero, the test will fail on the name's last character, and the statement following the body of the loop will continue.

> **NOTE:** A library function called `strlen()` determines the length of strings. You learn about this function in Chapter 23, "Character, String, and Numeric Functions."

4. The string-length program's `while` loop is not as efficient as it should be. A `while` loop fails when its *`test expression`* is zero, so there is no need for the inequality-to-zero test. By changing the *`test expression`*, as the following program shows, you can improve the efficiency of the string-length count.

```
// Filename: C14WHIL3.CPP
// Counts the number of letters in the user's first name

#include <iostream.h>

main()
     {
     char      name[ 15 ];     // Will hold user's first name
     int       count = 0;      // Will hold total characters in
                               // name

     // Get the user's first name
     cout << "What is your first name? ";
     cin >> name;

     while (name[ count ])     // Loop until the null zero
                               // is reached
          {
          count++;             // Add 1 to the count
          }

     cout << "Your name has " << count << " characters\n";
     return 0;
     }
```

The do-while Loop

The `do-while` statement controls the `do-while` loop. This loop is similar to the `while` loop, except that with `do-while` the relational test occurs at the *bottom* of the loop. This ensures that the body of the loop executes at least once. The `do-while` loop tests for a positive relational test; as long as the test is True, the body of the loop continues to execute.

The format of the `do-while` loop is

The body of the `do-while` loop executes at least once.

```
do
     {
          block of one or more C++ statements;
     }
while (test expression)
```

As with the `while` statement, the *`test expression`* must have parentheses around it.

Examples

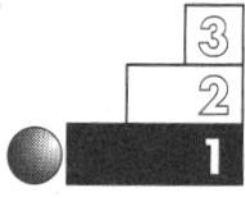

1. The following program is just like the earlier program with the `while` loop (C14WHIL1.CPP) except that a `do-while` loop is used instead. Notice the placement of the *`test expression`*. Because it is at the end of the loop, the user input does not have to appear before the loop and then again in the body of the loop.

```
// Filename: C14WHIL4.CPP
// Input routine to ensure that user types a correct response
// This routine might be part of a larger program.

#include <iostream.h>

main()
     {
     char     ans;
```

```
do
     {
     cout << "\nYou must type a Y or an N\n";
          // Warn and ask again
     cout << "Do you want to continue (Y/N) ?";
     cin >> ans;
     }     // Body of while loop ends here
while ((ans != 'Y') && (ans != 'N'));
return 0;
}
```

2. Suppose that you are entering sales amounts into the computer to calculate extended totals. You need the computer to print the quantity sold, part number, and extended total (quantity times the price per unit). The following program does that:

Compute extended inventory amount

```
// Filename: C14INV1.CPP
// Gets inventory information from user and prints
// an inventory detail listing with extended totals

#include <iostream.h>
#include <iomanip.h>

main()
     {
     int          part_no, quantity;
     float        cost, ext_cost;

     cout << "*** Inventory Computation ***\n\n";   // Title
     // Get inventory information
     do
          {
          cout << "What is the next part number ";
          cout << "(-999 to end)? ";
          cin >> part_no;
          if (part_no != -999)
               {
               cout << "How many were bought? ";
               cin >> quantity;
               cout << "What is the unit price ";
               cout << "of this item? ";
```

```
            cin >> cost;
            ext_cost = cost * quantity;
            cout << "\n" << quantity << " of # "
                 << part_no << " will cost "
                 << setprecision(2) << ext_cost;
            cout << "\n\n\n";     // Print two blank lines
            }
      }
   while (part_no != -999);         // Loop only if part
                                    // number is not -999

   cout << "End of inventory computation\n";
   return 0;
   }
```

Figure 14.1 shows the output from this program.

```
*** Inventory Computation ***

What is the next part number (-999 to end)? 123
How many were bought? 4
What is the unit price of this item? 5.43

4 of # 123 will cost 21.72


What is the next part number (-999 to end)? 523
How many were bought? 26
What is the unit price of this item? 1.25

26 of # 523 will cost 32.50


What is the next part number (-999 to end)? -999
End of inventory computation
```

Figure 14.1. Displaying extended inventory totals on the screen.

The `do-while` loop controls the entering of the customer sales information. Notice the trigger that ends the loop. If the user enters `-999` for the part number, the `do-while` loop quits because no part number –999 exists in the inventory.

This program can be improved in several ways. The invoice should be printed to the printer, not to the screen. You learn how to direct your output to a printer in Part V, "Character, Input, Output, and String Functions." The inventory total (the total amount of the entire order) should also be computed. You learn how to total such data in the section "Counters and Totals" later in this chapter.

The `if` Loop versus the `while` Loop

Some beginning programmers confuse the `if` statement with the loop constructs. The `while` and `do-while` loops repeat a section of code a number of times, depending on the condition being tested. The `if` statement may or may not execute a section of code, but if the section does execute, it executes only once.

Use an `if` statement when you want to conditionally execute a section of code once, and use a `while` or `do-while` loop if you want to execute the section of code more than once. Figure 14.2 shows the differences between the `if` statement and the two `while` loops.

`exit()` and `break`

C++ provides a way to leave a program early (before its natural finish) with the `exit()` function. The format of `exit()` is

```
exit(status);
```

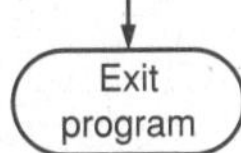

where *`status`* is an `int` variable or constant. In DOS, the *`status`* gets sent to the operating system's *error-level* environment variable where the *`status`* can be tested by batch files.

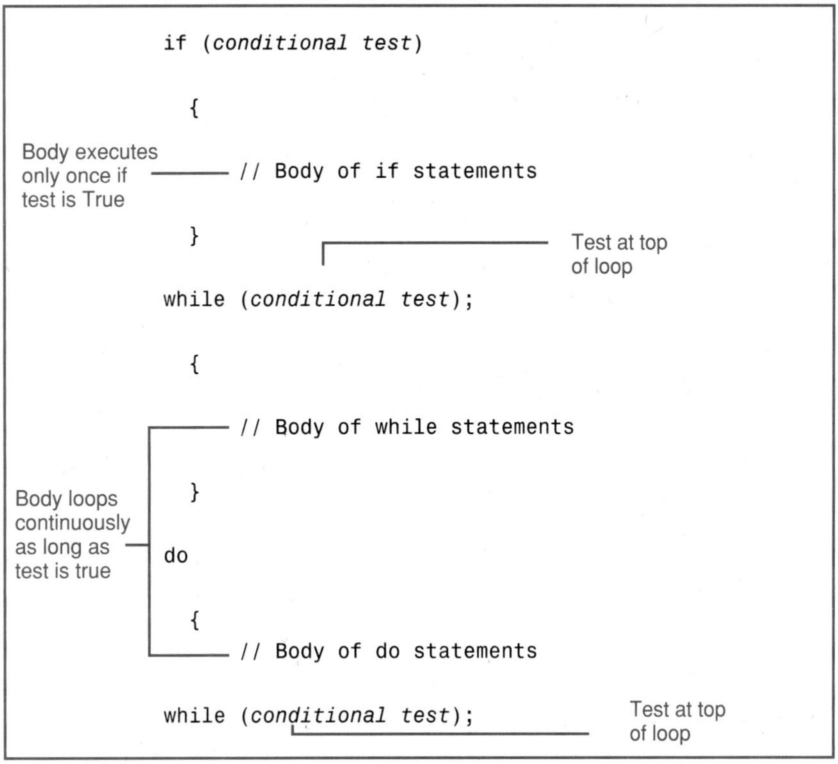

```
if (conditional test)
  {
    // Body of if statements
  }
while (conditional test);
  {
    // Body of while statements
  }
do
  {
    // Body of do statements
while (conditional test);
```


Figure 14.2. Differences between the `if` statement and the two `while` loops.

The `exit()` function provides an early exit from your programs.

Often something happens in a program that requires the program's termination. What occurs may be a major problem such as a disk drive error, or the user may simply indicate a desire to quit the program. (You can tell this by giving the user a special value to type in `cin` functions that triggers the user's intent.) You can put the `exit()` function on a line by itself or anywhere a C++ statement or function can appear. Typically, `exit()` is placed in the body of an `if` statement to end the program early, depending on the result of a relational test.

You should include the stdlib.h header file when using `exit()`. This file defines the operation of `exit()` to your program. Whenever you use a function in a program, you should know its corresponding `#include` header file, which is listed in the library reference manual.

Instead of exiting an entire program, you can use the `break` statement to exit the current loop. The format of `break` is

```
break;
```

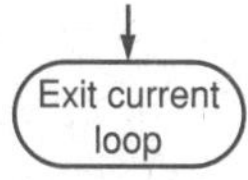

The `break` statement ends the current loop.

The `break` statement goes anywhere in a C++ program that another statement can go, but `break` typically appears in the body of a `while` or `do-while` loop so that you can leave the loop early. The following examples illustrate the `exit()` function and the `break` statement. The `break` statement is covered more extensively in Chapter 16.

> **NOTE:** The `break` statement exits only the most current loop. If you have a program with a `while` loop within another `while` loop, `break` exits only the internal loop.

Examples

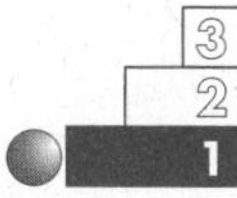

1. Here is a simple program that shows how the `exit()` function works. This program looks as if it prints several messages on the screen, but that is misleading. Because of the `exit()` early in the program, the program quits immediately after `main()`'s opening brace.

```
// Filename: C14EXIT1.CPP
// Quits very early because of exit() function

#include <iostream.h>
#include <stdlib.h>    // Required for exit()

main()
    {
    exit(0);          // Force program to end here

    cout << "C++ programming is fun.\n";
    cout << "I like learning Turbo C++ by example!\n";
    cout << "C++ is a powerful language ";
    cout << "that is not difficult to learn.";
```

```
     return 0;
     }
```

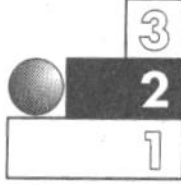

2. The `break` statement is not intended to be as strong a program exit as the `exit()` function. Whereas `exit()` ends the entire program, `break` quits only the loop that is active at the time. In other words, `break` is usually placed inside a `while` or `do-while` loop to make the program think that the loop is finished. The statement following the loop executes after a `break` occurs, but the program does not quit, as it does with `exit()`.

   The following program appears to print `C++ is fun!` until the user types `N` or `n` to stop it. The program prints the message only once, however, because the `break` statement forces an early exit from the loop.

```
// Filename: C14BRK.CPP
// Demonstrates the break statement

#include <iostream.h>

main()
     {
     char      user_ans;

     do
          {
          cout << "C++ is fun! \n";
          break;      // Cause early exit
          cout << "Do you want to see ";
          cout << "the message again (N/Y)? ";
          cin >> user_ans;
          }
     while (user_ans == 'N' && user_ans == 'n');

     cout << "That's all for now\n";
     return 0;
     }
```

This program always produces the following output:

```
C++ is fun!
That's all for now
```

You can tell from this program's output that the `break` statement does not allow the `do-while` loop to reach its natural conclusion but causes the loop to finish early. The final `cout` prints because the entire program does not exit with the `break` statement; only the current loop exits.

3. Unlike the `break` in the last program, `break` is usually placed after an `if` statement. This makes it a *conditional break*. The break occurs only if the relational test of the `if` statement is True.

   A good illustration of this is the inventory program you saw earlier (C14INV1.CPP). Even though the user enters `-999` to quit the program, an additional `if` test is needed inside the `do-while`. The `-999` ends the `do-while` loop, but the body of the `do-while` still needs an `if` test so that the remaining quantity and cost prompts are not given.

   If you insert a `break` after the test for the end of the user's input, as shown in the next program, the `do-while` does not need the `if` test. The `break` quits the `do-while` as soon as the user signals the end of the inventory by entering `-999` as the part number.

```
// Filename: C14INV2.CPP
// Gets inventory information from user and prints
// an inventory detail listing with extended totals

#include <iostream.h>
#include <iomanip.h>

main()

     {
     int          part_no, quantity;
     float        cost, ext_cost;

     cout << "*** Inventory Computation ***\n\n";   // Title
```

```
// Get inventory information
do
     {
     cout << "What is the next part number ";
     cout << "(-999 to end)? ";
     cin >> part_no;
     if (part_no == -999)
          {
          break;
          }    // Exit the loop if no more part numbers
     cout << "How many were bought? ";
     cin >> quantity;
     cout << "What is the unit price of this item? ";
     cin >> cost;
     ext_cost = quantity * cost
     cout << "\n" << quantity << " of # "
          << part_no << " will cost " << setprecision(2)
          << ext_cost;
     cout << "\n\n\n";      // Print two blank lines
     }
while (part_no != -999);   // Loop only if part number
                           // is not -999

cout << "End of inventory computation\n";
return 0;
}
```

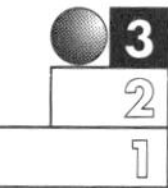

4. The following program might be used to control two other programs. It illustrates how C++ can pass information to DOS with `exit()`. This is your first example of a *menu* program. Like a menu in a restaurant, a menu program lists possible choices. The user decides which choice from the menu's options the computer is to perform. The mailing list application in Appendix F uses a menu for its user options.

   This program returns a 1 or 2 to its operating system, depending on the user's selection. The operating system then tests the exit value and handles the running of the appropriate program.

```
// Filename: C14EXIT2.CPP
// Asks user for selection and returns that selection
// to the operating system with exit()

#include <iostream.h>
#include <stdlib.h>

main()
     {
     int      ans;

     do
          {
          cout << "Do you want to:\n\n";
          cout << "\t1.  Run the word processor \n\n";
          cout << "\t2.  Run the database program \n\n";
          cout << "What is your selection? ";
          cin >> ans;
          }
     while ((ans != 1) && (ans != 2));          // Ensure that
                                                // user enters 1 or 2

     exit(ans);      // Return value to operating system
     return 0;
     }
```

Counters and Totals

Counting is important for many applications. For example, you might need to know how many customers you have or how many people scored above an average in a class. Or you might want to count how many checks you wrote last month with your computerized checkbook system.

Before developing C++ routines to count occurrences, think of how you count in your mind. If you were adding up a total number of items, such as the stamps in your stamp collection or the number of wedding invitations you sent out, you would do the following:

Start at 0 and add 1 to it for each item you are counting. When you finish, you have the total number (the total count) of items.

This is all you do when counting with C++. Assign 0 to a variable and add 1 to it every time you process another data value. The increment operator (++) is especially useful when counting.

Examples

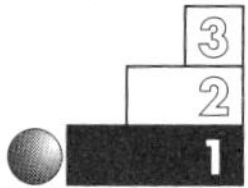

1. To illustrate the use of a counter, the following program prints `Computers are fun!` exactly 10 times on the screen. You could write a program that actually had 10 `cout` operators, but that would not be very elegant. It would also be too cumbersome to have 5,000 `cout` operators if you wanted to print that same message 5,000 times.

   By adding a `while` loop and a counter that stops after a certain total is reached, you can control the printing, as the following program shows:

```
// Filename: C14CNT1.CPP
// Program to print a message 10 times

#include <iostream.h>

main()
     {
     int      ctr = 0;    // Holds the number of times printed

     do
          {
          cout << "Computers are fun!\n";
          ctr++;     // Add one to the count, after each cout
          }
     while (ctr < 10); // Print again if fewer than 10 times
     return 0;
     }
```

   The following is the output from this program. Notice that the message prints exactly 10 times.

```
Computers are fun!
Computers are fun!
Computers are fun!
Computers are fun!
Computers are fun!
Computers are fun!
Computers are fun!
Computers are fun!
Computers are fun!
Computers are fun!
```

The heart of the counting process in this program is the following statement.

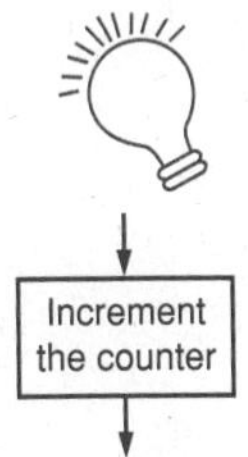

Increment the variable `ctr` *by 1.*

```
ctr++;
```

You learned earlier that the increment operator adds 1 to a variable. In this program, the counter variable is incremented each time the `do-while` loops. Because the only operation performed on this line is the increment of `ctr`, the prefix increment (`++ctr`) would produce the same result.

2. Notice that the last program not only added to the counter variable but also performed a loop a specific number of times. This is a common method of conditionally executing parts of a program a fixed number of times.

   The following program is a password program. A password is stored in an integer variable. The user must correctly enter the matching password in three attempts. If the user does not type the correct password in three tries, the program ends. This is a common method that dial-up computers use; they let the caller try the password a fixed number of times, and then hang up the phone if that limit is exceeded. This helps deter people from trying hundreds of different passwords at one sitting.

   If the user guesses the correct password within three tries, a secret message is displayed.

```
// Filename: C14PASS1.CPP
// Program to prompt for a password and check it against an
// internal one

#include <iostream.h>
#include <stdlib.h>

main()
     {
     int     stored_pass = 11862;
     int     num_tries = 0;          // The counter for
                                     // password attempts
     int     user_pass;

     while (num_tries < 3)           // Loop only 3 times
          {
          cout << "\nWhat is the password ";
          cout << "(You get 3 tries...)? ";
          cin >> user_pass;
          num_tries++;               // Add 1 to counter
          if (user_pass == stored_pass)
               {
               cout << "You entered the correct password.\n";
               cout << "The cash safe is behind ";
               cout << "the picture of the ship.\n";
               exit(0);
               }
          else
               {
               cout << "You entered the wrong password.\n";
               if (num_tries == 3)
                    {
                    cout << "Sorry, you get no more chances";
                    }
               else
                    {
                    cout << "You get " << 3 - num_tries
                         << " more tries...\n";
                    }
               }
          }     // End of while loop
```

```
exit(1);
}
```

This program gives the user three chances just in case one or two typing errors occur. Following three attempts, however, the program quits after refusing to let the user see the secret message.

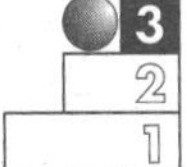

3. The following program is a letter-guessing game. It includes a message that tells the user how many tries were made before guessing the letter. A counter counts the number of tries.

```
// Filename: C14GUES.CPP
// Letter-guessing game

#include <iostream.h>

main()
     {
     int       tries = 0;
     char      comp_ans, user_guess;

     // Save the computer's letter
     comp_ans = 'T';     // Change to a different letter
                         // if desired

     cout << "I am thinking of a letter...";
     do
          {
          cout << "What is your guess? ";
          cin >> user_guess;
          tries++;            // Add 1 to the guess-counting
                              // variable
          if (user_guess > comp_ans)
               {
               cout << "Your guess was too high\n";
               cout << "\nTry again...\n";
               }
          if (user_guess < comp_ans)
               {
               cout << "Your guess was too low\n";
```

```
            cout << "\nTry again...\n";
            }
       }
  while (user_guess != comp_ans);      // Quit when match
                                       // found

  // User got it right, let the user know
  cout << "*** Congratulations!  You got it right! \n";
  cout << "It took you only " << tries
       << " tries to guess.";
  return 0;
  }
```

Figure 14.3 shows the output from this program.

```
I am thinking of a letter...What is your guess? A
Your guess was too low

Try again...What is your guess? Z
Your guess was too high

Try again...What is your guess? N
Your guess was too low

Try again...What is your guess? W
Your guess was too high

Try again...What is your guess? S
Your guess was too low

Try again...What is your guess? T
*** Congratulations!  You got it right!
It took you only 6 tries to guess.
```

Figure 14.3. Counting the number of guesses.

Producing Totals

Writing a routine that adds up values is as easy as counting. Instead of adding 1 to the counter variable, you add a value to the total variable. For instance, if you want to find the total dollar amount of checks you wrote in December, you would do the following: start at 0 (nothing) and add to that each check written in December. Instead of building a count, you are building a total.

When you want C++ to add up values, initialize a total variable to zero and add each value to the total until you have gone through all the values. The following examples show you how to produce totals.

Examples

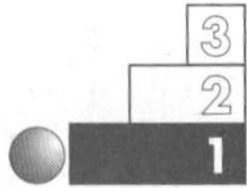

1. Suppose that you want to write a program to add your grades for a class you are taking. The teacher has informed you that if you get over 450 points, you will receive an A.

   The following program keeps asking you for values until you type -1. The -1 is a signal that you are finished entering grades and you want to see the total. The program also prints a congratulatory message if you earn an A.

Calculate total grade

```
// Filename: C14GRAD1.CPP
// Adds up grades and determines if an A was made

#include <iostream.h>
#include <iomanip.h>

main()
     {
     float     total_grade=0.0;
     float     grade;    // Holds individual grades

     do
          {
          cout << "What is your grade? (-1 to end) ";
          cin >> grade;
          if (grade >= 0.0)
               {
               total_grade += grade;
               }     // Add to total
          }
```

```
while (grade >= 0.0);     // Quit when -1 entered

// Control begins here if no more grades
cout << "\n\nYou made a total of "
     << setiosflags(ios::fixed) << setprecision(1)
     << total_grade << " points\n";
if (total_grade >= 450.00)
     {
     cout << "** You made an A!!";
     }

return 0;
}
```

Notice that the `-1` response does *not* get added into the total grade. The program checks for `-1` before adding to `total_grade`. Figure 14.4 shows the output from this program.

```
What is your grade? (-1 to end) 87
What is your grade? (-1 to end) 89
What is your grade? (-1 to end) 96
What is your grade? (-1 to end) 78
What is your grade? (-1 to end) 99
What is your grade? (-1 to end) 87
What is your grade? (-1 to end) 89
What is your grade? (-1 to end) -1


You made a total of 625.0 points
** You made an A!!
```

Figure 14.4. Computing the total grade.

2. The following program is an extension of the grade-calculation program. The program here not only totals the grades but also computes an average.

The program must know how many grades were entered before the average calculation can work. This is a subtle problem; the number of grades entered is unknown in advance. Therefore, every time the user enters a valid grade (not -1), the program must add 1 to a counter as well as add that grade to the total variable. This kind of routine, which combines a counter with totaling, is common in many programs.

```
// Filename: C14GRAD2.CPP
// Adds up grades, computes average, and determines if an
// A was made

#include <iostream.h>
#include <iomanip.h>

main()
     {
     float        total_grade = 0.0;
     float        grade_avg = 0.0;
     float        grade;
     int          grade_ctr = 0;

     do
          {
          cout << "What is your grade? (-1 to end) ";
          cin >> grade;
          if (grade >= 0.0)
               {
               total_grade += grade;      // Add to total
               grade_ctr ++;              // Add to count
               }
          }
     while (grade >= 0.0);      // Quit when -1 entered

     // Control begins here if no more grades
     if (grade_ctr != 0)
          {
          grade_avg = (total_grade / grade_ctr);  // Compute
                                                  // average
          cout << "\nYou made a total of "
```

```
                << setiosflags(ios::fixed) setprecision(1)
                << total_grade << " points.\n";
          cout << "Your average was " << setprecision(1)
                << grade_avg << " \n";
          if (total_grade >= 450.0)
                {
                cout << "** You made an A!!";
                }
          }
     return 0;
     }
```

Figure 14.5 shows the result of running this program. Congratulations! You are on your way to becoming a master C++ programmer!

```
What is your grade? (-1 to end) 88
What is your grade? (-1 to end) 98
What is your grade? (-1 to end) 97
What is your grade? (-1 to end) 87
What is your grade? (-1 to end) 94
What is your grade? (-1 to end) 96
What is your grade? (-1 to end) -1

You made a total of 560.0 points.
Your average was 93.3
** You made an A!!
```

Figure 14.5. Computing the total grade and the average.

Summary

This chapter shows you two ways to produce a C++ loop: the `while` loop and the `do-while` loop. The two variations of the `while` loop differ in how they test the end of the loop. The `while` loop tests at the top, and the `do-while` loop tests at the bottom. The end result is that the body of the `do-while` always executes at least once. To add to the `while` loop's flexibility, you learned the `exit()` function, which terminates a program, and the `break` statement, which terminates the current loop.

You learned also about counters and totals, which are two of the most important applications of loops. Your computer is a wonderful tool for adding and counting because of the repetitive capability of the `while` loop.

The next chapter extends your knowledge of loops by showing you how to create a *determinate* loop called the `for` loop. The `for` loop is useful when you want a section of code to loop for a specific number of times.

Review Questions

Answers to Review Questions are in Appendix B.

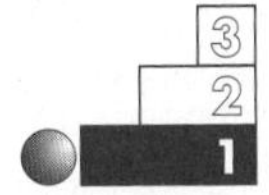

1. What is the difference between the `while` loop and the `do-while` loop?
2. What is the difference between a counter variable and a total variable?
3. Which C++ operator is most useful for counting?
4. True or false: The braces are not required around the body of `while` and `do-while` loops.

5. What is wrong with the following code?

```
while (sales > 50)
      cout << "Your sales are very good this month.\n";
      cout << "You will get a bonus for your high sales\n";
```

6. What file must you include as a header file if you use `exit()`?

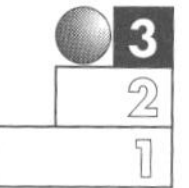

7. How many times will this `cout` print?

```
int     a = 0;
do
     {
     cout << "Careful \n";
     a++;
     }
while (a > 5);
```

8. How can you inform DOS of the program exit status?

9. What is printed in the following section of code?

```
a = 1;
while (a < 4)
        {
        cout << "This is the outer loop\n";
        a++;
        while (a <= 25)
                {
                break;
                cout << "This prints 25 times\n";
                }
        }
```

10. In program C14GRAD2.CPP, what could have happened if you hadn't checked for a grade counter of zero?

Review Exercises

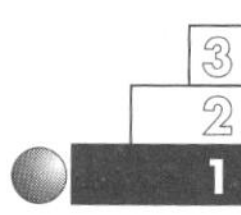

1. Write a program with a `while` loop that prints the numbers from 10 to 20, adding a blank line between the numbers.

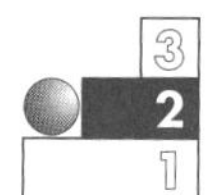

2. Write a weather-calculator program that asks for a list of the last 10 days' temperatures, computes the average, and prints the results. You will have to compute the total as the input occurs, and then divide that total by 10 to find the average. Use a `while` loop for the 10 repetitions.

3. Rewrite the program in exercise 1, using a `do-while` loop.
4. Write a program similar to the weather-calculator program in exercise 2 but make it a general-purpose program that computes the average of any number of days. You will have to count the number of temperatures entered so that you'll have that count when you compute the final average.
5. Write a program to produce your own ASCII table on the screen. Do not print the first 31 characters, because they are nonprintable.

15

for Loops

The `for` loop offers a way to repeat sections of your program a specific number of times. Unlike the `while` and `do-while` loops, the `for` loop is called a *determinate loop*. This means that at programming time you can usually determine exactly how many times the loop will take place. You saw that the `while` and `do-while` loops loop until a certain condition is met. The `for` loop does that and more; it continues looping until a specific count (up or down) is reached. Once the final `for` loop count is reached, execution continues at the next statement in the sequence.

This chapter introduces the following topics:

- The `for` loop
- Nested `for` loops

The `for` loop is a helpful way of looping through a section of code when you want to count or total amounts. Although the `for` loop does not replace the `while` and `do-while` loops, there are instances in which the `for` loop is more readable than a corresponding `while` loop.

The for Statement

The for statement encloses one or more C++ statements that form the body of the loop; the statements in the loop repeat continuously a certain number of times. You, as programmer, control the number of times the loop repeats.

The format of the for loop is

```
for (start expression; test expression; count expression)
    {
        Block of one or more C++ statements;

    }
```

The start expression is an expression that C++ evaluates before the loop begins. This expression is typically an assignment statement (such as `ctr = 1;`) but can be any legal expression you specify. C++ looks at and evaluates the start expression only once, at the top of the loop, and never evaluates the start expression again.

CAUTION: Do not put a semicolon after the right parenthesis. If you do, the for loop will think that the body of the loop is zero statements long! It will continue looping, doing nothing each time, until the test expression becomes False.

The for loop loops for a specific number of times.

Every time the body of the loop repeats, the count expression executes, typically incrementing or decrementing a variable. The test expression evaluates to True (nonzero) or False (zero) and determines whether the body of the loop will repeat again.

TIP: If only one C++ statement resides in the for loop's body, the braces are not required but are recommended. If you add more statements later, the braces will be there already, and you will not inadvertently leave them out.

The Concept of `for` Loops

You use the concept of `for` loops in day-to-day life. Whenever you have to repeat a certain procedure a specified number of times, it is a good candidate for a computerized `for` loop.

To illustrate further the concept of a `for` loop, suppose that you need to put up 10 new shutters on your house. You must do the following steps for each shutter:

Move the ladder to the location of the next shutter.
Take a shutter, hammer, and nails up the ladder.
Hammer the shutter to the side of the house.
Climb down the ladder.

Because you have 10 shutters, you must perform each of these steps exactly 10 times. After 10 times, the job is finished. You loop through a procedure that has several steps. These steps are the body of the loop. It is certainly not an endless loop because there is a fixed number of shutters; you run out of shutters after 10 of them.

For a less physical example that might be more easily computerized, suppose that you have to fill out three tax returns for each of your teenage children. For each child, you must perform the following steps:

Add up the total income.
Add up the total deductions.
Fill out a tax return.
Put it in an envelope.
Mail it.

You then must repeat this procedure two more times.

Notice how the sentence before these five steps begins: "For each child. . . ." This signals a construct similar to the `for` loop.

NOTE: The `for` loop tests at the top of the loop. If the *`test expression`* is False when the `for` loop begins, the body of the loop will never execute.

> **The Choice of Loops**
>
> You can write any loop construct with a `for` loop, `while` loop, or `do-while` loop. All these loop constructs are candidates for virtually any loop you need C++ to perform. The `for` loop is a good choice when you want to count or loop a specific number of times.
>
> Although the `while` and `do-while` loops continue looping until a certain condition is met, the `for` loop continues until a certain value is reached. Because of the close connection of C++'s True-False test to an expression's result (an expression is True if it is nonzero), any loop construct can be used for any loop your programs require.
>
> Generally, you will use `for` loops when you want a determinate loop that iterates until a specific incremented (or decremented) value is reached. You will reserve `while` loops for looping until a False condition is met.

Examples

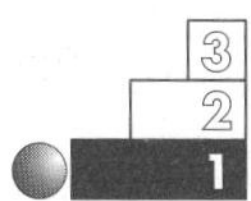

1. To give you a glimpse of the `for` loop's capabilities, the first program in this example contains a `for` loop, and the second program does not. The first program is a counting program. Look at the program and its output. The results basically speak for themselves and illustrate the `for` loop very well.

   Here is a program with a `for` loop.

   Comments to identify the program.
   Include the header file iostream.h.
   Start of the `main()` function.
   Declare the variable `ctr` as an integer.
   Start at the variable `ctr` equal to 1 and go through the loop, incrementing `ctr` by 1, while the variable `ctr` is less than or equal to 10.

Print to the screen the value of `ctr`.
Return from the `main()` *function.*

```
// Filename: C15FOR1.CPP
// Introduces the for loop

#include <iostream.h>

main()
     {
     int     ctr;

     for (ctr = 1; ctr <= 10; ctr++)      // Start ctr at 1,
                                         // increment through loop
          {
          cout << ctr << "\n";          // Body of for loop
          }
     return 0;
     }
```

Here is this program's output:

```
1
2
3
4
5
6
7
8
9
10
```

Now look at the same program with a `while` loop.

Comments to identify the program.
Include the header file stdio.h.
Begin the program by calling the `main()` *function.*
Initialize `ctr` *to 1.*
If `ctr <= 10` *is True, perform body of loop (do the* `cout` *operator and increment* `ctr` *by 1).*
If it is False (evaluates to 0), skip the loop and

continue with the rest of the program.
Return from the `main()` *function.*

```
// Filename: C15WHI1.CPP
// Simulating a for loop with a while loop

#include <iostream.h>

main()
     {
     int      ctr = 1;

     while (ctr <= 10)
          {
          cout << ctr << "\n";      // Body of while loop
          ctr++;
          }

     return 0;
     }
```

Notice that the `for` loop is a cleaner way of controlling the looping process. The `for` loop does several things that a `while` loop will not do unless you write extra statements.

With `for` loops, you do not have to write extra code to initialize variables and increment or decrement them. You can see at a glance (in the expressions within the `for` statement) exactly how the loop will execute. This is not the case with the `while` loop, which forces you to look inside the loop to see how it is controlled.

2. Both of the following programs add the numbers from 100 to 200. The first program uses a `for` loop, and the second program does not. The first example shows how using a *`start expression`* other than 1 starts the loop with a bigger *`count expression`*.

   Here is a program with a `for` loop:

```
// Filename: C15FOR2.CPP
// Demonstrates totaling by using a for loop

#include <iostream.h>

main()
     {
     int     total, ctr;

     total = 0;     // Will hold total of 100 to 200

     for (ctr = 100; ctr <= 200; ctr++)  // ctr is 100, 101,
                                         // 102, ..., 200
          {
          total += ctr;
          }          // Add value of ctr each iteration

     cout << "The total is " << total << "\n";
     return 0;
     }
```

Here is the same program without a for loop:

```
// Filename: C15WHI2.CPP
// A totaling program that uses a do-while loop
#include <iostream.h>

main()
     {
     int     total = 0;     // Initialize total
     int     num = 100;     // Starting value

     do
          {
          total += num;     // Add to total
          num++;            // Increment counter
          }
     while (num <= 200);
     cout << "The total is " << total << "\n";
     return 0;
     }
```

Both programs produce the following output:

```
The total is 15150
```

The body of the loop in both programs executes only 101 times. The starting value is 100, not 1 (as in the last example). Note that the `for` loop is less complex than the `do-while` loop because the initialization, testing, and incrementing are performed in the single `for` statement.

> **TIP:** Notice how the body of the `for` loop is indented. This is a good habit to develop; it makes the beginning and end of the loop's body easier to follow.

3. The body of the `for` loop can have more than one statement. The following program requests five pairs of data values: children's first names and their ages. It then prints the name of the child's teacher, based on the child's age. This program illustrates a `for` loop with `cout`s, a `cin`, and an `if` statement in its body. Because there are exactly five children to check, the `for` loop ensures that the program ends after the fifth child is checked.

Get child's name

Get child's age

Print name of child's teacher

```
// Filename: C15FOR3.CPP
// Program that receives input on five children and prints
// the names of their teachers inside a loop

#include <iostream.h>

main()
     {
     char      child[ 25 ];   // Holds child's first name
     int       age;           // Holds child's age
     int       ctr;           // The for loop counter variable

     for (ctr = 1; ctr <= 5; ctr++)
          {
          cout << "What is the next child's name? ";
          cin >> child;
          cout << "What is the child's age? ";
```

```
          cin >> age;
          if (age <= 5)
               {
               cout << "\n" << child
                    << " has Mrs. Jones for a teacher\n";
               }
          if (age == 6)
               {
               cout << "\n" << child
                    << " has Miss Smith for a teacher\n";
               }
          if (age >= 7)
               {
               cout << "\n" << child
                    << " has Mrs. Anderson for a teacher\n";
               }
          }      // Quits after 5 times

     return 0;
     }
```

Figure 15.1 shows the output from this program. You will be able to improve the program after you learn to use the `switch` statement in Chapter 17, "The `switch` and `goto` Statements."

```
What is the next child's name? Jim
What is the child's age? 5

Jim has Mrs. Jones for a teacher
What is the next child's name? Kerry
What is the child's age? 8

Kerry has Mrs. Anderson for a teacher
What is the next child's name? Julie
What is the child's age? 6

Julie has Miss Smith for a teacher
What is the next child's name? Ed
What is the child's age? 10

Ed has Mrs. Anderson for a teacher
What is the next child's name? Cherie
What is the child's age? 7

Cherie has Mrs. Anderson for a teacher
```

Figure 15.1. Input values inside a `for` loop.

4. The preceding examples use an increment as the *count expression*. You can make the for loop increment the loop variable by any value. It does not have to be a 1.

   The following program prints the even numbers from 1 to 20, followed by the odd numbers from 1 to 20. To do this, 2 (instead of 1) is added to the counter variable each time the loop executes.

```
// Filename: C15EVOD.CPP
// Prints the first few odd and even numbers

#include <iostream.h>

main()
     {
     int      num;      // The for loop variable

     cout << "Even numbers below 21\n";     // Title
     for (num = 2; num <= 20; num += 2)
          {
          cout << num << " ";
          }             // Print every other number

     cout << "\nOdd numbers below 20\n";    // A second title
     for (num = 1; num <= 20; num += 2)
          {
          cout << num << " ";
          }      // Print every other number
     cout << "\n";
     return 0;
     }
```

The first for loop variable, num, is 2 and not 1. If it were 1, the number 1 would print first, as it does in the odd-number section. There are two loops in this program. The body of each one consists of the single cout function.

Two of the couts, the titles, are not part of either loop. If they were, the titles would print before each number prints. Here is the result of running this program:

```
Even numbers below 21
2 4 6 8 10 12 14 16 18 20
Odd numbers below 20
1 3 5 7 9 11 13 15 17 19
```

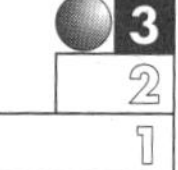

5. You can decrement the loop variable as well. If you do, the value is subtracted from the loop variable each time through the loop. The following example is a rewrite of the counting program, producing the reverse effect by showing a countdown:

```
// Filename: C15CNTD1.CPP
// Countdown to the lift-off

#include <iostream.h>

main()
     {
     int     ctr;

     for (ctr = 10; ctr != 0; ctr--)
          {
          cout << ctr << "\n";
          }     // Print ctr as it counts down
     cout << "*** Blast off! ***";
     return 0;
     }
```

When decrementing a loop variable, the initial value should be larger than the end value being tested for. In this case, 10 is counted down to 1. The loop variable, `ctr`, decrements each time. You can see how easy it is to control a loop by looking at this program's output:

```
10
 9
 8
 7
 6
 5
 4
```

```
3
2
1
*** Blast off! ***
```

TIP: This countdown program's `for` loop illustrates a redundancy you can eliminate in code, thanks to C++. The test expression, `ctr != 0;`, tells the `for` loop to continue looping until `ctr` equals zero. However, if `ctr` becomes zero, that is a False value in itself; there is no reason to add the additional `!= 0`, except for clarity. The `for` loop can be rewritten as

```
for (ctr = 10; ctr; ctr--)
```

without loss of meaning and with more efficiency. This technique is such an integral part of C++ that you should become comfortable with it. You have very little loss of clarity once you get used to writing your code this way.

6. You can make a `for` loop test for something other than a constant value. The following program combines much of what you have learned so far. It asks for student grades and computes an average. Because there may be a different number of students each semester, the program first asks the user for the number of students whose grades are about to be entered. The program then loops until the user enters that many scores, and computes the average based on the total and the number of grades entered.

```
// Filename: C15FOR4.CPP
// Computes a grade average with a for loop

#include <iostream.h>
#include <iomanip.h>
#include <stdlib.h>          // Why?...

main()
```

```
{
float        grade, avg;
float        total = 0.0;
int          num;           // Total number of grades
int          loopvar;       // Used to control for loop

cout << "\n*** Grade Calculation ***\n\n";     // Title
cout << "How many students are there? ";
cin >> num;     // Get total number to enter
if (num < 1)
     {
     exit(0);
     }

for (loopvar = 1; loopvar <= num; loopvar++)
     {
     cout << "\nWhat is the next student's grade? ";
     cin >> grade;
     total += grade;
     }     // Keep a running total

avg = total / num;
cout << "\n\nThe average of this class is: "
     << setprecision(1) << avg << "\n";
return 0;

}
```

Neither the total nor the average calculations have to be changed if the number of students changes, because of the way the `for` loop is set up.

7. Characters and integers are so closely associated in C++ that you can actually increment character variables in a `for` loop. The following program prints the letters A through Z with a simple `for` loop:

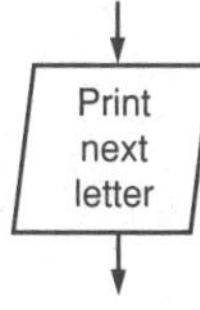


```
// Filename: C15FOR5.CPP
// Prints the alphabet with a simple for loop

#include <iostream.h>

main()
     {
     char     letter;

     cout << "Here is the alphabet\n";
     for (letter = 'A'; letter <= 'Z'; letter++)  // Loops
                                                  // 'A' through 'Z'
          {
          cout << letter << " ";
          }
     cout << "\n";
     return 0;
     }
```

The program produces the following output:

```
Here is the alphabet
A B C D E F G H I J K L M N O P Q R S T U V W X Y Z
```

8. You can leave any of the `for` loop's expressions blank. The following `for` loop leaves all the expressions blank (they are called *null expressions*):

```
for ( ; ; )
     {

     cout << "Over and over...";

     }
```

This executes forever in an infinite loop. Although you should avoid infinite loops, your program might dictate that you leave one expression or another in a `for` loop blank. If you already initialized the *`start expression`* earlier in the program, you would be wasting computer time to repeat that expression in the `for` loop, and C++ does not require it.

The following program leaves the *start expression* and the *count expression* blank, leaving only the for loop's *test expression*.

```
// Filename: C15FOR6.CPP
// Uses only the test expression in the for loop to count
// by 5s

#include <iostream.h>

main()
     {
     int     num = 5;                        // Starting value

     cout << "\nCounting by 5s: \n";      // Title
     for ( ; num <= 100; )  // Only contains test expression
          {
          cout << num << "\n";
          num += 5;  // Increment expression outside of loop
          }          // End of the loop's body
     return 0;
     }
```

Note the following output from this program, which illustrates the optional for loop expressions. Most of the time, you will need to leave out just one of them. If you find yourself using a for loop without two of its expressions, you might want to consider replacing it with a while or do-while loop.

```
Counting by 5s:
5
10
15
20
25
30
35
40
45
50
```

```
55
60
65
70
75
80
85
90
95
100
```

Nested for Loops

Any C++ statement can go inside the body of a for loop — even another for loop! When you put a loop within a loop, you are creating *nested loops*. The clock in a sporting event works like a nested loop. You might think that this is stretching an analogy a little far, but it truly works. A football game counts down from 15 minutes to 0. It does this 4 times. The first countdown is a loop going from 15 to 0 (for each minute), and that loop is nested within another loop counting from 1 to 4 (for each of the 4 quarters).

Use nested loops when you want to repeat a loop more than once.

Whenever your program needs to repeat a loop more than once, it is a good candidate for a nested loop. Figure 15.2 shows two outlines of nested loops. You can think of the inside loop as looping "faster" than the outside loop. In the first outline, the for loop, counting from 1 to 10, is the inside loop. It loops faster because the variable in goes from 1 to 10 before the outside loop, the variable out, finishes its first iteration. Because the outside loop does not repeat until the body of the loop ends, the inside for loop has a chance to finish in its entirety. When the outside loop finally does iterate a second time, the inside loop starts all over again.

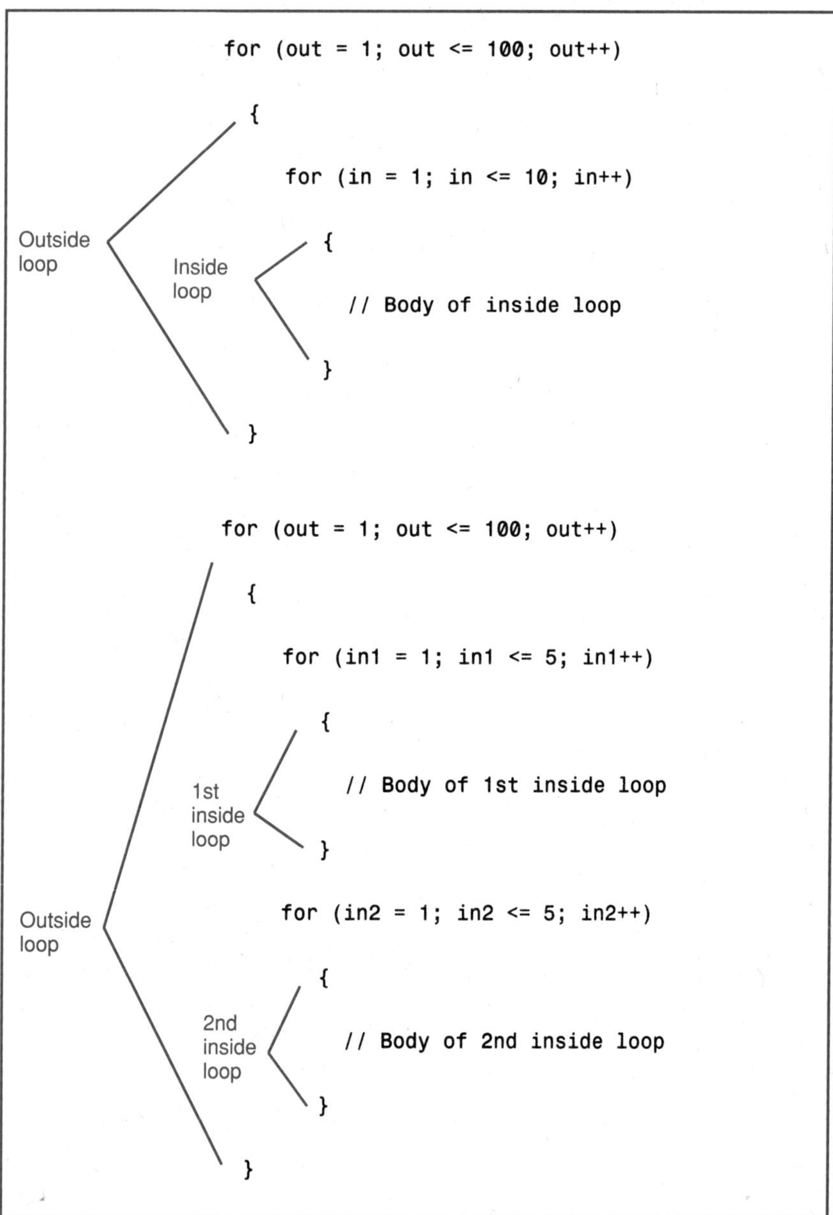
for (out = 1; out <= 100; out++)
{
for (in = 1; in <= 10; in++)
{
// Body of inside loop
}
}
Outside loop
Inside loop
for (out = 1; out <= 100; out++)
{
for (in1 = 1; in1 <= 5; in1++)
{
// Body of 1st inside loop
}
for (in2 = 1; in2 <= 5; in2++)
{
// Body of 2nd inside loop
}
}
Outside loop
1st inside loop
2nd inside loop

Figure 15.2. **Outlines of two nested loops.**

The second outline shows two loops within an outside loop. Both of the inside loops execute in their entirety before the outside loop finishes its first iteration. When the outside loop starts its second iteration, the two inside loops repeat all over again.

Notice the order of the braces in each of the outlines. The inside loop *always* finishes, and therefore its ending brace must come before the outside loop's ending brace. Indentation makes this much clearer because you can "line up" the braces of each loop.

To sum up nested loops, follow this rule of thumb:

In nested loops, the inside loop or loops execute completely before the outside loop's next iteration.

Nested loops become important later when you use them for array and table processing.

Examples

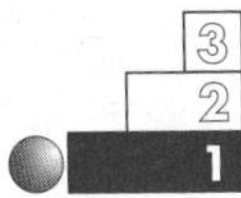

1. The following program contains a nested loop (a loop within a loop). The inside loop counts and prints from 1 to 5. The outside loop counts from 1 to 3. Therefore, the inside loop repeats, in its entirety, three times. In other words, this program prints the values 1 to 5 and prints them three times.

```
// Filename: C15NEST1.CPP
// Prints the numbers from 1 to 5 three times, using a
// nested loop

#include <iostream.h>

main()
     {
     int      times, num;     // Outer and inner for
                              // loop variables

     for (times = 1; times <= 3; times++)
          {
          for (num = 1; num <= 5; num++)
               {
               cout << num << "\n";
```

Here is the output:

```
What factorial do you want to see? 7
The factorial for 7 is 5040
```

You can run this program, entering different values when asked, and see various factorials. Be careful, however, because factorials multiply quickly, and a factorial of 11 or so will no longer fit in an `int` variable.

Summary

This chapter showed you how to control loops. Instead of writing extra code around a `while` loop, you can use the `for` loop to control the number of iterations at the time you define the loop. All `for` loops contain three parts: a *`start expression`*, a *`test expression`*, and a *`count expression`*.

You have now seen C++'s three loop constructs: the `while` loop, the `do-while` loop, and the `for` loop. These are similar but behave differently in the testing or initialization of loops. None of the three loops is better to use than another. Your programming problem should dictate which loop is appropriate.

The next chapter shows you additional ways to control the loops you write.

Review Questions

Answers to Review Questions are in Appendix B.

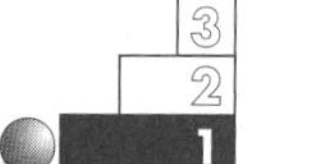

1. What is a loop?
2. True or false: The body of a `for` loop contains, at most, one statement.
3. What is a nested loop?

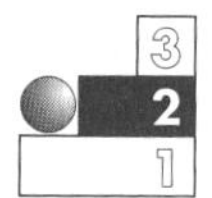

4. Why would you want to leave one or more expressions out of the `for` statement's parentheses?
5. Which loop "moves faster" — the inside loop or the outside loop?

6. What is the output from the following program?

```
for (ctr = 10; ctr >= 1; ctr -= 3)
     {

     cout << "ctr \n";

     }
```

7. True or false: A `for` loop is better to use than a `while` loop when you know in advance exactly how many iterations a loop requires.

8. What happens when the *`test expression`* becomes False in a `for` statement?

9. True or false: The following program contains a valid nested loop.

```
for (i = 1; i <= 10; i++);
     {
     for (j = 1; j <= 5; j++)
          {
          cout << i << "  " << j << "\n";
          }
     }
```

10. What is the output of the following section of code?

```
start = 1;
end = 5;
step = 1;

for ( ; start >= end; )
     {
     cout << i << "\n";
     start += step;
     end--;
     }
```

Review Exercises

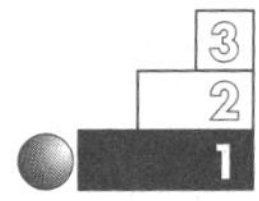

1. Write a program that prints the numbers from 1 to 15 on the screen. Use a `for` loop to control the printing.

2. Write a program that prints the values from 15 to 1 on the screen. Use a `for` loop to control the printing.

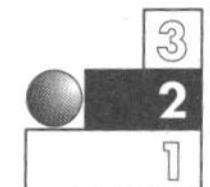

3. Write a program that uses a `for` loop to print every odd number from 1 to 100.

4. Write a program that asks for the user's age. Use a `for` loop to print `Happy Birthday!` for every year of the age.

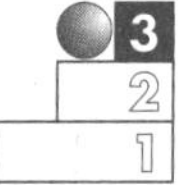

5. Write a program that uses a `for` loop to print the ASCII characters from 32 to 255 on the screen.

6. Using the ASCII table numbers, write a program that prints the following output, using a nested `for` loop:

```
A
AB
ABC
ABCD
ABCDE
```

HINT: The outside loop should loop from 1 to 5, and the inside loop's start variable should be 65 (the value of ASCII "A").

Advanced Control of `for` Loops: `break` and `continue`

This chapter focuses on two techniques for refining control of a `for` loop: the `break` statement and the `continue` statement. These statements allow you the power (depending on the data being processed) to break out of a `for` loop early or to skip processing the rest of the loop body.

This chapter covers the following topics:

- Using `break` inside a `for` loop
- Using the `continue` statement

The `break` and `for` Statements

The `for` loop was designed to execute a loop a specified number of times. However, there may be rare instances when the `for` loop should quit before the `for`'s counting variable has reached its final value. As with `while` loops, you can use the `break` statement to quit a `for` loop early.

The `break` statement goes in the body of the `for` loop. Programmers rarely put `break` on a line by itself; it almost always appears after an `if` test. If the `break` were on a line by itself, the loop would always quit early, defeating the purpose of the body of the `for` loop.

Examples

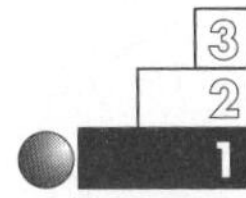

1. The following program shows what can happen when C++ encounters a break — that is, one *not* proceeded by an `if` statement.

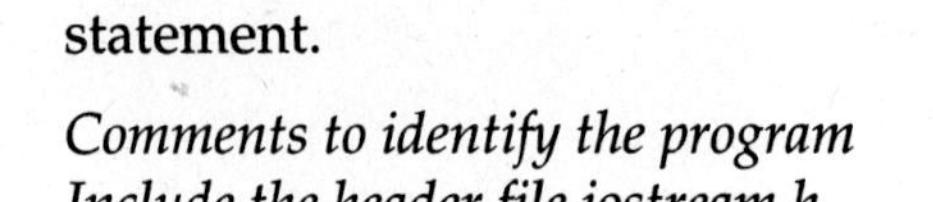

Comments to identify the program
Include the header file iostream.h.
Start of the `main()` *function.*
Declare the variable `num` *as an integer.*
Print `Here are the numbers from 1 to 20` *on the screen and return to the next line.*
The variable `num` *starts at 1 and is incremented by 1 while* `num` *is less than or equal to 20.*
Print the value of `num` *and return to the next line.*
Break immediately out of the `for` *loop.*
Print `That's all, folks!` *on the screen.*
Return out of the `main()` *function.*

```
// Filename: C16BRAK1.CPP
// A for loop defeated by the break statement

#include <iostream.h>

main()
     {
     int     num;


     cout << "Here are the numbers from 1 to 20\n";
     for (num = 1; num <= 20; num++)
          {
```

```
          cout << num << "\n";
          break;     // This exits the for loop immediately
          }

     cout << "That's all, folks!";
     return 0;
     }
```

Here is this program's output:

```
Here are the numbers from 1 to 20
1
That's all, folks!
```

Notice that the `break` immediately terminates the `for` loop before it has completed one cycle. The `for` loop might as well not be in this program.

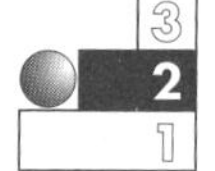

2. The following program is an improved version of the program in example 1. This program asks whether the user wants to see another number. If the user does, the `for` loop continues its next iteration. If the user does not, the `break` statement terminates the `for` loop.

```
// Filename: C16BRAK2.CPP
// A for loop running at the user's request

#include <iostream.h>

main()
     {
     int      num;          // Loop counter variable
     char     ans;

     cout << "Here are the numbers from 1 to 20\n";

     for (num = 1; num <= 20; num++)
          {
          cout << num << "\n";
          cout << "Do you want to see another (Y/N)? ";
          cin >> ans;
          if ((ans == 'N') || (ans == 'n'))
```

```
                {
                break;      // Will exit the for loop if
                            // user wants
                }
            }

    cout << "\nThat's all, folks!";
    return 0;
    }
```

Note the following sample run of this program. The `for` loop prints 20 numbers, as long as the user does not answer `N` or `n` to the prompt. Otherwise, the `break` takes over and terminates the `for` loop early. The statement after the body of the loop always executes next if the `break` occurs.

```
Here are the numbers from 1 to 20
1
Do you want to see another (Y/N)? Y
2
Do you want to see another (Y/N)? Y
3
Do you want to see another (Y/N)? Y
4
Do you want to see another (Y/N)? Y
5
Do you want to see another (Y/N)? Y
6
Do you want to see another (Y/N)? Y
7
Do you want to see another (Y/N)? Y
8
Do you want to see another (Y/N)? Y
9
Do you want to see another (Y/N)? Y
10
Do you want to see another (Y/N)? N
That's all, folks!
```

If you nest one loop inside another, the `break` terminates the "most active" loop — that is, the innermost loop in which the `break` statement resides.

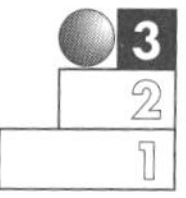

3. Use the *conditional* `break` (an `if` statement followed by a `break`) when you are missing data. When you process data files or large amounts of user data entry, you might expect 100 input numbers and get only 95; you could use a `break` to terminate the `for` loop before it cycles through its 96th iteration.

   Suppose, for example, that the teacher using C15FOR4.CPP, the grade-averaging program presented in the last chapter, entered an incorrect number of total students. Maybe she typed `16` when there were only 14 students. The preceding `for` loop would loop 16 times, no matter how many students there really were, because that loop relies on the teacher's count.

   The following grade-averaging program is more sophisticated. It asks the teacher for the total number of students, but if the teacher wants to, she can enter `-99` as a student's score. The –99 does not actually get averaged in but is used as a trigger value to break out of the `for` loop before its normal conclusion. A counter has to be placed in the loop as well, because the total number of grades entered may not match the number the teacher originally entered.

```
// Filename: C16BRAK3.CPP
// Computes a grade average with a for loop,
// allowing for an early exit with a break statement

#include <iostream.h>
#include <iomanip.h>

main()
     {
     float        grade, avg;
     float        total = 0.0;
     int          num, count = 0; // Total number of grades
                                  // and counter
     int          loopvar;        // Used to control for loop

     cout << "\n*** Grade Calculation ***\n\n";     // Title
     cout << "How many students are there? ";
     cin >> num;     // Get total number to enter
```

```
for (loopvar = 1; loopvar <= num; loopvar++)
     {
     cout << "\nWhat is the next student's grade? ";
     cout << "(-99 to quit) ";
     cin >> grade;
     if (grade < 0.0)    // A negative number triggers
                         // break
          {
          break;         // Leave the loop early
          }
     count++;
     total += grade;     // Keep a running total
     }

if (count != 0)
     {
     avg = total / count;
     cout << "\n\nThe average of this class is: "
          << setprecision(1) << avg << "\n";
     }
return 0;
}
```

Notice that the grade is tested for less than zero, not – 99.0. Floating-point values do not compare well for equality (because of their bit-level representations). No grade will be negative, so any negative number will trigger the break statement. Here is how this program works:

```
*** Grade Calculation ***

How many students are there? 10

What is the next student's grade? (-99 to quit) 87

What is the next student's grade? (-99 to quit) 97

What is the next student's grade? (-99 to quit) 67

What is the next student's grade? (-99 to quit) 89
```

```
What is the next student's grade? (-99 to quit) 94

What is the next student's grade? (-99 to quit) -99

The average of this class is: 86.8
```

The `continue` Statement

The `continue` statement causes C++ to skip the remaining statements in a loop.

The `continue` statement does the opposite of the `break`; instead of exiting a loop early, `continue` forces the computer to perform *another* iteration of the loop. If you put a `continue` statement in the body of a `for` or `while` loop, the computer ignores any statement in the loop that follows `continue`.

The format of `continue` is

```
continue;
```

Perform another loop iteration

You will use the `continue` statement when data in the body of the loop is bad, out of bounds, or unexpected. Instead of acting on the bad data, you might want to loop back to the top of the loop and get another data value. The following examples help illustrate the use of `continue`.

> **TIP:** The `continue` statement forces a new iteration of any of the three loop constructs: the `for` loop, the `while` loop, and the `do while` loop.

Figure 16.1 shows the difference between the `break` and `continue` statements.

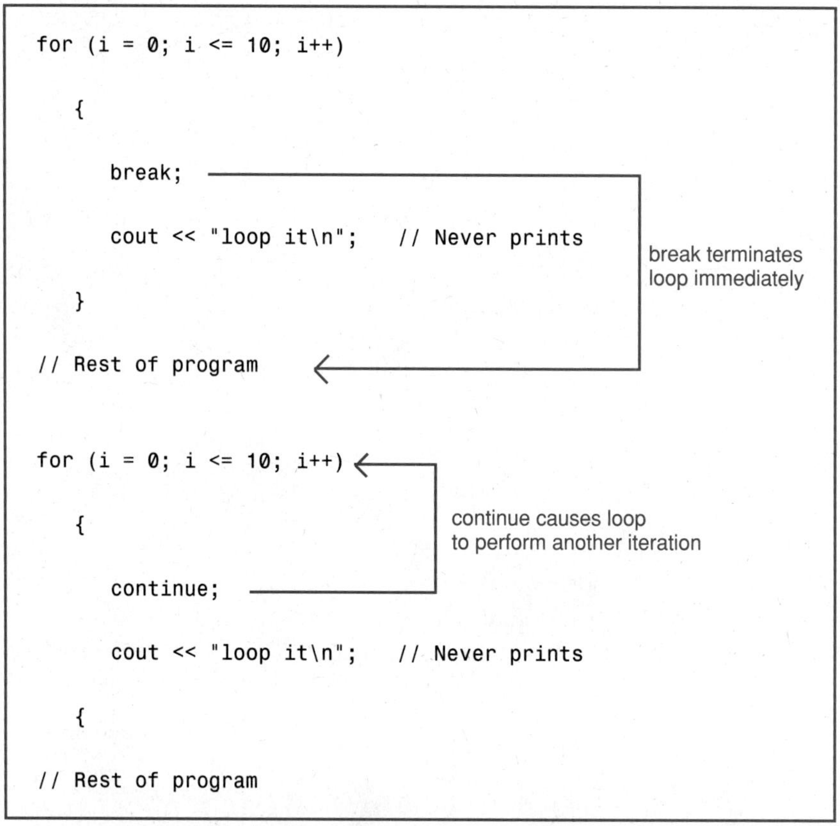
for (i = 0; i <= 10; i++)
{
break;
cout << "loop it\n"; // Never prints
}
// Rest of program
break terminates loop immediately
for (i = 0; i <= 10; i++)
{
continue;
cout << "loop it\n"; // Never prints
{
// Rest of program
continue causes loop to perform another iteration

Figure 16.1. The difference between `break` and `continue`.

Examples

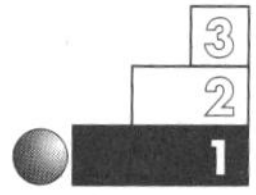

1. The following program appears to print the numbers 1 through 10, each followed by `C++ Programming`. It doesn't. The `continue` in the body of the `for` loop causes an early finish to the loop. The first `cout` in the `for` loop executes, but the second `cout` does not execute because of the `continue`.

```
// Filename: C16CON1.CPP
// Demonstrates use of continue statement

#include <iostream.h>

main()
     {
     int     ctr;

     for (ctr = 1; ctr <= 10; ctr++)     // Loop 10 times
          {
          cout << ctr << " ";
          continue;            // Cause body to end early
          cout << "C++ Programming\n";
          }
     cout << "\n";
     return 0;
     }
```

Note this program's output:

```
1 2 3 4 5 6 7 8 9 10
```

If you have such warnings enabled, Turbo C++ gives you a warning message when you compile this type of program. The compiler recognizes that the second `cout` is unreachable code since it will never execute because of the `continue`. Therefore, most programs do not use a `continue`, except after an `if` statement. This makes it a conditional `continue` statement, which is much more useful. The next two examples demonstrate the conditional use of `continue`.

2. The following program asks the user for five lowercase letters, one at a time, and prints their uppercase equivalents. The program uses the ASCII table to ensure that the user entered lowercase letters. (These are the letters whose ASCII numbers range from 97 to 122.) If the user does not type a lowercase letter, the program ignores it with the `continue` statement.

```
// Filename: C16CON2.CPP
// Prints uppercase equivalents of 5 lowercase letters

#include <iostream.h>

main()
     {
     char     letter;
     int      ctr;

     for (ctr = 1; ctr <= 5; ctr++)
          {
          cout << "Please enter a lowercase letter ";
          cin >> letter;
          if ((letter < 'a') || (letter > 'z')) // See if
                                                // out of range
               {
               continue;     // Go get another
               }
          letter -= 32;      // Subtract 32 from ASCII value
                             // to get uppercase
          cout << "The uppercase equivalent is: "
               << letter << "\n";
          }
     return 0;
     }
```

Because of the `continue` statement, only lowercase letters get converted to uppercase.

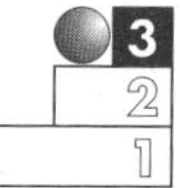

3. Suppose that you want to average the salaries of employees who made over $10,000 a year in your company, but you have only their monthly gross pay figures. The following program prompts for each employee's monthly salary, annualizes it (by multiplying it by 12), and computes an average. It does not average in any salary that is less than $10,000 a year. The `continue` ensures that those salaries are ignored in the average calculation, letting the other salaries fall through.

   If you enter `-1` as the monthly salary, the program quits and prints the result of the average.

```
// Filename: C16CON3.CPP
// Average salaries over $10,000 annually

#include <iostream.h>
#include <iomanip.h>

main()
     {
     float     month, year;    // Monthly and yearly salaries
     float     avg = 0.0, total = 0.0;
     int       count = 0;

     do
          {
          cout << "What is the next monthly salary ";
          cout << "(-1 to quit)? ";
          cin >> month;
          if ((year = month * 12.00) < 10000.00)   // Do not
                                                   // add low salaries
               {
               continue;
               }
          if (month < 0.0)
               {
               break;          // Quit if user entered -1
               }
          count++;             // Add 1 to valid counter
          total += year;       // Add yearly salary to total
```

```
     }
while (month > 0.0);

if (count)
     {
     avg = total / (float)count;     // Compute average
     cout << "\n\nThe average of high salaries is $"
          << setiosflags(ios::fixed) << setprecision(2)
          << avg << "\n";
     }
return 0;
}
```

Notice that this program uses both a `continue` statement and a `break` statement. The program does one of three things, depending on the user's input: adds to the total, continues another iteration if the salary is too low, or completely exits the `while` loop (and average calculation) if the user types a `-1`.

Here is the output from a sample run of this program:

```
What is the next monthly salary (-1 to quit)? 500.00
What is the next monthly salary (-1 to quit)? 2000.00
What is the next monthly salary (-1 to quit)? 750.00
What is the next monthly salary (-1 to quit)? 4000.00
What is the next monthly salary (-1 to quit)? 5000.00
What is the next monthly salary (-1 to quit)? 1200.00
What is the next monthly salary (-1 to quit)? -1

The average of high salaries is $36600.00
```

Summary

In this chapter, you learned several more ways to use and modify your program's loops. By adding `continue` statements and `break` statements, you can better control how the loop behaves. Being able to exit early (with the `break` statement) or continue the next loop iteration early (with the `continue` statement) allows more freedom in processing different types of data.

The next chapter shows you a construct of C++ that does not loop but relies on the `break` statement to work properly. This construct is the `switch` statement, which makes your program's choices much easier to program.

Review Questions

Answers to Review Questions are in Appendix B.

1. Why do `continue` and `break` statements rarely appear without an `if` statement controlling them?

2. What is the output from this section of code?

```
for (i = 1; i <= 10; i++)
     {
     continue;
     cout << "***** \n";
     }
```

3. What is the output from this section of code?

```
for (i = 1; i <= 10; i++)
     {
     cout << "***** \n";
     break;
     }
```

Review Exercises

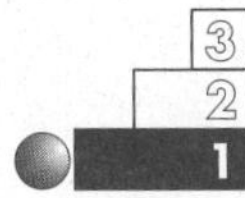

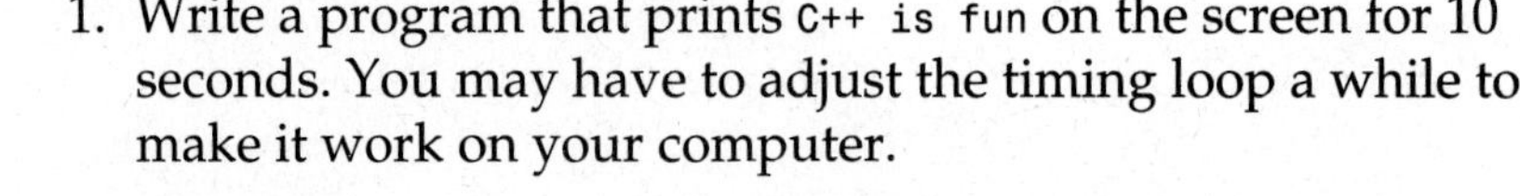

1. Write a program that prints `C++ is fun` on the screen for 10 seconds. You may have to adjust the timing loop a while to make it work on your computer.

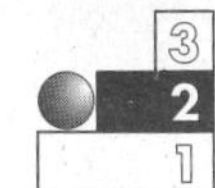

2. Make the program in exercise 1 flash the message `C++ is fun` on and off for 10 seconds. (HINT: You may have to use several timing loops.)

3. Write a grade-averaging program for a class of 20 students. Ignore any grade less than 0 and continue until all 20 student grades are entered, or until the user types `-99` to end early.

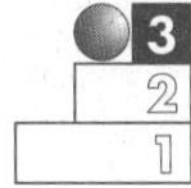

4. Write a program that prints the numbers from 1 to 15 in one column. To the right of each even number, print the square of that number. To the right of each odd number, print the cube (the number raised to the 3rd power) of that number.

17

The switch and goto Statements

The switch statement improves on the if and else-if constructs by streamlining the multiple-choice decisions your programs make. The switch statement does not replace the if statement but is better to use when your programs have to perform one of many different actions.

The switch and break statements work together. Almost every switch statement you use will include at least one break statement in its body. As a conclusion to Part III on C++ constructs, this chapter presents the goto statement for completeness, although you will use it rarely.

The following topics are introduced in this chapter:

- The switch statement
- The goto statement

If you have mastered the if statement, you should have little trouble with the concepts presented here. By learning the switch statement, you will be able to write menus and multiple-choice data-entry programs with ease.

The switch Statement

The switch statement, sometimes called the *multiple-choice statement*, lets your program choose from several alternatives. The format of the switch statement is a little longer than that of other statements you have seen. Here is its format:

Select a block of statements based on a condition

```
switch (expression)
{
case (expression1):
     one or more C++ statements;
case (expression2):
     one or more C++ statements;
case (expression3):
     one or more C++ statements;
  :
default:
     one or more C++ statements;
}
```

The *expression* can be any int or char expression, constant, or variable. The subexpressions — *expression1*, *expression2*, and so on — can be any other int or char constant. The number of case expressions following the switch line is determined by your application. The *one or more C++ statements* can be any block of C++ code.

Use the switch statement when your program makes a multiple-choice selection.

The default line is optional; not all switch statements include them, although most do. It does not have to be the last line of the switch body.

If the *expression* matches the first case *expression1*, the statements to the right of *expression1* execute. If the *expression* matches the second case *expression2*, the statements to the right of *expression2* execute. If none of the case expressions match that of the switch *expression*, the default case block executes.

The case expression does not have to have parentheses around it, but their use sometimes helps differentiate the value to make it easier to find.

> **TIP:** Use a `break` statement after each `case` block to keep execution from "falling through" to the rest of the `case` statements.

The use of the `switch` statement is easier than its format might lead you to believe. Anywhere an `if-else-if` combination of statements can go, you can usually use a clearer `switch` statement instead. The `switch` statement is much easier to follow than an `if` within an `if` within an `if`, as you had to write until now.

The `if` and `else-if` combinations of statements are not bad to use or that difficult to follow. When the relational test that determines the choice is complex and contains many `&&` and `||` operators, the `if` may be a better candidate. The `switch` statement is preferable when multiple-choice possibilities are based on a single constant, a variable, or an expression.

> **TIP:** To improve your program's speed, arrange the `cases` in decreasing order from those most often executed to those least often executed.

The following examples clarify the `switch` statement. They compare `switch` and `if` statements to help you see the difference.

Examples

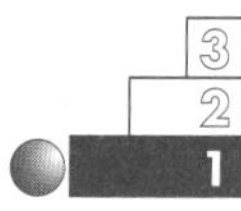

1. Suppose that you want to write a program to teach your child how to count. The program should ask the child for a number and then beep (ring the computer's alarm bell) that many times.

   The program assumes that the child enters a number from `1` to `5`. The following program uses the `if-else-if` combination to accomplish the beeping-counting program.

   Comments to identify the program.
   Include the header file iostream.h.
   Comment to identify what is about to happen in the program.
   Globally define `BEEP` *to print to the screen a control*

character that will make a beep and then move the cursor to a newline.

Start of the `main()` *function.*

Declare the variable `num` *as an integer.*

Comment to identify what is about to happen in the program.

Print to the screen `Please enter a number.`

Obtain an integer from the keyboard.

Comment to identify what is about to happen in the program.

If the variable obtained is equal to a 1, cause the computer to make a beep sound and return to a newline.

Otherwise, if the variable obtained is equal to a 2, cause the computer to make two beep sounds and return to a newline.

Otherwise, if the variable obtained is equal to a 3, cause the computer to make three beep sounds and return to a newline.

Otherwise, if the variable obtained is equal to a 4, cause the computer to make four beep sounds and return to a newline.

Otherwise, if the variable obtained is equal to a 5, cause the computer to make five beep sounds and return to a newline.

Return from the `main()` *function.*

```
// Filename: C17BEEP1.CPP
// Beeps a certain number of times

#include <iostream.h>

// Define a beep cout to save repetitiveness of the program
#define BEEP cout << "\a\n"
```

```
main()
     {
     int     num;

     // Get a number from the child (you may have to help
     // the child)
     cout << "Please enter a number ";
     cin >> num;

     // Use multiple if statements to beep
     if (num == 1)
          {
          BEEP;
          }
     else
          {
          if (num == 2)
               {
               BEEP;
               BEEP;
               }
          else
               {
               if (num == 3)
                    {
                    BEEP;
                    BEEP;
                    BEEP;
                    }
               else
                    {
                    if (num == 4)
                         {
                         BEEP;
                         BEEP;
                         BEEP;
                         BEEP;
                         }
```

```
// Define a beep cout to save repetitiveness of the program
#define BEEP cout << "\a\n"

main()
     {
     int     num;

     // Get a number from the child (you may have to help
     // the child)
     cout << "Please enter a number ";
     cin >> num;

     switch (num)
          {
          case 1:
               BEEP;
          case 2:
               BEEP;
               BEEP;
          case 3:
               BEEP;
               BEEP;
               BEEP;
          case 4:
               BEEP;
               BEEP;
               BEEP;
               BEEP;
          case 5:
               BEEP;
               BEEP;
               BEEP;
               BEEP;
               BEEP;
          default:
               cout << "You must enter a number ";
               cout << "from 1 to 5\n";
               cout << "Please run this program again\n";
               break;
          }
     return 0;
     }
```

If the child types a `1`, the program beeps *15* times! The `break` is there to stop the execution from falling through to the other `case`s. Unlike other programming languages, such as Pascal, C++'s `switch` statement requires that you handle the `case` code in this way.

This is not necessarily a drawback. The trade-off of having to specify `break`s gives more control in how you handle the specific `case`s, as shown in the next example.

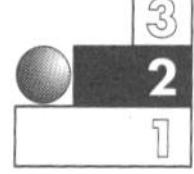

4. The following program controls the printing of end-of-day sales totals. The program first asks for the day of the week. If the day is Monday through Thursday, a daily total prints. If the day is a Friday, a weekly total, as well as a daily total, prints. If the day happens to be the end of the month, a monthly sales total prints.

In reality, these totals would come from the disk drive instead of being assigned at the top of the program. Furthermore, instead of individual sales figures being printed, a full daily, weekly, and monthly report of many sales totals would probably be printed. You are on your way to learning more about expanding the power of your C++ programs in the upcoming chapters. For now, concentrate on the `switch` statement and its possibilities.

The daily sales figures, the daily and weekly sales figures, and the daily, weekly, and monthly sales figures are handled through a hierarchy of `case`s. Because the daily amount is the last `case`, it is the only report printed if the day of the week is Monday through Thursday. If the day of the week is Friday, the second `case` executes, printing the weekly sales total and then falling through to the daily total (since Friday's total has to be printed as well). If it is the end of the month, the first `case` executes, falling through to the weekly total and then to the daily sales total. In this example, the use of a `break` statement would be harmful. Other languages that do not offer this "fall through" flexibility are more limiting.

```
// Filename: C17SALE.CPP
// Prints daily, weekly, and monthly sales totals
```

```
#include <iostream.h>
#include <iomanip.h>

main()
     {
     float     daily = 2343.34;     // Later these figures
// will come from a disk file instead of being so obviously
// assigned as they are here.
     float     weekly = 13432.65;
     float     monthly = 43468.97;
     char      ans;
     int       day;                      // Day value to trigger
                                         // correct case

// Month will be assigned 1 through 5 (for Mon - Fri)
// or 6 if it is the end of the month. Assume weekly AND
// daily prints if it is the end of month no matter what the
// day is.
     cout << "Is this the end of the month? (Y/N) ";
     cin >> ans;
     if ((ans=='Y') || (ans=='y'))
          {
          day = 6;     // Month value
          }
     else
          {
          cout << "What day number, 1 through 5 ";
          cout << "(for Mon-Fri) is it? ";
          cin >> day;
          }

     switch (day)
          {
          case 6:
               cout << "The monthly total is: $"
               << setiosflags(ios::fixed) << setprecision(2)
               << monthly << "\n";
          case 5:
               cout << "The weekly total is: $"
                    << setprecision(2) << weekly << "\n";
          default:
```

```
              cout << "The daily total is: $"
                   << setprecision(2) << daily << "\n";
         }
    return 0;
    }
```

5. The order of the case statements is not fixed. You can rearrange them to make them more efficient. If you know that most of the time only one or two cases will be selected, put those cases toward the top of the switch statement.

   For example, most of the company's employees in the last program are engineers, yet their option is third in the case statements. By rearranging the case statements so that Engineering is at the top, you will speed up this program. C++ will not have to scan two case expressions that it rarely executes.

```
// Filename: C17DEPT2.CPP
// Prints message, depending on the department entered

#include <iostream.h>

main()
     {
     char     choice;

     do      // Display menu and ensure that the user enters
             // a correct option
          {
          cout << "\nChoose your department:\n";
          cout << "S - Sales\n";
          cout << "A - Accounting\n";
          cout << "E - Engineering\n";
          cout << "P - Payroll\n";
          cout << "What is your choice? ";
          cin >> choice;
          // Convert choice to uppercase (if the user
          // entered lowercase) with the ASCII table
          if ((choice >= 'a') && (choice <= 'z'))
               {
```

```
                choice -= 32;       // Subtract enough to make
                                    // uppercase
            }
        }
    while ((choice != 'S') && (choice != 'A')
           && (choice != 'E') && (choice != 'P'));

        // Put the Engineering first since it occurs most
        // often

    switch (choice)
        {
        case 'E':
            cout << "\n Your meeting is at 2:30\n";
            break;
        case 'S':
            cout << "\n Your meeting is at 8:30\n";
            break;
        case 'A':
            cout << "\n Your meeting is at 10:00\n";
            break;
        case 'P':
            cout << "\n Your meeting has been canceled\n";
            break;
        }
    return 0;
    }
```

6. When you use menus, it is best to give the user a chance to do nothing. Perhaps the user started the program and then decided against continuing. If so, the user may not want to do *any* option on the menu. Most programmers give the user a chance to exit earlier than the normal conclusion of the program, as the following example shows. The menu now has a fifth option. If the user types `Q`, the program exits to the operating system early.

```
// Filename: C17DEPT3.CPP
// Prints message, depending on the department entered,
// giving the user a chance to stop the program early

#include <iostream.h>
#include <stdlib.h>
```

```
main()
     {
     char      choice;

     do      // Display menu and ensure that the user enters
             // a correct option
          {
          cout << "\nChoose your department:\n";
          cout << "S - Sales\n";
          cout << "A - Accounting\n";
          cout << "E - Engineering\n";
          cout << "P - Payroll\n";
          cout << "Q - Quit the program\n";
          cout << "What is your choice? ";
          cin >> choice;
          // Convert choice to uppercase (if the user
          // entered lowercase) with the ASCII table
          if ((choice >= 'a') && (choice <= 'z'))
               {
               choice -= 32;     // Subtract enough
                                 // to make uppercase
               }
          }
     while ((choice != 'S') && (choice != 'A')
            && (choice != 'E') && (choice != 'P')
            && (choice != 'Q'));

          // Put the Engineering first since it occurs most
          // often

     switch (choice)
          {
          case 'E':
               cout << "\n Your meeting is at 2:30\n";
               break;
          case 'S':
               cout << "\n Your meeting is at 8:30\n";
               break;
          case 'A':
               cout << "\n Your meeting is at 10:00\n";
               break;
```

```
        case 'P':
             cout << "\n Your meeting has been canceled\n";
             break;
        case 'Q':
             exit(0);        // Give the user a chance
                             // to change mind
             break;
     }
return 0;
}
```

The goto Statement

Early programming languages did not offer the flexible constructs that C++ gives you, such as `for` loops, `while` loops, and `switch` statements. The only means of looping and comparing was with the `goto` statement. C++ still includes a `goto`, but the other constructs are more powerful, more flexible, and easier to follow in a program.

The `goto` statement causes your program to jump to a different location, instead of executing the next statement in the sequence. The format of the `goto` statement is

```
goto statement label
```

The `goto` causes execution to jump to a statement other than the next one in order.

A *`statement label`* is named just as variables are (refer to Chapter 5, "Variables and Constants"). A *`statement label`* cannot have the same name as another variable being used in the program, or as a C++ command or function. If you use a `goto` statement, there must be elsewhere in the program a *`statement label`* to which the `goto` can branch. Execution then continues at the statement with the *`statement label`*.

The *`statement label`* precedes a line of code. Follow all such labels with a colon (:). C++ then knows that they are labels and will not get them confused with variables. You haven't seen such labels in the C++ programs so far in this book because none of the programs needed them. These labels are optional, unless you have a `goto` that branches to one.

Each of the following four lines of code has a different *`statement label`*. These lines are not a program, but individual lines that might be included in a program. Notice that each *statement label* goes to the left of its line:

```
pay:        cout << "Place checks in the printer \n;

Again:      cin >> name;

EndIt:      cout << "That is all the processing.\n";

CALC:       amount = (total / .5) * 1.15;
```

These labels are not intended to replace comments, although their label names should reflect something of the code that follows. Such labels give `goto` statements a tag to go to. When your program gets to the `goto`, it branches to the statement labeled by the *statement label*. The program then continues to execute sequentially until the next `goto` changes the order again (or until the program ends).

TIP: Use identifying line labels. A repetitive calculation deserves a label such as `CalcIt` and not `x15z`. Even though both are allowed, the first one is a better indication of the code's purpose.

Use `goto` Judiciously

The `goto` is not considered a good programming statement when overused. There is a tendency to include too many `goto`s in a program, especially for beginning programmers. When a program branches all over the place, following its execution becomes as difficult as trying to trace a single strand of spaghetti through a plate of noodles. This is called *spaghetti code.* Really.

Using a few `goto`s, here and there, is not necessarily a bad practice. Usually, however, you can substitute better code. To eliminate `goto`s and write more structured programs, you should use the other looping and `switch` constructs shown in the last few chapters. They are better alternatives to the `goto`.

> The `goto` should be used judiciously. Starting with the next chapter, you will begin to break your programs into smaller modules called functions, and the `goto` becomes less important as you write more and more functions.
>
> For now, become familiar with `goto` so that you can understand programs that use it. Some day, you might be called on to fix someone's code that contains the `goto`. The first thing you will probably do is substitute something else for the `goto`!

Examples

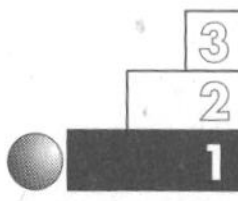

1. The following program has a problem, directly the result of the `goto`, but is one of the best illustrations of the `goto` statement. The program consists of an *endless loop* (sometimes called an *infinite loop*). The first three lines (after the opening brace) execute, and then the fourth line, the `goto`, causes execution to loop back to the beginning and repeat the first three lines. The `goto` continues to do this forever until you press the Ctrl-Break keys.

Comments to identify the program.
Include the header file iostream.h.
Start of the `main()` *function.*
Label the line as `Again:`
  and print `This message` *to the screen and return to the next line.*
  Tab over and print `keeps repeating` *and return to the next line.*
  Tab over twice and print `over and over` *and return to the next line.*
  Go to the line labeled as `Again:`.
  Return out of the `main()` *function.*

```
// Filename: C17GOTO1.CPP
// Program to show use of goto
// (This program ends only when user presses Ctrl-Break.)
```

```
#include <iostream.h>

main()
     {
Again:
     cout << "This message\n";
     cout << "\t keeps repeating\n";
     cout << "\t\t over and over\n";

     goto Again;     // Repeat continuously

     return 0;
     }
```

Figure 17.1 shows the result of running this program.

```
         keeps repeating
                 over and over
This message
         keeps repeating
                 over and over
This message
         keeps repeating
                 over and over
This message
         keeps repeating
                 over and over
This message
         keeps repeating
                 over and over
This message
         keeps repeating
                 over and over
This message
         keeps repeating
                 over and over
This message
         keeps repeating
                 over and over
This message
```

Figure 17.1. A repeat-printing program.

Of course, this is a silly example. You do not want to write programs with infinite loops. Because the `goto` is a statement best preceded with an `if`, eventually the `goto` will stop branching without intervention needed on the user's part.

2. The following program is one of the worst-written programs ever! It is the epitome of spaghetti code! However, do your best to follow it and understand its output. By understanding its flow, you will increase your understanding of the goto. You will also appreciate the fact that the rest of this book uses the goto only when needed to make the program clearer.

```
// Filename: C17GOTO2.CPP
// Program that demonstrates overuse of goto

#include <iostream.h>

main()
     {
     goto Here;
First:      cout << "A\n"; goto Final;
There:      cout << "B\n"; goto First;
Here:       cout << "C\n"; goto There;
Final:      return 0;
     }
```

At first glance, this program appears to print the first three letters of the alphabet, but the gotos make them print in reverse order: C, B, A. Although the program is not well designed, some indentation of the lines without *statement labels* will make the program a little more readable. Indenting lets you quickly separate the *statement labels* from the rest of the code, as you can see in the following program:

```
// Filename: C17GOTO3.CPP
// Program that demonstrates overuse of goto

#include <iostream.h>
main()
     {
     goto Here;

First:
     cout << "A\n";
     goto Final;
```

```
There:
     cout << "B\n";
     goto First;

Here:
     cout << "C\n";
     goto There;

Final:
     return 0;
     }
```

This program's listing is slightly easier to follow than the last one, even though they do the very same thing. In this book, the rest of the programs that use *statement labels* use indentation also.

You certainly realize that this output would be better produced by the following three lines:

```
cout << "C\n";
cout << "B\n";
cout << "A\n";
```

The goto warning is worth repeating: use goto sparingly and only when its use makes the program more readable and maintainable. Usually, there are better commands to use.

Summary

You have now seen the switch statement and its related options. It can help improve the readability of a complicated if-else-if selection. The switch is especially good when several outcomes are possible based on a certain choice. You can also use the exit() function (first mentioned in Chapter 14) to end a program earlier than its normal conclusion if the user prefers.

The goto statement causes an unconditional branch and can be difficult to follow at times. However, you should be acquainted with as much C++ as possible to prepare yourself to work on programs that others have written. The goto is not used much these days, and you can almost always find a better construct to use.

This ends the control section of the book. The next section introduces user-written functions. You have been using some of the library functions (such as cout and cin), and now you are ready to write your own.

Review Questions

Answers to Review Questions are in Appendix B.

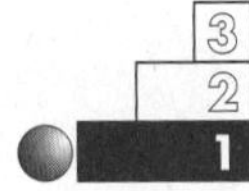

1. How does goto change the order in which parts of a program would normally execute?
2. What statement can substitute for an if-else-if construct?
3. What statement almost always ends each case statement in a switch?

4. True or false: The order of your case statements has no bearing on the efficiency of your program.
5. Rewrite the following section of code, using a switch statement:

```
if (num == 1)
     {
     cout << "Alpha";
     }
else if (num == 2)
     {
     cout << "Beta";
     }
else if (num == 3)
     {
     cout << "Gamma";
     }
else
     {

     cout << "Other";

     }
```

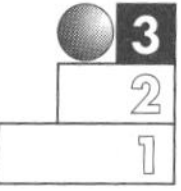

6. Rewrite the following program, using a `do-while` loop:

```
Ask:
     cout << "What is your first name? ";
     cin >> name);
     if ((name[0] < 'A') || (name[0] > 'Z'))
          {
          goto Ask;      // Keep asking until the user
                         // types a valid letter
          }
```

Review Exercises

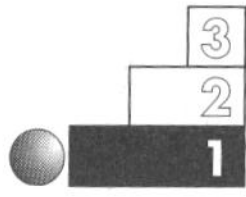

1. Write a program, using the `switch` statement, that asks for the user's age and prints a message saying `You can vote!` if the user is 18 or older, `You can adopt!` if the user is 21 or older, and `Are you REALLY that young?` for any other age.

2. Write a program, driven by a menu, for your local TV cable company. Here is how it charges:

   If you live within 20 miles outside the city limits, you pay $12.00 a month. If you live within 20 to 30 miles outside the city limits, you pay $23.00 a month. If you live within 30 to 50 miles outside the city limits, you pay $34.00 a month. No one living outside 50 miles gets the service. Use a menu to prompt for the user's living range from the city.

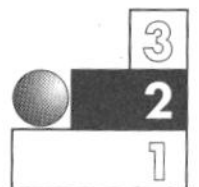

3. Write a program that calculates parking fees for a multilevel parking garage. Ask whether the driver is in a car or truck. Charge the driver $2.00 for parking the first hour, $3.00 for the second hour, and $5.00 for more than 2 hours. For a truck, add an extra $1.00 to the total fee. (HINT: Use one `switch` statement and one `if` statement.)

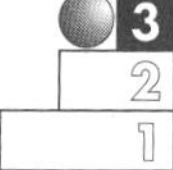

4. Modify the preceding program to charge depending on the time of day the car or truck is parked. If it is parked before 8 a.m., charge the fees given in exercise 3. If the car or truck is parked after 8 a.m. and before 5 p.m., charge an extra usage fee of 50 cents. If the car or truck is parked after 5 p.m.,

deduct 50 cents from the computed price. You will have to prompt the user for the starting time in a menu that includes the following:

A. Before 8 AM

B. Before 5 PM

C. After 5 PM

Part IV

Variable Scope and Modular Programming

Writing C++ Functions

A computer doesn't get bored. It performs the same input, output, and computations your programs require, as long as you want it to. You can take advantage of the computer's repetitive nature by looking at your programs in a new way: as a series of small routines that execute whenever you need them, as many times as necessary.

This chapter approaches its subject a little differently from the preceding chapters. It concentrates on teaching the need for writing your own *functions*, which are modules or sections of code that you execute and control from the `main()` function. So far, all programs in this book have consisted of one single, long function called `main()`. As you learn here, `main()`'s primary purpose is to control the execution of other functions that follow it.

This chapter covers the following topics:

- The need for functions
- Tracing functions
- Writing functions
- Calling functions

The chapter stresses the use of *structured programming*, sometimes called *modular programming*. C++ was designed to make it easy for you to write a program in several modules instead of as one long program. By breaking programs into several smaller routines (functions), you can better isolate problems, write correct programs faster, and produce programs that are much easier to maintain.

An Overview of Functions

When you approach an application problem that needs to be programmed, it's best not to sit down at the keyboard and start typing. Instead, you should think about the program and what it is to do. One of the best ways to attack a program is to start with the overall program's goal and then break it into several smaller tasks. You should never lose sight of the overall goal of the program, but you should try to think of how the individual pieces fit together to accomplish this goal.

When you finally do sit down to start coding the program, continue to think in terms of the pieces that fit together. Do not approach a program as if it were one giant program, but continue to write the small pieces individually.

This approach does not mean that you should write separate programs to do everything. You can keep individual pieces of the overall program together if you write functions.

C++ programs should consist of many small functions.

C++ programs are not like BASIC or FORTRAN programs. C++ was designed to force you to think in a modular, subroutine-like, functional style. Good C++ programmers write programs that consist of many small functions, even if their programs execute one or more of the functions only once. The functions work together to produce a program that solves an application problem.

TIP: You should not code one very long program. Instead, write several smaller routines, called functions. One of them has to be called `main()`, which is always the first function that executes.

`main()` does not have to be the first function in a program, but usually `main()` is.

Breaking a Program into Functions

If your program does very much, break it up into several functions. Each function should do one primary task. For instance, if you were writing a C++ program to get a list of characters from the keyboard, alphabetize them, and print them to the screen, you *could* write all of this in one big function — all in `main()`, as the C++ skeleton (program outline) in Listing 18.1 shows.

Listing 18.1. A nonstructured *`main()`* function skeleton.

```
main()
     {
     // :
     // C++ code to get a list of characters
     // :
     // C++ code to alphabetize the characters
     // :
     // C++ code to print the alphabetized list on screen
     // :

     return 0;
     }
```

The skeleton in Listing 18.1 is *not* a good way to write the program. Even though you could type this program in just a few lines of code, it would be much better to get in the habit of breaking up every program into distinct tasks. You should not use `main()` to do everything — in fact, you should use `main()` to do very little except call each of the other functions that actually do the work.

A better way to organize this program is to write separate functions for each task the program is to do. This does not mean that each function should be only one line long, but make sure that each function acts as a building block and performs only one distinct task in the program.

The skeleton in Listing 18.2 shows a much better way to write the program just described.

Figure 18.1 shows a trace of this program's execution. Notice that `main()` controls which of the other functions are called, as well as their order. Control *always* returns to the calling function once the called function finishes.

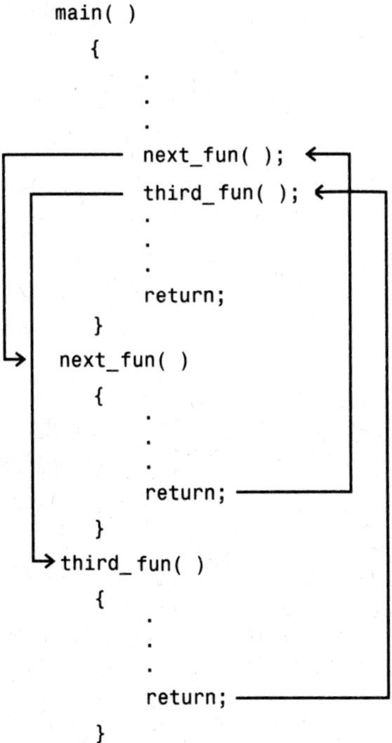

Figure 18.1. **Tracing the function calls.**

Notice that the user functions are preceded by `void` and include `void` inside the parentheses. C++, being a strongly typed language, requires this. Its meaning will be discussed in Chapter 21, "Function Return Values and Prototypes."

To call a function, you just type its name, including the parentheses, and then a semicolon. Remember that semicolons follow all executable statements in C++, and a function call (sometimes called a *function invocation*) is an executable statement. The execution is the function's code being called. Any function can call any other function. It just happens that `main()` is the only function that calls other user-written functions in this program.

You can tell that the following statement is a function call:

```
print_total();
```

Because `print_total` is not a C++ command or library function name, it must be the name of a variable or user-written function. Only function names end with the parentheses, so `print_total();` must be a function call or the start of a function's code. Of these two possibilities, it must be a call to a function because it ends with a semicolon. Without the semicolon, it would have to be the start of a function definition.

When you define a function—that is, when you type the function name and its subsequent code inside braces—you *never* follow the name with a semicolon. Notice in the previous program that `main()`, `next_fun()`, and `third_fun()` have no semicolons where these functions appear in the body of the program. Only in `main()`, where these two functions are called, does a semicolon follow the function names.

CAUTION: You cannot define a function within another one. All function code must be listed sequentially, throughout the program. A function's closing brace must appear before another function's code can be listed.

Examples

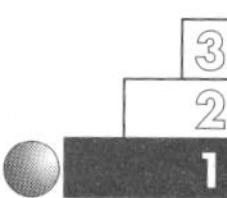

1. Suppose that you are writing a program to do the following:

   Ask for the user's department. If the user is in accounting, the user should receive the accounting department's report; if in engineering, the engineering department's report; and if in marketing, the marketing department's report.

Here is a skeleton of such a program. The code for `main()` is shown in its entirety. The `switch` statement is a perfect function-calling statement for such a multiple-choice selection. Only a skeleton of the other functions is shown.

```
// Skeleton of a departmental report program

#include <iostream.h>

void     acct_report(void)
     {
     // :
     // Accounting report code goes here
     // :

     return;
     }

void     eng_report(void)
     {
     // :
     // Engineering report code goes here
     // :

     return;
     }

void     mtg_report()
     {
     // :
     // Marketing report code goes here
     // :

     return;
     }

main()
     {
     int     choice;
```

```
do
      {
      cout << "Choose your department from ";
      cout << "the following list\n";
      cout << "\t1.  Accounting\n";
      cout << "\t2.  Engineering\n";
      cout << "\t3.  Marketing\n";
      cout << "What is your choice? ";
      cin >> choice;
      }
   while ((choice < 1) || (choice > 3)); // Ensure 1, 2,
                                          // or 3

   switch (choice)
      {
      case    1:
         acct_report();  // Call accounting function
         break;          // Don't fall through
      case    2:
         eng_report();   // Call engineering function
         break;
      case    3:
         mtg_report();   // Call marketing function
         break;
      }
   return 0;     // Program returns to DOS when done
   }
```

The body of `switch` statements usually contains function calls. You can tell that these `case` statements execute functions. For instance, `acct_report();`, which is the first line of the first `case`, is not a variable name or C++ command, but is the name of a function defined in the program. If the user enters a `1` at the menu, the function called `acct_report()` executes. Once it finishes, control returns to the first `case` body, whose `break;` statement causes the `switch` to end. The `main()` function returns to DOS (or to your integrated C++ environment if you are using it) when its `return` statement executes.

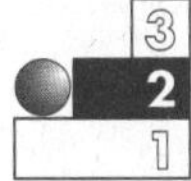

2. In the preceding example, the `main()` routine itself is not very modular. The displaying of the menu should be done in a separate function. Remember that `main()` should do very little except control other functions that do all the work.

   Here is a rewrite of this sample program, with a fourth function added that prints the menu to the screen. This is truly a modular example in which each function performs a single task. Three of the functions show only skeleton code because the goal of these examples is to illustrate function calling and returning.

```
// 2nd skeleton of a departmental report program

#include <iostream.h>

void     menu_print(void)
     {
     cout << "Choose your department from ";
     cout << "the following list\n";
     cout << "\t1.  Accounting\n";
     cout << "\t2.  Engineering\n";
     cout << "\t3.  Marketing\n";
     cout << "What is your choice? ";
     return;     // Return to main()
     }

void     acct_report(void)
     {
     // :
     // Accounting report code goes here
     // :

     return;
     }

void     eng_report(void)
     {
     // :
     // Engineering report code goes here
     // :
```

```
     return;
     }

void     mtg_report(void)
     {
     // :
     // Marketing report code goes here
     // :

     return;
     }

main()
     {
     int     choice;

     do
          {
          menu_print();     // Call a function to do printing
                            // of menu
          cin >> choice;
          }
     while ((choice < 1) || (choice > 3)); // Ensure 1, 2,
                                           // or 3

     switch (choice)
          {
          case     1:
               acct_report();  // Call accounting function
               break;          // Don't fall through
          case     2:
               eng_report();   // Call engineering function
               break;
          case     3:
               mtg_report();   // Call marketing function
               break;
          }
     return 0;     // Program returns to DOS when done
     }
```

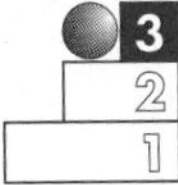

3. Because readability is the key, programs broken into separate functions result in better code that is easier to read. You can write and test each function, one at a time. Once you write a general outline of the program, you can list a bunch of function calls in `main()` and define their skeletons after `main()`.

   The body of each function will initially consist of `return` statements, so the program compiles in its skeleton format. As you complete each function, you can compile and test the program *as you write it*. This approach results in more accurate programs sooner. The separate functions let others who might later modify the program "zero in" on the code they need to change, without affecting the rest of the program.

   Another useful habit, popular with many C++ programmers, is to separate functions from each other with a comment consisting of a line of asterisks (*) or hyphens (-). This makes it easy, especially in longer programs, to see where a function begins and ends. Here is another listing of the preceding program but with separating comments that help break up the program listing, making it even easier to see the four separate functions:

```
// 3rd skeleton of a departmental report program

#include <iostream.h>

void      menu_print(void)
     {
     cout << "Choose your department from ";
     cout << "the following list\n";
     cout << "\t1.  Accounting\n";
     cout << "\t2.  Engineering\n";
     cout << "\t3.  Marketing\n";
     cout << "What is your choice? ";
     return;     // Return to main()
     }
```

```
//**********************************************************

void     acct_report(void)
     {
     // :
     // Accounting report code goes here
     // :

     return;
     }

//**********************************************************

void     eng_report(void)
     {
     // :
     // Engineering report code goes here
     // :

     return;
     }

//**********************************************************

void     mtg_report(void)
     {
     // :
     // Marketing report code goes here
     // :

     return;
     }

//**********************************************************

main()
     {
     int     choice;
```

```
do
     {
     menu_print();        // Call a function to do printing
                          // of menu
     cin >> choice;
     }
while ((choice < 1) || (choice > 3)); // Ensure 1, 2,
                                      // or 3

switch (choice)
     {
     case     1:
          acct_report();  // Call accounting function
          break;          // Don't fall through
     case     2:
          eng_report();   // Call engineering function
          break;
     case     3:
          mtg_report();   // Call marketing function
          break;
     }
return 0;      // Program returns to DOS when done
}
```

Because of space limitations, not all program listings in this book show functions separated in this manner. You might find, however, that your listings are easier to follow if you put the separating comments between your functions. The mailing list application in Appendix F uses these types of comments to separate its functions visually.

4. You can execute a function more than once simply by calling it from more than one place in a program. If you put a function call in the body of a loop, the function will execute repeatedly until the loop finishes.

   The following program uses functions to print the message `C++ is Fun!` both forward and backward several times on the screen. Notice that `main()` does not make every function call. The second function, `name_print()`, calls the function named `reverse_print()`. Trace the execution of the program's `cout`s. Figure 18.2 shows the output from the program to help you trace its execution.

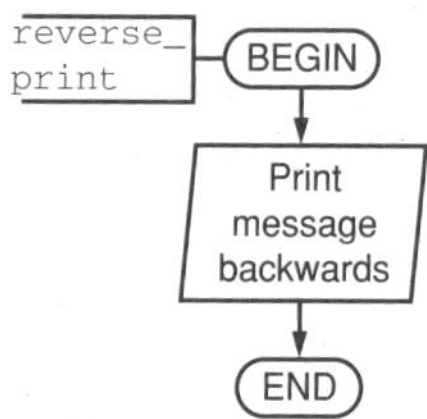


```
// Filename: C18FUN2.CPP
// Prints C++ is Fun! several times on the screen

#include <iostream.h>

//************************************************************

void     reverse_print(void)
     {
     // Print several C++ is Fun! messages, in reverse,
     // separated by tabs
     cout << "!nuF si ++C\t!nuF si ++C\t!nuF si ++C\t\n";
     return;     // Return to name_print()
     }

//************************************************************

void     name_print(void)
     {
     // Print C++ is Fun! across a line, separated by tabs
     cout << "C++ is Fun!\tC++ is Fun!\t";
     cout << "C++ is Fun!\tC++ is Fun!\n";
     cout << "C + +  i s  F u n !\tC + +  i s  F u n !\t";
     cout << "C + +  i s  F u n !\n";

     reverse_print();     // Call next function from here
     return;              // Return to main()
     }

//************************************************************

void     one_per_line(void)
     {
     // Print C++ is Fun! down the screen
     cout << "C\n+\n+\n \ni\ns\n \nF\nu\nn\n!\n";
     return;              // Return to main()
     }

main()
     {
     int     ctr;         // To control loops
```

```
for (ctr = 1; ctr <= 5; ctr++)
     {
     name_print();  // Call function 5 times
     }

one_per_line();      // Call last function once
return 0;
}
```

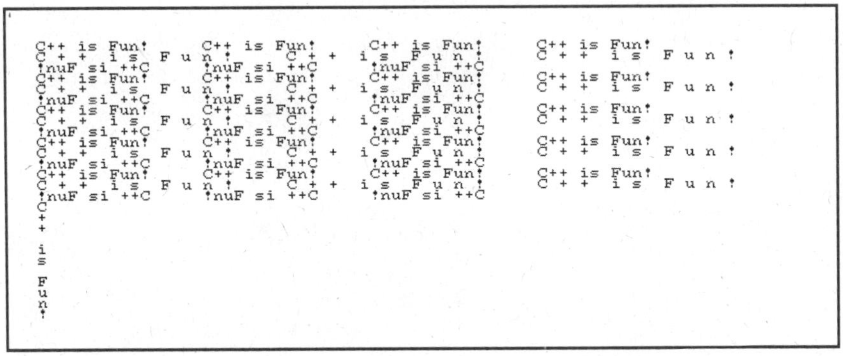

```
C++ is Fun!          C++ is Fun!          C++ is Fun!          C++ is Fun!
C + +   i s   F u n !          C + +   i s   F u n !          C + +   i s   F u n !
!nuF si ++C          !nuF si ++C          !nuF si ++C
C++ is Fun!          C++ is Fun!          C++ is Fun!          C++ is Fun!
C + +   i s   F u n !          C + +   i s   F u n !          C + +   i s   F u n !
!nuF si ++C          !nuF si ++C          !nuF si ++C
C++ is Fun!          C++ is Fun!          C++ is Fun!          C++ is Fun!
C + +   i s   F u n !          C + +   i s   F u n !          C + +   i s   F u n !
!nuF si ++C          !nuF si ++C          !nuF si ++C
C++ is Fun!          C++ is Fun!          C++ is Fun!          C++ is Fun!
C + +   i s   F u n !          C + +   i s   F u n !          C + +   i s   F u n !
!nuF si ++C          !nuF si ++C          !nuF si ++C
C++ is Fun!          C++ is Fun!          C++ is Fun!          C++ is Fun!
C + +   i s   F u n !          C + +   i s   F u n !          C + +   i s   F u n !
!nuF si ++C          !nuF si ++C          !nuF si ++C
C
+
+

i
s

F
u
n
!
```

Figure 18.2. A message printed several times on the screen.

Summary

You now have been exposed to truly structured programs. Instead of typing long programs, you can break them up into separate functions. That way, you can isolate your routines so that surrounding code doesn't get in the way when you are concentrating on a section of your program.

There is a little more complexity to functions that you should know, involving the way variable values are recognized by all the program's functions. The next chapter shows you how variables are handled between functions and helps strengthen your structured programming skills.

Review Questions

Answers to Review Questions are in Appendix B.

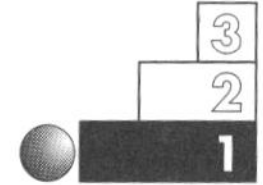

1. True or false: A function should always include a `return` statement as its last command.

2. What is the name of the first function executed in a C++ program?

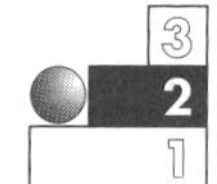

3. Which is better — one long function, or several smaller functions? Why?

4. How do function names differ from variable names?

5. How can you use comments to help visually separate functions from each other?

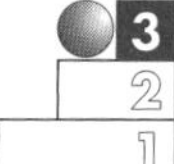

6. What is wrong with the following section of a program?

```
void     calc_it(void)
     {
     cout << "Getting ready to calculate the square of 25\n";

     sq_25()
          {
          cout << "The square of 25 is: "
               << (25 * 25) << "\n";
          return;
          }

     cout << "That is a big number!\n";
     return;
     }
```

7. Is the following a variable name, a function call, a function definition, or an expression?

```
scan_names();
```

19

Variable Scope

The concept of *variable scope* is most important when you write functions. Variable scope determines which functions recognize certain variables. If a function recognizes a variable, the variable is visible to that function. Variable scope protects variables in one function from other functions. If a function does not need access to a variable, that function should not be able to see or change the variable.

This chapter introduces the following topics:

- Local variables
- Global variables
- Passing arguments
- Receiving parameters
- Automatic and static variables

The concept introduced in the last chapter, multiple functions, is much more useful when you learn about local and global variable scope.

Global versus Local Variables

If you have programmed in BASIC only, the concept of local and global variables may be new to you. In many interpreted versions of BASIC, all variables are global. That is, the entire program knows what every variable is and has the capability to change any variable. If you use a variable called `SALES` at the top of the program, even the last line in the program can use `SALES`. (If you don't know BASIC, don't despair — this is one habit you won't have to break!)

Global variables can be dangerous. Parts of a program can inadvertently change a variable that shouldn't be changed. Suppose, for instance, that you need to write a program to keep track of grocery store inventory. You might keep track of sale percentages, discounts, retail prices, wholesale prices, produce prices, dairy prices, delivered prices, price changes, sales tax percentages, holiday markups, post-holiday markdowns, and so on.

The huge number of prices in such a system would be confusing. You would have to write a program to keep track of each kind of prices, and it would be easy to call the dairy prices `d_prices` but also call the delivered prices `d_prices`. Either C++ will disallow it (it will not let you define the same variable twice), or you will overwrite a value used for something else. Whatever happens, keeping track of all the different, but similarly named, prices will make the program confusing to write.

Global variables are visible across many program functions. Such variables can be dangerous because code can inadvertently overwrite a variable that has been initialized elsewhere in the program. It is better to have every variable local in your program; that way, only the functions that should be able to change the variables can do so.

A local variable can be seen (and changed) only from within the function in which the variable is defined. Therefore, if a function defines a variable as local, that variable's scope is protected. The variable cannot be used, changed, or erased from any other function without special programming that you learn about in Chapter 20, "Passing Values."

If you use only one function, `main()`, the question of global versus local variables is moot. You know, after reading the last chapter, that single-function programs are not recommended, however. It's best to write modular, structured programs made up of many smaller functions. When you type functions into your program, you must understand how to define variables to be local to the functions that need them.

Defining Variable Scope

When you first read about variables in Chapter 5, "Variables and Constants," you learned about two methods of defining variables:

- You can define a variable after the opening brace of a block of code (usually at the top of a function).
- You can define a variable before a function name, such as `main()`.

Until now, all the program examples in this book have contained variables defined with the first method. You have yet to see the second way used.

Because most of these programs consisted entirely of a single function called `main()`, there was no reason to distinguish the two methods. It is only when you use multiple functions in programs that these two variable definitions become critical.

Local variables are visible only in the block in which they are defined. These two methods of variable definitions describe the way local and global variables are defined. The following rules, specific to local and global variables, are very important:

- A variable is local if, and only if, you define it after an opening brace of a block, typically at the top of a function.
- A variable is global if, and only if, you define it outside a function.

All variables you have seen so far have been local. They were all defined immediately after the opening braces of `main()`; therefore, they were local to `main()`, and only `main()` could use them. Other functions would have no idea that these variables existed, as they

Make sure that you can recognize local and global variables before continuing. A little study here makes the rest of the chapter very easy.

5. Two variables, local to two different functions, can have the same name. They are distinct variables, even though their names are identical.

   The following short program uses two variables, both named `age`. They have two different values, and they are considered two very different variables. The first `age` is local to `main()`, and the second `age` is local to `get_age()`.

```
// Filename: C19LOC2.CPP
// Two different local variables with the same name

#include <iostream.h>

void get_age(void)
     {
     int  age;        // A different age - this one is local
                      // to get_age()

     cout << "What is your age again? ";
     cin >> age;
     return;
     }

main()
     {
     int  age;

     cout << "What is your age? ";
     cin >> age;

     get_age();      // Call the second function
     cout << "main()'s age is still: " << age << "\n";
     return 0;
     }
```

   The output of this program is shown next. Study it carefully. Notice that `main()`'s last `cout <<` does not print the newly changed age. Instead, cout << prints the only age known to main() — the age that is local to main(). Even though these variables have the same name, main()'s age has nothing to do with get_age()'s age. They might as well have different variable names.

```
What is your age? 28
What is your age again? 56
main()'s age is still 28
```

You should be careful when naming variables. Having two variables with the same name is misleading. It would be easy to get confused when changing this program later. If these variables truly need to be separate, name them differently, such as old_age and new_age, or ag1 and ag2. That convention helps you see immediately that they are quite different.

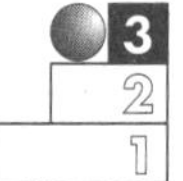

6. There are a few times when overlapping the names of local variables does not add to confusion, but you should be careful about overdoing it. Sometimes programmers use the same variable name as the name of the counter variable in a for loop. The following program illustrates an acceptable use of two local variables with the same name:

```
// Filename: C19LOC3.CPP
// Using two local variables with the same name as counting
// variables

#include <iostream.h>

void do_fun(void)
     {
     int  ctr;

     for (ctr = 10; ctr >= 0; ctr--)
          {
          cout << "do_fun()'s ctr is: " << ctr << "\n";
          }
     return;          // Return to main()
     }
```

```
main()
     {
     int  ctr;        // Loop counter

     for (ctr = 0; ctr <= 10; ctr++)
          {
          cout << "main()'s ctr is: " << ctr << "\n";
          }
     do_fun();        // Call second function
     return 0;
     }
```

Although this is a nonsense program that simply prints 0 through 10 and then prints 10 through 0, the use of `ctr` in both functions is not a problem. These variables do not hold important data that will be processed; instead, they serve as `for` loop counting variables. Calling them both `ctr` will cause little confusion as their use is limited to control `for` loops only. Because a `for` loop initializes and increments variables, neither function relies on the other's `ctr` to do anything.

7. Be very careful about creating local variables with the same names in the same function. If a local variable is defined early in a function and another local variable with the same name is defined again inside a new block, C++ uses only the innermost variable, until its block ends.

   The following example helps clarify this confusing problem. The program contains one function with three local variables. See if you can find the three variables.

```
// Filename: C19MULI.CPP
// Program with multiple local variables called i

#include <iostream.h>

main()
     {
     int  i;          // Outer i

     i = 10;
          {
```

```
          int  i;   // New block's i

          i = 20;   // Outer i STILL holds a 10
          cout << i << " " << i << "\n";     // Print 20 20
               {
               int  i;   // Another new block and local
                         // variable

               i = 30;   // Innermost i only
               cout << i << " " << i << " " << i << "\n";
                    // Print 30 30 30
               }    // Innermost i is now gone forever
          }    // Second i is gone forever (its block ended)
     cout << i << " " << i << " " << i << "\n";
          // Print 10 10 10
     return 0;
     }    // main() ends and so do its variables
```

All local variables are local to the block in which they are defined. This program has three blocks, each one nested within another. Because you can define local variables immediately after an opening brace of a block, there are three distinct `i` variables in this program.

The local `i` disappears completely when its block ends (that is, when the closing brace is reached). C++ always prints the variable it sees as the "most local."

Use Global Variables Rarely

You may be asking yourself, "So why do I need to know about global and local variables?" At this point, that's an understandable question, especially if you've programmed only in BASIC until now. Here is the bottom line: global variables can be dangerous. Code can inadvertently overwrite a variable that was initialized in another place in the program. It is better to have every variable in your program be local to the function that needs to access it.

Please read that last sentence once more. Even though you now know how to make variables global, you should not do so! Try to stay away from ever using another global variable. It may seem easier to use global variables when writing programs with more than one function; if you make every variable that is used by every function global, you never have to worry whether or not one is visible to a certain function. However, a function can accidentally change a global variable when the function has no right to do so. If you keep variables local to functions that need them, you protect their values and keep your programs, both the code and the data, fully modular.

The Need for Passing Variables

You just learned the difference between local and global variables. You saw that by making your variables local, you protect their values because the function that sees a variable is the only one that can modify the variable.

What do you do, though, if you have a local variable that you want to use in two or more functions? In other words, you may need a variable to be typed from the keyboard in one function, yet that same variable needs to be printed in another function. If the variable is local to the first function, how can the second function access it?

If two functions need to share a variable, you have two alternatives. One way is to declare the variable globally. This alternative is bad because you want only those two functions to "see" the variable, yet all functions could "see" it if it were global. The better way is to pass the local variable from one function to another. This alternative has a big advantage — the variable is known only to the two functions, and the rest of the program will not be able to access the variable.

> **CAUTION:** Never pass a global variable. C++ will get confused. There is no reason to pass global variables, as they are already visible to all functions.

You pass an argument when you pass one local variable to another function.

When you pass a local variable from one function to another, you are passing an argument from the first function to the next. You can pass more than one argument (variable) at a time if you want several local variables sent from one function to another. The receiving function receives parameters (variables) from the function that sent them. You should not worry too much about what you call these variables — either arguments or parameters. The important thing is that you are simply sending local variables from one function to another.

> **NOTE:** You already passed arguments to parameters when you passed data to the `cout` statement. The constants, variables, and expressions in the `cout` statement were arguments. The library `cout` function received those values (called parameters on its receiving end) and displayed them.

You need to know some additional terminology before you look at examples. When a function passes parameters, it is called the *calling function*. The function that receives those arguments (called parameters when they are received) is called the *receiving function*. Figure 19.2 shows a diagram that explains these new terms.

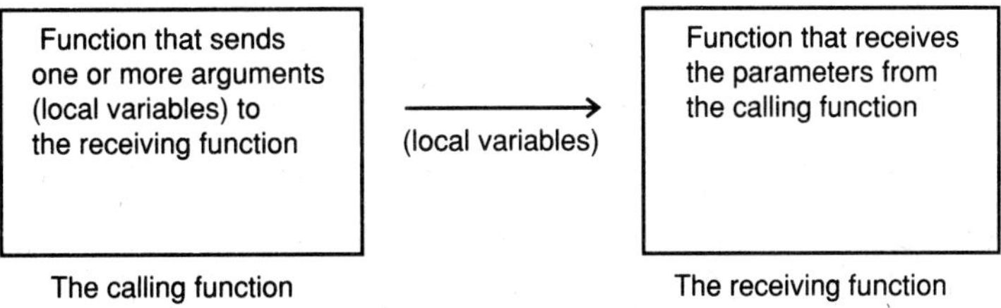

Figure 19.2. The calling and receiving functions.

To pass a local variable from one function to another, you must place the local variable in parentheses in both the calling and receiving functions. For example, the local and global examples presented earlier did not pass local variables from `main()` to `do_fun()`. If a function name has empty parentheses, nothing is being passed to it. Given this, the following line passes two variables, `total` and `discount`, to a function called `do_fun()`:

```
do_fun(total, discount);
```

It is sometimes said that a variable or function is defined. This has absolutely nothing to do with the `#define` preprocessor directive that defines constants. You define variables with such statements as these:

```
int         i, j;
int         m = 9;
float       x;
char        ara[ ] = "Tulsa";
```

These statements tell the program that these variables are needed and you want them reserved. A function is defined when the C++ compiler reads the function's first statement that describes the name and any variables that may have been passed to it. Never follow a function definition with a semicolon, but always follow the statement that calls a function with a semicolon.

NOTE: To some C++ purists, a variable is declared only when you write `int i;`, and it is truly defined only when you assign it a value such as `i = 7;`. They say that the variable is both declared and defined when you declare it and assign it a value at the same time, such as `int i = 7;`.

The following program contains two function definitions, `main()` and `pr_it()`.

The start of the `main()` *function.*
Initialize the integer variable `i` *to 5.*
Call the `pr_it` *function, passing the* `i` *variable with the value of 5.*
Jump down to the function `pr_it`.
Print the value of `i` *to the screen and return to the next line.*
Return to the `main()` *function.*
Return to DOS.

```
main()                     // The main() function definition
     {
     int  i = 5;           // Define an integer variable

     pr_it(i);             // Call the pr_it() function and
                           // pass it i
     return 0;             // Return to DOS
     }

void pr_it(int i)          // The pr_it() function definition
     {
     cout << i << "\n";  // Call the cout function
     return;               // Return to main()
     }
```

Because a passed parameter is treated like a local variable in the receiving function, the `cout` in `pr_it()` prints a `5`, even though `main()` was the function that initialized this variable.

When you pass arguments to a function, the receiving function has no idea of the data types of the incoming variables. Therefore, you must include each parameter's data type in front of the parameter's name. In the preceding example, the definition of `pr_it()` (the first line of the function) contains the type, `int`, of the incoming variable `i`. Notice that the `main()` calling function does not need to indicate the variable type. In this example, `main()` already knows what type of variable `i` is (an integer); only `pr_it()` needs to know that `i` is an integer.

> **TIP:** Always declare the type of the parameters in the receiving function. Precede each parameter in the function's parentheses with `int`, `float`, or whatever each passed variable's data type is.

Examples

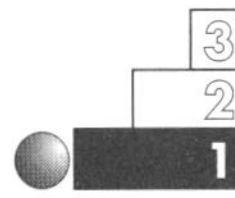

1. Here is a `main()` function that contains three local variables. `main()` passes one of the variables to the first function, and two of the variables to the second function.

```
// Filename: C19LOC1.CPP
// Passes 3 local variables to functions

#include <iostream.h>
#include <iomanip.h>

void pr_init(char initial)     // NEVER put a semicolon after
                               // a function definition
     {
     cout << "Your initial is really " << initial << "? \n";
     return;                   // Return to main()
     }

void pr_other(int age, float salary)    // MUST type BOTH
                                        // parameters
     {
     cout << "You look young for " << age << "\n";
     cout << "And $" << setprecision(2) << salary
          << " is a LOT of money!";
     return;                   // Return to main()
     }

main()
     {
     char      initial;        // 3 variables local to main()
     int       age;
     float     salary;

     // Fill these variables in main()
     cout << "What is your initial? ";
     cin >> initial;
     cout << "What is your age? ";
     cin >> age;
     cout << "What is your salary? ";
     cin >> salary;
     pr_init(initial);         // Call pr_init() and pass it
                               // initial
     pr_other(age, salary);    // Call pr_other() and pass
                               // it other 2
     return 0;
     }
```

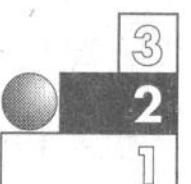

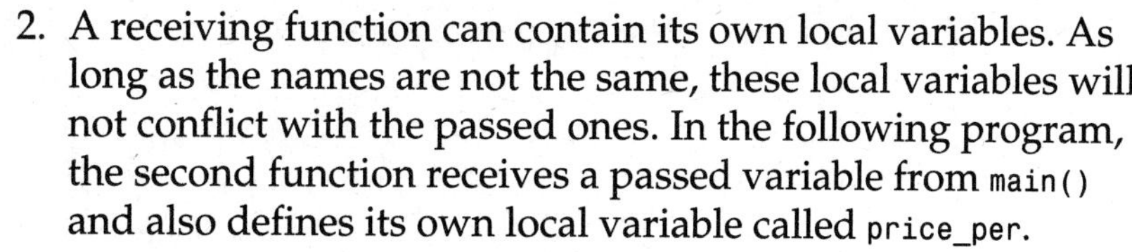

2. A receiving function can contain its own local variables. As long as the names are not the same, these local variables will not conflict with the passed ones. In the following program, the second function receives a passed variable from `main()` and also defines its own local variable called `price_per`.

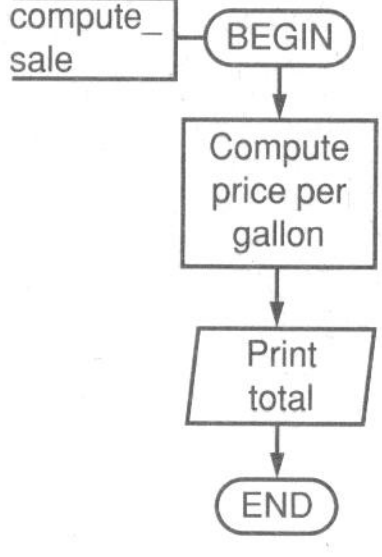


```
// Filename: C19LOC4.CPP
// Second function has its own local variable

#include <iostream.h>
#include <iomanip.h>

void compute_sale(int gallons)
     {
     float     price_per = 12.45;  // Local to
                                   // compute_sale()

     cout << "The total is: $" << setprecision(2)
          << (price_per * (float)gallons) << "\n";
     // Had to type cast gallons since it was integer
     return;                       // Return to main()
     }

main()
     {
     int  gallons;

     cout << "Richard's Paint Service\n";
     cout << "How many gallons of paint did you buy?";
     cin >> gallons;          // Get gallons in main()
     compute_sale(gallons);   // Compute total in function
     return 0;
     }
```

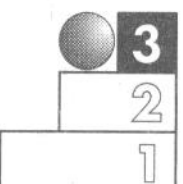

3. The following sample lines test your skill at recognizing calling and receiving functions. Being able to recognize the difference is half the battle of understanding them.

   ```
   do_it()
   ```

   The preceding code must be the first line of a new function because no semicolon appears at the end of the line.

```
do_it2(sales);
```

This calls a function called `do_it2()`. The calling function passes the variable called sales to `do_it2()`.

```
pr_it(float total)
```

This is the first line of a function that receives a floating-point variable from the calling function. All receiving functions must specify the type of each variable being passed.

```
pr_them(float total, int number)
```

This is the first line of a function that receives two variables; one is a floating-point variable, and the other is an integer. This line cannot be calling the function `pr_them` because no semicolon appears at the end of the line.

Automatic and Static Variables

The terms *automatic* and *static* describe what happens to local variables when a function returns to the calling procedure. By default, all local variables are automatic. This means that local variables are erased completely when their function ends. To declare a variable as an automatic variable, prefix its definition with the word `auto`. Because all local variables are automatic by default, the `auto` is optional. Look at the two statements after `main()`'s opening brace:

```
main()
    {
    int           i;
    auto float    x;
    // Rest of main() goes here
```

Both of these statements declare automatic local variables. Because `auto` is the default, `x` does not really need it. C++ programmers rarely use the `auto` keyword, as all local variables are automatic by default.

Automatic variables are local and disappear when their function ends. The opposite of an automatic variable is a static variable. All global variables are static. Local static variables are not erased when their functions end. If local, a static variable retains its value when its function ends, in case the function is ever called a second time. To declare a variable as static, place the keyword `static` in front of the variable when you define it. The following section of code defines three variables: `i`, `j`, and `k`. The variable `i` is automatic, but `j` and `k` are static.

```
my_fun()              // Start of new function definition
     {
     int              i;
     static int       j = 25;    // Both j and k are static
                                 // variables
     static int       k = 30;
```

If local variables are static, their values remain in case the function is called again. Always assign an initial value to a static variable when you declare it, as in the last two lines of the preceding code. That initial value will be placed there only the first time `my_fun()` executes. If you do not assign a static variable an initial value, C++ will initialize the static variable to zero.

> **TIP:** Static variables are good to use when you write functions that keep track of a count or that add to a total when called. If the counting or total variables were local and automatic, their values would disappear when the function ended, destroying the totals.

Rules for Automatic and Static Variables

A local automatic variable disappears when its block ends. All local variables are automatic by default. You can either prefix a variable (at its definition time) with the `auto` keyword or leave it off; the variable will still be automatic, and its value will be destroyed when the block in which the variable is local ends.

A local static variable does not lose its value when its function ends. The static variable remains local to that function. When the function is called after the first time, the static variable's value is still in place. As noted, you declare a static variable by placing the `static` keyword before a variable's definition.

Examples

1. Consider the following program:

```
// Filename: C19STA1.CPP
// Attempts to use a static variable without a static
// declaration
#include <iostream.h>

void triple_it(int ctr)
     {
     int  total, ans;    // Local automatic variables

     // Triple whatever value is passed to it and add up
     // the total

     total = 0;      // Will hold total of all numbers
                     // tripled

     ans = ctr * 3; // Triple number passed
     total += ans;  // Add up triple numbers as this is
                    // called

     cout << "The number " << ctr
          << ", multiplied by 3 is: " << ans << "\n";

     if (total > 300)
          {
          cout << "The total of the triple numbers ";
          cout << "is over 300\n";
          }
     return;
     }

main()
```

```
{
int  ctr;        // Used for the for loop to call
                 // a function 25 times

for (ctr = 1; ctr <= 25; ctr++)
     {
     triple_it(ctr);      // Pass function called
                          // triple_it() the ctr
     }
return 0;
}
```

This is a nonsense program that does not do much, yet if you look at it, you may sense that something is wrong. The program passes numbers from 1 to 25 to the function called `triple_it`. The function triples the number and prints it.

The variable called `total` is initially set to 0. The idea is to add up the triple numbers and print a message when the total of the triples goes over 300. However, that `cout` will never execute. Each of the 25 times this subroutine is called, `total` gets set back to 0 again. It is an automatic variable whose value is erased and initialized each time its procedure is called. The next example fixes this problem.

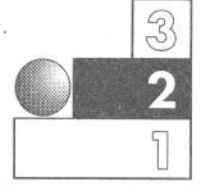

2. If you want `total` to retain its value, even after the procedure ends, you have to make it static. A local variable is automatic by default, so the `static` keyword overrides the default and makes the variable static. The variable's value is then retained each time the subroutine is called.

   The following program corrects the intent of the preceding program:

```
// Filename: C19STA2.CPP
// Uses a static variable with the static declaration

#include <iostream.h>

void triple_it(int ctr)
     {
     static int     total = 0;      // Local and static
```

```
     int            ans;           // Local and automatic

     // Triple whatever value is passed to it and add up
     // the total

     // total will be set to 0 only the FIRST time this
     // function is called

     ans = ctr * 3; // Triple number passed
     total += ans;  // Add up triple numbers as this is
                    // called

     cout << "The number " << ctr
          << ", multiplied by 3 is: " << ans << "\n";

     if (total > 300)
          {
          cout << "The total of the triple numbers ";
          cout << "is over 300\n";
          }
     return;
     }

main()
     {
     int  ctr;      // Used for the for loop to call
                    // a function 25 times

     for (ctr = 1; ctr <= 25; ctr++)
          {
          triple_it(ctr);     // Pass function called
                              // triple_it() the ctr
          }
     return 0;
     }
```

Figure 19.3 shows this program's output. Notice that the function's `cout` is triggered, even though `total` is a local variable. Because it is static, its value is not erased when the function finishes. When the function is called a second time by `main()`, `total`'s previous value (when you left the routine) is still there.

This does not mean that local static variables become global. The main program cannot refer to, use, print, or change `total` because it is local to the second function. *Static* simply means that the local variable's value will still be there if the program calls that function again.

```
The number 1, multiplied by 3 is: 3
The number 2, multiplied by 3 is: 6
The number 3, multiplied by 3 is: 9
The number 4, multiplied by 3 is: 12
The number 5, multiplied by 3 is: 15
The number 6, multiplied by 3 is: 18
The number 7, multiplied by 3 is: 21
The number 8, multiplied by 3 is: 24
The number 9, multiplied by 3 is: 27
The number 10, multiplied by 3 is: 30
The number 11, multiplied by 3 is: 33
The number 12, multiplied by 3 is: 36
The number 13, multiplied by 3 is: 39
The number 14, multiplied by 3 is: 42
The total of the triple numbers is over 300
The number 15, multiplied by 3 is: 45
The total of the triple numbers is over 300
The number 16, multiplied by 3 is: 48
The total of the triple numbers is over 300
The number 17, multiplied by 3 is: 51
The total of the triple numbers is over 300
The number 18, multiplied by 3 is: 54
The total of the triple numbers is over 300
The number 19, multiplied by 3 is: 57
The total of the triple numbers is over 300
The number 20, multiplied by 3 is: 60
The total of the triple numbers is over 300
The number 21, multiplied by 3 is: 63
The total of the triple numbers is over 300
The number 22, multiplied by 3 is: 66
The total of the triple numbers is over 300
The number 23, multiplied by 3 is: 69
The total of the triple numbers is over 300
The number 24, multiplied by 3 is: 72
The total of the triple numbers is over 300
The number 25, multiplied by 3 is: 75
The total of the triple numbers is over 300
```

Figure 19.3. Using a static variable.

Three Issues of Parameter Passing

To have a complete understanding of multiple functions, you need to learn three additional concepts:

1. Passing arguments (variables) by value (or "by copy")
2. Passing arguments (variables) by address (or "by reference")
3. Returning values from functions

The first two items deal with the way local variables are passed and received. The third item describes the way that receiving functions send values back to the calling functions. The next chapter focuses on these methods of passing parameters and returning values.

Summary

The concept of parameter passing is important to know because local variables are better than global ones; local variables are protected in their own functions but are shared among other functions. If the local data is to remain in those variables, in case the function is called again in the same program, the variables should be made static; if they are automatic, their values would disappear.

Most of the information in this chapter will become clearer as you use functions in your own programs. The next chapter provides more detail about the passing of parameters and shows two different ways to pass them.

Review Questions

Answers to Review Questions are in Appendix B.

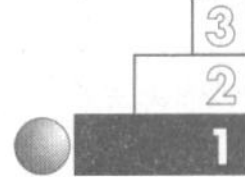

1. True or false: Even though it is not required, a function should always include a `return` statement as its last command.

2. What is a local variable called when it is passed — an argument or a parameter?

3. True or false: A function that is passed variables from another function cannot have its own local variables as well.

4. What must appear inside the receiving function's parentheses, besides the variables passed to it?

5. If a function keeps track of a total or count every time it is called, should the counting or total variable be automatic or static?

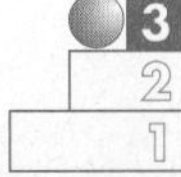

6. When would you pass a global variable to a function? (Be careful — this may be a trick question!)

7. How many arguments are there in the following statement?

```
cout << "The rain has fallen " << rainf << " inches.\n";
```

Review Exercises

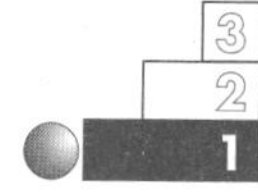

1. Write a program to ask for the following in `main()`:

   The age of the user's dog

   Write a second function, called `people()`, that computes the dog's age in "people" years (multiplying the dog's age by 7 to get the equivalent people years).

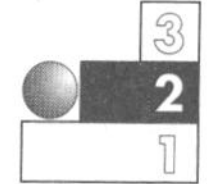

2. Write a function that counts the number of times the function is called. Name the function `count_it()`. Do not pass it anything. Print the following message in the body of `count_it()`:

   ```
   The number of times this function has been called is: ##
   ```

   ## is the actual number.

   (HINT: Because the variable must be local, make it static and initialize it to zero when you first define it.)

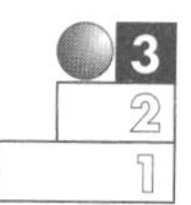

3. The following program contains several problems, some of which produce errors. One problem (for a hint, find all global variables) is not an error but is a bad location of a variable declaration. See if you can spot some of the problems in the program and rewrite it so that it works better.

```
// Filename: C19BAD.CPP
// Program with bad uses of variable declarations

#include <iostream.h>

#define NUM 10

char city[ ] = "Miami";
int  count;
```

```
main()
     {
     int  abc;

     count = NUM;
     abc = 5;
     do_var_fun();

     cout << abc << " " << count << " " << pgm_var << " "
          << xyz;
     return 0;
     }

int  pgm_var = 7;

void do_var_fun(void)
     {
     char xyz = 'A';

     xyz = 'b';
     cout << xyz << " " << pgm_var << " " << abc << " "
          << city;
     return;
     }
```

20

Passing Values

C++ provides two methods for passing variables between functions. This chapter explores both methods. The one you use depends on how you want the passed variables changed.

The concepts discussed here are not new to the C++ language. Other programming languages — such as Pascal, FORTRAN, and QBasic — pass parameters with similar techniques. A computer language must have the capability to pass information between functions in order to be truly structured.

This chapter introduces the following topics:

- Passing variables by value
- Passing arrays by address
- Passing nonarrays by address

Pay close attention to this chapter, as it explains these special passing issues. Most of the programs in the rest of the book rely on the methods described here.

Passing by Value (or by Copy)

The phrases "passing by value" and "passing by copy" mean the same thing in computer terms. Some textbooks and C++ programmers say that arguments are passed by value, and some say that they are passed by copy. Both describe one of the two methods by which arguments are passed to receiving functions. (The other method, covered later in this chapter, is called "passing by address" or "passing by reference.")

> **NOTE:** When an argument (local variable) is passed *by value*, a copy of the variable's value is assigned to the receiving function's parameter. If more than one variable is passed by value, a copy of each variable's value is assigned to the receiving function's parameters.

When passing by value, a copy of the variable's value is passed to the receiving function.

Figure 20.1 shows the action of passing an argument by value. The actual variable `i` is not passed, but the *value* of `i`, 5, is passed to the receiving function. There is not just one variable called `i`, but actually two variables. The first is local to `main()`, and the second is local to `pr_it()`. Both variables have the same name, but because they are local to their respective functions, no conflict exists. The variable does not have to be called `i` in both functions; the value of `i` is sent to the receiving function, so it does not matter what the receiving function called the variable that receives the value.

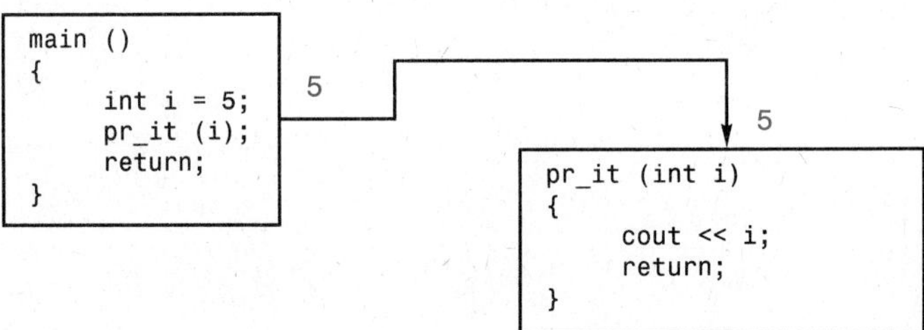

Figure 20.1. Passing the variable `i` by value.

In this case, when passing and receiving variables among functions, you should retain the *same* names. Even though they are not the same variables, they hold the same value. In this example, the value of 5 is passed from `main()`'s `i` to `pr_it()`'s `i`.

Because a copy of `i`'s value is passed to the receiving function (and *not* the actual variable), if `pr_it()` changed `i`, that function would be changing only its copy of `i`, not `main()`'s `i`. You have a technique to pass a copy of a variable to a receiving function, but the receiving function cannot modify the calling function's variable. Thus, you have true separation of functions and variables.

All C++'s nonarray variables that you have seen so far are passed by value. You do not have to do anything special to pass variables by value except to pass them in the calling function's argument list, and receive them in the receiving function's parameter list.

NOTE: The default method for passing parameters is by value, as just described, unless you pass arrays. Arrays are always passed by address, the other method described later in this chapter.

Examples

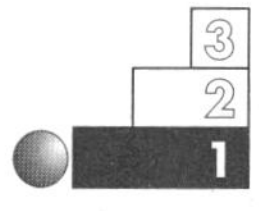

1. The following program asks for the user's weight. The program then passes the weight to a function that calculates the equivalent weight on the moon. Notice that the second function uses the passed value and calculates with it. Once the weight is passed to the second function, that function can treat it as though it were a local variable.

Comments to identify the program.
Include the header file iostream.h.
Start of the `moon()` *function.*
    Take the value of `weight` *and divide it by 6.*
    Print `You weigh only X pounds on the moon!` *to the screen.*
    Return out of the `moon()` *function.*

Start of the `main()` *function.*
    Declare the variable `weight` *as an integer.*
    Print `How many pounds do you weigh?` *to the screen.*

Obtain an integer from the keyboard.
Call the `moon()` *function and pass it the variable* `weight`.
Return out of the `main()` *function.*

```
// Filename: C20PASS1.CPP
// Calculates the user's weight in a second function

#include <iostream.h>

void     moon(int weight)     // Declare the passed parameter
     {
     // Moon weights are 1/6th that of Earth weights
     weight /= 6;              // Divide the weight by 6

     cout << "You weigh only " << weight
          << " pounds on the moon!\n";
     return;                   // Return to main()
     }

main()
     {
     int     weight;    // main()'s local weight

     cout << "How many pounds do you weigh? ";
     cin >> weight;
     moon(weight);         // Call the moon() function and pass
                           // it the weight
     return 0;             // Return to DOS
     }
```

Here is the output of this program:

```
How many pounds do you weigh? 120
You weigh only 20 pounds on the moon!
```

2. You can rename a passed variable in the receiving function. That variable is distinct from the calling function's variable. Here is the same program that is in example 1, except that the receiving function calls the passed variable `earth_weight`. A new variable, `moon_weight`, which is local to the receiving function, is used for the moon's equivalent weight.

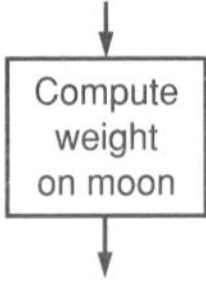


```
// Filename: C20PASS2.CPP
// Calculates the user's weight in a second function

#include <iostream.h>

void     moon(int earth_weight)       // Declare the passed
                                      // parameter
     {
     int     moon_weight;

     // Moon weights are 1/6th that of Earth weights
     moon_weight = earth_weight / 6;  // Divide the weight
                                      // by 6

     cout << "You weigh only " << moon_weight
          << " pounds on the moon!\n";
     return;                          // Return to main()
     }

main()
     {
     int     weight;   // main()'s local weight

     cout << "How many pounds do you weigh? ";
     cin >> weight;
     moon(weight);      // Call the moon() function and
                        // pass it the weight
     return 0;          // Return to DOS
     }
```

The resulting output is identical to that of the first program. Renaming the passed variable changes nothing.

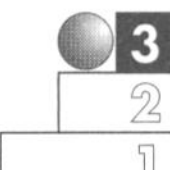

3. The following program passes three variables, of three different types, to the receiving function. In the receiving function's parameter list, each of these variable types must be declared.

   This program prompts the user for three values in the `main()` function. `main()` then passes those variables to the receiving function, which calculates and prints values related to those passed variables. Notice again that when the receiving function modifies a variable passed to it, it does *not* affect the calling function's variable. When variables are passed by value, the value — not the variable itself — is passed.

```
// Filename: C20PASS3.CPP
// Gets grade information for a student

#include <iostream.h>

void     check_grade(char lgrade, float average, int tests)
     {
     switch (tests)
          {
          case     0:
               cout << "You will get your current grade of "
                    << lgrade << "\n";
               break;
          case 1:
               cout << "You still have time to ";
               cout << "bring your average ";
               cout << "of " << average <<
                    " up.  Study hard!\n";
               break;
          default:
               cout << "Relax — You still have ";
               cout << "plenty of time.\n";
               break;
          }
     return;
     }

main()
     {
     char           lgrade;   // Letter grade
     int            tests;    // Number of tests yet taken
     float          average;  // Student's average based on
                              // 4.0 scale

     cout << "What letter grade do you want? ";
     cin >> lgrade;
     cout << "What is your current test average? ";
     cin >> average;
```

```
cout << "How many tests do you have left? ";
cin >> tests;

check_grade(lgrade, average, tests);  // Call function
                        // and pass 3 variables by value
return 0;
}
```

Passing by Address (or by Reference)

The phrases "passing by address" and "passing by reference" mean the *very same thing*. Some textbooks and C++ programmers say that arguments are passed by address, and some say that they are passed by reference. The first half of this chapter described the passing of arguments by value (or by copy). This section describes the passing of arguments by address (or by reference).

When a variable is passed by address, the address of the variable is passed to the receiving function.

When you pass an argument (local variable) by address, the variable's address is assigned to the receiving function's parameter. (If you pass more than one variable by address, each of their addresses is assigned to the receiving function's parameters.)

All variables in memory (RAM) are stored at memory addresses. Figure 20.2 illustrates addresses of memory. If you want more detail on your memory's internal representation, refer to Appendix A.

Memory
Address
0
1
2
.
.
.
655,358
655,359
655,360
(If you have 640K of RAM, as many microcomputers do, you have exactly 655,360 characters of RAM.
Each of those memory locations has a separate address, just as each house and building have separate addresses.)

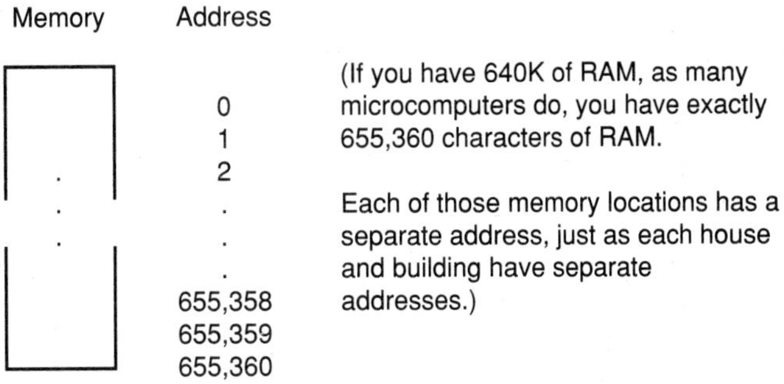

Figure 20.2. Memory addresses.

When you tell C++ to define a variable (such as `int i;`), you are requesting that C++ find a blank place in memory and assign that memory's address to `i`. When your program prints or uses the variable called `i`, C++ knows to go to `i`'s address and print what is there.

Note how five variables are defined:

```
int         i;
float       x = 9.8;
char        ara[ 2 ] = {'A', 'B'};
int         j = 8, k = 3;
```

C++ might arbitrarily place these variables in memory at the addresses shown in Figure 20.3.

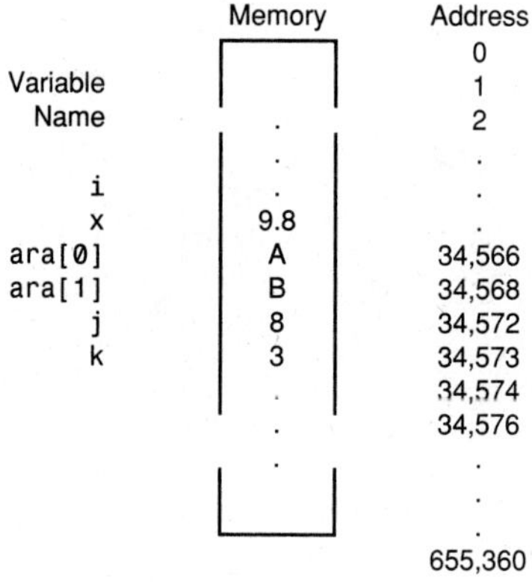

Figure 20.3. After variables are defined and placed in memory.

You don't know what is in the variable called `i` because you have not yet put anything in it. Before you use `i`, you should initialize it with a value. (All variables except character variables usually take more than one byte of memory.)

All C++ arrays are passed by address.

As noted, the address of the variable — not its value — is copied to the receiving function when you pass a variable by address. In C++, *all arrays are passed by address*. (Actually, a copy of the array's address is passed, but you will understand this better when you learn more about arrays and pointers in Part VI of this book.) The following important rule holds true for programs that pass by address:

Every time you pass a variable by address, if the receiving function changes the variable, it is also changed in the calling function.

Therefore, if you pass an array to a function and that function changes the array, the change will still be with the array when the function returns to the calling function. Unlike passing by value, passing by address gives you the ability to change a variable in the receiving function and keep the change in effect in the calling function. The following sample program will help illustrate this concept.

```
// Filename: C20ADD1.CPP
// Program that passes by address

#include <iostream.h>
#include <string.h>

void     change_it(char c[ 4 ]) // You MUST tell the
                               // function that c is an array
     {
     cout << c << "\n";       // Print as it is passed
     strcpy(c, "USA");        // Change the array, both here
                              // AND in main()
     return;
     }

main()
     {
     char     name[ 4 ] = "ABC";

     change_it(name);         // Pass by address since it is
                              // an array
     cout << name << "\n";    // Called function can change
                              // array
     return 0;
     }
```

Here is the output of this program:

```
ABC
USA
```

At this point, you should have no trouble understanding that the array is passed from `main()` to the function called `change_it()`. Even though `change_it()` calls the array `c`, that function refers to the same array passed to it, which was called `name` in the `main()` function.

Figure 20.4 shows how the array is passed. The value of the array is not passed from `name` to `c`, but both arrays are the same thing.

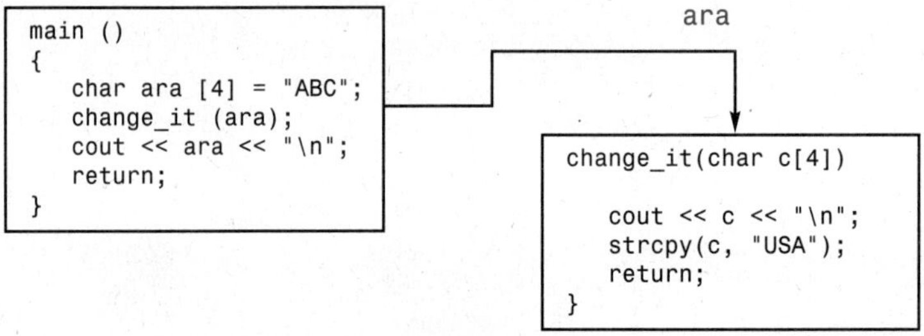

```
main ()
{
   char ara [4] = "ABC";
   change_it (ara);
   cout << ara << "\n";
   return;
}
```

ara

```
change_it(char c[4])

   cout << c << "\n";
   strcpy(c, "USA");
   return;
}
```

Figure 20.4. Passing an array by address.

Before going any further, a few additional comments are needed. Because the actual address of `name` is passed to the function, even though the array is called `c` in the receiving function, `c` is still the same array as `name`. Figure 20.5 shows how C++ accomplishes this at the memory address level.

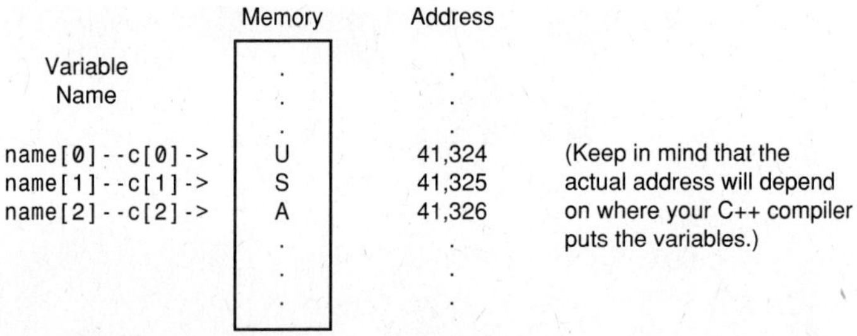

Variable Name	Memory	Address
	.	.
	.	.
	.	.
name[0]--c[0]->	U	41,324
name[1]--c[1]->	S	41,325
name[2]--c[2]->	A	41,326
	.	.
	.	.
	.	.

(Keep in mind that the actual address will depend on where your C++ compiler puts the variables.)

Figure 20.5. The array being passed is the same as that of the receiving function, despite the different names.

The variable array is referred to as `name` in `main()`, but as `c` in `change_it()`. The address of `name` is copied to the receiving function, so the variable gets changed no matter what it is called in either function. Because `change_it()` changes the array, it is also changed in `main()`.

Examples

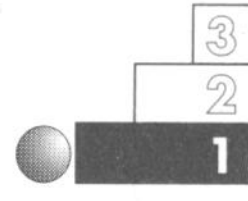

1. You can now use a function to fill an array with user input. The following program asks for the user's first name in the function called `get_name()`. As the user types the name in the array, the name is also being typed into `main()`'s array. `main()` then passes the array to `pr_name()`, where it is printed.

   You should realize that if arrays were passed by value, this program would not work. Only the array value would be passed to the receiving functions.

get_name: BEGIN → Get user's first name → END

print_name: BEGIN → Print user's name → END

```
// Filename: C20ADD2.CPP
// Gets a name in an array and then prints it,
// using separate functions

#include <iostream.h>

void     get_name(char name[ 25 ])    // Pass the array
                                      // by address
     {
     cout << "What is your first name? ";
     cin >> name;
     return;
     }

void     print_name(char name[ 25 ])
     {
     cout << "\n\n Here it is: " << name << "\n";
     return;
     }

main()
{
char     name[ 25 ];
```

```
get_name(name);      // Get the user's name
print_name(name);    // Print the user's name
return 0;
}
```

When you pass an array, be sure to specify the array's type in the receiving function's parameter list. If the preceding program declared the passed array with

```
get_name(char name)
```

the function `get_name()` would think that it were being passed a single-character variable, *not* a character array. You don't have to put the array size in brackets. The following statement would work as the first line of `get_name()`:

```
get_name(char name[ ])
```

Most C++ programmers put the array size in brackets even though it isn't needed.

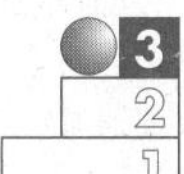

2. Many programmers pass character arrays to functions in order to erase the arrays. Here is a function called `clear_it()`. It expects two parameters: a character array and the total number of elements declared for that array. The array is passed by address (as all arrays are), and the number of elements, `num_els`, is passed by value (as all nonarrays are). When the function finishes, the array will be cleared (all its elements will be set to null zero). Subsequent functions that use the array will then have a fresh array.

Clear all elements in array

```
clear_it(char ara[ 10 ], int num_els)
     {
     int     ctr;

     for (ctr = 0; ctr <= num_els; ctr++)
          {
          ara[ ctr ] = '\0';
          }
     return;
     }
```

The `ara` brackets do not need to have a number, as indicated in the last example. The `10` in this example simply serves as a placeholder for the brackets. Any value (or no value) that you want to substitute will work too.

Passing Nonarrays by Address

You can pass nonarrays by address as well.

You should now understand the difference between passing variables by value and by address. You can pass arrays by address and pass nonarrays by value. You can override the default passing by value for nonarrays if you want. This is not always recommended because the called function can damage values in the calling function, but it is sometimes helpful.

If you want a nonarray variable changed in a receiving function, and you want the change also kept in the calling function, you must override C++'s default (passing by value) and pass the variable by address. (You will better understand this section once you learn how arrays and pointers relate.) To pass a nonarray by address, you must do the following:

1. Precede the variable in the calling function with an ampersand (`&`).

2. Precede the variable in the receiving function with an asterisk (`*`) everywhere the variable appears.

This technique might sound strange, and it is at this point. Not many C++ programmers override the default passing by value. When you learn about pointers, you will have little need for this technique. Most C++ programmers do not like to clutter their code with those extra ampersands and asterisks, but they know they can use them if necessary.

The following examples demonstrate how to pass nonarray variables by address.

Examples

1. The following program passes a nonarray variable by address from `main()` to a function. The function changes the variable and returns to `main()`. Because the variable is passed by address, `main()` recognizes the new value.

```
// Filename: C20ADD3.CPP
// Demonstrates passing nonarrays by address

#include <iostream.h>

void     do_fun(int *amt)      // Inform function of passing
                               // by address
     {
     *amt = 85;                // Assign new value to amt
     cout << "In do_fun(), amt is " << *amt << "\n";
     return;
     }


main()
     {
     int     amt;

     amt = 100;          // Assign a value in main()
     cout << "In main(), amt is " << amt << "\n";
     do_fun(&amt);       // The & means to pass it by address
     cout << "After return, amt is " << amt
          << " in main()\n";
     return 0;
     }
```

The output of this program is shown here:

```
In main(), amt is 100
In do_fun(), amt is 85
After return, amt is 85 in main()
```

Notice that `amt` changed in the receiving function. Because `amt` was passed by address, it gets changed also in the calling function.

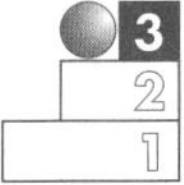

2. You can use a function to get the user's keyboard values, and `main()` will recognize those values as long as you pass them by address. The following program calculates the cubic feet in a swimming pool by requesting the length, width, and depth in one function; then calculates the cubic feet of water in another function; and then prints the answer in a third function. The purpose of `main()` is clearly to be a controlling function, passing variables between the functions by address.

Calculate pool's cubic feet

```
// Filename: C20POOL.CPP
// Calculates cubic feet in a swimming pool

#include <iostream.h>

void     get_values(int *length, int *width, int *depth)
     {
     cout << "What is the pool's length? ";
     cin >> *length;
     cout << "What is the pool's width? ";
     cin >> *width;
     cout << "What is the pool's average depth? ";
     cin >> *depth;
     return;
     }

void     calc_cubic(int *length, int *width,
                    int *depth, int *cubic)
     {
     // This may look confusing, but you MUST precede each
     // variable with an asterisk.
     *cubic = (*length) * (*width) * (*depth);
     return;
     }

void     print_cubic(int *cubic)
     {
     cout << "\nThe pool has " << *cubic << " cubic feet\n";
     return;
}
```

```
main()
     {
     int     length, width, depth, cubic;

     get_values(&length, &width, &depth);
     calc_cubic(&length, &width, &depth, &cubic);
     print_cubic(&cubic);
     return 0;
     }
```

Here is the output of the program:

```
What is the pool's length? 16
What is the pool's width? 32
What is the pool's average depth? 6
The pool has 3072 cubic feet
```

Summary

You now have a complete understanding of the various ways to pass data to functions. Because you will be using local variables as much as possible, you need to know how to pass them between functions so that they can share data, yet keep the data away from functions that don't need it.

There are two ways to pass data: by value and by address. When you pass data by value, which is the default method for nonarrays, only a copy of the variable's contents is passed. If the receiving function modifies its parameters, those variables are not modified in the calling function. When you pass data by address, as is done with arrays and nonarray variables preceded by an ampersand (`&`), the receiving function can change the data in both functions.

When passing values, you must ensure that they match in number and type. If you do not match them, you will have potential problems. For example, suppose that you pass an array and a floating-point variable, but in the receiving function, you receive a floating-point variable followed by an array. The data will not get to the receiving function properly because the parameter data types do not match the variables being passed. The next chapter shows you how to protect against such a disaster by prototyping all functions.

Review Questions

Answers to Review Questions are in Appendix B.

1. What kind of variable is always passed by address?
2. What kind of variable is always passed by value?
3. True or false: If a variable is passed by value, it is also passed by copy.

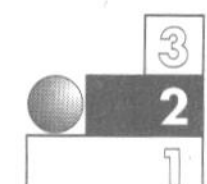

4. If a variable is passed to a function by value and the function changes that variable, will it be changed in the receiving function?
5. If a variable is passed to a function by address and the function changes that variable, will it be changed in the receiving function?

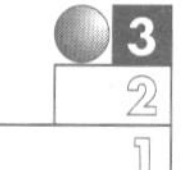

6. What is wrong with the following function?

```
do_fun(x, y, z)
     {
     cout << "The variables are: " << x << ", " << y
          << ", and " << z;
     return;
     }
```

7. If you pass an array *and* a nonarray variable to a function at the same time, which of the following is correct?

   A. Both variables are passed by address.

   B. Both variables are passed by value.

   C. One variable is passed by address, and the other variable is passed by value.

Review Exercises

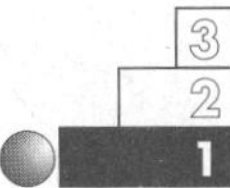

1. Write a `main()` function and a second function that `main()` calls. Ask for the user's income in `main()`. Pass the income to the second function and print a congratulatory message if the user makes more than $50,000 or an encouragement message if the user makes less.

2. Write a three-function program, consisting of the following functions:

```
main()
fun1()
fun2()
```

   Declare a 10-element character array in `main()`, fill it with the letters `A` through `J` in `fun1()`, and print that array backward in `fun2()`.

3. Write a program whose `main()` function passes a number to a function called `print_aster()`. The `print_aster()` function prints that many asterisks on a line, across the screen. If `print_aster()` is passed a number greater than 80, display an error, because most screens will not be able to print more than that. When finished, return control to `main()` and then return to the operating system.

4. Write a function that is passed two integer values by address. The function should declare a third local variable. Use the third variable as an intermediate variable and swap the values of both integers passed. In other words, if the calling function passes it `old_pay` and `new_pay`, as in

```
swap_it(old_pay, new_pay);
```

   the function `swap_it()` should reverse the two values so that the `old_pay` and `new_pay` values are swapped when control is returned to the calling function.

21

Function Return Values and Prototypes

So far, you have passed all variables to functions in one direction: a calling function passes data to a receiving function. You have yet to see how data is passed back *from* the receiving function to the calling function. When you pass variables by address, the data gets changed in both functions, but this is different from actually passing data back. This chapter shows you how to write function return values that improve your programming power.

Once you learn to pass and return values, you need to prototype every function you write. By prototyping your functions, you ensure accuracy of passed and return values.

In this chapter, you are introduced to the following topics:

- Returning values from functions
- Prototyping functions
- Understanding header files

This chapter concludes the coverage of functions. After you read the chapter, your programs will be truly modular. You will be writing better, more powerful, and more accurate programs once you complete your understanding of functions and how to use them.

Function Return Values

Until now, all functions in this book have been subroutines. A *subroutine* is a function that is called from another function but does not return any values. The difference between subroutines and functions that return values in C++ is not as critical as in other languages. All functions, whether they are subroutines or functions that return values, are defined in the same way. You can pass variables to each of them, as you have seen in this part of the book.

Put the return value at the end of the `return` statement.

Functions that return values offer a new approach to using functions. Instead of data being passed in one direction, from calling function to receiving function, you can pass data back from a function to its calling function. When you want to return a value from a function to its calling function, put the return value after the `return` statement. To make the return value clearer, many programmers put parentheses around the return value, as in

```
return (return value);
```

CAUTION: Do not return global variables. Not only will you confuse your compiler, but there is no need to do so because their values are already known throughout the code.

The calling function must have a use for the return value. Suppose, for example, that you wrote a function to calculate the average of three integer variables passed to it. If you return the average, the calling function will have to receive that return value. The following example helps illustrate this principle:

Calculate average

```
// Filename: C21AVG.CPP
// Calculates the average of three input values

#include <iostream.h>

int     calc_av(int num1, int num2, int num3)
     {
     int     local_avg;   // Holds average for these numbers

     local_avg = (num1 + num2 + num3) / 3;
     return (local_avg);
     }


main()
     {
     int     num1, num2, num3;
     int     avg;     // Will hold the return value

     cout << "Please type three numbers ";
     cout << "(such as 23, 54, 85) ";
     cin >> num1 >> num2 >> num3;

     // Call the function, passing the numbers, and accept
     // return value
     avg = calc_av(num1, num2, num3);
     cout << "\n\nThe average is " << avg << "\n";
     return 0;
     }
```

Note this sample output from the program:

```
Please type three numbers (such as 23, 54, 85) 30, 40, 50

The average is 40
```

Study this program carefully. It is like many programs you have seen, but a few additional points should be considered now that the function returns a value. It may help to walk through this program a few lines at a time.

The early part of `main()` is similar to that of many programs in previous chapters. It declares its local variables — three for the user input, and one for the calculated average. The `cout` and `cin` are familiar to you. The function call to `calc_av()` is familiar too; it passes three variables — `num1`, `num2`, and `num3` — to the `calc_av()` by value. (If the function passed them by address, an ampersand, `&`, would have to precede each argument, as discussed in the last chapter.)

Put the function's return type before its name.

The receiving function, `calc_av()`, looks like others you have seen except that the first line, the function's definition line, has one addition: the `int` before its name. This is the type of the return value. You must always precede a function name with its return data type. If you don't specify a type, C++ will assume that it is `int`. Without the return type indicated, this program would work just as well because an `int` return type would be assumed.

Since the variable `local_avg`, which is being returned from `calc_av()`, is an integer, the integer return type is placed before `calc_av()`'s name.

You can also see that the return statement of `calc_av()` includes the return value, `local_avg`. This is the variable being sent back to the calling function, `main()`. You can return only a single variable to a calling function. Note this rule for returning variables:

> Even though a function can receive more than one parameter, it can return only a single value to the calling function. If a receiving function is to modify more than one value from the calling function, you must pass the parameters by address; you cannot return multiple values by using a `return` statement.

Once the receiving function, `calc_av()`, returns the value, `main()` must do something with that returned value. So far, you have seen function calls on lines by themselves. Notice in `main()` that the function call appears on the right side of the following assignment statement:

```
avg = calc_av(num1, num2, num3);
```

When the `calc_av()` function returns its value (the average of the three numbers), that value *replaces* the function call. If the average computed in `calc_av()` is 40, the C++ compiler "sees" the following statement in place of the function call:

```
avg = 40;
```

You typed a function call to the right of the equal sign, but the program replaces the function call with its return value when the `return` takes place. In other words, a function that returns a value becomes that value. You *must* put such a function where you would put any variable or constant, usually to the right of an equal sign, or in an expression or `cout`. The following line is an incorrect way to call `calc_av()`:

```
calc_av(num1, num2, num3);
```

If you used this line, C++ would have nothing to do with the return value of 40 (or whatever it happens to be).

NOTE: Function calls that return values usually never appear on lines by themselves. Because the function call is replaced by the return value, you should do something with that return value — for example, assign it to a variable or use it in an expression. Return values can be ignored, but doing so usually defeats the purpose of using them.

Examples

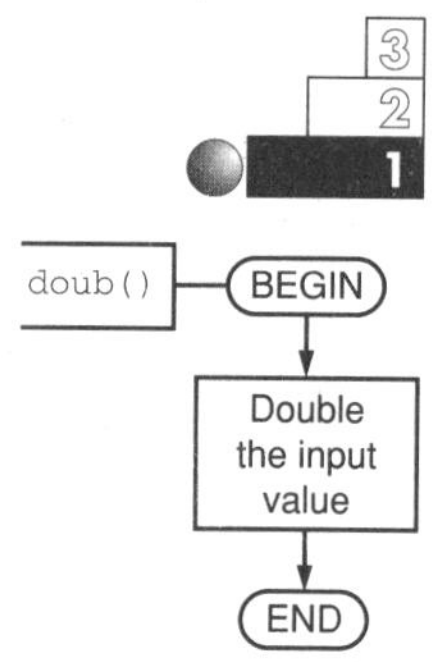

1. The following program passes a number to a function called `doub()`. The function doubles the number and returns the result.

```
// Filename: C21DOUB.CPP
// Doubles the user's number

#include <iostream.h>

int     doub(int num)
```

```
     {
     int     d_num;

     d_num = num * 2;       // Double the number
     return (d_num);        // Return the result
     }


main()
     {
     int     number;     // Holds user's input
     int     d_number;   // Will hold double the user's input

     cout << "What number do you want doubled? ";
     cin >> number;
     d_number = doub(number);      // Assign return value
     cout << number << " doubled is " << d_number << "\n";
     return 0;
     }
```

The program produces output like this:

```
What number do you want doubled? 5
5 doubled is 10
```

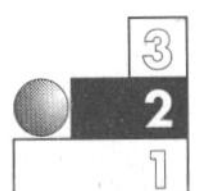

2. Function return values can be used anywhere that constants, variables, and expressions are used. Notice that the following program is quite similar to the preceding one. The difference is found in `main()`. The function call is performed, not on a line by itself, but from within a `cout`.

   This call is a nested function call. You call the `cout`, using the return value from one of the program's functions, named `doub()`. Because the call to `doub()` is replaced by its return value, the `cout` has enough information to proceed as soon as `doub()` returns. This keeps `main()` a little cleaner from the extra variable called `d_number`, although you must use your own judgment as to whether the program is easier to maintain. Sometimes it is wise to include function calls within other expressions. At other times, it may be clearer to call the function and assign its return value to a variable before using it.

```
// Filename: C21DOUB2.CPP
// Doubles the user's number

#include <iostream.h>

int     doub(int num)
     {
     int     d_num;

     d_num = num * 2;     // Double the number
     return (d_num);      // Return the result
     }


main()
     {
     int     number;      // Holds user's input

     cout << "What number do you want doubled? ";
     cin >> number;
     // The 3rd cout parameter is replaced with
     // a return value
     cout << number << " doubled is " << doub(number)
          << "\n";

     return 0;
     }
```

3. The following program asks the user for a number. The number is then passed to a function called `sum()`, which adds together the numbers from 1 to that number. In other words, if the user types `6`, the function returns the result of the following calculation:

   1 + 2 + 3 + 4 + 5 + 6

This is known as the *sum-of-the-digits calculation,* and it is sometimes used for depreciation in accounting.

```
// Filename: C21SUMD.CPP
// Computes the sum of the digits

#include <iostream.h>

int     sum(int num)
     {
     int     ctr;           // Local loop counter
     int     sumd = 0;      // Local to this function

     if (num <= 0) // Check to see if parameter is too small
          {
          sumd = num;       // Return parameter if too small
          }
     else
          {
          for (ctr = 1; ctr <= num; ctr++)
               {
               sumd += ctr;
               }
          }
     return (sumd);
     }


main()
     {
     int     num, sumd;

     cout << "Please type a number ";
     cin >> num;
     sumd = sum(num);
     cout << "The sum of the digits is " << sumd << "\n";
     return 0;
     }
```

Here is the output of this program:

```
Please type a number 6
The sum of the digits is 21
```

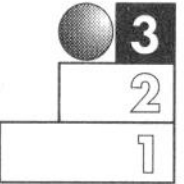

4. The following program contains two functions that return values. The first function, `maximum()`, returns the higher of two numbers entered by the user. The second function, `minimum()`, returns the lower number.

```
// Filename: C21MINMX.CPP
// Finds minimum and maximum values in functions

#include <iostream.h>

int     maximum(int num1, int num2)
     {
     int     max;     // Local to this function only

     max = (num1 > num2) ? (num1) : (num2);
     return (max);
     }

int     minimum(int num1, int num2)
     {
     int     min;     // Local to this function only

     min = (num1 < num2) ? (num1) : (num2);
     return (min);
     }


main()
     {
     int     num1, num2;     // User's 2 numbers
     int     min, max;

     cout << "Please type two numbers (such as 46, 75) ";
     cin >> num1 >> num2;
     max = maximum(num1, num2);  // Assign return value of
                                 // each function to variables
     min = minimum(num1, num2);
     cout << "The minimum number is " << min << "\n";
     cout << "The maximum number is " << max << "\n";
     return 0;
     }
```

Note the following output:

```
Please type two numbers (such as 46, 75) 72, 55
The minimum number is 55
The maximum number is 72
```

If the user types the same number twice, the minimum and maximum numbers will be the same.

These two functions can be passed any two integer values. In a simple example like this one, the user already knows which number is higher or lower. The purpose is to show how to code return values. You might want to use similar functions in a more useful application, such as finding the highest-paid employee from a payroll disk file.

Function Prototypes

The word *prototype* is sometimes defined as a model. In C++, a function prototype models the actual function. Before completing your study of functions, parameters, and return values, you must understand how to prototype each function in a program.

You should prototype all functions in your programs. By prototyping them, you inform C++ of the function's parameter types and its return value, if any. You do not always need to prototype functions, but it is always recommended. Sometimes a prototype is mandatory before your functions will work properly.

A simple example will help clarify the need for prototyping. Listing 21.1 contains a program that asks the user for a temperature in Celsius and then converts that temperature to Fahrenheit. The parameter and the return type are both floating-point values. You know the return type is a floating-point value because of the word *float* before the function `convert()`'s definition. See if you can follow this program. Except for the Celsius calculation, the program is similar to those you have seen.

Listing 21.1. A program that converts Celsius to Fahrenheit.

```
// Filename: C21TEMP.CPP
// Converts the user's Celsius to Fahrenheit

#include <iostream.h>
#include <iomanip.h>

main()
     {
     float     c_temp;    // Holds user's Celsius temperature
     float     f_temp;    // Holds converted temperature

     cout << "What is the Celsius temperature to convert? ";
     cin >> c_temp;

     f_temp = convert(c_temp);     // Convert the temperature

     cout << "The Fahrenheit equivalent is "
          << setprecision(1) << f_temp << "\n";
     return 0;
     }

float     convert(float c_temp)  // Return var and parameter
                                 // are both float
     {
     float     f_temp;           // Local variable

     f_temp = c_temp * (9.0 / 5.0) + 32.0;
     return (f_temp);
     }
```

You must prototype all functions that return a data type other than `int`.

If you run the preceding program, your C++ compiler will refuse to compile it, or you will get incorrect results, at best. Yet this program seems like many others you have seen. The primary difference is the return type; when you return a data type that is not `int`, you must prototype the function to ensure that it works.

Even though no prototypes are required for functions that return integers, you should prototype those functions as well. Taking this one step further, you should prototype *all* functions, whether or not they return a value.

To prototype a function, just copy the function's definition line to the top of your program. (Immediately before or after the `#include <stdio.h>` line is fine.) Place a semicolon at the end of the copied line, and you have the prototype. Because the definition line (the function's first line) contains the return type, the function name, and the type of each argument, the function prototype serves (to the program) as a model of the function that is to follow.

If a function does not return a value, or if that function has no arguments passed to it, you should still prototype it. Use the keyword `void` in place of a return type or parameters. Even `main()` can be prototyped. Listing 21.2 shows the preceding program corrected with the prototype lines. There are two functions, `main()` and `convert()`, so there are two prototypes.

Listing 21.2. Temperature-conversion program corrected with prototypes.

```
// Filename: C21TEMP.CPP
// Converts the user's Celsius to Fahrenheit

#include <iostream.h>
#include <iomanip.h>

int       main(void);
float     convert(float c_type);    // convert()'s prototype

int     main(void)
     {
     float     c_temp;   // Holds user's Celsius temperature
     float     f_temp;   // Holds converted temperature

     cout << "What is the Celsius temperature to convert? ";
     cin >> c_temp;

     f_temp = convert(c_temp);     // Convert the temperature
```

```
     cout << "The Fahrenheit equivalent is "
          << setprecision(1) << f_temp << "\n";
     return 0;
     }

float     convert(float c_temp)  // Return var and parameter
                                 // are both float
     {
     float     f_temp;           // Local variable

     f_temp = c_temp * (9.0 / 5.0) + 32.0;
     return (f_temp);
     }
```

All functions must match their prototypes. You don't have to list individual parameter names in the function's prototype parentheses, only the data types of each parameter.

You can look at a prototype and tell whether it is a prototype or function definition (the function's first line) by the semicolon at the end.

Prototyping Is Safe

Prototyping protects you from the possibility of your own programming mistakes. Suppose that you write a function which expects two arguments: an integer followed by a floating-point value. Here is the definition line of such a function:

```
my_fun(int num, float amount)
```

What if you were to pass `my_fun()` incorrect data types? If you called this function by passing it two constants, a floating-point value followed by an integer, as in

```
my_fun(23.43, 5);    // Call the my_fun() function
```

the function would *not* receive correct parameters. The function is expecting an integer followed by a floating-point value, but you did the opposite and sent it a floating-point value followed by an integer.

Prototyping protects your programs from function programming errors.

Despite the power of your C++ compiler, you will *not* get an error if you do this! C++ lets you pass such incorrect values if you do not prototype first. By prototyping such a function at the top of the program, as in

```
void     my_fun(int num, float amount);     // Prototype
```

you tell your compiler to check this function for accuracy. You inform the compiler to expect *nothing* after the `return` statement (because of the `void` keyword). You inform the compiler to expect an integer followed by a floating-point value in the parentheses.

If you fail to follow the usage defined by the prototype, your compiler informs you of the problem, and you can correct it. Without the prototype, the program would compile, but the results would be wrong. The program would be difficult to debug, at best.

Prototype All Functions

You should prototype every function in your program — even `main()`, as the earlier example showed. The prototype defines for the program which functions follow, their return types, and their parameter types.

Think about how you would prototype `cout`. You don't always pass it the same types of parameters, because you print different data with each `cout`. Prototyping functions that you write is easy; the prototype is basically the first line in the function. Prototyping functions that you don't write may seem difficult. It isn't — in fact, you have already done it in each program in this book!

The designers of C++ realized that all functions should be prototyped. They realized also that you cannot prototype library functions, so they did that for you by placing their prototypes in header files on your disk. You have been including the `cout` and `cin` prototype in each program with the following statement:

```
#include <iostream.h>
```

Header files contain library function prototypes.

Inside the file iostream.h is a prototype of many of C++'s input and output functions. By prototyping these functions, you ensure that you cannot pass bad values to such functions. If you do, C++ will catch the problem.

Prototyping is the primary reason why you should always include the matching header file when using one of C++'s library functions. The `strcpy()` function you saw in earlier chapters requires the following line:

```
#include <string.h>
```

This is the header file for the `strcpy()` function. Without this file, the program may or may not work, depending on how careful you were with the data you passed to `strcpy()`. It is best to be safe and to prototype. If you want values other than `int` returned from a function, a prototype is required.

Examples

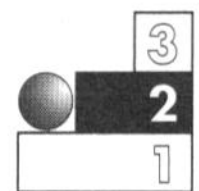

1. The following program asks the user for a number in `main()` and passes that number to `ascii()`. The `ascii()` function then returns the ASCII character of the user's number. This program illustrates a character return type. Functions can return any data type.

```
// Filename: C21ASC.CPP
// Prints the ASCII character of the user's number
// Prototypes follow

#include <iostream.h>

char     ascii(int num);

int     main(void)
     {
     int       num;
     char      asc_char;

     cout << "What is an ASCII number? ";
     cin >> num;

     asc_char = ascii(num);
     cout << "The ASCII character for " << num
          << " is " << asc_char << "\n";
     return 0;
     }
```

```
char     ascii(int num)
     {
     char     asc_char;

     asc_char = (char)num;
     return (asc_char);
     }
```

Here is the output of this program:

```
What is an ASCII number? 67
The ASCII character for 67 is C
```

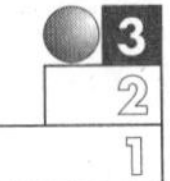

2. Suppose that you need to calculate net pay for a company. You will find yourself multiplying the hours worked by the hourly pay and then deducting taxes to compute the net pay. The following program includes a function that does these tasks. It requires three arguments: the hours worked, the hourly pay, and the tax rate (as a floating-point decimal, such as .30 for 30%). The function returns the net pay. The `main()` calling program tests this by sending three different payroll values to the function and then prints the three return values.

```
// Filename: C21NPAY.CPP
// Defines a function that computes net pay

#include <iostream.h>
#include <iomanip.h>

float     netpayfun(float hours, float rate, float taxrate);

int     main(void)
     {
     float     net_pay;

     net_pay = netpayfun(40.0, 3.50, .20);
     cout << "The pay for 40 hours at $3.50/hr., ";
     cout << "and a 20% tax rate is: ";
     cout << setprecision(2) << net_pay << "\n";
     net_pay = netpayfun(50.0, 10.00, .30);
```

```
     cout << "The pay for 50 hours at $10.00/hr., ";
     cout << "and a 30% tax rate is: ";
     cout << setprecision(2) << net_pay << "\n";
     net_pay = netpayfun(10.0, 5.00, .10);
     cout << "The pay for 10 hours at $5.00/hr., ";
     cout << "and a 10% tax rate is: ";
     cout << setprecision(2) << net_pay << "\n";
     return 0;
     }

float     netpayfun(float hours, float rate, float taxrate)
     {
     float     gross_pay, taxes, net_pay;

     gross_pay = (hours * rate);
     taxes = (taxrate * gross_pay);
     net_pay = (gross_pay - taxes);
     return (net_pay);
     }
```

Summary

You have now seen how to build your own collection of functions. When you write a function, you might want to use it in several programs; there is no need to reinvent the wheel. Many programmers write useful functions and use them in more than one program.

You now understand the importance of prototyping functions. You should prototype all your own functions and include the appropriate header file when using one of the library functions. When a function returns a value other than an integer, you must prototype the function in order for C++ to recognize the noninteger return value.

The rest of this book uses the concepts presented in Parts I through IV so that you can take advantage of separate, modular functions and local data. You are now ready to learn more about how C++ performs input and output. The next chapter shows you the theory behind C++'s I/O and introduces more library functions.

Review Questions

Answers to Review Questions are in Appendix B.

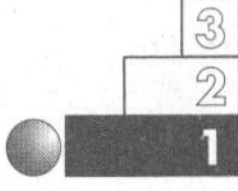

1. How do you declare a function return type?
2. What is the maximum number of return values a function can return?

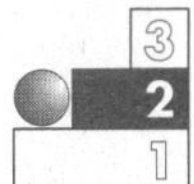

3. What are header files for?
4. What is the default function return type?
5. True or false: A function that returns a value can be passed only a single parameter.

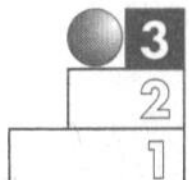

6. How do prototypes protect the programmer from bugs?
7. Why do you not need to return global variables?
8. Consider the following function prototype:

```
float my_fun(char a, int b, float c);
```

   What is the return type? How many parameters are being passed to `my_fun()`? What are their types?

Review Exercises

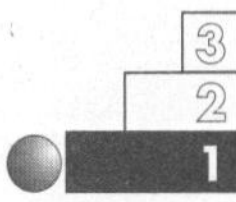

1. Write a program that contains two functions. The first function returns the square of the integer passed to it, and the second function returns the cube. As with all programs from this point on, prototype all functions, including `main()`.

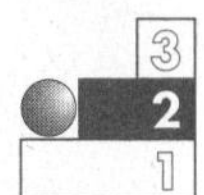

2. Write a function that returns the double-precision area of a circle, given the double-precision radius passed to it. The formula to calculate the radius of a circle is

   area = 3.14159 * radius * radius

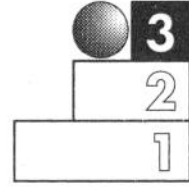

3. Write a function that returns the value of a polynomial (the return value), given this formula:

   $9x^4 + 15x^2 + x^1$

   Assume that `x` is passed from `main()` and was supplied by the user.

Part V

Character, Input, Output, and String Functions

Device and Character I/O

Unlike many programming languages, C++ contains no input or output commands. C++ is an extremely *portable* language; this means that a C++ program which compiles and runs on one computer will be able to compile and run on another type of computer. Most incompatibilities between computers reside in their input and output devices. Each device requires a different method of performing I/O (input/output).

By putting all I/O capabilities in common functions supplied with each computer's compiler instead of in C++ statements, the designers of C++ ensured that programs were not tied to specific hardware for input and output. A compiler has to be modified for every computer for which it is written. This ensures that the compiler works with the computer and all its devices. The compiler writers write I/O functions for each machine; when your C++ program writes a character to the screen, the program works whether you have a color PC screen or a UNIX X/Windows terminal.

This chapter shows you additional ways to perform input and output of data other than with the `cin` and `cout` operators you have seen so far. With its character-based I/O functions, C++ gives you the basic I/O functions needed for writing powerful data entry and printing routines.

This chapter introduces the following topics:

- Stream input and output
- Redirecting I/O
- Printing to the printer
- Character I/O functions
- Buffered and nonbuffered I/O

By the time you finish this chapter, you will understand the fundamental, built-in I/O functions available in C++. Performing character input and output, one character at a time, may sound like a slow method of I/O. You will soon see that character I/O actually gives you the ability to create more powerful I/O functions than are possible with the `cin` and `cout` operators.

Stream and Character I/O

C++ views all input and output as streams of characters. Whether your program gets input from the keyboard, a disk file, a modem, or a mouse, C++ sees only a stream of characters. C++ does not know (or care) what type of device is supplying the input. C++ lets the operating system take care of the device specifics. The designers of C++ want your programs to operate on characters of data without regard to the physical method that is taking place.

C++ views input and output from all devices as a stream of characters.

This stream I/O means that you can use the same functions to get input from the keyboard as from the modem. You can use the same functions to write to a disk file, printer, or screen. Of course, you need some way of routing that stream input or output to the proper device, but each program's I/O functions work similarly. Figure 22.1 illustrates this concept.

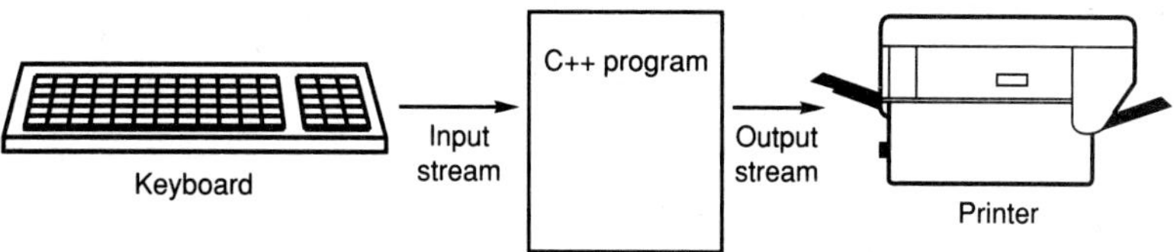

Figure 22.1. All I/O is viewed as a character stream to C++.

The Newline Special Character: `\n`

Portability is the key to C++'s success. Few companies have the resources to rewrite every program they use when changing computer equipment. They need a programming language that works on many platforms (hardware combinations). C++ achieves true portability better than almost any other programming language.

It is because of portability that C++ uses the generic newline character, `\n`, instead of the specific carriage return and linefeed sequences other languages use. This is why C++ uses `\t` for tab, as well as all the other control characters used in I/O functions.

If C++ relied on specific ASCII code to represent these special characters, your programs would not be portable. You would be writing a C++ program on one computer, using a carriage return value such as 12, but 12 may not be the carriage return value on another type of computer.

By using the newline character and the rest of the control characters available in C++, you ensure that your programs will work on any computer on which they are compiled. A specific compiler will substitute its computer's actual codes for the control codes in your programs.

Standard Devices

Table 22.1 shows a listing of standard I/O devices. C++ always assumes that input will come from `stdin`, meaning the *standard input device*. It is usually the keyboard, although you can reroute this default. C++ assumes that all output will go to `stdout`, or the *standard output device*. There is nothing magical in the words `stdin` and `stdout`; if you have never heard of them, that is fine because many people see them for the first time in C++.

Table 22.1. Standard devices in C++.

Description	*C++ Name*	*MS-DOS Name*
Screen	`stdout`	CON:
Keyboard	`stdin`	CON:
Printer	`stdprn`	PRN: or LPT1:
Serial port	`stdaux`	AUX: or COM1:
Error messages	`stderr`	CON:
Disk files	None	Filename

Take a moment to study Table 22.1. It may seem confusing that three devices are named CON:. MS-DOS knows the difference between the screen device called CON: (which stands for *con*sole) and the keyboard device called CON: from the context of the data stream. If you send an output stream (a stream of characters) to CON:, MS-DOS knows to route it to the screen. If you request input from CON:, MS-DOS knows to get it from the keyboard. (These defaults hold true as long as you have not redirected these devices, as explained next.) MS-DOS sends all error messages to the screen (CON:) as well.

NOTE: If you want to route I/O to a second printer or serial port, you learn that procedure in Chapter 32, "Sequential Files."

Redirecting Devices from MS-DOS

The reason why `cout` goes to the screen is simply that `stdout` is routed to the screen, by default, on most computers. The reason why `cin` gets input from the keyboard is that most computers consider the keyboard to be the standard input device, `stdin`. After compiling your program, C++ does *not* send data to the screen or get it from the keyboard. Instead, the program sends output to `stdout` and gets input from `stdin`. The operating system routes the data to the appropriate device.

The operating system gives you control over devices.

MS-DOS lets you reroute I/O from their default locations to other devices through the use of the output *redirection symbol* (>) and the *input redirection symbol* (<). The goal of this book is certainly not to delve deeply into operating system redirection. You might want to get a good book on MS-DOS to learn more about its handling of I/O, such as Que's *Using MS-DOS 5*.

Basically, the output redirection symbol informs the operating system that you want standard output to go to a device other than the default (the screen). The input redirection symbol routes input away from the keyboard to another input device. The following examples illustrate how to do this redirection in MS-DOS.

Examples

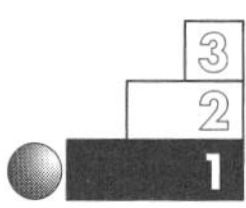

1. Suppose that you want to write a program which uses only `cin` and `cout` for input and output. Instead of sending output to the screen, you want the program to send output to a file called MYDATA. Because `cout` sends output to `stdout`, you must redirect `stdout`. After compiling the program into a file called MYPGM.EXE, you can redirect its output from the screen with the following DOS command:

   ```
   C:>MYPGM > MYDATA
   ```

   Of course, you can include a full path name before either the program name or filename. There is a danger in redirecting all output such as this, however. *All* output, including screen prompts for keyboard input, goes to MYDATA. This is probably not acceptable to you in most cases; you'll still want prompts and some messages to go to the screen. In the next section, you learn how to separate I/O — sending some output to one device such as the screen, and the rest to another device such as a file or printer.

2. You can also route the program's output to the printer by typing the following at the prompt.

Route MYPGM output to the printer.

```
C:>MYPGM > PRN:
```

3. If the program requires much input, which is stored in a file called ANSWERS, you can override the keyboard default device that `cin` uses, as shown here.

The program reads from the file named ANSWERS whenever `cin` *requires input.*

```
C:>MYPGM < ANSWERS
```

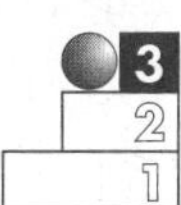

4. You can combine redirection symbols. For example, you might want to get input from the ANSWERS disk file and send output to the printer:

```
C:>MYPGM < ANSWERS > PRN:
```

TIP: You can route the output to a serial printer or second parallel printer port by substituting COM1: or LPT2: in place of PRN: in these examples.

Printing Formatted Output to the Printer

`ofstream` lets your program write to the printer.

Sending program output to the printer is easy with the `ofstream` function. The format of `ofstream` is

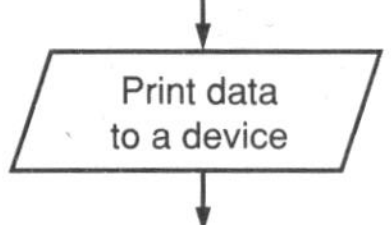


```
ofstream device(device_name);
```

NOTE: `ofstream` uses the fstream.h header file.

The next example shows how you can combine `cout` and `ofstream` to write to both the screen and the printer.

Example

The following program asks for the user's first and last names. It then prints the full name, last name first, on the printer.

```
// Filename: C22FPR1.CPP
// Prints a name on the printer

#include <fstream.h>

main()
     {
     char     first[ 20 ];
     char     last[ 20 ];

     cout << "What is your first name? ";
     cin >> first;
     cout << "What is your last name? ";
     cin >> last;

     // Send names to the printer
     ofstream prn("PRN");
     prn << "In a phone book, your name looks like this: \n";
     prn << last << ", " << first << "\n";
     return 0;
     }
```

Character I/O Functions

Because all I/O is actually character I/O, C++ provides many functions for performing character input and output. The `cout` and `cin` functions are called *formatted I/O operators*, which give you formatting control over your input and output. The `cout` and `cin` functions are not character I/O functions.

There's nothing wrong with using `cout` for formatted output, but `cin` has many problems, as you have seen. In this discussion, you see how to write character input routines that replace `cin`, as well as use character output functions to prepare you for Chapters 32 and 33 on disk files.

The get() and put() Functions

`get()` inputs characters from any standard devices; `put()` outputs characters to any standard devices.

The most fundamental character I/O functions are `get()` and `put()`. The `get()` function inputs a single character from the standard input device (the keyboard if you don't redirect it). The `put()` function outputs a single character to the standard output device (the screen if you don't redirect it from the operating system).

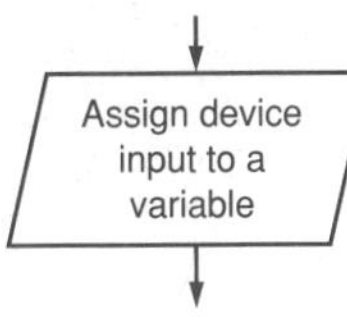

The format of `get()` is

```
device.get(char_var);
```

The *`device`* can be any standard input device. If you were getting character input from the keyboard, you would use `cin` as the device. If you had initialized your modem and wanted to receive characters from it, you would use `ifstream` to open the modem device and read from it.

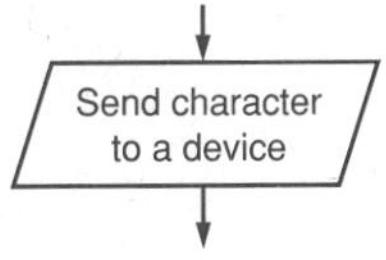

The format of `put()` is

```
device.put(char_val);
```

You output character data with `put()`. The *`char_val`* can be a character variable, expression, or constant. The *`device`* can be any standard output device. To write a character to your printer, you would open PRN with `ofstream`.

Examples

1. The following program asks for the user's initials, one character at a time. Notice that the program uses both `cout` and `put()`. The `cout` is still very useful for formatted output, such as messages to the user. Writing individual characters is best achieved with `put()`.

   The program has to call two `get()` functions for each character typed. When you answer a `get()` prompt, by typing a character and then pressing Enter, C++ sees that input as a stream of two characters. The `get()` first gets the letter you typed and then gets the `\n` (the newline character, supplied to C++ when you press Enter). Examples that follow fix this double `get()` problem.

```
// Filename: C22CH1.CPP
// Introduces get() and put()

#include <fstream.h>

main()
     {
     char     in_char;      // Holds incoming initial
     char     first, last; // Holds converted first and
                           // last initials

     cout << "What is your first name initial? ";
     cin.get(in_char);      // Wait for first initial
     first = in_char;
     cin.get(in_char);      // Ignore newline
     cout << "What is your last name initial? ";
     cin.get(in_char);      // Wait for last initial
     last = in_char;
     cin.get(in_char);      // Ignore newline
     cout << "\nHere they are: \n";
     cout.put(first);
     cout.put(last);
     return 0;
     }
```

Here is the output of this program:

```
What is your first name initial? G
What is your last name initial? P

Here they are:
GP
```

2. You can add carriage returns for better spacing of the output. To print the two initials on two separate lines, use `put()` to write a newline character to `cout`. The following program does this:

```
// Filename: C22CH2.CPP
// Introduces get() and put() and uses put() to output
// newline

#include <fstream.h>

main()
     {
     char     in_char;      // Holds incoming initial
     char     first, last;  // Holds converted first and
                            // last initials

     cout << "What is your first name initial? ";
     cin.get(in_char);      // Wait for first initial
     first = in_char;
     cin.get(in_char);      // Ignore newline
     cout << "What is your last name initial? ";
     cin.get(in_char);      // Wait for last initial
     last = in_char;
     cin.get(in_char);      // Ignore newline
     cout << "\nHere they are: \n";
     cout.put(first);
     cout.put('\n');
     cout.put(last);
     return 0;
     }
```

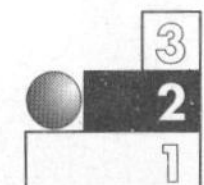

3. It may be clearer to define the newline character as a constant. At the top of the preceding program, you could use this:

```
#define NEWLINE '\n'
```

The `put()` could then read

```
cout.put(NEWLINE);
```

Some programmers prefer to define their character formatting constants and refer to them by name. It's up to you if you think that this is clearer, or if you want to continue using the `'\n'` character constant in `put()`.

Buffered and Unbuffered Character I/O

The `get()` function is a *buffered* input function. That is, as you type characters, the data does not immediately go into your program but instead goes into a buffer. The buffer is a section of memory managed by C++ (and has nothing to do with your PC's type-ahead buffers).

Figure 22.2 shows how a buffered input function works. When your program gets to a `get()`, the program temporarily waits as you type the input. The program doesn't see the characters at all, because they are going to the buffer of memory. There is practically no limit to the size of the buffer; it will keep filling up with input until you press Enter. When you press Enter, the computer releases the buffer to your program.

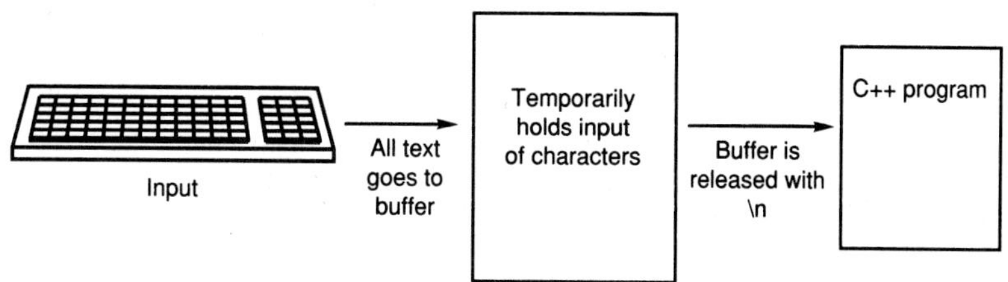

Figure 22.2. `get()` input goes to a buffer, which is released when you press Enter.

Most PCs allow either buffered or unbuffered input. The `getch()` function, discussed later in this chapter, is unbuffered. With `get()`, all input is buffered, which affects the timing of your program's input. The program receives no characters from `get()` until Enter is pressed. Therefore, if you ask a question, such as

```
Do you want to see the report again (Y/N)?
```

and use `get()` for input, the user can answer `Y`, but the program does not know it until the user presses Enter. The `Y` and the Enter keystroke are then sent, one character at a time, to the program where the input is processed. If you want immediate response to a user's typing (as with INKEY$, if you are familiar with BASIC), you will have to use `getch()`.

TIP: If you use buffered input, the user can type a string of characters, in response to a loop with `get()`, getting characters and correcting the input with a Backspace keystroke, if desired, before pressing Enter. If the input is unbuffered, the Backspace keystroke is treated as just another character of data.

Examples

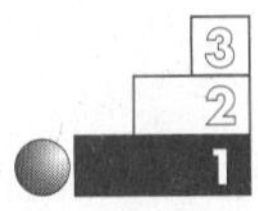

When getting characters, you may have to discard the newline keystroke.

1. C22CH2.CPP must discard the newline character. It did so by assigning the input character, from `get()`, to an extra variable. Obviously, the `get()` returns a value (the character typed). In this case, it's okay to ignore that return value by not using the character returned by `get()`. You know that the user will have to press Enter (to end the input), so discarding the character with an unused `get()` function call is acceptable.

2. `cin` is very limited when used for inputting strings, such as names and sentences. The `cin` operator allows only one word to be entered at a time. If you asked for a user's full name with the lines

```
cout << "What are your first and last names? ";
cin >> names;      // Get name into character array names
```

the array names would receive only the first name; cin ignores all data to the right of the first space.

3. You can build your own input function, using get(), which doesn't have a single-word limitation. When you want to get a string of characters from the user, such as first and last names, you can call the get_in_str() function, shown in the following program.

   The main() function defines an array and prompts the user for a name. After the prompt, the program calls the get_in_str() function and builds the input array, one character at a time, using get(). The function keeps looping, using the while loop, until the user presses Enter (signaled by the newline character, \n) *or* until the maximum number of characters are typed.

   You might want to use this function in your own programs. Be sure to pass it a character array and an integer that holds the maximum array size. (You don't want the input string to be longer than the character array that will hold it.) When control returns to main(), or to whatever function called get_in_str(), the array will have the user's full input, spaces and all.

```
// Filename: C22IN.CPP
// Program that builds an input string array, using get()

#include <fstream.h>

#define MAX 25     // Size of character array to be typed in

//**********************************************************
// The following function requires that a string and the
// maximum length of the string be passed to it. It accepts
// input from the keyboard and will send keyboard input into
// the string. On return, the calling routine has access to
// the string.
//**********************************************************
```

```
void    get_in_str(char str[ ], int len)
     {
     int      i = 0;          // Index
     char     input_char;     // Character typed

     cin.get(input_char);     // Get next character in string
     while (i < (len - 1) && (input_char != '\n'))
          {
          str[ i ] = input_char; // Build string a character
                                 // at a time
          i++;
          cin.get(input_char);   // Get next character in
                                 // string
          }
     str[ i ] = '\0';   // Make the char array into a string
     return;
     }


int     main(void)
     {
     char     input_str[ MAX ]; // Keyboard input will fill
                                // this
     cout << "What is your full name? ";
     get_in_str(input_str, MAX);     // String from keyboard
     cout << "After return, your name is " << input_str
          << "\n";
     return 0;
     }
```

NOTE: The loop checks for `len - 1` to save room for the null terminating zero at the end of the input string.

The getch() and putch() Functions

The functions `getch()` and `putch()` are slightly different from the preceding character I/O functions. Their formats are similar to those of `get()` and `put()`. `getch()` and `putch()` read from the keyboard and write to the screen, and they cannot be redirected, even from the operating system. Here are the formats of `getch()` and `putch()`:

```
int_var = getch();
putch(int_var);
```

`getch()` and `putch()` are not ANSI C standard functions but are unbuffered functions. The `putch()` character-output function is a mirror image of the `getch()` character-input function. Because almost every output device made (except for the screen and modem) are inherently buffered, `putch()` effectively does the same thing as `put()`.

`getch()` and `putch()` offer unbuffered input and output that grabs the user's characters immediately after the user types them.

Another difference between `getch()` and the other character-input functions is that `getch()` does not echo the input characters on the screen as it receives them. When you type characters in response to `get()`, you see the characters as you type them (as they are sent to the buffer). If you want to see on the screen the characters received by `getch()`, you must follow a `getch()` with a `putch()`. Echoing the characters on the screen enables the user to verify that what was entered was correct.

When you want your program to respond immediately to keyboard input, use `getch()`. Some programmers do not want to have the user press Enter after answering a prompt or selecting from a menu. Other programmers believe that the extra time given with buffered input provides users more time to decide whether they really want to give certain answers; a user can press Backspace and correct the input before pressing Enter.

NOTE: `getch()` and `putch()` use the conio.h header file.

Character input with `getch()` is not echoed to the screen as the user types the characters.

Other programmers like to grab the user's response to a single-character answer, such as a menu response, and act on it immediately. They think that pressing Enter is an added and unneeded burden for the user. The choice is yours. You should understand both buffered and unbuffered input, however, so that you can use either when you need it.

TIP: You can also use `getche()`. It is an unbuffered input identical to `getch()` except that the input characters are echoed (displayed) to the screen as the user types them. Using `getche()` instead of `getch()` sometimes keeps you from having to call a `putch()` to echo the user's input to the screen.

Example

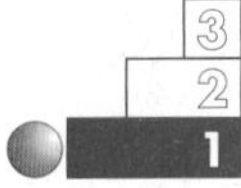

The following program shows the `getch()` and `putch()` functions. The user is asked to enter five letters, which are added to the character array name `letters`, using a `for` loop. As you run this program, notice that the characters are *not* echoed to the screen as you type them. Because `getch()` is unbuffered, the program actually receives each character, adds it to the array, and loops again, *as you type the characters*. (If this were buffered input, the program would not loop through the five iterations until you pressed Enter.)

A second loop prints the five letters, using `putch()`. A third loop prints the five letters to the printer, using `put()`.

```
// Filename: C22GCH1.CPP
// Uses getch() and putch() for input and output

#include <fstream.h>
#include <conio.h>

main()
     {
     int      ctr;           // for loop counter
     char     letters[ 5 ]; // Holds 5 input characters. No
                            // room is needed for the null
                            // zero since this array will
                            // never be treated as if it
                            // were a string.

     cout << "Please type five letters... \n";
     for (ctr = 0; ctr < 5; ctr++)
```

```
        {
        letters[ ctr ] = getch();   // Add input to array
        }
   for (ctr = 0; ctr < 5; ctr++)    // Print them to screen
        {
        putch(letters[ ctr ]);
        }
   ofstream prn("PRN");
   for (ctr = 0; ctr < 5; ctr++)    // Print them to printer
        {
        prn.put(letters[ ctr ]);
        }
   return 0;
   }
```

When you run this program, do not press Enter after supplying the five letters. The `getch()` function does not use the Enter keystroke. The loop ends automatically after the fifth letter (because of the `for` loop). This is possible only because of the unbuffered input allowed with `getch()`.

Summary

You should now understand the generic method that C++ programs use for input and output. By writing to standard I/O devices, you have portability with C++. If you write a program for one computer, it will work on another. If C++ were to write directly to specific hardware, programs would not work on every computer.

If you still want to use the formatted I/O functions, such as `cout`, you can do so. The `ofstream()` function lets you write formatted output to any device, including the printer.

Although the methods of character I/O may seem primitive (and they are), they provide flexibility because you can build on them to create your own input functions. One of the C++ functions used most often, a string-building character I/O function, was demonstrated in the C22IN.CPP program in this chapter.

The next two chapters introduce many character and string functions, including string I/O functions. The string I/O functions build on the principles presented here. You will be surprised at the extensive character- and string-manipulation functions available in the language as well.

Review Questions

Answers to Review Questions are in Appendix B.

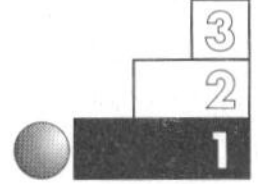

1. Why are there no input or output commands in C++?
2. True or false: If you use the character I/O functions to send output to `stdout`, the output always goes to the screen.

3. What is the difference between `getch()` and `get()`?
4. What function sends formatted output to devices other than the screen?
5. What are the MS-DOS redirection symbols?
6. What nonstandard function, which is most similar to `getch()`, echoes the input character to the screen as the user types it?

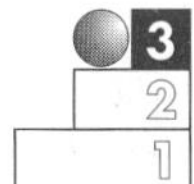

7. True or false: When using `get()`, the program receives your input as you type it.
8. Which keystroke releases the buffered input to the program?
9. True or false: Using devices and functions described in this chapter, you can write one program that sends some output to the screen, some to the printer, and some to the modem.

Review Exercises

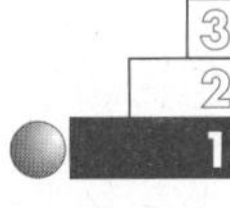

1. Write a program that asks the user for five letters and prints them backward, first to the screen and then to the printer.

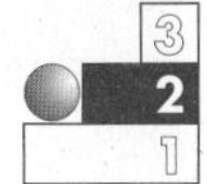

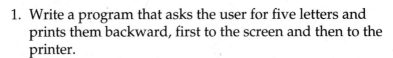

2. Write a miniature typewriter program, using `get()` and `put()`. Loop while getting a line of input (until the user presses Enter without typing any text) and then write that line to the printer. Because `get()` is buffered, nothing goes to the printer until the user presses Enter at the end of each line of text. (Use the string-building input function shown in C22IN.CPP.)

3. Add a `putch()` inside the first loop of C22CH1.CPP (this chapter's first `get()` program) so that the characters are echoed to the screen as the user types them.

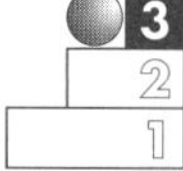

4. A *palindrome* is a word or phrase spelled the same forward and backward. Two sample palindromes are

```
Madam, I'm Adam
Golf? No sir, prefer prison flog!
```

Write a C++ program that asks the user for a phrase. Build the input, one character at a time, using a character input function such as `get()`. Once you have the full string (store it in a character array), test the phrase to see whether it is a palindrome. You will have to filter out special characters (nonalphabetic), storing only alphabetic characters to a second character array. You must also convert the characters, as you store them, to uppercase. The first palindrome becomes

```
MADAMIMADAM
```

Using one or more `for` or `while` loops, you can now test the phrase to see whether it is a palindrome. Print the result of the test on the printer. Sample output should look like this:

```
"Madam, I'm Adam" is a palindrome.
```

23

Character, String, and Numeric Functions

C++ provides many built-in functions in addition to the `strcpy()` function and the `cout` and `cin` operators presented in this book. These library functions increase your productivity and save you programming time. You do not have to write as much code because they perform many useful tasks for you.

This chapter introduces the following topics:

- Character-testing functions
- Character-conversion functions
- String-testing functions
- String-manipulation functions
- String I/O functions
- Mathematical functions
- Trigonometric functions
- Logarithmic and exponential functions
- Random number processing

Character Functions

This section explores many of the character functions available in the C++ language. Generally, you pass character arguments to the functions, and they return values you can store or print. By using these functions, you off-load a lot of work to C++, letting it do some of the tedious manipulation of your character and string data.

The character functions return True (nonzero) or False (0) results, based on characters you pass to them.

Several functions test for certain characteristics of your character data. With these functions, you can test whether your character data is alphabetic (uppercase or lowercase) or numeric, and much more. You must pass a character variable or constant argument to these functions (by placing the argument in the function parentheses) when calling them. All the functions return a True (nonzero) or False (0) result, so you can test their return values inside an `if` statement or a `while` loop.

NOTE: All character functions discussed here are prototyped in the ctype.h header file. Be sure to include ctype.h at the top of any program that uses these functions.

Alphabetic and Digit Testing

The following functions test for alphabetic conditions:

- `isalpha(c)`. Returns True (nonzero) if `c` is an uppercase or a lowercase letter. A False (0) value is returned if anything other than a letter is passed to this function.
- `islower(c)`. Returns True (nonzero) if `c` is a lowercase letter. A False (0) value is returned if anything other than a lowercase letter is passed to this function.
- `isupper(c)`. Returns True (nonzero) if `c` is an uppercase letter. A False (0) value is returned if anything other than an uppercase letter is passed to this function.

Remember that any nonzero value is considered to be True in C++, and 0 is always False. If you use these functions' return values in a relational test, the True return value is not always 1 (it might be any nonzero value), but it will always be considered True for the test.

The following functions test for numeric characters:

- `isdigit(c)`. Returns True (nonzero) if `c` is a digit from 0 through 9. A False (0) value is returned if anything other than a digit is passed to this function.

NOTE: Even though some of the character functions test for digits, the arguments are still considered to be character data and cannot be used in mathematical calculations, unless you want to calculate using ASCII values of characters.

- `isxdigit(c)`. Returns True (nonzero) if `c` is any of the hexadecimal digits 0 through 9, A through F, or *a* through *f*. A False (0) value is returned if anything other than a hexadecimal digit is passed to this function. (See Appendix A for more information on the hexadecimal numbering system.)

The following function tests for numeric or alphabetic arguments:

- `isalnum(c)`. Returns True (nonzero) if `c` is a digit from 0 through 9 or an alphabetic character (either uppercase or lowercase). A False (0) value is returned if anything other than a digit or letter is passed to this function.

CAUTION: You can pass only character values and integer values (holding ASCII values of characters) to these functions. You cannot pass an entire character array to character functions. If you want to test the elements of a character array, you must pass the array one element at a time.

Example

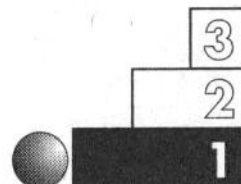

The following program asks for the user's initials. If the user types anything other than alphabetic characters, the program displays an error and asks again.

Comments to identify the program.
Include the header file iostream.h.
Include the header file ctype.h.
Start of the `main()` *function.*
    Declare the variable `initial` *to a character.*
    Print `What is your first initial?` *to the screen.*
    Obtain a character from the keyboard.
    While the character was not an alphabetic character, go through the loop.
        Print `That was not a valid initial!` *to the screen.*
        Print `What is your first initial?` *to the screen.*
        Obtain another character from the keyboard.
    Print `Thanks!` *to the screen.*
    Return from the `main()` *function.*

```
// Filename: C23INI.CPP
// Asks for initials and tests to ensure that they are
// correct

#include <iostream.h>
#include <ctype.h>

main()
     {
     char     initial;

     cout << "What is your first initial? ";
     cin >> initial;
     while (!isalpha(initial))
          {
          cout << "\nThat was not a valid initial!\n";
          cout << "\nWhat is your first initial? ";
          cin >> initial;
          }
```

```
cout << "\nThanks!\n";
return 0;
}
```

This is one use of the `!` (NOT) operator that is clear. The program continues to loop while the entered character is not alphabetic.

Special Character-Testing Functions

None of the character-testing functions change characters.

Some character functions are useful if you need to read from a disk file, a modem, or another operating system device from which you route input. These functions are not used as much as the character functions you saw in the last section, but these functions may be useful for testing specific characters for readability.

Here are the rest of the character-testing functions:

- `iscntrl(c)`. Returns True (nonzero) if `c` is a *control character* (any character numbered 0 through 31 from the ASCII table). A False (0) value is returned if anything other than a control character is passed to this function.

- `isgraph(c)`. Returns True (nonzero) if `c` is a printable character (a noncontrol character), except for a space. A False (0) value is returned if a space or anything other than a printable character is passed to this function.

- `isprint(c)`. Returns True (nonzero) if `c` is a printable character (a noncontrol character) from ASCII 32 to ASCII 127, including a space. A False (0) value is returned if anything other than a printable character is passed to this function.

- `ispunct(c)`. Returns True (nonzero) if `c` is any *punctuation character* (any printable character other than a space, letter, or digit). A False (0) value is returned if anything other than a punctuation character is passed to this function.

- `isspace(c)`. Returns True (nonzero) if `c` is a space, newline (`\n`), carriage return (`\r`), tab (`\t`), or vertical tab (`\v`) character. A False (0) value is returned if anything other than a space character is passed to this function.

Character-Conversion Functions

Two remaining character functions come in handy. Instead of testing characters, these functions can actually change characters to their lowercase or uppercase equivalents.

- `tolower(c)`. Converts `c` to lowercase. Nothing is changed if you pass `tolower()` a lowercase letter or a nonalphabetic character.
- `toupper(c)`. Converts `c` to uppercase. Nothing is changed if you pass `toupper()` an uppercase letter or a nonalphabetic character.

`tolower()` and `toupper()` return lowercase arguments and uppercase arguments, respectively.

These two functions return their changed character values. Typically, programmers change a character in the following ways:

```
c = tolower(c);
c = toupper(c);
```

In these two statements, the character variable named `c` gets changed to its lowercase and uppercase equivalents.

These functions are quite useful for user input. Suppose that you ask the user a yes or no question, such as

```
Do you want to print the checks (Y/N)?
```

Without knowing `toupper()` and `tolower()`, you would have to check for both `Y` and `y` before printing the checks. (The user may or may not type an uppercase letter for the answer.) Instead of testing for both conditions, you can convert the character to uppercase and then test for `Y`.

Example

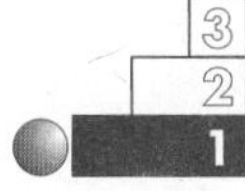

Here is a program that prints an appropriate message for a user who is a girl or a user who is a boy. The program tests for `G` or `B` after converting the user's input to uppercase. No check for lowercase has to be done.

Comments to identify the program.
Include the header file iostream.h.
Include the header file ctype.h.
Start of the `main()` *function.*

Declare the variables `ans` *and* `c` *as characters.*
Print `Are you a Girl or a Boy (G/B)?` *to the screen.*
Assign the variable `ans` *to the value entered from the keyboard.*
Accept the Enter from the keyboard.
Change the value of `ans` *to uppercase.*
If `ans` *is a G, print* `You look like a princess, today!` *to the screen and skip to the next line. Then break out of the switch.*
If `ans` *is a B, print* `You look handsome, today!` *to the screen and skip to the next line. Then break out of the switch.*
If a G or B is not entered, print `Your answer doesn't make sense!` *to the screen and skip to the next line. Then break out of the switch.*
Return from the main loop.

```
// Filename: C23GB.CPP
// Tests if a G or a B is entered by user

#include <iostream.h>
#include <ctype.h>

main()
     {
     char     ans;      // Holds user's response
     char     c;        // To catch newline

     cout << "Are you a Girl or a Boy (G/B)? ";
     cin.get(ans);      // Get answer
     cin.get(c);        // Discard newline
     ans = toupper(ans);      // Convert answer to uppercase
     switch (ans)
          {
          case     'G':
               cout << "You look like a princess, today!\n";
```

```
                    break;
               case      'B':
                    cout << "You look handsome, today!\n";
                    break;
               default:
                    cout << "Your answer doesn't make sense!\n";
                    break;
          }
     return 0;
     }
```

Here is the output from this program:

```
Are you a Girl or a Boy (G/B)? B
You look handsome, today!
```

String Functions

Some of the most powerful built-in C++ functions are the string functions. They perform much of the tedious work you have been writing code for so far, such as inputting strings from the keyboard and comparing strings.

As with the character functions, there is no need to reinvent the wheel by writing code for tasks when built-in functions will do them for you. Use these functions as much as possible. Now that you have a good grasp of the basics of C++, you can master the string functions. They let you concentrate on your program's primary purpose instead of spending time coding your own string functions.

String-Manipulation Functions

A handful of string functions can be used for string testing and conversion. You have already seen one of the string functions, `strcpy()`, which copies a string of characters into a character array.

> **NOTE:** All string functions presented in this section are prototyped in the string.h header file. Be sure to include string.h at the top of any program that uses the string functions.

The string-manipulation functions work on character arrays that contain strings or on string constants.

Here are some string functions that test or manipulate strings:

- `strcat(s1, s2)`. Concatenates (merges) the string `s2` onto the end of the character array `s1`. The array `s1` must have enough reserved elements to hold both strings.
- `strcmp(s1, s2)`. Compares the string `s1` with `s2` on an alphabetic, element-by-element basis. If `s1` alphabetizes before `s2`, `strcmp()` returns a negative value. If `s1` and `s2` are exactly the same, `strcmp()` returns a 0. If `s1` alphabetizes after `s2`, `strcmp()` returns a positive value.
- `strlen(s1)`. Returns the length of `s1`. Remember that the length of a string is the number of characters up to but not including the null zero. The number of characters actually defined for the character array has nothing to do with the length of the string.

TIP: Before using `strcat()` to concatenate (merge) strings, use `strlen()` to ensure that the target string (the string being contatenated to) is large enough to hold both strings.

String Input/Output Functions

In the last chapter, you used a character input function, `get()`, to build input strings. Now that you have seen a few string functions, you can begin to use the string input and output functions. Although the string-building functions show you the specifics of the language, these string I/O functions are much easier to use than writing character input functions.

Here are the string input and output functions:

- `gets(s)`. Stores input from `stdin` (usually directed to the keyboard) in a string named `s`.
- `puts(s)`. Outputs string `s` to `stdout` (usually directed to the screen by the operating system).

- `fgets(s, len, dev)`. Stores input from the standard device specified by *dev* (such as `stdin` or `stdaux`) in the string `s`. If more than *len* characters are input, `fgets()` discards the excess characters.

- `fputs(s, dev)`. Outputs string `s` to the standard device specified by *dev*.

These four functions make the input and output of strings easy. The functions work in pairs. That is, strings input with `gets()` are usually output with `puts()`. Strings input with `fgets()` are usually output with `fputs()`.

> **TIP:** `gets()` replaces the string-building input function you saw in earlier chapters.

`gets()` inputs strings, and `puts()` outputs strings.

When you get strings with `gets()` or `fgets()`, an Enter keystroke terminates the input. Each of these functions handles string-terminating characters in a slightly different manner. Table 23.1 shows the differences.

Table 23.1. String I/O functions handle newlines and nulls differently.

Function	*Newlines and Nulls*
`gets()`	A newline input becomes a null zero (`\0`).
`puts()`	A null at the end of string becomes a newline character (`\n`).
`fgets()`	A newline input stays, and a null zero is added after it.
`fputs()`	The null zero is dropped, and no newline character is added.

Therefore, when you enter strings with `gets()`, C++ places a string-terminating character in the string at the point where Enter is pressed. This creates the input string. (Without the null zero, the input would not be a string.) When you output a string, the null zero at the end of the string becomes a newline character. This is good because you typically prefer a newline at the end of a line of output (to put the cursor on the next line).

Because `fgets()` and `fputs()` can input and output strings from devices such as disk files and telephone modems, it may be critical that the incoming newline characters are retained for the data's integrity. When outputting strings to these devices, you do not want C++ to insert extra newline characters.

CAUTION: Neither `gets()` nor `fgets()` ensures that their input strings are large enough to hold the incoming data. It is up to you to make sure that enough characters are reserved in the character array to hold the complete input.

One final function, `fflush()`, is worth noting although it is not a string function. `fflush()` flushes (empties) whatever standard device is listed in its parentheses. To flush the keyboard of all its input, you code the following:

```
fflush(stdin);
```

When you are doing string input and output, sometimes an extra newline character gets into the keyboard buffer. A previous answer to `gets()` or `getc()` might have an extra newline that you forgot to discard. When a program seems to ignore a `gets()`, you might have to insert `fflush(stdin)` before the `gets()`.

Flushing the standard input device causes no harm, and using `fflush()` can clear the input stream so that your next `gets()` works properly. You can also flush standard output devices with `fflush()` to clear the output stream of any characters you may have sent to it.

NOTE: The header file for `fflush()` is stdio.h.

Example

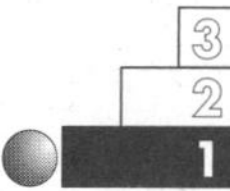

To show you how easy it is to use `gets()` and `puts()`, the following program requests the name of a book from the user with a single `gets()` function call. The program then prints the book title with `puts()`.

Identify the program with comments.
Include the header file iostream.h.
Include the header file stdio.h.
Include the header file string.h.
Start of the `main()` *function.*

> *Declare the character array* `book` *with 30 elements.*
> *Print* `What is a book title?` *to the screen.*
> *Assign the array* `book` *the string that is entered from the keyboard.*
> *Display the string that is stored in the array* `book` *to an output device, probably your screen.*
> *Print* `Thanks for the book!` *to the screen and move to the next line.*
> *Return from the* `main()` *function.*

```
// C23GPS1.CPP
// Gets and puts strings

#include <iostream.h>
#include <stdio.h>
#include <string.h>

main()
     {
     char     book[ 30 ];

     cout << "What is a book title? ";
     gets(book);      // Get an input string
     puts(book);      // Display the string
     cout << "Thanks for the book!\n";
     return 0;
     }
```

Here is the output of this program:

```
What is a book title? Mary and Her Lambs
Mary and Her Lambs
Thanks for the book!
```

Converting Strings to Numbers

At times, you will need to convert numbers stored in character strings to a numeric data type. C++ provides the following functions:

- `atoi(s)`. Converts `s` to an integer. The name stands for *a*lphabetic *to i*nteger.
- `atol(s)`. Converts `s` to a long integer. The name stands for *a*lphabetic *to l*ong integer.
- `atof(s)`. Converts `s` to a floating-point number. The name stands for *a*lphabetic *to f*loating-point.

NOTE: These three `ato()` functions are prototyped in the stdlib.h header file. Be sure to include stdlib.h at the top of any program that uses the `ato()` functions.

The string must contain a valid number. Here is a string that can be converted to an integer:

```
"1232"
```

The string must hold a string of digits short enough to fit in the target numeric data type. The following string cannot be converted to an integer with the `atoi()` function:

```
"-1232495.654"
```

This string can be converted to a floating-point number with the `atof()` function.

C++ cannot perform any mathematical calculations with such strings, even if they contain digits that represent numbers. Therefore, you must convert a string into its numeric equivalent before performing arithmetic with it.

> **NOTE:** If you pass a string to an `ato()` function and that string does not contain a valid representation of a number, the `ato()` function returns 0.

These functions will become more useful later, after you learn about disk files, pointers, and command-line arguments.

Numeric Functions

In this section, you are introduced to some of the C++ numeric functions. As with string functions, these library functions save you time by converting and calculating numbers so that you don't have to write functions to do such tasks. Many of these functions are trigonometric and advanced math functions. You may use some of them rarely, but they are available if you need them.

Mathematical Functions

There are several built-in numeric functions that return results based on numeric variables and constants passed to them. Even if you write very few science and engineering programs, some of these functions will be useful to you.

> **NOTE:** All mathematical and trigonometric functions are prototyped in the math.h header file. Be sure to include math.h at the top of any program that uses these functions.

These numeric functions return double-precision values.

Here are the mathematical functions:

- `ceil(x)`. Rounds up to the nearest integer. This function is sometimes called the *ceiling function*.
- `fabs(x)`. Returns the absolute value of `x`. The absolute value of a number is its positive equivalent.

TIP: Absolute value is used for distances (which are always positive), accuracy measurements, age differences, and other calculations that require a positive result.

- `floor(x)`. Rounds down to the nearest integer.
- `fmod(x, y)`. Returns the floating-point remainder of `(x` divided by `y)`, with the same sign as `x`. `y` cannot be zero. Because the modulus operator (`%`) works with integers only, this function was supplied to find the remainder of floating-point number divisions.
- `pow(x, y)`. Returns `x` raised to the `y` power, or `xy`. If `x` is less than or equal to zero, `y` must be an integer. If `x` equals zero, `y` cannot be negative.
- `sqrt(x)`. Returns the square root of `x`. `x` must be greater or equal to zero.

The *n*th Root

There are no functions that return the *n*th root of a number, only the square root. In other words, you cannot call a function that gives you the 4th root of 65,536. By the way, 16 is the 4th root of 65,536 because 16 times 16 times 16 times 16 equals 65,536.

You can use a mathematical trick to simulate the *n*th root, however. C++ lets you raise a number to a fractional power, so with the `pow()` function, you can raise a number to the *n*th root by raising it to the (1/*n*) power. For example, to find the 4th root of 65,536, you type something like

```
root = pow(65536.0, (1.0/4.0));
```

CAUTION: The decimal points keep the numbers in floating-point format. If you left them as integers, as in

```
root = pow(65536, (1/4));
```

C++ would produce incorrect results. The `pow()` and most of the other mathematical functions require floating-point values as arguments.

To store the 7th root of 78,125 in a variable called `root`, you type

```
root = pow(78125.0, (1.0/7.0));
```

This stores 5.0 in `root` since 5^7 equals 78,125.

Knowing how to compute the *n*th root comes in handy in scientific programs and financial applications, such as time value of money problems.

Example

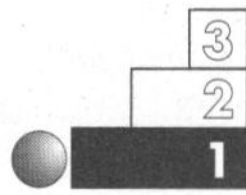

The following program uses the `fabs()` function to compute the difference between two ages.

```
// Filename: C23ABS.CPP
// Prints the difference between two ages

#include <iostream.h>
#include <math.h>

main()
     {
     float     age1, age2, diff;

     cout << "\nWhat is the first child's age? ";
     cin >> age1;
     cout << "What is the second child's age? ";
     cin >> age2;
```

```
// Calculate the positive difference
diff = fabs(age1 - age2);    // Determine the absolute
                             // value
cout << "\nThey are " << diff << " years apart.\n";
return 0;
}
```

Here is this program's output:

```
What is the first child's age? 10
What is the second child's age? 12

They are 2 years apart.
```

Because of `fabs()`, the order of the ages does not matter. Without absolute value, this program would produce a negative age difference if the first age were less than the second age. Because the ages are relatively small, floating-point variables are used in this example. C++ automatically converts floating-point arguments to double when passing them to `fabs()`.

Trigonometric Functions

The following functions are available for trigonometric applications:

- `cos(x)`. Returns the cosine of the angle *x*. *x* is expressed in radians.
- `sin(x)`. Returns the sine of the angle *x*. *x* is expressed in radians.
- `tan(x)`. Returns the tangent of the angle *x*. *x* is expressed in radians.

These are probably the least-used functions in most programs. This is not meant to belittle the work of scientific and mathematical programmers who need them; thank goodness that C++ supplies these functions! Otherwise, programmers would have to write their own functions to perform these three basic trigonometric calculations.

> **TIP:** If you need to pass an angle, expressed in *degrees*, to these functions, convert the angle in radians to degrees by multiplying the radians by (pi / 180.0). Pi is approximately 3.14159.

Logarithmic and Exponential Functions

Three highly mathematical functions are sometimes used in business and mathematics:

- `exp(x)`. Returns the base of the natural logarithm (e) raised to a power specified by *x* (e^x). e is approximately 2.718282.
- `log(x)`. Returns the natural logarithm of the argument *x*, mathematically written as `ln(x)`. *x* must be positive.
- `log10(x)`. Returns the base-10 logarithm of the argument *x*, mathematically written as `log10(x)`. *x* must be positive.

Random Number Processing

Random events happen every day of your life. You wake up, and it might be raining or sunny. You may have a good day or a bad day. You may get a phone call, or you may not. Your stock portfolio may go up or down in value. Random events are especially important in games; part of the fun of games is the luck involved with the roll of the dice or the draw of a card, when combined with your playing skills.

Simulating random events is important for a computer also. Computers, however, are finite machines. That is, given the same input, they always produce the same output. This can result in very boring game programs.

The `rand()` function produces random integer numbers.

The designers of C++ knew this and found a way to overcome it. They wrote a function, `rand()`, for generating random numbers. With it, you can get a random number to compute a dice roll or to draw a card randomly.

To call the `rand()` function and assign the returned random number to test, you use the following line.

Assign the variable `test` *a random number returned from the* `rand()` *function.*

```
test = rand();
```

The `rand()` function returns an integer from 0 to 32767. Never use an argument in the `rand()` parentheses. Each time you call `rand()` in the same program, you will get a different number.

If you run the *same* program that uses `rand()` over and over, `rand()` returns the same set of random numbers. One way to get a different set of random numbers is to call the `srand()` function. Its format is

```
srand(seed);
```

where *seed* is an integer variable or constant. If you don't call `srand()`, C++ assumes a *seed* value of 1. The *seed* value reseeds (resets) the random number generator, so the *next* random number is based on the new *seed* value. If you were to run a program that uses `rand()`, and you call `srand()` with a different *seed* value at the beginning of the program, `rand()` would return a different random number.

> **NOTE:** The `rand()` and `srand()` functions are prototyped in the stdlib.h header file. Be sure to include stdlib.h at the top of any program that uses `rand()` or `srand()`.

Why Do They Make Us Do This?

There is much debate among C++ programmers concerning the random number generator. Many of them think that random numbers should be *truly* random and that programmers should not have to seed the generator themselves. These programmers believe that C++ should do its own internal seeding when you ask for a random number, thereby taking the burden of *randomness* off the programmers' backs.

However, many applications would no longer work if the random number generator were seeded for you. Computer simulations are used all the time in business, engineering, and research to approximate the pattern of real-world events. Researchers need to be able to duplicate these simulations, over and over. Even though the events inside the simulations may be random to each other, the running of the simulations cannot be random if researchers are to study several different effects.

Mathematicians and statisticians also need to repeat random number patterns for their analyses, especially when working with risk, probability, and gaming theory.

Because so many computer users need to repeat their random number patterns, the designers of C++ have wisely chosen to give you, the programmer, the option of keeping the same random patterns or changing them. The advantages outweigh by far the burden of including an extra `srand()` function call!

If you do want to produce a different set of random numbers every time your program runs, you can use `randomize()` to initialize the random number generator randomly. It is implemented as a macro that calls the `time()` function, so you should include time.h.

Summary

By including the ctype.h header file, you can test and convert characters the user types. There are many useful purposes for these character functions, such as converting a user's responses to questions to uppercase letters. That way, you can easily test the user's answers.

The string I/O functions give you more ease and control over both string and numeric input. You can get a string of digits from the keyboard and convert the digits to a number with the `ato()` functions. The string-comparison and concatenation functions let you test and change the contents of more than one string.

Functions save you programming time because they do some of the computing tasks for you, leaving you time to concentrate on your programs. There are numeric functions that round numbers, manipulate numbers, produce trigonometric and logarithm results, and produce random numbers.

This chapter concludes the discussion of C++'s standard library functions. After mastering the concepts in this chapter, you will be ready to learn more about arrays and pointers, discussed in Part VI of this book.

Review Questions

Answers to Review Questions are in Appendix B.

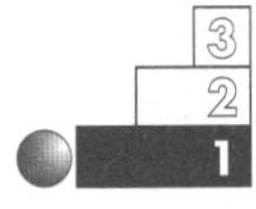

1. How do the character-testing functions differ from the character-conversion functions?
2. What are the two string input functions?
3. What is the difference between `floor()` and `ceil()`?

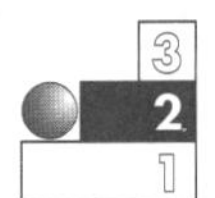

4. What will the following nested function return?

```
isalpha(islower('s'));
```

5. If the character array `str1` contains the string `Peter`, and the character array `str2` contains `Parker`, what does `str2` contain after the following line of code?

```
strcat(s2, s1);
```

6. What is the output of the following `cout`?

```
cout << floor(8.5) << " " << ceil(8.5);
```

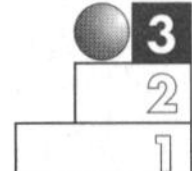

7. True or false: The `isxdigit()` and `isgraph()` functions could return the same value, depending on the character passed to them.

8. Assume that you declare a character array with the following statement:

```
char ara[5];
```

Now suppose that the user types `Programming` in response to the following statement:

```
fgets(ara, 5, stdin);
```

Would `ara` contain `Prog`, `Progr`, or `Programming`?

9. True or false: The following statements print the same results.

```
cout << pow(64.0, (1.0/2.0));
cout << sqrt(64.0);
```

Review Exercises

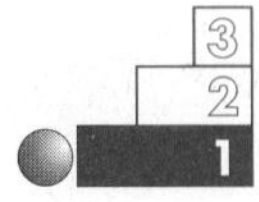

1. Write a program that asks for the user's age. If the user types anything other than two digits, display an error message.

2. Write a program that stores a password in a character array called `pass`. Ask the user for the password. Use `strcmp()` to let the user know whether the proper password was typed. Use the string I/O functions for all the program's input and output.

3. Write a program that rounds the numbers –10.5, –5.75, and 2.75 in two different ways (up and down).

4. Write a program that asks for the user's name. Print the name in reverse case; in other words, print the first letter of each name in lowercase and print the rest of the name in uppercase.

5. Write a program that asks the user for five movie titles. Print the longest title. Use only the string I/O functions and the string-manipulation functions shown in this chapter.

6. Write a program that computes the square root, cube root, and fourth root of the numbers from 10 to 25.

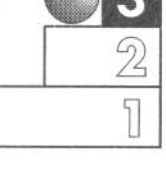

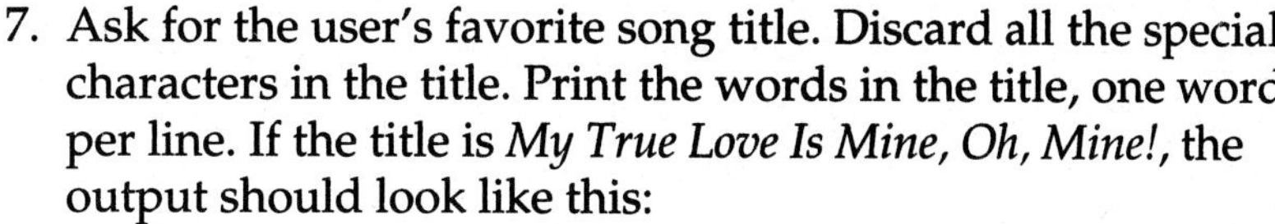

7. Ask for the user's favorite song title. Discard all the special characters in the title. Print the words in the title, one word per line. If the title is *My True Love Is Mine, Oh, Mine!*, the output should look like this:

```
My
True
Love
Is
Mine
Oh
Mine
```

8. Ask the user for 10 first names of children. Using `strcmp()` on each pair of names, write a program to print the name (in each pair) that comes first in the alphabet.

Part VI

Arrays and Pointers

24

Introducing Arrays

This chapter discusses different types of arrays. You are already familiar with the character array, which is the only way to store a string of characters in C++. Character arrays are not the only kind of arrays you can use, however. There is an array for every data type in C++. Learning how to process these arrays will improve the efficiency and power of your programs.

This chapter introduces the following topics:

- Array basics: names, data types, and subscripts
- Initializing an array at declaration time
- Initializing an array during program execution
- Selecting elements from arrays

The sample programs in this chapter and the next few chapters are some of the most advanced you will see in this book. Arrays are not difficult, but their power lends them to advanced programs.

Array Basics

An array is a list of two or more variables with the same name.

Although you have seen a special use of arrays as character strings, a little review of arrays is needed. An *array* is a list of two or more variables with the same name. Not every list of variables is an array. The following four variables do not count as an array:

```
sales
bonus_92
first_initial
ctr
```

This is a list of four variables, but they do not make up an array because each variable has a different name. You might wonder how more than one variable can have the same name; that seems to violate the rules of variables. If two variables have the same name, how will C++ know which one you want when you use the name of one of them?

Array variables are distinguished from each other by a *subscript*. A subscript is a number, inside brackets, that differentiates one *element* of an array from another. Elements are the individual variables in an array.

Suppose that you want to store a person's name in a character array called `name`. You can use either of the following definitions:

```
char name[ ] = "Ray Krebbs";
char name[ 11 ] = "Ray Krebbs";
```

Because C++ knows to reserve an extra element for the null zero at the end of every string, you don't have to specify the 11 as long as you initialize the array with a value. You know that the variable `name` is an array because brackets follow its name. The array has a single name called `name`, which contains 11 elements. The array is stored in memory (see Figure 24.1). Each element is a character. You can manipulate individual elements in the array by their subscripts.

	name
[0]	R
[1]	a
[2]	y
[3]	
[4]	K
[5]	r
[6]	e
[7]	b
[8]	b
[9]	s
[10]	\0

Figure 24.1. **Storing a character array in memory.**

> **NOTE:** All array subscripts begin with 0.

For instance, the following `cout` function prints Ray's initials.

Print the first and fifth elements of the array `name`.

```
cout << name[ 0 ] << ". " << name[ 4 ];
```

You can define an array as any data type in C++. You can have integer arrays, long integer arrays, double floating-point arrays, short integer arrays, and so on. C++ knows that you are defining an array instead of a single nonarray variable when you put brackets after the array name. For example, the following line defines an array, called `ages`, of five integers:

```
int  ages[ 5 ];
```

The first element in the `ages` array is `ages[ 0 ]`. The second element is `ages[ 1 ]`, and the last element is `ages[ 4 ]`. This declaration of `ages` does not assign values to the elements, so you do not know what is in `ages`, and your program cannot assume that it contains zeros or anything else.

Here are some more array definitions:

```
int  weights[ 25 ], sizes[ 100 ]; // Declare 2 integer arrays

float      salaries[ 8 ];    // Declare 1 floating-point array

double     temps[ 50 ];      // Declare 1 double floating-point
                             // array

char letters[ 15 ];          // Declare a character array
```

When you declare an array, you instruct C++ to reserve a specific number of memory locations for that array. C++ will protect those elements. In the preceding four lines of code, if you assign a value to `letters[ 2 ]`, you will not overwrite any data in `weights`, `sizes`, `salaries`, or `temps`. If you assign a value to `sizes[ 94 ]`, you will not overwrite data stored in `weights`, `salaries`, `temps`, or `letters`.

Each element in an array occupies the same amount of space as a nonarray variable of the same data type. In other words, each element in a character array occupies one byte of memory. Each element in an integer array occupies two bytes of memory. The same is true for every other data type.

In your programs, you can reference elements by using formulas for subscripts. As long as the subscript can evaluate to an integer, you can use a constant, a variable, or an expression for the subscript. All the following reference individual elements of arrays:

```
ara[ 4 ]

sales[ ctr + 1 ]

bonus[ month ]

salary[ month[ i ] * 2 ]
```

Array elements follow each other in memory, with nothing between them.

All array elements are stored in a contiguous, back-to-back fashion. This is important to remember, especially as you write more advanced programs. You can *always* count on an array's first element preceding the second, the second element placed immediately before the third, and so on. There is no "padding" of memory; that is, C++ ensures that there is no extra space between array elements. This holds true for character arrays, integer arrays, floating-point arrays, and every other array data type. If a floating-point value on your computer occupies four bytes of memory, the *next* element in a floating-point array *always* begins four bytes after the preceding element.

> **The Size of Arrays**
>
> The `sizeof()` function returns the number of bytes needed to hold its argument. If you use `sizeof()` to request the size of an array name, `sizeof()` returns the number of bytes *reserved* for the entire array.
>
> For instance, suppose that you declared an integer array of 100 elements called `scores`. If you were to produce the size of the array, as in
>
> ```
> n = sizeof(scores);
> ```
>
> `n` would hold 200. `sizeof()` always returns the reserved amount of storage, no matter what data is in the array. Therefore, a character array's contents, even if the array holds a very short string, do not affect the size of the array that was originally reserved in memory.
>
> If, however, you request the size of an individual array element, such as
>
> ```
> n = sizeof(scores[ 6 ]);
> ```
>
> `n` would hold 2.

You must never go out of bounds of an array. Suppose, for example, that you want to keep track of five employees' exemptions and their five salary codes. You can reserve two arrays to hold this data:

```
int  exemptions[ 5 ];    // Holds up to 5 employee exemptions
char sal_codes[ 5 ];     // Holds up to 5 employee codes
```

C++ protects only as many array elements as you specify.

Figure 24.2 shows how C++ reserves memory for these arrays. Notice that C++ knows to reserve five elements for `exemptions` from the array declaration. C++ starts reserving memory for `sal_codes` after it reserves all five elements for the `exemptions`. If you were to declare several more variables, either locally or globally, after these two lines, C++ would always protect the five elements for `exemptions` and `sal_codes`.

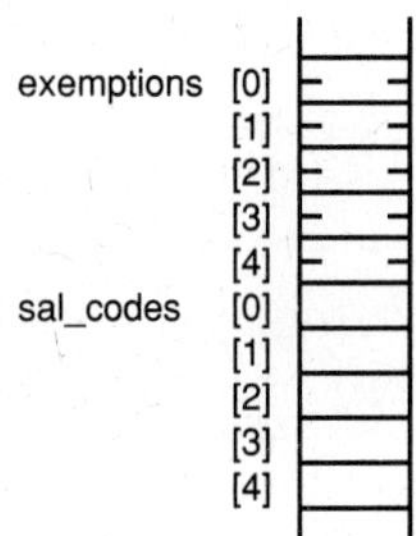

Figure 24.2. **Memory locations of two arrays.**

C++ does its part to protect your array data, so you must too. If you reserve five elements for `exemptions`, you have five integer array elements referred to as `exemptions[ 0 ]`, `exemptions[ 1 ]`, `exemptions[ 2 ]`, `exemptions[ 3 ]`, and `exemptions[ 4 ]`. *C++ will not protect more than five elements for* `exemptions`*!* If you were to put a value into an `exemptions` element that you did not reserve, such as

```
exemptions[ 6 ] = 4;      // Assign a value to an out-of-range
                          // element
```

C++ lets you do so, but the results are damaging! C++ overwrites other data — in this case, `sal_codes[ 2 ]` and `sal_codes[ 3 ]`, because they were reserved where the sixth element of the integer array `exemptions` would be placed. Figure 24.3 shows the damaging results of assigning a value to an out-of-range element.

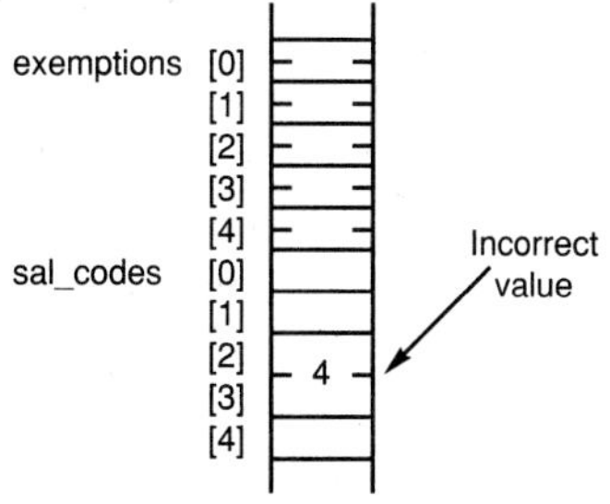

Figure 24.3. Memory storage after overwriting part of `sal_codes`.

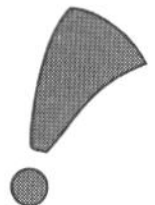

CAUTION: Unlike most programming languages, C++ lets you assign values to out-of-range (nonreserved) subscripts. You must be careful not to do this, because you will overwrite other data or code.

Although you can define an array of any data type, you cannot declare an array of strings. A string is not a C++ variable data type. You learn how to hold multiple strings in an arraylike structure in Chapter 28, "Pointers and Arrays."

Initializing Arrays

You must assign values to array elements before using them. Here are the two ways to initialize elements in an array:

- Initialize the elements at declaration time.
- Initialize the elements in the program.

NOTE: C++ automatically initializes global arrays to null zeros. All global character array elements are therefore null, and all numeric array elements contain zero. You should limit your use of global arrays. If you do use them, explicitly initialize them to zero, even though C++ does this for you, to clarify your intentions.

Initializing Elements at Declaration Time

You already know how to initialize character arrays that hold strings when you define the arrays. You simply assign the array a string. For example, the following declaration reserves six elements in a character array called `city`:

```
char city[ 6 ];       // Reserve space for city
```

Initialize arrays

If you also want to initialize `city` with a value, you can use the following code:

```
char city[ 6 ] = "Tulsa"; // Reserve space and initialize city
```

The `6` is optional because C++ counts the elements needed to hold `Tulsa`, plus an extra element for the null zero at the end of the quoted string.

You can reserve a character array and initialize it, a single character at a time, by using braces around the character data. The following line of code declares an array called `initials` and initializes it with eight characters:

```
char initials[ 8 ] =
     { 'Q', 'K', 'P', 'G', 'V', 'M', 'U', 'S' };
```

The array `initials` is *not a string!* Its data does not end in a null zero. There is nothing wrong with defining an array of characters like this one, but you must remember that you cannot treat the array as if it were a string. Do not use string functions with it, or attempt to print the array as a string.

Using the braces, you can initialize any type of array. For example, if you want to initialize an integer array that holds five children's ages, you can use the following declaration:

```
int  child_ages[ 5 ] =
     { 2, 5, 6, 8, 12 }; // Declare and initialize array
```

If you want to keep track of the last three years' total sales, you can declare an array and initialize it at the same time with this declaration:

```
double    sales[ ] =
    { 454323.43, 122355.32, 343324.96 };
```

As with character arrays, you do not have to state explicitly the array size when declaring and initializing an array of any type. C++ knows, in this case, to reserve three double floating-point array elements for `sales`. Figure 24.4 shows the memory representation of `child_ages` and `sales`.

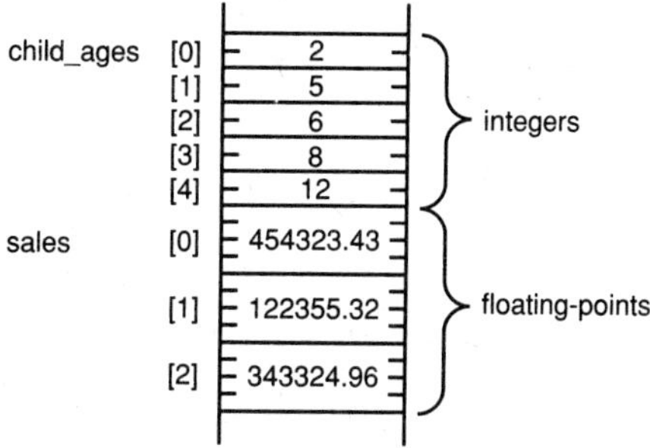

Figure 24.4. Memory representation of two arrays.

NOTE: You cannot initialize an array, using the assignment and braces, *after* you declare it. You can initialize arrays in this manner only when you declare them. If you want to fill an array with data after you declare the array, you must do so element by element, or by using functions as described later in this chapter.

C++ zeros all array values that you do not explicitly define at declaration time.

Although C++ does not automatically zero-out (or initialize to *any* value) array elements, if you initialize some but not all the elements when you declare the array, C++ will finish the job for you by assigning the rest of the elements to zero.

For instance, suppose that you need to reserve array storage for three preceding months of profit figures as well as the next three months of profit figures. You need to reserve six elements of storage, but you know values for only the first three elements. You can initialize the array in this way:

```
double    profit[ 6 ] =
     { 67654.43, 46472.34, 63451.93 };
```

Because you explicitly initialized the three elements, C++ initializes the rest of them to zero. If you were to print the entire array, one element per line, with an appropriate `cout`, you would get the following:

```
67654.43
46472.34
63451.93
00000.00
00000.00
00000.00
```

TIP: To initialize all elements of a large array to zero at the same time, declare the entire array and initialize its first value to zero. C++ finishes assigning the rest of the array to zero.

CAUTION: Always declare an array with the maximum number of subscripts, unless you initialize the array at the same time. The following array declaration is illegal:

```
int  count[ ];    // BAD array declaration!
```

C++ will not know how many elements to reserve for `count`, so it reserves *none*. If you then assign values to `count`'s nonreserved elements, you may (and probably will) inadvertently overwrite other data.

You can leave the brackets empty only when you assign values to the array, such as

```
int  count[ ] =
     { 15, 9, 22, -8, 12 };    // Good definition
```

C++ can tell, from the list of values, how many elements to reserve. In this case, C++ reserves five elements for `count`.

Examples

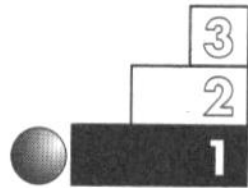

1. Suppose that you want to keep track of the stock market averages for the preceding 90 days. Instead of storing the averages in 90 different variables, you can easily store them in an array:

   ```
   float     stock[ 90 ];
   ```

   The rest of the program can assign values to the averages.

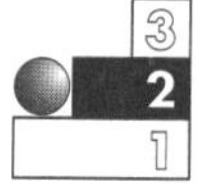

2. You just finished taking classes at a local university and want to average your six class scores. The following program initializes an array for the school name and for the six classes. The body of the program averages each of the six scores.

```
// Filename: C24ARA1.CPP
// Averages six test scores

#include <iostream.h>

main()
     {
     char      s_name[ ] = "Tri Star University";
     float     scores[ 6 ] =
          { 88.7, 90.4, 76.0, 97.0, 100.0, 86.7 };
     float     average = 0.0;
     int       ctr;

     // Compute total of scores
     for (ctr = 0; ctr < 6; ctr++)
          {
          average += scores[ ctr ];
          }
     // Compute the average
     average /= (float)6;
     cout << "At " << s_name << ", your class average is "
          << average << ".\n";
     return 0;
     }
```

Here is this program's output:

```
At Tri Star University, your class average is 89.8.
```

Notice that the use of arrays makes processing lists of information much easier. Instead of averaging six differently named variables, you can use a `for` loop to step through the array elements. The advantage to arrays is that you can average even 1,000 numbers with a simple `for` loop. If the 1,000 variables were not arrays but were individually named, you would have to write a lot of code just to add them together.

3. The following program is an expanded version of the preceding one. This program prints the six scores before computing the average. Notice that you have to print array elements individually; there is no way to print an entire array in a single `cout`. (Of course, you can print an entire character array, but only if it holds a null-terminated string of characters.)

```
// Filename: C24ARA2.CPP
// Prints and averages six test scores

#include <iostream.h>

void     pr_scores(float scores[ 6 ])
     {
     // Print the six scores
     int     ctr;

     cout << "Here are your scores:\n";     // Title
     for (ctr = 0; ctr < 6; ctr++)
          cout << scores[ ctr ] << "\n";
     return;
     }


int     main(void)
     {
     char      s_name[ ] = "Tri Star University";
     float     scores[ 6 ] =
```

```
          { 88.7, 90.4, 76.0, 97.0, 100.0, 86.7 };
     float     average = 0.0;
     int       ctr;

     // Call function to print scores
     pr_scores(scores);
     // Compute total of scores
     for (ctr = 0; ctr < 6; ctr++)
          {
          average += scores[ ctr ];
          }
     // Compute the average
     average /= (float)6;
     cout << "At " << s_name << ", your class average is "
          << average << ".\n";
     return 0;
     }
```

To pass any array to a function, you just specify the array's name. In the receiving function's parameter list, you must state the array type and provide brackets that tell the function it is an array.

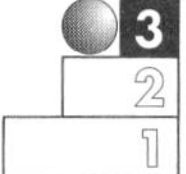

4. To improve the maintainability of your programs, define all array sizes with the `#define` preprocessor directive. What if you plan to take only four classes next semester but you want to use this same program? You can modify it by changing all the 6s to 4s, but if you have defined the array size with a defined constant, you will need to alter only one line to change the program's subscript limits. Notice how the following program uses a defined constant for the number of classes throughout the program:

```
// Filename: C24ARA3.CPP
// Prints and averages six test scores

#include <iostream.h>

#define      CLASS_NUM      (6)

void      pr_scores(float scores[ CLASS_NUM ])
     {
```

```
    int     ctr;

    cout << "Here are your scores:\n";      // Title
    for (ctr = 0; ctr < CLASS_NUM; ctr++)
        cout << scores[ ctr ] << "\n";
    return;
    }


int     main(void)
    {
    char        s_name[ ] = "Tri Star University";
    float       scores[ CLASS_NUM ] =
        { 88.7, 90.4, 76.0, 97.0, 100.0, 86.7 };
    float       average = 0.0;
    int         ctr;

    // Call function to print scores
    pr_scores(scores);
    // Compute total of scores
    for (ctr = 0; ctr < CLASS_NUM; ctr++)
        {
        average += scores[ ctr ];
        }
    // Compute the average
    average /= (float)CLASS_NUM;
    cout << "At " << s_name << ", your class average is "
        << average << ".\n";
    return 0;
    }
```

For a simple example like this, using a defined constant for the maximum subscript may not seem like a big advantage. However, if you were writing a larger program that processed several arrays, changing the defined constant at the top of the program is much easier than searching the program for each occurrence of that array reference.

Using defined constants for array sizes has the added advantage of protecting you from going out of the subscript bounds. You don't have to remember the subscript when looping through arrays; you can use the defined constant instead.

Initializing an Array in the Program

Rarely will you know the contents of arrays when you declare them. Usually, you fill an array with user input or from a disk file's data. The `for` loop is a perfect tool for looping through arrays when you fill them with values.

CAUTION: An array name cannot appear on the left side of an assignment statement.

You cannot assign one array to another. Suppose that you want to copy an array called `total_sales` to a second array called `saved_sales`. You *cannot* do this with the following assignment statement:

```
saved_sales = total_sales;      // INVALID!
```

Instead, you have to copy the arrays one element at a time, using a loop, as in the following section of code.

Initialize the variable `ctr` *to 0 and increment it by 1 while the variable* `ctr` *is less than* `ARRAY_SIZE`*.*
Write the `ctr`*'th element of the* `total_sales` *array to the* `ctr`*'th element of the* `saved_sales` *array.*

```
for (ctr = 0; ctr < ARRAY_SIZE; ctr++)
     {

     saved_sales[ ctr ] = total_sales[ ctr ];

     }
```

The following examples illustrate methods for initializing arrays within the program. After learning about disk processing later in the book, you will learn to read array values from a disk file.

Examples

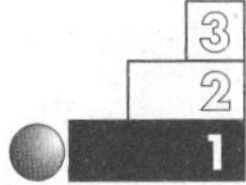

1. The following program uses the assignment operator to assign 10 temperatures to an array:

```
// Filename: C24ARA4.CPP
// Fills an array with 10 temperature values

#include <iostream.h>

#define NUM_TEMPS 10

main()
     {
     float         temps[ NUM_TEMPS ];
     int           ctr;

     temps[ 0 ] = 78.6;     // Subscripts ALWAYS begin at 0
     temps[ 1 ] = 82.1;
     temps[ 2 ] = 79.5;
     temps[ 3 ] = 75.0;
     temps[ 4 ] = 75.4;
     temps[ 5 ] = 71.8;
     temps[ 6 ] = 73.3;
     temps[ 7 ] = 69.5;
     temps[ 8 ] = 74.1;
     temps[ 9 ] = 75.7;
     // Print the temps
     cout << "Daily temperatures for the last "
          << NUM_TEMPS << " days:\n";
     for (ctr = 0; ctr < NUM_TEMPS; ctr++)
          {
          cout << temps[ ctr ] << "\n";
          }
     return 0;
     }
```

2. The following program uses a `for` loop to assign eight integers from the user's input, using `cin`. The program then prints the total of the numbers.

```
// Filename: C24TOT.CPP
// Totals 8 input values from the user
```

```
#include <iostream.h>

#define NUM 8

main()
     {
     int      nums[ NUM ];
     int      ctr;
     int      total = 0;    // Holds total of user's 8 numbers

     for (ctr = 0; ctr < NUM; ctr++)
          {
          cout << "Please enter the next number...";
          cin >> nums[ ctr ];
          total += nums[ ctr ];
          }
     cout << "The total of the numbers is " << total << "\n";
     return 0;
     }
```

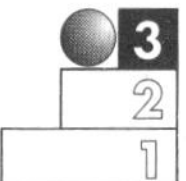

3. You don't have to access the elements of an array in the same order in which you initialized the array. The next chapter, "Array Processing," shows you how to change the order of an array. You can use the subscript to "pick out" items from a list (array) of values.

   The following program requests sales data for the last 12 months. The program then waits until another user types a month number. That month's sales are then printed, without the values for the surrounding months getting in the way. This is how you would begin to build a search program to find requested data: store the data in an array (or in a disk file that can be read into an array, as you see in Chapters 32 and 33) and then wait for a request from the user to see only specific pieces of that data.

```
// Filename: C24SAL.CPP
// Stores 12 months of sales and prints selected ones

#include <iostream.h>
#include <ctype.h>
```

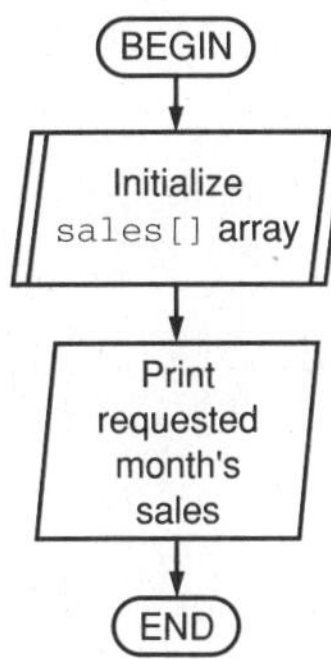


```
#include <conio.h>
#include <iomanip.h>
#define NUM 12

main()
     {
     float     sales[ NUM ];
     int       ctr, ans;
     int       req_month;     // Holds user's request

     cout.setf(ios::fixed);
     cout.setf(ios::showpoint);
     // Fill the array
     cout << "Please enter the twelve monthly "
          << "sales values\n";
     for (ctr = 0; ctr < NUM; ctr++)
          {
          cout << "What are sales for month number "
               << (ctr + 1) << "\n";
          cin >> sales[ ctr ];
          }
     // Wait for a requested month
     for (ctr = 0; ctr < 25; ctr++)
          cout << "\n";  // Clear the screen
     cout << "*** Sales Printing Program ***\n";
     cout << "Prints any sales from the last " << NUM
          << " months\n\n";
     do
          {
          cout << "\nWhat month (1-" << NUM
               << ") do you want to see a sales value for?";
          cin >> req_month;
          // Adjust for zero-based subscript
          cout << "Month " << req_month << "'s sales are "
               << setprecision(2) << sales[ req_month - 1 ]
               << "\n";
          cout << "\nDo you want to see another (Y/N)? ";
          ans = getch();
          ans = toupper(ans);
          }
     while (ans == 'Y');
     return 0;
     }
```

Figure 24.5 shows the second screen from this program. Once the 12 sales values are entered into the array, any or all of them can be requested, one at a time, simply by supplying the month number (the number of the subscript).

```
*** Sales Printing Program ***
Prints any sales from the last 12 months


What month (1-12) do you want to see a sales value for?1
Month 1's sales are 3233.45

Do you want to see another (Y/N)?
What month (1-12) do you want to see a sales value for?5
Month 5's sales are 6535.64

Do you want to see another (Y/N)?
What month (1-12) do you want to see a sales value for?2
Month 2's sales are 6434.67

Do you want to see another (Y/N)?
What month (1-12) do you want to see a sales value for?8
Month 8's sales are 4598.79

Do you want to see another (Y/N)?
```

Figure 24.5. Printing sales values entered into the array.

Notice the helpful screen-clearing routine that prints 25 newline characters. This routine scrolls the screen until it is blank.

Summary

You now know how to declare and initialize arrays of various data types. You can initialize an array when you declare it or in the body of your program. Array elements are much easier to process than many variables with different names.

Useful sorting and searching techniques are available to make your programs extremely powerful. The next chapter describes these techniques and shows you other ways to access array elements.

Review Questions

Answers to Review Questions are in Appendix B.

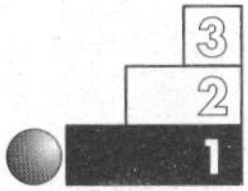

1. True or false: A single array can hold several values of different data types.
2. How do C++ programs tell one array element from another if the elements have identical names?

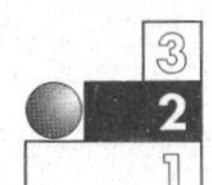

3. Why must you initialize an array before using it?
4. Look at the following definition of an array called weights:

```
int     weights[ 10 ] = { 5, 2, 4 };
```

What is the value of `weights[ 5 ]`?

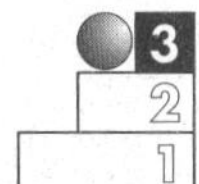

5. Recall how character arrays are passed to functions. If you change a passed integer array in a function, does the array change also in the calling function?
6. How does C++ initialize global array elements?

Review Exercises

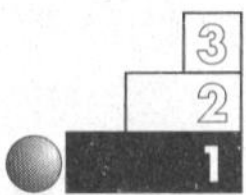

1. Write a program to store six of your friends' ages in a single array. Store each of the six ages by using the assignment operator. Print the ages on the screen.
2. Modify the preceding program to print the ages backward.

3. Write a simple data program to track a radio station's ratings (1, 2, 3, 4, or 5) for the last 18 months. Use `cin` to initialize the array with the ratings. Print the ratings on the screen with an appropriate title.
4. Write a program to store the numbers from 1 to 100 in an array of 100 integer elements. Remember that the subscripts begin at 0 and end at 99.

5. Write a program that a small business owner can use to track customers. Assign each customer a number (starting at 0). When a customer comes into the store, store that customer's

sales in an element that matches a number for that customer (the next, unused array element). When the store owner signals the end of the day, print a report of each customer number and matching sales, with the total sales at the bottom, along with the average sales per customer.

25

Array Processing

C++ provides many ways to access arrays. If you have programmed with other computer languages, some of C++'s array-indexing techniques will be unfamiliar to you. Arrays in the C++ language are closely linked with pointers. Chapter 27, "Pointers," describes the many ways that pointers and arrays interact.

Because pointers are so powerful, and because understanding arrays provides a good foundation for learning about pointers, this chapter describes in detail how to reference arrays and discusses the different types of array processing. You learn how to search an array for one or more values, find the highest and lowest values in an array, and sort an array into numeric or alphabetic order.

This chapter introduces the following topics:

- Searching arrays
- Finding the highest and lowest values in arrays
- Sorting arrays
- Advanced subscripting with arrays

Many programmers see the use of arrays as a turning point. Understanding array processing will make your programs not only more accurate but also more powerful.

Searching Arrays

Arrays are one of the primary means by which data is stored in C++ programs. Many types of programs lend themselves to processing lists (arrays) of data, such as an employee payroll program, scientific research of several chemicals, or customer account processing. As mentioned in Chapter 24, array data is usually read from a disk file. Upcoming chapters describe disk file processing. For now, you should know how to manipulate arrays so that you see the data exactly the way you want to see it.

Array elements do not always appear in the most appropriate order.

In the preceding chapter, you learned how to print the elements of arrays in the same order in which you entered the data. This is sometimes done but not always the best method for looking at data.

Suppose, for instance, that a high school uses C++ programs for its grade reports, and the principal wants to see the top 10 grade-point averages. You cannot print the first 10 grade-point averages in the list of student averages because the top 10 grade points may not (and probably do not) appear as the first 10 array elements. Because the grade points are not in any sequence, the program would have to sort the array elements into numeric order (from high to low grade points), or search the array for the 10 highest grade points.

You need a method for putting arrays in a specific order. This is called *sorting* an array. When you sort an array, you put that array's elements in a specific order, such as alphabetic order or numeric order. A dictionary is in alphabetic order, and so is a phone book.

You can also reverse the order of a sort, called a *descending sort*. For instance, if you wanted to look at a list of all employees in descending salary order, the names of the highest-paid employees would be printed first.

Figure 25.1 shows a list of 8 numbers in an array called `unsorted`. The middle list of numbers is an ascending sorted version of `unsorted`. The third list of numbers is a descending sorted version of `unsorted`.

Unsorted	Ascending order	Descending order
6	1	8
1	2	7
2	3	6
4	4	5
7	5	4
8	6	3
3	7	2
5	8	1

Figure 25.1. **A list of unsorted numbers sorted in both ascending and descending order.**

Before learning to sort, you need to know a preliminary step — how to search an array for a value. What if one of those students receives a grade change? The computer has to be able to access that student's grade in order to change it (without affecting the others). As the next section shows, programs can search for specific array elements.

NOTE: C++ provides a method for sorting and searching lists of strings, although you cannot understand how to do this until you learn about pointers, beginning in Chapter 27, "Pointers." The sorting and searching examples and algorithms in this chapter on array processing demonstrate sorting and searching arrays of numbers. The same concepts will apply (and will actually be much more usable for real-world applications) when you learn how to store lists of names in C++.

Searching for Values

You do not have to sort an array to find its extreme values.

You do not need to know any new commands to search an array for a value. Basically, the `if` and `for` loop statements are all you need. To search an array for a specific value, look at each element in the array, using the `if` statement to compare the elements to see whether they match. If they do not, keep searching down the array. If you run out of array elements before finding the value, it is not in the array.

You can perform several different kinds of searches. For example, you might need to find the highest or lowest value in a list of numbers. This is helpful when you have lots of data and you want to know the extremes of the data (such as the highest and lowest sales regions in your division). In addition, you can search an array to see whether it contains a matching value. For instance, you can determine whether an item is already in an inventory by searching a part number array for a match.

The following programs illustrate some of these array-searching techniques.

Examples

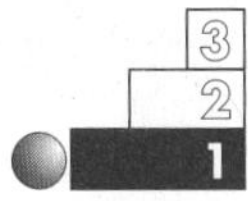

1. To find the highest number in an array, compare each element with the first one. If you find a higher value, it becomes the basis for the rest of the array. If you continue until you reach the end of the array, you will have the highest value, as the following program shows:

```
// Filename: C25HIGH.CPP
// Finds the highest value in the array

#include <iostream.h>

#define SIZE 15

main()
     {
     // Put a bunch of numbers in the array
     int     ara[ SIZE ] =
```

```
          { 5, 2, 7, 8, 36,
            4, 2, 86, 11, 43,
            22, 12, 45, 6, 85 };
     int     high_val, ctr;

     high_val = ara[ 0 ];      // Initialize with first array
                               // element
     for (ctr = 1; ctr < SIZE; ctr++)
          {     // Store current value if it is higher than
                // highest so far
          if (ara[ ctr ] > high_val)
               {
               high_val = ara[ ctr ];
               }
          }
     cout << "The highest number in the list is "
          << high_val << ".\n";
     return 0;
     }
```

Here is this program's output:

```
The highest number in the list is 86.
```

You save the element only if it is higher than the one you are comparing the element to. Finding the smallest number in an array is just as easy except that you compare the elements to see whether each succeeding array value is less than the lowest value found so far.

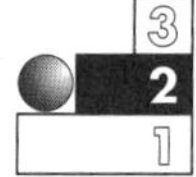

2. The following program finds the highest and lowest values. It stores the first array element in *both* the highest and lowest variables to begin the search. This ensures that each element, after that one, is tested to see whether it is higher or lower than the first.

   This example also uses the `rand()` function, discussed in Chapter 23, to fill the array with random values from 0 to 99.

The modulus operator (%) and 100 are applied to whatever value rand() produces. The program prints the entire array before starting the search for the highest and lowest values.

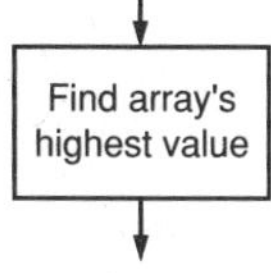


```
// Filename: C25HILO.CPP
// Finds the highest and lowest values in the array

#include <time.h>
#include <iostream.h>
#include <stdlib.h>

#define SIZE 15

main()
     {
     int     ara[ SIZE ];
     int     high_val, low_val, ctr;

     // Fill array with random numbers from 0 to 99
     randomize();
     for (ctr = 0; ctr < SIZE; ctr++)
          {
          ara[ ctr ] = rand() % 100;
          }
     // Print the array to the screen
     cout << "Here are the " << SIZE
          << " random numbers:\n";     // Title
     for (ctr = 0; ctr < SIZE; ctr++)
          {
          cout << ara[ ctr ] << "\n";
          }
     cout << "\n\n";            // Print a blank line
     high_val = ara[ 0 ];       // Initialize both high_val
                                // and low_val to 1st element
     low_val  = ara[ 0 ];
     for (ctr = 1; ctr < SIZE; ctr++)
          {     // Store current value if it is higher than
                // highest so far
          if (ara[ ctr ] > high_val)
              high_val = ara[ ctr ];
          if (ara[ ctr ] < low_val)
```

```
            low_val = ara[ ctr ];
        }
    cout << "The highest number in the list is "
        << high_val << ".\n";
    cout << "The lowest number in the list is "
        << low_val << ".\n";
    return 0;
    }
```

Figure 25.2 shows the output of this program.

```
Here are the 15 random numbers:
  46
  30
  82
  90
  56
  17
  95
  15
  48
  26
   4
  58
  71
  79
  92


The highest number in the list is 95.
The lowest number in the list is 4.
```

Figure 25.2. Printing the highest and lowest values in a list of random numbers.

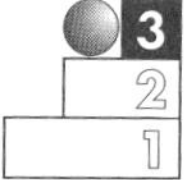

3. The following program fills an array with part numbers from an inventory. Use your imagination; the inventory array would normally fill more of the array, be initialized from a disk file, and be part of a larger set of arrays holding descriptions, quantities, costs, selling prices, and so on. For this example, assignment statements initialize the array. The important idea to learn from this program is not the array initialization but the method for searching the array.

NOTE: If the newly entered part number is already on file, the program tells the user. Otherwise, the part number is added to the end of the array.

```
// Filename: C25SERCH.CPP
// Searches a part number array for the input value. If
// the entered part number is not in the array, it is added.
// If the part number is in the array, a message is printed.

#include <iostream.h>

#define MAX 100


void      fill_parts(long int parts[ MAX ])
     {
     // Assign 5 part numbers to array for testing
     parts[ 0 ] = 12345;
     parts[ 1 ] = 24724;
     parts[ 2 ] = 54154;
     parts[ 3 ] = 73496;
     parts[ 4 ] = 83925;
     return;
     }


int      main(void)
     {
     long int     search_part;   // Holds user request
     long int     parts[ MAX ];
     int          ctr;
     int          num_parts = 5; // Beginning inventory count

     fill_parts(parts);     // Fill the first 5 elements
```

```
do
     {
     cout << "\n\nPlease type a part number ";
     cout << "...(-9999 ends program) ";
     cin >> search_part;
     if (search_part == -9999)
          break;      // Exit loop if user wants
     // Scan array to see if part is in inventory
     for (ctr = 0; ctr < num_parts; ctr++)
            // Check each item
          {
          if (search_part == parts[ctr])
               // If in inventory...
               {
               cout << "\nPart " << search_part
                    << " is already in inventory";
               break;
               }
          else
               {
               if (ctr == (num_parts - 1))
                    // If not there, add it
                    {
                    parts[ num_parts ] = search_part;
                    // Add to end of array
                    num_parts++;
                    cout << "\n" << search_part
                         << " was added to inventory\n";
                    break;
                    }
               }
          }
     }
while (search_part != -9999); // Loop until user
                              // signals end
return 0;
}
```

Figure 25.3 shows the output of this program.

```
Please type a part number...(-9999 ends program) 25432
25432 was added to inventory

Please type a part number...(-9999 ends program) 12345
Part 12345 is already in inventory
Please type a part number...(-9999 ends program) 65468
65468 was added to inventory

Please type a part number...(-9999 ends program) 25432
Part 25432 is already in inventory
Please type a part number...(-9999 ends program) 43234
```

Figure 25.3. Searching a table of part numbers.

Sorting Arrays

At times, you may need to sort one or more arrays. Suppose that you took a list of numbers, wrote each number on a separate piece of paper, and threw all the pieces into the air. The steps you would follow in trying to put the numbers in order, shuffling and changing the order of the pieces, are similar to what your computer goes through to sort numbers or character data.

Because sorting arrays requires exchanging values of elements, you should first learn the technique for swapping variables. Suppose that you have two variables named `score1` and `score2`. What if you wanted to reverse their values (putting `score2` into the `score1` variable, and `score1` into the `score2` variable? You could *not* use the following method:

```
score1 = score2;      // Does NOT swap the two values
score2 = score1;
```

Why doesn't this work? In the first line, the value of `score1` gets replaced with `score2`'s value; when the first line finishes, both `score1` and `score2` contain the same value. Therefore, the second line cannot work.

To swap two variables, you need to use a third variable to hold the intermediate result. (That's the only purpose of the third variable.) For instance, to swap `score1` and `score2`, use a third variable, called `hold_score`, as in the following code:

```
hold_score = score1;      // These 3 lines properly swap
score1 = score2;          // score1 and score2
score2 = hold_score;
```

This code exchanges the two values in the two variables.

There are several different ways to sort arrays. Some of the methods are the *bubble sort*, the *quick sort*, and the *shell sort*. The basic goal of each method is to compare each array element to another array element and then swap them if the higher one is less than the other one.

The lowest value in a list "floats" to the top with the bubble sort algorithm.

The theory behind these sorts is beyond the scope of this book; however, the bubble sort is one of the easiest methods to follow. Values in the array are compared to each other, a pair at a time, and swapped if they are not in back-to-back order. The lowest value eventually "floats" to the top of the array, like a bubble in a glass of soda.

Figure 25.4 shows a list of numbers before, during, and after a bubble sort. The bubble sort steps through the array, comparing pairs of numbers, to see whether they need to be swapped. Several passes may have to be made through the array before it is finally sorted (that is, no more passes are needed). Other types of sorts improve on the bubble sort; its procedure is easy to program but slower than many of the other methods.

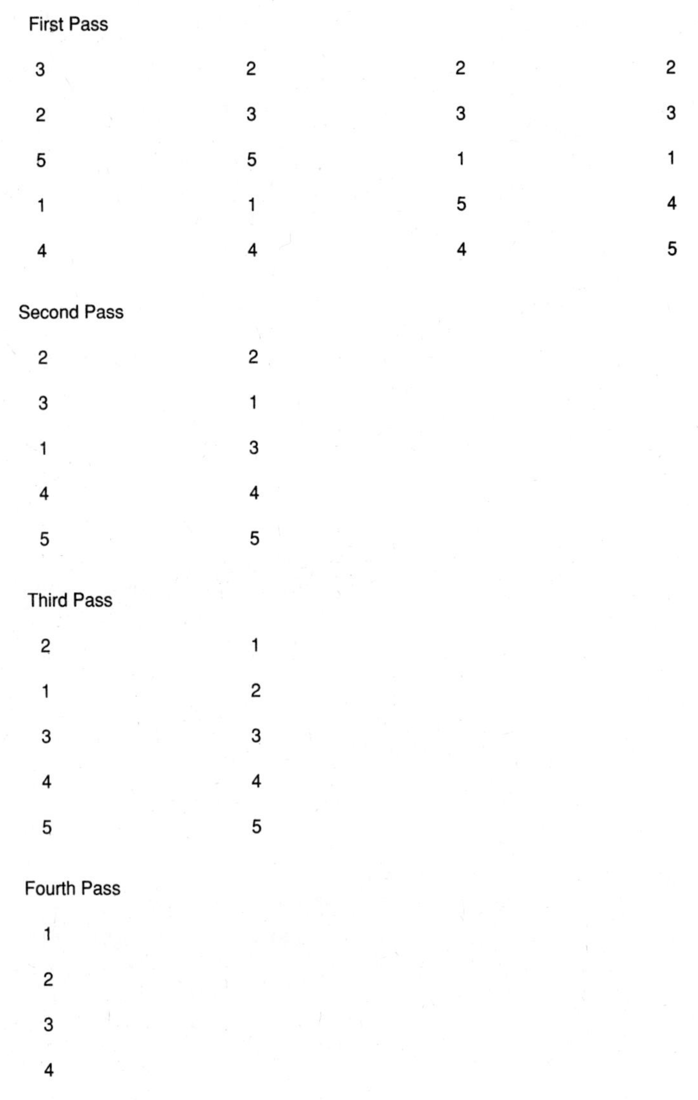

Figure 25.4. Sorting a list of numbers with the bubble sort.

The sample programs that follow show the bubble sort in action.

Examples

1. This program assigns 10 random numbers, between 0 and 99, to an array and then sorts it.

   A nested `for` loop, as shown in the `sort_array()` function, is perfect for sorting numbers in the array. Nested `for` loops provide a nice mechanism for working on pairs of values, swapping them if needed. As the outside loop counts down the list, referencing each element, the inside loop compares each of the remaining values with those array elements.

```
// Filename: C25SORT1.CPP
// Sorts and prints a list of numbers

#define MAX 10

#include <time.h>
#include <iostream.h>
#include <stdlib.h>


void     fill_array(int ara[ MAX ])
     {
     // Put random numbers in the array
     int     ctr;

     randomize();
     for (ctr = 0; ctr < MAX; ctr++)
          ara[ ctr ] = (rand() % 100);  // Force # to
                                        // 0-99 range
     return;
     }

void     print_array(int ara[ MAX ])
     {
     // Print the array
     int     ctr;
     for (ctr = 0; ctr < MAX; ctr++)
          cout << ara[ ctr ] << "\n";
     return;
     }
```

```
void     sort_array(int ara[ MAX ])
     {
     // Sort the array
     int     temp;          // Temporary variable to swap with
     int     ctr1, ctr2;    // Need 2 loop counters to swap
                            // pairs of numbers

     for (ctr1 = 0; ctr1 < (MAX - 1); ctr1++)
          {
          for (ctr2 = (ctr1 + 1); ctr2 < MAX; ctr2++)
               // Test pairs
               {
               if (ara[ ctr1 ] > ara[ ctr2 ])
                    // Swap if this pair
                    {
                    temp = ara[ ctr1 ]; // is not in order
                    ara[ ctr1 ] = ara[ ctr2 ];
                    ara[ ctr2 ] = temp; // "float" the
                                        // lowest to highest
                    }
               }
          }
     return;
     }


int     main(void)
     {
     int     ara[ MAX ];

     fill_array(ara);      // Put random numbers in the array
     cout << "Here are the unsorted numbers:\n";
     print_array(ara);     // Print the unsorted array
     sort_array(ara);      // Sort the array
     cout << "\n\nHere are the sorted numbers:\n";
     print_array(ara);     // Print the newly sorted array
     return 0;
     }
```

Figure 25.5 shows the output of this program. If any two randomly generated numbers are the same, the bubble sort will work properly, placing them next to each other in the list.

```
Here are the unsorted numbers:
46
30
82
90
56
17
95
15
48
26


Here are the sorted numbers:
15
17
26
30
46
48
56
82
90
95
```

Figure 25.5. **Printing a sorted list of numbers.**

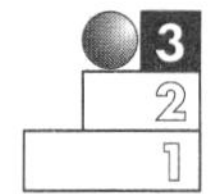

To produce a descending sort, use the < (less than) logical operator when swapping array elements.

2. The following program is just like the last one, except that this program prints the list of numbers in descending order.

   A descending sort is as easy to write as an ascending sort. With the ascending sort (from low to high values), you compare pairs of values, testing to see whether the first value is greater than the second one. With a descending sort, you test to see whether the first value is less than the second one.

```
// Filename: C25SORT2.CPP
// Sorts and prints a list of numbers in descending order

#define MAX 10

#include <time.h>
#include <iostream.h>
#include <stdlib.h>


void     fill_array(int ara[ MAX ])
     {
     // Put random numbers in the array
     int     ctr;

     randomize();
     for (ctr = 0; ctr < MAX; ctr++)
          ara[ ctr ] = (rand() % 100);     // Force # to
                                           // 0-99 range
     return;
     }

void     print_array(int ara[ MAX ])
     {
     // Print the array
     int     ctr;
     for (ctr = 0; ctr < MAX; ctr++)
          cout << ara[ ctr ] << "\n";
     return;
     }

void     sort_array(int ara[ MAX ])
     {
     // Sort the array
     int     temp;         // Temporary variable to swap with
     int     ctr1, ctr2;   // Need 2 loop counters to swap
                           // pairs of numbers

     for (ctr1 = 0; ctr1 < (MAX - 1); ctr1++)
          {
          for (ctr2 = (ctr1 + 1); ctr2 < MAX; ctr2++)
```

```
                // Test pairs
                // Notice the difference in descending (here)
                // and ascending
                {
                if (ara[ ctr1 ] < ara[ ctr2 ])
                    // Swap if this pair
                    {
                    temp = ara[ ctr1 ]; // is not in order
                    ara[ ctr1 ] = ara[ ctr2 ];
                    ara[ ctr2 ] = temp; // "float" the
                                        // highest to lowest
                    }
                }
            }
        return;
        }

int     main(void)
        {
        int     ara[ MAX ];

        fill_array(ara);      // Put random numbers in the array
        cout << "Here are the unsorted numbers:\n";
        print_array(ara);     // Print the unsorted array
        sort_array(ara);      // Sort the array
        cout << "\n\nHere are the sorted numbers:\n";
        print_array(ara);     // Print the newly sorted array
        return 0;
        }
```

TIP: You can save the preceding programs' sort functions in two files named `sort_ascend` and `sort_descend`. When you need to sort two different arrays, `#include` these files inside your own programs. Even better, compile each of these routines separately and link the one you need to your program.

You can sort character arrays as easily as you sort numeric arrays. C++ uses the ASCII table for its sorting comparisons. Look at the ASCII table in Appendix C, and you will see that numbers sort before letters and that uppercase letters sort before lowercase letters.

Advanced Referencing of Arrays

The array notation you have seen so far is common in computer programming languages. Most languages use subscripts inside brackets (or parentheses) to refer to individual array elements. For instance, you know that the following array references describe the first and fifth element of the array called `sales` (remember that the starting subscript is always 0):

```
sales[ 0 ]
sales[ 4 ]
```

C++ provides another approach to referencing arrays. Even though the title of this section includes the word *Advanced*, this array-referencing method is not difficult. It is very different, though, especially if you are familiar with another programming language's approach.

There is nothing wrong with referring to array elements in the manner you have seen. However, the approach described here, unique to C++, will be helpful when you learn about pointers in upcoming chapters. Actually, C++ programmers who have programmed for several years rarely use the subscript notation you have seen.

An array name is the address of the starting element of the array.

In C++, an array's name is not just a label for you to use in programs. To C++, the array name is the actual address where the first element begins in memory. Suppose that you define an array called `amounts` with the following statement:

```
int     amounts[ 6 ] =
    { 4, 1, 3, 7, 9, 2 };
```

Figure 25.6 shows how this array is stored in memory. The figure shows the array beginning at address 405,332. (The actual addresses of variables are determined by the computer when you load and run your compiled program.) Notice that the name of the array, `amounts`, is located somewhere in memory and contains the address of `amounts[ 0 ]`, or 405,332.

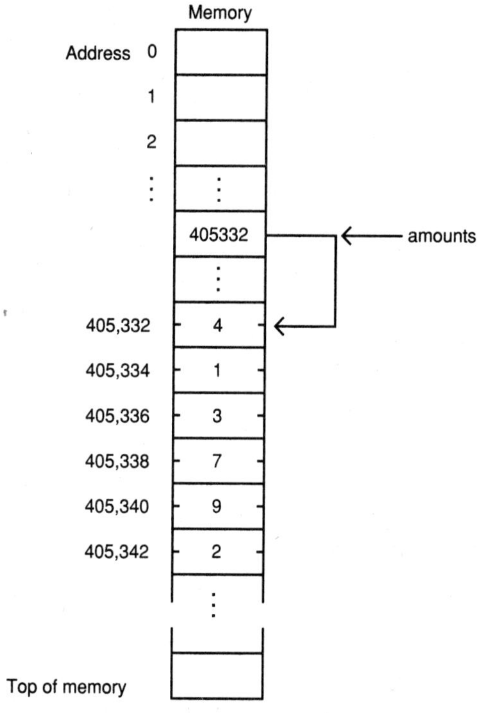

Figure 25.6. The array name `amounts` holds the address of `amounts[ 0 ]`.

You can refer to an array by using its regular subscript notation or modifying the address of the array. Both of the following items refer to the third element of `amounts`:

```
amounts[ 3 ]
(amounts + 3)[ 0 ]
```

Because C++ considers the array name to be an address in memory that contains the location of the first array element, nothing keeps you from using a different address as the starting address and referencing from there. Taking this one step further, each of the following *also* refers to the third element of `amounts`:

```
(amounts + 0)[ 3 ]
(amounts + 2)[ 1 ]
(amounts - 2)[ 5 ]
(1 + amounts)[ 2 ]
(3 + amounts)[ 0 ]
(amounts + 1)[ 2 ]
```

You can print any of these array elements with a `cout` function.

CAUTION: The hierarchy table in Appendix D shows that array subscripts have precedence over addition and subtraction. Therefore, you must enclose an array name in parentheses if you want to modify the name. The following examples are not equivalent:

```
(2 + amounts)[ 1 ]
2 + amounts[ 1 ]
```

The second example takes the value of amounts[1] (which is 1 in this sample array) and adds 2 to it (resulting in a value of 3).

This second method of array referencing might seem like more trouble than it is worth, but learning to reference arrays in this way will make your transition to pointers much easier. An array name is actually a pointer itself, because the array contains the address of the first array element (it "points" to the start of the array).

When printing strings inside character arrays, referencing the arrays by their modified addresses is more useful than referencing the arrays with integers. Suppose that you stored three strings in a single-character array. You could initialize the array with the following statement:

```
char names[ ] =
     { 'T', 'e', 'd', '\0',
       'E', 'v', 'a', '\0',
       'S', 'a', 'm', '\0' };
```

Figure 25.7 shows how this array might look in memory. The array name, `names`, contains the address of the first element, `names[0]` (the letter T).

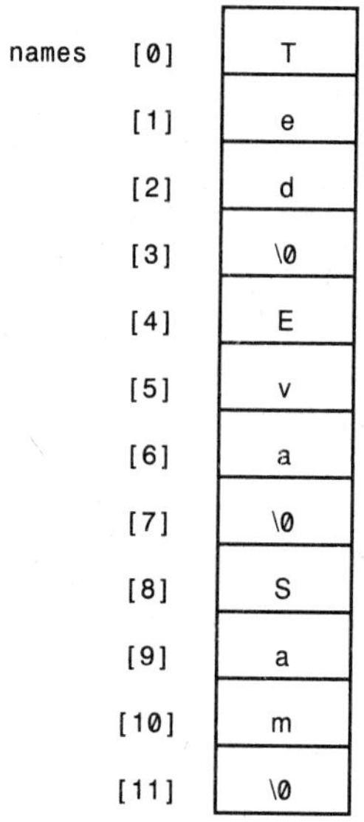

names	[0]	T
	[1]	e
	[2]	d
	[3]	\0
	[4]	E
	[5]	v
	[6]	a
	[7]	\0
	[8]	S
	[9]	a
	[10]	m
	[11]	\0

Figure 25.7. Storing more than one string in a single-character array.

You have yet to see a character array that holds more than one string, but C++ allows such an array. The problem is how you reference (especially how you print) the second and third strings. If you were to print this array (as you have been doing) with

```
cout << names;
```

C++ would print

```
Ted
```

cout prints characters starting at the array's address until the null zero is reached.

As mentioned in Chapter 8, "Simple Input and Output," `cout` prints the string starting at the address of the specified array. Without a different way to reference the array, you would have no method of printing the three strings inside the single array (without resorting to printing them one element at a time).

Because `cout` requires a starting address, you can print the three strings with the following `cout` function calls:

```
cout << names;          // Print Ted
cout << names + 4;      // Print Eva
cout << names + 8;      // Print Sam
```

To test your understanding, what will the following `cout` function calls print?

```
cout << names + 1;
cout << names + 6;
```

The first `cout` prints `ed`, the string starting at the address specified (`names + 1`), and stops printing when it gets to the null zero. The second `cout` prints `a`. Adding 6 to the address at `names` produces the address where the `a` is located. The "string" is only one character long because the null zero appears in the array immediately after the `a`.

In summary of character arrays, the following refer to individual array elements (single characters):

```
names[ 2 ]
(names + 1)[ 1 ]
```

You can print both of these elements as characters but *not* as strings.

The following refer to addresses only:

```
names
(names + 4)
```

You can print both of these elements as strings but *not* as characters.

The next sample program is a little different from most of those you have seen. This example does not perform real-world work but helps you become familiar with this new method of array referencing. The next few chapters expand on this method.

Example

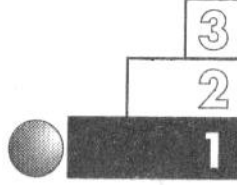

The following program stores the numbers from 100 to 600 in an array and then prints elements with the new method of array subscripting:

```
// Filename: C25REF1.CPP
// Prints elements of an integer array in different ways

#include <iostream.h>

main()
     {
     int      num[ 6 ] =
          { 100, 200, 300, 400, 500, 600 };

     cout << "num[0] is \t" << num[ 0 ] << "\n";
     cout << "(num + 0)[ 0 ] is \t" << (num + 0)[ 0 ]
          << "\n";
     cout << "(num - 2)[ 2 ] is \t" << (num - 2)[ 2 ]
          << "\n\n";
     cout << "num[ 1 ] is \t" << num[ 1 ] << "\n";
     cout << "(num + 1)[ 0 ] is \t" << (num + 1)[ 0 ]
          << "\n";
     cout << "(num - 5)[ 4 ] is \t" << (num - 5)[ 4 ]
          << "\n\n";
     cout << "num[ 5 ] is \t" << num[ 5 ] << "\n";
     cout << "(num + 5)[ 0 ] is \t" << (num + 5)[ 0 ]
          << "\n";
```

```
cout << "(num + 2)[ 3 ] is \t" << (num + 2)[ 3 ]
     << "\n\n";
cout << "(3 + num)[ 1 ] is \t" << (3 + num)[ 1 ]
     << "\n";
cout << "3 + num[ 1 ] is \t" << 3 + num[ 1 ] << "\n";
return 0;
}
```

Figure 25.8 shows this program's output.

```
num[0] is        100
(num+0)[0] is    100
(num-2)[2] is    100

num[1] is        200
(num+1)[0] is    200
(num-5)[4] is    200

num[5] is        600
(num+5)[0] is    600
(num+2)[3] is    600

(3+num)[1] is    500
3+num[1] is      203
```

Figure 25.8. The output of various array references.

Summary

You are beginning to see the true power of programming languages. Arrays enable you to search and sort lists of values. Sorting and searching are what computers do best; they can quickly scan hundreds and even thousands of values, looking for a match. Scanning files of paper by hand to look for just the right number takes much more time. By stepping through arrays, your programs can quickly scan, sort, calculate, or print a list of values. You now have the tools to sort lists of numbers as well as to search for values in a list.

You will use the concepts presented in this chapter to search and sort lists of string data as well, once you learn a little more about the way C++ manipulates strings and pointers. In building a solid foundation for this and other more advanced material, you now know how to reference array elements without using conventional subscripts.

Chapter 26, "Multidimensional Arrays," shows you how to keep track of arrays in a different format, called a *matrix*. Not all lists of data lend themselves to matrices, but you should be prepared when you need them.

Review Questions

Answers to Review Questions are in Appendix B.

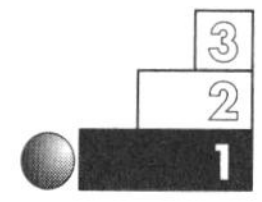

1. True or false: You must access an array in the same order in which you initialized it.
2. Where did the bubble sort get its name?
3. Are the following values sorted in ascending or descending order?

```
33  55  78  78  90  102  435  859  976  4092
```

4. How does C++ use the name of an array?
5. Look at this array definition:

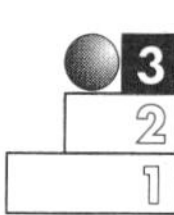

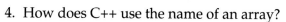

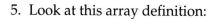

```
char teams[ ] =
     { 'E', 'a', 'g', 'l', 'e', 's', '\0',
       'R', 'a', 'm', 's', '\0' };
```

What is printed with each of the following statements?

A. `cout << teams;`

B. `cout << teams + 7;`

C. `cout << (teams + 3);`

D. `cout << teams[ 0 ];`

E. `cout << (teams + 0)[ 0 ];`

F. `cout << (teams + 5);`

G. `cout << (teams - 200)[ 202 ]);`

Review Exercises

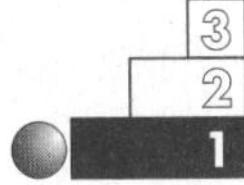

1. Write a program to store six of your friends' ages in a single array. Assign the ages in random order. Print the ages, from lowest to highest, on the screen.

2. Modify the preceding program to print the ages in descending order.

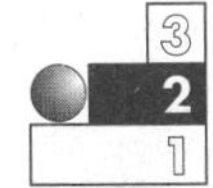

3. Using the new approach of subscripting arrays, rewrite the programs in exercises 1 and 2. Always put a 0 in the subscript brackets, modifying the address instead. Use `(ages + 3)[ 0 ]` instead of `ages[ 3 ]`.

4. Sometimes *parallel arrays* are used in programs that must track more than one list of values that are related. Suppose that you have to maintain an inventory, tracking the integer part numbers, prices, and quantities of each item. This task requires three arrays: an integer part-number array, a floating-point price array, and an integer quantity array. Each array has the same number of elements (the total number of parts in the inventory).

   Write a program to maintain such an inventory. Reserve enough elements for 100 parts in the inventory. Present the user with an input screen. When the user enters a part number, search the part number array. Once you locate the position of the part, print the corresponding price and quantity. If the part does not exist, let the user add it to the inventory, along with the matching price and quantity.

26

Multidimensional Arrays

Some data fits into lists, as shown in the preceding chapters; other data is better suited for tables of information. The preceding chapters focused on single-dimensional arrays — that is, an array that represents a list of values but has only one subscript. This chapter takes arrays one step further by covering *multidimensional arrays*. These arrays, sometimes called *tables* or *matrices*, have at least two dimensions: rows and columns. Sometimes they have even more dimensions.

This chapter covers the following topics:

- ♦ What multidimensional arrays are
- ♦ Reserving storage for multidimensional arrays
- ♦ Putting data into multidimensional arrays
- ♦ Using nested `for` loops to process multidimensional arrays

If you understood single-dimensional arrays, you should have no trouble understanding arrays with more than one dimension.

What Multidimensional Arrays Are

A multidimensional array has more than one subscript.

A *multidimensional array* is an array with more than one subscript. A single-dimensional array is a list of values, but a multidimensional array simulates a table of values, or even multiple tables of values. The most commonly used table is a two-dimensional table (an array with two subscripts).

Suppose that a softball team wants to keep track of its players' hits. The team played 10 games, and there are 15 players on the team. Table 26.1 shows the team's record of hits.

Table 26.1. A softball team's record of hits.

Player Name	*1*	*2*	*3*	*4*	*5*	*6*	*7*	*8*	*9*	*10*
Adams	2	1	0	0	2	3	3	1	1	2
Berryhill	1	0	3	2	5	1	2	2	1	0
Downing	1	0	2	1	0	0	0	0	2	0
Edwards	0	3	6	4	6	4	5	3	6	3
Franks	2	2	3	2	1	0	2	3	1	0
Grady	1	3	2	0	1	5	2	1	2	1
Howard	3	1	1	1	2	0	1	0	4	3
Jones	2	2	1	2	4	1	0	7	1	0
Martin	5	4	5	1	1	0	2	4	1	5
Powers	2	2	3	1	0	2	1	3	1	2
Smith	1	1	2	1	3	4	1	0	3	2
Smithtown	1	0	1	2	1	0	3	4	1	2
Townsend	0	0	0	0	0	0	1	0	0	0
Ulmer	2	2	2	2	2	1	1	3	1	3
Williams	2	3	1	0	1	2	1	2	0	3

Do you see that the softball table is a two-dimensional table? It has rows (the first dimension) and columns (the second dimension). Therefore, you would call this a two-dimensional table with 15 rows and 10 columns. (Generally, the number of rows is specified first.)

Each row has a player's name, and each column has a game number associated with it, but these are not part of the actual data. The data consists only of 150 values (15 rows times 10 columns equals 150 data values). The data in a two-dimensional table, just as with arrays, is always the same type of data; in this case, every value is an integer. If it were a table of salaries, every element would be a floating-point value.

A three-dimensional table has three dimensions: depth, rows, and columns.

The number of dimensions — in this case, two of them — corresponds to the dimensions in the physical world. The single-dimensional array is a line, or list of values. Two dimensions represent length and width. You write on a piece of paper in two dimensions; two dimensions represent a flat surface. Three dimensions represent length, width, and depth. You have seen 3-D movies. Not only do the images have length (height) and width, but they also (appear to) have depth. Figure 26.1 shows what a three-dimensional array looks like if it has a depth of four, six rows, and three columns. Notice that a three-dimensional table resembles a cube of blocks.

It is difficult to visualize more than three dimensions. However, you can think of each dimension after three as another occurrence. In other words, a list of one player's season hit record could be stored in an array. The team's hit record (as shown earlier) is two-dimensional. The league, made of up several teams' hit records would represent a three-dimensional table. Each team (the depth of the table) would have rows and columns of hit data. If there are two leagues, the second league could be considered another dimension (another set of data).

C++ gives you the capability to store several dimensions, although real-world data rarely requires more than two or three dimensions.

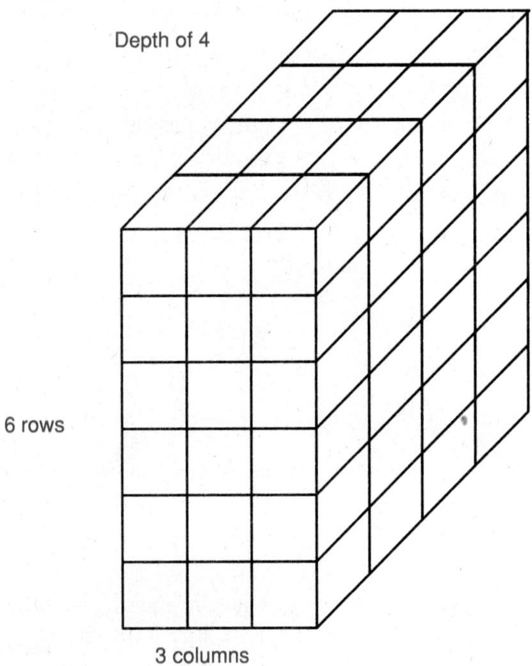

Figure 26.1. A represention of a three-dimensional table (a cube).

Reserving Multidimensional Arrays

When you reserve a multidimensional array, you must let C++ know that the array has more than one dimension. Put more than one subscript in brackets after the array name. You must put a different number, in brackets, for each dimension in the table. For example, to reserve the team data from Table 26.1, you use the following multidimensional array declaration.

Declare the integer array `teams` *with 15 rows and 10 columns.*

```
int  teams[ 15 ][ 10 ];     // Reserve a two-dimensional table
```

CAUTION: Unlike other programming languages, C++ requires that you enclose *each* dimension in brackets. Do not reserve multidimensional array storage like this:

```
int  teams[ 15, 10 ];     // INVALID table declaration
```

Properly reserving the `teams` table produces a table with 150 elements. The elements' subscripts look like those in Figure 26.2.

Columns

Rows

[0] [0]	[0] [1]	[0] [2]	[0] [3]	[0] [4]	[0] [5]	[0] [6]	[0] [7]	[0] [8]	[0] [9]
[1] [0]	[1] [1]	[1] [2]	[1] [3]	[1] [4]	[1] [5]	[1] [6]	[1] [7]	[1] [8]	[1] [9]
[2] [0]	[2] [1]	[2] [2]	[2] [3]	[2] [4]	[2] [5]	[2] [6]	[2] [7]	[2] [8]	[2] [9]
[3] [0]	[3] [1]	[3] [2]	[3] [3]	[3] [4]	[3] [5]	[3] [6]	[3] [7]	[3] [8]	[3] [9]
[4] [0]	[4] [1]	[4] [2]	[4] [3]	[4] [4]	[4] [5]	[4] [6]	[4] [7]	[4] [8]	[4] [9]
[5] [0]	[5] [1]	[5] [2]	[5] [3]	[5] [4]	[5] [5]	[5] [6]	[5] [7]	[5] [8]	[5] [9]
[6] [0]	[6] [1]	[6] [2]	[6] [3]	[6] [4]	[6] [5]	[6] [6]	[6] [7]	[6] [8]	[6] [9]
[7] [0]	[7] [1]	[7] [2]	[7] [3]	[7] [4]	[7] [5]	[7] [6]	[7] [7]	[7] [8]	[7] [9]
[8] [0]	[8] [1]	[8] [2]	[8] [3]	[8] [4]	[8] [5]	[8] [6]	[8] [7]	[8] [8]	[8] [9]
[9] [0]	[9] [1]	[9] [2]	[9] [3]	[9] [4]	[9] [5]	[9] [6]	[9] [7]	[9] [8]	[9] [9]
[10] [0]	[10] [1]	[10] [2]	[10] [3]	[10] [4]	[10] [5]	[10] [6]	[10] [7]	[10] [8]	[10] [9]
[11] [0]	[11] [1]	[11] [2]	[11] [3]	[11] [4]	[11] [5]	[11] [6]	[11] [7]	[11] [8]	[11] [9]
[12] [0]	[12] [1]	[12] [2]	[12] [3]	[12] [4]	[12] [5]	[12] [6]	[12] [7]	[12] [8]	[12] [9]
[13] [0]	[13] [1]	[13] [2]	[13] [3]	[13] [4]	[13] [5]	[13] [6]	[13] [7]	[13] [8]	[13] [9]
[14] [0]	[14] [1]	[14] [2]	[14] [3]	[14] [4]	[14] [5]	[14] [6]	[14] [7]	[14] [8]	[14] [9]

Figure 26.2. Subscripts for the softball team table.

array is an array of arrays, you can nest braces together when initializing them.

The following three array definitions fill the arrays `ara1`, `ara2`, and `ara3`, as shown in Figure 26.4:

```
int  ara1[ 5 ] =
     { 8, 5, 3, 25, 41 };     // 1-dimensional array
int  ara2[ 2 ][ 4 ] =
     {
          { 4, 3, 2, 1 },
          { 1, 2, 3, 4 }
     };
int  ara3[ 3 ][ 4 ] =

     {
          { 1, 2, 3, 4 },
          { 5, 6, 7, 8 },
          {9, 10, 11, 12 }
     };
```

TIP: To make a multidimensional array initialization match the array's subscripts, some programmers like to visualize how arrays are filled. Because C programs are free-form, you can initialize `ara2` and `ara3` as

```
int ara2[2][4]={{4, 3, 2, 1},        // Does exactly the
                {1, 2, 3, 4}};       // same thing as
                                     // before
int ara3[4][4]={{1, 2, 3, 4},
                {5, 6, 7, 8},
                {9, 10, 11, 12},
                {13, 14, 15, 16}};   // Visually more
                                     // obvious
```

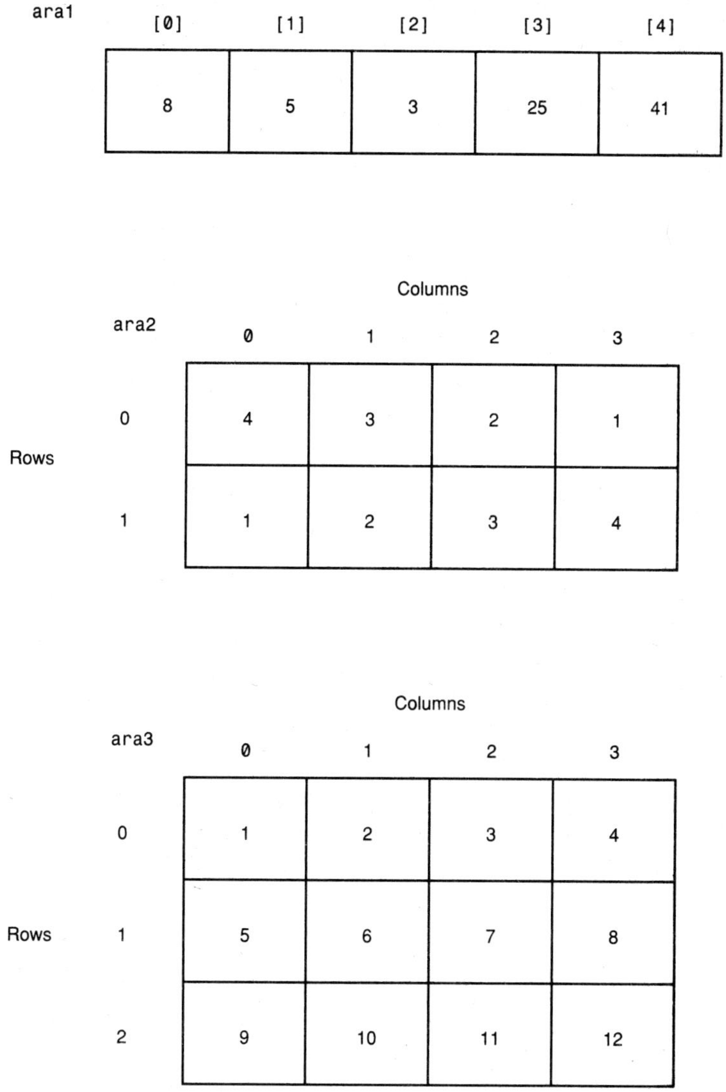

ara1

[0]	[1]	[2]	[3]	[4]
8	5	3	25	41

ara2

Rows		Columns 0	1	2	3
	0	4	3	2	1
	1	1	2	3	4

ara3

Rows		Columns 0	1	2	3
	0	1	2	3	4
	1	5	6	7	8
	2	9	10	11	12

Figure 26.4. Table contents after initialization.

Notice that the multidimensional arrays are stored in row order. In `ara3`, the first row gets the first four elements of the definition (`1`, `2`, `3`, and `4`).

C++ does not mind if you initialize a multidimensional array as if it were a single-dimensional array. You have to make sure that you keep track of the row order if you do this. For instance, the following two definitions reserve storage and initialize ara2 and ara3:

```
int      ara2[ 2 ][ 4 ] =
     { 4, 3, 2, 1, 1, 2, 3, 4 };
int      ara3[ 4 ][ 4 ] =
     { 1, 2, 3, 4, 5, 6, 7, 8, 9, 10, 11, 12, 13, 14,
       15, 16 };
```

There is no difference in initializing ara2 and ara3 with and without the nested braces. The nested braces seem to show the dimensions and how C++ fills them a little better, but the choice of using nested braces is yours.

TIP: Multidimensional arrays (unless they are global) are *not* initialized to specific values unless you assign them values at declaration time or in the program. As with single-dimensional arrays, if you initialize one or more of the elements, but not all of them, C fills the rest with zeros. If you want to zero-out an entire multidimensional array, you can use

```
float      sales[ 3 ][ 4 ][ 7 ][ 2 ] =
     { 0.0 };      // Fill all of sales with zeros
```

One last point to consider is how multidimensional arrays are viewed by your compiler. Many people program in C++ for years but never understand how tables are stored internally. As long as you use subscripts, a table's internal representation should not matter. Once you learn about pointer variables, however, you might need to know how C++ stores your tables in case you want to reference them with pointers (as shown in the next few chapters).

Figure 26.5 shows the way C++ stores a three-by-four table in memory. Unlike the elements of a single-dimensional array, each element is stored contiguously, but look at how C++ views the data. Because a table is an array of arrays, the array name contains the address of the start of the primary array. Each of those elements points to the array it contains (the data in each row). This coverage of table storage is for your information only. As you become more proficient in C++ and write more powerful programs that manipulate internal memory, you may want to review this method, used by C++ for table storage.

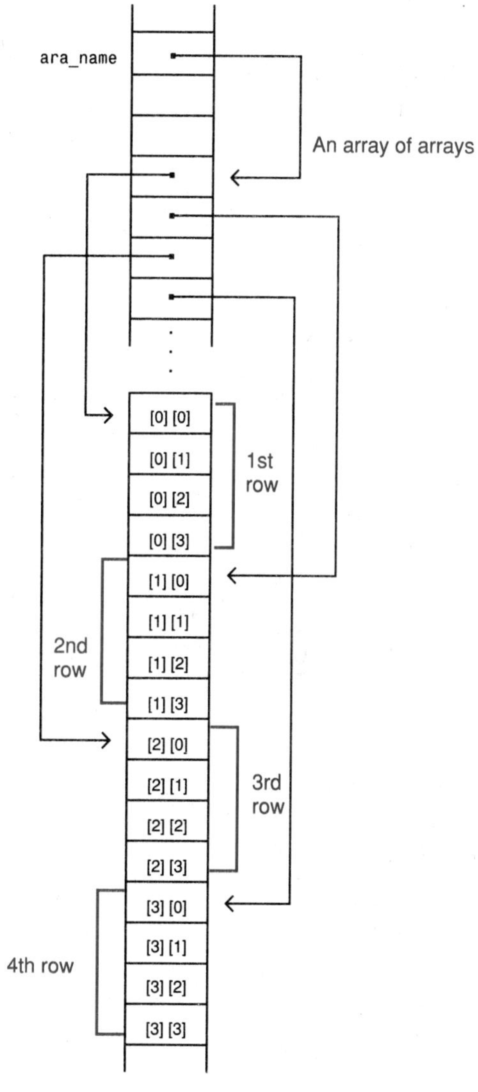

Figure 26.5. Internal representation of a two-dimensional table.

Tables and `for` Loops

Nested `for` loops are good candidates for looping through every element of a multidimensional table. For instance, the code

```
for (row = 0; row < 2; row++)
     {
     for (col = 0; col < 3; col++)
          cout << row << "   " << col << "\n";
     }
```

produces the following output:

```
0    0
0    1
0    2
1    0
1    1
1    2
```

These are exactly the subscripts, in row order, for a two-row by three-column table that is dimensioned with

```
int     table[ 2 ][ 3 ];
```

Nested loops work well with multidimensional arrays.

Notice that there are as many `for` loops as there are subscripts in the array (two). The outside loop represents the first subscript (the rows), and the inside loop represents the second subscript (the columns). The nested `for` loop steps through each element of the table.

You can use `cin()`, `get()`, and other input functions to fill a table, and you can assign values to the elements when declaring the table. Usually, the data comes from data files on disk. Regardless of what method actually stores values in multidimensional arrays, nested `for` loops are excellent control statements for stepping through the subscripts. The next examples illustrate how nested `for` loops work with multidimensional arrays.

Examples

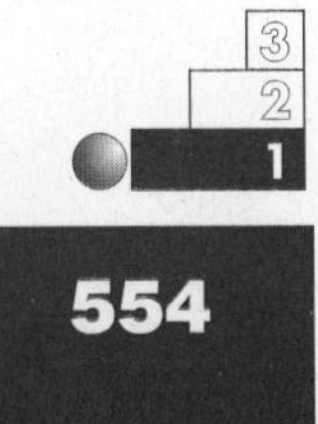

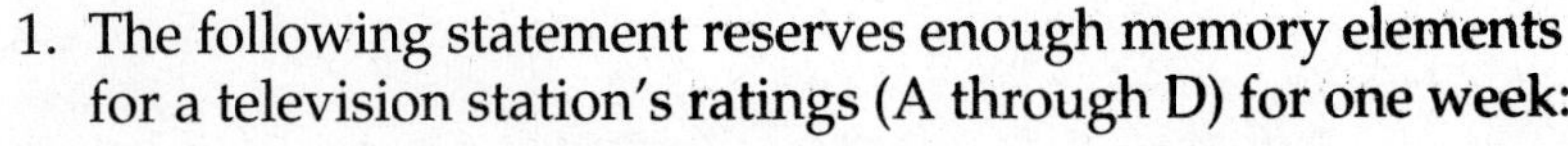

1. The following statement reserves enough memory elements for a television station's ratings (A through D) for one week:

```
char     shows[ 7 ][ 48 ];
```

This statement reserves enough elements to hold 7 days (the rows) of ratings for each 30-minute time slot (48 of them in a day).

Every element in a table is always the same type. In this case, each element is a character variable. Some of them can be initialized with the following assignment statements:

```
shows[ 3 ][ 12 ] = 'B';    // Store B in 4th row, 13th column
shows[ 1 ][ 5 ] = 'A';     // Store C in 2nd row, 6th column
cin.get(shows[ 6 ][ 20 ]);
```

2. A computer company sells two sizes of diskettes: 3 1/2 inch and 5 1/4 inch. Each diskette comes in one of four capacities: single-sided, double-density; double-sided, double-density; single-sided, high-density; and double-sided, high-density.

   The diskette inventory is well suited for a two-dimensional table. The company determined that the diskettes have the following retail prices:

	Single-sided, Double-density	*Double-sided, Double-density*	*Single-sided, High-density*	*Double-sided, High-density*
3 1/2"	2.30	2.75	3.20	3.50
5 1/4"	1.75	2.10	2.60	2.95

   The company wants to store the price of each diskette in a table for easy access. The following program does that with assignment statements:

BEGIN
Fill disk inventory table
Print table to screen
END

```
// Filename: C26DISK1.CPP
// Assigns diskette prices to a table

#include <iostream.h>

main()
     {
     float       disks[ 2 ][ 4 ];  // Table of disk prices
     int         row, col;
```

```
disks[ 0 ][ 0 ] = 2.30;      // Row 1, Column 1
disks[ 0 ][ 1 ] = 2.75;      // Row 1, Column 2
disks[ 0 ][ 2 ] = 3.20;      // Row 1, Column 3
disks[ 0 ][ 3 ] = 3.50;      // Row 1, Column 4
disks[ 1 ][ 0 ] = 1.75;      // Row 2, Column 1
disks[ 1 ][ 1 ] = 2.10;      // Row 2, Column 2
disks[ 1 ][ 2 ] = 2.60;      // Row 2, Column 3
disks[ 1 ][ 3 ] = 2.95;      // Row 2, Column 4
// Print the prices
for (row = 0; row < 2; row++)
     {
     for (col = 0; col < 4; col++)
          cout << "$" << disks[ row ][ col ] << "\n";
     }
return 0;
}
```

This program displays the following prices:

```
$2.30
$2.75
$3.20
$3.50
$1.75
$2.10
$2.60
$2.95
```

The program prints the prices one line at a time and without any descriptive titles. Although this output is not labeled, the program illustrates how you can use assignment statements to initialize a table and how nested `for` loops can print the elements.

3. The preceding diskette inventory would be displayed better if the output had descriptive titles. Before you add titles, you should know how to print a table in its native row-and-column format.

   Typically, you use a nested `for` loop, like the one in the preceding example, to print rows and columns. You should not output a newline character with every `cout`, however. If you do, you will see one value per line, as in the preceding output, which is not the row-and-column format of the table.

You do not want to see every diskette price on one line, but you want each row of the table printed on a separate line. You must insert a `cout << "\n";` to send the cursor to the next line each time the row number changes. Printing newlines after each row prints the table in its row-and-column format, as the following program shows:

```
// Filename: C26DISK2.CPP
// Assigns diskette prices to a table and prints them in a
// table format

#include <iostream.h>

main()
     {
     float        disks[ 2 ][ 4 ];  // Table of disk prices
     int          row, col;

     disks[ 0 ][ 0 ] = 2.30;     // Row 1, Column 1
     disks[ 0 ][ 1 ] = 2.75;     // Row 1, Column 2
     disks[ 0 ][ 2 ] = 3.20;     // Row 1, Column 3
     disks[ 0 ][ 3 ] = 3.50;     // Row 1, Column 4
     disks[ 1 ][ 0 ] = 1.75;     // Row 2, Column 1
     disks[ 1 ][ 1 ] = 2.10;     // Row 2, Column 2
     disks[ 1 ][ 2 ] = 2.60;     // Row 2, Column 3
     disks[ 1 ][ 3 ] = 2.95;     // Row 2, Column 4
     // Print the prices
     for (row = 0; row < 2; row++)
          {
          for (col = 0; col < 4; col++)
               cout << "$" << disks[row][col] << "\t";
          cout << "\n";     // Print a new line each row
          }
     return 0;
     }
```

Here is the output of the disk prices in their native table order:

```
$2.30     $2.75     $3.20     $3.50
$1.75     $2.10     $2.60     $2.95
```

4. To add descriptive titles, simply print a row of titles before the first row of values and then print a new column title before each column, as shown in this program:

```
// Filename: C26DISK3.CPP
// Assigns diskette prices to a table
// and prints them in a table format with titles

#include <iostream.h>
#include <iomanip.h>

main()
     {
     float     disks[ 2 ][ 4 ];    // Table of disk prices
     int       row, col;

     disks[ 0 ][ 0 ] = 2.30;  // Row 1, Column 1
     disks[ 0 ][ 1 ] = 2.75;  // Row 1, Column 2
     disks[ 0 ][ 2 ] = 3.20;  // Row 1, Column 3
     disks[ 0 ][ 3 ] = 3.50;  // Row 1, Column 4
     disks[ 1 ][ 0 ] = 1.75;  // Row 2, Column 1
     disks[ 1 ][ 1 ] = 2.10;  // Row 2, Column 2
     disks[ 1 ][ 2 ] = 2.60;  // Row 2, Column 3
     disks[ 1 ][ 3 ] = 2.95;  // Row 2, Column 4
     cout.setf(ios::fixed);
     cout.setf(ios::showpoint);
     // Print the top titles
     cout << "\tSingle-sided,\tDouble-sided,"
          << "\tSingle-sided,\tDouble-sided,\n";
     cout << "\tDouble-density\tDouble-density"
          << "\tHigh-density\tHigh-density\n";
     // Print the prices
     for (row = 0; row < 2; row++)
          {
          if (row == 0)
               cout << "3 1/2\"\t";
          else
               cout << "5 1/4\"\t";
          for (col = 0; col < 4; col++)
               cout << "$" << setprecision(2)
                    << disks[row][col] << "\t\t";
          cout << "\n"; // Print a new line each row
```

```
    }
return 0;
}
```

The output from this program in shown in Figure 26.6.

```
        Single-sided,    Double-sided,   Single-sided,   Double-sided,
        Double-density   Double-density  High-density    High-density
3 1/2"  $2.30            $2.75           $3.20           $3.50
5 1/4"  $1.75            $2.10           $2.60           $2.95
```

Figure 26.6. The table of disk prices with titles.

Summary

You now know how to create, initialize, and process multidimensional arrays. Although not all data fits into the compact format of tables, some data does. Using nested `for` loops makes stepping through a multidimensional array straightforward.

One of the limitations of a multidimensional array is that each element must be the same data type. This keeps you from being able to store several kinds of data in tables. Upcoming chapters show you how to store data in different ways to overcome this limitation of tables.

Review Questions

Answers to Review Questions are in Appendix B.

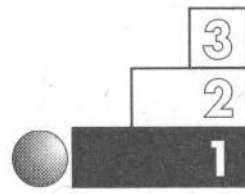

1. What statement reserves a two-dimensional table of integers, called `scores`, with five rows and six columns?
2. What statement reserves a 3-dimensional array of 4 tables of character variables, called `initials`, with 10 rows and 20 columns?
3. Consider the following statement:

```
int     weights[ 5 ][ 10 ];
```

   Which subscript (first or second) represents rows, and which represents columns?

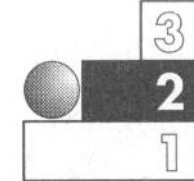

4. How many elements are reserved with the following statement?

```
int     ara[ 5 ][ 6 ];
```

5. Examine the following table of integers, called `ara`:

4	1	3	5	9
10	2	12	1	6
25	42	2	91	8

   What values do the following elements contain?

   A. `ara[ 2 ][ 2 ]`

   B. `ara[ 0 ][ 1 ]`

   C. `ara[ 2 ][ 3 ]`

   D. `ara[ 2 ][ 4 ]`

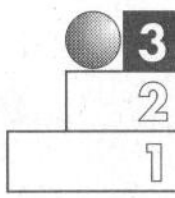

6. What control statement is best used for stepping through multidimensional arrays?

7. Consider this section of a program:

```
int     grades[ 3 ][ 5 ] = {80, 90, 96, 73, 65,
                            67, 90, 68, 92, 84,
                            70, 55, 95, 78, 100 };
```

What are the values of the following?

A. `grades[ 2 ][ 3 ]`

B. `grades[ 2 ][ 4 ]`

C. `grades[ 0 ][ 1 ]`

Review Exercises

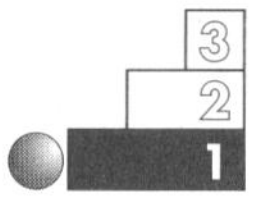

1. Write a program that stores and prints the numbers from 1 to 21 in a three-by-seven table. (HINT: Remember that C++ begins subscripts at 0.)
2. Write a program that reserves storage for three years' worth of sales data for five salespeople. Use assignment statements to fill the table with data and print it out, one value per line.

3. Instead of using assignment statements, use the `cin` function to fill the salespeople's data in the preceding exercise.
4. Write a program that tracks the grades for 5 classes, each having 10 students. Input the data, using the `cin` function. Print the table in its native row-and-column format.

27

Pointers

C++ reveals its true power through pointer variables. *Pointer variables* (or *pointers*, as they are generally called) are variables that contain addresses of other variables. All variables that you have seen so far have held data values. You understand that variables hold various data types: character, integer, floating-point, and so on. Pointer variables contain the location of regular data variables. In effect, a pointer variable *points* to the data because the variable holds the address of the data.

When first learning C++, students of the language tend to shy away from pointers, thinking that they will be difficult. But pointers don't have to be difficult. In fact, after you work with them for a while, you will think that pointers are easier to use than arrays (and much more flexible).

This chapter introduces the following topics:

- What pointers are
- Pointers of different data types
- The address-of (&) operator
- The dereferencing (*) operator
- Arrays of pointers

Pointers offer a highly efficient means of accessing and changing data. Because a pointer contains the actual address of data, your compiler has less work to do when finding that data in memory. Pointers do not have to link data to specific variable names. A pointer can point to an unnamed data value. With pointers, you gain a "different view" of your data.

Pointer Variables

Pointers are variables. They follow all the usual naming rules of regular, nonpointer variables. As with regular variables, you must declare pointer variables before you use them. There is a type of pointer for every data type in C++; there are integer pointers, character pointers, floating-point pointers, and so on. You can declare global pointers (although global pointers, as with regular variables, are not usually recommended) or local pointers, depending on where you declare them.

Pointers contain addresses of other variables.

About the only difference between pointer variables and regular variables is what they hold. Pointers do not contain data, but *addresses* of data. If you need a quick review of addresses and memory, see Appendix A.

C++ has two pointer operators:

```
&    The "address of" operator
*    The dereferencing operator
```

Don't let these operators throw you. You have seen them before! The `&` is the bitwise AND operator (see Chapter 13, "Bitwise Operators"), and the `*` means, of course, multiplication. These are called *overloaded* operators. They perform more than one function, depending on how you use them in your programs. C++ does not confuse `*` with multiplication when you use this symbol as a dereferencing operator with pointers.

Whenever you see `&` used with pointers, think of the phrase "address of." The `&` operator always produces the memory address of whatever it precedes. The `*` operator, when used with pointers, either declares a pointer or dereferences the pointer's value. The next sections explain these operators.

Declaring Pointers

Because you must declare all pointers before using them, the best way to begin learning about pointers is to see how to declare and define them. Actually, declaring pointers is almost as easy as declaring regular variables. After all, pointers are variables.

If you need to declare a variable that is to hold your age, you might use the following variable declaration:

```
int     age = 30;      // Declare a variable to hold my age
```

Declaring `age` like this does several things. Because C++ knows that you will need a variable called `age`, C++ reserves storage for that variable. C++ knows also that you will store only integers in `age`, not floating-point or double floating-point data. You also have requested that C++ store the value of 30 in `age` after it reserves storage for it.

Where did C++ store `age` in memory? You, as programmer, do not really care where C++ decided to store `age`. You do not need to know the variable's address because you will never refer to `age` by its address. If you want to calculate or print with `age`, you will call it by its name, `age`.

Suppose that you want to declare a pointer variable. This pointer variable will not hold your age but will *point* to `age`, the variable that holds your age. (Why you would want to do this will be made clear in this chapter and the next few chapters.) `p_age` might be a good name for this pointer variable. Figure 27.1 shows an illustration of what you want to do. It is assumed that C++ stored `age` at address 350,606, although your C++ compiler arbitrarily determines the address of `age`, and it could be anything.

TIP: Make your pointer variable names meaningful.

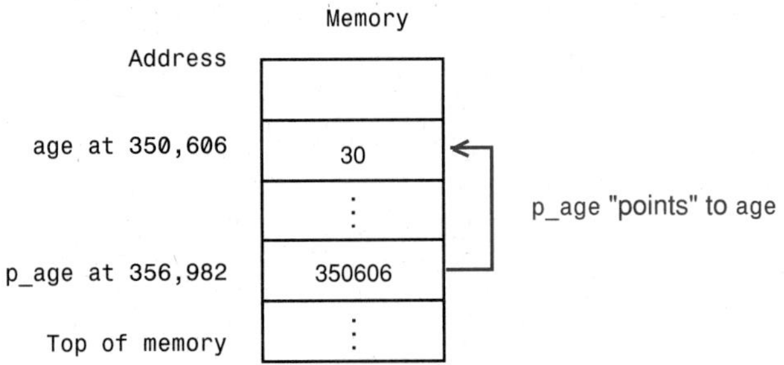

Figure 27.1. p_age contains the address of age; p_age points to the age variable.

The name p_age by itself has nothing to do with pointers except that it is the name selected for the pointer to age. p_age could just as easily be named house, x43344, space_trek, or whatever else you wanted to call it. You can name variables anything, as long as you follow the naming rules for variables. This reinforces the idea that a pointer is just a variable that you must reserve in your program. Make up meaningful variable names, even for pointer variables. p_age is a good name for a variable that points to age. The names ptr_age and ptr_to_age are appropriate too.

To declare the p_age pointer variable, you must do the following:

```
int     *p_age;      // Declare an integer pointer
```

As with the declaration for age, this line reserves a variable called p_age. It is not a normal integer variable, however. Because of the dereferencing operator, *, C++ knows that this is to be a pointer variable.

Remember that the * is *not* part of the variable name. When you later use p_age, you will not always prefix the name with the *, unless you are dereferencing it at the time (as later examples will show).

TIP: Whenever an * appears in a variable definition, the variable being declared is *always* a pointer variable.

Consider the declaration for p_age if the asterisk were not there; C++ would think that you were declaring a regular integer variable. The * is important because it tells C++ to interpret p_age as a pointer variable instead of as a normal, data variable.

Assigning Values to Pointers

Pointers point to data of their own type.

p_age is an integer pointer. This is very important. p_age can point only to integer values, never to floating-point values, double values, or even characters. If you needed to point to a floating-point variable, you might declare the pointer as

```
float     *point;     // Declare a floating-point pointer
```

As with any automatic variables, C++ does not initialize pointers when you declare them. If you declare p_age as previously described, and you want p_age to point to age, you have to explicitly assign p_age to the address of age:

```
p_age = &age;          // Assign the address of age to p_age
```

What value is now in p_age? You do not know exactly, but you do know that it is the address of age, wherever that is.

Instead of assigning the address of age to p_age with an assignment operator, you can declare and initialize pointers at the same time. The next two lines declare and initialize both age and p_age:

```
int      age = 30;          // Declare a regular integer
                            // variable, putting 30 in it
int      *p_age = &age;     // Declare an integer pointer,
                            // initializing it with the
                            // address of age
```

These two lines produce the variables described in Figure 27.1.

If you want to print the value of age, you can use the following cout:

```
cout << age;                // Print the value of age
```

Or you can print the value of age with this cout:

```
cout << *p_age;             // Dereference p_age
```

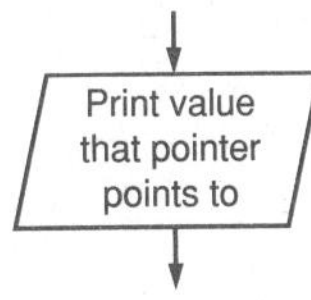

The dereferencing operator produces the value *where the pointer points to*. Without the `*`, the second `cout` would print an address (the address of `age`). The `*` means to print the value at that address.

You can assign `age` a different value with the following statement:

```
age = 41;            // Assign age a new value
```

Or you can assign `age` a value in this way:

```
*p_age = 41;
```

This line says, "Take the value being pointed to by `p_age` and assign it 41."

TIP: The `*` appears before a pointer variable in only two places: when you declare a pointer variable and when you dereference a pointer variable (to find the data it points to).

Pointers and Parameters

You may recall from Chapter 20, "Passing Values," that you can override C++'s normal default of passing by copy (also known as passing by value) by passing a variable preceded by an `&`, and putting an asterisk before the parameter everywhere it appears in the receiving function. The following function call passes `tries` by address to the receiving function called `pr_it()`:

```
pr_it(&tries);    // Pass integer tries to pr_it() by address
                  // (tries would normally pass by copy)
```

The function `pr_it()` receives the address of `tries`, in effect, receiving `tries` by address:

```
void     pr_it(int *tries)  // Receive tries by address
                            // (dereference its value)
    {
    *tries++;        // This changes tries in calling AND
                     // receiving functions.
    return;
    }
```

Now that you understand the & and * operators, you can understand the passing of nonarray parameters to functions by address. (Arrays default to passing by address without requiring that you use & and *.)

Examples

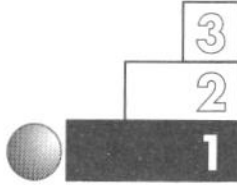

1. The following section of a program declares three regular variables of three different data types, as well as pointers that point to those variables:

```
char         initial= 'Q';  // Declare three regular
int          num = 40;      // variables of three
                            // different types
float    sales = 2321.59;

char         *p_initial = &initial;    // Declare three
int          *ptr_num = &num;          // pointers
float        *sales_add = &sales;
```

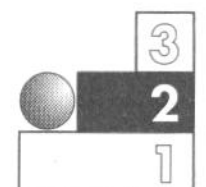

2. As with regular variables, you can initialize pointers with assignment statements. You do not have to initialize pointers when you declare them. The next few lines of code are equivalent to the code in the preceding example:

```
char         initial;     // Declare three regular variables
int          num;         // of three different types
float        sales;

char         *p_initial; // Declare three pointers but
int          *ptr_num;   // do not initialize them yet
float        *sales_add;

initial = 'Q';            // Initialize the regular
num = 40;                 // variables with values
sales = 2321.59;

p_initial = &initial;     // Initialize the pointers with
ptr_num = &num;           // the addresses of their
sales_add = &sales;       // corresponding variables
```

Notice that you do not put the * operator before the pointer variable names when assigning them values. You prefix a pointer variable with * only if you are dereferencing it.

NOTE: In this example, the pointer variables could have been assigned the addresses of the regular variables before they were assigned values. There would be no difference in the operation. The pointers are assigned the addresses of the regular variables no matter what data is in the regular variables.

Keep the data type of each pointer consistent. Do *not* assign a floating-point variable to an integer's address. For instance, you cannot make the assignment statement

```
p_initial = &sales;      // INVALID pointer assignment
```

because `p_initial` can point only to character data, not to floating-point data.

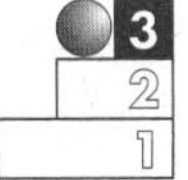

3. Examine the following program closely. It shows more about pointers and the pointer operators, & and *, than several pages of text could explain:

```
// Filename: C27POINT.CPP
// Demonstrates the use of pointer declarations and
// operators

#include <iostream.h>

main()
     {
     int     num = 123;        // A regular integer variable
     int     *p_num;           // Declare an integer pointer

     cout << "num is " << num << "\n";  // Print value of num
     cout << "The address of num is "
          << (unsigned long)&num << "\n";
```

```
p_num = &num;       // Put address of num in p_num,
                    // in effect, making p_num point
                    // to num (no * in front of p_num)
cout << "*p_num is " << *p_num << "\n"; // Print value
                                        // of num
cout << "p_num is " << (unsigned long)p_num << "\n";
                    // Print location of num
return 0;
}
```

Here is the output of this program:

```
num is 123
The address of num is 65522
*p_num is 123
p_num is 65522
```

If you run this program, you will probably get different results for the value of `p_num`, because your compiler will place `num` at a different location, depending on your memory setup. The actual address is moot, though. Because the pointer `p_num` will always contain the address of `num`, and because you can dereference `p_num` to get `num`'s value, the actual address is not critical.

4. The following program includes a function that swaps the values of any two integers passed to it. You may recall that a function can return only a single value. Therefore, you could not write, before now, a function that changed two different values and returned both values to the calling function.

   To swap two variables (reversing their values for sorting as you saw in Chapter 25, "Array Processing"), you need the ability to pass both variables by address. Then, when the function reverses the variables, the calling function's variables will also be swapped.

   Notice the function's use of dereferencing operators before each occurrence of `num1` and `num2`. You don't care which addresses `num1` and `num2` are stored at, but you have to make sure that you dereference whatever addresses were passed to the function.

Be sure to pass arguments with the prefix `&` to functions that receive by address, as shown here in `main()`.

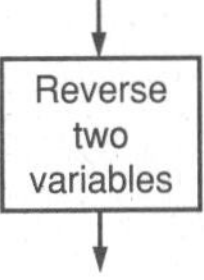


```
// Filename: C27SWAP.CPP
// Program that includes a function which swaps any two
// integers passed to it

#include <iostream.h>

void     swap_them(int *num1, int *num2)
     {
     int     temp;       // Variable that holds in-between
                         // swapped value

     temp = *num1;       // The asterisks ensure that the
                         // calling function's variables are
                         // ones worked on in this function
                         // and not copies of them.
     *num1 = *num2;
     *num2 = temp;
     return;
     }


int     main(void)
     {
     int i = 10, j = 20;

     cout << "\n\nBefore swap, i is " << i
          << " and j is " << j << "\n\n";
     swap_them(&i, &j);
     cout << "\n\nAfter swap, i is " << i
          << " and j is " << j << "\n\n";
     return 0;
     }
```

Arrays of Pointers

If you need to reserve many pointers for many different values, you might want to declare an *array of pointers*. You know that you can reserve an array of characters, integers, long integers, and floating-point values, as well as an array of every other data type available. You can also reserve an array of pointers, with each pointer being a pointer to a specific data type.

The following line reserves an array of 10 integer pointer variables:

```
int     *iptr[ 10 ];    // Reserve an array of 10 integer
                        // pointers
```

Figure 27.2 shows how C++ views this array. Each element holds an address (after being assigned values) that *points* to other values in memory. Each value pointed to must be an integer. You can assign an element from `iptr` an address, just as you would for nonarray pointer variables. You can make `iptr[ 4 ]` point to the address of an integer variable named `age` by assigning it, as shown here:

```
iptr[ 4 ] = &age;  // Make iptr[ 4 ] point to address of age
```

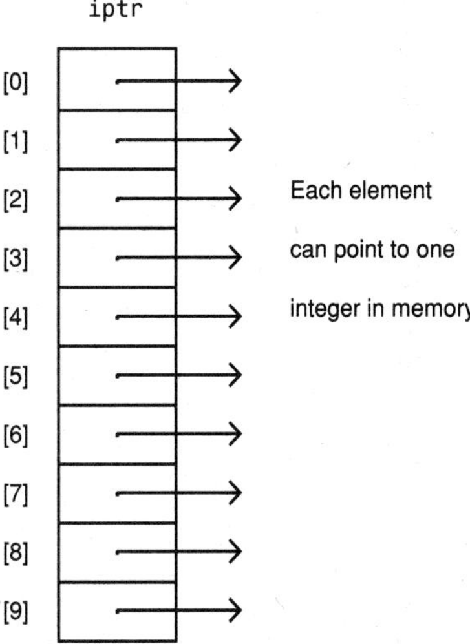

Figure 27.2. An array of 10 integer pointers.

The following line reserves an array of 20 character pointer variables:

```
char     *cpoint[ 20 ];     // Array of 20 character pointers
```

Again, the asterisk is not part of the array name. The asterisk serves to let C++ know that this is an array of character pointers and not just an array of characters.

Some beginning C++ students start getting confused when they see such a declaration. Pointers are one thing, but reserving storage for arrays of pointers tends to bog down students. Reserving storage for arrays of pointers is easy to understand. Take away the asterisk from the last declaration, as in

```
char     cpoint[ 20 ];
```

and what do you have? You have just reserved a simple array of 20 characters. Adding the asterisk informs C++ to go one step further: instead of wanting an array of character variables, you want an array of character-pointing variables. Instead of each element being a character variable, each element holds an address that points to characters.

Reserving arrays of pointers will be much more meaningful when you learn about structures in the next few chapters. As with regular, nonpointer variables, an array makes processing several variables much easier. You can use a subscript to reference each variable (element) without having to use a different variable name for each value.

Summary

Declaring and using pointers may seem like a lot of trouble at this point. Why assign `*p_num` a value when it is easier (and clearer) to assign a value directly to `num`? If you are asking yourself (and this book!) that question, you probably understand everything you should from this chapter, and you are ready to begin seeing the true power of pointers: combining array processing and pointers.

Review Questions

Answers to Review Questions are in Appendix B.

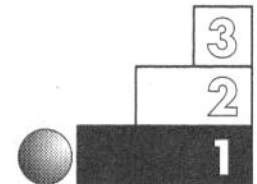

1. What kind of variable is reserved in each of the following?

   A. `int      *a;`

   B. `char     *cp;`

   C. `float    *dp;`

2. What words should spring to mind when you see the `&` operator?

3. What is the dereferencing operator?

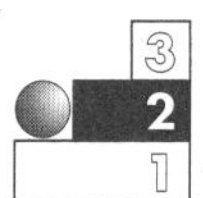

4. How would you assign the address of the floating-point variable `salary` to a pointer called `pt_sal`?

5. True or false: You must define a pointer with an initial value when declaring it.

6. Examine the following two sections of code:

```
int      i;
int      *pti;
i = 56;
pti = &i;

int      i;
int      *pti;
pti = &i;      // These two lines are reversed from the
i = 56;        // preceding example.
```

   Is the value of `pti` the same after the fourth line of each section?

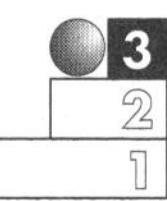

7. Now look at this section of code:

```
float     pay;
float     *ptr_pay;
pay = 2313.54;
ptr_pay = &pay;
```

   What is the value of each of the following (answer "Invalid" if it cannot be determined)?

A. `pay`

B. `*ptr_pay`

C. `*pay`

D. `&pay`

8. What does the following declare?

```
double     *ara[ 4 ][ 6 ];
```

A. An array of double floating-point values

B. An array of double floating-point pointer variables

C. An invalid declaration statement

NOTE: Because this is a theory-oriented chapter, exercises are saved until you master the next chapter, "Pointers and Arrays."

28

Pointers and Arrays

Arrays and pointers are closely related in the C++ programming language. You can address arrays as if they were pointers, and pointers as if they were arrays. Being able to store and access pointers and arrays means that you can store strings of data in array elements. Without pointers, you could not do this because there is no fundamental string data type in C++; there are no string variables, only string constants.

This chapter introduces the following topics:

- Array names and pointers
- Character pointers
- Pointer arithmetic
- Ragged-edge arrays of string data

You will use the concepts presented here for much of your future programming in C++. Pointer manipulation is very important to the C++ programming language.

Array Names as Pointers

An array name is just a pointer, nothing more. Suppose that you have the following array declaration:

```
int      ara[ 5 ] =
     { 10, 20, 30, 40, 50 };
```

If you printed ara[0], you would see 10. By now, you fully understand and expect this value to appear.

An array name is a pointer.

But what if you were to print *ara? Would that print anything? If so, what? If you thought that an error would print because ara is not a pointer but an array, you would be wrong. An array name is a pointer. If you print *ara, you would also see 10.

Recall how arrays are stored in memory. Figure 28.1 reviews how ara is mapped in memory. The array name, ara, is nothing more than a pointer that points to the first element of the array. If you dereference that pointer, you dereference the value stored at the first element of the array, which is 10. Dereferencing ara is exactly the same thing as referring to ara[0] because both produce the same value.

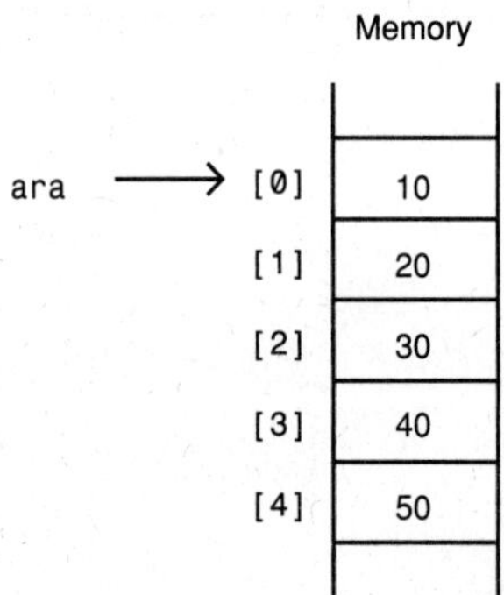

Figure 28.1. Storing the array ara in memory.

You now see that you can reference an array with subscripts or with pointer dereferencing. Can you use pointer notation to print the third element of ara? Yes, and you already have the tools to do so.

The following cout prints ara[2] (the third element of ara) without using a subscript:

```
cout << *(ara + 2);      // Print ara[ 2 ]
```

The expression *(ara + 2) is not vague at all, as long as you remember that an array name is just a pointer that always points to the array's first element. *(ara + 2) takes the address stored in ara, adds 2 to the address, and dereferences *that* location. All the following hold true:

ara + 0 points to ara[0]

ara + 1 points to ara[1]

ara + 2 points to ara[2]

ara + 3 points to ara[3]

ara + 4 points to ara[4]

Therefore, to print, store, or calculate with an array element, you can use either subscript notation or pointer notation. Because an array name contains the address of the array's first element, you must dereference the pointer to get the element's value.

Internal Locations

C++ knows the internal data-size requirements of characters, integers, floating-points, and the other data types on your computer. Therefore, because ara is an integer array and each element in an integer array consumes two bytes of storage, C++ adds 2 or 4 to the address if you reference arrays as just shown.

Even though you may write *(ara + 3) to refer to ara[3], C++ really adds 6 to the address of ara to get the third element. C++ does not add an actual 3. You don't have to worry about this because C++ handles these internals. When you write *(ara + 3), you are actually requesting that C++ add 3 integer addresses to the address of ara. If ara were a floating-point array, C++ would add 3 floating-point addresses to ara.

Pointer Advantages

An array name is a pointer constant.

Although arrays are really pointers in disguise, they are special types of pointers. An array name is a *pointer constant*, not a pointer variable. You cannot change the value of an array name because you cannot change constants. This explains why you cannot assign an array new values during a program's execution. For instance, even if `cname` is a character array, the following is not valid in C++:

```
cname = "Christine Chambers";     // INVALID array assignment
```

The array name, `cname`, cannot be changed because it is a constant. You would not attempt

```
5 = 4 + 8 * 2;                    // INVALID assignment
```

because you cannot change the constant `5` to any other value. C++ knows that you cannot assign anything to `5`, and will give you an error if you attempt to change `5`. C++ knows also that an array name is a constant and that you cannot change an array to another value. You can assign values to an array only at declaration time, one element at a time during execution, or by using functions such as `strcpy()`.

The most important reason to learn pointers is this: pointers (except arrays referenced as pointers) are variables. You *can* change a pointer variable, which makes processing virtually any data, including arrays, much more powerful and flexible.

Examples

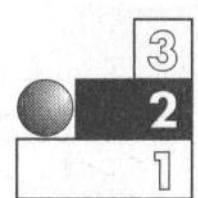

1. By changing pointers, you make them point to different values in memory. The following program shows how to change pointers. The program first defines two floating-point values. A floating-point pointer points to the first variable, `v1`, and is used in the `cout`. The pointer is then changed so that it points to the second floating-point variable, `v2`.

```
// C28PTRCH.CPP
// Changes the value of a pointer variable
```

```
#include <iostream.h>

main()
     {
     float     v1 = 676.54;      // Define 2 floating-point
                                 // variables
     float     v2 = 900.18;
     float     *p_v;       // Define a floating-point pointer

     p_v = &v1;                  // Make pointer point to v1
     cout << "The first value is " << *p_v << "\n";
          // Print 676.54
     p_v = &v2;      // Change the pointer so it points to v2
     cout << "The second value is " << *p_v << "\n";
          // Print 900.18
     return 0;
     }
```

Because they are able to change pointers, most C++ programmers use pointers instead of arrays. Sometimes, because arrays are easy to declare, programmers declare arrays and then use pointers to reference those arrays. If the array data changes, the pointer helps to change it.

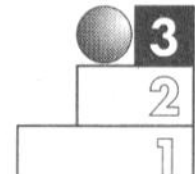

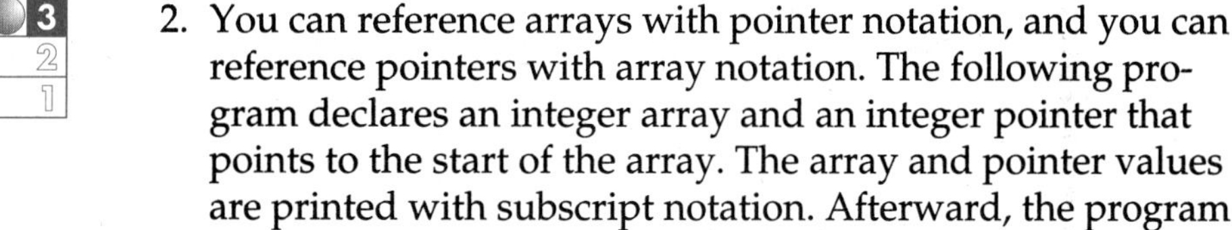

2. You can reference arrays with pointer notation, and you can reference pointers with array notation. The following program declares an integer array and an integer pointer that points to the start of the array. The array and pointer values are printed with subscript notation. Afterward, the program uses array notation to print the array and pointer values.

   Study this program carefully. You will see the inner workings of arrays and pointer notation.

```
// Filename: C28ARPTR.CPP
// References arrays like pointers and references pointers
// like arrays

#include <iostream.h>

main()
     {
```

```
int     ctr;
int     iara[ 5 ] =
     { 10, 20, 30, 40, 50 };
int     *iptr;

iptr = iara; // Make iptr point to array's first element
// This would also work: iptr = &iara[ 0 ];
cout << "Using array subscripts:\n";
cout << "iara\tiptr\n";
for (ctr = 0; ctr < 5; ctr++)
     cout << iara[ ctr ] << "\t" << iptr[ ctr ] << "\n";
cout << "\nUsing pointer notation:\n";
cout << "iara\tiptr\n";
for (ctr = 0; ctr < 5; ctr++)
     cout << *(iara + ctr) << "\t"
          << *(iptr + ctr) << "\n";
return 0;
}
```

This program's output is shown here:

```
Using array subscripts:
iara    iptr
10      10
20      20
30      30
40      40
50      50

Using pointer notation:
iara    iptr
10      10
20      20
30      30
40      40
50      50
```

Using Character Pointers

The ability to change pointers is useful when you are working with character strings in memory. You have the ability to store strings in character arrays or to point to strings with character pointers. Consider the following two string definitions:

```
char      cara[ ] = "C++ is fun";      // An array holding
                                       // a string
char      *cptr = "C++ By Example";    // A pointer to
                                       // the string
```

A character pointer can point to the first character of a string.

Figure 28.2 shows how C++ stores these two strings in memory. C++ stores them basically the same way. You are familiar with the array definition. When assigning a string to a character pointer, C++ finds enough free memory to hold the string, and assigns the address of the first character to the pointer. Apart from the changeability of the two pointers (the array name and the character pointers), the preceding two string definition statements do exactly the same thing.

Because `cout` prints strings, starting at the array or pointer name until the null zero is reached, you can print each of these strings with the following `cout` statements:

```
cout << "String 1: " << cara << "\n";
cout << "String 2: " << cptr << "\n";
```

Notice that you print strings in arrays and strings pointed to in the same way. Up to this point, you may have wondered what advantage one method of storing strings has over the other. The seemingly minor difference between these stored strings makes a big difference when you change them.

Suppose that you want to store the string `Hello` in the two strings. You *cannot* assign the string to the array in this way:

```
cara = "Hello";      // INVALID
```

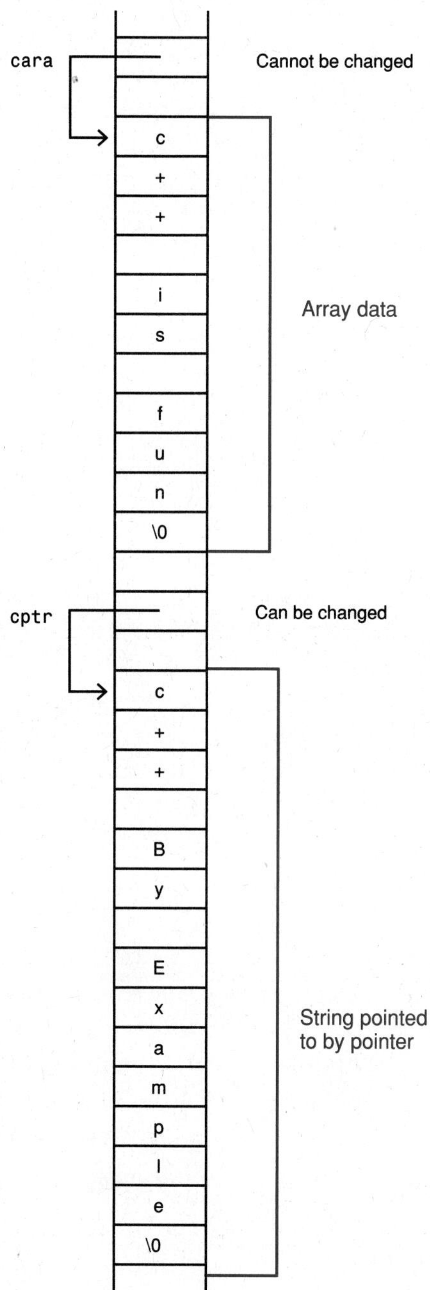

Figure 28.2. **Storing two strings as arrays.**

Because you cannot change the array name, you cannot assign it a new value. The only way to change the contents of the array is to assign characters from the string to the array, one element at a time, or to use a built-in function such as `strcpy()`. You can, however, make the character pointer point to the new string, as in

```
cptr = "Hello";       // Change the pointer so that it points
                      // to the new string
```

TIP: If you want to store user input in a string, pointed to by a pointer, you first must reserve enough storage for that input string. The easiest way to do this is to reserve a character array and then assign a character pointer to the beginning element of that array, like this:

```
char     input[ 81 ];    // Holds a string as long as
                         // 80 characters
char *iptr = input;      // Could also have done this:
                         // char *iptr = &input[ 0 ];
```

Now you can input a string by using the pointer, as in

```
cin >> iptr;             // Make sure that iptr points
                         // to the string typed by user
```

You can use pointer manipulation, arithmetic, and modification on the input string.

Examples

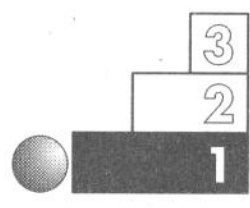

1. Suppose that you want to store your sister's full name and then print it. Instead of using arrays, you can use a character pointer. The following program does just that:

```
// Filename: C28CP1.CPP
// Stores a name in a character pointer
```

```
#include <iostream.h>

main()
     {
     char     *c = "Bettye Lou Horn";

     cout << "My sister's name is " << c << "\n";
     return 0;
     }
```

This program prints the following:

```
My sister's name is Bettye Lou Horn
```

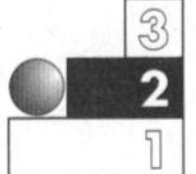

2. Now suppose that you need to change a string pointed to by a character pointer. If your sister married, changing her last name to Henderson, your program can show both strings:

```
// Filename: C28CP2.CPP
// Illustrates changing a character string

#include <iostream.h>

main()
     {
     char     *c = "Bettye Lou Horn";

     cout << "My sister's maiden name was " << c << "\n";
     c = "Bettye Lou Henderson";    // Assign new string to c
     cout << "My sister's married name is " << c << "\n";
     return 0;
     }
```

Here is the output:

```
My sister's maiden name was Bettye Lou Horn
My sister's married name is Bettye Lou Henderson
```

3. Do not use character pointers to change string constants. This can confuse the compiler, and you will probably not get the results you expect. The following program is similar to

those you just saw. Instead of making the character pointer point to a new string, this example attempts to change the contents of the original string.

```
// Filename: C28CP3.CPP
// Illustrates changing a character string improperly

#include <iostream.h>

main()
     {
     char     *c = "Bettye Lou Horn";

     cout << "My sister's maiden name was " << c << "\n";
     c += 11;     // Make c point to the last name
                  // (the 12th character)
     c = "Henderson";     // Assign new string to c
     cout << "My sister's married name is " << c << "\n";
     return 0;
     }
```

The program seems to change the last name from `Horn` to `Henderson`, but it does not. Here is the output of this program:

```
My sister's maiden name was Bettye Lou Horn
My sister's married name is Henderson
```

Why didn't the full string print? Because the address pointed to by `c` was incremented by 11, `c` still points to `Henderson`, so that was all that printed.

4. You might guess at a way to fix the preceding program. Instead of printing the string stored at `c` after assigning it to `Henderson`, you might want to decrement it by 11 so that it points to its original location, the start of the name. The code to do this is shown here, but it does not work as expected. Study the program before reading the explanation.

```
// Filename: C28CP4.CPP
// Illustrates changing a character string improperly

#include <iostream.h>
```

```
main()
     {
     char      *c = "Bettye Lou Horn";

     cout << "My sister's maiden name was " << c << "\n";
     c += 11;       // Make c point to the last name
                    // (the 12th character)
     c = "Henderson";      // Assign new string to c
     c -= 11;       // Make c point to its
                    // original location (???)
     cout << "My sister's married name is " << c << "\n";
     return 0;
     }
```

This program will produce garbage at the second `cout`. There are actually two string constants in this program. When you first assign `c` to `Bettye Lou Horn`, C++ reserves space in memory for the constant string and puts the starting address of the string in `c`.

When the program then assigns `c` to `Henderson`, C++ finds room for *another* character constant, as shown in Figure 28.3. If you subtract 11 from the location of `c`, after it points to the new string `Henderson`, `c` points to an area of memory that is not used by your program. There is no guarantee that printable data appears before the string constant `Henderson`. If you want to manipulate parts of the string, you will have to do so an element at a time, just as you would with arrays.

Pointer Arithmetic

You saw an example of pointer arithmetic when you accessed array elements with pointer notation. By now, you should be comfortable with the fact that both of these array/pointer references are identical:

```
ara[ sub ]
*(ara + sub)
```

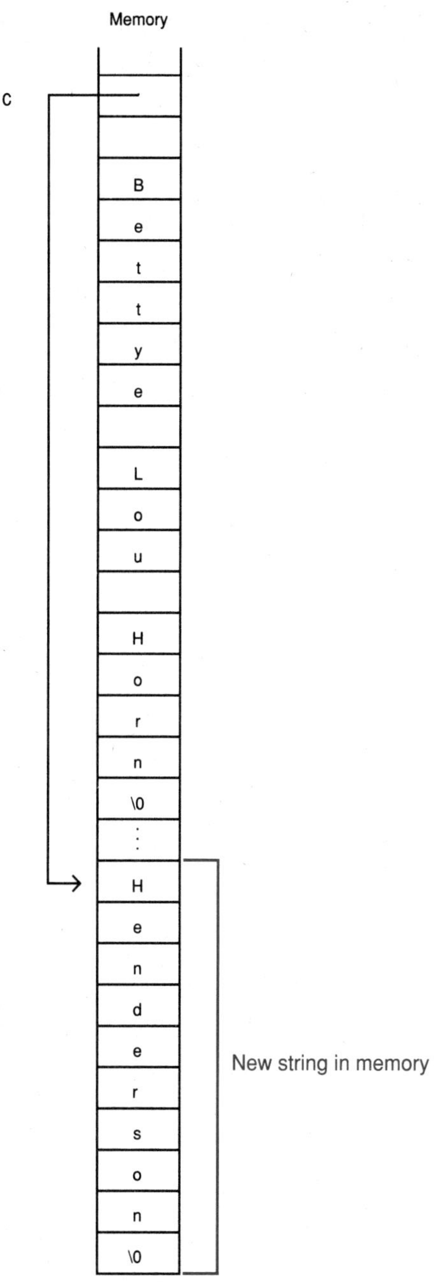

Figure 28.3. Two string constants appear in memory because two string constants are used in the program.

You can increment or decrement a pointer. If you increment a pointer, the address inside the pointer variable increments. The pointer does not always increment by 1, however.

Suppose that f_ptr is a floating-point pointer that points to the first element of an array of floating-point numbers. f_ptr might be initialized like this:

```
float     fara[ ] =
     { 100.5, 201.45, 321.54, 389.76, 691.34 };
f_ptr = fara;
```

Figure 28.4 shows what these variables look like in memory. Each floating-point value in this example takes four bytes of memory.

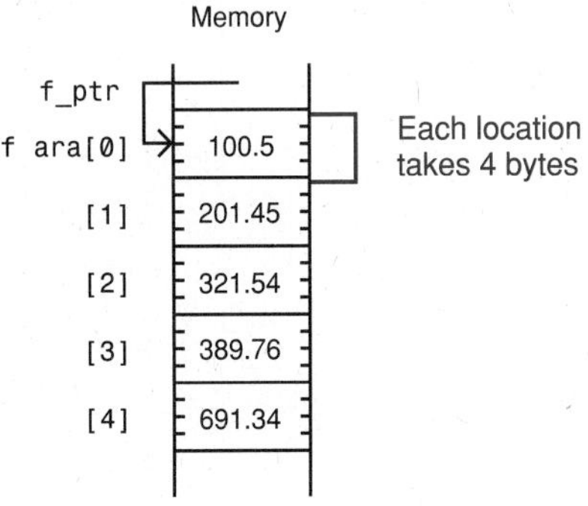

Figure 28.4. A floating-point array and a pointer.

If you print the value of *f_ptr, you will see 100.5. Suppose that you incremented f_ptr by one with the following statement:

```
f_ptr++;
```

Incrementing a pointer may add more than one byte to the pointer.

C++ does *not* add 1 to the address in f_ptr even though it seems as though 1 should be added. In this case, because floating-point values take four bytes each on this machine, C++ adds 4 to f_ptr. How does C++ know how many bytes to add to f_ptr? C++ knows from the pointer's declaration how many bytes of memory pointers take. This is why the data type of pointers is so important.

After incrementing f_ptr, if you were to print *f_ptr, you would see 201.45, the second element in the array. If C++ added only 1 to the address in `f_ptr`, `f_ptr` would point only to the second byte of `100.5`. This would print garbage to the screen.

> **NOTE:** When you increment a pointer, C++ adds one data type size (in bytes) to the pointer, not 1. When you decrement a pointer, C++ subtracts one data type size (in bytes) from the pointer.

Examples

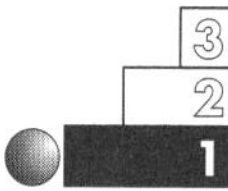

1. The following program defines an array with five values. An integer pointer is then initialized to point to the first element in the array. The rest of the program prints the dereferenced value of the pointer and then increments the pointer so that it points to the next integer in the array.

   So that you can see what is going on, the size of integer values is printed at the bottom of the program. Because integers take two bytes, C++ increments the pointer by 2 in order to point to the next integer. (The integers are two bytes apart from each other.)

```
// Filename: C28PTI.CPP
// Increments a pointer through an integer array

#include <iostream.h>

main()
     {
     int      iara[ ] =
          { 10, 20, 30, 40, 50 };
     int      *ip = iara;      // The pointer points to
                               // the start of the array

     cout << *ip << "\n";
     ip++;      // 2 is actually added
     cout << *ip << "\n";
     ip++;      // 2 is actually added
     cout << *ip << "\n";
```

```
     ip++;      // 2 is actually added
     cout << *ip << "\n";
     ip++;      // 2 is actually added
     cout << *ip << "\n\n";
     cout << "The integer size is " << sizeof(int)
          << " bytes on this machine";
     return 0;
     }
```

Here is the output of this program:

```
10
20
30
40
50
The integer size is 2 bytes on this machine
```

2. Here is the same program, but using a character array and a character pointer. Because a character takes only one byte of storage, incrementing a character pointer actually adds just 1 to the pointer; only 1 is needed since the characters are just one byte apart from each other.

```
// Filename: C28PTC.CPP
// Increments a pointer through a character array

#include <iostream.h>

main()
     {
     char     cara[ ] =
          { 'a', 'b', 'c', 'd', 'e' };
     char *cp = cara;     // The pointer points to
                          // the start of the array

     cout << *cp << "\n";
     cp++;      // 1 is actually added
     cout << *cp << "\n";
     cp++;      // 1 is actually added
     cout << *cp << "\n";
     cp++;      // 1 is actually added
```

```
     cout << *cp << "\n";
     cp++;     // 1 is actually added
     cout << *cp << "\n\n";
     cout << "The character size is " << sizeof(char)
          << " byte on this machine";
     return 0;
     }
```

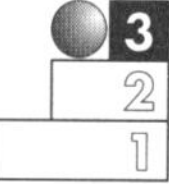

3. The following program shows the many ways you can add to, subtract from, and reference arrays and pointers. The program defines a floating-point array and a floating-point pointer. The body of the program prints the values from the array, using array and pointer notation.

```
// Filename: C28ARPT2.CPP
// Comprehensive reference of arrays and pointers

#include <iostream.h>

main()
     {
     float     ara[ ] =
          { 100.0, 200.0, 300.0, 400.0, 500.0 };
     float     *fptr;     // Floating-point pointer

     // Make pointer point to array's first value
     fptr = &ara[ 0 ];     // Could also have been this:
                           // fptr = ara;

     cout << *fptr << "\n";     // Print 100.0
     fptr++;     // Point to NEXT floating-point value
     cout << *fptr << "\n";     // Print 200.0
     fptr++;     // Point to NEXT floating-point value
     cout << *fptr << "\n";     // Print 300.0
     fptr++;     // Point to NEXT floating-point value
     cout << *fptr << "\n";     // Print 400.0
     fptr++;     // Point to NEXT floating-point value
     cout << *fptr << "\n";     // Print 500.0
     fptr = ara;     // Point back to first element again
     cout << *(fptr + 2) << "\n";  // Print 300.00 but do
                                   // NOT change fptr
     // Reference both array and pointer using subscripts
```

```
cout << (fptr + 0)[ 0 ] << "  " << (ara + 0)[ 0 ]
     << "\n"; // 100.0  100.0
cout << (fptr + 1)[ 0 ] << "  " << (ara + 1)[ 0 ]
     << "\n"; // 200.0  200.0
cout << (fptr + 4)[ 0 ] << "  " << (ara + 4)[ 0 ]
     << "\n"; // 500.0  500.0
// Reference both array and pointer, using subscripts
// Notice that subscripts are based from addresses that
// begin before the data in the array and pointer.
cout << (fptr - 1)[ 2 ] << "  " << (ara - 1)[ 2 ]
     << "\n"; // 200.0  200.0
cout << (fptr - 20)[ 23 ] << "  " << (ara - 20)[ 23 ]
     << "\n"; // 400.0  400.0
return 0;
}
```

Here is this program's output:

```
100.0
200.0
300.0
400.0
500.0
300.0
100.0  100.0
200.0  200.0
500.0  500.0
200.0  200.0
400.0  400.0
```

Arrays of Strings

You are now ready for one of the most useful applications of character pointers: storing arrays of strings. Actually, you cannot store an array of strings, but you can store an array of character pointers, and each character pointer can point to a string in memory.

An array of character pointers defines a ragged-edge array.

By defining an array of character pointers, you define a *ragged-edge array*. This array is similar to a two-dimensional table, with one exception: instead of each row being the same length (the same number of elements), each row contains a different number of characters.

The words *ragged-edge* derive from word processing. A word processor can typically print text fully justified or with a ragged-right margin. The columns in a newspaper are fully justified because both the left and the right columns align evenly. Letters you write by hand or type on typewriters (remember what a typewriter is?) generally have ragged-right margins. It is very difficult to type so that each line ends in exactly the same column on the right.

All two-dimensional tables you have seen so far have been the fully justified kind. For example, if you declared a character table with 5 rows and 20 columns, each row contains the same number of characters. You could define the table with the following statement:

```
char     names[ 5 ][ 20 ] =
     {
          { "George" },
          { "Michelle" },
          { "Joe" },
          { "Marcus" },
          { "Stephanie" }

     };
```

This table is shown in Figure 28.5. Notice that much of the table is wasted space. Each row takes 20 characters, even though the data in each row has far fewer characters. The unfilled elements contain null zeros because C++ zeros-out all elements you do not initialize in arrays. This type of table uses too much memory.

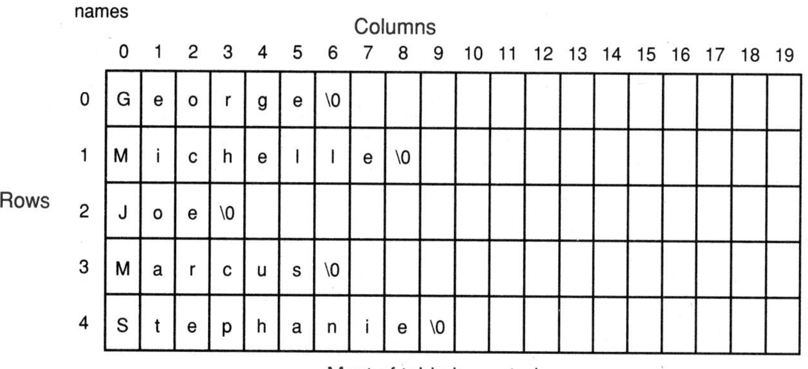

Figure 28.5. A fully justified table.

To fix the memory-wasting problem of fully justified tables, you should declare a single-dimensional array of character pointers. Each pointer points to a string in memory, and the strings do *not* have to be the same length.

Here is the definition for such an array:

```
char *names[ 5 ] =
     {
          { "George" },
          { "Michelle" },
          { "Joe" },
          { "Marcus" },
          { "Stephanie" }

     };
```

This array is single-dimensional. The definition should not confuse you, although it is something you have not seen. The asterisk before `names` makes this an array of pointers. The type of pointers is character. The strings are *not* being assigned to the array elements, but they are being *pointed to* by the array elements. Figure 28.6 shows this array of pointers. The strings are stored elsewhere in memory. Their actual locations are not critical because each pointer points to the starting character. The strings waste no data; each string takes only as much memory as needed by the string and its terminating zero. This gives the data its ragged-right appearance.

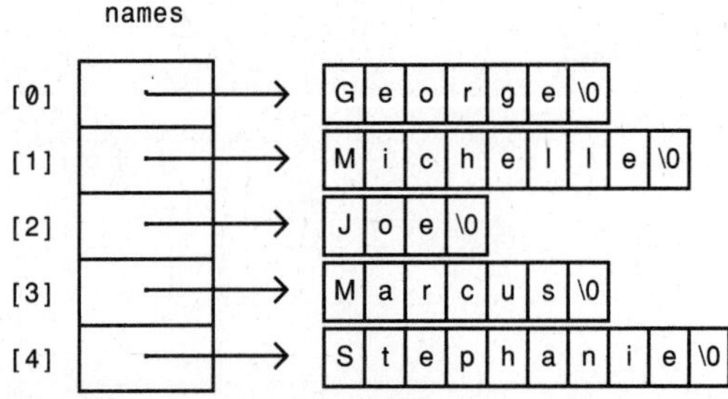

Figure 28.6. The array that points to each of the five strings.

To print the first string, you use the following `cout`:

```
cout << *names;          // Print George
```

To print the second string, you use this `cout`:

```
cout << *(names + 1);      // Print Michelle
```

Whenever you dereference any pointer element, using the `*` dereferencing operator, you access one of the strings in the array. You can use a dereferenced element anywhere you use a string constant or character array (with `strcpy()`, `strcmp()`, and so on).

> **TIP:** Working with pointers to strings is *much* more efficient than working with the strings. For instance, it takes a lot of time to sort a list of strings if they are stored as a fully justified table. It is much faster to sort strings pointed to by a pointer array. You just swap pointers during the sort, not entire strings.

Examples

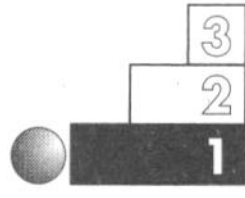

1. Here is a full program that uses the pointer array with five names. The `for` loop controls the `cout` function, printing each name in the string data. You can now see why learning about pointer notation for arrays pays off!

```
// Filename: C28PTST1.CPP
// Prints strings pointed to by an array

#include <iostream.h>

main()
     {
     char      *name[ 5 ] =
          {
               { "George" },   // Define a ragged-edge array
               { "Michelle" }, // of pointers to strings
               { "Joe" },
               { "Marcus" },
               { "Stephanie" }
          };
     int      ctr;

     for (ctr = 0; ctr < 5; ctr++)
```

```
          cout << "String #" << ctr + 1 << " is "
          << *(name + ctr) << "\n";
     return 0;
     }
```

The output of this program is shown here:

```
String #1 is George
String #2 is Michelle
String #3 is Joe
String #4 is Marcus
String #5 is Stephanie
```

2. The following program stores the days of the week in an array. When the user types a number from 1 to 7, the day of the week that matches that number (with Sunday being 1) is displayed. The program dereferences the pointer that points to that string.

BEGIN

Initialize days of week in array

Get day number from user

Print day of week

END

```
// Filename: C28PTST2.CPP
// Prints the day of the week based on an input value

#include <iostream.h>

main()
     {
     char      *days[ ] =
          {
          "Sunday",      // The seven separate sets
          "Monday",      // of braces are optional.
          "Tuesday",
          "Wednesday",
          "Thursday",
          "Friday",
          "Saturday"
          };
     int     day_num;

     do
          {
          cout << "What is a day number (from 1 to 7)? ";
          cin >> day_num;
          }
```

```
while ((day_num < 1) || (day_num > 7));
     // Ensure accurate number
day_num--;      // Adjust for subscript
cout << "The day is " << *(days + day_num) << "\n";
return 0;
}
```

Summary

You deserve a break! You now understand the foundation of C++'s pointers and array notation. Once you master this material, you are on your way to thinking in C++ as you design your programs. C++ programmers know that C++'s arrays are pointers in disguise, and program them accordingly.

Using ragged-edge arrays offers two advantages. You can hold arrays of string data without wasting extra space, and you can quickly change the pointers without having to move the string data around in memory.

As you progress into advanced C++ concepts, you will appreciate the time you spend on pointer notation. The next chapter introduces a new topic, *structures*. Structures let you store data in a more unified way than simple variables allow.

Review Questions

Answers to Review Questions are in Appendix B.

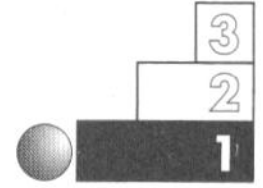

1. What is the difference between an array name and a pointer?
2. Assume that `ipointer` points to integers that take two bytes of memory. If you performed the statement

   ```
   ipointer += 2;
   ```

   how many bytes are added to `ipointer`?

3. Which of the following items are equivalent, assuming that `iary` is an integer array and that `iptr` is an integer pointer that points to the start of the array?

A. `iary` and `iptr`

B. `iary[ 1 ]` and `iptr + 1`

C. `iary[ 3 ]` and `*(iptr + 3)`

D. `(iary - 4)[ 9 ]` and `iary[ 5 ]`

E. `*iary` and `iary[ 0 ]`

F. `iary[ 4 ]` and `*iptr + 4`

4. Why is it more efficient to sort a ragged-edge character array than a fully justified string array?

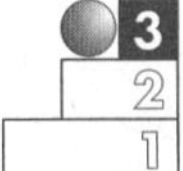

5. Look at the following array and pointer definition:

```
int      ara[ ] =
     { 1, 2, 3, 4, 5, 6, 7, 8, 9, 10 };
int      *ip1, *ip2;
```

Which of the following are allowed?

A. `ip1 = ara;`

B. `ip2 = ip1 = &ara[ 3 ];`

C. `ara = 15;`

D. `*(ip2 + 2) = 15; // Assuming ip2 and ara are equal`

Review Exercises

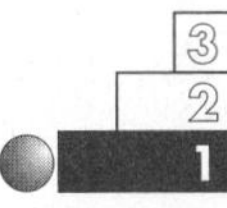

1. Write a program to store the names of your family members in a character array of pointers. Print the names.

2. Write a program that asks the user for 15 daily stock market averages and stores those averages in a floating-point array. Using only pointer notation, print the array forward and backward. Using only pointer notation, print the highest and lowest stock market quotes in the list.

3. Modify the bubble sort shown in Chapter 25, "Array Processing," so that it sorts with pointer notation. Add this

bubble sort to the program in exercise 2, printing the stock market averages in ascending order.

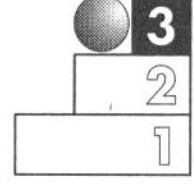

4. Write a program that requests 10 song titles from the user. Store the titles in an array of character pointers (a ragged-edge array). Print the original titles, print the alphabetized titles, and print the titles in reverse alphabetic order (from Z to A).

Part VII

Data Structures

29

Structures

Structures give you the ability to group data together but work with that data as a whole. Business data processing uses the concepts of structures in almost every program. Being able to manipulate several variables as a single group makes programs easier to manage.

This chapter introduces the following topics:

- Structure definitions
- Initializing structures
- The dot operator (.)
- Structure assignment
- Nested structures

This is one of the last chapters to present new concepts. The rest of the book builds on the structure concepts you learn in this chapter.

Structure Variables

Structures can have members of different data types.

A *structure* is a collection of one or more variable types. As you know, the elements in an array must be the same data type, and you must refer to the entire array by its name. Each element (called a *member*) in a structure can be a different data type.

Suppose that you want to use a structure to keep track of your CD music collection. You might want to track the following pieces of information about each CD:

Title
Artist
Number of songs
Cost
Date bought

This CD structure would have five members.

TIP: If you have programmed in other computer languages or used a database program, C++ structures are analogous to file records, and members are analagous to fields in those records.

After deciding on the members, you must decide what data types to use for the members. Both the title and the artist can be character arrays, the number of songs can be an integer, the cost can be a floating-point value, and the date can be another character array. This information is represented here:

Member Name	*Data Type*
Title	Character array of 25 characters
Artist	Character array of 20 characters
Number of songs	Integer
Cost	Floating-point
Date bought	Character array of 8 characters

A structure tag is a label for the structure's format.

Each structure you define can have an associated structure name, called a *structure tag*. Structure tags are not required in most cases, but generally it is best to define one for each structure in your program. The structure tag is *not* a variable name. Unlike array names that reference arrays as variables, a structure tag is just a label for the structure's format.

You name structure tags yourself, using the naming rules of variables. If you give the CD structure a structure tag named `cd_collection`, you are telling C++ that the tag called `cd_collection` looks like two character arrays, followed by an integer, a floating-point value, and a final character array.

A structure tag is actually a newly defined data type that you, the programmer, define. When you want to store an integer, you do not have to define to C++ what an integer is. C++ already knows. However, when you want to store a CD collection's data, C++ does not know what format your CD collection will take. You have to tell C++ (using the example described here) that you need a new data type. That data type will be your structure tag called `cd_collection`, and it will look like the structure just described (two character arrays, an integer, a floating-point value, and another character array).

NOTE: No memory is reserved for structure tags. A structure tag is your own data type. C++ does not reserve memory for the integer data type until you declare an integer variable. C++ does not reserve memory for a structure until you declare a structure variable.

Figure 29.1 contains the CD structure, graphically showing the data types within the structure. Notice that there are five members, and each member is a different data type. The entire structure is called `cd_collection`, which is the structure tag.

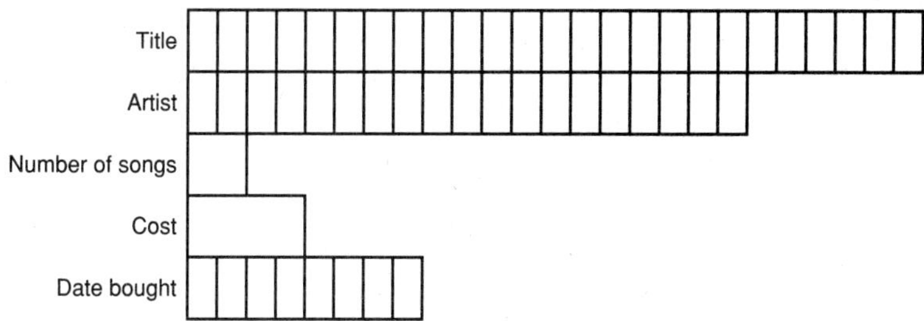

Figure 29.1. The look of the `cd_collection` structure.

NOTE: The mailing list application in Appendix F uses a structure to hold names, addresses, cities, states, and ZIP codes.

Examples

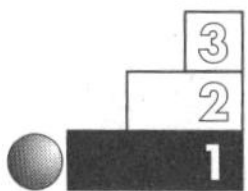

1. Suppose that you are asked to write a program for a company's inventory system. The company had been using a card-file inventory system that tracks the following items:

   Item name
   Quantity in stock
   Quantity on order
   Retail price
   Wholesale price

   This is a perfect use for a structure containing five members. Before defining the structure, you need to determine the data type of each member by asking questions about the range of data. For example, you must know the largest item name and the most quantity that will ever be on order to ensure that your data types will hold the data. You then decide to use the following structure tag and data types:

   Structure tag: `inventory`

Member	*Data Type*
Item name	Character array of 20 characters
Quantity in stock	long int
Quantity on order	long int
Retail price	double
Wholesale price	double

2. Suppose that the same company wants you to write a program to keep track of its monthly and annual salaries, printing a report at the end of the year that shows each month's individual salaries and the annual salaries at the end of the year.

What would the structure look like? Be careful! This type of data probably does not need a structure. Because all the monthly salaries will be the same data type, a floating-point or double floating-point array will hold the monthly salaries nicely without the complexity of a structure.

Structures are useful for keeping track of data that must be grouped together, such as inventory data, a customer's name and address data, or an employee data file.

Defining Structures

To define a structure, you must use the `struct` statement. `struct` defines for your program a new data type with more than one member. The format of the `struct` statement is

```
struct [structure tag]
     {
     member definition;
     member definition;
     member definition;
     :
     } [one or more structure variables];
```

As mentioned earlier, the *structure tag* is optional (hence, the brackets in the format). Each *member definition* is a normal variable definition, such as `int i;` or `float sales[ 20 ];` or any other valid variable definition, including variable pointers if the structure requires a pointer as a member. At the end of the structure's definition and before the final semicolon, you can specify one or more structure variables.

If you specify a structure variable, you request C++ to reserve space for that variable. C++ knows that the variable is not an integer, character, or any other internal data type; C++ knows that the variable will be a type that looks like the structure. It may seem strange that the members themselves do not reserve storage, but they don't. The structure variables do. This will be made clear in the examples that follow.

Here is how you declare the CD structure:

```
struct cd_collection
    {
    char           title[ 25 ];
    char           artist[ 20 ];
    int            num_songs;
    float          price;
    char           date_bought[ 8 ];
    } cd1, cd2, cd3;
```

Before going any further, you should be able to answer the following questions about this structure:

1. What is the structure tag?
2. How many members are there?
3. What are the member data types?
4. What are the member names?
5. How many structure variables are there?
6. What are their names?

The structure tag is called `cd_collection`. There are five members: two character arrays, an integer, a floating-point value, and a character array. The member names are `title`, `artist`, `num_songs`, `price`, and `date_bought`. The three structure variables are `cd1`, `cd2`, and `cd3`.

TIP: Often you can visualize structure variables as looking like a card-file inventory system. Figure 29.2 shows how you might keep your CD collection in a 3-by-5 card file, each CD taking one card (representing each structure variable). The information about the CD (the structure members) is on each card.

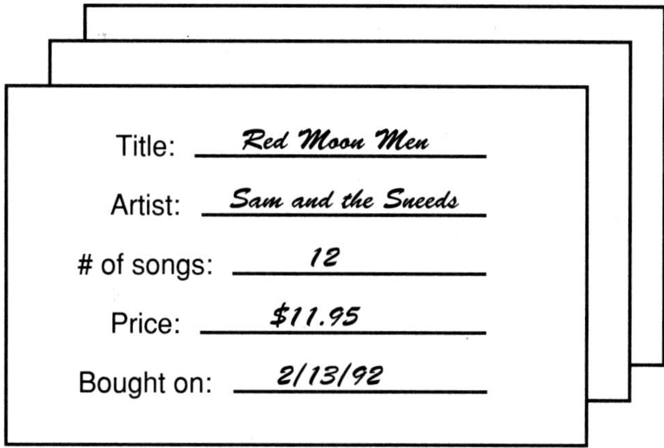

Figure 29.2. Using a card-file CD inventory system.

If you had 1,000 CDs, you would have to declare 1,000 structure variables. Obviously, you would not want to list that many structure variables at the end of a structure definition. To help define structures for a large number of occurrences, you must define an *array of structures*. The next chapter, "Arrays of Structures," shows you how to do that. For now, just familiarize yourself with structure definitions.

Examples

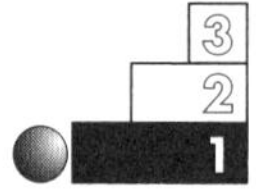

1. Here is a structure definition of the inventory application described earlier in this chapter:

```
struct inventory
     {
     char          item_name[ 20 ];
     long int      in_stock;
     long int      order_qty;
     float         retail;
     float         wholesale;
     } item1, item2, item3, item4;
```

Four inventory structure variables are defined. Each structure variable — `item1`, `item2`, `item3`, and `item4` — looks like the structure.

no structure variables. In each function, local structure variables are declared through references to the structure tag. The structure tag keeps you from having to redefine the structure members every time you define a new structure variable.

```
// Filename: C29ST3.CPP
// Structure input with student data passed to functions

#include <iostream.h>
#include <stdio.h>
#include <string.h>

struct     students    // A global structure
     {
     char          name[ 25 ];
     int           age;
     float         average;
     };                // No memory reserved yet

struct students     fill_structs(struct students student_var)
     {
     // Get students' data
     fflush(stdin);     // Clear input buffer for next input
     cout << "What is student's name? ";
     gets(student_var.name);
     cout << "What is the student's age? ";
     cin >> student_var.age;
     cout << "What is the student's average? ";
     cin >> student_var.average;
     return (student_var);
     }

void     pr_students(struct students student_var)
     {
     cout << "Name:    " << student_var.name << "\n";
     cout << "Age:     " << student_var.age << "\n";
     cout << "Average: " << student_var.average << "\n";
     return;
     }
```

```
int     main(void)
     {
     struct students     student1, student2;     // Define 2
                                                 // local variables

     // Call function to fill structure variables
     student1 = fill_structs(student1);  // student1 is
                                         // passed by copy, so it
                                         // must be returned for
                                         // main() to recognize it.
     student2 = fill_structs(student2);
     // Print the data
     cout << "\n\nHere is the student ";
     cout << "information you entered:\n\n";
     pr_students(student1);   // Print first student's data
     pr_students(student2);   // Print second student's data
     return 0;
     }
```

The prototype and definition of the `fill_structs()` function may seem complicated but follow the same pattern you have seen throughout this book. Before a function name, you must declare `void` or put the return data type if the function returns a value. `fill_structs()` does return a value, and the type of value it returns is `struct students`.

4. Because structure data is nothing more than regular variables grouped together, feel free to calculate with structure members. As long as you use the dot operator, you can treat structure members like other variables.

   The following example asks for a customer's balance and uses a discount rate (included in the customer's structure) to calculate a new balance. To keep the example short, the structure's data is initialized at variable declaration time.

   This program does not actually require structures because only one customer is used. Individual variables could be used, but they do not illustrate calculating with structures.

```
// Filename: C29CUST.CPP
// Updates a customer balance in a structure
```

```
#include <iostream.h>

struct     customer_rec
     {
     char           cust_name[ 25 ];
     double         balance;
     float          dis_rate;
     };

main()
     {
     struct customer_rec     customer =
          { "Steve Thompson", 2431.23, .25 };

     cout << "Before the update, " << customer.cust_name;
     cout << " has a balance of " << customer.balance
          << "\n";
     // Update the balance
     customer.balance *= (1.0 - customer.dis_rate);
     cout << "After the update, " << customer.cust_name;
     cout << " has a balance of " << customer.balance
          << "\n";
     return 0;
     }
```

5. You can copy the members of one structure variable to those of another structure variable as long as both structures have the same format. Some older versions of C++ required that you copy each member individually when you wanted to copy one structure variable to another, but ANSI C makes duplicating structure variables easy.

   Being able to copy one structure variable to another will be more meaningful in the next chapter, "Arrays of Structures," but the concept is very easy to apply.

   The following program declares three structure variables but initializes only the first one with data. The other two structure variables are then initialized when the first structure variable is assigned to them.

```
// Filename: C29STCPY.CPP
// Demonstrates assigning one structure to another

#include <iostream.h>

struct     student
     {
     char          st_name[ 25 ];
     char          grade;
     int           age;
     float         average;
     };

main()
     {
     struct student     std1 =
          { "Joe Brown", 'A', 13, 91.4 };
     struct student     std2, std3;     // Not initialized

     std2 = std1;    // Copy each member of std1 to std2
     std3 = std1;    // and std3
     cout << "The contents of std2:\n";
     cout << std2.st_name << ", " << std2.grade << ", ";
     cout << std2.age << ", " << std2.average << "\n\n";
     cout << "The contents of std3:\n";
     cout << std3.st_name << ", " << std3.grade << ", ";
     cout << std3.age << ", " << std3.average << "\n\n";
     return 0;
     }
```

Copy members of one structure to another

Here is this program's output:

```
The contents of std2
Joe Brown, A, 13, 91.4

The contents of std3
Joe Brown, A, 13, 91.4
```

Notice that each member of `std1` is assigned to `std2` and `std3` with two single assignments.

Nested Structures

C++ enables you to nest one structure definition within another. This saves time when you are writing programs that use similar structures. You have to define the common members only once in their own structure and then use that structure as a member in another structure.

Consider the following two structure definitions:

```
struct     employees
     {
     char          emp_name[ 25 ];     // Employee full name
     char          address[ 30 ];      // Employee address
     char          city[ 10 ];
     char          state[ 2 ];
     long int      zip;
     double        salary;             // Annual salary
     };

struct     customers
     {
     char          cust_name[ 25 ];    // Customer full name
     char          address[ 30 ];      // Customer address
     char          city[ 10 ];
     char          state[ 2 ];
     long int      zip;
     double        balance;     // Balance owed to company
     };
```

These structures hold very different data. One structure is for employee data, and the other structure is for customer data. Even though the data should be kept separate (you don't want to send a customer a paycheck!), the structure definitions have a lot of overlap and can be consolidated if you create a third structure:

```
struct     address_info
     {
     char          address[ 30 ];    // Common address
                                     // information
     char          city[ 10 ];
```

```
    char          state[ 2 ];
    long int      zip;
    };
```

This structure can then be used *as a member* in the other structures in this way:

```
struct     employees
    {
    char                        emp_name[ 25 ];    // Employee
                                                   // full name
    struct address_info e_address;       // Employee address
    double                  salary;      // Annual salary
    };

struct     customers
    {
    char                        cust_name[ 25 ];   // Customer
                                                   // full name
    struct address_info c_address;       // Customer address
    double                  balance;     // Balance owed
                                         // to company
    };
```

You must realize that there is a total of three structures, with the tags `address_info`, `employees`, and `customers`. How many members does the `employees` structure have? If you answered three, you are correct. There are three members in both `employees` and `customers`. `employees` has the structure of a character array, followed first by the `address_info` structure and then by the double floating-point member `salary`.

Figure 29.4 shows how these structures look graphically.

Once you define a structure, it is then a new data type in the program and can be used anywhere that a data type (such as `int`, `float`, and so on) can appear.

You can assign values to members by using the dot operator. To assign the customer balance a number, you can type something like this:

```
customer.balance = 5643.24;
```

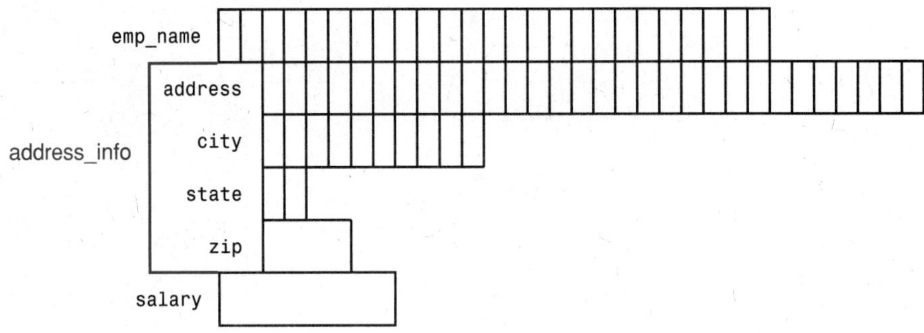

customers:

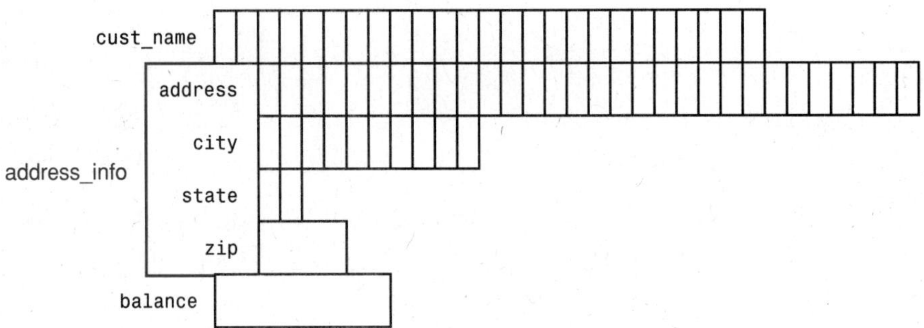

Figure 29.4. Defining a nested structure.

The nested structure might appear to pose a problem. How can you assign a value to one of the nested members? When you use the dot operator, you must nest it just as you nest the structure definitions. To assign a value to the customer's ZIP code, you use the following:

```
customer.c_address.zip = 34312;
```

To assign a value to the employee's ZIP code, you use this:

```
employee.e_address.zip = 59823;
```

Summary

Structures enable you to group data together in more flexible ways than arrays allow. The structures can contain members of different data types. You can initialize the structures either at declaration time or during the program with the dot operator (.).

Structures become even more powerful when you declare arrays of structure variables. The next chapter shows you how to declare several structure variables without giving each one a different name. This lets you step through structures more quickly with loop constructs.

Review Questions

Answers to Review Questions are in Appendix B.

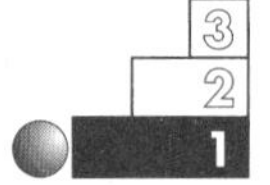

1. What is the difference between structures and arrays?
2. What are the individual elements of a structure called?
3. What are the two ways to initialize members of a structure?
4. Do you pass structures by copy or by address?
5. True or false: The following structure definition reserves storage in memory.

```
struct     crec
{
char          name[ 25 ];
int           age;
float         sales[ 5 ];
long          int num;
     }
```

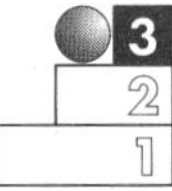

6. Should you declare a structure globally or locally?
7. Should you declare a structure variable globally or locally?

8. How many members does the following structure declaration contain?

```
struct     item
     {
     int                      quantity;
     struct part_rec          item_desc;
     float                    price;
     char                     date_bought[8];
     };
```

Review Exercises

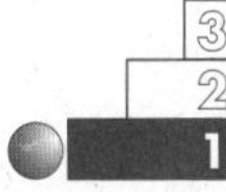

1. Write a structure that a video store can use in a program to track the video tape inventory. Make sure that the structure includes the tape's title, length of the tape (in minutes), cost of the tape, rental price of the tape, and date of the movie's release.

2. Write a program that uses the structure declared in the preceding exercise. Define three structure variables and initialize them *when you declare the variables* with data. Print the data to the screen.

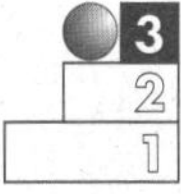

3. Write a teacher's program that keeps track of 10 student names, ages, letter grades, and IQs. Use 10 different structure variable names and get the data for the students in a `for` loop from the keyboard. Print the data on the printer when the teacher finishes entering the information for all the students.

Arrays of Structures

This chapter builds on the preceding one by showing you how you can create many structures for your data. After creating an array of structures, you can store multiple occurrences of your data values.

Arrays of structures are good for storing a complete employee file, an inventory file, or any other set of data that fits within the structure format. Whereas arrays provide a handy way to store several values of the same type, arrays of structures let you store together several values of different types, grouped as structures.

This chapter introduces the following topics:

- Creating arrays of structures
- Initializing arrays of structures
- Referencing elements from a structure array
- Arrays as members

Many C++ programmers use arrays of structures as a prelude to storing data in a disk file. You can input and calculate your disk data in arrays of structures and then store those structures in memory. Arrays of structures also provide a means of holding data you read from the disk.

Declaring Arrays of Structures

Declaring an array of structures is easy. You specify the number of reserved structures inside array brackets when you declare the structure variable. Consider the following structure definition:

```
struct     stores
    {
    int          employees;
    int          registers;
    double       sales;
    } store1, store2, store3, store4, store5;
```

This structure is easy to understand because no new commands are used in the structure declaration, which creates five structure variables. Figure 30.1 shows how C++ stores these five structures in memory. Each of the structure variables has three members — two integers followed by a double floating-point value.

If the fourth store increases its employees by three, you can update the store's employee count with the following assignment statement:

```
store4.employees += 3;      // Add 3 to this store's
                            // employee count
```

Suppose that the fifth store just opened and you want to initialize its members with data. If the stores are a chain and the new store is similar to one of the others, you might begin initializing the store's data by assigning each of its members the same data as that of another store:

```
store5 = store2;            // Define initial values for the
                            // store5 members
```

Arrays of structures make working with large numbers of structure variables manageable.

Such structure declarations are fine for a small number of structures, but if the stores are a national chain, five structure variables will not be enough. What if there are 1,000 stores? You would not want to create 1,000 different store variables and work with each one individually. It would be much easier to create an array of store structures.

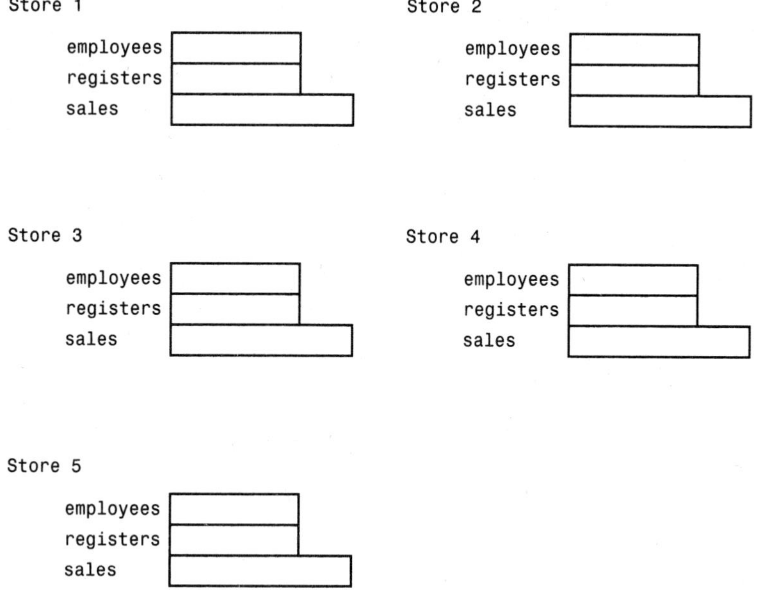

Figure 30.1. The structure of five stores.

Consider the following structure declaration:

```
struct      stores
    {
    int           employees;
    int           registers;
    double        sales;
    } store[ 1000 ];
```

In one quick declaration, this code creates 1,000 store structures, each containing three members. Figure 30.2 shows how these structure variables appear in memory. Notice the name of each individual structure variable: `store[ 0 ]`, `store[ 1 ]`, `store[ 2 ]`, and so on.

CAUTION: Be careful that you do not run out of memory when creating a large number of structures. Arrays of structures quickly consume valuable memory. You may have to create fewer structures, storing more data in disk files and less data in memory.

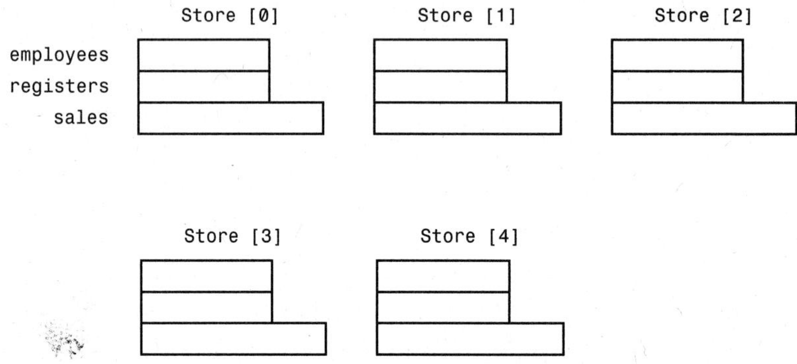

Figure 30.2. An array of the store structures.

The element `store[ 2 ]` is an array element. This element, unlike the others you have seen, is a structure variable. Therefore, it contains three members, each of which you can reference with the dot operator (.).

The dot operator works the same way for structure array elements as for regular structure variables. If the number of employees for the fifth store (`store[ 4 ]`) increases by three, you can update the structure variable like this:

```
store[ 4 ].employees += 3;      // Add 3 to this store's
                                // employee count
```

You can assign complete structures to one another by using array notation also. To assign all the members of the 20th store to the 45th store, you can do this:

```
store[ 44 ] = store[ 19 ];      // Copy all members from the
                                // 20th store to the 45th
```

The rules of arrays are still in force here. The elements of the array called store are the *very same data type*. The data type of store is struct stores. As with any array, the elements have to be the same data type; you cannot mix data types within the same array. This array's data type happens to be a structure you created, containing three members. The data type for store[316] is exactly the same for store[981] and store[74].

The name of the array, store, is a pointer constant to the starting element of the array, store[0]. Therefore, you can use pointer notation to reference the stores. To assign store[60] the same value as store[23], you can reference the two elements like this:

```
*(store + 60) = *(store + 23);
```

You can also mix array and pointer notation, as in

```
store[ 60 ] = *(store + 23);
```

and get the same results.

You can increase the sales of store[8] by 40 percent with pointer or subscript notation as well:

```
store[ 8 ].sales = (*(store + 8)).sales * 1.40;
```

The extra pair of parentheses is required because the dot operator has precedence over the dereferencing symbol in C++'s hierarchy of operators (see Appendix D). Of course, in this case, the code is not helped by the pointer notation, and the following is a much clearer way to increase the sales by 40 percent:

```
store[ 8 ].sales *= 1.40;
```

Keep Your Array Notation Straight

You would never access the member sales like this:

```
store.sales[ 8 ] = 3234.54;      // INVALID
```

Array subscripts follow array elements only. sales is not an array; it was declared as being a double floating-point number. store can never be used *without* a subscript (unless you are using pointer notation).

Here is a corrected version of the preceding assignment statement:

```
store[ 8 ].sales = 3234.54;      // Correctly assigns
                                  // the value
```

The following examples build an inventory data-entry system for a mail order firm, using an array of structures. There is very little new that you have to know when working with arrays of structures. Concentrate on the notation for accessing arrays of structures and their members so that you can get comfortable with this notation.

Examples

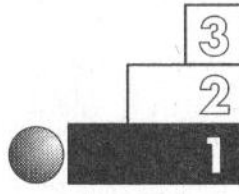

1. Suppose that you work for a mail order company that sells disk drives. You are given the task of writing a tracking program for the 125 different drives you sell. You must keep track of the following information:

   Storage capacity in megabytes
   Access time in milliseconds
   Vendor code (A, B, C, or D)
   Cost
   Price

   Because there are 125 different disk drives in the inventory, the data will fit nicely into an array of structures. Each array element is a structure containing the five members described in this list.

   The following structure definition defines the inventory:

```
struct      inventory
     {
     long int   storage;
     int        access_time;
     char       vendor_code;
     double     code;
     double     price;
     } drive[ 125 ];      // Define 125 occurrences
                          // of the structure
```

2. When working with a large array of structures, your first concern should be how the data will be input into the array elements. The application will determine the best method of data entry.

   For instance, if you are converting from an older computerized inventory system, you will have to write a conversion program that reads the inventory file in its native format and saves it to a new file in the format needed by your C++ programs. This is no easy task, requiring that you have extensive knowledge of the system you are converting from.

   If you are writing a computerized inventory system for the first time, your job is a little easier because you do not need to worry about converting the old files. You must still realize that someone has to type the data into the computer. You will have to write a data entry program that receives each inventory item from the keyboard and saves the item to a disk file. You should give the user a chance to edit inventory data to correct any data that may have been typed incorrectly.

   One of the reasons that this book does not introduce disk files until the last chapters is that disk file formats and structures share a common bond. Once you store data in a structure, or more often in an array of structures, you can easily write that data to a disk file with straightforward disk I/O commands.

   The following program takes the array of disk drive structures shown in the preceding example and adds a data entry function so that the user can enter data into the array of structures. The program is menu-driven. The user has a choice, when starting the program, to add data, print data to the screen, or exit the program. Because you have yet to see disk I/O commands, the data in the array of structures goes away when the program ends. As noted, saving those structures to disk will be an easy task after you learn C++'s disk I/O commands. For now, concentrate on the manipulation of the structures.

This program is longer than many you have seen in this book, but if you have followed the discussion of structures and the dot operator, you should have little trouble following the code.

```
// Filename: C30DSINV.CPP
// Data entry program for a disk drive company

#include <iostream.h>
#include <stdio.h>
#include <stdlib.h>

struct     inventory     // Global structure definition
     {
     long int  storage;
     int       access_time;
     char      vendor_code;
     float     cost;
     float     price;
     };     // No structure variables defined globally

void     disp_menu(void)
     {
     cout << "\n\n*** Disk Drive Inventory System ***\n\n";
     cout << "Do you want to:\n\n";
     cout << "\t1. Enter new item in inventory\n\n";
     cout << "\t2. See inventory data\n\n";
     cout << "\t3. Exit the program\n\n";
     cout << "What is your choice? ";
     return;
     }

struct inventory     enter_data(void)
     {
     struct inventory     disk_item; // Local variable to
                                     // fill with input

     cout << "\n\nWhat is the next drive's ";
     cout << "storage in bytes? ";
     cin >> disk_item.storage;
     cout << "What is the drive's access time in ms? ";
```

```
     cin >> disk_item.access_time;
     cout << "What is the drive's vendor code ";
     cout << "(A, B, C, or D)? ";
     fflush(stdin);     // Discard input buffer before
                        // getting character
     cin.get(disk_item.vendor_code);
     fflush(stdin);     // Discard carriage return
     cout << "What is the drive's cost? ";
     cin >> disk_item.cost;
     cout << "What is the drive's price? ";
     cin >> disk_item.price;
     return (disk_item);
     }

void     see_data(struct inventory disk[ 125 ],
                  int num_items)
     {
     int     ctr;

     cout << "\n\nHere is the inventory listing:\n\n";
     for (ctr = 0; ctr < num_items; ctr++)
          {
          cout << "Storage: " << disk[ ctr ].storage
               << "\t";
          cout << "Access time: " << disk[ ctr ].access_time
               << "\n";
          cout << "Vendor code: " << disk[ ctr ].vendor_code
               << "\t";
          cout << "Cost: $" << disk[ ctr ].cost << "\t";
          cout << "Price: $" << disk[ ctr ].price << "\n";
          }
     return;
     }

int     main(void)
     {
     struct inventory     disk[ 125 ];   // Local array
                                         // of structures
     int                    ans;
     int                    num_items = 0;      // Number of
                             // total items in the inventory
```

```
do
     {
     do
          {
          disp_menu();  // Display menu of user choices
          cin >> ans;   // Get user's request
          }
     while ((ans < 1) || (ans > 3));
     switch (ans)
          {
          case 1:
               // Enter disk data
               disk[ num_items ] = enter_data();
               num_items++; // Increment number of items
               break;
          case 2:
               // Display disk data
               see_data(disk, num_items);
               break;
          default:
               break;
          }
     }
while (ans != 3);  // Quit program when user is through
return 0;
}
```

Figure 30.3 shows an item being entered into the inventory file. Figure 30.4 shows the inventory listing being displayed to the screen. There are many features and error-checking functions you can add, but this program is the building block to a more comprehensive inventory system. You can easily adapt the program to a different type of inventory — such as a video tape collection, a coin collection, or any other tracking system — just by changing the structure definition and the member names throughout the program.

```
*** Disk Drive Inventory System ***

Do you want to:

        1. Enter new item in inventory

        2. See inventory data

        3. Exit the program

What is your choice? 1


What is the next drive's storage in bytes? 120000
What is the drive's access time in ms? 17
What is the drive's vendor code (A, B, C, or D)? A
What is the drive's cost? 121.56
What is the drive's price? 240.00
```

Figure 30.3. Entering inventory information.

```
What is your choice? 2


Here is the inventory listing:

Storage: 120000 Access time: 17
Vendor code: A  Cost: $121.56   Price: $240.00
Storage: 320000 Access time: 21
Vendor code: D  Cost: $230.85   Price: $409.57
Storage: 280000 Access time: 19
Vendor code: C  Cost: $210.84   Price: $398.67


*** Disk Drive Inventory System ***

Do you want to:

        1. Enter new item in inventory

        2. See inventory data

        3. Exit the program

What is your choice? 3
```

Figure 30.4. Displaying inventory data.

Arrays as Members

Members of structures can themselves be arrays. Array members pose no new problem, but you have to be careful when you access individual array elements. Keeping track of arrays of structures that contain array members might seem like a lot of work on your part, but there is really nothing to it.

Consider the following structure definition. This statement declares an array of 100 structures, each structure holding payroll information for a company. Two of the members, `name` and `department`, are arrays.

```
struct     payroll
     {
     char           name[ 25 ];        // Employee name array
     int            dependents;
     char           department[ 10 ]; // Department name array
     float          salary;
     } employee[ 100 ];      // An array of 100 employees
```

Figure 30.5 shows what these structures look like. The first and third members are arrays. `name` is an array of 25 characters, and `department` is an array of 10 characters.

Suppose that you need to save the 25th employee's initial in a character variable. Assuming that `initial` is already declared as a character variable, the following statement assigns the employee's initial to `initial`:

```
initial = employee[ 24 ].name[ 0 ];
```

The double subscripts may look confusing, but the dot operator requires a structure variable on its left (`employee[ 24 ]`) and a member on its right (`name`'s first array element). Being able to refer to member arrays makes the processing of character data in structures simple.

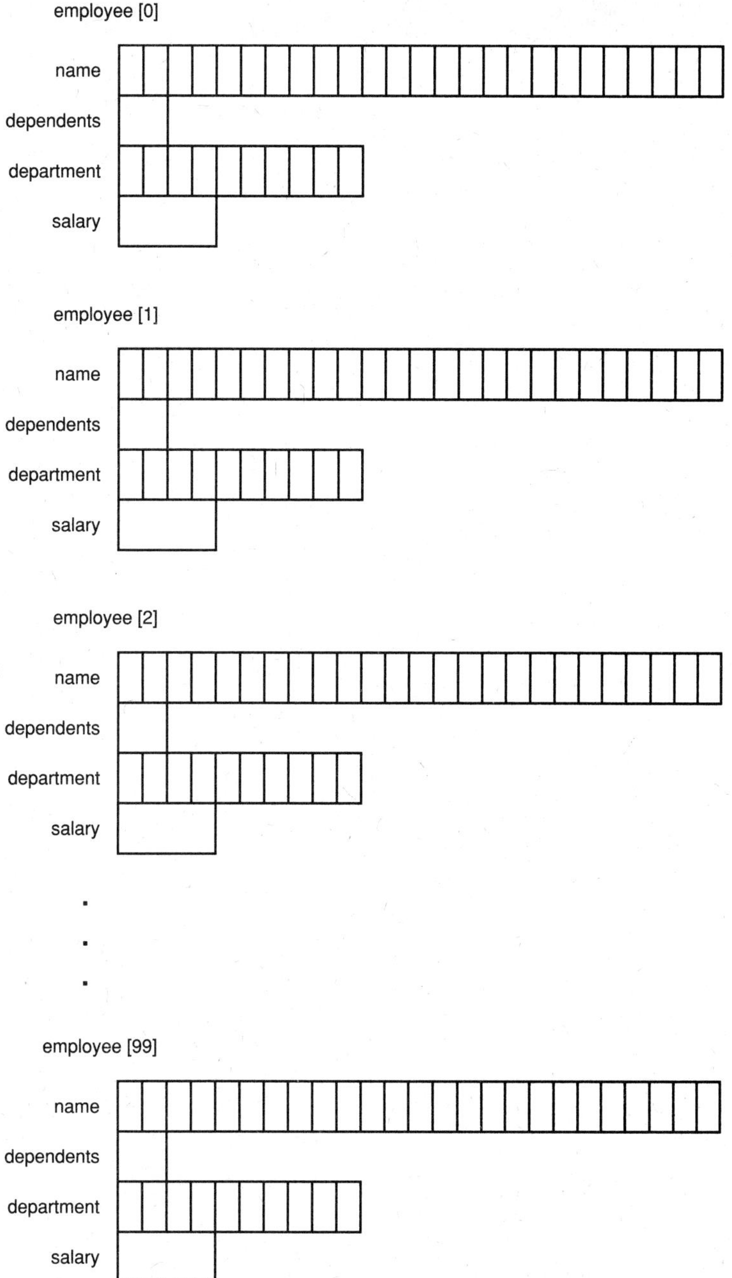

Figure 30.5. The payroll data.

Examples

1. Suppose that an employee gets married and wants her name changed in the payroll file. (She happens to be the 45th employee in the array of structures.) Given the payroll structure just described, the following assigns a new name to her structure:

```
// Assign a new name
strcpy(employee[ 44 ].name, "Mary Larson");
```

When you refer to a structure variable with the dot operator, you can use regular commands and functions to process the data in the structures.

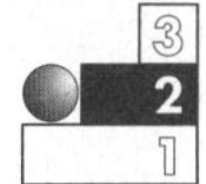

2. A bookstore wants to catalog its inventory of books. The following program creates an array of 100 structures. Each structure contains several types of variables, including arrays. This program is the data entry portion of a larger inventory system. Study the references to the members to see how member arrays are used.

```
// Filename: C30BOOK.CPP
// Bookstore data entry program

#include <iostream.h>
#include <stdio.h>
#include <ctype.h>

struct     inventory
    {
    char         title[ 25 ];          // Book's title
    char         pub_date[ 19 ];       // Publication date
    char         author[ 20 ];         // Author's name
    int          num;                  // Number in stock
    int          on_order;             // Number on order
    float        retail;               // Retail price
    };

main()
    {
    struct inventory     book[ 100 ];
```

```
int                      total = 0;  // Total books
                                     // in inventory
char                      ans;

do     // Program enters data into the structures
     {
     cout << "Book #" << (total + 1) << ":\n";
     cout << "What is the title? ";
     gets(book[ total ].title);
     cout << "What is the publication date? ";
     gets(book[ total ].pub_date);
     cout << "Who is the author? ";
     gets(book[ total ].author);
     cout << "How many books of this title are there? ";
     cin >> book[ total ].num;
     cout << "How many are on order? ";
     cin >> book[ total ].on_order;
     cout << "What is the retail price? ";
     cin >> book[ total ].retail;
     fflush(stdin);
     cout << "\nAre there more books? (Y/N) ";
     cin >> ans;
     fflush(stdin);          // Discard carriage return
     ans = toupper(ans);     // Convert to uppercase
     if (ans == 'Y')
          {
          total++;
          continue;
          }
     }
while (ans == 'Y');
return 0;
}
```

There is a lot more needed to make this a usable inventory program. An exercise at the end of this chapter recommends ways you can improve this program (adding a printing routine and an author and title search). One of the first things you should do is put the data entry routine in a separate function to make the code more modular. Because this example is so short and the program performs only one task (data entry), there is no advantage to putting the data entry task in a separate function.

3. Here is a comprehensive example of the steps you might go through to write a C++ program. You are getting to the point where you understand enough of the C++ language to start writing some advanced programs.

Assume that you are hired to write a magazine inventory system by a local bookstore. You need to track the following:

Magazine title (maximum of 25 characters)
Publisher (maximum of 20 characters)
Month (1, 2, 3, ..., 12)
Publication year
Number of copies in stock
Number of copies on order
Price of magazine (dollars and cents)

Suppose that there is a projected maximum of 1,000 magazine titles that the store will ever carry. This means that you need 1,000 occurrences of the structure, not a total of 1,000 magazines. Here is a good structure definition for such an inventory:

```
struct     mag_info
    {
    char           title[ 25 ];
    char           pub[ 25 ];
    int            month;
    int            year;
    int            stock_copies;
    int            order_copies;
    float          price;
    } mags[ 1000 ];      // Define 1,000 occurrences
```

Because this program will consist of more than one function, it is best to declare the structure globally and the structure variables locally within the functions that need them.

This program needs three basic functions: a `main()` controlling function, a data entry function, and a data printing function. There is a lot more you can add, but this is a good start for an inventory system. To keep the length of this example reasonable, assume that the user wants to enter several magazines and then print them out. (To make the program more usable, you would want to add a menu so that the user can control when to add and print the information, as well as add more error-checking and editing capabilities.)

Here is an example of the complete data entry and printing program with prototypes. The arrays of structures are passed between the functions from `main()`.

```
// C30MAG.CPP
// Magazine inventory program for adding and displaying
// a bookstore's magazines

#include <iostream.h>
#include <stdio.h>
#include <ctype.h>

struct     mag_info
     {
     char         title[ 25 ];
     char         pub[ 25 ];
     int          month;
     int          year;
     int          stock_copies;
     int          order_copies;
     float        price;
     };


struct mag_info     fill_mags(struct mag_info mag)
     {
     cout << "\n\nWhat is the title? ";
     gets(mag.title);
     cout << "Who is the publisher? ";
     gets(mag.pub);
     cout << "What is the month (1, 2, ..., 12)? ";
     cin >> mag.month;
     cout << "What is the year? ";
```

```
     cin >> mag.year;
     cout << "How many copies in stock? ";
     cin >> mag.stock_copies;
     cout << "How many copies on order? ";
     cin >> mag.order_copies;
     cout << "How much is the magazine? ";
     cin >> mag.price;
     return (mag);
     }


void     print_mags(struct mag_info mags[], int mag_ctr)
     {
     int     i;

     for (i = 0; i <= mag_ctr; i++)
          {
          cout << "\n\nMagazine " << (i + 1) << "\n";
          cout << "\nTitle: " << mags[ i ].title << "\n";
          cout << "\tPublisher: " << mags[ i ].pub << "\n";
          cout << "\tPub. Month: "
               << mags[ i ].month << "\n";
          cout << "\tPub. Year: "
               << mags[ i ].year << "\n";
          cout << "\tIn-stock: "
               << mags[ i ].stock_copies << "\n";
          cout << "\tOn order: "
               << mags[ i ].order_copies << "\n";
          cout << "\tPrice: " << mags[ i ].price << "\n";
          }
     return;
     }

int     main(void)
     {
     struct mag_info     mags[ 1000 ];
     int                    mag_ctr = 0; // Number of
                                         // magazine titles
     char                    ans;

     do
          {     // Assume that there will be at least
```

```
          // one magazine filled
      mags[ mag_ctr ] = fill_mags(mags[ mag_ctr ]);
      cout << "Do you want to enter another magazine? ";
      fflush(stdin);
      cin.get(ans);
      fflush(stdin);     // Discard carriage return
      if (toupper(ans) == 'Y')
         mag_ctr++;
      }
   while (toupper(ans) == 'Y');
   print_mags(mags, mag_ctr);
   return 0;     // Return to operating system
   }
```

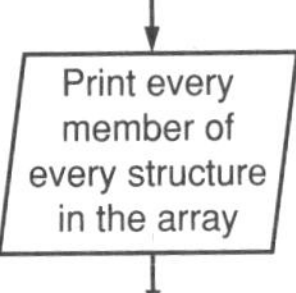

Summary

You have now mastered structures and arrays of structures. There are many useful inventory and tracking programs ready to be written by you, using structures. By being able to create arrays of structures, you can now create multiple occurrences of data.

The next step in the process of learning C++ is to master classes. The next chapter explores the C++ class concept.

Review Questions

Answers to Review Questions are in Appendix B.

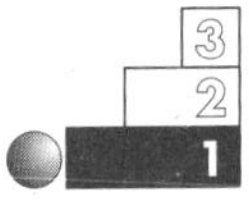

1. True or false: All elements in an array of structures must be the same type.
2. What is the advantage of creating an array of structures instead of using individual variable names for each structure variable?

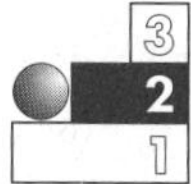

3. Consider the following structure declaration:

```
struct      item
     {
     char           part_no[ 8 ];
     char           descr[ 20 ];
     float          price;
     int            in_stock;
     } inventory[ 100 ];
```

   A. How would you assign a price of 12.33 to the 33rd item's in-stock quantity?

   B. How would you assign the first character of the 12th item's part number the value of `'X'`?

   C. How would you assign the 97th inventory item the same value as the 63rd?

4. Now look at this structure declaration:

```
struct      item
     {
     char           desc[ 20 ];
     int            num;
     float          cost;
     } inventory[ 25 ];
```

   What is wrong with each of the following statements?

   A. `item[ 1 ].cost = 92.32;`

   B. `strcpy(inventory.desc, "Widgets");`

   C. `inventory.cost[ 10 ] = 32.12;`

Review Exercises

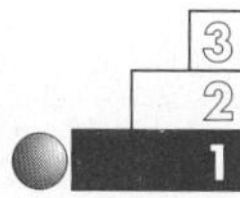

1. Write a program that stores an array of friends' names, phone numbers, and addresses and then prints them two ways: the full name and address, and just the name and phone number for a phone listing.

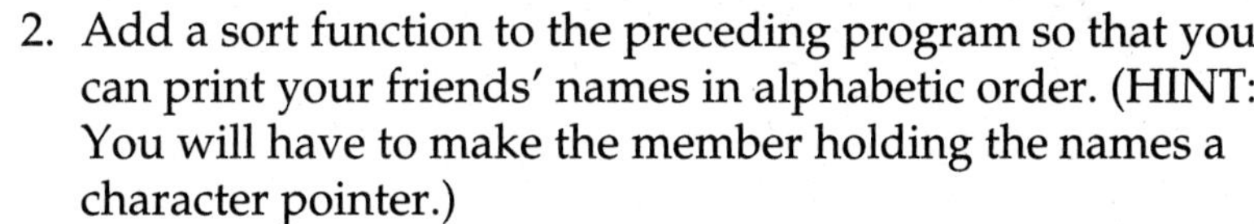

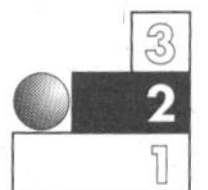

2. Add a sort function to the preceding program so that you can print your friends' names in alphabetic order. (HINT: You will have to make the member holding the names a character pointer.)

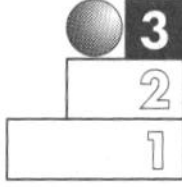

3. Expand the data entry program (C30BOOK.CPP) by adding features to make it more usable, such as searching books by author and title, and printing an inventory of books on order.

31

Classes

Classes are a powerful part of Turbo C++. They distinguish C++ from C. In fact, before the name C++ was coined, the language was called "C with classes."

What Is a Class?

As a user-defined data type, a class can have data members and member functions. The data members can be of any type, whether defined by the language or the user. The member functions can manipulate the data members, create and destroy class variables, and even redefine C++'s operators to act on the class objects.

This chapter introduces the following topics:

- Class members
- Class member visibility

Members

Like a structure, a class has one or more variable types. These variable types are called *members*, and there are two kinds of members: data members and member functions. Class members also have a new attribute that hasn't been seen before: visibility. Just as global variables are visible to all functions yet variables declared inside a function are not, individual members of a class can be made visible everywhere or not.

> **NOTE:** If this sounds like something discussed earlier in this book, it should. A class of nothing but data members, all of which are visible outside the class, has another name: a structure.

Data Members

Data members of a class are exactly like the variables in a structure. If you wanted to describe a sphere, you would need to know the sphere's radius and the coordinates describing its center. This is what a sphere class would look like:

```
// A sphere class
class Sphere
     {
public:
     float     r;         // Radius of sphere
     float     x, y, z;   // Coordinates of sphere
     };
```

The `Sphere` class has four data members: `r`, `x`, `y`, and `z`. So far, there isn't much to distinguish the sphere class from a `struct`, however. Notice that there appears to be a label — the word `public:` in the class. This label is explained a little later in the chapter. For now, pay no attention to it.

Member Functions

Member functions are functions defined within a class that act on the data members in the class. The use of member functions distinguishes a `class` from a `struct`. In the following code, some member functions have been added to the `Sphere` class:

```
#include  <math.h>
// M_PI (value of pi) is defined in MATH.H

// A sphere class
class Sphere
     {
public:
     float     r;          // Radius of sphere
     float     x, y, z;  // Coordinates of sphere
     Sphere(float xcoord, float ycoord,
            float zcoord, float radius)
       { x = xcoord; y = ycoord; z = zcoord; r = radius; }
     ~Sphere() { }
     float volume()
       {
       return (r * r * r * 4 * M_PI / 3);
       }
     float surface_area()
       {
       return (r * r * 4 * M_PI);
       }
     };
```

The member functions added to the `Sphere` class are `Sphere`, `~Sphere`, `volume`, and `surface_area`. The `class` is definitely not a `struct` anymore.

One of the functions is a very special function: `Sphere`. `Sphere` is a constructor function, and its name is always the same as its class. It is used primarily in declaring a new instance of the class. A *constructor function* is one that allows you to create a class variable and initialize it all at once. Class variables can be relatively complex to create and initialize; class constructors automate the procedure of creating and initializing the class variable, eliminating the likelihood of missing a step or performing a step incorrectly.

The following program shows the `Sphere` class constructor creating and initializing a `Sphere` class variable `s`:

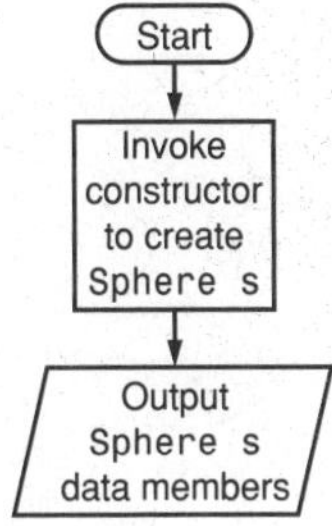


```
// Filename: C31CON.CPP
// Demonstrates use of a class constructor function

#include  <iostream.h>
#include  <math.h>
// M_PI (value of pi) is defined in MATH.H

// A sphere class
class Sphere
     {
public:
     float     r;         // Radius of sphere
     float     x, y, z;  // Coordinates of sphere
     Sphere(float xcoord, float ycoord,
            float zcoord, float radius)
       { x = xcoord; y = ycoord; z = zcoord; r = radius; }
     ~Sphere() { }
     float volume()
       {
       return (r * r * r * 4 * M_PI / 3);
       }
     float surface_area()
       {
       return (r * r * 4 * M_PI);
       }
     };

int  main(void)
     {
     Sphere    s(1.0, 2.0, 3.0, 4.0);

     cout << "X = " << s.x
          << " Y = " << s.y
          << " Z = " << s.z
          << " R = " << s.r
          << "\n";
     }
```

Figure 31.1 shows the output of this program.

X = 1 Y = 2 Z = 3 R = 4
Press a key when ready...

Figure 31.1. A class constructor in use.

The other special function is `~Sphere`. This is the destructor function. Note that it also has the same name as the class, but with a *tilde* (~) as a prefix.

Whereas the constructor function allocates memory to create a class variable, the *destructor function* gives back the memory, effectively destroying the class variable. The destructor may perform other activities, such as print out the final values of the class data members (useful for debugging).

The destructor function takes no arguments and returns no value. You'll notice also that this destructor doesn't do anything, which is true of most destructors. If your destructor function does nothing, you don't have to create one; as soon as the class variable is no longer in existence, the memory allocated for it is returned to the system. Similarly, if you don't need to do anything specific for a constructor, you don't need one; Turbo C++ will allocate memory for a class variable when you create it.

Just to show you that a destructor does do something, the following program's destructor announces that it is being called:

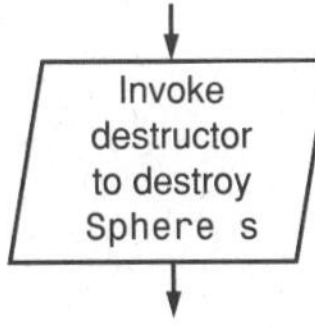


```
// Filename: C31DES.CPP
// Demonstrates use of a class destructor function

#include  <iostream.h>
#include  <math.h>
// M_PI (value of pi) is defined in MATH.H

// A sphere class
class Sphere
     {
public:
     float     r;          // Radius of sphere
     float     x, y, z;    // Coordinates of sphere
     Sphere(float xcoord, float ycoord,
            float zcoord, float radius)
       { x = xcoord; y = ycoord; z = zcoord; r = radius; }
     ~Sphere()
          {
          cout << "Sphere (" << x << ", " << y << ", "
               << z << ", " << r << ") destroyed\n";
          }
     float volume()
       {
       return (r * r * r * 4 * M_PI / 3);
       }
     float surface_area()
       {
       return (r * r * 4 * M_PI);
       }
     };

int  main(void)
     {
     Sphere    s(1.0, 2.0, 3.0, 4.0);

     cout << "X = " << s.x
          << " Y = " << s.y
          << " Z = " << s.z
          << " R = " << s.r << "\n";
     }
```

Figure 31.2 shows the output of this program. Note that `main()` does not explicitly call the destructor function.

```
"C:\>c30des"
X = 1 Y = 2 Z = 3 R = 4
Sphere (1, 2, 3, 4) destroyed
Press a key when ready...
```

Figure 31.2. A class destructor in use.

You can also use the `volume` and `surface_area` functions, as in this version of the program:

Invoke Sphere member functions

```
// Filename: C31MEM.CPP
// Demonstrates use of class member functions

#include  <iostream.h>
#include  <math.h>
// M_PI (value of pi) is defined in MATH.H

// A sphere class
class Sphere
     {
public:
     float     r;        // Radius of sphere
     float     x, y, z;  // Coordinates of sphere
     Sphere(float xcoord, float ycoord, float zcoord,
            float radius)
       { x = xcoord; y = ycoord; z = zcoord; r = radius; }
     ~Sphere()
          {
```

```
"C:\>c30mem1"
X = 1 Y = 2 Z = 3 R = 4
The volume is 268.082581
The surface area is 201.061935
Sphere (1, 2, 3, 4) destroyed
Press a key when ready...
```

Figure 31.4. Inline class member in use.

You can create a sphere with the following instructions:

Invoke Sphere constructor to use defaults

```
Sphere    s(1.0);                      // Use all defaults
Sphere    t(1.0, 1.1);                 // Override y coord
Sphere    u(1.0, 1.1, 1.2);            // Override y and z
Sphere    v(1.0, 1.1, 1.2, 1.3);       // Override all defaults
// This is seen in the following code; the results are
// displayed in Figure 31.5.
// Filename: C31DEF.CPP
// A program that demonstrates use of default arguments in
// class member functions

#include  <iostream.h>
#include  <math.h>
// M_PI (value of pi) is defined in MATH.H

// A sphere class
class Sphere
     {
public:
     float     r;        // Radius of sphere
```

```
     float     x, y, z;  // Coordinates of sphere
     Sphere(float xcoord,
            float ycoord = 2.0,
            float zcoord = 2.5,
            float radius = 1.0)
       { x = xcoord; y = ycoord; z = zcoord; r = radius; }
     ~Sphere()
          {
          cout << "Sphere (" << x << ", " << y << ", "
               << z << ", " << r << ") destroyed\n";
          }
     inline float volume()
       {
       return (r * r * r * 4 * M_PI / 3);
       }
     float surface_area()
       {
       return (r * r * 4 * M_PI);
       }
     };

int  main(void)
     {
     Sphere    s(1.0);                  // Use all defaults
     Sphere    t(1.0, 1.1);             // Override y coord
     Sphere    u(1.0, 1.1, 1.2);        // Override y and z
     Sphere    v(1.0, 1.1, 1.2, 1.3);   // Override all
                                        // defaults

     cout << "s: X = " << s.x
          << " Y = " << s.y
          << " Z = " << s.z
          << " R = " << s.r << "\n";
     cout << "The volume of s is " << s.volume() << "\n";
     cout << "The surface area of s is "
          << s.surface_area() << "\n";
     cout << "t: X = " << t.x
          << " Y = " << t.y
          << " Z = " << t.z
          << " R = " << t.r << "\n";
     cout << "The volume of t is " << t.volume() << "\n";
     cout << "The surface area of t is "
```

```
         << t.surface_area() << "\n";
    cout << "u: X = " << u.x
         << " Y = " << u.y
         << " Z = " << u.z
         << " R = " << u.r << "\n";
    cout << "The volume of u is " << u.volume() << "\n";
    cout << "The surface area of u is "
         << u.surface_area() << "\n";
    cout << "v: X = " << v.x
         << " Y = " << v.y
         << " Z = " << v.z
         << " R = " << v.r << "\n";
    cout << "The volume of v is " << v.volume() << "\n";
    cout << "The surface area of v is "
         << v.surface_area() << "\n";
}
```

Figure 31.5 shows the output of this program.

```
"C:\>c30def"
s: X = 1 Y = 2 Z = 2.5 R = 1
The volume of s is 4.18879
The surface area of s is 12.566371
t: X = 1 Y = 1.1 Z = 2.5 R = 1
The volume of t is 4.18879
The surface area of t is 12.566371
u: X = 1 Y = 1.1 Z = 1.2 R = 1
The volume of u is 4.18879
The surface area of u is 12.566371
v: X = 1 Y = 1.1 Z = 1.2 R = 1.3
The volume of v is 9.202771
The surface area of v is 21.237165
Sphere (1, 1.1, 1.2, 1.3) destroyed
Sphere (1, 1.1, 1.2, 1) destroyed
Sphere (1, 1.1, 2.5, 1) destroyed
Sphere (1, 2, 2.5, 1) destroyed
Press a key when ready...
```

Figure 31.5. Various defaults in use; all four spheres are destroyed.

Notice that once you elect to use a default value, you are stuck with using all the other values to the right. Similarly, once you define a function's parameter as having a default value, every parameter to the right must have a default value as well.

You can also have more than one constructor; this is called *overloading the constructor*. Overloading is the technique of giving a function more than one thing to do while using the same function name for each of the different things it does. How do you (and the C++ compiler) know what the overloaded function is doing? You create a different *context* for each of the different purposes.

With more than one constructor, each of which must have the name of the class, you have to give the constructors different parameter lists so that the compiler can figure out which constructor you intend to use. This supplies the context to the compiler and lets the compiler know which constructor you intend to use. A common purpose is to create an uninitialized object to be on the receiving end of an assignment, as in the following program:

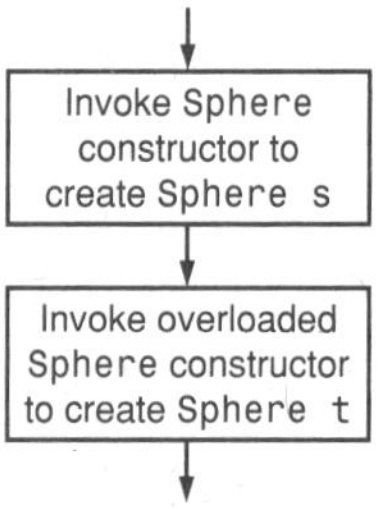

Invoke Sphere constructor to create Sphere s

Invoke overloaded Sphere constructor to create Sphere t

```
// Filename: C31OVCON.CPP
// Demonstrates use of overloaded constructors

#include  <iostream.h>
#include  <math.h>
// M_PI (value of pi) is defined in MATH.H

// A sphere class
class Sphere
     {
public:
     float     r;         // Radius of sphere
     float     x, y, z;  // Coordinates of sphere
     Sphere() { // doesn't do anything...   }
     Sphere(float xcoord, float ycoord,
            float zcoord, float radius)
       { x = xcoord; y = ycoord; z = zcoord; r = radius; }
     ~Sphere()
          {
          cout << "Sphere (" << x << ", " << y << ", "
               << z << ", " << r << ") destroyed\n";
          }
     inline float volume()
       {
```

```
            return (r * r * r * 4 * M_PI / 3);
            }
        float surface_area()
            {
            return (r * r * 4 * M_PI);
            }
        };

int     main(void)
        {
        Sphere    s(1.0, 2.0, 3.0, 4.0);
        Sphere    t;    // No parameters - an uninitialized
                        // sphere

        cout << "X = " << s.x
             << " Y = " << s.y
             << " Z = " << s.z
             << " R = " << s.r << "\n";
        t = s;
        cout << "The volume of t is " << t.volume() << "\n";
        cout << "The surface area of t is "
             << t.surface_area() << "\n";
        }
```

Figure 31.6 shows the output of this program.

Class Member Visibility

Recall that this class contains the label `public:`. The label is necessary because, by default, all members of a class are *private*. This means that they cannot be accessed by anything but a member function. In order for data or member functions to be used by other programs, they must be explicitly declared *public*. In the case of the `Sphere` class, you would probably want to hide the actual data from other programs. And (just to say that you did it) you can add `cube` and `square` functions to do some of the work of the `volume` and `surface_area` functions. There is no need for other functions to use the `cube` and `square` functions, either.

```
"C:\>c30ovcon"
X = 1 Y = 2 Z = 3 R = 4
The volume of t is 268.082581
The surface area of t is 201.061935
Sphere (1, 2, 3, 4) destroyed
Sphere (1, 2, 3, 4) destroyed
Press a key when ready...
```

Figure 31.6. Overloaded constructors in use.

Here is the modified program:

```
// Filename: C31VISIB.CPP
// Demonstrates use of class visibility labels

#include  <iostream.h>
#include  <math.h>
// M_PI (value of pi) is defined in MATH.H

// A sphere class
class Sphere
     {
private:
     float    r;         // Radius of sphere
     float    x, y, z;  // Coordinates of sphere
     float cube() { return (r * r * r); }
     float square() { return (r * r); }
public:
     Sphere(float xcoord, float ycoord,
            float zcoord, float radius)
       { x = xcoord; y = ycoord; z = zcoord; r = radius; }
```

```
    ~Sphere()
        {
        cout << "Sphere (" << x << ", " << y << ", "
            << z << ", " << r << ") destroyed\n";
        }
    float volume()
      {
      return (cube() * 4 * M_PI / 3);
      }
    float surface_area()
      {
      return (square() * 4 * M_PI);
      }
    };

int  main(void)
    {
    Sphere    s(1.0, 2.0, 3.0, 4.0);

    cout << "The volume is " << s.volume() << "\n";
    cout << "The surface area is "
        << s.surface_area() << "\n";
    }
```

Notice that the line showing the data members had to be removed from `main()`. The data members are no longer directly accessible except by a member function of class `Sphere`.

The output of this program appears in Figure 31.7.

Summary

This chapter introduced you to classes, class members, and member functions. To expand your knowledge of C++ further, you may want to read Que's *Using Borland C++*. The coverage there is compatible with Turbo C++.

The next two chapters discuss file I/O. Once you have covered that material, you will possess the tools to write your own programs with Turbo C++.

```
"C:\>c30visib"
The volume is 268.082581
The surface area is 201.061935
Sphere (1, 2, 3, 4) destroyed
```

Figure 31.7. Class visibility labels in use.

Review Questions

Answers to Review Questions are in Appendix B.

1. What are the two types of class members?
2. Is a constructor always necessary?
3. Is a destructor always necessary?
4. What is the default visibility of a class member?
5. How do you make a class member visible outside its class?

Review Exercise

Construct a class for handling personnel records. Use the following data members and keep them private:

```
char      name[ 25 ];
float     salary;
char      data_of_birth[ 9 ];
```

Create a constructor to initialize the record with its necessary values, and a constructor that simply creates an uninitialized record. Create member functions to alter the individual's name, salary, and date of birth.

32

Sequential Files

So far, every example in this book has processed data that resided inside the program listing or came from the keyboard. You assigned constants and variables to other variables and created new data values from expressions. The programs also received input with `cin`, `gets()`, and the character input functions.

The data that is created by the user and assigned to variables with assignment statements is sufficient for some applications. With the large volumes of data that most real-world applications need to process, however, you need a better way of storing that data. For all but the smallest computer programs, disk files offer the solution.

After storing data on disk, the computer helps you enter, find, change, and delete the data. The computer and C++ are simply tools to help you manage and process data. This chapter focuses on disk file processing concepts and shows you the first of two methods of disk access: *sequential file access.*

This chapter introduces the following topics:

- An overview of disk files
- The types of files
- Processing data on the disk
- Sequential file access
- File I/O functions

After reading this chapter, you will be ready to tackle the more advanced methods of accessing random files, covered in the next chapter. If you have programmed computerized data files with another programming language, you might be surprised at how C++ borrows from other programming languages, especially BASIC, when working with disk files. If you are new to disk file processing, disk files are simple to create and read.

Why Use a Disk?

Disks hold more data than can fit in computer memory.

The typical computer system has much less memory storage than hard disk storage. Your disk drive holds more data than can fit in your computer's RAM. This is the primary reason for using the disk for your data. The disk memory, because it is nonvolatile, also lasts longer; when you power-off your computer, the disk memory is not erased, whereas RAM is erased. Furthermore, when your data changes, you (or more important, your users) do not have to edit the program and look for a set of assignment statements. Instead, the users run previously written programs that make changes to the disk data.

All of this makes programming more difficult at first because programs have to be written to change the data on the disk. However, nonprogrammers can then use the programs and modify the data without knowing how to program.

The capacity of your disk makes it a perfect place to store your data as well as your programs. Think about what would happen if all data had to be stored with a program's assignment statements. What if the Social Security office in Washington, D.C., asked you to write a C++ program to compute, average, filter, sort, and print each person's name and address in its files? Would you want your program to include millions of assignment statements? Not only would you not want the program to hold that much data, but the program could not do so because only relatively small amounts of data fit in a program before you run out of RAM.

By storing data on your disk, you are much less limited because you have more storage. Your disk can hold as much data as you have disk capacity. If your disk requirements grow, you can usually increase your disk space, whereas you cannot always add more RAM to your computer.

NOTE: C++ cannot access the special extended or expanded memory that some computers have.

When working with disk files, C++ does not have to access much RAM because C++ reads data from your disk drive and processes it only parts at a time. Not all your disk data has to reside in RAM for C++ to process it. C++ reads some data, processes it, and then reads some more. If C++ requires disk data a second time, it rereads that place on the disk.

Types of Disk File Access

Your programs can access files in two ways: through sequential access and random access. Your application determines the method you should choose. The access mode of a file determines how you read, write, change, and delete data from the file. Some of your files can be accessed in both ways, sequentially and randomly, as long as your programs are written properly and the data lends itself to both types of file access.

A sequential file has to be accessed in the same order in which the file was written. This is analogous to cassette tapes: you play music in the same order it was recorded. (You can quickly fast-forward or rewind songs that you do not want to listen to, but the order of the songs dictates what you do to play the song you want.) It is difficult, and sometimes impossible, to insert data in the middle of a sequential file. How easy is it to insert a new song in the middle of two other songs on a tape? The only way to add or delete records from the middle of a sequential file is to create a completely new file that combines both old and new songs. It may seem that sequential files are limiting, but it turns out that many applications lend themselves to sequential file processing.

Unlike sequential files, random access files can be accessed in any order you want. Think of data in a random access file as you would songs on a compact disc or record; you can go directly to any song you want without having to play or fast-forward the other songs. If you want to play the first song, the sixth song, and then the fourth song, you can do so. The order of play has nothing to do with the order in which the songs were originally recorded. Random file access sometimes takes more programming but rewards that effort with a more flexible file access method. Chapter 33, "Random Access Files," discusses how to program for random access files.

Sequential File Concepts

You can perform the following operations on sequential disk files:

- Create disk files
- Add to disk files
- Read from disk files

Again, your application determines what you need to do. If you are creating a disk file for the first time, you must create the file and write the initial data to it. Suppose that you want to create a customer data file. You need to create a new file and write your current customers to that file. The customer data might originally be in arrays, arrays of structures, pointed to with pointers, or typed into regular variables by the user.

As your customer base grows, you can add new customers to the file. When you add to the end of a file, you *append* to that file. As customers enter the store, you read their information from the customer data file.

Customer disk processing brings up one disadvantage of sequential files. Suppose that a customer moves and wants you to change his or her address in your files. Sequential access files do not lend themselves well to changing data stored in them. It is also difficult to remove information from sequential files. Random files, described in the next chapter, provide a much easier approach to changing and removing data. The primary approach to changing or removing data from a sequential access file is to create a new one from the old one, using the updated data. Because of the ease of updating provided with random access files, this chapter concentrates on creating, reading, and adding to sequential files.

Opening and Closing Files

Before you can create, write to, or read from a disk file, you must open the file. This is analogous to opening a file cabinet before working with a file stored in the cabinet. Once you are done with a cabinet's file, you close the file door. You must also close a disk file when you finish with it.

When you open a disk file, you just have to inform C++ of the file name and what you want to do (write to, add to, or read from). C++ and MS-DOS work together to make sure that the disk is ready and to create an entry in your file directory (if you are creating a file) for the filename. When you close a file, C++ writes any remaining data to the file, releases the file from the program, and updates the file directory to reflect the file's new size.

> **CAUTION:** You must ensure that the `FILES=` statement in your CONFIG.SYS file is large enough to hold the maximum number of disk files you will have open, with one file left over for your C++ program itself. If you are unsure about how to do this, check your DOS reference manual or a beginner's book on DOS.

To open a file, you call the `open()` function. To close a file, you call the `close()` function. Here are the formats of these two function calls:

```
file_ptr.open(file_name, access);

file_ptr.close();
```

The *`file_ptr`* is a special type of pointer that points only to files, not to data variables.

Your operating system handles the exact location of your data in the disk file. You don't want to worry about the exact track and sector number of your data on the disk. Therefore, you will let the *`file_ptr`* point to the data you are reading and writing. Your program has only to manage the *`file_ptr`* while C++ and MS-DOS take care of locating the actual physical data.

The *`file_name`* is a string (or a character pointer that points to a string) containing a valid filename for your computer. The *`file_name`* can contain a complete disk and directory pathname. You can specify the filename in uppercase or lowercase letters. The `access` can be one of the values from Table 32.1.

Table 32.1. Possible access modes.

Mode	*Description*
`app`	Open the file for appending (adding to it)
`ate`	Seek to end of file on opening it
`in`	Open file for reading
`out`	Open file for writing
`binary`	Open file in binary mode
`trunc`	Discard contents if file exists
`nocreate`	If file doesn't exist, open fails
`noreplace`	If file exists, open fails unless appending or seeking to end of file on opening

The default mode for file access is text. A text file is an ASCII file, compatible with most other programming languages and applications. Text files do not always contain text in the word processing sense of the word. Any data you need to store can go in a text file. Programs that read ASCII files can read data you create as C++ text files.

Binary Modes

If you specify binary access, C++ creates or reads the file in a binary format. Binary data files are "squeezed." That is, they take less space than text files. The disadvantage of using binary files is that other programs cannot always read the data files. Only C++ programs that are written to access binary files can read and write to them. The advantage of binary files is that you save disk space because your data files are more compact. Other than including the access mode in the `open()` function, you use no additional commands to access binary files with your C++ programs.

> The binary format is a system-specific file format. In other words, not all computers will be able to read a binary file created on another computer.
>
> If you open a file for writing, C++ creates the file. If a file by that name *already* exists, C++ overwrites the old file with no warning. You must be careful when opening files so that you do not overwrite existing data you want to save.

If an error occurs during the opening of a file, C++ will not create a valid file pointer. Instead, C++ creates a file pointer equal to zero. For example, if you open a file for output but use a disk name that is invalid, C++ will not be able to open the file and will make the file pointer equal to zero. Always check the file pointer when writing disk file programs in order to ensure that the file opened properly.

> **TIP:** Beginning programmers like to open all files at the beginning of their programs and close them at the end. This is not always best. Open files immediately before you access them and close them when you are done with them. This protects the files, keeping them open only as long as needed. A closed file is more likely to be protected in the unlikely (but possible) event of a power failure or computer breakdown.

This part of the chapter has included a lot of file access theory. The following examples help illustrate these concepts.

Examples

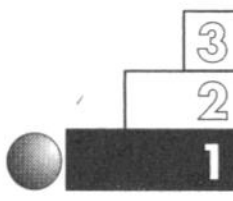

1. Suppose that you want to create a file for storing your house payment records for the last year. Here are the first few lines in the program, which would create a file called HOUSE.DAT on your disk:

```
#include <fstream.h>

main()
     {
     ofstream     file_ptr;      // Declare a file pointer
                                 // for writing
     file_ptr.open("house.dat", ios::out); // Create the file
```

The rest of the program writes data to the file. The program never has to refer to the filename again but will use the `file_ptr` variable to refer to the file. Examples in the next few sections illustrate how this is done. There is nothing special about `file_ptr`, other than its name (although the name is meaningful in this case). You can name file pointer variables XYZ or a908973 if you like, but these names would not be meaningful.

You must include the fstream.h header file because it contains the definition for the `ofstream` and `ifstream` declarations. You don't have to worry about the physical specifics. The `file_ptr` will "point" to data in the file, as you write it. Put the declarations in your programs where you declare other variables and arrays.

TIP: Because files are not part of your program, you might find it useful to declare file pointers globally. Unlike data in variables, file pointers usually don't need to be kept local.

Before finishing with the program, you should close the file. The following `close()` function closes the house file:

```
file_ptr.close();     // Close the house payment file
```

2. If you like, you can put the complete pathname in the file's name. The following line opens the household payment file in a subdirectory on the `d:` disk drive:

```
file_ptr.open("d:\mydata\house.dat", ios::out);
```

3. You can store a filename in a character array or point to it with a character pointer. Each of the following sections of code are equivalent:

```
char     fn[ ] = "house.dat"; // Filename in character array
file_ptr.open(fn, ios::out);         // Create the file

char     *myfile = "house.dat";      // Filename pointed to
file_ptr.open(myfile, ios::out);     // Create the file

// Let the user enter the filename
cout << "What is the name of the household file? ";
gets(filename);       // Filename must be an array
                      // or character pointer
file_ptr.open(filename, ios::out);  // Create the file
```

No matter how you specify the filename when opening the file, close the file with the file pointer. The following `close()` function closes the open file, no matter which method you used to open the file:

```
file_ptr.close();     // Close the house payment file
```

4. You should check the return value from `open()` to ensure that the file opened properly. Here is code after `open()` that checks for an error:

Check to see if an error occurred

```
#include <fstream.h>

main()
     {
     ofstream     file_ptr;        // Declare a file pointer

     file_ptr.open("house.dat", ios::out); // Create the file
     if (!file_ptr)
          cout << "Error opening file.\n");
     else
          {

          // Rest of output commands go here

          }
```

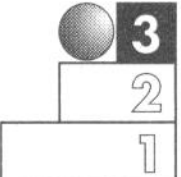

5. You can open and write to several files in the same program. Suppose that you want to read data from a payroll file and create a backup payroll data file. You would have to open the current payroll file by using the `in` reading mode, and the backup file in the `out` output mode.

For each open file in your program, you must declare a different file pointer. The file pointers that your input and output statements use determine which file they operate on. If you have to open many files, you can declare an array of file pointers.

Here is a way you can open the two payroll files:

```
#include <fstream.h>

ifstream     file_in;      // Input file
ofstream     file_out;     // Output file

main()
     {
     file_in.open("payroll.dat", ios::in);  // Existing file
     file_out.open("payroll.BAK", ios::out);   // New file
```

When you finish with these files, be sure to close them with the following two `close()` function calls:

```
file_in.close();
file_out.close();
```

Writing to a File

Any input or output function that requires a device will perform input and output with files. You have seen most of these functions already. The most common file I/O functions are

```
get()
put()

gets()
puts()
```

You can also use the `file_ptr` as you use `cout` or `cin`.

The following function call reads three integers from a file pointed to by `file_ptr`:

```
file_ptr >> num1 >> num2 >> num3;    // Read three variables
```

There is always more than one way to write data to a disk file. Most of the time, more than one function will work. For instance, if you write a bunch of names to a file, both `puts()` and `file_ptr <<` will work. You can also write the names by using `put()`. You should use whichever function you are most comfortable with for the data being written. If you want a newline character (`\n`) at the end of each line in your file, the `file_ptr <<` and `puts()` are probably easier to use than `put()`, but any of these three will do the job.

> **TIP:** Each line in a file is called a *record*. By putting a newline character at the end of file records, you make the input of those records easier.

Examples

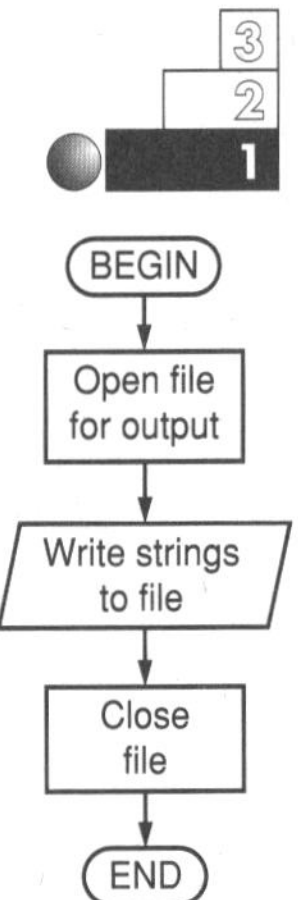

1. The following program creates a file called NAMES.DAT. The program writes five names to a disk file, using `fp <<`.

```
// Filename: C32WR1.CPP
// Writes 5 names to a disk file

#include <fstream.h>

ofstream     fp;

main()
     {
     fp.open("NAMES.DAT", ios::out);    // Create a new file

     fp << "Michael Langston\n";
     fp << "Sally Redding\n";
     fp << "Jane Kirk\n";
     fp << "Stacy Grady\n";
     fp << "Paula Hiquet\n";
     fp.close();                        // Release the file
     return 0;
     }
```

For simplicity, no error checking was done on the `open()`. The next few examples check for the error.

NAMES.TXT is a text data file. If you like, you can read this file into your word processor (use the word processor's command for reading ASCII files), or you can use the MS-DOS TYPE command to display this file on the screen. If you display NAMES.TXT, you see the following:

```
Michael Langston
Sally Redding
Jane Kirk
Stacy Grady
Paula Hiquet
```

2. The following file writes the numbers from 1 to 100 to a file called NUMS.1:

```
// Filename: C32WR2.CPP
// Writes 1 to 100 to a disk file

#include <fstream.h>

ofstream     fp;

main()
     {
     int      ctr;

     fp.open("NUMS.1", ios::out);      // Create a new file
     if (!fp)
          cout << "Error opening file.\n";
     else
          {
          for (ctr = 1; ctr < 101; ctr++)
               fp << ctr << " ";
          }
     fp.close();
     return 0;
     }
```

The numbers are not written one per line, but with a space between them. The format of the `fp <<` determines the format of the output data. When writing data to disk files, keep in mind that you will have to read the data later. You will have to use "mirror image" input functions to read the data you output to files.

Writing to a Printer

The `open()` function and other output functions were not designed just to write to files. They were designed to write to any device, including files, the screen, and the printer. If you need to write data to a printer, you can treat it as if it were a file. The following program opens a file pointer, using the MS-DOS name for a printer located at LPT1 (the first parallel printer port):

```
// Filename: C32PRNT.CPP
// Prints to the printer device

#include <fstream.h>

ofstream     prnt;     // Will point to the printer

main()
     {
     prnt.open("LPT1", ios::out);
     prnt << "Printer line 1\n";     // 1st line printed
     prnt << "Printer line 2\n";     // 2nd line printed
     prnt << "Printer line 3\n";     // 3rd line printed
     prnt.close();
     return 0;
     }
```

Make sure that your printer is turned on and has paper before you run this program. When you run it, the following lines are printed on the printer:

```
Printer line 1
Printer line 2
Printer line 3
```

Adding to a File

You can easily add data to an existing file or create new files by opening the file in append access mode. Data files on the disk are rarely static; they grow almost daily as business increases. Being able to add to data already on the disk is very useful indeed.

A file you open for append access (using `ios::app`) does not have to exist. If the file exists, C++ appends data to the end of the file when you write the data. If the file does not exist, C++ creates the file (just as when you open a file for write access).

Example

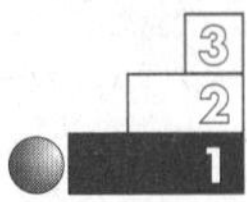

The following program adds three more names to the NAMES.DAT file created earlier:

```
// Filename: C32AP1.CPP
// Adds 3 names to a disk file

#include <fstream.h>

ofstream     fp;

main()
     {
     fp.open("NAMES.DAT", ios:app);      // Add to file
     fp << "Johnny Smith\n";
     fp << "Laura Hull\n";
     fp << "Mark Brown\n";
     fp.close();     // Release the file
     return 0;
     }
```

Here is what the file now looks like:

```
Michael Langston
Sally Redding
Jane Kirk
Stacy Grady
Paula Hiquet
Johnny Smith
```

```
Laura Hull
Mark Brown
```

NOTE: If the file did not exist, C++ would create it and store the three names in the file.

Basically, you have to change only the `open()` function's access mode to turn a file-creation program into a file-appending program.

Reading from a File

Once the data is in a file, you need to be able to read that data. You must open the file in a read access mode. There are several ways to read data. You can read character data a character at a time or a string at a time. The choice depends on the format of the data.

Files must exist if you open them for read access.

Files you open for read access (using `ios::in`) must exist already; otherwise, C++ gives you an error. You cannot read a file that does not exist. `open()` returns zero if the file does not exist when you open it for read access.

Another event happens when reading files. Eventually, you read *all* the data. Subsequent reading produces errors because there is no more data to read. C++ provides a solution to the end-of-file occurrence. If you have read all the data from a file and then try to read the file again, C++ returns the value of zero. To find the end-of-file condition, be sure to check for zero when performing input from files.

Examples

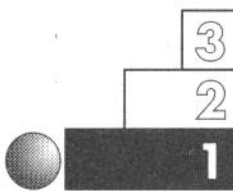

1. The following program asks the user for a filename and prints the contents of the file to the screen. If the file does not exist, the program displays an error message.

```
// Filename: C32RE1.CPP
// Reads and displays a file
```

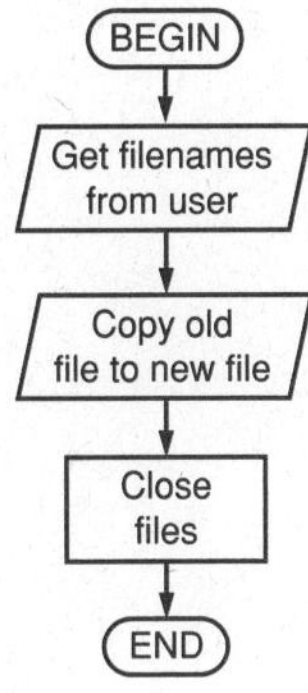


```
#include <fstream.h>
#include <stdlib.h>

ifstream     fp;

main()
     {
     char     filename[ 12 ];     // Will hold user's filename
     char     in_char;            // Input character

     cout << "What is the name of the file ";
     cout << "you want to see? ";
     cin >> filename;
     fp.open(filename, ios::in);
     if (!fp)
          {
          cout << "\n\n*** That file does not exist ***\n";
          exit(0);     // Exit program
          }
     while (fp.get(in_char))
          cout << in_char;
     fp.close();
     return 0;
     }
```

Figure 32.1 shows what happens when the NAMES.DAT file is requested. Because newline characters are in the file at the end of each name, the names appear on the screen, one name per line. If you attempt to read a file that does not exist, the program displays the following message:

```
*** That file does not exist ***
```

2. The following program reads one file and copies it to another file. You might want to use such a program to back up important data in case the original file gets damaged.

   This program must open two files, the first for reading and the second for writing. The file pointer determines which of the two files is being accessed.

```
What is the name of the file you want to see? names.dat
Michael Langston
Sally Redding
Jane Kirk
Stacy Grady
Paula Hiquet
Johnny Smith
Laura Hull
Mark Brown
```

Figure 32.1. Reading and displaying a disk file.

```
// Filename: C32RE2.CPP
// Makes a copy of a file

#include <fstream.h>
#include <stdlib.h>

ifstream     in_fp;
ofstream     out_fp;

main()
     {
     char     in_filename[ 12 ];  // Will hold original
                                  // filename
     char     out_filename[ 12 ]; // Will hold backup
                                  // filename
     char     in_char;            // Input character

     cout << "What is the name of the file ";
     cout << "you want to back up? ";
     cin >> in_filename;
     cout << "What is the name of the file ";
```

```
cout << "you want to copy " << in_filename
     << " to? ";
cin >> out_filename;
in_fp.open(in_filename, ios::in);
if (!in_fp)
     {
     cout << "\n\n*** file does not exist ***\n";
     exit(0);     // Exit program
     }
out_fp.open(out_filename, ios::out);
if (!out_fp)
     {
     cout << "\n\n*** Error opening file ***\n";
     exit(0);     // Exit program
     }
cout << "\nCopying...\n";     // Waiting message
while (in_fp.get(in_char))
     out_fp.put(in_char);
cout << "\nThe file is copied.\n";
in_fp.close();
out_fp.close();
return 0;
}
```

Summary

This chapter showed you how to perform two of the most important requirements of data processing: writing and reading to and from disk files. Before now, you could only store data in variables. The short life of variables (they last only as long as your program is running) made long-term storage of data impossible. Now you can save large amounts of data in disk files for processing later.

Reading and writing sequential files involve learning more concepts than actual commands or functions. The `open()` and `close()` functions are the most important ones discussed in this chapter. You are already familiar with most of the I/O functions needed to get data to and from disk files.

The next chapter, which concludes this book's discussion of disk files, shows you how to create and use random access files. By programming with such files, you will be able to read selected data from a file, as well as change data without having to rewrite the entire file.

Review Questions

Answers to Review Questions are in Appendix B.

1. What are the three ways to access sequential files?
2. What advantages do disk files have over holding data in memory?
3. How do sequential files differ from random access files?

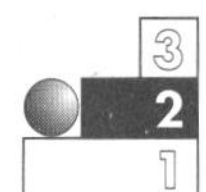

4. What happens if you open a file for read access and the file does not exist?
5. What happens if you open a file for write access and the file already exists?
6. What happens if you open a file for append access and the file does not exist?

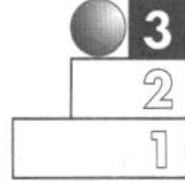

7. How does C++ inform you that you have reached the end-of-file condition?

Review Exercises

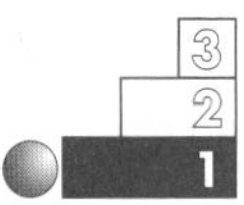

1. Write a program that creates a file containing the following data:

   Your name
   Your address
   Your phone number
   Your age

2. Write a second program that reads and prints the data file created in the preceding exercise.

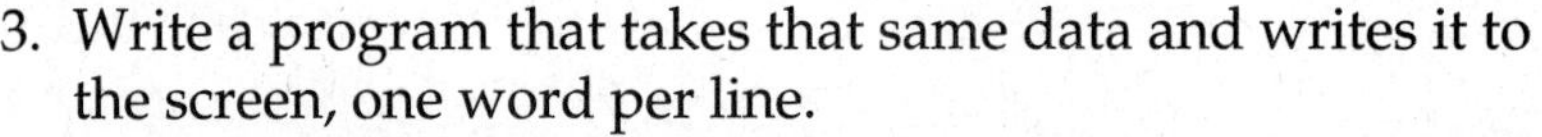

3. Write a program that takes that same data and writes it to the screen, one word per line.

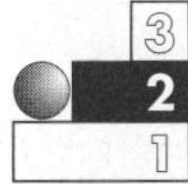

4. Write a program for PCs that backs up two important files: AUTOEXEC.BAT and CONFIG.SYS. Call the backup files AUTOEXEC.SAV and CONFIG.SAV.

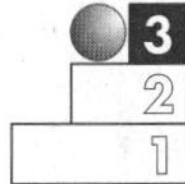

5. Write a program that reads a file and creates a new file with the same data, with one exception: reverse the case on the second file. Everywhere uppercase letters appear in the first file, write lowercase letters to the new file. Everywhere lowercase letters appear in the first file, write uppercase letters to the new file.

33

Random Access Files

Random file access enables you to read or write any data in a disk file without having to read or write every piece of data before it. You can quickly search for, add, retrieve, change, and delete information in a random access file. Although you need a few new functions to access files randomly, you will find that the extra effort pays off in flexibility, power, and speed of disk access.

In this chapter, you learn about the following topics:

- Random access files
- File records
- The `seekg()` function
- Special-purpose file I/O functions

This chapter concludes *Turbo C++ By Example*. With C++'s sequential and random access files, you can do everything you would ever want to do with disk data.

Random File Records

Random files exemplify the power of data processing with C++. Sequential file processing is slow unless you read the entire file into arrays and process them in memory. As explained in the preceding chapter, however, you have much more disk space than RAM, and most disk files do not even fit in your RAM at one time. Therefore, you need a way to quickly read individual pieces of data from a file in any order needed and to process them one at a time.

A record to a file is like a structure to variables.

Generally, you read and write file records. A record to a file is analogous to a C++ structure. A *record* is a collection of one or more data values (called *fields*) that you read and write to disk. Generally, you store data in structures and write the structures to disk, where they are called records. When you read a record from disk, you generally read that record into a structure variable and process it with your program.

Unlike most programming languages, C++ does not require that all disk data be stored in record format. Typically, you write a stream of characters to a disk file and access that data either sequentially or randomly by reading it into variables and structures.

The process of randomly accessing data in a file is simple. Think about the data files of a large credit card organization. When you make a purchase, the store calls the credit card company to get an authorization. There are millions of people in the credit card company's files. There is no way that the credit card company could read from the disk in a timely manner every record that comes before yours. Sequential files do not lend themselves to quick access. It is not feasible in many instances to look up individual records in a data file with sequential access.

The credit card company must use a random file access so that its computers can go directly to your record, just as you go directly to a song on a compact disk or record album. The functions you use are different from the sequential functions, but the power that results from learning the added functions is worth the effort.

You do not have to rewrite the entire file to change random access file data.

Reading and writing files randomly are similar to thinking of the file as a big array. With arrays, you know that you can add, print, or remove values in any order. You do not have to start at the first array element, sequentially looking at the next one, until you get to array element, sequentially looking at the next one, until you get to the element you need. You can view your random access file in the same way, accessing the data in any order.

Most random file records are fixed-length records. That is, each record (usually a row in the file) takes the same amount of disk space. Most of the sequential files you read and wrote in the preceding chapter were variable-length records. When you are reading or writing sequentially, there is no need for fixed-length records because you input each value one character, word, string, or number at a time, looking for the data you want. With fixed-length records, your computer can better calculate exactly where the search record is located on the disk.

Although you waste some disk space with fixed-length records (because of the spaces that pad some of the fields), the advantages of random file access make up for the "wasted" disk space.

TIP: With random access files, you can read or write records in any order. Therefore, even if you want to perform sequential reading or writing of the file, you can use random access processing and "randomly" read or write the file in sequential record number order.

Opening Random Access Files

Just as with sequential files, you must open random access files before reading or writing to them. You can use any of the read access modes mentioned in the preceding chapter (such as `ios::in`) if you will *only* read a file randomly. However, to modify data in a file, you must open the file in one of the update modes listed in the last chapter and repeated in Table 33.1.

Table 33.1. Random access update modes.

Mode	*Description*
`app`	Open the file for appending (adding to it)
`ate`	Seek to end of file on opening it
`in`	Open file for reading
`out`	Open file for writing
`binary`	Open file in binary mode
`trunc`	Discard contents if file exists
`nocreate`	If file doesn't exist, open fails
noreplace	If file exists, open fails unless appending or seeking to end of file on opening

There is really no difference between sequential files and random files in C++. The difference between the files is not physical but lies in the method you use to access and update them.

Examples

1. Suppose that you want to write a program to create a file of friends' names. The following `open()` function call does the job, assuming that `fp` is declared as a file pointer:

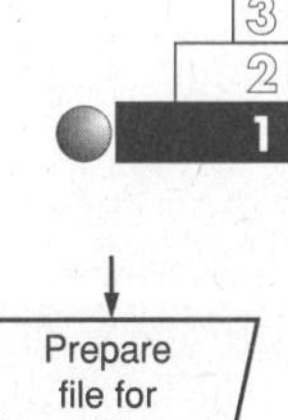


```
fp.open("NAMES.DAT", ios::out);
if (!fp)
cout << "\n*** Cannot open file ***\n");
```

No update `open()` access mode is needed if you are only creating the file. However, what if you wanted to create the file, write names to it, and give the user a chance to change any of the names before closing the file? You would then have to open the file like this:

```
fp.open("NAMES.DAT", ios::in | ios::out);
if (!fp)
cout << "\n*** Cannot open file ***\n");
```

This lets you create the file and then change the data you wrote to the file.

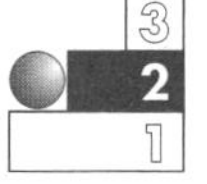

2. As with sequential files, with random files the only difference in using a binary `open()` access mode is that the file you create will be more compact and will save disk space. You will not, however, be able to read that file from other programs as an ASCII text file. The preceding `open()` function can be rewritten to create and allow updating of a binary file. All other file-related commands and functions work for binary files just as they do for text files. Here is the modified code:

```
fp.open("NAMES.DAT", ios::in ¦ ios::out ¦ ios::binary);
if (!fp)
cout << "\n*** Cannot open file ***\n");
```

The seekg() Function

C++ provides a function that allows you to read to a specific point in a random access data file. This is the `seekg()` function. The format of `seekg()` is

```
file_ptr.seekg(long_num, origin);
```

You can use `seekg()` to read forward or backward from any point in a file.

The *`file_ptr`* is the pointer to the file you want to access, initialized with an `open()` statement. *`long_num`* is the number of bytes in the file you want to skip. C++ will not read this many bytes but will literally skip the data by the number of bytes specified in *`long_num`*. Skipping the bytes on the disk is much faster than reading them. If *`long_num`* is negative, C++ skips backward in the file (allowing for rereading of data several times). Because data files can be large, you must declare *`long_num`* as a long integer to hold a large amount of bytes.

The *`origin`* is a value that tells C++ where to begin the skipping of bytes specified by *`long_num`*. The *`origin`* can be any of the three values shown in Table 33.2.

Table 33.2. Possible `origin` values.

Description	*Value*
Beginning of file	`SEEK_SET`
Current file position	`SEEK_CUR`
End of file	`SEEK_END`

The words `SEEK_SET`, `SEEK_CUR`, and `SEEK_END` are defined in stdio.h.

NOTE: Actually, the file pointer plays a much more important role than just "pointing to the file" on the disk. The file pointer continually points to the exact location of the *next byte to read or write*. In other words, as you read data, from either a sequential file or a random access file, the file pointer increments with each byte read. By using `seekg()`, you can move the file pointer forward or backward in the file.

Examples

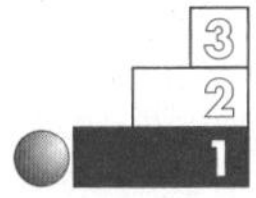

1. No matter how far into a file you have read, the following `seekg()` function positions the file pointer back to the beginning of a file:

```
fp.seekg(0L, SEEK_SET);  // Position the file pointer
                         // at the beginning
```

The constant `0L` passes a long integer `0` to the `seekg()` function. Without the `L`, C++ would pass a regular integer, and this would not match the prototype for `seek()` that is located in fstream.h. Chapter 5, "Variables and Constants," explained the use of data type suffixes on numeric constants, but the suffixes have not been used again until now.

This `seekg()` function literally reads, "move the file pointer 0 bytes from the beginning of the file."

2. The following example reads a file named MYFILE.TXT twice, once to send the file to the screen and once to send the file to the printer. Three file pointers are used, one for each device (the file, the screen, and the printer).

```
// Filename: C33TWIC.CPP
// Writes a file to the printer, rereads it, and sends it
// to the screen

#include <fstream.h>
#include <stdlib.h>
#include <stdio.h>

ifstream     in_file;  // Input file pointer
ofstream     scrn;     // Screen pointer
ofstream     prnt;     // Printer pointer

main()
     {
     char     in_char;

     in_file.open("MYFILE.TXT", ios::in);
     if (!in_file)
          {
          cout << "\n*** Error opening MYFILE.TXT ***\n";
          exit(0);
          }
     scrn.open("CON", ios::out);   // Open screen device
     while (in_file.get(in_char))
          scrn << in_char;         // Output characters
                                   // to the screen
     scrn.close();                 // Close screen since
                                   // it is no longer needed
     in_file.seekg(0L, SEEK_SET);  // Reposition file pointer
     prnt.open("LPT1", ios::out);  // Open printer device
     while (in_file.get(in_char))
          prnt << in_char;         // Output characters
                                   // to the printer
     prnt.close();                 // Always close all
                                   // open files
     in_file.close();
```

```
    return 0;
    }
```

You can also close and then reopen a file to position the file pointer back at the beginning, but using `seekg()` is a more efficient method.

Of course, regular I/O functions could be used to write to the screen, instead of opening the screen as a separate device.

3. The following `seekg()` function positions the file pointer at the 30th byte in the file. (The next byte read will be the 31st byte.)

```
file_ptr.seekg(30L, SEEK_SET);     // Position file pointer
                                   // at the 30th byte
```

This `seekg()` function literally reads, "move the file pointer 30 bytes from the beginning of the file."

If you write structures to a file, you can quickly seek any structure in the file by using the `sizeof()` function. Suppose that you want the 123rd occurrence of the structure tagged with `inventory`. You would search with this `seekg()` function:

```
file_ptr.seekg((123L * sizeof(struct inventory)), SEEK_SET);
```

4. The following program writes the letters of the alphabet to a file called ALPH.TXT. The `seekg()` function is then used to read and display the 9th and 17th letters (I and Q).

```
// Filename: C33ALPH.CPP
// Stores the alphabet in a file and then reads 2 letters
// from it

#include <fstream.h>
#include <stdlib.h>
#include <stdio.h>

ofstream    fp;

main()
    {
```

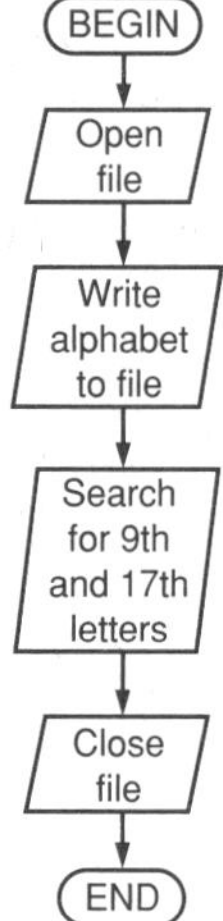


```
char     ch;     // Will hold A through Z

// Open in update mode so that you can read
// file after writing to it
fp.open("alph.txt", ios::in | ios::out);
if (!fp)
     {
     cout << "\n*** Error opening file ***\n";
     exit(0);
     }
for (ch = 'A'; ch <= 'Z'; ch++)
     fp << ch;     // Write letters
fp.seekg(8L, SEEK_SET);   // Skip 8 letters, point to I
fp >> ch;
cout << "The first character is " << ch << "\n";
fp.seekg(16L, SEEK_SET);  // Skip 16 letters, point to Q
fp >> ch;
cout << "The second character is " << ch << "\n";
fp.close();
return 0;
}
```

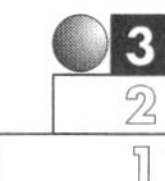

5. To point to the end of a data file, you can use the `seekg()` function to position the file pointer at the last byte. Subsequent `seekg()`s should then use a negative *`long_num`* value to skip backward in the file. The following `seekg()` function makes the file pointer point to the end of the file:

```
file_ptr.seekg(0L, SEEK_END);     // Position file pointer
                                  // at the end
```

This `seekg()` function literally reads, "move the file pointer 0 bytes from the end of the file." The file pointer now points to the end-of-file marker, but you can then `seekg()` backward to get to other data in the file.

6. The following program reads the ALPH.TXT file (created in example 4) backward, printing each character as it skips back in the file:

```
// Filename: C33BACK.CPP
// Reads and prints a file backward
```

```
#include <fstream.h>
#include <stdlib.h>
#include <stdio.h>

ifstream     fp;

main()
     {
     int       ctr;     // Step through the 26 letters
                        // in the file
     char      in_char;

     fp.open("ALPH.TXT", ios::in);
     if (!fp)
          {
          cout << "\n*** Error opening file ***\n";
          exit(0);
          }
     fp.seekg(0L, SEEK_END);      // Point to last byte
                                  // in the file
     for (ctr = 0; ctr <= 26; ctr++)
          {
          fp >> in_char;
          fp.seekg(-2L, SEEK_CUR);
          cout << in_char;
          }
     fp.close();
     return 0;
     }
```

This program also uses `SEEK_CUR` for *origin*. The last `seekg()` in the program seeks two bytes backward from the *current* position — not the beginning or end, as in the previous examples. The `for` loop toward the end of the program performs a "skip two bytes back, read one byte forward" method to skip backward through the file.

7. The following program performs the same actions as example 4 (C33ALPH.CPP), but with one addition. When the letters `I` and `Q` are found, the letter `X` is written over the `I` and `Q`. The `seekg()` must be used to back up one byte in the file to overwrite the letter just read.

```
// Filename: C33CHANG.CPP
// Stores the alphabet in a file, reads 2 letters from it,
// and changes each of them to x

#include <fstream.h>
#include <stdlib.h>
#include <stdio.h>

fstream     fp;

main()
     {
     char     ch;     // Will hold A through Z

     // Open in update mode so that you can read file
     // after writing to it
     fp.open("alph.txt", ios::in | ios::out);
     if (!fp)
          {
          cout << "\n*** Error opening file ***\n";
          exit(0);
          }
     for (ch = 'A'; ch <= 'Z'; ch++)
          fp << ch;     // Write letters
     fp.seekg(8L, SEEK_SET);   // Skip 8 letters, point to I
     fp >> ch;
     // Change the I to an x
     fp.seekg(-1L, SEEK_CUR);
     fp << 'x';
     cout << "The first character is " << ch << "\n";
     fp.seekg(16L, SEEK_SET);  // Skip 16 letters, point to Q
     fp >> ch;
     cout << "The second character is " << ch << "\n";
     // Change the I to an x
     fp.seekg(-1L, SEEK_CUR);
     fp << 'x';
     fp.close();
     return 0;
     }
```

The file named ALPH.TXT now looks like this:

```
ABCDEFGHxJKLMNOPxRSTUVWXYZ
```

This program forms the basis of a more complete data file management program. After you master the `seekg()` function and become more familiar with disk data files, you can begin to write programs that store more advanced data structures and access them.

The mailing list application in Appendix F is a good example of what you can do with random file access. The user is given a chance to change name and address information for people already in the file. The program uses random access seeks and writes to change selected data without having to rewrite the entire disk file.

Other Helpful I/O Functions

Several more disk I/O functions are available that you might find useful. They are mentioned here for completeness. As you write more powerful programs in C++, you will find a use for many of these functions when performing disk I/O. Each of the following functions is prototyped in the fstream.h header file:

- `read(`*`array`*`, `*`count`*`)`. Reads the amount of data specified by the integer *`count`* into the array or pointer specified by *`array`*. `read()` is called a *buffered I/O* function. `read()` lets you read a lot of data with a single function call.
- `write(`*`array`*`, `*`count`*`)`. Writes *`count array`* bytes to the file specified. `write()` is a buffered I/O function. `write()` lets you write a lot of data in a single function call.
- `remove(`*`filename`*`)`. Erases the file named by *`filename`*. `remove()` returns a 0 if the file was successfully erased or –1 if an error occurred.

Many of these built-in I/O functions, as well as others you will learn in your C++ programming career, are helpful functions that you can duplicate by using what you already know.

The buffered I/O file functions let you read and write entire arrays (including arrays of structures) to the disk in a single function call.

Examples

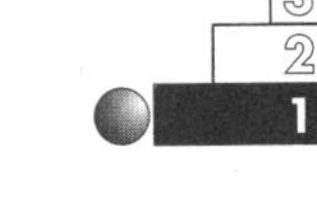

1. The following program requests a filename from the user and erases the file from the disk, using the `remove()` function.

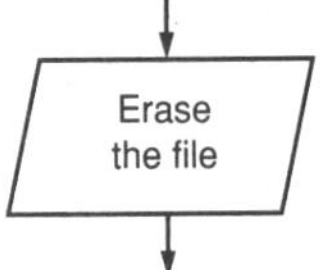


```
// Filename: C33ERAS.CPP
// Erases the file specified by the user

#include <stdio.h>
#include <iostream.h>

main()
     {
     char     filename[ 12 ];

     cout << "What is the filename you want me to erase? ";
     cin >> filename;
     if (remove(filename) == -1)
          cout << "\n*** I could not remove the file ***\n";
     else
          cout << "\nThe file " << filename <<
               " is now removed\n";
     return 0;
     }
```

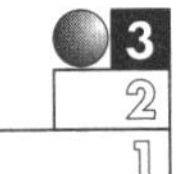

2. The following function could be part of a larger program that gets inventory data, in an array of structures, from the user. This function is passed the array name and the number of elements (structure variables) in the array. The `write()` function then writes the complete array of structures to the disk file pointed to by `fp`.

```
void write_str(struct inventory items[ ], int inv_cnt)
     {
     fp.write(items, inv_cnt * sizeof(struct inventory);
     return;
     }
```

If the inventory array had 1,000 elements, this one-line function would still write the entire array to the disk file. The `read()` function can be used to read the entire array of structures from the disk in a single function call.

Summary

C++ supports random access files with several functions. These include error checking, file pointer positioning, opening of files, and closing of files. You now have the tools you need to save your C++ program data to the disk for storage and retrieval.

The mailing list application in Appendix F offers a complete example of random access file manipulation. The program lets the user enter names and addresses, store them to disk, edit them, change them, and print them from the disk file. The mailing list program combines almost every topic from this book into a complete application that "puts it all together."

Review Questions

Answers to Review Questions are in Appendix B.

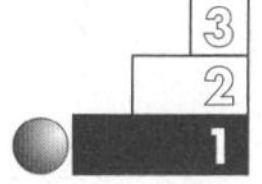

1. What is the difference between records and structures?
2. True or false: You have to create a random access file before reading from it randomly.
3. What happens to the file pointer as you read from a file?

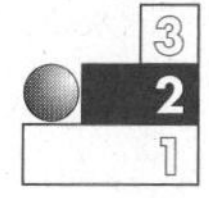

4. What are the two buffered file I/O functions?
5. What are two methods for positioning the file pointer at the beginning of a file?

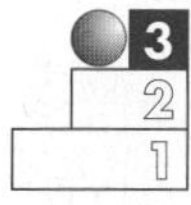

6. What are the three starting positions (the *origin*s) in the `seekg()` function?
7. What is wrong with the following program?

```
#include <fstream.h>

ifstream     fp;

main()
     {
     char     in_char;

     fp.open(ios::in ¦ ios::binary);
     if fp.get(in_char))
          cout << in_char;     // Write to the screen
     fp.close();
     return 0;
     }
```

Review Exercises

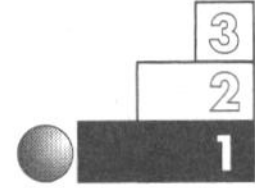

1. Write a program that asks the user for a list of five names and writes the names to a file. Rewind the file and display its contents on the screen, using the `seekg()` and `get()` functions.

2. Rewrite the preceding program so that it displays every other character in the file of names.

3. Write a program that reads characters from a file. If the input character is a lowercase letter, change it to uppercase. If the input character is uppercase, change it to lowercase. Do not change other characters in the file.

4. Write a program that displays the number of nonalphabetic characters in a file.

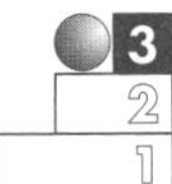

5. Write a grade-keeping program for a teacher. Let the teacher enter up to 10 students' grades. Each student has 3 grades for the semester. Store the student names and their 3 grades in an array of structures and store the data on the disk. Make the program menu-driven. Let the teacher have the options of adding more students, looking at the file's data, or printing the grades to the printer with a calculated class average.

Part VIII

Appendixes

A

Memory Addressing, Binary, and Hexadecimal Review

You do not have to understand the concepts in this appendix to become well versed in C++. The only way you can master C++, however, is to spend some time learning about the "behind the scenes" roles played by binary numbers. The material presented here is not difficult, but many programmers do not take the time to study it. Hence, there are a handful of C++ masters who learn this material and understand how C++ works "under the hood," and there are those who will never be as expert in the language as they could be.

You should take the time to learn about addressing, binary numbers, and hexadecimal numbers. These fundamental principles are presented here for you to learn, and although a working knowledge of C++ is possible without understanding them, they will greatly enhance your C++ skills (and your skills in every other programming language).

After reading this appendix, you will better understand why different C++ data types hold different ranges of numbers. You will also see the importance of being able to represent hexadecimal numbers in C++, and you will better understand C++ array and pointer addressing.

Computer Memory

Each memory location inside your computer holds a single character called a *byte*. A byte is any character, whether it is a letter of the alphabet, a digit, or a special character such as a period, question mark, or even a space (a blank character). If your computer contains 640K of memory, it can hold a total of approximately 640,000 bytes of memory. This means that once you fill your computer's memory with 640K, there will be no room for an additional character unless you overwrite something else.

Before describing the physical layout of your computer's memory, it may be best to take a detour and explain what 640K means.

Memory and Disk Measurements

K means approximately 1,000 and exactly 1,024.

By appending the *K* (from the metric word *Kilo*) to memory measurements, the manufacturers of computers do not have to attach as many zeros to the end of numbers for disk and memory storage. The K stands for approximately 1,000 bytes. As you are about to see, almost everything inside your computer is based on a power of 2. Therefore, the K of computer memory measurements actually equals the power of 2 closest to 1,000, which is 2 to the 10th power, or 1,024. Because 1,024 is very close to 1,000, computerists often think of K as meaning 1,000, even though they know it equals *approximately* 1,000.

Think for a moment what 640K exactly equals. Practically speaking, 640K is about 640,000 bytes. To be exact, however, 640K equals 640 times 1,024, or 655,360. This explains why the PC DOS command CHKDSK returns 655,360 as your total memory (assuming that you have 640K of RAM) instead of 640,000.

M means approximately 1,000,000 and exactly 1,048,576.

Because extended memory and many disk drives can hold such a large amount of data (typically several million characters), there is an additional memory measurement shortcut used, called *M*, which stands for *Meg*, or *Megabytes*. The M is a shortcut for approximately one million bytes. Therefore, 20M is approximately 20,000,000 characters, or bytes, of storage. As with K, the M literally stands for 1,048,576 because that is the closest power of 2 (2 to the 20th power) to one million.

How many bytes of storage is 60 megabytes? It is approximately 60 million characters, or 62,914,560 characters to be exact.

Memory Addresses

Like each house in your town, each memory location in your computer has a unique *address*. A memory address is simply a sequential number, starting at 0, that labels each memory location. Figure A.1 shows a diagram of how your computer memory addresses are numbered if you have 640K of RAM.

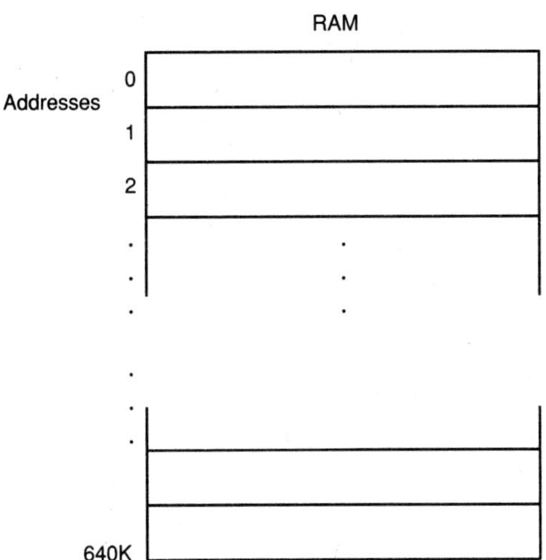

Figure A.1. Memory addresses for a 640K computer.

By using unique addresses, your computer can keep track of memory. When the computer stores a result of a calculation in memory, it finds an empty address, or one matching the data area where the result is to go, and stores the result at that address.

Your C++ programs and data share computer memory with DOS. DOS must always reside in memory while you operate your computer; otherwise, your programs would have no way to access disks, printers, the screen, or the keyboard. Figure A.2 shows computer memory being shared by DOS and a C++ program. The exact amount of memory taken by DOS and a C++ program is determined by the version of DOS you use, how many DOS extras (such as device drivers and buffers) your computer uses, and the size and needs of your C++ program and data.

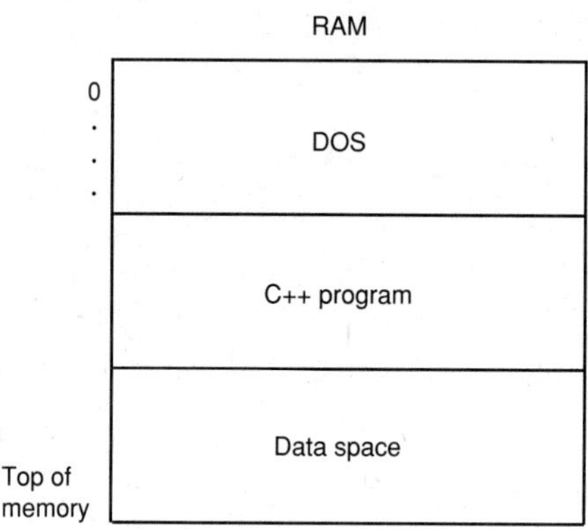

Figure A.2. DOS, your C++ program, and your program's data share the same memory.

Bits and Bytes

You now know that a single address of memory might contain any character, called a byte. You know that your computer holds many bytes of information, but it does not store those characters in the same way that humans think of characters. For example, if you press the letter W on your keyboard while working in your C++ editor, you will see the `W` on the screen, and you also know that the

W is stored in a memory location at some unique address. Actually, your computer does not store the letter W; it stores electrical impulses that stand for the letter W.

Electricity, which is what runs through the components of your computer to make it understand and execute your programs, can exist in only two states: on and off. As with a light bulb, electricity is either flowing (it is on) or not flowing (it is off). Even though you can dim some lights, the electricity is still either on or off.

Today's modern digital computers use this on/off concept. Your computer is nothing more than millions of on and off switches. You may have heard about integrated circuits, transistors, and even vacuum tubes that computers over the years have contained. These electrical components are nothing more than switches that rapidly turn electrical impulses on and off.

The binary digits 1 and 0 (called bits) represent on and off states of electricity.

This two-state (on and off) mode of electricity is called a *binary* state of electricity. Computer people use a 1 to represent an on state (a switch in the computer that is on) and a 0 to represent an off state (a switch that is off). These numbers, 1 and 0, are called binary digits. The term *binary digits* is usually shortened to *bits*. A bit is either a 1 or a 0, representing an on or off state of electricity. Different combinations of bits represent different characters.

Several years ago, someone listed every single character that might be represented on a computer, including all uppercase letters, all lowercase letters, the digits 0 through 9, the many other characters (such as %, *, {, and +), and some special control characters. When you add up the total number of characters that a PC can represent, you will get 256 of them. These are listed in Appendix C's ASCII (pronounced "ask-ee") table.

The order of the ASCII table's 256 characters is basically arbitrary, just as the radio's Morse code table is arbitrary. With Morse code, different sets of long and short beeps represent different letters of the alphabet. In the ASCII table, a different combination of bits (1s and 0s strung together) represents each of the 256 ASCII characters. The ASCII table is a standard table used by almost every PC in the world. Its letters form the acronym for American Standard Code for Information Interchange. (There is a similar table that some minicomputers and mainframes use, called the EBCDIC table.)

It turns out that if you take every different combination of eight 0s strung together all the way to eight 1s strung together (that is, from 00000000, 00000001, 00000010, and so on, until you get to 11111110, and last, 11111111), you will have a total of 256 of them! (256 is 2 to the 8th power.) Each memory location in your computer holds eight bits. These bits can be any combination of eight 1s and 0s. This brings you to the following fundamental rule of computers:

> Because it takes a combination of eight 1s and 0s to represent a character, and because each byte of computer memory can hold exactly one character, it holds true that eight bits equal one byte.

For a better perspective on this, consider that the bit pattern needed for the uppercase letter A is 01000001. No other character in the ASCII table "looks" like this to the computer because each of the 256 characters is assigned a unique bit pattern.

Suppose that you press the A key on your keyboard. Your keyboard does *not* send a letter A to the computer; instead, it looks in its ASCII table for the on and off states of electricity that represent the letter A. As Figure A.3 shows, when you press the A key, the keyboard actually sends 01000001 (as on and off impulses) to the computer. Your computer simply stores this bit pattern for A in a memory location. Even though you can think of the memory location as holding an A, it really holds the byte 01000001.

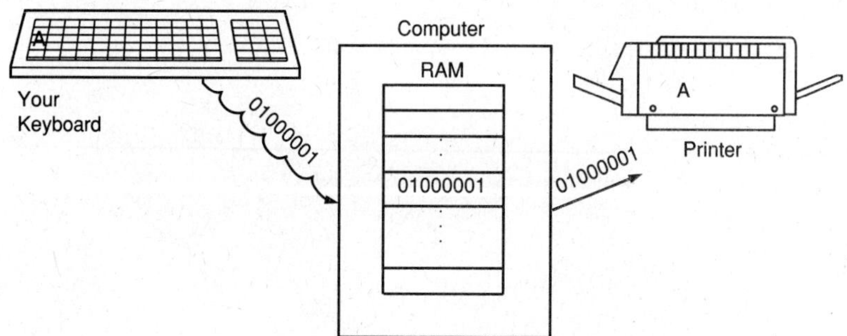

Figure A.3. Your computer keeps track of characters by their bit patterns.

If you were to print that A, your computer does not send an A to the printer but sends the 01000001 bit pattern for an A. The printer receives that bit pattern, looks up the correct letter in the ASCII table, and prints an A.

From the time you press the A until the time you see it on the printer, it is *not* the letter A! It is the ASCII pattern of bits the computer uses to represent an A. Because a computer is electrical and electricity is easily turned on and off, this is a very nice way for the computer to manipulate and move characters, and it can do so very quickly. Actually, if it were up to the computer, you would enter everything by its bit pattern and look at all the results in their bit patterns! This would not be good, so devices such as the keyboard, screen, and printer work part of the time with letters as we know them. That is why the ASCII table is such as integral part of a computer.

There are times when your computer treats two bytes as a single value. Even though memory locations are typically eight bits wide, many CPUs access memory two bytes at a time. In that case, the two bytes are called a *word* of memory. On other computers (commonly mainframes), the word size may be four bytes (32 bits) or even eight bytes (64 bits).

A Summary of Bits and Bytes

A bit is either a 1 or a 0 that represents an on or off state of electricity.

Eight bits represent a byte.

A byte, or eight bits, represents one character.

Each memory location of your computer is eight bits (a single byte) wide. Therefore, each memory location can hold one character of data. A list of all possible characters can be found in the ASCII table in Appendix C.

If the CPU accesses memory two bytes at a time, those two bytes are called a word of memory.

The Order of Bits

To further understand memory, you should know how programmers refer to individual bits. Figure A.4 shows a byte and a two-byte word. Notice that the far right bit is called bit 0. From bit 0, keep counting by 1s as you move left. For a byte, the bits are numbered 0 to 7, from right to left. For a double byte (a 16-bit word), the bits are numbered from 0 to 15, from right to left.

Bit 0 is called the *least-significant bit*, or sometimes the *low-order bit*. Bit 7 (or bit 15 for a 2-byte word) is called the *most-significant bit*, or sometimes the *high-order bit*.

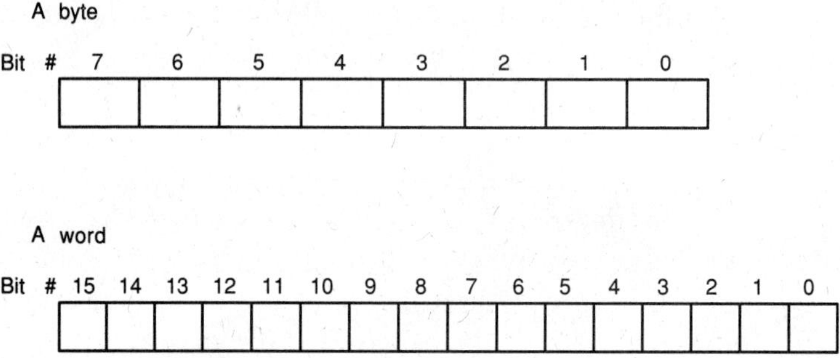

Figure A.4. The order of bits in a byte and a two-byte word.

Binary Numbers

Because a computer works best with 1s and 0s, its internal numbering method is limited to a *base-2* (binary) numbering system. People work in a *base-10* numbering system in the real world. The base-10 numbering system is sometimes called the decimal numbering system. There are always as many different digits as the base in a numbering system. For example, in the base-10 system, there are 10 digits, 0 through 9. As soon as you count to 9 and run out of digits, you have to combine some that you already used. The number 10 is a representation of 10 values but combines the digits 1 and 0.

The same is true of base 2. There are only two digits, 0 and 1. As soon as you run out of digits, after the second one, you have to reuse digits. The first 7 binary numbers are

0 1 10 11 100 101 110

If you do not understand how these numbers were derived, that is okay; you will see how in a moment. For the time being, you should realize that no more than two digits, 0 and 1, can be used to represent any base-2 number, just as no more than 10 digits, 0 through 9, can be used to represent any base-10 number in the regular "real world" numbering system.

You should know that a base-10 number, such as 2,981, does not really mean anything by itself. You must assume what base it is. You get very used to working with base-10 numbers because that is what the world uses. However, the number 2,981 actually represents a quantity based on powers of 10. For example, Figure A.5 shows what the number 2,981 represents. Notice that each digit in the number stands for a certain number of a power of 10.

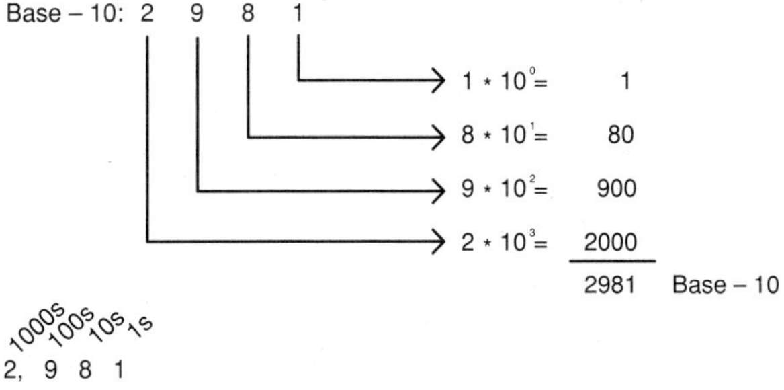

Figure A.5. The base-10 breakdown of the number 2,981.

This same concept applies when you work in a base-2 numbering system. Your computer uses this numbering system, so the power of 2 is just as common to your computer as the power of 10 is to you. The only difference is that the digits in a base-2 number represent powers of 2 and not powers of 10. Figure A.6 shows what the binary numbers 10101 and 10011110 are in base-10. This is how you convert any binary number to its base-10 equivalent.

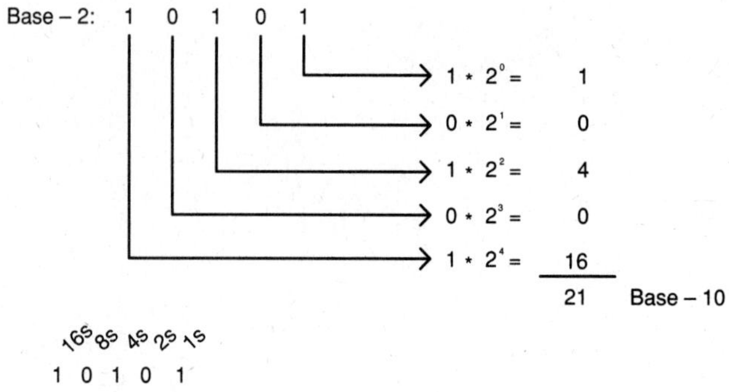

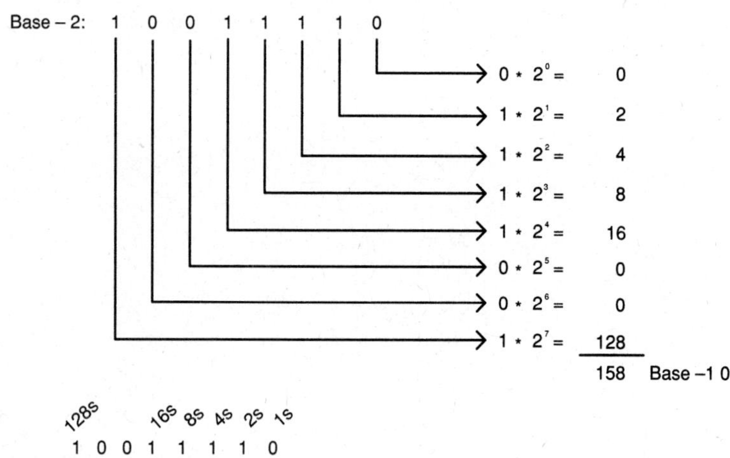

Figure A.6. The base-2 breakdown of the numbers 10101 and 10011110.

A binary number can contain only the digits 1 and 0.

A base-2 number contains only 1s and 0s. To convert any base-2 number to base-10, add each power of 2 everywhere a 1 appears in the number. The base-2 number 101 represents the base-10 number 5; there are two 1s in the number — one in the 2 to the 0th power (which equals 1), and one in the 2 to the 2nd power (which equals 4). Table A.1 shows the first 17 base-10 numbers, and their matching base-2 numbers.

Table A.1. The first 17 base-10 (decimal) and base-2 (binary) numbers.

Base-10	*Base-2*	*Base-10*	*Base-2*
0	0	9	1001
1	1	10	1010
2	10	11	1011
3	11	12	1100
4	100	13	1101
5	101	14	1110
6	110	15	1111
7	111	16	10000
8	1000	17	10001

You do not have to memorize this table; you should be able to figure the base-10 numbers from their matching binary numbers by adding the powers of 2 over each 1 (on bit). Many programmers do memorize the first several binary numbers, however, which can come in handy in advanced programming techniques.

What is the largest binary number a byte can hold? The answer is all 1s, or 11111111. If you add the first 8 powers of 2, you will get 255.

A byte holds either a number or an ASCII character, depending on how it is accessed. For example, if you were to convert the base-2 number 01000001 to a base-10 number, you would get 65. However, this also happens to be the ASCII bit pattern for an uppercase letter A. Check out the ASCII table, and you will see that the A is ASCII code 65. Because the ASCII table is so closely linked with the bit patterns, the computer knows (by the context of how they are used) to work with a number 65, or a letter A.

Unlike an ASCII character, a binary number is not limited to a byte. Sixteen or 32 bits at a time can represent a binary number (and usually do). There are more powers of 2 to add when converting that number to a base-10 number, but the process is the same. You ought to be able to figure out by now (although it may take a little time to calculate) that 1010101010101010 is 43,690 in the base-10 decimal numbering system.

To convert from decimal to binary takes a little more effort. Luckily, you rarely need to convert in that direction. Converting from base-10 to base-2 is not covered here.

Binary Arithmetic

At their lowest level, computers can only add and convert binary numbers to their negative equivalents. Computers are not truly able to subtract, multiply, and divide, although they simulate these operations through judicious use of the addition and negative-conversion techniques.

If a computer were to add the numbers 7 and 6, it can do so (at the binary level). The result will be 13. If the computer is instructed to subtract 7 from 13, it cannot do so. However, it can take the negative value of 7 and add that to 13. Because −7 plus 13 equals 6, the result is a simulated subtraction.

To multiply, computers perform repeated addition. To multiply 6 by 7, the computer adds seven 6s together and gets a 42 as the answer. To divide 42 by 7, a computer keeps subtracting 7 from 42 repeatedly until it gets to a 0 answer (or less than 0 if there is a remainder), and then counts the number of times it took to reach 0.

All math is done at the binary level, so the following additions are possible in binary arithmetic:

0 + 0 = 0

0 + 1 = 1

1 + 0 = 1

1 + 1 = 10

Because these are binary numbers, the last result is not the number 10, but the binary number 2. (Just as the binary 10 means "no ones, and carry an additional power of two," the decimal number 10 means "no ones, carry a power of ten.") There is not a binary digit to represent a 2, so you have to combine the 1 and the 0 to form the new number.

Since binary addition is the foundation of all other math, you should learn how to add binary numbers. You will then understand how computers do the rest of their arithmetic.

Using the binary addition rules previously shown, consider the following binary calculation:

```
  01000001  (65 decimal)
+ 00101100  (44 decimal)
  --------
  01101101  (109 decimal)
```

The first number, 01000001, is 65 decimal. This also happens to be the bit pattern for the ASCII A, but if you add with it, the computer knows to interpret it as the number 65 instead of the character A.

The following binary addition requires a carry into bit 4 and bit 6:

```
 00101011  (43 decimal)
+00100111  (39 decimal)
 --------
 01010010  (82 decimal)
```

Typically, you have to ignore bits that carry past bit 7, or bit 15 for double-byte arithmetic. For example, both of the following binary additions produce incorrect positive results:

```
 10000000 (128 decimal)  +1000000000000000 (65536 decimal)
+10000000 (128 decimal)  +1000000000000000 (65536 decimal)
 --------                 ----------------
 00000000 (0 decimal)     0000000000000000 (0 decimal!)
```

There is no 9th or 17th bit for the carry, so both of these additions produce incorrect results. Because the byte and 16-bit word cannot hold the answers, the magnitude of both of these additions is not possible. The computer must be programmed, at the bit level, to perform *multiword arithmetic*, which is beyond the scope of this book.

Binary Negative Numbers

Because subtracting requires understanding binary negative numbers, you need to learn how computers represent them. The computer uses *2's complement* to represent negative numbers in binary form. To convert a binary number to its 2's complement (to its negative) you must do the following:

1. Reverse the bits (the 1s to 0s, and the 0s to 1s).
2. Add 1.

Negative binary numbers are stored in their 2's complement format.

This may seem a little strange at first, but it works very well for binary numbers. To represent a binary −65, you need to take the binary 65 and convert it to its 2's complement, such as

```
01000001      (65 decimal)
10111110      (Reverse the bits)
      +1      (Add 1)
--------
10111111      (−65 binary)
```

By converting the 65 to its 2's complement, you produce −65 in binary. You might wonder what makes 10111111 mean the negative 65, but by the 2's complement definition, it means −65.

If you were told that 10111111 is a negative number, how would you know which binary number it is? You perform the 2's complement on it. Whatever number you produce is the positive of that negative number. Note the following example:

```
10111111      (−65 decimal)
01000000      (Reverse the bits)
      +1      (Add 1)
--------
01000001      (65 decimal)
```

Something might seem wrong at this point. You just saw that 10111111 is the binary −65, but isn't 10111111 *also* 191 decimal (adding the powers of 2 marked by the 1s in the number, as explained in a previous section)? It depends on whether the number is *signed* or *unsigned*. If a number is signed, the computer looks at the most-significant bit (the leftmost bit) called the *sign bit*. If the most-significant bit is a 1, the number is negative. If it is 0, the number is positive.

Most numbers are 16 bits in length. That is, two-byte words are used to store most integers. This is not always the case for all computers, but it is true for most PCs.

In the C++ programming language, you can designate numbers as either signed integer or unsigned integers (they are signed by default if you do not specify otherwise). If you designate a variable as a signed integer, the computer will interpret the high-order bit as a sign bit. If the high-order bit is on (1), the number is negative. If the high-order bit is off (0), the number is positive. If, however, you designate a variable as an unsigned integer, the computer uses the high-order bit as just another power of 2. That is why the range of unsigned integer variables goes higher (generally from 0 to 65536, but it depends on the computer) than for signed integer variables (generally from −32768 to +32767).

After so much description, a little review is in order. Assume that the following 16-bit binary numbers are unsigned:

0011010110100101   1001100110101010   1000000000000000

These numbers are unsigned, so bit 15 is not the sign bit, but just another power of 2. You should practice converting these large 16-bit numbers to decimal. The decimal equivalents are

13733   39338   32768

If, however, these numbers are signed numbers, the high-order bit (bit 15) indicates the sign. If the sign bit is 0, the number is positive, and you convert the numbers to decimal in the usual manner. If the sign bit is 1, you must convert the numbers to their 2's complement in order to find what they equal. Their decimal equivalents are

+13733   −26198   −32768

To compute the last two binary numbers to their decimal equivalents, take their 2's complement and convert it to decimal. Put a minus sign in front of the result, and you find what the original number represents.

TIP: To make sure that you convert a number to its 2's complement correctly, you can add the 2's complement to its original positive value. If the answer is 0 (ignoring the extra carry to the left), you know that the 2's complement number is correct. This is just like saying that decimal opposites, such as −72 + 72, add up to zero.

Hexadecimal Numbers

All those 1s and 0s get confusing to people. If it were up to your computer, you would enter *everything* as 1s and 0s! This is unacceptable because people don't like to keep track of all those 1s and 0s. Therefore, a *hexadecimal* numbering system (sometimes called *hex*) was devised. The hexadecimal numbering system is based on base-16 numbers. As with other bases, there are 16 unique digits in the base-16 numbering system. Here are the first 19 hexadecimal numbers:

0 1 2 3 4 5 6 7 8 9 A B C D E F 10 11 12

Hexadecimal numbers use 16 unique digits, 0 through F.

Because there are only 10 unique digits as we know them (0 through 9), we must use the letters A through F to represent the remaining six digits. (Anything could have been used, but the designers of the hexadecimal numbering system decided to use the first six letters of the alphabet.)

To understand base-16 numbers, you should know how to convert them to base-10, so that they represent numbers people are familiar with. You perform the conversion to base-10 from base-16 in the same way that you did with base-2, but instead of representing powers of 2, each hexadecimal digit represents powers of 16. Figure A.7 shows how to convert the number 3C5 to decimal.

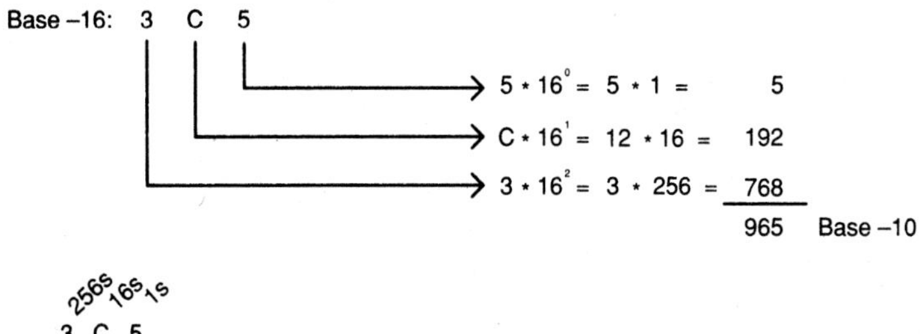

Figure A.7. Converting hexadecimal 3C5 to its decimal equivalent.

TIP: There are calculators available for programmers to do conversions between numbers in base-16, base-10, and base-2, as well as perform 2's complement arithmetic.

You ought to be able to convert 2B to its decimal 43 equivalent and convert E1 to decimal 225 in the same manner. Table A.2 shows the first 20 decimal, binary, and hexadecimal numbers.

Table A.2. The first 20 base-10 (decimal), base-2 (binary), and base-16 (hexadecimal) numbers.

Base-10	*Base-2*	*Base-16*	*Base-10*	*Base-2*	*Base-16*
1	1	1	11	1011	A
2	10	2	12	1100	B
3	11	3	13	1101	C
4	100	4	14	1110	D
5	101	5	15	1111	E
6	110	6	16	10000	F
7	111	7	17	10001	10
8	1000	8	18	10010	11
9	1001	9	19	10011	12
10	1010	A	20	10100	13

Why Learn Hexadecimal?

Hexadecimal notation is extremely efficient for describing memory locations and values because of its close association to the actual binary numbers your computer uses. It is much easier for you (and more important at this level, for your *computer*) to convert from base-16 to base-2 than from base-10 to base-2. Therefore, you sometimes want to represent data at the bit level, but using hexadecimal notation is easier (and requires less typing) than using binary numbers.

To convert from hexadecimal to binary, convert each hex digit to its 4-bit binary number. You can use Table A.2 as a guide for this. For example, the hexadecimal number

5B75

can be converted to binary by taking each digit and converting it to four binary numbers. If you need leading zeros to "pad" the four digits, use them. The number becomes

0101 1011 0111 0101

It turns out that the binary number 0101101101110101 is equal to the hexadecimal number 5B75. This was much easier than converting them both to decimal first.

To convert from binary to hexadecimal, reverse this process. If you are given the binary number

1101000011110111111010

you can convert it to hexadecimal by grouping the bits into groups of four, starting with the right bit. Since there is not an even number of groups of four, pad the leftmost one with 0s. You will then have the following:

0011 0100 0011 1101 1111 1010

Now you just have to convert each group of four binary digits into their hexadecimal number equivalents. You can refer to Table A.2 for help. You then get the following base-16 number:

343DFA

The C++ programming language also supports the base-8 *octal* representation of numbers. Because octal numbers are rarely used much in today's computers, they are not covered here.

How This Relates to C++

The material presented here may seem foreign to many programmers. The binary and 2's complement arithmetic resides deep in your computer and is shielded from most programmers (except assembly language programmers). Understanding this level of your computer, however, explains everything else you learn.

Many C++ programmers learn C++ before delving into binary and hexadecimal representation. For them, there is much about the C++ language that seems strange but could be explained very easily if they understood these basic concepts.

For example, a signed integer holds a different range of numbers from that of an unsigned integer. You now know the reason for this: the sign bit is used in two different ways, depending on whether the number is designated as signed or unsigned.

The ASCII table should make more sense to you after this discussion as well. The ASCII table is an integral part of your computer. Characters are not actually stored in memory and variables; instead, their ASCII bit patterns are. That is why C++ is able to move between characters and integers with ease. The following two C++ statements are allowed, although they probably would not be in another programming language:

```
char c = 65;      // Put the ASCII letter A in c
int ci = 'A';     // Put the number 65 in ci
```

The hexadecimal notation taught to a lot of C++ programmers also makes more sense when they truly understand base-16 numbers. For example, if you saw the line

```
char a = '\x041';
```

you would be able to convert the hex 41 to decimal (65 decimal) if you wanted to know what was really being assigned. In addition, C++ systems programmers find that they can better interface with assembly language programs if they understand the concepts presented here.

If you gain only a cursory knowledge of this material at this point, you will be very much ahead of the game when you program in C++.

Answers to Review Questions

Chapter 1 Answers

1. Low-level languages express a problem and its solution in a language that is very close to the computer's native machine language. High-level languages allow you to express a problem and its solution in a language you can readily understand.
2. It has aspects of both.
3. C++ embodies some of the object-oriented models and allows the user to define data types not possible under C++.
4. It offers an integrated programming environment, providing both the compiler and the source code editor in one program.
5. DOS and Windows
6. BIOS calls are faster. Operating system calls are more portable.

Chapter 2 Answers

1. False
2. The text window
3. Clicking means to press a mouse button once quickly. Double-clicking means to press a mouse button twice rapidly. Dragging means to press a mouse button and hold it down while you move the mouse.
4. No. The menus are there so that you don't have to memorize commands.
5. Click **H**elp and then **C**ontents. Or press Alt+F+C.
6. It means that the help screen you bring up is a response to whatever the cursor is on.
7. To save any modified files
8. Pressing F1 or clicking the **H**elp menu item
9. C
10. They are used to automate some features of Turbo C++, such as allowing the compiler to be used in a batch file.
11. You use the shortcut keys as an alternative to having to go through the levels of menus.

Chapter 3 Answers

1. A set of detailed instructions that tells the computer what to do
2. Buy one or write it yourself.
3. False
4. The program produces the output.
5. A program editor
6. .CPP

7. You must first plan the program by determining the steps you will take to produce the final program.
8. To get the errors out of your program
9. False. You must compile a program before linking it. Most compilers link the program automatically.

Chapter 4 Answers

1. `/*` before and `*/` after
2. A holding place for data that can be changed
3. A value that cannot be changed
4. False
5. `+`, `-`, `*`, and `/`
6. `=` (the assignment operator)
7. False. There can be floating-point, double floating-point, short integers, long integers, and many more variable data types.
8. `cout`
9. `city` must be a variable name because it is not enclosed in quotation marks.
10. All C++ statements must be in lowercase.

Chapter 5 Answers

1. `my_name` and `sales_89`
2. Characters: `'X'` and `'0'`

   Strings: `"2.0"` and `"X"`

   Integer: `0` and `-708`

   Floating-point constants: `-12.0` and `65.4`

3. Seven variables are declared — 3 integers, 3 characters, and 1 floating-point variable.
4. A null zero, also called a binary zero
5. True
6. 1
7. As a series of ASCII values, representing the characters and blanks in the string, ending in a binary 0
8. As a single binary 0

Chapter 6 Answers

1. `char my_name[ ] = "This is C++";`
2. 11
3. 12
4. Binary zero
5. Two character arrays are declared, each with 25 elements.
6. False. The keyword `char` must precede the variable name.
7. True. The binary zero terminates the string.
8. False. The characters do not represent a string because there is no terminating zero.

Chapter 7 Answers

1. False. You can define constants only with the `#define` preprocessor directive.
2. `#include`
3. `#define`
4. True

5. The preprocessor changes your source code before the compiler sees the source code.

6. Use angle brackets when the include files reside in the compiler's include subdirectory. Use quotation marks when the include file resides in the same subdirectory as the source program.

7. Defined constants are easier to change because you just have to change the line with `#define`, not several other lines in the program.

8. iostream.h

9. False. You cannot define constants enclosed in quotation marks (as `"MESSAGE"` is in the `cout` operator).

10. `Amount is 4`

Chapter 8 Answers

1. `cout` sends output to the screen, and `cin` gets input from the keyboard.

2. The prompt informs the user of what is expected.

3. Four values will be entered.

4. The `cin` function gets its value(s) from the keyboard, and the assignment statement gets its value from data in the program.

5. `The backslash, "\" character is special`

6. The following value prints (with one leading space):

   ```
   123.456
   ```

Chapter 9 Answers

1. A. `5`

   B. `6`

   C. `5`

2. A. `2`

   B. `7`

3. A. `a = (3 + 3) / (4 + 4);`

   B. `x = (a - b) * ((a - c) * (a - c));`

   C. `f = (a1 / 2) / (b1 / 3);`

   D. `d = ((8 - x * x) / (x - 9)) - ((4 * 2 - 1) / (x * x * x));`

4.

```
#include <iostream.h>
#define PI 3.14159
int  main(void)
     {
     cout << (PI * (4 * 4));
     return 0;
     }
```

5.

```
r = 100 % 4;
cout << r;
```

Chapter 10 Answers

1. `==`
2. A. False

   B. True

   C. True

   D. True
3. True
4. The `if` statement determines what code executes if the relational test is true. The `if-else` statement determines what happens for both the true and the false relational tests.

5. No
6. A. True

   B. False

   C. True

Chapter 11 Answers

1. `&&`, `||`, and `!`
2. A. False

   B. False

   C. True

   D. True
3. A. True

   B. 11

   C. True
4. `g is 25 and f got changed to 35`

Chapter 12 Answers

1. The `if-else` statement
2. The conditional operator is the only C++ operator with three arguments.
3.
```
if (a == b)
   ans = c + 2;
else
   ans = c + 3;
```
4. True

5. The increment and decrement operators compile into single assembly instructions.
6. A comma (,) operator that forces a left-to-right execution of the statements on either side
7. The output cannot reliably be determined. Do not pass an increment operator as an argument.
8. `The size of name is 20`

Chapter 13 Answers

1. `!`, `&`, `^`, `¦`, `&=`, `^=`, `¦=`, `<<`, and `>>`
2. A. `1`

   B. `1`

   C. `0`

   D. `0`
3. True
4. The 2's complement converts a number to its negative; the 1's complement simply reverses the bit pattern.

Chapter 14 Answers

1. The `while` loop tests for a true condition at the top of the loop, and the `do-while` loop tests at the bottom.
2. A counter variable increments by one, and a total variable increments by the addition to the total you are performing.
3. `++`
4. True. The braces are not required if the body of the loop is a single statement, but the braces are always recommended.
5. There are no braces. The second `cout` will always execute no matter what the `while` loop's relational test results in.

6. stdlib.h
7. One time
8. By returning a value inside the `exit()` function's parentheses
9. ```
   This is the outer loop
   This is the outer loop
   This is the outer loop
   This is the outer loop
   ```
10. The program could have executed a divide by zero.

Chapter 15 Answers

1. A sequence of one or more instructions executed repeatedly
2. False
3. A loop within a loop
4. The expressions may be initialized elsewhere, such as before the loop or in the body of the loop.
5. The inside loop
6. ```
   10
   7
   4
   1
   ```
7. True
8. The body of the `for` loop stops repeating.
9. False, because of the semicolon after the first `for` loop
10. There is no output. The value of `start` is already less than `end` when the loop begins; therefore, the `for` loop's test is immediately false.

Chapter 16 Answers

1. If the `continue` and `break` statements are unconditional, there would be little use for them.
2. There is no output because of the unconditional `continue` statement.
3. *****

Chapter 17 Answers

1. The program does not execute sequentially, as it would without `goto`.
2. The `switch` statement
3. The `break` statement
4. False
5.

```
switch (num)
     {
     case 1:
          cout << "Alpha";
          break;
     case 2:
          cout << "Beta";
          break;
     case 3:
          cout << "Gamma";
          break;
     default:
          cout << "Other";
          break;
     }
```

6.

```
do
     {
     cout << "What is your first name? ";
     cin >> name;
     }
while ((name[ 0 ] < 'A') || (name[ 0 ] > 'Z'));
```

Chapter 18 Answers

1. True
2. `main()`
3. Several smaller functions, so that each function performs a single task
4. Function names always end with a set of parentheses.
5. By putting separating comments between functions
6. The function `sq_25()` cannot be nested within `calc_it()`.
7. A function call

Chapter 19 Answers

1. True
2. A local variable is passed as an argument.
3. False
4. The variable data types
5. Static
6. You should never pass global variables; they do not need to be passed.
7. Three

Chapter 20 Answers

1. Arrays are always passed by address.
2. Nonarray variables are always passed by value (unless you override the default with `&` before each variable name).
3. True
4. No
5. Yes
6. The data types of variables `x`, `y`, and `z` are not declared in the receiving parameter list.
7. C

Chapter 21 Answers

1. By putting the return type to the left of the function name
2. One
3. To prototype library functions
4. `int`
5. False
6. Prototypes ensure that the correct number and type of parameters are being passed.
7. Global variables are known across functions already.
8. The return type is float. Three parameters are being passed—a character, an integer, and a floating-point variable.

Chapter 22 Answers

1. To achieve portability between different computers
2. False. The standard output can be redirected to any device through the operating system.

3. `get()` assumes `stdin` for the input device.
4. `cout`
5. `>` and `<`
6. `getche()`
7. False. The input from `get()` goes to a buffer as you type it.
8. Enter
9. True

Chapter 23 Answers

1. The character-testing functions do not change the characters passed to them.
2. `gets()` and `fgets()`
3. `floor()` rounds down, and `ceil()` rounds up.
4. False (the inner function returns 1)
5. `ParkerPeter`
6. `8 9`
7. True
8. `Prog` with a null zero at the end
9. True

Chapter 24 Answers

1. False
2. The array subscripts differentiate array elements from one another.
3. C++ does not initialize or zero-out arrays for you.
4. `0`

5. Yes. All arrays are passed by address because an array name is nothing more than an address to that array.

6. C++ initializes all global variables (and every other static variable in your program) to zero or null zero.

Chapter 25 Answers

1. False

2. From the low numbers "floating" to the top of the array like bubbles

3. Ascending order

4. The name of an array is an address to the starting element of that array.

5. A. `Eagles`

   B. `Rams`

   C. `les`

   D. `E`

   E. `E`

   F. `s`

   G. `g`

Chapter 26 Answers

1. `int scores[ 5 ][ 6 ];`

2. `char initials[ 4 ][ 10 ][ 20 ]`

3. The first subscript represents rows, and the last subscript represents columns.

4. 30

5. A. 2

   B. 1

   C. 91

   D. 8

6. Nested `for` loops step through multidimensional tables very easily.

7. A. 78

   B. 100

   C. 90

Chapter 27 Answers

1. A. Integer pointer

   B. Character pointer

   C. Floating-point pointer

2. Address of

3. `*`

4. `pt_sal = &salary;`

5. False

6. Yes

7. A. 2313.54

   B. 2313.54

   C. Invalid

   D. Invalid

8. B

Chapter 28 Answers

1. Array names are pointer constants, not pointer variables.
2. Four
3. A, C, D, and E. (Parentheses are needed around `iptr + 4` to make F valid.)
4. You just have to move pointers, not entire strings.
5. A, B, and D

Chapter 29 Answers

1. Structures hold groups of more than one value, each of which can be a different data type.
2. Members
3. At declaration time and at runtime
4. Structures are passed by copy.
5. False. Memory is reserved only when structure variables are declared.
6. Globally
7. Locally
8. Four

Chapter 30 Answers

1. True
2. Arrays are easier to manage.
3. A. `inventory[32].price = 12.33;`

   B. `inventory[11].part_no[0] = 'X';`

   C. `inventory[96] = inventory[62];`

4. A. `item` is not a structure variable.
   B. `inventory` is an array and must have a subscript.
   C. `inventory` is an array and must have a subscript.

Chapter 31 Answers

1. Data members and member functions
2. No
3. No
4. Private
5. Place the label `public:` before it in the class.

Chapter 32 Answers

1. Write, append, and read
2. Disks hold more data than can fit in memory.
3. You can access sequential files only in the order in which they were originally written.
4. An error condition occurs.
5. The old file is overwritten.
6. The file is created.
7. The `eof()` function returns True when an end-of-file condition is met.

Chapter 33 Answers

1. Records are stored in files, and structures are stored in memory.
2. False

3. The file pointer continually updates to point to the next byte to read.
4. `write()` and `read()`
5. `rewind()` and `seekg(0, beg);`
6. `beg` (or 0), `cur` (or 1), and `end` (or 2)
7. No filename is specified.

ASCII Table

(Including IBM Extended Character Codes)

Dec X_{10}	*Hex* X_{16}	*Binary* X_2	*ASCII Character*
000	00	0000 0000	null
001	01	0000 0001	☺
002	02	0000 0010	☻
003	03	0000 0011	♥
004	04	0000 0100	♦
005	05	0000 0101	♣
006	06	0000 0110	♠
007	07	0000 0111	●
008	08	0000 1000	■
009	09	0000 1001	○
010	0A	0000 1010	■
011	0B	0000 1011	♂
012	0C	0000 1100	♀
013	0D	0000 1101	♪
014	0E	0000 1110	♫
015	0F	0000 1111	☼
016	10	0001 0000	►

Dec X_{10}	*Hex* X_{16}	*Binary* X_2	*ASCII Character*
017	11	0001 0001	◄
018	12	0001 0010	↕
019	13	0001 0011	!!
020	14	0001 0100	¶
021	15	0001 0101	§
022	16	0001 0110	–
023	17	0001 0111	↨
024	18	0001 1000	↑
025	19	0001 1001	↓
026	1A	0001 1010	→
027	1B	0001 1011	←
028	1C	0001 1100	FS
029	1D	0001 1101	GS
030	1E	0001 1110	RS
031	1F	0001 1111	US
032	20	0010 0000	SP
033	21	0010 0001	!
034	22	0010 0010	"
035	23	0010 0011	#
036	24	0010 0100	$
037	25	0010 0101	%
038	26	0010 0110	&
039	27	0010 0111	'
040	28	0010 1000	(
041	29	0010 1001	)
042	2A	0010 1010	*
043	2B	0010 1011	+
044	2C	0010 1100	'
045	2D	0010 1101	-
046	2E	0010 1110	.
047	2F	0010 1111	/

Dec X_{10}	*Hex* X_{16}	*Binary* X_2	*ASCII Character*
048	30	0011 0000	0
049	31	0011 0001	1
050	32	0011 0010	2
051	33	0011 0011	3
052	34	0011 0100	4
053	35	0011 0101	5
054	36	0011 0110	6
055	37	0011 0111	7
056	38	0011 1000	8
057	39	0011 1001	9
058	3A	0011 1010	:
059	3B	0011 1011	;
060	3C	0011 1100	<
061	3D	0011 1101	=
062	3E	0011 1110	>
063	3F	0011 1111	?
064	40	0100 0000	@
065	41	0100 0001	A
066	42	0100 0010	B
067	43	0100 0011	C
068	44	0100 0100	D
069	45	0100 0101	E
070	46	0100 0110	F
071	47	0100 0111	G
072	48	0100 1000	H
073	49	0100 1001	I
074	4A	0100 1010	J
075	4B	0100 1011	K
076	4C	0100 1100	L
077	4D	0100 1101	M
078	4E	0100 1110	N

Dec X_{10}	*Hex* X_{16}	*Binary* X_2	*ASCII Character*
079	4F	0100 1111	O
080	50	0101 0000	P
081	51	0101 0001	Q
082	52	0101 0010	R
083	53	0101 0011	S
084	54	0101 0100	T
085	55	0101 0101	U
086	56	0101 0110	V
087	57	0101 0111	W
088	58	0101 1000	X
089	59	0101 1001	Y
090	5A	0101 1010	Z
091	5B	0101 1011	[
092	5C	0101 1100	\
093	5D	0101 1101	]
094	5E	0101 1110	^
095	5F	0101 1111	_
096	60	0110 0000	`
097	61	0110 0001	a
098	62	0110 0010	b
099	63	0110 0011	c
100	64	0110 0100	d
101	65	0110 0101	e
102	66	0110 0110	f
103	67	0110 0111	g
104	68	0110 1000	h
105	69	0110 1001	i
106	6A	0110 1010	j
107	6B	0110 1011	k
108	6C	0110 1100	l
109	6D	0110 1101	m

Dec X_{10}	*Hex* X_{16}	*Binary* X_2	*ASCII Character*
110	6E	0110 1110	n
111	6F	0110 1111	o
112	70	0111 0000	p
113	71	0111 0001	q
114	72	0111 0010	r
115	73	0111 0011	s
116	74	0111 0100	t
117	75	0111 0101	u
118	76	0111 0110	v
119	77	0111 0111	w
120	78	0111 1000	x
121	79	0111 1001	y
122	7A	0111 1010	z
123	7B	0111 1011	{
124	7C	0111 1100	¦
125	7D	0111 1101	}
126	7E	0111 1110	~
127	7F	0111 1111	DEL
128	80	1000 0000	Ç
129	81	1000 0001	ü
130	82	1000 0010	é
131	83	1000 0011	â
132	84	1000 0100	ä
133	85	1000 0101	à
134	86	1000 0110	å
135	87	1000 0111	ç
136	88	1000 1000	ê
137	89	1000 1001	ë
138	8A	1000 1010	è
139	8B	1000 1011	ï
140	8C	1000 1100	î

Dec X_{10}	*Hex* X_{16}	*Binary* X_2	*ASCII Character*
141	8D	1000 1101	ì
142	8E	1000 1110	Ä
143	8F	1000 1111	Å
144	90	1001 0000	É
145	91	1001 0001	æ
146	92	1001 0010	Æ
147	93	1001 0011	ô
148	94	1001 0100	ö
149	95	1001 0101	ò
150	96	1001 0110	û
151	97	1001 0111	ù
152	98	1001 1000	ÿ
153	99	1001 1001	Ö
154	9A	1001 1010	Ü
155	9B	1001 1011	¢
156	9C	1001 1100	£
157	9D	1001 1101	¥
158	9E	1001 1110	₧
159	9F	1001 1111	ƒ
160	A0	1010 0000	á
161	A1	1010 0001	í
162	A2	1010 0010	ó
163	A3	1010 0011	ú
164	A4	1010 0100	ñ
165	A5	1010 0101	Ñ
166	A6	1010 0110	ª
167	A7	1010 0111	º
168	A8	1010 1000	¿
169	A9	1010 1001	⌐
170	AA	1010 1010	¬
171	AB	1010 1011	½

Dec X_{10}	Hex X_{16}	Binary X_2	ASCII Character
172	AC	1010 1100	¼
173	AD	1010 1101	¡
174	AE	1010 1110	«
175	AF	1010 1111	»
176	B0	1011 0000	░
177	B1	1011 0001	▒
178	B2	1011 0010	▓
179	B3	1011 0011	│
180	B4	1011 0100	┤
181	B5	1011 0101	╡
182	B6	1011 0110	╢
183	B7	1011 0111	╖
184	B8	1011 1000	╕
185	B9	1011 1001	╣
186	BA	1011 1010	║
187	BB	1011 1011	╗
188	BC	1011 1100	╝
189	BD	1011 1101	╜
190	BE	1011 1110	╛
191	BF	1011 1111	┐
192	C0	1100 0000	└
193	C1	1100 0001	┴
194	C2	1100 0010	┬
195	C3	1100 0011	├
196	C4	1100 0100	─
197	C5	1100 0101	┼
198	C6	1100 0110	╞
199	C7	1100 0111	╟
200	C8	1100 1000	╚
201	C9	1100 1001	╔
202	CA	1100 1010	╩

Dec X_{10}	*Hex* X_{16}	*Binary* X_2	*ASCII Character*
203	CB	1100 1011	╦
204	CC	1100 1100	╠
205	CD	1100 1101	═
206	CE	1100 1110	╬
207	CF	1100 1111	╧
208	D0	1101 0000	╨
209	D1	1101 0001	╤
210	D2	1101 0010	╥
211	D3	1101 0011	╙
212	D4	1101 0100	╘
213	D5	1101 0101	╒
214	D6	1101 0110	╓
215	D7	1101 0111	╫
216	D8	1101 1000	╪
217	D9	1101 1001	┘
218	DA	1101 1010	┌
219	DB	1101 1011	█
220	DC	1101 1100	▄
221	DD	1101 1101	▌
222	DE	1101 1110	▐
223	DF	1101 1111	▀
224	E0	1110 0000	α
225	E1	1110 0001	β
226	E2	1110 0010	Γ
227	E3	1110 0011	π
228	E4	1110 0100	Σ
229	E5	1110 0101	σ
230	E6	1110 0110	µ
231	E7	1110 0111	τ
232	E8	1110 1000	Φ
233	E9	1110 1001	θ

Dec X_{10}	*Hex* X_{16}	*Binary* X_2	*ASCII Character*
234	EA	1110 1010	Ω
235	EB	1110 1011	δ
236	EC	1110 1100	∞
237	ED	1110 1101	ø
238	EE	1110 1110	∈
239	EF	1110 1111	∩
240	F0	1111 0000	≡
241	F1	1111 0001	±
242	F2	1111 0010	≥
243	F3	1111 0011	≤
244	F4	1111 0100	⌠
245	F5	1111 0101	⌡
246	F6	1111 0110	÷
247	F7	1111 0111	≈
248	F8	1111 1000	°
249	F9	1111 1001	•
250	FA	1111 1010	·
251	FB	1111 1011	
252	FC	1111 1100	η
253	FD	1111 1101	2
254	FE	1111 1110	■
255	FF	1111 1111	

D

C++ Precedence Table

Precedence Level	*Symbol*	*Description*	*Associativity*
1	++	Prefix increment	Left to right
	--	Prefix decrement	
	()	Function call and subexpression	
	[]	Array subscript	
	->	Structure pointer	
	.	Structure member	
2	!	Logical negation	Right to left
	~	1's complement	
	-	Unary negation	
	+	Unary plus	

Precedence Level	*Symbol*	*Description*	*Associativity*
	(type)	Type cast	
	*	Pointer dereference	
	&	Address of	
	sizeof	Size of	
3	*	Multiplication	Left to right
	/	Division	
	%	Modulus (int remainder)	
4	+	Addition	Left to right
	-	Subtraction	
5	<<	Bitwise left shift	Left to right
	>>	Bitwise right shift	
6	<	Less than	Left to right
	<=	Less than or equal to	
	>	Greater than	
	>=	Greater than or equal to	
7	==	Equal test	Left to right
	!=	Not equal test	
8	&	Bitwise AND	Left to right
9	^	Bitwise exclusive OR	Left to right

Precedence Level	*Symbol*	*Description*	*Associativity*
10	`¦`	Bitwise inclusive OR	Left to right
11	`&&`	Logical AND	Left to right
12	`¦¦`	Logical inclusive OR	Left to right
13	`?:`	Conditional test	Right to left
14	`=`	Assignment	Right to left
	`+=`	Compound add	
	`-+`	Compound subtract	
	`*=`	Compound multiply	
	`/=`	Compound divide	
	`%=`	Compound modulus	
	`<<=`	Compound bitwise left shift	
	`>>=`	Compound bitwise right shift	
	`&=`	Compound bitwise AND	
	`^=`	Compound bitwise exclusive OR	
	`¦=`	Compound bitwise inclusive OR	
15	`,`	Sequence point	Left to right
	`++`	Postfix increment	
	`--`	Postfix decrement	

Keyword and Function Reference

Here are the 64 Turbo C++ keywords:

asm	_ds	interrupt	short
auto	else	_loadds	signed
break	enum	long	sizeof
case	_es	_near	_ss
catch	_export	near	static
_cdecl	extern	new	struct
cdecl	_far	operator	switch
char	far	_pascal	template
class	float	pascal	this
const	for	private	typedef
continue	friend	protected	union
_cs	goto	public	unsigned
default	huge	register	virtual
delete	if	return	void
do	inline	_saveregs	volatile
double	int	_seg	while

The following are the library function prototypes, listed by their header files. The prototypes describe how you use them in your programs.

<alloc.h>

```
int brk (void *);
void *calloc (size_t, size_t);
unsigned coreleft (void);
unsigned long coreleft (void);
void far *farcalloc (unsigned long, unsigned long);
unsigned long farcoreleft (void);
void farfree (void far *);
int farheapcheck (void);
int farheapcheckfree (unsigned int);
int farheapchecknode (void far *);
int farheapfillfree (unsigned int);
int farheapwalk (struct farheapinfo *);
void far *farmalloc (unsigned long);
void far *farrealloc (void far *, unsigned long);
void free (void *);
int heapcheck (void);
int heapcheckfree (unsigned int);
int heapchecknode (void *);
int heapchecknode (void far *);
int heapfillfree (unsigned int);
int heapwalk (struct heapinfo *);
int heapwalk (struct farheapinfo far *);
void *malloc (size_t);
void *realloc (void *, size_t);
void *sbrk (int);
```

<assert.h>

```
void assert(int p);
void __assertfail(char *, char *, char *, int);
```

<bcd.h>

```
bcd abs (bcd&);
bcd acos (bcd&);
bcd asin (bcd&);
bcd atan (bcd&);
bcd cos (bcd&);
bcd cosh (bcd&);
bcd exp (bcd&);
bcd log (bcd&);
bcd log10 (bcd&);
bcd pow (bcd&, bcd&);
long double real (bcd&);
bcd sin (bcd&);
bcd sinh (bcd&);
bcd sqrt (bcd&);
bcd tan (bcd&);
bcd tanh (bcd&);
long double pascal __bcd_log10(bcd far *);
void pascal __bcd_pow10(int n, bcd far *);
long double pascal __bcd_tobinary(const bcd far *);
void pascal __bcd_todecimal(long double, int, bcd far *);
```

<bios.h>

```
int bioscom(int, char, int);
int biosdisk(int, int, int, int, int, int, void *);
int biosequip(void);
int bioskey(int);
int biosmemory(void);
int biosprint(int, int, int);
long biostime(int, long);
```

<complex.h>

```
double abs(complex&);
complex acos(complex&);
double arg(complex&);
complex asin(complex&);
```

```
complex atan(complex&);
complex conj(complex&);
complex cos(complex&);
complex cosh(complex&);
complex exp(complex&);
double imag(complex&);
complex log(complex&);
complex log10(complex&);
double norm(complex&);
complex polar(double, double);
complex pow(complex&, double);
complex pow(double, complex&);
complex pow(complex&, complex&);
double real(complex&);
complex sin(complex&);
complex sinh(complex&);
complex sqrt(complex&);
complex tan(complex&);
complex tanh(complex&);
```

<conio.h>

```
char cgets (char *);
void clreol (void);
void clrscr (void);
int cprintf (const char *, ...);
int cputs (const char *);
int cscanf (const char *, ...);
void delline (void);
int getch (void);
int getche (void);
char getpass (const char *);
int gettext (int, int, int, int, void *);
void gettextinfo (struct text_info *);
void gotoxy (int, int);
void highvideo (void);
void insline (void);
int kbhit (void);
void lowvideo (void);
int movetext (int, int, int, int, int, int);
```

```
void normvideo (void);
int putch (int);
int puttext (int, int, int, int, void *);
void textattr (int);
void textbackground (int);
void textcolor (int);
void textmode (int);
int ungetch (int);
int wherex (void);
int wherey (void);
void window (int, int, int, int);
void _setcursortype (int);
```

<ctype.h>

```
int isalnum (int);
int isalpha (int);
int isascii (int);
int iscntrl (int);
int isdigit (int);
int isgraph (int);
int islower (int);
int isprint (int);
int ispunct (int);
int isspace (int);
int isupper (int);
int isxdigit (int);
int toascii (int);
int tolower (int);
int toupper (int);
```

<dir.h>

```
int chdir (const char *);
int findfirst (const char *, struct ffblk *, int);
int findnext (struct ffblk *);
void fnmerge (char *, const char *, const char *, const char *,
              const char *);
int fnsplit (const char *, char *, char *, char *, char *);
```

```
int getcurdir (int, char *);
char getcwd (char *, int);
int getdisk (void);
int mkdir (const char *);
char mktemp (char *);
int rmdir (const char *);
char searchpath (const char *);
int setdisk (int);
```

<dos.h>

```
int absread (int, int, long, void *);
int abswrite (int, int, long, void *);
int allocmem (unsigned, unsigned *);
int bdos (int, unsigned, unsigned);
int bdosptr (int, void *, unsigned);
struct COUNTRY *country (int, struct COUNTRY *);
void ctrlbrk (int (*)(void));
void delay (unsigned);
void disable (void);
int dosexterr (struct DOSERROR *);
long dostounix (struct date *, struct time *);
void enable (void);
unsigned FP_OFF (void far *);
unsigned FP_SEG (void far *);
int freemem (unsigned);
void geninterrupt (int);
int getcbrk (void);
void getdate (struct date *);
void getdfree (unsigned char, struct dfree *);
char far *getdta (void);
void getfat (unsigned char, struct fatinfo *);
void getfatd (struct fatinfo *);
unsigned getpsp (void);
int getswitchar (void);
void gettime (struct time *);
void interrupt (far *getvect(int))(void);
int getverify (void);
void harderr (int(*)());
void hardresume (int);
void hardretn (int);
```

```
unsigned char inp (int);
int inport (int);
unsigned char inportb (int);
int int86 (int, union REGS *, union REGS *);
int int86x (int, union REGS *, union REGS *, struct SREGS *);
int intdos (union REGS *, union REGS *);
int intdosx (union REGS *, union REGS *, struct SREGS *);
void intr (int, struct REGPACK *);
void keep (unsigned char, unsigned);
void far *MK_FP (void _seg *, void near *)
void nosound (void);
void outp (int, unsigned char);
void outport (int, int);
void outportb (int, unsigned char);
char *parsfnm (const char *, struct fcb *, int);
int peek (unsigned, unsigned);
char peekb (unsigned, unsigned);
void poke (unsigned, unsigned, int);
void pokeb (unsigned, unsigned, char);
int randbrd (struct fcb *, int);
int randbwr (struct fcb *, int);
void segread (struct SREGS *);
int setblock (unsigned, unsigned);
int setcbrk (int);
void setdate (struct date *);
void setdta (char far *);
void setswitchar (char);
void settime (struct time *);
void setvect (int, void interrupt (far *)());
void setverify (int);
void sleep (unsigned);
void sound (unsigned);
void unixtodos (long, struct date *, struct time *);
int unlink (const char *);
int far _OvrInitEms (unsigned, unsigned, unsigned);
int far _OvrInitExt (unsigned long, unsigned long);
void __cli__ (void);
void __emit__ (int);
unsigned char __inportb__ (int);
void __int__ (int);
void __outportb__ (int, unsigned char);
void __sti__ (void);
```

<float.h>

```
unsigned int _clear87 (void);
unsigned int _control87 (unsigned int, unsigned int);
void _fpreset( void);
unsigned int _status87 (void);
```

<fstream.h>

```
filebuf* attach (int);
void attach (int);
filebuf* close ();
void close ();
int fd ();
int is_open ();
filebuf* open (const char*, int, int);
void open (const char*, int, int);
virtual int overflow (int);
filebuf* rdbuf ();
virtual streampos seekoff (streamoff, seek_dir, int);
virtual streambuf* setbuf (char*, int);
void setbuf (char*, int);
virtual int sync ();
virtual int underflow ();
```

<graphics.h>

```
void far arc (int, int, int, int, int);
void ATT_driver (void);
void far bar (int, int, int, int);
void far bar3d (int, int, int, int, int, int);
void CGA_driver (void);
void far circle (int, int, int);
void far cleardevice (void);
void far clearviewport (void);
void far closegraph (void);
void far detectgraph (int far *, int far *);
void far drawpoly (int, int far *);
void EGAVGA_driver (void);
```

```
void far ellipse (int, int, int, int, int, int);
void far fillellipse (int, int, int, int);
void far fillpoly (int, int far *);
void far floodfill (int, int, int);
void far getarccoords (struct arccoordstype far *);
void far getaspectratio (int far *, int far *);
int far getbkcolor (void);
int far getcolor (void);
struct palettetype far *far getdefaultpalette (void);
char *far getdrivername (void);
void far getfillpattern (char far *);
void far getfillsettings (struct fillsettingstype far *);
int far getgraphmode (void);
void far getimage (int, int, int, int, void far *);
void far getlinesettings (struct linesettingstype far *);
int far getmaxcolor (void);
int far getmaxmode (void);
int far getmaxx (void);
int far getmaxy (void);
char *far getmodename (int);
void far getmoderange (int, int far *, int far *);
void far getpalette (struct palettetype far *);
int far getpalettesize (void);
unsigned far getpixel (int, int);
void far gettextsettings (struct textsettingstype far *);
void far getviewsettings (struct viewporttype far *);
int far getx (void);
int far gety (void);
void gothic_font (void);
void far graphdefaults (void);
char *far grapherrormsg (int);
int far graphresult (void);
void Herc_driver (void);
void IBM8514_driver (void);
unsigned far imagesize (int, int, int, int);
void far initgraph (int far *, int far *, char far *);
int far installuserdriver (char far *, int huge (*)(void));
int far installuserfont (char far *);
void far line (int, int, int, int);
void far linerel (int, int);
void far lineto (int, int);
void far moverel (int, int);
```

```
void far moveto (int, int);
void far outtext(char far *);
void far outtextxy (int, int, char far *);
void PC3270_driver (void);
void far pieslice (int, int, int, int, int);
void far putimage (int, int, void far *, int);
void far putpixel (int, int, int);
void far rectangle (int, int, int, int);
int registerbgidriver (void (*)(void));
int registerbgifont (void (*)(void));
int far registerfarbgidriver (void far *);
int far registerfarbgifont (void far *);
void far restorecrtmode (void);
void sansserif_font (void);
void far sector (int, int, int, int, int, int);
void far setactivepage (int);
void far setallpalette (struct palettetype far *);
void far setaspectratio (int, int);
void far setbkcolor (int);
void far setcolor (int);
void far setfillpattern (char far *, int);
void far setfillstyle (int, int);
unsigned far setgraphbufsize (unsigned);
void far setgraphmode (int);
void far setlinestyle (int, unsigned, int);
void far setpalette (int, int);
void far setrgbpalette (int, int, int, int);
void far settextjustify (int, int);
void far settextstyle (int, int, int);
void far setusercharsize (int, int, int, int);
void far setviewport (int, int, int, int, int);
void far setvisualpage (int);
void far setwritemode (int);
void small_font (void);
int far textheight (char far *);
int far textwidth (char far *);
void triplex_font (void);
void far _graphfreemem (void far *, unsigned);
void far *far _graphgetmem (unsigned);
```

<io.h>

```
int access (const char *, int);
int chmod (const char *, int);
int chsize (int, long);
int close (int);
int creat (const char *, int);
int creatnew (const char *, int);
int creattemp (char *, int);
int dup (int);
int dup2 (int, int);
int eof (int);
long filelength (int);
int getftime (int, struct ftime *);
int ioctl (int, int, ...);
int isatty (int);
int lock (int, long, long);
long lseek (int, long, int);
int open (const char *, int, ...);
int read (int, void *, unsigned);
int setftime (int, struct ftime *);
int setmode (int, int);
int sopen (const char *, int, int, unsigned);
long tell (int);
unsigned umask (unsigned);
int unlink (const char *);
int unlock (int, long, long);
int write (int, void *, unsigned);
int _chmod (const char *, int, ...);
int _close (int);
int _creat (const char *, int);
int _open (const char *, int);
int _read (int, void *, unsigned);
int _write (int, void *, unsigned);
```

<iostream.h>

```
int allocate ();
int bad ();
char* base ();
```

```
int blen ();
void clear (int);
void dbp ();
ios& dec (ios&);
virtual int doallocate ();
signed char do_get ();
int do_ipfx (int);
int do_opfx ();
void do_osfx ();
virtual int do_sgetn (char*, int);
int do_snextc ();
virtual int do_sputn (const char*, int);
void eatwhite ();
char* eback ();
char* ebuf ();
char* egptr ();
ostream& endl (ostream&);
ostream& ends (ostream&);
int eof ();
char* epptr ();
int fail ();
char fill (char);
long flags (long);
ostream& flush ();
ostream& flush (ostream&);
void gbump (int);
int gcount ();
int get ();
istream& get (signed char&);
istream& get (signed char*, int, char);
istream& get (streambuf&, char);
istream& get (unsigned char&);
istream& get (unsigned char*, int, char);
istream& getline (signed char*, int, char);
istream& getline (unsigned char*, int, char);
int good ();
char* gptr ();
ios& hex (ios&);
istream& ignore (int, int);
void init (streambuf*);
int in_avail ();
int ipfx (int);
```

```
int ipfx0 ();
int ipfx1 ();
long & iword (int);
ios& oct (ios&);
int opfx ();
void osfx ();
void outstr (const signed char*, const signed char*);
int out_waiting ();
virtual int overflow (int);
virtual int pbackfail (int);
char* pbase ();
void pbump (int);
int peek ();
char* pptr ();
int precision (int);
ostream& put (char);
istream& putback (char);
void* & pword (int);
streambuf* rdbuf ();
int rdstate ();
istream& read (signed char*, int);
istream& read (unsigned char*, int);
int sbumpc ();
istream& seekg (streampos);
istream& seekg (streamoff, seek_dir);
virtual streampos seekoff (streamoff, seek_dir, int);
ostream& seekp (streamoff, seek_dir);
ostream& seekp (streampos);
virtual streampos seekpos (streampos, int);
void setb (char*, char*, int);
streambuf* setbuf (unsigned char*, int);
long setf (long, long);
void setg (char*, char*, char*);
void setp (char*, char*);
void setstate (int);
int sgetc ();
int sgetn (char*, int);
int skip (int);
int snextc ();
int sputbackc (char);
int sputc (int);
int sputn (const char*, int);
```

```
void stossc ();
virtual int sync ();
int sync ();
streampos tellg ();
streampos tellp ();
ostream* tie (ostream*);
int unbuffered ();
void unbuffered (int);
virtual int underflow ();
long unsetf (long);
void usersize (int);
int width (int);
ostream& write (const signed char*, int);
ostream& write (const unsigned char*, int);
istream& ws (istream&);
```

<locale.h>

```
struct lconv *localeconv (void);
char *setlocale (int, const char *);
```

<math.h>

```
int abs (int);
double acos (double);
double asin (double);
double atan (double);
double atan2 (double, double);
double atof (const char *);
double cabs (struct complex);
double ceil (double);
double cos (double);
double cosh (double);
double exp (double);
double fabs (double);
double floor (double);
double fmod (double, double);
double frexp (double, int *);
double hypot (double, double);
```

```
long labs (long);
double ldexp (double, int);
double log (double);
double log10 (double);
int matherr (struct exception *);
double modf (double, double *);
double poly (double, int, double[]);
double pow (double, double);
double pow10 (int);
double sin (double);
double sinh (double);
double sqrt (double);
double tan (double);
double tanh (double);
double _matherr (_mexcep, char *, double *, double *, double);
```

<mem.h>

```
void *memccpy (void *, const void *, int, size_t);
void *memchr (const void *, int, size_t);
int memcmp (const void *, const void *, size_t);
void *memcpy (void *, const void *, size_t);
int memicmp (const void *, const void *, size_t);
void *memmove (void *, const void *, size_t);
void *memset (void *__s, int __c, size_t __n);
void movedata (unsigned, unsigned, unsigned, unsigned, size_t);
void movmem (void *, void *, unsigned);
void setmem (void *, unsigned, char);
```

<process.h>

```
void abort (void);
int execl (char *, char *, ...);
int execle (char *, char *, ...);
int execlp (char *, char *, ...);
int execlpe (char *, char *, ...);
int execv (char *, char *[]);
int execve (char *, char *[], char **);
int execvp (char *, char *[]);
```

```
int execvpe (char *, char *[], char **);
void exit (int);
int spawnl (int, char *, char *, ...);
int spawnle (int, char *, char *, ...);
int spawnlp (int, char *, char *, ...);
int spawnlpe (int, char *, char *, ...);
int spawnv (int, char *, char *[]);
int spawnve (int, char *, char *[], char **);
int spawnvp (int, char *, char *[]);
int spawnvpe (int, char *, char *[], char **);
int system (const char *);
void _exit (int);
```

<setjmp.h>

```
void longjmp (jmp_buf, int);
int setjmp (jmp_buf);
```

<signal.h>

```
int raise(int);
void (*signal(int, void (*)(int)))(int);
```

<stdio.h>

```
void clearerr (FILE *);
int fclose (FILE *);
int fcloseall(void);
FILE *fdopen (int, char *);
int feof (FILE *);
int ferror (FILE *);
int fflush (FILE *);
int fgetc (FILE *);
int fgetchar (void);
int fgetpos (FILE *, fpos_t *);
char *fgets (char *, int, FILE *);
int fileno (FILE *);
int flushall (void);
```

```
FILE *fopen (const char *, const char *);
int fprintf (FILE *, const char *, ...);
int fputc (int, FILE *);
int fputchar (int);
int fputs (const char *, FILE *);
size_t fread (void *, size_t, size_t, FILE *);
FILE *freopen (const char *, const char *, FILE *);
int fscanf (FILE *, const char *, ...);
int fseek (FILE *, long, int);
int fsetpos (FILE *, const fpos_t *);
long ftell (FILE *);
size_t fwrite (const void *, size_t, size_t, FILE *);
int getc (FILE *);
int getchar (void);
char *gets (char *);
int getw (FILE *);
void perror (const char *);
int printf (const char *, ...);
int putc (const int, FILE *);
int putchar (const int);
int puts (const char *);
int putw (int, FILE *);
int remove (const char *);
int rename (const char *, const char *);
void rewind (FILE *);
int scanf (const char *__format, ...);
void setbuf (FILE *, char *);
int setvbuf (FILE *, char *, int, size_t);
int sprintf (char *, const char *, ...);
int sscanf (const char *, const char *, ...);
char *strerror (int);
FILE *tmpfile (void);
char *tmpnam (char *);
int ungetc (int, FILE *);
int unlink (const char *);
int vfprintf (FILE *, const char *, void *);
int vfscanf (FILE *, const char *, void *);
int vprintf (const char *, void *);
int vscanf (const char *, void *);
int vsprintf (char *, const char *, void *);
int vsscanf (const char *, const char *, void *);
int _fgetc (FILE *);
```

```
int _fputc (char, FILE *);
char *_strerror (const char *);
```

<stdiostr.h>

```
virtual int overflow (int);
virtual int pbackfail (int);
stdiobuf *rdbuf ();
virtual streampos seekoff (streamoff, seek_dir, int);
FILE *stdiofile ();
virtual int sync ();
virtual int underflow ();
```

<stdlib.h>

```
void abort (void);
int abs (int);
int atexit (atexit_t);
double atof (const char *);
int atoi (const char *);
long atol (const char *);
void *bsearch (const void *, const void *, size_t, size_t, int
              (*)(const void *, const void *));
void *calloc (size_t, size_t);
div_t div (int, int);
char ecvt (double, int, int *, int *);
void exit (int);
char *fcvt (double, int, int *, int *);
void free (void *);
char *gcvt (double, int, char *);
char getenv (const char *);
char itoa (int, char *, int);
long labs (long);
ldiv_t ldiv (long, long);
void *lfind (const void *, const void *, size_t *, size_t, int
            (*)(const void *, const void *));
void *lsearch (const void *, void *, size_t *, size_t, int
              (*)(const void *, const void *));
char *ltoa (long, char *, int);
```

```
void *malloc (size_t);
int max (int, int);
int mblen (const char *, size_t);
size_t mbstowcs (wchar_t *, const char *, size_t);
int mbtowc (wchar_t *, const char *, size_t);
int min (int, int);
int putenv (const char *);
void qsort (void *, size_t, size_t, int (*)(const void *,
            const void *));
int rand (void);
int random(int);
void randomize(void);
void *realloc (void *, size_t);
void srand (unsigned);
double strtod (const char *, char **);
long strtol (const char *, char **, int);
unsigned long strtoul (const char *, char **, int);
void swab (char *, char *, int);
int system (const char *);
char *ultoa (unsigned long, char *, int);
size_t wcstombs (char *, const wchar_t *, size_t);
int wctomb (char *, wchar_t);
void _exit (int);
unsigned long _lrotl (unsigned long, int);
unsigned long _lrotr (unsigned long, int);
unsigned _rotl (unsigned, int);
unsigned _rotr (unsigned, int);
int __abs__ (int);
```

<stream.h>

```
int allocate ();
int bad ();
void checkskip (int&, int&);
char *chr (int, int);
void clear (int);
int close ();
char *dec (long, int);
void eatwhite (istream&);
int eof ();
```

```
int fail ();
ostream& flush ();
char *form (char * ...);
istream& get (char&);
istream& get (char *, int, int);
long get_long (int);
int good ();
char *hex (long, int);
char *oct (long, int);
filebuf *open ( char *, int );
virtual int overflow ();
ostream& put (char);
void putback (char);
int rdstate ();
streambuf *setbuf ( char *, int, unsigned);
int skip (int);
int snextc ();
virtual int snextc ();
virtual void sputbackc (char);
void sputbackc (char);
int sputc (int);
virtual int sputc (int);
char *str (const char *, int);
virtual void terminate ();
void terminate ();
ostream *tie (ostream *);
virtual int underflow ();
```

<string.h>

```
void *memccpy (void *, const void *, int, size_t);
void *memchr (const void *, int, size_t);
int memcmp (const void *, const void *, size_t);
void *memcpy (void *, const void *, size_t);
int memicmp (const void *, const void *, size_t);
void *memmove (void *, const void *, size_t);
void *memset (void *, int, size_t);
void movedata (unsigned, unsigned, unsigned, unsigned, size_t);
char *stpcpy (char *, const char *);
char *strcat (char *, const char *);
char *strchr (const char *, int);
```

```
int strcmp (const char *, const char *);
int strcmpi (const char *, const char *);
int strcoll (const char *, const char *);
char *strcpy (char *, const char *);
size_t strcspn (const char *, const char *);
char *strdup (const char *);
char *strerror (int);
int stricmp (const char *, const char *);
size_t strlen (const char *);
char *strlwr (char *);
char *strncat (char *, const char *, size_t);
int strncmp (const char *, const char *, size_t);
int strncmpi (const char *, const char *, size_t);
char *strncpy (char *, const char *, size_t);
int strnicmp (const char *, const char *, size_t);
char *strnset (char *, int, size_t);
char *strpbrk (const char *, const char *);
char *strrchr (const char *, int);
char *strrev (char *);
char *strset (char *, int);
size_t strspn (const char *, const char *);
char *strstr (const char *, const char *);
char *strtok (char *, const char *);
char *strupr (char *);
size_t strxfrm (char *, const char *, size_t);
char *_strerror (const char *);
```

<strstrea.h>

```
void *(*allocf) (long);
virtual int doallocate ();
void (*freef) (void *);
void freeze (int);
void init (signed char *, int, signed char *);
virtual int overflow (int);
int pcount ();
strstreambuf *rdbuf ();
virtual streampos seekoff (streamoff, seek_dir, int);
virtual streambuf *setbuf (char*, int);
char *str ();
virtual int underflow ();
```

<time.h>

```
char *asctime (const struct tm *);
char *ctime (const time_t *);
clock_t clock (void);
double difftime (time_t, time_t);
struct tm *gmtime (const time_t *);
struct tm *localtime (const time_t *);
time_t mktime (struct tm *);
int stime (time_t *);
size_t strftime (char *, size_t, const char *,
                 const struct tm *);
time_t time (time_t *);
void tzset (void);
```

<sys\stat.h>

```
int fstat (int, struct stat *);
int stat (char *, struct stat *);
```

<sys\timeb.h>

```
void ftime (struct timeb *);
```

The Mailing List Application

This appendix collects *in one complete program* most of the commands and functions you learned throughout the book. This program manages a mailing list for your personal or business needs.

When you run the program, you are presented with a menu of choices that guides you through the program's operation. Comments throughout the program offer suggested improvements you might want to make. As your knowledge and practice of Turbo C++ improves, you might want to expand this mailing list application into your entire database of contacts.

Note that a code continuation character (arrow) appears on a few of the code lines in this program. This character indicates a continuing line of code that should *not* be broken when you type the program. These lines have been broken here because of the book's margin restrictions. When you encounter this character in your typing, simply leave one space and continue typing the second line.

Here is the listing of the complete program:

```
// Filename: MAILING.CPP
// Mailing list application
// ------------------------
```

```
// This program lets the user enter, edit, maintain, and print a
// mailing list of names and addresses.

// All commands and concepts included in this program are
// explained throughout the text of Turbo C++ By Example.

// These are items you might want to add or change:
// 1. Find your compiler's clear-screen function to
//    improve on the screen-clearing function.
// 2. Add an entry for the 'code' member to track different types
//    of names and addresses (such as business codes, personal
//    codes, and so on).
// 3. Search for a partial name (for example, typing "Sm" finds
//    "Smith" and "Smitty" and "Smythe" in the file).
// 4. When searching for name matches, ignore case (for example,
//    typing "smith" finds "Smith" in the file).
// 5. Print mailing labels on your printer.
// 6. Allow for sorting a listing of names and addresses by name
//    or ZIP code.

// Header files used by the program

#include <conio.h>
#include <ctype.h>
#include <fstream.h>
#include <iostream.h>
#include <string.h>

#define   FILENAME  "ADDRESS.DAT"

// Prototype all of this program's functions

char get_answer(void);
void disp_menu (void);
void clear_sc (void);
void change_na (void);
void print_na (void);
void err_msg (char err_msg[ ]);
void pause_sc (void);

#define   NAME_SIZE (25)
#define   ADDRESS_SIZE (25)
```

```
#define   CITY_SIZE (12)
#define   STATE_SIZE (4)
#define   ZIPCODE_SIZE (7)
#define   CODE_SIZE (7)

// Class of a name and address
class     Mail
     {
private:
     char name[ NAME_SIZE ];  // Name stored here, should be
                              // last, first order
     char address[ ADDRESS_SIZE ];
     char city[ CITY_SIZE ];
     char state[ STATE_SIZE ];     // Save room for null zero
     char zipcode[ ZIPCODE_SIZE ];
     char code[ CODE_SIZE ];  // For additional expansion. You
                              // might want to use this member
                              // for customer codes, vendor
                              // codes, or holiday card codes.
public:

void pr_data(Mail *item)
     {
     // Print the name and address sent to it
     cout << "\nName   : " << (*item).name << "\n";
     cout << "Address: " << (*item).address << "\n";
     cout << "City   : " << (*item).city << "\tState: "
          << (*item).state << "  ZIP code: " << (*item).zipcode
          << "\n";
     }

void get_new_item(Mail *item)
     {
     Mail temp_item;     // Holds temporary changed input

     cout << "\nEnter new name and address information below\n"
          << "(Press the Enter key without typing data to "
          << "retain old information)\n\n";
     cout << "What is the new name? ";
     cin.getline(temp_item.name, NAME_SIZE);
     if (strlen(temp_item.name))    // Save new data only if user
                                    // types something
```

```
          strcpy((*item).name, temp_item.name);
     cout << "What is the address? ";
     cin.getline(temp_item.address, ADDRESS_SIZE);
     if (strlen(temp_item.address))
          strcpy((*item).address, temp_item.address);
     cout << "What is the city? ";
     cin.getline(temp_item.city, CITY_SIZE);
     if (strlen(temp_item.city))
          strcpy((*item).city, temp_item.city);
     cout << "What is the state? (2 letter abbreviation only) ";
     cin.getline(temp_item.state, STATE_SIZE);
     if (strlen(temp_item.state))
          strcpy((*item).state, temp_item.state);
     cout << "What is the ZIP code? ";
     cin.getline(temp_item.zipcode, ZIPCODE_SIZE);
     if (strlen(temp_item.zipcode))
          strcpy((*item).zipcode, temp_item.zipcode);
     (*item).code[ 0 ] = 0;    // Null out the code member
                               // (unused here)
     }

void add_to_file(Mail *item);
void change_na(void);
void enter_na(Mail *item);
void getzip(Mail *item);
     };

void Mail::change_na(void)
     {
     // This search function can be improved by using the code
     // member to assign a unique code to each person in the
     // list. Names are difficult to search for because there
     // are so many variations (such as Mc and Mac and St. and
     // Saint).

     Mail item;
     fstream   file;
     int  ans;
     int  s;         // Holds size of structure
     int  change_yes = 0;      // Will be TRUE if user finds a
                               // name to change
     char test_name[ 25 ];
```

```
cout << "\nWhat is the name of the person you want to "
     << "change? ";
cin.getline(test_name, NAME_SIZE);
s = sizeof(Mail);   // To ensure that fread() reads properly
file.open(FILENAME, ios::in | ios::out);
if (!file)
     {
     err_msg("*** Read error - Ensure file exists before
     reading it ***");
     return;
     }
do
     {
     file.read((unsigned char *)&item, sizeof(Mail));
     if (file.gcount() != s)
          {
          if (file.eof())
               break;
          }
     if (strcmp(item.name, test_name) == 0)
          {
          item.pr_data(&item);     // Print name and address
          cout << "\nIs this the name and address to "
               << "change? (Y/N) ";
          ans = get_answer();
          if (toupper(ans) == 'N')
               break;              // Get another name
          get_new_item(&item);     // Let user type new
                                   // information
          file.seekg((long)-s, ios::cur);    // Back up one
                                             // structure
          file.write((const unsigned char *)(&item),
               sizeof(Mail));   // Rewrite information
          change_yes = 1;       // Changed flag
          break;    // Finished
          }
     }
while (!file.eof());
if (!change_yes)
     err_msg("*** End of file encountered before finding
     the name ***");
}
```

```
void Mail::getzip(Mail *item) // Ensure that ZIP code is all
                              // digits
     {
     int  ctr;
     int  bad_zip;

     do
          {
          bad_zip = 0;
          cout << "What is the ZIP code? ";
          cin.getline((*item).zipcode, ZIPCODE_SIZE);
          for (ctr = 0; ctr < 5; ctr++)
               {
               if (isdigit((*item).zipcode[ ctr ]))
                    continue;
               else
                    {
                    err_msg("*** The ZIP code must consist
                    of digits only ***");
                    bad_zip = 1;
                    break;
                    }
               }
          }
     while (bad_zip);
     }

void Mail::add_to_file(Mail *item)
     {
     ofstream  file;

     file.open(FILENAME, ios::app);     // Open file in append
                                        // mode
     if (!file)
          {
          err_msg("*** Disk error - please check disk drive ***");
          return;
          }
     // Add structure to file
```

```
     file.write((const unsigned char *)(item), sizeof(Mail));
     }

void Mail::enter_na(Mail *item)
     {
     char ans;

     do
          {
          cout << "\n\n\n\n\nWhat is the name? ";
          cin.getline((*item).name, NAME_SIZE);
          cout << "What is the address? ";
          cin.getline((*item).address, ADDRESS_SIZE);
          cout << "What is the city? ";
          cin.getline((*item).city, CITY_SIZE);
          cout << "What is the state? (2 letter abbreviation "
               << "only)";
          cin.getline((*item).state, STATE_SIZE);
          getzip(item);  // Ensure that ZIP code is all digits
          strcpy((*item).code, " ");     // Null out the code
                                         // member
          add_to_file(item);  // Write new information to disk
                              // file
          cout << "\n\nDo you want to enter another name and "
               << "address? (Y/N)";
          ans = get_answer();
          }
     while (toupper(ans) == 'Y');
     }

//*****************************************************************

// Defined constants
// MAX is total number of names allowed in memory for reading
// mailing list

#define   MAX  250
#define   BELL '\x07'

//*****************************************************************
```

```
int  main(void)
     {
     char ans;
     Mail item;

     do
          {
          disp_menu();   // Display the menu for the user
          ans = get_answer();
          switch (ans)
               {
               case '1':
                    item.enter_na(&item);
                    break;
               case '2':
                    item.change_na();
                    break;
               case '3':
                    print_na();
                    break;
               case '4':
                    break;
               default:
                    err_msg("*** You need to enter
                    1 through 4 ***");
                    break;
               }
          }
     while (ans != '4');
     return 0;
     }

//*****************************************************************

void disp_menu(void)     // Display the main menu of program
     {
     clear_sc();    // Clear the screen
     cout << "\t\t*** Mailing List Manager ***\n";
     cout << "\t\t    --------------------\n\n\n\n";
     cout << "Do you want to:\n\n\n";
     cout << "\t1. Add names and addresses to the list\n\n\n";
     cout << "\t2. Change names and addresses in the list\n\n\n";
```

```
     cout << "\t3. Print names and addresses in the list\n\n\n";
     cout << "\t4. Exit this program\n\n\n";
     cout << "What is your choice? ";
     }

//*****************************************************************

void clear_sc()      // Clear the screen by sending 25 blank lines
                     // to it
     {
     int  ctr; // Counter for the 25 blank lines

     for (ctr = 0; ctr < 25; ctr++)
          cout << "\n";
     }

//*****************************************************************

void print_na(void)
     {
     Mail      item;
     ifstream  file;
     int       s;
     int       linectr = 0;

     s = sizeof(Mail);   // To ensure that fread() reads properly
     file.open(FILENAME);
     if (!file)
          {
          err_msg("*** Read error - Ensure file exists
          before reading it ***");
          return;
          }
     do
          {
          file.read((signed char *)&item, s);
          if (file.gcount() != s)
               {
               if (file.eof())     // If EOF, quit reading
                    break;
               }
          if (linectr > 20)   // Screen is full
               {
```

```
                pause_sc();
                linectr = 0;
                }
            item.pr_data(&item);     // Print the name and address
            linectr += 4;
            }
        while (!file.eof());
        cout << "\n- End of list -";
        pause_sc();     // Give user a chance to see names remaining
                        // on screen
        }

//*****************************************************************

void err_msg(char err_msg[ ])
        {
        cout << "\n\n" << err_msg << BELL << "\n";
        }

//*****************************************************************

void pause_sc()
        {
        cout << "\nPress the Enter key to continue...";
        while (getch() != '\r')
            ;
        }

//*****************************************************************

char get_answer(void)
        {
        char ans;

        ans = getch();
        while (kbhit())
            getch();
        putch(ans);
        return ans;
        }
```

Glossary

address Each memory (RAM) location (each byte) has a unique address. The first address in memory is 0, the second address is 1, and so on, until the last address (which comes thousands of bytes later).

argument The value sent *to* a function or procedure. This can be either a constant or a variable and is enclosed in parentheses.

array A list of variables, sometimes called a table of variables.

ASCII Acronym for *A*merican *S*tandard *C*ode for *I*nformation *I*nterchange.

ASCII file A file containing characters that can be used by any program on most computers. Sometimes the file is called a text file or an ASCII text file.

AUTOEXEC.BAT A batch file in PCs that executes a series of commands whenever you start or reset the computer.

backup file A duplicate copy of a file that preserves your work in case you damage the original file. Files on a hard disk are commonly backed up onto floppy disks or tapes.

binary A numbering system based on only two digits. The only valid digits in a binary system are 0 and 1. See also *bit*.

binary zero Another name for null zero.

bit Binary digit, the smallest unit of storage on a computer. Each bit can have a value of 0 or 1, indicating the absence or presence of an electrical signal. See also *binary*.

bitwise operators C++ operators that manipulate the binary representation of values.

block Two or more statements treated as though they are a single statement. A block is always enclosed in braces (`{ }`).

boot To start a computer with the operating system software in place. You must boot your computer before using it.

bubble sort A type of sorting routine.

bug An error in a program that prevents it from running correctly. Originated when a moth short-circuited a connection in one of the first computers, preventing the computer from working!

byte A basic unit of data storage and manipulation. A byte is equivalent to 8 bits and can contain a value ranging from 0 through 255.

cathode ray tube (CRT) The television-like screen, also called the *monitor*. It is one place to which the output of the computer can be sent.

central processing unit (CPU) The controlling circuit responsible for operations within the computer. These operations generally include system timing, logical processing, and logical operations. The central processing unit controls every operation of the computer system. On PCs, the central processing unit is called a microprocessor and is stored on a single integrated circuit chip.

class A unit of related information and functions containing one or more members and functions that act on those members. See also *structure*.

code A set of instructions written in a programming language. See *source code*.

compile Process of translating a program written in a programming language such as C++ into machine code that your computer understands.

concatenation The process of attaching one string to the end of another or combining two or more strings into a longer string.

conditional loop A series of C++ instructions that occurs a fixed number of times.

constant Data that remains the same during a program run.

constructor The function executed when the program declares an instance of a class.

CPU See *central processing unit.*

CRT See *cathode ray tube.*

data Information stored in the computer as numbers, letters, and special symbols such as punctuation marks. Data also refers to the characters you input into your program so that it can produce meaningful information.

data member A data component of a class or structure.

data processing This is what computers really do. They take data and manipulate it into meaningful output, which is called *information.*

data validation The process of testing the values input into a program—for instance, testing for a negative number when you know the input cannot be negative, or ensuring that a number is within a certain range.

debug Process of locating an error (bug) in a program and removing it.

declaration A statement that declares the existence of a data object or function. A declaration reserves memory.

default A predefined action or command that the computer chooses unless you specify otherwise.

definition A statement that defines the format of a data object or function. A definition reserves no memory.

demodulate To convert an analog signal into a digital signal for use by a computer. See also *modulate.*

dereference The process of finding a value pointed to by a pointer variable.

destructor The function called when a class instance goes out of scope.

digital computer A computer that operates on binary (on and off) digital impulses of electricity.

directory A list of files stored on a disk. Directories within existing directories are called subdirectories.

disk A round, flat magnetic storage medium. Floppy disks are made of flexible material enclosed in 5 1/4-inch or 3 1/2-inch protective cases. Hard disks consist of a stack of rigid disks housed in a single unit. A disk is sometimes called *external memory.* Disk storage is nonvolatile. When you turn off your computer, the disk's contents do not go away.

disk drive Device that reads and writes data to a floppy or hard disk.

diskette Another name for a removable floppy disk.

display A screen or monitor.

display adapter Located in the system unit, the display adapter determines the amount of *resolution* and the possible number of colors on the screen.

DOS Acronym for *D*isk *O*perating *S*ystem.

dot-matrix printer One of the two most common PC printers. (The *laser* printer is the other.) A dot-matrix printer is inexpensive and fast; it uses a series of small dots to represent printed text and graphics.

element An individual variable in an array.

execute To run a program.

expanded memory RAM that is above and beyond the standard 640K. It is accessed with special software and can be copied in and out of memory below 1M. Expanded memory can be obtained through special hardware or through emulation by extended memory drives.

extended memory RAM that is above and beyond the standard 640K. It is accessed with special software and is found only on PCs with 80286, 80386, and 80486 microprocessors.

external modem A modem that sits in a box outside your computer. See also *internal modem*.

file A collection of data stored as a single unit on a floppy or hard disk. A file always has a filename that identifies it.

file extension Used by PCs and consists of a period followed by one to three characters. The file extension follows the filename.

filename A unique name that identifies a file. Filenames can contain up to eight characters and may have a period followed by an extension (usually three characters long).

fixed disk See *hard disk*.

fixed-length record Each of this record's fields takes the same amount of disk space, even if that field's data value does not fill the field.

floppy disk See *disk*.

format Process of creating on the disk a "map" that tells the operating system how the disk is structured. This is how the operating system keeps track of where files are stored.

function A self-contained coding segment designed to do a specific task. All C++ programs must have at least one function called `main()`. Some functions are library routines that manipulate numbers, strings, and output.

function keys The keys labeled F1 through F12 (some keyboards go to F10 only).

global variable A variable that can be seen from (and used by) every statement in the program.

hard copy The printout of a program (or its output); also a safe backup copy for a program in case the disk is erased.

hard disk Sometimes called a *fixed disk*, they hold much more data and are many times faster than floppy disks. See also *disk*.

hardware The physical parts of the machine. Hardware has been defined as "anything you can kick" and consists of the things you can see.

hexadecimal A numbering system based on 16 elements. Digits are numbered 0 through F (0, 1, 2, 3, 4, 5, 6, 7, 8, 9, A, B, C, D, E, and F).

hierarchy of operators See *order of operators*.

indeterminate loop Unlike the `for` loop, a loop whose number of cycles is not known in advance.

infinite loop The never-ending repetition of a block of C++ statements.

information The meaningful product from a program. Data goes *into* a program to produce meaningful output (information).

inline function A function that compiles as inline code each time the function is called.

input The entry of data into a computer through a device such as the keyboard.

input-process-output This model is the foundation of everything that happens in your computer. Data is input, it is then processed by your program in the computer, and finally information is output.

I/O Acronym for *I*nput/*O*utput.

integer variable A variable that can hold an integer.

internal modem A modem that resides inside the system unit. See also *external modem*.

kilobyte (K) A unit of measurement that is 1,024 bytes.

laser printer A type of printer that is generally faster than a dot-matrix printer. Laser printer output is much sharper than that of a dot-matrix printer because a laser beam actually burns toner ink into the paper. Laser printers are more expensive than dot-matrix printers.

least significant bit The rightmost bit of a byte. For example, a binary 00000111 would have a 1 as the least significant bit.

line printer Another name for your printer.

local variable A variable that can be seen from (and used by) only the block in which it is defined.

loop The repeated execution of one or more statements.

machine language The series of binary digits that a microprocessor executes to perform individual tasks. People seldom, if ever, program in machine language. Instead, they program in assembly language, and an assembler translates their instructions into machine language.

main module The first function of a modular program, called `main()`, which controls the execution of the other functions.

maintainability The computer industry's word for the ability to change and update programs that were written in a simple style.

manipulator A value used by a program to tell the stream to modify one of its modes.

math operator A symbol used for addition, subtraction, multiplication, division, or other calculations.

megabyte (M) A unit of measurement that is approximately a million bytes (1,048,576 bytes).

member A piece of a structure variable that holds a specific type of data, a piece of a class variable that holds a specific type of data, or a class variable function acting on class data.

member function A function of a class.

memory Storage area inside the computer, used to store data temporarily. The computer's memory is erased when the power is turned off.

menu A list of commands or instructions displayed on the screen. A menu organizes commands and makes a program easier to use.

menu-driven Describes a program that provides menus for choosing commands.

microchip A small wafer of silicon that holds computer components and occupies less space than a postage stamp.

microcomputer A small computer, such as a PC, that can fit on a desktop. The microchip is the heart of the microcomputer. Microcomputers are much less expensive than their larger counterparts.

microprocessor The chip that does the calculations for PCs. Sometimes this chip is called the central processing unit (CPU).

modem A piece of hardware that modulates and demodulates signals so that your computer can communicate with other computers over telephone lines. See also *external modem* and *internal modem*.

modular programming The process of writing your programs in several modules rather than as one long program. By breaking a program into several smaller program-like routines, you can isolate problems better, write correct programs faster, and produce programs that are easier to maintain.

modulate Before your computer can transmit data over a telephone line, the information to be sent must be converted (modulated) into analog signals. See also *demodulate.*

modulus The integer remainder of division.

monitor A television-like screen that lets the computer display information. The monitor is an output device.

mouse A hand-held device that you move across the desktop to move a corresponding indicator, called a mouse pointer, across the screen. Used instead of the keyboard to select and move items (such as text or graphics), execute commands, and perform other tasks.

MS-DOS An operating system for IBM and compatible PCs.

multidimensional array An array with more than one dimension. Two-dimensional arrays are sometimes called tables or matrices, which have rows and columns.

nested loop A loop within a loop.

null string An empty string whose first character is the null zero and whose length is zero.

null zero The string-terminating character. All C++ string constants and strings stored in character arrays end in null zero. The ASCII value for the null zero is 0.

numeric functions Library routines that work with numbers.

object code A "halfway step" between source code and executable machine language. Object code consists mostly of machine language but is not directly executable by the computer. Such code must first be linked in order to resolve external references and address references.

operator An operator works on data and might perform math calculations or change data to other data types. Examples include `+`, `-`, and `sizeof()`.

order of operators Sometimes called the *hierarchy of operators* or the *precedence of operators*, this order determines exactly how C++ computes formulas.

output device The device where the results of a program are output, such as the screen, the printer, or a disk file.

parallel arrays Two arrays working side by side. Each element in each array corresponds to an element in the other array.

parallel port A connector used to plug a device, such as a printer, into the computer. Transferring data through a parallel port is much faster than through a serial port.

parameter A list of variables enclosed in parentheses that follow the name of a function or procedure. Parameters indicate the number and type of arguments that will be sent to the function or procedure.

passing by address Also called passing by reference. When an argument (a local variable) is passed by address, the variable's address in memory is sent to and assigned to the receiving function's parameter list. (If more than one variable is passed by address, each variable's address is sent to and assigned to the receiving function's parameters.) A change made to the parameter within the function will also change the value of the argument variable.

passing by copy Another name for *passing by value*.

passing by reference Another name for *passing by address*.

passing by value By default, all C++ variable arguments are passed *by value*. When the value contained in a variable is passed to the parameter list of a receiving function, changes made to the parameter within the routine will *not* change the value of the argument variable. Also called *passing by copy*.

path The route that the computer "travels" from the root directory to any subdirectories when locating a file. The path refers also to the subdirectories that MS-DOS examines when you type a command that requires the operating system to find and access a file.

peripheral A device attached to the computer, such as a modem, disk drive, mouse, or printer.

personal computer A microcomputer that is sometimes called a PC, which stands for *p*ersonal *c*omputer.

pointer A variable that holds the address of another variable.

precedence of operators See *order of operators*.

preprocessor directive A command, preceded by a `#`, that you place in your source code to direct the compiler to modify the source code in some way. The two most common preprocessor directives are `#define` and `#include`.

printer A device that prints data from the computer to paper.

private class member A class member that is inaccessible except to the class's member functions.

program A group of instructions that tells the computer what to do.

programming language A set of rules for writing instructions for the computer. Popular programming languages include BASIC, Visual Basic, C, C++, and Pascal.

prototype The definition of a function. The prototype includes the function's name, return type, and parameter list.

public class member A class member that is accessible to any functions.

RAM Acronym for *R*andom *A*ccess *M*emory.

random access file A file in which records can be accessed in any order you want.

random access memory (RAM) What your computer uses to store data and programs temporarily. RAM is measured in kilobytes and megabytes. Generally, the more RAM a computer has, the more powerful programs it can run.

read-only memory (ROM) A permanent type of computer memory. It contains the BIOS (*B*asic *I*nput/*O*utput *S*ystem), a special chip used to provide instructions to the computer when you turn it on.

real numbers Numbers that have decimal points and a fractional part to the right of the decimal.

record An individual row in a file.

relational operators Operators that compare data, telling how two variables or constants relate to each other. Relational operators can tell whether two variables are equal or not equal, or which variable is less than or more than the other.

ROM Acronym for *R*ead-*O*nly *M*emory.

scientific notation A shortcut method of representing numbers of extreme values.

sectors A pattern of pie-shaped wedges on a disk. Formatting creates a pattern of tracks and sectors where your data and programs are stored.

sequential file A file that has to be accessed one record at a time, beginning with the first record.

serial port A connector used to plug in serial devices, such as a modem or mouse.

single-dimensional array An array that has only one subscript. A single-dimensional array represents a list of values.

software The data and programs that interact with your hardware. The C++ language is an example of software.

sorting A method of putting data in a specific order (such as alphabetical or numerical order), even if that order is not the same order in which the elements were entered.

source code The C++ language instructions, written by humans, that the C++ compiler translates into object code.

spaghetti code Term used when there are too many `goto`s in a program. If a program branches all over the place, it is difficult to follow, and trying to follow the logic resembles a "bowl of spaghetti."

stream A stream of characters, one following another, flowing between devices in the computer.

string constant One or more groups of characters that end in a null zero.

string literal Another name for a *string constant*.

structure A unit of related information containing one or more members, such as an employee number, employee name, employee address, employee pay rate, and so on. See also *class*.

subscript A number inside brackets that differentiates one element of an array from another element.

syntax error An error that is the result of an incorrect statement in the code.

system unit The large box component of the computer. The system unit houses the PC's microchip (the CPU).

tracks A pattern of paths on a disk. Formatting creates a pattern of tracks and sectors where your data and programs are stored.

truncation The fractional part of a number (the part of the number to the right of the decimal point) is taken off the number. No rounding is done.

two's complement A method your computer uses to take the negative of a number. This method, when used with addition, allows the computer to simulate subtraction.

unary operator The addition or subtraction operator used before a single variable or constant.

user-friendliness A program is user-friendly if it makes the user comfortable and simulates what the user is already familiar with.

variable Data that can change as the program runs.

variable-length records This record's fields take up no wasted space on the disk. As soon as a field's data value is saved to the file, the next field's data value is stored immediately after it. There is usually a special separating character between the fields so that your program knows where the fields begin and end.

variable scope Sometimes called the *visibility of variables*, this describes how variables are "seen" by your program. See also *global variable* and *local variable.*

volatile Temporary. For example, when you turn the computer off, all the RAM is erased.

word In PC usage, two consecutive bytes (16 bits) of data.

Index

Symbols

A

B

D

E

F

G

H

I

J-K

L

M

N

O

P

Q

R

S

T

U

V

W

X-Y-Z

Computer Books from Que Mean PC Performance!

Spreadsheets

3 Beyond the Basics $24.95
3 for DOS Release 2.3 Quick Reference $ 9.95
3 for DOS Release 2.3 QuickStart $19.95
3 for DOS Release 3.1+ Quick Reference $ 9.95
for DOS Release 3.1+ QuickStart $19.95
for Windows Quick Reference $ 9.95
for Windows QuickStart $19.95
Personal Money Manager $29.95
Power Macros $39.95
Release 2.2 QueCards $19.95
1-2-3 $19.95
Excel $19.95
Quattro Pro $19.95
3 for Windows QuickStart $19.95
for Windows Quick Reference $ 9.95
Your Best with 1-2-3 $24.95
o Pro 3 QuickStart $19.95
o Pro Quick Reference $ 9.95
1-2-3 for DOS Release 2.3, Special Edition $29.95
1-2-3 for Windows $29.95
1-2-3 for DOS Release 3.1+, Special Edition $29.95
Excel 4 for Windows, Special Edition $29.95
Quattro Pro 4, Special Edition $27.95
Quattro Pro for Windows $24.95
SuperCalc5, 2nd Edition $29.95

Databases

III Plus Handbook, 2nd Edition $24.95
IV 1.1 Qiuck Reference $ 9.95
IV 1.1 QuickStart $19.95
ction to Databases $19.95
3.5 Quick Reference $ 9.95
Quick Reference, 2nd Edition $ 9.95
lphaFOUR $24.95
lipper, 3rd Edition $29.95
ataEase $24.95
BASE IV $29.95
xPro 2 $29.95
RACLE $29.95
aradox 3.5, Special Edition $29.95
aradox for Windows $26.95
aradox, Special Edition $29.95
C-File $24.95
BASE $29.95

Business Applications

e Quick Reference $ 9.95
cken $19.95
Works Quick Reference $ 9.95
tilities 6 Quick Reference $ 9.95
7 Quick Reference $ 9.95
atabase Techniques $29.95
uick Reference $ 9.95
uickStart $19.95
ue Cards $19.95
mputer User's Dictionary, 2nd Edition $10.95
ng Enable $29.95
Quick Reference $ 9.95
e Tips, Tricks, and Traps, 2nd Edition $26.95
Easy, 2nd Edition $24.95
rosoft Money $19.95
rosoft Works: IBM Version $22.95
rosoft Works for Windows, Special Edition $24.95
neyCounts $19.95
oli 2000 $19.95
ton Utilities 6 $24.95
Tools Deluxe 7 $24.95
First Choice $22.95
WindowWorks $24.95
4 $27.95
ken 5 $19.95
ken for Windows $19.95
t $29.95
Line $24.95
oTax: 1992 Edition $19.95

CAD

Quick Reference, 2nd Edition $ 8.95
CAD, 3rd Edition $29.95

Word Processing

erfect $19.95
erfect for Windows $19.95
Look Your Best with WordPerfect 5.1 $24.95
Look Your Best with WordPerfect forWindows $24.95
Microsoft Word Quick Reference $ 9.95
Using Ami Pro $24.95
Using LetterPerfect $22.95
Using Microsoft Word 5.5: IBM Version, 2nd Edition $24.95
Using MultiMate $24.95
Using PC-Write $22.95
Using Professional Write $22.95
Using Professional Write Plus for Windows $24.95
Using Word for Windows 2, Special Edition $27.95
Using WordPerfect 5 $27.95
Using WordPerfect 5.1, Special Edition $27.95
Using WordPerfect for Windows, Special Edition $29.95
Using WordStar 7 $19.95
Using WordStar, 3rd Edition $27.95
WordPerfect 5.1 Power Macros $39.95
WordPerfect 5.1 QueCards $19.95
WordPerfect 5.1 Quick Reference $ 9.95
WordPerfect 5.1 QuickStart $19.95
WordPerfect 5.1 Tips, Tricks, and Traps $24.95
WordPerfect for Windows Power Pack $39.95
WordPerfect for Windows Quick Reference $ 9.95
WordPerfect for Windows Quick Start $19.95
WordPerfect Power Pack $39.95
WordPerfect Quick Reference $ 9.95

Hardware/Systems

Batch File and Macros Quick Reference $ 9.95
Computerizing Your Small Business $19.95
DR DOS 6 Quick Reference $ 9.95
Easy DOS $19.95
Easy Windows $19.95
Fastback Quick Reference $ 8.95
Hard Disk Quick Reference $ 8.95
Hard Disk Quick Reference, 1992 Edition $ 9.95
Introduction to Hard Disk Management $24.95
Introduction to Networking $24.95
Introduction to PC Communications $24.95
Introduction to Personal Computers, 2nd Edition $19.95
Introduction to UNIX $24.95
Laplink Quick Reference $ 9.95
MS-DOS 5 Que Cards $19.95
MS-DOS 5 Quick Reference $ 9.95
MS-DOS 5 QuickStart $19.95
MS-DOS Quick Reference $ 8.95
MS-DOS QuickStart, 2nd Edition $19.95
Networking Personal Computers, 3rd Edition $24.95
Que's Computer Buyer's Guide, 1992 Edition $14.95
Que's Guide to CompuServe $12.95
Que's Guide to DataRecovery $29.95
Que's Guide to XTree $12.95
Que's MS-DOS User's Guide, Special Edition $29.95
Que's PS/1 Book $22.95
TurboCharging MS-DOS $24.95
Upgrading and Repairing PCs $29.95
Upgrading and Repairing PCs, 2nd Edition $29.95
Upgrading to MS-DOS 5 $14.95
Using GeoWorks Pro $24.95
Using Microsoft Windows 3, 2nd Edition $24.95
Using MS-DOS 5 $24.95
Using Novell NetWare, 2nd Edition $29.95
Using OS/2 2.0 $24.95
Using PC DOS, 3rd Edition $27.95
Using Prodigy $19.95
Using UNIX $29.95
Using Windows 3.1 $26.95
Using Your Hard Disk $29.95
Windows 3 Quick Reference $ 8.95
Windows 3 QuickStart $19.95
Windows 3.1 Quick Reference $ 9.95
Windows 3.1 QuickStart $19.95

Desktop Publishing/Graphics

CorelDRAW! Quick Reference $ 8.95
Harvard Graphics 3 Quick Reference $ 9.95
Harvard Graphics Quick Reference $ 9.95
Que's Using Ventura Publisher $29.95
Using DrawPerfect $24.95
Using Freelance Plus $24.95
Using Harvard Graphics 3 $29.95
Using Harvard Graphics for Windows $24.95
Using Harvard Graphics, 2nd Edition $24.95
Using Microsoft Publisher $22.95
Using PageMaker 4 for Windows $29.95
Using PFS: First Publisher, 2nd Edition $24.95
Using PowerPoint $24.95
Using Publish It! $24.95

Macintosh/Apple II

Easy Macintosh $19.95
HyperCard 2 QuickStart $19.95
PageMaker 4 for the Mac Quick Reference $ 9.95
The Big Mac Book, 2nd Edition $29.95
The Little Mac Book $12.95
QuarkXPress 3.1 Quick Reference $ 9.95
Que's Big Mac Book, 3rd Edition $29.95
Que's Little Mac Book, 2nd Edition $12.95
Que's Mac Classic Book $24.95
Que's Macintosh Multimedia Handbook $24.95
System 7 Quick Reference $ 9.95
Using 1-2-3 for the Mac $24.95
Using AppleWorks, 3rd Edition $24.95
Using Excel 3 for the Macintosh $24.95
Using FileMaker Pro $24.95
Using MacDraw Pro $24.95
Using MacroMind Director $29.95
Using MacWrite Pro $24.95
Using Microsoft Word 5 for the Mac $27.95
Using Microsoft Works: Macintosh Version, 2nd Edition $24.95
Using Microsoft Works for the Mac $24.95
Using PageMaker 4 for the Macintosh $24.95
Using Quicken 3 for the Mac $19.95
Using the Macintosh with System 7 $24.95
Using Word for the Mac, Special Edition $24.95
Using WordPerfect 2 for the Mac $24.95
Word for the Mac Quick Reference $ 9.95

Programming/Technical

Borland C++ 3 By Example $21.95
Borland C++ Programmer's Reference $29.95
C By Example $21.95
C Programmer's Toolkit, 2nd Edition $39.95
Clipper Programmer's Reference $29.95
DOS Programmer's Reference, 3rd Edition $29.95
FoxPro Programmer's Reference $29.95
Network Programming in C $49.95
Paradox Programmer's Reference $29.95
Programming in Windows 3.1 $39.95
QBasic By Example $21.95
Turbo Pascal 6 By Example $21.95
Turbo Pascal 6 Programmer's Reference $29.95
UNIX Programmer's Reference $29.95
UNIX Shell Commands Quick Reference $ 8.95
Using Assembly Language, 2nd Edition $29.95
Using Assembly Language, 3rd Edition $29.95
Using BASIC $24.95
Using Borland C++ $29.95
Using Borland C++ 3, 2nd Edition $29.95
Using C $29.95
Using Microsoft C $29.95
Using QBasic $24.95
Using QuickBASIC 4 $24.95
Using QuickC for Windows $29.95
Using Turbo Pascal 6, 2nd Edition $29.95
Using Turbo Pascal for Windows $29.95
Using Visual Basic $29.95
Visual Basic by Example $21.95
Visual Basic Programmer's Reference $29.95
Windows 3.1 Programmer's Reference $39.95

For More Information,
Call Toll Free!
1-800-428-5331

All prices and titles subject to change without notice. Non-U.S. prices may be higher. Printed in the U.S.A.

Order Your Program Disk Today!

You can save yourself hours of tedious, error-prone typing by ordering the companion disk to *Turbo C++ By Example*. This disk contains the source code for all complete programs and all sample code in the book, as well as Appendix F's complete mailing list application.

You will get code that shows you how to use all the beginning and advanced features of C++. Samples include code for keyboard and screen control, file I/O, control construct statements, structures, pointers, and more. Every complete program in this book is included on one disk, giving you over 200 programs that help you learn C++.

Each 3½-inch disk is $10.

Just make a copy of this page, fill in the blanks, and mail it with your check or money order to:

Greg Perry
Turbo C++ Diskette
P.O. BOX 35752
Tulsa, OK 74153-0752

Please **print** the following information:

3½-inch only

Name: ____

Street Address: ________________________________

City: ______________________ State: ____________

ZIP code: __________________

For foreign orders, please use a separate page to give your exact mailing address in the format required by your post office and add $5 (U.S. currency only) to cover the additional postage.

Make checks and money orders payable to:

Greg Perry

(This offer is made by Greg Perry, not by Que Corporation.)